MAIMONIDES

MISHNEH TORAH

ספר שופטים

SEFER SHOFTIM

The Book of Judges

Hilchot Sanhedrin V'Haonshin Hamesurim Lahem
The Laws of the Courts and the Penalties Placed under their Jurisdiction
הלכות סנהדרין והענשין המסורין להם

Hilchot Edut
The Laws of Witnesses
הלכות עדות

Hilchot Mamrim
The Laws of the Rebellious Ones
הלכות ממרים

Hilchot Evel
The Laws of Mourning
הלכות אבל

Hilchot Melachim UMilchamotehem
The Laws of Kings and their Wars
הלכות מלכים ומלחמותיהם

MAIMONIDES

MISHNEH TORAH

SEFER SHOFTIM
The Book of Judges

Hilchot Sanhedrin V'Haonshin Hamesurim Lahem
The Laws of the Courts and the Penalties Placed under their Jurisdiction

and

Hilchot Edut
The Laws of Witnesses

and

Hilchot Mamrim
The Laws of the Rebellious Ones

and

Hilchot Evel
The Laws of Mourning

and

Hilchot Melachim UMilchamotehem
The Laws of Kings and their Wars

A new translation with commentaries and notes.

by
Rabbi Eliyahu Touger

MOZNAIM PUBLISHING CORPORATION
NEW YORK / JERUSALEM

רמב"ם
משנה תורה

ספר שופטים
הלכות סנהדרין והענשין המסורין להם
הלכות עדות
הלכות ממרים
הלכות אבל
הלכות מלכים ומלחמותיהם

תורגם מחדש לאנגלית
עם מקורות, הערות ודיאגרמות

מאת
הרב אליהו תגר

בית הוצאת ספרים
מאזנים
ירושלים — ניו יארק
תשס"א

For information write:
Moznaim Publishing Corporation
4304 12th Avenue
Brooklyn, New York 11219
Tel. (718) 438-7680, 853-0525

ISBN 1-885220-28-6

Printed and bound in Jerusalem, Israel
by Vagshal Ltd.
Typesetting by Vagshal Ltd.
Jerusalem

Printed in Israel

TABLE OF CONTENTS

Hilchot Edut

Hilchot Mamrim

Hilchot Eval

Hilchot Melachim U'Milchamoteihem

Translator's Introduction

It would be an understatement to say that the Rambam carefully structured the order of the *Mishneh Torah*. Anyone even slightly familiar with the work appreciates how it is carefully planned and how the order of the presentation of the laws is representative of a comprehensive understanding and a carefully weighed, didactic approach to the Oral Law. As the Rambam himself states:

> I sought to compose a work which would include... the Torah's laws all in clear and concise terms, so that the entire Oral Law could be ordered in a person's mouth without questions or objections.

Accordingly, we can appreciate why the Book of Judges concludes this magnum opus. For:

a) it is only after all the laws are recorded that a judge can apply Torah Law in practice;

b) as stated in *Hilchot Mamrim* 1:1, "The Supreme *Sanhedrin* in Jerusalem are the essence of the Oral Law. They are the pillars of instruction from whom statutes and judgments issue forth for the entire Jewish people." Implied is that the judges are the repository of knowledge for the Oral Law and perhaps, more important, they are the medium throughout which the Oral Law is kept current. For they possess the authority to interpret the law and apply it to the circumstances we face in our day-to-day lives.

* * *

This volume focuses primarily on the explanation of the makeup of a court, the judicial process, and the laws pertaining to the qualification and examination of witnesses. It also includes a discussion of the judgment of those who rebel against the court's authority. As a corollary to the latter concepts, it also discusses the laws governing honoring one's parents. And as a corollary to the laws governing execution, it also discusses the laws concerning burial and mourning. It concludes with *Hilchot Melachim* which describes the laws pertaining to a Jewish monarch. More particularly, its final chapters focus on the ultimate monarch, *Mashiach*.

As explained in the introduction to that section, a Jewish king's function is to uphold the laws of the Torah and create a society centered around these laws. In this manner, he will create a culture that reflects God's desire for humanity. The consummate expression of a monarch's execution of this function - and thus the ultimate expression of God's intent - will be realized by *Mashiach*. For this reason, these are the concluding subjects of the Rambam's work.

In the many centuries since the Rambam completed the *Mishneh Torah*, his work has been debated and discussed, and thus, with regard to *halachah limaaseh*, Jewish law as it is actually applied, his text does not serve as a final authority. Nevertheless, the study of the *Mishneh Torah* still has much relevance for the average Jew, for it provides him with a comprehensive overview and a basic understanding of the fundamental halachic issues involved.

* * *

As were the other volumes in the Moznaim *Mishneh Torah* series, the composition of this text was a team effort, made possible by the combined efforts of many individuals. The full list of all those involved is too long to mention. At the very least, however, recognition must be granted to the following individuals:

Rabbi Moshe Weiner for checking the sources and the accuracy of the translation;

Rabbi Nosson Vogel for his editorial contributions;

Avraham Eisenbach, Dov Schwartz, Michah Witzel, and the entire staff of Moznaim publications for the layout and typography which greatly enhance the text;

Finally, my publisher, Rabbi Menachem Wagshall, whose cooperation, support and dedication to the spread of Torah has made working with him a pleasure.

* * *

The *Zohar* states: "The Holy One, blessed be He, looked into the Torah and created the world. A man looks into the Torah and maintains the world." The commentaries explain that a process of spiritual causation is implied. Through a person's study of a subject in the Torah, he evokes spiritual forces that will enable the subject of his study to become actual reality.

May our study of these laws help bring about the renewal of the *Sanhedrin* and then the ultimate redemption of our people with coming of *Mashiach* and the dawning of the age when "the occupation of the entire world will be solely to know God.... And 'the earth will be filled with the knowledge of God as the waters cover up the ocean bed.'"

Shvat 10, 5760 — *Rabbi Eliyahu Touger*
Jerusalem

"Open your mouth, judge righteously, and render justice for the poor and indigent" (Proverbs 31:9)

The Fourteenth Book
SEFER SHOFTIM
The Book of Judges

It contains five *halachot*. They are:
Hilchot Sanhedrin V'Haonshin Hamesurim Lahem - The Laws of the Courts and the Penalties Placed under their Jurisdiction
Hilchot Edut - The Laws of Witnesses
Hilchot Mamrim - The Laws of the Rebellious Ones
Hilchot Evel - The Laws of Mourning
Hilchot Melachim UMilchamotehem - The Laws of Kings and their Wars

פְּתַח פִּיךָ שְׁפָט צֶדֶק, וְדִין עָנִי וְאֶבְיוֹן:

סֵפֶר שׁוֹפְטִים

וְהוּא

סֵפֶר אַרְבָּעָה עָשָׂר

הִלְכוֹתָיו חָמֵשׁ. וְזֶהוּ סִדּוּרָן:

הִלְכוֹת סַנְהֶדְרִין וְהָעֳנָשִׁין הַמְּסוּרִין לָהֶם

הִלְכוֹת עֵדוּת

הִלְכוֹת מַמְרִים

הִלְכוֹת אֵבֶל

הִלְכוֹת מְלָכִים וּמִלְחֲמוֹתֵיהֶם

HILCHOT SANHEDRIN V'HAONSHIN HAMESURIM LAHEM

THE LAWS OF THE COURTS AND THE PENALTIES PLACED UNDER THEIR JURISDICTION

[These laws] contain 30 mitzvot: Ten positive commandments and twenty negative commandments. They are:
1. To appoint judges,
2. Not to appoint a judge who does not know the [proper] manner of judgment
3. To follow the majority if there is a difference of opinion among the judges
4. Not to issue a death sentence if there is a majority of only one condemning the defendant; rather, a majority of at least two is necessary,
5. For a judge who argued in favor of acquittal in a capital case not to argue for a conviction,
6. To execute by stoning [the condemned to death],
7. To execute by burning [the condemned to death],
8. To execute by decapitation,
9. To execute by strangulation,
10. To hang [the corpses of certain sinners who were executed],
11. To bury the executed person on the day of his execution,
12. Not to allow his corpse to remain unburied overnight,
13. Not to allow a sorcerer to live,
14. To [punish] a sinner with lashes,
15. Not to add blows when lashing a sinner,
16. Not to punish a person forced [to commit a sin],
17. Not to kill an innocent person based on an apparent conclusion,
18. Not to have mercy on a person who killed or injured a colleague,
19. Not to have mercy on a poor person in judgment,
20. Not to honor a man of stature in judgment,
21. Not to pervert judgment against a sinner even though he is [known to be] a transgressor,
22. Not to act deceitfully in judgment,
23. Not to pervert the justice due converts or orphans,
24. To render a righteous judgment,
25. For a Judge not to fear rendering [a just] judgment because of a powerful person,
26. Not to accept a bribe,
27. Not to curse the judges,
28. Not to accept a false report,
29. Not to curse the nasi,
30. Not to curse any other Jew of moral repute.

The explanation of these mitzvot is [found] in the coming chapters.

הִלְכוֹת סַנְהֶדְרִין וְהָעֳנָשִׁין הַמְּסוּרִין לָהֶם

יֵשׁ בִּכְלָלָן שְׁלֹשִׁים מִצְוֹת: עֶשֶׂר מִצְוֹת עֲשֵׂה, וְעֶשְׂרִים מִצְוֹת לֹא תַעֲשֶׂה, וְזֶה הוּא פְּרָטָן:

א) לְמַנּוֹת שׁוֹפְטִים.

ב) שֶׁלֹּא לְמַנּוֹת דַּיָּן שֶׁאֵינוֹ יוֹדֵעַ דֶּרֶךְ הַמִּשְׁפָּט.

ג) לִנְטוֹת אַחֲרֵי רַבִּים אִם נֶחְלְקוּ הַשּׁוֹפְטִים.

ד) שֶׁלֹּא לַהֲרֹג אִם רַבּוּ הַמְחַיְּבִין בְּאִישׁ אֶחָד, עַד שֶׁיִּהְיוּ יָתֵר שְׁנַיִם.

ה) שֶׁלֹּא יְלַמֵּד חוֹבָה מִי שֶׁלִּמֵּד זְכוּת בְּדִינֵי נְפָשׁוֹת.

ו) לַהֲרֹג בִּסְקִילָה.

ז) לַהֲרֹג בִּשְׂרֵפָה.

ח) לַהֲרֹג בְּסַיִף.

ט) לַהֲרֹג בְּחֶנֶק.

י) לִתְלוֹת.

יא) לִקְבֹּר הַנֶּהֱרָג בְּיוֹם הֲרִיגָתוֹ.

יב) שֶׁלֹּא תָּלִין נִבְלָתוֹ.

יג) שֶׁלֹּא לְהַחֲיוֹת מְכַשֵּׁף.

יד) לְהַלְקוֹת רָשָׁע.

טו) שֶׁלֹּא יוֹסִיף בְּהַכָּאַת הַלּוֹקֶה.

טז) שֶׁלֹּא לַעֲנֹשׁ אָנוּס.

יז) שֶׁלֹּא לַהֲרֹג דָּם נָקִי בְּאֹמֶד הַדַּעַת.

יח) שֶׁלֹּא לָחוּס עַל הוֹרֵג חֲבֵרוֹ אוֹ חוֹבֵל בּוֹ.

יט) שֶׁלֹּא לְרַחֵם אֶת הַדַּל בַּדִּין.

כ) שֶׁלֹּא לְהַדֵּר גָּדוֹל בַּדִּין.

כא) שֶׁלֹּא לְהַטּוֹת הַדִּין עַל בַּעֲלֵי עֲבֵרוֹת, אַף עַל פִּי שֶׁהוּא חוֹטֵא.

כב) שֶׁלֹּא לְעַוֵּת מִשְׁפָּט.

כג) שֶׁלֹּא לְהַטּוֹת מִשְׁפַּט גֵּר וְיָתוֹם.

כד) לִשְׁפֹּט בְּצֶדֶק.

כה) שֶׁלֹּא לִירֹא בַּדִּין מֵאִישׁ זְרוֹעַ.

כו) שֶׁלֹּא לִקַּח שֹׁחַד.

כז) שֶׁלֹּא לְקַלֵּל הַדַּיָּנִים.

כח) שֶׁלֹּא לִשָּׂא שֵׁמַע שָׁוְא.

כט) שֶׁלֹּא לְקַלֵּל הַנָּשִׂיא.

ל) שֶׁלֹּא לְקַלֵּל אָדָם מִשְּׁאָר בְּנֵי יִשְׂרָאֵל הַכְּשֵׁרִים.

וּבֵאוּר מִצְוֹת אֵלּוּ בִּפְרָקִים אֵלּוּ:

CHAPTER ONE

1. It is a positive Scriptural commandment[1] to appoint judges and enforcement officers in every city[2] and in every region,[3] as [Deuteronomy 16:18] states: "Appoint judges and enforcement officers in all your gates."

The term "Judges" refers to magistrates whose [attendance] is fixed in court, before whom the litigants appear. "Enforcement officers" refers to those equipped with a billet and a lash who stand before the judges and patrol the market places and the streets [to inspect] the stores and to regulate the prices and the measures.[4] They inflict corporal punishment on all offenders. Their deeds are controlled entirely by the judges.[5]

Whenever a person is seen perpetrating injustice, they should bring him to the court, where he will be judged according to his wickedness.

2. We are obligated to appoint courts in every region and in every city only in *Eretz Yisrael*. In the diaspora, by contrast, we are not obligated to appoint courts in every region.[6] [This is derived from the continuation of the above] verse: "Appoint... in all your gates which God your Lord is giving you for your tribes."

3. How many established courts[7] should there be among the Jewish people and how many judges should there be in each court?

1. *Sefer HaMitzvot* (positive commandment 176) and *Sefer HaChinuch* (mitzvah 491) count this as one of the 613 mitzvot of the Torah.
2. The Radbaz states that this mitzvah applies both in *Eretz Yisrael* and in the Diaspora. Even when our people live outside our native land, there is a Scriptural (not merely a Rabbinic) commandment to establish Torah authority for the Jewish community. The Ramban (see his commentary to Deuteronomy, ch. 16) maintains that the Rambam differs and asserts that the mitzvah applies only in *Eretz Yisrael*.

The *Tur* (*Choshen Mishpat* 1) and the Ramban (*ibid.*) state that this mitzvah applies only to judges who possess the *semichah* (ordination) described in Chapter 4. At present, although we carry out the charge of the judges of the previous generations and appoint courts to adjudicate certain legal complaints, the appointment of these courts is not within the scope of the Biblical commandment.
3. The *Kessef Mishneh* notes that *Sanhedrin* 16b mentions an obligation for every tribe to establish a court for itself and questions why the Rambam does not include this point. The *Chasdei David* in his commentary to *Sanhedrin* explains that this is the Rambam's intent with the words "in every region." For since judges will be appointed in every city in *Eretz Yisrael*, there seemingly is no need for there to be judges appointed for the region. What is meant by regional judges? Judges for each tribe. This conception appears to be reinforced by the Rambam's statements in Chapter 5, Halachah 1, which speaks of appointing courts for each tribe (*Lechem Mishneh*).

It would appear that these regional [or tribal] courts served as appeals courts for that region. Alternatively, they help clarify problems which the lower courts do not know how to solve.
4. To check the accuracy of the weights, the volume of the liquid measures, and the like. See *Hilchot Geneivah* 8:20.

פֶּרֶק רִאשׁוֹן

א מִצְוַת עֲשֵׂה שֶׁל תּוֹרָה לְמַנּוֹת שׁוֹפְטִים וְשׁוֹטְרִים בְּכָל מְדִינָה וּמְדִינָה וּבְכָל פֶּלֶךְ וָפֶלֶךְ. שֶׁנֶּאֱמַר: שֹׁפְטִים וְשֹׁטְרִים תִּתֶּן לְךָ בְּכָל שְׁעָרֶיךָ.

שׁוֹפְטִים – אֵלּוּ הַדַּיָּנִים הַקְּבוּעִין בְּבֵית דִּין, וּבַעֲלֵי דִינִין בָּאִים לִפְנֵיהֶם.

שׁוֹטְרִים – אֵלּוּ בַּעֲלֵי מַקֵּל וּרְצוּעָה, וְהֵם עוֹמְדִים לִפְנֵי הַדַּיָּנִין, הַמְסַבְּבִין בַּשְּׁוָקִים וּבָרְחוֹבוֹת וְעַל הַחֲנֻיּוֹת, לְתַקֵּן הַשְּׁעָרִים וְהַמִּדּוֹת וּלְהַכּוֹת כָּל מְעֻוָּת.

וְכָל מַעֲשֵׂיהֶם עַל פִּי הַדַּיָּנִים.

וְכֹל שֶׁיִּרְאוּ בּוֹ עִוּוּת דָּבָר – מְבִיאִין אוֹתוֹ לְבֵית דִּין, וְדָנִין אוֹתוֹ כְּפִי רִשְׁעוֹ.

ב אֵין אָנוּ חַיָּבִין לְהַעֲמִיד בָּתֵּי דִינִים בְּכָל פֶּלֶךְ וָפֶלֶךְ וּבְכָל עִיר וָעִיר אֶלָּא בְּאֶרֶץ יִשְׂרָאֵל בִּלְבַד; אֲבָל בְּחוּצָה לָאָרֶץ – אֵינָן חַיָּבִין לְהַעֲמִיד בֵּית דִּין בְּכָל פֶּלֶךְ וָפֶלֶךְ. שֶׁנֶּאֱמַר: תִּתֶּן לְךָ בְּכָל שְׁעָרֶיךָ אֲשֶׁר יְיָ אֱלֹהֶיךָ נוֹתֵן לְךָ לִשְׁבָטֶיךָ.

ג כַּמָּה בָּתֵּי דִינִין קְבוּעִין יִהְיוּ בְּיִשְׂרָאֵל? וְכַמָּה יִהְיֶה מִנְיָנָן?

5. With this statement, perhaps the Rambam is alluding to the fact that the appointment of the enforcement officers is not considered a separate mitzvah. Since they are merely the arm which apply the judges' decisions, their appointment is not considered as a different charge.

6. Even in the Diaspora, however, we are obligated to appoint judges in every city. From Numbers 35:29: "And these will be the statutes of judgment for you... in all of your settlements," *Makkot* 7a understands that we are obligated to operate courts in the Diaspora as well.

The commentaries have, nevertheless, noted that the Rambam's statements seem to be in direct contradiction to his source. For *Makkot, loc. cit.*, states that in the Diaspora, courts should be appointed in every region, but not in every city. *Chok UMishpat* reinforces this question, noting that with regard to establishing courts for gentiles, the Rambam states (*Hilchot Melachim* 9:14) that courts should be established "in every region."

In resolution, the *Lechem Mishneh* maintains that the text should be reversed to read as in *Makkot*, for one should first establish the minimal necessity, a regional court. The Radbaz maintains that the Rambam's conception is derived from the words "in all your settlements," i.e., wherever there is a Jewish community, there should be a Jewish court. In this manner, the Torah will govern the public and private matters of the Jewish people. If there would be only regional courts, the Torah's influence would not be felt as powerfully in every local community.

The Ramban (in his commentary to Deuteronomy *loc. cit.*) states, however, that there is no obligation to establish courts in the Diaspora at all. Instead, the disputes should be brought to the courts of *Eretz Yisrael*. He maintains that the Rambam would also accept this ruling.

7. I.e., courts that hold regular sessions and whose existence is mandated by the principle stated in the previous halachot. At any given time, two litigants may establish an *ad hoc* court.

First, a supreme court is established in the Temple.[8] This is called the Great *Sanhedrin*.[9] It was composed of 71 judges. [This is derived from Numbers 11:16 which] states: "Gather for Me seventy men from the elders of Israel." And Moses presided over them, as [the verse continues]: "And they shall stand there with you." Thus there are 71.

The one who possesses the most knowledge is placed at their head. He acts as the *Rosh Yeshivah*,[10] and he is called the *nasi*[11] by the Sages in all sources. He assumes the position of Moses our teacher.

The greatest among the [remaining] 70 is appointed as an assistant to the head. He sits at his right and is called *av beit din*.[12] The remaining judges of the 70 sit before them and are seated according to their age and according to their stature.[13] Whoever possesses greater wisdom than his colleague is seated closer than his colleagues to the *nasi* on his left.[14] [The members of the *Sanhedrin*] sit in a semi-circle[15] so that the *nasi* and the *av beit din* can see all of them.

In addition, two courts of 23 judges each are appointed. One [holds sessions] at the entrance to the Temple courtyard.[16] and the other at the entrance to the Temple Mount.[17]

[In addition,] we appoint a minor *Sanhedrin* in every city in Israel in which their are 120[18] or more [adult males].[19] They hold court at the entrance to the city, as [implied by Amos 5:15]: "And you shall establish judgment in your gates." How many judges should be in such a court? 23.[20] The one who possesses the greatest wisdom is the chief justice and the remainder sit in a semi-circle so that the chief justice can see all of them.

4. In a city where there are less than 120 [adult males], we appoint a court of three judges.[21] For a court should never be less than three.[22] In that way, there will be a majority and a minority[23] if there is a difference of opinion in any particular judgment.

8. The *Sanhedrin* would hold sessions in the Chamber of Hewn Stone, inside Temple courtyard, one portion was consecrated and one was not. The *Sanhedrin* would sit in the outer portion. See the notes to Chapter 14, Halachah 12.

9. The word *Sanhedrin* is a Greek term meaning "council" or "assembly."

10. Literally, "the head of the academy."

11. The term *nasi* literally means "upraised one," and is also translated as "prince."

12. Literally, "the father of the court."

13. The commentaries have questioned the Rambam's intent, for if they are seated according to their age, how can they be seated according to their wisdom? The *Kessef Mishneh* explains that age was the determining factor, but if they were equal in age, wisdom determined priority. Rav Kappach, based on his Yemenite manuscripts of the *Mishneh Torah* explains that there is a printing error in the text. Instead of *lifneihem kifei shanim*, "before them, according to their years," but rather *lifnei shneihem*, "in front of both of them." According to this version, wisdom is the sole determining factor. Age is not significant. This approach is borne out by the continuation of the Rambam's wording: "Whoever possesses greater wisdom than his colleague..." and by the wording he employs in Halachah 7.

14. I.e., next to the *nasi*, to his left, in the center of the semi-circle (Radbaz).

קוֹבְעִין בַּתְּחִלָּה בֵּית דִּין הַגָּדוֹל בַּמִּקְדָּשׁ, וְהוּא הַנִּקְרָא סַנְהֶדְרֵי גְדוֹלָה. וּמִנְיָנָם שִׁבְעִים וְאֶחָד. שֶׁנֶּאֱמַר: אֶסְפָה לִּי שִׁבְעִים אִישׁ מִזִּקְנֵי יִשְׂרָאֵל; וּמֹשֶׁה עַל גַּבֵּיהֶן, שֶׁנֶּאֱמַר: וְהִתְיַצְּבוּ שָׁם עִמָּךְ – הֲרֵי שִׁבְעִים וְאֶחָד. הַגָּדוֹל בְּחָכְמָה שֶׁבְּכֻלָּן – מוֹשִׁיבִין אוֹתוֹ רֹאשׁ עֲלֵיהֶן, וְהוּא רֹאשׁ הַיְשִׁיבָה. וְהוּא שֶׁקּוֹרִין אוֹתוֹ הַחֲכָמִים נָשִׂיא בְּכָל מָקוֹם, וְהוּא הָעוֹמֵד תַּחַת מֹשֶׁה רַבֵּנוּ. וּמוֹשִׁיבִין הַגָּדוֹל שֶׁבַּשִּׁבְעִים מִשְׁנֶה לָרֹאשׁ, וְיוֹשֵׁב מִימִינוֹ. וְהוּא הַנִּקְרָא אַב בֵּית דִּין. וּשְׁאָר הַשִּׁבְעִים יוֹשְׁבִין לְפָנָיו כְּפִי שְׁנֵיהֶם וּכְפִי מַעֲלָתָם. כָּל הַגָּדוֹל מֵחֲבֵרוֹ בְּחָכְמָה – יִהְיֶה קָרוֹב לַנָּשִׂיא מִשְּׂמֹאלוֹ יוֹתֵר מֵחֲבֵרוֹ. וְהֵם יוֹשְׁבִין כְּמוֹ חֲצִי גֹּרֶן בְּעִגּוּל, כְּדֵי שֶׁיִּהְיֶה הַנָּשִׂיא עִם אַב בֵּית דִּין רוֹאִין כֻּלָּן.

וְעוֹד מַעֲמִידִין שְׁנֵי בָּתֵּי דִינִין שֶׁל עֶשְׂרִים וּשְׁלֹשָׁה עֶשְׂרִים וּשְׁלֹשָׁה: אֶחָד עַל פֶּתַח הָעֲזָרָה, וְאֶחָד עַל פֶּתַח הַר הַבַּיִת. וּמַעֲמִידִין בְּכָל עִיר וָעִיר מִיִּשְׂרָאֵל, שֶׁיֵּשׁ בָּהּ מֵאָה וְעֶשְׂרִים אוֹ יוֹתֵר, סַנְהֶדְרֵי קְטַנָּה. וְיוֹשֶׁבֶת בְּשַׁעַר הָעִיר, שֶׁנֶּאֱמַר: וְהַצִּיגוּ בַשַּׁעַר מִשְׁפָּט. וְכַמָּה יִהְיֶה מִנְיָנָם? עֶשְׂרִים וּשְׁלֹשָׁה דַיָּנִים. וְהַגָּדוֹל בְּחָכְמָה שֶׁבְּכֻלָּן רֹאשׁ עֲלֵיהֶן. וְהַשְּׁאָר יוֹשְׁבִין בְּעִגּוּל כְּמוֹ חֲצִי גֹּרֶן, כְּדֵי שֶׁיְּהֵא הָרֹאשׁ רוֹאֶה אֶת כֻּלָּן.

ד עִיר שֶׁאֵין בָּהּ מֵאָה וְעֶשְׂרִים – מַעֲמִידִין בָּהּ שְׁלֹשָׁה דַיָּנִים. שֶׁאֵין בֵּית דִּין פָּחוֹת מִשְּׁלֹשָׁה, כְּדֵי שֶׁיְּהֵא בָּהֶן רַב וּמְעוּט, אִם הָיְתָה בֵּינֵיהֶן מַחֲלֹקֶת בְּדִין מִן הַדִּינִין.

A Depiction of the Supreme Sanhedrin

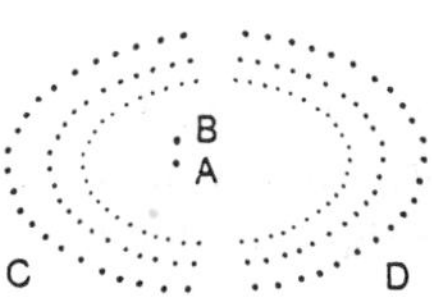

A - The seat of the Nasi
B - The seat of the Av Beis Din
C - 3 rows of 23 seats for the judges
D - 3 rows of 23 seats for students

15. *Sanhedrin* 37a interprets Song of Songs 7:3: "Your navel is like a moon-shaped basin" as a reference to this shape. The verse is interpreted as an allusion to the *Sanhedrin* who sit "at the center of the world," i.e., in the Temple. They should be seated in a semi-circle, like the crescent of the moon.

A Depiction of the Temple and its Courtyards

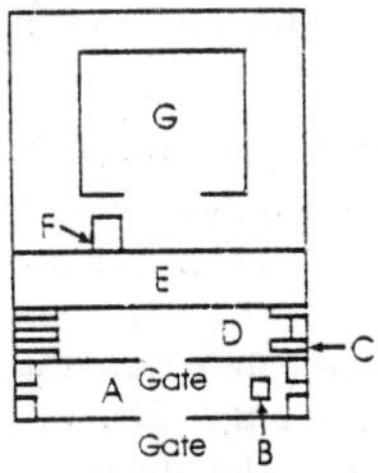

A - The Women's Courtyard
B - The Small Sanhedrin
C - The Chamber of Hewn Stone
D - The Courtyard of the Israelites
E - The Courtyard of the Priests
F - The Altar
G - The Sanctuary

16. I.e., within the Women's Courtyard, before the Nikanor Gates that lead to the Temple Courtyard.

17. Near the entrance to the Chuldah gates through which most of the visitors to the Temple entered.

18. See Halachah 10.

19. For as stated in Halachah 1, the commandment is to appoint judges in every city.

20. See Chapter 3, Halachah 5, which explains the derivation of this number of judges.

21. For any city, regardless of how small it is should have a Torah authority to regulate the social interaction among its inhabitants (*Kessef Mishneh*). According to *Sefer HaMitzvot, loc. cit.*, this obligation is also included in the mitzvah to appoint judges.

22. See Chapter 5, Halachah 18, and notes.

23. Instead of there being an even number of judges (see *Sanhedrin* 3b).

5. When a city does not possess two sages of great knowledge - one fit to teach and issue rulings with regard to the entire Torah and one who knows how to listen [diligently] and knows how to raise questions and arrive at solutions[24] - a court should not be appointed for it even though thousands of Jews live there.[25]

6. When a court has two [judges of this caliber]: one capable of listening [with regard to the entire Torah], and one capable of expounding, it is a valid court.[26] If there are three, it is of intermediate esteem. If [the court] possess four judges who can expound [upon the entire Torah], it is a wise court.

7. We seat three rows of Torah scholars before every minor *Sanhedrin.* In each row, there are 23 men.[27] The first row is seated next to the *Sanhedrin,* the second row below it, and the third row below it. In each row, the scholars are seated in the order of their level of wisdom.[28]

8. If there is a difference of opinion among the judges and it is necessary to grant *semichah* to one student to add to the number,[29] the scholar of the greatest stature from the first row is granted *semichah.* The first scholar in the second row advances and sits in the first row[30] to make up for the deficiency, and the first scholar in the third row advances and sits in the second row to make up for the deficiency. One of the remaining people is chosen and is seated in the third row. Similarly, if they must grant *semichah* to a second or third judge, they follow this pattern.

9. Whenever a *Sanhedrin* functions, two legal scribes should stand before them: one at the right and one at the left. One writes the arguments of those who seek to hold the defendant liable, and the other writes the arguments of those who seek to exonerate him.[31]

10. Why is a *Sanhedrin* appointed only in a city with a population of 120? So that there will be a *Sanhedrin* of 23 judges, three rows of 23 students each,

In his Commentary to the Mishnah (*Sanhedrin* 1:1), the Rambam describes the derivation of the need for three judges in a court as follows. Exodus 22:8 states that "the words of both of them should be brought to the judges." Since the word for judges, *elohim* is written in the plural, we derive that there must be at least two judges. And to prevent the court from being evenly balanced, we add a third judge.

24. The other judges must also be wise men of stature. It is not necessary, however, that their knowledge encompass the entire Torah. This explanation helps resolve the difficulty raised by Rav Moshe Cohen and others who question the Rambam's statements as follows: If the other judges are not knowledgeable in the Torah, of what benefit is their presence on the court?

25. The Rambam's statements in this and the following halachah are based on *Sanhedrin* 17b. It must be emphasized that Rashi and others interpret that passage differently.

26. I.e., after the fact, it is acceptable.

27. From Rashi, *Sanhedrin* 37a, it appears that the reason this number of scholars was chosen was because - as stated in the following halachah - there are times when we add

ה כָּל עִיר שֶׁאֵין בָּהּ שְׁנֵי חֲכָמִים גְּדוֹלִים, אֶחָד רָאוּי לְלַמֵּד וּלְהוֹרוֹת בְּכָל הַתּוֹרָה כֻּלָּהּ, וְאֶחָד יוֹדֵעַ לִשְׁמֹעַ וְיוֹדֵעַ לִשְׁאֹל וּלְהָשִׁיב – אֵין מוֹשִׁיבִין בָּהּ סַנְהֶדְרִין, אַף עַל פִּי שֶׁיֵּשׁ בָּהּ אֲלָפִים מִיִּשְׂרָאֵל.

ו סַנְהֶדְרִין שֶׁיֵּשׁ בָּהּ שְׁנַיִם אֵלּוּ, אֶחָד רָאוּי לִשְׁמֹעַ וְאֶחָד רָאוּי לְדַבֵּר – הֲרֵי זוֹ סַנְהֶדְרִין. הָיוּ בָּהּ שְׁלֹשָׁה – הֲרֵי זוֹ בֵּינוֹנִית. הָיוּ בָּהּ אַרְבָּעָה יוֹדְעִים לְדַבֵּר – הֲרֵי זוֹ סַנְהֶדְרֵי חָכְמָה.

ז כָּל סַנְהֶדְרֵי קְטַנָּה מוֹשִׁיבִין לִפְנֵיהֶן שָׁלֹשׁ שׁוּרוֹת שֶׁל תַּלְמִידֵי חֲכָמִים, בְּכָל שׁוּרָה וְשׁוּרָה עֶשְׂרִים וּשְׁלֹשָׁה אִישׁ. שׁוּרָה רִאשׁוֹנָה קְרוֹבָה לַסַּנְהֶדְרִין, וְשׁוּרָה שְׁנִיָּה לְמַטָּה הֵימֶנָּה, וּשְׁלִישִׁית לְמַטָּה הֵימֶנָּה. וְכָל שׁוּרָה וְשׁוּרָה יוֹשְׁבִין בָּהּ לְפִי מַעֲלָתָן בְּחָכְמָה.

ח אִם נֶחְלְקוּ הַסַּנְהֶדְרִין, וְהֻצְרְכוּ לִסְמֹךְ אֶחָד לְהוֹסִיף עַל מִנְיָנָן – סוֹמְכִין מִן הָרִאשׁוֹנָה גָּדוֹל שֶׁבָּהּ; וְהָרִאשׁוֹן שֶׁבְּשׁוּרָה שְׁנִיָּה בָּא וְיוֹשֵׁב בְּסוֹף שׁוּרָה הָרִאשׁוֹנָה, כְּדֵי לְמַלֹּאת חֶסְרוֹנָהּ,
וְהָרִאשׁוֹן שֶׁבַּשְּׁלִישִׁית בָּא וְיוֹשֵׁב בְּסוֹף שׁוּרָה שְׁנִיָּה;
וּבוֹרְרִין לָהֶן אֶחָד מִשְּׁאָר הַקָּהָל, וּמוֹשִׁיבִין אוֹתוֹ בְּסוֹף שׁוּרָה שְׁלִישִׁית.
וְכֵן אִם צָרְכוּ לִסְמֹךְ שֵׁנִי אוֹ שְׁלִישִׁי – עַל הַסֵּדֶר הַזֶּה הֵם עוֹשִׂים.

ט כָּל מָקוֹם שֶׁיֵּשׁ בּוֹ סַנְהֶדְרִין, יִהְיוּ שָׁם שְׁנֵי סוֹפְרֵי דַיָּנִים עוֹמְדִין לִפְנֵיהֶם, אֶחָד מִן הַיָּמִין וְאֶחָד מִן הַשְּׂמֹאל.
אֶחָד כּוֹתֵב דִּבְרֵי הַמְחַיְּבִין, וְאֶחָד כּוֹתֵב דִּבְרֵי הַמְזַכִּים.

י וְלָמָּה אֵין סַנְהֶדְרִין אֶלָּא בְּעִיר שֶׁיֵּשׁ בָּהּ מֵאָה וְעֶשְׂרִים?
כְּדֵי שֶׁיִּהְיֶה מֵהֶן סַנְהֶדְרִין שֶׁל עֶשְׂרִים וּשְׁלֹשָׁה, וְשָׁלֹשׁ שׁוּרוֹת שֶׁל עֶשְׂרִים וּשְׁלֹשָׁה,

judges to the court. Now the most that are added are 48, for a court is never larger than 71. Nevertheless, it is not appropriate for the rows of scholars to be larger or smaller than the rows of judges. Hence there are three rows of scholars.

28. Each one had a designated place as stated in *Sanhedrin, loc. cit.*.

29. See Chapter 9, Halachah 2, which explains a situation where judges are added to a minor *Sanhedrin*. See also Chapter 8, Halachah 2. In those sources, however, the Rambam speaks of adding two judges, not only one.

See also the notes to Chapter 2, Halachah 8, which note the apparent contradiction between these halachot and the explanation why the Rambam's statements in this halachah apply only when there is a difference of opinion within the court, and not when one of the members of the court dies.

30. We tell him "It is preferable to be a tail to lions than a head to foxes" (*Sanhedrin, loc. cit.*).

31. See Chapter 12, Halachah 3, which describes the function of these scribes.

ten sitters in the synagogue,[32] two scribes,[33] two court officers,[34] two litigants, two witnesses,[35] two witnesses who seek to invalidate the testimony of the witnesses,[36] two witnesses who seek to invalidate the testimony of the second pair of witnesses and restore the validity of the first, two charity collectors, and a third to distribute these collections,[37] a doctor who is a bloodletter,[38] a scribe,[39] and a teacher for young children.[40] This reaches a total of 120.

CHAPTER TWO

1. We appoint to a *Sanhedrin* - both to the Supreme *Sanhedrin* and to a minor *Sanhedrin* - only men of wisdom and understanding,[1] of unique distinction in their knowledge of the Torah and who possess a broad intellectual potential. [They should also] have some knowledge concerning other intellectual disciplines, [2] e.g., medicine,[3] mathematics, the fixation of the calendar, astronomy, astrology, and [also] the practices of fortune-telling,[4] magic,[5] sorcery,[6] and the hollow teachings of idolatry, so that they will know how to judge them.[7]

We appoint to the *Sanhedrin* only priests, Levites, and Israelites of lineage of fine repute who can marry into the priesthood.[8] [This is derived from Number 11:16]: "And they shall stand there with you." [Implied is that] they should resemble you, [Moses] in wisdom, the fear [of heaven], and in lineage.[9]

32. The Hebrew term *batlanim* literally means "idle ones." These individuals are referred to with this term, because - as the Rambam's Commentary to the Mishnah (*Megilah* 1:3) states - these have "no occupation except communal affairs, Torah study, and [caring] diligently for the synagogue." In *Hilchot Megilah* 1:8, the Rambam refers to them as "ten people who have no other occupation, but instead attend the synagogue in a fixed manner, concerning themselves with communal affairs."
33. As mentioned in the previous halachah.
34. Who are responsible for giving subpoenas to litigants and administering lashes if necessary.
35. For the testimony of one witness is not significant.
36. See *Hilchot Edut*, chs. 18-19, which discuss the invalidation of testimony through *hazamah*, the term used by the Rambam.

The *Kessef Mishneh* explains that it is necessary to have people in the city to serve in this capacity. Otherwise, witnesses will not be afraid to lie. Similarly, if there are no witnesses to disqualify this second pair, they will not be afraid to lie.
37. For charity should be collected by a minimum of two people and a third should help in its distribution (*Hilchot Matanot Aniyim* 9:5).
38. See *Hilchot De'ot* 4:23 which appears to view the doctor and the bloodletter as different from each other. It is not, however, necessary to say there is a contradiction between the two sources. Here the Rambam is counting heads, and the doctor and the bloodletter could be the same person. In *Hilchot De'ot*, he is speaking about functions and the functions performed by the two are distinct (*Lechem Mishneh, Hilchot De'ot*).
39. Not a court scribe, but one who writes documents for the community (Radbaz).
40. See *Hilchot Talmud Torah* 2:1 which states: "When a city does not have children who study Torah, the city's populace should be placed under a ban of ostracism until they employ teachers. If they do not employ teachers, the city deserves to be destroyed."

וַעֲשָׂרָה בַּטְלָנִין שֶׁל בֵּית הַכְּנֶסֶת, וּשְׁנֵי סוֹפְרִים, וּשְׁנֵי חַזָּנִים, וּשְׁנֵי בַּעֲלֵי דִינִין, וּשְׁנֵי עֵדִים, וּשְׁנֵי זוֹמְמִין, וּשְׁנֵי זוֹמְמֵי זוֹמְמִין, וּשְׁנֵי גַבָּאֵי צְדָקָה, וְעוֹד אֶחָד כְּדֵי שֶׁיִּהְיוּ שְׁלֹשָׁה לְחַלֵּק צְדָקָה, וְרוֹפֵא אֻמָּן, וְלַבְלָר, וּמְלַמֵּד תִּינוֹקוֹת. הֲרֵי מֵאָה וְעֶשְׂרִים.

פֶּרֶק שֵׁנִי

א אֵין מַעֲמִידִין בְּסַנְהֶדְרִין, בֵּין בִּגְדוֹלָה בֵּין בִּקְטַנָּה, אֶלָּא אֲנָשִׁים חֲכָמִים וּנְבוֹנִים, מֻפְלָגִין בְּחָכְמַת הַתּוֹרָה, בַּעֲלֵי דֵעָה מְרֻבָּה, יוֹדְעִים קְצָת מִשְּׁאָר חָכְמוֹת, כְּגוֹן רְפוּאוֹת וְחֶשְׁבּוֹן וּתְקוּפוֹת וּמַזָּלוֹת וְאִצְטַגְנִינוּת וְדַרְכֵי הַמְעוֹנְנִים וְהַקּוֹסְמִים וְהַמְכַשְּׁפִים וְהַבְלֵי עֲבוֹדָה זָרָה וְכַיּוֹצֵא בָּאֵלּוּ, כְּדֵי שֶׁיִּהְיוּ יוֹדְעִים לָדוּן אוֹתָם.

וְאֵין מַעֲמִידִין בְּסַנְהֶדְרִין אֶלָּא כֹּהֲנִים לְוִיִּם וְיִשְׂרְאֵלִים הַמְיֻחָסִים הָרְאוּיִים לְהַשִּׂיא לִכְהֻנָּה.

שֶׁנֶּאֱמַר: וְהִתְיַצְּבוּ שָׁם עִמָּךְ – בְּדוֹמִין לְךָ בְּחָכְמָה וּבְיִרְאָה וּבְיַחַס.

1. Cf. Deuteronomy 1:13. Commenting on that verse, the *Sifri* explains that the term "men of understanding" refers to persons who have the ability to derive new and original concepts from those already taught.
2. For familiarity with these other disciplines of knowledge is necessary in order to deliver certain Torah rulings. For example, medical knowledge is required to know whether a sick person may eat on Yom Kippur or which practices may be performed in violation of the Sabbath laws. The laws of astronomy are necessary to calculate the fixation of the calendar (*Merkevat HaMishneh* in resolution to the question asked by Rav Moshe Cohen, as cited in the *Kessef Mishneh*).
3. Among other reasons, medical knowledge is also important to the judges, because it is their responsibility to evaluate the number of lashes a convicted person can bear.
4. See *Hilchot Avodat Kochavim* 11:8-9.
5. See *ibid.*:6-7.
6. See *ibid.*:15. See also the Rambam's statements (*ibid.*:16):

> All of the above matters (fortune-telling, witchcraft, and the like) are falsehood and lies which the original idolaters deceived the gentile nations in order to lead them after them....
>
> Whoever believes in [occult arts] of this nature and.... thinks that they are true and words of wisdom, but are forbidden by the Torah, is foolish and feebleminded....
>
> The masters of wisdom... know... that all these crafts which the Torah forbade are not reflections of wisdom, but rather emptiness and vanity which attracted the feebleminded....

7. I.e., since cases involving such matters may be brought to the court, the court must know some of the particulars concerning these rites, so they can determine whether the person worshipped a false deity in a forbidden manner or not (Rabbenu Nissim).
8. Implied is that for four generations, we know that the person's lineage is acceptable.
9. The *Kessef Mishneh* notes that *Sanhedrin* 36b offers this prooftext, but then rejects it, because of a question and then offers another prooftext. The *Kessef Mishneh* explains that

2. It is a mitzvah for there to be priests and Levites in the Supreme *Sanhedrin*, as [Deuteronomy 17:9] states: "And you shall come to the priests and to the Levites. If [appropriate ones] are not found, it is permissible for all [the judges] to be Israelites.[10]

3. We should not appoint to a *Sanhedrin* a man of very old age[11] or one who does not possess male physical attributes,[12] for they possess [the trait of] cruelty,[13] nor a man who is childless, so that [the judges] should be merciful.

4. A king of Israel[14] may not be included in the *Sanhedrin*, for we are forbidden to disagree with him and repudiate his words.[15] The High Priest, by contrast, may be included in the *Sanhedrin*[16] if his knowledge makes him fitting.[17]

5. Although the kings of the House of David may not be included in the *Sanhedrin*,[18] they may sit in judgment over the people.[19] Conversely, they may be called to judgment if a person has a complaint against them.[20] The Kings of Israel, by contrast, may not serve as judges, nor may they be called to judgment. [The rationale is that] they do not humble themselves before the words of the Torah,[21] and [letting them serve as a judge or issuing a judgment against them] may lead to disaster.[22]

the Rambam maintains that the question asked by the Talmud stemmed from a minority opinion and that the prooftext originally suggested is acceptable to the majority view.
10. The *Sifri* to the above verse notes that the verse continues "to the judge," implying the court is acceptable even if there are no priests and Levites fit to sit on it.
11. For such a person has already forgotten the difficulty and trials of raising children (Rashi, *Sanhedrin* 36b). The Meiri states that this refers to a man who is past the age when he is capable of fathering children.

See the Responsa of the Rashba (Vol. VI, Responsum 191) which states that even if a person had already served in the *Sanhedrin*, when he reaches a very old age, he should be removed from his position. The *K'nesset HaGedolah* in his gloss to *Hilchot Sanhedrin* maintains that the Rambam does not follow this approach and instead maintains that a judge who has been serving on the *Sanhedrin* should be allowed to continue in that capacity even if he becomes old or loses his male qualities.
12. And thus will never have fathered children.
13. Note the exceptions mentioned in Chapter 11, Halachah 5.
14. This refers both to the kings of the ten tribes and the kings of Judah.
15. Thus if the king would condemn a person, the court would not be able to vindicate him (*Sanhedrin* 18b).
16. The Jerusalem Talmud (*Sanhedrin* 1:2) interprets the description of the exile and execution of Sariah, the High Priest (Jeremiah 52:24) as an indication that he was a member of the *Sanhedrin* at the time the First Temple was destroyed by the Babylonians. Similarly, Ezra the scribe and Shimon the Just were High Priests and also served as the heads of the *Sanhedrin.*
17. I.e., in the Second Temple period, the office of the High Priesthood was sold by the Romans and not all of the purchasers were paradigms of wisdom and observance.
18. As stated in the previous halachah.

ב וּמִצְוָה לִהְיוֹת בְּסַנְהֶדְרִין גְּדוֹלָה כֹּהֲנִים וּלְוִיִּם, שֶׁנֶּאֱמַר: וּבָאתָ אֶל הַכֹּהֲנִים הַלְוִיִּם. וְאִם לֹא מָצְאוּ, אֲפִלּוּ הָיוּ כֻּלָּם יִשְׂרְאֵלִים - הֲרֵי זֶה מֻתָּר.

ג אֵין מַעֲמִידִין בְּכָל הַסַּנְהֶדְרִין לֹא זָקֵן מֻפְלָג בַּשָּׁנִים וְלֹא סָרִיס, מִפְּנֵי שֶׁיֵּשׁ בָּהֶן אַכְזָרִיּוּת. וְלֹא מִי שֶׁאֵין לוֹ בָּנִים, כְּדֵי שֶׁיְּהֵא רַחֲמָן.

ד וְאֵין מוֹשִׁיבִין מֶלֶךְ יִשְׂרָאֵל בְּסַנְהֶדְרִין, שֶׁאָסוּר לַחֲלֹק עָלָיו וְלַמְרוֹת אֶת דְּבָרוֹ. אֲבָל מוֹשִׁיבִין כֹּהֵן גָּדוֹל, אִם הָיָה רָאוּי בְּחָכְמָה.

ה מַלְכֵי בֵּית דָּוִד, אַף עַל פִּי שֶׁאֵין מוֹשִׁיבִין אוֹתָם בְּסַנְהֶדְרִין - יוֹשְׁבִין וְדָנִים הֵם אֶת הָעָם. וְדָנִים אוֹתָם, אִם יֵשׁ עֲלֵיהֶן דִּין. אֲבָל מַלְכֵי יִשְׂרָאֵל - אֵין דָּנִין וְאֵין דָּנִין אוֹתָם; לְפִי שֶׁאֵין נִכְנָעִים לְדִבְרֵי תּוֹרָה, שֶׁמָּא תָּבוֹא מֵהֶן תְּקָלָה.

19. See *Berachot* 4a where King David is praised for involving himself in the details of halachic judgments for the sake of his people. Similarly, King Solomon is renowned for his wisdom in adjudicating the dispute of the two harlots who came to him with one baby (I Kings, ch. 3). *Sanhedrin* 19a derives this concept based on Jeremiah 21:12 which declares: "House of David... execute judgment in the morning."

20. *Sanhedrin, ibid.*, derives this from our Sages' charge: "Correct yourself and afterwards correct others." Were the kings themselves not accountable to the scrutiny of a court of law, they would have no right to judge others.

21. The term "King of Israel" refers to the kings of the Ten Tribes. As reflected in the narratives of the Book of Kings, by and large, they were neither righteous nor God-fearing.

22. *Sanhedrin, ibid.*, states that this law was enacted because of the conduct of Yannai, one of the later Hasmonean kings. One of Yannai's servants slew another person. The Sages summoned Yannai to give testimony at his trial. Yannai complied with their request and appeared in court. He, however, seated himself before the judges.

Shimon ben Shetach, the presiding judge ordered Yannai to stand. "Don't think of yourself as standing before us," he told him. "Think of yourself as standing before God."

Yannai responded: "What do your colleagues say? I will follow their directives and not yours."

He turned to the other judges to see their reaction. They all lowered their heads, unwillingly to challenge the king. When Shimon ben Shetach saw this, he declared: "You are all concerned with your own thoughts. May the Master of thought repay you." At that moment, all of them died. After this event, our Sages declared: "A king does not judge, nor is he judged."

There is, however, a slight difficulty with the Rambam's wording. The expression, "the kings of Israel," refers to the kings of the Ten Tribes. They lived centuries before Yannai. Why were they mentioned in our Sages' decree? Also, the question from which dynasty the king came is seemingly insignificant. What is important is whether or not he is righteous.

The *Kessef Mishneh* (in his gloss to *Hilchot Melachim* 3:7) explains the Rambam's intent as follows: The kings of Israel were not automatically disqualified from rendering judgment. If, however, an incident similar to that involving Yannai occurred, the Sages

6. Just as the [judges of] a court must be on the highest level of righteousness; so, too, must they be unsullied by any physical blemishes.[23]

An effort should be made[24] that they all be white-haired,[25] of impressive height, and of dignified appearance,[26] men who understand whispered matters,[27] who understand many different languages[28] so that the *Sanhedrin* will not need to hear [testimony] from an interpreter.

7. We are not particular [to demand] that [a judge for] a court of three possess all these qualities. He must, however, possess seven attributes:[29] wisdom, humility, the fear [of God], a loathing for money, a love for truth; he must be a person who is beloved by people at large, and must have a good reputation.

All of these qualities are mentioned explicitly in the Torah. [When relating Moses' statements concerning the appointment of judges, Deuteronomy 1:13] mentions: "Men of wisdom and understanding." This refers to wisdom.

[The verse continues:] "Beloved[30] by your tribes." This refers to those who are appreciated by people at large. What will make them beloved by people? Conducting themselves with a favorable eye and a humble spirit, being good company, and speaking and conducting their business with people gently.[31]

[When relating Jethro's advice to Moses to appoint judges, Exodus 18:21] speaks of "men of power." [This refers to people who] are mighty in their observance of the mitzvot, who are very demanding of themselves and who overcome their evil inclination until they possess no unfavorable qualities and no trace of an unpleasant reputation; even during their early manhood, they were spoken of highly.[32] The phrase "men of power" also implies that they should have a courageous heart to save an oppressed person from the one oppressing him, as [Exodus 2:17] states: "And Moses arose and delivered them."[33]

had the right to disqualify him. In contrast, since the above-mentioned verse from Jeremiah specifically associates the House of David with judgment, even in the event of such a tragedy, they were not disqualified.

Chok UMishpat questions why the Rambam mentions this law. The kings of Israel are merely historical figures and the ultimate king, *Mashiach*, will be from the House of David and will be righteous. That text explains that it refers to a situation when, as in the instance of Bar Kochba, the Jewish people appointed a king over themselves. Such a monarch is bound by these laws.

23. *Sanhedrin* 36b cites as an allusion, Song of Songs 4:7: "You are perfectly beautiful, my beloved, there is no blemish upon you."

24. The implication is that these qualities are desirable, but that if a qualified judge does not possess them, he may fill a vacancy on the *Sanhedrin* (*Kessef Mishneh*).

25. Though not of extreme old age, as stated in Halachah 3.

26. So that the litigants and the witnesses will be in awe of them (Rashi, *Sanhedrin* 17a).

27. The Rambam's words are borrowed from Isaiah 3:3. *Chagigah* 14a interprets the term as referring to a person who can understand the words of the Torah which are communicated in whispers. From the statements of *Chagigah* 13a, it would appear that this refers to the Torah's mystic secrets that should be communicated only in private. See also the Guide to the Perplexed, Vol. 1, ch. 34.

ו כְּשֵׁם שֶׁבֵּית דִּין מְנֻקִּין בְּצֶדֶק, כָּךְ צְרִיכִין לִהְיוֹת מְנֻקִּין מִכָּל מוּמֵי הַגּוּף. וְצָרִיךְ לְהִשְׁתַּדֵּל וְלִבְדֹּק וּלְחַפֵּשׂ, שֶׁיִּהְיוּ כֻּלָּן בַּעֲלֵי שֵׂיבָה, בַּעֲלֵי קוֹמָה, בַּעֲלֵי מַרְאֶה, נְבוֹנֵי לַחַשׁ, וְשֶׁיֵּדְעוּ בְּרֹב הַלְּשׁוֹנוֹת, כְּדֵי שֶׁלֹּא תְּהֵא סַנְהֶדְרִין שׁוֹמַעַת מִפִּי הַתֻּרְגְּמָן.

ז בֵּית דִּין שֶׁל שְׁלֹשָׁה, אַף עַל פִּי שֶׁאֵין מְדַקְדְּקִין בָּהֶן בְּכָל אֵלּוּ הַדְּבָרִים – צָרִיךְ שֶׁיְּהֵא בְּכָל אֶחָד מֵהֶן שִׁבְעָה דְּבָרִים. וְאֵלּוּ הֵן: חָכְמָה, וַעֲנָוָה, וְיִרְאָה, וְשִׂנְאַת מָמוֹן, וְאַהֲבַת הָאֱמֶת, וְאַהֲבַת הַבְּרִיּוֹת לָהֶן, וּבַעֲלֵי שֵׁם טוֹב. וְכָל אֵלּוּ הַדְּבָרִים מְפֹרָשִׁין הֵן בַּתּוֹרָה. הֲרֵי הוּא אוֹמֵר: אֲנָשִׁים חֲכָמִים וּנְבֹנִים – הֲרֵי בַּעֲלֵי חָכְמָה אָמוּר. וִידֻעִים לְשִׁבְטֵיכֶם – אֵלּוּ שֶׁרוּחַ הַבְּרִיּוֹת נוֹחָה מֵהֶם. וּבַמֶּה יִהְיוּ אֲהוּבִים לַבְּרִיּוֹת? בִּזְמַן שֶׁיִּהְיוּ בַּעֲלֵי עַיִן טוֹבָה, וְנֶפֶשׁ שְׁפָלָה, וְחֶבְרָתָן טוֹבָה, וְדִבּוּרָן וּמַשָּׂאָן בְּנַחַת עִם הַבְּרִיּוֹת.
וּלְהַלָּן הוּא אוֹמֵר: אַנְשֵׁי חַיִל – אֵלּוּ שֶׁהֵן גִּבּוֹרִים בְּמִצְוֹת, וּמְדַקְדְּקִים עַל עַצְמָם, וְכוֹבְשִׁין אֶת יִצְרָן, עַד שֶׁלֹּא יְהֵא לָהֶן שׁוּם גְּנַאי וְלֹא שֵׁם רַע, וִיהֵא פִּרְקָן נָאֶה.
וּבִכְלַל אַנְשֵׁי חַיִל, שֶׁיִּהְיֶה לָהֶן לֵב אַמִּיץ לְהַצִּיל עָשׁוּק מִיַּד עוֹשְׁקוֹ. כָּעִנְיָן שֶׁנֶּאֱמַר: וַיָּקָם מֹשֶׁה וַיּוֹשִׁעָן.

28. *Sanhedrin* 17a speaks of a judge having knowledge "in the 70 languages." The *Kessef Mishneh* questions that statement, noting that it is very rare for a person to know that many languages. The *Lechem Mishneh* explains that the intent is not that a judge should know all 70 languages, but some of the 70.

29. The Radbaz asks: "And what should be done if it is impossible to find judges in a particular city who possess these qualities?" He explains that we should seek out the individuals who possess as many of these qualities as possible and appoint them as judges, choosing even the lesser of the evils. In no event, however, should a city be left without a Torah court. The *Mabit* (Responsum 280), however, states that at least one of the judges must have all the seven qualities listed.

Kin'at Eliyahu notes that Halachah 13: "All the judges who sit in court must be Torah scholars and of appropriate [character]," seems to imply that a person who does not possess these qualities should not sit on a court.

30. The translation of *yeduim* as "beloved" has parallels in Genesis 18:19 where God describes Abraham *ki yedativ*, which Rashi renders as "because I cherished him."

31. See *Hilchot Yesodei HaTorah* 5:11 which speaks of the mitzvah of sanctifying God's name, explaining that it does not mean only dying to affirm His being, but also living a life which makes all others respect the Torah and its students. There the Rambam mentions similar character traits as evoking such a response on behalf of others.

32. This relates to the quality of having a good reputation mentioned by the Rambam previously. The *Derishah* (*Choshen Mishpat* 7) explains that, at the outset, the Rambam does not follow the order mentioned in the verse, to make a distinction between the qualities that involve a person's relationship with God and those which concern the manner with which he relates to others.

Note the Introduction to the Rambam's Commentary on the Mishnah where he explains that the tractate of *Avot* which teaches proper character traits is included in the Order of *Nezikin* after the laws applying to judges to emphasize that the judges must be of fine character.

33. I.e., he saved Jethro's daughters who were being mistreated by the people of Midian.

Just as we see that Moses was humble;[34] so, too, every judge should be humble. [Exodus 18:21 continues:] "God-fearing" - the intent is obvious. [It mentions:] "men who hate profit," i.e., people who do not become overly concerned even about their own money. They do not pursue the accumulation of money, for anyone who is overly concerned about wealth will [ultimately] be overcome by want.[35]

[The verse continues:] "men of truth," i.e., people who pursue justice because of their own inclination; they love truth, hate crime, and flee from all forms of crookedness.

8. Our Sages relate:[36] From the Supreme *Sanhedrin*, they would send [emissaries] throughout the entire land of Israel[37] to seek out [judges].[38] Whenever they found a person who was wise, sin-fearing, humble, modest, with a good reputation, and beloved by people at large, they have him appointed as a judge in his own city. From there, they promote him to the court[39] [which holds sessions] at the entrance to the Temple Mount.[40] From there, he is promoted to the court [which holds sessions] at the entrance to the Temple Courtyard, and from there, to the Supreme *Sanhedrin*.

9. When one of the judges of a court of three is a convert, the court is disqualified.[41] His mother[42] must be a [native-born] Jewess. If, by contrast, one of the judges is a *mamzer*,[43] even if all three of them are *mamzerim*, they are acceptable to pass judgment.[44]

34. As Numbers 12:3 states: "And the man Moses was more humble than every person on the face of the earth."
35. Cf. Proverbs 28:22.
36. *Sanhedrin* 88b; Jerusalem Talmud, *Sanhedrin* 1:4.
37. The Jerusalem Talmud states that the search is conducted throughout *Eretz Yisrael*. The Babylonian Talmud, by contrast, mentions that the search is conducted in all places.
38. I.e., the selection of members of the courts was not by popular vote, nor by appointment of the king, but by the judges themselves. *Kiryat Sefer* quotes as a source for this concept, the appointment of judges by Moses. Moses was the head of the court and he appointed the judges under him.
39. *Chasdei David* notes that in Chapter 1, Halachah 8, the Rambam states that if a necessity arises to appoint a new judge, the most appropriate candidate from the students who sit before the judges is chosen. If so, how could a judge from another place be appointed to the courts of Jerusalem? Seemingly, that appointment would come from the students sitting in that court.

Moreover, he explains, we cannot say that a judge from outside Jerusalem would be appointed merely as a student, for that would be a decline in his standing. He explains that the intent is that if the judge from outside Jerusalem surpasses the student in knowledge, the judge is appointed.

Kin'at Eliyahu notes that in Chapter 1, the Rambam mentions increasing judges when an unresolved question is being debated in court. In such circumstances, there is no time to wait, and the appointment is made from the ranks of the students. In this halachah, we

וּמַה מֹּשֶׁה רַבֵּנוּ עָנָו, אַף כָּל דַּיָּן צָרִיךְ לִהְיוֹת עָנָו. יִרְאֵי אֱלֹהִים – כְּמַשְׁמָעוֹ. שֹׂנְאֵי בָצַע – אַף מָמוֹן שֶׁלָּהֶם אֵינָן נִבְהָלִין עָלָיו, וְלֹא רוֹדְפִין לְקַבֵּץ הַמָּמוֹן. שֶׁכָּל מִי שֶׁהוּא נִבְהָל לַהוֹן – חֶסֶר יְבֹאֶנּוּ.

אַנְשֵׁי אֱמֶת – שֶׁיִּהְיוּ רוֹדְפִין אַחַר הַצֶּדֶק מֵחֲמַת עַצְמָן בְּדַעְתָּן. אוֹהֲבִין אֶת הָאֱמֶת, וְשׂוֹנְאִין אֶת הֶחָמָס, וּבוֹרְחִין מִכָּל מִינֵי הָעָוֶל.

ח אָמְרוּ חֲכָמִים: שֶׁמִּבֵּית דִּין הַגָּדוֹל הָיוּ שׁוֹלְחִים בְּכָל אֶרֶץ יִשְׂרָאֵל וּבוֹדְקִין. כָּל מִי שֶׁיִּמְצָאוּהוּ חָכָם, וִירֵא חֵטְא, וְעָנָו, וְשָׁפוּי, וּפִרְקוֹ נָאֶה, וְרוּחַ הַבְּרִיּוֹת נוֹחָה הֵימֶנּוּ – עוֹשִׂין אוֹתוֹ דַּיָּן בְּעִירוֹ.

וּמִשָּׁם מַעֲלִין אוֹתוֹ לְפֶתַח הַר הַבַּיִת, וּמִשָּׁם מַעֲלִין אוֹתוֹ לְפֶתַח הָעֲזָרָה, וּמִשָּׁם מַעֲלִין אוֹתוֹ לְבֵית דִּין הַגָּדוֹל.

ט בֵּית דִּין שֶׁל שְׁלֹשָׁה שֶׁהָיָה אֶחָד מֵהֶן גֵּר – הֲרֵי זֶה פָּסוּל, עַד שֶׁתִּהְיֶה אִמּוֹ מִיִּשְׂרָאֵל. הָיָה אֶחָד מַמְזֵר, אֲפִלּוּ שְׁלָשְׁתָּן מַמְזֵרִים – הֲרֵי אֵלּוּ כְּשֵׁרִין לָדוּן.

are talking about an appointment made after the death, incapacitation, or resignation of one of the judges. In such circumstances, the matter can be thought over and a successor chosen from another city.

40. *Kin'at Eliyahu* questions why he is not first promoted to the regional (or tribal) courts.

41. Deuteronomy 17:15 states: "You shall surely appoint a king from among your brethren," excluding a gentile. *Yevamot* 45b states: "All your appointments should come from 'among your brethren.'"

The commentaries note that *Sanhedrin* 36b states that a convert is acceptable to serve as a judge. Nevertheless, the Rambam apparently interprets that statement as meaning that he may judge another convert, as stated in Chapter 11, Halachah 11 (Radbaz, *Kessef Mishneh*).

The commentaries have raised questions concerning the Rambam's ruling, noting that even judges of the Supreme *Sanhedrin* were converts, e.g., Shamayah and Avtalion. The gloss of the *Baalei Tosafot* to the Torah (*Parshat Mishpatim*) raises this questions and explains that the exclusion applies only when there are native-born Jews who possess the same level of Torah knowledge. If, however, a convert's knowledge surpasses that of a native born Jew, he is given the appointment. The *Chidah* (*Birkai Yosef, Choshen Mishpat* 7:7) offers a similar explanation.

The *K'neset HaGedolah* maintains that Shamayah and Avtalion were accepted by the entire Jewish people and appointed by them to positions of authority. Hence, an exception could be made. The *Tumim* states that they lived in the era of the Hasmonean kings and were appointed by the king. And a king has the authority to act and make decisions even if they run contrary to Torah law.

42. *Tosafot* (*Yevamot* 102a) states that if his father is a native-born Jew, he is acceptable, even if his mother is a convert. The *Kessef Mishneh* and the Ramah (*Choshen Mishpat* 7:1) quote this ruling.

43. A person born from an incestuous or adulterous union.

44. See *Hilchot Talmud Torah* 3:2 which states that a *mamzer* who is a Torah scholar receives precedence over a High Priest who is unlearned.

Similarly, if all of the members [of a court of three] were blind in one eye, it is acceptable. This does not apply with regard to a *Sanhedrin*.[45] If, however, [a judge] is blind in both eyes, he is unacceptable [to serve] on any [court].[46]

10. Although a court requires no less than three [judges], it is permissible for one [judge] to adjudicate a case[47] according to Scriptural Law, as [Leviticus 19:15] states: "Judge[48] your fellow countryman with righteousness." According to Rabbinic Law, however, there should be three judges.[49] When two [judges] adjudicate [a case], their ruling is not binding.[50]

11 When a judge is an expert[51] and he is known by many [to possess such knowledge][52] or if he[53] was granted permission by the court,[54] he may adjudicate a case alone.[55] Nevertheless, he is not considered as a court.[56]

Even though it is permitted for [such a person to issue judgments alone], it is a mitzvah from the Sages[57] for him to have others sit [in judgment] with him, for [our Sages] said:[58] "Do not act as a judge alone, for there is only One who judges alone."[59]

12. A person[60] may execute judgment himself if he has the power to do so.[61] If he acts according to the dictates of our faith and according to law, he is not obligated to take the trouble to come to the court. [This applies] even if he

45. For as stated in Halachah 6, the judges of a *Sanhedrin* may not have physical blemishes. See also Chapter 4, Halachah 10.

Similarly, a *mamzer* and a convert may not serve on such a court, because, as stated in Halachah 1, the judges of the *Sanhedrin* must come from distinguished lineage.

46. Because he is incapacitated in this manner, he is not acceptable as a witness (*Hilchot Edut* 9:12). And as stated in *Niddah* 49b, anyone who is disqualified as a witness is also disqualified as a judge.

47. Moreover, according to Scriptural Law, such a judge need not be an "expert" (see the following halachah), it is sufficient that he be moderately knowledgeable (*Kessef Mishneh*).

48. The conjugation of the verb is singular.

49. See Chapter 1, Halachah 4; see also the following halachah and notes.

50. *Sanhedrin* 3a states that we fear that both of the two judges chosen will be unlearned. If, however, there are three judges, at least one is likely to have Torah knowledge (Rashi, *ibid.*).

Chapter 22, Halachah 6, states that even after the fact, the litigants are not obligated to accept their decision. If, however, the litigants agree to accept the judgment of a two man court, they cannot retract their consent. Similarly, if the judges are experts, their judgment is binding (*Kessef Mishneh*).

51. I.e., he has studied the laws and knows how to derive concepts through logical deduction (*Kessef Mishneh*, based on *Sanhedrin* 4b,5a). The *Sefer Me'irat Einayim* 3:5 also notes that the term *mumchah* has the connotation, possessing experience.

52. Our translation is based on the Rambam's Commentary to the Mishnah (*Sanhedrin* 1:1). Such a person may serve as a judge even if he was not granted permission by the ruling authority to act in this capacity (*Kessef Mishneh*).

53. I.e., a judge who has the same degree of knowledge as an "expert," but his reputation has not spread throughout the Jewish community (*Kessef Mishneh*).

וְכֵן אִם הָיָה כָּל אֶחָד מֵהֶם סוּמָא בְּאֶחָד מֵעֵינָיו - כָּשֵׁר. מַה שֶּׁאֵין כֵּן בְּסַנְהֶדְרִין. אֲבָל הַסּוּמָא בִּשְׁתֵּי עֵינָיו - פָּסוּל לַכֹּל.

י אַף עַל פִּי שֶׁאֵין בֵּית דִּין פָּחוּת מִשְּׁלֹשָׁה - מֻתָּר לְאֶחָד לָדוּן מִן הַתּוֹרָה; שֶׁנֶּאֱמַר: בְּצֶדֶק תִּשְׁפֹּט עֲמִיתֶךָ. וּמִדִּבְרֵי סוֹפְרִים, עַד שֶׁיִּהְיוּ שְׁלֹשָׁה; וּשְׁנַיִם שֶׁדָּנוּ - אֵין דִּינֵיהֶן דִּין.

יא אֶחָד שֶׁהָיָה מֻמְחֶה לָרַבִּים, אוֹ שֶׁנָּטַל רְשׁוּת מִבֵּית דִּין - הֲרֵי זֶה מֻתָּר לוֹ לָדוּן יְחִידִי, אֲבָל אֵינוֹ חָשׁוּב בֵּית דִּין.
וְאַף עַל פִּי שֶׁהוּא מֻתָּר, מִצְוַת חֲכָמִים הוּא שֶׁמּוֹשִׁיב עִמּוֹ אֲחֵרִים; שֶׁהֲרֵי אָמְרוּ: אַל תְּהִי דָן יְחִידִי, שֶׁאֵין דָּן יְחִידִי אֶלָּא אֶחָד.

יב יֵשׁ לְאָדָם לַעֲשׂוֹת דִּין לְעַצְמוֹ, אִם יֵשׁ בְּיָדוֹ כֹּחַ. הוֹאִיל וְכַדָּת וְכַהֲלָכָה הוּא עוֹשֶׂה, אֵינוֹ חַיָּב לִטְרֹחַ וְלָבוֹא לְבֵית דִּין.

54. By a court within *Eretz Yisrael*, as stated in Chapter 4, Halachah 14.

55. I.e., such a person has the authority to summon litigants to judgment against their will.

As indicated by Chapter 5, Halachah 18 (and *Sanhedrin* 30a), a judge need not have received *semichah* to be considered "an expert, known by many [to possess this knowledge]." What is necessary is that he have that degree of knowledge. For that reason, even in Babylonia, the Sages were granted this authority.

The Ramah (*Choshen Mishpat* 3:2) states that there is no concept of such an "expert" in the present age. The *Tur*, by contrast, appears to maintain that even in the present era, a learned and experienced judge can be given such distinction and authority.

56. I.e., an admission made in the presence of such a judge is not equivalent to an admission made in court (Chapter 5, Halachah 18) and a litigant can retract his statements *Shulchan Aruch* (*loc. cit.*).

57. This is an ethical directive and guidance for pious conduct beyond the letter of the law. There is no prohibition according to law (the Rambam's Commentary to the Mishnah).

58. *Avot* 4:8.

59. Only God has the wisdom to make unilateral decisions that are always correct. A mortal, by contrast, will always benefit from the give and take of debate and from hearing other perspectives.

The Jerusalem Talmud notes that Rabbi Abahu would act as a judge alone. His students respectfully questioned his conduct. He explained to them that since the litigants came to him on their own volition, it is as if they accepted him as a judge. And when litigants consent, it is permissible for one person to act as a judge.

These concepts are echoed by the later authorities, including Rav Ovadiah Bartenura in his commentary on the Mishnah (*Avot, loc. cit.*) and the Radbaz, in his notes to this halachah. They note that on this basis, throughout Jewish history, it has been common for one judge to serve as the legal authority for an entire community.

60. The Radbaz states that this license is given to any person, not only to a Torah scholar. If he knows the law, he may apply it.

61. I.e., if he sees his property in the hands of another person, he may take it, even if he must use physical force to do so (*Lechem Mishneh*)

would not suffer any financial loss if he would delay and bring the matter to the court.[62]

Consequently, should the other litigant lodge a complaint against him and bring him to court, if the court investigates and discovers that he acted according to law, i.e., the decision which he arrived at was true, we do not abrogate his decision.[63]

13. Although a court of three is considered as a complete entity, whenever there are more [judges], it is praiseworthy.[64] It is preferable to make a decision with 11 judges than with ten. All the judges who sit in court must be Torah scholars and of appropriate [character].[65]

14. It is forbidden for a wise man to sit in judgment until he knows with whom he will be sitting.[66] [This restraint is observed] lest he be coupled with men who are unsuitable.[67] Thus he will be part of "a band of traitors,"[68] and not part of a court.

CHAPTER THREE

1. Until when should the judges hold session? A minor *Sanhedrin* and a court of three should hold sessions from after the morning service[1] until the end of the sixth hour of the day.[2] The supreme *Sanhedrin*, by contrast, would hold sessions from the time of the slaughter of the morning sacrifice[3] until [the offering of] the afternoon sacrifice.[4] On Sabbaths and on festivals they would hold sessions in the House of Study on the Temple Mount.[5]

2. The High Court of 71 judges was not required to sit all together in their place in the Temple.[6] Instead, when it was necessary for them to gather

62. See the comments of the Ramah (*Choshen Mishpat* 4:1) which add many details concerning the license granted by this halachah.
63. If, however, he erred and did not act according to law, he must return the article and pay damages for hitting his colleague (*Lechem Mishneh*).
64. For the discussion of the subject with others will enable a judge to arrive at a clearer conception.
65. As stated in Halachah 7. Otherwise, the inclusion of them in the court will be detrimental.
66. I.e., who are the other judges.
67. Chapter 22, Halachah 10, quotes *Sanhedrin* 23a which states that the men of pure character in Jerusalem would not participate in a court until they knew the identity of the other judges. Indeed, they would not enter a feast or sign a legal document until they knew who else would be present or who else would sign.
68. *Sanhedrin* 26a uses the expression "a band of wicked people." The Rambam mentions "traitors," perhaps alluding to Jeremiah 9:1: "a company of traitors."

1. The morning service begins at day break.

אַף עַל פִּי שֶׁלֹּא הָיָה שָׁם הֶפְסֵד בִּנְכָסָיו אִלּוּ נִתְאַחֵר וּבָא לְבֵית דִּין.
לְפִיכָךְ, אִם קִבֵּל עָלָיו בַּעַל דִּינוֹ וֶהֱבִיאוֹ לְבֵית דִּין, וְדָרְשׁוּ וּמָצְאוּ שֶׁעָשָׂה כַּהֲלָכָה, וְדִין אֱמֶת דָּן לְעַצְמוֹ – אֵין סוֹתְרִין אֶת דִּינוֹ.

יג אַף עַל פִּי שֶׁבֵּית דִּין שֶׁל שְׁלֹשָׁה בֵּית דִּין שָׁלֵם הוּא, כָּל זְמַן שֶׁהֵן רַבִּים – הֲרֵי זֶה מְשֻׁבָּח. וּמוּטָב שֶׁיֵּחָתֵךְ הַדִּין בְּאַחַד עָשָׂר יוֹתֵר מֵעֲשָׂרָה.
וּצְרִיכִין שֶׁיִּהְיוּ הַיּוֹשְׁבִים כֻּלָּם שָׁם בְּבֵית דִּין תַּלְמִידֵי חֲכָמִים וּרְאוּיִין.

יד וְאָסוּר לְאָדָם חָכָם שֶׁיֵּשֵׁב בְּדִין עַד שֶׁיֵּדַע עִם מִי יֵשֵׁב. שֶׁמָּא יִצְטָרֵף עִם אֲנָשִׁים שֶׁאֵינָן הֲגוּנִים, וְנִמְצָא בִּכְלַל קֶשֶׁר בּוֹגְדִים, וְלֹא בִּכְלַל בֵּית דִּין.

פֶּרֶק שְׁלִישִׁי

א עַד אֵימָתַי יוֹשְׁבִין הַדַּיָּנִים בְּדִין? סַנְהֶדְרֵי קְטַנָּה וּבֵית דִּין שֶׁל שְׁלֹשָׁה – יוֹשְׁבִין מֵאַחַר תְּפִלַּת הַשַּׁחַר עַד סוֹף שֵׁשׁ שָׁעוֹת בַּיּוֹם.
אֲבָל בֵּית דִּין הַגָּדוֹל הָיוּ יוֹשְׁבִין מִתָּמִיד שֶׁל שַׁחַר עַד תָּמִיד שֶׁל בֵּין הָעַרְבַּיִם.
וּבְשַׁבָּתוֹת וְיָמִים טוֹבִים הָיוּ יוֹשְׁבִין בְּבֵית הַמִּדְרָשׁ שֶׁבְּהַר הַבַּיִת.

2. I.e., until after noon. The *Shulchan Aruch* (*Choshen Mishpat* 5:3) states that the court would hold session until the end of the fifth hour. Both opinions have their source in *Shabbat* 10a which states that the sages would hold court until the time came to partake of their meals, which is the sixth hour. The Rambam (and similarly, the *Tur*) interpret this as referring to the end of the sixth hour, while the *Shulchan Aruch* interprets it as referring to the beginning of the sixth hour.

Note, however, the commentary of the *Nitziv* to the *Sh'ilitot* that states that the judges would eat breakfast beforehand. Nevertheless, the court would stop after the seventh hour, because they were concerned that during lunch either the judges or the litigants might consume alcohol.

3. Which was offered at day break.
4. Which was offered nine and a half seasonal hours after sunrise.
5. On the Sabbath, it is forbidden to sit in judgment regarding monetary law (*Hilchot Shabbat* 23:14). Hence, they would hold sessions in this chamber, to make a distinction in the eyes of people at large (Rashi, *Sanhedrin* 88b). On these holy days, they would deal with questions concerning the priesthood and other matters of this nature.
6. See *Tana d'Bei Eliyahu Rabbah,* ch. 11, which explains that the members of the Sanhedrin should "gird their loins with iron garters and lift their robes above their knees and trek throughout the villages of Israel... to teach the Jews... so that the name of the Holy One, blessed be He, would be magnified... throughout the entire world."

together,[7] they would all gather together. At other times, whoever had private affairs would tend to his concerns and then return.

[The above applies] provided there would be no less than 23 judges in attendance whenever they were sitting.[8] If a judge needs to leave, he should look at his colleagues who remain. If there are 23 remaining, he may leave. If not, he should not leave until another comes.

3. [A court] should not begin adjudicating a case at night. According to the Oral Tradition, [this concept] was derived [as follows: Based on Deuteronomy 21:5 which mentions]: "Every dispute and every blemish,"[9] [an equation is established between] the adjudication of disputes and blemishes. Just as blemishes are viewed only during the day;[10] so, too, disputes should be adjudicated only during the day.[11]

4. Similarly, we do not listen to the testimony of witnesses or validate the authenticity of legal documents[12] at night.[13] With regard to cases involving monetary law,[14] if [the judges] began hearing the matter during the day,[15] it is permitted for them to conclude the judgment at night.[16]

5. [The division of] an inheritance resembles a judgment,[17] for with regard to them, [Numbers 35:29] states: "For the statutes of judgment." Therefore inheritances are not divided at night.[18]

6. When two people enter to visit a person[19] who is [deathly] ill, if he makes

7. In the case of situations which require 71 judges, as listed in Chapter 5, Halachah 1.
8. *Sanhedrin* 37a derives this concept from the exegesis of Song of Songs 7:3: "Your navel is like a moon-shaped basin; mixed wine should not be lacking." This verse is interpreted as a reference to the *Sanhedrin* who sit "at the center of the world," and in a semi-circle, like the crescent of the moon. It is explained that mixed wine is 2/3 water and 1/3 wine; so, too, the that ratio - at least 1/3 - should apply with regard to the judges. At least 1/3 should be present at all times (*Kessef Mishneh*).

More simply, since there are 23 judges in a minor *Sanhedrin*, as long as that number of judges are present, any matters that do not specifically require the presence of the entire *Sanhedrin* may be adjudicated.
9. A blemish of *tzara'at*, an affliction similar to leprosy, but stemming from spiritual rather than physical causes. A person with such a blemish must show it to a priest to determine whether it causes him to become ritually impure or not.
10. As Leviticus 13:14 states: "On the day when... appears." See *Hilchot Tumat Tzara'at* 9:5.
11. Note, however, the following halachah. See also the *Sefer Me'irat Einayim* 5:7 which rules that if both sides agree, cases involving monetary law can be heard at night.

Chok UMishpat notes that the prooftext cited by the Rambam does not involve monetary laws, but rather the measurement required to determine which city must bring a calf to atone for a murder in a situation where the murderer is not known. On that basis, it explains that this halachah refers only to laws involving capital punishment and does not deal with monetary law at all.
12. For as the Rambam states in *Hilchot Edut* 6:1, the validation of a legal document is

ב אֵין בֵּית דִּין שֶׁל שִׁבְעִים וְאֶחָד צְרִיכִין שֶׁיִּהְיוּ יוֹשְׁבִין כֻּלָּן כְּאֶחָד בִּמְקוֹמָן שֶׁבַּמִּקְדָּשׁ; אֶלָּא בָּעֵת שֶׁיְּהוּ צְרִיכִין לְהִתְקַבֵּץ – מִתְקַבְּצִין כֻּלָּן, וּבִשְׁאָר הָעִתּוֹת – כָּל מִי שֶׁהָיָה לוֹ עֵסֶק, יָצָא לַעֲשׂוֹת חֶפְצוֹ וְחוֹזֵר.
וְהוּא שֶׁלֹּא יִפְחֲתוּ מֵעֶשְׂרִים וּשְׁלֹשָׁה יוֹשְׁבִין תָּמִיד כָּל זְמַן יְשִׁיבָתָן. הֻצְרַךְ אֶחָד מֵהֶן לָצֵאת – הֲרֵי זֶה מִסְתַּכֵּל בַּחֲבֵרָיו הַנִּשְׁאָרִים: אִם יִשָּׁאֲרוּ שָׁם עֶשְׂרִים וּשְׁלֹשָׁה – יֵצֵא; וְאִם לָאו – לֹא יֵצֵא עַד שֶׁיָּבוֹא אַחֵר.

ג אֵין מַתְחִילִין אֶת הַדִּינִין בַּלַּיְלָה. מִפִּי הַשְּׁמוּעָה לָמְדוּ, שֶׁהַדִּינִין כִּנְגָעִים. שֶׁנֶּאֱמַר: כָּל רִיב וְכָל נָגַע; מָה רְאִיַּת נְגָעִים בַּיּוֹם בִּלְבַד, אַף הַדִּינִין בַּיּוֹם בִּלְבַד.

ד וְכֵן אֵין מְקַבְּלִין עֵדוּת וְאֵין מְקַיְּמִין שְׁטָרוֹת בַּלַּיְלָה. וּבְדִינֵי מָמוֹנוֹת, אִם הִתְחִילוּ בַּיּוֹם – מֻתָּר לִגְמֹר הַדִּין בַּלַּיְלָה.

ה הַנְּחָלוֹת – כַּדִּינִין; שֶׁנֶּאֱמַר בָּהֶן: לְחֻקַּת מִשְׁפָּט. לְפִיכָךְ אֵין מַפִּילִין נְחָלוֹת בַּלַּיְלָה.

ו שְׁנַיִם שֶׁנִּכְנְסוּ לְבַקֵּר אֶת הַחוֹלֶה, וְצִוָּה בִּפְנֵיהֶם – כּוֹתְבִים וְאֵין עוֹשִׂין דִּין.

equivalent to a judgment. Even after the fact, the validation is not acceptable (*Siftei Cohen* 46:5), but if both litigants agree, the validation may be performed at night (*Sefer Me'irat Einayim* 46:6; *Siftei Cohen* 46:4).

13. In his *Kessef Mishneh* and in his *Shulchan Aruch* (*Choshen Mishpat* 28:24, Rav Yosef Karo states that, even after the fact, testimony given at night is not acceptable. The Ramah adds, however, that if both litigants agree, testimony given at night is acceptable.

14. Cases involving capital punishment, by contrast, may be concluded only during the day (Chapter 11, Halachah 1).

15. From the wording of the *Shulchan Aruch* (*Choshen Mishpat* 5:2), the commentaries infer that if a court began hearing a case at night, the judgment is invalidated, even after the fact. The Ramah differs and maintains that, after the fact, the judgment is binding. The *Siftei Cohen* 5:5 mentions the opinions of the several *Rishonim* and rules that the judgment should be invalidated. The *Kitzot HaChoshen* 5:2 differs and maintains that since the conclusion of the judgment is acceptable at night, the fact that the judgment was started in an unacceptable manner is not of consequence.

16. *Sanhedrin* 34b states: Exodus 18:22 states: "And they shall judge the nation at all times," implying that judgment can be rendered during the day and at night. Deuteronomy 21:16, by contrast, states: "On the day when he conveys his inheritance to his sons," indicating that matters involving a court must be performed during the day. In resolution, we begin during the day, but may conclude at night.

17. I.e., it is not considered as a compromise or a division of property among partners which could be carried out at night.

18. The Radbaz states that just as is true with regard to cases involving monetary law, if one began during the day, one may conclude at night.

19. In his *Kessef Mishneh*, Rav Yosef Karo quotes opinions which maintain that the wording of the halachah is carefully chosen. If the men came as visitors, they may have the option of serving as judges later. If, however, they were invited with the intent that

statements [dividing his estate][20] in their presence, they may record his statements,[21] but they may not adjudicate [the division of the estate].[22] If they were three, if they desire, they may record his statements[23] or they may adjudicate [the division of the estate].[24]

When does the above apply? During the day. During the night, they may record his statements, but they may not adjudicate [the division of the estate].[25]

7. Whenever a suitable court among the Jewish people [sits in judgment], the Divine Presence [rests] among them.[26] Accordingly, the judges must sit in awe and fear, wrapped [in *tallitot*],[27] and [conduct themselves with] reverence.[28] It is forbidden to act frivolously, to joke, or to speak idle matters in court. Instead, one may speak only words of Torah and wisdom.

8. Whenever a *Sanhedrin*, a king,[29] or an exilarch[30] appoints a judge who is not fitting[31] and/or is not learned in the wisdom of the Torah and is not suitable to be a judge - even if he is entirely a delight[32] and possesses other [positive] qualities - the person who appoints him violates a negative commandment,[33] as [Deuteronomy 1:17] states: "Do not show favoritism in judgment." According to the Oral Tradition, we learn that [this command] is addressed to those who appoint judges.

Our Sages declare:[34] "Perhaps a person will say: 'So and so is attractive, I will appoint him as a judge,' 'So and so is strong, I will appoint him as a judge,' 'So and so is my relative, I will appoint him as a judge,' or 'So and so knows all the languages, I will appoint him as a judge.' " [This will lead to] those who are liable being vindicated and those who should be vindicated held liable, not because [the judge] is wicked, but because he does not know [Torah law]. Therefore the Torah states: 'Do not show favoritism in judgment.' "

they serve as witnesses, they cannot serve as judges. He also, however, quotes other opinions which do not accept this distinction and maintain that even if he originally intended to serve as a witness, if asked to receive the testimony as a judge, he may accept that role. See *Shulchan Aruch* (*Choshen Mishpat* 7:5) which quotes both perspectives without determining which one should be followed.

20. Using the legal convention of a *tzava'at shchiv mera*, an oral will. See *Hilchot Zechiyah UMatanah*, Chapter 8, and onward.

21. And use their notes as basis for testimony before a court.

22. For a case may not be determined by two judges, as stated in Chapter 2, Halachah 10.

23. And act as witnesses before another court.

24. For any three men who are acceptable witnesses are acceptable as judges for such a matter. They may confirm the transfer of the property to all the prospective recipients. If the recipients claim, "We would like the matter adjudicated by another court," their claim is not accepted [Ramah (*Choshen Mishpat* 353:1)].

As alluded to in the gloss of the *Kessef Mishneh*, this halachah sheds light on an issue of greater scope. If the visitors hear the statements of the dying man themselves, they do not need other witnesses to testify before them, their own knowledge is sufficient. Similarly, the *Nimukei Yosef* maintains, in other cases of business, when the judges have firsthand knowledge, they may issue a ruling without hearing the testimony of witnesses.

וְאִם הָיוּ שְׁלֹשָׁה – רָצוּ כּוֹתְבִין, רָצוּ עוֹשִׂין דִּין.
בַּמֶּה דְּבָרִים אֲמוּרִים? בַּיּוֹם; אֲבָל בַּלַּיְלָה – כּוֹתְבִין וְאֵין עוֹשִׂין דִּין.

ז כָּל בֵּית דִּין שֶׁל יִשְׂרָאֵל שֶׁהוּא הָגוּן – שְׁכִינָה עִמָּהֶם.
לְפִיכָךְ צְרִיכִין הַדַּיָּנִים לֵישֵׁב בְּאֵימָה וְיִרְאָה וַעֲטִיפָה וְכֹבֶד רֹאשׁ.
וְאָסוּר לְהָקֵל רֹאשׁ אוֹ לְשַׂחֵק אוֹ לְסַפֵּר בְּשִׂיחָה בְּטֵלָה בְּבֵית דִּין, אֶלָּא בְּדִבְרֵי תּוֹרָה וְחָכְמָה.

ח כָּל סַנְהֶדְרִין אוֹ מֶלֶךְ אוֹ רֹאשׁ גּוֹלָה שֶׁהֶעֱמִידוּ לָהֶן לְיִשְׂרָאֵל דַּיָּן שֶׁאֵינוֹ הָגוּן, וְאֵינוֹ חָכָם בְּחָכְמַת הַתּוֹרָה וְרָאוּי לִהְיוֹת דַּיָּן, אַף עַל פִּי שֶׁהוּא כֻּלּוֹ מַחֲמַדִּים וְיֵשׁ בּוֹ טוֹבוֹת אֲחֵרוֹת – הֲרֵי זֶה שֶׁהֶעֱמִידוֹ עוֹבֵר בְּלֹא תַעֲשֶׂה.
שֶׁנֶּאֱמַר: לֹא תַכִּירוּ פָּנִים בַּמִּשְׁפָּט. מִפִּי הַשְּׁמוּעָה לָמְדוּ, שֶׁזֶּה מְדַבֵּר כְּנֶגֶד הַמְמַנֶּה לְהוֹשִׁיב דַּיָּנִין.
אָמְרוּ חֲכָמִים: שֶׁמָּא תֹאמַר: אִישׁ פְּלוֹנִי נָאֶה, אוֹשִׁיבֶנּוּ דַּיָּן; אִישׁ פְּלוֹנִי גִּבּוֹר, אוֹשִׁיבֶנּוּ דַּיָּן; אִישׁ פְּלוֹנִי קְרוֹבִי, אוֹשִׁיבֶנּוּ דַּיָּן; אִישׁ פְּלוֹנִי יוֹדֵעַ בְּכָל לָשׁוֹן, אוֹשִׁיבֶנּוּ דַּיָּן. נִמְצָא מְזַכֶּה אֶת הַחַיָּב וּמְחַיֵּב אֶת הַזַּכַּאי. לֹא מִפְּנֵי שֶׁהוּא רָשָׁע, אֶלָּא מִפְּנֵי שֶׁאֵינוֹ יוֹדֵעַ. לְכָךְ נֶאֱמַר: לֹא תַכִּירוּ פָּנִים בַּמִּשְׁפָּט.

The *Kessef Mishneh* brings other opinions which differ and maintain that the dying man's statements are considered equivalent to the testimony of witnesses and in other cases, testimony is required. In his *Shulchan Aruch* (*Choshen Mishpat* 7:5), Rav Yosef Karo follows the opinion of the *Nimukei Yosef* and rules that judges may adjudicate a case based on their own firsthand knowledge. The testimony of witnesses is not necessary.

25. For as stated in the previous halachah, estates may not be divided at night.

26. *Sanhedrin* 7a derives this concept from Psalms 82:1: "God stands among the congregation of the Almighty; He renders judgment in the midst of judges." This indicates that the Divine Presence rests among a court and is involved in the judgment they render. See also *Berachot* 6a and Chapter 23, Halachah 9.

27. As a sign of their deference to the Divine presence (see Rashi, *Shabbat* 10a). See also *Hilchot Tefilah* 6:6. The *Pitchei Teshuvah* 7:4 quotes several authorities who explain that this practice is not followed at present.

28. See Chapter 23, Halachah 8.

29. The judges in *Eretz Yisrael* were appointed by the *Sanhedrin* (see Chapter 2, Halachah 8) or by royal edict.

30. Descendants of the Davidic dynasty who were the secular heads of the Jewish community in Babylonia. They had the right to judge the people themselves and appoint judges. See Chapter 4, Halachah 13.

31. I.e., lacks proper character.

32. Cf. Song of Songs 5:16. 33. *Sefer HaMitzvot* (negative commandment 284) and *Sefer HaChinuch* (mitzvah 414) count this as one of the 613 mitzvot of the Torah. See also Chapter 4, Halachah 15.

34. *Sifri* to the above verse.

Our Sages also declare:[35] "Whoever appoints a judge who is not appropriate for the Jewish people is considered as if he erected a monument, as [implied by Deuteronomy 16:22]: 'Do not erect a monument which is hated by God, your Lord.'[36] [If he is appointed] instead of a Torah scholar, it is as if one planted an *asherah*,[37] as [*Ibid.*:21] states: 'Do not plant an *asherah* [or] any other tree next to God's altar.'"[38]

And our Sages[39] interpreted [Exodus 20:23]: "Do not make gods of silver and gods of gold together with Me" to mean "Do not appoint a judge[40] because of silver and gold." This refers to a judge who was appointed because of his wealth[41] alone.[42]

9. Whenever a judge pays money in order to be appointed, it is forbidden to stand in his presence.[43] Our Sages commanded[44] that he be denigrated and derided. And our Sages declare: "Consider the *tallit* with which he wraps himself[45] as the saddle blanket of a donkey."

10. This was the manner of conduct of the sages of the previous generations. They would flee from being appointed [to a court][46] and would undergo extreme pressure not to sit in judgment until they knew that there was no other person as appropriate as they were and that the quality [of the legal system] would be impaired if they would refrain from participating in the judgment.[47] Even so, they would not sit in judgment until the people at large and the elders would compel them and implore them [to do so].

CHAPTER FOUR

1. At least one[1] of the members of the Supreme *Sanhedrin*, a minor *Sanhedrin*, or a court of three must have received *semichah* (ordination) from a teacher who himself had been given *semichah*.[2]

35. There is a similar, but not exact quote in *Sanhedrin* 7b. The *Maharik* (Responsum 117) explains that since the verses cited as prooftexts follow the command to appoint judges, the Rambam interpreted them in this context even though the Talmud derived these concepts in another way. Without discounting the *Maharik's* explanation, the *Kessef Mishneh* states that the Rambam does not often offer independent interpretations of Biblical verses. Hence he postulates that the Rambam possessed other Midrashic sources which are not available to us at present.

The Radbaz follows a similar line of thought, explaining that these charges are not considered as part of the 613 mitzvot of the Torah, for the purpose of these verses is primarily to teach their straightforward meanings and the association with judges is a secondary, homiletic interpretation.

36. Since such a judge is hated by God, appointing him as a judge is equivalent to erecting a monument (the *Targum* of Yonason ben Uziel to the verse).

37. A tree worshipped as a false deity.

38. The Torah scholar is comparable to God's altar. Thus the appointment of the improper judge in his place is considered as planting an *asherah* near him.

וְעוֹד אָמְרוּ: כָּל הַמַּעֲמִיד לְיִשְׂרָאֵל דַּיָּן שֶׁאֵינוֹ הָגוּן – כְּאִלּוּ הֵקִים מַצֵּבָה. שֶׁנֶּאֱמַר: וְלֹא תָקִים לְךָ מַצֵּבָה אֲשֶׁר שָׂנֵא יְיָ אֱלֹהֶיךָ. וּבִמְקוֹם תַּלְמִידֵי חֲכָמִים – כְּאִלּוּ נָטַע אֲשֵׁרָה. שֶׁנֶּאֱמַר: לֹא תִטַּע לְךָ אֲשֵׁרָה כָּל עֵץ אֵצֶל מִזְבַּח יְיָ אֱלֹהֶיךָ. וְכֵן אָמְרוּ חֲכָמִים: לֹא תַעֲשׂוּן אִתִּי אֱלֹהֵי כֶסֶף – אֱלוֹהַּ הַבָּא בִּשְׁבִיל כֶּסֶף וְזָהָב. זֶה הַדַּיָּן שֶׁמִּנּוּהוּ מִפְּנֵי עָשְׁרוֹ בִּלְבַד.

ט כָּל דַּיָּן שֶׁנָּתַן מָמוֹן כְּדֵי שֶׁיִּתְמַנֶּה – אָסוּר לַעֲמֹד מִפָּנָיו. וְצִוּוּ חֲכָמִים לְהָקֵל אוֹתוֹ וּלְזַלְזֵל בּוֹ. וְאָמְרוּ חֲכָמִים: שֶׁהַטַּלִּית שֶׁמִּתְעַטֵּף בָּהּ, תְּהִי בְּעֵינֶיךָ כְּמַרְדַּעַת שֶׁל חֲמוֹר.

י כָּךְ הָיָה דֶּרֶךְ חֲכָמִים הָרִאשׁוֹנִים: בּוֹרְחִין מִלְּהִתְמַנּוֹת, וְדוֹחֲקִין עַצְמָן הַרְבֵּה שֶׁלֹּא יֵשְׁבוּ בַּדִּין, עַד שֶׁיֵּדְעוּ שֶׁאֵין שָׁם רָאוּי כְּמוֹתָם, וְשֶׁאִם יִמָּנְעוּ מִן הַדִּין – תְּקַלְקֵל הַשּׁוּרָה. אַף עַל פִּי כֵן לֹא הָיוּ יוֹשְׁבִין בַּדִּין אֶלָּא עַד שֶׁמַּכְבִּידִין עֲלֵיהֶם אֶת הָעָם וְהַזְּקֵנִים וּפוֹצְרִים בָּהֶן.

פֶּרֶק רְבִיעִי

א אֶחָד בֵּית דִּין הַגָּדוֹל וְאֶחָד סַנְהֶדְרִין קְטַנָּה אוֹ בֵּית דִּין שֶׁל שְׁלֹשָׁה, צָרִיךְ שֶׁיִּהְיֶה אֶחָד מֵהֶן סָמוּךְ מִפִּי הַסָּמוּךְ.

39. *Sanhedrin, loc. cit.*.
40. The term *Elohim* can be rendered both as "God" and as "judge."
41. Rashi (*Sanhedrin, loc. cit.*) interprets this as meaning that the judge bribed the king to appoint him. From the words of the *Rivosh* (the conclusion of Responsum 271), it would appear that the intent is that he was appointed in appreciation of his wealth. *Kin'at Eliyahu* also favors this interpretation, noting that otherwise, it would have been more appropriate to mention this clause in the following halachah.
42. I.e., it is desirable that a judge be wealthy because then he will not covet money belonging to others. This, however, should not be his fundamental virtue.
43. Implied is both that one should not stand before him as a litigant in court and that one should not stand in his honor.
44. Jerusalem Talmud, *Bikkurim* 3:3. Similarly, the *Shulchan Aruch* (*Choshen Mishpat* 8:1 states that it is a mitzvah to denigrate and deride him.
45. As is customary for a judge, as stated in Halachah 7.
46. *Horiot* 10a relates that Rabban Gamliel sought to appoint two of his students, Rabbi Elazar ben Chisma and Rabbi Yochanan ben Gudgada, to the High Court. When he summoned them, they initially refused to come, for they sought to avoid the appointment. Similarly, *Sanhedrin* 14a relates that Rabbi Zeira sought to hide to avert being given *semichah*.
47. For others who were less qualified would seek the appointment.

1. This is the version found in the standard printed text of the *Mishneh Torah*. Based on authentic manuscripts, early printings, and the Rambam's Commentary to the Mishnah (*Sanhedrin* 1:3), it would appear that the proper version is "Every member of...."
2. The *Lechem Mishneh* states that here, the Rambam's statements apply with regard to

Our teacher, Moses ordained Joshua by [placing his] hands upon him, as [Numbers 27:23] states: "And he placed his hands upon him and commanded him." Similarly, Moses ordained the 70 judges and the Divine presence rested upon them.[3] Those elders ordained others, and the others still others [in later generations]. [This tradition continued until the Talmudic era, when the Sages] had received ordination one from the other [in a change] extending back to the court of Joshua, and to the court of Moses.

A person who is ordained by the *nasi*[4] and one ordained by another ordained judge [have the same status], even if that ordained judge never served in a *Sanhedrin*.[5]

2. How is the practice of *semichah* practiced for all time?[6] [The person conveying ordination does] not rest his hands[7] on the elder's[8] head. Instead, he is addressed by the title of Rabbi and is told: "You are ordained and you have the authority to render judgment, even in cases involving financial penalties."[9]

3. The *semichah* which ordains elders as judges may be conveyed only by three individuals. One of the three must have received *semichah* from others as explained.[10]

4. The term *Elohim*[11] can be applied only to a court which received *semichah* in *Eretz Yisrael* alone.[12] They are wise men who are fit to render judgment[13] who were scrutinized by a court within *Eretz Yisrael* which appointed them and conveyed *semichah* upon them.[14]

5. At first, whoever had received *semichah* would convey *semichah* on his students. [Afterwards,] as an expression of honor to Hillel,[15] the elder, the Sages ordained that *semichah* would not be conveyed upon anyone unless license had been granted by the *nasi*.[16]

conveying *semichah*. In other contexts, all the members of a *Sanhedrin* must have been granted *semichah*.

3. As related in the Biblical narrative, Numbers, Ch. 11, Moses called the elders together to share with them the burden of leading the people. A certain measure of the Divine spirit that rested on Moses was imparted to them.

4. The head of the Supreme *Sanhedrin*, as stated in Chapter 1, Halachah 3.

5. For we find that the practice of *semichah* continued even after the nullification of the *Sanhedrin*.

6. I.e., aside from the appointment of Joshua and the elders by Moses.

7. As Moses did to Joshua, and as might be construed from the term *semichah*. See the commentary of the Ramaz to *Sanhedrin* 1:3 which states that Moses placed his hands on Joshua to impart to him the spirit of prophecy.

8. I.e., the person receiving *semichah*. He is called a *zekein*, "elder," for the Hebrew word *zekein* is interpreted as an allusion to the phrase *zeh shekanah chochmah* - "the one who acquired wisdom."

9. *Kenasot*. As explained in Chapter 5, Halachah 8, such cases may be adjudicated only by judges possessing *semichah*.

וּמשֶׁה רַבֵּנוּ סָמַךְ יְהוֹשֻׁעַ בַּיָּד, שֶׁנֶּאֱמַר: וַיִּסְמֹךְ אֶת יָדָיו עָלָיו וַיְצַוֵּהוּ. וְכֵן הַשִּׁבְעִים זְקֵנִים – משֶׁה רַבֵּנוּ סְמָכָם, וְשָׁרְתָה עֲלֵיהֶן שְׁכִינָה. וְאוֹתָן הַזְּקֵנִים סָמְכוּ לַאֲחֵרִים, וַאֲחֵרִים לַאֲחֵרִים. וְנִמְצְאוּ הַסְּמוּכִין אִישׁ מִפִּי אִישׁ, עַד בֵּית דִּינוֹ שֶׁל יְהוֹשֻׁעַ וְעַד בֵּית דִּינוֹ שֶׁל משֶׁה רַבֵּנוּ. וְאֶחָד הַנִּסְמָךְ מִפִּי הַנָּשִׂיא אוֹ מִפִּי אֶחָד מִן הַסְּמוּכִין, אֲפִלּוּ לֹא הָיָה אוֹתוֹ סָמוּךְ בְּסַנְהֶדְרִין לְעוֹלָם.

ב וְכֵיצַד הִיא הַסְּמִיכָה לְדוֹרוֹת? לֹא שֶׁיִּסְמְכוּ יְדֵיהֶן עַל רֹאשׁ הַזָּקֵן, אֶלָּא שֶׁקּוֹרִין לוֹ רַבִּי, וְאוֹמְרִים לוֹ: הֲרֵי אַתְּ סָמוּךְ, וְיֵשׁ לְךָ רְשׁוּת לָדוּן אֲפִלּוּ דִּינֵי קְנָסוֹת.

ג וְאֵין סוֹמְכִין סְמִיכָה שֶׁהִיא מִנּוּי הַזְּקֵנִים לְדַיָּנוּת אֶלָּא בִּשְׁלֹשָׁה.
וְהוּא שֶׁיִּהְיֶה הָאֶחָד מֵהֶן סָמוּךְ מִפִּי אֲחֵרִים, כְּמוֹ שֶׁבֵּאַרְנוּ.

ד אֵין קְרוּיִ אֱלֹהִים אֶלָּא בֵּית דִּין שֶׁנִּסְמַךְ בְּאֶרֶץ יִשְׂרָאֵל בִּלְבַד.
וְהֵם הָאֲנָשִׁים הַחֲכָמִים הָרְאוּיִין לָדוּן, שֶׁבָּדְקוּ אוֹתָן בֵּית דִּין שֶׁל אֶרֶץ יִשְׂרָאֵל וּמִנּוּ אוֹתָם וְסָמְכוּ אוֹתָן.

ה בָּרִאשׁוֹנָה הָיָה כָּל מִי שֶׁנִּסְמַךְ סוֹמֵךְ לְתַלְמִידָיו.
וַחֲכָמִים חָלְקוּ כָּבוֹד לְהִלֵּל הַזָּקֵן, וְהִתְקִינוּ שֶׁלֹּא יְהֵא אָדָם נִסְמָךְ אֶלָּא בִּרְשׁוּת הַנָּשִׂיא.
וְשֶׁלֹּא יְהֵא הַנָּשִׂיא סוֹמֵךְ אֶלָּא אִם כֵּן הָיָה אַב בֵּית דִּין עִמּוֹ.

10. In Halachah 1. The other two, however, need not have received such ordination. In his Commentary to the Mishnah (*Sanhedrin* 1:3), the Rambam states that there is a doubt whether all three ordaining judges must have been ordained themselves or only one. He states, however, that he favors the opinion recorded here.

As support for the Rambam's ruling, the Radbaz points to the story of Rabbi Yehudah ben Bava who sacrificed his life to convey *semichah* on five elders (*Sanhedrin* 14a). Only Rabbi Yehudah is mentioned in the narrative, indicating that the other judges who joined him did not possess *semichah* themselves. See also Halachah 11.

11. Which refers to God, the supreme Judge, but which is also the term used by the Bible (Exodus 22:8) for a court.

12. I.e., and not in the Diaspora, as stated in Halachah 6.

13. I.e., who have the appropriate character traits explained in Chapter 2, Halachah 7.

14. See Chapter 5, Halachah 8.

15. The authoritative Yemenite manuscripts of the *Mishneh Torah* speak of the honor being granted to "the House of Hillel," i.e., not to him as an individual alone, but as a representative of the family who stemmed from the Davidic dynasty. This version is borne out by the source for this teaching, the Jerusalem Talmud (*Sanhedrin* 1:2) which speaks of the honor granted to "the house of the *nasi*."

16. I.e., the *nasi* would have to give his approval before *semichah* was conveyed upon the candidate. From the Jerusalem Talmud (*ibid.*), it appears that, even after the fact, *semichah* that was granted without the *nasi's* approval is not binding.

[They also ordained that] the *nasi* should not convey *semichah* unless he is accompanied by the *av beit din*, and that the *av beit din* should not convey *semichah* unless he was accompanied by the *nasi*.[17] The other elders could convey *semichah* themselves after receiving license from the *nasi*, provided they were accompanied by two others. For *semichah* cannot be conveyed by fewer than three [judges].

6. *Semichah* may not be conveyed upon elders in the diaspora even if [the judges] conveying *semichah* received *semichah* in *Eretz Yisrael*.[18] Even if [the judges] conveying *semichah* were in *Eretz Yisrael* and [the elders to receive] *semichah* were in the diaspora, they should not convey *semichah*. Needless to say, this applies if [the judges] conveying *semichah* were in the diaspora and [the elders to receive] *semichah* were in *Eretz Yisrael*.

If both of them were in *Eretz Yisrael*, *semichah* may be conveyed even though [the recipients] are not in the same place as those conveying *semichah*.[19] Instead, [the judges conveying *semichah*] send to [the elder] or write to him that he has been given *semichah* and that he has permission to adjudicate cases involving financial penalties.

[This is acceptable,] because both of them are located in *Eretz Yisrael*. The entire area of *Eretz Yisrael* which the Jews who left Egypt took possession of[20] is fit to have *semichah* conveyed within it.

17. These regulations were instituted to insure that these sages offered the appropriate measures of respect to each other.
18. From Isaiah 2:3: "Out of Zion shall come forth the Torah," we learn that the fundamental decisions regarding the Torah leadership of our people must be made in the land upon which God's holiness rests. This concept is also explicitly stated in the Jerusalem Talmud (*Bikkurim* 3:3):

> Elders may not be appointed in the Diaspora. Rabbi Levi states: "There is an explicit verse [which can serve as a source, Ezekiel 3:17] states: 'The House of Israel is dwelling (*yoshvim*) on their land.' Implied is that every *yeshivah*, 'sitting of consequence,' must be 'on their land.'"

In his Commentary to the Mishnah (*Bechorot* 4:3, the Rambam explains that the authority for the appointment of judges lies among the inhabitants of *Eretz Yisrael*, for only they are called a *kahal*, "community."
19. As the Rambam continues to explain, the ordination may be conveyed verbally by an agent or in writing. *Sanhedrin* 14a states that the ability to convey *semichah* over distances can be derived from the fact that it is necessary to disqualify the ordination when the ordaining judges are in *Eretz Yisrael* and the recipients in the Diaspora or vice versa. Although the two are not in the same place, that is not considered a disqualifying difficulty, only the fact that one is in the Diaspora (*Kessef Mishneh*). [Note, however, the *Minchat Chinuch* (mitzvah 491) who rejects the support offered by the *Kessef Mishneh*.]
20. When the Jews entered *Eretz Yisrael* after the exodus from Egypt, they conquered the Holy Land and settled within. After the Babylonian conquest, they were exiled and the holiness of the land was nullified. After conquering Babylon, Cyrus, King of Persia, gave the Jews the right to return to *Eretz Yisrael* and led by Ezra, they resettled and reconsecrated the land. The area which they resettled was, however, smaller than that

וְשֶׁלֹּא יִהְיֶה אַב בֵּית דִּין סוֹמֵךְ אֶלָּא אִם כֵּן הָיָה הַנָּשִׂיא עִמּוֹ.
אֲבָל שְׁאָר הַחֲבוּרָה – יֵשׁ לְכָל אֶחָד מֵהֶם לִסְמֹךְ בִּרְשׁוּת הַנָּשִׂיא.
וְהוּא שֶׁיִּהְיוּ שְׁנַיִם עִמּוֹ, שֶׁאֵין סְמִיכָה פָּחוֹת מִשְּׁלֹשָׁה.

ו אֵין סוֹמְכִין זְקֵנִים בְּחוּצָה לָאָרֶץ, וְאַף עַל פִּי שֶׁאֵלּוּ הַסּוֹמְכִין נִסְמְכוּ בְּאֶרֶץ יִשְׂרָאֵל.
אֲפִלּוּ הָיוּ הַסּוֹמְכִין בָּאָרֶץ, וְהַנִּסְמָךְ חוּצָה לָאָרֶץ – אֵין סוֹמְכִין.
וְאֵין צָרִיךְ לוֹמַר אִם הָיוּ הַסּוֹמְכִין בְּחוּצָה לָאָרֶץ וְהַנִּסְמָכִין בָּאָרֶץ.
הָיוּ שְׁנֵיהֶם בָּאָרֶץ – סוֹמְכִין אוֹתוֹ, אַף עַל פִּי שֶׁאֵינוֹ עִם הַסּוֹמְכִים בְּמָקוֹם אֶחָד; אֶלָּא שׁוֹלְחִין לוֹ אוֹ כּוֹתְבִין לוֹ שֶׁהוּא סָמוּךְ, וְנוֹתְנִין לוֹ רְשׁוּת לָדוּן דִּינֵי קְנָסוֹת, הוֹאִיל וּשְׁנֵיהֶם בָּאָרֶץ. וְכָל אֶרֶץ יִשְׂרָאֵל שֶׁהֶחֱזִיקוּ בָּהּ עוֹלֵי מִצְרַיִם רְאוּיָה לִסְמִיכָה.

originally possessed by the Jewish people. See *Hilchot Terumot* 1:6-7 for a description of the boundaries of the lands.

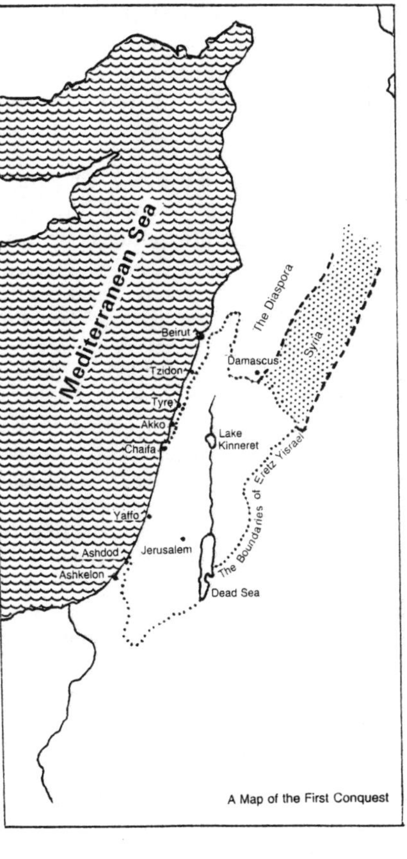

A Map of the First Conquest

A Map of the Second Conquest

7. Judges who themselves were granted *semichah* may convey *semichah* on [many individuals] - even 100 - at one time. King David once conveyed *semichah* on 30,000 individuals on one day.[21]

8. [Such judges] may appoint anyone they desire for particular matters, provided he is fit to [adjudicate] all matters.

What is implied? A court has the authority to give *semichah* to a remarkable judge who is fit to issue rulings with regard to the entire Torah and [limit] his authority to the adjudication of financial matters, but not to what is forbidden and permitted.[22] Conversely, they may grant him authority with regard to what is forbidden and permitted, but not to adjudicate cases involving financial matters. Or they may give him license with regard to adjudicate both such matters, but not laws involving financial penalties,[23] or to rule with regard to financial penalties, but not to rule that a blemish [disqualifies] a firstborn animal.[24] Or they may give him license merely to absolve vows,[25] to judge stains,[26] or [to rule only] within other similarly [limited parameters].

9. Similarly, the judges conveying *semichah* have permission to give the person receiving *semichah* license to judge only for a specific time, telling him: "You have permission to judge or issue rulings until the *nasi* arrives here," or "...as long as you are together with us in this city," or [to issue] other similar restrictions.[27]

10. When a sage of remarkable [knowledge] is blind in one eye, he is not given *semichah* with regard to matters of financial law[28] although he may adjudicate such cases.[29] [The rationale is that] he is not fit to judge all matters.[30] Similar principles apply in all analogous situations.

Although with regard to the agricultural laws and other issues (see *ibid.*:5, *Hilchot Beit HaBechirah* 6:16), the area settled by the Jews on their return from Babylonia is of primary importance, in this context, emphasis is placed on the area settled by the Jews originally. The *Kessef Mishneh* draws support for this concept from the fact that *Sanhedrin* 5a relates that Rabbah bar Chanah was granted ordination to judge in the border cities that were outside the bounds of *Eretz Yisrael* proper. If *semichah* is effective there, he concludes, it is certainly effective in the areas conquered by the Jews ascending from Egypt. The *Kaftor ViPerach* explains that the holiness of *Eretz Yisrael* and the sanctity of the land with regard to the agricultural laws are two separate factors. From the time God promised the land to Abraham, it was endowed with holiness and that holiness remains until the present day. Because of that holiness, the power of the Divine presence can be conveyed to judges. The sanctity of the land with regard to the agricultural laws, by contrast, is associated with particular ritual obligations. Even when that sanctity is not intact, the essential holiness of the land is.

21. The Jerusalem Talmud (*Sanhedrin* 10:2) derives this concept through the exegesis of II Samuel 6:1 which speaks of David's desire to transport the ark to Jerusalem. Albeit the Rambam's version of that text was apparently different from the standard printed version (*Lechem Mishneh*).

22. In his Commentary to the Mishnah (*Bechorot* 4:4), the Rambam cites proof for his thesis that to be granted license to adjudicate any questions of law, a judge must possess knowledge of the entire Torah from the Jerusalem Talmud (*Chagigah* 1:8).

ז יֵשׁ לַסּוֹמְכִין לִסְמֹךְ אֲפִלּוּ מֵאָה בְּפַעַם אַחַת. וְדָוִד הַמֶּלֶךְ סָמַךְ שְׁלֹשִׁים אֶלֶף בְּיוֹם אֶחָד.

ח וְיֵשׁ לָהֶן לְמַנּוֹת כָּל מִי שֶׁיִּרְצוּ לִדְבָרִים יְחִידִים. וְהוּא שֶׁיִּהְיֶה רָאוּי לְכָל הַדְּבָרִים. כֵּיצַד? חָכָם מֻפְלָא שֶׁרָאוּי לְהוֹרוֹת לְכָל הַתּוֹרָה כֻּלָּהּ – יֵשׁ לְבֵית דִּין לִסְמֹךְ אוֹתוֹ וְלִתֵּן לוֹ רְשׁוּת לָדוּן, וְלֹא לְהוֹרוֹת בְּאִסּוּר וְהֶתֵּר. אוֹ יִתְּנוּ לוֹ רְשׁוּת בְּאִסּוּר וְהֶתֵּר, וְלֹא לָדוּן דִּינֵי מָמוֹנוֹת. אוֹ יִתְּנוּ רְשׁוּת לָזֶה וְלָזֶה, אֲבָל לֹא לָדוּן דִּינֵי קְנָסוֹת. אוֹ לָדוּן דִּינֵי קְנָסוֹת, אֲבָל לֹא לְהַתִּיר בְּכוֹרוֹת בְּמוּמִין. אוֹ יִתְּנוּ לוֹ רְשׁוּת לְהַתִּיר נְדָרִים בִּלְבַד, אוֹ לִרְאוֹת כְּתָמִים. וְכֵן כֹּל כַּיּוֹצֵא בָּהֶן.

ט וְכֵן יֵשׁ לַסּוֹמְכִין לִתֵּן רְשׁוּת עַד זְמַן, וְלוֹמַר לַנִּסְמָךְ: יֵשׁ לְךָ רְשׁוּת לָדוּן אוֹ לְהוֹרוֹת עַד שֶׁיָּבוֹא הַנָּשִׂיא לְכָאן, אוֹ כָּל זְמַן שֶׁאֵין אַתָּה עִמָּנוּ בַּמְּדִינָה. וְכֵן כֹּל כַּיּוֹצֵא בָּזֶה.

י חָכָם מֻפְלָא שֶׁהוּא סוּמָא בְּעֵינוֹ אַחַת, אַף עַל פִּי שֶׁהוּא רָאוּי לְדִינֵי מָמוֹנוֹת – אֵין סוֹמְכִין אוֹתוֹ לְדִינֵי מָמוֹנוֹת, מִפְּנֵי שֶׁאֵינוֹ רָאוּי לְכָל הַדְּבָרִים. וְכֵן כֹּל כַּיּוֹצֵא בָּזֶה.

The *Minchat Chinuch* (mitzvah 491) objects to the Rambam's ruling, maintaining that the matter is the subject of a difference of opinion between the Babylonian Talmud and the Jerusalem Talmud. For the Babylonian Talmud (*Sanhedrin* 5b) offers a supposition that Rabbi Chiyya did not give Rav permission to judge the blemishes of firstborn animals, because he was not knowledgeable in that regard. Although this supposition is rejected, for Rav in fact possessed such knowledge, the fact that such a supposition was suggested indicates that a judge could be given authority for certain matters although he did not possess knowledge regarding the entire Torah. The *Minchat Chinuch* concludes, however, that the supposition could have been rejected also because of the principle stated by the Rambam. It was not necessary for the Talmud to state that, because Rav did in fact possess the required knowledge.

23. *Kenasot*, which as stated in Chapter 4, Halachah 9, may only be adjudicated by judges possessing *semichah*.

24. As stated in *Hilchot Bechorot* 2:1, a firstborn animal may be used for non-sacramental purposes only if it has a permanent blemish. And as stated (*ibid.* 3:1), the determination of what is a permanent blemish can be made only by an expert judge who was given license to rule regarding such matters.

25. Which can be absolved only by a distinguished judge (*Hilchot Nedarim* 4:5).

26. To determine whether they render a woman ritually impure or not. See *Hilchot Issurei Bi'ah* 9:36. As stated in the Jerusalem Talmud (*Chagigah* 1:8), special authority must be given to a sage to issue such rulings.

27. See *Sanhedrin* 5b which gives examples of this principle.

28. See the Jerusalem Talmud (*loc. cit.*) which states that Rabbi Yehoshua ben Levi suffered anguish because he had a student of outstanding abilities whom he could not grant *semichah*, because the student was blind in one eye.

29. As Chapter 2, Halachah 9, states, a judge with this physical disability may rule with regard to such matters. Since he is not given *semichah*, however, he is not absolved of financial responsibility in the event of error as he would be if he possessed such ordination. See Chapter 6, Halachah 2.

30. For as stated in Chapter 2, Halachah 9, he may not serve in the *Sanhedrin*.

11. If there was only one judge in *Eretz Yisrael* who possessed *semichah*, he should call two other [judges] to sit with him[31] and they should convey *semichah* on 70 [judges] at one time or one after the other.[32] Afterwards, he and these 70 should [join together to] make up the Supreme *Sanhedrin* and grant *semichah* [to others] to make up other courts.

It appears to me[33] that if all the all the wise men[34] in *Eretz Yisrael*[35] agree to appoint judges and convey *semichah* upon them, the *semichah* is binding and [these judges] may adjudicate cases involving financial penalties and convey *semichah* upon others.[36]

If so, why did the Sages suffer anguish[37] over [the institution] of *semichah*, so that the judgment of cases involving financial penalties would not be nullified among the Jewish people?[38] Because the Jewish people were dispersed,[39] and it is impossible that all could agree.[40] If, by contrast, there was a person who had received *semichah* from a person who had received *semichah*, he does not require the consent of all others. Instead, he may adjudicate cases involving financial penalties for everyone, for he received *semichah* from a court.

[The question whether *semichah* can be renewed] requires resolution.[41]

12. When a court received *semichah* in *Eretz Yisrael* and then departed to the diaspora, they may judge cases involving financial penalties in the diaspora in

31. As stated in Halachah 3, a quorum of three judges is required to convey *semichah.*
32. As *Sanhedrin* 14a relates the Romans tried to stamp out the Jewish court system by preventing the sages from conveying *semichah* on their students. They were almost successful, but Rabbi Yehudah ben Bava sacrificed his life and conveyed *semichah* on five students. They in turn conveyed *semichah* on others and were able to reconstruct the court system.
33. This preface introduces a concept for which the Rambam has no explicit source in previous Rabbinic literature.
34. I.e., wise men who do not possess *semichah.*
35. For *semichah* cannot be conveyed in the Diaspora as stated in Halachah 4.
36. In this way, the process of *semichah* could be renewed and all the judicial prerogatives possessed only by judges who received *semichah* could be continued. See the notes at the conclusion of the halachah.
37. And actually sacrifice their lives, as in the story of Rabbi Yehudah ben Bava cited previously.
38. I.e., if *semichah* could be renewed so easily, why was their such anguish and such self-sacrifice to perpetuate it? Let it be nullified temporarily in the face of persecution and renewed afterwards.
39. Geographically, and communication was difficult.
40. The simple meaning of the Rambam's words is that because of the geographic distance, it would be difficult to arrange a meeting where the Sages could gather together and agree on a court. There is, however, an implication that our people suffered from centrifugal force with regard to their inner feelings and because of their lack of unity, the possibility of achieving consensus was challenging.

יא הֲרֵי שֶׁלֹּא הָיָה בְּאֶרֶץ יִשְׂרָאֵל אֶלָּא סוֹמֵךְ אֶחָד – מוֹשִׁיב שְׁנַיִם בְּצִדּוֹ, וְסוֹמֵךְ שִׁבְעִים כְּאֶחָד, אוֹ זֶה אַחַר זֶה, וְאַחַר כָּךְ יַעֲשֶׂה הוּא וְהַשִּׁבְעִים בֵּית דִּין הַגָּדוֹל, וְיִסְמְכוּ בָּתֵּי דִינִין אֲחֵרִים.

נִרְאִין לִי הַדְּבָרִים: שֶׁאִם הִסְכִּימוּ כָּל הַחֲכָמִים שֶׁבְּאֶרֶץ יִשְׂרָאֵל לְמַנּוֹת דַּיָּנִים וְלִסְמֹךְ אוֹתָם – הֲרֵי אֵלּוּ סְמוּכִים, וְיֵשׁ לָהֶן לָדוּן דִּינֵי קְנָסוֹת, וְיֵשׁ לָהֶן לִסְמֹךְ לַאֲחֵרִים.

אִם כֵּן, לָמָּה הָיוּ הַחֲכָמִים מִצְטַעֲרִין עַל הַסְּמִיכָה כְּדֵי שֶׁלֹּא יִבָּטְלוּ דִּינֵי קְנָסוֹת מִיִּשְׂרָאֵל? לְפִי שֶׁיִּשְׂרָאֵל מְפֻזָּרִין, וְאִי אֶפְשָׁר שֶׁיַּסְכִּימוּ כֻּלָּן.

וְאִם הָיָה שָׁם סָמוּךְ מִפִּי סָמוּךְ – אֵינוֹ צָרִיךְ דַּעַת כֻּלָּן, אֶלָּא דָן דִּינֵי קְנָסוֹת לַכֹּל, שֶׁהֲרֵי נִסְמַךְ מִפִּי בֵּית דִּין.

וְהַדָּבָר צָרִיךְ הֶכְרֵעַ.

יב בֵּית דִּין שֶׁנִּסְמְכוּ בְּאֶרֶץ יִשְׂרָאֵל וְיָצְאוּ חוּצָה לָאָרֶץ – הֲרֵי הֵם דָּנִים דִּינֵי קְנָסוֹת

41. I.e., the Rambam was uncertain whether his ruling should be accepted or not. His equivocation on this matter represents somewhat of a change of thinking on this subject. In his Commentary to the Mishnah (*Sanhedrin* 1:3), the Rambam explains his rationale for this ruling and outlines similar ideas. In that source, however, he does not speak of the need for resolution. To quote:

> If you do not say [that *semichah* can be renewed in the above manner], there will never be the possibility for the Supreme *Sanhedrin* to exist [again], for it will be necessary that there be a judge who received *semichah* [and this is not so].... And God has promised [the Jewish people] on their return [to *Eretz Yisrael*] (Isaiah 1:26): "I will restore your judges as in the previous era."

This issue was debated not only by the Rambam, but by many other sages. Moreover, the debate was not merely theoretical. In the year 5298 (1538), Rav Ya'akov bei Rav, the Chief Rabbi of Tsfat, acted on the Rambam's ruling. Convening his yeshivah which included such luminaries as Rav Yosef Karo and Rav Moshe of Turin, he desired to be granted *semichah* himself, then to convey *semichah*, and in this way, to renew the *Sanhedrin*.

The Chief Rabbi of Jerusalem, the Ralbach, opposed this concept vehemently, composing a text *Kuntres HaSemichah* to explain his opposition to the concept. For resolution, the two sides turned to the Radbaz, Chief Rabbi of Egypt, who sided with the Ralbach. In his gloss to this halachah, the Radbaz reveals some of the thinking that motivated his decision. Firstly, he questions the Rambam's statements about the difficulty of collecting all the judges together and suggests that the appointments could be done by correspondence. Alternatively, he notes that if one requires all the judges of *Eretz Yisrael* to gather together, that was not done in Tsfat. Secondly, he notes that to receive *semichah*, a sage must be able to rule with regard to the entire Torah, and questions whether such sages exist at present.

And with regard to the Rambam's statements in his Commentary to the Mishnah, that in the Messianic era, there will be a *Sanhedrin* and that *Sanhedrin* must be made up of judges with *semichah*, the Radbaz answers that Elijah the prophet will arrive before *Mashiach*. He possesses *semichah* and he can grant that ordination to others.

the same manner as they judge [such cases] in *Eretz [Yisrael]*. For the *Sanhedrin* exercises judicial authority in *Eretz [Yisrael]* and in the diaspora, provided the judges have received *semichah* in *Eretz [Yisrael]*.[42]

13. The exiliarchs in Babylon function instead of the kings. They have the authority to impose their rule over the Jewish people in all places and to judge them whether they consent or not.[43] [This is derived from Genesis 49:10:] "The staff[44] will not depart from Judah" - this refers to the exiliarchs of Babylon.[45]

14. Any judge who is fit to adjudicate [cases][46] and was given license to serve as a judge by the exiliarch has the authority to act as a judge throughout the entire world, whether in *Eretz Yisrael* or in the diaspora.[47] Even though [either or both of] the litigants do not desire [to argue the case before him], [they are required to do so][48] despite the fact that he does not have the authority to adjudicate cases involving financial penalties.[49]

Any judge who is fit to adjudicate [cases] and was given license to serve as a judge by the court in *Eretz Yisrael* has the authority to act as a judge throughout *Eretz Yisrael* and in the cities which are located on its boundaries[50] even though the litigants do not desire [to argue the case before him]. In the diaspora, by contrast, the license [granted him] does not afford him the authority to compel the litigants [to appear before him]. Although he has the sanction to adjudicate cases involving financial penalties in the diaspora,[51] he may adjudicate [such cases] only when the litigants consent for him to judge. He does not have the authority to compel the litigants to accept his rulings unless he is granted such authority by the exiliarch.[52]

15. When a person is not fit to act as a judge because he is not knowledgeable or because he lacks proper character and an exiliarch transgressed[53] and granted him authority or the court erred[54] and granted him authority, the authority granted him is of no consequence unless he is fit. [To cite a parallel:] When a person consecrates an animal with a physical blemish [to be sacrificed] on the altar, the holiness does not encompass it.[55]

42. This last phrase is not included in the standard printed texts of the *Mishneh Torah* and was added on the basis of authoritative manuscripts.
43. I.e., when summoned to court a litigant must appear and he must carry out the judgment of the court.
44. I.e., the ruling authority.
45. The exiliarchs were descendants of King David, son after son. As such, they were granted authority over the Jewish people. As the Rambam states in his Commentary to the Mishnah (*Bechorot* 4:4), their authority was not an outgrowth of their wisdom - indeed, not all of them were Torah sages - but rather of their lineage and the acceptance of them by people at large.
46. I.e., his wisdom and his character fit the criteria described in the beginning of Chapter 2. The following halachah discusses judges who are unfit.
47. I.e., the authority of the exiliarch is also effective in *Eretz Yisrael*. As reflected in the

בְּחוּצָה לָאָרֶץ כְּדֶרֶךְ שֶׁדָּנִים בָּאָרֶץ; שֶׁסַּנְהֶדְרִין נוֹהֶגֶת בָּאָרֶץ וּבְחוּצָה לָאָרֶץ, וְהוּא שֶׁיִּהְיוּ סְמוּכִים.

יג רָאשֵׁי גָּלֻיּוֹת שֶׁבְּבָבֶל – בִּמְקוֹם מֶלֶךְ הֵן עוֹמְדִים. וְיֵשׁ לָהֶן לִרְדּוֹת אֶת יִשְׂרָאֵל בְּכָל מָקוֹם, וְלָדוּן עֲלֵיהֶן בֵּין רָצוּ בֵּין לֹא רָצוּ. שֶׁנֶּאֱמַר: לֹא יָסוּר שֵׁבֶט מִיהוּדָה – אֵלּוּ רָאשֵׁי גָּלֻיּוֹת שֶׁבְּבָבֶל.

יד וְכָל דַּיָּן הָרָאוּי לָדוּן, שֶׁנָּתַן לוֹ רֹאשׁ גָּלוּת רְשׁוּת לָדוּן – יֵשׁ לוֹ רְשׁוּת לָדוּן בְּכָל הָעוֹלָם אַף עַל פִּי שֶׁלֹּא רָצוּ בַּעֲלֵי דִינִין, בֵּין בָּאָרֶץ בֵּין בְּחוּצָה לָאָרֶץ, אַף עַל פִּי שֶׁאֵינוֹ דָן דִּינֵי קְנָסוֹת.

וְכָל דַּיָּן הָרָאוּי לָדוּן, שֶׁנָּתְנוּ לוֹ בֵּית דִּין שֶׁבְּאֶרֶץ יִשְׂרָאֵל רְשׁוּת לָדוּן – יֵשׁ לוֹ רְשׁוּת לָדוּן בְּכָל אֶרֶץ יִשְׂרָאֵל וּבָעֲיָרוֹת הָעוֹמְדוֹת עַל הַגְּבוּלִים אַף עַל פִּי שֶׁלֹּא רָצוּ בַּעֲלֵי דִינִין; אֲבָל בְּחוּצָה לָאָרֶץ – אֵין רְשׁוּתָן מוֹעֶלֶת לוֹ לָכֹף אֶת בַּעֲלֵי דִינִין. אַף עַל פִּי שֶׁיֵּשׁ לוֹ לָדוּן דִּינֵי קְנָסוֹת בְּחוּצָה לָאָרֶץ – אֵינוֹ דָן אֶלָּא לְמִי שֶׁרוֹצֶה לָדוּן אֶצְלוֹ; אֲבָל לָכֹף אֶת בַּעֲלֵי דִינִין וְלָדוּן לָהֶם – אֵין לוֹ רְשׁוּת, עַד שֶׁיִּטֹּל רְשׁוּת מֵרֹאשׁ גָּלוּת.

טו מִי שֶׁאֵינוֹ רָאוּי לָדוּן, מִפְּנֵי שֶׁאֵינוֹ יוֹדֵעַ אוֹ מִפְּנֵי שֶׁאֵינוֹ הָגוּן, שֶׁעָבַר רֹאשׁ גָּלוּת וְנָתַן לוֹ רְשׁוּת, אוֹ שֶׁטָּעוּ בֵּית דִּין וְנָתְנוּ לוֹ רְשׁוּת – אֵין הָרְשׁוּת מוֹעֶלֶת לוֹ כְּלוּם עַד שֶׁיְּהֵא רָאוּי. שֶׁהַמַּקְדִּישׁ בַּעַל מוּם לַמִּזְבֵּחַ – אֵין הַקְּדֻשָּׁה חָלָה עָלָיו.

continuation of the halachah, his authority thus surpasses that of the *nasi* in *Eretz Yisrael* (*Sanhedrin* 5a).

48. I.e., at times, litigants may desire to have their cases heard by judges whom they desire and at times, they may use this as a means of procrastinating and preventing a case from being brought to court. Since these judges have been appointed by the ruling authority, they need not heed such requests and may compel the litigants to come to court to settle a dispute.

49. Because he was not granted *semichah*.

50. For they are governed by the legal system of *Eretz Yisrael*.

51. Which judges appointed in the Diaspora did not possess.

52. Although *semichah* can be given only by the judges of *Eretz Yisrael* and this empowers a judge to adjudicate a wider variety of cases, *semichah* does not carry with it the authority to compel a litigant to appear in court. In the Diaspora, that is dependent on the authority granted by the exiliarch alone.

53. For appointing such a judge violates a Scriptural commandment as stated in Chapter 3, Halachah 8. Although the exiliarchs have authority over the people, that authority is not strong enough to countermand the Torah's law.

54. As stated above, not all the exiliarchs were paradigms of righteousness. Hence it is possible that an unfit judge was intentionally given authority to adjudicate cases. We do not suspect that the court will intentionally appoint an improper judge. There is, however, a possibility that they will err.

55. None of the prohibitions that apply to consecrated animals apply to it. See *Hilchot Issurei Mizbeach* 1:10.

CHAPTER FIVE

1. A king may not be enthroned except by the [High] Court of 71 judges.[1] A minor *Sanhedrin* for every tribe and every city may be appointed only by the [High] Court of 71 judges.[2] A tribe that has been led to apostasy in its entirety,[3] a false prophet,[4] or a case in which the High Priest might be liable for capital punishment,[5] may be judged only by the [High] Court of 71 judges. Financial cases involving a High Priest, by contrast, may be adjudicated by a court of three.[6]

Similarly, [the determination of] a rebellious elder[7] or a city led to apostasy[8] and [the decision] to cause a woman suspected of adultery to drink [the waters which test her][9] may only be done by the High Court. Similarly, [the decisions to] extend the city limits of Jerusalem and the limits of the Temple Courtyard,[10] to enter a voluntary war,[11] and to measure [the distance between a corpse and the nearby cities][12] may be done only by the [High] Court of 71 judges. [These concepts are derived from Exodus 18:22]: "All the major matters will be brought to you."

2. Cases involving capital punishment may not be judged by a court with less than 23 judges, i.e., a minor *Sanhedrin.*[13] This applies not only to instances where humans are judged with regard to capital punishment, but also when animals face such judgment. Therefore an ox which must be stoned to death[14] and an animal used in bestial sexual practices[15] is [condemned to death only] by a court of 23 judges. Even when a lion, a bear, or a cheetah that have been domesticated and which have owners kill [a human], they are executed [based on the judgment of a court] of 23. When, however, a snake kills [a human], even one [ordinary] person may kill him.[16]

1. See *Hilchot Melachim* 1:3 which states that the appointment must be made by a prophet, as Moses appointed Joshua and Samuel appointed Saul and David. Afterwards, that appointment must be affirmed by the High Court.
2. *Sanhedrin* 16b derives this from the fact that it was Moses who appointed all the courts for the Jewish people. And Moses had the authority of a court of 71 judges.
3. The intent is not necessarily that every member of the tribe was led astray. If the majority was led astray these rules apply.

Deuteronomy, ch. 13, speaks of a city that is influenced to worship false divinities. *Sanhedrin* 16b-17a also applies these laws if a tribe is led astray. There is, however, a difference with regard to the application of these laws vis-a-vis a tribe and a city. As the Rambam (*Hilchot Avodat Kochavim* 4:2) states: "If, however, the majority of a tribe is led astray, they are judged as individuals." Based on *Sanhedrin, loc. cit.*, that statement means "They are executed as individuals." Nevertheless, the judgment of the people is held under the auspices of the High Court.

4. See *Hilchot Avodat Kochavim* 5:8 which explains that we are referring to a person who claims to be communicating a prophecy from God, when he never received such a revelation. *Sanhedrin, loc. cit.*, establishes an association between such a prophet and a rebellious elder. Just as a rebellious elder is judged by the High Court as will be explained; so, too, such a prophet is brought to judgment before them.

פֶּרֶק חֲמִישִׁי

א אֵין מַעֲמִידִין מֶלֶךְ אֶלָּא עַל פִּי בֵּית דִּין שֶׁל שִׁבְעִים וְאֶחָד. וְאֵין עוֹשִׂין סַנְהֶדְרֵי קְטַנָּה לְכָל שֵׁבֶט וָשֵׁבֶט וּלְכָל עִיר וָעִיר אֶלָּא עַל פִּי בֵּית דִּין שֶׁל שִׁבְעִים וְאֶחָד. וְאֵין דָּנִין לֹא אֶת הַשֵּׁבֶט שֶׁהֻדַּח כֻּלּוֹ וְלֹא אֶת נְבִיא הַשֶּׁקֶר וְלֹא אֶת כֹּהֵן גָּדוֹל בְּדִינֵי נְפָשׁוֹת אֶלָּא בְּבֵית דִּין הַגָּדוֹל; אֲבָל דִּינֵי מָמוֹנוֹת [שֶׁל כֹּהֵן גָּדוֹל] – בִּשְׁלֹשָׁה.

וְכֵן אֵין עוֹשִׂין זָקֵן מַמְרֵא, וְלֹא עוֹשִׂין עִיר הַנִּדַּחַת, וְלֹא מַשְׁקִין אֶת הַסּוֹטָה, אֶלָּא בְּבֵית דִּין הַגָּדוֹל. וְאֵין מוֹסִיפִין עַל הָעִיר וְעַל הָעֲזָרוֹת, וְלֹא מוֹצִיאִין לְמִלְחֶמֶת הָרְשׁוּת וְלִמְדִידַת הֶחָלָל, אֶלָּא עַל פִּי בֵּית דִּין הַגָּדוֹל. שֶׁנֶּאֱמַר: כָּל הַדָּבָר הַגָּדֹל יָבִיאוּ אֵלֶיךָ.

ב אֵין דָּנִין דִּינֵי נְפָשׁוֹת בְּפָחוֹת מֵעֶשְׂרִים וּשְׁלֹשָׁה, שֶׁהֵן סַנְהֶדְרֵי קְטַנָּה. בֵּין דִּינֵי נְפָשׁוֹת שֶׁל אָדָם, בֵּין דִּינֵי נְפָשׁוֹת שֶׁל בְּהֵמָה. לְפִיכָךְ, אֵין דָּנִין שׁוֹר הַנִּסְקָל וְלֹא הַבְּהֵמָה הַנִּרְבַּעַת אוֹ הָרוֹבֵעַ אֶלָּא בְּבֵית דִּין שֶׁל עֶשְׂרִים וּשְׁלֹשָׁה. אֲפִלּוּ אֲרִי וְדֹב וּבַרְדְּלָס, שֶׁהֵן בְּנֵי תַּרְבּוּת וְיֵשׁ לָהֶן בְּעָלִים, שֶׁהֵמִיתוּ – מִיתָתָן בְּעֶשְׂרִים וּשְׁלֹשָׁה. אֲבָל נָחָשׁ שֶׁהֵמִית – אֶחָד הוֹרֵג אוֹתוֹ.

5. *Gadol*, the Hebrew term translated as "major" in the prooftext cited by the Rambam at the conclusion of the halachah, is also part of the title given to the High Priest. Hence *Sanhedrin, loc. cit.*, maintains that this is also one of the "major matters" brought to the High Court.

6. For monetary matters are not considered as being "major" in scope (*Sanhedrin, loc. cit.*).

7. For in this context, Deuteronomy 17:8 speaks of "aris[ing] and ascend[ing] to that place," i.e, to Jerusalem, the seat of the Supreme *Sanhedrin*.

8. *Sanhedrin* 16a states that individuals are judged by their local courts. Implied is that communal judgments must be made be a higher body.

9. *Sotah* 7b explains that their is an association made between the judgment of such a woman and that of a rebellious elder.

10. See *Hilchot Beit HaBechirah* 6:10-14 for a discussion and description of these acts. Moses' participation in the delineation of the borders or the Courtyard of the Tent of Meeting and the Camp of Israel serve as a precedent for the High Court's involvement (Rashi, *Sanhedrin* 16b).

11. See *Hilchot Melachim* 5:1 which distinguishes between a *milchemet mitzvah*, a war which we are obligated to fight, and a *milchement reshut*, a voluntary war which a king may undertake to expand the territory of the Jewish people or to add its renown among the nations. *Sanhedrin* 16b derives the need for the *Sanhedrin's* involvement from the description (I Chronicles 27:34) of David's advisers.

12. In order to determine which city is required to bring a calf which is decapitated. I.e., a corpse is found between two cities and the one which is closest is required to bring the calf. Here it appears that the entire High Court should be involved in the measurement to determine which city is closest. In *Hilchot Rotzeach* 9:1, however, the Rambam states that five judges are appointed to supervise this task. See Halachah 5.

13. The rationale is stated in the following halachah.

14. For goring a person to death, as stated in Exodus 21:29.

15. Which is executed as stated in Leviticus 20:15-16.

16. I.e., a trial is not necessary. Instead, the snake should be slain by any person.

3. When a person who spreads a malicious report [concerning his wife],[17] at the outset, [the case] is judged by a court of 23. For there is the possibility of a capital case arising if [the husband's claim] proves true and the woman is to be stoned to death. If the husband's claim is not substantiated,[18] and [the woman's] father comes to demand payment of the fine,[19] the matter may be judged by a court of three.[20]

What is the source which teaches that capital cases may be judged only by [a court] of 23? Although this is a matter conveyed by the Oral Tradition, [there is an allusion to it in the Torah]. [Numbers 35:24-25] states: "And the congregation shall judge... and the congregation shall save...." [Implied is that there must be the possibility of] a congregation judging - and condemning him to death - and a congregation saving - and seeking his acquittal. Now a congregation is no less than ten.[21] Thus there are at least 20 [judges]. We add three [judges] so that there not be an equally balanced court and to allow the possibility of "follow[ing] after the inclination of the majority."[22]

4. Lashes[23] are [decided upon by a court] of three [judges]. Even though the person may die when lashes are administered to him.

5. Decapitating the calf[24] is performed by five judges.

6. The enlargement of the month[25] is decided upon by three [judges].

7. The enlargement of the year[26] is decided upon by seven [judges].[27] All of the [above] must possess *semichah* as we explained.

8. [Cases involving] financial penalties,[28] robbery, personal injury, the payment of double [for a stolen article], the payment of four and five times [the value of

The Ra'avad notes that the Rambam's ruling follows the position of Rabbi Akiva in *Sanhedrin* 2a, even though it appears to be a minority ruling. The *Kessef Mishneh* explains that there are three positions in the Mishnah. Since the first opinion stated by the Mishnah and Rabbi Akiva agree that the other animals should be tried by a court of 23, this is the majority view and the view of Rabbi Eliezer is a minority opinion. Hence it is accepted. But with regard to a snake, since both Rabbi Eliezer and Rabbi Akiva agree that a killer snake should be slain without a trial, their view is the majority. The Radbaz notes that *Bava Kama* 15b appears to support Rabbi Akiva's view. Hence it is given priority. A responsum attributed to the Rambam also provides the resolution offered by the *Kessef Mishneh*.

17. As stated in Deuteronomy, ch. 22, and explained in *Hilchot Na'arah Betulah*, ch. 3, this is speaking about a man who claimed that his wife was not a virgin on her wedding night. Now in that age, a woman was consecrated (*erusin*) before being married (*nisuin*). While consecrated, relations with any other man are considered adultery and punishable by death. Hence even though he is primarily suing to free himself from the obligation to pay the woman the money due her by virtue of her *ketubah* (ante-nuptial contract), the husband's claim could result in the execution of the woman if in fact it were proven that she committed adultery after being consecrated.

18. E.g., it is proven that the witnesses whom he brought to support his claim lied.

ג הַמּוֹצִיא שֵׁם רַע – אֵין דָּנִין אוֹתוֹ תְּחִלָּה אֶלָּא בְּבֵית דִּין שֶׁל עֶשְׂרִים וּשְׁלֹשָׁה, מִפְּנֵי שֶׁיֵּשׁ בְּדִינוֹ צַד דִּינֵי נְפָשׁוֹת, שֶׁמָּא יִהְיֶה הַדָּבָר אֱמֶת וְתִסָּקֵל הַבַּת. לֹא נֶאֶמְנוּ דִּבְרֵי הַבַּעַל, וּבָא הָאָב לְתוֹבְעוֹ בַּקְּנָס – דִּינוֹ בִּשְׁלֹשָׁה.

וּמִנַּיִן שֶׁאֵין דָּנִין דִּינֵי נְפָשׁוֹת אֶלָּא בְּעֶשְׂרִים וּשְׁלֹשָׁה?

אַף עַל פִּי שֶׁדִּבְרֵי קַבָּלָה הֵן, הֲרֵי הוּא אוֹמֵר: וְשָׁפְטוּ הָעֵדָה וְהִצִּילוּ הָעֵדָה – עֵדָה שׁוֹפֶטֶת וְעֵדָה מַצֶּלֶת; עֵדָה שׁוֹפֶטֶת – וְהֵן הַמְחַיְּבִין, וְעֵדָה מַצֶּלֶת – וְהֵן הַמְזַכִּין; וְאֵין עֵדָה פָּחוֹת מֵעֲשָׂרָה – הֲרֵי עֶשְׂרִים; וּמוֹסִיפִין שְׁלֹשָׁה, כְּדֵי שֶׁלֹּא יְהֵא בֵּית דִּין שָׁקוּל, וְיִהְיֶה בּוֹ אַחֲרֵי רַבִּים לְהַטּוֹת.

ד מַכּוֹת – בִּשְׁלֹשָׁה, וְאַף עַל פִּי שֶׁאֶפְשָׁר שֶׁיָּמוּת כְּשֶׁמַּלְקִין אוֹתוֹ.

ה עֲרִיפַת הָעֶגְלָה – בַּחֲמִשָּׁה.

ו עִבּוּר הַחֹדֶשׁ – בִּשְׁלֹשָׁה.

ז עִבּוּר הַשָּׁנָה – בְּשִׁבְעָה. וְכָל אֵלּוּ סְמוּכִין כְּמוֹ שֶׁבֵּאַרְנוּ.

ח דִּינֵי קְנָסוֹת, כְּגוֹן גְּזֵלוֹת וְחַבָּלוֹת, וְתַשְׁלוּמֵי כֶּפֶל וְתַשְׁלוּמֵי אַרְבָּעָה וַחֲמִשָּׁה, וְהָאוֹנֵס

19. 100 silver *shekalim*, as stated in the sources mentioned above.
20. For this is an ordinary *knas*, financial penalty.
21. This is derived from Numbers 14:27: "Until when [must I bear] this evil congregation," which refers to the spies. There were 12 spies, since Joshua and Caleb were righteous, they were not included in "the evil congregation," leaving ten.
22. Exodus 23:2. As explained in Chapter 8, Halachah 1, *Sanhedrin* 2a interprets this verse to mean that the manner in which we follow the bias of the majority is different when they desire to obligate a person for capital punishment than when they wish to exonerate him. A majority of at least two judges are necessary.
23. I.e., trying a person for the violation of transgressions punishable by lashes and the determination of how many lashes the person can bear.
24. The *Kessef Mishneh* maintains that this refers to measuring which city is closest to the corpse. The Radbaz, however, maintains that the entire court of 71 must supervise the measurement as stated in Halachah 1. This refers to the actual sacrifice of the calf in the wadi.
25. I.e., the decision whether or not to add a day to the month or not. Three judges are sufficient. See *Hilchot Kiddush HaChodesh* 1:5-7.
26. The decision whether to add another month to the year or not, as described by *ibid.*, ch. 4.
27. As *Hilchot Kiddush HaChodesh* explains, three judges begin discussion of the matter. It is then debated among five and the final decision is reached with seven.
28. In *Hilchot Nizkei Mammon* 2:8, the Rambam defines a *k'nas*, financial penalty, as a situation where the person pays more or less than the actual monetary damage that he caused. This indicates that the monetary issues between one man and another are not the primary matters at stake, but rather the person's relationship with God. Therefore such cases must be adjudicated by a court of three judges possessing *semichah*.

a stolen sheep or ox], rape, seduction, and the like may be adjudicated only by three expert judges who have received *semichah* in *Eretz Yisrael*,

Other cases of financial law, e.g., admissions [of financial liability] and loans, do not require an expert judge. Even three ordinary people, or even one expert judge[29] may adjudicate them. For this reason, cases involving admissions [of financial liability],[30] loans,[31] and the like[32] may be adjudicated in the diaspora. Although a court in the diaspora is not referred to as *Elohim*,[33] they carry out the charge of the court of *Eretz Yisrael*.[34] This charge does not, however, give them license to adjudicate cases involving financial penalties.

9. The courts of the diaspora adjudicate only cases that commonly occur and which involve financial loss, e.g., admissions of liability, loans,[35] and property damage.[36] Matters that occur only infrequently, by contrast, even though they involve financial loss, e.g., an animal that injures another,[37] or events that commonly occur, but do not involve financial loss, e.g., a double payment [for theft],[38] are not adjudicated by the judges of the diaspora.

Similarly, all the financial penalties which our Sages imposed against a person who punches a colleague, slaps a colleague, or the like[39] are not adjudicated by the judges of the diaspora. Whenever a person is required to pay half the damages [for the destruction of property][40] [the matter] is not adjudicated by the judges of the diaspora, with the exception of the half payment for damages caused by pebbles propelled by one's animals.[41] For that is a reimbursement for financial loss and is not a financial penalty.

10. Whenever [the injuries a person suffers] are evaluated by calculating his worth as one calculates the worth of a servant, [the payment] is not expropriated by the judges of the diaspora.[42] Therefore if a person injures a

29. See Chapter 2, Halachah 10. The Rambam's wording indicates that it is preferable for three ordinary judges to adjudicate a case rather than one expert judge.

30. I.e., the plaintiff brings witnesses who testify that the defendant acknowledged a debt in their presence.

31. Witnesses testify that they observed a loan being given.

32. E.g., property disputes, laws involving sales and presents, inheritances and wills, divorce settlements.

33. See Chapter 4, Halachah 4.

34. The Rambam clarifies the matters given over to the jurisdiction of the judges of the Diaspora and those withheld from their jurisdiction in the following halachot.

Rav Moshe Cohen asks: Since, as te Rambam states in Chapter 2, Halachah 10, one judge is acceptable according to Scriptural Law, why is it necessary to say that the judges of the Diaspora are carrying out the charge of the judges of *Eretz Yisrael* in judging loans and the like? Independently, they have the authority to judge such cases.

The *Or Sameach* explains that according to Scriptural Law, it is necessary to have at least one judge on the court with *semichah*. Since that is not possible in the Diaspora, it is necessary to rely on the charge given by the judges of *Eretz Yisrael*.

וְהַמְפַתֶּה וְכַיּוֹצֵא בָּהֶן - אֵין דָּנִין אוֹתָם אֶלָּא שְׁלֹשָׁה מֻמְחִים, וְהֵם הַסְּמוּכִין בְּאֶרֶץ יִשְׂרָאֵל.

אֲבָל שְׁאָר דִּינֵי מָמוֹנוֹת, כְּגוֹן הוֹדָאוֹת וְהַלְוָאוֹת - אֵינָן צְרִיכִין מֻמְחֶה, אֶלָּא אֲפִלּוּ שְׁלֹשָׁה הֶדְיוֹטוֹת, וַאֲפִלּוּ אֶחָד מֻמְחֶה דָּן אוֹתָן. לְפִיכָךְ דָּנִין בְּהוֹדָאוֹת וְהַלְוָאוֹת וְכַיּוֹצֵא בָּהֶן בְּחוּצָה לָאָרֶץ. אַף עַל פִּי שֶׁאֵין בֵּית דִּין שֶׁל חוּצָה לָאָרֶץ אֱלֹהִים, שְׁלִיחוּת בֵּית דִּין שֶׁל אֶרֶץ יִשְׂרָאֵל עוֹשִׂין; וְאֵין לָהֶן רְשׁוּת לָדוּן דִּינֵי קְנָסוֹת בִּשְׁלִיחוּתָן.

ט אֵין דָּנִין בֵּית דִּין שֶׁל חוּצָה לָאָרֶץ אֶלָּא דְּבָרִים הַמְּצוּיִין תָּמִיד וְיֵשׁ בָּהֶן חֶסְרוֹן כִּיס, כְּגוֹן הוֹדָאוֹת וְהַלְוָאוֹת וּמַזִּיק מָמוֹן חֲבֵרוֹ; אֲבָל דְּבָרִים שֶׁאֵין מְצוּיִין, אַף עַל פִּי שֶׁיֵּשׁ בָּהֶן חֶסְרוֹן כִּיס, כְּגוֹן בְּהֵמָה שֶׁחָבְלָה בַּחֲבֶרְתָּהּ; אוֹ דְּבָרִים הַמְּצוּיִין, אֲבָל אֵין בָּהֶן חֶסְרוֹן כִּיס, כְּגוֹן תַּשְׁלוּמֵי כֶפֶל - אֵין דָּנִין אוֹתָן דַּיָּנֵי חוּצָה לָאָרֶץ.

וְכֵן כָּל הַקְּנָסוֹת שֶׁקָּנְסוּ חֲכָמִים בְּתוֹקֵעַ לַחֲבֵרוֹ וּבְסוֹטֵר אֶת חֲבֵרוֹ וְכַיּוֹצֵא בָּהֶן - אֵין גּוֹבִין אוֹתָן דַּיָּנֵי חוּצָה לָאָרֶץ.

וְכָל הַמְשַׁלֵּם חֲצִי נֶזֶק - אֵין גּוֹבִין אוֹתוֹ דַּיָּנֵי חוּצָה לָאָרֶץ; חוּץ מֵחֲצִי נֶזֶק צְרוֹרוֹת, מִפְּנֵי שֶׁהוּא מָמוֹן וְאֵינוֹ קְנָס.

י כָּל הַנִּשּׁוֹם כְּעֶבֶד - אֵין גּוֹבִין אוֹתוֹ דַּיָּנֵי חוּצָה לָאָרֶץ.

35. As explained above, both of these types of cases involve loans. If cases of this nature were not adjudicated in the Diaspora, a person would never lend his colleague money, for if he did not repay him, he would have no way of seeking financial redress (*Bava Kama* 84b).
36. For if people knew that they would not be held liable for property damage, they would be careless and allow damage to occur (*ibid.*).
37. To exemplify this category, the *Tur* (*Choshen Mishpat* 1) mentions a person who injures a colleague.
38. Compensation for the stolen article is, however, granted as stated in Halachah 13.
39. See *Hilchot Chovel UMazik* 3:9 which states that our Sages assigned specific financial penalties for certain actions which involve a moderate amount of pain, but great embarrassment.
40. When an ox which is not wont to gore other ox injures another by goring, the owner is required to pay only half the damages. Similarly, whenever damage is caused by an animal which deviates from its natural pattern, only half the damages are paid. Since the person is not required to pay the entire amount of the damages, this is considered a *k'nas* and cannot be levied by judges who do not possess *semichah.*
41. As the Rambam states in *Hilchot Nizkei Mammon* 2:7, this is a unique instance where although the person is required to pay only half the damages, it is considered as financial restitution and not as a *k'nas*.
42. Our Rabbis explain that no person would willingly undergo a loss of limb, embarrassment, or pain. Since any financial redress is less than the value to the person, the assessment is considered as a *k'nas* and is not made by the judges of the Diaspora. Moreover, injuries of this nature are not frequent occurrences. Hence there is no need to establish provisions for them.

colleague, [compensation for] the damages, the pain, and the embarrassment[43] for which he is liable is not expropriated by the judges of the diaspora. [Compensation] for the inability to work and medical expenses is, by contrast, expropriated [in the diaspora], because they involve a financial loss.[44] The *Geonim*[45] ruled in this manner and stated that it is a commonplace matter to expropriate [compensation] for the inability to work and medical expenses in the diaspora.

11. The judges of the diaspora do not exact payment when an animal injures a person, because this is an uncommon occurrence. When, by contrast, a person damages an animal belonging to a colleague,[46] he must pay the complete damages [to his colleague] regardless of where this takes place, just as he is responsible if he ripped his garments, broke his utensils, or cut down his produce.

Similarly, when an animal causes damage by eating or by treading, since its owner is forewarned[47] that this is its inherent natural tendency, it is a common matter and [the damages] are expropriated by the judges of the diaspora. [This applies] whether it damaged another animal, e.g., it rubbed against it,[48] it consumed produce that it would naturally[49] eat or the like, or it damaged food or utensils [by treading upon them] in which instance he is obligated to [pay] full damages. [Payment for] all of these [damages] can be expropriated by the judges of the diaspora.

If, however, an animal was not prone to cause damage, [then it caused damages to the extent that the owner] was warned, and then it caused damage again, e.g., it bit, it butted with its body, it lay down, it kicked, or it gored, these damages are not expropriated by the judges of the diaspora. [The rationale is] that there is no concept [of the owner] of an animal being forewarned in the diaspora.[50] Even if [an animal caused its owner to be] forewarned in *Eretz Yisrael*, and then it was taken to the diaspora where it caused damage, the damages are not expropriated, because this is an uncommon occurrence.

12. Why is there no concept of warning [an owner] in the diaspora? Because testimony[51] must be given against [the owner] in the presence of a court.[52] And the concept of a court applies only with regard to judges who have been given *semichah* in *Eretz Yisrael*.[53]

43. In the latter two instances, there is no financial loss suffered at all.
44. They are also semi-frequent occurrences. Injuries that cause permanent loss of limbs are not common, but those which cause unemployment and require medical attention occur more frequently (Radbaz).
45. The *Hagahot Ashurei* attribute such a ruling to Rabbenu Chananel and the *Tur* (*Choshen Mishpat* 1) to Rav Hai Gaon. The Rabbis note that in the Rambam's Commentary to the Mishnah (*Bava Kama* 8:1), the Rambam states that in the Diaspora, a person who causes a colleague injury should be placed under a ban of ostracism until he agrees to settle the issue. He does not, however, mention the concept of receiving restitution for unemployment and medical expenses. This indicates the possibility that at

לְפִיכָךְ, אָדָם שֶׁחָבַל בַּחֲבֵרוֹ – אֵין גּוֹבִין הַנֶּזֶק וְהַצַּעַר וְהַבֹּשֶׁת שֶׁהוּא חַיָּב בָּהֶן דַּיָּנֵי חוּצָה לָאָרֶץ; אֲבָל שֶׁבֶת וְרִפּוּי – גּוֹבִין, מִפְּנֵי שֶׁיֵּשׁ בָּהֶן חֶסְרוֹן כִּיס. וְכֵן הוֹרוּ הַגְּאוֹנִים, וְאָמְרוּ: שֶׁמַּעֲשִׂים בְּכָל יוֹם לִגְבּוֹת שֶׁבֶת וְרִפּוּי בְּבָבֶל.

יא בְּהֵמָה שֶׁהִזִּיקָה אֶת הָאָדָם – אֵין גּוֹבִין נִזְקוֹ דַּיָּנֵי חוּצָה לָאָרֶץ, מִפְּנֵי שֶׁהוּא דָּבָר שֶׁאֵינוֹ מָצוּי. אֲבָל אָדָם שֶׁהִזִּיק בֶּהֱמַת חֲבֵרוֹ – מְשַׁלֵּם נֶזֶק שָׁלֵם בְּכָל מָקוֹם, כְּמִי שֶׁקָּרַע כְּסוּתוֹ אוֹ שִׁבֵּר כֵּלָיו אוֹ קִצֵּץ נְטִיעוֹתָיו.

וְכֵן בְּהֵמָה שֶׁהִזִּיקָה בְּשֵׁן וָרֶגֶל, הוֹאִיל וְהִיא מוּעֶדֶת לָהֶן מִתְּחִלָּתָהּ – הֲרֵי זֶה דָּבָר מָצוּי, וְגוֹבִין אוֹתוֹ דַּיָּנֵי חוּצָה לָאָרֶץ. בֵּין שֶׁהִזִּיקָה בְּהֵמָה אַחֶרֶת, כְּגוֹן שֶׁנִּתְחַכְּכָה בָּהּ, אוֹ אָכְלָה פֵּרוֹת שֶׁדַּרְכָּהּ לְאָכְלָן, וְכַיּוֹצֵא בָּזֶה, בֵּין שֶׁהִזִּיקָה אֳכָלִין וְכֵלִים שֶׁהִיא חַיֶּבֶת עֲלֵיהֶן נֶזֶק שָׁלֵם – הַכֹּל גּוֹבִין דַּיָּנֵי חוּצָה לָאָרֶץ.

אֲבָל אִם הָיְתָה תַּמָּה וְהוּעֲדָה וְהִזִּיקָה, כְּגוֹן שֶׁנָּשְׁכָה אוֹ נָגְפָה אוֹ רָבְצָה אוֹ בָּעֲטָה אוֹ נָגְחָה – אֵין גּוֹבִין הַנֶּזֶק הַזֶּה הַשָּׁלֵם דַּיָּנֵי חוּצָה לָאָרֶץ, שֶׁאֵין מוּעָד בְּחוּצָה לָאָרֶץ. וַאֲפִלּוּ הוּעַד בָּאָרֶץ וְיָצָא לְחוּצָה לָאָרֶץ וְהִזִּיק – אֵין גּוֹבִין נִזְקוֹ, מִפְּנֵי שֶׁאֵינוֹ דָּבָר מָצוּי.

יב מִפְּנֵי מָה אֵין מוּעָד בְּחוּצָה לָאָרֶץ?

לְפִי שֶׁצָּרִיךְ לְהָעִיד בּוֹ בִּפְנֵי בֵּית דִּין, וְאֵין שָׁם בֵּית דִּין אֶלָּא הַסְּמוּכִין בָּאָרֶץ.

that time, the Rambam held a different position than that stated here in the *Mishneh Torah*.

We find that the *Tur* and Rabbenu Asher offer such a dissenting view. Although the *Shulchan Aruch* (*Choshen Mishpat* 1:2) states the Rambam's view, the Ramah follows the other opinion.

46. This is a more common occurrence. Hence it is given over to the jurisdiction of the judges of the Diaspora.

47. I.e., in contrast to goring, which is considered against the animal's nature, these are the animal's natural tendencies. Hence it is not necessary for the court to warn its owner that it has caused damage, before he is held responsible for it. On the contrary, from the outset, the owner must take precautions.

48. I.e., different rules apply if an animal injures another by goring, as the Rambam proceeds to explain. He is seeking an example of one animal injuring another that is considered a derivative of eating. Now just as eating is an activity performed by the animal for its own comfort, so is rubbing. Hence, damages caused by rubbing against another object or animal are considered a derivative of eating.

49. If the animal would not naturally eat such produce, doing so would be a departure from the norm, and the owner would not be held liable.

50. See the following halachah.

51. That the ox gored three times.

52. The phrase (Exodus 21:29): "And his owner was warned," could also be rendered "And testimony was given against his owner."

53. As stated in Chapter 4, Halachah 4.

Accordingly, if a court [of judges from *Eretz Yisrael*] were in the diaspora, just as they have the authority to judge laws involving financial penalties in the diaspora;[54] so, too, testimony regarding an animal can be delivered in their presence in the diaspora.

13. When a person steals or robs, the principal can be expropriated by the judges of the diaspora.[55] They do not, however, expropriate the double payment.[56]

14. The judges of the diaspora do not expropriate [payment] in every [situation] where a person would be liable to make compensation based on his own statements.[57] For [the payment to a maiden's father for] blemishing [her virginity] and for the embarrassment [she suffers],[58] and [a person who must pay] an atonement fee [because his ox killed another person][59] are situations where a person must make compensation, because of his statements. For example, he said: "I seduced so-and-so's daughter,"[60] or "My ox killed so-and-so."[61] Nevertheless, such payments are not expropriated by the judges of the diaspora.[62]

15. Judgments involving situations where a person's actions served as a direct cause of damage[63] are not equivalent to laws involving *k'nasot* and they may be adjudicated by the judges of the diaspora.[64]

16. Similarly, the laws applying to a person who gives money belonging to a colleague to gentiles[65] - even if he [merely threatens] to do so - may be adjudicated by the judges of the diaspora.[66]

17. The custom of the *yeshivot* of the diaspora[67] is that even though they do not expropriate [money due as] *k'nasot*, they place [the person who causes the damage] under a ban of ostracism[68] until he satisfies the plaintiff[69] or goes with him to *Eretz Yisrael* to have the case adjudicated.[70]

54. As stated in Chapter 4, Halachah 12.
55. For theft is common, unfortunately, and involves monetary loss. In his gloss to *Bava Kama*, Chapter 4, the *Nimukei Yosef* explains that the type of robbery that is common is a person who seeks to steal an article entrusted to him, or a shepherd who misappropriates animals given to him for safekeeping.
56. For as stated in Halachah 9, the double payment does not represent a monetary loss. Similarly, the extra fifth which a robber must pay is not expropriated by the judges of the Diaspora.
57. This halachah is intended to correct a misconception that might arise. Generally, we follow the conception that a person who admits that he is liable for a *k'nas* before witnesses testify is exonerated, as explained in *Hilchot Na'arah Betulah* 2:12. Since in these situations, a person is liable to pay on the basis of his own admission, one might think they are not *k'nasot*, and hence, payment may be expropriated by the judges of the Diaspora. This is not the case, as the Rambam continues to state (*Kessef Mishneh*).

לְפִיכָךְ, אִם הָיוּ בֵּית דִּין בְּחוּצָה לָאָרֶץ – כְּשֵׁם שֶׁהֵן דָּנִים דִּינֵי קְנָסוֹת בְּחוּצָה לָאָרֶץ, כָּךְ מְעִידִים אֶת הַבְּהֵמָה בִּפְנֵיהֶם בְּחוּצָה לָאָרֶץ.

יג מִי שֶׁגָּנַב אוֹ גָּזַל – גּוֹבִין מִמֶּנּוּ הַקֶּרֶן דַּיָּנֵי חוּצָה לָאָרֶץ, אֲבָל אֵין גּוֹבִין אֶת הַכֶּפֶל.

יד וְלֹא כָּל הַמְשַׁלֵּם עַל פִּי עַצְמוֹ גּוֹבִין מִמֶּנּוּ דַּיָּנֵי חוּצָה לָאָרֶץ. שֶׁהֲרֵי הַפְּגָם וְהַבֹּשֶׁת וְהַכֹּפֶר מְשַׁלֵּם אָדָם עַל פִּי עַצְמוֹ, כְּגוֹן שֶׁאָמַר: פִּתִּיתִי בִּתּוֹ שֶׁל פְּלוֹנִי וְהֵמִית שׁוֹרִי אֶת פְּלוֹנִי, וְאֵין גּוֹבִין אוֹתוֹ דַּיָּנֵי חוּצָה לָאָרֶץ.

טו דִּינֵי גְרָמוֹת – אֵינָן כִּקְנָסוֹת, וְגוֹבִין אוֹתָן וְדָנִין בָּהֶן בְּחוּצָה לָאָרֶץ.

טז וְכֵן דִּין הַמּוֹסֵר מָמוֹן חֲבֵרוֹ, אַף עַל פִּי שֶׁלֹּא עָשָׂה מַעֲשֶׂה – גּוֹבִין אוֹתוֹ דַּיָּנֵי חוּצָה לָאָרֶץ.

יז מִנְהַג הַיְשִׁיבוֹת בְּחוּצָה לָאָרֶץ: אַף עַל פִּי שֶׁאֵין גּוֹבִין שָׁם קְנָס, מְנַדִּין אוֹתוֹ עַד שֶׁיְּפַיֵּס לְבַעַל דִּינוֹ, אוֹ יַעֲלֶה עִמּוֹ לְדִין לְאֶרֶץ יִשְׂרָאֵל.

58. See *Hilchot Chovel UMazik* 5:7-8 which explains that a person is liable to pay for embarrassment even if his liability is created by his own statements alone. The rationale is that those statements alone are a source of embarrassment.
59. Since the atonement fine causes the owner of the ox to be pardoned for the responsibility for the other person's death, he is required to pay even if it is his statements alone that create the liability.
60. In which instance he is obligated to pay for the blemish to her virginity and the embarrassment she suffered.
61. In which instance, he is liable to pay an atonement fine.
62. The Radbaz states that our Sages considered these situations as either (- or both -) infrequent occurrences or situations where there is no financial loss involved. Hence, they are not adjudicated by the judges of the Diaspora.
63. See *Hilchot Chovel UMazik* 7:7,9 which gives as examples of this principle: a person who removes pillows from under an object thrown from a height, thus causing the object to be broken and a person who burns promissory notes belonging to a colleague.
64. *Bava Kama* 98b gives an example of such cases being adjudicated in Babylon.
65. See *Hilchot Chovel UMazik*, ch. 8, which describes these type of cases.
66. *Bava Kama* 117a-b gives an examples of such cases being adjudicated in Babylon.
67. I.e., this was the practice in Sura and Pumpedita, the two leading *yeshivot* of Babylon.
68. See *Hilchot Talmud Torah*, chs. 6-7, which describes the nature of this ban.
69. Paying him the amount that he would receive were the cases to be adjudicated by a court.
70. By judges who have been given *semichah*.

In his gloss to *Bava Kama*, ch. 8, Rabbenu Asher quotes the explanation of this practice offered by Rav Tzemach *Gaon*: "In this way, [the knowledge that] cases involving *k'nasot* are not adjudicated in Babylon will not cause the sinner to profit from the situation and the Jewish people will not be uninhibited with regard to causing damage." See *Siftei Cohen* 1:14 that this practice applies only with regard to damages due because of injury and the

Once [the person who causes the damage] pays the amount that he would be held liable for,[71] the ban of ostracism is lifted whether [the person who suffered the injury] is appeased or not. Similarly, if [the person who suffered the injury] seizes an amount [of property belonging to the person who causes the damage] equivalent to the amount he would be awarded [by the court],[72] we do not expropriate it from his possession.

18. When one person is an expert judge and he is known by many [to possess such knowledge],[73] although he is allowed to judge cases involving financial law alone, an admission of liability made in his presence is not considered as an admission made in the presence of a court.[74] [This applies] even if he possesses *semichah*.[75]

When, by contrast, [a court is composed of] three [judges], even though they do not possesses *semichah*, [and even if] they are ordinary men and are not referred to as *Elohim*, an admission made in their presence is considered as an admission made in a court of law.[76] Similarly, if a person denies [an obligation] in their presence and witnesses come [and testify against him], he is established as one who has lied. He cannot offer another claim, as we have explained.[77]

The general principle is: With regard to the admission [of financial responsibility], [cases involving] debts, and the like, their authority is the same as that of a court composed of judges possessing *semichah* with regard to all matters.

CHAPTER SIX

1. [The following laws apply] whenever a judge[1] adjudicates a case involving financial matters and errs. If his error involves matters that are revealed and known - e.g., a law that is explicitly stated in the Mishnah or the Gemara,[2] the ruling is reversed. The situation is returned to its original status and the

like where a person suffers a real loss. It does not apply with regard to the double payment for theft and similar additional monetary awards.

71. The *Sefer Me'irat Einayim* 1:17 states that this law applies even if the person does not make full payment, but instead pays a substantial sum, close to the amount for which he would be held liable.

72. The *Sefer Me'irat Einayim* 1:18 states that even if the plaintiff seizes a double payment for theft, he is allowed to maintain possession, for that amount is in effect due him.

73. See Chapter 2, Halachah 11.

74. Accordingly, there are certain leniencies involved. Among them, when a person admits liability before such a judge, he may retract his claim. Making statements before such a judge[s] is like making them before other witnesses.

This concept is not accepted by the *Tur*. He follows Rabbenu Asher's approach and maintains that an admission made before an expert judge is considered as having been made in court. The *Shulchan Aruch* (*Choshen Mishpat* 3:2) follows the Rambam's view,

וְכֵיוָן שֶׁיִּתֵּן לוֹ שִׂעוּר הָרָאוּי לוֹ – מַתִּירִין נִדּוּיוֹ, בֵּין שֶׁנִּתְפַּיֵּס בַּעַל דִּינוֹ בֵּין שֶׁלֹּא נִתְפַּיֵּס. וְכֵן אִם תָּפַשׂ הַנִּזָּק שִׂעוּר מַה שֶּׁרָאוּי לוֹ לִטֹּל – אֵין מוֹצִיאִין אוֹתוֹ מִיָּדוֹ.

יח יָחִיד שֶׁהוּא מֻמְחֶה לָרַבִּים, אַף עַל פִּי שֶׁהוּא דָּן דִּינֵי מָמוֹנוֹת יְחִידִי – אֵין הַהוֹדָאָה בְּפָנָיו הוֹדָאָה בְּבֵית דִּין, וַאֲפִלּוּ הָיָה סָמוּךְ.
אֲבָל הַשְּׁלשָׁה, אַף עַל פִּי שֶׁאֵינָן סְמוּכִין, וַהֲרֵי הֵן הֶדְיוֹטוֹת, וְאֵין אֲנִי קוֹרֵא בָּהֶן אֱלֹהִים – הֲרֵי הַהוֹדָאָה בִּפְנֵיהֶם הוֹדָאָה בְּבֵית דִּין. וְכֵן הַכּוֹפֵר בִּפְנֵיהֶם, וְאַחַר כָּךְ בָּאוּ עֵדִים – הֻחְזַק כַּפְרָן, וְאֵינוֹ יָכוֹל לַחֲזֹר וְלִטְעֹן, כְּמוֹ שֶׁבֵּאַרְנוּ.
כְּלָלוֹ שֶׁל דָּבָר: הֲרֵי הֵן לְעִנְיַן הוֹדָאוֹת וְהַלְוָאוֹת וְכַיּוֹצֵא בָּהֶן כְּבֵית דִּין הַסָּמוּךְ לְכָל הַדְּבָרִים.

פֶּרֶק שִׁשִּׁי

א כָּל דַּיָּן שֶׁדָּן דִּינֵי מָמוֹנוֹת וְטָעָה: אִם טָעָה בִּדְבָרִים הַגְּלוּיִים וְהַיְּדוּעִים, כְּגוֹן דִּינִין הַמְפֹרָשִׁין בַּמִּשְׁנָה אוֹ בַּגְּמָרָא – חוֹזֵר הַדִּין, וּמַחֲזִירִין הַדָּבָר כְּשֶׁהָיָה, וְדָנִין בּוֹ כַּהֲלָכָה.

while the Ramah appears to follow the perspective of the *Tur*. See the *Siftei Cohen* 3:8 who substantiates the Rambam's view.
75. If, however, the litigants accepted one judge as the legal authority, an admission made in his presence is considered as an admission made in court [Ramah (*Choshen Mishpat* 3:2)].
76. And cannot be retracted.
77. *Hilchot Toen ViNitan* 6:1 states that when a defendant denies the existence of an obligation at first, he cannot afterwards claim "I paid the debt," if witnesses testify concerning the existence of such an obligation in the interim.

1. This applies whenever a judge or a court have the jurisdiction to issue judgment, including an expert judge who rules alone and a court of three ordinary people.
2. The expression used by *Sanhedrin* 33a is "err[ing] with regard to a matter of the Mishnah." The intent is not necessarily a statement from the Mishnah itself, but any definitive halachic statement that has been universally accepted. For this reason, the Rambam mentions the rulings of the Gemara, for in his era, these too were universally accepted Halachic rulings. Similarly, in later eras, this status was conferred on other works of Halachah such as the works of Rabbenu Yitzchak Alfasi (Radbaz, *Kessef Mishneh*). In the present age, the *Shulchan Aruch* and the works of the later authorities were placed in this category.

In this context, the *Tur* and the Ramah (*Choshen Mishpat* 25:1) quote the opinion of Rabbenu Asher who maintains that if a law derived by logical analysis (in contrast to a point stated to be part of the accepted tradition) is stated in a text which is universally revered, a later halachic authority may, nevertheless, take issue with it. As long as the point in question was not stated explicitly in the Talmud, if the sages in his generation accept his understanding, he can rule accordingly, despite the fact that previously a different conception had been accepted. Support for that concept can also be derived from the Rambam's statements, *Hilchot Mamrim* 2:1.

judgment required by halachah is rendered. If it is impossible to return the matter to its original status, e.g., the person who unwarrantedly received the money traveled overseas, or he was a stubborn and strong person, [the judge] is not liable. Although he caused a loss, he did not have the intent of doing so.[3] [Similar laws apply if a judge] ruled that a substance that was pure was impure,[4] that [an animal] that was kosher was unacceptable and had it fed to the dogs,[5] or the like.

2. [Different principles apply if the judge] errs in [a case requiring a decision to be made by using] one's logic to weigh [alternative positions],[6] for example, [a case arose involving] the subject of a difference of opinion among the Sages of the Mishnah or the Sages of the Gemara where it was not explicitly stated whose opinion the halachah follows. [The judge decided] to follow one opinion without knowing it had already been universally established practice [within the Torah community] to follow the other view.

[In such a situation,] if the judge was an expert who had been given license to adjudicate cases by the exiliarch,[7] or even if he had not been given such license, but the litigants [voluntarily] accepted him [as their judicial authority],[8] the ruling is reversed.[9] [The rationale is that] he is an expert.

If the ruling cannot be reversed, he is not liable to make restitution.[10] [This applies] both to [a judge] who received permission from the exiliarch or one received permission from a Jewish court [to adjudicate cases] in *Eretz Yisrael*, but not [to serve as judge] in the diaspora, as explained.[11]

3. [Different rules apply if] the person who erred in a question of logical deduction was an expert [judge], but he had not received license [to adjudicate cases], nor was he accepted by the litigants as an authority, or was not an expert, but was accepted by the litigants to adjudicate their case according to Torah law.[12] If he personally took [property from one litigant] and gave [it to

3. A person is held liable for being a cause of damage, even though he does not bring about the damage with his own hands (*dina degarmei*; see *Hilchot Chovel UMazik* 7:7). Nevertheless, in this situation, since the judge did not have the intent of causing damage, he is absolved of responsibility. Compare to the conclusion of Halachah 4.

The *Sefer Me'irat Einayim* 25:6 states that generally a person is held responsible even if he inadvertently causes damage, because "a person must always be forewarned [about the consequences of his behavior]." Nevertheless, in this instance, were a judge to be held liable, no one would ever desire to accept this responsibility. Hence, since the judge is acting with the authority vested in him by the court or the communal authorities - in contrast to the situation mentioned at the conclusion of Halachah 4 - he is released from liability.

The Rambam's position is accepted by the *Shulchan Aruch* (*Choshen Mishpat* 25:1). Rabbenu Asher differs with this approach and maintains that since the judge's ruling caused financial loss, the judge should be held responsible. His conception is cited by the Tur and the Ramah (loc. cit.).

4. One might ask: What is the difficulty? Since the judge was informed of the error, he

וְאִם אִי אֶפְשָׁר לְהַחֲזִיר, כְּגוֹן שֶׁהָלַךְ זֶה שֶׁנָּטַל הַמָּמוֹן שֶׁלֹּא כַּדִּין לִמְדִינַת הַיָּם, אוֹ שֶׁהָיָה אַלָּם, אוֹ שֶׁטִּמֵּא דָּבָר טָהוֹר, אוֹ שֶׁהוֹרָה בִּכְשֵׁרָה שֶׁהִיא טְרֵפָה וְהֶאֱכִילָהּ לַכְּלָבִים, וְכַיּוֹצֵא בָּזֶה – הֲרֵי זֶה פָּטוּר מִלְּשַׁלֵּם;
אַף עַל פִּי שֶׁגָּרַם לְהַזִּיק, לֹא נִתְכַּוֵּן לְהַזִּיק.

ב טָעָה בְּשִׁקּוּל הַדַּעַת, כְּגוֹן דָּבָר שֶׁהוּא מַחֲלֹקֶת תַּנָּאִים אוֹ אָמוֹרָאִים, וְלֹא נִפְסְקָה הֲלָכָה כְּאֶחָד מֵהֶן בְּפֵרוּשׁ, וְעָשָׂה כְּאֶחָד מֵהֶן, וְלֹא יָדַע שֶׁכְּבָר פָּשַׁט הַמַּעֲשֶׂה בְּכָל הָעוֹלָם כְּדִבְרֵי הָאַחֵר:
אִם הָיָה זֶה הַדַּיָּן מֻמְחֶה וְנָטַל רְשׁוּת מֵרֹאשׁ גָּלוּת, אוֹ שֶׁלֹּא הָיָה נוֹטֵל רְשׁוּת אֲבָל קִבְּלוּ אוֹתוֹ בַּעֲלֵי דִינִין עֲלֵיהֶן, הוֹאִיל וְהוּא מֻמְחֶה – חוֹזֵר הַדִּין, וְאִם אִי אֶפְשָׁר לְהַחֲזִיר – פָּטוּר מִלְּשַׁלֵּם.
אֶחָד הַנּוֹטֵל רְשׁוּת מֵרֹאשׁ גָּלוּת אוֹ הַנּוֹטֵל רְשׁוּת מִבֵּית דִּין שֶׁל אֶרֶץ יִשְׂרָאֵל בְּאֶרֶץ יִשְׂרָאֵל, אֲבָל לֹא בְּחוּצָה לָאָרֶץ, כְּמוֹ שֶׁבֵּאַרְנוּ.

ג הָיָה הַטּוֹעֶה מֻמְחֶה וְלֹא נָטַל רְשׁוּת וְלֹא קִבְּלוּ אוֹתוֹ בַּעֲלֵי דִינִין עֲלֵיהֶן, אוֹ שֶׁלֹּא הָיָה מֻמְחֶה אֲבָל קִבְּלוּ אוֹתוֹ בַּעֲלֵי דִינִין עֲלֵיהֶן לָדוּן לָהֶן כַּדִּין, וְטָעָה בְּשִׁקּוּל הַדַּעַת:

could merely reverse his ruling? For this reason, the *Sefer Me'irat Einayim* 25:3 explains that we are speaking about a situation where the judge ruled that a substance that was in fact pure was impure, and because of that ruling, the owner placed it in a setting where actually became impure.

5. The *Kessef Mishneh* explains that the Rambam's words are carefully weighed out. If the person merely had the animal fed to the dogs, he is not liable. If, however, he personally fed it to the dogs, he is held responsible. This is also the approach of the Remo. [Note, however, the *Sefer Me'irat Einayim* 25:4,7 which understands the wording chosen by the Rambam as indicating that the judge personally made the article impure or fed it to the dogs in order to teach his students (- albeit mistakenly -) a point of Torah law.]

6. We have given an almost literal translation to the term *shikul hadaat*. The intent is a judgment call, rather than a decision for which there is an explicit Talmudic ruling. In the future, we will translate it as "logical deduction."

7. In which instance, he has the authority to compel the litigants to allow him to judge their dispute and they must abide by his rulings.

8. See Chapter 7, Halachah 2.

9. And the opinion which is commonly accepted is followed.

10. I.e., he is not held liable. Since he is an expert judge and either he has permission to compel the litigants to accept his judgment or they agreed to do so, he is not held responsible. The rationale is that the sages have the power to confiscate property belonging to others even when the halachah does not support their rulings (*Kessef Mishneh*, based on Rashi, *Sanhedrin* 5a).

11. See Chapter 4, Halachah 14.

12. I.e., not just to negotiate a compromise, but to rule according to Torah law, which was not the ultimate result.

the other], his actions are irreversible[13] and he should pay [the damages] from his own resources.[14] If, however, he did not personally take [the property from one] and give [it to the other],[15] the decision should be reversed. If the decision cannot be reversed,[16] he should pay [the damages] from his own resources.[17]

4. When, however, a person who is not an expert and was not accepted by the litigants[18] adjudicates [a case], even though he was given permission [to act as a judge],[19] he is considered as one of the men of force and not as a [proper] judge. Therefore, the judgment he renders is of no consequence.[20] [This applies] whether he erred[21] or whether he did not err. Either one of the litigants may withdraw and have the case adjudicated by a proper court.[22]

If such a judge erred and personally gave [property] from one [litigant] to the other, he is obligated to pay from his own resources. He may then regain [the money] from the litigant to whom he gave property unlawfully. If [one litigant paid the other because of the ruling of such a judge[23] and the recipient][24] is unable to return [the money][25] or if [the judge] rendered [an object] ritually impure[26] or gave [meat] that was kosher to the dogs to eat, [the judge] must bear the loss as is the law regarding anyone who causes damages. For such a person has the intent of causing damages.[27]

5. When a judge errs and obligates a person who is not required to take an oath to do so, and in order to free himself from the obligation to take the

13. Since there is not an explicit ruling otherwise, the litigant whose claim was vindicated can claim: "The verdict was just. The money I received was due me." Hence he is not required to return it. When, by contrast, the error is made with regard to an explicit ruling, the litigant whose claim was vindicated will accept that an error was made (Rashi, *Sanhedrin* 6a).

14. I.e., he is considered as a person who caused damages. With regard to an expert judge, since he did not have the authority to call the litigants to judgment or their consent for judging them, he is held liable. For deciding to adjudicate a case in such a situation is equivalent to accepting responsibility in the event of error.

A judge who is not an expert has a more encompassing responsibility. Since he knows that he is not an expert, the very fact that he consents to judge involves accepting responsibility for his mistakes. For he is aware of his limitations and knows that he might err. Nevertheless, he is not held liable for a mistake regarding an explicit law. The rationale is that this is considered like an *ones*, a factor beyond his control. Since he would not be expected to make an error concerning such a matter, it is not taken for granted that he accepts responsibility (*Lechem Mishneh*).

15. But merely ordered that the money be given.

16. E.g., the litigant who was given the money journeyed overseas.

17. The *Kessef Mishneh* questions the Rambam's decision, explaining that his statements are based on the rulings of the *Halachot* of Rabbenu Yitzchak Alfasi with one exception. With regard to the liability imposed on the judges in this halachah, Rabbenu Yitzchak Alfasi frees the judges of liability because they do not intentionally cause damage, while in certain instances, the Rambam holds them responsible.

The *Kessef Mishneh* explains that the Rambam's ruling depends on the principle *hefker*

אִם נָשָׂא וְנָתַן בַּיָּד – מַה שֶּׁעָשָׂה עָשׂוּי, וִישַׁלֵּם מִבֵּיתוֹ; אִם לֹא נָשָׂא וְנָתַן בַּיָּד – יַחֲזֹר הַדִּין, וְאִם אִי אֶפְשָׁר לְהַחֲזִיר – יְשַׁלֵּם מִבֵּיתוֹ.

ד אֲבָל מִי שֶׁאֵינוֹ מֻמְחֶה וְלֹא קִבְּלוּ אוֹתוֹ בַּעֲלֵי דִינִין, אַף עַל פִּי שֶׁנָּטַל רְשׁוּת – הֲרֵי זֶה בִּכְלַל בַּעֲלֵי זְרוֹעַ, וְאֵינוֹ בִּכְלַל הַדַּיָּנִין. לְפִיכָךְ אֵין דִּינוֹ דִּין, בֵּין טָעָה בֵּין לֹא טָעָה; וְכָל אֶחָד מִבַּעֲלֵי דִינִין, אִם רָצָה, חוֹזֵר וְדָן בִּפְנֵי בֵּית דִּין. וְאִם טָעָה, וְנָשָׂא וְנָתַן בַּיָּד – חַיָּב לְשַׁלֵּם מִבֵּיתוֹ, וְחוֹזֵר וְלוֹקֵחַ מִבַּעַל דִּין זֶה שֶׁנָּתַן לוֹ שֶׁלֹּא כַּהֲלָכָה. וְאִם אֵין לוֹ לְהַחֲזִיר, אוֹ שֶׁטִּמֵּא, אוֹ שֶׁהֶאֱכִיל דָּבָר הַמֻּתָּר לַכְּלָבִים – יְשַׁלֵּם, כְּדִין כָּל גּוֹרֵם לְהַזִּיק; שֶׁזֶּה מִתְכַּוֵּן לְהַזִּיק הוּא.

ה דַּיָּן שֶׁטָּעָה וְחִיֵּב שְׁבוּעָה לְמִי שֶׁאֵינוֹ חַיָּב בָּהּ, וְעָשָׂה זֶה פְּשָׁרָה עִם בַּעַל דִּינוֹ כְּדֵי שֶׁלֹּא

beit din hefker, that the court has the right to expropriate property from an individual. When is that principle applied, however? When expert judges are empowered to act as a court or explicitly asked to do so by the litigants. Hence when they are not so empowered and when consent was not granted them by the litigants, they are personally responsible.

Rabbenu Asher mentions a third perspective, that as long as a judge is not empowered or was not accepted by the litigants, he is always personally responsible for his errors whether or not he took the property from one and gave it to the other. Even if it is possible for a judgment to be reversed, it is allowed to stand and the judge must make good the error. The *Shulchan Aruch* (*Choshen Mishpat* 25:3) quotes the Rambam's ruling, while the *Tur* and the Ramah quote that of Rabbenu Asher.

18. The laws that apply when the litigants accept a judge who is not fit are described in Chapter 7, Halachah 2.

19. This is possible, because the exiliarchs were not necessarily paradigms of ethical excellence.

20. As stated in Chapter 4, Halachah 15, license to adjudicate cases is of consequence only when the person to whom license was granted is fit for this responsibility. See also Chapter 3, Halachah 8.

21. Similarly, it makes no difference if his error is concerning an explicitly stated law or a question requiring weighing the different perspectives.

22. The *Siftei Cohen* 25:43 questions: What advantage is there in having the case judged a second time if the ruling was in fact correct? He quotes certain opinions which explain that this is referring to a situation where the litigant is not certain whether the judgment was rendered correctly or not and hence seeks to have the matter clarified again. The *Siftei Cohen* himself explains that the litigant's intent could be procrastination. Until the judgment is reached by the proper court, he has the right to benefit from the property.

23. But the judge did not personally take the money from him as in the previous clause.

24. Our translation is based on the gloss of the *Kessef Mishneh* and supported by the commentary of the *Siftei Cohen* 25:44. Note the *Bayit Chadish* and the *Sefer Me'irat Einayim* 25:28 who offer different interpretations.

25. If, however, the recipient is capable of returning the money, he is obligated to do so (*Kessef Mishneh*).

26. I.e., he personally caused the object to contract ritual impurity.

27. Since he is unfit to serve as a judge and yet acts in that capacity, he is willfully putting

oath,[28] this person negotiated a compromise with the other litigant, [the compromise may be revoked].[29] Even though he affirmed the compromise with a *kinyan*, it is of no substance. He agreed to pay or to waive [the other person's liability][30] only to free himself from the oath to which the judge who erred obligated him. And whenever a *kinyan* is carried out on the basis of an error, it is annulled.[31] Similar laws apply in all analogous situations.

6. When two people are involved in a dispute concerning a judgment, one states: "Let us have the matter judged here,"[32] and the other says, "Let us ascend to the Supreme Court, lest these judges err and expropriate money contrary to the law," we compel [the latter litigant] to have the matter adjudicated locally.[33]

If he asks [the judges]: "Write down the rationale why you have rendered this judgment against me and give it to me, lest you have erred," [they must] write down [their rationale] and give him [the transcript].[34] Afterwards, they expropriate [what he owes].[35] If [the local judges] feel the need to ask [for clarification] regarding a matter from the Supreme Court in Jerusalem, they should write down [their question] and send it.[36] [After] their inquiry, the judgment should be rendered in the local [court] on the basis of the answer written to them by the Supreme Court.[37]

7. When does the above[38] apply? With regard to judgments dependent on claims issued by both litigants[39] or a situation when a lender desires to have the case adjudicated locally and the borrower says: "Let us go to the Supreme Court." If, by contrast, the lender says: "Let us go to the Supreme Court," we compel the borrower to ascend with the lender, as [implied by Proverbs 22:7]: "A borrower is a servant to the lender."

himself in a situation where he knows that he may expropriate money contrary to Torah law. This is causing damage intentionally.

28. For because of the severity involved in taking an oath, many people would rather give in slightly and negotiate a compromise, rather than invoke God's name, even when their claim is justified.

29. If he agreed to pay a plaintiff a sum, he is not bound by his commitment, and if he waived money due to him, the waiver is not binding.

30. Partially or fully depending on the terms of the compromise.

31. See *Hilchot Mechirah* 15:2.

32. I.e., in the local court, whether it is a court of three or a court of twenty-three.

33. This reflects consideration of the other litigant's position. He is not required to undertake the time or the expense of a journey which he feels is unnecessary.

The Maharik (Responsum 90) questions what would be the ruling if the other litigant would be traveling to the place of the Supreme Court (- or in contemporary terms, the place of a more renowned court, see Halachah 9 -) regardless: Could he be compelled to have the matter adjudicated there, or does he still have the right to leave the case under the jurisdiction of the local court.

34. See Chapter 22, Halachah 8. The Radbaz explains that any litigant may make such a request of the judges. The *Kessef Mishneh*, by contrast, quotes many authorities which

יִשָּׁבַע, וְאַחַר כָּךְ יָדַע שֶׁאֵינוֹ בֶּן שְׁבוּעָה, אַף עַל פִּי שֶׁקָּנוּ מִיָּדוֹ עַל הַפְּשָׁרָה – אֵינָהּ כְּלוּם; שֶׁלֹּא קִבֵּל עָלָיו לִתֵּן לוֹ אוֹ לִמְחֹל לוֹ אֶלָּא כְּדֵי שֶׁיִּפָּטֵר מִשְּׁבוּעָה שֶׁחִיְּבוּ בָהּ הַטּוֹעֶה, וְכָל קִנְיָן בְּטָעוּת – חוֹזֵר. וְכֵן כֹּל כַּיּוֹצֵא בָּזֶה.

ו שְׁנַיִם שֶׁנִּתְעַצְּמוּ בְּדִין, אֶחָד אוֹמֵר: נָדוּן כָּאן, וְאֶחָד אוֹמֵר: נַעֲלֶה לְבֵית דִּין הַגָּדוֹל, שֶׁמָּא יִטְעוּ אֵלּוּ הַדַּיָּנִין וְיוֹצִיאוּ מָמוֹן שֶׁלֹּא כַּדִּין – כּוֹפִין אוֹתוֹ וְדָן בְּעִירוֹ.
וְאִם אָמַר: כִּתְבוּ וּתְנוּ לִי מֵאֵי זֶה טַעַם דַּנְתּוּנִי, שֶׁמָּא טְעִיתֶם – כּוֹתְבִים וְנוֹתְנִין לוֹ, וְאַחַר כָּךְ מוֹצִיאִין מִמֶּנּוּ. וְאִם הֻצְרַךְ לִשְׁאֹל דָּבָר מִבֵּית דִּין הַגָּדוֹל שֶׁבִּירוּשָׁלַיִם – כּוֹתְבִים וְשׁוֹלְחִין וְשׁוֹאֲלִין, וְדָנִין לָהֶם בְּעִירָם כְּפִי מַה שֶּׁיָּבֹא בִּכְתַב בֵּית דִּין הַגָּדוֹל.

ז בַּמֶּה דְּבָרִים אֲמוּרִים? בִּשְׁאָר הַדִּינִין שֶׁזֶּה טוֹעֵן וְזֶה טוֹעֵן, אוֹ כְּשֶׁאָמַר הַמַּלְוֶה: נָדוּן כָּאן, וְהַלֹּוֶה אוֹמֵר: נֵלֵךְ לְבֵית דִּין הַגָּדוֹל;
אֲבָל אִם אָמַר הַמַּלְוֶה: נֵלֵךְ לְבֵית דִּין הַגָּדוֹל – כּוֹפִין אֶת הַלֹּוֶה וְעוֹלֶה עִמּוֹ, שֶׁנֶּאֱמַר: עֶבֶד לֹוֶה לְאִישׁ מַלְוֶה.

maintain that this ruling applies only when a litigant desired to have the matter adjudicated by a higher court and was forced to enter judgment in a local court. If he suspects that an error arose, he - and not litigants in ordinary situations - may request an explanation. See also the gloss of the *Hagahot Maimoniot* which mentions both positions.

The *Beit Yosef* (*Choshen Mishpat* 14) writes that an explanation of the motivating principles can be demanded only of a lower court. The Supreme Court, by contrast, is not required to supply such an explanation, because we do not suspect that they will err. Similarly, in the present time, when a case is adjudicated by one of the leading courts of the generation, there is no need for that court to write up a position paper explaining its ruling. This concept is also quoted by the Ramah (*loc. cit.*).

The *Sefer Me'irat Einayim* 14:25 interprets the statements of the Ramah (*Choshen Mishpat* 14:4) as implying that he agrees that any litigant has the right to ask a judge to provide the rationale for his ruling. The judge, however, may be required to provide only a verbal explanation, he is not required to write down his explanations.

35. The litigant may show the transcript to other authorities and if they discover an error, the judges' ruling may be reversed according to the principles stated in the previous halachot.

36. Both litigants must share the cost of sending the inquiry [*Shulchan Aruch* (*Choshen Mishpat* 14:1)].

37. The Supreme Court is not rendering judgment - for a judgment may be rendered only in the presence of both litigants - they see the situation as described by the local court and write an abstract analysis of what the judgment should be. On the basis of their opinion, the judgment is rendered by the local court (*Kessef Mishneh*).

38. That one litigant can compel another to have a case adjudicated locally.

39. E.g., disputes concerning the ownership of property, or other instances where there is neither a plaintiff and a defendant, but two litigants with neither having established a claim of ownership with regard to a property or a privilege.

Similarly, if a person claims that his colleague injured or damaged his person or his property or stole from him, and the plaintiff desires to ascend [to the Supreme Court], the local court compels the defendant to ascend together with him. Similar laws apply in all analogous situations.[40]

8. When does the above[41] apply? When the person from whom property was stolen, the person who suffered injury or damage, or the lender has witnesses or proof [that support his claim]. When, however, his claim is unsupported, we do not obligate the defendant to leave [his locale]. Instead, he takes an oath[42] there and is freed of obligation.[43]

9. Similar [concepts apply] in the present age, when there is no Supreme Court, but there are places where there are great sages whose expertise is renowned and there are other places where there are scholars who are not on that level. If the lender says: "Let us go to this-and-this place in this-and-this land to have the case adjudicated by so-and-so, the great [sage]," we compel the borrower to go with him.[44] This was the practice continually in Spain.

CHAPTER SEVEN

1. [The following law applies when] one of the litigants says: "Let so-and-so act as a judge for me," and the other litigant says: "Let so-and-so act as a judge for me."[1] [Together] the two judges who were chosen by each of the litigants [respectively] choose a third judge[2] and the three of them adjudicate the case for the two litigants. In this manner, a true judgment will emerge.[3]

40. The *Tur* and the Ramah (*Choshen Mishpat* 14:1) quote the opinion of Rabbenu Chananel who differs and maintains that the borrower may also compel the lender to accompany him.
41. That we compel a defendant to ascend with the plaintiff.
42. A *sh'vuat hesset* as is required when a person denies an obligation that is not supported by witnesses.
43. For otherwise people will lodge spurious claims against the rich and demand that they ascend to the Supreme Court with them in the hope that, rather than undertake the journey, the defendant will seek to negotiate a compromise (Radbaz, *Kessef Mishneh*).
44. The Radbaz and the *Kessef Mishneh* cite *Sanhedrin* 32b which interprets the injunction (Deuteronomy 16:20): "Righteousness! Righteousness, shall you pursue" as implying that people should take their disputes to an accomplished court. As an example, they cite the court of Rabbi Eliezer in Lod and Rabbi Matia ben Cheresh in Rome, which were the leading courts of their generations.

In his *Kessef Mishneh* [and this is apparently his perspective in his *Shulchan Aruch* (*Choshen Mishpat* 14:1)], Rav Yosef Karo maintains that this law should be followed today as well, for in every generation, there are Rabbinic courts that are profound in their expertise. The Ramah differs and cites other authorities who maintain that in the present era, there are no courts whose erudition and authority is such that they should be given this standing.

וְכֵן אִם טָעַן זֶה שֶׁהִזִּיקוֹ אוֹ גְזָלוֹ, וְרָצָה הַטּוֹעֵן לַעֲלוֹת - כּוֹפִין בֵּית דִּין שֶׁבְּעִירוֹ אֶת הַנִּטְעָן לַעֲלוֹת עִמּוֹ. וְכֵן כֹּל כַּיּוֹצֵא בָּזֶה.

ח בַּמֶּה דְּבָרִים אֲמוּרִים? כְּשֶׁיִּהְיוּ שָׁם עֵדִים אוֹ רְאָיָה לַגְּזֵלָה אוֹ לַנֵּזֶק אוֹ לַמִּלְוֶה; אֲבָל טַעֲנָה רֵיקָנִית - אֵין מְחַיְּבִין אֶת הַנִּטְעָן לָצֵאת כְּלָל, אֶלָּא נִשְׁבָּע בִּמְקוֹמוֹ וְנִפְטָר.

ט וְכֵן הַדִּין בִּזְמַן הַזֶּה, שֶׁאֵין שָׁם בֵּית דִּין גָּדוֹל, אֲבָל יֵשׁ מְקוֹמוֹת שֶׁיֵּשׁ בָּהֶן חֲכָמִים גְּדוֹלִים מֻמְחִין לָרַבִּים, וּמְקוֹמוֹת שֶׁיֵּשׁ בָּהֶן תַּלְמִידִים שֶׁאֵינָן כְּמוֹתָן,
אִם אָמַר הַמַּלְוֶה: נֵלֵךְ לִמְקוֹם פְּלוֹנִי שֶׁבְּאֶרֶץ פְּלוֹנִית לִפְלוֹנִי וּפְלוֹנִי הַגָּדוֹל וְנָדוּן לְפָנָיו בְּדִין זֶה - שֶׁכּוֹפִין אֶת הַלֹּוֶה וְהוֹלֵךְ עִמּוֹ.
וְכֵן הָיוּ מַעֲשִׂים בְּכָל יוֹם בִּסְפָרַד.

פֶּרֶק שְׁבִיעִי

א אֶחָד מִבַּעֲלֵי דִינִין שֶׁאָמַר: אִישׁ פְּלוֹנִי יָדוּן לִי, וְאָמַר בַּעַל דִּינוֹ: פְּלוֹנִי יָדוּן לִי - הֲרֵי אֵלּוּ שְׁנֵי הַדַּיָּנִים, שֶׁבֵּרֵר זֶה אֶחָד וְזֶה אֶחָד, הֵם בּוֹרְרִים לָהֶן דַּיָּן שְׁלִישִׁי, וּשְׁלָשְׁתָּן דָּנִין לִשְׁנֵיהֶן; שֶׁמִּתּוֹךְ כָּךְ יֵצֵא הַדִּין לַאֲמִתּוֹ.

1. The *Sefer Me'irat Einayim* 13:3 states that this law applies when neither of the two litigants desire to have the case adjudicated by the local court. If, however, one of them has that intent, the case should be adjudicated by that court, and not by a court made up through this selection process.
2. The litigants themselves, however, have no say in the selection of the third judge. Instead, the judges themselves select an authority whomthey feel is fitting to adjudicate the case. *Sanhedrin* 23a quotes a difference of opinion regarding this matter between the Sages and Rabbi Meir. The opinion quoted above follows the perspective of the Sages, while Rabbi Meir maintains that the litigants chose the third judge. Although there are editions of the *Mishneh Torah* which follow a version which appears to follow Rabbi Meir's opinion, the version above is both corroborated by the ancient manuscripts and accepted by the later Rabbis.
3. The Jerusalem Talmud (*Sanhedrin* 3:1) states that each of the judges selected by the litigants will protect the interest of the party who appointed him, and the third judge will discern which of the positions should be accepted. Rabbenu Asher (in his halachic gloss to *Sanhedrin*, ch. 3) emphasizes that these judges are judges, not lawyers. The litigants who chose them are not their clients whose case they are obligated to argue. Instead, they are objective authorities. That said, they have a greater tendency to look out for the interest of the litigant who selected them and bring out the positive points in his argument. Since each of the judges selected will thus present a clear picture of the two litigants' claims, arguments, and defenses, together with the guidance of the third judge, they will be able to clarify whose position is vindicated by the Torah. See *Kessef Mishneh* who elaborates on this issue.

Even if the [judge] chosen by [one of] the litigants is a great sage who has received *semichah*, the [one litigant] cannot compel the other litigant to have him adjudicate the case.[4] Instead, he also chooses [a judge] he desires.

2. [The following rules apply when a litigant] accepts [his own or an opposing litigant's] relative[5] or another person who is unacceptable to serve as a judge or a witness [in his case].[6] If he affirms his commitment with a *kinyan*, he cannot retract [his consent].[7] If he did not affirm his commitment with a *kinyan*, he can retract [his consent] until the case is concluded.[8] Once the verdict is rendered and the unacceptable [judge ruled] in his verdict - or [a verdict was rendered on the basis of] the testimony of an unacceptable [witness] - that money should be expropriated,[9] [the litigant] may not retract.[10]

[The above laws also apply] if [a litigant] accepted a person who is disqualified because he committed a transgression[11] as two witnesses to testify concerning him or as a court of three judges to rule concerning his interests.[12] Similarly, [it applies] regardless of whether he gave his consent [at the risk of] forfeiting rights and waiving a claim that he is pressing or he gave his consent [at the risk of] having to pay what the plaintiff demands of him because of the testimony of this unacceptable [witness] or because of the ruling of this unacceptable [judge].

3. Similarly, [the following rules apply when a person] was obligated by a court to take an oath to a colleague and [the person to whom the oath must be given] states: "Take an oath on your own life,[13] and be freed of liability," or "Take an oath on your own life [that your claim is justified] and I will give you everything that you claim." If he affirms his commitment with a *kinyan*, he cannot retract [his consent]. If he did not affirm his commitment with a *kinyan*, he can retract [his consent] until the case is concluded.[14] Once the case is concluded and he took an oath as stipulated, he cannot retract and is obligated to pay.

4. Similar laws apply when a person was obligated to take a *sh'vuat hesset* and he reversed it [and obligated the plaintiff].[15] If he affirmed his consent with a *kinyan* or [the plaintiff] took the oath, [the defendant] cannot retract.

4. The Radbaz emphasizes that the judge chosen by the second litigant must be more or less comparable to the first. A sage of great eminence cannot be required to sit on a court together with a commonplace individual.
5. The disqualification of relatives as witnesses is discussed in *Hilchot Edut*, Chapter 13.
6. The *Siftei Cohen* 22:1 explains at length that this law applies when the litigant makes this commitment before an acceptable court.
7. Ordinarily, he would not be bound by such a commitment. Nevertheless, since he performed a specific act to affirm his willingness to accept such a witness or judge, he is obligated to abide by his commitment. The act performed - a *kinyan suder* - involves the transfer of a handkerchief or another piece of movable property from one litigant to the other. As explained in *Hilchot Mechirah*, the latter portion of Chapter 5, a *kinyan* indicates the sincerity of a person's commitment and his willingness to obligate himself in a binding manner. See also Chapter 22, Halachah 6.

אֲפִלּוּ הָיָה הָאֶחָד שֶׁבֵּרְרוּ בַּעֲלֵי הַדִּין חָכָם גָּדוֹל וְסָמוּךְ, אֵינוֹ יָכוֹל לָכֹף אֶת בַּעַל דִּינוֹ שֶׁיָּדוּן אֵצֶל זֶה, אֶלָּא גַּם הוּא בּוֹרֵר מִי שֶׁיִּרְצֶה.

ב מִי שֶׁקִּבֵּל עָלָיו קָרוֹב אוֹ פָּסוּל, בֵּין לִהְיוֹתוֹ דַּיָּן בֵּין לִהְיוֹתוֹ עֵד עָלָיו, אֲפִלּוּ קִבֵּל אֶחָד מִן הַפְּסוּלִים בַּעֲבֵרָה כִּשְׁנֵי עֵדִים כְּשֵׁרִים לְהָעִיד עָלָיו אוֹ כִּשְׁלֹשָׁה בֵּית דִּין מֻמְחִין לָדוּן לוֹ, בֵּין שֶׁקִּבֵּל עַל עַצְמוֹ לְאַבֵּד זְכֻיּוֹתָיו וְלִמְחֹל מַה שֶּׁהָיָה טוֹעֵן עַל פִּיהֶן, בֵּין שֶׁקִּבֵּל שֶׁיִּתֵּן כָּל מַה שֶּׁיִּטְעַן עָלָיו חֲבֵרוֹ בְּעֵדוּת זוֹ הַפָּסוּל אוֹ בְּדִינוֹ: אִם קָנוּ מִיָּדוֹ עַל זֶה – אֵינוֹ יָכוֹל לַחֲזֹר בּוֹ; וְאִם לֹא קָנוּ מִיָּדוֹ – יָכוֹל לַחֲזֹר בּוֹ עַד שֶׁיִּגָּמֵר הַדִּין. נִגְמַר הַדִּין, וְהוֹצִיא הַמָּמוֹן בְּדִין זֶה הַפָּסוּל אוֹ בְעֵדוּתוֹ – אֵינוֹ יָכוֹל לַחֲזֹר.

ג וְכֵן מִי שֶׁנִּתְחַיֵּב לַחֲבֵרוֹ שְׁבוּעָה בְּבֵית דִּין, וְאָמַר לוֹ: הִשָּׁבַע לִי בְּחַיֵּי רֹאשְׁךָ וְהִפָּטֵר, אוֹ הִשָּׁבַע לִי בְּחַיֵּי רֹאשְׁךָ וְאֶתֵּן לְךָ כָּל מַה שֶּׁתִּטְעַן: אִם קָנוּ מִיָּדוֹ – אֵינוֹ יָכוֹל לַחֲזֹר בּוֹ; וְאִם לֹא קָנוּ מִיָּדוֹ – יָכוֹל לַחֲזֹר בּוֹ עַד שֶׁיִּגָּמֵר הַדִּין. נִגְמַר הַדִּין וְנִשְׁבַּע כְּמוֹ שֶׁאָמַר לוֹ – אֵינוֹ יָכוֹל לַחֲזֹר, וְחַיָּב לְשַׁלֵּם.

ד וְהוּא הַדִּין לְמִי שֶׁנִּתְחַיֵּב שְׁבוּעַת הֶסֵּת וַהֲפָכָהּ, אִם קָנוּ מִיָּדוֹ אוֹ אִם נִשְׁבַּע זֶה שֶׁנֶּהֶפְכָה עָלָיו – אֵינוֹ יָכוֹל לַחֲזֹר בּוֹ.

8. I.e., the verdict is rendered. The exact wording used by the judge when rendering the verdict - e.g., "Go out and give it to him," or "You are obligated to give it to him" - is not significant. Since a verdict has been rendered, the case is considered as concluded.

9. Our translation is based on the interpretation of the Radbaz (see his gloss and see also Vol. V of his Responsa, Responsum 82) and the *Kessef Mishneh*. A literal translation of the version in the printed text of the *Mishneh Torah* would be: "If he expropriated money in this judgment...."

10. For if he could retract even then, there would be no point in having the matter judged at all.

11. See *Hilchot Edut*, Chapter 10, which describes the violation of which transgressions render a person to be considered as unacceptable to serve as a witness or a judge.

12. I.e., not only is the person who is unacceptable allowed to function as a judge, he is allowed to serve in that capacity alone, although generally, the matter would be adjudicated by three judges. The *Tur* and the Ramah (*Choshen Mishpat* 22:1) differ with regard to the latter point, explaining that if a litigant accepts an unacceptable person as one judge, his commitment is binding, but if he accepts him as three judges, he may retract. For making two extensions beyond the norm is considered excessive. Hence, if the litigant did not affirm his commitment with a *kinyan*, he is allowed to retract even after the judgment was rendered.

13. This represents a reduction in the severity of the oath. As *Hilchot Sh'vuot* 11:8-9 states, generally an oath must be taken "on God, the Lord of Israel."

14. The Radbaz interprets the conclusion of the case as meaning that the judges obligated the litigant to take an oath and the oath was taken. The *Sefer Me'irat Einayim* 22:17,22 quotes the opinion of Rabbenu Asher who interprets it as meaning "when the litigants left court," i.e. they left court without taking the oath. They are then obligated to pay

15. A defendant who claims to be totally free of obligation to the plaintiff was required by

5. Similarly, when a person was not obligated to take an oath[16] and [yet] he says: "I will take an oath [in response] to your [claim]," he cannot retract if he affirms [his statement] with a *kinyan*. If he does not affirm his statement with a *kinyan*, he has the right to retract until the judgment is concluded and he actually takes the oath,[17] even though he made his commitment in court.

6. When a person was obligated by a court, and then brought witnesses or proof[18] to vindicate himself, the judgment is rescinded and the case should be tried again. Although the judgment was already rendered, whenever he brings support [for his claim], the judgment is rescinded.[19]

Even if the judges tell him: "Bring all the proofs that you have within 30 days," [a litigant] may have the judgment rescinded although he brings proof after 30 days. What can he do if he did not discover the proof within 30 days, but found it afterwards?

7. If, however, [the litigant] completed [stating] his claims, he cannot have the judgment rescinded.

What is implied? [The judges] asked him: "Do you have witnesses [supporting your claim]?"

He replied: "I do not have witnesses."

"Do you have proof [of your position]?"

"I do not have proof," he answered.[20]

[In such a situation,] if [the court] judged him and held him liable, [the judgment is not rescinded]. [Although] when he sees that he was being held liable, he declared: "So-and-so and so-and-so come forward and testify on my behalf" or he produced [written] proof from his money-belt, it is not significant.[21] We do not pay any attention to his witnesses or his proof.[22]

8. When does the above apply? When[23] the proof was in his possession[24] and the witnesses were together with him in the country. If, however, he said: "I have neither witnesses, nor proof," and afterwards, witnesses came from overseas or a leather satchel belonging to his father[25] where legal documents were held had been entrusted to another person and that person came and supplied him with proof, he may call on these witnesses and/or this proof and have [the ruling] rescinded.

our Sages to take a less severe oath. Moreover, our Sages ruled that, if he desired, the defendant could give the plaintiff the option of taking the oath and then the plaintiff could collect his claim. See *Hilchot To'en ViNitan* 1:6.

16. The Yemenite manuscripts of the *Mishneh Torah* state "a severe oath," i.e., an oath that must be taken while holding a sacred article. This is likely the Rambam's intent (- whether or not the text reads that way or not). For there are few occasions when a defendant is released without having to take an oath at all. Hence the intent is rather than be required to take only a *sh'vuat hesset*, he offers to take a severe oath.

17. Our translation is based on the gloss of the *Sefer Me'irat Einayim* 22:22 who explains that since the oath is not required of the person, he has the option of retracting until he takes the oath. The delivery of the judgment by the court is not significant.

18. A written document.

ה וְהוּא הַדִּין בְּמִי שֶׁלֹּא הָיָה חַיָּב שְׁבוּעָה, וְאָמַר אֶשָּׁבַע לְךָ שְׁבוּעָה: אִם קָנוּ מִיָּדוֹ – אֵינוֹ יָכוֹל לַחֲזֹר בּוֹ; וְאִם לֹא קָנוּ מִיָּדוֹ, אַף עַל פִּי שֶׁקִּבֵּל בְּבֵית דִּין – חוֹזֵר עַד שֶׁיִּגָּמֵר הַדִּין וְיִשָּׁבַע.

ו מִי שֶׁנִּתְחַיֵּב בְּבֵית דִּין, וְהֵבִיא עֵדִים אוֹ רְאָיָה לִזְכוּתוֹ – סוֹתֵר אֶת הַדִּין, וְחוֹזֵר הַדִּין. אַף עַל פִּי שֶׁכְּבָר נִגְמַר הַדִּין, כָּל זְמַן שֶׁהוּא מֵבִיא רְאָיָה – סוֹתֵר.
אָמְרוּ לוֹ הַדַּיָּנִים: כָּל רְאָיוֹת שֶׁיֵּשׁ לְךָ, הָבֵא מִכָּאן וְעַד שְׁלֹשִׁים יוֹם! אַף עַל פִּי שֶׁהֵבִיא רְאָיָה לְאַחַר שְׁלֹשִׁים יוֹם – סוֹתֵר אֶת הַדִּין. מַה יַּעֲשֶׂה אִם לֹא מָצָא בְּתוֹךְ שְׁלֹשִׁים וּמָצָא לְאַחַר שְׁלֹשִׁים?

ז אֲבָל אִם סָתַם אֶת טַעֲנוֹתָיו – אֵינוֹ סוֹתֵר. כֵּיצַד? אָמְרוּ לוֹ: יֵשׁ לְךָ עֵדִים? אָמַר: אֵין לִי עֵדִים. יֵשׁ לְךָ רְאָיָה? אָמַר: אֵין לִי רְאָיָה. וְדָנוּ אוֹתוֹ וְחִיְּבוּהוּ. כֵּיוָן שֶׁרָאָה שֶׁנִּתְחַיֵּב, אָמַר: קִרְבוּ פְּלוֹנִי וּפְלוֹנִי וְהָעִידוּנִי! אוֹ שֶׁהוֹצִיא רְאָיָה מִתּוֹךְ אֲפֻנְדָּתוֹ – אֵין זֶה כְּלוּם, וְאֵין מַשְׁגִּיחִין עַל עֵדָיו וְעַל רְאָיָתוֹ.

ח בַּמֶּה דְּבָרִים אֲמוּרִים? כְּשֶׁהָיְתָה הָרְאָיָה אֶצְלוֹ וְהָעֵדִים עִמּוֹ בַּמְּדִינָה;
אֲבָל אִם אָמַר: אֵין לִי עֵדִים וְאֵין לִי רְאָיָה, וּלְאַחַר מִכָּן בָּאוּ לוֹ עֵדִים מִמְּדִינַת הַיָּם, אוֹ שֶׁהָיְתָה הַחֵמֶת שֶׁל אָבִיו שֶׁיֵּשׁ שָׁם הַשְּׁטָרוֹת מֻפְקֶדֶת בְּיַד אֲחֵרִים, וּבָא זֶה שֶׁהַפִּקָּדוֹן אֶצְלוֹ וְהוֹצִיא לוֹ רְאָיָתוֹ – הֲרֵי זֶה מֵבִיא וְסוֹתֵר.

19. The *Shulchan Aruch* (*Choshen Mishpat* 20:1) states that even if a defendant has already paid a plaintiff, if the support he brings appears substantial, the judgment should be rescinded.

20. In his *Kessef Mishneh* and his *Shulchan Aruch* (*Choshen Mishpat* 20:1), Rav Yosef Karo points to the text of *Sanhedrin* 31a and on that basis restates this clause as follows:

> If they told him to bring witnesses or proof and he said: "I do not have," even though he discovers them afterwards, they are of no consequence. Needless to say, it applies if they asked him: "Do you have witnesses?" and he replied: "I do not have witnesses."

21. *Sanhedrin, loc. cit.*, records this point as a difference of opinion between Rabban Shimon ben Gamliel and the Sages. Generally, in such situations the halachah follows Rabbi Shimon ben Gamliel's approach. This and two other situations are exceptions and the Sages' opinion is followed.

22. For the fact that he denied having witnesses or proof when asked to produce them creates a suspicion that he is lying. If he knew about the possibility of these witnesses testifying or using this support, he should have stated so. Hence we assume that until he knew that he would be held liable, he was not willing to risk falsehood. After he was held liable, he tried to perpetrate deception to exonerate himself (*Sefer Me'irat Einayim* 20:4-5).

23. At the time he made his statements.

24. The *Sefer Me'irat Einayim* 20:6 states that even if the proof was not in his possession, if it is easily accessible to him, he must have acknowledged it at the outset.

25. Or even his own satchel with his own legal documents [Ramah (*Choshen Mishpat* 20:6].

Why may he have [the ruling] rescinded? Because he could claim: "The reason I said: 'I don't have any witnesses' and 'I don't have any proof,' is because they were not available to me." Whenever he could make such a claim and there is substance to his words,[26] he is not considered to have completed [stating] his claims [when he originally stated]: "I have no witnesses...." He may [bring the witnesses and/or proof and] have the judgment rescinded.

Accordingly, if he explicitly states: "I have no witnesses at all, neither here or overseas, nor any [written] proof, neither in my possession or in the possession of others," he cannot have [the judgment] rescinded.

9. When does the above[27] apply? With regard to an adult who was held liable[28] and then brought [written] proof or witnesses after completing the statement of his arguments.[29]

[Different concepts apply, however, with regard to] an heir who was a minor when the person whose estate he inherited died and a suit was lodged against him because of that person[30] after he came of age.[31] Even though he stated: "I have neither witnesses, nor proof," and after he departed from the court after being held liable, others told him: "We know testimony that favors your father that will cause this judgment to be rescinded," or "The person whose estate you inherited entrusted this [written] proof [to me]," he may bring [the testimony or the proof] immediately and have the judgment rescinded. [The rationale is that] a minor is not aware of all the proofs possessed by the person whose estate he inherited.

10. [The following rules apply when a person] affirmed [his consent to the following agreement] with a *kinyan*:[32] If he does not come on this-and-this day and take an oath, his colleague's[33] claim would be accepted and [that colleague] could take whatever he claims without taking an oath. Alternatively, if he does not come on this-and-this day, take an oath, and collect his due, he forfeits his right [to the claim]. Nothing is to be granted him and his colleague[34] is released of liability. Should that day pass and he not come, the stipulation is binding and he forfeits his rights.[35]

26. I.e., there is evidence that indicates to the court that he is telling the truth. The Ramah (*loc. cit.*) states that witnesses must corroborate his statements.
27. That the judgment cannot be rescinded.
28. In a suit involving his own property or liability.
29. If he did not bring or at least mention the proofs or witnesses at the outset, it is a clear indication that he had no proof and is in fact forging the documents or bringing witnesses who lie.
30. I.e., a complaint was lodged that the person was not the legitimate owner of the property.
31. For until he comes of age, no suits can be lodged against him. Although *Sanhedrin* 31a, speaks of this situation with regard to a *yanuka*, "a young child," the Rambam interprets that as meaning that the child was young at the time he inherited the property, but came of age before the suit was brought to court (Radbaz; *Kessef Mishneh*).

Tosafot and Rabbenu Asher interpret the passage as applying even when the child was

וּמִפְּנֵי מָה סוֹתֵר? מִפְּנֵי שֶׁיָּכוֹל לִטְעֹן וְלוֹמַר: זֶה שֶׁאָמַרְתִּי אֵין לִי עֵדִים וְאֵין לִי רְאָיָה, מִפְּנֵי שֶׁלֹּא הָיוּ מְצוּיִין אֶצְלִי.

וְכָל זְמַן שֶׁיָּכוֹל לִטְעֹן וְלוֹמַר: זֶה שֶׁאָמַרְתִּי אֵין לִי עֵדִים וְאֵין לִי רְאָיָה, מִפְּנֵי שֶׁלֹּא הָיוּ מְצוּיִין אֶצְלִי, אוֹ מִפְּנֵי כַּךְ וְכַךְ אָמַרְתִּי אֵין לִי עֵדִים וְאֵין לִי רְאָיָה, וְהָיָה מַמָּשׁ בִּדְבָרָיו – הֲרֵי זֶה לֹא סָתַם טַעֲנוֹתָיו, וְסוֹתֵר.

לְפִיכָךְ, אִם פֵּרֵשׁ וְאָמַר: אֵין לִי עֵדִים כְּלָל, לֹא הֵנָּה וְלֹא בִּמְדִינַת הַיָּם, וְלֹא רְאָיָה כְּלָל, לֹא בְּיָדִי וְלֹא בְּיַד אֲחֵרִים – אֵינוֹ יָכוֹל לִסְתֹּר.

ט בַּמֶּה דְּבָרִים אֲמוּרִים? בְּגָדוֹל שֶׁנִּתְחַיֵּב, וְהֵבִיא רְאָיוֹת וְהֵבִיא עֵדִים אַחַר שֶׁסָּתַם טַעֲנוֹתָיו;

אֲבָל יוֹרֵשׁ שֶׁהוּא קָטָן כְּשֶׁמֵּת מוֹרִישׁוֹ, וּבָאוּ עָלָיו טְעָנוֹת מֵחֲמַת מוֹרִישׁוֹ אַחַר שֶׁהִגְדִּיל, וְאָמַר: אֵין לִי עֵדִים וְאֵין לִי רְאָיָה, וְאַחַר שֶׁיָּצָא מִבֵּית דִּין חַיָּב אָמְרוּ לוֹ אֲחֵרִים: אָנוּ יוֹדְעִים לְאָבִיךָ עֵדוּת שֶׁתִּסְתֹּר בָּהּ דִּין זֶה, אוֹ אָמַר לוֹ אֶחָד: מוֹרִישְׁךָ הִפְקִיד רְאָיָה זוֹ – הֲרֵי זֶה מֵבִיא מִיָּד וְסוֹתֵר, שֶׁאֵין הַיּוֹרֵשׁ קָטָן יוֹדֵעַ כָּל רְאָיוֹת מוֹרִישׁוֹ.

י מִי שֶׁקָּנוּ מִיָּדוֹ, שֶׁאִם לֹא יָבוֹא בְּיוֹם פְּלוֹנִי וְיִשָּׁבַע – יִהְיֶה חֲבֵרוֹ נֶאֱמָן בְּטַעֲנָתוֹ וְיִטֹּל כָּל מַה שֶּׁטָּעַן בְּלֹא שְׁבוּעָה,

אוֹ שֶׁאִם לֹא יָבוֹא בְּיוֹם פְּלוֹנִי וְיִשָּׁבַע וְיִטֹּל – אִבֵּד אֶת זְכוּתוֹ וְאֵין לוֹ כְּלוּם וְיִפָּטֵר חֲבֵרוֹ, וְעָבַר הַיּוֹם וְלֹא בָּא – נִתְקַיְּמוּ הַתְּנָאִים, וְאִבֵּד אֶת זְכוּתוֹ.

still a minor, e.g., the case involved a promissory note, in which instance, the case can be prosecuted even against a minor.

Rabbenu Asher takes the issue a step further and differs with Rambam, explaining that if the minor indeed came of age, he can no longer protest. For we assume that since he knew he was being sued, he familiarized himself with his father's affairs before the matter was brought to court. The *Kessef Mishneh* explains that this is not necessarily the case. It is possible that he was unaware of the matter entirely and did not know how to begin investigating the matter. The *Shulchan Aruch* (*Choshen Mishpat* 20:6) quotes the Rambam's view. The Ramah states that if it is known that the minor turned adult had knowledge of the witnesses or the proof beforehand, yet did not mention this at the outset, he cannot have the judgment rescinded.

32. The *Sefer Me'irat Einayim* 21:1,6 states that in the first instance, the *kinyan* must be undertaken in an important court, while in the second instance, that is not necessary. The *Siftei Cohen* 21:5 quotes both more lenient and more stringent views.

33. The plaintiff.

34. The defendant.

35. Since he affirmed his commitment with a *kinyan*, we assume that he sincerely agreed to the stipulation. We do not consider it as an *asmachta*, a commitment which the person never intended to keep (see *Hilchot Mechirah* 11:13).

The Ramah (*Choshen Mishpat* 21:1) emphasizes that the *kinyan* must be made at the time of the stipulation. Otherwise, it is considered as an *asmachta*, and is not binding.

If, however, he brings proof that he was held back by forces beyond his control on that day,[36] he is not bound by his agreement. He may take an oath against the claim issued by his colleague as before.[37] Similar laws apply in all analogous situations.

CHAPTER EIGHT

1. When a court reaches a split decision - some say that [the defendant] is not liable, and others say that he is liable, we follow the majority. This is a positive mitzvah of Scriptural origin,[1] as [Exodus 23:2] states: "Follow after the inclination of the majority."[2]

When does the above apply? With regard to financial matters and with regard to laws involving questions of what is forbidden and what is permitted, what is impure and what is pure, and the like. With regard to cases involving capital punishment, [different laws apply] if there is a difference of opinion whether the transgressor should be executed or not.[3] If the majority [rule] to exonerate him, he is exonerated. If, however, the majority [rules] that he is guilty, he should not be executed until there are [at least] two more [judges] who hold him guilty than who exonerate him.

According to the Oral Tradition, we learned that the Torah warned against this, saying [*ibid.*]: "Do not follow the majority to do harm."[4] That is to say that if the majority are inclined "to do harm," i.e., to execute [the defendant], you should not follow them until there is a significant inclination, and there [is a majority of] two judges who rule that he is guilty.

[This is implied by (*ibid.*):] "to follow the inclination of the majority [and] influence [the judgment]." A positive inclination may be made on the basis [of a majority] of one, a harmful inclination, on the basis [of a majority] of two. All of these concepts are [based on] the Oral Tradition.

2. [The following laws apply when] there is a difference of opinion within a court of three [judges with regard to a monetary issue]: If two say [the defendant's] claim should be vindicated and one says that he is liable, his claim is vindicated. If two say that he is liable and one says his claim should be vindicated, he is held liable. If one says that his claim should be vindicated and one says he is liable, or two say that his claim should be vindicated or that he is liable and the third [judge] says: "I do not know," we add[5] another two[6] judges. Thus five [judges] debate the matter.[7]

36. The commentaries note that this law applies even if he was held back by forces beyond his control only on that day. Although he could have fulfilled his commitment beforehand, since he was not able to do on the last day, he is not held liable.

This relates to a halachic issue of a general scope: Is the fact that a person is held back by forces beyond his control only on the last day significant or not? See the comments of the Ramah (*Yoreh De'ah* 232:12) and the glosses of the *Ketzot HaChoshen* and the *Netivot HaMishpat* 55:1 which discuss this issue.

וְאִם הֵבִיא רְאָיָה שֶׁהָיָה אָנוּס בְּאוֹתוֹ הַיּוֹם - הֲרֵי זֶה פָּטוּר מִקִּנְיָן זֶה, וְיִשָּׁבַע כְּשֶׁיִּתְבָּעֶנּוּ חֲבֵרוֹ, כְּשֶׁהָיָה מִקֹּדֶם. וְכֵן כֹּל כַּיּוֹצֵא בָּזֶה.

פֶּרֶק שְׁמִינִי

א בֵּית דִּין שֶׁנֶּחְלְקוּ, מִקְצָתָם אוֹמְרִים זַכַּאי, וּמִקְצָתָם אוֹמְרִים חַיָּב - הוֹלְכִין אַחַר הָרֹב. וְזוֹ מִצְוַת עֲשֵׂה שֶׁל תּוֹרָה, שֶׁנֶּאֱמַר: אַחֲרֵי רַבִּים לְהַטּוֹת.

בַּמֶּה דְּבָרִים אֲמוּרִים? בְּדִינֵי מָמוֹנוֹת וּבִשְׁאָר דִּינֵי אָסוּר וּמֻתָּר וְטָמֵא וְטָהוֹר וְכַיּוֹצֵא בָּהֶן; אֲבָל בְּדִינֵי נְפָשׁוֹת, אִם נֶחְלְקוּ בְּזֶה הַחוֹטֵא אִם יֵהָרֵג אוֹ לֹא יֵהָרֵג: אִם הָיוּ הָרֹב מְזַכִּים - זַכַּאי, וְאִם הָיוּ הָרֹב מְחַיְּבִין - אֵינוֹ נֶהֱרָג עַד שֶׁיִּהְיוּ הַמְחַיְּבִין יָתֵר עַל הַמְזַכִּים שְׁנַיִם. מִפִּי הַשְּׁמוּעָה לָמְדוּ, שֶׁעַל זֶה הִזְהִירָה תּוֹרָה וְאָמְרָה: לֹא תִהְיֶה אַחֲרֵי רַבִּים לְרָעֹת. כְּלוֹמַר: אִם הָרֹב נוֹטִים לְרָעָה לַהֲרֹג - לֹא תִהְיֶה אַחֲרֵיהֶם, עַד שֶׁיִּטּוּ הַטָּיָה גְּדוֹלָה וְיוֹסִיפוּ הַמְחַיְּבִין שְׁנַיִם. שֶׁנֶּאֱמַר: לִנְטֹת אַחֲרֵי רַבִּים לְהַטֹּת. הַטָּיָתְךָ לְטוֹבָה - עַל פִּי אֶחָד, לְרָעָה - עַל פִּי שְׁנַיִם. וְכָל אֵלּוּ הַדְּבָרִים קַבָּלָה הֵם.

ב בֵּית דִּין שֶׁל שְׁלֹשָׁה שֶׁנֶּחְלְקוּ: שְׁנַיִם אוֹמְרִים זַכַּאי, וְאֶחָד אוֹמֵר חַיָּב - הֲרֵי זֶה זַכַּאי. שְׁנַיִם אוֹמְרִים חַיָּב, וְאֶחָד אוֹמֵר זַכַּאי - הֲרֵי זֶה חַיָּב.

אֶחָד אוֹמֵר זַכַּאי, וְאֶחָד אוֹמֵר חַיָּב, וְאֶחָד אוֹמֵר אֵינִי יוֹדֵעַ, אוֹ שֶׁאָמְרוּ שְׁנַיִם זַכַּאי אוֹ חַיָּב, וְהַשְּׁלִישִׁי אוֹמֵר אֵינִי יוֹדֵעַ - יוֹסִיפוּ הַדַּיָּנִים שְׁנַיִם. נִמְצְאוּ חֲמִשָּׁה נוֹשְׂאִים וְנוֹתְנִים בַּדָּבָר.

37. Since he was held back by forces beyond his control, we do not cause him to forfeit his rights because he did not keep his commitment.

Similarly, he may take an oath and collect the property that was due him (*Siftei Cohen* 21:4).

1. *Sefer HaMitzvot* (positive commandment 175) and *Sefer HaChinuch* (mitzvah 78) count this as one of the 613 mitzvot of the Torah.
2. See *Hilchot Mamrim* 1:3 which describes the process of reaching a majority decision.
3. See Chapter 5, Halachah 3, where this subject is also discussed.
4. *Sefer HaMitzvot* (negative commandment 282) and *Sefer HaChinuch* (mitzvah 76) count this as one of the 613 mitzvot of the Torah.
5. Since the third judge says that he does not know, it is considered as if he is not present.
6. An even number of judges is always added so that there will not be an even number of judges sitting on the court. Although the judge who says "I don't know" is considered as if he is not present, he is not disqualified from the court. Instead, he can change his mind at any time. Thus if only one judge were added, it would be possible that the court would ultimately be evenly balanced (Radbaz).
7. Rav Moshe Cohen (as quoted by the *Kessef Mishneh*) notes that in cases involving capital punishment, a judge who says "I don't know" is not allowed to take part in the

If three say [the defendant's] claim should be vindicated and two say[8] that he is liable, his claim is vindicated. If three say that he is liable and two say his claim should be vindicated, he is held liable. If two say that his claim should be vindicated and two say he is liable, and the fifth [judge] says: "I do not know," we add another two judges. If, however, four say his claim should be vindicated or that he is liable and one says: "I don't know," or three say his claim should be vindicated and one says that he is liable, and the fifth says: "I don't know," we follow the majority.[9] [This applies] whether the judge who says: "I don't know" is the same who said "I don't know" at the outset or another individual.

If, in this situation as well, the opinions are evenly balanced and one says: "I don't know," or [in any situation] that there is a doubt, we continue to add two more judges until we reach 71 [judges].[10] If, [after] reaching 71, [the issue is still unresolved], [i.e.,] 35 hold him liable, 35 wish to vindicate his claim and one says: "I don't know," they debate the matter until [the judge who has not made up his mind] sides with one of the opinions and thus there will be 36 who vindicate him or 36 who hold him liable. If neither [that judge] nor another[11] changes his opinion, the matter remains unresolved and the money is allowed to remain in the possession of its owner.[12]

3. Whenever a judge says: "I don't know," he is not[13] required to explain the rationale for his statements and explain the reason why he is in doubt. [In contrast, a judge] who rules that [a litigant's claim] is vindicated must state why he vindicates [the claim], or if he holds him liable, he must state why he holds him liable.[14]

CHAPTER NINE

1. When all [the judges of] a *Sanhedrin*[1] begin their judgment of a case involving capital punishment and say that [the defendant] is liable, he is exonerated. There must be some who seek to exonerate him and argue on his behalf,[2] and yet the majority hold him liable. [Only] then he is executed.

debate further if he desires to convict the defendant. Making such a statement does not, however, prevent a judge from judging financial cases or even judging cases involving capital punishment if he discovers a rationale to exonerate the defendant.

8. I.e., the judge who originally said: "I don't know" now took a position.

9. Similarly, if three hold the defendant liable, one supports his claim, and one says "I don't know," the defendant is held liable.

If, however, two hold the defendant liable, one supports his claim and two say "I don't know," there is a difference of opinion among the Rabbis. The Rashba states that the defendant is held liable. Rav Shlomo Luria explains that since the Rambam counts the judges who say "I don't know" as part of the court, the matter is considered as undecided and more judges are added. For there is not a majority of the court that holds the defendant liable.

10. For 71, the number of judges on the Supreme *Sanhedrin* is the maximum number of judges that are ever included on a court.

אָמְרוּ שְׁלשָׁה מֵהֶם זַכַּאי, וּשְׁנַיִם אוֹמְרִים חַיָּב – הֲרֵי זֶה זַכַּאי. אָמְרוּ שְׁלשָׁה חַיָּב, וּשְׁנַיִם זַכַּאי – הֲרֵי זֶה חַיָּב. אָמְרוּ שְׁנַיִם מֵהֶם זַכַּאי, וּשְׁנַיִם מֵהֶם חַיָּב, וְאֶחָד אוֹמֵר אֵינִי יוֹדֵעַ – מוֹסִיפִין שְׁנַיִם. אֲבָל אִם אָמְרוּ אַרְבָּעָה זַכַּאי אוֹ חַיָּב, וְאֶחָד אוֹמֵר אֵינִי יוֹדֵעַ, אוֹ שֶׁאָמְרוּ שְׁלשָׁה זַכַּאי, וְאֶחָד חַיָּב, וְאָמַר אֶחָד אֵינִי יוֹדֵעַ, בֵּין שֶׁהָיָה זֶה שֶׁאָמַר אֵינִי יוֹדֵעַ הוּא שֶׁאָמַר אֵינִי יוֹדֵעַ בַּתְּחִלָּה, בֵּין שֶׁאָמַר אַחֵר – הוֹלְכִים אַחַר הָרֹב.

הָיוּ מֶחֱצָה לְמֶחֱצָה וְאֶחָד אוֹמֵר אֵינִי יוֹדֵעַ – הֲרֵי אֵלּוּ מוֹסִיפִין שְׁנַיִם אֲחֵרִים. וְכֵן אִם נִסְתַּפֵּק הַדָּבָר – מוֹסִיפִין וְהוֹלְכִין עַד שִׁבְעִים וְאֶחָד. הִגִּיעוּ לְשִׁבְעִים וְאֶחָד, וְאָמְרוּ שְׁלשִׁים וַחֲמִשָּׁה חַיָּב, וּשְׁלשִׁים וַחֲמִשָּׁה זַכַּאי, וְאֶחָד אוֹמֵר אֵינִי יוֹדֵעַ – נוֹשְׂאִים וְנוֹתְנִים עִמּוֹ עַד שֶׁיַּחֲזֹר לְדִבְרֵי הַצַּד הָאֶחָד, וְנִמְצְאוּ שְׁלשִׁים וְשִׁשָּׁה מְזַכִּים אוֹ מְחַיְּבִין.

וְאִם לֹא חָזַר לֹא הוּא וְלֹא אֶחָד מֵהֶן – הֲרֵי הַדָּבָר סָפֵק, וּמַעֲמִידִין אֶת הַמָּמוֹן בְּחֶזְקַת בְּעָלָיו.

ג כָּל מִי שֶׁאָמַר אֵינִי יוֹדֵעַ – אֵינוֹ צָרִיךְ לָתֵת טַעַם לִדְבָרָיו וּלְהוֹדִיעַ מֵאֵי זֶה טַעַם בָּא לוֹ הַסָּפֵק, כְּדֶרֶךְ שֶׁמַּרְאֶה הַמְזַכֶּה מֵאֵי זֶה טַעַם מְזַכֶּה, וְהַמְחַיֵּב מֵאֵי זֶה טַעַם מְחַיֵּב.

פֶּרֶק תְּשִׁיעִי

א סַנְהֶדְרִין שֶׁפָּתְחוּ כֻּלָּם בְּדִינֵי נְפָשׁוֹת תְּחִלָּה, וְאָמְרוּ כֻּלָּן חַיָּב – הֲרֵי זֶה פָּטוּר, עַד שֶׁיִּהְיוּ שָׁם מִקְצָת מְזַכִּין שֶׁיֵּהָפְכוּ בִּזְכוּתוֹ, וְיִרְבּוּ הַמְחַיְּבִין, וְאַחַר כָּךְ יֵהָרֵג.

11. For if one of the other judges change their opinion, there will still be a majority even if the other judge remains undecided.
12. We follow the principle: "A person who desires to expropriate property from a colleague must prove his claim." Since the plaintiff cannot prove the validity of his claim, for it is not supported by the majority of judges, the money is allowed to remain in the possession of the defendant.
13. In the Yemenite manuscripts of the *Mishneh Torah*, the version is "Whenever a judge says: 'I don't know,' he is required... to explain the reason why he is in doubt, just like [a judge] who rules that [a litigant's claim] is vindicated must state why he vindicates [the claim]." This version allows for an easier flow of the Hebrew. The commentaries and the *Shulchan Aruch* (*Choshen Mishpat* 18:3) follow the version stated in the standard printed text.
14. See Chapter 10, Halachot 1,4.

1. From the comparison to the wording of the following halachah, one might think that this applies only with regard to the Supreme *Sanhedrin*. The Radbaz clarifies that this is not the case and the law applies to an ordinary *Sanhedrin* as well.
2. And in such a situation, this is unlikely to happen, for all of the judges rule that he is

2. [The following rules apply when there is] a difference of opinion in a minor *Sanhedrin*. If twelve judges say that he should be exonerated and eleven say that he should be held liable, he is exonerated.[3] If twelve say that he is liable and eleven say that he should be exonerated[4] or eleven say that he should be exonerated and eleven say that he is liable, and one says: "I don't know," we add two [judges].[5] Even if there are twelve who wish to exonerate him and twelve who hold him liable, and one who one says: "I don't know," we add two [judges]. [The rationale is that the judge] who says: "I don't know," is considered as if he does not exist,[6] for he cannot change his mind and explain why [the defendant] should be held liable.[7] Thus after the addition, there are 24 judges aside from the person who says: "I don't know."

If twelve say that he should be exonerated and twelve say that he is liable, he is exonerated.[8] If eleven say that he should be exonerated and thirteen say that he is liable, he is liable. [This applies] even if one of the original judges says: "I don't know."[9] For there are two more judges who rule that he is liable.

If twelve say that he should be exonerated and twelve say that he is liable,[10] we add two judges. And similarly, [if the balance is not broken,] we continue to add [two judges] until there is at least one more judge who rules that he should be exonerated or at least two more judges who rule that he should be held liable. If there are an even number of judges on both sides, and one says: "I don't know," or if the number [of judges] who rule that he is liable is only one more [than those who rule that he should be exonerated], we continue to add judges until we reach 71.

[The following rules apply when the court] reaches [that size]. If 36 say that he should be exonerated and 35 say that he is liable, he should be exonerated. If 36 say that he is liable and 35 say that he should be exonerated, they debate back and forth against each other until one of them sees the other's perspective and either exonerates him or holds him liable. If such a change in perspective does not take place, the judge of the greatest stature declares: "This judgment has become aged," and he is released.[11]

liable. Since the Torah's criteria for execution - that there be "a congregation that saves," i.e., judges who argue on the defendant's behalf are not met, he is exonerated (*Likkutei Sichot*, Vol. 29, p. 166ff.).

3. For a majority of one is enough to exonerate a defendant (Chapter 8, Halachah 1).

4. For a majority of one is not enough to convict him (*Ibid.*).

5. One judge is not added, so that the court will not have an even number of judges.

6. Since it is as if this judge does not exist, it is as if there are only 22 judges on the court and 23 are necessary. Therefore, we make an addition.

7. The Radbaz and the *Kessef Mishneh* state that this judge can change his mind and decide to acquit the defendant, but cannot rule to convict him. From Chapter 10, Halachah 2, it appears that he can also, however, vote with those who hold the defendant liable at the time of the final judgment. Since he can change his mind, two judges are added and not only one.

8. The twenty-fifth judge says: "I don't know." This ruling has aroused the attention of the commentaries who a) question why the defendant is acquitted when there is not a majority

ב סַנְהֶדְרֵי קְטַנָּה שֶׁנֶּחְלְקוּ בְּדִינֵי נְפָשׁוֹת, שְׁנֵים עָשָׂר אוֹמְרִים זַכַּאי, וְאַחַד עָשָׂר אוֹמְרִים חַיָּב – הֲרֵי זֶה זַכַּאי. שְׁנֵים עָשָׂר אוֹמְרִים חַיָּב, וְאַחַד עָשָׂר אוֹמְרִים זַכַּאי, אוֹ שֶׁאָמְרוּ אַחַד עָשָׂר זַכַּאי, וְאַחַד עָשָׂר חַיָּב, וְאֶחָד אוֹמֵר אֵינִי יוֹדֵעַ, אֲפִלּוּ עֶשְׂרִים וּשְׁנַיִם מְזַכִּין אוֹ מְחַיְּבִין, וְהָאֶחָד אוֹמֵר אֵינִי יוֹדֵעַ – יוֹסִיפוּ שְׁנַיִם. זֶה שֶׁאָמַר אֵינִי יוֹדֵעַ – הֲרֵי הוּא כְּמִי שֶׁאֵינוֹ, שֶׁהֲרֵי אֵינוֹ חוֹזֵר וּמְלַמֵּד חוֹבָה. וְנִמְצְאוּ אַחַר הַתּוֹסֶפֶת עֶשְׂרִים וְאַרְבָּעָה חוּץ מִזֶּה הַמִּסְתַּפֵּק. אָמְרוּ שְׁנֵים עָשָׂר זַכַּאי, וּשְׁנֵים עָשָׂר חַיָּב – הֲרֵי זֶה זַכַּאי. אַחַד עָשָׂר אוֹמְרִים זַכַּאי, וּשְׁלֹשָׁה עָשָׂר אוֹמְרִים חַיָּב, אַף עַל פִּי שֶׁהָאֶחָד מִן הָרִאשׁוֹנִים אוֹמֵר אֵינִי יוֹדֵעַ – הֲרֵי זֶה חַיָּב, שֶׁהֲרֵי הַמְחַיְּבִין רַבּוּ בִּשְׁנַיִם. אָמְרוּ שְׁנֵים עָשָׂר זַכַּאי, וּשְׁנֵים עָשָׂר חַיָּב, וְאֶחָד אוֹמֵר אֵינִי יוֹדֵעַ – מוֹסִיפִין שְׁנַיִם אֲחֵרִים.

וְכֵן מוֹסִיפִין וְהוֹלְכִין עַד שֶׁיִּרְבּוּ הַמְזַכִּין אֶחָד וִיהֵא זַכַּאי, אוֹ יִרְבּוּ הַמְחַיְּבִין שְׁנַיִם אוֹ יוֹתֵר וִיהֵא חַיָּב.

הָיוּ אֵלּוּ כְּנֶגֶד אֵלּוּ וְאֶחָד אוֹמֵר אֵינִי יוֹדֵעַ, אוֹ שֶׁהָיוּ הַמְחַיְּבִין יוֹתֵר אֶחָד בִּלְבַד – מוֹסִיפִין וְהוֹלְכִין עַד שִׁבְעִים וְאֶחָד.

הִגִּיעוּ לְשִׁבְעִים וְאֶחָד, שְׁלֹשִׁים וְשִׁשָּׁה אוֹמְרִים זַכַּאי, וּשְׁלֹשִׁים וַחֲמִשָּׁה אוֹמְרִים חַיָּב – הֲרֵי זֶה זַכַּאי.

שְׁלֹשִׁים וְשִׁשָּׁה אוֹמְרִים חַיָּב, וּשְׁלֹשִׁים וַחֲמִשָּׁה אוֹמְרִים זַכַּאי – דָּנִים אֵלּוּ כְּנֶגֶד אֵלּוּ, עַד שֶׁיִּרְאֶה אֶחָד מֵהֶן דִּבְרֵי חֲבֵרוֹ וּמְזַכִּין אוֹתוֹ אוֹ מְחַיְּבִין אוֹתוֹ.

וְאִם לֹא רָאָה – גָּדוֹל שֶׁבַּדַּיָּנִים אוֹמֵר: נִזְדַּקֵּן הַדִּין! וּפוֹטְרִין אוֹתוֹ.

of judges issuing such a verdict, and b) note that it appears to contradict his ruling a few lines later.

The *Lechem Mishneh* explains that since there are an ample number of judges who seek to acquit him, the fact that there are an equal number who wish to convict him is not significant. We follow the principle: With regard to doubt in cases involving capital punishment, we rule leniently.

The *Tosafot Yom Tov* (*Sanhedrin* 5:5) maintains that there is a printing error in the text of the *Mishneh Torah* and it should read: "Thirteen say that he should be exonerated and twelve say that he is liable...."

9. I.e., either the judge who originally said: "I don't know" still maintains that position, or he changed his mind and adapted a different position, but another judge became doubtful.

10. And the twenty-fifth judge says: "I don't know." As mentioned above, this clause appears to contradict the Rambam's previous statements. Some explain that in this instance, we are speaking about a situation where at the outset, there were twelve judges who ruled that he was liable and eleven who ruled that he should be acquitted. From the two judges who were added, one ruled that he should be exonerated, while the other said: "I don't know." In this instance, since originally, there was a majority voting in favor of conviction, the defendant is not exonerated because of the doubt and more judges are added (Radbaz, according to one interpretation).

11. I.e., we are unable to reach a resolution.

If 35 say that he is liable and 35 say that he should be exonerated, and one says "I don't know," we release him.[12] If 34 say that he should be exonerated and 36 say that he is liable, and one says: "I don't know," he is held liable. For there is a majority of two judges who hold him liable.

3. When there is a difference of opinion in the Supreme *Sanhedrin*, whether with regard to [a law involving][13] capital punishment, monetary law, or other matters of Torah law, we do not add judges.[14] Instead, they debate against each other and the ruling follows the majority. If their difference of opinion involves whether a person will be executed, they should debate against each other until they either exonerate him or hold him liable.

CHAPTER TEN

1. When one of the judges in a case involving capital punishment[1] rules to acquit the defendant or to hold him liable, not because this is his own opinion which he arrived upon the basis of his own decision, but rather because he was swayed by his colleague's words, he commits a transgression, as [implied by Exodus 23:2]: "Do not respond to a dispute with an inclination."[2] According to the Oral Tradition,[3] [this command is interpreted to mean that,] when the judges are determining the verdict, a person should not say: "It is sufficient for me to adopt so-and-so's [understanding]."[4] Instead, he should say what he thinks [himself].

2. Included in this interdiction is a prohibition against [a judge] who had [first] proposed a rationale to exonerate a defendant in a capital case proposing a rationale to convict him. [This is also implied by:] "Do not respond to a dispute with an inclination."[5]

When does the above apply? In the give and take [among the judges]. At the time of the verdict even [a judge] who had proposed a rationale for acquittal may join the others who vote for conviction.[6]

12. Since there is a doubt, we rule leniently and release him. The Meiri and others rule that the judges should continue debating until they come to a resolution.
13. This addition is made on the basis of one of the responsa of the Radbaz (Vol. V, Responsum 1690) who explains that this clause refers to a theoretical issue that relates to capital punishment, while the latter clause refers to an actual case involving a suspect brought before the court.
14. For we never make a court larger than 71, as stated above.

1. Although the mitzvah *per se* applies only with regard to cases involving capital punishment, the prohibition applies in all cases, even with regard to matters of financial law. For this reason, it is not one of the distinctions between cases involving capital punishment and those involving financial law mentioned in the following chapter (*Minchat Chinuch,* mitzvah 77).
2. *Sefer HaMitzvot* (negative commandment 283) and *Sefer HaChinuch* (mitzvah 77)

שְׁלשִׁים וַחֲמִשָּׁה אוֹמְרִים חַיָּב, וּשְׁלשִׁים וַחֲמִשָּׁה אוֹמְרִים זַכַּאי, וְאֶחָד אוֹמֵר אֵינִי יוֹדֵעַ – פּוֹטְרִין אוֹתוֹ. אַרְבָּעָה וּשְׁלשִׁים אוֹמְרִים זַכַּאי, וְשִׁשָּׁה וּשְׁלשִׁים אוֹמְרִים חַיָּב, וְאֶחָד אוֹמֵר אֵינִי יוֹדֵעַ – חַיָּב, שֶׁהֲרֵי רַבּוּ הַמְחַיְּבִין שְׁנַיִם.

ג בֵּית דִּין הַגָּדוֹל שֶׁבָּא לָהֶם מַחֲלֹקֶת, בֵּין בְּדִינֵי נְפָשׁוֹת בֵּין בְּדִינֵי מָמוֹנוֹת בֵּין בְּדִינֵי תּוֹרָה – אֵין מוֹסִיפִין עֲלֵיהֶן, אֶלָּא דָּנִין אֵלּוּ כְּנֶגֶד אֵלּוּ, וְהוֹלְכִין אַחַר הָרֹב שֶׁלָּהֶן. וְאִם בְּדִין אֶחָד מִן הַנֶּהֱרָגִין נֶחְלְקוּ – דָּנִין אֵלּוּ כְּנֶגֶד אֵלּוּ, עַד שֶׁיִּפְטְרוּהוּ אוֹ יִתְחַיֵּב.

פֶּרֶק עֲשִׂירִי

א אֶחָד מִן הַדַּיָּנִים בְּדִינֵי נְפָשׁוֹת שֶׁהָיָה מִן הַמְזַכִּין אוֹ מִן הַמְחַיְּבִין, לֹא מִפְּנֵי שֶׁאָמַר דָּבָר הַנִּרְאֶה לוֹ בְּדַעְתּוֹ, אֶלָּא נָטָה אַחַר דִּבְרֵי חֲבֵרוֹ – הֲרֵי זֶה עוֹבֵר בְּלֹא תַעֲשֶׂה. וְעַל זֶה נֶאֱמַר: וְלֹא תַעֲנֶה עַל רִב לִנְטֹת. מִפִּי הַשְּׁמוּעָה לָמְדוּ, שֶׁלֹּא תֹאמַר בִּשְׁעַת מִנְיָן: דַּי שֶׁאֶהְיֶה כְּאִישׁ פְּלוֹנִי! אֶלָּא אֱמֹר מַה שֶּׁלְּפָנֶיךָ.

ב וּבִכְלַל לָאו זֶה: שֶׁלֹּא יַחֲזֹר הַמְלַמֵּד זְכוּת בְּדִינֵי נְפָשׁוֹת לְלַמֵּד חוֹבָה, שֶׁנֶּאֱמַר: לֹא תַעֲנֶה עַל רִב לִנְטֹת. בַּמֶּה דְּבָרִים אֲמוּרִים? בִּשְׁעַת מַשָּׂא וּמַתָּן; אֲבָל בִּשְׁעַת גְּמַר דִּין – יֵשׁ לִמְלַמֵּד זְכוּת לַחֲזֹר וּלְהִתְמַנּוֹת עִם הַמְחַיְּבִים.

count this as one of the 613 mitzvot of the Torah. Significantly, when listing the mitzvot at the beginning of this section, the Rambam mentions only the dimension of the prohibition described in the following halachah.

With regard to that dimension of the mitzvah, the Ra'avad (in his gloss to the listing of the mitzvot at the beginning of the *Mishneh Torah*) objects, explaining that since the judge may ultimately change his mind, the fact that he cannot reverse his position in the debate is not sufficient to be considered as a mitzvah.

3. *Tosefta, Sanhedrin* 3:4; Jerusalem Talmud, *Sanhedrin* 4:7; *Mechilta d'Rabbi Yishmael* to the above verse.

4. In the Torah, the word *riv*, translated as "dispute," is written in a short form, lacking a *yud*. This enables it to be read as *rav*, "great one." According to that meaning, the verse could be interpreted "Do not respond to the great one," i.e., do not follow his thinking blindly. Instead, weigh the matter yourself and arrive at a decision. See Halachah 6.

Alternatively, *rav* can be interpreted as "the majority." In that vein, the intent of the prohibition is that if a judge sees the majority leaning in a particular direction, he should not follow without making his own decision independently (*Sefer HaMitzvot, loc. cit.*).

5. In this context, the verse could be interpreted: "Do not go against your [first] inclination in a dispute" (Radbaz).

6. I.e., if a judge offered a rationale for acquittal, he may ultimately decide that he made an error and hence, reverse his initial position. He may not, however, voice this concern in the debate. This measure - and the others which follow in this chapter - was instituted by the Torah as a safeguard for the rights of a defendant.

3. When a scholar[7] offers a rationale for acquittal[8] and then dies, we consider it as if he is [alive] and advocating this position.[9]

4. If a judge[10] says: "I can offer a rationale to acquit him" and then lost the power of speech or died before he could explain the rationale for acquittal, it is as if he does not exist.[11]

5. When two [judges] mention one rationale, even if they cite different prooftexts,[12] they are only counted as one.

6. According to the Oral Tradition, we learned that with regard to cases involving capital punishment,[13] we do not [ask the judge] of the highest stature[14] to render judgment first,[15] lest the remainder rely on his opinion and do not see themselves as worthy to argue against him.[16] Instead, every judge must state what appears to him, according to his own opinion.

7. Similarly, with regard to cases involving capital punishment,[17] we do not begin with a condemnatory statement, but rather one which points towards acquittal.

What is implied? We tell the [presumed] transgressor: "If you did not commit the transgression concerning which testimony was given concerning you, do not fear the words [of the witnesses].[18]

8. When one of the scholars[19] makes a statement with regard to a case involving capital punishment: "I can teach a rationale which would convict him," we silence him.[20] If he states: "I can teach a rationale which will

The rationale for this prohibition can be explained as follows: Since the judge cannot retract his initial opinion in the debate, even if he erred, he will seek other - and this time, more correct - rationales to support his initial concept and exonerate him [Rashi (*Sanhedrin* 32a)].

7. I.e., one of the scholars who sit before the judges (see Chapter 1, Halachah 7). As mentioned in Halachah 8, even though these scholars are not judges of the court, if one of them advances a rationale that could be used to acquit the defendant, he is included as a judge.

8. The *Kessef Mishneh* states that if, however, a judge advances an opinion holding the defendant liable and then dies, another judge is appointed before the vote is taken.

9. I.e., even though he has already died, when the opinions are tallied, his vote to acquit the defendant is counted.

10. Significantly, *Sanhedrin* 43a, the Rambam's source, states this concept with regard to "one of the scholars," and not one of the judges.

11. Although we desire to rule leniently and offer the defendant the maximum opportunity for acquittal, since the judge did not state his rationale, he is ignored.

It would appear that if the judge could write out his opinion, that would be significant and he would be included in the reckoning (*Kin'at Eliyahu*).

12. The intent is that the Torah uses only one prooftext to teach a rationale, and not two. Therefore if two judges each cite a different prooftext, one of them is making an error (*Kessef Mishneh*). See also Chapter 12, Halachah 3, where the Rambam mentions this concept.

ג תַּלְמִיד שֶׁהָיָה מְזַכֶּה וָמֵת - רוֹאִין אוֹתוֹ כְּאִלּוּ הוּא מְזַכֶּה בִּמְקוֹמוֹ.

ד אָמַר אֶחָד: יֵשׁ לִי לְלַמֵּד עָלָיו זְכוּת, וְנִשְׁתַּתֵּק אוֹ מֵת קֹדֶם שֶׁיְּלַמֵּד זְכוּת וְיֹאמַר מֵאֵי זֶה טַעַם מְזַכֶּה - הֲרֵי הוּא כְּמִי שֶׁאֵינוֹ.

ה שְׁנַיִם שֶׁאָמְרוּ טַעַם אֶחָד, אֲפִלּוּ מִשְּׁנֵי מִקְרָאוֹת - אֵין נִמְנִין אֶלָּא כְּאֶחָד.

ו וּמִפִּי הַשְּׁמוּעָה לָמְדוּ, שֶׁאֵין מַתְחִילִין בְּדִינֵי נְפָשׁוֹת מִן הַגָּדוֹל.
שֶׁמָּא יִסְמְכוּ הַשְּׁאָר עַל דַּעְתּוֹ, וְלֹא יִרְאוּ עַצְמָן כְּדָאִין לַחֲלֹק עָלָיו.
אֶלָּא יֹאמַר כָּל אֶחָד דָּבָר הַנִּרְאֶה לוֹ בְּדַעְתּוֹ.

ז וְכֵן אֵין פּוֹתְחִין בְּדִינֵי נְפָשׁוֹת לְחוֹבָה, אֶלָּא לִזְכוּת. כֵּיצַד? אוֹמְרִים לָזֶה שֶׁחָטָא: אִם לֹא עָשִׂיתָ דָּבָר זֶה שֶׁהֵעִידוּ בוֹ עָלֶיךָ - אַל תִּירָא מִדִּבְרֵיהֶם.

ח אָמַר אֶחָד מִן הַתַּלְמִידִים בְּדִינֵי נְפָשׁוֹת: יֵשׁ לִי לְלַמֵּד עָלָיו חוֹבָה - מְשַׁתְּקִין אוֹתוֹ.

Rav Moshe Cohen and the *Siftei Cohen* 25:19 protest the use of the word "even," for it implies that certainly if they base their ruling on the same prooftext, they are counted as one. This would imply that each judge must come up with an independent rationale. That is illogical. If one judges says: "So-and-so" should be executed, because he violated the commandment: 'Do not kill,'" there is no need for the other judges to find different rationales.

13. As mentioned in Chapter 11, Halachah 4, this and the principles mentioned in the following halachot also apply with regard to cases involving convictions for lashes and for exile.

14. As is the practice with regard to other judgments. See Chapter 11, Halachah 6.

15. As Chapter 11, Halachah 6, states: "With regard to [cases involving] capital punishment, we begin from the side." As stated in Chapter 1, Halachah 3, the judges are seated in a semi-circle and the judges of the highest stature are seated in the center. Beginning from the side means asking the judge of the lowest stature to state his opinion first.

16. This relates to the prohibition against relying on another sage's opinion which is mentioned in Halachah 1 (Radbaz).

17. Note the contrast to financial law, as mentioned in Chapter 11, Halachah 1, and Chapter 12, Halachah 3.

18. *Sanhedrin* 32b derives this concept from the oath administered to a *sotah*, a woman suspected of adultery. Numbers 5:19 states: "The priest administers the oath to her, saying: "...If a man did not lie with you... you will be held blameless by these waters." Although the oath then continues to mention the severe punishment the woman will suffer if she transgressed, it begins with reassurance if she is innocent. The same pattern is followed here.

19. This refers to the students who sit in observation of the court proceedings, as stated in Chapter 1, Halachah 7.

20. One of the fundamental points of the Torah's approach to capital punishment is that ultimately man's future is in God's hands. The court must do what it can to judge the matter, but it need not work overzealously to convict the defendant, for even if he is not

exonerate him," he is raised up and included in the *Sanhedrin*.[21] If his words are of substance, we heed his statements and he never descends.[22] If his words are not of substance, he does not descend from [the court] for that entire day.[23]

Even if the defendant himself says: "I can teach a rationale which will exonerate myself," we heed his statements and he is counted [among the judges],[24] provided his words are of substance.

9. When a court errs with regard to a case involving capital punishment and convicts an innocent person, ruling that he is guilty, and [later] they discover a rationale that would require that the ruling be nullified and he be vindicated, they nullify the ruling and retry the case.[25] If, however, they erred and acquitted a person liable to be executed, the judgment is not nullified and the case is not retried.[26]

When does the above apply? When they erred with regard to a matter that the Sadducees[27] would not acknowledge. If, however, they erred with regard to a matter that the Sadducees acknowledge, we retry the case to convict him.

What is implied? If they said that a person who has adulterous or incestuous anal intercourse is not liable and they released him, he is retried and executed.[28] If, however, they said a person who merely inserted the corona of his organ into the woman's anus[29] is not liable and they released him, he is not retried. Similar principles apply in all analogous situations.

CHAPTER ELEVEN

1. What are the differences between [cases involving] financial matters and [cases involving] capital punishment? [Cases involving] financial matters are adjudicated by three judges,[1] while [cases involving] capital punishment are adjudicated by 23.[2] [In cases involving] financial matters, we begin the

executed by the court, God will administer justice (see *Sanhedrin* 37b). Hence, even though there is a possibility that the student's rationale would be substantial, since he is not a judge, he is not given a chance to decide the defendant's fate. Indeed, he is not even given the opportunity to state his point.

21. I.e., to participate in the debate.

22. But instead becomes part of the court.

Kin'at Eliyahu states that it would appear that another judge is also added to the court together with him, so that there will not be the possibility of an evenly balanced court. He also questions what will happen in the future, for the court will have an extra judge.

23. For that would be embarrassing for him.

24. The *Lechem Mishneh* (and similarly, many commentaries to *Sanhedrin* 40a, the Rambam's source) maintain that this phrase is an error. The intent is that his opinion is considered. He himself is not considered a judge, for a relative - and certainly, the defendant himself - cannot serve as a judge.

25. *Sanhedrin* 33b derives this concept from the adjuration (Exodus 23:7): "Do not execute the guiltless or the righteous." Implied is that if he is innocent, even if he was not deemed righteous by the court, he should not be executed.

אָמַר: יֵשׁ לִי לְלַמֵּד עָלָיו זְכוּת – מַעֲלִין אוֹתוֹ עִמָּהֶן לַסַּנְהֶדְרִין. אִם יֵשׁ מַמָּשׁ בִּדְבָרָיו – שׁוֹמְעִין לוֹ, וְאֵינוֹ יוֹרֵד מִשָּׁם לְעוֹלָם; וְאִם אֵין מַמָּשׁ בִּדְבָרָיו – אֵינוֹ יוֹרֵד מִשָּׁם כָּל הַיּוֹם כֻּלּוֹ. אֲפִלּוּ אָמַר הַנִּדּוֹן עַצְמוֹ: יֵשׁ לִי לְלַמֵּד עַל עַצְמִי זְכוּת – שׁוֹמְעִין לוֹ וְעוֹלֶה לַמִּנְיָן; וְהוּא שֶׁיִּהְיֶה מַמָּשׁ בִּדְבָרָיו.

ט בֵּית דִּין שֶׁטָּעוּ בְּדִינֵי נְפָשׁוֹת וְחִיְּבוּ אֶת הַפָּטוּר וְגָמְרוּ דִּינוֹ לְחוֹבָה, וְנִרְאָה לָהֶם הַטַּעַם שֶׁיִּסְתְּרוּ בּוֹ אֶת דִּינוֹ כְּדֵי לְזַכּוֹתוֹ – סוֹתְרִין, וְחוֹזְרִין וְדָנִין אוֹתוֹ. אֲבָל אִם טָעוּ וּפָטְרוּ אֶת הַמְחֻיָּב הֲרִיגָה – אֵין סוֹתְרִין אֶת דִּינוֹ, וְאֵין מַחֲזִירִין אוֹתוֹ. בַּמֶּה דְּבָרִים אֲמוּרִים? בְּשֶׁטָּעוּ בְּדָבָר שֶׁאֵין הַצְּדוּקִין מוֹדִין בּוֹ; אֲבָל אִם טָעוּ בְּדָבָר שֶׁהַצְּדוּקִין מוֹדִין בּוֹ – מַחֲזִירִין אוֹתוֹ לְחוֹבָה.

כֵּיצַד? אָמְרוּ: הַבָּא עַל הָעֶרְוָה שֶׁלֹּא כְּדַרְכָּהּ – פָּטוּר, וּפְטָרוּהוּ – מַחֲזִירִין אוֹתוֹ וּמְמִיתִין אוֹתוֹ; אֲבָל אִם אָמְרוּ: הַמְעָרֶה שֶׁלֹּא כְּדַרְכָּהּ – פָּטוּר, וּפְטָרוּהוּ – אֵין מַחֲזִירִין אוֹתוֹ. וְכֵן כֹּל כַּיּוֹצֵא בָּזֶה.

פֶּרֶק אַחַד עָשָׂר

א מַה בֵּין דִּינֵי מָמוֹנוֹת לְדִינֵי נְפָשׁוֹת?
דִּינֵי מָמוֹנוֹת – בִּשְׁלֹשָׁה; דִּינֵי נְפָשׁוֹת – בְּעֶשְׂרִים וּשְׁלֹשָׁה.

26. As *Sanhedrin, loc. cit.*, continues: If he was deemed righteous, even though he is not innocent, he should not be executed.

27. The Sadducees were followers of Tzadok, one of the students of Antigonus of Socho, who abandoned traditional Jewish practice and started a new sect. Although their intent was to assimilate among the Greek and Roman societies, they professed to maintain adherence to Judaism and disguised their assimilationist tendencies by protesting that it is only to the Oral Law that they were rejecting. The Written Law, by contrast, they would agree to keep. If a matter was thus accepted by the Sadducees, it is quite obvious and everyone would realize the error. Hence, the judgment is discarded. If, however, the judgment was not a point accepted by the Sadducees, even though it concerns an explicit statement of the Mishnah, the error is not as obvious, and the judgment is allowed to stand.

28. When speaking about the prohibition against forbidden sexual relations, a plural term, *mishkavei ishah*, is used in Leviticus 20:13, indicating that there are two types of forbidden intercourse, vaginal and anal (*Sanhedrin* 54a). *Horiot* 4a states that even the Sadducees would accept this concept.

29. I.e., without inserting the entire organ. According to *Sanhedrin* 33b, this is considered as intercourse. Nevertheless, this point is not accepted by the Sadducees. See *Hilchot Issurei Bi'ah* 1:10 and commentaries.

1. See Chapter 2, Halachah 10.
2. See Chapter 5, Halachah 3.

judgment either with a statement to the defendant's detriment or his advantage,[3] while with regard to [cases involving] capital punishment, we begin with a statement which points towards acquittal, as we explained, and we don't begin with one which points toward his conviction.[4]

[In cases involving] financial matters, we make a decision based on a majority of one whether it is to the defendant's detriment or in his support, while with regard to [cases involving] capital punishment, we acquit him on the basis of a majority of one, but convict him only when there is a majority of two.[5] [In cases involving] financial matters, we retry a judgment whether doing so is to the defendant's detriment or his advantage,[6] while with regard to [cases involving] capital punishment, we retry a judgment if it will lead to acquittal, but not if it will lead to conviction, as we explained.[7]

[In cases involving] financial matters, everyone - both the judges or the scholars[8] - is entitled to advance any rationale whether it is [to the defendant's] detriment or in his support. With regard to [cases involving] capital punishment, by contrast, everyone - even the students - may advance a rationale leading to acquittal, but only the judges may advance a rationale leading to conviction.[9] [In cases involving] financial matters, a person who advanced a rationale [to the defendant's] detriment may [change his mind and] advance a rationale in his support. Conversely, one who advanced a rationale [in the defendant's] support may [change his mind and] advance a rationale to his detriment. With regard to [cases involving] capital punishment, by contrast, a judge who advanced a rationale for conviction may advance a rationale for acquittal, but a judge who advanced a rationale for acquittal may not [change his mind and] advance a rationale for conviction. At the time the judgment is being rendered, however, he may vote to be counted among those favoring conviction, as we explained.[10]

[Cases involving] financial matters are adjudicated during the day, but the verdict may be rendered at night.[11] [Cases involving] capital punishment are adjudicated during the day and the verdict must also be rendered during the day.[12] The verdict in [cases involving] financial matters is rendered on that very day, whether it is [to the defendant's] detriment or in his support. With regard to [cases involving] capital punishment, by contrast, a verdict of acquittal is rendered on that very day, but a verdict of conviction is [not] rendered [until] the following day.[13]

2. For this reason,[14] we do not adjudicate cases [involving] capital punishment on Fridays, nor on the days preceding festivals. [The rationale is that the defendant] may be convicted and it is impossible to execute him on the following day,[15] but it is forbidden to postpone his [execution] until after the Sabbath.[16] [Hence,] we imprison him and begin his trial on Sunday.[17]

3. For since there are two litigants involved, what is to the detriment of one is to the advantage of the other.
4. Chapter 10, Halachah 7.
5. See Chapter 8, Halachah 1.

דִּינֵי מָמוֹנוֹת – פּוֹתְחִין בֵּין לִזְכוּת בֵּין לְחוֹבָה; דִּינֵי נְפָשׁוֹת – פּוֹתְחִין לִזְכוּת, כְּמוֹ שֶׁבֵּאַרְנוּ, וְאֵין פּוֹתְחִין לְחוֹבָה.

דִּינֵי מָמוֹנוֹת – מַטִּין עַל פִּי אֶחָד בֵּין לִזְכוּת בֵּין לְחוֹבָה; דִּינֵי נְפָשׁוֹת – מַטִּין עַל פִּי אֶחָד לִזְכוּת, וְעַל פִּי שְׁנַיִם לְחוֹבָה. דִּינֵי מָמוֹנוֹת – מַחֲזִירִין בֵּין לִזְכוּת בֵּין לְחוֹבָה; וְדִינֵי נְפָשׁוֹת – מַחֲזִירִין לִזְכוּת, וְאֵין מַחֲזִירִין לְחוֹבָה, כְּמוֹ שֶׁבֵּאַרְנוּ. דִּינֵי מָמוֹנוֹת – הַכֹּל רְאוּיִין לְלַמֵּד זְכוּת אוֹ חוֹבָה, בֵּין הַדַּיָּנִים בֵּין הַתַּלְמִידִים; וְדִינֵי נְפָשׁוֹת – הַכֹּל מְלַמְּדִין זְכוּת, וַאֲפִלּוּ הַתַּלְמִידִים, וְאֵין מְלַמֵּד חוֹבָה אֶלָּא הַדַּיָּנִים.

דִּינֵי מָמוֹנוֹת – הַדַּיָּן הַמְלַמֵּד חוֹבָה חוֹזֵר וּמְלַמֵּד זְכוּת, וְהַמְלַמֵּד זְכוּת חוֹזֵר וּמְלַמֵּד חוֹבָה; דִּינֵי נְפָשׁוֹת – הַמְלַמֵּד חוֹבָה חוֹזֵר וּמְלַמֵּד זְכוּת, אֲבָל הַמְלַמֵּד זְכוּת אֵינוֹ יָכוֹל לַחֲזוֹר וּלְלַמֵּד חוֹבָה, אֶלָּא בִּשְׁעַת גְּמַר דִּין יֵשׁ לוֹ לַחֲזוֹר וּלְהִמָּנוֹת עִם הַמְחַיְּבִין, כְּמוֹ שֶׁבֵּאַרְנוּ.

דִּינֵי מָמוֹנוֹת – דָּנִין בַּיּוֹם וְגוֹמְרִין בַּלַּיְלָה; דִּינֵי נְפָשׁוֹת – דָּנִין בַּיּוֹם וְגוֹמְרִין בַּיּוֹם.

דִּינֵי מָמוֹנוֹת – גּוֹמְרִין בּוֹ בַּיּוֹם בֵּין לִזְכוּת בֵּין לְחוֹבָה; דִּינֵי נְפָשׁוֹת – גּוֹמְרִין בּוֹ בַּיּוֹם לִזְכוּת, וּבַיּוֹם שֶׁלְּאַחֲרָיו לְחוֹבָה.

ב לְפִיכָךְ אֵין דָּנִין דִּינֵי נְפָשׁוֹת לֹא עֶרֶב שַׁבָּת וְלֹא עֶרֶב יוֹם טוֹב; שֶׁמָּא יִתְחַיֵּב, וְאִי אֶפְשָׁר לְהָרְגוֹ לְמָחָר, וְאָסוּר לְעַנּוֹת אֶת דִּינוֹ וּלְהַנִּיחוֹ אַחַר הַשַּׁבָּת. אֶלָּא אוֹסְרִין אוֹתוֹ עַד אֶחָד בַּשַּׁבָּת, וּמַתְחִילִין בְּדִינוֹ.

6. If a court realizes that it made an error, the judgment is rescinded and a new judgment is rendered. See Chapter 6.
7. Chapter 10, Halachah 9.
8. Who sit and observe the court.
9. See Chapter 10, Halachah 8.
10. Chapter 10, Halachah 2.
11. See Chapter 3, Halachah 4.
12. *Sanhedrin* 34b derives this concept based on Numbers 25:4: "Hang them before God before the sun."
13. If the court sees that the judges desire to convict the defendant, a final judgment is not rendered. Instead, the judges debate the matter throughout the entire night in the hope of finding a basis for acquittal. On the following day, they gather together and they are polled again (*Sanhedrin* 32a, 35a, see Chapter 12, Halachah 3).
14. I.e., because two successive sittings of the court might be necessary.
15. For doing so involves the transgression of one of the Torah's commandments. As stated in *Hilchot Shabbat* 24:7, one of the 613 mitzvot of the Torah is not to execute a guilty person on the Sabbath.
16. For once a person is convicted, he should be executed immediately. It is considered as agonizing to allow him to live with the sword of death hanging over him.
17. From this ruling, we can see that ordinarily a person was not imprisoned before his trial began. Instead, he would be arrested and tried on that very same day.

3. According to Scriptural Law, cases involving financial law can be adjudicated at all times, as [Exodus 18:22] states: "They shall judge the people at all times." According to Rabbinic Law, cases are not adjudicated on Fridays.[18]

4. All of the same laws[19] that apply to cases involving capital punishment apply also to cases involving lashes[20] and exile,[21] except that cases involving lashes are adjudicated by three judges.[22] None of these [distinctions] are made with regard to the judgment of an ox that is stoned except for one, that the judgment is adjudicated by 23 [judges].[23]

5. The laws which pertain to a *mesit*, a person who entices others [to serve false divinities],[24] differ from those pertaining to others liable for capital punishment. We hide witnesses [to observe his act].[25] He does not need a warning[26] as [must be given] to others who are executed.[27] If he departed from the court after being acquitted, and someone said: "I know a rationale that will lead to his conviction," he is returned [and retried]. If he was sentenced [to death] and someone said: "I know a rationale that will lead to his release," he is not retried.[28] [The court does not] advance arguments in defense of a *mesit*.[29] An elderly person, a eunuch, and a person who does not have sons are placed on the court which judges him,[30] so that they will not have mercy on him. For cruelty to those who sway the people after emptiness [brings] mercy to the world,[31] as [implied by Deuteronomy 13:19]: "so that God will turn away from His fierce anger and grant you mercy."[32]

6. [With regard to] cases involving monetary matters and similarly [questions of] ritual purity and impurity, the judge of the greatest stature gives his ruling

18. To enable the litigants and the judges to carry out their preparations for the Sabbath [*P'nei Moshe* (Jerusalem Talmud, *Sanhedrin* 4:6)]. Alternatively, a judgment must be made patiently, with peace of mind, and that would be difficult on Friday because of the necessary Sabbath preparations (*Sefer Me'irat Einayim* 5:3). See also Chapter 25, Halachah 9.

The *Shulchan Aruch* (*Choshen Mishpat* 5:2) writes that it is also forbidden to hold court on the day preceding a festival. The Ramah quotes opinions which maintain that in the present age, judgments may be rendered on Fridays and on the days preceding festivals.

As mentioned in *Hilchot Shabbat* 23:14, although one would be allowed to hold court and render a judgment on the Sabbath or a festival itself according to Scriptural Law, our Sages forbade doing so as a safeguard, lest one write.

19. I.e., all the distinctions mentioned in Halachah 1 between cases involving financial matters and cases involving capital punishment.

20. The punishment granted for the violation of one of the Torah's prohibition that involves a deed, and is not punishable by execution. See Chapters 18 and 19. See also Chapter 16, Halachah 1, which draws an equation between lashes and execution.

21. The punishment given for accidental murder. See *Hilchot Rotzeach*, chs. 5 and 6.

22. And not 23 as is the case with regard to laws involving capital punishment.

ג דִּינֵי מָמוֹנוֹת, אַף עַל פִּי שֶׁדָּנִין אוֹתָן בְּכָל יוֹם מִן הַתּוֹרָה, שֶׁנֶּאֱמַר: וְשָׁפְטוּ אֶת הָעָם בְּכָל עֵת, מִדִּבְרֵיהֶם לָמְדוּ שֶׁאֵין דָּנִין בְּעֶרֶב שַׁבָּת.

ד אֶחָד דִּינֵי נְפָשׁוֹת וְאֶחָד דִּינֵי מַלְקִיּוֹת וְאֶחָד דִּינֵי גָלוּת – הַדִּינִים הָאֵלּוּ שָׁוִים בָּהֶן, אֶלָּא שֶׁהַמַּלְקוּת בִּשְׁלֹשָׁה. וְאֵין אֶחָד מֵהֶן בְּשׁוֹר הַנִּסְקָל, חוּץ מִדָּבָר אֶחָד: שֶׁדִּינוֹ בְּעֶשְׂרִים וּשְׁלֹשָׁה.

ה הַמֵּסִית – אֵין דִּינָיו כִּשְׁאָר דִּינֵי נְפָשׁוֹת:
מְכַמְּנִין לוֹ אֶת הָעֵדִים, וְאֵינוֹ צָרִיךְ הַתְרָאָה כִּשְׁאָר הַנֶּהֱרָגִין. וְאִם יָצָא מִבֵּית דִּין זַכַּאי, וְאָמַר אֶחָד: יֵשׁ לִי לְלַמֵּד עָלָיו חוֹבָה – מַחֲזִירִין אוֹתוֹ. יָצָא חַיָּב, וְאָמַר אֶחָד: יֵשׁ לִי לְלַמֵּד עָלָיו זְכוּת – אֵין מַחֲזִירִין אוֹתוֹ. וְאֵין טוֹעֲנִין לְמֵסִית. וּמוֹשִׁיבִין בְּדִינוֹ זָקֵן וְסָרִיס וּמִי שֶׁאֵין לוֹ בָּנִים, כְּדֵי שֶׁלֹּא יְרַחֲמוּ עָלָיו. שֶׁהָאַכְזָרִיּוּת עַל אֵלּוּ שֶׁמַּטְעִין אֶת הָעָם אַחֲרֵי הַהֶבֶל – רַחֲמִים הוּא בָּעוֹלָם; שֶׁנֶּאֱמַר: לְמַעַן יָשׁוּב יְיָ מֵחֲרוֹן אַפּוֹ וְנָתַן לְךָ רַחֲמִים.

ו דִּינֵי מָמוֹנוֹת, וְכֵן הַטֻּמְאוֹת וְהַטְּהָרוֹת – מַתְחִילִין מִן הַגָּדוֹל שֶׁבַּדַּיָּנִים, וְשׁוֹמְעִין

23. On the basis of Exodus 21:19, *Sanhedrin* 2a states that an ox is condemned to death in the same manner as its master, i.e., by a court of 23 judges. See Chapter 5, Halachah 2.
24. See Deuteronomy 13:2-12 and *Hilchot Avodat Kochavim*, Chapter 5, where the laws governing such a transgressor are explained.
25. I.e., the person who he has been enticed should inform the court. Together they contrive a plan so that the *mesit* will make his statements in the presence of witnesses who can see and hear him even though he cannot see them. See *Hilchot Avodat Kochavim* 5:3.
26. The person whom he seeks to proselytize should, however, tell him: "How can we forsake our God in heaven and serve stone and wood?" (*ibid.*). As *Tosafot, Sanhedrin* 8b, explains, this statement impresses the *mesit* with the severity of his actions. If the *mesit* does not repeat his statements after receiving this warning, he is not executed.
27. See Chapter 12, Halachah 2, which states that, to be executed for other transgressions, a person must receive a warning from two witnesses and acknowledge that warning.
28. This is the direct opposite of the laws that apply with regard to others tried for sins punishable by execution, as stated in Chapter 10, Halachah 9. The rationale for these stringencies is that Deuteronomy 13:9 states: "Do not have pity and do not cover up for him."
29. Instead, he must offer his own defense. In contrast, in other instances, the court and even the students observing the court (see Chapter 10, Halachah 8) are encouraged to offer defenses.
30. Although because of their tendency to cruelty, they are not fit to judge other cases involving capital punishment, as stated in Chapter 2, Halachah 3.
31. Compare also to the Guide to the Perplexed, Vol. II, Ch. 39, which states: "Mercy to the cruel is cruelty to the merciful."
32. Although this verse is stated with regard to an *ir hanidachat*, a city that was led astray, i.e., after idol worship, its motivating rationale also applies with regard to a *mesit*.

first[33] and [the other judges] hear his ruling. With regard to laws involving capital punishment, we begin from the side.[34] The words [of the judge] of the highest stature are not heard until the end.[35]

7. [With regard to] cases involving monetary matters and similarly [questions of] ritual purity and impurity, a father and his son and a teacher and his student[36] are counted as two judges.[37] With regard to cases involving capital punishment, lashes, the sanctification of the moon and the declaration of a leap year, a father and his son and a teacher and his student are counted as one.

8. The concept that a father and a son are counted as one or as two applies when one is a member of the *Sanhedrin* and the other was one of the students [attending the court who] said: "I can contribute a rationale that will lead to his vindication," or "...to his being held liable." We listen to his words and enable him to participate in the debate, and he is counted [in the polling of the judges].[38]

9. At the time of the final judgment,[39] relatives are not included. For judges who are related to each other are not acceptable to rule [together], as will be explained.[40]

10 When a student was wise and understanding[41] but is lacking [sufficient] knowledge of the tradition,[42] his master may convey to him the tradition which he requires with regard to these laws and then he may serve as a judge [even] in cases regarding capital punishment.[43]

33. This is an act of deference and respect for that judge. Nevertheless, if that judge desires, as an expression of humility, he may forgo this token of respect. *Sanhedrin* 36a relates that this was the practice of Rabbi Yehudah HaNasi who began by asking the judges of the lowest stature (Radbaz).

34. As stated in Chapter 1, Halachah 3, the judges are seated in a semi-circle and the judges of the highest stature are seated in the center. Beginning from the side means asking the judge of the lowest stature to state his opinion first.

35. As stated in Chapter 10, Halachah 6, we fear that otherwise, the judges of lesser stature will be intimidated and will fear to contradict the opinions of the judge of greater stature.

36. The *Shulchan Aruch* (*Choshen Mishpat* 18:5) interprets this as referring to an instance where the student relies on the teacher and has not developed sufficient independent thinking processes to consider the laws abstractly and apply them to different situations on his own. See also Halachah 10.

37. The Rambam's ruling is based on *Sanhedrin* 36a. His version of that text was apparently different from the standard printed text. The standard printed version includes cases involving financial laws in the same category as cases involving capital punishment. For this reason, the Ra'avad objects to the Rambam's ruling.

Rashi explains that with regard to rulings concerning ritual purity, it is not necessary

אֶת דְּבָרָיו; וְדִינֵי נְפָשׁוֹת - מַתְחִילִין מִן הַצַּד, וְאֵין שׁוֹמְעִין דִּבְרֵי הַגָּדוֹל אֶלָּא בָּאַחֲרוֹנָה.

ז דִּינֵי מָמוֹנוֹת, וְכֵן הַטֻּמְאוֹת וְכֵן הַטְּהָרוֹת - הָאָב וּבְנוֹ הָרַב וְתַלְמִידוֹ מוֹנִין אוֹתָן בִּשְׁנַיִם; וְדִינֵי נְפָשׁוֹת וּמַכּוֹת, וְקִדּוּשׁ הַחֹדֶשׁ וְעִבּוּר הַשָּׁנָה - אָב וּבְנוֹ אוֹ הָרַב וְתַלְמִידוֹ מוֹנִין אוֹתָן בְּאֶחָד.

ח זֶה שֶׁאָנוּ מוֹנִין הָאָב עִם הַבֵּן בֵּין בְּאֶחָד בֵּין בִּשְׁנַיִם, כְּגוֹן שֶׁהָיָה הָאֶחָד מֵהֶן בַּסַּנְהֶדְרִין, וְהַשֵּׁנִי הָיָה מִן הַתַּלְמִידִים שֶׁאָמַר: יֵשׁ לִי לְלַמֵּד זְכוּת אוֹ חוֹבָה.
שׁוֹמְעִין דְּבָרָיו, וְנוֹשְׂאִין וְנוֹתְנִין עִמּוֹ, וְנִמְנִין עִמּוֹ.

ט וּבִשְׁעַת גְּמַר דִּין - אֵין גּוֹמְרִין אֶת הַדִּין בִּקְרוֹבִים; שֶׁהַדַּיָּנִין הַקְּרוֹבִים פְּסוּלִין לְדִין, כְּמוֹ שֶׁיִּתְבָּאֵר.

י תַּלְמִיד שֶׁהָיָה חָכָם וּמֵבִין, וְהָיָה מְחֻסַּר קַבָּלָה - הֲרֵי רַבּוֹ מוֹסֵר לוֹ הַקַּבָּלָה שֶׁהוּא צָרִיךְ לָהּ בְּדִין זֶה, וְהוּא דָן עִמּוֹ בְּדִינֵי נְפָשׁוֹת.

that a question be judged by any minimum amount of judges. Hence, every person's opinion is counted equally. With regard to cases involving capital punishment and the other types of judgment mentioned, the Torah requires a specific number of judges at the outset. This implies that every judge is important and hence, a father and a son may not be counted together.

According to Rabbinic Law, there is no minimum amount of judges necessary to adjudicate questions of financial law. Hence the version of *Sanhedrin* possessed by the Rambam places these laws together with the laws of ritual purity.

38. I.e., he is given the status of a member of the court. He participates in the debate and he is counted in the reckoning of the opinions of the judges (*Kessef Mishneh*).

39. According to the Rambam, this refers to the pronouncement of the verdict: "So-and-so, you are liable," or "So-and-so, you are vindicated" (*Kessef Mishneh*). The Ra'avad differs and maintains that this refers to the polling of the judges. Hence he objects to the Rambam's statements.

40. See *Hilchot Edut* 16:5.

41. And thus capable of developing insightful rationales.

42. I.e., the laws received from the previous generation regarding a particular issue.

Sanhedrin 36b cites as an example Rav Kahaneh and Rav Assi who were students of Rav. They were highly intelligent and capable of reasoning with the greatest sages of the age. They lacked, however, the knowledge of certain laws. Rav would convey these laws to them and they would participate as full members of the court.

43. I.e., the students are then considered as judges in their own right, independent of their teacher.

Rashi explains the rationale for this ruling. Ultimately, the entire Jewish people received the body of Torah knowledge from Moses. What difference does it make on which level of the chain a person is? What is significant is that they can assimilate the knowledge and apply it to the particulars of a given situation.

11. All individuals are acceptable to judge cases involving financial laws, even a convert, provided his mother is a native-born Jewess.[44]

A convert may judge a fellow convert even if his mother is not a native-born Jewess. Similarly, a *mamzer*[44] and a person who is blind in one eye[45] are acceptable to adjudicate financial disputes. Cases involving capital punishment, however, may be judged only by priests, Levites, and Israelites with [lineage acceptable to] marry into the priesthood.[46] Not one of them may be blind even in one of his eyes, as we explained.[47]

CHAPTER TWELVE

1. How are [cases involving] capital punishment judged? When the witnesses come to the court and say: "We saw this[1] person violate such-and-such a transgression," [the judges] ask them: "Do you recognize him?[2] Did you give him a warning?"[3]

If they answer: "We do not recognize him," "We are unsure of his identity," or "We did not warn him," the defendant is exonerated.

2. Both a Torah scholar and a common person need a warning, for [the obligation for] a warning was instituted only to make a distinction between a person who transgresses inadvertently and one who transgresses intentionally,[4] lest the person say: "I transgressed inadvertently."

How is a warning administered? We tell him: "Desist..." or "Do not do it. It is a transgression and you are liable to be executed by the court"[5] or "to receive lashes for it." If he ceases, he is not liable.[6] Similarly, if he remains silent or nods his head, he is not liable [for punishment].[7] Even if he says: "I know," he is not liable [for punishment] until he accepts death upon himself, saying: "It is for this reason that I am doing this." [In such a situation,] he is executed.

He must commit the transgression directly after receiving the warning, within the time to offer a salutation.[8] If he [waits] longer than that, a second warning is necessary.[9]

44. See Chapter 2, Halachah 9, where this concept is explained at length.
45. If, however, he is blind in both eyes, he is not acceptable to serve as a judge at all (*ibid.*).
46. Implied is that for four generations, we know that the person's lineage is acceptable.
47. Chapter 2, Halachah 9.

1. For the testimony must be given in the presence of the defendant.
2. I.e., are you certain of his identity? Perhaps you are confusing him with someone else. This is the Rambam's interpretation of *Sanhedrin* 40a. Rashi interprets that passage differently (*Lechem Mishneh*).
3. See the following halachah.
4. The Rambam's ruling reflects a unique instance in which he uses the wording of a Talmudic passage for the opposite intent. *Sanhedrin* 8b quotes Rabbi Yossi bar Rabbi Yehudah as coining the expression the Rambam employs: "A warning was instituted only

יא הַכֹּל כְּשֵׁרִים לָדוּן דִּינֵי מָמוֹנוֹת, אֲפִלּוּ גֵר; וְהוּא שֶׁתִּהְיֶה אִמּוֹ מִיִּשְׂרָאֵל.
וְגֵר דָּן אֶת חֲבֵרוֹ הַגֵּר, אַף עַל פִּי שֶׁאֵין אִמּוֹ מִיִּשְׂרָאֵל.
וְכֵן הַמַּמְזֵר וְהַסּוּמָא בְּאַחַת מֵעֵינָיו – כָּשֵׁר לָדוּן דִּינֵי מָמוֹנוֹת.
אֲבָל בְּדִינֵי נְפָשׁוֹת – אֵין דָּנִין אוֹתָן אֶלָּא כֹּהֲנִים לְוִיִּם וְיִשְׂרְאֵלִים הַמַּשִּׂיאִין לִכְהֻנָּה, וְלֹא יִהְיֶה אֶחָד מֵהֶן סוּמָא אֲפִלּוּ בְּאַחַת מֵעֵינָיו, כְּמוֹ שֶׁבֵּאַרְנוּ.

פֶּרֶק שְׁנֵים עָשָׂר

א כֵּיצַד דָּנִין דִּינֵי נְפָשׁוֹת? כְּשֶׁיָּבוֹאוּ עֵדִים לְבֵית דִּין וְאוֹמְרִים: רָאִינוּ פְּלוֹנִי זֶה שֶׁעָבַר עֲבֵרָה פְּלוֹנִית – אוֹמְרִין לָהֶן: מַכִּירִין אַתֶּם אוֹתוֹ? הִתְרֵיתֶם בּוֹ? אִם אָמְרוּ: אֵין אָנוּ מַכִּירִין אוֹתוֹ, אוֹ נִסְתַּפֵּק לָנוּ, אוֹ שֶׁלֹּא הִתְרוּ בּוֹ – הֲרֵי זֶה פָּטוּר.

ב אֶחָד תַּלְמִיד חָכָם וְאֶחָד עַם הָאָרֶץ צָרִיךְ הַתְרָאָה; שֶׁלֹּא נִתְּנָה הַתְרָאָה אֶלָּא לְהַבְחִין בֵּין שׁוֹגֵג לְמֵזִיד, שֶׁמָּא שׁוֹגֵג הָיָה. וְכֵיצַד מַתְרִין בּוֹ? אוֹמְרִין לוֹ: פְּרֹשׁ, אוֹ אַל תַּעֲשֶׂה, שֶׁזּוֹ עֲבֵרָה הִיא, וְחַיָּב אַתָּה עָלֶיהָ מִיתַת בֵּית דִּין אוֹ מַלְקוּת.
אִם פֵּרַשׁ – פָּטוּר. וְכֵן אִם שָׁתַק אוֹ הִרְכִּין בְּרֹאשׁוֹ – פָּטוּר. וַאֲפִלּוּ אָמַר: יוֹדֵעַ אֲנִי – פָּטוּר. עַד שֶׁיַּתִּיר עַצְמוֹ לְמִיתָה וְיֹאמַר: עַל מְנָת כֵּן אֲנִי עוֹשֶׂה, וְאַחַר כָּךְ יֵהָרֵג.
וְצָרִיךְ שֶׁיַּעֲבֹר וְיַעֲשֶׂה תֵּכֶף לַהַתְרָאָה בְּתוֹךְ כְּדֵי דִבּוּר; אֲבָל אַחַר כְּדֵי דִבּוּר – צָרִיךְ הַתְרָאָה אַחֶרֶת.

to make a distinction between a person who transgresses inadvertently and one who transgresses intentionally." Rabbi Yossi, however, used this concept as support for his contention that a Torah scholar does not need a warning. Since he is knowledgeable, we assume that he is familiar with the laws. If he is transgressing, we can conclude that he is doing so as a conscious act of rebellion. Hence, he is deserving of punishment.

The Rambam differs, maintaining that even a Torah scholar might not be aware that his act violates a particular prohibition. We do not suspect that he did not know the law, it was however possible that he was aware of the prohibition, but did not know that it applied in this instance, e.g., he knew that fat is forbidden, but did not know that a particular piece of meat contained forbidden fat. The warning will clarify that for him (*Kessef Mishneh*; *Maggid Mishneh, Hilchot Issurei Bi'ah* 1:3).

5. He does not, however, need to be told the type of execution he will receive.

6. For he did not transgress.

7. By an earthly court. Although it appears that he acknowledged the warning and transgressed intentionally, we do not execute him for we are not certain that this is so unless he makes an explicit statement to this effect. We are not concerned that a person who is obligated to be executed may be released. For even if he is not punished by an earthly court, God will execute judgment upon him.

8. I.e., the time it takes to say *Shalom Alecha Rebbe Umori* (*Hilchot Sh'vuot* 2:17).

9. Otherwise, it is possible that he forgot the warning (*Sanhedrin* 40b). Although this is

The warning is acceptable whether it was administered by one of the witnesses or by another individual, even a woman or a servant.[10] Even if [the transgressor] hears the voice of the person administering the warning, but does not see him,[11] and even if he himself[12] administers the warning, he should be executed.

3. If the witnesses say: "He was given a warning and we recognize him," the court intimidates them.[13]

How do they intimidate them in cases involving capital punishment? [They] say: "Maybe you are speaking on the basis of supposition,[14] or on the basis of hearsay, one witness from another witness, or maybe you heard from a trustworthy person?"[15] "Maybe you do not know that ultimately we will subject you to questions and crossexamination?"[16]

"Know that cases involving capital punishment do not resemble those involving financial matters. With regard to financial matters, [if there is any deceit,] a person can make financial restitution and receive atonement. With regard to capital punishment, [the victim's] blood and the blood of his [unborn] descendants are dependent on [the murderer] until eternity. As it is said with regard to Cain, 'The voice of the blood of your brother is crying out.' [The Torah uses the plural form of the word blood, implying] his blood and the blood of his descendants.[17]

"For this reason, man was created alone[18] in the world. This teaches us that a person who eliminates one soul from the world is considered as if he eliminated an entire world. [Conversely,] a person who saves one soul is considered as if he saved an entire world.

"All the inhabitants of the world are created in the image of Adam, the first man, and yet no one person's face resembles the face of his colleague. Therefore each person can say: 'The world was created for me.'[19]

"If you might say: 'Why should we enter this difficulty?'[20] It is written [Leviticus 5:1]: 'If he witnessed, observed, or knew....'[21] If you will say: 'Why should we become responsible for [shedding the defendant's] blood?' It is already said: 'At the destruction of the wicked, there is joy.'"[22]

If they stand by their word,[23] the witness of the greater stature is brought into the court [alone] and he is questioned and cross-examined, as will be explained in *Hilchot Edut*.[24] If his testimony appears to be factual,[25] the

highly unlikely, this is another one of the leniencies given to insure that an innocent person is never executed.

10. Who are not acceptable to serve as witnesses.

11. *Makkot* 6b states that even if the person heard the warning from a demon, it is sufficient. The Rambam, who maintained that demons no longer exist in the present time, however, omitted this concept (Radbaz).

12. I.e., the person committing the transgression (*Kessef Mishneh*). Rashi (*Makkot* 6b) interprets this as referring to the victim.

13. I.e., administers a severe warning, so that if a person was considering giving false testimony, he will recant. *Hilchot Edut* 17:2 describes a warning given with regard to financial matters, but it is not as severe.

14. Something that you did not actually see, but presume to be true. For example, a person

וּבֵין שֶׁהִתְרָה בּוֹ אֶחָד מִן הָעֵדִים וּבֵין שֶׁהִתְרָה בּוֹ אַחֵר בִּפְנֵי עֵדִים, אֲפִלּוּ אִשָּׁה אוֹ עֶבֶד, אֲפִלּוּ שָׁמַע קוֹל הַמַּתְרֶה וְלֹא רָאָהוּ, וַאֲפִלּוּ הִתְרָה בְּעַצְמוֹ – הֲרֵי זֶה נֶהֱרָג.

ג אָמְרוּ הָעֵדִים: הָיְתָה לוֹ הַתְרָאָה וּמַכִּירִין אָנוּ אוֹתוֹ – מְאַיְּמִין בֵּית דִּין עֲלֵיהֶן. וְכֵיצַד מְאַיְּמִין עַל עִסְקֵי נְפָשׁוֹת? אוֹמְרִים לָהֶן: שֶׁמָּא תֹּאמְרוּ מֵאֹמֶד וּמִשְּׁמוּעָה, עֵד מִפִּי עֵד, מִפִּי אָדָם נֶאֱמָן שְׁמַעְתֶּם? אוֹ שֶׁמָּא אֵין אַתֶּם יוֹדְעִים שֶׁסּוֹפֵנוּ לִבְדֹּק אֶתְכֶם בִּדְרִישָׁה וַחֲקִירָה? הֱווּ יוֹדְעִים, שֶׁלֹּא כְּדִינֵי מָמוֹנוֹת דִּינֵי נְפָשׁוֹת. דִּינֵי מָמוֹנוֹת – אָדָם נוֹתֵן מָמוֹנוֹ וּמִתְכַּפֵּר לוֹ; דִּינֵי נְפָשׁוֹת – דָּמוֹ וְדַם זַרְעוֹ תְּלוּיִין בּוֹ עַד סוֹף כָּל הָעוֹלָם. שֶׁהֲרֵי בְּקַיִן נֶאֱמַר: קוֹל דְּמֵי אָחִיךָ צֹעֲקִים – דָּמוֹ וְדַם זַרְעוֹ.
לְפִיכָךְ נִבְרָא אָדָם יְחִידִי בָּעוֹלָם, לְלַמֵּד: שֶׁכָּל הַמְאַבֵּד נֶפֶשׁ אַחַת מִן הָעוֹלָם – מַעֲלִין עָלָיו כְּאִלּוּ אִבֵּד עוֹלָם מָלֵא; וְכָל הַמְקַיֵּם נֶפֶשׁ אַחַת בָּעוֹלָם – מַעֲלִין עָלָיו כְּאִלּוּ קִיֵּם עוֹלָם מָלֵא.
הֲרֵי כָּל בָּאֵי עוֹלָם בְּצוּרַת אָדָם הָרִאשׁוֹן הֵם נִבְרָאִים, וְאֵין פְּנֵי כָּל אֶחָד מֵהֶן דּוֹמִין לִפְנֵי חֲבֵרוֹ. לְפִיכָךְ, כָּל אֶחָד וְאֶחָד יָכוֹל לוֹמַר: בִּשְׁבִילִי נִבְרָא הָעוֹלָם.
שֶׁמָּא תֹּאמְרוּ: מַה לָּנוּ וּלְצָרָה זוֹ? הֲלוֹא כְּבָר נֶאֱמַר: וְהוּא עֵד אוֹ רָאָה אוֹ יָדָע.
אוֹ שֶׁמָּא תֹּאמְרוּ: מַה לָּנוּ לָחוּב בְּדָמוֹ שֶׁל זֶה? וַהֲלוֹא כְּבָר נֶאֱמַר: וּבַאֲבֹד רְשָׁעִים רִנָּה.
אִם עָמְדוּ בְּדִבְרֵיהֶן – מַכְנִיסִין אֶת הַגָּדוֹל שֶׁבָּעֵדִים וּבוֹדְקִים אוֹתוֹ בִּדְרִישָׁה וַחֲקִירָה, כְּמוֹ שֶׁיִּתְבָּאֵר בְּהִלְכוֹת עֵדוּת.

walked out of a room with a bloody knife and a victim was found slain inside. Although the likelihood is great that the person carrying the knife was the murderer, this is considered as circumstantial evidence and may not be used to convict the defendant.
15. Hearsay evidence, even from a totally reliable source, is inadmissible. Instead, the person who saw the crime being committed must testify himself.
16. The precise meaning of the Hebrew words *derishah vichakirah* is discussed in *Hilchot Edut*, Chapters 1 and 2.
17. God was holding Cain responsible, not only for the death of Abel, but for the destruction of all his descendants.
18. I.e., in contrast to all the animals which were created in pairs, Adam was created alone.
19. Implied by the above are two concepts: a) the importance of every life; that the witnesses should take seriously the consequences involved in having the defendant executed; b) the responsibility the witnesses have upon them, for "the entire world" depends on them.
20. With these statements, the judges counsel the witnesses against refraining from testifying. They might feel that even though they know incriminating evidence, they will refrain from testifying, because of the difficulty and the responsibility involved.
21. I.e., the Torah commands a person to give testimony if he saw a colleague commit a transgression. This is one of the 613 mitzvot of the Torah, as stated in *Hilchot Edut* 1:1.
22. I.e., God will be happy because of their execution. See also *Hilchot Evel* 1:10.
23. And still desire to testify despite hearing this warning.
24. Chapter 1, Halachah 4.
25. I.e., he describes the event, the date, and the time at which it took place (*ibid.*:5).

second witness is brought into the court, and he is questioned as the first one was. Even if there are 100 witnesses, each one is questioned and cross-examined.[26]

If the testimony of all the witnesses is accurate, we begin the judgment with a statement that tends to acquittal as stated.[27] We tell him: "If you did not transgress, do not fear their words." [Then] we judge him. If grounds for acquittal are found, he is released. If they do not find grounds for acquittal, [the defendant] is imprisoned until the following day.[28]

On that day, the *Sanhedrin* divides itself into pairs and they examine the judgment. They eat little and do not drink wine throughout that entire day.[29] They debate the matter throughout the night, each one with his comrade or alone. On the morrow, they come to the court early. [Each of] those who voted for acquittal state: "I am the one who voted for acquittal [yesterday], and I still favor that ruling." [Each of] those who voted for conviction state: "I am the one who voted for conviction [yesterday], and I still favor that ruling," or "...I have changed my mind and I vote for acquittal." If they erred in that regard, or did not know who voted for conviction or who voted for acquittal on the basis of one rationale and hence are considered only as one, as we explained,[30] the two scribes of the court[31] remind them, for they write down the rationale given by each one of them.

We begin the judgment. If they find a rationale to acquit him, they acquit him. If it is necessary to add judges,[32] they add. If there is a majority of judges who seek to convict him, and he is convicted, he is taken out to be executed [immediately].[33]

The place where the court conducts the execution is outside the court and removed from it,[34] as [implied by Leviticus 24:14]: "Take the blasphemer outside the camp...."[35] It appears to me that it should be approximately 6 *mil*,[36] the distance between the court of Moses our teacher which was before the entrance of the Tent of Meeting and the extremities of the camp of the Jewish people.[37]

4. After [a defendant] has been convicted, we do not delay [the matter], but instead execute him immediately. Even if [a woman] is pregnant, we do not wait until she gives birth.[38] Instead, we give her a blow against the womb so

26. If there is a discrepancy between the testimony of any of the witnesses, the testimony of all of them is nullified (*Hilchot Edut* 2:3).
27. Chapter 10, Halachah 7.
28. As a source, the *Or Sameach* cites Numbers 15:34 which relates how the person who collected sticks on the Sabbath was imprisoned until God revealed how he would be executed.
29. They do not fast, so that their minds will be clear, but they are careful not to overindulge. This is a sign of deference to the seriousness of the judgment they are undertaking. For this reason, they do not drink at all. Needless to say, they would not eat and drink to the extent that their thoughts would be blurred.

Sanhedrin 42a derives this concept based on Proverbs 31:4: "The princes should not [partake of] strong drink." The Hebrew for princes, *roznim*, shares the same root as the

אִם נִמְצֵאת עֵדוּתוֹ מְכֻוֶּנֶת – מַכְנִיסִין אֶת הַשֵּׁנִי וּבוֹדְקִין אוֹתוֹ כָּרִאשׁוֹן. אֲפִלּוּ הָיוּ מֵאָה עֵדִים – בּוֹדְקִין כָּל אֶחָד וְאֶחָד בִּדְרִישָׁה וַחֲקִירָה. נִמְצְאוּ דִבְרֵי כָּל הָעֵדִים מְכֻוָּנִים – פּוֹתְחִין לִזְכוּת, כְּמוֹ שֶׁבֵּאַרְנוּ, וְאוֹמְרִים: אִם לֹא חָטָאתָ – אַל תִּירָא מִדִּבְרֵיהֶם. וְדָנִין אוֹתוֹ.

אִם מָצְאוּ לוֹ זְכוּת – פְּטָרוּהוּ; וְאִם לֹא מָצְאוּ לוֹ זְכוּת – אוֹסְרִין אוֹתוֹ עַד לְמָחָר.

וּבוֹ בַּיּוֹם מִזְדַּוְּגִין הַסַּנְהֶדְרִין זוּגוֹת זוּגוֹת לְעַיֵּן בְּדִינוֹ. וּמְמַעֲטִין בְּמַאֲכָל וְאֵין שׁוֹתִין יַיִן כָּל אוֹתוֹ הַיּוֹם. וְנוֹשְׂאִין בַּדָּבָר כָּל הַלַּיְלָה כָּל אֶחָד וְאֶחָד עִם זוּג שֶׁלּוֹ אוֹ עִם עַצְמוֹ בְּבֵיתוֹ. וְלַמָּחֳרָת מַשְׁכִּימִין לְבֵית דִּין. הַמְזַכֶּה אוֹמֵר: אֲנִי הוּא הַמְזַכֶּה, וּמְזַכֶּה אֲנִי בִּמְקוֹמִי; וְהַמְחַיֵּב אוֹמֵר: אֲנִי הוּא הַמְחַיֵּב, וּמְחַיֵּב אֲנִי בִּמְקוֹמִי, אוֹ חָזַרְתִּי בִּי וַאֲנִי מְזַכֶּה.

וְאִם טָעוּ בַּדָּבָר וְלֹא יָדְעוּ מִי הֵם שֶׁחִיְּבוּ אוֹ זִכּוּ מִטַּעַם אֶחָד, שֶׁאֵינָן נֶחְשָׁבִין אֶלָּא כְּאֶחָד כְּמוֹ שֶׁבֵּאַרְנוּ – הֲרֵי סוֹפְרֵי הַדַּיָּנִין מַזְכִּירִין אוֹתָן, שֶׁהֲרֵי כּוֹתְבִין טַעַם שֶׁל כָּל אֶחָד וְאֶחָד.

וּמַתְחִילִין בְּדִינוֹ. אִם מָצְאוּ לוֹ זְכוּת – פְּטָרוּהוּ; וְאִם הֻצְרְכוּ לְהוֹסִיף – מוֹסִיפִין.

רַבּוּ הַמְחַיְּבִין וְנִתְחַיֵּב – מוֹצִיאִין אוֹתוֹ לְהָרְגוֹ.

וּמָקוֹם שֶׁהוֹרְגִין בּוֹ בֵּית דִּין הָיָה חוּץ לְבֵית דִּין וְרָחוֹק מִבֵּית דִּין, שֶׁנֶּאֱמַר: הוֹצֵא אֶת הַמְקַלֵּל אֶל מִחוּץ לַמַּחֲנֶה.

וְיֵרָאֶה לִי, שֶׁיִּהְיֶה רָחוֹק כְּמוֹ שִׁשָּׁה מִילִין, כְּמוֹ שֶׁהָיָה בֵּין בֵּית דִּינוֹ שֶׁל מֹשֶׁה רַבֵּנוּ, שֶׁהָיָה לִפְנֵי פֶּתַח אֹהֶל מוֹעֵד, וּבֵין מַחֲנֵה יִשְׂרָאֵל.

ד מִשֶּׁנִּגְמַר דִּינוֹ אֵין מַשְׁהִין אוֹתוֹ, אֶלָּא יֵהָרֵג בְּיוֹמוֹ.

אֲפִלּוּ הָיְתָה עֻבָּרָה – אֵין מַמְתִּינִין לָהּ עַד שֶׁתֵּלֵד. וּמַכִּין אוֹתָהּ כְּנֶגֶד בֵּית הַהֵרָיוֹן עַד

Hebrew word *raz*, meaning "secret." "Those involved in the secrets of the world [- i.e., questions of life and death -] should not partake of strong drink."

30. Chapter 10, Halachah 5.
31. See Chapter 1, Halachah 9.
32. As explained in Chapter 9, Halachot 2-3.
33. He is not left to languish under the distress of a death sentence as stated in the following halachah.
34. As evident from Chapter 13, Halachah 1, one of the reasons for this was to allow the possibility of a rationale acquitting the defendant to be discovered. Another rationale is mentioned by *Sanhedrin* 42b: so that the judges will not appear to be anxious to carry out the execution.
35. The verse concludes describing how the blasphemer would be stoned to death there.
36. A *mil* is 2000 cubits, approximately a kilometer in contemporary measure.
37. The camp of the Jewish people was 12 *mil* long and the Tent of Meeting was in the center. Thus the distance from Moses' tent to the camp's periphery was slightly less than 6 *mil*.
38. In this context, the fetus is considered as part of the mother's body and not as an independent entity (*Arachin* 7a).

that the fetus will die first.[39] If, by contrast, she is already in the throes of labor, we wait until she gives birth.[40]

Whenever a woman is executed, it is permitted to benefit from her hair.[41]

5. When a person is being taken out to be executed and a sacrifice of his has already been slaughtered, we do not execute him until the blood of his sin offering or guilt offering[42] has been sprinkled [on the altar] for his sake. If, however, he was already convicted and the [animal designated as a] sacrifice has not been slaughtered already, we do not wait until the sacrifice is brought, for we do not prolong his judgment.[43]

CHAPTER THIRTEEN

1. When a person is sentenced to death, he is taken out of the court [and led to the place of execution]. One person stands at the entrance to the court with flags in his hands and a horse distant from him.[1] An announcement is made before him: "So-and-so is being taken to be executed in this-and-this manner, because he violated this prohibition, in this place at this time. So-and-so and so-and-so are the witnesses.[2] If there is anyone who knows a rationale leading to his acquittal, let them come and tell us."

If a person says: "I know a rationale that leads to his acquittal," the person with the flags waves them and the rider on the horse races to bring the defendant back to the court. If a factor leading to his acquittal is found, he is released. If not, he is taken back for execution.

If the defendant himself says: "I know a rationale that leads to my acquittal," even though there is no substance to his words,[3] he is returned [to the court] once or twice. [We suspect that] perhaps out of fear, he could not present his arguments and when he is returned to the court, he will be composed and will state a [substantial] reason [for acquittal].

If they return him to the court, and it is discovered that his words are without substance, for a third time, he is taken [to be executed]. If on this third

39. If the fetus is not killed first, it may emerge after the woman's death and that would result in the denigration of her corpse (Rashi, *Arachin, loc. cit.*).

40. For the fetus has already taken on the status of an independent entity (*ibid.*).

41. As the Rambam states in *Hilchot Evel* 14:21, it is forbidden to benefit from a corpse. Nevertheless, an exception exists with regard to the hair of the corpse, for it is not considered as part of the corpse. *Arachin* 7b explains the rationale for this exception: Every other portion of the corpse will change after death; the hair, by contrast, will remain the same.

In the Rambam's Commentary to the Mishnah (*Arachin* 1:4), he states that this exception applies when before her death, the woman said that her hair should be given to another person. If she did not make such a statement, it is forbidden to benefit from her hair as well. He does not, however, make such a stipulation in *Hilchot Evel*.

It must be mentioned that the Rambam's ruling in *Hilchot Evel* has been questioned by

שֶׁיָּמוּת הַוָּלָד תְּחִלָּה. אֲבָל אִם יָשְׁבָה עַל הַמַּשְׁבֵּר – מַמְתִּינִין לָהּ עַד שֶׁתֵּלֵד. וְכָל אִשָּׁה שֶׁתֵּהָרֵג – מֻתָּר לֵהָנוֹת בִּשְׂעָרָהּ.

ה מִי שֶׁיָּצָא לֵהָרֵג וְהָיָה זִבְחוֹ זָבוּחַ – אֵין הוֹרְגִין אוֹתוֹ עַד שֶׁמַּזִּין עָלָיו מִדַּם חַטָּאתוֹ וַאֲשָׁמוֹ. וְאִם נִגְמַר דִּינוֹ וַעֲדַיִן לֹא נִשְׁחַט הַזֶּבַח – אֵין מַמְתִּינִין לוֹ עַד שֶׁיַּקְרִיבוּ עָלָיו קָרְבָּנוֹ, שֶׁאֵין מְעַנִּין אֶת דִּינוֹ.

פֶּרֶק שְׁלֹשָׁה עָשָׂר

א מִי שֶׁנִּגְמַר דִּינוֹ לְמִיתָה – מוֹצִיאִין אוֹתוֹ מִבֵּית דִּין, וְאֶחָד עוֹמֵד עַל פֶּתַח בֵּית דִּין וְהַסּוּדָרִין בְּיָדוֹ, וְהַסּוּס רָחוֹק מִמֶּנּוּ. וְהַכָּרוֹז יוֹצֵא לְפָנָיו: פְּלוֹנִי יוֹצֵא לֵהָרֵג בְּמִיתָה פְּלוֹנִית, עַל שֶׁעָבַר עֲבֵרָה פְּלוֹנִית בְּמָקוֹם פְּלוֹנִי בִּזְמַן פְּלוֹנִי, וּפְלוֹנִי וּפְלוֹנִי עֵדָיו. מִי שֶׁיּוֹדֵעַ לוֹ זְכוּת – יָבוֹא וִילַמֵּד עָלָיו. אָמַר אֶחָד: יֵשׁ לִי לְלַמֵּד עָלָיו זְכוּת – זֶה מֵנִיף בַּסּוּדָרִין, וְזֶה הָרוֹכֵב עַל הַסּוּס רָץ וּמַחֲזִיר אֶת הַנִּדּוֹן לְבֵית דִּין.

אִם נִמְצָא לוֹ זְכוּת – פּוֹטְרִין אוֹתוֹ; וְאִם לָאו – יַחֲזֹר וְיֵצֵא לַהֲרִיגָה.

אָמַר הוּא בְּעַצְמוֹ: יֵשׁ לִי לְלַמֵּד עַל עַצְמִי זְכוּת, אַף עַל פִּי שֶׁאֵין מַמָּשׁ בִּדְבָרָיו – מַחֲזִירִין אוֹתוֹ פַּעַם רִאשׁוֹנָה וּשְׁנִיָּה; שֶׁמָּא מִפְּנֵי הַפַּחַד נִסְתַּתְּמוּ טַעֲנוֹתָיו, וּכְשֶׁיַּחֲזֹר לְבֵית דִּין – תִּתְיַשֵּׁב דַּעְתּוֹ וְיֹאמַר טַעַם. הֶחֱזִירוּהוּ וְלֹא נִמְצָא מַמָּשׁ בִּדְבָרָיו – מוֹצִיאִין אוֹתוֹ פַּעַם שְׁלִישִׁית.

the commentaries. In his *Kessef Mishneh*, Rav Yosef Karo raises objections, and in his *Shulchan Aruch* (*Yoreh De'ah* 349:2), he states that it is forbidden to benefit from the hair of a corpse. According to his interpretation, the leniency derived from *Arachin, loc. cit.*, with regard to the hair of a condemned woman is that, even though she has been condemned to death, until she is executed her hair may be cut off and used.

42. A burnt offering, by contrast, is offered even after the person's death (*Arachin* 7b).

43. Our assumption is that it is more desirable for him to be executed immediately than to wait for the sacrificed to be offered. We do not offer such sacrifices after his death, for once a person has passed away, these sacrifices cannot procure atonement for him. These laws are restated in *Hilchot Shegagot* 3:12.

1. I.e., far removed from him, but in a place and at a distance where the rider can see the person with the flags clearly.

2. All these particulars are mentioned so that if a person was present at that place, at that time, and did not see the crime take place or was with the witnesses in another place at that time, he could come to court and nullify the testimony that served as the basis for the conviction.

3. I.e., even if the people who accompany him feel that his words are not substantial, they bring him back to the court. Since he is brought back to the court regardless, scholars who

[occasion], he also says: "I know a rationale that leads to my acquittal," we return him to the court - even several times - if his words are substantial. For this reason, two scholars are sent to accompany him and listen to his statements on the way. If his words are of substance, he is returned to the court. If not, he is not returned.

If an argument leading to his acquittal is not discovered, he is brought out for execution. The witnesses are the ones who execute him[4] in the manner[5] for which he is liable.[6] When a murderer is not executed by his witnesses, all other people are obligated to execute him.[7]

Approximately ten cubits from the place of execution,[8] he is told to confess. For all those who are executed should confess. For if they confess, they receive a portion in the world to come. If he does not know how to confess, we tell him: "Say 'may my death atone for my sins.'" Even if he knows that he was the victim of false testimony, he should confess in this manner.[9]

2. After he confessess,[10] he is given a granule of frankincense [dissolved] in a cup of wine, so that he will lose control of his mind and become drunk.[11] Afterwards, he is executed in the manner for which he is liable.

3. The wine, the frankincense, the stone used to execute a person stoned to death,[12] the sword used to decapitate a defendant,[13] the cloth use for strangulation,[14] the pole on which [a blasphemer or an idolater] is hung [after being executed],[15] the flags that are waved before those being executed, and the horse[16] that runs to save him all are paid for from communal funds. Anyone who wants to donate them may donate them.[17]

4. The court does not attend the funeral of the executed person.[18] Whenever a court has a person executed, they are forbidden to eat [for the remainder of] that entire day.. This [prohibition] is included in [the interdiction (Leviticus 19:26)]: "Do not eat upon the blood."[19] A meal of comfort[20] is not given the

can evaluate the substance of his words are not sent with him the first two times (*Sanhedrin* 43a).

4. In his Commentary to the Mishnah (*Sanhedrin* 7:3), the Rambam explains that the execution is placed in the hands of the witnesses, because they are the only ones who have firsthand knowledge of the transgression. Since everyone else knows only because of them, they are given the responsibility to carry out the execution.

5. One of the four types of death: stoning, burning, decapitation, or strangling.

6. As Deuteronomy 17:7 states: "And the hand of the witnesses shall be the first against him."

7. With regard to others condemned to death, by contrast, it is the witnesses who must execute them. See Halachah 7, and Chapter 14, Halachah 8.

8. We fear that if he is asked to confess at the place of execution itself, he will be overcome by fear and will not be able to confess properly [the Rambam's Commentary to the Mishnah (*Sanhedrin* 6:2)].

9. For certainly he has other sins, for which he is liable.

Sanhedrin 43a suggests that, in such a situation, a person should say: "May my death be

אָמַר בַּשְּׁלִישִׁית: יֵשׁ לִי לְלַמֵּד עַל עַצְמִי זְכוּת, אִם יֵשׁ מַמָּשׁ בִּדְבָרָיו – מַחֲזִירִין אוֹתוֹ אֲפִלּוּ כַּמָּה פְּעָמִים. לְפִיכָךְ מוֹסְרִין לוֹ שְׁנֵי תַּלְמִידֵי חֲכָמִים שֶׁשּׁוֹמְעִין דְּבָרָיו בַּדֶּרֶךְ. אִם יֵשׁ מַמָּשׁ בִּדְבָרָיו – מַחֲזִירִין אוֹתוֹ; וְאִם לָאו – אֵין מַחֲזִירִין אוֹתוֹ. אִם לֹא נִמְצָא לוֹ זְכוּת – מוֹצִיאִין אוֹתוֹ. וְעֵדָיו הֵם הַהוֹרְגִין אוֹתוֹ בְּכָל מִיתָה שֶׁיִּתְחַיֵּב בָּהּ. וְרוֹצֵחַ שֶׁלֹּא הֲרָגוּהוּ עֵדָיו – חַיָּבִין לַהֲמִיתוֹ בְּיַד כָּל אָדָם.

רָחוֹק מִמְּקוֹם הַהֲרִיגָה כְּעֶשֶׂר אַמּוֹת אוֹמְרִים לוֹ: הִתְוַדֵּה! שֶׁכֵּן דֶּרֶךְ כָּל הַמּוּמָתִין מִתְוַדִּין. וְכָל הַמִּתְוַדֶּה – יֵשׁ לוֹ חֵלֶק לָעוֹלָם הַבָּא. אִם אֵינוֹ יוֹדֵעַ לְהִתְוַדּוֹת – אוֹמְרִים לוֹ: אֱמֹר: תְּהֵא מִיתָתִי כַּפָּרָה עַל כָּל עֲוֹנוֹתַי. אֲפִלּוּ יָדַע בְּעַצְמוֹ שֶׁשֶּׁקֶר הֵעִידוּ עָלָיו, כָּךְ הוּא מִתְוַדֶּה.

ב וְאַחַר שֶׁמִּתְוַדֶּה מַשְׁקִין אוֹתוֹ קֹרֶט שֶׁל לְבוֹנָה בְּכוֹס שֶׁל יַיִן, כְּדֵי שֶׁתִּטָּרֵף דַּעְתּוֹ עָלָיו וְיִשְׁתַּכֵּר, וְאַחַר כָּךְ יֵהָרֵג בַּמִּיתָה שֶׁהוּא חַיָּב בָּהּ.

ג זֶה הַיַּיִן וְהַלְּבוֹנָה, וְהָאֶבֶן שֶׁיִּסָּקֵל בָּהּ הַנִּסְקָל, וְהַסַּיִף שֶׁיֵּהָרֵג בּוֹ הַנֶּהֱרָג, וְהַסּוּדָר שֶׁחוֹנְקִין בּוֹ הַנֶּחֱנָק, וְהָעֵץ שֶׁתּוֹלִין עָלָיו הַנִּתְלֶה, וְהַסּוּדָרִין שֶׁמְּנִיפִין בָּהֶן לִפְנֵי הֲרוּגֵי בֵּית דִּין, וְהַסּוּס שֶׁרָץ לְהַצִּילוֹ – הַכֹּל בָּאִין מִשֶּׁל צִבּוּר. וּמִי שֶׁיִּרְצֶה לְהִתְנַדֵּב – יָבוֹא וְיִתְנַדֵּב.

ד אֵין בֵּית דִּין יוֹצְאִין אַחַר הַנֶּהֱרָג. וְכָל בֵּית דִּין שֶׁהָרְגוּ נֶפֶשׁ – אֲסוּרִים לֶאֱכֹל כָּל אוֹתוֹ הַיּוֹם. הֲרֵי זֶה בִּכְלַל לֹא תֹאכְלוּ עַל הַדָּם.

atonement for all my sins except this one." It, however, rejects that option lest all the executed adopt that version to create the impression that they were framed.

Significantly, in *Sefer HaMitzvot* (positive mitzvah 73), the Rambam writes that if a person knows that he is being framed, he should not confess. *Mayim Chayim* explains that in *Sefer HaMitzvot*, the Rambam is speaking according to Scriptural Law, while here he is speaking according to Rabbinic decree.

10. But not before, so that he will be of sound mind when he confesses (*Torat Chayim*).

11. I.e., he is not required to face his death with a clear mind. *Sanhedrin* 43a draws support from Proverbs 31:6: "Give strong drink to one who is lost and wine to the bitter of soul."

12. See Chapter 15, Halachah 1.

13. *Ibid.*:4.

14. *Ibid.*:5.

15. *Ibid.*:7.

16. See Halachah 1.

17. *Sanhedrin* 43a states that "the precious women of Jerusalem would donate the wine and the frankincense."

18. This might create the impression that the court desired to see him executed (*Sanhedrin* 43a).

19. See Chapter 18, Halachah 3, and notes which explain that this interdiction includes within it several prohibitions involving different subjects.

20. The meal brought to the mourners after the burial. See *Hilchot Evel* 14:9.

relatives of those executed by the court.[21] [This too is derived from the above verse.] These acts are forbidden, but they are not punishable by lashes.[22]

5. When a person is held liable for the death penalty during *Chol HaMoed*, the court [prolong] their analysis of his judgment. The judges eat and drink.[23] Afterwards, shortly before sunset, they conclude the judgment and have him executed.

6. Mourning rites are not held for those executed by the court.[24] Their relatives come and inquire about the well-being of the witnesses and the well-being of the judges to show that they have no [bad feelings] against them in their hearts and that they [acknowledge] that their judgment was true. Although they do not observe the mourning rites, they do observe *aninut*.[25] For *aninut* is solely [a reflection] of the feeling in one's heart.[26]

7. When a person was sentenced in one court, fled, and brought to another court,[27] we do not reopen his case. Instead, wherever two people will arise and state: "We testify that this person was sentenced to death in this court and that so-and-so and so-and-so are those who testified against him," he is executed.

When does the above apply? To a murderer.[28] Other people who are obligated to be executed are not [given that punishment] until the witnesses who originally testified against them come and testify that they were sentenced to death. [The witnesses] must then execute [the convicted] themselves.[29] The above applies provided testimony is given in a court of 23 judges.[30]

8. When a person was sentenced to death by a court in the Diaspora[31] and fled to a court in *Eretz Yisrael*, we reopen his case at least.[32] If [he comes before]

21. *Sanhedrin* 63a states that this act diminishes the honor of the executed person and thus helps bring him atonement.

22. As stated in Chapter 18, *loc. cit.*, this prohibition is considered as being "inclusive in nature." Although all of the forbidden acts included within it are forbidden by Scriptural Law, nevertheless, because of the general nature of the prohibition, their violation is not punishable by lashes. See *Sefer HaMitzvot*, General Principle 9.

23. Since *Chol HaMoed* are festive days, it is improper for the judges to be forbidden to eat. Hence the judgment is prolonged. Since the sentence was not delivered, this is not considered as prolonging the condemned person's suffering.

The implication is that the judges are permitted also to drink wine. Although they have not delivered their ruling and a person who is intoxicated is forbidden to deliver a ruling, no restriction is given. Some suggest that since they have already made their decisions and the hesitation in delivering the ruling is merely a technical factor, there is no necessity for a restriction. *Kin'at Eliyahu* suggests that the awe of dealing with a case involving capital punishment will prevent them from losing self-control.

24. As mentioned above, this failure to show them respect conveys atonement upon them (*Sanhedrin* 46b). In his Commentary to the Mishnah (*Sanhedrin* 6:8), the Rambam writes

וְאֵין מַבְרִין הַקְּרוֹבִים עַל הֲרוּגֵי בֵּית דִּין, מִשּׁוּם לֹא תֹאכְלוּ עַל הַדָּם. וּדְבָרִים אֵלּוּ אֲסוּרִין וְאֵין בָּהֶן מַלְקוּת.

ה מִי שֶׁנִּתְחַיֵּב מִיתָה בְּחֻלּוֹ שֶׁל מוֹעֵד – מְעַיְּנִין בְּדִינוֹ, וְאוֹכְלִין בֵּית דִּין וְשׁוֹתִין, וְאַחַר כָּךְ גּוֹמְרִין אֶת דִּינוֹ סָמוּךְ לִשְׁקִיעַת הַחַמָּה, וְהוֹרְגִין אוֹתוֹ.

ו הֲרוּגֵי בֵּית דִּין – אֵין מִתְאַבְּלִין עֲלֵיהֶן. וּבָאִין קְרוֹבֵיהֶן וְשׁוֹאֲלִים אֶת שְׁלוֹם הָעֵדִים וְאֶת שְׁלוֹם הַדַּיָּנִים, לְהוֹדִיעַ שֶׁאֵין בְּלִבָּם עֲלֵיהֶן כְּלוּם, שֶׁדִּין אֱמֶת דָּנוּ. וְאַף עַל פִּי שֶׁאֵין נוֹהֲגִין אֲבֵלוּת – הֲרֵי הֵן אוֹנְנִים עֲלֵיהֶם; שֶׁאֵין אֲנִינוּת אֶלָּא בַּלֵּב.

ז מִי שֶׁנִּגְמַר דִּינוֹ וּבָרַח, וּבָא לְבֵית דִּין אַחֵר – אֵין סוֹתְרִין אֶת דִּינוֹ.
אֶלָּא כָּל מָקוֹם שֶׁיַּעַמְדוּ שְׁנַיִם וְיֹאמְרוּ: מְעִידִין אָנוּ אֶת אִישׁ פְּלוֹנִי שֶׁנִּגְמַר דִּינוֹ בְּבֵית דִּין פְּלוֹנִי, וּפְלוֹנִי וּפְלוֹנִי עֵדָיו – הֲרֵי זֶה יֵהָרֵג.
בַּמֶּה דְּבָרִים אֲמוּרִים? בְּרוֹצֵחַ; אֲבָל שְׁאָר חַיָּבֵי מִיתוֹת – עַד שֶׁיָּבוֹאוּ עֵדָיו הָרִאשׁוֹנִים וְיָעִידוּ שֶׁנִּגְמַר דִּינוֹ, וְיַהַרְגוּהוּ בְּיָדָם. וְהוּא שֶׁיָּעִידוּ בְּבֵית דִּין שֶׁל עֶשְׂרִים וּשְׁלֹשָׁה.

ח מִי שֶׁנִּגְמַר דִּינוֹ בְּבֵית דִּין שֶׁהָיָה בְּחוּצָה לָאָרֶץ, וּבָרַח לְבֵית דִּין שֶׁבְּאֶרֶץ יִשְׂרָאֵל – סוֹתְרִין אֶת דִּינוֹ עַל כָּל פָּנִים.

that the atonement for these individuals is not granted until their corpses begin to decompose. Hence at the time of the funeral, it is not fit to mourn for them. See also *Hilchot Evel* 1:9 where this law is repeated.

25. *Aninut* refers to the severe feelings of mourning - and appropriate practices - experienced on the day a close relative dies. There is a difference of opinion among the Rabbis whether *aninut* applies only up until the burial or afterwards as well. From *Hilchot Bi'at HaMikdash* 2:9, it would appear that the Rambam maintains that the classification of *aninut* applies after the burial as well.

There are two contexts in which *aninut* is mentioned in the Torah: the prohibition against partaking of sacrificial offerings (Leviticus 10:19) and the prohibition against partaking of the second tithe (Deuteronomy 26:14). Other mourning practices associated with *aninut* are mentioned in *Hilchot Evel* 4:6.

26. These feelings do not detract from the atonement to be granted the person executed.

27. See also the following halachah.

28. For if he is not executed by the witnesses, the entire Jewish people are obligated to execute him (*Sanhedrin* 45b).

29. As Deuteronomy 17:7 states: "And the hand of the witnesses shall be the first against him." See Halachah 1 and Chapter 14, Halachah 8.

30. For only such a court may deal with cases involving capital punishment.

31. This refers to a court of judges who received *semichah* in *Eretz Yisrael*, but who were found in the diaspora either temporarily or permanently (Chapter 14, Halachah 14).

32. Maybe the merit of *Eretz Yisrael* will make it possible that a rationale to acquit him will be found (*Makkot* 7a).

the same court who sentenced him [in the Diaspora], we do not reopen his case,[33] even though they sentenced him in the Diaspora and now they are in *Eretz Yisrael.*

CHAPTER FOURTEEN

1. Four types of execution were given to the court: stoning, burning, decapitation with a sword, and strangulation. Stoning and burning are explicitly mentioned in the Torah.[1] Moses our teacher taught[2] that whenever the Torah mentions the death sentence without any further description, the intent is strangulation. When a person kills a colleague, he should be decapitated.[3] Similarly, the inhabitants of a city that goes astray[4] are executed by decapitation.[5]

2. Every one of these forms of execution involves a positive commandment for the court to execute a person with the form of death for which he is liable.[6] A king has permission to execute using only one of them - by decapitation.[7]

3. Whenever a person is obligated to be executed and the court did not execute him, [the judges] negated the observance of a positive commandment,[8] but do not transgress a negative commandment. There is one exception: a sorcerer. If they do not kill him, they violate a negative commandment,[9] as [Exodus 22:17] states: "Do not allow a sorcerer to live."

4. Stoning to death is a more severe form of execution than burning.[10] Burning is a more severe form than decapitation,[11] and decapitation is more sever than strangulation.[12]

When a person is liable to be executed with two different forms of execution,[13] he should be executed with the more severe form. [This applies] whether he committed two transgressions, one after the other, or he committed one transgression which involved two death penalties.[14] Even if he was sentenced to be executed for the less severe form of execution and afterwards, committed a transgression punishable by the more severe form, should he be convicted, he is executed in the more severe manner.[15]

33. For once they judged him and sentenced him to death, there is little likelihood of them changing their minds.

1. Stoning is mentioned in Leviticus 20:27 *et al* and burning in *ibid.*:14 *et al.*
2. I.e., this was part of the received tradition of the Oral Law.
3. This is also part of the Oral Tradition as stated in *Hilchot Rotzeach* 1:1.
4. I.e., a city where the majority of the inhabitants worship idols.
5. Deuteronomy 13:16 states that the inhabitants of such a city should be "struck... by the blade of the sword."
6. *Sefer HaMitzvot* (positive commandments 326-329) and *Sefer HaChinuch* (mitzvot 555, 261, 50, 47) include these mitzvot in their reckoning of the 613 mitzvot of the Torah
7. See *Hilchot Melachim* 3:2,8 which explains that a king has the right to decapitate people who rebel against him.

וְאִם הָיוּ אוֹתָן בֵּית דִּין עַצְמָן שֶׁנִּגְמַר דִּינוֹ בִּפְנֵיהֶם – אֵין סוֹתְרִין אֶת דִּינוֹ, אַף עַל פִּי שֶׁגְּמָרוּהוּ בְּחוּצָה לָאָרֶץ וְהֵם עַתָּה בְּאֶרֶץ יִשְׂרָאֵל.

פֶּרֶק אַרְבָּעָה עָשָׂר

א אַרְבַּע מִיתוֹת נִמְסְרוּ לְבֵית דִּין: סְקִילָה, וּשְׂרֵפָה, וַהֲרִיגָה בְּסַיִף, וָחֶנֶק.
סְקִילָה וּשְׂרֵפָה – מְפֹרָשִׁין הֵן בַּתּוֹרָה; וּמִפִּי מֹשֶׁה רַבֵּנוּ לָמְדוּ, שֶׁכָּל מִיתָה הָאֲמוּרָה בַּתּוֹרָה סְתָם – הִיא חֶנֶק, וְהַהוֹרֵג אֶת חֲבֵרוֹ – מִיתָתוֹ בְּסַיִף.
וְכֵן אַנְשֵׁי עִיר הַנִּדַּחַת – מִיתָתָן בְּסַיִף.

ב כָּל מִיתָה מֵהֶם – מִצְוַת עֲשֵׂה הִיא לְבֵית דִּין לַהֲרֹג בָּהּ מִי שֶׁנִּתְחַיֵּב בָּהּ.
וְאֵין רְשׁוּת לַמֶּלֶךְ לַהֲרֹג בְּאַחַת מֵהֶן, אֶלָּא בְּסַיִף בִּלְבַד.

ג כָּל מְחֻיַּב מִיתַת בֵּית דִּין שֶׁלֹּא הֱמִיתוּ אוֹתוֹ בֵּית דִּין – בִּטְּלוּ מִצְוַת עֲשֵׂה, וְלֹא עָבְרוּ עַל מִצְוַת לֹא תַעֲשֶׂה. חוּץ מִן הַמְכַשֵּׁף, שֶׁאִם לֹא הֱמִיתוּהוּ – עָבְרוּ עַל מִצְוַת לֹא תַעֲשֶׂה, שֶׁנֶּאֱמַר: מְכַשֵּׁפָה לֹא תְחַיֶּה.

ד סְקִילָה חֲמוּרָה מִן הַשְּׂרֵפָה, וּשְׂרֵפָה חֲמוּרָה מִן הַסַּיִף, וְהַסַּיִף חֲמוּרָה מִן הַחֶנֶק.
וְכָל מִי שֶׁנִּתְחַיֵּב בִּשְׁתֵּי מִיתוֹת – נִדּוֹן בַּחֲמוּרָה. בֵּין שֶׁעָבַר שְׁתֵּי עֲבֵרוֹת זוֹ אַחַר זוֹ, בֵּין שֶׁעָבַר עֲבֵרָה אַחַת שֶׁחַיָּב עָלֶיהָ שְׁתֵּי מִיתוֹת.
אֲפִלּוּ נִגְמַר דִּינוֹ לַקַּלָּה, וְאַחַר כָּךְ עָבַר עַל הַחֲמוּרָה וְנִגְמַר דִּינוֹ – נִדּוֹן בַּחֲמוּרָה.

8. I.e., the appropriate positive commandment mentioned in the previous halachah.
9. *Sefer HaMitzvot* (negative commandment 310) and *Sefer HaChinuch* (mitzvah 62) count this as one of the 613 mitzvot of the Torah.
10. As proof of this, *Sanhedrin* 49b cites the fact that this is the manner in which a person who blasphemes God's name or one who worships idols is executed. Since these are the most severe transgressions, it follows that the punishment for them is also more severe.
11. *Sanhedrin* 50a concludes that this is a more severe form of execution, because it is the manner in which a priest's daughter is executed. Her transgression is considered more severe for it disgraces the honor of the priesthood.
12. From the fact that this is the manner in which the inhabitants of an idolatrous city are executed - and their property is also destroyed - we conclude that this is more severe than strangulation (*ibid.*).
13. I.e., he violated two transgressions, each punishable by execution.
14. E.g., a person engaged in relations with his mother-in-law while she was married. He is liable to be executed by burning for having relations with his mother-in-law, and to be executed by strangulation for having relations with a married woman. He is punished by the more severe of the two transgressions.
15. We do not say that since he has been sentenced to death, it is as if he was already executed and hence, he is not liable for his transgressions (*Sanhedrin* 81a).

5. Both men and women are executed in these four manners.[16]

6. Whenever people who are all liable to be executed are mixed together,[17] each one of them is executed in the less severe manner.[18]

7. When a person who has been sentenced to death becomes mixed together with others and it is impossible to distinguish him from them, and similarly, when a person who was not convicted becomes mixed together with others who have been convicted and sentenced to death and it is impossible to distinguish him from them, they are all released from liability. [The rationale[19] is that] we complete the judgment of a person only when he is present.[20]

8. When a convicted person[21] fights for his life and it is impossible for the court to have him bound so that he can be executed in the manner in which he is obligated to die, the witnesses should kill him in any manner they can, for he has been sentenced to death. No one else, however, has the right to kill him first.[22]

For this reason, if the hands of the witnesses are cut off,[23] [the convicted person] is released.[24] If, however, at the outset, the witnesses did not have hands, [the convicted person] should be executed by others.[25]

When does the above[26] apply? To all people who are liable to be executed by the court with the exception of a murderer. When, however, a murderer has been sentenced by the court every person should pursue him using any means possible [to kill him] until he is executed.[27]

9. All of the people executed by the court should not be buried in their family plots together with the entire Jewish people.[28] Instead, the court sets aside two different burial plots:[29] one for those who are stoned and those who are burnt, and the other for those who are decapitated and strangled. This[30] is a halachah conveyed by the Oral Tradition.

16. As the Rambam states in *Hilchot Issurei Bi'ah* 13:5: "There is no difference between men and women with regard to punishment, except with regard to a pledged maid-servant."
17. And the court is unable to differentiate the person who was sentenced to be executed in a less severe manner from one liable to be executed in a more severe manner.
18. It is improper to give the person a more severe punishment than that for which he is liable. Hence, since there is the possibility that each person is liable only for the lesser punishment, that is the punishment which is given to him (Rashi, *Sanhedrin* 79b).
19. For the latter instance. The rationale for the first instance is obvious. Since the other people did not commit a sin punishable by death, there is no reason why they should be executed. Hence even the convicted person is released (*Kessef Mishneh*).
20. Since the person cannot be identified, it is as if he is not present (Rashi, *Sanhedrin* 79b).

If a murderer who has not been sentenced becomes mixed together with other murderers, none are executed. They are not released, however. Instead, they are imprisoned for life (*Hilchot Rotzeach* 4:7).
21. Any person sentenced to death, not only a murderer.

ה וְאֶחָד הָאִישׁ וְאֶחָד הָאִשָּׁה דָּנִין אוֹתָן בְּאַרְבַּע מִיתוֹת.

ו כָּל חַיָּבֵי מִיתוֹת שֶׁנִּתְעָרְבוּ זֶה בָּזֶה – נִדּוֹן כָּל אֶחָד מֵהֶן בַּקַּלָּה שֶׁבָּהֶן.

ז מִי שֶׁנִּגְמַר דִּינוֹ שֶׁנִּתְעָרֵב עִם שְׁאָר הָעָם וְלֹא נוֹדַע מִי הוּא מֵאֵלּוּ,
אוֹ מִי שֶׁלֹּא נִגְמַר דִּינוֹ שֶׁנִּתְעָרֵב עִם מִי שֶׁנִּגְמַר דִּינוֹ וְלֹא נוֹדַע מִי הוּא – כֻּלָּן פְּטוּרִין.
לְפִי שֶׁאֵין גּוֹמְרִין דִּינוֹ שֶׁל אָדָם אֶלָּא בְּפָנָיו.

ח מִי שֶׁעָמַד עַל נַפְשׁוֹ וְלֹא יָכְלוּ בֵּית דִּין לְאָסְרוֹ עַד שֶׁיְּמִיתוּהוּ בַּמִּיתָה שֶׁהוּא חַיָּב בָּהּ –
הוֹרְגִין אוֹתוֹ עֵדָיו בְּכָל מִיתָה שֶׁיְּכוֹלִין לַהֲמִיתוֹ בָּהּ, מֵאַחַר שֶׁנִּגְמַר דִּינוֹ.
וְאֵין רְשׁוּת לִשְׁאָר הָעָם לַהֲמִיתוֹ תְּחִלָּה. לְפִיכָךְ, אִם נִקְטְעָה יַד הָעֵדִים – פָּטוּר.
וְאִם הָיוּ הָעֵדִים גִּדְמִין מִתְּחִלָּה – יֵהָרֵג בְּיַד אֲחֵרִים.
בַּמֶּה דְּבָרִים אֲמוּרִים? בִּשְׁאָר מְחֻיְּבֵי מִיתוֹת בֵּית דִּין חוּץ מִן הָרוֹצֵחַ; אֲבָל הוֹרֵג נֶפֶשׁ
שֶׁנִּגְמַר דִּינוֹ – רוֹדְפִין אַחֲרָיו בְּכָל דָּבָר וּבְיַד כָּל אָדָם עַד שֶׁמְּמִיתִין אוֹתוֹ.

ט כָּל הֲרוּגֵי בֵּית דִּין – אֵין קוֹבְרִין אוֹתָן בְּקִבְרֵי אֲבוֹתֵיהֶם בִּכְלַל יִשְׂרָאֵל,
אֶלָּא שְׁנֵי קְבָרוֹת מְתַקְּנִין לָהֶן בֵּית דִּין: אֶחָד לַנִּסְקָלִין וְלַנִּשְׂרָפִין, וְאֶחָד לַנֶּהֱרָגִין
וְלַנֶּחֱנָקִין. וְדָבָר זֶה הֲלָכָה מִפִּי הַשְּׁמוּעָה.

22. As Deuteronomy 17:7 states: "The hand of the witness shall be raised against him first..., and the hand of the entire nation afterwards." Until the hand of the witnesses are raised against the convicted person, the people at large may not execute him (*Sanhedrin* 45b).
23. After they testified.
24. For the charge to execute the convicted cannot be fulfilled as prescribed by the Torah.
25. Since the witnesses did not have hands before they testified, the execution is performed by others. For no where did the Torah disqualify people without hands from testifying (Rashi, *Sanhedrin, loc. cit.*).

The *Kessef Mishneh* questions why the Rambam mentions the laws in this clause in connection with the convicted person fighting for his life. Seemingly, they apply in all situations, whether or not he fights for his life.
26. That a person should be executed by the witnesses and not by others.
27. *Sanhedrin, loc. cit.*, derives this concept through the techniques of Biblical exegesis. The Radbaz emphasizes that the exegesis is supported by logic: a murderer is a threat to society, for he may kill others. See *Hilchot Rotzeach* 1:4.
28. As a rationale, *Sanhedrin* 47a states: It is improper to bury a wicked person next to a righteous man.
29. The sins of those in first category are considered far more severe than the sins of those in the second category, to the extent that it would be inappropriate to bury the one next to the other (*ibid.*).
30. I.e., the Oral Tradition teaches that there are two plots and not four - one for each category (*ibid.*).

When the flesh [of the corpse] decomposes, they would gather the bones and rebury them in their ancestral plots.[31] The relatives may make a coffin and shrouds [in which to rebury the bones].[32]

10. The court must be very patient with regard to laws involving capital punishment and ponder the matter without being hasty. Whenever a court executes a person once in seven years, it is considered a savage court. Nevertheless, if it happens that they must execute a person every day, they do.[33] They do not, however, judge two [cases involving capital punishment] on the same day.[34] Instead, one is judged immediately, and the other on the following day.

If, however, the two people committed the same sin and are punished with the same form of execution, e.g., a man and a woman who committed adultery,[35] we judge both of them on the same day.[36] It follows that if an adulterer had relations with the daughter of a priest, since he is executed by strangulation and she is burnt to death, they are not executed on the same day.[37]

11. Cases involving capital punishment are adjudicated only when the Temple is standing.[38] It is also necessary that the High Court hold its sessions in the Chamber [of Hewn Stone] in the Temple. This is derived from the statements [of Deuteronomy 17:12] with regard to a rebellious elder: "who refuses to heed the priest." According to the Oral Tradition,[39] it was taught: "At a time when there is a priest offering sacrifices on the altar, cases involving capital punishment are adjudicated."[40] This applies provided the court is holding sessions in its place.[41]

12. At the outset, when the Temple was constructed, the Supreme *Sanhedrin* would hold session in the Chamber of Hewn Stone in the Courtyard of the Israelites. The place where [the judges] would sit was not consecrated.[42] For only kings of the House of David were permitted to sit in the Temple Courtyard.

31. The decomposition of the flesh is a sign that the soul has received atonement for its sins.

32. From the Rambam's words, it appears that, at the outset, it is forbidden for the relatives to bury the corpse of the executed person in shrouds and a coffin (Radbaz).

33. For they are obligated to carry out their mission as charged by the Torah. *Sanhedrin* 45b relates that Shimon ben Shetach executed 80 witches in one day. Although that was obviously an exception to the rule as indicated by its lack of conformity to the laws that follow, it nevertheless shows that a court need not restrict itself when the need for execution arises.

34. For it will be difficult to give each one proper thought and consideration in an attempt to find rationales to acquit the defendant (see Rashi, *Sanhedrin* 46a).

35. Rashi (*ibid.*) states that this applies even if two people violated the Sabbath laws. It is questionable whether the Rambam would accept that view (*Or Sameach*).

נִתְאַכֵּל הַבָּשָׂר – הָיוּ מְלַקְּטִין אֶת הָעֲצָמוֹת וְקוֹבְרִין אוֹתָן בְּקִבְרוֹת אֲבוֹתֵיהֶן. וְיֵשׁ לִקְרוֹבֵיהֶן לַעֲשׂוֹת לָהֶן אָרוֹן וְתַכְרִיכִין.

י צְרִיכִין בֵּית דִּין לְהִתְיַשֵּׁב בְּדִינֵי נְפָשׁוֹת וּלְהַמְתִּין, וְלֹא יָאִיצוּ. וְכָל בֵּית דִּין שֶׁהָרְגוּ נֶפֶשׁ בְּשֶׁבַע שָׁנִים – הֲרֵי אֵלּוּ חַבְּלָנִין. אַף עַל פִּי כֵן, אִם אֵרַע לָהֶם לַהֲרֹג בְּכָל יוֹם וָיוֹם – הוֹרְגִין. אֲבָל אֵין דָּנִין לְעוֹלָם שְׁנַיִם בְּיוֹם אֶחָד, אֶלָּא דָנִין זֶה הַיּוֹם וְהַשֵּׁנִי לְמָחָר. הָיוּ שְׁנֵיהֶם בַּעֲבֵרָה אַחַת וּמִיתָה אַחַת, כְּגוֹן נוֹאֵף עִם נוֹאֶפֶת – דָּנִין שְׁנֵיהֶם בְּיוֹם אֶחָד. לְפִיכָךְ, אִם הָיָה הַנּוֹאֵף בּוֹעֵל בַּת כֹּהֵן, הוֹאִיל וְהוּא בְּחֶנֶק וְהִיא בִּשְׂרֵפָה – אֵין הוֹרְגִין שְׁנֵיהֶן בְּיוֹם אֶחָד.

יא אֵין דָּנִין דִּינֵי נְפָשׁוֹת אֶלָּא בִּפְנֵי הַבַּיִת. וְהוּא שֶׁיִּהְיֶה בֵּית דִּין הַגָּדוֹל שָׁם בַּלִּשְׁכָּה שֶׁבַּמִּקְדָּשׁ. שֶׁנֶּאֱמַר בְּזָקֵן מַמְרֵא: לְבִלְתִּי שְׁמֹעַ אֶל הַכֹּהֵן וְגוֹמֵר. וּמִפִּי הַשְּׁמוּעָה לָמְדוּ, שֶׁבִּזְמַן שֶׁיֵּשׁ כֹּהֵן מַקְרִיב עַל גַּבֵּי הַמִּזְבֵּחַ – יֵשׁ דִּינֵי נְפָשׁוֹת. וְהוּא שֶׁיִּהְיֶה בֵּית דִּין הַגָּדוֹל בִּמְקוֹמוֹ.

יב בַּתְּחִלָּה, כְּשֶׁנִּבְנָה בֵּית הַמִּקְדָּשׁ, הָיוּ בֵּית דִּין הַגָּדוֹל יוֹשְׁבִין בְּלִשְׁכַּת הַגָּזִית שֶׁהָיְתָה בְּעֶזְרַת יִשְׂרָאֵל. וְהַמָּקוֹם שֶׁהָיוּ יוֹשְׁבִין בּוֹ – חֹל הָיָה, שֶׁאֵין יְשִׁיבָה בָּעֲזָרָה אֶלָּא לְמַלְכֵי בֵּית דָּוִד.

36. For the rationale used with regard to one will also apply with regard to the other (*ibid.*).
37. Similarly, when one person violated the Sabbath laws and another person served idols, they are not judged together. Although the sins are punished by the same form of execution, they are different and each requires its own process of analysis.
38. *Sanhedrin* 37b emphasizes that even when the court's license to execute no longer applies, God will punish wrongdoers. He has many ways to kill those who are liable.

It must be emphasized that when the court feels it necessary, even in the present age, it may have a person killed without the full judicial process. See Chapter 24, Halachah 4, and *Hilchot Chovel UMazik* 8:10.
39. Curiously, the Rambam quotes a different portion of the verse cited as a proof-text than his source, *Sanhedrin* 52b. The portion cited by the Rambam is, however, more closely related to the concept of execution (Radbaz).
40. I.e., from the laws involving a rebellious elder, our Sages (*ibid.*) establish an association with all other individuals to be executed by capital punishment.
41. For when speaking about the *Sanhedrin*, Deuteronomy 17:8, speaks of "ris[ing] up and ascend[ing] to the place which God your Lord will choose" (*Kessef Mishneh*).
42. From the drawings that accompany the Rambam's Commentary to the Mishnah (the conclusion of *Middot*) and the Rambam's statements there, it appears that he maintains that the entire Chamber of Hewn Stone was situated inside the Temple Courtyard. Nevertheless, since it had an entrance leading outside the Temple Courtyard, that portion

When the moral character of the Jewish people declined, [the *Sanhedrin*] went into exile.[43] They traveled to ten different places in exile, the last being Tiberias. Afterwards, until the present age, the Supreme *Sanhedrin* has never been convened. And it is an accepted tradition, that in the future, the *Sanhedrin* will first convene in Tiberias,[44] and from there, they will proceed to the Temple.

13. 40 years before the destruction of the Temple, capital punishment was abolished among the Jewish people. Although the Temple was still standing, since the *Sanhedrin* went into exile and were not in their place in the Temple, [these laws could not be enforced].

14. In the era when cases involving capital punishment were adjudicated in *Eretz Yisrael*, such cases could also be adjudicated in the Diaspora, provided the members of that court received *semichah* in *Eretz Yisrael*. As we have already stated,[45] the *Sanhedrin* exercises judicial authority in *Eretz [Yisrael]* and in the Diaspora.

CHAPTER FIFTEEN

1. How is the mitzvah of stoning carried out? Four cubits from the place of execution, we remove the clothes of the person to be stoned;[1] we do, however, cover his sexual organ in front.[2] A woman is not executed naked.[3] Instead, she is allowed to wear one cloak.

The place of execution was two storeys high.[4] [The convicted person]

was not consecrated, as stated in *Hilchot Beit HaBechirah* 6:7. This is also indicated by his statements in Chapter 1, Halachah 3, above, that the Supreme *Sanhedrin* would hold sessions in the Temple. See also *Hilchot Beit HaBechirah* 5:17. There are other commentaries who explain that the major portion of this chamber protruded outside the walls of the Temple Courtyard.

The Position of the Chamber of Hewn Stone

A - The Chamber of the Wood
B - The Chamber of Hewn Stone
C - The Courtyard of the Israelites
D - The Wall Surrounding the Temple Courtyard

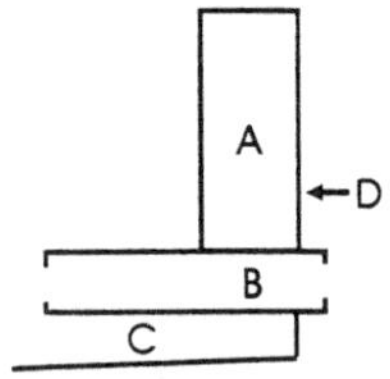

43. Voluntarily. There was a proliferation of murderers among the Jewish people and the Sages were not able to bring them to judgment. They decided that they would move the High Court from the Chamber of Hewn Stone. In this manner, the responsibility would no longer rest upon them, for it would not be possible to carry out executions (*Avodah Zarah* 8a).

44. *Rosh HaShanah* 31a derives this from Isaiah 52:2: "Shake yourself off from the dust; arise," i.e., arise from the very dust in which you fell."

The Radbaz (here and in his commentary to Chapter 4, Halachah 11) writes that our

וּכְשֶׁנִּתְקַלְקְלָה הַשּׁוּרָה, גָּלוּ מִמָּקוֹם לְמָקוֹם. וְלַעֲשָׂרָה מְקוֹמוֹת גָּלוּ, וְסוֹפָן לְטְבֶרְיָא, וּמִשָּׁם לֹא עָמַד בֵּית דִּין גָּדוֹל עַד עַתָּה. וְקַבָּלָה הִיא, שֶׁבִּטְבֶרְיָא עֲתִידִין לַחֲזֹר תְּחִלָּה, וּמִשָּׁם נֶעְתָּקִין לַמִּקְדָּשׁ.

יג אַרְבָּעִים שָׁנָה קֹדֶם חֻרְבַּן בַּיִת שֵׁנִי בָּטְלוּ דִּינֵי נְפָשׁוֹת מִיִּשְׂרָאֵל, אַף עַל פִּי שֶׁהָיָה הַמִּקְדָּשׁ קַיָּם; מִפְּנֵי שֶׁגָּלוּ הַסַּנְהֶדְרִין, וְלֹא הָיוּ שָׁם בִּמְקוֹמָן בַּמִּקְדָּשׁ.

יד בִּזְמַן שֶׁדָּנִין דִּינֵי נְפָשׁוֹת בְּאֶרֶץ יִשְׂרָאֵל – דָּנִין דִּינֵי נְפָשׁוֹת בְּחוּצָה לָאָרֶץ. וְהוּא שֶׁיִּהְיוּ הַסַּנְהֶדְרִין סְמוּכִין בָּאָרֶץ, כְּמוֹ שֶׁבֵּאַרְנוּ. שֶׁהַסַּנְהֶדְרִין נוֹהֶגֶת בָּאָרֶץ וּבְחוּצָה לָאָרֶץ.

פֶּרֶק חֲמִשָּׁה עָשָׂר

א כֵּיצַד מִצְוַת הַנִּסְקָלִין? רָחוֹק מִבֵּית הַסְּקִילָה אַרְבַּע אַמּוֹת מַפְשִׁיטִין אֶת הַמְחֻיָּב סְקִילָה בְּגָדָיו, וּמְכַסִּין עֶרְוָתוֹ מִלְּפָנָיו. וְאֵין הָאִשָּׁה נִסְקֶלֶת עֲרֻמָּה, אֶלָּא בְּחָלוּק אֶחָד. וּבֵית הַסְּקִילָה גָּבוֹהַּ שְׁתֵּי קוֹמוֹת.

Sages prophesied that Mashiach will be revealed in the Galillee. He will then be hidden for a time and then appear in Jerusalem. Perhaps, he continues, before he will become hidden, the prophet Elijah who will accompany him will grant *semichah* to 70 eleders and they will reconvene the *Sanhedrin* in Tiberias.

The later Rabbis have noted that the Rambam is buried in Tiberias (and that came about by unique providence). Referring to the *Midrash* that states that the righteous will be resurrected at the very beginning of the Messianic Redemption, they make an association. The Rambam will be among the first to be resurrected and he will take his place in the *Sanhedrin* to be convened in Tiberias.

45. Chapter 4, Halachah 12. The *Kessef Mishneh* states that this halachah was included only to teach that during the 40 years that the *Sanhedrin* was exiled, the courts in the diaspora could not employ capital punishment despite the fact that the Temple was standing.

1. As *Sanhedrin* 44b relates, this is a kindness for the person being stoned. In this way, his clothes will not cushion his fall and/or the impact of the stone against him. Thus he will die quickly and not suffer over an extended period of time.

2. For the embarrassment of being executed while naked will be more aggravating than the physical pain he might suffer. We consider the feelings of the person being executed, as *Sanhedrin* 45a explains, the command (Leviticus 19:19): "Love your fellow-man as yourself," applies even to a person being executed. We must choose for him the best possible manner of execution.

3. Women are more sensitive to being seen unclothed than men, and she would be shamed and embarrassed greatly.

4. Our Sages calculated that a fall from such a height would kill a person quickly, but

ascends there with his hands tied,[5] together with his witnesses.[6] One of the witnesses pushes him at his loins from behind, he falls over, landing on his heart on the ground.[7] If he dies because of this, they have fulfilled their obligation,[8] for [Exodus 19:13] states: "Or he will be cast down or stoned," creating an equation between a person who has a stone fall upon him with one who himself falls on the earth.

If he does not die after this fall, the witnesses pick up a stone that is so large it requires two people to carry it. The second witness lets go[9] and [the first] casts the stone on [the convicted person's] heart.[10] If he dies because of this, they have fulfilled their obligation. If not, he should be stoned by the entire Jewish people, as [Deuteronomy 17:7] states: "The hand of the witnesses shall be raised up against him first to execute him, and the hand of the entire nation afterwards."

2. An idolater should be stoned at the gateway to the place where he performed the transgression. If the majority of the population of a city are gentiles, he should be stoned at the entrance to the court.[11] This concept has been conveyed by the Oral Tradition. The term "to your gates" [where Deuteronomy 17:8 states that an idolater should be executed] refers to the gate where he performed the transgression and not the gate where he was sentenced.[12]

3. The mitzvah [of executing a person] by burning [is performed as follows]:[13] [The convicted] is placed in fertilizer until his knees.[14] A firm cloth is placed within a soft cloth[15] and they are wound around his neck. The two witnesses [are positioned on either side] and each pull [the cloths] toward himself until [the convicted] opens his mouth.[16] Tin, lead, and the like are melted down and then poured into his mouth.[17] The [molten metal] descends and burns his innards.

4. The mitzvah of decapitation [is performed as follows]: We cut of his head with a sword as the kings do.[18]

5. The mitzvah [of executing a person] by strangulation [is performed as follows]: [The convicted] is placed in fertilizer until his knees. A firm cloth is placed within a soft cloth and they are wound around his neck. Each [of the two witnesses] pulls [the cloths] toward himself[19] until [the convicted] expires.

would not cause his corpse to rupture. Thus within the context of the punishment decreed for him, it is the best manner of execution possible.

5. Lest he attack the witnesses.

6. For as stated in Chapter 13, Halachah 7, and Chapter 14, Halachah 8, it is the witnesses whose responsibility it is to execute him.

7. For lying on his back is more embarrassing (Rashi, *Sanhedrin* 45a).

8. Even though he was not stoned at all, the witnesses fulfill their obligation.

9. Because it will be impossible for either person to cast the stone with his full strength if the other is holding on (Rashi, *Sanhedrin* 45b).

10. Therefore he must be turned over on his back so that the stone will fall on his heart (*Kessef Mishneh*).

עוֹלֶה לְשָׁם הוּא וְעֵדָיו, וְיָדָיו אֲסוּרוֹת. וְאֶחָד מִן הָעֵדִים דּוֹחֲפוֹ עַל מָתְנָיו מֵאֲחוֹרָיו, וְהוּא נֶהְפָּךְ וְנוֹפֵל עַל לִבּוֹ לָאָרֶץ. אִם מֵת בָּהּ – יָצָא. שֶׁהֲרֵי נֶאֱמַר: סָקוֹל יִסָּקֵל אוֹ יָרֹה יִיָּרֶה. הִנֵּה הִשְׁוָה הַנִּסְקָל שֶׁנָּפַל אֶת הָאֶבֶן עָלָיו עִם הַנִּדְחָף שֶׁנָּפַל הוּא בְּעַצְמוֹ עַל הָאָרֶץ. וְאִם לֹא מֵת מִדְּחִיפָה זוֹ – מַגְבִּיהִין הָעֵדִים אֶבֶן שֶׁהָיְתָה מֻנַּחַת שָׁם, מַשָּׂא שְׁנֵי בְּנֵי אָדָם, וְהָעֵד הַשֵּׁנִי מַרְפֶּה אֶת יָדוֹ וּמַשְׁלִיךְ הָאֶבֶן עַל לִבּוֹ. אִם מֵת בּוֹ – יָצָא, וְאִם לָאו – רְגִימָתוֹ בְּכָל יִשְׂרָאֵל. שֶׁנֶּאֱמַר: יַד הָעֵדִים תִּהְיֶה בּוֹ בָרִאשֹׁנָה לַהֲמִיתוֹ, וְיַד כָּל הָעָם בָּאַחֲרֹנָה.

ב עוֹבֵד עֲבוֹדָה זָרָה – אֵין סוֹקְלִין אוֹתוֹ אֶלָּא עַל שַׁעַר שֶׁעָבַד בּוֹ. וְאִם הָיְתָה עִיר שֶׁרֻבָּהּ עוֹבְדֵי כּוֹכָבִים – סוֹקְלִין אוֹתוֹ עַל פֶּתַח בֵּית דִּין. וְדָבָר זֶה קַבָּלָה מִפִּי הַשְּׁמוּעָה: אֶל שְׁעָרֶיךָ – זֶה שַׁעַר שֶׁעָבַד בּוֹ, וְלֹא שֶׁנִּגְמַר דִּינוֹ בּוֹ.

ג מִצְוַת הַנִּשְׂרָפִין: הָיוּ מְשַׁקְּעִין אוֹתוֹ בְּזֶבֶל עַד אַרְכֻּבּוֹתָיו, וְנוֹתְנִים סוּדָר קָשֶׁה לְתוֹךְ הָרַךְ וְכוֹרְכִין עַל צַוָּארוֹ. וּשְׁנֵי עֵדָיו – זֶה מוֹשֵׁךְ אֶצְלוֹ, וְזֶה מוֹשֵׁךְ אֶצְלוֹ, עַד שֶׁהוּא פּוֹתֵחַ אֶת פִּיו. וּמַתִּיכִים אֶת הַבְּדִיל וְאֶת הָעוֹפֶרֶת וְכַיּוֹצֵא בָּהֶן, וְהוּא זוֹרֵק לְתוֹךְ פִּיו, וְהִיא יוֹרֶדֶת וְשׂוֹרֶפֶת אֶת בְּנֵי מֵעָיו.

ד מִצְוַת הַנֶּהֱרָגִין: מַתִּיזִין אֶת רֹאשׁוֹ בְּסַיִף, כְּדֶרֶךְ שֶׁהַמְּלָכִים עוֹשִׂים.

ה מִצְוַת הַנֶּחֱנָקִין: מְשַׁקְּעִין אֶת הַמְחֻיָּב בְּזֶבֶל עַד אַרְכֻּבּוֹתָיו, וְנוֹתְנִין סוּדָר קָשֶׁה לְתוֹךְ הָרַךְ וְכוֹרְכִין עַל צַוָּארוֹ. זֶה מוֹשֵׁךְ אֶצְלוֹ, וְזֶה מוֹשֵׁךְ אֶצְלוֹ, עַד שֶׁתֵּצֵא נַפְשׁוֹ.

11. Lest the fact that the Jews execute a person at the gate to their city arouse their ire. As stated in Chapter 12, Halachah 3, the intent is not the gateway of the court itself, but a place somewhat removed from it.
12. Even if he was judged in another city, he is returned to the city where he performed the transgression to be executed.
13. I.e., he is not burnt at the stake. *Sanhedrin* 52a derives this concept by the Torah's description (Leviticus 10:6) of Aaron's sons as being burnt although the fire entered their body and did not harm their flesh at all.
14. To prevent him from squirming when the lead is being poured down his throat. This is undesirable, because perhaps the lead will spill and burn his body, causing him unnecessary pain.
15. A soft cloth would not strangle the person effectively and a firm cloth would harm his neck. Hence the firm cloth is put inside the soft cloth so that the execution will be performed with the least pain possible.
16. While gasping for breath.
17. *Shoshanim LiDavid* states that one of the witnesses pours the molten metal down his throat. That is, however, slightly difficult, because the witnesses are holding on to the cloth that strangles the convicted. Perhaps after his throat is opened another person takes the witness' place and he pours the molten liquid.
18. When executing those who rebel against them (see *Hilchot Melachim* 2:8).
19. With regard to this entire halachah, see the notes to Halachah 3.

6. It is a positive commandment to hang a blasphemer and an idolater[20] [after they have been executed],[21] as [implied by Deuteronomy 21:23]: "A person who is hung is cursing God." This refers to the blasphemer. With regard to an idolater, [Numbers 15:30] states: "He blasphemes God."[22]

A man is hung, but a woman is not hung,[23] [as implied by Deuteronomy 21:22]: "When a man[24] has sinned and is condemned to die, [after] he is executed, you shall hang him...."

7. How is the mitzvah of hanging carried out? After [the convicted] is stoned, a beam is implanted in the ground with a rafter protruding from it. The two hands of [the corpse] are intercrossed and he is hung[25] close to sunset.

He is released immediately. If not, a negative commandment is transgressed, as [*ibid.*:23] states: "Do not let his corpse tarry overnight on the beam."[26]

8. It is a positive mitzvah[27] to bury the persons executed by the court on the day of their execution, as [*ibid.*] states: "For you shall surely bury him on that day."

Not only those executed by the court, but anyone who leaves a deceased overnight without burying him transgresses a negative commandment.[28] If, however, a burial is delayed overnight to honor [the deceased], [e.g.,] to bring a coffin or shrouds,[29] there is no transgression.

9. We do not hang a person on a tree that is [still] growing from the ground, only from one which has been detached. In this way, [the tree] will not have to be chopped down [before the person's burial]. For the tree on which [the executed] is hung is buried with him,[30] so that it will not be an unfavorable remembrance, [causing people] to say: "This is the tree on which so-and-so was hung."

Similarly, the stone, the sword, and the cloths used for execution are all buried near the deceased,[31] but not in his actual grave.

20. *Sefer HaMitzvot* (positive commandment 230) and *Sefer HaChinuch* (mitzvah 535) count this as one of the 613 mitzvot of the Torah.
21. I.e., their corpses are hung as sign of degradation.
22. And therefore he is worthy of the same punishment given a blasphemer.
23. Even if she violates the above commandments.
24. I.e., a man and not a woman (*Sanhedrin* 46a).
25. By his hands, and not by his neck as the gentile kings do (Radbaz).
26. *Sefer HaMitzvot* (negative commandment 66) and *Sefer HaChinuch* (mitzvah 536) count this as one of the 613 mitzvot of the Torah. The Torah explains the rationale for this prohibition with verse cited above: "A person who is hung is cursing God." For since every man is created in God's image, leaving a corpse hanging is a disgrace not only to the corpse itself, but to the One in whose image the corpse was made.

ו מִצְוַת עֲשֵׂה לִתְלוֹת אֶת הַמְגַדֵּף וְעוֹבֵד עֲבוֹדַת כּוֹכָבִים. שֶׁנֶּאֱמַר: כִּי קִלְלַת אֱלֹהִים תָּלוּי – הֲרֵי מְגַדֵּף אָמוּר. וּבְעוֹבֵד עֲבוֹדַת כּוֹכָבִים נֶאֱמַר: אֶת יְיָ הוּא מְגַדֵּף. וְהָאִישׁ נִתְלֶה, וְאֵין הָאִשָּׁה נִתְלֵית. שֶׁנֶּאֱמַר: כִּי יִהְיֶה בְאִישׁ חֵטְא מִשְׁפַּט מָוֶת וְהוּמָת וְתָלִיתָ אֹתוֹ.

ז כֵּיצַד מִצְוַת הַנִּתְלִין? אַחַר שֶׁסּוֹקְלִין אוֹתָן מְשַׁקְּעִין אֶת הַקּוֹרָה בָּאָרֶץ, וְעֵץ יוֹצֵא מִמֶּנָּה, וּמַקִּיפִין שְׁתֵּי יָדָיו זוֹ לָזוֹ, וְתוֹלֵהוּ סָמוּךְ לִשְׁקִיעַת הַחַמָּה, וּמַתִּירִין אוֹתוֹ מִיָּד. וְאִם לָן – עוֹבְרִין עָלָיו בְּלֹא תַעֲשֶׂה, שֶׁנֶּאֱמַר: לֹא תָלִין נִבְלָתוֹ עַל הָעֵץ.

ח וּמִצְוַת עֲשֵׂה לִקְבֹּר אֶת כָּל הֲרוּגֵי בֵּית דִּין בְּיוֹם הַהֲרִיגָה. שֶׁנֶּאֱמַר: כִּי קָבוֹר תִּקְבְּרֶנּוּ בַּיּוֹם הַהוּא.

וְלֹא הֲרוּגֵי בֵּית דִּין בִּלְבַד, אֶלָּא כָּל הַמֵּלִין אֶת מֵתוֹ – עוֹבֵר עָלָיו בְּלֹא תַעֲשֶׂה.

הֱלִינוֹ לִכְבוֹדוֹ לְהָבִיא לוֹ אָרוֹן וְתַכְרִיכִין – אֵינוֹ עוֹבֵר עָלָיו.

ט אֵין תּוֹלִין עַל אִילָן הַמְחֻבָּר לַקַּרְקַע, אֶלָּא עַל הַתָּלוּשׁ, כְּדֵי שֶׁלֹּא יְהֵא מְחֻסַּר קְצִיצָה. שֶׁהָעֵץ שֶׁנִּתְלֶה עָלָיו נִקְבָּר עִמּוֹ, שֶׁלֹּא יְהֵא לוֹ זִכָּרוֹן רַע וְיֹאמְרוּ: זֶה הָעֵץ שֶׁנִּתְלָה עָלָיו פְּלוֹנִי.

וְכֵן הָאֶבֶן שֶׁנִּסְקַל בָּהּ, וְהַסַּיִף שֶׁנֶּהֱרַג בּוֹ הַנֶּהֱרָג, וְהַסּוּדָרִין שֶׁחוֹנְקִין בָּהֶן – הַכֹּל נִקְבָּרִים בִּתְפִיסַת הַנֶּהֱרָג, אֲבָל לֹא בַּקֶּבֶר עַצְמוֹ.

See, however, *Hilchot Melachim* 3:10 which states that a king may hang the persons he executes for a longer period.

27. *Sefer HaMitzvot* (positive commandment 231) and *Sefer HaChinuch* (mitzvah 537) count this as one of the 613 mitzvot of the Torah.

28. I.e., the negative commandment cited in the previous halachah. *Sanhedrin* 46b derives this concept from the repetition of the Hebrew verb in the prooftext cited above. There is a debate among the commentaries if the delay in the burial of persons other than executed criminals is included in the scope of the Biblical command or not (i.e., all agree, that delay is forbidden; the question is whether the prohibition is Scriptural or Rabbinic in origin). Significantly, in *Sefer HaMitzvot, loc. cit.*, when discussing this negative commandment, the Rambam mentions only the mitzvah of burying an executed person. When discussing the positive commandment, by contrast, he also mentions other deceased individuals. See also *Hilchot Evel* 12:1.

29. These contribute to the honor of the deceased. Hence it is preferable to wait until these are prepared before burying him. Similar concepts apply with regard to other factors which will add dignity to his funeral (*Sanhedrin* 46a). See *Hilchot Evel* 4:7-8 for a discussion of this issue.

30. The intent is not in the actual grave of the executed, but in proximity to it (*Sanhedrin* 45b).

31. I.e., within four cubits of the corpse (Rashi, *Sanhedrin, loc. cit.*).

10. The Torah [mentions]18 people who are executed by stoning. They are:[32] a) a person who engages in relations with his mother,[33] b) ...with his father's wife,[34] c) ...his daughter-in-law, d) ...a maiden who was consecrated,[35] e) a man involved in homosexual relations, f) a man who sodomizes an animal, g) a woman who has relations with an animal,[36] h) a blasphemer, i) an idolater, j) a person who gives his descendants to *Molech*, k) a person who divines with an *ov*, l) a person who divines with an *yidoni*, m) a person who entices others to worship idols, n) the people who lead a city to idol worship, o) a sorcerer,[37] p) a person who desecrates the Sabbath,[38] q) a person who curses his father or his mother, and r) a wayward and rebellious son.[39]

11. There are 10 people who are executed by burning: a) a priest's daughter[40] who commits adultery, b) a person who has relations with his daughter,[41] c) ...with his daughter's daughter, d) ...with his son's daughter, e) ...with his wife's daughter,[42] f) ...with the daughter of his wife's daughter, g) ...with the daughter of his wife's son, h) ...with his mother-in-law, i) ...with the mother of his mother-in-law, and j) ...with the mother of his father-in-law.[43]

The latter prohibitions apply if [the man] has relations with them during his wife's lifetime. After his wife's death, these relations are punishable by *kerait*[44] alone like other incestuous relationships.

12. There are two who are decapitated: a murderer, and the inhabitants of a city enticed to idolatry.[45]

13. There are six who are executed by strangulation: a) an adulterer,[46] b) a person who wounds his father or mother,[47] c) a person who kidnaps a fellow Jew,[48] d) a rebellious elder,[49] e) a false prophet, and f) a person who prophesies in the name of a false deity.[50]

Thus the court executes individuals for a totality of 36 prohibitions.

32. The *Tosafot Yom Tov* (*Sanhedrin* 7:4) notes that the Rambam does not mention the prohibitions in the same order as the Mishnah which is his source.
33. Even if she was never married to his father, i.e., he was born out of wedlock.
34. Even if she is not his mother.
35. But not married. I.e., Jewish marriage is a two stage process including consecration, where a woman is designated as a man's wife and forbidden to other men, and marriage, when the couple begins living together. This punishment is given to a man who has relations with a woman after she was consecrated, but before she was married.
36. All the above prohibitions are detailed in *Hilchot Issurei Bi'ah.*
37. All the above prohibitions are detailed in *Hilchot Avodat Kochavim.*
38. By performing a forbidden labor.
39. The latter two prohibitions are described in *Hilchot Mamrim.*
40. In contrast to others who commit adultery, she receives this punishment, because she "desecrates her father" (Leviticus 21:9). Even the man with whom she commits adultery does not receive this punishment.

י כָּל הַנִּסְקָלִין שֶׁבַּתּוֹרָה שְׁמוֹנָה עָשָׂר, וְאֵלּוּ הֵן:

הַבָּא עַל הָאֵם,
וְעַל אֵשֶׁת אָב,
וְעַל כַּלָּתוֹ,
וְעַל נַעֲרָה הַמְאֹרָסָה,
וְעַל הַזְּכוּר.
וְהַשּׁוֹכֵב עִם בְּהֵמָה.
וְהָאִשָּׁה הַמְּבִיאָה אֶת הַבְּהֵמָה עָלֶיהָ.
וְהַמְגַדֵּף.
וְעוֹבֵד עֲבוֹדַת כּוֹכָבִים.
וְהַנּוֹתֵן מִזַּרְעוֹ לַמֹּלֶךְ.
וּבַעַל אוֹב.
וּבַעַל יִדְּעוֹנִי.
וְהַמֵּסִית.
וְהַמַּדִּיחַ.
וְהַמְכַשֵּׁף.
וְהַמְחַלֵּל אֶת הַשַּׁבָּת.
וּמְקַלֵּל אָבִיו אוֹ אִמּוֹ.
וּבֵן סוֹרֵר וּמוֹרֶה.

יא כָּל הַנִּשְׂרָפִין עֲשָׂרָה, וְאֵלּוּ הֵן:

בַּת כֹּהֵן שֶׁזָּנְתָה תַּחַת בַּעְלָהּ.
וּבָא עַל בִּתּוֹ,
וְעַל בַּת בִּתּוֹ,
וְעַל בַּת בְּנוֹ.
וְעַל בַּת אִשְׁתּוֹ,
וְעַל בַּת בִּתָּהּ,
וְעַל בַּת בְּנָהּ.
וְעַל חֲמוֹתוֹ,
וְעַל אֵם חֲמוֹתוֹ,
וְעַל אֵם חָמִיו.

וְהוּא שֶׁבָּא עֲלֵיהֶן בְּחַיֵּי אִשְׁתּוֹ; אֲבָל לְאַחַר מִיתַת אִשְׁתּוֹ – הֲרֵי הֵן בְּכָרֵת בִּלְבַד, בִּכְלַל הָעֲרָיוֹת.

יב הַנֶּהֱרָגִין שְׁנַיִם: הָרוֹצֵחַ וְהַנִּדָּח.

יג הַנֶּחֱנָקִין שִׁשָּׁה, וְאֵלּוּ הֵן: הַבָּא עַל אֵשֶׁת אִישׁ. הַחוֹבֵל בְּאָבִיו אוֹ בְּאִמּוֹ. וְגוֹנֵב נֶפֶשׁ מִיִּשְׂרָאֵל. וְזָקֵן מַמְרֵא. וּנְבִיא הַשֶּׁקֶר. וְהַמִּתְנַבֵּא בְּשֵׁם עֲבוֹדָה זָרָה. נִמְצְאוּ כָּל הֲרוּגֵי בֵּית דִּין שִׁשָּׁה וּשְׁלֹשִׁים.

41. Even if she was born out of wedlock.
42. Even if she is not his daughter.
43. All of these prohibitions are detailed in *Hilchot Issurei Bi'ah*.
44. Premature death at the hand of heaven alone. There are many authorities who maintain that such relations are not even punishable by *kerait*. See the commentaries to *Hilchot Issurei Bi'ah* 2:7.
45. These prohibitions are described in *Hilchot Rotzeach* and *Hilchot Avodat Kochavim*, ch. 4, respectively.
46. See *Hilchot Issurei Bi'ah*, ch. 1.
47. See *Hilchot Mamrim*, ch. 5.
48. See *Hilchot Genevah*, ch. 9.
49. See *Hilchot Mamrim*, ch. 3.
50. The latter two prohibitions are discussed in *Hilchot Avodat Kochavim*, ch. 5.

CHAPTER SIXTEEN

1. Just as it is a mitzvah to execute a person who is obligated to be executed; so, too, it is a positive commandment[1] to give lashes to a person who is obligated to receive lashes, as [Deuteronomy 25:2] states: "And the judge should cause him to fall and will have him beaten in his presence." Although [transgressions punishable by] lashes are adjudicated by three judges,[2] [lashes] are equivalent to execution.[3]

2. Lashes are administered in the present age[4] in any place,[5] according to Scriptural Law in the presence of three judges who were given *semichah*.[6] [This punishment] is not, however, [administered] in the presence of three ordinary people.[7]

3. All the lashes that are administered by the judges of the diaspora[8] in every place are "stripes for rebellious conduct."[9]

4. A person is not punished by lashes unless his transgression was observed by witnesses and they administered a warning to him.[10] The witnesses are questioned and cross-examined in the same manner as they are in cases involving capital punishment.[11]

[The following laws apply when a] person transgresses a negative commandment that can be corrected by a positive commandment.[12] [Before the transgressor violates the negative commandment, witnesses must] administer a warning, telling him: "Do not perform this activity. If you perform it and do not fulfill the positive commandment associated with it, you will receive lashes." [If, after receiving such a warning, the transgressor] violates the commandment and does not fulfill the positive commandment, he receives lashes. Although the warning involved uncertainty,[13] - for if he fulfills the positive commandment, he will be released [unpunished] - an uncertain warning is considered as a warning.[14]

1. *Sefer HaMitzvot* (positive commandment 224) and *Sefer HaChinuch* (mitzvah 594) consider this as one of the 613 mitzvot of the Torah.
2. See Chapter 5, Halachah 4.
3. I.e., the judges must have *semichah*. The witnesses must have given a warning to the transgressor before he violated the commandment, and the witnesses are thoroughly questioned and cross-examined (*Kessef Mishneh*). Note the explanation in Halachah 4.
4. I.e., the matter is not dependent on whether or not the Temple is standing, or whether or not the High Court holds session in the Chamber of Hewn Stone.

This concept is not accepted by all authorities. The *Sefer Mitzvot Gadol* and the *Sefer Yirayim* differ and maintain that lashes are administered only during the time the High Court holds session.
5. I.e., not only in *Eretz Yisrael*.
6. For the prooftext cited in the previous verse speaks of "the judge," i.e., a judge who has been granted *semichah*. See also the Introduction to the Rambam's Commentary to the Mishnah which explains the order of the tractates of the Talmud and states that *Sanhedrin*

פֶּרֶק שִׁשָּׁה עָשָׂר

א כְּשֵׁם שֶׁמִּצְוָה לְהָמִית אֶת הַמְחֻיָּב מִיתָה, כָּךְ מִצְוַת עֲשֵׂה לְהַלְקוֹת אֶת הַמְחֻיָּב מַלְקוּת. שֶׁנֶּאֱמַר: וְהִפִּילוֹ הַשֹּׁפֵט וְהִכָּהוּ לְפָנָיו. וְאַף עַל פִּי שֶׁמַּלְקוּת בִּשְׁלֹשָׁה – בִּמְקוֹם מִיתָה הִיא עוֹמֶדֶת.

ב מַלְקִין בִּזְמַן הַזֶּה בְּכָל מָקוֹם מִן הַתּוֹרָה בִּפְנֵי שְׁלֹשָׁה סְמוּכִין, אֲבָל לֹא בִּפְנֵי הֶדְיוֹטוֹת.

ג וְכָל מַלְקֻיּוֹת שֶׁמַּלְקִין דַּיָּנֵי חוּצָה לָאָרֶץ בְּכָל מָקוֹם, אֵינָהּ אֶלָּא מַכַּת מַרְדּוּת.

ד אֵין אָדָם לוֹקֶה אֶלָּא בְּעֵדִים וְהַתְרָאָה. וּבוֹדְקִין הָעֵדִים בִּדְרִישָׁה וּבַחֲקִירָה, כְּדֶרֶךְ שֶׁעוֹשִׂים בְּדִינֵי נְפָשׁוֹת. עָבַר עַל לָאו שֶׁנִּתַּק לַעֲשֵׂה, וְהִתְרוּ בוֹ וְאָמְרוּ לוֹ: אַל תַּעֲשֶׂה דָבָר זֶה, שֶׁאִם תַּעֲשֶׂנּוּ וְלֹא תְקַיֵּם עֲשֵׂה שֶׁבּוֹ – תִּלְקֶה, וְעָבַר וְלֹא קִיֵּם הָעֲשֵׂה – הֲרֵי זֶה לוֹקֶה. אַף עַל פִּי שֶׁהַתְרָאָה בְּסָפֵק הִיא, שֶׁאִם יְקַיֵּם – יִפָּטֵר, הַתְרָאַת סָפֵק הַתְרָאָה הִיא.

is followed by *Makkot*, "for it is not within the province of any man other than the judges to administer punishment and lashes."

7. I.e., judges who did not receive *semichah*. Thus in the present age, lashes are not administered, because there are no longer any judges who have been granted *semichah*, as explained in Chapter 4.

8. I.e., judges who have not received *semichah*.

9. As reflected by the Rambam's statements in Chapter 24, Halachot 4-9, all judges have the right to administer punishments that are not mandated by the Torah if they think that it is necessary to do so. One of the punishments that was traditionally given by the Rabbis - even during the time when the judges possessed *semichah* was "stripes for rebellious conduct." This punishment is given to individuals who violate a Scriptural commandment without acknowledging a warning, disobey a Rabbinic commandment, fail to fulfill a positive commandment, or perform other undesirable acts. Unlike the lashes administered by Scriptural decree, there are no firm and fast rules governing this Rabbinic punishment.

10. In a manner similar to the warning issued for transgressions punishable by execution. See Chapter 12, Halachah 2.

11. See *Hilchot Edut* 3:2.

12. To cite an example of a negative commandment that can be corrected by a positive commandment: It is forbidden to take a mother bird while she is sitting on her chicks. Instead, one must first drive the mother bird away and then take the chicks. Even if one transgresses and takes the mother bird together with the chicks, it is possible to correct one's transgression by fulfilling the positive commandment and sending the mother bird away. If the transgressor in fact corrects his violation, he is not punished by lashes (Radbaz, *Kessef Mishneh*).

13. I.e., the witnesses administering the warning can never be certain that the violator will receive punishment.

14. The *Kessef Mishneh* notes that in *Hilchot Sh'vuot* 5:2, the Rambam issues an opposite ruling concerning an instance when a warning that is delivered with uncertainty.

5. [The following rules apply when] a person performs a prohibited act that is punishable both by lashes and execution by the court, e.g., he slaughtered an animal and its offspring [on the same day as a sacrifice] to a false divinity.[15] If he was warned that [his act is punishable] by execution, he is stoned to death and is not given lashes, for he is obligated for a more severe judgment.[16] If he was given a warning only for lashes, he receives lashes.[17]

6. There is no need for the two witnesses [who obligate a person for] lashes, [to observe] other than at the time [the transgression] is committed. The prohibition itself, by contrast, can be established on the basis of one witness.

What is implied? One witness said: "This [substance] is fat from the kidneys,[18] "These [grapes] were grown together [with grain] in a vineyard,[19] "This woman is a divorcee or a *zonah*."[20] If a person partook [of this food] or had relations [with these women] after he was warned, he receives lashes, despite the fact that the essence of the prohibition was [established] by one witness.[21]

When does the above apply? When he did not contradict the witness when he established the prohibition. If, however, he said: "This is not fat," "She is not a divorcee," and then he partook [of the food] or had relations [with the woman] after his denial, he does not receive lashes until the prohibition was established through the testimony of two witnesses.[22]

7. If [the person] remained silent when the one witness testifies to establish the prohibition, and after he violated the transgression and was warned, he issued a claim to contradict the witness, his words are not accepted.[23] Instead, he receives lashes.

8. How are lashes administered? [The transgressor's] two hands are bound to a pillar[24] on either side. The community attendant takes hold of his clothes[25] [and pulls downward]. If they tear at the front, that is satisfactory; if the tear at the sides,[26] that is satisfactory. [He continues] until he uncovers his heart. [The

For example, a person takes an oath dependent on the actions of others, in which instance, the witnesses can never give a warning with certainty, because the others may carry out the actions mentioned in the oath. The Rambam explains the distinction between the two cases as follows. In the instance mentioned in this halachah, the prohibition is explicitly mentioned in the Torah. With regard to *Hilchot Sh'vuot*, by contrast, there is no such explicit prohibition. The *Kessef Mishneh* questions the Rambam's source for making such a distinction.

The Radbaz explains the Rambam's position as follows: In other cases, when a warning is delivered with uncertainty, the uncertainty involves whether the transgression will be violated or not. In this instance, the transgression will certainly be violated, the question is whether the person will correct the violation or not.

15. As Leviticus 22:28 states, it is forbidden to sacrifice an animal and its offspring on the same day. That prohibition is punishable by lashes. When, however, the animal(s) are sacrificed to a false divinity, the same act involves a greater transgression. See also *Hilchot Shechitah* 12:7.

ה עָבַר עֲבֵרָה שֶׁיֵּשׁ בָּהּ מַלְקוּת וּמִיתַת בֵּית דִּין כְּאַחַת, כְּגוֹן שֶׁשָּׁחַט אוֹתוֹ וְאֶת בְּנוֹ לַעֲבוֹדָה זָרָה: אִם הִתְרוּ בּוֹ לְמִיתָה - סוֹקְלִין אוֹתוֹ וְאֵינוֹ לוֹקֶה, שֶׁהֲרֵי נִתְחַיֵּב בְּדִין גָּדוֹל מִזֶּה; וְאִם הִתְרוּ בּוֹ לְמַלְקוּת בִּלְבַד - לוֹקֶה.

ו אֵינוֹ צָרִיךְ שְׁנֵי עֵדִים לְמַלְקוּת אֶלָּא בִּשְׁעַת מַעֲשֶׂה; אֲבָל הָאִסּוּר עַצְמוֹ - בְּעֵד אֶחָד יֶחְזַק. כֵּיצַד? אָמַר עֵד אֶחָד: חֵלֶב כְּלָיוֹת הוּא זֶה, כִּלְאֵי הַכֶּרֶם הֵם פֵּרוֹת אֵלּוּ, גְּרוּשָׁה אוֹ זוֹנָה אִשָּׁה זוֹ, וְאָכַל אוֹ בָּעַל בְּעֵדִים אַחַר שֶׁהִתְרוּ בּוֹ - הֲרֵי זֶה לוֹקֶה, אַף עַל פִּי שֶׁעִקַּר הָאִסּוּר בְּעֵד אֶחָד.

בַּמֶּה דְּבָרִים אֲמוּרִים? שֶׁלֹּא הִכְחִישׁ הָעֵד בְּעֵת שֶׁקָּבַע הָאִסּוּר; אֲבָל אִם אָמַר: אֵינוֹ חֵלֶב זֶה, וְזוֹ אֵינָהּ גְּרוּשָׁה, וְאָכַל אוֹ בָּעַל אַחַר שֶׁהִכְחִישׁ - אֵינוֹ לוֹקֶה, עַד שֶׁיִּקְבְּעוּ הָאִסּוּר שְׁנֵי עֵדִים.

ז שָׁתַק בְּעֵת שֶׁהֵעִיד הָעֵד הָאֶחָד בִּקְבִיעוּת הָאִסּוּר, וְאַחַר שֶׁעָבַר וְהִתְרוּ בּוֹ טָעַן לְהַכְחִישׁ הָעֵד - אֵין שׁוֹמְעִין לוֹ, אֶלָּא לוֹקֶה.

ח כֵּיצַד מַלְקִין אוֹתוֹ? כּוֹפֵת שְׁתֵּי יָדָיו עַל הָעַמּוּד אֵילָךְ וְאֵילָךְ, וְחַזַּן הַכְּנֶסֶת אוֹחֵז בִּבְגָדָיו. אִם נִקְרְעוּ - נִקְרְעוּ, וְאִם נִפְרְמוּ - נִפְרְמוּ. עַד שֶׁהוּא מְגַלֶּה אֶת לִבּוֹ.

16. *Makkot* 13b interprets Deuteronomy 25:2 as teaching that a person is responsible for only one type of punishment for every transgression he performs.
17. Since he was not given a warning for execution, that punishment cannot be administered. Hence, it is as if he performed an act that was punishable only by lashes.
18. Which is forbidden by Leviticus 3:17 in contrast to other types of fat that may be eaten.
19. In which they are forbidden, as stated in Deuteronomy 22:9.
20. The term *zonah* refers to a woman who engaged in relations with a person prohibited to her. A priest is forbidden to engage in relations with such a woman, as stated by Leviticus 21:7.
21 . For as *Gittin* 2b states, the word of one witness is accepted with regard to prohibitions. See also *Hilchot Shegagot* 3:2.
22. Whenever there is a contradiction, the testimony of two witnesses is necessary to establish a prohibition.
23. After his transgression, his denial of the prohibition is of no consequence. If, however, he remains silent originally, but afterwards protests before he transgresses, the protest is of consequence (*Kessef Mishneh*).
24. The pillar was two cubits (a little more than a yard) high. Thus the transgressor is required to bend over when receiving the lashes as stated in Halachah 10. See *Makkot* 22b.
25. At the collar.
26. Our translation is based on the Rambam's Commentary to the Mishnah (*Sotah* 1:5). Others translate *nifrimu* as "bursts at the seams."

rationale is that] he should not administer lashes on his garment, [as indicated by Deuteronomy 25:2]: "And he shall strike him," [i.e., "him,"] and not his garment.

A stone is placed behind him. The attendant who administers the lashes stands on it. He holds a strap of calf's leather[27] that is folded into two, and a second one, making four, and two straps of donkey leather[28] [attached to it] that rise and descend with it.

The strap is a handbreadth wide and it is long enough to reach the transgressor's belly. The handle of the strap is a handbreadth wide.

9. The man administering the lashes should be heavily endowed with knowledge and minimally endowed with physical power.[29] He should lift up the strap with both his hands and strike [him] with one hand, with all his power.

He should strike him with a third of the lashes on his front, i.e., on his breast, between his nipples, and two thirds of the lashes on his back,[30] one third on one shoulder and the other third on the other shoulder.

10. The person receiving the lashes should not stand, nor should he sit. Instead, he should bend over [as Deuteronomy 25:2] states: "The judge shall cast him down."

[The verse continues:] "And he shall strike him before him." [This implies that] the attention of the judge should be focused upon him.[31] He should not look at other matters [while] having him lashed. From this, we learn that two people are never lashed at the same time.[32]

11. Throughout the time the person is being lashed, the judge of the highest stature reads[33] the passage [Deuteronomy 28:58ff]: "If you are not careful to heed and to perform... in an extraordinary way, God [will increase] the blows [against] you and your offspring...." He should have the intent to complete the passage[34] with the lashes. If the lashes are not completed,[35] he should return to the beginning of the passage and read it again - and again [if necessary] until all the lashes are administered.

The judge of intermediate stature counts [the lashes] and the third judge tells the attendant [before each blow]: "Strike him." Throughout the entire time he administers the lashes, he does so following [the judge's] instruction.

27. *Makkot* 23a derives this concept from the fact that directly after mentioning the obligation to give lashes, the Torah mentions the prohibition against muzzling an ox.
28. *Makkot, loc. cit.*, derives this from Isaiah 1:3: "An ox knows its owner and a donkey, its master's feeding trough." Let one who recognizes his master's feeding trough take retribution from one who does not.
29. In his Commentary to the Mishnah, the Rambam writes that the person administering the lashes should not be an abuser with sadistic tendencies.
30. *Makkot* 23a derives this concept from the exegesis of Deuteronomy 25:2: "He shall strike him before him according to his wickedness with the appropriate number." *Lifanav* translated as "before him" can also mean "on his front." And *bimispar*, translated as "with the

שֶׁאֵינוֹ מַכֵּהוּ עַל כְּסוּתוֹ, שֶׁנֶּאֱמַר: וְהִכָּהוּ – וְלֹא לִכְסוּתוֹ. וְהָאֶבֶן נְתוּנָה מֵאֲחוֹרָיו, שֶׁהַחַזָּן הַמַּכֶּה עוֹמֵד עָלֶיהָ. וּרְצוּעָה שֶׁל עֵגֶל בְּיָדוֹ, כְּפוּלָה לִשְׁנַיִם וּשְׁנַיִם לְאַרְבָּעָה. וּשְׁתֵּי רְצוּעוֹת שֶׁל חֲמוֹר עוֹלוֹת וְיוֹרְדוֹת בָּהּ.

וְרֹחַב הָרְצוּעָה טֶפַח, וְאָרְכָּהּ כְּדֵי שֶׁתְּהֵא מַגַּעַת עַד פִּי כְּרֵסוֹ. וְיָד שֶׁל רְצוּעוֹת שֶׁאוֹחֵז בָּהּ אָרְכָּהּ טֶפַח.

ט הָאִישׁ הַמַּכֶּה צָרִיךְ לִהְיוֹת יָתֵר בְּדֵעָה וְחָסֵר בְּכֹחַ. וּמַגְבִּיהַּ אֶת הָרְצוּעוֹת בִּשְׁתֵּי יָדָיו, וּמַכֶּה בְּיָדוֹ אַחַת בְּכָל כֹּחוֹ.

וּמַלְקֵהוּ שְׁלִישׁ מִלְּפָנָיו [עַל חָזֵהוּ] בֵּין דַּדָּיו, וּשְׁנֵי שְׁלִישִׁים מֵאֲחוֹרָיו: שְׁלִישׁ עַל כָּתֵף זֶה, וּשְׁלִישׁ עַל כָּתֵף זֶה.

י הַמַּכֶּה אֵינוֹ עוֹמֵד וְלֹא יוֹשֵׁב, אֶלָּא מֻטֶּה. שֶׁנֶּאֱמַר: וְהִפִּילוֹ הַשֹּׁפֵט וְהִכָּהוּ לְפָנָיו – שֶׁיְּהוּ עֵינָיו שֶׁל שׁוֹפֵט בּוֹ, לֹא שֶׁיִּהְיֶה מַבִּיט בְּדָבָר אַחֵר וּמַכֵּהוּ. מִכָּאן, שֶׁאֵין מַכִּים שְׁנַיִם כְּאֶחָד.

יא הַגָּדוֹל שֶׁבַּדַּיָּנִים קוֹרֵא כָּל זְמַן שֶׁזֶּה לוֹקֶה: אִם לֹא תִשְׁמֹר לַעֲשׂוֹת, וְהִפְלָא יְיָ אֶת מַכֹּתְךָ. וּמִתְכַּוֵּן שֶׁיִּגְמֹר הַפְּסוּקִים עִם הַמַּלְקִיּוֹת.

וְאִם לֹא גָמַר – חוֹזֵר לִתְחִלַּת הַמִּקְרָא, וְקוֹרֵא וְחוֹזֵר וְקוֹרֵא עַד שֶׁתִּגָּמֵר כָּל הַהַכָּאָה.

וְהַשֵּׁנִי שֶׁבַּדַּיָּנִים מוֹנֶה, וְהַשְּׁלִישִׁי אוֹמֵר לַחַזָּן: הַכֵּה! כָּל זְמַן שֶׁמַּכֶּה – עַל פִּיו הוּא מַכֶּה.

appropriate number" can be interpreted as "with a double number." Thus the verse can be understood as intimating that the person receives lashes on his front and twice that number elsewhere, i.e., on his back (see *Torah Temimah*).

31. Some have explained that this is required for the safety of the person receiving the lashes. The judge must pay attention and make sure that the person receiving the lashes is not endangered. Others explain this as a measure of empathy. Even though the punishment the judge ordained is justified, he must himself see the pain it causes.

32. For then, the judge would not be able to focus on either of them.

Our translation and explanation follow the standard printed texts of the *Mishneh Torah*. There are, however, other versions of the text which view this as a separate clause. They read: "'And he shall strike him' - This teaches...." According to this version, the concept is derived from the use of a singular form for the object. Significantly, the *Sifri* derives this concept through a similar process of exegesis, but focuses on a different verse.

33. *Keritot* 11a derives this concept from the exegesis of Leviticus 19:20. That verse refers to lashes. One of the words in it, *bikoret*, can be interpreted as meaning "while reciting."

34. The passage begins with the verse the Rambam cites and continues, concluding at Deuteronomy 29:8. In the standard published text of the Talmud, the Mishnah (*Makkot* 22b) also mentions that the judge should recite the verse (Psalms 78:38): "He, being merciful, pardons sin...." The Rambam does not mention this concept here and it is not included in his version of the Mishnah. (Nor is it present in the version of the Mishnah found in the Jerusalem Talmud.)

35. By the time he finishes the passage.

12. If [the person receiving the lashes] dies while receiving them, [the attendant administering them] is not liable.[36] If he added another blow to the estimate[37] [arrived at by the judges] and [the person receiving the lashes] dies, the attendant is exiled.[38] If he does not die, the attendant [is held liable for] transgressing a negative commandment,[39] as [Deuteronomy 25:3] states: "Do not add."

Similarly, any other person who strikes a colleague violates a negative commandment. If a person who was given permission by the Torah to strike a colleague is [warned] not to strike him more than [is required to punish] his wickedness, certainly, this applies with regard to other people. For this reason, whenever a person strikes a colleague - even a servant[40] - with a blow for which [the victim] would not receive a *p'rutah* [in damages], [the offender] should be lashed.[41] If, however, the blow is worth a *p'rutah* [in damages], [the offender] is not lashed. [The rationale is that] he is obligated to make financial restitution, and a person never [both] receives lashes and is required to make financial restitution,[42] as explained [previously] in several places.[43]

CHAPTER SEVENTEEN

1. How are lashes administered to a person liable to receive them? According to his strength,[1] as [indicated by Deuteronomy 25:2]: "According to his wickedness by number."[2] The number 40 [stated in the following verse is mentioned to teach that] more than 40 lashes are never administered even if the person is as healthy and as strong as Samson. When, by contrast, a person is weak, [the amount of lashes] is reduced. For if a weak person is given too many lashes, he will certainly die.[3] Therefore our Sages said:[4] that even a

36. Needless to say, he is not liable for intentional murder, for he had no intent to kill him. He is not even liable for exile for unintentional killing. As *Makkot* 8a explains, from Deuteronomy 19:5, it is evident that a person is liable for exile when he performs an activity that he has the choice to perform or not. Implied is that if he is commanded to perform that activity - as in the present instance - he is not liable if a person dies as a result.

37. See the first halachot of the following chapter.

38. Since he is not commanded to administer this blow, the principle stated in the previous halachah does not apply. He is nevertheless only exiled and not judged for capital punishment, because he did not intend to kill the person receiving the lashes. Hence, it is a case of accidental death.

39. *Sefer HaMitzvot* (negative commandment 300) and *Sefer HaChinuch* (mitzvah 495) count this as one of the 613 mitzvot of the Torah.

40. But not a gentile. Since a servant is obligated to perform some of the mitzvot, he is placed in this category (*Hilchot Chovel UMazik* 5:3).

41. A *p'rutah* is the smallest amount of money that is considered significant. The court will not deal with any smaller amount of funds (see *Hilchot Gezeilah* 7:3; *Hilchot Toen ViNitan* 3:6). Hence if the damages are not worth that amount, there is no financial penalty and the offender receives lashes instead.

יב מֵת תַּחַת יָדוֹ – פָּטוּר. וְאִם הוֹסִיף רְצוּעָה אַחַת עַל הָאֹמֶד וָמֵת – הֲרֵי הַחַזָּן גּוֹלֶה. וְאִם לֹא מֵת – הֲרֵי הַחַזָּן עָבַר עַל מִצְוַת לֹא תַעֲשֶׂה, שֶׁנֶּאֱמַר: לֹא יֹסִיף.
וְהוּא הַדִּין לְכָל מַכֶּה אֶת חֲבֵרוֹ, שֶׁהוּא בְּלֹא תַעֲשֶׂה. וּמָה אִם זֶה, שֶׁנָּתְנָה תּוֹרָה רְשׁוּת לְהַכּוֹתוֹ, צִוָּה הַכָּתוּב שֶׁלֹּא לְהַכּוֹתוֹ עַל רִשְׁעוֹ; קַל וָחֹמֶר לִשְׁאָר כָּל הָאָדָם. לְפִיכָךְ, כָּל הַמַּכֶּה אֶת חֲבֵרוֹ, אֲפִלּוּ הִכָּה עֶבֶד, הַכָּאָה שֶׁאֵין בָּהּ שָׁוֶה פְּרוּטָה – לוֹקֶה. אֲבָל אִם יֵשׁ בָּהּ שָׁוֶה פְּרוּטָה, הוֹאִיל וְהוּא חַיָּב לְשַׁלֵּם מָמוֹן – אֵין אָדָם מְשַׁלֵּם וְלוֹקֶה, כְּמוֹ שֶׁבֵּאַרְנוּ בְּכַמָּה מְקוֹמוֹת.

פֶּרֶק שִׁבְעָה עָשָׂר

א כֵּיצַד מַלְקִין אֶת הַמְחֻיָּב מַלְקוֹת? כְּפִי כֹחוֹ. שֶׁנֶּאֱמַר: כְּדֵי רִשְׁעָתוֹ בְּמִסְפָּר. וְזֶה שֶׁנֶּאֱמַר: אַרְבָּעִים – שֶׁאֵין מוֹסִיפִין עַל הָאַרְבָּעִים, אֲפִלּוּ הָיָה חָזָק וּבָרִיא כְּשִׁמְשׁוֹן. אֲבָל פּוֹחֲתִין לְחַלָּשׁ; שֶׁאִם יַכֶּה לְחַלָּשׁ מַכָּה רַבָּה – בְּוַדַּאי הוּא מֵת.

42. Of the two penalties, *Ketubot* 32b states that he should be required to make financial restitution rather than receive lashes. This concept is derived from the exegesis of Leviticus 24:19 which uses the term *yinatein*, meaning "be given." Implied is that the punishment involves "something given from hand to hand," i.e., money. This concept applies not only in this instance, but in every case where a person is liable for both lashes and financial payment for the same act.

This is a Scriptural decree. Even if the victim states: "I don't desire financial reimbursement. I want to see him receive lashes," the offender must make financial reimbursement and is not lashed (Radbaz).

43. *Hilchot Na'arah Betulah* 1:11; *Hilchot Chovel UMazik* 4:9.

1. I.e., the court makes an estimation how many lashes he personally can bear as the Rambam continues to explain.
2. In his Commentary to the Mishnah (*Makkot* 3:12, according to Rav Kappach's translation in contrast to the version of the standard text), the Rambam explains that this wording indicates that an individual assessment should be made for each person.
3. *Sanhedrin* 10b states: "The Torah says (Deuteronomy 25:3): 'And your brother will be humiliated before your eyes.' [Implied is that] even after he is lashed [and 'humiliated'], 'your brother' will remain alive 'before your eyes.'"
4. *Makkot* 22a. The Rambam's wording indicates that the reduction of the number of lashes to 39 is a Rabbinic decree. According to Scriptural Law, according to this understanding, a person capable of bearing the full measure of 40 lashes would be given that amount, our Rabbis, however, reduced that number. This interpretation is strengthened by the continuation of that passage (*ibid.*b) which states: "How foolish are people? They rise before a Torah scroll, but do not rise before a sage of stature. For the Torah states: 'Strike him 40 [times],' and our Sages came and reduced the number by one." This quote indicates that the Sages made the reduction on their own initiative.

The commentaries, however, question that interpretation, noting that the Sages (*Makkot, ibid.*) base their ordinance on the phrase: "by number 40..." which they interpret very healthy person is given only 39 lashes. For if [accidentally] an extra [blow] is administered, he will still not have been given more than the 40 which he was required to receive.[5]

2. When [the court][6] estimates how many [lashes the condemned] is able to bear, the estimation is made in numbers that are divisible by three.[7] If it was estimated that he could bear 20, we do not say that he should be given 21,[8] so that the number [of lashes] will be divisible by three. Instead, he is given 18 lashes.[9]

If [the court] estimated that he could bear 40[10] lashes, but when they began lashing him, they saw that he was weak and that he would not be able to bear more than the nine or twelve lashes that he already received, he is released.[11] If they estimated that he could bear twelve and after he was lashed, they saw that he was strong and could bear more, he is released. He is not lashed more than the original estimate.[12]

3. If, on a specific day, it was estimated that he could bear twelve lashes [to be given on that day], but he was not lashed until the following day, and on the following day, he is able to bear eighteen, he receives only twelve.[13]

If it was estimated [on one day] that if he was lashed on the following day, he could bear twelve and he was not lashed until the third day, at which time he was strong enough to bear eighteen, he should be given eighteen lashes. [The rationale is] that at the time the estimation was made, it was reckoned that he would not be lashed until a later date.[14] Similar laws apply in all analogous situations.

4. [The following rules apply when a person] was obligated to receive several sets of lashes whether for the transgression of several sins,[15] or he performed one deed [that involved several transgressions and hence, caused him] to be liable for several sets of lashes.[16] [Everything depends on the judges.] If they

to mean: "a number close to 40." [Had the verse stated "40 by number," the implication would have been exactly 40. The reverse order leaves the matter open to interpretation.] The implication is that the reduction is mandated by Scriptural decree.

The Radbaz explains that, according to the Rambam, the Sages are explaining the rationale for the Torah's ruling. The *Kessef Mishneh* explains that the exegesis is merely an *asmachta*, i.e., an allusion created by the Sages, but the ordinance is their own. Alternatively, the intent is that the Rambam refers to any concept derived through the principles of exegesis as *midivrei sofrim*, "from the words of the Sages," even though concepts derived in that manner have the strength of Scriptural decree, as explained with regard to the consecration of a woman through a gift of money (see *Hilchot Ishut* 1:1 and commentaries).

5. For this reason, if the person is given a fortieth blow and dies, the attendant is not exiled (see the conclusion of the previous chapter), for he did not give him more than he was originally ordained to receive by the Torah (Radbaz).

6. This is one of the reasons why, as stated in Chapter 2, Halachah 1, it is desirable for the

לְפִיכָךְ אָמְרוּ חֲכָמִים: שֶׁאֲפִלּוּ הַבָּרִיא בְּיוֹתֵר מַכִּין אוֹתוֹ שְׁלֹשִׁים וָתֵשַׁע; שֶׁאִם יוֹסִיף לוֹ אַחַת, נִמְצָא שֶׁלֹּא הִכָּהוּ אֶלָּא אַרְבָּעִים הָרְאוּיוֹת לוֹ.

ב כְּשֶׁאוֹמְדִין אֶת הַחוֹטֵא כַּמָּה הוּא יָכוֹל לְקַבֵּל, אֵין אוֹמְדִין אֶלָּא בְּמַכּוֹת הָרְאוּיוֹת לְהִשְׁתַּלֵּשׁ. אֲמָדוּהוּ שֶׁיָּכוֹל לְקַבֵּל עֶשְׂרִים – אֵין אוֹמְרִין: יִלְקֶה עֶשְׂרִים וְאַחַת כְּדֵי שֶׁיִּהְיוּ יְכוֹלִין לְהִשְׁתַּלֵּשׁ, אֶלָּא יִלְקֶה שְׁמוֹנֶה עֶשְׂרֵה. אֲמָדוּהוּ לְקַבֵּל אַרְבָּעִים, וּמִשֶּׁהִתְחִיל לִלְקוֹת רָאוּהוּ חַלָּשׁ, וְאָמְרוּ: אֵינוֹ יָכוֹל לְקַבֵּל יוֹתֵר עַל אֵלּוּ הַתֵּשַׁע אוֹ הַשְּׁתֵּים עֶשְׂרֵה שֶׁלָּקָה – הֲרֵי זֶה פָּטוּר. אֲמָדוּהוּ לְקַבֵּל שְׁתֵּים עֶשְׂרֵה, וְאַחַר שֶׁלָּקָה רָאוּהוּ חָזָק וְיָכוֹל לְקַבֵּל יוֹתֵר – הֲרֵי זֶה פָּטוּר, וְאֵינוֹ לוֹקֶה יוֹתֵר עַל הָאֹמֶד.

ג אֲמָדוּהוּ הַיּוֹם שֶׁיִּלְקֶה שְׁתֵּים עֶשְׂרֵה, וְלֹא הִלְקוּהוּ עַד לְמָחָר, וַהֲרֵי הוּא לְמָחָר יָכוֹל לְקַבֵּל שְׁמוֹנֶה עֶשְׂרֵה – אֵינוֹ לוֹקֶה אֶלָּא שְׁתֵּים עֶשְׂרֵה.
אֲמָדוּהוּ שֶׁיִּלְקֶה לְמָחָר שְׁתֵּים עֶשְׂרֵה, וְלֹא לָקָה עַד יוֹם שְׁלִישִׁי, וַהֲרֵי הוּא חָזָק לְקַבֵּל שְׁמוֹנֶה עֶשְׂרֵה – לוֹקֶה שְׁמוֹנֶה עֶשְׂרֵה; שֶׁהֲרֵי בִּשְׁעַת הָאֹמֶד לֹא אֲמָדוּהוּ לִלְקוֹת אֶלָּא לְאַחַר זְמַן. וְכֵן כֹּל כַּיּוֹצֵא בָּזֶה.

ד מִי שֶׁנִּתְחַיֵּב מַלְקֻיּוֹת הַרְבֵּה, בֵּין עַל עֲבֵרוֹת הַרְבֵּה בֵּין עַל מַעֲשֶׂה אֶחָד שֶׁחַיָּבִין עָלָיו מַלְקֻיּוֹת הַרְבֵּה:

judges to have a certain amount of medical knowledge (Radbaz in his gloss to that halachah).

7. For lashes are administered in sets of three, one on his front and one on each of his shoulders, as stated in Chapter 16, Halachah 9.

8. For the extra lash might endanger his life.

9. In all cases, the number is rounded off to the lower figure, lest giving him the greater number of lashes endanger his life.

10. I.e., 39.

11. In this instance, as well, the additional lashes endanger his life. Moreover, we do not say that he should be given time for his wounds to heal and then be given the remainder of the lashes. Instead, he is released entirely.

12. Once he has already been humiliated by being lashed, his sin is atoned. There is no need for a second estimation and lashing (*Makkot* 22b).

13. Even if he was not lashed at all, since he was judged to be lashed on that day, that judgment is binding (*Makkot, ibid.*). This explanation follows the *Kessef Mishneh's* understanding of the way the Rambam interprets that passage. Other commentaries differ with the Rambam and offer alternative explanations.

14. Hence it is implicit that if his physical state changes, the ruling should also be adjusted. Needless to say, this ruling also applies if he becomes weaker and fewer lashes must be administered.

15. E.g., he ate non-kosher meat and shaved his beard. Alternatively, he shaved his beard several times.

16. E.g., he plowed a field with a donkey and ox together in the Sabbatical year.

made one estimation [for both transgressions], he receives the lashes and is absolved. If not,[17] he is given lashes, [given time] to recuperate, and then given lashes again.

What is implied? He was held liable for two [transgressions punishable by] lashes. [If the court] estimated that he [could bear] 45 lashes,[18] once he receives these 45, he is absolved from further punishment. If, however, they estimated [the amount of] lashes [he could bear for] one [transgression], and they gave him three, nine, or thirty lashes according to their estimation, [we wait until] he is healed, and estimate how many lashes he can bear for the second lashing until he is given all the lashings[19] for which he is obligated.

5. When it was estimated that a person [could bear a specific number] of lashes, they began lashing him and he became discomfited because of the power of the blows and either defecated or urinated, he is not given any more lashes. [This is derived from Deuteronomy 25:3]: "and your brother will be degraded before your eyes." Since he was discomfited, he is absolved.[20]

If, however, he became discomfited from fear before being beaten, even if he became discomfited when he was taken out from the court to be lashed, and even if [he became discomfited] on the previous evening,[21] he is given all the lashes that it was estimated that he could bear.[22]

If one estimation was made for two [transgressions punishable by] lashes,[23] and he becomes discomfited, whether in the midst of the first [set of 40] or the second [set of 40], he is absolved.[24] If the lash became severed in the midst of the second lashing, he is absolved.[25] If it became severed in the midst of the first lashing, he is absolved from the first set of lashes, but is given the lashes of the second set.[26]

6. If they bound him to the pillar to be lashed,[27] and he severed the ties and fled, he is absolved.[28] We do not force him to return.

7. Whenever a person sins and is lashed, he returns to his [original state of] acceptability,[29] as [implied by] the verse: "And your brother will be degraded before your eyes." Once he is lashed, he is "your brother."[30]

17. But instead, they considered each transgression individually.

18. The commentaries note that the Rambam changes the wording of his source, *Makkot* 22b which speaks of 42 lashes. Significantly, in his Commentary to the Mishnah (*Makkot* 3:12), the Rambam follows the wording of that source.

Among the explanations offered is that the Rambam does not accept that number, because he maintains that according to Scriptural Law, a person is obligated to receive 40 lashes for a transgression; it is only Rabbinic decree that caused the number to be reduced to 39 (see the notes to Halachah 1). Therefore when 40 is deducted from 42, only 2 are left. Now two lashes cannot be divided in groups of 3. Hence no additional lashes would be given him. Similarly, with regard to 43 and 44, since they cannot be divided into groups of three, they could not be the number of lashes the Sages intended. Instead, the lowest number which allows for a set of three above 40 and is itself divisible by three is 45 (*Or Sameach*).

19. I.e., not only two, but as many sets of lashes for which he is obligated.

20. I.e., the shame he feels at losing control of his excretory functions in public is sufficient for him to receive atonement.

אִם אֲמָדוּהוּ אֹמֶד אֶחָד – לוֹקֶה וּפָטוּר; וְאִם לָאו – לוֹקֶה וּמִתְרַפֵּא, וְחוֹזֵר וְלוֹקֶה. כֵּיצַד? נִתְחַיֵּב שְׁתֵּי מַלְקִיּוֹת, וְאָמְדוּ שֶׁיָּכוֹל הוּא לְקַבֵּל אַרְבָּעִים וְחָמֵשׁ – כֵּיוָן שֶׁלָּקָה אַרְבָּעִים וְחָמֵשׁ נִפְטַר. אֲבָל אִם אֲמָדוּהוּ לְמַלְקוּת אַחַת, וְהִכָּהוּ שָׁלֹשׁ אוֹ תֵּשַׁע אוֹ שְׁלֹשִׁים כְּמוֹ הָאֹמֶד – הֲרֵי זֶה מִתְרַפֵּא, וְחוֹזְרִין וְאוֹמְדִין אוֹתוֹ לְמַלְקוּת שְׁנִיָּה, עַד שֶׁיִּלְקֶה לְכָל מַלְקִיּוֹת שֶׁהוּא חַיָּב בָּהֶן.

ה מִי שֶׁאֲמָדוּהוּ, וּכְשֶׁהִתְחִיל לִלְקוֹת נִתְקַלְקֵל מִכֹּחַ הַהַכָּאָה, בֵּין בְּרְעִי בֵּין בְּמֵימֵי רַגְלַיִם – אֵין מַכִּין אוֹתוֹ יוֹתֵר. שֶׁנֶּאֱמַר: וְנִקְלָה אָחִיךָ לְעֵינֶיךָ – כֵּיוָן שֶׁנִּקְלָה פָּטוּר. אֲבָל אִם נִתְקַלְקֵל מִן הַפַּחַד מִקֹּדֶם הַהַכָּאָה, אֲפִלּוּ נִתְקַלְקֵל מִשֶּׁיָּצָא מִבֵּית דִּין לִלְקוֹת, וַאֲפִלּוּ מִבָּעֶרֶב – הֲרֵי זֶה לוֹקֶה כָּל הָאֹמֶד שֶׁאֲמָדוּהוּ. אֲמָדוּהוּ לִשְׁתֵּי מַלְקִיּוֹת, וְלָקָה וְנִתְקַלְקֵל, בֵּין בָּרִאשׁוֹנָה בֵּין בַּשְּׁנִיָּה – פָּטוּר. נִפְסְקָה הָרְצוּעָה בַּשְּׁנִיָּה – פּוֹטְרִין אוֹתוֹ; נִפְסְקָה בָּרִאשׁוֹנָה – נִפְטַר מִמַּלְקוּת רִאשׁוֹנָה, וְלוֹקֶה הָאֹמֶד הַשֵּׁנִי.

ו כְּפָתוּהוּ עַל הָעַמּוּד לִלְקוֹת, וְכָרַת אֶת הַמֵּיתָרִים וּבָרַח – פָּטוּר, וְאֵין מַחֲזִירִין אוֹתוֹ.

ז כָּל מִי שֶׁחָטָא וְלָקָה – חוֹזֵר לְכַשְׁרוּתוֹ. שֶׁנֶּאֱמַר: וְנִקְלָה אָחִיךָ לְעֵינֶיךָ – כֵּיוָן שֶׁלָּקָה הֲרֵי הוּא אָחִיךָ.

21. I.e., we do not say that since he lost control of his faculties because of weakness, he will certainly not be able to bear the lashes. Instead, we give him the amount of lashes it was estimated that he could bear (Radbaz).
22. The verse cited states: "And he shall be beaten... and your brother shall be degraded...." Implied is that only when the degradation comes about because of the beating itself is he absolved (*Makkot* 23a). The Radbaz explains the rationale for this concept. There are certain people who cannot control themselves because of fright. That, however, is not proof that they are unable to bear the pain of lashes.
23. As explained in the previous halachah.
24. He is not given any further lashes. Even though one might think that he would be absolved for only one transgression, since the two were combined together, once he is discomfited, he is absolved for both.
25. For by being lashed, he has already been publicly disgraced. If Divine Providence saw to it that the lash became severed, we assume that he has already received sufficient punishment.
26. In this instance, we do not say that both sets of lashes are considered as a single unit.
27. See Chapter 16, Halachah 8.
28. For his fleeing in disgrace and fear is sufficient degradation to atone for his transgression. Even though the lashing had not started before he fled, he is absolved entirely. The fact that he fled is shameful enough to absolve him.
29. The commentaries question what is the "state of acceptability" to which the Rambam is referring. It would appear that the intent is that the person is now considered as acceptable as a witness or to take an oath. There is, however, a question if repentance is also required for him to become acceptable for these matters. See *Hilchot Edut* 12:4 and notes.
30. On the above verse, the *Sifri* comments: "Throughout the entire day, [the Torah] calls him 'the wicked one.' After he is lashed, he is called 'your brother.'"
31. Premature death in this world and the soul being "cut off" in the world to come, as stated in *Hilchot Teshuvah* 8:2.

Similarly, all those obligated for *kerait*[31] who received lashes are absolved for *kerait*.[32]

8. When a High Priest sins, he is lashed [on the basis of the judgment of a court] of three like people at large.[33] Afterwards, he returns to [his position of] eminence.[34]

9. When, by contrast, the head of the academy[35] transgresses, he is given lashes in the presence [of a court] of three, but does not return to [his position of] authority.[36] He also is not reinstated as one [of the other judges] of the *Sanhedrin*. [The rationale is that] we ascend higher in matters of holiness, and do not descend.[37]

CHAPTER EIGHTEEN

1. These are the individuals who receive lashes:
a) anyone who transgresses a negative commandment punishable by *kerait*,[1] but which is not punishable by execution by the court,[2] e.g., a person who eats either fats, blood, or *chametz* on Passover,
b) anyone who transgresses a negative commandment punishable by death at the hand of heaven,[3] e.g., a person who eats *tevel*,[4] or a priest who eats *terumah*[5] that is ritually pure, while he is in a state of ritual impurity,
c) anyone who transgresses a negative prohibition that involves a deed, e.g., a person who eats milk and meat or who wears *sha'atnez*.[6]

When, however, a prohibition does not involve a deed, i.e., a gossiper,[7] a person who takes revenge, or who bears a grudge, and [a judge] who hears a false report,[8] [a violator] does not receive lashes.[9]

2. Whenever a prohibition does not involve a deed, it is not punishable by lashes except for a person who takes a false oath,[10] a person who transfers the

32. In his Commentary to the Mishnah (*Makkot* 3:16), the Rambam writes: "Lashes and repentance atone for [a sin punishable by] *kerait*.
33. We do not say that as a measure of respect for his position, he should be judged by a court of 23 judges. For if he is held liable, he will be lashed in their presence and this will be a public dishonor [Jerusalem Talmud (*Sanhedrin* 2:1)].
34. The Jerusalem Talmud (*loc. cit.*) explains that this comes as a result of the holiness with which the High Priest is endowed. It is a microcosm of God's holiness and hence, like His holiness cannot be nullified.
35. The *nasi* (see Chapter 1, Halachah 3).
36. The Jerusalem Talmud (*loc. cit.*) suggests that this is because he will take revenge and kill the judges who ordered his punishment. The *Kessef Mishneh* advances a different version of that text which states that they will be killing him, i.e., the shame of having to stand before the judges who humiliated him will be too great.

The Radbaz (Responsum 2001) cites one of the Rambam's responsa which states that a judge from the *Sanhedrin* is never removed from his position unless he violates a

אַף כָּל מְחֻיְּבֵי כָּרֵת שֶׁלָּקוּ – נִפְטְרוּ מִידֵי כְּרִיתָתָן.

ח כֹּהֵן גָּדוֹל שֶׁחָטָא – לוֹקֶה בִּשְׁלֹשָׁה, כִּשְׁאָר כָּל הָעָם, וְחוֹזֵר לִגְדֻלָּתוֹ.

ט אֲבָל רֹאשׁ הַיְשִׁיבָה שֶׁחָטָא – מַלְקִין אוֹתוֹ, וְאֵינוֹ חוֹזֵר לִשְׂרָרוּתוֹ. גַּם אֵינוֹ חוֹזֵר לִהְיוֹת כְּאֶחָד מִשְּׁאָר הַסַּנְהֶדְרִין, שֶׁמַּעֲלִין בַּקֹּדֶשׁ וְלֹא מוֹרִידִין.

פֶּרֶק שְׁמוֹנָה עָשָׂר

א אֵלּוּ הֵן הַלּוֹקִין: כָּל הָעוֹבֵר עַל לֹא תַעֲשֶׂה שֶׁחַיָּבִין עָלָיו כָּרֵת וְאֵין בּוֹ מִיתַת בֵּית דִּין, כְּגוֹן אוֹכֵל חֵלֶב וָדָם וְחָמֵץ בְּפֶסַח. וְכֵן כָּל הָעוֹבֵר עַל לֹא תַעֲשֶׂה שֶׁחַיָּבִין עָלָיו מִיתָה בִּידֵי שָׁמַיִם, כְּגוֹן אוֹכֵל טֶבֶל וְכֹהֵן טָמֵא שֶׁאָכַל תְּרוּמָה טְהוֹרָה. וְכֵן כָּל הָעוֹבֵר עַל לָאו שֶׁיֵּשׁ בּוֹ מַעֲשֶׂה, כְּגוֹן אוֹכֵל בָּשָׂר בְּחָלָב אוֹ לוֹבֵשׁ שַׁעַטְנֵז. אֲבָל לָאו שֶׁאֵין בּוֹ מַעֲשֶׂה, כְּגוֹן הוֹלֵךְ רָכִיל וְנוֹקֵם וְנוֹטֵר וְנוֹשֵׂא שֵׁמַע שָׁוְא – אֵינוֹ לוֹקֶה.

ב כָּל לָאו שֶׁאֵין בּוֹ מַעֲשֶׂה – אֵין לוֹקִין עָלָיו, חוּץ מִנִּשְׁבָּע וּמֵמֵר וּמְקַלֵּל אֶת חֲבֵרוֹ בְּשֵׁם.

prohibition in public. The Radbaz, however, explains that for a *nasi*, any transgression is equivalent to a transgression in public.

37. Hence he should not be given the lesser position. This principle applies, not only in this context, but in others. See *Hilchot Beit HaBechirah* 3:16, *Hilchot Klei HaMikdash* 4:21.

1. The person is not absolved from punishment by an earthly court because he will later receive *kerait*, because if he repents he will not suffer those punishments (*Makkot* a,b).
2. For if the transgression is punishable by execution, even if the person is not executed, he does not receive lashes for it. Indeed, even if he does not receive a warning that the prohibition is punishable by execution, but rather that it is punishable by lashes, he does not receive lashes (*ibid.*).
3. In contrast to *kerait*, the soul of a person who violates such a prohibition is not "cut off" in the afterlife [the Rambam's Commentary to the Mishnah (*Sanhedrin* 9:6)].
4. Produce from which *terumah* and the tithes were not separated.
5. The heap offering taken from crops which must be eaten when both the *terumah* and the person partaking of it are ritually pure.
6. A mixture of wool and linen in the same garment.
7. For, in this context, speech is not considered a deed.
8. See Chapter 21, Halachah 7.
9. *Makkot* 13b derives the above concepts from the fact that the punishment of lashing is followed directly by the prohibition (Deuteronomy 25:4): "Do not muzzle an ox while threshing." Just as muzzling an ox is a prohibition that involves a deed, so, too, all other prohibitions punishable by lashes must involve a deed.
10. In this instance, a explicit prooftext teaches us to make the exception. Exodus 20:7

sanctity of one sacrificial animal to another,[11] and one who curses a colleague using God's name.[12] [Similarly,] any prohibition punishable by execution by the court, e.g., "Do not commit adultery," or "Do not perform labor on the Sabbath" is not punishable by lashes.[13]

Whenever a prohibition requires financial recompense, e.g., "Do not rob," or "Do not steal," it is not punishable by lashes.[14] Whenever a prohibition can be corrected by the performance of a positive commandment, e.g., "Do not take the mother together with the offspring,"[15] or "Do not complete [the reaping of] the corners of your field,"[16] it is not punishable by lashes, unless one does not perform the positive commandment.[17]

[Similarly,] a prohibition of a general nature[18] is not punishable by lashes. All other Scriptural prohibitions are punishable by lashes.[19]

3. What is meant by a prohibition of a general nature? A prohibition that includes many matters, e.g., [Leviticus 19:26,]: "Do not eat over the blood."[20] Similarly, if [the Torah] states: "Do not do this and this," since a prohibition was not explicitly stated with regard to each deed, [these prohibitions] are not punishable by lashes unless [the Torah] divides them into separate prohibitions or it is conveyed via the Oral Tradition that they have been divided.

What is implied? [Exodus 12:9] states: "Do not partake of it[21] partially roasted or cooked." [If a person partakes of a portion of the Paschal sacrifice while it is] partially roasted and [another portion that] has been cooked [at the same time], he does not receive two [sets of] lashes, only one.[22]

states: "God will not absolve anyone who swears by His Name in vain." *Sh'vuot* 21a interprets the verse as implying that God will not absolve such a transgression on His own. Nevertheless, if an earthly court punishes a transgressor, this sin may be absolved.

11. In this instance, lashes are given because the person's words have an effect comparable to deed. Through his statements, the sanctity of the offering is transferred from one animal to another (*Temurah* 3b).

12. *Temurah, loc. cit.*, explains that the obligation for lashes is derived from Deuteronomy 28:58-59 which states: "If you will not be careful... to fear the glorious and awesome name God... God will render awesome blows upon you." Through exegesis, the latter phrase is interpreted as referring to lashes. If a person does not fear God's name - as evidenced by his using it to curse a colleague - he is punished by lashes.

The enumeration of the transgressions that do not involve deed and yet are punishable by lashes is quoted from *Sh'vuot* 21a. On that passage, *Tosafot* notes that lying witnesses and a person who spreads a malicious report about his virgin wife are also punished by lashes.

13. As mentioned above, this applies even if the transgressor received a warning that the transgression is punishable by lashes.

14. As mentioned by *Makkot* 4b and *Ketubot* 32b, whenever an act is punishable by both a financial obligation and lashes, the person is held obligated financially and is not lashed.

15. After stating that prohibition, Deuteronomy 22:6 continues: "You shall certainly send forth the mother." This is interpreted, not only as advice to be applied before taking the chicks, but also a means to correct and atone for one's conduct (Rashi, *Makkot* 17a).

16. After stating that prohibition, Leviticus 19:9 continues: "Leave them for the poor and

וְכָל לָאו שֶׁנִּתַּן לְאַזְהָרַת מִיתַת בֵּית דִּין, כְּגוֹן לֹא תִנְאָף, לֹא תַעֲשֶׂה מְלָאכָה בְּשַׁבָּת - אֵין לוֹקִין עָלָיו.

וְכָל לָאו שֶׁנִּתַּן לְתַשְׁלוּמִין, כְּגוֹן לֹא תִגְזֹל וְלֹא תִגְנֹב - אֵין לוֹקִין עָלָיו.

וְכָל לָאו שֶׁנִּתַּק לַעֲשֵׂה, כְּגוֹן לֹא תִקַּח הָאֵם עַל הַבָּנִים, לֹא תְכַלֶּה פְּאַת שָׂדְךָ - אֵין לוֹקִין עָלָיו, אֶלָּא אִם לֹא קִיֵּם עֲשֵׂה שֶׁבָּהֶן.

וְעַל לָאו שֶׁבִּכְלָלוֹת - אֵין לוֹקִין עָלָיו.

וּשְׁאָר כָּל הַלָּאוִין שֶׁבַּתּוֹרָה - לוֹקִין עֲלֵיהֶן.

ג אֵי זֶהוּ לָאו שֶׁבִּכְלָלוֹת? זֶה לָאו אֶחָד שֶׁכּוֹלֵל עִנְיָנִים הַרְבֵּה, כְּגוֹן לֹא תֹאכְלוּ עַל הַדָּם. וְכֵן אִם נֶאֱמַר: לֹא תַעֲשֶׂה דָּבָר פְּלוֹנִי וּפְלוֹנִי, הוֹאִיל וְלֹא יִחֵד לוֹ לָאו לְכָל אֶחָד וְאֶחָד מֵהֶן - אֵין לוֹקִין עַל כָּל אֶחָד וְאֶחָד, אֶלָּא אִם כֵּן חִלֵּק אוֹתָהּ בְּלָאוִין אֲחֵרִים, אוֹ נֶאֱמַר מִפִּי הַשְּׁמוּעָה שֶׁנֶּחְלְקוּ.

כֵּיצַד? כְּגוֹן זֶה שֶׁנֶּאֱמַר: אַל תֹּאכְלוּ מִמֶּנּוּ נָא וּבָשֵׁל מְבֻשָּׁל - אֵינוֹ לוֹקֶה עַל הַנָּא וְהַמְּבֻשָּׁל שְׁתַּיִם אֶלָּא אַחַת.

the stranger." This also is not merely advice to be fulfilled at the outset, but a means of compensating and atoning for transgression.

17. The wording is slightly misleading. The intent is that one is no longer able to fulfill the positive commandment, e.g., the mother bird died, or the grain from the corners was consumed. As long as it is possible to perform that commandment, the person is not lashed even if he shows no inclination of performing that commandment. For the possibility always exists that he will change his mind.

18. This term is defined in the following halachah.

19. Lashes are not administered, however, when a prohibition is understood from a positive commandment, but is not mentioned explicitly, e.g., marriage between a High Priest and a non-virgin. He is commanded to marry a virgin (Leviticus 21:13). Hence we assume he should not marry a non-virgin (see *Hilchot Ishut* 1:8). Since that prohibition is not mentioned by the Torah, its violation is not punishable by lashes. See Chapter 19, Halachah 3.

20. This prohibition forbids several unconnected matters, including:
a) not to partake of the meat of an animal until it is dead;
b) not to partake of the meat of a sacrifice before its blood was offered on the altar;
c) not to bring the meal of consolation to the relatives of a person who was executed;
d) that a court who condemned a person to die should not eat on the day of his execution;
e) that a "wayward and rebellious son" should not partake of the food purchased from the money he stole from his parents (see *Sanhedrin* 63a) .

Since it includes so many different matters, it does not resemble the prohibition against muzzling an ox, which as stated above is the archetype for prohibitions punishable by lashes. That prohibition is explicit and focused on one deed. Any prohibition that is not does not receive the same punishment (*Pesachim* 41b).

21. The Paschal sacrifice.

22. Thus there is no difference whether the person ate partially roasted meat, cooked meat, or both together. He receives only one set of lashes. The Ramban in his *Hasagot* to the *Sefer HaMitzvot*, General Principle 9, differs and maintains that the person is given

With regard to *chadash*,[23] [Leviticus 22:14] states: "You shall not partake of bread, roasted grain, or fresh grain...." A violator is liable for three sets of lashes for these three transgressions. According to the Oral Tradition, we learned that a distinction is to be made.

It is also written: "There shall not be found among you one who passes his son or daughter through the fire, one who divines...." Even though all the matters[24] are included in one prohibition,[25] [in other places, the Torah] distinguishes them as separate prohibitions, as [Leviticus 19:26] states: "Do not augur and do not read omens."[26] This teaches that each one is a separate prohibition. Similar principles apply in all analogous situations.[27]

4. [The following rules apply when a person] receives lashes in a court because of [the violation of] a prohibition punishable by *kerait*, and then received lashes a second time for [the violation of] that same prohibition - e.g., he ate forbidden fat, received lashes for it, and then ate forbidden fat again and received lashes for it. If he eats [such fat] a third time, he is not given lashes. Instead, he is compelled to enter a *kipah*,[28] a narrow place of his own height where he cannot lie down. He is given meager portions of bread and water until his digestive tract contracts and he becomes ill.[29] Afterwards, we feed him barley[30] until his stomach bursts.[31]

5. When a person violates a prohibition punishable by *kerait* or by execution by the court and received a warning beforehand, if he nodded his head,[32] or remained silent and did not acknowledge the warning,[33] we do not execute him, as explained above,[34] nor do we give him lashes. If he repeats this transgression, receives a warning, nods his head, or remains silent, we neither execute him or give him lashes. If he repeats this transgression a third time, receives a warning, even though he [merely] nodded his head or remained silent,[35] he is placed in a *kipah* until he dies.[36]

two sets of lashes if he eats partially roasted meat and cooked meat together. He considers the two as separate prohibitions.

In contrast to the prohibition: "Do not eat upon the blood," a person is liable for lashes for transgressing the prohibition against partaking of the Paschal sacrifice in this manner. It is not entirely a prohibition of a general nature, for both dimensions are explicitly mentioned in the Torah.

23. Fresh grain that may not be eaten before the offering of the *Omer* on the sixteenth of Nisan. See *Hilchot Ma'acholot Assurot*, Ch. 10.

24. The various different prohibitions against black magic and occult arts mentioned in the verse.

25. And hence, one might think that one would receive only one set of lashes even though one violated all the transgressions. This, however, is not so, as the Rambam proceeds to explain.

26. Although there are not separate prohibitions for all the different occult arts mentioned in the verse in Deuteronomy, since there are separate prohibitions for these two - and they are mentioned in the midst of the verse, we assume that similar concepts apply with

וּבְחָדָשׁ הוּא אוֹמֵר: וְלֶחֶם וְקָלִי וְכַרְמֶל לֹא תֹאכְלוּ, וְחַיָּב עַל שְׁלָשְׁתָּן שָׁלֹשׁ מַלְקִיּוֹת. מִפִּי הַשְּׁמוּעָה לָמְדוּ שֶׁזֶּה לְחַלֵּק.

הֲרֵי נֶאֱמַר: לֹא יִמָּצֵא בְךָ מַעֲבִיר בְּנוֹ וּבִתּוֹ בָּאֵשׁ, קֹסֵם קְסָמִים. וְאַף עַל פִּי שֶׁכָּלַל כָּל הָעִנְיָנִים בְּלָאו אֶחָד, הֲרֵי חִלֵּק אוֹתָם בְּלָאוִין אֲחֵרִים, וְאָמַר: לֹא תְנַחֲשׁוּ וְלֹא תְעוֹנֵנוּ. מְלַמֵּד, שֶׁכָּל אֶחָד מֵהֶן בְּלָאו בִּפְנֵי עַצְמוֹ. וְכֵן כֹּל כַּיּוֹצֵא בָּזֶה.

ד מִי שֶׁלָּקָה בְּבֵית דִּין עַל אִסּוּר כָּרֵת, וְלָקָה פַּעַם שְׁנִיָּה עַל אוֹתוֹ כָּרֵת עַצְמוֹ, כְּגוֹן שֶׁאָכַל חֵלֶב וְלָקָה עָלָיו, וְאָכַל חֵלֶב פַּעַם שְׁנִיָּה וְלָקָה עָלָיו, אִם אָכַל פַּעַם שְׁלִישִׁית – אֵין מַלְקִין אוֹתוֹ.

אֶלָּא מַכְנִיסִין אוֹתוֹ לְכִפָּה, וְהוּא מָקוֹם צַר כְּפִי קוֹמָתוֹ וְאֵינוֹ יָכוֹל לִשְׁכַּב בּוֹ, וְנוֹתְנִין לוֹ לֶחֶם צַר וּמַיִם לַחַץ, עַד שֶׁיֵּצָרוּ מֵעָיו וְיִחְלֶה. וְאַחַר כָּךְ מַאֲכִילִין אוֹתוֹ שְׂעוֹרִים, עַד שֶׁכְּרֵסוֹ נִבְקַעַת.

ה מִי שֶׁעָבַר עַל אִסּוּר כָּרֵת אוֹ מִיתַת בֵּית דִּין, וְהִתְרוּ בוֹ, וְהִרְכִּין בְּרֹאשׁוֹ אוֹ שָׁתַק וְלֹא קִבֵּל עָלָיו הַתְרָאָה – אֵין הוֹרְגִין אוֹתוֹ, כְּמוֹ שֶׁבֵּאַרְנוּ, וְאֵין מַלְקִין אוֹתוֹ.

חָזַר וְעָשָׂה כָּךְ, וְהִתְרוּ בוֹ, וְהִרְכִּין בְּרֹאשׁוֹ אוֹ שָׁתַק – אֵין מְמִיתִין אוֹתוֹ וְאֵין מַלְקִין אוֹתוֹ.

חָזַר פַּעַם שְׁלִישִׁית וְעָבַר, וְהִתְרוּ בוֹ, אַף עַל פִּי שֶׁהִרְכִּין בְּרֹאשׁוֹ אוֹ שָׁתַק – כּוֹנְסִין אוֹתוֹ לְכִפָּה עַד שֶׁיָּמוּת.

regard to the other prohibitions [*Sefer Mitzvot* (General Principle 9), based on the Jerusalem Talmud (*Sanhedrin* 7:5).]

27. E.g., the prohibition against a priest marrying woman unfit for him (Leviticus 21:7; *Hilchot Issurei Bi'ah* 17:2).

28. The word *kipah* literally means "dome," i.e., a small room with a dome.

29. Our translation follows the version found in authentic manuscripts and early printings of the *Mishneh Torah*. The standard published text has a different and more difficult to understand version.

30. Which will swell in his digestive tract.

31. And he dies.

Since he brazenly violated a prohibition punishable by *kerait* time after time, the court causes him to die. This applies only when he violates the same prohibition repeatedly, but not when he violates different prohibitions punishable by *kerait*.

32. In apparent acquiescence to the warning.

33. I.e., stating that he is committing the transgression in full awareness of the punishment involved.

34. See Chapter 12, Halachah 2; see also Chapter 16, Halachah 4 with regard to lashes.

35. And thus he is not considered as having accepted the warning.

36. In the manner described in the previous halachah.

As an allusion to this practice, *Sanhedrin* 81b cites Psalms 34:22 which Rashi interprets as meaning "the evil of the wicked will cause him to die." Since the person is a

All these individuals who did not acknowledge the warning [they received] are given "stripes for rebellious behavior"[37] for they did at least commit a sin.[38] Even a person who violates a Rabbinic prohibition[39] is given "stripes for rebellious behavior."[40]

6. When a person steals one of the sacrificial vessels from the Temple,[41] curses God's name using the name of a false divinity,[42] or has relations with an idolatrous gentile[43] woman,[44] the court does not deal with this matter.[45] Instead, the zealous strike them. Whoever slays them is worthy of merit. Similarly, when a priest served [in the Temple] while ritually impure, his priestly brethren would not bring him to court.[46] Instead, the young priests take him out of the Temple Courtyard[47] and crack his head open with logs.[48]

It is a Scriptural decree[49] that the court does not execute a person or have him lashed because of his own admission.[50] Instead, the punishments are given on the basis of the testimony of two witnesses. Joshua's execution of Achan[51] and David's execution of the Amalekite[52] convert because of their own statements was a directive of immediate relevance only[53] or was by royal[54] fiat.[55] The *Sanhedrin*, however, may not execute or lash a person who admits committing a transgression, lest he have become crazed concerning this matter. Perhaps he is one of those embittered people who are anxious to

repeated sinner, he is considered as worthy of death. See also *Hilchot Rotzeach* 4:8 which speaks about a killer being placed in a *kipah.*

37. See the notes to Chapter 16, Halachah 3, for a definition of this term.

38. And since they were given a warning, the transgression was at least partially intentional.

39. In this instance, a warning is not necessary. If the court is convinced that the violation was intentional, it may administer this punishment without a warning having been given.

40. As reflected by the discussion of this practice by the *Sefer Me'irat Einayim* 73:17 and the *Siftei Cohen* 73:16, this punishment may also be given in the present age, and in fact, was used as a deterrent in previous generations. Today, however, it is no longer employed by most courts.

41. *Sanhedrin* 81b cites a non-literal interpretation of Numbers 4:20 as an allusion to this concept.

42. The prohibition against blaspheming God's name is described in *Hilchot Avodat Kochavim*, Chapter 2. In this instance, since the transgressor involves the name of a false divinity, he is not liable for the violation of that prohibition. Instead, he is punished in this manner.

43. If, however, the woman observes the seven universal laws commanded to Noah and his descendants, this punishment does not apply [*Hilchot Issurei Bi'ah* 12:5; the Rambam's Commentary to the Mishnah (*Sanhedrin* 9:6).]

44. The Rambam deals with the question of relations with an idolatrous gentile woman at length in *Hilchot Issurei Bi'ah*, Chapter 12. There he explains that if a Jew marries such a woman, their relations are punishable by lashes. If the relations are carried out in public (i.e., they seclude themselves in the presence of ten Jews), while the couple are in the midst of relations - but not afterwards - a zealous person may slay them. The classic example of such actions is the slaying of Zimri by Pinchas, as related in Numbers, Ch. 25.

וְכָל אֵלּוּ שֶׁלֹּא קִבְּלוּ עֲלֵיהֶן הַהַתְרָאָה – מַכִּין אוֹתָן מַכַּת מַרְדּוּת, הוֹאִיל וְחָטְאוּ מִכָּל מָקוֹם. אֲפִלּוּ עַל אִסּוּר שֶׁל דִּבְרֵי סוֹפְרִים – מַכִּין אוֹתוֹ מַכַּת מַרְדּוּת.

ו הַגּוֹנֵב כְּלִי שָׁרֵת מִן הַמִּקְדָּשׁ, וְהַמְקַלֵּל בְּקוֹסֵם, וְהַבּוֹעֵל אֲרַמִּית – אֵין בֵּית דִּין נִזְקָקִין לָהֶן; אֶלָּא הַקַּנָּאִין פּוֹגְעִין בָּהֶן, וְכֹל שֶׁהוֹרְגָן – זָכָה. וְכֵן כֹּהֵן שֶׁשִּׁמֵּשׁ בְּטֻמְאָה – לֹא הָיוּ אֶחָיו הַכֹּהֲנִים מְבִיאִין אוֹתוֹ לְבֵית דִּין, אֶלָּא פִּרְחֵי כְּהֻנָּה הָיוּ מוֹצִיאִין אוֹתוֹ חוּץ לָעֲזָרָה וּפוֹצְעִין אֶת מֹחוֹ בִּגְזִירִין.

גְּזֵרַת הַכָּתוּב הִיא, שֶׁאֵין מְמִיתִין בֵּית דִּין וְלֹא מַלְקִין אֶת הָאָדָם בְּהוֹדָאַת פִּיו, אֶלָּא עַל פִּי שְׁנַיִם עֵדִים. וְזֶה שֶׁהָרַג יְהוֹשֻׁעַ לְעָכָן וְדָוִד לְגֵר עֲמָלֵקִי בְּהוֹדָאַת פִּיהֶם – הוֹרָאַת שָׁעָה הָיְתָה, אוֹ דִּין מַלְכוּת הָיָה.

אֲבָל הַסַּנְהֶדְרִין – אֵין מְמִיתִין וְלֹא מַלְקִין הַמּוֹדֶה בַּעֲבֵרָה. שֶׁמָּא נִטְרְפָה דַּעְתּוֹ בְּדָבָר זֶה.

45. Indeed, if the court is asked what to do, they should not respond. The action must be the result of the spontaneous feelings of the zealous person who cannot bear the knowledge that such an act is taking place (*ibid.*:5).
46. This transgression is punishable by death at the hand of heaven. Hence the violator would be given lashes by the court (see Chapter 19, Halachah 2).
47. So that there will be no impurity in that holy place.
48. This punishment is derived from an extension of the interpretation of Leviticus 22:9: "They will die... because they have defiled it."
49. As indicated by Deuteronomy 19:15: "According to the testimony of two witnesses... will a matter be established."
50. Instead, we follow the principle (*Yevamot* 25b) that a person is considered to be an involved party and his own testimony should not be used against him. Only with regard to financial matters, do we follow the principle (*Bava Metzia* 3b): "The admission of a witness is equivalent to the testimony of 100 witnesses."

The Radbaz explains the difference between the two realms of judgment as follows: A person's life - and even his physical body - are not his own possessions, but God's. Hence he is not making an admission concerning what belongs to him. His financial resources, by contrast, are his own and he may do with them what he desires.
51. For benefiting from the spoil of Jericho (Joshua, Ch. 7).
52. For killing King Saul (II Samuel, Ch. 15).
53. I.e., he was instructed to do so by a Divine order which he received through the prophetic spirit (*Bamidbar Rabbah* 23:6). Thus this practice should not be emulated in the future.
54. Joshua is also considered as a king (see *Hilchot Melachim* 1:3).
55. As stated in *Hilchot Melachim* 3:8-10, a king has the right to execute people even when they are not liable for execution by the court. The commentaries have raised a question with this explanation, because as stated in that source, a king may only execute violators through decapitation, and Joshua had Achan stoned to death. The *Minchat Chinuch* states that when the king executes a person to strengthen Torah observance, his fiat is not limited and he may use any means of execution he desires.

die and pierce their reins with swords or throw themselves from the rooftops. [Similarly, we fear] that such a person may come and admit committing an act that he did not perform, so that he will be executed. The general principle is [the disqualification of a person's own testimony] is a decree of the King.[56]

CHAPTER NINETEEN

1. There are a total of 21 negative commandments[1] that are punishable by *kerait*, but which are not punishable by execution by the court,[2] for which lashes are administered. They are:
1) a person who has relations with his sister;[3]
2) ...with his father's sister;
3) ...with his mother's sister;
4) ...with the sister of his wife;
5) ...with his brother's wife;
6) ...with the wife of the brother of his father;
7) ...with a woman in the *niddah* state;
8) a person who eats forbidden fat;[4]
9) ...blood;[5]
10) ...leaven on Passover;[6]
11) ...on Yom Kippur;[7]
12) a person who performs forbidden labor on Yom Kippur;[8]
13) a person who partakes of sacrificial meat after the designated time;[9]
14) ...of sacrificial meat disqualified as *piggul*;[10]
15) ...of sacrificial meat while ritually impure;[11]
16) a person who enters the Temple Courtyard while ritually impure;[12]
17) a person who slaughters a consecrated animal outside the Temple;[13]
18) a person who burns a consecrated animal as a sacrifice outside the Temple;[14]
19) a person who prepares the [anointing] oil [for personal use];[15]
20) a person who anoints himself with the anointing oil [for his own benefit][16]
21) a person who prepares the incense offering [for his personal use];[17]

56. I.e., although one might question the above explanation - for it does not necessarily apply with regard to lashes - one must realize that the ruling is not dependent on the explanation, but is instead a Divine decree, which we may or may not comprehend intellectually.

1. The Rambam is not mentioning the number of negative commandments specifically, but rather the acts punishable by lashes. As will be explained, there are times when two acts are included in the same negative commandment, and other times when one deed will involve the transgression of two or more commandments (*Ner Mitzvah*).
2. For if they are punishable by execution, a person is never punished by lashes for their transgression. This applies even if he is not executed and indeed, even if he was given a warning for lashes, rather than a warning for execution, as explained in Chapter 18, Halachah 2, and notes.
3. This and the following six commandments are mentioned in Leviticus, Ch. 18, and in

שֶׁמָּא מִן הָעֲמֵלִין מָרֵי נֶפֶשׁ הוּא, הַמְחַכִּים לָמוּת, שֶׁתּוֹקְעִין הַחֲרָבוֹת בְּבִטְנָם וּמַשְׁלִיכִין עַצְמָן מֵעַל הַגַּגּוֹת. שֶׁמָּא כָּךְ זֶה יָבוֹא וְיֹאמַר דָּבָר שֶׁלֹּא עָשָׂה, כְּדֵי שֶׁיֵּהָרֵג. וּכְלָלוֹ שֶׁל דָּבָר: גְּזֵרַת מֶלֶךְ הִיא.

פֶּרֶק תְּשְׁעָה עָשָׂר

א כָּל לֹא תַעֲשֶׂה שֶׁיֵּשׁ בּוֹ כָּרֵת וְאֵין בּוֹ מִיתַת בֵּית דִּין שֶׁלּוֹקִין עֲלֵיהֶן - אֶחָד וְעֶשְׂרִים. וְאֵלּוּ הֵן:

א) הַבָּא עַל אֲחוֹתוֹ.
ב) הַבָּא עַל אֲחוֹת אָבִיו.
ג) הַבָּא עַל אֲחוֹת אִמּוֹ.
ד) הַבָּא עַל אֲחוֹת אִשְׁתּוֹ.
ה) הַבָּא עַל אֵשֶׁת אָחִיו.
ו) הַבָּא עַל אֵשֶׁת אֲחִי אָבִיו.
ז) הַבָּא עַל הַנִּדָּה.
ח) הָאוֹכֵל חֵלֶב.
ט) הָאוֹכֵל דָּם.
י) הָאוֹכֵל חָמֵץ בַּפֶּסַח.
יא) הָאוֹכֵל בְּיוֹם הַכִּפּוּרִים.
יב) הָעוֹשֶׂה מְלָאכָה בְּיוֹם הַכִּפּוּרִים.
יג) הָאוֹכֵל הַנּוֹתָר.
יד) הָאוֹכֵל פִּגּוּל.
טו) הַטָּמֵא שֶׁאָכַל בְּשַׂר קֹדֶשׁ.
טז) הַטָּמֵא שֶׁנִּכְנַס לָעֲזָרָה.
יז) הַשּׁוֹחֵט קָדָשִׁים בַּחוּץ.
יח) הַמַּעֲלֶה קָדָשִׁים בַּחוּץ.
יט) הַמְפַטֵּם אֶת הַשֶּׁמֶן.
כ) הַסָּךְ בְּשֶׁמֶן הַמִּשְׁחָה.
כא) הַמְפַטֵּם אֶת הַקְּטֹרֶת.

Hilchot Issurei Bi'ah. A person who has relations with his sister violates two negative commandments, for there is a separate commandment prohibiting relations with the daughter of one's father (*Ner Mitzvah*).

4. As forbidden by Leviticus 7:23; *Hilchot Ma'achalot Assurot* 7:2.
5. As forbidden by Leviticus 7:26; *Hilchot Ma'achalot Assurot* 6:1. *Derech Mitzvotecho* questions why the Rambam does not mention in this chapter the prohibitions against partaking of blood that are not punishable by *kerait*, but which are punishable by lashes, as explained in *Hilchot Ma'achalot Assurot* 6:4.
6. As forbidden by Exodus 13:3; *Hilchot Chametz UMatzah* 1:1.
7. As forbidden by Leviticus 23:29; *Hilchot Sh'vitat Esor* 1:4.
8. As forbidden by Leviticus 23:25; *Hilchot Sh'vitat Esor* 1:1.
9. As forbidden by Leviticus 19:8; *Hilchot Pesulei HaMukdashim* 18:10.
10. As forbidden by Leviticus 7:18; *Hilchot Pesulei HaMukdashim* 18:6.
11. As forbidden by Leviticus 7:20; *Hilchot Pesulei HaMukdashim* 18:13.
12. As forbidden by Numbers 5:3; *Hilchot Bi'at HaMikdash* 3:12.
13. As forbidden by Leviticus 17:3-4; *Hilchot Ma'aseh HaKorbanot* 18:2.
14. As forbidden by Deuteronomy 12:13; *Hilchot Ma'aseh HaKorbanot* 18:3.
15. As forbidden by Exodus 30:32; *Hilchot Klei HaMikdash* 1:4.
16. As forbidden by Exodus 30:32; *Hilchot Klei HaMikdash* 1:5.
17. As forbidden by Exodus 30:37; *Hilchot Klei HaMikdash* 2:9.

2. There are a total of 18 negative commandments that are punishable by death by the hand of heaven,[18] whose transgression involve a deed,[19] for which lashes are administered. They are:
1) a person other than a priest[20] who partakes of primary *terumah* whether it was ritually pure or ritually impure;[21]
2) a person other than a priest who partakes of *terumat ma'aser*;[22]
3) a person other than a priest who partakes of the first fruits after they entered Jerusalem;[23]
4) a person other than a priest who partakes of *challah*;
5) a person who partakes of *tevel* before the primary *terumah* and *terumat ma'aser* were separated from it;[24]
6) a person who partakes [of the product] of dough from which *challah* was not separated;[25]
7) a priest who partakes of *terumah* that was ritually pure while he was in a state of ritual impurity;[26]
8) a priest who entered the Holy of Holies for a purpose other than sacrificial worship;[27]
9) a priest who departed from the Temple in the midst of the sacrificial worship;[28]
10) a Levite who performed the service of the priests;[29]
11) a person other than a priest who performs service in the Temple;[30]
12) a person who does not wear all the priestly garments; he is considered as if he is not a priest[31] and receives lashes if he serves [in the Temple];[32]
13) a priest who serves [in the Temple] while in a state of ritual impurity;[33]
14) a person who was intoxicated from wine who served [in the Temple];[34]
15) a person who immersed himself [to emerge from a state of ritual impurity] but must still wait until the end of the day [to attain a state of purity] who served [in the Temple];[35]
16) [a priest] who served [in the Temple] although he did not yet bring the required sacrifices to attain atonement;[36]

18. Like transgressions punishable by *kerait*, violation of these transgressions causes a person to die prematurely. Unlike *kerait*, however, such transgressors receive atonement through their death [the Rambam's Commentary to the Mishnah (*Sanhedrin* 9:6)].
19. I.e., there are transgressions which warrant this punishment that do not involve a deed. Lashes are not, however, given for such transgressions, as stated in Chapter 18, Halachah 2.
20. By using this term, the Rambam includes two negative commandments [*Sefer HaMitzvot* (negative commandments 133-134)], the prohibition against an Israelite partaking of *terumah* and the prohibition against a worker or a servant of a priest partaking of it.
21. As forbidden by Leviticus 22:9-10; *Hilchot Terumot* 6:6.
22. This and the following two prohibitions are included in the prohibition mentioned in Leviticus 22:9-10. The *Lechem Mishneh* explains that even though this prohibition includes these four substances, it is not considered as being general in nature (and hence, not punishable by lashes as stated in Chapter 18, Halachah 2), because all of these substances are called *terumah*.

ב כָּל מְחֻיָּבִין מִיתָה בִּידֵי שָׁמַיִם, שֶׁהֵן בְּלֹא תַעֲשֶׂה וְיֵשׁ בָּהֶן מַעֲשֶׂה, שֶׁלּוֹקִין עֲלֵיהֶן – שְׁמוֹנָה עָשָׂר. וְאֵלּוּ הֵן:

א) זָר שֶׁאָכַל תְּרוּמָה גְדוֹלָה, בֵּין טְהוֹרָה בֵּין טְמֵאָה.

ב) זָר שֶׁאָכַל תְּרוּמַת מַעֲשֵׂר.

ג) זָר שֶׁאָכַל בִּכּוּרִים אַחַר שֶׁנִּכְנְסוּ לִירוּשָׁלַיִם.

ד) זָר שֶׁאָכַל חַלָּה.

ה) הָאוֹכֵל טֶבֶל שֶׁלֹּא הוּרַם מִמֶּנּוּ תְּרוּמָה גְדוֹלָה וּתְרוּמַת מַעֲשֵׂר.

ו) הָאוֹכֵל עִסָּה שֶׁלֹּא הוּרְמָה חַלָּתָהּ.

ז) כֹּהֵן טָמֵא שֶׁאָכַל תְּרוּמָה טְהוֹרָה.

ח) כֹּהֵן שֶׁנִּכְנַס לְקֹדֶשׁ הַקֳּדָשִׁים שֶׁלֹּא לַעֲבוֹדָה.

ט) כֹּהֵן שֶׁיָּצָא מִן הַמִּקְדָּשׁ בִּשְׁעַת עֲבוֹדָה.

י) לֵוִי שֶׁעָבַד בַּעֲבוֹדַת כֹּהֲנִים.

יא) זָר שֶׁשִּׁמֵּשׁ בַּמִּקְדָּשׁ.

יב) מְחֻסַּר בְּגָדִים – הֲרֵי הוּא כְּזָר, וְלוֹקֶה אִם עָבַד.

יג) כֹּהֵן טָמֵא שֶׁשִּׁמֵּשׁ.

יד) שְׁתוּי יַיִן שֶׁשִּׁמֵּשׁ.

טו) טְבוּל יוֹם שֶׁשִּׁמֵּשׁ.

טז) מְחֻסַּר כִּפּוּרִים שֶׁשִּׁמֵּשׁ.

יז) פְּרוּעַ רֹאשׁ שֶׁשִּׁמֵּשׁ.

23. See *Hilchot Bikurim* 3:1.
24. As forbidden by Leviticus 22:15; *Hilchot Ma'achalot Assurot* 2:3.
25. See *Hilchot Bikkurim* 8:5. The dough is also considered *tevel* and forbidden, because of the prohibition mentioned in the previous note.
26. As forbidden by Leviticus 22:4; *Hilchot Terumot* 7:1.
27. As forbidden by Leviticus 16:2; *Hilchot Bi'at HaMikdash* 10:19. See also Halachah 4, prohibition 27.
28. As forbidden by Leviticus 10:7; *Hilchot Bi'at HaMikdash* 2:5.
29. As forbidden by Numbers 18:3; *Hilchot Klei HaMikdash* 3:11.
30. As forbidden by Numbers 18:4; *Hilchot Bi'at HaMikdash* 9:1.
31. *Sanhedrin* 83b derives this concept from the exegesis of Exodus 29:9.
32. Hence he is included in the above prohibition. See *Hilchot Klei HaMikdash* 10:4.
33. As forbidden by Leviticus 22:2; *Hilchot Bi'at HaMikdash* 4:1. See Chapter 18, Halachah 6, which states that such a person would not be brought to court for lashes. Instead, he would be killed by the young priests.
34. As forbidden by Leviticus 10:9; *Hilchot Bi'at HaMikdash* 1:1.
35. As forbidden by Leviticus 21:6; *Hilchot Bi'at HaMikdash* 4:4.
36. As forbidden by Leviticus 15:13-15. See the Radbaz and the *Kessef Mishneh* who cite *Hilchot Bi'at HaMikdash* 4:4 where the Rambam states that a person who commits this transgression is not liable for punishment. For this reason, the Maharik states that the wording here should be "a person who wears additional garments." See *Hilchot K'lei HaMikdash* 10:5.

17) a person who let his hair grow long who served [in the Temple];[37]
18) a person whose clothes are ripped who served [in the Temple];[38]

3. When, however, a person serves [in the Temple] without sanctifying his hands and feet, although he is worthy of death,[39] he does not receive lashes, because [he has violated] only a positive commandment.[40] Similarly, the [following] three - a prophet who withheld his prophecy[41] or transgressed his own [prophecy][42] and a person who violated the words of a prophet - although they all are worthy of death[43] - they do not receive lashes. For their transgression stems from a positive commandment, as [Deuteronomy 18:15] states: "And you shall listen to him." [In all contexts,][44] a prohibition that stems from a positive commandment has the status of a positive commandment and lashes are not administered because of it.

4. There are a total of 168 negative commandments that are neither punishable by *kerait*, nor by execution by the court, for which lashes are administered. They are:
1) a person who fashions an idol;[45]
2) a person who makes an image for artistic purposes;[46]
3) a person who turns to idolatry with any deed;[47]
4) a person who erects a monument;[48]
5) a person who plants a tree in the Temple;[49]
6) a person who places down an engraved stone [on which to prostrate himeself];[50]
7) a person who takes a vow in the name of a false divinity;[51]
8) a person who takes an oath in the name [of a false divinity];[52]
9) a person who derives benefit from [a false divinity];[53]
10) a person who rebuilds a city [destroyed because] it was swayed [to idolatry];[54]

37. As forbidden by Leviticus 10:6; *Hilchot Bi'at HaMikdash* 1:8.
38. As forbidden by Leviticus 10:6; *Hilchot Bi'at HaMikdash* 1:14.
39. At the hand of God.
40. Exodus 30:21 states: "They shall wash their hands and feet so that they do not die." Implied is that if a priest does not wash his hands, he will receive that punishment. There is, however, no explicit negative commandment warning one not to do so. See *Hilchot Bi'at HaMikdash* 9:10-11.
41. E.g., the prophet Jonah who tried to flee to Tarshish rather than deliver his prophecy against Nineveh. See Jonah, Ch. 1.
42. E.g., Ido, the prophet, who was commanded to prophesy against the altar established by Jeroboam. God told him not to eat or drink until he returned. He disobeyed this command, and was therefore slain by a lion (I Kings, Ch. 13).
43. As Deuteronomy 18:19 states: "And a person who will not heed My words which he speaks in My name, I will seek [retribution] from him." See *Hilchot Yesodei HaTorah* 9:2-3.
44. See, for example, *Hilchot Ishut* 1:8 with regard to the prohibitions against marrying Egyptian and Edomite converts.

יח) קְרוּעַ בְּגָדִים שֶׁשִּׁמֵּשׁ.

ג אֲבָל הַמְשַׁמֵּשׁ בְּלֹא קִדּוּשׁ יָדַיִם וְרַגְלַיִם, אַף עַל פִּי שֶׁהוּא חַיָּב מִיתָה – אֵינוֹ לוֹקֶה, מִפְּנֵי שֶׁהִיא מִצְוַת עֲשֵׂה.

וְכֵן נָבִיא שֶׁכָּבַשׁ נְבוּאָתוֹ, אוֹ שֶׁעָבַר עַל דִּבְרֵי עַצְמוֹ, וְהָעוֹבֵר עַל דִּבְרֵי נָבִיא, אַף עַל פִּי שֶׁשְּׁלָשְׁתָּן בְּמִיתָה – אֵינוֹ לוֹקֶה.

שֶׁהֵן בָּאִין מִכְּלַל עֲשֵׂה, שֶׁנֶּאֱמַר: אֵלָיו תִּשְׁמָעוּן; וְלָאו הַבָּא מִכְּלַל עֲשֵׂה – הֲרֵי הוּא כַּעֲשֵׂה, וְאֵין לוֹקִין עָלָיו.

ד כָּל לֹא תַעֲשֶׂה שֶׁבַּתּוֹרָה, שֶׁאֵין בָּהֶן לֹא כָּרֵת וְלֹא מִיתַת בֵּית דִּין, שֶׁלּוֹקִין עֲלֵיהֶן – מֵאָה שִׁשִּׁים וּשְׁמוֹנָה. וְאֵלּוּ הֵן:

א) הָעוֹשֶׂה אֱלִיל.

ב) הָעוֹשֶׂה אֱלִיל לְנוֹי.

ג) הַפּוֹנֶה אֶל אֱלִילִים בְּאֶחָד מִן הַמַּעֲשִׂים.

ד) הַמֵּקִים מַצֵּבָה.

ה) הַנּוֹטֵעַ אִילָן בַּמִּקְדָּשׁ.

ו) הַנּוֹתֵן אֶבֶן מַשְׂכִּית.

ז) הַנּוֹדֵר בְּשֵׁם עֲבוֹדָה זָרָה.

ח) הַנִּשְׁבָּע בִּשְׁמָהּ.

ט) הַנֶּהֱנֶה בָּהּ.

י) הַבּוֹנֶה עִיר הַנִּדַּחַת.

45. As forbidden by Exodus 20:4 and Leviticus 19:4. As explained in *Hilchot Avodat Kochavim* 3:9, the first prohibition applies when a person fashions an idol for himself. The second when he makes an idol for a gentile without the intent of worshipping it himself.

46. As forbidden by Exodus 20:23; *Hilchot Avodat Kochavim* 3:10.

47. As forbidden by Leviticus 19:4; *Hilchot Avodat Kochavim* 2:3.

48. Even for the worship of God. This is forbidden by Deuteronomy 16:22; *Hilchot Avodat Kochavim* 6:6.

49. As forbidden by Deuteronomy 16:21; *Hilchot Avodat Kochavim* 6:9.

50. Even for the sake of heaven, as forbidden by Leviticus 26:1; *Hilchot Avodat Kochavim* 6:6.

51. As forbidden by Exodus 23:13; *Hilchot Avodat Kochavim* 5:11.

52. This is forbidden by the prohibition mentioned in the previous note. The *Lechem Mishneh* questions why lashes are given, for seemingly these are prohibitions that do not involve a deed.

53. As forbidden by Deuteronomy 7:26; *Hilchot Avodat Kochavim* 7:2. As mentioned in *Hilchot Avodat Kochavim, loc. cit.*, a person who benefits from a false divinity also violates prohibition 11 and is given lashes on both counts.

54. As forbidden by Deuteronomy 13:17; *Hilchot Avodat Kochavim* 4:8.

11) a person who benefits from [the property of such a city];[55]
12) a person who follows the statutes of the gentiles;[56]
13) a diviner;[57]
14) an augurer;[58]
15) a reader of omens;[59]
16) a person who casts spells;[60]
17) a necromancer;[61]
18) a person who erases [God's] name, or the like, e.g., he destroys a stone from the altar or destroys wood [consecrated to] the Sanctuary;[62]
19) a person who extinguishes fire from the altar;[63]
20) a person who ascends [the altar] with steps;[64]
21) a person who enters the Temple Courtyard with impure garments;[65]
22) a *zav*[66] and the like[67] who enters the Temple Mount;[68]
23) a person who removes the staves of the ark;[69]
24) a person who removes the [High Priest's] breastplate from his *ephod*;[70]
25) a person who tears the collar of the [High Priest's] cloak;[71]
26) a person who offers [anything else than the commanded offerings][72] on the golden altar;[73]
27) a priest who enters the Sanctuary while not in the midst of sacrificial worship;[74]
28) [a priest with] a physical deformity who enters [the Sanctuary];[75]
29) [a priest with] who enters [the Sanctuary] while intoxicated;[76]
30) [a priest with] a physical deformity who performs sacrificial worship;[77]
31) an uncircumcised [priest] who performs sacrificial worship;[78]

55. As forbidden by Deuteronomy 13:18; *Hilchot Avodat Kochavim* 4:7.
56. As forbidden by Leviticus 20:23; *Hilchot Avodat Kochavim* 11:1.
57. As forbidden by Deuteronomy 18:10; *Hilchot Avodat Kochavim* 11:6. See Chapter 18:3 which explains why this and the following prohibitions are not considered as prohibitions of a general nature.
58. As forbidden by Deuteronomy 18:10; *Hilchot Avodat Kochavim* 11:8.
59. As forbidden by Leviticus 19:26; *Hilchot Avodat Kochavim* 11:4.
60. As forbidden by Deuteronomy 18:10; *Hilchot Avodat Kochavim* 11:10.
61. As forbidden by Deuteronomy 18:10; *Hilchot Avodat Kochavim* 11:13.
62. As forbidden by Deuteronomy 12:3-4. *Hilchot Yesodei HaTorah* 6:1 discusses the prohibition against erasing God's name. *Ibid.*:7 discusses the extension of the principle to include stones from the altar and wood consecrated to the Sanctuary.
63. As forbidden by Leviticus 6:6; *Hilchot Temidim UMusafim* 2:6.
64. As forbidden by Exodus 20:23; *Hilchot Beit HaBechirah* 1:17.
65. As forbidden by Leviticus 17:16; *Hilchot Bi'at HaMikdash* 3:16-17.
66. A urological condition which produces a secretion similar to that which results from gonorrhea.
67. I.e., a *zavah*, a woman in the *niddah* state, or a woman who has given birth. In all these instances, the ritual impurity is a result of a physical condition.
68. As forbidden by Deuteronomy 23:11; *Hilchot Bi'at HaMikdash* 3:3-4. The commentaries note that as stated in *Hilchot Bi'at HaMikdash* 3:8, a *metzora* who enters

יא) הַנֶּהֱנֶה מִמֶּנָּה.

יב) הָעוֹשֶׂה כְּחֻקּוֹת הָעוֹבְדֵי כּוֹכָבִים.

יג) הַקּוֹסֵם.

יד) הַמְעוֹנֵן.

טו) הַמְנַחֵשׁ.

טז) הַחוֹבֵר.

יז) הַדּוֹרֵשׁ אֶל הַמֵּתִים.

יח) הַמּוֹחֵק שֵׁם וְכַיּוֹצֵא בּוֹ, כְּגוֹן הוֹרֵס אֶבֶן מִן הַמִּזְבֵּחַ אוֹ שׂוֹרֵף עֵץ מִן הַמִּקְדָּשׁ.

יט) הַמְכַבֶּה אֵשׁ מִן הַמִּזְבֵּחַ.

כ) הָעוֹלֶה עָלָיו בְּמַעֲלוֹת.

כא) הַנִּכְנָס לָעֲזָרָה בִּבְגָדִים טְמֵאִים.

כב) זָב וְכַיּוֹצֵא בּוֹ שֶׁנִּכְנַס לְהַר הַבַּיִת.

כג) הַמֵּסִיר בַּדֵּי אָרוֹן.

כד) הַמֵּזִיחַ חשֶׁן מֵעַל הָאֵפוֹד.

כה) הַקּוֹרֵעַ פִּי הַמְּעִיל.

כו) הַמַּקְרִיב עַל מִזְבַּח הַזָּהָב.

כז) כֹּהֵן שֶׁנִּכְנַס לַהֵיכָל שֶׁלֹּא בִּשְׁעַת הָעֲבוֹדָה.

כח) בַּעַל מוּם שֶׁנִּכְנַס לְשָׁם.

כט) שָׁתוּי שֶׁנִּכְנַס לְשָׁם.

ל) בַּעַל מוּם שֶׁשִּׁמֵּשׁ.

לא) עָרֵל שֶׁשִּׁמֵּשׁ.

Jerusalem is also worthy of receiving lashes. They question why the Rambam does not mention this prohibition here.

69. As forbidden by Exodus 25:15; *Hilchot Klei HaMikdash* 2:13.

70. As forbidden by Exodus 28:28; *Hilchot Klei HaMikdash* 9:10.

71. As forbidden by Exodus 28:32; *Hilchot Klei HaMikdash* 9:3. As explained in that source, this prohibition also applies to the other priestly garments.

72. I.e., anything other than incense and the blood from the bull and the goat that was brought into the Holy of Holies.

73. As forbidden by Exodus 30:9; *Hilchot Klei HaMikdash* 2:11.

74. As forbidden by Leviticus 16:2; *Hilchot Bi'at HaMikdash* 2:4. As mentioned in the notes to Halachah 2, this same prohibition forbids the High Priest from entering the Holy of Holies, except during the sacrificial worship.

75. As forbidden by Leviticus 21:23; *Hilchot Bi'at HaMikdash* 6:1. As the latter source states, this prohibition also applies if such a priest proceeds beyond the altar in the Temple Courtyard.

76. As forbidden by Leviticus 10:9; *Hilchot Bi'at HaMikdash* 1:1-2.

77. As forbidden by Leviticus 21:17; *Hilchot Bi'at HaMikdash* 6:1.

78. As forbidden by Leviticus 44:9; *Hilchot Bi'at HaMikdash* 6:8.

32) a priest who performs the tasks of the Levites;[79]
33) a priest who enters [the Sanctuary] with uncut hair;[80]
34) a priest who enters [the Sanctuary] with torn clothes;[81]
35) a person who consecrates an animal with a physical deformity;[82]
36) a person who slaughters [such an animal as an offering];[83]
37) a person who sprinkles the blood [of such animals on the altar];[84]
38) a person who burns the fats [of such animals on the altar];[85]
39) a person who offers an animal with a physical deformity on behalf of gentile;[86]
40) a person who produces a blemish in a consecrated animal at the time the Temple is standing;[87]
41) a person who performs labor with consecrated animals;[88]
42) a person who shears [consecrated animals][89]
43) a person who makes a fire-offering of yeast or honey;[90]
44) a person who allows the remainder of the meal-offerings to leaven;[91]
45) a person who offers a sacrifice without salt;[92]
46) a person who offers a present [given to a prostitute] or an animal given in exchange for a dog;[93]
47) a person who adds oil to the meal-offering of a sinner;[94]
48) a person who adds frankincense to such an offering;[95]
49) a person who adds oil to the meal-offering of a *sotah*;[96]
50) a person who adds frankincense to such an offering;[97]
51) a person who separates [the head of] a bird brought as a sin offering [from its trunk];[98]
52) a person who transfers the holiness of one animal to another;[99]
53) a person who partakes of sacrificial meat after it became ritually impure;[100]
54) a person who partakes of sacrifices that have been disqualified;[101]
55) a priest who partakes of the meat of sacrifices of the most sacred order outside the Temple courtyard;[102]

79. As forbidden by Numbers 18:3; *Hilchot Klei HaMikdash* 3:11.
80. As forbidden by Leviticus 10:6; *Hilchot Bi'at HaMikdash* 1:16.
81. As forbidden by the above sources. As mentioned in Halachah 2, if a priest performs sacrificial service with torn clothes, he is worthy of death at the hand of God.
82. As forbidden by Leviticus 22:20; *Hilchot Issurei Mizbeach* 1:2.
83. As forbidden by Leviticus 22:22; *Hilchot Issurei Mizbeach* 1:4.
84. As forbidden by Leviticus 22:24; *Hilchot Issurei Mizbeach, loc. cit.*.
85. As forbidden by Leviticus 22:22; *Hilchot Issurei Mizbeach* 1:4.
86. As forbidden by Leviticus 22:25; *Hilchot Issurei Mizbeach* 1:6.
87. This prohibition is derived from the exegesis of Leviticus 22:21; see *Hilchot Issurei Mizbeach* 1:7-8.
88. As forbidden by Deuteronomy 15:19; *Hilchot Me'ilah* 1:7.
89. As forbidden by the above sources.
90. As forbidden by Leviticus 2:11; *Hilchot Issurei Mizbeach* 5:1. If a person offers both these forbidden substances at one time, he receives only one set of lashes, because they are both mentioned in the same prohibition.
91. As forbidden by Leviticus 6:10; *Hilchot Ma'aseh HaKorbanot* 1:6.

לב) כֹּהֵן שֶׁעָבַד בַּעֲבוֹדַת הַלְוִיִּם.
לג) כֹּהֵן שֶׁנִּכְנַס לַמִּקְדָּשׁ פְּרוּעַ רֹאשׁ.
לד) כֹּהֵן שֶׁנִּכְנַס לַמִּקְדָּשׁ קְרוּעַ בְּגָדִים.
לה) הַמַּקְדִּישׁ בַּעֲלֵי מוּמִין.
לו) הַשּׁוֹחֲטָן.
לז) הַזּוֹרֵק דְּמֵיהֶן.
לח) הַמַּקְטִיר אֵמוּרֵיהֶן.
לט) הַמַּקְרִיב קָרְבְּנוֹת עוֹבְדֵי כּוֹכָבִים בַּעֲלֵי מוּמִין.
מ) הַמַּטִּיל מוּם בְּקָדָשִׁים בִּזְמַן הַמִּקְדָּשׁ.
מא) הָעוֹבֵד בְּקָדָשִׁים.
מב) הַגּוֹזֵז אוֹתָן.
מג) הַמַּקְטִיר שְׂאוֹר אוֹ דְּבַשׁ.
מד) הָעוֹשֶׂה שְׁיָרֵי מְנָחוֹת מֵחָמֵץ.
מה) הַמַּקְרִיב בְּלֹא מֶלַח.
מו) הַמַּקְרִיב אֶתְנַן אוֹ מְחִיר כֶּלֶב.
מז) הַנּוֹתֵן שֶׁמֶן עַל מִנְחַת חוֹטֵא.
מח) הַנּוֹתֵן עָלֶיהָ לְבוֹנָה.
מט) הַנּוֹתֵן שֶׁמֶן בְּקָרְבַּן סוֹטָה.
נ) הַנּוֹתֵן עָלָיו לְבוֹנָה.
נא) הַמַּבְדִּיל בְּחַטַּאת הָעוֹף.
נב) הַמֵּמֵר בְּקָדְשֵׁי מִזְבֵּחַ.
נג) הָאוֹכֵל בְּשַׂר קֹדֶשׁ שֶׁנִּטְמָא.
נד) הָאוֹכֵל מִפְּסוּלֵי הַמֻּקְדָּשִׁין.
נה) כֹּהֵן שֶׁאָכַל בְּשַׂר קָדְשֵׁי קָדָשִׁים חוּץ לָעֲזָרָה.

92. As forbidden by Leviticus 2:13; *Hilchot Issurei HaMizbeach* 5:11.
93. As forbidden by Deuteronomy 23:19; *Hilchot Issurei HaMizbeach* 3:7, 4:8. In this instance as well, since the prohibition against these two subjects is mentioned in the same verse, if a person violates them both at the same time, he receives only one set of lashes.
94. As forbidden by Leviticus 5:11; *Hilchot Ma'aseh HaKorbanot* 12:7.
95. As forbidden by Leviticus 5:11; *Hilchot Ma'aseh HaKorbanot* 12:8.
96. As forbidden by Numbers 5:15; *Hilchot Ma'aseh HaKorbanot* 12:7-8.
97. As forbidden by the above sources.
98. As forbidden by Leviticus 5:8; *Hilchot Ma'aseh HaKorbanot* 7:6.
99. As forbidden by Leviticus 27:10; *Hilchot Temurah* 1:1.
100. As forbidden by Leviticus 7:19; *Hilchot Pesulei HaMukdashim* 18:12.
101. This prohibition is also included in the warning of Deuteronomy 14:3; see *Hilchot Pesulei HaMukdashim* 18:3-5.
102. *Makkot* 17a derives this prohibition from Deuteronomy 12:17; see *Hilchot Ma'aseh HaKorbonot* 11:5.

56) a non-priest who partakes of the meat of sacrifices of the most sacred order after their blood has been sprinkled on the altar;[103]
57) a non-priest who partakes of the meat of a firstborn animal;[104]
58) a daughter of a priest who married a non-priest who partakes of the breast and the foreleg [given to the priests]; [this applies] even after the death of her husband;[105]
59) a *chalalah*[106] who partakes of *terumah*;[107]
60) a person who partakes of sacrifices of lesser sanctity outside of Jerusalem;[108]
61) a person who partakes of sacrifices of lesser sanctity before their blood is sprinkled [on the altar][109]
62) a person who partakes of an [unblemished] firstborn animal outside of Jerusalem;[110]
63) a person who partakes of the second tithe after it had entered Jerusalem [once it had been taken] outside Jerusalem [again];[111]
64) a priest who partakes of the first fruits after they entered Jerusalem, [but] before they were placed down in the Temple Courtyard;[112]
65) a priest who partakes of the first fruits after they were placed down in the Temple Courtyard and [were then taken] outside Jerusalem [again];[113]
66) a person who partakes of *ma'aser sheni* in Jerusalem after it became impure, before it was redeemed;[114]
67) a person who is ritually impure who partakes of *ma'aser sheni* which was pure in Jerusalem;[115]
68) a person who partakes of *ma'aser sheni* - and similarly, any other consecrated food[116] - while in a state of acute mourning;[117]
69) an uncircumcised person who partakes of sacrificial meal or *terumot*;[118]
70) a person who partakes of a meal offering brought by a priest or any other sacrifice that should be totally consumed by the fire [of the altar];[119]
71) a person who partakes of the meat of the sin-offerings that are burned and any other [sacrifices] that must be burnt;[120]
72) a person who slaughters the Paschal sacrifice while [he possesses] *chametz*;[121]
73) a person who breaks a bone [from the Paschal sacrifice]; this applies with regard to the first [sacrifice][122] or the second [sacrifice];[123]
74) a person who removes meat from [the Paschal sacrifice] outside the company [of people partaking of it];[124]

103. As forbidden by Exodus 29:33; *Hilchot Ma'aseh HaKorbanot* 7:8.
104. Such animals must be offered as sacrifices and their meat given to the priests. The prohibition is stated in Deuteronomy 12:17; *Hilchot Bechorot* 1:16.
105. As forbidden by Leviticus 22:12; *Hilchot Terumot* 6:7.
106. A woman born from relations forbidden to a priest, or a woman who is forbidden to a priest who has relations with one.
107. This prohibition is also inferred from the above verse. See *Hilchot Terumot, loc. cit.*.
108. As inferred from Deuteronomy 12:17; *Hilchot Ma'aseh HaKorbanot* 11:5.
109. This prohibition is also derived from the above verse; see *Hilchot Ma'aseh HaKorbanot* 4:5.

נו) זָר שֶׁאָכַל בְּשַׂר קָדְשֵׁי קָדָשִׁים אַחַר מַתַּן דָּמִים.
נז) זָר שֶׁאָכַל בְּשַׂר בְּכוֹר.
נח) כֹּהֶנֶת שֶׁנִּשֵּׂאת לְזָר שֶׁאוֹכֶלֶת חָזֶה וָשׁוֹק, אֲפִלּוּ לְאַחַר מִיתַת בַּעְלָהּ.
נט) חֲלָלָה שֶׁאָכְלָה תְּרוּמָה.
ס) הָאוֹכֵל קָדָשִׁים קַלִּים חוּץ לִירוּשָׁלַיִם.
סא) הָאוֹכֵל קָדָשִׁים קַלִּים קֹדֶם זְרִיקַת דָּמִים.
סב) הָאוֹכֵל בְּכוֹר חוּץ לִירוּשָׁלַיִם.
סג) הָאוֹכֵל מַעֲשֵׂר שֵׁנִי אַחַר שֶׁרָאָה פְּנֵי הַבַּיִת חוּץ לִירוּשָׁלַיִם.
סד) כֹּהֵן שֶׁאָכַל בִּכּוּרִים מִשֶּׁנִּכְנְסוּ לִירוּשָׁלַיִם קֹדֶם הֲנָחָה בָּעֲזָרָה.
סה) כֹּהֵן שֶׁאָכַל בִּכּוּרִים חוּץ לִירוּשָׁלַיִם אַחַר שֶׁהִנִּיחוּ בָּעֲזָרָה.
סו) הָאוֹכֵל מַעֲשֵׂר שֵׁנִי שֶׁנִּטְמָא בִּירוּשָׁלַיִם קֹדֶם שֶׁיִּפָּדֶה.
סז) טָמֵא שֶׁאָכַל מַעֲשֵׂר שֵׁנִי הַטָּהוֹר בִּירוּשָׁלַיִם.
סח) הָאוֹכֵל מַעֲשֵׂר שֵׁנִי בַּאֲנִינוּת, וְכֵן כָּל הַקֳּדָשִׁים.
סט) עָרֵל שֶׁאָכַל בְּשַׂר קֹדֶשׁ אוֹ תְּרוּמוֹת.
ע) הָאוֹכֵל מִמִּנְחַת כֹּהֵן, וְכֵן מִכָּל דָּבָר שֶׁהוּא כָּלִיל לָאִשִּׁים.
עא) הָאוֹכֵל מִבְּשַׂר חַטָּאוֹת הַנִּשְׂרָפוֹת, וְכֵן מִכָּל הַטָּעוּן שְׂרֵפָה.
עב) הַשּׁוֹחֵט פֶּסַח עַל הֶחָמֵץ.
עג) הַשּׁוֹבֵר בּוֹ עֶצֶם, בֵּין בָּרִאשׁוֹן בֵּין בַּשֵּׁנִי.
עד) הַמּוֹצִיא מִבְּשָׂרוֹ חוּץ לַחֲבוּרָתוֹ.

110. This prohibition is also derived from the above verse; see *Hilchot Bechorot* 1:16.
111. This prohibition is also derived from the above verse; see *Hilchot Ma'aser Sheni* 2:5-6.
112. This prohibition is also derived from the above verse; see *Hilchot Bikkurim* 3:3-4.
113. This prohibition is also derived from the above verse; see *Hilchot Bikkurim* 3:3.
114. As inferred from Deuteronomy 26:14; *Hilchot Ma'aser Sheni* 3:1.
115. This prohibition is also derived from the same sources.
116. See Leviticus 10:19.
117. This prohibition is also derived from the same verse; see *Hilchot Ma'aser Sheni* 3:5-7.
118. *Yevamot* 70a derives this prohibition from Exodus 12:48. See *Hilchot Terumot* 7:10, *Hilchot Ma'aseh HaKorbanot* 10:9, and *Hilchot Korban Pesach* 9:8.
119. As forbidden by Leviticus 6:16; *Hilchot Ma'aseh HaKorbanot* 11:3.
120. As forbidden by Leviticus 22:23; *Hilchot Ma'aseh HaKorbanot, loc. cit.*
121. As forbidden by Exodus 23:18; *Hilchot Korban Pesach* 1:5.
122. Brought on the fourteenth of Nisan.
123. Brought on the fourteenth of Iyar by a person who did not bring a sacrifice in Nisan. This prohibition is forbidden by Exodus 12:46; Numbers 9:12; *Hilchot Korban Pesach* 6:1.
124. As forbidden by Exodus 12:46; *Hilchot Korban Pesach* 9:1.

75) a person who partakes of meat from [the Paschal sacrifice] outside of that company;[125]
76) a person who partakes of meat from [the Paschal sacrifice] partially roasted or cooked;[126]
77) a person who purposely derives benefit from consecrated property;[127]
78) a person who partakes of *tevel* from which the tithes, even the tithe for the poor, has not been separated, even though the *terumot* have been separated;[128]
79) a person who partakes of the meat of an animal that was condemned to be stoned to death, even if [the condemned animal] was slaughtered [correctly];[129]
80) a person who eats [meat from] a non-kosher animal;[130]
81) ... a non-kosher fowl;[131]
82) ... a non-kosher fish;[132]
83) a person who partakes of a flying teeming animal;[133]
84) ... an earthbound teeming animal;[134]
85) ... an aquatic teeming animal;[135]
86) ... an animal that crawls on the earth even though it does not reproduce;[136]
87) ... worms from fruit after they emerged [from the fruit];[137]
88) a person who eats carrion;[138]
89) ... an animal that was critically injured;[139]
90) ... a limb from a living animal;[140]
91) ... the sciatic nerve;[141]
92) ... meat [cooked] with milk;[142]
93) a person who cooks meat with milk;[143]
94) a person who partakes of fresh grain before the bringing of the *omer*;[144]
95) a person who partakes of *orlah*;[145]

125. This prohibition is derived from Exodus 22:30. Although that verse speaks about other subjects entirely, this prohibition is also included. See *Hilchot Ma'achalot Assurot* 5:9, *Hilchot Ma'aseh HaKorbanot* 11:6, and *Hilchot Korban Pesach* 9:2.
126. As forbidden by Exodus 12:9; *Hilchot Korban Pesach* 8:6. See Chapter 18:3 which explains that if a person violates both of these prohibitions at the same time, he receives only one set of lashes.
127. This prohibition is also derived from Deuteronomy 12:17; see *Hilchot Meilah* 1:3.
128. A person who partakes of food from which the *terumot* have not been separated, by contrast, is liable for death at the hand of heaven as mentioned in Halachah 2. The prohibition against partaking of food from which tithes have not been separated is also derived from Deuteronomy, *loc. cit.*. See *Hilchot Ma'achalot Assurot* 10:20-21.
129. As forbidden by Exodus 21:25; *Hilchot Ma'achalot Assurot* 4:22.
130. As forbidden by Deuteronomy 14:6-8; *Hilchot Ma'achalot Assurot* 2:1-2.
131. As forbidden by Leviticus 11:13; *Hilchot Ma'achalot Assurot* 2:4.
132. As forbidden by Leviticus 11:11; *Hilchot Ma'achalot Assurot* 2:4.
133. E.g., a fly or a mosquito; as forbidden by Deuteronomy 14:19; *Hilchot Ma'achalot Assurot* 2:5-6.
134. E.g., snakes, scorpions; as forbidden by Leviticus 11:29, 41; *Hilchot Ma'achalot Assurot* 2:6.

עה) הָאוֹכֵל מִבְּשָׂרוֹ חוּץ מֵחֲבוּרָתוֹ.

עו) הָאוֹכֵל מִבְּשָׂרוֹ נָא אוֹ מְבֻשָּׁל.

עז) הַנֶּהֱנֶה מִן הַהֶקְדֵּשׁ בְּמֵזִיד.

עח) הָאוֹכֵל טֶבֶל שֶׁעֲדַיִן לֹא הֻפְרַשׁ מִמֶּנּוּ מַעֲשֵׂר, אֲפִלּוּ מַעְשַׂר עָנִי, אַף עַל פִּי שֶׁהוּרְמוּ תְּרוּמוֹתָיו.

עט) הָאוֹכֵל מִבְּשַׂר נֶפֶשׁ חַיָּה שֶׁנִּגְמַר דִּינָהּ לִסְקִילָה, אַף עַל פִּי שֶׁנִּשְׁחֲטָה.

פ) הָאוֹכֵל בְּהֵמָה טְמֵאָה.

פא) הָאוֹכֵל עוֹף טָמֵא.

פב) הָאוֹכֵל דָּג טָמֵא.

פג) הָאוֹכֵל שֶׁרֶץ הָעוֹף.

פד) הָאוֹכֵל שֶׁרֶץ הָאָרֶץ.

פה) הָאוֹכֵל שֶׁרֶץ הַמַּיִם.

פו) הָאוֹכֵל רֶמֶשׂ הָאֲדָמָה, אַף עַל פִּי שֶׁאֵינוֹ רָבֶה.

פז) הָאוֹכֵל תּוֹלָעִים שֶׁבַּפֵּרוֹת אַחַר שֶׁפֵּרְשׁוּ.

פח) הָאוֹכֵל נְבֵלָה.

פט) הָאוֹכֵל טְרֵפָה.

צ) הָאוֹכֵל אֵיבָר מִן הַחַי.

צא) הָאוֹכֵל גִּיד הַנָּשֶׁה.

צב) הָאוֹכֵל בָּשָׂר בְּחָלָב.

צג) הַמְבַשֵּׁל בָּשָׂר בְּחָלָב.

צד) הָאוֹכֵל מִתְּבוּאָה חֲדָשָׁה קֹדֶם הֲבָאַת הָעֹמֶר.

צה) הָאוֹכֵל עָרְלָה.

135. I.e., any aquatic animal that is not a fish; as forbidden by Leviticus 11:43; *Hilchot Ma'achalot Assurot* 2:12.
136. But rather comes into being from filth; as forbidden by Leviticus 11:44; *Hilchot Ma'achalot Assurot* 2:13.
137. This refers to worms that come into being from fruit as it decays. While they are in the fruit, they may be eaten. After they emerge, they are forbidden, as stated by Leviticus 11:42; *Hilchot Ma'achalot Assurot* 2:14.
138. As forbidden by Deuteronomy 14:21; *Hilchot Ma'achalot Assurot* 4:1.
139. As forbidden by Exodus 22:30; *Hilchot Ma'achalot Assurot* 4:6.
140. As forbidden by Deuteronomy 12:23; *Hilchot Ma'achalot Assurot* 4:10, 5:1-3.
141. As forbidden by Genesis 32:33; *Hilchot Ma'achalot Assurot* 8:2.
142. As forbidden by Exodus 23:19; *Hilchot Ma'achalot Assurot* 9:1-2.
143. As forbidden by Exodus 34:26; *Hilchot Ma'achalot Assurot, loc. cit.*.
144. As forbidden by Leviticus 23:14; *Hilchot Ma'achalot Assurot* 10:2. As explained in that source, there are three different negative commandments involved.
145. Fruit which grows within three years of a tree's being planted; as forbidden by Leviticus 19:23; *Hilchot Ma'achalot Assurot* 10:10-11.

96) a person who partakes of *kilai hakerem;*[146]
97) a person who partakes of *chametz* in a mixture on Pesach;[147]
98) ...after midday [on the fourteenth of Nissan];[148]
99) a person who maintains possession of *chametz* [on Pesach], e.g., he causes his dough to leaven;[149]
100) a person who drinks wine used as a libation for false deities;[150]
101) a nazarite who partakes of the products of the vine;[151]
102) ... cuts his hair,[152]
103) ...who contracts impurity imparted by a corpse;[153]
104) a person who shaves [the hair] next to a blemish [of *tzara'at*][154]
105) a person who cuts off signs of *tzara'at* or removes them with fire;[155]
106) a person who tills a wadi where the neck of a calf was broken [to atone for an unsolved murder];[156]
107) a person who sows [in] *Eretz Yisrael* in the Sabbatical year;[157]
108) a person who trims a tree in the Sabbatical year;[158]
109) a person who reaps freely growing produce [in the Sabbatical year] without deviating from his ordinary pattern;[159]
110) a person who harvests fruit [in the Sabbatical year] without deviating from his ordinary pattern;[160]
111) a person who sows in the Jubilee year;[161]
112) a person who reaps in the Jubilee year without deviating from his ordinary pattern;[161]
113) a person who harvests fruit in the Jubilee year without deviating from his ordinary pattern;[161]
114) a person who destroys [the produce from] the corners of his harvest without giving it to a poor person;[162]
115) a person who collects the grapes that grow individually in his vineyard and does not give them to a poor person;[163]
116) a person who collects the grain that falls from the reapers and does not give it to a poor person;[164]
117) a person who collects the grapes that grow in underdeveloped clusters in his vineyard and does not give them to a poor person;[165]

146. Grain or vegetables that grow in a vineyard; as forbidden by Deuteronomy 22:9; *Hilchot Ma'achalot Assurot* 10:7.
147. As forbidden by Exodus 12:20; *Hilchot Chametz UMatzah* 1:6.
148. As forbidden by Deuteronomy 16:3; *Hilchot Chametz UMatzah* 1:8. A person who partakes of *chametz* on Pesach itself is liable for *kerait*, as stated in Halachah 1.
149. As forbidden by Exodus 12:19; *Hilchot Chametz UMatzah* 1:2-3. There are two prohibitions involved in possessing *chametz* and the person is worthy for lashes for violating each of them.

This refers to grain products that we caused to leaven on Pesach itself. If, however, a person leaves *chametz* in his possession before the beginning of the holiday, he violates these prohibitions, but is not punished by lashes.
150. As forbidden by Deuteronomy 32:38; *Hilchot Ma'achalot Assurot* 11:1-2.
151. As forbidden by Numbers 6:3-4; *Hilchot Nazirut* 1:2;5:2-3. Included by this wording are five negative commandments, as explained in those sources.
152. As forbidden by Numbers 6:5; *Hilchot Nazirut* 5:11.

צו) הָאוֹכֵל כִּלְאֵי הַכֶּרֶם.

צז) הָאוֹכֵל תַּעֲרֹבֶת חָמֵץ בַּפֶּסַח.

צח) הָאוֹכֵל חָמֵץ אַחַר חֲצוֹת.

צט) הַמְקַיֵּם חָמֵץ בִּרְשׁוּתוֹ, וּכְגוֹן שֶׁחִמֵּץ עִסָּתוֹ.

ק) הַשּׁוֹתֶה יֵין נֶסֶךְ.

קא) נָזִיר שֶׁאָכַל מִגֶּפֶן הַיַּיִן.

קב) נָזִיר שֶׁגִּלַּח.

קג) נָזִיר שֶׁנִּטְמָא לְמֵת.

קד) הַמְגַלֵּחַ אֶת הַנֶּתֶק.

קה) הַחוֹתֵךְ סִימָנֵי צָרַעַת אוֹ שֶׁכְּוָאָן בָּאֵשׁ.

קו) הָעוֹבֵד בַּנַּחַל שֶׁנִּתְעָרְפָה בּוֹ הָעֶגְלָה.

קז) הַזּוֹרֵעַ אֶרֶץ יִשְׂרָאֵל בַּשְּׁבִיעִית.

קח) הַזּוֹמֵר אֶת הָאִילָן בַּשְּׁבִיעִית.

קט) הַקּוֹצֵר סָפִיחַ בְּלֹא שִׁנּוּי.

קי) הַבּוֹצֵר בְּלֹא שִׁנּוּי.

קיא) הַזּוֹרֵעַ בִּשְׁנַת הַיּוֹבֵל.

קיב) הַקּוֹצֵר בָּהּ בְּלֹא שִׁנּוּי.

קיג) הַבּוֹצֵר בָּהּ בְּלֹא שִׁנּוּי.

קיד) הַמְכַלֶּה פְּאַת שָׂדֶה וְלֹא נְתָנָהּ לְעָנִי.

קטו) הַמְעוֹלֵל כַּרְמוֹ וְלֹא נְתָנָהּ לְעָנִי.

קטז) הַמְלַקֵּט לֶקֶט וְלֹא נְתָנוֹ לְעָנִי.

קיז) פָּרַט כַּרְמוֹ וְלֹא נְתָנוֹ לְעָנִי.

153. As forbidden by Numbers 6:7; *Hilchot Nazirut* 5:15-18. Included by this wording are two negative commandments, as explained in those sources.
154. As forbidden by Leviticus 13:33; *Hilchot Tuma'at Tzara'at* 10:1.
155. As forbidden by Deuteronomy 24:8; *Hilchot Tuma'at Tzara'at, loc. cit.*
156. As forbidden by Deuteronomy 21:4; *Hilchot Rotzeach* 10:9.
157. As forbidden by Leviticus 25:4; *Hilchot Shemitah ViYovel* 1:1-2.
158. As forbidden by Leviticus 25:4; *Hilchot Shemitah ViYovel* 1:2-3.
159. As forbidden by Leviticus 25:5; *Hilchot Shemitah ViYovel* 5:1.
160. As forbidden by Leviticus 25:5; *Hilchot Shemitah ViYovel* 4:22-23.
161. As forbidden by Leviticus 25:11; *Hilchot Shemitah ViYovel* 10:16.
162. As forbidden by Leviticus 23:22; *Hilchot Matanot Aniyim* 1:3. If, however, the produce is not destroyed, the violator may correct his transgression and avoid lashes by giving that produce to the poor, as stated in Chapter 18, Halachah 2. Similar concepts apply with regard to the next six transgressions the Rambam mentions.
163. As forbidden by Leviticus 19:10; *Hilchot Matanot Aniyim* 4:17-18.
164. As forbidden by Leviticus 19:9; *Hilchot Matanot Aniyim* 1:4.
165. As forbidden by Leviticus 19:10; *Hilchot Matanot Aniyim* 4:16.

118) a person who takes a forgotten sheaf and does not give it to a poor person;[166]
119) a person who takes a mother bird together with her young and does not send away the mother bird;[167]
120) a person who sows mixed species of seeds together [while] sowing in *Eretz [Yisrael]*;[168]
121) a person who sows mixed species in a vineyard in *Eretz [Yisrael]*;[169]
122) a person who grafts mixed species of trees; [this prohibition applies] in every place;[170]
123) a person who mates mixed species of animals; [this prohibition applies] in every place;[171]
124) a person who leads mixed species of animals; [this prohibition applies] in every place;[172]
125) a person who muzzles an animal while it is working; [this prohibition applies] in every place;[173]
126) a person who slaughters an animal and its offspring [on the same day]; [this prohibition applies] in every place;[174]
127) a person who takes security from a colleague and does not return it to him [when he requires it];[175]
128) a person who takes security from a widow and does not return it to her;[176]
129) a person who takes utensils used in the preparation of food as security;[177]
130) a lying witness who is not penalized financially;[178]
131) a person who strikes a colleague with a blow that does not require a *p'rutah* to be paid as compensation;[179]
132) a wayward and rebellious son after the first testimony was delivered against him;[180]
133) a person who spreads a libelous report about his wife who is discovered to have lied;[181]
134) a person who curses a colleague using God's name;[182]
135) a person who takes a false oath[183]
136) a person who takes an unnecessary oath[184]
137) a person who abrogates his vow;[185]
138) a person who goes beyond the Sabbath limits on the Sabbath;[186]
139) a person who performs a forbidden labor on a festival;[187]

166. As forbidden by Deuteronomy 24:19; *Hilchot Matanot Aniyim* 1:6.
167. As forbidden by Deuteronomy 22:6; *Hilchot Shechitah* 13:1.
168. As forbidden by Leviticus 19:19; *Hilchot Kelayim* 1:1-3.
169. As forbidden by Deuteronomy 22:9; *Hilchot Kelayim* 5:1.
170. As forbidden by the above verse; *Hilchot Kelayim* 1:5.
171. As forbidden by the above verse; *Hilchot Kelayim* 9:1.
172. As forbidden by Deuteronomy 22:10; *Hilchot Kelayim* 9:7-8.
173. As forbidden by Deuteronomy 25:4; *Hilchot Sechirut* 13:2.
174. As forbidden by Leviticus 22:28; *Hilchot Shechitah* 12:1.
175. As forbidden by Deuteronomy 24:12; *Hilchot Malveh V'Loveh* 3:5.

קיח) הַלּוֹקֵחַ עֹמֶר הַשִּׁכְחָה וְלֹא נְתָנוֹ לְעָנִי.
קיט) הַלּוֹקֵחַ אֵם עַל בָּנִים וְלֹא שִׁלַּח הָאֵם.
קכ) הַזּוֹרֵעַ כִּלְאַיִם בָּאָרֶץ בִּזְרָעִים.
קכא) הַזּוֹרֵעַ כִּלְאֵי הַכֶּרֶם בָּאָרֶץ.
קכב) הַמַּרְכִּיב אִילָנוֹת כִּלְאַיִם בְּכָל מָקוֹם.
קכג) הַמַּרְבִּיעַ בְּהֵמָה כִּלְאַיִם בְּכָל מָקוֹם.
קכד) הַמַּנְהִיג בְּכִלְאַיִם בְּכָל מָקוֹם.
קכה) הַחוֹסֵם בְּהֵמָה בְּעֵת מְלָאכָה בְּכָל מָקוֹם.
קכו) הַשּׁוֹחֵט אוֹתוֹ וְאֶת בְּנוֹ בְּכָל מָקוֹם.
קכז) הַמְמַשְׁכֵּן חֲבֵרוֹ בְּיָדוֹ וְלֹא הֶחֱזִיר לוֹ הָעֲבוֹט.
קכח) הַחוֹבֵל אַלְמָנָה וְלֹא הֶחֱזִיר הַמַּשְׁכּוֹן.
קכט) הַחוֹבֵל כֵּלִים שֶׁעוֹשִׂין בָּהֶן אֹכֶל נֶפֶשׁ.
קל) עֵד זוֹמֵם שֶׁאֵין בּוֹ תַּשְׁלוּמִין.
קלא) הַמַּכֶּה חֲבֵרוֹ הַכָּאָה שֶׁאֵין בָּהּ שָׁוֶה פְּרוּטָה.
קלב) בֵּן סוֹרֵר וּמוֹרֶה בְּעֵדוּת רִאשׁוֹנָה.
קלג) הַמּוֹצִיא שֵׁם רַע שֶׁנִּמְצָא דְבָרוֹ שֶׁקֶר.
קלד) הַמְקַלֵּל אֶת חֲבֵרוֹ בְּשֵׁם.
קלה) הַנִּשְׁבָּע לַשֶּׁקֶר.
קלו) הַנִּשְׁבָּע לַשָּׁוְא.
קלז) הַמְחַלֵּל נִדְרוֹ.
קלח) הַיּוֹצֵא חוּץ לַתְּחוּם בְּשַׁבָּת.
קלט) הָעוֹשֶׂה מְלָאכָה בְּיוֹם טוֹב.

176. As forbidden by Deuteronomy 24:17; *Hilchot Malveh V'Loveh* 3:1.
177. As forbidden by Deuteronomy 24:6; *Hilchot Malveh V'Loveh* 3:2.
178. As forbidden by Exodus 20:15; *Hilchot Edut* 20:8-9. If, however, there is a financial penalty, he is required to make financial reimbursement and does not receive lashes. This applies with regard to the following halachah as well. See Chapter 18, Halachah 2.
179. As forbidden by Deuteronomy 25:3; *Hilchot Sanhedrin* 16:12.
180. As mentioned by Deuteronomy 21:18; *Hilchot Mamrim* 7:1,7.
181. As mentioned by Deuteronomy 22:18; *Hilchot Na'arah Betulah* 3:1,6.
182. As forbidden by Leviticus 19:14; *Hilchot Sanhedrin* 26:1. Included in this are also the prohibitions against cursing a judge and cursing a *nasi*.
183. As forbidden by Leviticus 19:12; *Hilchot Sh'vuot* 1:2-3.
184. As forbidden by Exodus 20:6; *Hilchot Sh'vuot* 1:4-7.
185. As forbidden by Numbers 30:3; *Hilchot Nedarim* 1:5.
186. As forbidden by Exodus 16:29; *Hilchot Shabbat* 27:1.
187. As forbidden by Exodus 12:18; *Hilchot Sh'vitat Yom Tov* 1:1-2. There is a separate prohibition, forbidding the performance of work on each of the festivals.

140) a person who [removes the hair] at the corner of his head;[188]
141) a person who [removes the hair] at the corner of his beard;[188]
142) a person who gouges [his flesh] because of a person's death;[189]
143) a person who shaves [his head] because of a person's death;[190]
144) a person who tatoos himself;[191]
145) a person who wears *shaatnez*;[192]
146) a person who chops down a fruit tree for a destructive purpose;[193]
147) a man who wears the garments of a woman;[194]
148) a woman who wears the garments of a man;[195]
149) a priest who contracts impurity because of contact with a corpse;[196]
150) a priest who consecrates a woman classified as a *zonah*[197] and has relations with her;[198]
151) a priest who consecrates a divorcee and has relations with her;[199]
152) a priest who consecrates a woman classified as a *challalah*[200] and has relations with her;[201]
153) a High Priest who had relations with a widow even though he did not consecrate her;[202]
154) a person who remarries his divorcee after she has been consecrated [by another man];[203]
155) a person who marries a woman who is obligated to perform *yibbum*;[204]
156) a man who has relations with a woman outside the context of marriage;[205]
157) a *mamzer*[206] who marries a native-born Jewess and has relations with her;[207]
158) a person with crushed testicles who marries a native-born Jewess and has relations with her;[208]
159) a person who castrates another man, or a male animal, beast, or fowl;[209]
160) a rapist who divorces his victim and does not remarry her;[210]
161) a person who spreads a libelous report about his wife, divorces her without remarrying her;[211]

188. As forbidden by Leviticus 19:27; *Hilchot Avodat Kochavim* 12:1,6.
189. As forbidden by Leviticus 19:25; *Hilchot Avodat Kochavim* 12:12.
190. As forbidden by Deuteronomy 14:1; *Hilchot Avodat Kochavim* 12:15.
191. As forbidden by Leviticus 19:28; *Hilchot Avodat Kochavim* 12:11.
192. As forbidden by Deuteronomy 22:11; *Hilchot Kelayim* 10:30.
193. As forbidden by Deuteronomy 20:19; *Hilchot Melachim* 6:8.
194. As forbidden by Deuteronomy 22:5; *Hilchot Avodat Kochavim* 12:10.
195. As forbidden by Deuteronomy 22:5; *Hilchot Avodat Kochavim* 12:10.
196. As forbidden by Leviticus 21:1; *Hilchot Eivel* 3:1-3. As explained in these sources, by contracting ritual impurity, a priest violates three prohibitions. Each one is punishable by lashes.
197. This term is defined as referring to any woman who is not a native-born Jewess or who has engaged in sexual relations with a man whom she is forbidden to marry.
198. As forbidden by Leviticus 21:7; *Hilchot Issurei Bi'ah* 17:1-2.
199. As forbidden by Leviticus 21:7; *Hilchot Issurei Bi'ah* 17:1-2.
200. This term is defined as referring to any woman who was forbidden to a priest and

קמ) הַמַּקִּיף פְּאַת הָרֹאשׁ.

קמא) הַמַּקִּיף פְּאַת זָקָן.

קמב) הַשּׂוֹרֵט עַל מֵת.

קמג) הַקּוֹרֵחַ רֹאשׁוֹ עַל הַמֵּת.

קמד) הַכּוֹתֵב כְּתֹבֶת קַעֲקַע.

קמה) הַלּוֹבֵשׁ שַׁעַטְנֵז.

קמו) הַקּוֹצֵץ אִילָנֵי מַאֲכָל דֶּרֶךְ הַשְׁחָתָה.

קמז) אִישׁ שֶׁלָּבַשׁ מַלְבּוּשׁ אִשָּׁה.

קמח) אִשָּׁה שֶׁלָּבְשָׁה מַלְבּוּשׁ אִישׁ.

קמט) כֹּהֵן שֶׁנִּטְמָא לְמֵת.

קן) כֹּהֵן שֶׁקִּדֵּשׁ אִשָּׁה זוֹנָה וּבְעָלָהּ.

קנא) כֹּהֵן שֶׁקִּדֵּשׁ גְּרוּשָׁה וּבְעָלָהּ.

קנב) כֹּהֵן שֶׁקִּדֵּשׁ חֲלָלָה וּבְעָלָהּ.

קנג) כֹּהֵן גָּדוֹל שֶׁבָּעַל אַלְמָנָה אַף עַל פִּי שֶׁלֹּא קִדְּשָׁהּ.

קנד) הַמַּחֲזִיר גְּרוּשָׁתוֹ אַחַר שֶׁנִּתְקַדְּשָׁה.

קנה) הַנּוֹשֵׂא זְקוּקָה לְיָבָם.

קנו) הַבָּא עַל הַקְּדֵשָׁה.

קנז) מַמְזֵר שֶׁנָּשָׂא בַּת יִשְׂרָאֵל וּבָעַל.

קנח) פְּצוּעַ דַּכָּא שֶׁנָּשָׂא בַּת יִשְׂרָאֵל וּבָעַל.

קנט) הַמְסָרֵס אִישׁ, וְכֵן שְׁאָר זִכְרֵי בְּהֵמָה חַיָּה וָעוֹף.

קס) אוֹנֵס שֶׁגֵּרֵשׁ אֲנוּסָתוֹ וְלֹא הֶחֱזִירָהּ.

קסא) הַמּוֹצִיא שֵׁם רַע שֶׁגֵּרֵשׁ אִשְׁתּוֹ וְלֹא הֶחֱזִירָהּ.

afterwards had relations with a priest or a woman fathered by a priest through relations that are forbidden to him.

201. As forbidden by Leviticus 21:7; *Hilchot Issurei Bi'ah* 17:1-2.

202. As forbidden by Leviticus 21:15; *Hilchot Issurei Bi'ah* 17:3.

203. As forbidden by Deuteronomy 24:4; *Hilchot Gerushin* 11:12.

204. As forbidden by Deuteronomy 25:5; *Hilchot Yibbum* 2:18. *Yibbum* refers to a person's marriage to the childless widow of his deceased brother.

205. As forbidden by Deuteronomy 23:18; *Hilchot Ishut* 1:4.

206. A person born from an adulterous or incestuous relationship.

207. As forbidden by Deuteronomy 23:3; *Hilchot Issurei Bi'ah* 1:2. The Ra'avad questions why marriage is mentioned. Seemingly, the prohibition is violated by any sexual relations, within or without the context of marriage. In his gloss to *Hilchot Issurei Bi'ah* 15:2, the *Maggid Mishneh* quotes a responsa attributed to the Rambam which deals with this question.

208. As forbidden by Deuteronomy 23:2; *Hilchot Issurei Bi'ah* 16:1-3.

209. As forbidden by Leviticus 22:24; *Hilchot Issurei Bi'ah* 16:9-10.

210. As forbidden by Deuteronomy 22:29; *Hilchot Na'arah Betulah* 1:7.

211. As forbidden by Deuteronomy 22:19; *Hilchot Na'arah Betulah* 3:4.

162) a person who enjoys intimacy with a woman forbidden him even though he did not engage in sexual relations; such a person is suspect of forbidden sexual activity;[212]
163) a person who marries out of the faith;[213]
164) an Ammonite convert who marries a native-born Jewess and had relations with her;[214]
165) a Moabite convert who marries a native-born Jewess and had relations with her;[215]
166) a king who takes more wives [than allowed by the Torah];[216]
167) a king who acquires more horses [than allowed by the Torah];[217]
168) a king who acquires more wealth than necessary;[218]

Thus there are a total of 207 violations which are punishable by lashes. An acronym for them is ילקו זרים [The strangers will be lashed.][219]

CHAPTER TWENTY

1. A court does not inflict punishment on the basis of conclusions which it draws,[1] only on the basis [of the testimony] of witnesses with clear proof. Even if witnesses saw a person pursuing a colleague, they gave him a warning,[2] but then diverted their attention, [punishment is not inflicted on the basis of their testimony]. Or [to give a graphic example,] the pursuer entered into a ruin, following the pursued and the witnesses followed him. They saw the victim slain, in his death throes, and the sword dripping blood in the hand of the killer, since they did not see him strike him, the court does not execute [the killer] based on this testimony. Concerning this and the like, [Exodus 23:7] states: "Do not kill an innocent and righteous person."[3]

Similarly, if two people testified that a person served a false deity [in different circumstances, e.g.,] one saw him serve the sun and warned him, while the other saw him serve the moon and warned him, their testimonies are not combined.[4] [This can also be inferred from] the verse: "Do not kill an innocent and righteous person." Since there is a rationale on which basis he could be held innocent and righteous, he should not be executed.[5]

212. As forbidden by Leviticus 18:6; *Hilchot Issurei Bi'ah* 21:1-2.
213. As forbidden by Deuteronomy 7:3; *Hilchot Issurei Bi'ah* 12:1.
214. As forbidden by Deuteronomy 23:4; *Hilchot Issurei Bi'ah* 12:17.
215. This prohibition is mentioned in the same sources.
216. As forbidden by Deuteronomy 17:17; *Hilchot Melachim* 3:2.
217. As forbidden by Deuteronomy 17:16; *Hilchot Melachim* 3:3.
218. As forbidden by Deuteronomy 17:17; *Hilchot Melachim* 3:4.
219. This acronym is found in the manuscript copies of the *Mishneh Torah* indicating it was included by the Rambam himself.

1. Different rules apply with regard to cases of financial responsibility. In such instances,

קסב) הַקָּרֵב אֶל הָעֲרָיוֹת בְּדֶרֶךְ מִדַּרְכֵי הַזְּנוּת, אַף עַל פִּי שֶׁלֹּא גִלָּה עֶרְוָה. וְזֶהוּ הֶחָשׁוּד עַל הָעֲרָיוֹת.

קסג) הַמִּתְחַתֵּן בְּעוֹבְדֵי כּוֹכָבִים.

קסד) גֵּר עַמּוֹנִי שֶׁנָּשָׂא בַּת יִשְׂרָאֵל וּבָעַל.

קסה) גֵּר מוֹאָבִי שֶׁנָּשָׂא בַּת יִשְׂרָאֵל וּבָעַל.

קסו) מֶלֶךְ שֶׁהִרְבָּה נָשִׁים.

קסז) מֶלֶךְ שֶׁהִרְבָּה סוּסִים.

קסח) מֶלֶךְ שֶׁהִרְבָּה כֶּסֶף וְזָהָב.

נִמְצְאוּ כָּל הַלּוֹקִים מָאתַיִם וְשִׁבְעָה. וְסִימָן לָהֶם: יִלְקוּ זָרִים.

פֶּרֶק עֶשְׂרִים

א אֵין בֵּית דִּין עוֹנְשִׁין בְּאֹמֶד הַדַּעַת, אֶלָּא עַל פִּי עֵדִים בִּרְאָיָה בְּרוּרָה. אֲפִלּוּ רָאוּהוּ הָעֵדִים רוֹדֵף אַחַר חֲבֵרוֹ, וְהִתְרוּ בּוֹ, וְהֶעְלִימוּ עֵינֵיהֶם, אוֹ שֶׁנִּכְנַס אַחֲרָיו לְחֻרְבָּה וְנִכְנְסוּ אַחֲרָיו, וּמְצָאוּהוּ הָרוּג וּמְפַרְפֵּר וְהַסַּיִף מְנַטֵּף דָּם בְּיַד הַהוֹרֵג, הוֹאִיל וְלֹא רָאוּהוּ בְּעֵת שֶׁהִכָּהוּ – אֵין בֵּית דִּין הוֹרְגִין בְּעֵדוּת זוֹ.

וְעַל זֶה וְכַיּוֹצֵא בּוֹ נֶאֱמַר: וְנָקִי וְצַדִּיק אַל תַּהֲרֹג.

וְכֵן אִם הֵעִידוּ עָלָיו שְׁנַיִם שֶׁעָבַד עֲבוֹדָה זָרָה, זֶה רָאָהוּ שֶׁעָבַד אֶת הַחַמָּה וְהִתְרָה בּוֹ, וְזֶה רָאָהוּ שֶׁעָבַד אֶת הַלְּבָנָה וְהִתְרָה בּוֹ – אֵין מִצְטָרְפִין.

שֶׁנֶּאֱמַר: וְנָקִי וְצַדִּיק אַל תַּהֲרֹג. הוֹאִיל וְיֵשׁ שָׁם צַד לְנַקּוֹתוֹ וְלִהְיוֹתוֹ צַדִּיק – אַל תַּהַרְגֵהוּ.

firm circumstantial evidence is accepted, as the Rambam states in Chapter 24, Halachah 1; *Hilchot Chovel UMazik* 5:4 and other sources.

2. For otherwise no punishment would be given, as stated in Chapter 16, Halachah 4.

3. I.e., no matter how strong the circumstantial evidence, unless the witnesses actually see the crime, the killer is not executed. *Sefer HaMitzvot* (negative commandment 290) and *Sefer HaChinuch* (mitzvah 82) count this as one of the 613 mitzvot of the Torah.

In *Sefer HaMitzvot*, the Rambam explains the rationale for this mitzvah. Once the matter is left to human choice and logic, there is ultimately the possibility of error. The Torah feared that a judge would consider certain evidence as conclusive and sentence an innocent person to death.

4. For in neither instance did two witnesses observe a transgression. The Ramban (*Hasagot* to *Sefer HaMitzvot*) notes that similar concepts also apply with regard to financial laws. See *Hilchot Edut*, Chapter 4.

5. The *Mechilta* cites the conclusion of the verse: "For I (God) will not justify the wicked." Implied is that the court need not worry if it releases a killer because there is not sufficient evidence to have him executed. For ultimately, he and all existence is in God's hands and He will find a means to have retribution exacted. See the Jerusalem Talmud (*Sanhedrin* 4:3).

2. Whenever a person violates a prohibition punishable by execution by the court under duress, the court should not execute him. Even in situations where [the transgressor] was commanded to sacrifice his life and not transgress,[6] if he sinned under duress, although he desecrated God's name, he should not be executed. [This is derived from Deuteronomy 22:26]: "To the maiden, you should not do anything."[7] This verse is a warning to the court not to punish a person who transgresses under duress.[8]

3. When a man is compelled to engage in relations with a woman forbidden to him, he is liable for execution by the court. [The rationale is that] an erection can only come about willingly.[9] When a woman is raped, by contrast, she is absolved.[10] [This applies] even if, in the midst of the rape, she says: "Allow him to continue."[11] It is her natural inclination that overcame her.

4. It is forbidden for the court to have compassion for the killer.[12] [The judges] should not say: "Since this person has already been killed, what advantage is there in killing another person," and thus be lax in executing him. [This is implied by Deuteronomy 19:13]: "Do not allow your eyes to take pity. You shall eliminate innocent blood[shed]."[13]

Similarly, it is forbidden for the court to take pity on a person who was obligated to pay a fine.[14] They should not say: "He is poor. He acted unintentionally." Instead, they should exact the entire payment from him without compassion, as [*ibid.*:21] states: "You shall not take pity."

Similarly, in questions of monetary law, one should not show mercy to the poor, saying: "He is indigent and the other litigant is wealthy. Since both I and the wealthy man are obligated to provide for [the poor person's] livelihood, I will vindicate him in judgment and thus he will derive his livelihood with honor." With regard to this, the Torah warned [Exodus 23:3]: "Do not glorify the indigent in his dispute," and [Leviticus 19:15]: "Do not show favor to the poor."[15]

It is forbidden to show favor to a person of stature. What is implied? Two people come before one for judgment, one a wise man of stature and one, an

6. See *Hilchot Yesodei HaTorah*, Chapter 5, which outlines the situations in which a person is obligated to sacrifice his life to sanctify God's name.

7. The verse speaks of the rape of a maiden who has already been consecrated. Although she is party to a sin, since she was not willfully involved, she is absolved of responsibility. Similarly, *Nedarim* 27a mentions the general principle: "The Torah absolves a person acting under duress (an *oness*). This principle also applies in financial law.

8. *Sefer HaMitzvot* (negative commandment 294) and *Sefer HaChinuch* (mitzvah 556) count this as one of the 613 mitzvot of the Torah. The Ramban disputes this classification, stating that although the Torah does not hold the person liable, this is not considered as a mitzvah.

9. Hence he is considered to have acted on his own volition. The *Kessef Mishneh* explains

ב כָּל מִי שֶׁעָשָׂה דָבָר שֶׁחַיָּבִין עָלָיו מִיתַת בֵּית דִּין בְּאֹנֶס – אֵין בֵּית דִּין מְמִיתִין אוֹתוֹ.
וְאַף עַל פִּי שֶׁהָיָה מְצֻוֶּה שֶׁיֵּהָרֵג וְאַל יַעֲבֹר.
אַף עַל פִּי שֶׁחִלֵּל אֶת הַשֵּׁם וְהוּא אָנוּס – אֵינוֹ נֶהֱרָג.
שֶׁנֶּאֱמַר: וְלַנַּעֲרָה לֹא תַעֲשֶׂה דָבָר. זוֹ אַזְהָרָה לְבֵית דִּין, שֶׁלֹּא יַעַנְשׁוּ אֶת הָאָנוּס.

ג אִישׁ שֶׁאֲנָסוּהוּ עַד שֶׁבָּא עַל הָעֶרְוָה – חַיָּב מִיתַת בֵּית דִּין; שֶׁאֵין קִשּׁוּי אֶלָּא לְדַעַת.
אֲבָל הָאִשָּׁה הַנִּבְעֶלֶת בְּאֹנֶס, אֲפִלּוּ אָמְרָה אַחַר שֶׁנֶּאֶנְסָה: הַנִּיחוּ לוֹ – הֲרֵי הִיא פְּטוּרָה,
מִפְּנֵי שֶׁיִּצְרָהּ נִתְגַּבֵּר עָלֶיהָ.

ד אָסוּר לְבֵית דִּין לָחוּס עַל הַהוֹרֵג. שֶׁלֹּא יֹאמְרוּ: כְּבָר נֶהֱרַג זֶה, וּמַה תּוֹעֶלֶת יֵשׁ בַּהֲרִיגַת הָאַחֵר? וְנִמְצְאוּ מִתְרַשְּׁלִין בַּהֲרִיגָתוֹ. שֶׁנֶּאֱמַר: לֹא תָחוֹס עֵינְךָ עָלָיו, וּבִעַרְתָּ דַם הַנָּקִי.
וְכֵן אָסוּר לְבֵית דִּין לָחוּס עַל מִי שֶׁנִּתְחַיֵּב קְנָס. שֶׁלֹּא יֹאמְרוּ: עָנִי הוּא זֶה, שֶׁלֹּא בְּכַוָּנָה עָשָׂה. אֶלָּא מַגְבִּין מִמֶּנּוּ כֹּל שֶׁיֵּשׁ לוֹ בְּלֹא חֲנִינָה. שֶׁנֶּאֱמַר: וְלֹא תָחוֹס עֵינֶךָ.
וְכֵן בְּדִינֵי מָמוֹנוֹת אֵין מְרַחֲמִין עַל הַדַּל. שֶׁלֹּא תֹאמַר: עָנִי הוּא זֶה, וּבַעַל דִּינוֹ עָשִׁיר; הוֹאִיל וַאֲנִי וְהֶעָשִׁיר חַיָּבִין לְפַרְנְסוֹ – אֲזַכֶּנּוּ בַּדִּין, וְנִמְצָא מִתְפַּרְנֵס בְּכָבוֹד. עַל זֶה הִזְהִירָה תּוֹרָה: וְדָל לֹא תֶהְדַּר בְּרִיבוֹ. וְנֶאֱמַר: לֹא תִשָּׂא פְנֵי דָל.
אָסוּר לְהַדֵּר פְּנֵי גָדוֹל. כֵּיצַד? הֲרֵי שֶׁבָּאוּ לְפָנֶיךָ שְׁנַיִם לְדִין, אֶחָד חָכָם גָּדוֹל וְאֶחָד הֶדְיוֹט

that the intent is not that he was forced into having an erection, but that having an erection comes as a result of his own pleasure and desire. Hence he is considered to have acted totally willingly.

The Radbaz and the *Kessef Mishneh* ask: How is it possible for the man to be liable for execution? If he did not consent to the relations, he would not have accepted the warning that he was given. The *Kessef Mishneh* explains that the intent is not that he is executed, but that he is considered as having acted willingly. See also the gloss of the *Maggid Mishneh* to *Hilchot Issurei Bi'ah* 1:9 which quotes opinions which differ with the Rambam and maintain that a person who is compelled to engage in relations is not liable.

10. For at the outset, she is being forced against her will.

11. *Ketubot* 51a states graphically: "Even if the woman says, 'Had he not raped me, I would have hired him,' she is not liable." Since initially she was forced, she is not held responsible if her natural inclination takes control of her.

12. See the *Minchat Chinuch* (mitzvah 521) who states that it appears that this prohibition applies only with regard to a killer and not to others condemned to death by the court.

13. *Sefer HaMitzvot* (negative commandment 279) and *Sefer HaChinuch* (mitzvah 521) count this as one of the 613 mitzvot of the Torah.

14. The intent appears to be monetary compensation for injury which is considered as a *k'nas*, "fine," as stated in Chapter 5, Halachah 8. As indicated by the Rambam in his listing of mitzvot at the beginning of these laws, he includes this as one facet of the above mitzvah. See also *Hilchot Chovel UMazik* 1:4 where the Rambam refers to this prohibition in the context of the laws regarding compensation for personal injury.

15. *Sefer HaMitzvot* (negative commandment 277) and *Sefer HaChinuch* (mitzvah 79) count this as one of the 613 mitzvot of the Torah.

ordinary person. One may not ask about the welfare of the person of stature first, nor treat him with favor, nor show him honor,[16] lest this cause the other [litigant] to become tongue-tied.[17] Instead, [the judge] should not turn to either of them [in a personal manner] until the judgment is concluded. [This is derived from [*ibid.*]: "Do not glorify the countenance of a person of stature."[18] Our Sages said:[19] One should not say: "This man is affluent; he is the son of people of stature, how can I embarrass him and witness his humiliation." With regard to this, it is written: "Do not glorify the countenance of a person of stature."

5. If two people come before [a judge] one observant and one wicked, he should not say : "Since he is wicked and it can be presumed that he is lying and conversely, it can be assumed that the other [litigant] does not falsify his statements, I will be biased against the wicked[20] in judgment." With regard to this, [Exodus 23:7] states: "Do not be biased in the judgment of the poor person."[21] [The intent is] even if [a person] is poor in [the observance of] mitzvot, do not be biased in his judgment.[22]

6. [Leviticus 19:15:] "Do not act perversely in judgment" [refers to a person who] distorts the judgment and vindicates the [litigant who should be held] liable and obligates the [litigant who should be] vindicated.[23] Similarly, a person who delays rendering judgment[24] and extends [his deliberations even though] the matter is clear-cut in order to aggravate one of the litigants is also considered as one who acts perversely.

7. A person who is haughty when rendering judgment and hurries to deliver a judgment before he examines the matter in his own mind until it is as clear as the sun to him[25] is considered a fool, wicked, and conceited. Our Sages commanded:[26] "Be patient in judgment." And similarly, Job [29:16] states: "When I did not understand a complaint, I would investigate."

8. A judge who begins comparing a judgment that is brought before him to a judgment that was already rendered with which he was familiar is considered as wicked and haughty when rendering judgment if there is [a scholar] in his city[27] who is wiser than him and he fails to consult him. Our Sages comment: "May evil upon evil befall him." For these and similar concepts [stem] from haughtiness which leads to the perversion of justice.[28]

16. The *Sefer Me'irat Einayim* 17:21 states that if one of the litigants is a Torah scholar of great stature, the judge must stand in deference to him. This should not confound the other litigant, for he should realize that this is an obligation due because of the person's scholarship alone. See also Chapter 21, Halachah 4.
17. I.e., seeing the judge show this courtesy to the other person may cause the litigant to become flustered to the extent that he forgets the arguments he wished to present.
18. *Sefer HaMitzvot* (negative commandment 275) and *Sefer HaChinuch* (mitzvah 234) count this as one of the 613 mitzvot of the Torah.

– לֹא תַקְדִּים לִשְׁאֹל בִּשְׁלוֹמוֹ שֶׁל גָּדוֹל, וְלֹא תַּסְבִּיר לוֹ פָּנִים, וְלֹא תְכַבְּדֶנּוּ, כְּדֵי שֶׁלֹּא יִסְתַּתְּמוּ טַעֲנוֹתָיו שֶׁל אַחֵר; אֶלָּא אֵינוֹ נִפְנֶה לְאֶחָד מֵהֶן עַד שֶׁיִּגָּמֵר הַדִּין. שֶׁנֶּאֱמַר: לֹא תֶהְדַּר פְּנֵי גָדוֹל. אָמְרוּ חֲכָמִים: אַל תֹּאמַר: עָשִׁיר הוּא זֶה, בֶּן גְּדוֹלִים הוּא זֶה, הֵיאַךְ אֲבַיְּשֶׁנּוּ וְאֶרְאֶה בְּבָשְׁתּוֹ? לְכָךְ נֶאֱמַר: לֹא תֶהְדַּר פְּנֵי גָדוֹל.

ה בָּאוּ לְפָנֶיךָ שְׁנַיִם, אֶחָד כָּשֵׁר וְאֶחָד רָשָׁע – אַל תֹּאמַר: הוֹאִיל וְרָשָׁע הוּא וְחֶזְקָתוֹ מְשַׁקֵּר, וְחֶזְקַת זֶה שֶׁאֵינוֹ מְשַׁנֶּה בִּדְבָרוֹ, אַטֶּה הַדִּין עַל הָרָשָׁע. עַל זֶה נֶאֱמַר: לֹא תַטֶּה מִשְׁפַּט אֶבְיֹנְךָ בְּרִיבוֹ – אַף עַל פִּי שֶׁהוּא אֶבְיוֹן בְּמִצְוֹת, לֹא תַטֶּה דִּינוֹ.

ו לֹא תַעֲשׂוּ עָוֶל בַּמִּשְׁפָּט – זֶה הַמְעַוֵּת אֶת הַדִּין, וּמְזַכֶּה אֶת הַחַיָּב וּמְחַיֵּב אֶת הַזַּכַּאי. וְכֵן הַמְעַנֶּה אֶת הַדִּין, וּמַאֲרִיךְ בִּדְבָרִים בְּרוּרִים כְּדֵי לְצַעֵר אֶחָד מִבַּעֲלֵי דִינִים – הֲרֵי זֶה בִּכְלַל עָוֶל.

ז הַגַּס לִבּוֹ בְּהוֹרָאָה, וְקוֹפֵץ וְחוֹתֵךְ אֶת הַדִּין קֹדֶם שֶׁיַּחְקְרֶהוּ בֵּינוֹ לְבֵין עַצְמוֹ עַד שֶׁיְּהֵא לוֹ בָּרוּר כַּשֶּׁמֶשׁ – הֲרֵי זֶה שׁוֹטֶה, רָשָׁע וְגַס רוּחַ. כָּךְ צִוּוּ חֲכָמִים: הֱווּ מְתוּנִים בַּדִּין. וְכֵן אִיּוֹב הוּא אוֹמֵר: וְרִב לֹא יָדַעְתִּי אֶחְקְרֵהוּ.

ח כָּל דַּיָּן שֶׁבָּא לְפָנָיו דִּין, וְהִתְחִיל לְדַמּוֹתוֹ בְּדִין פָּסוּק שֶׁכְּבָר יָדַע אוֹתוֹ, וְיֵשׁ בַּמְּדִינָה גָּדוֹל מִמֶּנּוּ בְּחָכְמָה וְאֵינוֹ הוֹלֵךְ וְנִמְלָךְ בּוֹ – הֲרֵי זֶה בִּכְלַל הָרְשָׁעִים שֶׁלִּבָּם גַּס בְּהוֹרָאָה. וְאָמְרוּ חֲכָמִים: רָעָה עַל רָעָה תָּבוֹא לוֹ. שֶׁכָּל אֵלּוּ הַדְּבָרִים וְכַיּוֹצֵא בָּהֶן – מִגַּסּוּת הָרוּחַ הֵן, הַמְּבִיאוֹת לִידֵי עִוּוּת הַדִּין.

19. *Sifra* to the above verse.
20. I.e., accept the other litigant's statements without diligent cross-examination.
21. *Sefer HaMitzvot* (negative commandment 278) and *Sefer HaChinuch* (mitzvah 81) count this as one of the 613 mitzvot of the Torah.
22. In this context, the *Shulchan Aruch* (*Choshen Mishpat* 17:10) quotes the advice of the mishnah (*Avot* 1:8): "When the litigants stand before you, regard them both as guilty." See Chapter 23, Halachah 10.
23. *Sefer HaMitzvot* (negative commandment 273) and *Sefer HaChinuch* (mitzvah 233) count this as one of the 613 mitzvot of the Torah.
24. Our translation is based on the Rambam's Commentary to the Mishnah (*Avot* 5:8).
25. Although as stated in the previous halachah, a judge must not delay rendering judgment, he should not be hasty in doing so either. Instead, he should patiently review the matter before coming to a decision.
26. *Avot* 1:1.
27. In the present age, when the breakthroughs in communication have made the world a global village, this advice applies not only to scholars located in the same city, but throughout the world.
28. His haughtiness will prevent him from realizing his errors and lead to a perversion of justice (Radbaz).

[Proverbs 7:26:] "She cast down[29] many corpses" refers to a student who has not reached the level where he can deliver rulings, but does so. "Awesome[30] are all she has slain" [*ibid.*] refers to [a scholar] who has reached the level where he can deliver rulings, but does not do so.

[The latter denunciation applies] provided his generation requires his [services]. If, however, he knows that there is [another scholar] capable of rendering decisions, and [therefore] he refrains from doing so, he is praiseworthy. Whenever a person refrains from [becoming involved in] a judgment,[31] he removes [the responsibility for] antagonism, theft, and false oaths from himself. A person who is haughty in rendering judgment is foolish, wicked, and arrogant.[32]

9. A student should not give a ruling in the presence of his teacher[33] unless he is three *parseot*[34] removed from him.[35] [This distance is the length of] the encampment of the Jews [in the desert].[36]

10. A person should not say: "All of the above applies with regard to a judgment that involves the expropriation of a large sum of money from one person to another." [Instead,] a judgment involving 1000 *maneh*[37] and one involving a *p'rutah*[38] should be regarded as identical with regard to all matters.[39]

11. Judges should not sit down to adjudicate a case involving less than a *p'rutah*.[40] If, however, they were required to adjudicate a complaint involving a *p'rutah*, they render a judgment even if [ultimately,] the outcome concerns less than a *p'rutah*.[41]

12. Anyone who perverts a judgment against another Jew transgresses a negative commandment, as [Leviticus 19:15] states: "Do not act perversely in judgment."[42] If the litigant was a convert, he transgresses two negative

29. *Hepilah*, translated as "cast down" also has the connotation "miscarried." I.e., the student is like a fetus who emerges from the womb too early (Rashi, *Avodah Zarah* 19b).
30. *Atzumim*, translated as "awesome," also has the connotation to "those who hold back." On this basis, our Sages advance this interpretation (Rashi, *Ibid.*). See also *Hilchot Talmud Torah* 5:4 where the Rambam quotes the same concepts.
31. And instead defers to another, allowing him to judge the case. This appears to be the Rambam's interpretation. The *Perisha* (*Choshen Mishpat* 10) offers an alternate perspective, explaining that rather than render a judgment, the judge convinces the litigants to accept a compromise.
32. The *Sefer Me'irat Einayim* 10:3 explains: "foolish," because he thinks he is wise, but is not, "wicked," for he perverts judgment, and "arrogant," because due to his haughtiness, he thinks that a person of his stature need not be patient in judgment.
33. I.e., a teacher who has taught him the majority of his knowledge (*Hilchot Talmud Torah* 5:2-3).

כִּי רַבִּים חֲלָלִים הִפִּילָה – זֶה תַּלְמִיד שֶׁלֹּא הִגִּיעַ לְהוֹרָאָה וּמוֹרֶה; וַעֲצֻמִים כָּל הֲרֻגֶיהָ – זֶה שֶׁהִגִּיעַ לְהוֹרָאָה וְאֵינוֹ מוֹרֶה. וְהוּא שֶׁיִּהְיֶה הַדּוֹר צָרִיךְ לוֹ; אֲבָל אִם יָדַע שֶׁיֵּשׁ לְשָׁם רָאוּי לְהוֹרָאָה, וּמָנַע עַצְמוֹ מִן הַהוֹרָאָה – הֲרֵי זֶה מְשֻׁבָּח. וְכָל הַמּוֹנֵעַ עַצְמוֹ מִן הַדִּין – מוֹנֵעַ מִמֶּנּוּ אֵיבָה וְגָזֵל וּשְׁבוּעַת שָׁוְא; וְהַגַּס לִבּוֹ בְּהוֹרָאָה – שׁוֹטֶה, רָשָׁע וְגַס רוּחַ.

ט תַּלְמִיד אַל יוֹרֶה הֲלָכָה לִפְנֵי רַבּוֹ, אֶלָּא אִם כֵּן הָיָה רָחוֹק מִמֶּנּוּ שָׁלֹשׁ פַּרְסָאוֹת – כְּנֶגֶד מַחֲנֵה יִשְׂרָאֵל.

י אַל תֹּאמַר: שֶׁכָּל אֵלּוּ הַדְּבָרִים בְּדִין שֶׁיֵּשׁ בּוֹ הוֹצָאַת מָמוֹן הַרְבֵּה מִזֶּה וּנְתִינָתוֹ לָזֶה. לְעוֹלָם יְהִי דִין אֶלֶף מָנֶה וְדִין פְּרוּטָה אַחַת שָׁוִין בְּעֵינֶיךָ לְכָל דָּבָר.

יא אֵין הַדַּיָּנִין יוֹשְׁבִין לָדוּן בְּדִין פָּחוּת מִשָּׁוֶה פְּרוּטָה. וְאִם הֻזְקְקוּ לְשָׁוֶה פְּרוּטָה – גּוֹמְרִין אֶת דִּינוֹ אֲפִלּוּ לְפָחוּת מִשָּׁוֶה פְּרוּטָה.

יב כָּל הַמַּטֶּה מִשְׁפַּט אֶחָד מִיִּשְׂרָאֵל – עוֹבֵר בְּלָאו אֶחָד, שֶׁנֶּאֱמַר: לֹא תַעֲשׂוּ עָוֶל בַּמִּשְׁפָּט.

34. A *parsa* is twelve *mil*, and a *mil* is approximately a kilometer in modern measure.
35. When, by contrast, a person renders a ruling in the presence of his teacher, he is liable for death at the hand of heaven (*Hilchot Talmud Torah, loc. cit.*).
36. Anyone in the camp could approach Moses with his halachic questions. If, however, the teacher grants him permission - as Moses granted to the other judges whom he appointed - the student may also render judgment (*Hilchot Talmud Torah, loc. cit.*).
37. A *maneh* is 100 silver pieces.
38. A copper coin of minimal value, worth less than any other coinage in the Talmudic age.
39. *Sanhedrin* 8a states that this means that if a case involving a *p'rutah* is brought to a judge before one involving a large sum, the judge must adjudicate the smaller case first. The Radbaz qualifies that statement, explaining that if the smaller case involves patient judgment and the larger matter is straightforward and can be settled quickly, the larger matter should be adjudicated first.
40. For anything less than a *p'rutah* is not considered financially significant. See the *Siftei Cohen* 6:1 who explains that if a judgment concerns utensils that are worth less than a *p'rutah*, the judges must hear the case. Note the parallel to *Hilchot To'ain ViNitan* 3:5-6.
41. Rashi (*Bava Metzia* 55b) interprets this as referring to an instance where after a judge renders a judgment concerning a *p'rutah*, the defendant tries to exonerate himself from part of the responsibility by citing a claim that is worth less than a *p'rutah*.

Rabbenu Asher disputes the Rambam's decision, ruling that whenever a case does not concern a *p'rutah*, it is not heard by the judges regardless of the circumstances. Although the *Shulchan Aruch* (*Choshen Mishpat* 6:1, quotes the Rambam's view, the *Sefer Me'irat Einayim* 6:3 favors Rabbenu Asher's perspective.
42. As mentioned in Halachah 6.

commandments,[43] as [Deuteronomy 24:17] states: "Do not distort the judgment of a convert." If he[44] was an orphan, [the transgressor] violates three negative commandments[45] as [that verse] continues: "...the judgment of an orphaned convert."

CHAPTER TWENTY ONE

1. It is a positive commandment[1] for a judge to adjudicate righteously, as [Leviticus 19:15] states: "Judge your colleagues with righteousness."

What is meant by a righteous judgment? Equating the litigants with regard to all matters. One should not be allowed to speak to the full extent he feels necessary while the other is told to speak concisely.[2] One should not treat one favorably and speak gently to him and treat the other harshly and speak sternly to him.

2. When there are two litigants, one wearing precious garments and the other degrading garments, we tell [the litigant who carries himself] honorably: "Either clothe him as you are clothed for the duration of your judgment or dress like him, so that you will be equal. Afterwards, stand judgment."[3]

3. One of the litigants should not be allowed to sit, while the other stands.[4] Instead, they both should stand.[5] If the court desires to seat both of them, they may.[6] One should not be seated on a higher plane than the other. Instead, they should sit on the same level.

When does this[7] apply? During the give and take of the arguments. When, however, the judgment is being delivered, both [litigants] must stand, as [Exodus 18:13] states: "And the people stood before Moses."

What is meant by the delivery of the judgment? [The announcement:] "So and so, you are vindicated." "So and so, you are liable."

43. *Sefer HaMitzvot* (negative commandment 280) and *Sefer HaChinuch* (mitzvah 590) count this as one of the 613 mitzvot of the Torah. See note 45.

44. I.e., the convert.

45. From the Rambam's wording here, it appears that there are two prohibitions involved, one for a convert, and a second, if the convert is an orphan. Nevertheless, in *Sefer HaMitzvot* (and in the mitzvot mentioned at the beginning of these halachot), he considers wronging the two as one prohibition. From *Sefer HaMitzvot*, it appears that a person violates the same prohibition whether he perverts the judgment of a convert or a convert who is an orphan. The intent of "three prohibitions" is not that the person has violated three separate prohibitions, but that the deed involves the spiritual severity of violating God's decree three times. If a person perverts the judgment of a native-born Jewish orphan, however, he is not considered to have violated this commandment (Radbaz).

The *Minchat Chinuch* (mitzvah 590) notes that every convert is an "orphan," for he no longer has any connection to his natural father. He explains that if the convert is young and unable to manage on his own, he is considered an orphan. Once he can fend for himself, he is no longer placed in that category.

וְאִם הָיָה גֵר – עוֹבֵר בִּשְׁנֵי לָאוִין, שֶׁנֶּאֱמַר: לֹא תַטֶּה מִשְׁפַּט גֵּר. וְאִם הָיָה יָתוֹם – עוֹבֵר בִּשְׁלֹשָׁה לָאוִין, שֶׁנֶּאֱמַר: מִשְׁפַּט גֵּר יָתוֹם.

פֶּרֶק אֶחָד וְעֶשְׂרִים

א מִצְוַת עֲשֵׂה לִשְׁפֹּט הַשּׁוֹפֵט בְּצֶדֶק. שֶׁנֶּאֱמַר: בְּצֶדֶק תִּשְׁפֹּט עֲמִיתֶךָ.
אֵי זֶהוּ צֶדֶק הַמִּשְׁפָּט? זוֹ הַשְׁוָיַת שְׁנֵי בַּעֲלֵי דִינִין בְּכָל דָּבָר.
לֹא יְהֵא אֶחָד מְדַבֵּר כָּל צָרְכּוֹ, וְאֶחָד אוֹמֵר לוֹ: קַצֵּר דְּבָרֶיךָ!
וְלֹא יַסְבִּיר פָּנִים לְאֶחָד וִידַבֵּר לוֹ רַכּוֹת, וְיֵרַע פָּנָיו לְאַחֵר וִידַבֵּר לוֹ קָשׁוֹת.

ב שְׁנֵי בַּעֲלֵי דִינִין, שֶׁהָיָה אֶחָד מֵהֶם מְלֻבָּשׁ בִּגְדֵי יְקָרִים, וְהַשֵּׁנִי מְלֻבָּשׁ בְּגָדִים בְּזוּיִין – אוֹמֵר לַמְכֻבָּד: אוֹ הַלְבִּישֵׁהוּ כְּמוֹתְךָ עַד שֶׁתָּדוּן עִמּוֹ, אוֹ לְבַשׁ כְּמוֹתוֹ עַד שֶׁתִּהְיוּ שָׁוִין, אַחַר כָּךְ תַּעַמְדוּ בְּדִין.

ג לֹא יִהְיֶה אֶחָד יוֹשֵׁב וְאֶחָד עוֹמֵד, אֶלָּא שְׁנֵיהֶם עוֹמְדִים. וְאִם רָצוּ בֵּית דִּין לְהוֹשִׁיב אֶת שְׁנֵיהֶם – מוֹשִׁיבִין. וְלֹא יֵשֵׁב אֶחָד לְמַעְלָה וְאֶחָד לְמַטָּה, אֶלָּא זֶה בְּצַד זֶה.
בַּמֶּה דְּבָרִים אֲמוּרִים? בִּשְׁעַת מַשָּׂא וּמַתָּן; אֲבָל בִּשְׁעַת גְּמַר דִּין – שְׁנֵיהֶם בַּעֲמִידָה. שֶׁנֶּאֱמַר: וַיַּעֲמֹד הָעָם עַל מֹשֶׁה. וְאֵי זֶהוּ גְּמַר דִּין? אִישׁ פְּלוֹנִי אַתָּה זַכַּאי, אִישׁ פְּלוֹנִי אַתָּה חַיָּב.

1. *Sefer HaMitzvot* (positive commandment 177) and *Sefer HaChinuch* (mitzvah 235) count this as one of the 613 mitzvot of the Torah.
2. A judge may, however, instruct both litigants to speak concisely.
3. For the manner in which a person is dressed creates an impression and influences the way a judge will look at the case. Moreover, this may cause the litigant who is poorly dressed to be disconcerted and prevent him from presenting his arguments articulately (Rashi, *Sh'vuot* 31a).

The *Sefer Me'irat Einayim* 17:2 states that when there is not a radical difference in the litigants' manner of dress, even though one's clothes are more elegant than the other's, there is no necessity for the court to equate them entirely. The *Siftei Cohen* 17:2 extends this principle, stating that at present, since it is not customary for anyone to wear the extremely expensive clothing that some wore in the Talmudic age, this law is not practiced.
4. For this would indicate favoritism.
5. As indicated by Deuteronomy 19:17: "And the two men who have the dispute shall stand before God."
6. This is the custom at present, as stated in Halachah 5.
7. The license to sit.

When does the above[7] apply? To the litigants. The witnesses, by contrast, must always stand,[8] as [Deuteronomy 19:17] states: "And the two men shall stand."[9]

4. When a Torah scholar and a common person come to adjudicate a dispute, the Torah scholar is seated.[10] And the common person is instructed to sit.[11] If, however, he does not sit, it is of no consequence.[12]

A student who wishes to have a dispute adjudicated should not come early and sit before his teacher if he desires to have him adjudicate the case.[13] If, however, [each one of the judge's students] had a fixed time to read before the judge and one of them came to read at the time [of his judgment],[14] it is permitted [for the judge to hear the case].[15]

5. It has already become customary in all the courts throughout Israel after the era of Talmud, in all the *yeshivot*,[16] to have the litigants and the witnesses sit so that there will be no controversy.[17] For we do not have the power to establish the judgments of our faith in a firm manner.

6. If there were many litigants before the judges, precedence should be give to a case involving an orphan to one involving a widow, as [implied by Isaiah 1:17]: "Judge an orphan, enter in a dispute on behalf of a widow."[18] A case involving a widow receives precedence over a case involving a Torah scholar.[19] A case involving a Torah scholar takes precedence over a case involving a common person.[20] And a case involving a woman takes precedence over one involving a man, because the shame felt by a woman[21] is greater.[22]

7. It is forbidden for a judge to hear the words of one of the litigants before the other comes or outside the other's presence.[23] Even hearing one word is

8. The *Sefer Me'irat Einayim* 17:5 states that after the fact, if the witnesses sit, their testimony is not invalidated. Moreover, he cites authorities who maintain that even at the outset, the requirement applies only to judges who possess *semichah*. Before judges of the present era, the litigants may sit.
9. Although literally, the verse is speaking about the litigants, *Sh'vuot* 30a states that the words "who have the dispute" refer to the litigants. Who then are "the two men"? The witnesses.
10. For it is a mitzvah to show deference to a Torah scholar (see *Hilchot Talmud Torah* 6:1).
11. So that they appear equal.
12. For everyone realizes that the scholar is given this respect in appreciation of his scholarship. That does not necessarily mean that the judges will favor him in judgment.
13. For it will appear that he told him his perspective concerning the dispute. See also Halachah 7.
14. Our translation follows the version found in the manuscripts and early printings of the *Mishneh Torah*. The standard published text has a slightly different version.

בַּמֶּה דְּבָרִים אֲמוּרִים? בְּבַעֲלֵי דִינִין; אֲבָל הָעֵדִים – לְעוֹלָם בַּעֲמִידָה. שֶׁנֶּאֱמַר: וְעָמְדוּ שְׁנֵי הָאֲנָשִׁים.

ד תַּלְמִיד חָכָם וְעַם הָאָרֶץ שֶׁבָּאוּ לְדִין – מוֹשִׁיבִין אֶת הֶחָכָם, וְאוֹמְרִים לְעַם הָאָרֶץ: שֵׁב! אִם לֹא יָשַׁב – אֵין מַקְפִּידִין עַל כָּךְ.
וְלֹא יַקְדִּים הַתַּלְמִיד כְּשֶׁיָּבוֹא לְדִין וְיֵשֵׁב לִפְנֵי רַבּוֹ כְּרוֹצֶה לָדוּן לְפָנָיו.
וְאִם הָיָה קָבוּעַ לוֹ זְמַן לִקְרוֹת, וּבָא זְמַנּוֹ – מֻתָּר.

ה כְּבָר נָהֲגוּ כָּל בָּתֵּי דִינֵי יִשְׂרָאֵל מֵאַחַר הַגְּמָרָא בְּכָל הַיְשִׁיבוֹת, שֶׁמּוֹשִׁיבִין בַּעֲלֵי דִינִין וּמוֹשִׁיבִין הָעֵדִים, כְּדֵי לְסַלֵּק הַמַּחֲלֹקֶת. שֶׁאֵין בָּנוּ כֹּחַ לְהַעֲמִיד מִשְׁפְּטֵי הַדָּת עַל תִּלָּם.

ו הָיוּ לִפְנֵי הַדַּיָּנִים בַּעֲלֵי דִין הַרְבֵּה – מַקְדִּימִין אֶת דִּין הַיָּתוֹם לְדִין הָאַלְמָנָה. שֶׁנֶּאֱמַר: שִׁפְטוּ יָתוֹם רִיבוּ אַלְמָנָה. וְדִין אַלְמָנָה קוֹדֵם לְדִין תַּלְמִיד חָכָם. וְדִין תַּלְמִיד חָכָם קוֹדֵם לְדִין עַם הָאָרֶץ. וְדִין הָאִשָּׁה קוֹדֵם לְדִין הָאִישׁ; שֶׁבֹּשֶׁת הָאִשָּׁה מְרֻבָּה.

ז אָסוּר לַדַּיָּן לִשְׁמֹעַ דִּבְרֵי אֶחָד מִבַּעֲלֵי דִינִין קֹדֶם שֶׁיָּבוֹא חֲבֵרוֹ אוֹ שֶׁלֹּא בִּפְנֵי חֲבֵרוֹ.

15. For it is obvious that he came at the time he usually comes and not to provide him with information concerning the dispute.
16. We have left the term in its Hebrew original in which instance, it connotes Talmudic academies, i.e., the courts sanctioned by all the Talmudic academies. It could, however, be interpreted as meaning "settlements," i.e., throughout the international Jewish community, this practice was accepted.
17. I.e., common people might begin arguing if they were asked to stand. The *Siftei Cohen* 17:7 quotes the *Bayit Chadash* who states that although this dispensation is granted, it is proper for the litigants and the witnesses not to accept it and stand when delivering testimony.
18. I.e., the sequence of the verse implies the order of precedence.
19. Since widows have experienced grief and suffering, their spirits are weak and we undertake this and other measures to alleviate their anguish.
20. This is one of the expressions of deference for Torah scholars, as stated in *Hilchot Talmud Torah* 6:10.
21. *Yevamot* 100a states that women are rarely involved in judicial disputes and hence, having to appear in court would be very embarrassing. *Kina'at Eliyahu* questions if the changes in the socio-economic norms and the wider role women have in society today would cause this ruling to be altered.
22. The *Shulchan Aruch* (*Choshen Mishpat* 15:2 quotes these principles. It also states (*loc. cit.*:1) that generally a judge should hear the cases in the order that the litigants appear in court.
23. For in this way, the other litigant can challenge the statement if he maintains that it is false. Moreover, we assume that a person will have greater difficulty lying in the presence of the person he is trying to mistreat.

forbidden,[24] as [implied by Deuteronomy 1:16]: "Listen among your brethren." A judge who listens to [only] one litigant violates a negative commandment, as [Exodus 23:1] states: "Do not bear a false report."[25] Included in this prohibition is a warning to a person who listens to malicious gossip, one who speaks malicious gossip, and one who bears false testimony.

Similarly, [each] litigant is warned not to tell his arguments to a judge before the other litigant comes. With regard to this and similar matters,[26] [Exodus 23:7] states: "Keep distant from words of falsehood."

8. A judge should not hear from a translator.[27] If he understands the language of the litigants and listens to their arguments, but is not fluent in their language in order to respond to them, he should appoint a translator to inform them of the ruling and the rationale why this person's claim was vindicated and the other was held liable.

9. A judge must listen to the arguments of the litigants and restate their claims,[28] as [evident from I Kings 3:23 which] states: "And the king said: 'This one says: "Mine is the son who lives and your son is the one who is dead."...' "

He should determine the just resolution of the judgment in his heart and then pronounce judgment.

10. What is the source which teaches that a judge should not justify the arguments of one of the litigants?[29] "Keep distant from words of falsehood." Instead, [the litigant] should tell [the judge] what appears [correct] to him and [the judge] should remain silent.[30]

He should not teach one of the litigants an argument at all.[31] Even if [the plaintiff] brings [only] one witness, [the judge] should not say: "We do not accept the testimony of one witness." Instead, he should tell the defendant: "[See,] he has testified against you." Preferably, he will acknowledge [the other's claim], saying: "He testified truthfully." [The judge should not ignore the witness's testimony] unless [the other litigant] says: "He is only one witness and I do not accept his [testimony]." Similar principles apply in all analogous situations.

11. If a judge sees a vindicating argument for one of the litigants [and realizes] that the litigant is seeking to state it, but does not know how to articulate the matter, sees that one was painfully trying to extricate himself with a true claim, but because of his anger and rage, he lost touch of the argument, or sees that one became confused because of his intellectual inadequacy, he may

24. The Rambam's apparent source is the *Zohar*, Vol. I, p. 179b. This is significant, because there are questions whether or not he was ever exposed to the teachings of the Kabbalah.

25. *Sefer HaMitzvot* (negative commandment 281) and *Sefer HaChinuch* (mitzvah 74) count this as one of the 613 mitzvot of the Torah.

וַאֲפִלּוּ דָּבָר אֶחָד – אָסוּר. שֶׁנֶּאֱמַר: שָׁמֹעַ בֵּין אֲחֵיכֶם. וְכָל הַשּׁוֹמֵעַ מֵאֶחָד – עוֹבֵר בְּלֹא תַעֲשֶׂה, שֶׁנֶּאֱמַר: לֹא תִשָּׂא שֵׁמַע שָׁוְא. וּבִכְלַל לָאו זֶה: אַזְהָרָה לִמְקַבֵּל לָשׁוֹן הָרָע, וּמְסַפֵּר לָשׁוֹן הָרָע, וּמֵעִיד עֵדוּת שֶׁקֶר. וְכֵן בַּעַל דִּין מֻזְהָר שֶׁלֹּא יַשְׁמִיעַ דְּבָרָיו לַדַּיָּן קֹדֶם שֶׁיָּבוֹא בַּעַל דִּין חֲבֵרוֹ. וְגַם עַל זֶה וְכַיּוֹצֵא בוֹ נֶאֱמַר: מִדְּבַר שֶׁקֶר תִּרְחָק.

ח לֹא יִהְיֶה הַדַּיָּן שׁוֹמֵעַ מִפִּי הַתֻּרְגְּמָן, אֶלָּא אִם כֵּן הָיָה מַכִּיר לְשׁוֹן בַּעֲלֵי דִינִין וְשׁוֹמֵעַ טַעֲנוֹתֵיהֶם. וְאִם אֵינוֹ מָהִיר בִּלְשׁוֹנָם כְּדֵי לְהָשִׁיב לָהֶם – יַעֲמֹד הַתֻּרְגְּמָן לְהוֹדִיעַ אוֹתָם פְּסַק הַדִּין, וּמֵאֵי זֶה טַעַם חִיֵּב זֶה וְזִכָּה זֶה.

ט צָרִיךְ הַדַּיָּן לִשְׁמֹעַ טַעֲנוֹת בַּעֲלֵי דִינִין וְלִשְׁנוֹת טַעֲנוֹתֵיהֶן. שֶׁנֶּאֱמַר: וַיֹּאמֶר הַמֶּלֶךְ, זֹאת אוֹמֶרֶת זֶה בְּנִי הַחַי וּבְנֵךְ הַמֵּת. וּמְצַדֵּק אֶת הַדִּין בְּלִבּוֹ, וְאַחַר כָּךְ חוֹתְכוֹ.

י מִנַּיִן לַדַּיָּן שֶׁלֹּא יַעֲשֶׂה מֵלִיץ לִדְבָרָיו שֶׁל בַּעַל דִּין? שֶׁנֶּאֱמַר: מִדְּבַר שֶׁקֶר תִּרְחָק. אֶלָּא יֹאמַר מַה שֶּׁנִּרְאֶה לוֹ וְיִשְׁתֹּק. וְלֹא יְלַמֵּד אֶחָד מִבַּעֲלֵי דִינִין טְעָנָה כְּלָל. אֲפִלּוּ הֵבִיא עֵד אֶחָד – לֹא יֹאמַר לוֹ: אֵין מְקַבְּלִין עֵד אֶחָד! אֶלָּא יֹאמַר לַנִּטְעָן: הֲרֵי זֶה הֵעִיד עָלֶיךָ! הַלְוַאי שֶׁיּוֹדֶה וְיֹאמַר: אֱמֶת הֵעִיד! עַד שֶׁיִּטְעַן הוּא וְיֹאמַר: עֵד אֶחָד הוּא, וְאֵינוֹ נֶאֱמָן עָלַי. וְכֵן כֹּל כַּיּוֹצֵא בָזֶה.

יא רָאָה הַדַּיָּן זְכוּת לְאֶחָד מֵהֶן, וּבַעַל דִּין מְבַקֵּשׁ לְאָמְרָהּ וְאֵינוֹ יוֹדֵעַ לְחַבֵּר הַדְּבָרִים, אוֹ שֶׁרָאָהוּ מִצְטַעֵר לְהַצִּיל עַצְמוֹ בְּטַעֲנַת אֱמֶת, וּמִפְּנֵי הַחֵמָה וְהַכַּעַס נִסְתַּלֵּק מִמֶּנּוּ, אוֹ נִשְׁתַּבֵּשׁ מִפְּנֵי הַסִּכְלוּת –

26. See Halachah 10, and see Chapter 22, Halachot 2-3. This warning is also applied to judges, see Chapter 23, Halachah 10, and Chapter 24, Halachah 3.
27. For the judge must hear the words of the litigants and the witnesses [*Shulchan Aruch* (*Choshen Mishpat* 28:6)] directly. See the *Sefer Me'irat Einayim* 17:14 who states that at present, leniency is taken in this regard and it has become customary for litigants to give others power of attorney to argue their cases.
28. This clarifies that he understood them correctly. Implied is that he should restate their statements in their presence, so that they can correct him if he errs (*Sefer Me'irat Einayim* 17:15).
29. Saying "He appears to have made a proper argument" or the like (*Kessef Mishneh*).
30. Our translation is based on the interpretation of the *Sefer Me'irat Einayim* 17:18.
31. *Avot* 1:8 states: "Do not accept the role of a counselor." In his commentary to that mishnah, the Rambam writes:

> One should not advise a litigant to assert a claim that will benefit him or [teach him] to defend himself... This applies even when [the judge] knows that he is being exploited and that the other litigant is making a false claim. It is, nevertheless, forbidden to teach [the litigant] a claim that will advance his interests.

assist him somewhat to grant him an initial understanding of the matter, as [indicated by Proverbs 31:8]: "Open your mouth for the dumb person." One must reconsider the matter amply, lest one become like a legal counselor.[32]

CHAPTER TWENTY TWO

1. When two people come before [a judge], one soft and one harsh[1] - before he hears their words, or [even] after he hears their words, but does not know the direction in which the judgment is leaning - he has the license to tell them: "I will not involve myself with you," lest the harsh [litigant] be held liable and seek vengeance from the judge.

After he hears their words and knows in which direction the judgment is leaning, he does not have the license to tell them: "I will not involve myself with you," as [Deuteronomy 1:18] states: "Do not be intimidated by any person."[2] [That verse implies that] one should not say: "So-and-so is wicked, maybe he will kill my son, set fire to my crops, or cut down my trees." If he was an expert [appointed to judge] the many, he is obligated to involve himself with them [in all circumstances].[3]

2. Similarly, if a student was sitting before his master[4] and became aware of a factor that would vindicate a poor person and obligate his rich [adversary],[5] he transgresses the above commandment if he remains silent.[6] Concerning such matters, [Exodus 23:7] states: "Keep distant from words of falsehood."

What is the source which teaches that a judge should not have an underdeveloped student sit before him?[7] It is written: "Keep distant from words of falsehood."

3. What is the source which teaches that a student who sees his teacher erring with regard to a judgment should not say: "I will wait until he renders judgment. Then I will refute his ruling and then construct[8] [a new one] so that the judgment will be quoted in my name"? It is written: "Keep distant from words of falsehood."[9]

As explained in the next halachah and notes, there is room for leniency in certain situations. Nevertheless, this is the general rule.

32. The *Tur* (*Choshen Mishpat* 17) differs with the Rambam's ruling, maintaining that a judge can take greater leniency and advise a litigant with regard to a just claim. In that vein, he cites the example of Rav Huna stated by the Jerusalem Talmud who would offer assistance when he saw a litigant who did not know how to state his claims.

Ketubot 52b cites an example of Rabbi Yochanan who did offer such assistance to a litigant, but then regretted it stating: "I have conducted myself like a legal counselor." The Rambam himself states in *Hilchot Shemitah ViYovel* 9:24: "When a creditor brings the promissory note... we tell the defendant: 'Pay him.' If the defendant protests: 'Where is your *pruzbol*?' [The judge] may ask the plaintiff: 'Did you have a *pruzbol* and lose it?'"

The issue is a very delicate one and the Rabbis (see the *Sefer Me'irat Einayim* 17:19 and the *Turei Zahav*) have debated it extensively. Ultimately, as the Rambam states, every judge must employ his own discretion.

הֲרֵי זֶה מֻתָּר לְסַעֲדוֹ מְעַט, לַהֲבִינוֹ תְּחִלַּת הַדָּבָר, מִשּׁוּם פְּתַח פִּיךָ לְאִלֵּם. וְצָרִיךְ לְהִתְיַשֵּׁב בְּדָבָר זֶה הַרְבֵּה, שֶׁלֹּא יִהְיֶה כְּעוֹרְכֵי הַדַּיָּנִין.

פֶּרֶק שְׁנַיִם וְעֶשְׂרִים

א שְׁנַיִם שֶׁבָּאוּ לְפָנֶיךָ לְדִין, אֶחָד רַךְ וְאֶחָד קָשֶׁה: עַד שֶׁלֹּא תִּשְׁמַע אֶת דִּבְרֵיהֶם, אוֹ מִשֶּׁתִּשְׁמַע אֶת דִּבְרֵיהֶם וְאִי אַתָּה יוֹדֵעַ לְהֵיכָן הַדִּין נוֹטֶה – אַתָּה רַשַּׁאי לוֹמַר לָהֶם: אֵינִי נִזְקָק לָכֶם! שֶׁמָּא יִתְחַיֵּב הַקָּשֶׁה, וְנִמְצָא רוֹדֵף אַחַר הַדַּיָּן.

אֲבָל מִשֶּׁתִּשְׁמַע אֶת דִּבְרֵיהֶם וְתֵדַע לְהֵיכָן הַדִּין נוֹטֶה – אִי אַתָּה רַשַּׁאי לוֹמַר: אֵינִי נִזְקָק לָכֶם! שֶׁנֶּאֱמַר: לֹא תָגוּרוּ מִפְּנֵי אִישׁ. שֶׁלֹּא תֹּאמַר: אִישׁ פְּלוֹנִי רָשָׁע הוּא, שֶׁמָּא יַהֲרֹג אֶת בְּנִי, שֶׁמָּא יַדְלִיק אֶת גְּדִישִׁי, שֶׁמָּא יְקַצֵּץ נְטִיעוֹתַי. וְאִם הָיָה מְמֻנֶּה לָרַבִּים – חַיָּב לְהִזָּקֵק לָהֶם.

ב וְכֵן תַּלְמִיד שֶׁהָיָה יוֹשֵׁב לִפְנֵי רַבּוֹ, וְרָאָה זְכוּת לֶעָנִי וְחוֹבָה לֶעָשִׁיר, אִם שָׁתַק – הֲרֵי זֶה עוֹבֵר מִשּׁוּם לֹא תָגוּרוּ מִפְּנֵי אִישׁ. וְעַל זֶה נֶאֱמַר: מִדְּבַר שֶׁקֶר תִּרְחָק.

וּמִנַּיִן לְדַיָּן שֶׁלֹּא יוֹשִׁיב תַּלְמִיד בּוּר לְפָנָיו? תַּלְמוּד לוֹמַר: מִדְּבַר שֶׁקֶר תִּרְחָק.

ג וּמִנַּיִן לְתַלְמִיד שֶׁרָאָה רַבּוֹ שֶׁטּוֹעֶה בַּדִּין, שֶׁלֹּא יֹאמַר: אַמְתִּין לוֹ עַד שֶׁיִּגָּמֵר הַדִּין וְאֶסְתְּרֶנּוּ וְאֶבְנֶנּוּ, כְּדֵי שֶׁיִּקָּרֵא הַדִּין עַל שְׁמִי? תַּלְמוּד לוֹמַר: מִדְּבַר שֶׁקֶר תִּרְחָק.

1. The Rambam chooses such an instance because if both litigants are harsh, the one vindicated will defend the judge against the other litigant (see *Tosafot, Sanhedrin* 6b). The Radbaz explains that this is unlikely; no litigant will risk his own welfare to defend a judge. Instead the Rambam is referring to a common situation. The same principles apply if both litigants are harsh. The Ramah (*Choshen Mishpat* 12:1) differs and maintains that if both litigants are harsh, the judge is obligated to adjudicate the case.

2. The verse continues: "for the judgment is God's." Implied is that the command applies at the time of judgment (*Sefer Me'irat Einayim* 12:2).

Sefer HaMitzvot (negative commandment 276) and *Sefer HaChinuch* (mitzvah 415) count this as one of the 613 mitzvot of the Torah.

3. For the community will protect him (Radbaz).

4. See Chapter 1, Halachah 7, which states that students should sit before the court.

5. Similarly, the law applies in a situation when both litigants are poor or both rich (*Sefer Me'irat Einayim* 9:18).

6. And allows the judge to decide the case without considering that factor.

7. For in this way, the student will not be able to inform him if he deviates from the proper path [*Shulchan Aruch* (*Choshen Mishpat* 9:6)].

8. Our translation is based on authoritative manuscripts and early printings of the *Mishneh Torah*. The version in the standard printed text is slightly different.

9. Instead, in a reverent manner, he should ask: "Master, did you not teach us such and such?" [*Shulchan Aruch* (*Choshen Mishpat* 9:8)]. See also *Hilchot Talmud Torah 5:9.*

4. At the outset, it is a mitzvah to ask the litigants: "Do you desire a judgment or a compromise?" If they desire a compromise, a compromise is negotiated.[10] Any court that continuously negotiates a compromise is praiseworthy.[11] Concerning [this approach, Zechariah 8:16] states: "Adjudicate a judgment of peace in your gates." Which judgment involves peace?[12] A compromise. Similarly, with regard to King David it is stated: "And David carried out justice and charity for his entire people." When does justice involve charity?[13] When a compromise [is made].[14]

When does the above apply? Before a judgment is rendered. Even though [the judge] has already heard their arguments and knows the direction in which the judgment is heading, it is a mitzvah to negotiate a compromise. Once the judgment is rendered and he declares: "So-and-so, your claim is vindicated; so-and-so, you are liable," he may not negotiate a compromise. Instead, let the judgment pierce the mountain.[15]

5. Although the litigants agreed to a compromise in court, [the judges] have the authority to demand a judgment until the litigants confirm their commitment [to the compromise] with a *kinyan*.[16]

6. A compromise has greater legal power than a judgment. If two[17] ordinary people rendered a judgment, their judgment is not binding and the litigants need not accept it. If, however, [such individuals[18]] negotiated a compromise and the litigants affirmed [their agreement] with a *kinyan*, they may not retract.

7. After leaving the court, it is forbidden for any of the judges to say: "I was the one who vindicated [you] or held [you] liable and my colleagues differed with me. What could I do? They outnumbered me." If he says this, he is among those [to whom the words of censure, Proverbs 11:13,]: "He proceeds gossiping, revealing secrets" is applied. An incident occurred with regard to one student who revealed the [private] conversations in the House of Study 22 years later. The court had him removed from the House of Study and denounced him as "a revealer of secrets."[19]

10. *Pesharah*, the Hebrew term for compromise, is derived from *poshrin*, meaning "lukewarm water." Just as water is brought to that temperature by mixing hot and cold water together, the court negotiates a compromise by taking into consideration the perspectives of both litigants (the Rambam's Commentary to the Mishnah, *Ketubot* 10:5). It must, however, be emphasized that a compromise is negotiated through the guiding influence of a judge who knows the legal principles involved. Unlike a judgment which must remain true to those principles without bending an inch, in a compromise, there is room for flexibility. Nevertheless, the basis for the compromise is the Torah's guidelines.
11. See the Introduction to the Rambam's Commentary to the Mishnah where he mentions similar concepts.
12. For generally, judgment does not lead to peace. The litigant who loses the case will think that he has been wronged.
13. For generally, a judgment is not charitable. Instead it should be executed without consideration of the situation of the litigant who loses.
14. The *Sefer Me'irat Einayim* 12:9 states that even though the litigant whose claim

ד מִצְוָה לוֹמַר לְבַעֲלֵי דִינִים בַּתְּחִלָּה: בְּדִין אַתֶּם רוֹצִים אוֹ בִּפְשָׁרָה? אִם רָצוּ בִּפְשָׁרָה – עוֹשִׂין בֵּינֵיהֶן פְּשָׁרָה. וְכָל בֵּית דִּין שֶׁעוֹשִׂין פְּשָׁרָה תָּמִיד – הֲרֵי זֶה מְשֻׁבָּח. וְעָלָיו נֶאֱמַר: מִשְׁפַּט שָׁלוֹם שִׁפְטוּ בְּשַׁעֲרֵיכֶם. אֵי זֶהוּ מִשְׁפָּט שֶׁיֵּשׁ עִמּוֹ שָׁלוֹם? הֱוֵי אוֹמֵר: זֶה בִּצּוּעַ. וְכֵן בְּדָוִד הוּא אוֹמֵר: וַיְהִי דָוִד עֹשֶׂה מִשְׁפָּט וּצְדָקָה לְכָל עַמּוֹ. אֵי זֶהוּ מִשְׁפָּט שֶׁיֵּשׁ עִמּוֹ צְדָקָה? הֱוֵי אוֹמֵר: זֶהוּ בִּצּוּעַ. וְהִיא הַפְּשָׁרָה.

בַּמֶּה דְבָרִים אֲמוּרִים? קֹדֶם גְּמַר דִּין. אַף עַל פִּי שֶׁשָּׁמַע דִּבְרֵיהֶם וְיָדַע לְהֵיכָן הַדִּין נוֹטֶה – מִצְוָה לְבַצֵּעַ. אֲבָל אַחֲרֵי שֶׁגָּמַר הַדִּין וְאָמַר: אִישׁ פְּלוֹנִי אַתָּה זַכַּאי, אִישׁ פְּלוֹנִי אַתָּה חַיָּב – אֵינוֹ רַשַּׁאי לַעֲשׂוֹת פְּשָׁרָה בֵּינֵיהֶן, אֶלָּא יִקֹּב הַדִּין אֶת הָהָר.

ה אַף עַל פִּי שֶׁרָצוּ בַּעֲלֵי הַדִּין בִּפְשָׁרָה בְּבֵית דִּין – יֵשׁ לָהֶם לַחֲזֹר וְלִתְבֹּעַ אֶת הַדִּין, עַד שֶׁיִּקְנוּ מִיַּד שְׁנֵיהֶם.

ו יָפֶה כֹּחַ פְּשָׁרָה מִכֹּחַ הַדִּין. שֶׁשְּׁנֵי הֶדְיוֹטוֹת שֶׁדָּנוּ – אֵין דִּינֵיהֶן דִּין, וְיֵשׁ לְבַעֲלֵי דִינִין לַחֲזֹר בָּהֶן; וְאִם עָשׂוּ פְּשָׁרָה וְקָנוּ מִיָּדָן – אֵין יְכוֹלִין לַחֲזֹר בָּהֶן.

ז אָסוּר לְאֶחָד מִן הַדַּיָּנִים, כְּשֶׁיֵּצֵא מִבֵּית דִּין, לוֹמַר: אֲנִי הוּא הַמְזַכֶּה אוֹ הַמְחַיֵּב, וַחֲבֵרַי חוֹלְקִין עָלַי; אֲבָל מָה אֶעֱשֶׂה שֶׁהֵם רַבּוּ עָלַי? וְאִם אָמַר כֵּן – הֲרֵי הוּא בִּכְלַל הוֹלֵךְ רָכִיל מְגַלֶּה סּוֹד. וּמַעֲשֶׂה בְּתַלְמִיד אֶחָד, שֶׁהוֹצִיא דְּבָרִים שֶׁנֶּאֶמְרוּ בְּבֵית הַמִּדְרָשׁ לְאַחַר שְׁתַּיִם וְעֶשְׂרִים שָׁנָה, וְהוֹצִיאוּהוּ בֵּית דִּין מִבֵּית הַמִּדְרָשׁ, וְהִכְרִיזוּ עָלָיו: זֶה מְגַלֶּה סוֹד הוּא!

would have been vindicated will forgo a certain amount of financial gain, it is considered to his advantage to negotiate a compromise. For the benefits of peace and goodwill outweigh the financial loss.

15. I.e., the judgment should be executed regardless of the difficulties.

The Radbaz and the *Shulchan Aruch* (*Choshen Mishpat* 12:2) state that a compromise can be negotiated even after the judgment has been rendered if an oath is involved and the judges fear that a false oath might be taken. The *Siftei Cohen* quotes the *Shiltei Giborim* who rules that the judges cannot impose an arbitrated compromise settlement after the judgment has been rendered. Nevertheless, if the judges suggest a settlement and it is accepted by the litigants, it is binding.

16. Although the litigants agreed to a compromise, if they did not affirm their agreement with a *kinyan*, their agreement is not binding and they can retract [*Shulchan Aruch* (*Choshen Mishpat* 12:7)]. Hence the judges have the authority to push towards a judgment in the hope that this will compel the parties to agree on a compromise.

17. But a judgment rendered by three ordinary people is binding in most instances as stated in Chapter 2, Halachah 10.

18. The Rambam uses a plural form. The Radbaz explains that this form was employed only for literary reasons, so that the second clause will parallel the first. If, however, one expert judge negotiated a compromise, it is also binding. In his *Kessef Mishneh*, however, Rav Yosef Caro cites opinions that require two judges and in his *Shulchan Aruch* (*Choshen Mishpat* 12:7), he cites both views.

19. The narrative is related in *Sanhedrin* 31a.

8. If either of the litigants asks [the court] to compose a record of the judgment,[20] they write it for him in the following manner: "So-and-so came to this-and-this court with so-and-so, the opposing litigant, claiming this-and-this. He was vindicated" or "...held liable." The record is given to him without it mentioning the names of those who vindicated him or those who held him liable. Instead, [it says merely] "From the statements of the court of such-and-such,[21] so-and-so was vindicated."

9. This was the custom of the men of Jerusalem: They would bring the litigants into [the court] and listen to their statements and claims. They would [then] bring in the witnesses and listen to their statements. [Afterwards,] the judges would have all others[22] removed[23] and would debate the matter among themselves [until] they came to a decision. Afterwards, they would call the litigants in and the judge of the greatest stature[24] declares: "So-and-so, your claim is vindicated; so-and-so, you are liable." In this way, the litigants do no know which judge vindicated him and which judge held him liable.

10. When a judge knows that a colleague is a robber or a wicked person, it is forbidden for him to [sit in judgment] with him,[25] as it is stated: "Keep distant from words of falsehood."

This is the practice that would be followed by Jerusalem's men of refined character: They would not sit to participate in a judgment unless they knew who would sit with them.[26] They would not sign a legal document unless they knew who would sign with them.[27] And they would not enter a feast until they knew who would be joining them.[28]

CHAPTER TWENTY THREE

1. [Deuteronomy 16:19 states:] "Do not take a bribe." Needless to say, [this command applies if the intent is] to pervert judgment.[1] [The verse is teaching

20. So that he has the possibility of taking it a higher court for review; see Chapter 6, Halachah 6, and notes. In this halachah, the Rambam is focusing only on the manner in which the text of the record is composed, emphasizing how - in keeping with the statements of the previous halachah - the opinions should not be associated with the judges by name.
21. This wording indicates that there was a difference of opinion among the judges, but allows each to preserve his anonymity. The *Sefer Me'irat Einayim* 19:3 states that if the judges of the court are unanimous in their decision, it is sufficient to say: "So-and-so was vindicated" or "So-and-so was held liable."
22. The *Bayit Chadash* (*Choshen Mishpat* 18) states that this refers to the litigants and the witness. Others, however, may stay. Indeed, it is desirable for the students of the judges to remain to listen to the debate and offer suggestions as indicated by Halachot 2 and 3. The *Pitchei Teshuvah* (*Choshen Mishpat* 18:1) clarifies the intent of the *Bayit Chadash*,

ח שָׁאַל אֶחָד מִבַּעֲלֵי דִינִים לִכְתֹּב לוֹ פְּסַק דִּין – כּוֹתְבִין לוֹ כָּךְ: בָּא פְּלוֹנִי לְבֵית דִּין שֶׁל פְּלוֹנִי עִם פְּלוֹנִי בַּעַל דִּינוֹ שֶׁטְּעָנוֹ בְּכָךְ, וְיָצָא זַכַּאי אוֹ חַיָּב. וְנוֹתְנִין לוֹ. וְאֵין מַזְכִּירִין שֵׁם הַמְזַכִּין וְלֹא שֵׁם הַמְחַיְּבִין, אֶלָּא: בֵּית דִּין שֶׁל פְּלוֹנִי, מִדִּבְרֵיהֶם נִזְדַּכֶּה פְּלוֹנִי.

ט כָּךְ הָיָה מִנְהָגָם שֶׁל אַנְשֵׁי יְרוּשָׁלַיִם: מַכְנִיסִין בַּעֲלֵי דִינִין וְשׁוֹמְעִים דִּבְרֵיהֶם וְטַעֲנוֹתֵיהֶם, וּמַכְנִיסִים הָעֵדִים וְשׁוֹמְעִים דִּבְרֵיהֶם. וּמוֹצִיאִין כָּל אָדָם לַחוּץ, וְהַדַּיָּנִים נוֹשְׂאִים וְנוֹתְנִים בֵּינֵיהֶם בַּדָּבָר, וְגוֹמְרִין אֶת הַדָּבָר. וְאַחַר כָּךְ מַכְנִיסִין בַּעֲלֵי דִינִים, וְגָדוֹל שֶׁבַּדַּיָּנִים אוֹמֵר: אִישׁ פְּלוֹנִי אַתָּה זַכַּאי, אִישׁ פְּלוֹנִי אַתָּה חַיָּב. כְּדֵי שֶׁלֹּא יֵדַע אֶחָד מִבַּעֲלֵי דִינִים אֵי זֶה דַּיָּן הוּא מִי שֶׁזִּכָּה אוֹתוֹ, וְלֹא אֵי זֶה דַּיָּן הוּא שֶׁחִיְּבוֹ.

י דַּיָּן שֶׁהוּא יוֹדֵעַ בַּחֲבֵרוֹ שֶׁהוּא גַזְלָן אוֹ רָשָׁע – אָסוּר לְהִצְטָרֵף עִמּוֹ. שֶׁנֶּאֱמַר: מִדְּבַר שֶׁקֶר תִּרְחָק. וְכָךְ הָיוּ נְקִיֵּי הַדַּעַת שֶׁבִּירוּשָׁלַיִם עוֹשִׂין: אֵין יוֹשְׁבִים בְּדִין עַד שֶׁיֵּדְעוּ עִם מִי הֵם יוֹשְׁבִים, וְלֹא חוֹתְמִים אֶת הַשְּׁטָר עַד שֶׁיֵּדְעוּ מִי חוֹתֵם עִמָּהֶם, וְלֹא נִכְנָסִים לִסְעֻדָּה עַד שֶׁיֵּדְעוּ מִי מֵסֵב עִמָּהֶן.

פֶּרֶק שְׁלֹשָׁה וְעֶשְׂרִים

א לֹא תִקַּח שֹׁחַד. אֵין צָרִיךְ לוֹמַר לְעַוֵּת אֶת הַדִּין, אֶלָּא אֲפִלּוּ לְזַכּוֹת אֶת הַזַּכַּאי וּלְחַיֵּב

stating that people are not allowed to remain indiscriminately. Instead, the court considers whether the presence of a person will be valuable or not and asks all others to leave.

23. To preserve their anonymity as above, and also to make sure that the judges will not try to curry favor with the litigants [the Rambam's Commentary to the Mishnah (*Sanhedrin* 3:7)].

24. Since he would always be the spokesman, there is no way of knowing which of the judges supported either of the litigants. If, however, this was not the case, one might think that the judge announcing the verdict was the one who pushed for its acceptance (*Sefer Me'irat Einayim* 19:1).

25. This applies even when he knows that he will deliver an honest and just judgment (*Sefer Me'irat Einayim* 7:26).

26. See Chapter 2, Halachah 14.

27. Lest an unacceptable witness sign with them, the document be nullified, and they become embarrassed (*Sanhedrin* 23a).

28. For it is humiliating for a sage to sup together with common people (*Berachot* 43b). See *Hilchot Deot* 5:2.

1. For that is forbidden under all circumstances as stated in Chapter 20, Halachah 6.

See also *Hilchot Teshuvah* 4:3 which states that taking a bribe to pervert judgment is one of the transgressions for which it is impossible to achieve full-hearted repentance.

When a person receives payment - or even a favor - from another person, he will be predisposed to support him in his claim. We are not speaking necessarily about a that] it is forbidden [for a bribe to be given] even to vindicate the just and to obligate the one who is liable. [In such an instance, the judge] transgresses a negative commandment.[2] Such a person is included in [the malediction, Deuteronomy 27:25]: "Cursed by he who takes a bribe." He is required to return the bribe if he is demanded to by the giver.[3]

2. Just as the recipient transgresses a negative commandment; so, too, does the giver, as [Leviticus 19:14] states: "Do not place a stumbling block before the blind."[4]

3. Any judge who sits and seeks to amplify his reputation in order to cause the wages of his attendants and scribes to be enhanced[5] is included among those who seek after profit. This is what the sons of Samuel did. Hence [I Samuel 8:3] describes them as being "inclined to profit and tak[ing] bribery."[6]

[The above applies] not only to a bribe of money, but a bribe of all things.[7] An incident occurred concerning [a judge] who stood up in a small boat, as he was crossing a river.[8] A person extended his hand and helped him as he was standing. [Later that person came before] the judge [with a case]. The judge told him: "I am unacceptable to serve as a judge for you."

Another incident took place where a person removed a feather from a fowl from a judge's scarf and another person covered some spittle that was lying before the judge and the judge told [them]: "I am unacceptable to serve as a judge for you." Another incident took place concerning a person who brought one of the presents given to priests[9] to a judge who as a priest. The judge told him: "I am unacceptable to serve as a judge for you."

And another incident took place concerning a sharecropper of [a field belonging to] a judge who would bring him figs from his field every Friday. Once he came earlier and brought him the figs on Thursday, because he had a judgment [over which he desired that the judge preside]. The judge told him: "I am unacceptable to serve as a judge for you." [This applies] although the figs belonged to the judge. Since he brought them earlier than the ordinary time, [that favor] caused him to be disqualified as a judge.

4. Whenever a judge borrows [an article], he is unacceptable to serve as a judge for the person who lent him the article.[10] When does the above apply?

conscious desire to act on that person's behalf. Instead, the intent is that in the judge's unconscious - in his cognitive processes over which he does not usually exercise control - there will be a motivation to help his benefactor. This is the rationale for all the stringencies the Rambam mentions in Halachah 3.

2. *Sefer HaMitzvot* (negative commandment 274) and *Sefer HaChinuch* (mitzvah 83) count this as one of the 613 mitzvot of the Torah.

3. As a source, the commentaries cite I Samuel 12:3 which relates that Samuel told the people: "From whom have I taken money that I will turn my eyes away from him? [Tell me,] and I will make restitution." See also the *Minchat Chinuch* (mitzvah 83) who writes that even if the giver does not demand restitution, the judge is obligated to return it.

אֶת הַחַיָּב – אָסוּר, וְעוֹבֵר בְּלֹא תַעֲשֶׂה, וַהֲרֵי הוּא בִּכְלַל אָרוּר לֹקֵחַ שֹׁחַד. וְחַיָּב לְהַחֲזִיר הַשֹּׁחַד כְּשֶׁיִּתְבָּעֶנּוּ הַנּוֹתֵן.

ב וּכְשֵׁם שֶׁהַלּוֹקֵחַ עוֹבֵר בְּלֹא תַעֲשֶׂה, כַּךְ הַנּוֹתֵן. שֶׁנֶּאֱמַר: וְלִפְנֵי עִוֵּר לֹא תִתֵּן מִכְשֹׁל.

ג כָּל דַּיָּן שֶׁיּוֹשֵׁב וּמְגַדֵּל מַעֲלָתוֹ, כְּדֵי לְהַרְבּוֹת שָׂכָר לְחַזָּנָיו וּלְסוֹפְרָיו – הֲרֵי הוּא בִּכְלַל הַנּוֹטִים אַחֲרֵי הַבֶּצַע. וְכֵן עָשׂוּ בְּנֵי שְׁמוּאֵל. וּלְכַךְ נֶאֱמַר לָהֶם: וַיִּטּוּ אַחֲרֵי הַבָּצַע וַיִּקְחוּ שֹׁחַד. וְלֹא שֹׁחַד מָמוֹן בִּלְבַד, אֶלָּא אֲפִלּוּ שֹׁחַד דְּבָרִים.

וּמַעֲשֶׂה בְּדַיָּן אֶחָד, שֶׁהָיָה עוֹלֶה בְּדוּגִית קְטַנָּה לַעֲבֹר בַּנָּהָר, וּפָשַׁט אֶחָד יָדוֹ וְסִיְּעוֹ בַּעֲלִיָּתוֹ, וְהָיָה לוֹ דִין, וְאָמַר לוֹ הַדַּיָּן: הֲרֵינִי פָּסוּל לְךָ לְדִין.

וּמַעֲשֶׂה בְּאֶחָד, שֶׁהֶעֱבִיר אֶבְרָה – נוֹצָה שֶׁל עוֹף – מֵעַל רְדִיד הַדַּיָּן, וְאַחֵר כִּסָּה רֹק מִלִּפְנֵי הַדַּיָּן, וְאָמַר לוֹ: הֲרֵינִי פָּסוּל לְךָ לְדִין.

וּמַעֲשֶׂה בְּאֶחָד, שֶׁהֵבִיא מַתָּנָה אַחַת מִמַּתְּנוֹת כְּהֻנָּה לְדַיָּן כֹּהֵן, וְאָמַר לוֹ: פָּסוּל אֲנִי לְךָ לְדִין.

וּמַעֲשֶׂה בַּאֲרִיס אֶחָד שֶׁל דַּיָּן, שֶׁהָיָה מֵבִיא לוֹ תְּאֵנִים מִתּוֹךְ שָׂדֵהוּ מֵעֶרֶב שַׁבָּת לְעֶרֶב שַׁבָּת. פַּעַם אַחַת הִקְדִּים וְהֵבִיא בַּחֲמִישִׁי בַּשַּׁבָּת, מִפְּנֵי שֶׁהָיָה לוֹ דִין. וְאָמַר לוֹ הַדַּיָּן: הֲרֵינִי פָּסוּל לְךָ לְדִין. אַף עַל פִּי שֶׁהַתְּאֵנִים מִשֶּׁל דַּיָּן, הוֹאִיל וֶהֱבִיאָן שֶׁלֹּא בִּזְמַנָּן – נִפְסַל לוֹ לְדִין.

ד כָּל דַּיָּן שֶׁשָּׁאַל שְׁאֵלָה – פָּסוּל לְדִין לָזֶה שֶׁהִשְׁאִילוֹ.

4. As the Rambam states in *Hilchot Rotzeach* 12:14, this prohibition forbids placing moral stumbling blocks in a person's path.
5. I.e., even though he does not take the profit for himself, causing his attendants to be rewarded is also considered as resembling receiving bribery.
6. *Shabbat* 56a offers this interpretation of Scripture's words of censure.
7. We have offered an interpretation of the Hebrew term *devarim* that fits the examples cited by the Rambam. It must, however, be noted that the term *devarim* can also be interpreted as meaning "words." The *Sefer Me'irat Einayim* 9:4 explains that words - e.g., giving a judge a greeting when one would not ordinarily do so, praising him, or speaking on his behalf - can also be considered a bribe, just as it can be considered as interest (see *Hilchot Malveh ViLoveh* 5:12).
8. All these examples are cited in *Ketubot* 105b. The *Kessef Mishneh* states that according to the Rambam, all the examples that follow reflect conduct mandated by law. They are not merely illustrations of pious behavior that would be desirable to emulate, as suggested by *Tosafot, Sanhedrin* 8a.
9. E.g., *Terumah*, the offering of grain given to the priests, *challah*, a portion of dough, or the first of a sheep's shearings. See Hilchot Bikkurim, Ch. 1, where the 24 presents given the priests are mentioned.
10. We fear that the fact that the judge borrowed from the lender will cause him to feel indebted to him and hence - knowingly or unknowingly - show favoritism to him.

When the judge does not have [articles] to lend him [in return]. If, however, the judge [possesses articles] to lend [in return], it is acceptable [for him to serve as a judge], for that person will also borrow from him.[11]

5. Whenever a judge takes a wage for adjudicating a case,[12] his judgments[13] are nullified. [This applies] only when it is not evident [that he is receiving compensation for losing his] wages.[14] If, however, he was involved in his profession and two people came to him for a judgment and he told them: "Provide me with a person who will work instead of me and I will adjudicate your case or pay me for the wages that I will forfeit," this is permitted.[15]

[This leniency] is permitted provided it is evident that the wage is merely in lieu of his hire, but no more, and he takes equal payment from both of the litigants, [receiving payment from each one] in the presence of the other.[16]

6. A judge may not[17] adjudicate the case of a friend. [This applies] even if the person is not a member of his wedding party[18] or one of his more intimate companions. [Similarly, he may not adjudicate the case of] one he hates. [This applies] even if the person is not his enemy and one whose misfortune he seeks. Instead, the two litigants must be looked upon equally in the eyes and in the hearts of the judges. If the judge does not know either of them and is not familiar with their deeds, this is the fairest judgment that could be.

7. Whenever two Torah scholars hate each other, they are forbidden to act as judges together.[19] For this will lead to a contorted judgment. The hatred each one of them bears for the other will cause him to overturn his colleague's words.

8. A judge should always see himself as if a sword is drawn on his neck[20] and Hell is open before him.[21] He should know who he is judging,[22] before Whom he is judging, and Who will ultimately exact retribution from him if

The Ramah (*Choshen Mishpat* 9:1 states that this applies in a situation when the judge borrows from the person frequently. Borrowing from him only on occasion is not considered a significant enough factor to have him disqualified as a judge.

11. Thus there is no sense of the judge being indebted to the lender. For one favor will be repaid by another favor.

12. He may, however, accept a wage for negotiating a compromise (*Siftei Cohen* 9:7).

13. I.e., not only the judgment for which he took a wage, but all of his previous judgments are also nullified (Rabbenu Nissim in his gloss to *Kiddushin*, Ch. 2). The *Shulchan Aruch* (*Choshen Mishpat* 9:5) quotes this concept as law.

14. Compare to *Hilchot Gezelah ViAvedah* 12:4.

15. *Ketubot* 105a cites the examples of the Sages Karna and Rav Huna who would conduct themselves in this manner.

In his gloss to *Hilchot Talmud Torah* 3:10, the *Kessef Mishneh* states that if the judge has no profession other than this, he may be paid a salary. For were he not to accept work as a judge, he would have to find another profession. On the basis of this rationale, from the Talmudic age onward, communities have paid judges salaries from communal funds even though the judges have no other professions.

בַּמֶּה דְּבָרִים אֲמוּרִים? בְּשֶׁלֹּא הָיָה לוֹ לַדַּיָּן לְהַשְׁאִיל; אֲבָל הָיָה לוֹ לְהַשְׁאִיל - כָּשֵׁר, שֶׁהֲרֵי גַם זֶה שׁוֹאֵל מִמֶּנּוּ.

ה כָּל דַּיָּן שֶׁנּוֹטֵל שְׂכָרוֹ לָדוּן - דִּינָיו בְּטֵלִים. וְהוּא שֶׁלֹּא יִהְיֶה שָׂכָר הַנִּכָּר; אֲבָל אִם הָיָה עוֹסֵק בִּמְלַאכְתּוֹ, וּבָאוּ לְפָנָיו שְׁנַיִם לְדִין, וְאָמַר לָהֶן: תְּנוּ לִי מִי שֶׁיַּעֲשֶׂה תַּחְתַּי עַד שֶׁאָדוּן לָכֶם, אוֹ תְּנוּ לִי שְׂכַר בַּטָּלָתִי - הֲרֵי זֶה מֻתָּר.
וְהוּא שֶׁיִּהְיֶה הַדָּבָר נִכָּר שֶׁהוּא שְׂכַר הַבַּטָּלָה בִּלְבַד וְלֹא יוֹתֵר, וְיִטֹּל מִשְּׁנֵיהֶם בְּשָׁוֶה זֶה בִּפְנֵי זֶה - כְּגוֹן זֶה מֻתָּר.

ו אָסוּר לַדַּיָּן לָדוּן לְמִי שֶׁהוּא אוֹהֲבוֹ, אַף עַל פִּי שֶׁאֵינוֹ שׁוֹשְׁבִינוֹ וְלֹא רֵעוֹ אֲשֶׁר כְּנַפְשׁוֹ; וְלֹא לְמִי שֶׁשּׂוֹנְאוֹ, אַף עַל פִּי שֶׁאֵינוֹ אוֹיֵב לוֹ וְלֹא מְבַקֵּשׁ רָעָתוֹ; אֶלָּא צָרִיךְ שֶׁיִּהְיוּ שְׁנֵי בַּעֲלֵי דִינִים שָׁוִין בְּעֵינֵי הַדַּיָּנִים וּבְלִבָּם. וְאִם לֹא הָיָה מַכִּיר אֶת אֶחָד מֵהֶם וְלֹא מַעֲשָׂיו - אֵין לְךָ דַּיָּן צֶדֶק כָּמוֹהוּ.

ז כָּל שְׁנֵי תַּלְמִידֵי חֲכָמִים שֶׁשּׂוֹנְאִים זֶה אֶת זֶה - אֲסוּרִין לֵישֵׁב בְּדִין זֶה עִם זֶה.
שֶׁדָּבָר זֶה גּוֹרֵם לִיצִיאַת מִשְׁפָּט מְעֻקָּל, מִפְּנֵי הַשִּׂנְאָה שֶׁבֵּינֵיהֶן דַּעַת כָּל אֶחָד נוֹטָה לִסְתֹּר דִּבְרֵי חֲבֵרוֹ.

ח לְעוֹלָם יִרְאֶה דַּיָּן עַצְמוֹ כְּאִלּוּ חֶרֶב מֻנַּחַת לוֹ עַל צַוָּארוֹ, וְגֵיהִנֹּם פְּתוּחָה לוֹ מִתַּחְתָּיו.
וְיֵדַע אֶת מִי הוּא דָן, וְלִפְנֵי מִי הוּא דָן, וּמִי עָתִיד לְהִפָּרַע מִמֶּנּוּ אִם נָטָה מִקַּו הָאֱמֶת.

16. For if one pays the judge outside the other's presence, the other litigant may think that the one paid the other more as a bribe. Alternatively, the one paying may think that the judge is taking payment only from him (*Kessef Mishneh*).
17. The Radbaz states that from the Talmudic sources (*Ketubot* 105b; *Sanhedrin* 27b), it appears that although it is forbidden for a judge to adjudicate such cases, if he violates this prohibition and acts as a judge, his judgment is binding. He maintains that the Rambam's linking of this issue with bribery indicates, however, that he maintains that the judgment is unacceptable. This is also indicated by the Rambam's wording in his Commentary to the Mishnah (*Sanhedrin* 3:5). The *Beit Yosef* and the Ramah (*Choshen Mishpat* 7:7), however, follow the initial view.
18. It was customary for a person to invite his closest friends to share in his wedding celebrations with him. See *Hilchot Zechiyah UMatanah*, ch. 7, where the Aramaic term the Rambam uses, *shushvinin*, is discussed.
19. The *Bayit Chadash* (*Choshen Mishpat* 8) rules that if the two judges truly hate each other, the judgment is not binding, even after the fact.
20. The Rambam follows Rabbenu Yitzchak Alfasi's version of *Sanhedrin* 7a. The standard printed text follows a slightly different version.
21. The sword refers to retribution that is exacted in this world, and Hell to retribution exacted in the world to come (*Sefer Me'irat Einayim* 8:7-8).
22. For every Jew has a soul which is an actual part of God.

he deviates from the path of truth, as [indicated by Psalms 82:1]: "God stands among the congregation of the Almighty." And [II Chronicles 19:6] states: "See what you are doing. For you are not judging for man's sake, but for God's."[23]

9. Whenever a judge does not render a genuinely true judgment, he causes the Divine presence to depart from Israel. Whenever a judge expropriates money from one litigant and gives it to the other unlawfully, God exacts retribution from his life, as [Proverbs 22:23] states: "He will exact payment from the soul of one who exacts payment."

[Conversely,] when a judge adjudicates a case in a genuinely true manner for even one moment, it is as if he has corrected the entire world and he causes the Divine Presence to rest within Israel, as [implied by] the verse: "God stands among the congregation of the Almighty." If a judge will ask: "Why should involve myself in this difficulty?" [He should know that] it is written: [II Chronicles, *loc. cit.*]: "He is with you in the matter of judgment." [Nor should the judge worry about erring.] A judge may only base his judgment on what his eyes see.

10. [At the outset, a judge] should always look upon the litigants[24] as if they were wicked and operate under the presumption that both of them are lying. He should adjudicate according to his perception of the situation. When they depart, having accepted the judgment, he should view them both as righteous, seeing each of them in a favorable light.[25]

CHAPTER TWENTY FOUR

1. A judge may adjudicate cases involving monetary law[1] based on factors that he is inclined to regard as true and concerning which he feels strongly in his heart are correct even though he does not have proof of the matters. Needless to say, if he personally knows that a matter is true, he may judge the case according to his knowledge.

What is implied? A person was obligated to take an oath by the court.[2] A person whom the judge regards as trustworthy and upon whose word the judge relies tells him[3] that this person is suspect to take a false oath.[4] The judge may reverse the obligation for the oath and place it on the other litigant, [allowing him] to take an oath and collect his claim because the judge relied on the statements of this person.

[Moreover,] even if he regards a woman or a servant[5] as trustworthy, should he feel strongly that the matter [about which they are speaking] is correct, he may rely on their statement and judge [accordingly]. Needless to say, if he

23. This was part of the charge King Yehoshafat administered to the judges whom he appointed.
24. I.e., even if the litigant is a person of stature, the judge must regard him with suspicion and scrutinize his statements carefully.

שֶׁנֶּאֱמַר: אֱלֹהִים נִצָּב בַּעֲדַת אֵל. וְאוֹמֵר: רְאוּ מָה אַתֶּם עֹשִׂים, כִּי לֹא לְאָדָם תִּשְׁפְּטוּ כִּי לַיְיָ.

ט כָּל דַּיָּן שֶׁאֵינוֹ דָּן דִּין אֱמֶת לַאֲמִתּוֹ – גּוֹרֵם לַשְּׁכִינָה שֶׁתִּסְתַּלֵּק מִיִּשְׂרָאֵל. וְכָל דַּיָּן שֶׁנּוֹטֵל מִזֶּה וְנוֹתֵן לָזֶה שֶׁלֹּא כַּדִּין – הַקָּדוֹשׁ בָּרוּךְ הוּא גּוֹבֶה מִמֶּנּוּ נְפָשׁוֹת. שֶׁנֶּאֱמַר: וְקָבַע אֶת קֹבְעֵיהֶם נָפֶשׁ.

וְכָל דַּיָּן שֶׁדָּן דִּין אֱמֶת לַאֲמִתּוֹ, אֲפִלּוּ שָׁעָה אַחַת – כְּאִלּוּ תִּקֵּן אֶת כָּל הָעוֹלָם כֻּלּוֹ, וְגוֹרֵם לַשְּׁכִינָה שֶׁתִּשְׁרֶה בְּיִשְׂרָאֵל. שֶׁנֶּאֱמַר: אֱלֹהִים נִצָּב בַּעֲדַת אֵל. וְשֶׁמָּא יֹאמַר הַדַּיָּן: מַה לִּי וְלַצָּרָה הַזֹּאת? תַּלְמוּד לוֹמַר: וְעִמָּכֶם בִּדְבַר מִשְׁפָּט – אֵין לַדַּיָּן אֶלָּא מַה שֶּׁעֵינָיו רוֹאוֹת.

י וּלְעוֹלָם יִהְיוּ בַּעֲלֵי דִינִין לְפָנֶיךָ כִּרְשָׁעִים, וּבְחֶזְקַת שֶׁכָּל אֶחָד מֵהֶן טוֹעֵן שֶׁקֶר, וְדוּן לְפִי מַה שֶּׁתִּרְאֶה מִן הַדְּבָרִים. וּכְשֶׁיִּפָּטְרוּ מִלְּפָנֶיךָ – יִהְיוּ בְעֵינֶיךָ כְּצַדִּיקִים, כְּשֶׁקִּבְּלוּ עֲלֵיהֶם אֶת הַדִּין, וְדוּן כָּל אֶחָד מֵהֶם לְכַף זְכוּת.

פֶּרֶק אַרְבָּעָה וְעֶשְׂרִים

א יֵשׁ לַדַּיָּן לָדוּן בְּדִינֵי מָמוֹנוֹת עַל פִּי הַדְּבָרִים שֶׁדַּעְתּוֹ נוֹטָה לָהֶן שֶׁהֵן אֱמֶת, וְהַדָּבָר חָזָק בְּלִבּוֹ שֶׁהוּא כֵּן, אַף עַל פִּי שֶׁאֵין שָׁם רְאָיָה בְּרוּרָה. וְאֵין צָרִיךְ לוֹמַר, אִם הָיָה יוֹדֵעַ בְּוַדַּאי שֶׁהַדָּבָר כֵּן הוּא, שֶׁהוּא דָן כְּפִי מַה שֶּׁיּוֹדֵעַ.

כֵּיצַד? הֲרֵי שֶׁנִּתְחַיֵּב אָדָם שְׁבוּעָה בְּבֵית דִּין, וְאָמַר לַדַּיָּן אָדָם שֶׁהוּא נֶאֱמָן אֶצְלוֹ וְשֶׁדַּעְתּוֹ סוֹמֶכֶת עַל דְּבָרָיו, שֶׁזֶּה הָאִישׁ חָשׁוּד עַל הַשְּׁבוּעָה – יֵשׁ לַדַּיָּן לַהֲפֹךְ הַשְּׁבוּעָה עַל שֶׁכְּנֶגְדּוֹ, וְיִשָּׁבַע וְיִטֹּל; הוֹאִיל וְסָמְכָה דַעְתּוֹ שֶׁל דַּיָּן עַל דִּבְרֵי זֶה.

אֲפִלּוּ הָיְתָה אִשָּׁה אוֹ עֶבֶד נֶאֱמָנִים אֶצְלוֹ, הוֹאִיל וּמָצָא הַדָּבָר חָזָק וְנָכוֹן בְּלִבּוֹ – סוֹמֵךְ עָלָיו וְדָן.

25. I.e., even when he holds a person liable, he should not view him as wicked, but rather a person who committed a misdeed inadvertently, for various reasons.

1. In contrast to laws involving capital punishment, as stated in Chapter 20, Halachah 1.
2. I.e., he denied a claim and was required to take an oath to substantiate his denial.
3. I.e., although generally, the word of one witness is not accepted, an exception is made in this case.
4. This term has a specific halachic meaning: A person who is disqualified from taking an oath, because he is known to have taken a false oath in the past or to have been disqualified to serve as a witness (*Hilchot Toen ViNitan* 2:2).
5. Although these individuals are not acceptable as formal witnesses, a judge may choose

himself knows that a person is suspect [to take a false oath, he may judge accordingly].

Similarly, when a promissory note comes before him and a person upon whom he relies - even a woman or a relative[6] - says that it has been repaid, if he trusts his word, he may tell [the bearer of the note]: "Payment [will be required only] when an oath is taken."[7] Similarly, if [the alleged debtor] is also indebted to another person, [the judge] may have the debtor pay the creditor whose promissory note was not impugned at all and leave the promissory note that was impugned by the person's testimony [unpaid].[8] Or he may reject the promissory note and not consider it in judgment if he sees fit.[9]

Similar [laws apply] if a person comes and claims that he entrusted an article to so-and-so who died[10] and identified [the article] with extremely precise descriptive marks. If the claimant did not frequent the home of the deceased,[11] and if the judge knows that the deceased did not have the means to own such an article and he firmly believes that the article did not belong to the deceased, the article may be expropriated from the heirs[12] and given to the person [provided] he has the means to own it[13] and identified it with descriptive marks. Similar laws apply in all analogous situations.

These matters are solely given over to the heart of the judge [to decide] according to what he perceives as being a true judgment. Why then did the Torah require two witnesses?[14] Because when two witnesses appear before a judge, he must judge according to their testimony whether or not he knows it to be true.[15]

2. All of the matters mentioned above are the fundamental standard of law. Nevertheless, when courts which were not fitting - not necessarily [courts which] were not upright, but even those whose deeds were just, but [whose judges] were not sufficiently wise and masters of understanding - proliferated, the majority of the courts among the Jewish people agreed not to reverse oaths unless there was clear proof [that a litigant was suspect of taking a false oath].[16] [Similarly, they agreed] not to disqualify a promissory note on the basis of the testimony of a woman or an unacceptable [witness], nor [accept their

to rely on their word if he so desires. *Ketubot* 85a relates that Ravva accepted the word of his wife with regard to such a matter, for he was confident that she would not lie.

6. Whose testimony is not acceptable. The Rambam mentions only the testimony of non-acceptable witnesses in this instance, for if one acceptable witness testifies that a promissory note has been paid, the bearer must take an oath before expropriating payment even if the judge does not have feelings of certainty that his testimony is true (*Hilchot Malveh ViLoveh* 14:1).

7. The Ra'avad objects to this ruling, maintaining that the alleged creditor should not be given the opportunity to collect his claim, even with an oath. The *Kessef Mishneh* explains that the Rambam's perspective is also reflected in the rulings of Rabbenu Chananel and *Tosafot* (*Ketubot* 85a). According to this view, the unique dimension of this teaching is that based on the judge's trust, the woman or servant is given the same status as an acceptable witness. They are not, however, given greater credibility than that.

וְאֵין צָרִיךְ לוֹמַר, אִם יָדַע הוּא עַצְמוֹ שֶׁזֶּה חָשׁוּד. וְכֵן אִם יָצָא שְׁטַר חוֹב לְפָנָיו, וְאָמַר לוֹ אָדָם שֶׁסָּמַךְ עָלָיו, אֲפִלּוּ אִשָּׁה אוֹ קָרוֹב: זֶה פָּרוּעַ הוּא! אִם סָמְכָה דַעְתּוֹ עַל דְּבָרָיו – יֵשׁ לוֹ לוֹמַר לָזֶה: לֹא תִפָּרַע אֶלָּא בִשְׁבוּעָה. אוֹ אִם הָיָה עָלָיו שְׁטַר חוֹב לְאַחֵר – יִתֵּן לָזֶה שֶׁלֹּא נִפְגַּם שְׁטָרוֹ כְּלָל, וְיַנִּיחַ זֶה שֶׁנִּפְגַּם שְׁטָרוֹ בְּדִבְרֵי הָאֶחָד. אוֹ יַשְׁלִיךְ הַשְּׁטָר בְּפָנָיו וְלֹא יָדוּן בּוֹ. כְּפִי מַה שֶּׁיֵּרָאֶה.

וְכֵן מִי שֶׁבָּא וְטָעַן שֶׁיֵּשׁ לוֹ פִּקָּדוֹן אֵצֶל פְּלוֹנִי שֶׁמֵּת בְּלֹא צַוָּאָה, וְנָתַן סִימָנִין מֻבְהָקִין, וְלֹא הָיָה זֶה הַטּוֹעֵן רָגִיל לְהִכָּנֵס בְּבֵית זֶה הָאִישׁ שֶׁמֵּת, אִם יָדַע הַדַּיָּן שֶׁזֶּה הַמֵּת אֵינוֹ אָמוּד לִהְיוֹת לוֹ חֵפֶץ זֶה, וְסָמְכָה דַעְתּוֹ שֶׁאֵין זֶה הַחֵפֶץ שֶׁל מֵת – מוֹצִיאוֹ מִן הַיּוֹרְשִׁין וְנוֹתְנוֹ לָזֶה הָאָמוּד בּוֹ וְנָתַן סִימָנִים. וְכֵן כֹּל כַּיּוֹצֵא בָּזֶה.

שֶׁאֵין הַדָּבָר מָסוּר אֶלָּא לְלִבּוֹ שֶׁל דַּיָּן, לְפִי מַה שֶּׁיֵּרָאֶה לוֹ שֶׁהוּא דִין הָאֱמֶת.

אִם כֵּן, לָמָּה הִצְרִיכָה תוֹרָה שְׁנֵי עֵדִים? שֶׁבִּזְמַן שֶׁיָּבוֹאוּ לִפְנֵי הַדַּיָּן שְׁנֵי עֵדִים – יָדוּן עַל פִּי עֵדוּתָן, אַף עַל פִּי שֶׁאֵינוֹ יוֹדֵעַ אִם בֶּאֱמֶת הֵעִידוּ אוֹ בְּשֶׁקֶר.

ב כָּל אֵלּוּ הַדְּבָרִים הֵן עִקַּר הַדִּין. אֲבָל מִשֶּׁרַבּוּ בָּתֵּי דִינִין שֶׁאֵינָן הֲגוּנִים, וַאֲפִלּוּ הָיוּ הֲגוּנִים בְּמַעֲשֵׂיהֶם – אֵינָן חֲכָמִים כָּרָאוּי וּבַעֲלֵי בִינָה, הִסְכִּימוּ רֹב בָּתֵּי דִינֵי יִשְׂרָאֵל: שֶׁלֹּא יַהַפְכוּ שְׁבוּעָה אֶלָּא בִרְאָיָה בְּרוּרָה. וְלֹא יִפְגְּמוּ שְׁטָר וְיַפְסִידוּ חֶזְקָתוֹ בְּעֵדוּת אִשָּׁה אוֹ פָּסוּל. וְכֵן בִּשְׁאָר כָּל הַדִּינִין.

8. I.e., the debtor has sufficient financial resources to pay only one of the promissory notes.

9. He may not, however, destroy the promissory note and thus the bearer may take it to another judge who may decide to act upon it.

10. Without informing his family that the article had been entrusted to him (*Ketubot* 85b).

11. For if he would frequent the deceased's home, the fact that he could identify the article is not significant. He could have seen it during his visits.

12. Generally, heirs are given the benefit of the doubt. Although the heirs are not aware of the details, the court presents any argument that the deceased could have advanced on their behalf. Thus we might think that since the deceased could have claimed that the article belonged to him, that claim would be advanced on behalf of the heirs. This, however, is not the case, because the deceased did not have the means to own the article (*Kessef Mishneh*). The above ruling applies even when there are no witnesses that the alleged owner entrusted the article.

13. If, however, he does not have the means to own such an article, it is not given to him even though he identifies it, stating precise descriptive characteristics. Compare to *Hilchot Sha'alah UPikadon* 6:4, *Hilchot Nachalot* 11:1.

14. I.e., if we rely on the judges' discernment, why did the Torah require witnesses?

15. The Radbaz states that the Rambam's wording implies that if the judge feels strongly that witnesses are lying, he may refuse to accept their testimony even if he has no firm proof to substantiate his assumptions. He may not say: "The perversion of justice is the witnesses' responsibility; I am merely acting upon their testimony." Instead, he must act according to his own scruples. See Halachah 3.

16. The Radbaz states that the Rambam's statements are based on the rulings of Rabbenu

testimony] with regard to all other judgments, nor to judge according to the inclinations of one's thoughts without [firm] knowledge.

[The rationale for this stringency is to] prevent any simple person from saying: "My heart trusts this person's words and my mind relies on this." Similarly, we do not expropriate [property] from orphans unless there is clear proof.[17] [We] do not [rely on] the judge's opinion, the evaluation of the deceased's [financial capacity], or that of the claimant. Even though a trustworthy person delivered testimony concerned a certain matter and the mind of the judge was inclined to believe that he was telling the truth, he should hesitate in judgment.[18] He should not reject his testimony. Instead, he should mediate between the litigants until they accept the testimony of the witness or agree to a compromise.[19] [Alternatively,] the judge may withdraw from the case.[20]

3. What is the source which teaches that a judge who knows that a claim is contrived[21] should not say: "I will deliver a judgment and the responsibility will lie with the witnesses"? It is written [Exodus 23:7]: "Keep distant from words of falsehood."

What shall he do? He should question and cross-examine the witnesses exceedingly, following [the cross-examination] process employed in cases involving capital punishment.[22] If it appears to him according to his understanding that there is no deception,[23] he should deliver a judgment. If, however,

a) he [still] has hesitations [because he feels that] deception is involved,

b) he does not rely on the testimony of the witnesses although he cannot disqualify them,

c) he feels that [one of] the litigants is a deceiver and a beguiler and misled the witnesses even though they are fit to testify and testified honestly, it is only that [the litigant] led them astray, or

d) that from the things that were said, he feels that there are hidden factors which they do not desire to reveal,

in these and in all similar matters, it is forbidden for him to deliver a ruling. Instead, he should withdraw from this judgment and allow it to be decided by someone whose heart is at peace with the matter.[24] These matters are given

Yitzchak Alfasi and the *Geonim* who preceded him. They are quoted by the *Shulchan Aruch* (*Choshen Mishpat* 15:5. It must, however, be noted that in a responsa (Responsum 108), the Maharik writes that even in the present age, a judge should rely on his own appreciation of the truth. His words are cited by the *Sefer Me'irat Einayim* 15:15.

17. I.e., the testimony of at least two acceptable witnesses. In his *Kessef Mishneh*, Rav Yosef Karo writes that, in contrast to the concepts mentioned previously, the reservation against expropriating property from orphans is not mentioned by Rabbenu Yitzchak Alfasi. Neither is it mentioned by Rabbenu Asher or the *Tur*. In his *Shulchan Aruch* (*Choshen Mishpat* 15:5), Rav Yosef Karo quotes the Rambam, but the *Sefer Me'irat Einayim* 15:16 questions why the Ramah does not cite the other view.

18. I.e., because he is only one witness, the judge could not decide the case according to

וְלֹא יָדוּן הַדַּיָּן בִּסְמִיכַת דַּעְתּוֹ וְלֹא בִּידִיעָתוֹ, כְּדֵי שֶׁלֹּא יֹאמַר כָּל הֶדְיוֹט: לִבִּי מַאֲמִין לְדִבְרֵי זֶה, וְדַעְתִּי סוֹמֶכֶת עַל זֶה. וְכֵן אֵין מוֹצִיאִין מִן הַיְתוֹמִים אֶלָּא בִּרְאָיָה בְּרוּרָה, לֹא בְּדַעַת הַדַּיָּן וְלֹא בְּאֻמְדַּן הַמֵּת אוֹ הַטּוֹעֵן. וְאַף עַל פִּי כֵן, אִם הֵעִיד אָדָם נֶאֱמָן בְּדָבָר מִכָּל הַדְּבָרִים, וְנָטְתָה דַעַת הַדַּיָּן שֶׁאֱמֶת הוּא אוֹמֵר – מַמְתִּין בַּדִּין, וְאֵינוֹ דוֹחֶה עֵדוּתוֹ, וְנוֹשֵׂא וְנוֹתֵן עִם בַּעֲלֵי דִינִין עַד שֶׁיּוֹדוּ לְדִבְרֵי הָעֵד, אוֹ יַעֲשׂוּ פְּשָׁרָה, אוֹ יִסְתַּלֵּק מִן הַדִּין.

ג וּמִנַּיִן לַדַּיָּן שֶׁהוּא יוֹדֵעַ בְּדִין שֶׁהוּא מְרֻמֶּה, שֶׁלֹּא יֹאמַר: אֶחְתְּכֶנּוּ, וְיִהְיֶה הַקּוֹלָר תָּלוּי בְּצַוְּארֵי הָעֵדִים? תַּלְמוּד לוֹמַר: מִדְּבַר שֶׁקֶר תִּרְחָק. כֵּיצַד יַעֲשֶׂה? יִדְרשׁ בּוֹ וְיַחְקֹר הַרְבֵּה בִּדְרִישָׁה וּבַחֲקִירָה שֶׁל דִּינֵי נְפָשׁוֹת. אִם נִרְאֶה לוֹ לְפִי דַעְתּוֹ [שֶׁאֵין בּוֹ רַמָּאוּת – חוֹתֵךְ אֶת הַדִּין עַל פִּי הָעֵדוּת.

אֲבָל אִם הָיָה לִבּוֹ נוֹקְפוֹ] שֶׁיֵּשׁ בּוֹ רַמָּאוּת;

אוֹ שֶׁאֵין דַּעְתּוֹ סוֹמֶכֶת עַל דִּבְרֵי הָעֵדִים, אַף עַל פִּי שֶׁאֵינוֹ יָכוֹל לְפָסְלָן;

אוֹ שֶׁדַּעְתּוֹ נוֹטָה שֶׁבַּעַל דִּין זֶה רַמַּאי וּבַעַל עָרְמָה, וְהִשִּׂיא אֶת הָעֵדִים, אַף עַל פִּי שֶׁהֵם כְּשֵׁרִים וּלְפִי תֻּמָּם הֵעִידוּ, וְזֶה הִטְעָם;

אוֹ שֶׁנִּרְאֶה לוֹ מִכְּלַל הַדְּבָרִים, שֶׁיֵּשׁ שָׁם דְּבָרִים אֲחֵרִים מְסֻתָּרִין, וְאֵינָן רוֹצִים לְגַלּוֹתָם – כָּל אֵלּוּ הַדְּבָרִים וְכַיּוֹצֵא בָּהֶן אָסוּר לוֹ לַחְתֹּךְ אוֹתוֹ הַדִּין, אֶלָּא יְסַלֵּק עַצְמוֹ מִדִּין זֶה,

his testimony unless he used the license mentioned in the previous halachah and, as stated above, this is not the practice at present. Hence, the judge should follow one of the courses of action mentioned by the Rambam.

19. See Chapter 22, Halachot 4-6, which explain the virtues of negotiating a compromise. These concepts are particularly relevant in the present age because of the decline in the level of the courts. See the *Hagahot Maimoniot* which elaborates on this issue; see also the notes to the following halachah.

20. As stated in the following halachah.

21. And is based on the testimony of witnesses who are lying.

22. See *Hilchot Edut* 1:4-5. Although generally, this cross-examination procedure is suspended in cases involving monetary law (*Ibid.* 3:1-2), a judge has the right to make an exception and employ these measures.

23. I.e., the cross-examination of the witnesses resolved the doubts that had initially troubled him.

24. The *Hagahot Maimoniot* and the *Shulchan Aruch* (*Choshen Mishpat* 15:4) state this ruling applies when the plaintiff is a deceiver. Different rules apply if, however, it is the defendant who is a deceiver - and thus by withdrawing himself, the judge will allow the transgressor to get his way. For the money claimed will remain in the defendant's possession. Instead, the judge should continue the process of cross-examination until the truth comes to the fore. Moreover, if he is a judge of stature, he may expropriate the funds from the defendant even if he has no proof that his assumptions are correct.

Even when it is the plaintiff who is the deceiver, Rabbenu Asher [and his conduct is cited as law by the *Shulchan Aruch* (*Choshen Mishpat* 15:3)] would compose a court decision exonerating the defendant and preventing the plaintiff from pursuing the matter in other courts. The *Sefer Me'irat Einayim* 15:12 understands this to be a direct contradiction to the Rambam's approach.

over to [a person's] heart. Concerning these [Deuteronomy 1:17] states: "Judgment is God's."[25]

4. A court[26] has the authority to administer lashes to a person who is not required to receive lashes and to execute a person who is not liable to be executed.[27] [This license was] not [granted] to overstep the words of the Torah, but rather to create a fence around the words of the Torah. When the court sees that the people[28] have broken the accepted norms with regard to a matter, they may establish safeguards to strengthen the matter according to what appears [necessary] to them. All [the above] applies with regard to establishing directives for the immediate time, and not with regard to the establishment of halachah for all time.

An incident occurred where they had a man lashed for engaging in relations with his wife under a tree.[29] And an incident occurred concerning a person who rode on a horse on the Sabbath in the era of the Greeks[30] and they brought him to the court and had him stoned to death. And an incident occurred and Shimon ben Shetach hung 80 women[31] on one day in Ashkelon. All of the required processes of questioning, cross-examination, and warnings were not followed, nor was the testimony unequivocal.[32] Instead, [their execution] was a directive for that immediate time according to what he perceived as [necessary].

5. Similarly, at any time, and in any place, a court has the license to give a person lashes if he has a reputation for immorality and people gossip about him, [saying] that he acts licentiously. [This applies] provided the rumor is heard continuously, as we explained,[33] and he does not have any known enemies who would spread this unfavorable report. Similarly, a person with such an unsavory reputation may be humiliated and scorn may be heaped on his mother in his presence.

6. Similarly, at all times, a court has the prerogative to declare money belonging to others as ownerless. It may destroy [those funds] or give them to whomever they see fit so as to close any breaches in the faith and to strengthen its observance or to penalize a stubborn and difficult person. The Book of Ezra [10:8] states: "Whoever fails to come in three days according to the advice of the officers and the elders will have all of his property confiscated." From this we learn that when a court declares property ownerless, [their declaration is effective].

7. Similarly, a judge may apply a ban of ostracism or excommunication[34] to a

25. The *Sefer Me'irat Einayim* 15:11 offers two interpretations of this conclusion:
a) God will assist him in delivering a just judgment and perceiving whether or not deception is involved.
b) God sees into the person's heart. Therefore he cannot excuse himself by saying: "I did not perceive any injustice" when in fact he did.

26. According to the *Shulchan Aruch* (*Choshen Mishpat* 2:1), this applies even with

וִידִינֶנּוּ מִי שֶׁלִּבּוֹ שָׁלֵם בַּדָּבָר. וַהֲרֵי הַדְּבָרִים מְסוּרִים לַלֵּב. וְהַכָּתוּב אוֹמֵר: כִּי הַמִּשְׁפָּט לֵאלֹהִים הוּא.

ד יֵשׁ לְבֵית דִּין לְהַלְקוֹת מִי שֶׁאֵינוֹ מְחֻיָּב מַלְקוּת, וְלַהֲרֹג מִי שֶׁאֵינוֹ מְחֻיָּב מִיתָה. וְלֹא לַעֲבֹר עַל דִּבְרֵי תּוֹרָה, אֶלָּא לַעֲשׂוֹת סְיָג לַתּוֹרָה. וְכֵיוָן שֶׁרוֹאִים בֵּית דִּין שֶׁפָּרְצוּ הָעָם בַּדָּבָר, יֵשׁ לָהֶן לִגְדֹּר וּלְחַזֵּק הַדָּבָר כְּפִי מַה שֶּׁיֵּרָאֶה לָהֶם. הַכֹּל הוֹרָאַת שָׁעָה, לֹא שֶׁיִּקָּבַע הֲלָכָה לְדוֹרוֹת.
מַעֲשֶׂה וְהִלְקוּ אָדָם שֶׁבָּעַל אִשְׁתּוֹ תַּחַת אִילָן.
וּמַעֲשֶׂה בְּאֶחָד שֶׁרָכַב עַל סוּס בְּשַׁבָּת בִּימֵי יְוָנִים, וֶהֱבִיאוּהוּ לְבֵית דִּין וּסְקָלוּהוּ. וּמַעֲשֶׂה וְתָלָה שִׁמְעוֹן בֶּן שֶׁטַח שְׁמוֹנִים נָשִׁים בְּיוֹם אֶחָד בְּאַשְׁקְלוֹן. וְלֹא הָיוּ שָׁם כָּל דַּרְכֵי הַדְּרִישָׁה וַחֲקִירָה וְהַהַתְרָאָה, וְלֹא בְּעֵדוּת בְּרוּרָה, אֶלָּא הוֹרָאַת שָׁעָה כְּפִי מַה שֶּׁרָאָה.

ה וְכֵן יֵשׁ לְבֵית דִּין בְּכָל מָקוֹם וּבְכָל זְמַן לְהַלְקוֹת אָדָם שֶׁשְּׁמוּעָתוֹ רָעָה, וְהָעָם מְרַנְּנִים עָלָיו שֶׁהוּא עוֹבֵר עַל הָעֲרָיוֹת. וְהוּא שֶׁיִּהְיֶה קוֹל שֶׁאֵינוֹ פּוֹסֵק, כְּמוֹ שֶׁבֵּאַרְנוּ, וְלֹא יִהְיוּ אֵלּוּ אוֹיְבִים יְדוּעִים שֶׁמּוֹצִיאִין עָלָיו שְׁמוּעָה רָעָה. וְכֵן מְבַזִּין אֶת זֶה שֶׁשְּׁמוּעָתוֹ רָעָה, וּמְחָרְפִין אֶת יוֹלַדְתּוֹ בְּפָנָיו.

ו וְכֵן יֵשׁ לַדַּיָּן תָּמִיד לְהַפְקִיר מָמוֹן שֶׁיֵּשׁ לוֹ בְּעָלִים, וּמְאַבֵּד וְנוֹתֵן כְּפִי מַה שֶּׁיִּרְאֶה לִגְדֹּר פִּרְצוֹת הַדָּת וּלְחַזֵּק הַבֶּדֶק, אוֹ לִקְנֹס אַלָּם זֶה.
וַהֲרֵי הוּא אוֹמֵר בְּעֶזְרָא: וְכֹל אֲשֶׁר לֹא יָבוֹא לִשְׁלֹשֶׁת הַיָּמִים כַּעֲצַת הַשָּׂרִים וְהַזְּקֵנִים יָחֳרַם כָּל רְכוּשׁוֹ. מִכָּאן, שֶׁהֶפְקֵר בֵּית דִּין – הֶפְקֵר.

ז וְכֵן יֵשׁ לַדַּיָּן לְנַדּוֹת וּלְהַחֲרִים מִי שֶׁאֵינוֹ בֶּן נִדּוּי, כְּדֵי לִגְדֹּר פֶּרֶץ, כְּפִי מַה שֶּׁיֵּרָאֶה לוֹ

regard to the courts of the present age. Some commentaries have questioned that ruling based on a comparison to the wording of the following halachah.
27. Similarly, they have right to impose fines (*Ibid.*; see Halachah 6).
28. The *Sefer Me'irat Einayim* 2:3 states that such decrees can be enforced even if the conduct of people at large is appropriate and it is only one individual who oversteps the ordinary bounds.
29. Allowing such licentious behavior would lead to immorality (*Hilchot Issurei Bi'ah* 21:14).
30. The Greeks forbade the observance of the Sabbath. Our Sages feared that any laxity in its observance might have widespread repercussions among the people.
31. Who practiced witchcraft.
32. For all these reasons, we cannot say that Shimon ben Shetach sentenced them to death according to the requirements of law. Instead, he exercised the special dispensation granted judges, as the Rambam states.
33. Hilchot Sotah 2:14.
34. See *Hilchot Talmud Torah*, Chapter 7, which describes the nature of these bans and the restrictions they involve.

person to whom these measures would not ordinarily be applied[35] according to his perception of what is necessary at that time. He should state that he is ostracizing him or excommunicating him on his own conviction[36] and should publicize his transgression in public. [This is indicated by Judges 5:23]: " 'Curse Meroz,' said the angel of G-d. 'Curse [him]. Those who dwell with him are cursed, because they did not come to the aid of God['s people].' "[37]

8. Similarly, a judge may enter into a controversy with a person with whom it is necessary to enter into controversy, cursing him, having him beaten, having his hair pulled out, and compelling him to take an oath to God against his will so that he will not perform or that he did not perform a specific action, as [Nechemiah 13:25] states: "I entered into controversy with them; I cursed them; I beat people among them; I tore their hair out, and I made them take an oath to God."[38]

9. Similarly, he may have a person's hands and feet bound. He may imprison him[39] and have him pushed to the ground and dragged, as [Ezra 7:26] states: "[Judgment will be speedily administered to him,] to be executed, to be uprooted, to be punished by [a loss of] property, and to be imprisoned."[40]

10. All of the above measures should be applied according to the judge's perception that it is appropriate that the violator be punished in this manner or[41] the situation at large requires it. All of his deeds should be for the sake of heaven[42] and the honor of people at large should be precious in his eyes. For [consideration of their honor] overrides [the observance of] a Rabbinic prohibition.[43] Certainly, this applies with regard to the descendants of Abraham, Isaac, and Jacob who uphold the Torah. He must take care not to ruin their honor and act only to increase the honor of the Omnipresent. For whenever a person debases the Torah, his person will be degraded for people at large. [Conversely,] when a person honors the Torah,[44] his person will be honored by people at large. And there is no other honor for the Torah except to follow its statutes and judgments.

35. See *Ibid.*, the conclusion of Chapter 6.
36. The court attendant should convey this message to the person being ostracized or being excommunicated, so that he will realize that the action was taken by a judge of stature and hence, he will hurry to amend his conduct (*Kessef Mishneh*).
37. This malediction was pronounced by the prophetess Deborah in her song of victory after the defeat of the Canaanites. She cursed Meroz, an important personage of that time, because although he lived near the battlefield, he did not join Barak's troops (Radak). The Rambam cites this (quoting *Mo'ed Kattan* 16a) as an example of the fact that the transgression performed by the person must be publicized.

וְהַשָּׁעָה צְרִיכָה לְכָךְ. וְיֹאמַר, שֶׁנִּדָּהוּ וְהֶחֱרִימָהוּ עַל דַּעְתּוֹ. וִיפַרְסֵם חֶטְאוֹ בָּרַבִּים. שֶׁנֶּאֱמַר: אוֹרוּ מֵרוֹז אָמַר מַלְאַךְ יְיָ, אֹרוּ אָרוֹר יֹשְׁבֶיהָ, כִּי לֹא בָאוּ לְעֶזְרַת יְיָ.

ח וְכֵן יֵשׁ לַדַּיָּן לַעֲשׂוֹת מְרִיבָה עִם הָרָאוּי לָרִיב עִמּוֹ, וּלְקַלְּלוֹ וּלְהַכּוֹתוֹ וְלִתְלֹשׁ שְׂעָרוֹ, וּלְהַשְׁבִּיעוֹ בֵּאלֹהִים בְּעַל כָּרְחוֹ שֶׁלֹּא יַעֲשֶׂה אוֹ שֶׁלֹּא עָשָׂה. שֶׁנֶּאֱמַר: וָאָרִיב עִמָּם וָאֲקַלְלֵם, וָאַכֶּה מֵהֶם אֲנָשִׁים וָאֶמְרְטֵם, וָאַשְׁבִּיעֵם בֵּאלֹהִים.

ט וְכֵן יֵשׁ לוֹ לִכְפּוֹת יָדַיִם וְרַגְלַיִם, וְלֶאֱסֹר בְּבֵית הָאֲסוּרִים, וְלִדְחֹף וְלִסְחֹב עַל הָאָרֶץ. שֶׁנֶּאֱמַר: הֵן לְמוֹת הֵן לִשְׁרשִׁי, הֵן לַעֲנָשׁ נִכְסִין וְלֶאֱסוּרִין.

י כָּל אֵלּוּ הַדְּבָרִים – לְפִי מַה שֶּׁיִּרְאֶה הַדַּיָּן שֶׁזֶּה רָאוּי לְכָךְ וְשֶׁהַשָּׁעָה צְרִיכָה. וּבְכֹל יִהְיוּ מַעֲשָׂיו לְשֵׁם שָׁמַיִם. וְאַל יִהְיֶה כְּבוֹד הַבְּרִיּוֹת קַל בְּעֵינָיו, שֶׁהֲרֵי הוּא דוֹחֶה אֶת לֹא תַעֲשֶׂה שֶׁל דִּבְרֵיהֶם. וְכָל שֶׁכֵּן כְּבוֹד בְּנֵי אַבְרָהָם יִצְחָק וְיַעֲקֹב, הַמַּחֲזִיקִין בְּתוֹרַת הָאֱמֶת, שֶׁיִּהְיֶה זָהִיר שֶׁלֹּא יֶהֱרֹס כְּבוֹדָם; אֶלָּא לְהוֹסִיף בִּכְבוֹד הַמָּקוֹם בִּלְבַד. שֶׁכָּל הַמְבַזֶּה אֶת הַתּוֹרָה – גּוּפוֹ מְחֻלָּל עַל הַבְּרִיּוֹת; וְהַמְכַבֵּד אֶת הַתּוֹרָה – גּוּפוֹ מְכֻבָּד עַל הַבְּרִיּוֹת. וְאֵין כְּבוֹד הַתּוֹרָה אֶלָּא לַעֲשׂוֹת עַל פִּי חֻקֶּיהָ וּמִשְׁפָּטֶיהָ.

38. These activities were performed by Nechemiah to influence the people to send away the gentile wives they had taken.
39. This is a somewhat unique ruling on the Rambam's part, for no where else in the Torah literature is the concept of imprisonment mentioned. Although the Rambam's ruling is based on the interpretation of the verse from Ezra in *Mo'ed Kattan* 16a, Rashi - in both his commentary on the Tanach and on the Talmud - interprets the phrase as referring to binding a person to the pillar against which he is lashed. See also *Hilchot Malveh ViLoveh* 2:1 which states that a person should not be imprisoned for financial matters and the Ramah (*Choshen Mishpat* 97:15) who allows such a practice.
40. The king of Persia granted Ezra permission to punish transgressors as he saw fit. The Rambam's ruling is based on the interpretation of the verse in *Mo'ed Kattan, loc. cit.*
41. Our translation is based on the gloss of the *Bayit Chadash* (*Choshen Mishpat* 2) who explains that at times, such measures are employed because of the severity of the individual's actions and at times, because of the climate in the society at large.
42. I.e., there should not be any sense of personal vendetta, heaven forbid.
43. For example, see *Hilchot Evel* 3:14 which states that in order to show honor to people at large, a priest is granted license to enter into an area which is ordinarily forbidden for him according to Rabbinic Law as a safeguard to the prohibitions involving ritual impurity. See also *Hilchot Kilayim* 10:29.
44. Avos 4:8. In his Commentary to the Mishnah, the Rambam interprets the phrase "honors the Torah" as meaning "honors its commandments by showing eagerness to fulfill them, honors its scholars who carry its [standard], and honors the texts composed about it."

CHAPTER TWENTY FIVE

1. It is forbidden for a judge to assert himself in a lordly and haughty manner over his community. Instead, he should conduct himself with humility and awe. Any leader who casts unnecessary fear upon the community without [intentions] for the sake of heaven will be punished.[1] And he will not see a son who is a Torah scholar, as [implied by a non-literal reading of Job 37:24]: "Therefore people fear him - he will never see anyone with a wise heart."[2]

2. Similarly, a judge may not treat them with capriciousness even though they are common people.[3] He should not step over the heads of the holy people.[4] Even though they are simple people and lowly, they are the descendants of Abraham, Isaac, and Jacob and the hosts of God whom He led out of Egypt with great power and a strong hand. He should patiently bear the difficulty of the community and their burden like Moses our teacher, as [Numbers 11:12] states concerning him: "As a nursemaid will carry an infant." And [Deuteronomy 1:16] states: "And I commanded your judges." This is a admonition to the judges to bear the community like a nursemaid carries an infant.

Take an example from Moses, the master of all prophets whom the Holy One, blessed be He, sent to Egypt, [about whom Exodus 6:12] states: "And I commanded them concerning the children of Israel." The Oral Tradition relates[5] that [God] told Moses and Aaron [to accept this mission] even though the people would curse them and stone them.

3. Just as a judge is commanded to fulfill this mitzvah; so, too, the community is commanded to show honor to a judge, as [Deuteronomy 1:18] states: "And I commanded you...."[6] This is a command to the community that they should treat a judge with awe. He should not act in a demeaning manner in their presence, nor should he conduct himself in a frivolous manner.

4. When a person is given a position of leadership over the community, he is forbidden to perform work in the presence of three people, lest he be demeaned in their eyes.[7] Now if performing work in public is forbidden to him, certainly, it is forbidden for him to eat and drink or to become intoxicated in the presence of people at large[8] and in the gatherings of the common people and in friendly get-togethers.[9] Woe to those judges who

1. By the hand of heaven. See *Hilchot Teshuvah* 3:13 which includes leaders who cast fear upon the community unnecessarily among those who will not receive a portion in the world-to-come.
2. Elihu was rebuking Job, telling him that perhaps he suffered his misfortune, because as the leader of the community, he imposed fear upon the people (Rashi's commentary to the verse).
3. See *Nedarim* 81a who mentions that Torah sages will be punished for referring to people at large in a derogatory manner.

פֶּרֶק חֲמִשָּׁה וְעֶשְׂרִים

א אָסוּר לְאָדָם לִנְהֹג בִּשְׂרָרָה עַל הַצִּבּוּר וּבְגַסּוּת הָרוּחַ, אֶלָּא בַּעֲנָוָה וְיִרְאָה. וְכָל פַּרְנָס הַמֵּטִיל אֵימָה יְתֵרָה עַל הַצִּבּוּר שֶׁלֹּא לְשֵׁם שָׁמַיִם - נֶעֱנָשׁ, וְאֵינוֹ רוֹאֶה לוֹ בֵּן תַּלְמִיד חָכָם. שֶׁנֶּאֱמַר: לָכֵן יְרֵאוּהוּ אֲנָשִׁים, לֹא יִרְאֶה כָּל חַכְמֵי לֵב.

ב וְכֵן אָסוּר לוֹ לִנְהֹג בָּהֶן קַלּוּת רֹאשׁ, אַף עַל פִּי שֶׁהֵן עַמֵּי הָאָרֶץ. וְלֹא יַפְסִיעַ עַל רָאשֵׁי עַם הַקֹּדֶשׁ. אַף עַל פִּי שֶׁהֵן הֶדְיוֹטוֹת וּשְׁפָלִים - בְּנֵי אַבְרָהָם יִצְחָק וְיַעֲקֹב הֵם, וְצִבְאוֹת הַשֵּׁם שֶׁהוֹצִיא מֵאֶרֶץ מִצְרַיִם בְּכֹחַ גָּדוֹל וּבְיָד חֲזָקָה. וְסוֹבֵל טֹרַח הַצִּבּוּר וּמַשָּׂאָן. כְּמֹשֶׁה רַבֵּנוּ, שֶׁנֶּאֱמַר בּוֹ: כַּאֲשֶׁר יִשָּׂא הָאֹמֵן אֶת הַיֹּנֵק. וַהֲרֵי הוּא אוֹמֵר: וָאֲצַוֶּה אֶת שֹׁפְטֵיכֶם. זוֹ אַזְהָרָה לַדַּיָּן, שֶׁיִּסְבֹּל אֶת הַצִּבּוּר כַּאֲשֶׁר יִשָּׂא הָאוֹמֵן אֶת הַיּוֹנֵק.
צֵא וּלְמַד מִמֹּשֶׁה, רַבָּן שֶׁל כָּל הַנְּבִיאִים. כֵּיוָן שֶׁשְּׁלָחוֹ הַקָּדוֹשׁ בָּרוּךְ הוּא בְּמִצְרַיִם, וְנֶאֱמַר: וַיְצַוֵּם אֶל בְּנֵי יִשְׂרָאֵל. אָמְרוּ מִפִּי הַקַּבָּלָה, שֶׁאָמַר לָהֶם לְמֹשֶׁה וּלְאַהֲרֹן: עַל מְנָת שֶׁיִּהְיוּ מְקַלְּלִים אֶתְכֶם וְסוֹקְלִין אֶתְכֶם בָּאֲבָנִים.

ג כְּדֶרֶךְ שֶׁנִּצְטַוָּה הַדַּיָּן לִנְהֹג בְּמִצְוָה זוֹ, כָּךְ נִצְטַוּוּ הַצִּבּוּר לִנְהֹג כָּבוֹד בַּדַּיָּן. שֶׁנֶּאֱמַר: וָאֲצַוֶּה אֶתְכֶם. זוֹ אַזְהָרָה לַצִּבּוּר שֶׁתִּהְיֶה אֵימַת הַדַּיָּן עֲלֵיהֶן. וְלֹא יִתְבַּזֶּה בִּפְנֵיהֶם, וְלֹא יִנְהַג קַלּוּת רֹאשׁ בְּעַצְמוֹ.

ד כֵּיוָן שֶׁנִּתְמַנָּה אָדָם פַּרְנָס עַל הַצִּבּוּר, אָסוּר בַּעֲשִׂיַּת מְלָאכָה בִּפְנֵי שְׁלֹשָׁה, כְּדֵי שֶׁלֹּא יִתְבַּזֶּה בִּפְנֵיהֶם.
אִם הַמְּלָאכָה בָּרַבִּים אֲסוּרָה עָלָיו, קַל וָחֹמֶר לֶאֱכֹל וְלִשְׁתּוֹת וּלְהִשְׁתַּכֵּר בִּפְנֵי רַבִּים וּבִכְנִיסַת עַמֵּי הָאָרֶץ וּבִסְעֻדַּת מֵרֵעוּת.

4. I.e., when entering a room, he should not enter where the people are seated, so that it appears that he is stepping over their heads. Note the *Sefer Me'irat Einayim* 8:19 which states that in the present age when it is customary to sit on benches or chairs and not on the ground, this prohibition applies only when the judge walks on a table in front of the community. Only then would it appear that he is "stepping over their heads." See also *Hilchot Talmud Torah* 6:7 which states that a Torah scholar should not enter the house of study last, so as not to inconvenience the people.
5. The *Sifri* to Numbers 11:12.
6. I.e., Moses relayed God's command to honor the judges to the people.
7. Rashi, *Kiddushin* 70a states that it is degrading for a community to have a leader who does not have anyone to perform ordinary tasks on his behalf.
8. See *Hilchot De'ot* 5:2; *Hilchot Talmud Torah* 4:5.
9. Our translation follows the interpretation of the *Bayit Chadash* who explains that it is forbidden for such a person to attend a feast of common people even if it is held in honor of a mitzvah, and it is forbidden for him to attend an ordinary friendly get-together even if Torah scholars will be in attendance.

conduct themselves in this manner, disgracing the Torah of Moses. They debase its judgments and lower them to the earth, casting them in the dust, bringing about harm to them and their descendants in this world and in the world to come.

5. It is forbidden to conduct oneself capriciously in relation to the agent sent by the court. For [the word of the court's] agent is accepted as that of two witnesses with regard to the question of ostracism.[10] Were he to say: "So-and-so disgraced me," "...disgraced the judge," or "...refused to appear in court," [that person] is ostracized on the basis of his statements. We do not, however, have a document recording the ban of ostracism composed until two witness come and testify that he refused to appear in the court.[11]

6. An agent of the court is not liable for relating unfavorable gossip for telling the court [about these matters[12]]. Whenever anyone causes aggravation to the agent of the court, the court has the license to have "stripes for rebellious conduct"[13] administered to him.

7. When the agent of the court [orders a person to appear in court,] saying: "So-and-so sent me," and mentioning the name of only one of the judges, a document declaring his ostracism cannot be composed against the litigant unless the agent [summons him] in the name of all three [judges].[14]

When does the above apply? When the agent went [and conveyed this message] on a day on which it was not known that the court was to hold session. On a day on which it is known to hold session, by contrast, everyone knows that all of the judges gather together. Even though the agent came [and conveyed the message] in the name of only one [judge], it is as if he came in the name of all three.[15]

8. When a person is summoned by the court and does not appear in court, a ban of ostracism is pronounced against him. This ban is recorded in a legal document; he is liable to pay the fee of the scribe [who composes the document].[16] When he comes to court, this document is torn.

If such a document was composed because a litigant did not accept a judgment, it may be torn up when he states that he is willing to accept it.[17] When a court summons a litigant to appear on a certain day and he does not appear at all that day, a document recording the ban of ostracism is composed that evening.[18]

10. I.e., the court pronounces a ban of ostracism on that basis.
11. *Bava Kama* 112b states that the testimony of witnesses is required, because the person against whom the ban is pronounced is required to pay the scribe's fee for the composition of the legal document (see Halachah 8). Since money is never expropriated from a person unless two witnesses testify to his obligation, witnesses must testify for that document to be composed.

אוֹי לָהֶם לְאוֹתָן הַדַּיָּנִים שֶׁנָּהֲגוּ בְּכָךְ מֵעֶלְבּוֹן תּוֹרַת מֹשֶׁה! שֶׁבָּזוּ דִּינֶיהָ, וְהִשְׁפִּילוּהָ עַד אָרֶץ, וְהִגִּיעוּהָ עַד עָפָר, וְגָרְמוּ רָעָה לָהֶן וְלִבְנֵי בְנֵיהֶם בָּעוֹלָם הַזֶּה וְלָעוֹלָם הַבָּא.

ה אָסוּר לִנְהֹג קַלּוּת רֹאשׁ בִּשְׁלִיחַ בֵּית דִּין.
וַהֲרֵי הַשָּׁלִיחַ נֶאֱמָן כִּשְׁנַיִם לְעִנְיַן הַנִּדּוּי. שֶׁאִם אָמַר: פְּלוֹנִי הִקְלַנִי, אוֹ הִקְלָה הַדַּיָּן, אוֹ לֹא רָצָה לָבוֹא לְדִין – מְשַׁמְּתִין אוֹתוֹ עַל פִּיו.
אֲבָל אֵין כּוֹתְבִין פִּתְחָא עָלָיו עַד שֶׁיָּבוֹאוּ שְׁנַיִם וְיָעִידוּ עָלָיו שֶׁנִּמְנַע לָבוֹא לְבֵית דִּין.

ו אֵין שְׁלִיחַ בֵּית דִּין חַיָּב בַּאֲמִירַת דְּבָרִים מִשּׁוּם לָשׁוֹן הָרָע.
וְכָל הַמְצַעֵר שְׁלִיחַ בֵּית דִּין – יֵשׁ לְבֵית דִּין רְשׁוּת לְהַכּוֹתוֹ מַכַּת מַרְדּוּת.

ז שָׁלִיחַ שֶׁאָמַר: פְּלוֹנִי שְׁלָחַנִי בְּשֵׁם אֶחָד מִן הַדַּיָּנִים, וְלֹא רָצָה בַּעַל דִּין לָבוֹא – אֵין כּוֹתְבִין עָלָיו פִּתְחָא שֶׁל שַׁמְתָּא, עַד שֶׁיֹּאמַר מִשֵּׁם שְׁלָשְׁתָּן.
בַּמֶּה דְּבָרִים אֲמוּרִים? שֶׁהָלַךְ הַשָּׁלִיחַ בְּיוֹם שֶׁאֵינוֹ יָדוּעַ לִישִׁיבַת הַדַּיָּנִים;
אֲבָל בְּיוֹם הַיָּדוּעַ שֶׁהַדַּיָּנִים יוֹשְׁבִים בּוֹ לְדִין – הַכֹּל יוֹדְעִים שֶׁכָּל הַדַּיָּנִים מְקֻבָּצִין, וְאַף עַל פִּי שֶׁבָּא הַשָּׁלִיחַ בְּשֵׁם אֶחָד – כְּאִלּוּ בָּא בְּשֵׁם שְׁלָשְׁתָּן.

ח מִי שֶׁשָּׁלְחוּ לוֹ בֵּית דִּין לָבוֹא, וְלֹא בָּא לְדִין – מְנַדִּין אוֹתוֹ, וְכוֹתְבִין עָלָיו פִּתְחָא, וְנוֹתֵן שְׂכַר הַסּוֹפֵר. וּבְעֵת שֶׁיָּבוֹא קוֹרְעִין הַפִּתְחָא.
כָּתְבוּ לוֹ פִּתְחָא מִפְּנֵי שֶׁלֹּא קִבֵּל הַדִּין, כֵּיוָן שֶׁאָמַר: הֲרֵינִי מְקַבֵּל הַדִּין – קוֹרְעִין נִדּוּיוֹ.
קָבְעוּ לוֹ בֵּית דִּין זְמַן שֶׁיָּבוֹא הַיּוֹם, וְלֹא בָּא כָּל אוֹתוֹ הַיּוֹם – כּוֹתְבִין עָלָיו פִּתְחָא לָעֶרֶב.

12. I.e., negative statements the litigant made against him or against the judges.
13. See Chapter 18, Halachah 5. See also *Hilchot Rotzeach* 5:6 where the Rambam states that the agent of the court himself is allowed to administer blows. See also the Ramah (*Choshen Mishpat* 8:5) which echoes these statements.
14. The Ramah (*Choshen Mishpat* 11:2) states that if one of the judges is of exceptional renown, as a token of respect, the summons should always be conveyed in his name.
15. The *Siftei Cohen* 11:3 states that if the agent comes in the name of a judge of lower stature, the litigant is not judged as if he disobeyed the commandment of the entire court.
16. I.e., when he seeks to have the ban of ostracism annulled, he must pay for the composition of the document.
17. We do not wait until he actually pays the settlement imposed upon him. As long as he makes a commitment to do so, we lift the ban of ostracism (see Rashi, *Bava Kama* 113a). In *Hilchot Talmud Torah* 6:14, the Rambam writes that the ban is not lifted until the litigant pays. In his gloss to that halachah, the *Kessef Mishneh* states that in *Hilchot Talmud Torah*, the Rambam was speaking in more general terms.
18. When quoting this law, the *Shulchan Aruch* (*Choshen Mishpat* 11:1) deviates from the Rambam's ruling and states that the ban of ostracism is composed the following day. The *Sefer Me'irat Einayim* 11:13 states that it is possible to explain that there is no contradiction between the two, because in the evening, the new day begins. The point of both rulings is that the ban of ostracism is not issued until the day of the summons passes.

When does the above apply? When he [lived] in the city[19] and stubbornly refused to come. If, however, he [lived] in the outlying villages and would go in and go out [from the city at times], we summon him to appear [in court] on Monday, Thursday, and [the following] Monday.[20] If the second Monday passes without him appearing, we do not compose a ban of ostracism until the following day.[21]

9. We do not summon [a person to court] during the month of Nissan, nor during the month of Tishrei,[22] because the people are occupied with [the preparations for] the festivals.[23] Nor is a summons issued for Friday, or for the day preceding a festival. We do, however, issue a summons in Nissan, for him to appear after Nissan, and a summons in Tishrei, for him to appear after Tishrei. We do not, however, issue a summons on Friday for a litigant to appear after the Sabbath. [The rationale is that] everyone is busy on Friday.[24]

10 When a person was located in a city and the agent of the court went [to summon him], but could not find him, a court date is not set until the agent finds him and conveys this information.[25]

[Different rules apply] if he lives in a village outside the city. If he is accustomed to coming on that day, the agent may tell one of his neighbors, even a woman:[26] "If so-and-so comes, inform him that the court summoned him to appear at this time." If he does not come [that day], he is placed under a ban of ostracism that evening.[27]

When does the above apply? When the way which he is wont to follow does not pass the place of the court. If, however, his path passes [the court], he is not placed under a ban of ostracism until the agent notifies him himself. For perhaps the neighbors will not notify him. For they will rationalize: "His path passes past the entrance to the court. Certainly, he visited them and was released."[28] Similarly, if he will not come into the city until the following day, we do not rely on the neighbors, for perhaps they will forget and fail to notify him.[29]

19. Where the court was located. In such a situation, it is obvious that his refusal stems from stubbornness.
20. I.e., he is given three separate summonses [*Shulchan Aruch* (*Choshen Mishpat* 11:1)]. These are the days when the courts would hold session in the Talmudic era. If the courts hold sessions on other days, the times for the ban of ostracism should be adjusted accordingly. If the court has a fixed day on which they hold sessions, they do not have the authority to summon him on any other day.
21. Since he does not live in the city, he is give this additional measure of consideration.
22. Even on the ordinary weekdays of these months.

Hilchot Sh'vitat Yom Tov 7:12 states that the court may adjudicate a case during *Chol HaMoed*. This does not, however, necessarily represent a contradiction. The intent could be that when both litigants agree, the hearing may be held on *Chol HaMoed* - and needless to say, on the days before or after the festival. If, however, a litigant must be summoned against his will, he should not be summoned in these months.

בַּמֶּה דְּבָרִים אֲמוּרִים? כְּשֶׁהָיָה בַּמְּדִינָה, וּמָרַד וְלֹא בָּא; אֲבָל אִם הָיָה בַּכְּפָרִים וְיוֹצֵא וְנִכְנָס – קוֹבְעִים לוֹ זְמַן שֵׁנִי וַחֲמִישִׁי וְשֵׁנִי. וְאִם שָׁלַם יוֹם שֵׁנִי וְלֹא בָּא – אֵין כּוֹתְבִין עָלָיו פִּתְחָא עַד לְמָחָר.

ט אֵין קוֹבְעִין זְמַן לֹא בִּימֵי נִיסָן וְלֹא בִּימֵי תִּשְׁרֵי, מִפְּנֵי שֶׁהָעָם טְרוּדִין בַּמּוֹעֲדוֹת. וְלֹא בְּעֶרֶב שַׁבָּת וְלֹא בְּעֶרֶב יוֹם טוֹב. אֲבָל קוֹבְעִין בְּנִיסָן שֶׁיָּבוֹא אַחַר נִיסָן, וּבְתִשְׁרֵי שֶׁיָּבוֹא אַחַר תִּשְׁרֵי. אֲבָל לֹא קוֹבְעִין בְּעֶרֶב שַׁבָּת שֶׁיָּבוֹא אַחַר שַׁבָּת, מִפְּנֵי שֶׁהַכֹּל טְרוּדִין בְּעֶרֶב שַׁבָּת.

י מִי שֶׁהוּא בַּמְּדִינָה, וְהָלַךְ שְׁלִיחַ בֵּית דִּין וְלֹא מְצָאוֹ – אֵין קוֹבְעִין לוֹ זְמַן עַד שֶׁיִּמְצָא אוֹתוֹ הַשָּׁלִיחַ וְיֹאמַר לוֹ.

הָיָה בִּכְפָר חוּץ לַמְּדִינָה, אִם דַּרְכּוֹ לָבוֹא בְּאוֹתוֹ הַיּוֹם – אוֹמֵר הַשָּׁלִיחַ אֲפִלּוּ לְאֶחָד מִן הַשְּׁכֵנִים, אֲפִלּוּ לְאִשָּׁה: אִם יָבוֹא פְּלוֹנִי, הוֹדִיעוּהוּ שֶׁבֵּית דִּין קָבְעוּ לוֹ זְמַן שֶׁיָּבוֹא לְבֵית דִּין. וְאִם לֹא בָּא – מְנַדִּין אוֹתוֹ לָעֶרֶב.

בַּמֶּה דְּבָרִים אֲמוּרִים? כְּשֶׁאֵין הַדֶּרֶךְ שֶׁדַּרְכּוֹ לֵילֵךְ בָּהּ עַל מְקוֹם בֵּית דִּין; אֲבָל אִם דַּרְכּוֹ עֲלֵיהֶן – אֵין מְנַדִּין אוֹתוֹ עַד שֶׁיּוֹדִיעוֹ הַשָּׁלִיחַ בְּעַצְמוֹ; שֶׁמָּא לֹא אָמְרוּ לוֹ הַשְּׁכֵנִים, שֶׁהֲרֵי הֵם אוֹמְרִין: דַּרְכּוֹ עַל פֶּתַח בֵּית דִּין, וּכְבָר הָלַךְ אֲלֵיהֶם וְנִפְטַר.

וְכֵן אִם לֹא בָּא בַּמְּדִינָה עַד לְמָחָר – אֵין סוֹמְכִין עַל הַשְּׁכֵנִים, שֶׁמָּא שָׁכְחוּ וְלֹא אָמְרוּ לוֹ.

23. Rashi, *Bava Kama* 113a, gives a different reason: During these months, the people are occupied with the harvest.

The *Sefer Me'irat Einayim* 5:5 states that no restrictions are placed on the month of Sivan. Since the holiday of Shavuos is only one (or in the diaspora, two) day(s) and there are no unique mitzvot associated with its observance, extensive preparation is not necessary.

Similarly, after the festivals, the hustle and bustle of the holiday season still leaves its impression and it is not appropriate to summon a person to court (Rabbi Akiva Eiger).

24. Because he could excuse himself, saying: "Because of my preoccupation with the preparations for the Sabbath, I forgot about the summons" (*Bava Kama* 113a).

25. In this instance, the agent does not convey the message to the neighbors, relying on them to communicate it to the litigant. The rationale is that since the litigant is in the city, the neighbors will not feel responsible to communicate the message to him. They will feel that sooner or later, the court agent will meet the person and convey the message to him (*Sefer Me'irat Einayim* 11:12).

26. Although a woman is not accepted as a witness, we rely on her to communicate this message.

27. We assume that he received the message and willfully did not heed it. Hence, he is ostracized in punishment for refusing to obey the court's summons.

28. Since it is possible that the message was not delivered, the person cannot be held responsible for failing to appear in court.

29. In this instance, as well, since it is possible that he did not receive the message, the person cannot be held responsible for failing to appear in court.

11. [The following laws apply when] a person comes to the court and accepts the judgment [issued against him],[30] he is told to make financial restitution, but does not do so.[31] He is not placed under a ban of ostracism until he is given a warning on Monday, Thursday, and the following Monday. [If he does not pay by that time,] he is placed under a ban of ostracism until he pays what he is liable. If he waits 30 days and does not seek to have the ban of ostracism lifted, he is excommunicated.[32]

CHAPTER TWENTY SIX

1. Anyone who curses one of the judges of Israel transgresses a negative commandment,[1] as [Exodus 22:27] states: "Do not curse a judge."[2] Similarly, if a person curses a *nasi*, whether the head of the Supreme *Sanhedrin* or a king,[3] he transgresses a negative commandment,[4] as [the verse] continues: "Do not curse a prince among your nation."

[This prohibition] does not apply only to a judge or a *nasi*. Instead, anyone who curses any other Jew[5] receives lashes,[6] as [Leviticus 19:14] states: "Do not curse a deaf-mute."[7] Why does the verse mention a deaf-mute? To teach you that even when a person cannot hear and thus will not be bothered by being cursed,[8] [the person pronouncing] the curse is lashed. It appears to me[9] that a person who curses a child who is embarrassed receives lashes;[10] [the child] resembles a deaf-mute.

2. A person who curses a deceased person is not liable.[11]

Since a person who curses any Jewish person is liable, why did [the Torah] set aside a special prohibition for a judge and for a *nasi*? For the person to be liable for two transgressions. Thus we learn that a person who curses any

30. If, however, he refuses to accept the court's judgment, he is placed under a ban of ostracism immediately [*Kessef Mishneh*; Ramah (*Choshen Mishpat* 19:3)].
31. I.e., he does not brazenly refuse to uphold the court's ruling, but procrastinates and does not pay.
32. I.e., placed under a more severe ban.

1. *Sefer HaMitzvot* (negative commandment 315) and *Sefer HaChinuch* (mitzvah 69) count this as one of the 613 mitzvot of the Torah.
2. The verse uses the word *Elohim* which can also be interpreted as a reference to the Almighty. Nevertheless, *Sanhedrin* 66a states that in this instance, the reference is to a mortal judge.

In *Sefer HaMitzvot* (negative commandment 60), the Rambam notes that this verse is also used as one of the sources for the prohibition against cursing God. Nevertheless, the verse is not considered as a prohibition of a general nature, because a specific punishment is mentioned for the latter transgression. See also the gloss of Rabbi Akiva Eiger which cites a similar issue.

The *Tumim* (*Choshen Mishpat* 2) states that the term *Elohim* refers to a judge possessing the unique *semichah* passed down from master to disciple originating with Moses. Hence this law does not apply in the present age when our judges no longer possess such a *semichah*.

יא מִי שֶׁבָּא לְבֵית דִּין וְקִבֵּל הַדִּין, וְאָמְרוּ לוֹ לְשַׁלֵּם, וְהָלַךְ וְלֹא שִׁלֵּם – אֵין מְנַדִּין אוֹתוֹ עַד שֶׁיַּתְרוּ בּוֹ שֵׁנִי וַחֲמִישִׁי וְשֵׁנִי, וְאַחַר כָּךְ מְנַדִּין אוֹתוֹ עַד שֶׁיִּתֵּן מַה שֶּׁהוּא חַיָּב.
וְאִם עָמַד שְׁלֹשִׁים יוֹם וְלֹא תָּבַע לְהַתִּיר נִדּוּיוֹ – מַחֲרִימִין אוֹתוֹ.

פֶּרֶק שִׁשָּׁה וְעֶשְׂרִים

א כָּל הַמְקַלֵּל דַּיָּן מִדַּיָּנֵי יִשְׂרָאֵל – עוֹבֵר בְּלֹא תַעֲשֶׂה, שֶׁנֶּאֱמַר: אֱלֹהִים לֹא תְקַלֵּל.
וְכֵן אִם קִלֵּל הַנָּשִׂיא, אֶחָד רֹאשׁ סַנְהֶדְרֵי גְדוֹלָה אוֹ הַמֶּלֶךְ – הֲרֵי זֶה עוֹבֵר בְּלֹא תַעֲשֶׂה, שֶׁנֶּאֱמַר: וְנָשִׂיא בְעַמְּךָ לֹא תָאֹר.
וְלֹא דַּיָּן וְנָשִׂיא בִּלְבַד, אֶלָּא כָּל הַמְקַלֵּל אֶחָד מִיִּשְׂרָאֵל – לוֹקֶה, שֶׁנֶּאֱמַר: לֹא תְקַלֵּל חֵרֵשׁ.
וְלָמָּה נֶאֱמַר חֵרֵשׁ? שֶׁאֲפִלּוּ זֶה שֶׁהוּא אֵינוֹ שׁוֹמֵעַ וְלֹא נִצְטַעֵר בִּקְלָלָה זוֹ – לוֹקֶה עַל קִלְלָתוֹ. וְיֵרָאֶה לִי, שֶׁהַמְקַלֵּל אֶת הַקָּטָן הַנִּכְלָם – לוֹקֶה. (הֲרֵי הוּא כְּחֵרֵשׁ.)

ב הַמְקַלֵּל אֶת הַמֵּת – פָּטוּר.
הוֹאִיל וּמְקַלֵּל כָּל אָדָם מִיִּשְׂרָאֵל – חַיָּב, לָמָּה יִחֵד לָאו עַל דַּיָּן וְלָאו עַל נָשִׂיא? לְחַיְּבוֹ שְׁתַּיִם.

3. The term *nasi* can have both these connotations. *Sefer HaMitzvot* (negative commandment 316) states that it refers to a person "in whom authority is vested and who is on the highest level, whether with regard to civic authority or Torah authority."
4. *Sefer HaMitzvot* (*Ibid.*) and *Sefer HaChinuch* (mitzvah 71) count this as one of the 613 mitzvot of the Torah.
5. Or even oneself (Halachah 3). One is, however, not liable for cursing a gentile (*Sofrim* 4:9). The Radbaz and the *Hagahot Maimoniot* also cite *Bava Kama* 94b which states that one is liable only for cursing an observant Jew.
6. The punishment given for the violation of a negative commandment (see Chapter 18, Halachah 2). *Sefer HaMitzvot* (negative commandment 317) and *Sefer HaChinuch* (mitzvah 231) count the prohibition against cursing a fellow Jew as one of the 613 mitzvot of the Torah.
7. These transgressions are cumulative as stated in the following halachah.
8. *Sefer HaMitzvot* (*Ibid.*) states that we take into consideration, "not only the situation of the person being cursed, but also that of the one pronouncing the curse. He was warned not to arouse his soul towards revenge or to habituate it towards anger."
9. This expression introduces a law derived by the Rambam through his process of deduction for which he has no explicit prior source in the Rabbinic literature.
10. The *Kessef Mishneh* cites *Bava Kama* 86b which states that one is liable for shaming a minor. Accordingly, one is also liable for cursing him. The *Kessef Mishneh* also notes that the *Tur* (*Choshen Mishpat* 27) quotes the *Mishneh Torah* as stating that a person who curses a person who is sleeping is liable. This, the *Kessef Mishneh* maintains, is the proper version of this halachah.
11. The *Sifra* derives this concept from the exegesis of Leviticus, *loc. cit.*. Although one is not liable for cursing a deceased person, it is forbidden to do so [Ramah (*Choshen Mishpat* 27:2)].

Jew, whether a man, woman, or child receives one set of lashes. If he curses a judge, he receives two sets of lashes. If he curses a *nasi*, he receives three sets of lashes. And if the son[12] of a *nasi* curses his father, he is liable for four transgression, the three for which all others are liable and one for [cursing] his father.[13]

3. A person who curses himself receives lashes just as one who curses others, as [Deuteronomy 4:9] states: "Take heed and guard your soul."[14]

Whether a person curses himself, a colleague, a *nasi*, or a judge, he does not receive lashes unless he curses using one of God's names: *Yaw, Elohim, Shaddai*, or the like,[15] or with one of the descriptive terms used to characterize [God], e.g., the Merciful One, the Vengeful One, or the like.[16] Since a person is liable if he cursed [a colleague] with any of these descriptive terms, he is also liable if he cursed him in any other language. For the names with which the gentiles refer to the Holy One, blessed be He, are comparable to all of these descriptive terms.[17]

The term *arur* ("cursed") can imply an oath, a curse, and a ban of ostracism.[18]

4. A person is not punished by lashing unless he is given a warning in the presence of two witnesses as applies with regard to the transgression of any other negative commandment.[19] If, however, a warning was not issued, a curse was uttered without mentioning God's name or a descriptive term, e.g., he said [merely]: "Cursed be so-and-so," the curse was uttered indirectly, e.g., he said: "May so-and-so not be blessed unto God," or "May God not bless so-and-so," or the like, he is not lashed.[20]

5. Even though he is not lashed,[21] a person who curses a Torah scholar is placed under a ban of ostracism. And[22] if the judges desire to have "stripes for rebellious conduct" administered to him, they can have him beaten and punished as they see fit, for he disgraced a learned elder.[23]

If he denounces a common person, the judges may punish him as they see necessary according to the needs of the situation, depending on the person who gave the verbal abuse and the one who receives it.[24]

12. Our translation follows the authoritative manuscripts of the *Mishneh Torah*. There is a printing error in the standard published text.
13. See *Hilchot Mamrim* 5:1-4 for a description of this prohibition.
14. The term "Take heed" is understood as implying a negative commandment (*Sh'vuot* 36b).
15. See *Hilchot Yesodei HaTorah* 6:2 which lists the seven names of God.

The Ra'avad differs with the Rambam and maintains that one is liable for punishment only when one issues a curse using God's ineffable name, Y-H-V-H. Although his statements appear to be based on the Jerusalem Talmud (*Sh'vuot* 4:10), it is possible to explain that those statements refer to a son's cursing of his parents. He is liable for execution, only when he uses God's ineffable name (Radbaz).
16. Although lashes are not given, it is forbidden to curse a colleague even without using

נִמְצֵאתָ לָמֵד: שֶׁהַמְקַלֵּל אֶחָד מִיִּשְׂרָאֵל, בֵּין אִישׁ בֵּין אִשָּׁה, בֵּין גָּדוֹל בֵּין קָטָן – לוֹקֶה אַחַת; וְאִם קִלֵּל דַּיָּן – לוֹקֶה שְׁתַּיִם; וְאִם קִלֵּל נָשִׂיא – לוֹקֶה שָׁלֹשׁ. וּבֶן נָשִׂיא שֶׁקִּלֵּל אָבִיו – חַיָּב מִשּׁוּם אַרְבָּעָה שֵׁמוֹת: שְׁלֹשָׁה שֶׁל כָּל אָדָם, וְאֶחָד מִשּׁוּם הָאָב.

ג הַמְקַלֵּל עַצְמוֹ – לוֹקֶה, כְּמוֹ שֶׁקִּלֵּל אֲחֵרִים. שֶׁנֶּאֱמַר: הִשָּׁמֶר לְךָ וּשְׁמֹר נַפְשְׁךָ.
וְאֶחָד הַמְקַלֵּל עַצְמוֹ אוֹ חֲבֵרוֹ אוֹ נָשִׂיא אוֹ דַּיָּן – אֵינוֹ לוֹקֶה עַד שֶׁיְּקַלֵּל בְּשֵׁם מִן הַשֵּׁמוֹת, כְּגוֹן יָהּ וֵאלֹהִים וְשַׁדַּי וְכַיּוֹצֵא בָּהֶן, אוֹ בְּכִנּוּי מִן הַכִּנּוּיִים, כְּגוֹן חַנּוּן וְקַנָּא וְכַיּוֹצֵא בָּהֶן. הוֹאִיל וְהוּא חַיָּב אִם קִלֵּל בְּכָל הַכִּנּוּיִים, כָּךְ אִם קִלֵּל בְּכָל לָשׁוֹן – חַיָּב; שֶׁהַשֵּׁמוֹת שֶׁקּוֹרְאִין בָּהֶן הַגּוֹיִם לְהַקָּדוֹשׁ בָּרוּךְ הוּא – הֲרֵי הֵן כְּכָל הַכִּנּוּיִים. וְאָרוּר – בּוֹ שְׁבוּעָה, בּוֹ קְלָלָה, בּוֹ נִדּוּי.

ד אֵינוֹ לוֹקֶה עַד שֶׁיַּתְרוּ בוֹ בִּפְנֵי עֵדִים, כִּשְׁאָר כָּל חַיָּבֵי לָאוִין. אֲבָל אִם לֹא הָיְתָה שָׁם הַתְרָאָה; אוֹ שֶׁקִּלֵּל בְּלֹא שֵׁם וּבְלֹא כִנּוּי, כְּגוֹן שֶׁאָמַר: אָרוּר פְּלוֹנִי; אוֹ שֶׁהָיְתָה הַקְּלָלָה בָּאָה מִכְּלַל הַדְּבָרִים, כְּגוֹן שֶׁאָמַר: אַל יְהִי פְלוֹנִי בָּרוּךְ לַיְיָ, אוֹ אַל יְבָרְכֵהוּ אֵל, וְכַיּוֹצֵא בִּדְבָרִים אֵלּוּ – אֵינוֹ לוֹקֶה.

ה אַף עַל פִּי שֶׁאֵינוֹ לוֹקֶה, אִם חֵרֵף תַּלְמִיד חָכָם – מְנַדִּין אוֹתוֹ. וְאִם רָצוּ הַדַּיָּנִים לְהַכּוֹתוֹ מַכַּת מַרְדּוּת – מַכִּין. וְעוֹנְשִׁין אוֹתוֹ כְּפִי מַה שֶּׁיִּרְאוּ, שֶׁהֲרֵי בָּזָה אֶת הַזָּקֵן.
וְאִם חֵרֵף עַם הָאָרֶץ – עוֹנְשִׁין הַדַּיָּנִים בַּדָּבָר כְּפִי מַה שֶּׁהַשָּׁעָה צְרִיכָה לוֹ לְפִי הַמְחָרֵף וּלְפִי זֶה שֶׁנִּתְחָרֵף.

God's name [*Shulchan Aruch* (*Choshen Mishpat* 27:2)]. If the court desires, they may decree a suitable punishment (Halachah 5).

17. Thus if one utters a curse in English, using the name God, one is liable.

18. I.e., depending on the circumstance it is used.

19. See Chapter 15, Halachah 4. The *Kessef Mishneh* explains that since cursing is unique in that it is one of the few prohibitions for which one is liable for lashes although one does not perform a deed, one might think that a warning is also not required. Alternatively, since a person issues a curse in anger, one might think that a warning is not necessary, because it would go unheeded regardless.

20. Issuing such a curse is, however, forbidden [*Shulchan Aruch* (*loc. cit.*)]. 21. I.e., he issues the curse in one of the ways that is not punishable by lashes.

22. I.e., in addition to the ban of ostracism; alternatively, if he would look at the ban of ostracism lightly, but would suffer from the beating, we give him the beating (*Sefer Me'irat Einayim* 27:9).

23. See *Hilchot Talmud Torah* 6:11-12 which states that a person who disgraces a sage is fined a *litra* of gold. Moreover, he will receive punishment in the afterlife, and will be denied a portion in the world-to-come. See also *Hilchot Chovel UMazik* 3:5.

24. *Hilchot Chovel UMazik, Ibid.* 25. This refers to a *nasi* who is the head of the

6. Although a judge or a *nasi*[25] has the right to overlook [affronts to] his honor, he cannot overlook being cursed.[26] Similarly, with regard to other people, even though the person who was cursed is prepared to overlook the matter, the person who uttered the curse is lashed, for he committed a transgression and incurred liability.

If, however, a person is obligated to be placed under a ban of ostracism, because he conducted himself in an unbridled manner in court, and the judges desire to overlook[27] [the affront to] their honor and not impose a ban of ostracism, they have that license,[28] provided it will not lead to a decline in the honor of the Creator. For example, people at large were repudiating the words of the Torah and the judges.[29] Since the people overstepped the bounds, the court must act firmly and punish as they see necessary.

7. When any person has a judgment adjudicated by gentile judges and their courts, he is considered a wicked person. It is as if he disgraced, blasphemed, and lifted up his hand against the Torah of Moses our teacher.[30] [This applies] even if their laws are the same as the laws of the Jewish people.[31] [This is indicated by Exodus 21:1]: "These are the judgments that you shall place before them." "Before them" and not before gentiles; "before them" and not before ordinary people.

[The following procedure should be carried out] if the gentiles have a powerful law enforcement system and the opposing litigant is a stubborn and powerful person from whom one cannot expropriate property through the judicial system of the Jewish people. One should summon him before the Jewish judges first. If he did not desire to come, one may receive license from the court and salvage [one's property] from the litigant by having the case tried in a gentile court.

Blessed be God who provides assistance.

Talmudic academy (see *Hilchot Talmud Torah* 6:6). A king, by contrast, may not waive the respect due him and must zealously protect his honor. See *Hilchot Melachim* 2:5-6.

26. For it is not the person's individual honor alone that is involved. What is of concern is the violation of the Torah's commandments. And that, no mortal has the right to forgo (*Kessef Mishneh*). The *Or Sameach* brings support for this concept, noting that a person who curses himself is punished by lashes (Halachah 3). Now this person would surely forgo the affront to his honor rather than receive the lashes. Nevertheless, he is lashed, because he violated the Torah's prohibitions. Similarly, when the curse is directed to another person, that person does not have the power to absolve him from punishment.

27. The *Kessef Mishneh* states that the Rambam's wording implies that when a person is obligated to be placed under a ban of ostracism for offending a sage, if that sage does not forgive him, he must be placed under that ban even if he repents and expresses regret for his actions publicly.

ו אַף עַל פִּי שֶׁיֵּשׁ לוֹ לַדַּיָּן אוֹ לַנָּשִׂיא לִמְחֹל עַל כְּבוֹדוֹ - אֵינוֹ יָכוֹל לִמְחֹל עַל קִלְלָתוֹ. וְכֵן שְׁאָר הָעָם, אַף עַל פִּי שֶׁמָּחַל הַמְקֻלָּל - מַלְקִין אֶת הַמְקַלֵּל; שֶׁכְּבָר חָטָא וְנִתְחַיֵּב. אֲבָל מִי שֶׁנִּתְחַיֵּב נִדּוּי מִפְּנֵי שֶׁהִפְקִיר בְּבֵית דִּין, וְרָצוּ בֵּית דִּין לִמְחֹל עַל כְּבוֹדָן וְלֹא נִדּוּהוּ - הָרְשׁוּת בְּיָדָן.

וְהוּא שֶׁלֹּא יִהְיֶה בַּדָּבָר הֶפְסֵד בִּכְבוֹד הַבּוֹרֵא. כְּגוֹן שֶׁהָיוּ הָעָם מְבַעֲטִין בְּדִבְרֵי תּוֹרָה וּבַדַּיָּנִים, הוֹאִיל וּפָקְרוּ הָעָם בַּדָּבָר - צְרִיכִין לְחַזֵּק וְלַעֲנֹשׁ כְּפִי מַה שֶּׁיֵּרָאֶה לָהֶם.

ז כָּל הַדָּן בְּדַיָּנֵי עוֹבְדֵי כּוֹכָבִים וּבְעַרְכָּאוֹת שֶׁלָּהֶן, אַף עַל פִּי שֶׁהָיוּ דִּינֵיהֶם כְּדִינֵי יִשְׂרָאֵל - הֲרֵי זֶה רָשָׁע, וּכְאִלּוּ חֵרֵף וְגִדֵּף וְהֵרִים יָד בְּתוֹרַת מֹשֶׁה רַבֵּנוּ. שֶׁנֶּאֱמַר: וְאֵלֶּה הַמִּשְׁפָּטִים אֲשֶׁר תָּשִׂים לִפְנֵיהֶם. לִפְנֵיהֶם - וְלֹא לִפְנֵי עוֹבְדֵי כּוֹכָבִים; לִפְנֵיהֶם - וְלֹא לִפְנֵי הֶדְיוֹטוֹת. הָיְתָה יַד הָעוֹבְדֵי כּוֹכָבִים תַּקִּיפָה, וּבַעַל דִּינוֹ אַלָּם, וְאֵינוֹ יָכוֹל לְהוֹצִיא מִמֶּנּוּ בְּדַיָּנֵי יִשְׂרָאֵל - יִתְבָּעֶנּוּ לְדַיָּנֵי יִשְׂרָאֵל תְּחִלָּה. אִם לֹא רָצָה לָבוֹא - נוֹטֵל רְשׁוּת מִבֵּית דִּין, וּמַצִּיל בְּדַיָּנֵי עוֹבְדֵי כּוֹכָבִים מִיַּד בַּעַל דִּינוֹ.

בְּרִיךְ רַחֲמָנָא דְּסַיְּיעָן

28. *Kiddushin* 32b relates that Rabbi Yehoshua ben Korcha summoned a person to him three times and that person did not come. He then sent him a message: "Were it not that I had never placed a person under a ban of ostracism, I certainly would have placed you under such a ban."

See *Hilchot Talmud Torah* 7:13 : "Although a sage has license to place a person under a ban of ostracism, because of [an affront to] his honor, it is not praiseworthy for a Torah scholar to act in this manner.... This was the practice of the pious men of the previous generations. They would hear their shame, but they would not reply. Moreover, they would pardon and forgive the person who insulted them."

29. As *Hilchot Talmud Torah, Ibid.* continues: "When does the above apply? When [the person] disgraced or embarrassed [the sage] in private. If he disgraced or embarrassed the sage in public, it is forbidden for the sage to waive [the affront to] his honor... because the disrespect of the Torah is involved."

30. For abandoning the Torah's court system is a repudiation of God who structured it.

The *Shulchan Aruch* (*Choshen Mishpat* 26:1) states that this applies even if both litigants are willing to have the case tried in the gentile court. The Ramah states that if a plaintiff brought a case against a fellow Jew to a gentile court, the Jewish court should place him under a ban of ostracism until he withdraws the claim from the gentile court.

31. Thus even in the present day when there are just gentile courts, complaints should be brought to a Rabbinic judge and not to them.

HILCHOT EDUT

THE LAWS OF WITNESSES

[These laws] contain 8 mitzvot: Three positive commandments and five negative commandments. They are:
1. For a person who knows testimony to testify in court,
2. To question and interrogate the witnesses,
3. For a witness who testified in a case involving capital punishment not to serve as a judge,
4. Not to carry out a judgment based on the testimony of one witness,
5. Not to accept a person who is a transgressor as a witness,
6. Not to accept a relative as a witness,
7. Not to testify falsely,
8. To punish an *ed zomaim*[1] in the manner he wished to have [the defendant] punished.
These mitzvot are explained in the coming chapters.

1. See the definition of this term in Chapter 18.

הִלְכוֹת עֵדוּת

יֵשׁ בִּכְלָלָן שְׁמוֹנֶה מִצְוֹת: שָׁלֹשׁ מִצְוֹת עֲשֵׂה, וְחָמֵשׁ מִצְוֹת לֹא תַעֲשֶׂה, וְזֶה הוּא פְּרָטָן:

א) לְהָעִיד לְבֵית דִּין לְמִי שֶׁיֵּשׁ לוֹ עֵדוּת.
ב) לִדְרֹשׁ וְלַחְקֹר הָעֵדִים.
ג) שֶׁלֹּא יוֹרֶה הָעֵד בְּדִין זֶה שֶׁהֵעִיד עָלָיו בְּדִינֵי נְפָשׁוֹת.
ד) שֶׁלֹּא יָקוּם דָּבָר בְּעֵד אֶחָד.
ה) שֶׁלֹּא יָעִיד בַּעַל עֲבֵרָה.
ו) שֶׁלֹּא יָעִיד קָרוֹב.
ז) שֶׁלֹּא לְהָעִיד בְּשֶׁקֶר.
ח) לַעֲשׂוֹת לְעֵד זוֹמֵם כַּאֲשֶׁר זָמַם.

וּבֵאוּר מִצְוֹת אֵלּוּ בִּפְרָקִים אֵלּוּ:

CHAPTER ONE

1. A witness is commanded to testify in court[1] with regard to all pertinent testimony that he knows.[2] [This applies both to] testimony that will cause his colleague[3] to be held liable or testimony that will vindicate him.[4] With regard to financial cases,[5] this applies [only] when he is summoned to testify.[6] [The source for this commandment is Leviticus 5:1]: "And should he witness, see, or know [of the matter], if he does not testify, he will bear his sin."[7]

2. If the witness was a wise man of great stature and [the judges of] the court did not possess the same degree of wisdom, he may refrain from testifying. [8] [The rationale is that] it is not becoming to his dignity for him to go [to testify] before them. Hence, the positive commandment of honoring the Torah[9] takes precedence.

When does the above apply? With regard to testimony concerning financial matters. With regard to testimony that safeguards a person from a prohibition,[10] by contrast,[11] or testimony in cases involving capital punishment or lashes,[12] he must go and testify. [This is derived from Proverbs 21:30]: "There is no wisdom or understanding... before God." [Implied is that] whenever the desecration of God's name is involved,[13] honor is not granted to a master.

3. A High Priest is not obligated to testify.[14] [An exception is made] only with regard to matters involving a king.[15] In such an instance, [the High Priest] should go to the Supreme *Sanhedrin* and testify. With regard to other testimony, he is not obligated.

1. I.e., it is statements made in court that are significant. Statements made outside the court, by contrast, are of no consequence (*Kessef Mishneh*).
2. *Sefer HaMitzvot* (positive commandment 178) and *Sefer HaChinuch* (mitzvah 122) count this as one of the 613 mitzvot of the Torah.
3. I.e., one's fellow Jew. If, however, one knows of testimony that will benefit a gentile, one is not obligated to testify in court (*Sefer Me'irat Einayim* 28:2). See *Shulchan Aruch* (*Choshen Mishpat* 28:3) which discusses the concept of testifying on behalf of a gentile at length.
4. If a person does not testify and as a result, his colleague loses money, the recalcitrant witness has a moral and spiritual obligation (*chayav bidinei shamayim*) to reimburse his colleague for his loss [*Bava Kama* 55b; *Shulchan Aruch* (*Choshen Mishpat* 28:1)].
5. With regard to testimony involving the Torah's prohibitions and cases involving capital punishment or lashes, by contrast, a witness is obligated to testify even when he is not summoned (*Kessef Mishneh*).
6. If, however, the litigant does not summon him, he is not required to volunteer the information on his own initiative. *Sh'vuot* 35a derives this concept from the exegesis of the verse from Leviticus which the Rambam cites.
7. From the Rambam's wording, it can be implied that even when there is only one witness, he is obligated to testify in court (*Kessef Mishneh*). Although his testimony does not have the power to cause money to be expropriated from the litigant, it may require

פֶּרֶק רִאשׁוֹן

א הָעֵד מְצֻוֶּה לְהָעִיד בְּבֵית דִּין בְּכָל עֵדוּת שֶׁיּוֹדֵעַ. בֵּין בְּעֵדוּת שֶׁיְּחַיֵּב בָּהּ אֶת חֲבֵרוֹ, בֵּין בְּעֵדוּת שֶׁיְּזַכֵּהוּ בּוֹ. וְהוּא שֶׁיִּתְבָּעֶנּוּ לְהָעִיד בְּדִינֵי מָמוֹנוֹת. שֶׁנֶּאֱמַר: וְהוּא עֵד אוֹ רָאָה אוֹ יָדָע אִם לֹא יַגִּיד וְנָשָׂא עֲוֹנוֹ.

ב הָיָה הָעֵד חָכָם גָּדוֹל, וְהָיָה בְּבֵית דִּין פָּחוּת מִמֶּנּוּ בְּחָכְמָה, הוֹאִיל וְאֵין כְּבוֹדוֹ שֶׁיֵּלֵךְ לִפְנֵיהֶם – עֲשֵׂה שֶׁל כְּבוֹד תּוֹרָה עָדִיף, וְיֵשׁ לוֹ לְהִמָּנַע.
בַּמֶּה דְּבָרִים אֲמוּרִים? בְּעֵדוּת מָמוֹן; אֲבָל בְּעֵדוּת שֶׁמַּפְרִישׁ בָּהּ מִן הָאִסּוּר, וְכֵן בְּעֵדוּת נְפָשׁוֹת אוֹ מַכּוֹת – הוֹלֵךְ וּמֵעִיד. שֶׁנֶּאֱמַר: אֵין חָכְמָה וְאֵין תְּבוּנָה לְנֶגֶד יְיָ. כָּל מָקוֹם שֶׁיֵּשׁ חִלּוּל הַשֵּׁם – אֵין חוֹלְקִין כָּבוֹד לָרַב.

ג כֹּהֵן גָּדוֹל – אֵינוֹ חַיָּב לְהָעִיד. אֶלָּא עֵדוּת שֶׁהִיא לְמֶלֶךְ יִשְׂרָאֵל בִּלְבַד – הוֹלֵךְ לְבֵית דִּין הַגָּדוֹל וּמֵעִיד בָּהּ. אֲבָל בִּשְׁאָר הָעֵדֻיּוֹת – פָּטוּר.

him to take an oath or intimidate him into admitting his obligation. See also Chapter 21, Halachah 10.

8. The Ramah (*Choshen Mishpat* 28:5) states that the court should send three representatives to him and he should testify in their presence. In that manner, the testimony is delivered in the presence of a court and the scholar's honor is preserved.

9. See *Hilchot Talmud Torah* 6:1 which describes the mitzvah to honor the Sages.

10. E.g., a woman who seeks permission from the court to remarry and the witness knows whether or not her husband is alive (Rashi, *Sh'vuot* 30b). The scholar is obligated to testify if the court wishes to grant leniency and he knows that there is a prohibition involved. If, however, the court seeks to rule stringently and he knows that there is no need for a prohibition, he is not required to testify (*Kessef Mishneh*). The *Sefer Me'irat Einayim* 28:28 explains that there are even times when the court seeks to be stringent that the person should testify, because the stringency may lead to leniency indirectly.

11. When there is only one witness, he is obligated to testify only when his testimony will prevent a person from transgressing (or continuing to transgress). If, however, the transgression has been performed and his testimony will be of no consequence, he should not testify. Indeed, doing so resembles malicious gossip (*Hagahot Maimoniot* to Chapter 5, Halachah 1).

12. He must testify regardless of whether his testimony will lead to conviction or acquittal (*Kessef Mishneh*).

13. And every transgression involves the desecration of God's name.

14. For being forced to testify would represent a deprecation of his honor (see *Sanhedrin* 18b).

15. I.e., the kings of the House of David. The kings of the Kingdom of Israel and the like, by contrast, should not be brought to court (*Hilchot Sanhedrin* 2:5). Alternatively, it could refer also to the King of Israel and be referring to a case involving the king's son (Radbaz).

Note the gloss of Rav Moshe HaCohen who asks why the Rambam does not mention an instance where the High Priest's testimony is necessary to prevent a transgression, for in such an instance, even the High Priest is required to testify. For it appears that the Rambam would not require a High Priest to testify in such circumstances.

4. It is a positive commandment[16] to question the witnesses and to interrogate them, asking many questions and weighing [their replies] exactingly. They should divert [their attention] from one matter to another while questioning them, so that they will refrain from speaking or retract their testimony if [there appears to] be flaws in it, as [Deuteronomy 13:15 states]: "And you shall inquire and research thoroughly."

The judges must show extreme care when questioning the witnesses, lest [from their questions] the witnesses learn to lie. They ask them seven questions:[17]

a) In which seven year cycle [the event] occurred?
b) In which year?
c) In which month?
d) On which day of the month?
e) On which day of the week?
f) At what time?
g) In which place?

Even if [a witness] says: "He killed him today," or "He killed him yesterday," we ask him all the above questions.[18] In addition to these seven questions which are asked universally, [the judges inquire into the fundamental issues involved]. For example, if the witnesses testify that a person worshipped false deities, [the judges] ask them: "Which deity did he worship?" "What service did he perform?" If they testified that he desecrated the Sabbath, [the judges] ask them: "Which forbidden labor did he perform?" "How did he perform it?" If they testify that he ate on Yom Kippur, [the judges] ask them: "Which food did he eat?" "How much did he eat?"[19] If they testified that he killed someone, [the judges] ask them: "With what did he kill him?" Inquiries of this type are considered as fundamental questions (*chakirot*).

5. The *derishot* and the *chakirot* involve the matters that constitute the essence of the testimony. On their basis, the person will either be held liable or released. They include defining the deed that was performed, the time when it was performed, and the place where it was performed. On this basis, the testimony of the witnesses will or will not be refuted through *hazamah*.[20] For we cannot refute the testimony of the witnesses unless they define the time and place [of the deed involved].[21]

6. In addition, [the judges] question the witnesses exceedingly with regard to matters that do not involve the fundamental aspects of the testimony and their testimony is not dependent on them. These [questions] are called *bedikot*.[22] The more [a judge questions the witnesses] with *bedikot*, the more praiseworthy it is.

16. *Sefer HaMitzvot* (positive commandment 179) and *Sefer HaChinuch* (mitzvah 463) count this as one of the 613 mitzvot of the Torah. As stated in Chapter 3, Halachah 1, according to Scriptural Law, this obligation applies with regard to all matters brought to court, cases involving financial matters as well as those involving capital punishment.

ד מִצְוַת עֲשֵׂה לִדְרֹשׁ אֶת הָעֵדִים וּלְחָקְרָן וּלְהַרְבּוֹת בִּשְׁאֵלָתָן. וּמְדַקְדְּקִין עֲלֵיהֶן, וּמַסִּיעִין אוֹתָן מֵעִנְיָן לְעִנְיָן בְּעֵת הַשְּׁאֵלָה, כְּדֵי שֶׁיִּשְׁתְּקוּ אוֹ יַחְזְרוּ בָּהֶן אִם יֵשׁ בְּעֵדוּתָן דֹּפִי. שֶׁנֶּאֱמַר: וְדָרַשְׁתָּ וְחָקַרְתָּ וְשָׁאַלְתָּ הֵיטֵב.

וּצְרִיכִין הַדַּיָּנִים לְהִזָּהֵר בְּעֵת חֲקִירַת הָעֵדִים, שֶׁמָּא מִתּוֹכָהּ יִלְמְדוּ לְשַׁקֵּר.

וּבְשֶׁבַע חֲקִירוֹת בּוֹדְקִין אוֹתָם: בְּאֵי זֶה שָׁבוּעַ? בְּאֵי זוֹ שָׁנָה? בְּאֵי זֶה חֹדֶשׁ? בְּכַמָּה בַּחֹדֶשׁ? בְּאֵי זֶה יוֹם מִימֵי הַשַּׁבָּת? וּבְכַמָּה שָׁעוֹת בַּיּוֹם? וּבְאֵי זֶה מָקוֹם?

אֲפִלּוּ אָמַר: הַיּוֹם הֲרָגוֹ, אוֹ אֶמֶשׁ הֲרָגוֹ – שׁוֹאֲלִין לָהֶן: בְּאֵי זֶה שָׁבוּעַ? בְּאֵי זוֹ שָׁנָה? בְּאֵי זֶה חֹדֶשׁ? בְּכַמָּה בַּחֹדֶשׁ? בְּאֵי זֶה יוֹם? בְּאֵי זוֹ שָׁעָה?

וּמִכְּלַל הַחֲקִירוֹת, יָתֵר עַל הַשֶּׁבַע הַשָּׁווֹת בַּכֹּל:

שֶׁאִם הֵעִידוּ עָלָיו שֶׁעָבַד עֲבוֹדָה זָרָה – שׁוֹאֲלִין לָהֶן: אֶת מָה עָבַד? וּבְאֵי זוֹ עֲבוֹדָה עָבַד?

הֵעִידוּ שֶׁחִלֵּל אֶת הַשַּׁבָּת – שׁוֹאֲלִין אוֹתָן: אֵי זוֹ מְלָאכָה עָשָׂה? וְהֵיאַךְ עָשָׂה? הֵעִידוּ שֶׁאָכַל בְּיוֹם הַכִּפּוּרִים – שׁוֹאֲלִין אוֹתָן: אֵי זֶה מַאֲכָל אָכַל? וְכַמָּה אָכַל? הֵעִידוּ שֶׁהָרַג אֶת הַנֶּפֶשׁ – שׁוֹאֲלִין אוֹתָן: בַּמֶּה הֲרָגוֹ? וְכֵן כֹּל כַּיּוֹצֵא בָּזֶה – הֲרֵי הוּא מִכְּלַל הַחֲקִירוֹת.

ה הַחֲקִירוֹת וְהַדְּרִישׁוֹת הֵן הַדְּבָרִים שֶׁהֵן עִקַּר הָעֵדוּת, וּבָהֶן יִתְחַיֵּב אוֹ יִפָּטֵר. וְהֵן כַּוָּנַת הַמַּעֲשֶׂה שֶׁעָשָׂה, וְכִוּוּן הַזְּמַן וְכִוּוּן הַמָּקוֹם, שֶׁבָּהֶן יָזֹמּוּ הָעֵדִים אוֹ לֹא יָזֹמּוּ; שֶׁאֵין אָנוּ יְכוֹלִים לַהֲזֵם הָעֵדִים עַד שֶׁיְּכַוְּנוּ הַזְּמַן וְהַמָּקוֹם.

ו וְעוֹד מַרְבִּין לִבְדֹּק הָעֵדִים בִּדְבָרִים שֶׁאֵינָן עִקַּר בָּעֵדוּת וְאֵינָהּ תְּלוּיָה בָּהֶם. וְהֵם הַנִּקְרָאִים בְּדִיקוֹת. וְכָל הַמַּרְבֶּה בִּבְדִיקוֹת – הֲרֵי זֶה מְשֻׁבָּח.

17. *Sanhedrin* 40a derives the need for these seven fundamental questions from the exegesis of three verses (Deuteronomy 13:15, 17:4, and 19:18) which deal with the judges' examination of the witnesses.

18. The reason for these questions is to divert the witnesses' attention and cause them to let down their guard, lest they have prepared false testimony (Rashi, *Sanhedrin* 32a).

19. I.e., did it have the minimum amount necessary for him to be liable (see *Hilchot Sh'vitat Asor* 2:1-5).

20. See the definition of this term in Chapter 18. As explained there, *hazamah* involves other witnesses stating that these witnesses were with them in another place at the time they claim to have observed the transgression taking place.

21. *Sanhedrin* 41a states: "Whenever there is no possibility of refuting testimony through *hazamah*, the testimony is of no consequence." For testimony must include the definition of the essential factors involved in a case. Otherwise, there is no way of proving its authenticity.

22. See the following chapter which elaborates on the differences between the *bedikot* and the *chakirot*.

What are examples of *bedikot*? [Witnesses] testified that a person killed [a colleague]. [The witnesses] were questioned with the seven *chakirot* which we mentioned which define the time and the place of the act. Similarly, they were interrogated with regard to the deed and they defined the deed and the murder weapon. [The judges] continue to interrogate them. They ask: What were the murderer and the victim wearing, white clothes or black clothes? Was the earth where he was killed white or red? These and similar questions are called *bedikot*.

An incident once occurred when witnesses stated that a murder took place under a fig tree. The judges questioned the witnesses: "Were the figs black or white?", "Were their stems long or short?" The more [a judge questions the witnesses] with *bedikot* like these, the more praiseworthy it is.

CHAPTER TWO

1. What is the difference between the *chakirot* and the *derishot* and the *bedikot*?[1] With regard to the *chakirot* and the *derishot*, if one witness gave specific testimony and the second said: "I do not know," their testimony is of no consequence. With regard to the *bedikot*, by contrast, even if both of them say: "I don't know," their testimony is allowed to stand. If, however, they contradict each other, even with regard to the *bedikot*, their testimony is nullified.

What is implied? [The witnesses] testified that one person killed another. One of the witnesses specified the seven year cycle, the year, the month, the date, [the day of the week,] Wednesday, [the time,] 12 noon, and the place of the murder. Similarly, they asked him: "With what did he kill him?", and he answered: "With a sword." If the second witnesses outlined his testimony in the same manner except for the time, i.e., he said: "I do not know the time of day at which [the murder] took place," or he was able to specify the time, but said: "I don't know what he used to kill him. I did not take notice of the murder weapon,"[2] their testimony is nullified. If, however, they outlined all [the above factors identically,] but were asked: "Was he dressed in black or white?" their testimony is allowed to stand if they replied: "We don't know. We did not pay attention to factors like these which are of no consequence."[3]

2. If one of the witnesses said: "He was wearing black clothes," and the second one said: "That is not so," he was wearing white clothes, their testimony is nullified. It is as if one said: "It took place on Wednesday," and the other said: "It took place on Thursday," in which instance, the testimony is of no consequence. Or [it can be compared to a situation where] one said: "He killed him with a sword," and the other says: "He killed him with a lance." [The need for corroboration of the witnesses' testimony is derived from Deuteronomy 13:15 which] states: "And the matter is precise." If they contradicted each other in any matter, [their testimony] is not precise.[4]

כֵּיצַד הֵן הַבְּדִיקוֹת? הֲרֵי שֶׁהֵעִידוּ עָלָיו שֶׁהָרַג, וְנֶחְקְרוּ בְּשֶׁבַע חֲקִירוֹת שֶׁמָּנִינוּ, שֶׁהֵן בְּכַוָּנַת הַזְּמַן וְכַוָּנַת הַמָּקוֹם, וְנִדְרְשׁוּ בְּכַוָּנַת הַמַּעֲשֶׂה, וְכִוְּנוּ הַמַּעֲשֶׂה וְכִוְּנוּ הַכְּלִי שֶׁהֲרָגוֹ בּוֹ, בּוֹדְקִין אוֹתָן עוֹד וְאוֹמְרִים לָהֶן: מֶה הָיָה לָבוּשׁ הַנֶּהֱרָג אוֹ הַהוֹרֵג, בְּגָדִים לְבָנִים אוֹ שְׁחֹרִים? עֲפַר הָאָרֶץ שֶׁנֶּהֱרַג עָלֶיהָ — לָבָן אוֹ אָדֹם? אֵלּוּ וְכַיּוֹצֵא בָּהֶן הֵם הַבְּדִיקוֹת.

מַעֲשֶׂה שֶׁאָמְרוּ הָעֵדִים: הֲרָגוֹ בְּמָקוֹם פְּלוֹנִי תַּחַת הַתְּאֵנָה. וּבָדְקוּ הָעֵדִים וְאָמְרוּ לָהֶם: תְּאֵנִים שֶׁלָּהּ שְׁחוֹרוֹת הָיוּ אוֹ לְבָנוֹת? עֻקְצִין שֶׁל אוֹתָם הַתְּאֵנִים אֲרֻכּוֹת הָיוּ אוֹ קְצָרוֹת? וְכָל הַמַּרְבֶּה בִּבְדִיקוֹת וְכַיּוֹצֵא בָּהֶן — הֲרֵי זֶה מְשֻׁבָּח.

פֶּרֶק שֵׁנִי

א מַה בֵּין חֲקִירוֹת וּדְרִישׁוֹת לִבְדִיקוֹת?

בַּחֲקִירוֹת וּדְרִישׁוֹת, אִם כִּוֵּן הָאֶחָד אֶת עֵדוּתוֹ, וְהַשֵּׁנִי אוֹמֵר: אֵינִי יוֹדֵעַ — עֵדוּתָן בְּטֵלָה; אֲבָל בִּבְדִיקוֹת, אֲפִלּוּ שְׁנֵיהֶן אוֹמְרִין: אֵין אָנוּ יוֹדְעִין — עֵדוּתָן קַיֶּמֶת.

וּבִזְמַן שֶׁהֵן מַכְחִישִׁין זֶה אֶת זֶה, אֲפִלּוּ בַּבְּדִיקוֹת — עֵדוּתָן בְּטֵלָה.

כֵּיצַד? הֵעִידוּ שֶׁהָרַג זֶה אֶת זֶה, וְאָמַר הָאֶחָד כְּשֶׁנֶּחְקַר: בִּשָׁבוּעַ פְּלוֹנִי, בְּשָׁנָה פְּלוֹנִית, בְּחֹדֶשׁ פְּלוֹנִי, בְּכַךְ וְכַךְ בַּחֹדֶשׁ, בָּרְבִיעִי בַּשַּׁבָּת, בְּשֵׁשׁ שָׁעוֹת בַּיּוֹם, בְּמָקוֹם פְּלוֹנִי הֲרָגוֹ. וְכֵן כְּשֶׁדְּרָשׁוּ: בַּמֶּה הֲרָגוֹ? אָמַר: הֲרָגוֹ בְּסַיִף. וְכֵן הָעֵד הַשֵּׁנִי כִּוֵּן עֵדוּתוֹ בַּכֹּל, חוּץ מִן הַשָּׁעוֹת, שֶׁאָמַר: אֵינִי יוֹדֵעַ בְּכַמָּה שָׁעוֹת הָיָה בַּיּוֹם; אוֹ שֶׁכִּוֵּן אֶת הַשָּׁעוֹת, וְאָמַר: אֵינִי יוֹדֵעַ בַּמֶּה הֲרָגוֹ, וְלֹא הֵבַנְתִּי בַּכְּלִי שֶׁהָיָה בְּיָדוֹ — הֲרֵי עֵדוּתָן בְּטֵלָה.

אֲבָל אִם כִּוְּנוּ הַכֹּל, וְאָמְרוּ לָהֶן הַדַּיָּנִים: כֵּלָיו הָיוּ שְׁחֹרִים אוֹ לְבָנִים? וְאָמְרוּ: אֵין אָנוּ יוֹדְעִים, וְלֹא שַׂמְנוּ לִבֵּנוּ לִדְבָרִים אֵלּוּ שֶׁאֵין לָהֶן מַמָּשׁ — הֲרֵי עֵדוּתָן קַיֶּמֶת.

ב אָמַר אֶחָד: כֵּלִים שְׁחֹרִים הָיָה לָבוּשׁ, וְהַשֵּׁנִי אָמַר: לֹא כֵן, אֶלָּא לְבָנִים הָיָה לָבוּשׁ — הֲרֵי עֵדוּתָן בְּטֵלָה; וּכְאִלּוּ אָמַר אֶחָד בָּרְבִיעִי בְּשַׁבָּת, וְהַשֵּׁנִי בַּחֲמִישִׁי, שֶׁאֵין כָּאן עֵדוּת; אוֹ שֶׁאָמַר הָאֶחָד בְּסַיִף הֲרָגוֹ, וְהַשֵּׁנִי אָמַר בְּרֹמַח, שֶׁאֵין כָּאן עֵדוּת. שֶׁנֶּאֱמַר: נָכוֹן הַדָּבָר, וְכֵיוָן שֶׁהִכְחִישׁוּ זֶה אֶת זֶה בְּאֵי זֶה מִכָּל הַדְּבָרִים — אֵין זֶה נָכוֹן.

1. See the conclusion of the previous chapter for a definition of these terms.
2. For the identification of the murder weapon is considered an essential element of his testimony.
3. The fundamental dimension of the testimony is communicated through the *chakirot*. They provide sufficient basis for *hazamah*. The other particulars discovered through the *bedikot* are secondary. Hence as long as there is no contradiction with regard to them, the testimony is allowed to stand. See *Sanhedrin* 41b.
4. This applies with regard to laws involving capital punishment. Different laws apply with regard to matters of financial law, as stated in Chapter 3, Halachah 3.

3. [The following rules apply if] there were many witnesses. If two of them testified in a like manner with regard to the *chakirot* and the *derishot*, their testimony is allowed to stand and the defendant is executed, even though the third witness says: "I don't know."[5] If, however, [that witness] contradicts the other two, even with regard to the *bedikot*, their testimony is nullified.[6]

4. If one witness says: "[The murder took place] on Wednesday, the second of the month," and another says: "[It took place] on Wednesday,[7] the third of the month," their testimony is allowed to stand. [Although there is a contradiction between them, we assume] that one knew that an extra day had been added to the [previous] month, and one did not know.[8]

[Until when] does the above apply? Until the middle of the month. After the middle of the month, by contrast, if, for example, one said: "[It took place] on the sixteenth[9] of the month," and the second said: "[It took place] on the seventeenth of the month," their testimony is nullified even though both of them spoke about the same day of the week. [The rationale is that] by the middle of the month, every one knows when Rosh Chodesh was commemorated.

5. If, however, one witness says: "[It took place] on the third of the month," and the other says: "[It took place] on the fifth of the month," their testimony is nullified.[10]

If one witness says: "[It took place] during the second hour of the day,"[11] and the other says: "[It took place] during the third hour," their testimony is allowed to stand.[12] [The rationale is that] it is common for people to err with regard to one hour. If, however, one says: "[It took place] during the third hour," and the other says: "[It took place] during the fifth hour," their testimony is nullified.[13]

5. Since the witness does not know the fundamental dimensions of the testimony, his testimony is of no consequence, and he is not considered as part of the same group of witnesses as the other two.

Note the *Lechem Mishneh* and others who question the Rambam's ruling based on his ruling in Chapter 5, Halachah 3, which states that when one of three witnesses is discovered to be a relative or otherwise disqualified, the entire testimony is nullified. For *Sanhedrin* 41a, the source for this halachah, considers the two concepts to be interrelated.

The *Lechem Mishneh* offers a possible resolution, explaining that in Chapter 5, the Rambam is speaking about an instance where the witnesses testified directly after each other. In this halachah, by contrast, there was an interruption between their testimony. Hence, there is the potential to consider each witness as a separate entity.

6. In this instance, the three witnesses are considered as a single group. And since there is a contradiction in their testimony, it is disqualified, for it is not "precise."

7. If, however, there is a contradiction between them with regard to the day of the week, even if there is only a one day difference with regard to the date, their testimony is nullified (*Kessef Mishneh*).

8. In order to juxtapose the lunar and solar calendars, an extra day is added to several months. At present, this is done according to a fixed calendar. In the time of the Temple

ג הָיוּ הָעֵדִים מְרֻבִּים, שְׁנַיִם מֵהֶן כִּוְּנוּ עֵדוּתָן בַּחֲקִירוֹת וּבַדְּרִישׁוֹת, וְהַשְּׁלִישִׁי אוֹמֵר: אֵינִי יוֹדֵעַ – תִּתְקַיֵּם הָעֵדוּת בִּשְׁנַיִם, וְיֵהָרֵג. אֲבָל אִם הִכְחִישׁ אֶת שְׁנֵיהֶן, אֲפִלּוּ בַּבְּדִיקוֹת – עֵדוּתָן בְּטֵלָה.

ד עֵד אֶחָד אוֹמֵר: בָּרְבִיעִי בַּשַּׁבָּת, בִּשְׁנַיִם לַחֹדֶשׁ, וְהַשֵּׁנִי אוֹמֵר: בָּרְבִיעִי בַּשַּׁבָּת, בִּשְׁלֹשָׁה לַחֹדֶשׁ – עֵדוּתָן קַיֶּמֶת; שֶׁזֶּה יוֹדֵעַ בְּעִבּוּרוֹ שֶׁל חֹדֶשׁ, וְזֶה אֵינוֹ יוֹדֵעַ.
בַּמֶּה דְּבָרִים אֲמוּרִים? עַד חֲצוֹת הַחֹדֶשׁ; אֲבָל אַחַר חֲצוֹת הַחֹדֶשׁ, כְּגוֹן שֶׁאָמַר הָאֶחָד: בְּשִׁשָּׁה עָשָׂר בַּחֹדֶשׁ, וְהַשֵּׁנִי אוֹמֵר: בְּשִׁבְעָה עָשָׂר בַּחֹדֶשׁ, אַף עַל פִּי שֶׁכִּוְּנוּ שְׁנֵיהֶם יוֹם אֶחָד מִימֵי הַשַּׁבָּת – עֵדוּתָן בְּטֵלָה; שֶׁאֵין חֲצִי הַחֹדֶשׁ בָּא וּכְבָר יָדְעוּ הַכֹּל אֵימָתַי הָיָה רֹאשׁ הַחֹדֶשׁ.

ה אָמַר הָאֶחָד: בִּשְׁלֹשָׁה, וְהַשֵּׁנִי אוֹמֵר: בַּחֲמִשָּׁה – עֵדוּתָן בְּטֵלָה. אָמַר עֵד אֶחָד: בִּשְׁתֵּי שָׁעוֹת בַּיּוֹם, וְהַשֵּׁנִי אוֹמֵר: בְּשָׁלֹשׁ שָׁעוֹת – הֲרֵי עֵדוּתָן קַיֶּמֶת; שֶׁדֶּרֶךְ הָעָם לִטְעוֹת בְּשָׁעָה אַחַת. אֲבָל אִם אָמַר הָאֶחָד: בְּשָׁלֹשׁ שָׁעוֹת, וְהַשֵּׁנִי אוֹמֵר: בְּחָמֵשׁ – עֵדוּתָן בְּטֵלָה.

and for several hundred years thereafter, the question of whether or not to add a month was dependent on the Supreme *Sanhedrin*'s acceptance of the testimony of witnesses who claimed to have sighted the moon on the appropriate night. Although this news was spread rather rapidly, it is possible that a person would be uninformed.

Moreover, even in the present era, when we have a fixed calendar, since the amount of days in a month vary from month to month, it is possible that a person might err at the beginning of the month. Hence this law still applies [*Shulchan Aruch* (*Choshen Mishpat* 30:7)].

9. If, however, one witness mentioned the fifteenth and the other, the sixteenth, we still give them the benefit of the doubt (Radbaz).

10. For a two day error is too great to attribute to the above factor. As mentioned in the previous halachah, by the middle of the month every one already knows when Rosh Chodesh was commemorated. Also, it is very rare that there are two 30 day months one after the other.

11. I.e., the second hour after sunrise.

12. *Pesachim* 12a states that a person will err in a little bit less than two hours. On that basis, the *Kessef Mishneh* questions the Rambam's ruling. In resolution, he explains that when the witness states "the second hour," the possibility is that he meant any time from the beginning of that hour until the end. The same is true with regard to the third hour. Thus there can be up to a two hour discrepancy between the two testimonies.

The commentaries mention that we are speaking about *shaot zemaniot*, seasonal hours (i.e., one twelfth of the time from sunrise to sunset), for everything is dependent on the position of the sun in the sky. *Kin'at Eliyahu* raises the question if similar laws apply today when most people use watches or clocks to tell time.

13. For it is unlikely that people will make an error of more than two hours.

If one witness says: "[It took place] before sunrise," and the other says: "[It took place] at sunrise," their testimony is nullified. Even though [the discrepancy between them is less than] one hour, the matter is evident to all.[14] Similar concepts apply with regard to sunset.

CHAPTER THREE

1. The questioning and interrogation[1] [of witnesses is required with regard to cases] involving both monetary law and capital punishment, as [Leviticus 24:22] states: "You shall have one judgment."[2] Nevertheless, our Sages ordained that witnesses [in cases] involving financial law not be questioned or interrogated, lest this prevent loans from being given.[3]

What is implied? If witnesses say: "So-and-so lent so-and-so a *maneh*[4] in this year," their testimony is allowed to stand even though they did not specify the month or the place in which the *maneh* was given, nor did they say of which coinage the *maneh* was.

2. When does the above apply? With regard to admissions of liability,[5] loans, presents, sales,[6] and the like.[7] [Cases involving] fines,[8] by contrast, require the full process of questioning and interrogation.[9] Needless to say, this applies with regard to cases involving [the penalties of] lashes and exile.[10] Similarly, if a judge perceives that a claim may be contrived and his suspicions are aroused,[11] questioning and interrogation is necessary [even with regard to cases involving financial matters].

3. Although there is no requirement to subject witnesses in [cases] involving monetary law to [the full process of] questioning and interrogation, if the witnesses contradict each other with regard to the *derishot* or the *chakirot*, their testimony is nullified.[12] If the witnesses contradict each other with regard to the *bedikot*, their testimony is allowed to stand.[13]

14. Before sunrise and at sunrise are factors concerning which a person will not err.

1. The process of *derishah* and *chakirah* mentioned in the previous chapter.
2. Hence the obligation for questioning and interrogation that applies with regard to cases involving capital punishment (Chapter 1, Halachah 4) also applies with regard to cases involving monetary law.
3. I.e., prospective lenders will fear that the witnesses to the loan will not be able to respond correctly to questioning and their testimony will be nullified. Hence the loan will be nullified and they will lose their money. Out of concern for such a possibility, the lenders may withhold granting loans. To avoid such a situation from arising, our Sages lifted the requirement for a full process of questioning and interrogation.
4. 100 *zuz*.
5. Witnesses testify that so-and-so admitted a debt in their presence.
6. Witnesses testify that a loan or a present was given or a sale was made in their presence. The Talmud states this concept with regard to admissions of liability and loans. Our Rabbis extended it to presents and sales, because they are matters that continually

אָמַר עֵד אֶחָד: קֹדֶם הֶנֵּץ הַחַמָּה, וְאֶחָד אוֹמֵר: בְּהֶנֵּץ הַחַמָּה – עֵדוּתָן בְּטֵלָה, אַף עַל פִּי שֶׁהִיא שָׁעָה אַחַת; שֶׁהַדָּבָר נִכָּר לַכֹּל. וְכֵן אִם נֶחְלְקוּ בִּשְׁקִיעָתָהּ.

פֶּרֶק שְׁלִישִׁי

א אֶחָד דִּינֵי מָמוֹנוֹת וְאֶחָד דִּינֵי נְפָשׁוֹת בִּדְרִישָׁה וַחֲקִירָה. שֶׁנֶּאֱמַר: מִשְׁפַּט אֶחָד יִהְיֶה לָכֶם. אֲבָל אָמְרוּ חֲכָמִים: כְּדֵי שֶׁלֹּא תִּנְעַל דֶּלֶת בִּפְנֵי לֹוִין, אֵין עֵדֵי מָמוֹן צְרִיכִין דְּרִישָׁה וַחֲקִירָה. כֵּיצַד? אָמְרוּ הָעֵדִים: בְּפָנֵינוּ הִלְוָה זֶה אֶת זֶה מָנֶה בְּשָׁנָה פְּלוֹנִית, אַף עַל פִּי שֶׁלֹּא כִּוְּנוּ אֶת הַחֹדֶשׁ, וְלֹא אֶת הַמָּקוֹם שֶׁהִלְוָה בּוֹ, וְלֹא אֶת הַמָּנֶה אִם הָיָה מִמַּטְבֵּעַ פְּלוֹנִי אוֹ מִמַּטְבֵּעַ פְּלוֹנִי – עֵדוּתָן קַיֶּמֶת.

ב בַּמֶּה דְּבָרִים אֲמוּרִים? בְּהוֹדָאוֹת וְהַלְוָאוֹת, מַתָּנוֹת וּמְכִירוֹת וְכַיּוֹצֵא בָּהֶן;
אֲבָל בְּדִינֵי קְנָסוֹת – צְרִיכִין דְּרִישָׁה וַחֲקִירָה. וְאֵין צָרִיךְ לוֹמַר בְּמַלְקוּת וּבְגָלוּת.
וְכֵן אִם רָאָה הַדַּיָּן שֶׁהַדִּין מְרֻמֶּה וְחָשַׁשׁ לוֹ – צָרִיךְ דְּרִישָׁה וַחֲקִירָה.

ג אַף עַל פִּי שֶׁאֵין עֵדֵי מָמוֹנוֹת צְרִיכִין דְּרִישָׁה וַחֲקִירָה, אִם הִכְחִישׁוּ הָעֵדִים זֶה אֶת זֶה בַּדְּרִישׁוֹת אוֹ בַּחֲקִירוֹת – עֵדוּתָן בְּטֵלָה. וְאִם הִכְחִישׁוּ הָעֵדִים זֶה אֶת זֶה בַּבְּדִיקוֹת – עֵדוּתָן קַיֶּמֶת.

arise and are necessary for the maintenance of ordinary commercial activity, for if they are not dealt with, the plaintiff will suffer financial loss.

7. E.g., inheritances (*Sefer Me'irat Einayim* 30:1).

8. Financial penalties in which the defendant is obligated to pay more or less than the damages involved, e.g., cases involving personal injury. See *Hilchot Sanhedrin* 5:8; *Hilchot Nizkei Mammon* 2:8.

9. Since these matters are uncommon and some do not involve financial loss, our Sages left the situation as prescribed by Scriptural Law and required the full process of questioning and interrogation (*Sanhedrin* 32b).

10. The punishments given for the violation of negative commandments and accidental murders. Since the failure to administer these punishments will not interrupt the normal commercial activity of society, our Sages did not alter the prescriptions of Scriptural Law. As stated in *Hilchot Sanhedrin* 11:4, all the requirements for cases involving capital punishment apply in these instances as well.

11. I.e., he suspects that the claim is contrived, but does not have definite indications of such. Were he to feel definitively that the case was contrived, he would have to withdraw from the case as stated in *Hilchot Sanhedrin* 24:3 (*Kessef Mishneh*).

12. Since these are essential matters on which the testimony is based and which are required by Scriptural Law, if there is a discrepancy in the testimony of the witnesses, the testimony is nullified. Although are Sages were lenient and did not require the full process of interrogation, if a discrepancy arises, it is considered significant and the testimony disqualified (Radbaz).

13. Since these are secondary matters, the testimony is allowed to stand. The Radbaz

What is implied? One witness says: "He borrowed from him in Nissan," and the other witness says: "No, he borrowed in Iyar," their testimony is nullified.[14] Or one says: "[The loan was given] in Jerusalem," and the second says: "No; we were in Lod," their testimony is nullified. Similarly, if one says: "He lent him a barrel of wine," and the other says: "It contained oil," their testimony is nullified, for they contradicted themselves with regard to the [fundamental] questions.[15]

If, by contrast, one said: "[He lent him] a black *maneh*,"[16] while the other said: "It was a white *maneh*.[17] One said: "They were in the upper storey when he made the loan," and the other said: "They were in the lower storey," their testimony is allowed to stand.[18] Moreover, even if one said: "He lent him a *maneh* and the other, "He lent him two hundred," [the defendant] is obligated to pay him at least a *maneh*, because 200 contains 100.[19] Similarly, if one said: "He owes him the cost of a barrel of wine," and the other says: "...a barrel of oil," [the defendant is required to] pay the lesser amount of the two. Similar concepts apply in all analogous situations.[20]

4. According to Scriptural Law, we do not accept testimony - neither in cases involving financial matters, nor in cases involving capital punishment - except orally from the witnesses, as [implied by Deuteronomy 17:6]: "On the basis of two witnesses...."[21] [Implied is that testimony is accepted] only orally, and not on the basis of their written statements.

According to Rabbinic Law, however, we decide cases involving financial matters on the basis of testimony recorded in a legal document[22] even if the witnesses are no longer alive. [This measure was enacted] lest [the alternative] prevent loans from being given.[23] We do not adjudicate cases involving fines

raises a question, noting that as the Rambam rules in Chapter 2, Halachah 3, if there is a discrepancy in the testimony of the witnesses, their testimony is nullified even if the discrepancy involves the *bedikot*. As explained, the rationale is that it is necessary for testimony to be "precise," and when there is even a slight discrepancy, that requirement is not met. The Radbaz resolves this difficulty by explaining that the requirement for precise testimony applies only with regard to cases involving capital punishment (the subject of the prooftext cited in the previous chapter) and not ordinary business matters.

14. Based on the ruling of the *Sefer Me'irat Einayim* 30:6, it appears that the Rambam's decision applies not only when the plaintiff claims that only one loan was given, but even when he claims to have lent him money in both Nisan and Iyar.

15. The *Sefer Me'irat Einayim* 30:9 and Rabbi Akiva Eiger note that the testimony of the witnesses is disregarded entirely. We do not even consider it as equivalent to the testimony of one witness, in which instance the defendant is required to take an oath to free himself of obligation.

16. I.e., the silver was so old that it became tarnished and black.

17. I.e., the silver was new and had not changed color.

The *Tur* and the Ramah (*Choshen Mishpat* 30:2) state that this law applies only when the plaintiff demands payment for both these loans. If, however, he demands payment for only one, the claim is not accepted, for his own statements contradict the testimony of the

כֵּיצַד? אֶחָד אוֹמֵר: בְּנִיסָן לָוָה מִמֶּנּוּ, וְהַשֵּׁנִי אוֹמֵר: לֹא כִּי, אֶלָּא בְּאִיָּר; אוֹ שֶׁאָמַר הָאֶחָד: בִּירוּשָׁלַיִם, וְהַשֵּׁנִי אוֹמֵר: לֹא כִּי, אֶלָּא בְּלֹד הָיִינוּ – עֵדוּתָן בְּטֵלָה.

וְכֵן אִם אָמַר הָאֶחָד: חָבִית שֶׁל יַיִן הִלְוָהוּ, וְהַשֵּׁנִי אוֹמֵר: שֶׁל שֶׁמֶן הָיְתָה – עֵדוּתָן בְּטֵלָה; שֶׁהֲרֵי הִכְחִישׁוּ בַּדְּרִישָׁה.

אֲבָל אִם אָמַר הָאֶחָד: מָנֶה שָׁחֹר, וְהַשֵּׁנִי אוֹמֵר: מָנֶה לָבָן הָיָה; זֶה אוֹמֵר: בַּדְּיוֹטָא הָעֶלְיוֹנָה הָיוּ כְּשֶׁהִלְוָהוּ, וְהַשֵּׁנִי אוֹמֵר: בַּדְּיוֹטָא הַתַּחְתּוֹנָה הָיוּ – עֵדוּתָן קַיֶּמֶת. אֲפִלּוּ אָמַר הָאֶחָד: מָנֶה הִלְוָהוּ, וְהַשֵּׁנִי אוֹמֵר: מָאתַיִם – חַיָּב לְשַׁלֵּם מָנֶה; שֶׁיֵּשׁ בִּכְלַל מָאתַיִם מָנֶה. וְכֵן אִם אָמַר הָאֶחָד: דְּמֵי חָבִית שֶׁל יַיִן יֵשׁ לוֹ בְּיָדוֹ, וְזֶה אוֹמֵר: דְּמֵי חָבִית שֶׁל שֶׁמֶן – מְשַׁלֵּם בַּפָּחוֹת שֶׁבַּדָּמִים. וְכֵן כֹּל כַּיּוֹצֵא בָּזֶה.

ד דִּין תּוֹרָה: שֶׁאֵין מְקַבְּלִין עֵדוּת, לֹא בְּדִינֵי מָמוֹנוֹת וְלֹא בְּדִינֵי נְפָשׁוֹת, אֶלָּא מִפִּי הָעֵדִים. שֶׁנֶּאֱמַר: עַל פִּי שְׁנַיִם עֵדִים – מִפִּיהֶם וְלֹא מִכְּתָב יָדָן.

אֲבָל מִדִּבְרֵי סוֹפְרִים: שֶׁחוֹתְכִין דִּינֵי מָמוֹנוֹת בְּעֵדוּת שֶׁבִּשְׁטָר, אַף עַל פִּי שֶׁאֵין הָעֵדִים קַיָּמִים, כְּדֵי שֶׁלֹּא תִּנְעַל דֶּלֶת בִּפְנֵי לֹוִין.

other witness. The *Sefer Me'irat Einayim* 30:11 explains that there is a difference of opinion between the *Rishonim* whether this perspective should be followed or not. These principles also apply with regard to the other instances mentioned in this halachah.

18. The *Kessef Mishneh* explains that we are referring to a situation where an observer could see both storeys at the same time. If that is not the case, the testimony is nullified, because it is considered a discrepancy involving the place where the loan was given and that is significant.

19. Thus included in the testimony that the defendant owed 200 was the fact that he owed 100 (a *maneh*). The fact that there is a discrepancy between the two testimonies is not significant.

20. The Ramah (*loc. cit.*) concludes his discussion of this halachah with the statement: "Whenever we can resolve the statements of the witnesses so that they will not be in contradiction to each other, we do."

21. *Al pi*, translated as "on the basis of," literally means "on the mouths of," implying that the testimony must be delivered orally by the witnesses.

22. The *Sefer Me'irat Einayim* 28:43 emphasizes that the legal document must be composed according to all the rules governing such archives; a personal note is not sufficient.

23. I.e., a person might refuse to give a loan out of fear that the witnesses will die or be unavailable and he will have no way of compelling the debtor to acknowledge the debt. If, however, the testimony of witnesses recorded on a legal document is deemed acceptable, that document could serve as proof and there would be no need for hesitation.

This concept applies not only to loans, but to sales, presents, and acknowledgments of responsibility as mentioned in Halachah 2. In all these and similar instances, our Sages enacted the acceptance of legal documents as testimony so that ordinary commercial activity could continue unhampered.

on the basis of testimony recorded in a legal document.[24] Needless to say, cases involving lashes or exile are decided only on the basis of verbal testimony, not on the basis of a written document.[25]

5. Both in cases involving financial matters and in cases involving capital punishment, once a witness has testified and has been questioned[26] in court,[27] he cannot retract.[28]

What is implied? If [the witness] states: "I [testified] in error,"[29] "I inadvertently [forgot the details] and [now] remembered that it was not so," or "I [testified only] out of fear of him"[30] we do not heed him,[31] even if he provides an explanation for his statements. Similarly, he cannot add that [any of the matters he mentioned in] his testimony were conditional.[32]

The general principle is: Any statement made by a witness after his testimony was [delivered and] questioned that will lead to the nullification of that testimony or that adds a condition [to the points stated] is not heeded.

6. Witnesses who sign a legal document are considered as if their testimony was [delivered and] questioned by a court of law.[33] They cannot retract it.

When does the above apply? When the authenticity of the document can be verified[34] without their testimony, e.g., other witness who could testify that it was their signatures were present[35] or their signatures were found on other

24. For ordinary commercial activity will continue even if these cases are not adjudicated.
25. According to Rashi (in his commentary to the above verse), if the witnesses do not testify orally, their testimony is nullified according to Scriptural Law. *Tosafot, Yevamot* 31b, however, rules that as long as witnesses are capable of testifying orally, their testimony is acceptable even if it is recorded in a legal document and sent to the court. Similarly, in his *Kessef Mishneh*, Rav Yosef Karo cites the opinions of Rabbenu Yitzchak Alfasi and the Rashbatz who admit such testimony. In support of this approach, they cite Jeremiah 32:44: "Purchase fields with silver, record [the sale] in a scroll, seal it, and have the witnesses testify," which appears to indicate that written testimony is acceptable.

Rav Yosef Karo explains that since the verse is based on the words of the prophets, it is not able to serve as a proof of the Scriptural Law. Nevertheless, he cites a Talmudic passage (*Ketubot* 21a) which appears to indicate that according to Scriptural Law, testimony recorded in a legal document is acceptable. [Similar concepts are stated by the Ramban in his *Hasagot* to (*Sefer HaMitzvot* (mitzvah 178).]

Despite the above, in his *Shulchan Aruch* (*Choshen Mishpat* 28:11), Rav Karo quotes the Rambam's ruling. The *Siftei Cohen* 28:14, however, protests this decision, explaining at length that written testimony is acceptable according to Scriptural Law. Similarly, the *Sefer Me'irat Einayim* 28:42 states that there are sages who allow Torah scholars to convey their testimony in writing rather than appear in person in court.
26. I.e., the judges asked them the basic questions that determine the accuracy of their testimony.
27. If, however, a witness makes certain statements outside the court, he can change his mind and testify differently in court. When he provides a feasible explanation, the statements made outside the court are of no consequence whatsoever (*Kessef Mishneh*).
28. *Ketubot* 18b derives this concept from Leviticus 5:1, the source for the mitzvah to

וְאֵין דָּנִין בְּעֵדוּת שֶׁבִּשְׁטָר בְּדִינֵי קְנָסוֹת, וְאֵין צָרִיךְ לוֹמַר בְּמַכּוֹת וּבְגָלוּת; אֶלָּא מִפִּיהֶן, וְלֹא מִכְּתַב יָדָן.

ה כָּל עֵד שֶׁנֶּחְקְרָה עֵדוּתוֹ בְּבֵית דִּין, בֵּין בְּדִינֵי מָמוֹנוֹת בֵּין בְּדִינֵי נְפָשׁוֹת – אֵין יָכוֹל לַחֲזוֹר בּוֹ.

כֵּיצַד? אָמַר: מֻטְעֶה הָיִיתִי, שׁוֹגֵג הָיִיתִי, וְנִזְכַּרְתִּי שֶׁאֵין הַדָּבָר כֵּן, לְפַחְדּוֹ עָשִׂיתִי – אֵין שׁוֹמְעִין לוֹ, אֲפִלּוּ נָתַן טַעַם לִדְבָרָיו. וְכֵן אֵינוֹ יָכוֹל לְהוֹסִיף בְּעֵדוּתוֹ תְּנַאי. כְּלָלוֹ שֶׁל דָּבָר: כָּל דְּבָרִים שֶׁיֹּאמַר הָעֵד אַחַר שֶׁנֶּחְקְרָה עֵדוּתוֹ, שֶׁיָּבוֹא מִכְּלָלָן בִּטּוּל הָעֵדוּת אוֹ הוֹסָפַת תְּנַאי בָּהּ – אֵין שׁוֹמְעִין לוֹ.

ו עֵדִים הַחֲתוּמִים עַל הַשְּׁטָר – הֲרֵי זֶה כְּמִי שֶׁנֶּחְקְרָה עֵדוּתָן בְּבֵית דִּין, וְאֵין יְכוֹלִין לַחֲזוֹר בָּהֶן. בַּמֶּה דְּבָרִים אֲמוּרִים? כְּשֶׁאֶפְשָׁר לְקַיֵּם הַשְּׁטָר שֶׁלֹּא מִפִּיהֶן, כְּגוֹן שֶׁהָיוּ שָׁם עֵדִים שֶׁזֶּה כְּתַב יָדָן, אוֹ שֶׁהָיָה כְּתַב יָדָן יוֹצֵא מִמָּקוֹם אַחֵר;

testify. That verse states: "If he does not testify, he will bear his sin." Since the verse mentions testifying only once, the implication is that once he testifies, he cannot retract.

The Radbaz explains that if the intent of the witnesses' original statements are not clear and they make additional statements that elucidate them, they are not considered to have retracted their statements.

The *Sefer Me'irat Einayim* 29:2 states that if a witnesses corrects himself in the midst of - or directly after the conclusion of - his testimony or even directly after the testimony of the other witness, the change in testimony is allowed to stand.

29. The *Lechem Mishneh* and the *Shulchan Aruch* (*Choshen Mishpat* 29:1) state that if it was apparent that a witness erred when testifying, he can correct his error.

30. I.e., I gave false testimony out of fear that the defendant would harm me.

31. The *Kessef Mishneh* explains that one might think that the witnesses' retraction would not be accepted in situations where their second testimony would cause them to be considered as wicked, e.g., they state that we lied because of fear. In which case the rationale would be that a person's own testimony can never be used to incriminate him.

The *Kessef Mishneh* states that this is not the case. Even when the witnesses' second testimony does not incriminate them, it is not acceptable if it involves a retraction of the first testimony.

32. If the witnesses were to state that the contract was made conditional to the fulfillment of a stipulation, they would be in effect retracting their initial testimony, for were the stipulation not to be fulfilled, the contract would not be binding.

The *Tur* and the Ramah differ with this ruling and maintain that witnesses may amend their testimony and state that a condition was involved. The *Siftei Cohen* 29:2 elaborates in support of the Rambam's position.

33. I.e., we assume that they signed the legal document with the same seriousness with which they approach testifying in court.

34. See Chapter 6 which explains in detail the processes of validating the authenticity of a legal document.

35. This ruling applies even if the other witnesses appeared after the witnesses made the statements that raised questions concerning the validity of the legal document. See Chapter 8, Halachah 4.

[legal documents].[36] If, however, the authenticity of the document could not be verified without their testimony and they said: "This is our handwriting, but we were compelled to do it,"[37] "...We were below majority at the time,"[38] "...We were related [to the litigants],"[39] "...We were deceived,"[40] their statements are accepted and the legal document is nullified.

7. If [the witnesses] say: "We were not acceptable as witnesses because of a transgression [we violated],"[41] or "We took a bribe to testify [on this document],"[42] their word is not accepted. [The rationale is that] a person's own testimony can never [be used] to have him considered as wicked.[43] [Instead,] two witnesses must testify that he is wicked.

Similarly, if [the witnesses] say: "Our words were given on faith,[44] their words are not accepted. For a person who [signs as] a witness on a promissory note given on faith is considered as if[45] he gave false testimony.[46]

8. If witnesses say: "A protest was made by the seller to us with regard to this deed of sale,"[47] their word is accepted even though their signatures were found on other [legal documents].

9. When the witnesses [who signed a document] say: "The legal document was composed conditionally,"[48] their word is not accepted if their signatures were

36. This and the clause that follows are dependent on two halachic principles: a) *miggo*, and b) that we do not apply the principle of *miggo* in a situation where witnesses are present.

To explain: *Miggo* means that a person's statements are accepted, because we say that had he desired to lie, he would have told a more effective lie. For example, with regard to the second clause of this halachah, had the witnesses desired to lie, instead of offering the arguments which they did offer, they could have claimed that the signatures are forgeries. Nobody could have disproved their statements, for no one else was familiar with their signatures. Since their word would have been accepted with regard to that statement, it is also accepted with regard to the other claims.

When does this concept apply? When there are no other witnesses involved. When, as in the present clause, there are other witnesses involved and they corroborate the original statement of the witnesses, we do not say: "Had they desired to lie...." For they do not have the option of lying. Even if they would desire to lie, their statements would be contradicted by the other witnesses. Hence, their word is not accepted with regard to other claims.

37. I.e., "we were compelled to sign because of danger to our lives, but the transaction never took place." If they said that they were compelled to sign because of financial loss, their word is not accepted. The rationale is that it is forbidden to sign a legal document under such circumstances. Thus by making such an admission, they are acknowledging committing a transgression. In such an instance, their word is not accepted as stated in the following halachah.

38. And a minor's testimony is unacceptable.

39. And a relative's testimony is unacceptable. This could be speaking about a situation where the relationship came about through marriage. Hence it is possible that at the time the document was composed a family connection existed, but afterwards, because of divorce, it was broken (*Sefer Me'irat Einayim* 46:100).

אֲבָל אִם אִי אֶפְשָׁר לְקַיֵּם אֶת הַשְּׁטָר אֶלָּא מִפִּיהֶן, וְאָמְרוּ: כְּתַב יָדֵנוּ הוּא זֶה, אֲבָל אֲנוּסִים הָיִינוּ, קְטַנִּים הָיִינוּ, קְרוֹבִים הָיִינוּ, מֻטְעִים הָיִינוּ – הֲרֵי אֵלּוּ נֶאֱמָנִים, וְיִבָּטֵל הַשְּׁטָר.

ז אָמְרוּ: פְּסוּלֵי עֵדוּת הָיִינוּ בַּעֲבֵרָה, אוֹ שֹׁחַד לָקַחְנוּ עַל עֵדוּת זוֹ – אֵין נֶאֱמָנִים; שֶׁאֵין אָדָם מֵשִׂים עַצְמוֹ רָשָׁע, עַד שֶׁיָּעִידוּ עָלָיו עֵדִים שֶׁהוּא רָשָׁע. וְכֵן אִם אָמְרוּ: אֲמָנָה הָיוּ דְבָרֵינוּ – אֵין נֶאֱמָנִים; שֶׁהַמֵּעִיד עַל שְׁטַר אֲמָנָה – כְּמֵעִיד בְּשֶׁקֶר.

ח אָמְרוּ הָעֵדִים: שְׁטַר מֶכֶר זֶה מוֹדָעָה נִמְסְרָה לָנוּ עָלָיו, אַף עַל פִּי שֶׁכְּתַב יָדָן יוֹצֵא מִמָּקוֹם אַחֵר – הֲרֵי אֵלּוּ נֶאֱמָנִין.

ט אָמְרוּ: עַל תְּנַאי הָיָה שְׁטָר זֶה: אִם הָיָה כְּתַב יָדָן יוֹצֵא מִמָּקוֹם אַחֵר – אֵין נֶאֱמָנִין;

40. And thus unknowingly made our statements in error.
41. I.e., we committed a transgression punishable by lashes. Hence we are disqualified as witnesses. See Chapter 10.
42. And we testified falsely. Alternatively, even if they say that they testified truly, but were paid for testifying, their statements are not accepted and the legal document is valid. For the testimony of a person who takes payment for testifying must be disqualified. Thus even in such a situation, their testimony would disqualify them as witnesses (*Merkevat HaMishneh*).

In his Commentary to the Mishnah [*Ketubot* 2:3; see also *Shulchan Aruch* (*Choshen Mishpat* 46:37)], the Rambam states this ruling applies if they were threatened with financial loss and saved their property by delivering false testimony.
43. The rationale is that for his testimony to be accepted, the person would have to testify against himself. This is unacceptable, because he is an involved party and thus unacceptable as a witness, as stated in Chapter 12, Halachah 2.
44. I.e., the witnesses say that the lender promised to give the loan and on the basis of his promise, they signed the promissory note even though they did not witness the loan actually being given. This is considered as giving false testimony, for they state that the loan was given when in fact it was not. See *Ketubot* 19a, *Hilchot Malveh ViLoveh* 14:5.
45. The Radbaz emphasizes that the Rambam's choice of wording is exact. It is only "as if" the witnesses gave false testimony. Although they should not have signed the legal document, they are not considered as having committed perjury, nor are they disqualified as witnesses in the future.
46. The *Shulchan Aruch* (*Choshen Mishpat* 46:37) states that in both the clauses mentioned in this halachah, the legal document is allowed to stand and a judgment is rendered on its basis. This applies even if the witnesses repented for giving improper testimony. Nevertheless, since the witnesses admitted that they gave improper testimony, they are required to reimburse the litigant who suffered the loss.
47. As the Rambam states in *Hilchot Mechirah*, Chapter 10, when a person compels a person to sell property, the seller can nullify the sale by issuing a protest in which he states that he sold the property under duress. According to the Rambam, even if the witnesses know of that protest beforehand, it was still legitimate for them to have signed the deed of sale. Hence even if the validation of their signatures is not dependent on their word, their statements are accepted.
48. Thus if the condition is not fulfilled, the document will be nullified. Thus in effect,

found on other [legal documents].[49] If, however, the authenticity of the document could not be verified without their testimony, their statement is accepted[49] and we tell the litigants: "Fulfill the condition and then bring the matter to judgment."

10. If one of the witnesses says: "The transaction was made conditionally," and the other says, "There was no condition involved," there is [only] one witness who is [testifying].[50]

11. Also in laws involving financial matters,[51] we receive testimony only in the presence of the litigants.[52] If, however, the plaintiff was deathly ill[53] or the witnesses desired to travel overseas and the defendant was summoned[54] and yet did not come, we receive the testimony in his absence.[55]

When does the above[56] apply? To testimony given orally. The authenticity of the signatures of a legal document, by contrast, may be verified in the defendant's absence.[57] [Moreover,] even if the defendant is present and protests vociferously: "This document is a forgery," "They are false witnesses," or "They are unacceptable witnesses," we pay no heed to him. Instead, we verify the authenticity of the document. If [the defendant] brings proof[58] which disqualifies the document, it is disqualified.[59]

their testimony is nullifying the legal power of the document. Since the condition is not stated in the document, we assume that such a stipulation was not made and we accept their testimony only in the specific instance the Rambam mentions.

This reflects the opinion of the Rambam and his teacher's master, Rabbenu Yitzchak Alfasi. The Ra'avad takes issue with the matter, noting that other authorities ruled that the statements of the witnesses are accepted in all instances, even when the authenticity of the document could be verified without their testimony. The Radbaz notes that *Ketubot* 19b appears to support the Ra'avad's approach although it could be interpreted in a manner that fits the Rambam's interpretation. The *Shulchan Aruch* (*Choshen Mishpat* 46:37) quotes the Rambam's view. (In *Choshen Mishpat* 82:12, however, the *Shulchan Aruch* quotes the view of the Ra'avad. See the *Siftei Cohen* 82:34 who discusses the matter.)

49. Following the rationale explained in Halachah 6.

50. I.e., this is speaking about a situation where the authenticity of the document could be verified without the testimony of the witnesses. Therefore it is considered as if there are two witnesses who testify to the veracity of the legal document and one who states that a condition was involved. The statement of that witness is not of consequence (Radbaz).

The *Kessef Mishneh*, however, states that this is speaking about a situation where there are no other witnesses to verify the signatures of the witnesses. Hence, everything depends on the testimony of those witnesses. Since one of them does not testify that the legal document is valid - for he claims there is a condition involved - the document cannot be substantiated.

Thus there is one witness who claims that the transaction was ordinary and did not involve a condition (thus he supports the plaintiff's claim) and one who claims that it did. Since there is one witness in support of the plaintiff's claim, the defendant is required to take an oath to deny it. We do not free the defendant from that responsibility because of the testimony of the witness who claims that a condition was involved.

Although the *Shulchan Aruch* (*Choshen Mishpat* 46:37) quotes the Rambam's words

וְאִם אֵין הַשְּׁטָר מִתְקַיֵּם אֶלָּא מִפִּיהֶם – נֶאֱמָנִים. וְאוֹמֵר לְבַעֲלֵי הַדִּין: קַיְּמוּ הַתְּנַאי וּבוֹאוּ לָדוּן.

י אָמַר אֶחָד מִן הָעֵדִים: עַל תְּנַאי הָיוּ הַדְּבָרִים, וְהַשֵּׁנִי אוֹמֵר: לֹא הָיָה שָׁם תְּנַאי – הֲרֵי כָּאן עֵד אֶחָד.

יא גַּם בְּדִינֵי מָמוֹנוֹת אֵין מְקַבְּלִין עֵדוּת אֶלָּא בִּפְנֵי בַּעַל דִּין. אִם הָיָה בַּעַל דִּין חוֹלֶה, אוֹ שֶׁהָיוּ הָעֵדִים מְבַקְשִׁים לֵילֵךְ לִמְדִינַת הַיָּם וְשָׁלְחוּ לְבַעַל דִּין וְלֹא בָּא – הֲרֵי אֵלּוּ מְקַבְּלִים עֵדִים שֶׁלֹּא בְּפָנָיו.
בַּמֶּה דְּבָרִים אֲמוּרִים? בְּעֵדוּת עַל פֶּה; אֲבָל בִּשְׁטָר – מְקַיְּמִין בֵּית דִּין אֶת עֵדָיו שֶׁלֹּא בִּפְנֵי בַּעַל דִּין. וַאֲפִלּוּ הָיָה עוֹמֵד וְצוֹוֵחַ וְאוֹמֵר: שְׁטָר מְזֻיָּף הוּא! עֵדֵי שֶׁקֶר הֵן! פְּסוּלֵי עֵדוּת הֵן! – אֵין מַשְׁגִּיחִין בּוֹ; אֶלָּא מְקַיְּמִין אֶת הַשְּׁטָר, וְאִם יֵשׁ לוֹ רְאָיָה לִפְסֹל – יִפְסֹל.

when discussing these laws, both the *Sefer Me'irat Einayim* 46:101 and the *Siftei Cohen* 46:109 explain that he relies on his ruling (*Choshen Mishpat* 82:12) in which he states that if one witness states that there was a condition and the other says there was not, the defendant is required to take only a *sh'vuat hesset*.

51. I.e., the principle to be stated applies not only in cases involving capital punishment, but also with regard to those involving monetary law. Although there are differences with regard to other matters, with regard to this point, there is an equation between the two.

52. With regard to an ox suspected of killing a person, Exodus 21:29 states: "And testimony must be brought against its owner," i.e., in his presence. From that instance, we extrapolate to others (*Bava Kama* 112b). In an ordinary situation, if testimony is received in the absence of the opposing litigant, it is unacceptable [*Kessef Mishneh*; *Shulchan Aruch* (*Choshen Mishpat* 28:15)].

53. Testimony is received so that the case can be tried in the plaintiff's lifetime. In this way, he will be able to hear the testimony of the witnesses and point out certain factors. The *Shulchan Aruch* (*Choshen Mishpat* 28:16) states this leniency also applies when the witnesses are deathly ill. If the defendant is deathly ill, by contrast, we do not take this leniency. Even though this may require the suit to be pressed against the defendant's heirs (and thus there will be certain difficulties for the plaintiff), we do not allow the witnesses to testify in the defendant's absence.

54. I.e., first the defendant must be summoned. There is no concept of having testimony offered without him having the opportunity to be there and hear it firsthand.

55. The Radbaz states that if a summons was given him and he did not appear, the witnesses may testify in his absence even if they are not planning to travel overseas.

56. That ordinarily testimony must be given in the litigant's presence.

57. I.e., in all instances, even if the defendant is not sick or does not refuse to come to court. For as stated in Halachah 6, when witnesses sign on a legal document, it is as if their testimony was delivered in court. Hence their testimony is a closed issue. It makes no difference whether the defendant was present or not.

58. Witnesses who support his claim.

59. In *Hilchot Malveh ViLoveh* 22:2, the Rambam writes:

> [The following rules apply when the borrower] claims: "The promissory note concerning which [the signatures of the witnesses] was validated is a forgery. I will

12. Whenever [a plaintiff] has witnesses [who will testify] to prove [his claim], he must tend to the witnesses until he brings them to court. If the court knows that the defendant is a strong and stubborn person and the plaintiff claims that the witnesses are afraid[60] to come and testify on behalf of [the plaintiff], the court compels the defendant to bring the witnesses.[61] We adjudicate cases involving strong and stubborn people according to these and other analogous principles.[62]

CHAPTER FOUR

1. Both witnesses in cases involving capital punishment must see the person committing the transgression at the same time. They must deliver their testimony together, in the same court. These requirements do not apply with regard to cases involving financial matters.

What is implied? If while looking from one window, a [witness] saw [the person] commit the transgression and the other witness saw him from another window, their testimonies can be combined if they can see each other. If they cannot [see each other],[1] their testimonies cannot be combined. If a person who administered the warning[2] sees the witnesses and the witnesses see him,[3] even though [the witnesses] do not see each other, their testimony may be combined [because of] the person administering the warning.

[If they do not see the transgression at the same time, their testimony is not combined. For example,] the two witnesses were in one house and one stuck his head out of the window and saw [a person] perform a forbidden labor on the Sabbath and another person issue a warning. He then withdrew his head and the other witness stuck his head out of the same window and saw [the person commit the transgression]. Their [testimonies] cannot be combined[4] unless they both see [the transgression] at the same time.[5]

[The following laws apply when] two witnesses see [the transgressor] from one window, two other witnesses see him from another window, and there is a person who gives a warning in between. If some of them see each other, they are considered as one group of witnesses.[6] If they do not see each other

bring proof and nullify [the matter]. The witnesses are located in this and this place and their names are so and so and so and so." If it appears to the judges that there is substance to his words, a time is established in which he must bring his witnesses [to court]. If it appears to them that he is merely raising deceptive arguments and fallacious claims, they should tell him: "Pay." Afterwards, if he brings proof of his claim, [the money] should be returned to him.

60. The *Kessef Mishneh* explains that the Rambam's wording is precise. For this ruling to be followed the court must know that the defendant is strong and stubborn and the plaintiff must claim that the witnesses are afraid. The *Tur* and the Ramah (*Choshen Mishpat* 28:5) are more stringent and require the plaintiff to prove his claim that the witnesses are afraid.

61. Although we suspect that the witnesses will refrain from testifying out of dread, we do not suspect that they will lie on behalf of the defendant (*Bava Metzia* 39b).

יב כָּל מִי שֶׁיֵּשׁ לוֹ רְאָיָה בְּעֵדִים – מְטַפֵּל בָּעֵדִים עַד שֶׁיְּבִיאֵם לְבֵית דִּין.
וְאִם יָדְעוּ בֵּית דִּין שֶׁבַּעַל דִּינוֹ אַלָּם, וְטָעַן הַתּוֹבֵעַ שֶׁהָעֵדִים מִתְפַּחֲדִים מִבַּעַל דִּינוֹ שֶׁיָּבוֹאוּ וְיָעִידוּ לוֹ – הֲרֵי בֵּית דִּין כּוֹפִין אֶת בַּעַל דִּינוֹ שֶׁיָּבִיא הוּא הָעֵדִים.
וְכֵן כֹּל כַּיּוֹצֵא בִּדְבָרִים אֵלּוּ דָּנִין בָּהֶן לְאַלָּם.

פֶּרֶק רְבִיעִי

א עֵדֵי נְפָשׁוֹת צְרִיכִין שֶׁיִּהְיוּ שְׁנֵיהֶם רוֹאִים אֶת הָעוֹשֶׂה עֲבֵרָה כְּאֶחָד.
וּצְרִיכִין לְהָעִיד כְּאֶחָד, וּבְבֵית דִּין אֶחָד. אֲבָל דִּינֵי מָמוֹנוֹת אֵין צְרִיכִין לְכָךְ.
כֵּיצַד? הָיָה אֶחָד רוֹאֵהוּ מֵחַלּוֹן זֶה כְּשֶׁעָבַר הָעֲבֵרָה, וְהָעֵד הָאַחֵר רוֹאֵהוּ מֵחַלּוֹן אַחֵר: אִם הָיוּ שְׁנֵי הָעֵדִים רוֹאִין זֶה אֶת זֶה – מִצְטָרְפִין, וְאִם לָאו – אֵין מִצְטָרְפִין.
הָיָה זֶה הַמַּתְרֶה בּוֹ רוֹאֶה הָעֵדִים, וְהָעֵדִים רוֹאִין אוֹתוֹ, אַף עַל פִּי שֶׁאֵין רוֹאִין זֶה אֶת זֶה – הַמַּתְרֶה מְצָרְפָן.
הָיוּ שְׁנֵי הָעֵדִים בְּבַיִת אֶחָד, וְהוֹצִיא אֶחָד מֵהֶן רֹאשׁוֹ מִן הַחַלּוֹן, וְרָאָהוּ זֶה שֶׁעוֹשֶׂה מְלָאכָה בְּשַׁבָּת וְאֶחָד מַתְרֶה בּוֹ, וְהִכְנִיס רֹאשׁוֹ, וְחָזַר הָעֵד הַשֵּׁנִי וְהוֹצִיא רֹאשׁוֹ מֵאוֹתוֹ הַחַלּוֹן וְרָאָהוּ – אֵין מִצְטָרְפִין, עַד שֶׁיִּרְאוּ שְׁנֵיהֶם כְּאֶחָד.
הָיוּ שְׁנֵי עֵדִים רוֹאִין אוֹתוֹ מֵחַלּוֹן זֶה, וּשְׁנֵי עֵדִים רוֹאִין אוֹתוֹ מֵחַלּוֹן אַחֵר, וְאֶחָד מַתְרֶה בּוֹ בָּאֶמְצַע: בִּזְמַן שֶׁמִּקְצָתָן רוֹאִין אֵלּוּ אֶת אֵלּוּ – הֲרֵי זוֹ עֵדוּת אַחַת;

In his commentary to that passage, Rashi states that unless the witnesses testify in support of the defendant, the plaintiff's claim is vindicated. *Tosafot* (*Ketubot* 27b) differs and maintains that unless the witnesses support the plaintiff's claim, the defendant is released from obligation.

62. The *Kessef Mishneh* states that although this ruling is somewhat discriminatory, for it puts the strong and stubborn people at a disadvantage, it is desirable that they feel this compulsion, so that they repent and give up their undesirable paths of conduct.

1. Even if they both see the violator perform the transgression.
2. For capital punishment to be administered, a person must administer a warning and the transgressor must acknowledge it as stated in *Hilchot Sanhedrin* 12:2.
3. The standard version of *Makkot, loc. cit.*, reads: "If [the witnesses] see the person administering the warning or the person administering the warning sees the witnesses." It appears, however, that the Rambam's version of the text stated "and" instead of "or."
4. Despite the fact that they both saw the person commit the same transgression.
5. *Makkot* 6b derives this concept from the exegesis of Deuteronomy 17:6: "One should not die on the basis of the testimony of one witness." Implied is that seeing the transgression one by one is also insufficient.
6. And if one of the witnesses is disqualified, the entire testimony is nullified, even though there are two acceptable witnesses who observed the transgression.

and the person giving the warning does not include them together, they are considered as two groups of witnesses. Therefore if one group are discovered to be *zomamim*,[7] [the transgressor] and [the witnesses] are executed. For [the transgressor] is executed on the basis of the testimony of the second group [of witnesses].

2. With regard to cases involving financial matters, by contrast, even though they did not see each other, their testimony can be combined.[8]

What is implied? One witness said: "In my presence, he lent him [money] on this-and-this day" or "In my presence, he acknowledged [a debt]," and the second witness says: "I also testify that he lent him money" or "...acknowledged [a debt]" on a different day, their testimony can be combined.[9]

3. Similarly, if one witness states: "He gave a loan in my presence," and the other said: "He acknowledged [a debt] in my presence,"[10] or the first said: "He acknowledged [a debt] in my presence," and the other testified afterwards, saying: "He gave a loan in my presence," their testimony can be combined.[11]

4. Similar concepts [apply with regard to] the time of their testimony in court. One may come on one day and [the court] will hear his testimony and the other may come at a later date and have his testimony heard. The testimonies may be combined and money expropriated on this basis.

5. Similarly, if the testimony of one witness was recorded [in a legal document] and the other testified orally, their testimony may be combined.[12] If the witness who did not record his testimony states: "I entered into an act of contract with him concerning this matter,[13] but the lender did not come and ask me to record my testimony [in a legal document]," the two can join together to [give the claim the status of] a loan backed by a promissory note.[14] [The borrower] may not claim: "I repaid the debt."

6. [The following laws apply in cases involving financial matters.] If one witness delivered testimony[15] in one court and the other witness delivered testimony in a second court, the two courts should come together and

7. Witnesses who conspire and testify falsely. When their testimony is disproved, they are given the punishment that they intended to have given the intended victim.
8. This concept also applies with regard to testimony regarding prohibitions [Ramah (*Choshen Mishpat* 30:6)].
9. For both of them are testifying that he owes him money.

As the *Shulchan Aruch* (*Choshen Mishpat* 30:7) states, their testimony is combined only when the plaintiff claims to have given two loans. If, however, he claims to have given only one loan, their testimony is unacceptable, as evident from Chapter 3, Halachah 3.

10. In this instance, it is possible that the two witnesses are speaking about the same debt.
11. Here it appears that although the testimony was given afterwards, the loan concerning

וְאִם לֹא הָיוּ רוֹאִין אֵלּוּ אֶת אֵלּוּ וְלֹא צֵרַף אוֹתָן הַמַּתְרֶה - הֲרֵי אֵלּוּ שְׁתֵּי עֵדֻיּוֹת. לְפִיכָךְ, אִם נִמְצֵאת כַּת אַחַת מֵהֶן זוֹמְמִין - הוּא וָהֵן נֶהֱרָגִין, שֶׁהֲרֵי הוּא נֶהֱרָג בְּעֵדוּת הַכַּת הַשְּׁנִיָּה.

ב אֲבָל בְּדִינֵי מָמוֹנוֹת, אַף עַל פִּי שֶׁלֹּא רָאוּ אֵלּוּ אֶת אֵלּוּ - עֵדוּתָן מִצְטָרֶפֶת. כֵּיצַד? אָמַר הָאֶחָד: בְּפָנַי הִלְוָהוּ בְּיוֹם פְּלוֹנִי, אוֹ בְּפָנַי הוֹדָה לוֹ, וְאָמַר הָעֵד הַשֵּׁנִי: וְכֵן אֲנִי מֵעִיד שֶׁהִלְוָהוּ בְּפָנַי אוֹ הוֹדָה בְּיוֹם אַחֵר - הֲרֵי אֵלּוּ מִצְטָרְפִין.

ג וְכֵן אִם אָמַר הָאֶחָד: בְּפָנַי הִלְוָהוּ, וְהַשֵּׁנִי אוֹמֵר: בְּפָנַי הוֹדָה לוֹ; אוֹ שֶׁאָמַר הָרִאשׁוֹן: בְּפָנַי הוֹדָה, וְהַשֵּׁנִי שֶׁהֵעִיד אַחַר זְמַן אָמַר: בְּפָנַי הִלְוָהוּ - הֲרֵי אֵלּוּ מִצְטָרְפִין.

ד וְכֵן בְּעֵת שֶׁמְּעִידִין בְּבֵית דִּין - יָבוֹא אֶחָד וְשׁוֹמְעִין דְּבָרָיו הַיּוֹם, וּכְשֶׁיָּבוֹא הָעֵד הַשֵּׁנִי לְאַחַר זְמַן - שׁוֹמְעִין דְּבָרָיו. וּמִצְטָרְפִין זֶה לָזֶה, וּמוֹצִיאִין בָּהֶן הַמָּמוֹן.

ה וְכֵן אִם הָיָה עֵד אֶחָד בִּכְתָב וְאֶחָד עַל פֶּה - מִצְטָרְפִין. וְאִם אָמַר זֶה שֶׁלֹּא כָּתַב עֵדוּתוֹ: אֲנִי קָנִיתִי מִיָּדוֹ עַל דָּבָר זֶה, וְלֹא בָּא הַמַּלְוֶה הַזֶּה וְלֹא שָׁאַל מִמֶּנִּי לִכְתֹּב - שְׁנֵיהֶם מִצְטָרְפִין לַעֲשׂוֹת הַמִּלְוָה בִּשְׁטָר, וְאֵינוֹ יָכוֹל לוֹמַר פָּרַעְתִּי.

ו הֵעִיד הָאֶחָד בְּבֵית דִּין זֶה, וְהָעֵד הַשֵּׁנִי בְּבֵית דִּין אַחֵר - יָבוֹא בֵּית דִּין אֵצֶל בֵּית דִּין וְיִצְטָרְפוּ עֵדוּתָן.

which he testifies must have been given before the first admission of the debt. Otherwise, the plaintiff must demand payment of two accounts as above (*Kessef Mishneh*).
12. And the borrower's word is not accepted if he claims never to have made the loan.
13. For when an act of contract is performed, the witness would have the right to record his statements in a legal document at any time; see *Hilchot Malveh ViLoveh* 23:5-6.
14. In his *Kessef Mishneh*, Rav Yosef Karo notes that the *Tur* (*Choshen Mishpat* 51) states that the document composed has the full status of a promissory note and can be used to expropriate landed property from people who purchased it from the borrower. The *Kessef Mishneh* differs and maintains that since neither the act of contract nor the original document was witnessed by two people, the document ultimately composed does not have the full power of a legal document and cannot be used to expropriate property. It is valuable only to negate the claim of the borrower if he asserts that he paid the debt. Significantly, in his *Shulchan Aruch* (*Choshen Mishpat* 51:1), Rav Yosef Karo rules according to the perspective of the *Tur*.
The *Perishah* (*Choshen Mishpat* 51) notes a difficulty with the *Kessef Mishneh's* interpretation, for in *Hilchot Malveh ViLoveh* 14:10, the Rambam writes that even when only one witness signs a promissory note, we do not accept the borrower's word if he claims to have repaid the debt. In resolution, the *Perishah* explains that in *Hilchot Malveh ViLoveh*, the borrower's word is accepted if he takes an oath to support his claim, while in this halachah, he is not given that option.
15. Concerning a loan, an admission of debt, or the like.

combine the testimonies.[16] Similarly, if two witnesses delivered testimony in one court[17] and then delivered testimony in another court, a member of either court can join together [with a member of the other court].[18] [The statements of] a witness and a judge before whom two witnesses testified[19] may not be combined.[20]

7. Although testimony [of two witnesses] may be combined in matters of financial law,[21] each of the witnesses must deliver testimony concerning an entire matter, as we explained.[22] If, by contrast, one witness testifies concerning a portion of a matter and the other witness testifies concerning another portion of the matter, we do not establish the matter on the basis of their testimony, as [indicated by Deuteronomy 19:15]: "According to the testimony of two witnesses shall the matter be established."

What is implied? One witness testifies that a person benefited from a field one year, another testifies that he benefited in the following year, and a third testifies that he benefited in the third year, the testimonies of the three cannot be linked together to say that he benefited for three years. For each of them testified only about a portion of the matter.[23]

Similarly, if one witness testifies: "I saw one hair on [the person's] right side," and another witness testifies: "I saw one hair on the person's left side," their testimonies are not linked together so that we can say that two people testified that [the person concerned] manifested signs of physical maturity on that particular day. For each of them testified only about a portion of the physical signs [required].[24] Even if two witnesses testified that [they saw] one hair and two other witnesses testified that they saw another hair, [their testimony is of no consequence]. Since they both testified about only half the matter,[25] this is not [acceptable] testimony.

If, however, one [witness] testified that he saw two hairs on [the person's] right side and another witness testified that he saw two hairs on [the person's] left side, their testimony can be linked together.[26] Similar concepts apply in all analogous situations.

16. Since each witness delivered his testimony before a court of law, it is acceptable. The courts, however, must come together as an entire body. It is not sufficient for some members of one court to join together with some members of the other. Nor is it sufficient for witnesses to testify that they heard these witnesses testify, for that would be indirect testimony which is unacceptable [Ramah (*Choshen Mishpat* 30:11)].

17. *Bava Batra* 165b interprets this as referring to an instance when witnesses testified concerning the validity of a promissory note, but the judges journeyed overseas before rendering a decision.

18. More specifically, one member of one court may join together with two members of another court. *Bava Batra, loc. cit.*, and the *Shulchan Aruch* (*Choshen Mishpat* 30:12) speak of the witnesses offering testimony in three different courts. Thus the expression "one judge from each court can join together" is more appropriate.

The judges from the different courts can join together, because each court heard testimony from two witnesses and thus has enough evidence on which to base a ruling. In the first clause, by contrast, each court heard only the testimony of one witness and thus does not have sufficient evidence on which to base a ruling (*Sefer Me'irat Einayim* 30:34).

וְכֵן אִם הֵעִידוּ שְׁנֵי הָעֵדִים בְּבֵית דִּין זֶה, וְחָזְרוּ וְהֵעִידוּ בְּבֵית דִּין אַחֵר – יָבוֹא אֶחָד מִכָּל בֵּית דִּין וְיִצְטָרְפוּ. אֲבָל הָעֵד עִם הַדַּיָּן שֶׁהֵעִידוּ שְׁנֵי הָעֵדִים בְּפָנָיו – אֵין מִצְטָרְפִין.

ז אַף עַל פִּי שֶׁמִּצְטָרְפִין הָעֵדוּת בְּדִינֵי מָמוֹנוֹת, צָרִיךְ שֶׁיָּעִיד כָּל אֶחָד מִשְּׁנֵיהֶם בְּכָל דָּבָר, כְּמוֹ שֶׁבֵּאַרְנוּ. אֲבָל אִם הֵעִיד עֵד אֶחָד בְּמִקְצָת דָּבָר, וְהֵעִיד הַשֵּׁנִי בְּמִקְצָתוֹ – אֵין מְקַיְּמִין הַדָּבָר מֵעֵדוּת שְׁנֵיהֶם. שֶׁנֶּאֱמַר: עַל פִּי שְׁנַיִם עֵדִים יָקוּם דָּבָר. כֵּיצַד? זֶה אוֹמֵר: פְּלוֹנִי אָכַל שָׂדֶה זוֹ שָׁנָה פְּלוֹנִית, וְזֶה הֵעִיד שֶׁאֲכָלָהּ שָׁנָה שְׁנִיָּה, וְזֶה הֵעִיד שֶׁאֲכָלָהּ שָׁנָה שְׁלִישִׁית – אֵין מִצְטָרְפִין עֵדוּת שְׁלָשְׁתָּן וְאוֹמְרִים: הֲרֵי אֲכָלָהּ שָׁלֹשׁ שָׁנִים; שֶׁכָּל אֶחָד וְאֶחָד הֵעִיד בְּמִקְצָת הַדָּבָר. וְכֵן אִם הֵעִיד זֶה: אֲנִי רָאִיתִי שַׂעֲרָה אַחַת בְּצַד יְמִינוֹ שֶׁל זֶה, וְזֶה אוֹמֵר: אֲנִי רָאִיתִי שַׂעֲרָה אַחַת בְּצַד שְׂמֹאלוֹ שֶׁל זֶה בְּאוֹתוֹ הַיּוֹם – אֵין מִצְטָרְפִין דִּבְרֵי שְׁנֵיהֶם כְּדֵי שֶׁנֹּאמַר: הֲרֵי הֵעִידוּ שְׁנֵיהֶם שֶׁהָיָה זֶה גָּדוֹל בְּיוֹם פְּלוֹנִי; לְפִי שֶׁכָּל אֶחָד מֵהֶם לֹא הֵעִיד אֶלָּא בְּמִקְצָת הַסִּימָנִין. אֲפִלּוּ הֵעִידוּ שְׁנַיִם בְּשַׂעֲרָה אַחַת, וְהֵעִידוּ שְׁנַיִם בְּשַׂעֲרָה אַחֶרֶת; שֶׁהֲרֵי כָּל כַּת מֵהֶם הֵעִידָה עַל חֲצִי דָּבָר, וְאֵין זוֹ עֵדוּת. אֲבָל אִם הֵעִידָה הָאַחַת שֶׁרָאֲתָה שְׁתֵּי שְׂעָרוֹת בְּצַד יָמִין, וְהֵעִידָה הַשְּׁנִיָּה שֶׁרָאֲתָה שְׁתֵּי שְׂעָרוֹת בְּצַד שְׂמֹאל – מִצְטָרְפִין. וְכֵן כֹּל כַּיּוֹצֵא בּוֹ.

19. The witness will testify before the new court which will include one of the judges from the old court.
20. For all of the judges on the court rendering the decision did not hear two witnesses offer testimony concerning the debt. Instead, the witness is testifying concerning the debt and the judge is testifying that he heard witnesses testifying concerning the debt [Rashi (*Ketubot* 21a)].
21. From this preface, the *Kessef Mishneh* concludes that the principles the Rambam states apply only with regard to financial matters, and not with regard to questions concerning marriage and divorce, nor with regard to cases involving capital punishment.
22. *Hilchot Toein ViNitan* 15:2.
23. For a claim of possession to landed property to be established, witnesses must testify that the person benefited from the property for three consecutive years (*Hilchot Toein ViNitan* 11:2). In this instance, none of the witnesses can testify about the entire three year period. Hence their testimony is of no consequence.
24. For a person to be considered an adult, a woman of 12 years and one day and a man of 13 years and one day must manifest signs of physical maturity, i.e., they must have two pubic hairs. If they do not manifest such signs of maturity, they are still considered minors. This concept has manifold consequences with regard to the laws concerning financial matters. Needless to say, it is also significant with regard to the laws concerning marriage and divorce and the laws involving punishment for transgression (*Kessef Mishneh*).

Two witnesses must testify that the person in question did in fact manifest such signs of physical maturity. In the instance cited by the Rambam, the testimony of the witnesses is not acceptable, because neither of them gave testimony that could serve as the basis to say that the person manifested signs of physical maturity. They mentioned only half the required information. See also Chapter 21, Halachah 7, and notes.
25. For one hair in and of itself is of no consequence.
26. For each of them is delivering testimony that is, in and of itself, complete. Compare to Halachah 3 and Chapter 3, Halachah 3.

CHAPTER FIVE

1. A ruling is never delivered in any judgment on the basis of the testimony of one witness, neither in cases involving financial law, nor in cases involving capital punishment, as [Deuteronomy 19:15] states: "One witness should not stand up against any person with regard to any transgression or any sin."[1] According to the Oral Tradition,[2] we learned that his testimony is effective with regard to an oath,[3] as stated in *Hilchot Toein ViNitan*.[4]

2. In two situations, the Torah accepted the testimony of one witness:
a) with regard to a *sotah*,[5] so that she does not drink the bitter waters;[6] and
b) with regard to a calf whose neck is broken,[7] to prevent its neck from being broken, as we explained.[8]

Similarly, according to Rabbinic Law, [we accept the testimony of one witness] with regard to testimony concerning a woman, if he testifies that her husband died.[9]

3. Whenever the testimony of one witness is effective, a woman and a person disqualified [as a witness][10] may also testify.[11] [There is, however,] an exception: a witness who requires that an oath be taken. We do not require that an oath be taken except on the basis of testimony that is acceptable and fit to be joined with the testimony of another person to obligate the person taking the oath to make financial restitution.[12]

1. *Sefer HaMitzvot* (negative commandment 288) and *Sefer HaChinuch* (mitzvah 523) count this as one of the 613 mitzvot of the Torah.
2. See *Sifri* to the above verse; *Sh'vuot* 40a.
3. If the plaintiff's claim is supported by the testimony of one witness, the defendant is required to take an oath if he denies the claim.
4. Chapter 1, Halachah 1.
5. A woman suspected of adultery. See Numbers, ch. 5; *Hilchot Sotah*.
6. I.e., if one witness testifies that he observed her infidelity, she is forced to accept a divorce. She may not drink the waters to prove her innocence. The commentaries explain the rationale for this exception as follows: Since a warning was issued and disobeyed, there is a great likelihood that she was indeed guilty of infidelity. Therefore all testimony is acceptable.
7. To atone for a murder when the identity of the murderer is unknown. See Deuteronomy, ch. 21; *Hilchot Rotzeach*, ch. 9.
8. As *Hilchot Rotzeach* 9:12 states, if one witness says that he saw the murder, we do not bring this unique atonement offering. For that offering was ordained only when no one at all knew the identity of the murderer, as indicated by Deuteronomy 21:1 (Radbaz).
9. A woman may not remarry until it is established that her previous husband died. The testimony of one witness is acceptable regarding this matter. As the Rambam states in *Hilchot Gerushin* 12:15: "If one witness comes and testifies that a woman's husband died, she is granted permission to marry by virtue of his testimony, because [the truth of] the matter will ultimately be revealed," i.e., if the husband is alive, that fact will surface in the near future. Hence there is no fundamental need for testimony.

פֶּרֶק חֲמִישִׁי

א אֵין חוֹתְכִין דִּין מִן הַדִּינִין עַל פִּי עֵד אֶחָד, לֹא דִינֵי מָמוֹנוֹת וְלֹא דִינֵי נְפָשׁוֹת. שֶׁנֶּאֱמַר: לֹא יָקוּם עֵד אֶחָד בְּאִישׁ לְכָל עָוֹן וּלְכָל חַטָּאת. וּמִפִּי הַשְּׁמוּעָה לָמַדְנוּ שֶׁקָּם הוּא לִשְׁבוּעָה, כְּמוֹ שֶׁבֵּאַרְנוּ בְּהִלְכוֹת טוֹעֵן.

ב בִּשְׁנֵי מְקוֹמוֹת הֶאֱמִינָה תּוֹרָה עֵד אֶחָד: בְּסוֹטָה שֶׁלֹּא תִּשְׁתֶּה מֵי מָרִים, וּבְעֶגְלָה עֲרוּפָה שֶׁלֹּא תֵּעָרֵף, כְּמוֹ שֶׁבֵּאַרְנוּ. וְכֵן מִדִּבְרֵיהֶן, בְּעֵדוּת אִשָּׁה שֶׁיָּעִיד לָהּ שֶׁמֵּת בַּעְלָהּ.

ג וְכָל מָקוֹם שֶׁעֵד אֶחָד מוֹעִיל, אִשָּׁה וּפָסוּל כְּמוֹ כֵן מְעִידִים. חוּץ מֵעֵד אֶחָד שֶׁל שְׁבוּעָה, שֶׁאֵין מְחַיְּבִין שְׁבוּעָה אֶלָּא בְּעֵדוּת כָּשֵׁר, הָרָאוּי לְהִצְטָרֵף עִם אַחֵר וְיִתְחַיֵּב זֶה הַנִּשְׁבָּע מָמוֹן עַל פִּיו.

The Rambam's statements here, however, appear to be slightly contradictory to his statements at the conclusion of *Hilchot Gerushin* (13:5):

> Do not wonder at the fact that our Sages released the prohibition [against marriage to a married woman]... on the basis of the testimony of a woman, a servant or a maidservant.... [These leniencies were instituted] because the Torah requires the testimony of two witnesses... only with regard to matters that cannot be verified definitively except via witnesses and their testimony, e.g., one person killed another or one person lent money to another.
>
> When, by contrast, the matter may be verified definitively without the testimony of a witness and the witness cannot justify [his statements] if they are not true, e.g., in an instance such as this when one testifies that a person died, the Torah did not require [formal testimony].
>
> For this reason, our Sages ruled leniently with regard to this matter and accepted the testimony of one witness that is based on the testimony of a maidservant, [testimony] from a written document, and [testimony] that was not investigated by the ordinary process of interrogation. [These leniencies were instituted] so that the daughters of Israel will not be forced to remain unmarried.

The *Noda BiY'hudah* (*Even HaEzer*, Vol. I, Responsa 27 and 33) interprets the Rambam's statements as meaning that according to Scriptural Law, the testimony of one witness is sufficient (as in *Hilchot Kiddush HaChodesh* 3:14 and *Hilchot Yibbum VaChalitzah* 4:31). Our Sages extended that leniency and also accepted the testimony of one witness based on the testimony of another witness and even one witness based on the testimony of a maid-servant. For as the Rambam states, in these instances, formal testimony is not necessary. His interpretation is, however, difficult to accept in the light of the Rambam's statements here.

10. See Chapters 9-16 which describe the reasons why a person may be disqualified from testifying as a witness.

11. When the testimony of one witness is effective, the requirements of formal testimony are not enforced. Hence, even persons who are otherwise disqualified may offer that information. There are, however, restrictions. A person who is known to be a robber is not accepted as a witness even in these circumstances (*Hilchot Gerushin* 12:17).

12. For the obligation to take an oath mandated by the testimony of one witness is

[Deuteronomy 19:15] states:[13] "On [the basis of] the testimony of two witnesses or on [the basis of] the testimony of three witnesses...," establishing [an equation between] three witnesses and two witnesses. Just as when there are two witnesses, if one of them is discovered to be a relative[14] or unfit to deliver testimony, the entire testimony is nullified; so, too, if there are three - or even 100 - witnesses and one of them is discovered to be a relative or unfit to deliver testimony, the entire testimony is nullified.[15] [This applies] both in matters involving financial law and in cases involving capital punishment.

4. When does the above apply? When all of the [potential] witnesses had the intent of delivering testimony. If, however, they did not all intend to deliver testimony, [the testimony will not be nullified]. What should two brothers do when they are together with other people and they and the others see a person murder a colleague, injure him, or grab an article from his hand?[16]

5. How do we investigate the matter? When many witnesses come to the court as a single group, we ask them: "When you saw this person kill or injure was your intent to serve as a witness or merely to observe?"[17] All those who say that their intent was not to serve as a witness, but instead they came merely to observe the matter as part of people at large are set aside.[18] And all those who say: "I stood [and took notice] solely for the purpose of serving as a witness and being precise in my testimony," are set aside. If a relative or an unacceptable witness is found among those who intended to deliver testimony, the entire testimony is nullified.[19]

When does the above apply? When a relative or an unacceptable witness was present. If, however, they are all acceptable to serve as witnesses, their testimony is [taken into account] whether they intended to serve as witnesses or not. Since they observed the matter, related the particulars of the testimony, and a warning was given [the transgressor],[20] the matter is adjudicated on this basis.[21] [This applies] both in matters involving financial law and in cases involving capital punishment.

comparable to the financial obligation created by the testimony of two witnesses. Hence all the requirements of formal testimony are required.

13. In some manuscript copies and early printings of the *Mishneh Torah*, this marks the beginning of Halachah 4.

14. I.e., related to the other witnesses or to one of the involved parties.

15. For the witnesses are considered as a single group.

16. I.e., certainly the fact that the brothers were both present should not prevent justice from being done and the offender from being prosecuted.

17. The *Sefer Me'irat Einayim* 36:2 states that according to the Rambam [and the *Shulchan Aruch* (*Choshen Mishpat* 36:1)], this question is addressed to all the witnesses who come to testify, not only the relatives. In this way, the unacceptable witnesses will not feel that they are under suspicion and will answer genuinely. Rashi and the *Tur* (*Choshen Mishpat* 36) differ and maintain that this question is asked only of the unacceptable witnesses.

עַל פִּי שְׁנַיִם עֵדִים אוֹ עַל פִּי שְׁלֹשָׁה עֵדִים – לַעֲשׂוֹת שְׁלֹשָׁה כִּשְׁנַיִם: מַה שְּׁנַיִם, נִמְצָא אֶחָד מֵהֶן קָרוֹב אוֹ פָּסוּל – בָּטְלָה הָעֵדוּת; אַף שְׁלֹשָׁה, וְהוּא הַדִּין לְמֵאָה, נִמְצָא אֶחָד מֵהֶן קָרוֹב אוֹ פָּסוּל – בָּטְלָה הָעֵדוּת. בֵּין בְּדִינֵי מָמוֹנוֹת, בֵּין בְּדִינֵי נְפָשׁוֹת.

ד בַּמֶּה דְּבָרִים אֲמוּרִים? בִּזְמַן שֶׁנִּתְכַּוְּנוּ כֻּלָּן לְהָעִיד; אֲבָל אִם לֹא נִתְכַּוְּנוּ כֻּלָּם לְהָעִיד – מַה יַּעֲשׂוּ שְׁנֵי אַחִים בִּכְלַל הָעָם, וְרָאוּ הָעָם כְּשֶׁהָרַג זֶה אֶת זֶה, אוֹ כְּשֶׁחָבַל בּוֹ, אוֹ כְּשֶׁחָטַף חֵפֶץ מִיָּדוֹ.

ה וְכֵיצַד בּוֹדְקִין אֶת הַדָּבָר? כְּשֶׁיָּבוֹאוּ לְבֵית דִּין עֵדִים מְרֻבִּין כַּת אַחַת, אוֹמֵר לָהֶם: כְּשֶׁרְאִיתֶם זֶה שֶׁהָרַג אוֹ חָבַל, לְהָעִיד בָּאתֶם אוֹ לִרְאוֹת? כָּל מִי שֶׁאוֹמֵר: לֹא לְהָעִיד עָלָיו, אֶלָּא לִרְאוֹת מָה הַדָּבָר, וּבִכְלַל הָעָם בָּאתִי – מַפְרִישִׁין אוֹתוֹ. וְכָל מִי שֶׁאוֹמֵר: לֹא הָיִיתִי עוֹמֵד אֶלָּא לְהָעִיד וּלְכַוֵּן הָעֵדוּת – מַפְרִישִׁין אוֹתוֹ. אִם נִמְצָא בְּאֵלּוּ שֶׁנִּתְכַּוְּנוּ לְהָעִיד קָרוֹב אוֹ פָּסוּל – עֵדוּת כֻּלָּם בְּטֵלָה. בַּמֶּה דְּבָרִים אֲמוּרִים? כְּשֶׁהָיָה בָּהֶן קָרוֹב אוֹ פָּסוּל; אֲבָל אִם כֻּלָּם כְּשֵׁרִים – אֶחָד שֶׁנִּתְכַּוֵּן לְהָעִיד אוֹ שֶׁלֹּא נִתְכַּוֵּן לְהָעִיד, הוֹאִיל וְרָאָה הַדָּבָר וְכִוֵּן עֵדוּתוֹ וְהָיָה שָׁם הַתְרָאָה, חוֹתְכִין הַדִּין עַל פִּיו. בֵּין בְּדִינֵי מָמוֹנוֹת, בֵּין בְּדִינֵי נְפָשׁוֹת.

18. Rabbenu Asher and the *Tur* (*loc. cit.*) follow a slightly different perspective and maintain that relatives are not disqualified unless they both observed the matter and came to court with the intent of testifying. If, however, they merely observed the matter with the intent of testifying, that is not sufficient to disqualify the testimony.

The *Shulchan Aruch* (*loc. cit.*) quotes both of these views without indicating which is to be given precedence. It also states that if acceptable witnesses are set aside for that purpose by the involved parties, they are not disqualified even if there are non-acceptable witnesses who observed the event with the intent to testify.

According to all views, there is a difficulty, for seemingly, the relatives of a killer could protect him by coming to court with the acceptable witnesses and saying they observed the matter with the intent of serving as witnesses. In this way, they would disqualify the acceptable witnesses and enable the killer to be released. Although several resolutions to this difficulty have been offered, the matter remains problematic.

19. I.e., even if the non-acceptable witnesses did not actually testify. Since they intended to testify, all of the witnesses are considered part of a single group. Hence they are all disqualified (*Sefer Me'irat Einayim* 36:4).

The Ramah (*Choshen Mishpat* 36:1) states that this restriction applies even when the witnesses do not know of each other's existence. The *Sefer Me'irat Einayim* 36:5 questions if the Rambam would also accept this ruling.

20. See *Hilchot Sanhedrin* 12:2.

21. Thus according to the Rambam [and his opinion is accepted by the *Shulchan Aruch* (*loc. cit.*)], it is not necessary for a person who observes an event to watch with the intent of serving as a witness. Even if he decides to serve as a witness afterwards, as long as he can describe the particulars precisely, his testimony is acceptable.

6. [The following laws apply when there is] a legal document with many witnesses and one of them is discovered to be a relative[22] or unacceptable or two of them are related to each other and the witnesses are not alive so that they could be asked [whether they intended to sign as witnesses or not].[23] If there is definitive testimony that they all sat down with the intent of signing - i.e., they intended to give testimony - [the document] is unacceptable.[24] If not, the testimony may be maintained on the basis of the other witnesses.

Why may the testimony be maintained on the basis of the other witnesses?[25] Because it is possible that the acceptable witnesses signed and left a place for a person of stature to sign and the relative or the unacceptable witness signed without them knowing.[26]

7. Even though an unacceptable witness is the first whose signature appears on the legal document, the document is acceptable.[27]

8. Whenever a witness delivers testimony in a case involving capital punishment, he may not rule [as a judge] with regard to this murder.[28] He may not offer an opinion in favor of [the accused's] acquittal or conviction. If he states: "I have a rationale that should lead to his acquittal, he is silenced, as [implied by Numbers 35:30]: "One witness shall not make a statement with regard to a case involving capital punishment," [i.e., his words are not accepted] neither for acquittal, nor for conviction.[29]

What is the intent of the phrase "involving capital punishment"? That once a witness testifies with regard to capital punishment, he should make no further statements. He should deliver his testimony and be silent. With regard to cases involving financial matters, he may, however, offer an opinion leading to the defendant being released from financial liability or being held liable. He may not, however, be counted among the judges or serve as a judge.[30] For a witness may not serve as a judge.[31] [This applies even] in cases involving financial matters.

22. Of either of the principles.

23. For as is evident from the continuation of the Rambam's statements, it is possible that the unacceptable witnesses signed merely to fill up the space on the legal document without intending to serve as witnesses. Hence if the witnesses say that they all signed together, the legal document is nullified. If they say that the unacceptable witness signed afterwards, the document is acceptable.

The *Kessef Mishneh* questions how the statements of the witnesses can be used to nullify the legal document. Seemingly, this contradicts the decision rendered previously in Chapter 3, Halachah 7, that once the validity of the signatures on a legal document have been verified, the witnesses cannot nullify the document through their testimony. The *Kessef Mishneh* explains that in this instance, the statements of the witnesses are accepted, because a question was already raised concerning the validity of the legal document.

24. Because the unacceptable witnesses signed with the intent of testifying.

25. After all, non-acceptable witnesses signed the document.

26. Hence the later signatures are not considered part of the original testimony and do not

ו שְׁטָר שֶׁהָיוּ עֵדָיו מְרֻבִּין, וְנִמְצָא אֶחָד מֵהֶן קָרוֹב אוֹ פָּסוּל, אוֹ שֶׁהָיוּ בָּהֶם שְׁנַיִם קְרוֹבִים זֶה לָזֶה, וַהֲרֵי אֵין הָעֵדִים קַיָּמִין כְּדֵי לִשְׁאֹל אוֹתָן: אִם יֵשׁ שָׁם עֵדוּת בְּרוּרָה שֶׁכֻּלָּם יָשְׁבוּ לַחְתֹּם, שֶׁהֲרֵי נִתְכַּוְּנוּ לְהָעִיד - הֲרֵי זֶה בָּטֵל; וְאִם לָאו - תִּתְקַיֵּם הָעֵדוּת בַּשְּׁאָר. וְלָמָּה מְקַיְּמִין הָעֵדוּת בַּשְּׁאָר? שֶׁהֲרֵי אֶפְשָׁר שֶׁחָתְמוּ הַכְּשֵׁרִים וְהִנִּיחוּ מָקוֹם לַגָּדוֹל לַחְתֹּם, וּבָא זֶה הַקָּרוֹב אוֹ הַפָּסוּל וְחָתַם שֶׁלֹּא מִדַּעְתָּם.

ז אַף עַל פִּי שֶׁהָעֵד שֶׁחָתוּם מִתְּחִלָּה בַּשְּׁטָר הוּא הַפָּסוּל - הֲרֵי הַשְּׁטָר כָּשֵׁר.

ח כָּל עֵד שֶׁהֵעִיד בְּדִינֵי נְפָשׁוֹת - אֵינוֹ מוֹרֶה בְּדִין זֶה הַנֶּהֱרָג, וְלֹא יְלַמֵּד עָלָיו לֹא זְכוּת וְלֹא חוֹבָה. וְאִם אָמַר: יֵשׁ לִי לְלַמֵּד עָלָיו זְכוּת - מְשַׁתְּקִין אוֹתוֹ. שֶׁנֶּאֱמַר: וְעֵד אֶחָד לֹא יַעֲנֶה בְנֶפֶשׁ לָמוּת - בֵּין לִזְכוּת בֵּין לְחוֹבָה. וּמַהוּ זֶה שֶׁנֶּאֱמַר לָמוּת? כְּלוֹמַר: עֵד שֶׁהֵעִיד בְּנֶפֶשׁ לָמוּת - לֹא יַעֲנֶה דָבָר, אֶלָּא יָעִיד וְיִשְׁתֹּק. אֲבָל בְּדִינֵי מָמוֹנוֹת - יֵשׁ לוֹ לְלַמֵּד עָלָיו זְכוּת אוֹ חוֹבָה. אֲבָל לֹא יִמָּנֶה עִם הַדַּיָּנִים, וְלֹא יֵעָשֶׂה דַּיָּן; שֶׁאֵין עֵד נַעֲשֶׂה דַּיָּן אֲפִלּוּ בְּדִינֵי מָמוֹנוֹת.

disqualify it. If all of the witnesses sit down together and sign, their signatures are considered as part of one testimony. If, by contrast, signatures were added afterwards, they do not have bearing on the status of the original signatures. See also the *Kessef Mishneh* who compares the Rambam's ruling here to his ruling in *Hilchot Gerushin* 9:27.

27. For in actual fact, it is possible that another witness signed before him and the unacceptable witness signed merely to fill in the space.

The Ramah (*Choshen Mishpat* 45:12) states that at the outset, relatives and unacceptable witnesses should never sign a legal document. Moreover, he also cites the opinion of the *Tur* who states that the document is not acceptable unless the signatures of the last two witnesses who appear are those of acceptable witnesses. Note the *Siftei Cohen* 45:23 who elaborates in disputing the conception that the last signatures are those of primary importance.

28. *Sefer HaMitzvot* (negative commandment 291) and *Sefer HaChinuch* (mitzvah 411) count this as one of the 613 mitzvot of the Torah.

29. Rashi (*Sanhedrin* 34a) explains the rationale for this prohibition. It appears that he is trying either to support or to retract his original testimony with these statements. This is unnecessary and undesirable. Once a witness delivers testimony, he can no longer retract it or add to it.

30. The rationale is that all testimony must be able to be disqualified through *hazomah*. If the witness serves as the judge, he will never disqualify his own testimony [*Tosafot (Bava Kama* 90b); see also *Sefer HaMitzvot, loc. cit.*]. The Rashbam (*Bava Batra* 114a) derives this concept from Deuteronomy 19:17: "And the two men will stand... before God." "Before God" refers to the judges. The two witnesses must stand before the judges, they cannot become judges themselves.

As evident from *Hilchot Sanhedrin* 3:6 and *Hilchot Kiddush HaChodesh* 6:2, if there is no necessity to deliver testimony, the judges can execute the matter themselves, e.g., judges who saw the new moon can consecrate the coming month.

31. As the *Shulchan Aruch* (*Choshen Mishpat* 7:5) emphasizes, this applies when the

9. When does the above apply? With regard to matters that, according to Scriptural Law, require testimony and adjudication by judges. In matters of Rabbinic Law, by contrast, a witness may serve as a judge.

What is implied? A person brought a bill of divorce and stated: "It was written and signed in my presence."[32] He and two other individuals [may serve as a court and] give the woman the bill of divorce. It is as if she received it in a court.[33] Similar laws apply in all analogous situations.[34]

CHAPTER SIX

1. As explained,[1] the verification [of the authenticity of the signatures of the witnesses to] legal documents is a Rabbinic provision so that loans will be given freely.[2] Nevertheless, we do not verify [the authenticity of] a legal document except in a court of three judges, for it is a judgment.[3] Ordinary people, however, are acceptable [to serve as the judges].[4] For this reason,[5] the authenticity of legal documents may not be verified at night, as we explained.[6]

2. [The authenticity of the signatures of the witnesses to] legal documents may be verified in any of five ways:
a) the judges recognize the handwriting of the witnesses [and know] that this is so-and-so's signature and that this is so-and-so's signature;
b) the witnesses sign the legal document in their presence;[7]
c) the witnesses who signed come and each testifies in the presence of the judges saying, "This is my signature and I am a witness to this matter";[8]

person testifies as a witness. If, however, a person observes a matter - even if he had the intent to serve as a witness - but does not actually testify, he may serve as a judge.
32. As *Hilchot Gerushin* 7:5 states, a person who brings a bill of divorce from the diaspora is required to make this statement before presenting the woman with the document.
33. And from this time onward, the husband cannot protest that the bill of divorce was a forgery. Since the necessity to validate the signature of witnesses on a legal document is a Rabbinic requirement, our Sages did not prevent a witness from serving as a judge in such an instance.
34. See also Chapter 7, Halachah 6.

1. Chapter 3, Halachah 4.
2. According to Scriptural Law, witnesses who sign on a legal document are considered as if they gave testimony in court. Nevertheless, were we not to require the verification of the signatures of witnesses, there is the possibility that there would be forgeries and no one would rely on a legal document (*Lechem Mishneh*).

The Radbaz (in his gloss to Chapter 7, Halachah 1) questions how it's possible that Scriptural Law would accept any signed legal document as valid. That would leave the possibility open for forgeries. He explains that the Torah does not suspect that a Jew will ever lie. It is only after our people became assimilated among the gentiles and learned dishonesty that there arose a need for such safeguards.

ט בַּמֶּה דְּבָרִים אֲמוּרִים? בְּדָבָר שֶׁצָּרִיךְ עֵדִים מִן הַתּוֹרָה, וְצָרִיךְ דַּיָּנִים לָדוּן בְּאוֹתוֹ הַדָּבָר מִן הַתּוֹרָה; אֲבָל בְּשֶׁל דִּבְרֵיהֶם – עֵד נַעֲשֶׂה דַּיָּן.
כֵּיצַד? אֶחָד שֶׁהֵבִיא הַגֵּט, וְאָמַר: בְּפָנַי נִכְתַּב וּבְפָנַי נֶחְתַּם – הוּא וּשְׁנַיִם נוֹתְנִין אוֹתוֹ לָהּ, וְנִמְצָא כְּאִלּוּ נְטָלוּהוּ מִבֵּית דִּין. וְכֵן כֹּל כַּיּוֹצֵא בָּזֶה.

פֶּרֶק שִׁשִּׁי

א כְּבָר בֵּאַרְנוּ, שֶׁקִּיּוּם שְׁטָרוֹת מִדִּבְרֵיהֶם, כְּדֵי שֶׁלֹּא תִּנְעַל דֶּלֶת בִּפְנֵי לֹוִין.
אַף עַל פִּי כֵן, אֵין מְקַיְּמִין שְׁטָרוֹת אֶלָּא בִּשְׁלֹשָׁה, אֲפִלּוּ שְׁלָשְׁתָּן הֶדְיוֹטוֹת, מִפְּנֵי שֶׁהוּא דִּין. וּלְפִיכָךְ אֵין מְקַיְּמִין שְׁטָרוֹת בַּלַּיְלָה, כְּמוֹ שֶׁבֵּאַרְנוּ.

ב בְּאֶחָד מֵחֲמִשָּׁה דְּרָכִים מִתְקַיֵּם הַשְּׁטָר בְּבֵית דִּין.
הַדֶּרֶךְ הָאֶחָד: שֶׁיִּהְיוּ דַּיָּנִים מַכִּירִין כְּתַב יְדֵי הָעֵדִים, שֶׁזּוֹ עֵדוּת פְּלוֹנִי וְזוֹ עֵדוּת פְּלוֹנִי.
הַדֶּרֶךְ הַשֵּׁנִי: שֶׁיַּחְתְּמוּ הָעֵדִים בִּפְנֵיהֶם.
הַדֶּרֶךְ הַשְּׁלִישִׁי: שֶׁיָּבוֹאוּ הָעֵדִים הַחֲתוּמִים בִּפְנֵיהֶם, וְיֹאמַר כָּל אֶחָד וְאֶחָד: זֶה כְּתַב יָדִי, וַאֲנִי עֵד בַּדָּבָר הַזֶּה.

3. According to law, if only two judges presided over the verification of the authenticity of a legal document, their actions are of no consequence. Nevertheless, it has become customary to allow a leading local Rabbinic authority to verify the authenticity of legal documents alone [Ramah (*Choshen Mishpat* 46:4)].
4. I.e., we do not require the unique *semichah* necessary to take part in a formal court. Since the verification of the authenticity of a legal document is a Rabbinic requirement, our Sages sanctioned even a court that is acceptable only by Rabbinic decree to perform this process (*Ketubot* 28a).
5. I.e., since it is considered as a judgment.
6. *Hilchot Sanhedrin* 3:4. The *Sefer Me'irat Einayim* 46:6 states that if both litigants agree, the verification may be made at night.
7. In this and the previous instance, since the judges have firsthand knowledge of the witnesses' signature, there is no need for further testimony.

There is a debate among the commentaries with regard to the rationale for this concept. Some explain that with regard to questions of Rabbinic Law (and the verification of the authenticity of the signatures of the witnesses is a question of Rabbinic Law), a witness can serve as a judge. Hence after seeing the signatures of the witnesses, the judges can serve as both witnesses and judges.

Others explain that the rationale for this law is that, when testimony is not required, as in this instance, the judges can act on their knowledge without the necessity for testimony.
8. In this instance, the witnesses are testifying that the event described in the legal document took place; we are not validating their signatures. What in fact the witnesses are saying is "By seeing the document and my signature, I recall that this event transpired" (*Lechem Mishneh*, based on Chapter 8, Halachah 1; *Sefer Me'irat Einayim* 46:15).

Accordingly, there is no necessity for another person to join the witness and testify

d) if the witnesses to the legal document died or they were in another locale,[9] [other] witnesses may come and testify to the authenticity of their signatures;[10] e) [if the witnesses'] signatures were found on other legal documents,[11] the court compares these signatures to the signatures on those documents, seeing that they resemble each other and the signatures on these [documents] match these signatures.

3. [The authenticity of the signatures of the witnesses to] legal documents should not be verified from documents other than:
a) two deeds of sale from two fields whose owners benefited from them for three years[12] in a proper and conspicuous manner without fear or dread from any claim in the world as all the owners of fields benefit from their properties; or b) two *ketubot*.[13]

These two legal documents must be in the possession of another person and not in the possession of the person who seeks to validate his legal document, for it is possible he forged all [the signatures].[14] Similarly, we may validate a legal document [by comparing the signatures of the witnesses to those on a] legal document whose authenticity was challenged and then verified by a court of law.[15] Such a legal document alone can be used to verify the authenticity [of the signatures to] a legal document just as a legal document can be validated by comparing it to the deeds of sale for two fields or two *ketubot*.[16]

4. When a court writes [on a legal document]: "In a sitting of three [judges], [the authenticity of] this legal document was validated in our presence," it is validated even though they did not state in which of the five ways it was validated. For we do not suspect that the court erred. [Nevertheless,] it has already become accepted practice for all the courts which we have seen and about whom we have heard [for the judges] to describe the manner in which the document was validated.[17]

concerning his signature. See also the notes to Chapter 7, Halachah 4. See also the *Tur* (*Choshen Mishpat* 46) who states that if the witnesses do not remember that the event took place, but can identify their signatures, each of them together with another witness may validate their signatures.

9. Based on Chapter 3, Halachah 6, it appears that this principle applies even if the witnesses are in the city and do not come to court for other reasons (*Kessef Mishneh*). The Rambam was mentioning the more likely situation. For if the witnesses were present, it would be probable that they would appear in court themselves. Moreover, it is preferable that if the witnesses are available, they testify in court themselves [*Bayit Chadash* (*Choshen Mishpat* 46)].

10. The Ramah (*Choshen Mishpat* 46:7) quotes a responsa of the Rivosh (Responsum 382) who states that the witnesses do not have to testify in the presence of the judges. It is sufficient for them to write a document acknowledging that they recognize the signatures in the original legal document.

11. Which had already been validated as authentic by the court [*Shulchan Aruch* (*Choshen Mishpat* 46:7)]. See also the following halachah.

הַדֶּרֶךְ הָרְבִיעִי: שֶׁאִם מֵתוּ עֵדֵי הַשְּׁטָר אוֹ שֶׁהָיוּ בִּמְדִינָה אַחֶרֶת - יָבוֹאוּ עֵדִים וְיָעִידוּ עַל כְּתַב יָדָן שֶׁהוּא זֶה. הַדֶּרֶךְ הַחֲמִישִׁי: שֶׁיִּהְיֶה כְּתַב יָדָן יוֹצֵא מִשְּׁטָרוֹת אֲחֵרִים, וְעוֹרְכִין בֵּית דִּין זֶה הַכְּתָב לְאוֹתוֹ הַכְּתָב שֶׁבִּשְׁטָרוֹת אֲחֵרִים, וְיִהְיֶה דּוֹמֶה זֶה לָזֶה, וְיֵרָאֶה לָהֶם בְּיַחַד שֶׁכְּתַב יְדֵי אֵלּוּ הוּא כְּתַב יְדֵי אֵלּוּ.

ג אֵין מְקַיְּמִין אֶת הַשְּׁטָר מִשְּׁטָרוֹת אֲחֵרִים, אֶלָּא מִשְּׁנֵי שְׁטָרוֹת שֶׁל שְׁתֵּי שָׂדוֹת שֶׁאֲכָלוּם בַּעֲלֵיהֶן שָׁלֹשׁ שָׁנִים אֲכִילָה גְלוּיָה, נְכוֹנָה, בְּלֹא שׁוּם יִרְאָה וְלֹא פַּחַד מִתְּבִיעָה בָּעוֹלָם, כְּדֶרֶךְ שֶׁאוֹכְלִין כָּל בַּעֲלֵי שָׂדוֹת שְׂדוֹתֵיהֶן. אוֹ מִשְּׁתֵּי שִׁטְרֵי כְתֻבּוֹת.
וְהוּא שֶׁיָּצְאוּ שְׁנֵי הַשְּׁטָרוֹת מִתַּחַת יְדֵי אַחֵר, לֹא מִתַּחַת יְדֵי זֶה שֶׁרוֹצֶה לְקַיֵּם שְׁטָרוֹ, שֶׁמָּא הוּא זִיֵּף הַכֹּל. וְכֵן מְקַיְּמִין הַשְּׁטָר מִשְּׁטָר שֶׁקָּרָא עָלָיו עַרְעָר וְהֻחְזַק בְּבֵית דִּין. מְקַיְּמִין מִמֶּנּוּ לְבַדּוֹ, כְּמוֹ שֶׁמְּקַיְּמִין מִשִּׁטְרֵי שְׁתֵּי שָׂדוֹת אוֹ מִשְּׁתֵּי כְתֻבּוֹת.

ד בֵּית דִּין שֶׁכָּתְבוּ: בְּמוֹשַׁב שְׁלֹשָׁה הָיִינוּ וְנִתְקַיֵּם שְׁטָר זֶה בְּפָנֵינוּ - הֲרֵי זֶה מְקֻיָּם, אַף עַל פִּי שֶׁלֹּא פֵּרְשׁוּ בְּאֵי זֶה דֶּרֶךְ מֵחֲמִשָּׁה דְּרָכִים נִתְקַיֵּם; שֶׁאֵין חוֹשְׁשִׁין לְבֵית דִּין שֶׁמָּא יִטְעוּ. וּכְבָר נָהֲגוּ כָּל בָּתֵּי דִּינִין שֶׁרָאִינוּ וְשָׁמַעְנוּ, שֶׁיִּכְתְּבוּ הַדֶּרֶךְ שֶׁנִּתְקַיֵּם בָּהּ לִפְנֵיהֶם.

12. For once a person benefits from property for three years, he has a *chazzakah* on that land; i.e., it is presumed that he is the legal owner unless a claimant presents proof to the contrary (*Hilchot Toein ViNitan*, Ch. 11).

13. A woman's ante-nuptial contract. These *ketubot* must belong to women who are presently married. The *Tur* ((*Choshen Mishpat* 46) adds that they must have been married for at least three years.

14. Rashi (*Ketubot* 20a) gives a different rationale: Perhaps the possessor of the documents looked carefully at the signatures of the witnesses and learned to forge these signatures. According to this rationale, even if the signatures on one of the legal documents has been validated by a court of law, this suspicion still applies (*Kessef Mishneh*). The Rambam, by contrast, would not cast suspicion over such a legal document. See the Ramah (*Choshen Mishpat* 46:7) who quotes both views.

15. For example, a promissory note which the debtor challenged, claiming it to be a forgery. To collect his debt, the creditor had the authenticity of the signatures to that promissory note verified. Obviously, the judges presiding over that case were careful in verifying the authenticity of the signatures. Hence that document can be used as a standard from which signatures on other documents can be verified.

16. When the signatures to those documents were not verified by the court.

The Ra'avad had a different version of *Ketubot* 20a (the standard published text follows the Rambam's version). According to his version, two documents are always necessary even if they have been validated by a court of law. The *Shulchan Aruch* (*Choshen Mishpat* 46:7) rules according to the Rambam's view. The Ramah adds that even when the debtor did not challenge the authenticity of a promissory note, if for whatever reason, the creditor had the authenticity of the witnesses' signatures verified, that document alone may be used to verify the witnesses' signatures. The *Sefer Me'irat Einayim* 46:23 and the *Siftei Cohen* 46:25 state that it is likely that the Rambam would also accept this ruling.

17. The *Sefer Me'irat Einayim* 46:27 explains that although we do not suspect the court

5. A court never checks whether another court [validated a legal document in a correct manner]. Instead, we act under the presumption that they were knowledgeable and did not err. We do, however, check the witnesses.[18]

6. When three [judges] sit to validate the authenticity of a legal document and one of them dies,[19] [the remaining judges] should write: "We sat in a session of three [judges], one of [the judges] exists no longer," lest an observer say: "A court of two judges validated it."[20] Even if [the validation] states that it was performed by a court,[21] [it would be insufficient], lest an observer say: "Perhaps they thought that two [judges] could constitute a court." If [their wording] implied that there were three judges, there is no need to mention [the death of the other judge].[22]

7. [The following principles apply when there is a question if one of the judges was acceptable to serve in his position. For example,] three [judges] sat to validate the authenticity of a legal document. Two witnesses came and challenged [the propriety] of one of the judges, [saying that] he was a robber or the like.[23] Two others came[24] and testified that he repented.[25] If, before [the judges] signed, they testified that he had repented,[26] he may sign with them.[27] For there were three [acceptable judges at the time of the signing]. If it was not until after the other two judges signed that the witnesses testified that he had repented, [the third judge] may not sign together with them. For it is as if he did not exist at the time the other two signed.[28]

When does the above apply? When [his propriety] was challenged because of a transgression. [Different rules apply, however, when,] however, his propriety was challenged because of a blemish in his lineage, e.g., they said: "His mother was never freed, and he is a servant,"[29] or "[His mother] never converted and he is a gentile." If after the other two [judges] signed, it was discovered that he does not have this type of blemished lineage and he is fit [to serve as a judge], he may sign together with the other two. [The rationale is that] this is merely the revelation of a fact that existed previously.[30]

erred, by stating how the court validated the signatures we give the other litigant the opportunity to argue his claim if he maintains that the document is a forgery. The *Siftei Cohen* 46:29, however, states that it is not customary to state how the document was validated.

18. *Bava Batra* 138b, the source for the Rambam's ruling, states that if witnesses compose a record of a dying man's statements, we suspect that they transcribed his words without checking the validity of his claims. Hence we investigate the matter before accepting their statements.

19. After validating the document, but before signing it.

20. In which case, the validation is not binding, as implied by Halachah 1.

21. And by stating "a court," they are implying that three judges were present.

22. The *Shulchan Aruch* (*Choshen Mishpat* 46:29) quotes the Rambam's opinion, but also the opinion of Rabbenu Asher who states that if the judges write that they sat in session with three judges, it is not necessary to mention that one no longer exists.

23. See Chapter 10 which explains the disqualification of witnesses because of the violation of transgressions. Similar principles apply with regard to a judge.

ה וּלְעוֹלָם אֵין בֵּית דִּין בּוֹדְקִין אַחַר בֵּית דִּין אַחֵר, אֶלָּא מַחֲזִיקִין אוֹתוֹ שֶׁהֵן בְּקִיאִין וְלֹא יִטְעוּ. אֲבָל בּוֹדְקִין אַחַר הָעֵדִים.

ו שְׁלֹשָׁה שֶׁיָּשְׁבוּ לְקַיֵּם אֶת הַשְּׁטָר, וּמֵת אֶחָד מֵהֶם – צְרִיכִין לִכְתֹּב: בְּמוֹשַׁב שְׁלֹשָׁה הָיִינוּ וְהָאֶחָד אֵינֶנּוּ. שֶׁמָּא יֹאמַר הָרוֹאֶה: בֵּית דִּין בִּשְׁנַיִם קִיְּמוּהוּ. אֲפִלּוּ הָיָה כָּתוּב בּוֹ 'בְּבֵית דִּין', יֹאמַר: שֶׁמָּא דִמּוּ שֶׁשְּׁנַיִם בֵּית דִּין הֵם. וְאִם יֵשׁ בּוֹ מַשְׁמָע שֶׁהָיוּ שְׁלֹשָׁה – אֵינוֹ צָרִיךְ.

ז שְׁלֹשָׁה שֶׁיָּשְׁבוּ לְקַיֵּם אֶת הַשְּׁטָר, וּבָאוּ שְׁנֵי עֵדִים וְעִרְעֲרוּ עַל אֶחָד מֵהֶן שֶׁהוּא גַּזְלָן וְכַיּוֹצֵא בּוֹ, וּבָאוּ שְׁנַיִם אֲחֵרִים וְהֵעִידוּ שֶׁחָזַר בִּתְשׁוּבָה: אִם עַד שֶׁלֹּא חָתְמוּ הֵעִידוּ שֶׁחָזַר – הֲרֵי זֶה חוֹתֵם עִמָּהֶם, שֶׁהֲרֵי שְׁלֹשָׁה הָיוּ; וְאִם אַחַר שֶׁחָתְמוּ הַשְּׁנַיִם הֵעִידוּ עָלָיו שֶׁחָזַר בִּתְשׁוּבָה – אֵינוֹ חוֹתֵם עִמָּהֶן, שֶׁהֲרֵי הוּא כְּמִי שֶׁאֵינוֹ בְּעֵת חֲתִימַת הַשְּׁנַיִם. בַּמֶּה דְּבָרִים אֲמוּרִים? כְּשֶׁעִרְעֲרוּ עָלָיו בַּעֲבֵרָה; אֲבָל עִרְעֲרוּ עָלָיו בִּפְגַם מִשְׁפָּחָה, כְּמוֹ שֶׁאָמְרוּ: אִמּוֹ לֹא נִשְׁתַּחְרְרָה וְעֶבֶד הוּא, אוֹ לֹא נִתְגַּיְּרָה וְעוֹבֵד כּוֹכָבִים הוּא, וְנוֹדַע אַחַר שֶׁחָתְמוּ הַשְּׁנַיִם שֶׁאֵין בְּמִשְׁפַּחְתּוֹ פְּגַם וְשֶׁהוּא כָּשֵׁר – הֲרֵי זֶה חוֹתֵם עִמָּהֶם, שֶׁזֶּה גִּלּוּי דָּבָר שֶׁהָיָה מִקֹּדֶם הוּא.

24. The *Sefer Me'irat Einayim* 46:61 states that, before they sign on the legal document, the other two judges may testify that the third judge has repented and is fit to serve in that capacity.
25. Before accepting the appointment and thus was fit to serve in that capacity.
26. If, however, they testify that he never robbed, the matter is considered unresolved and he is not acceptable as a judge (*Kessef Mishneh*; *Sefer Me'irat Einayim* 46:62).
27. Even though he was not acceptable as a judge beforehand, since he became acceptable before the others signed, we do not say that the entire sitting was nullified.
28. When it is discovered that a person committed a transgression that disqualifies him as a judge, he is disqualified until witnesses testify that he repented. Even if he repented beforehand, until such testimony is delivered in court, he is unacceptable (*Kessef Mishneh*).

For this reason, even if he had already repented, if the judges signed the document before the witnesses testified to that effect, the validation is unacceptable. For at the time they signed, the third judge was unacceptable and their entire sitting was nullified. For the document to be validated, the judges must reconvene their sitting and discuss the matter again. Indeed, the *Sefer Me'irat Einayim* 46:63 suggests that it might even be necessary to rehear the testimony of the witnesses who authenticated the signatures of the witnesses on the legal document.

The *Siftei Cohen* 46:66 notes that Rashi differs with the interpretation advanced by Rabbenu Yitzchak Alfasi and accepted by the Rambam. According to Rashi, after signing the validation of the legal document, the two judges may not give testimony concerning the propriety of the third judge. Others may, however, give such testimony and if they do, that judge may sign the validation of the legal document. The *Siftei Cohen* 46:66 argues at length in favor of Rashi's interpretation.
29. And thus unfit to serve as a judge.
30. I.e., it is revealed that, even during the time the judge was under suspicion, he was actually fit to serve in that capacity.

8. It is permitted to write the validation on the document before [the signatures on] the document are validated. For it is [the judges'] signing of the validation, not the writing of it that is of fundamental importance.[31]

The judges do not have to read the legal document[32] when they validate its authenticity.[33] Instead, they validate it based on [the signatures of] the witnesses even if they do not know what was written in it.[34]

CHAPTER SEVEN

1. A relative may give testimony with regard to his relative's signature.[1]

What is implied? There was a legal document which Reuven and Shimon [signed as] witnesses. They died or traveled overseas. Reuven's son came and testified: "This is my father's signature," and Shimon's son came and testified: "This is my father's signature." It is as if they are two acceptable witnesses who are not related [to the witnesses who have signed].[2] If a third witness[3] joins together with them and testifies with regard to the two signatures,[4] [the authenticity of] the legal document is validated.

2. The statements of the following individuals are acceptable when, as adults, they testify with regard to what they observed as minors.[5] A person's words is accepted when, as an adult, he states: "This is the signature of my father....", "This is the signature of my teacher...", "This is the signature of my brother which I [learned to] recognize when I was a minor."[6]

[The above applies,] provided he is joined by another person who [learned to] recognize these signatures while an adult.[7]

31. And the judges will not sign until it has in fact been validated.

The *Shulchan Aruch* (*Choshen Mishpat* 46:24) quotes the Rambam's opinion, but also quotes other views which differ and forbid writing these statements before the testimony is actually given. The *Siftei Cohen* 46:60 elaborates in support of the Rambam's position.

32. Witnesses, by contrast, must read the contents of a legal document and know them to be true before signing (*Ketubot* 109a,b).

33. See a practical application of this ruling in *Hilchot Toein ViNitan* 16:2.

34. For the judges are not testifying with regard to the contents of the legal document. Their statements concern only the authenticity of the signatures of the witnesses. Nevertheless, they must know the identity of the principals involved so that they are not their relatives. For that would disqualify the validation (Rabbenu Nissim; see the notes to Chapter 7, Halachah 1).

In his *Kessef Mishneh* and his *Shulchan Aruch* (*Choshen Mishpat* 46:20), Rav Yosef Karo quotes Rabbenu Nissim's view, but in his *Shulchan Aruch*, he also cites the view of the Rambam which he interprets as implying that the judges need not read the legal document at all.

1. The two witnesses may not, however, be related to each other (*Sefer Me'irat Einayim* 46:46). They may, however, both be related to the witnesses to the legal document

ח מֻתָּר לִכְתֹּב הַקִּיּוּם בַּשְּׁטָר קֹדֶם שֶׁיִּתְקַיֵּם הַשְּׁטָר; שֶׁאֵין הַכְּתִיבָה עִקָּר, אֶלָּא הַחֲתִימָה. וְאֵין הַדַּיָּנִים צְרִיכִין לִקְרוֹת הַשְּׁטָר שֶׁמְּקַיְּמִין אוֹתוֹ, אֶלָּא מְקַיְּמִין אוֹתוֹ מֵעֵדָיו, אַף עַל פִּי שֶׁלֹּא יָדְעוּ מַה כָּתוּב בּוֹ.

פֶּרֶק שְׁבִיעִי

א מֵעִיד קָרוֹב עַל כְּתַב קְרוֹבוֹ.
כֵּיצַד? שְׁטָר שֶׁעֵדָיו רְאוּבֵן וְשִׁמְעוֹן, וּמֵתוּ אוֹ שֶׁהָלְכוּ לִמְדִינַת הַיָּם, וּבָא בְּנוֹ שֶׁל רְאוּבֵן וְאָמַר: זֶה כְּתַב יָדוֹ שֶׁל אָבִי, וּבָא בְּנוֹ שֶׁל שִׁמְעוֹן וְאָמַר: זֶה כְּתַב יָדוֹ שֶׁל אָבִי – הֲרֵי אֵלּוּ כִּשְׁנֵי עֵדִים כְּשֵׁרִים שֶׁאֵינָן קְרוֹבִים; וְאִם יִצְטָרֵף עִמָּהֶם שְׁלִישִׁי וְהֵעִיד עַל כְּתַב יָדָן שֶׁל שְׁנֵיהֶם – הֲרֵי נִתְקַיֵּם הַשְּׁטָר.

ב וְאֵלּוּ מִדְּבָרִים שֶׁנֶּאֱמָנִים הַגְּדוֹלִים לְהָעִיד בְּגָדְלָם מַה שֶּׁרָאוּ בְּקָטְנָם: נֶאֱמָן אָדָם לוֹמַר כְּשֶׁהוּא גָּדוֹל: זֶהוּ כְּתַב יָדוֹ שֶׁל אָבִי, זֶהוּ כְּתַב יָדוֹ שֶׁל רַבִּי, זֶהוּ כְּתַב יָדוֹ שֶׁל אָחִי, שֶׁהָיִיתִי מַכִּיר בִּכְתַב יָדָם כְּשֶׁהָיִיתִי קָטָן. וְהוּא שֶׁיִּצְטָרֵף עִמּוֹ אַחֵר שֶׁמַּכִּיר כְּתַב יָדָן כְּשֶׁהוּא גָּדוֹל.

(Rabbenu Nissim, as quoted by the *Sefer Me'irat Einayim* 46:46). Needless to say, a relative's testimony is not accepted with regard to the signatures of the principals to a legal document (*Siftei Cohen* 46:47).

The *Shulchan Aruch* (*Choshen Mishpat* 46:18) quotes a difference of opinion among the Rabbis if it is acceptable for them to be related to the judges or not.

2. The rationale is that the two testimonies are considered to involve separate matters entirely. The father's testimony concerns the subject mentioned in the promissory note, while the son's testimony concerns his father's signature and not the subject of the note. Hence one is not affected by the other.

3. For the testimony of two witnesses is necessary to validate each of the signatures, as stated in Halachah 3.

4. Alternatively, if each one is familiar with the signature of the other father, the document can be validated (Maharshal).

5. As *Ketubot* 28a explains, since the necessity for validating the authenticity of the signatures of the witnesses is a Rabbinic requirement, our Sages showed leniency and accepted testimony which is otherwise inadmissible (Radbaz; *Kessef Mishneh*). When, by contrast, Scriptural Law requires testimony, a witness must be acceptable both when he observes and when he delivers his testimony (see Chapter 14, Halachah 3).

6. The *Shulchan Aruch* (*Choshen Mishpat* 46:17) quotes a difference of opinion among the Rabbis if these concepts apply only with regard to the signatures of these three individuals - for these are the three signatures with which a person is most likely to be familiar, or if they apply with regard to any individual and the Rambam was merely citing the most likely examples.

7. If, however, both witnesses require this leniency, their testimony is unacceptable.

3. When there is a legal document on which Reuven and Shimon signed as witnesses and two others came and testified to the authenticity of the signatures of both Reuven and Shimon,[8] the legal document is validated. If, however, one testified to the authenticity of Reuven's signature and the other testified to the authenticity of Shimon's signature, the document is not validated. [The rationale is that] two witnesses must testify with regard to both witnesses' signature. If there is a third witness who testifies with regard to the authenticity of both Reuven's and Shimon's signature, the document is validated.

4. When one witness says: "This is my signature,"[9] and he and another witness testify with regard to the signature of the other witness, the document is not validated, for three fourths of the money mentioned in the legal document is dependent on the testimony of one person.[10] Similarly,[11] if the son or the brother of the first witness testifies with another person with regard to the signature of the second witness, the document is not validated, because three fourths of the money is dependent on the testimony of relatives.

5. When two witnesses sign a legal document and one of them dies,[12] it is necessary that two witnesses testify with regard to the authenticity of the witness who died. If there is only one other witness [who recognizes his signature] in addition to the witness who is alive, the latter should write his signature, even on a shard,[13] in the presence of two witnesses and send it to the court so that his signature will be validated.[14] In that instance, it is not necessary for him to declare that it is his signature. Accordingly, he and another person can testify with regard to the signature of the deceased person so that his signature will be validated even though he is not present.[15]

6. [The following principles apply if] three [judges] sit together to validate the authenticity of a legal document, two of them recognize the signatures of the witnesses and one of them does not. Before [the judges] sign [the validation], [the two witnesses who recognize the signatures] may deliver testimony before [the third judge].[16] Then they may sign [the validation], for witnesses may serve as judges in a matter that is a Rabbinic ordinance, as we explained.[17]

[If the two witnesses who recognize the signatures] sign [the validation before testifying], they may not testify in the presence [of the third judge] and have him sign. For at the time they signed, only [those] two recognized the signature of the witnesses.[18] [A legal document] may be validated only when [all] three [judges] recognize the signatures or witnesses deliver testimony on the signatures before each one of them.

8. I.e., both witnesses testify to the validity of both signatures.
9. In which instance, his word is accepted, for he is testifying to the matters stated in the legal document, not validating his signature, as stated in the notes to Chapter 6, Halachah 2.
10. I.e., the effect of the witnesses' testimony must be equally balanced, as implied by

ג שְׁטָר שֶׁעֵדָיו רְאוּבֵן וְשִׁמְעוֹן, וּבָאוּ שְׁנַיִם וְהֵעִידוּ שֶׁזֶּה כְּתַב יָדוֹ שֶׁל רְאוּבֵן וְזֶה כְּתַב יָדוֹ שֶׁל שִׁמְעוֹן – נִתְקַיֵּם הַשְּׁטָר. אֲבָל אִם הֵעִיד זֶה עַל כְּתַב יָדוֹ שֶׁל רְאוּבֵן, וְהַשֵּׁנִי הֵעִיד עַל כְּתַב יָדוֹ שֶׁל שִׁמְעוֹן – לֹא נִתְקַיֵּם הַשְּׁטָר; לְפִי שֶׁצָּרִיךְ שְׁנֵי עֵדִים עַל כְּתַב כָּל אֶחָד מִשְּׁנֵיהֶם. וְאִם יֵשׁ שְׁלִישִׁי מֵעִיד עַל כְּתַב רְאוּבֵן וְשִׁמְעוֹן כְּאֶחָד – נִתְקַיֵּם.

ד אָמַר הָרִאשׁוֹן: זֶה כְּתַב יָדִי, וְהֵעִיד הוּא וְאַחֵר עַל כְּתַב יְדֵי הַשֵּׁנִי – לֹא נִתְקַיֵּם; לְפִי שֶׁנִּמְצָא שְׁלֹשֶׁת רִבְעֵי הַמָּמוֹן שֶׁבַּשְּׁטָר תָּלוּי בְּעֵדוּת הָאֶחָד. וְכֵן אִם הֵעִיד אָחִיו אוֹ בְּנוֹ שֶׁל רִאשׁוֹן עִם אַחֵר עַל כְּתַב יְדֵי הַשֵּׁנִי – לֹא נִתְקַיֵּם; שֶׁהֲרֵי שְׁלֹשֶׁת רִבְעֵי הַמָּמוֹן תָּלוּי בְּעֵדוּת הַקְּרוֹבִים.

ה שְׁנַיִם שֶׁחֲתוּמִין עַל הַשְּׁטָר, וּמֵת אֶחָד מֵהֶן – צָרִיךְ שְׁנֵי עֵדִים לְהָעִיד עַל כְּתַב יָדוֹ שֶׁל מֵת. וְאִם לֹא נִמְצָא אֶלָּא עֵד אֶחָד עִם זֶה הָעֵד הַחַי – כּוֹתֵב חֲתִימַת יָדוֹ בִּפְנֵי עֵדִים, אֲפִלּוּ עַל הַחֶרֶס, וּמַשְׁלִיכוֹ בְּבֵית דִּין, עַד שֶׁתֻּחְזַק כְּתַב יָדוֹ בְּבֵית דִּין, וְלֹא יִהְיֶה צָרִיךְ לוֹמַר שֶׁזֶּה כְּתַב יָדוֹ, וְיָעִיד הוּא וְאַחֵר עַל כְּתַב יְדֵי הַמֵּת, וְיִתְקַיֵּם כְּתַב יָדוֹ שֶׁלֹּא בְּפָנָיו.

ו שְׁלֹשָׁה שֶׁיָּשְׁבוּ לְקַיֵּם אֶת הַשְּׁטָר, שְׁנַיִם מֵהֶן מַכִּירִין חֲתִימַת יְדֵי עֵדִים, וְאֶחָד אֵינוֹ מַכִּיר: עַד שֶׁלֹּא חָתְמוּ – מְעִידִין בְּפָנָיו וְחוֹתֵם; שֶׁהָעֵדִים נַעֲשִׂים דַּיָּנִים בְּדָבָר שֶׁהוּא מִדִּבְרֵיהֶם, כְּמוֹ שֶׁבֵּאַרְנוּ. אֲבָל אַחַר שֶׁחָתְמוּ – אֵין מְעִידִין בְּפָנָיו וְחוֹתֵם; [שֶׁהֲרֵי בְּעֵת שֶׁחָתְמוּ לֹא הָיוּ מַכִּירִין אֶלָּא הַשְּׁנַיִם], וְאֵין מְקַיְּמִין אֶלָּא עַד שֶׁיִּהְיוּ שְׁלָשְׁתָּן מַכִּירִין, אוֹ יָעִידוּ הָעֵדִים עַל הַכְּתָב בִּפְנֵי כָּל אֶחָד וְאֶחָד.

Deuteronomy 19:15: "The matter will be established on the basis of the testimony... of two witnesses." *Ketubot* 21a states: "Half on the basis of one and half on the basis of the other."

11. When the first witness testifies with regard to his own signature.
12. Or travels overseas (*Sefer Me'irat Einayim* 46:35).
13. The commentaries state that there is an advantage to signing on a shard, because afterwards, that shard could not be used for a legal document. If, however, he would sign on a piece of paper or parchment, that paper could be misappropriated and a legal document illicitly written on top of it. See *Lechem Mishneh* and others.
14. I.e., these witnesses will compare his signature on the shard to his signature on the legal document and on that basis, validate the signature on the legal document.
15. Since he is not testifying with regard to his own signature, that half of the money is not considered to be dependent upon his testimony.
16. Since the necessity for the validation of the signatures of the witnesses is a Rabbinic ordinance, our Sages were lenient and accepted the testimony even though it was delivered in the presence of only one judge (*Kessef Mishneh*).
17. Chapter 5, Halachah 9.
18. Thus they signed the validation in error. For at that time, the third judge was unable to validate the document.

7. [The following law applies when] the two [witnesses] who signed a legal document died[19] and two others came [and testified], saying: "This is their signature, but they signed under duress," "...they were minors," or "...they were unacceptable as witnesses."[20] Even though there were other witnesses who testify with regard to their signatures[21] or their signatures [could be recognized] from another legal document concerning which a protest was raised and afterwards, it was validated by the court,[22] the legal document is not validated.[23] Instead, the two witnesses [who signed] the document are balanced against the two who testified that they were unacceptable [as witnesses], and the legal document may not be used to expropriate money.[24]

CHAPTER EIGHT

1. [The following law applies when] a person who signed on a promissory note comes to testify with regard to his signature in a court of law. If he recognizes that the signature is definitely his, but does not remember the matter of concern at all and does not have any recollection that this person ever borrowed from the other, it is forbidden for him to testify with regard to his signature in court. For a person is not testifying about his signature, but instead about the money mentioned in the legal document, that one person is obligated to the other. His signature serves merely to remind him of the matter. If he does not remember, he may not testify.[1]

2. Whether a person remembers his testimony [at the outset], [remembers it after] seeing his signature, or remembers it after being reminded by others - even if he is reminded by the other witness - if he [in truth] remembers, he may testify. If, however, it is the plaintiff who reminds him,[2] he may not testify. For it appears to the other litigant that he is testifying falsely concerning a matter about which he does not know.

19. If, however, the witnesses are alive, they certainly can be challenged. And if they are challenged and proven to be unacceptable as witnesses, the legal document is nullified and torn up [Ramah, (*Choshen Mishpat* 46:37)]. There are, however, other opinions which maintain that even if the witnesses are personally disqualified, their signatures on the legal document still have weight. See *Sefer Me'irat Einayim* 46:96.

20. Because of transgressions they committed. I.e., they attempt to nullify the effectiveness of the legal document with their testimony.

21. If, however, there is no proof to the validity of their signatures except the witnesses who maintain that they were unacceptable, the legal document is nullified and is torn up by the court [*Shulchan Aruch* (*Choshen Mishpat* 46:37)].

22. See Chapter 6, Halachah 3.

23. Since there is a pair of witnesses who testify that the legal document is invalid, the matter is considered as deadlocked. For whenever the testimony of two sets of witnesses contradicts each other, we consider the matter as unresolved.

24. Since the question is unresolved, we follow the principle: "Whenever a person seeks to expropriate money, the burden of proof is on him." The bearer of the legal document must prove that it is valid. Since he cannot do so, because of the unresolved doubt

ז שְׁנַיִם שֶׁהָיוּ חֲתוּמִין עַל הַשְּׁטָר וָמֵתוּ, וּבָאוּ שְׁנַיִם וְאָמְרוּ: כְּתַב יָדָן הוּא זֶה, אֲבָל אֲנוּסִים הָיוּ, קְטַנִּים הָיוּ, פְּסוּלֵי עֵדוּת הָיוּ,

אַף עַל פִּי שֶׁיֵּשׁ שָׁם עֵדִים אֲחֵרִים שֶׁזֶּה כְּתַב יָדָן, אוֹ שֶׁהָיָה כְּתַב יָדָן יוֹצֵא מִשְּׁטָר אַחֵר שֶׁקָּרָא עָלָיו עַרְעָר וְהֻחְזַק בְּבֵית דִּין – הֲרֵי זֶה לֹא נִתְקַיֵּם;

אֶלָּא מַעֲמִידִין הַשְּׁנַיִם שֶׁבַּשְּׁטָר כְּנֶגֶד הַשְּׁנַיִם שֶׁהֵעִידוּ עֲלֵיהֶן שֶׁהֵן פְּסוּלִין, וְאֵין גּוֹבִין בּוֹ כְּלוּם.

פֶּרֶק שְׁמִינִי

א מִי שֶׁחָתַם עַל הַשְּׁטָר, וּבָא לְהָעִיד עַל כְּתַב יָדוֹ בְּבֵית דִּין, וְהִכִּיר כְּתַב יָדוֹ שֶׁזֶּהוּ בְּוַדַּאי, אֲבָל אֵינוֹ זוֹכֵר הָעֵדוּת כְּלָל, וְלֹא יִמָּצֵא בְּלִבּוֹ זִכָּרוֹן כְּלָל שֶׁזֶּה לָוָה מִזֶּה לְעוֹלָם – הֲרֵי זֶה אָסוּר לְהָעִיד עַל כְּתַב יָדוֹ שֶׁהוּא זֶה בְּבֵית דִּין.

שֶׁאֵין אָדָם מֵעִיד עַל כְּתַב יָדוֹ שֶׁהוּא זֶה, אֶלָּא עַל הַמָּמוֹן שֶׁבַּשְּׁטָר הוּא מֵעִיד שֶׁזֶּה חַיָּב לָזֶה;

וּכְתַב יָדוֹ הוּא כְּדֵי לְהַזְכִּירוֹ הַדָּבָר, אֲבָל אִם לֹא נִזְכַּר – לֹא יָעִיד.

ב אֶחָד הַזּוֹכֵר אֶת הָעֵדוּת וְאֶחָד שֶׁרָאָה כְּתַב יָדוֹ אוֹ שֶׁהִזְכִּירוּהוּ אֲחֵרִים וְנִזְכַּר, אֲפִלּוּ הִזְכִּירוֹ הָעֵד הַשֵּׁנִי שֶׁהֵעִיד, אִם נִזְכַּר – הֲרֵי זֶה מֵעִיד.

אֲבָל אִם הִזְכִּיר אוֹתוֹ הַתּוֹבֵעַ עַצְמוֹ, אַף עַל פִּי שֶׁנִּזְכַּר – אֵינוֹ מֵעִיד; מִפְּנֵי שֶׁזֶּה דּוֹמֶה בְּעֵינֵי בַּעַל דִּין כְּאִלּוּ הֵעִיד שֶׁקֶר בְּדָבָר שֶׁלֹּא יָדַע.

described above, the defendant is allowed to retain possession of the funds. Nevertheless, if the claim involves movable property and the bearer of the document seizes property belonging to the defendant, the bearer may keep that property. The rationale is that the property is now in his possession and the original owner must sue to expropriate it. And he also is unable to prove his claim definitively [*Tur*, Ramah (*Choshen Mishpat* 46:37)].

1. Rashi, *Ketubot* 20a, explains that this concept is derived from the exegesis of Deuteronomy 19:15: "The matter will be established on the basis of the testimony... of two witness." *Al pi*, translated as "on the basis of the testimony," literally means "on the mouth." Testimony must come from the mouths of the witnesses and not from their written statements.

The Rambam's principle is not accepted by all authorities. The Ra'avad (gloss to Halachah 4) and Rabbenu Asher state that if there is another witness who recognizes the signature of the first witness, the two of them may testify that the signature is authentic and the legal document is validated. The *Shulchan Aruch* (*Choshen Mishpat* 46:10) quotes both of these views without saying which is favored. The *Siftei Cohen* 46:32 elaborates in support of the Rambam's position. See also Halachah 4 and notes.

2. According to the Rambam, this applies even if the witness is a Torah scholar. See the notes to the following halachah.

3. Accordingly, if the plaintiff was a Torah scholar and the plaintiff reminded the witness of the matter, he may testify. [The rationale is that] a Torah scholar knows that if [the witness] did not remember the matter, he would not testify.[3] This is a leniency which was granted with regard to cases involving financial law.[4] Even though [a witness] forgot a matter for many years and it was the written record that reminded him, he may testify.

4. Since this is true, [the following law applies when] a legal document is presented to the court and the witnesses come and say: "These are our signatures, but we never knew anything about this matter. We do not remember that this person borrowed anything from the other or sold anything to him." The legal document is not validated; the witnesses are considered as deaf-mutes[5] unless they remember their testimony. Whoever does not rule in this manner does not know between his right hand and his left hand with regard to matters of financial law.[6]

If, however, there was other evidence of their signatures or there were other witnesses who recognize their signatures, we pay no attention to their statements that they do not remember the matter [stated in the document]. [We suspect that] they may desire to retract [their testimony][7] and they say: "We don't remember," in order to nullify the legal document. This is just as if they said: "We were minors," or "We were not acceptable witnesses."[8] Their testimony is not accepted, and the legal document is validated independent of their testimony.

For this reason, we validate all legal documents without calling the witnesses and asking them if they remember the matter or not. Even if they say: "We do not remember the matter," we do not heed their statements since it is possible to validate the legal document without their testimony.

5. [The following laws apply whether] a person writes his testimony as a legal document or merely finds a note in his records in his handwriting,[9] stating: "So-and-so had me observe testimony concerning him on this-and-this date with regard to these-and-these matters." If he remembers the matter on his own initiative or if others remind him and he remembers, he may testify. If not, he may not testify. The situation is comparable to one in which a trustworthy person tells him: "So-and-so owes so-and-so such-and-such an amount," and [the listener] goes and testifies that one borrowed from the other although he has no [firsthand] knowledge of the matter, but instead merely hears from another person and testifies.

3. After discussing the question of reminding witnesses, *Ketubot* 20b states: "If he is a Torah scholar, even [the litigant] himself may remind him." The Rambam interprets the pronoun "he" as referring to the plaintiff. Rashi, by contrast, interprets it as referring to the witness; if the witness is a Torah scholar, even the litigant may remind him. For we assume a Torah scholar will not lie. The *Shulchan Aruch* (*Choshen Mishpat* 28:14) quotes Rashi's view. The *Sefer Me'irat Einayim* 28:46 also mentions the Rambam's view.
4. Implied is that in cases involving capital punishment, such testimony is not acceptable.

ג לְפִיכָךְ, אִם הָיָה הַתּוֹבֵעַ תַּלְמִיד חָכָם, וְהִזְכִּיר הַתּוֹבֵעַ הַזֶּה אֶת הָעֵד וְנִזְכַּר – הֲרֵי זֶה יָעִיד לוֹ;
שֶׁתַּלְמִיד חָכָם יוֹדֵעַ, שֶׁאִלּוּ לֹא זָכַר הַדָּבָר – לֹא הָיָה מֵעִיד.
וְקַל הוּא שֶׁהֵקֵלּוּ בְּדִינֵי מָמוֹנוֹת, שֶׁאַף עַל פִּי שֶׁשָּׁכַח הַדָּבָר מִכַּמָּה שָׁנִים, וְהַכְּתָב הוּא שֶׁהִזְכִּירוֹ – הֲרֵי זֶה מֵעִיד.

ד הוֹאִיל וְהַדָּבָר כֵּן, שְׁטָר שֶׁיָּצָא לְבֵית דִּין, וּבָאוּ עֵדִים וְאָמְרוּ: כְּתַב יָדֵנוּ הוּא זֶה, אֲבָל מֵעוֹלָם לֹא יָדַעְנוּ עֵדוּת זוֹ, וְאֵין אָנוּ זוֹכְרִים שֶׁזֶּה לָוָה מִזֶּה אוֹ מָכַר לוֹ – לֹא נִתְקַיֵּם הַשְּׁטָר, וַהֲרֵי הֵן כְּחֵרְשִׁים עַד שֶׁיִּזְכְּרוּ עֵדוּתָן.
וְכָל מִי שֶׁאֵינוֹ דָּן כֵּן – לֹא יָדַע בְּדִינֵי מָמוֹנוֹת בֵּין יְמִינוֹ לִשְׂמֹאלוֹ.
אֲבָל אִם הָיָה כְּתַב יָדָן יוֹצֵא מִמָּקוֹם אַחֵר, אוֹ שֶׁהָיוּ שָׁם עֵדִים שֶׁזֶּה כְּתַב יָדָן – מְקַיְּמִין אֶת הַשְּׁטָר, וְאֵין מַשְׁגִּיחִין עַל דִּבְרֵיהֶן שֶׁאוֹמְרִין: אֵין אָנוּ זוֹכְרִין עֵדוּת זוֹ; שֶׁמָּא חָזְרוּ בָּהֶן, וְזֶה שֶׁאָמְרוּ: אֵין אָנוּ זוֹכְרִין – כְּדֵי לְבַטֵּל הַשְּׁטָר. וּכְאִלּוּ אָמְרוּ: קְטַנִּים הָיִינוּ, פְּסוּלֵי עֵדוּת הָיִינוּ – שֶׁאֵינָן נֶאֱמָנִים, הוֹאִיל וּמִתְקַיֵּם הַשְּׁטָר שֶׁלֹּא עַל פִּיהֶם.
וּמִפְּנֵי טַעַם זֶה מְקַיְּמִין כָּל הַשְּׁטָרוֹת, וְאֵין אָנוּ צְרִיכִין לְהָבִיא עֵדִים וְלִשְׁאֹל אוֹתָם אִם הֵם זוֹכְרִים עֵדוּת זוֹ אוֹ אֵינָם זוֹכְרִים אוֹתָהּ;
שֶׁאֲפִלּוּ בָּאוּ וְאָמְרוּ: אֵין אָנוּ זוֹכְרִים אוֹתָהּ – אֵין שׁוֹמְעִין לָהֶן, הוֹאִיל וְאֶפְשָׁר לְקַיְּמוֹ שֶׁלֹּא מִפִּיהֶן.

ה אֶחָד הַכּוֹתֵב עֵדוּתוֹ עַל הַשְּׁטָר, אוֹ שֶׁנִּמְצָא אֶצְלוֹ כָּתוּב בְּפִנְקָסוֹ בִּכְתַב יָדוֹ: פְּלוֹנִי הֵעִיד אוֹתִי עָלָיו בְּיוֹם פְּלוֹנִי בְּכָךְ וָכָךְ:
אִם זָכַר מֵעַצְמוֹ, אוֹ הִזְכִּירוּהוּ אֲחֵרִים וְנִזְכַּר – מֵעִיד; וְאִם לָאו – אָסוּר לְהָעִיד.
שֶׁאֵין זֶה דּוֹמֶה אֶלָּא לְמִי שֶׁאָמַר לוֹ אָדָם נֶאֱמָן: פְּלוֹנִי יֵשׁ לוֹ אֵצֶל פְּלוֹנִי כָּךְ וָכָךְ, וְהֵעִיד הוּא שֶׁיֵּשׁ לָזֶה אֵצֶל זֶה, וְהוּא אֵינוֹ יוֹדֵעַ מִן הַדָּבָר כְּלוּם, אֶלָּא מִפִּי הָאַחֵר שָׁמַע וְהֵעִיד.

5. Who are unacceptable as witnesses (Chapter 9, Halachah 1). Others interpret the words as meaning "the legal document is like a useless shard."
6. The Ra'avad responds just as caustically, stating: "There are those who rule in this manner who are just as knowledgeable in law as he." As mentioned in the notes to Halachah 1, there is a difference of opinion among the later authorities which opinion should be followed.
7. Which is not acceptable. As stated in Chapter 3, Halachah 6, once witnesses sign a legal document, their testimony is binding.
8. See Chapter 7, Halachah 7.
9. With this halachah, the Rambam is emphasizing that there is no difference in this regard between a private note a person records for himself and an official legal document signed by another witness as well. If he remembers the matter, he may testify; if he does not, he may not.

CHAPTER NINE

1. There are ten categories of disqualifications. Any person belonging to one of them is not acceptable as a witness.[1] They are:
a) women;[2]
b) servants;[3]
c) minors;[4]
d) mentally or emotionally unstable individuals;[5]
e) deaf-mutes;[6]
f) the blind;[7]
g) the wicked;[8]
h) debased individuals;[9]
i) relatives;[10]
j) people who have a vested interest in the matter;[11] a total of ten.

2. Women are unacceptable as witnesses according to Scriptural Law,[12] as [Deuteronomy 17:6] states: "According to the testimony of two witnesses." [The verse uses] a male form and not a female form.[13]

3. A *tumtum*[14] and an *androgynus*[15] are also unacceptable, for there is an unresolved doubt whether they are considered as women. Whenever there is an unresolved doubt whether or not a person is acceptable as a witness, he is not accepted.[16] [The rationale is that] a witness is coming to expropriate money [from a defendant] based on his testimony or to cause [a defendant] to be held liable [for punishment].[17] And according to Scriptural Law, money may not be expropriated when there is a doubt involved,[18] nor do we inflict punishment when there is a doubt involved.[19]

4. Servants are not acceptable to offer testimony according to Scriptural Law, as [can be inferred from Deuteronomy 19:19:][20] "And you shall do unto him as he conspired to do unto his brother." Implied is that his brother is like him. Just as his brother is a member of the covenant; so, too, the witness must be a member of the covenant.[21]

[By extension,] we can infer that a gentile is certainly not acceptable. If servants who are obligated in certain mitzvot are unacceptable, certainly, this would apply with regard to gentiles.

1. As the Rambam proceeds to explain, some of these individuals are disqualified on the basis of Scriptural Law, and others on the basis of Rabbinic decree.
2. See Halachah 2.
3. I.e., Canaanite servants. See Halachot 3-6.
4. See Halachot 7-8.
5. See Halachot 9-10.
6. See Halachah 11.
7. See Halachah 12.
8. See Chapters 10 and 12.
9. See Chapter 11, Halachah 5.

פֶּרֶק תְּשִׁיעִי

א עֲשָׂרָה מִינֵי פְּסָלוֹת הֵם. כָּל מִי שֶׁנִּמְצָא בּוֹ אֶחָד מֵהֶן – הֲרֵי הוּא פָּסוּל לְעֵדוּת. וְאֵלוּ הֵן. הַנָּשִׁים, וְהָעֲבָדִים, וְהַקְּטַנִּים, וְהַשּׁוֹטִים, וְהַחֵרְשִׁים, וְהַסּוּמִים, וְהָרְשָׁעִים, וְהַבְּזוּיִין, וְהַקְּרוֹבִין, וְהַנּוֹגְעִין בְּעֵדוּתָן. הֲרֵי אֵלוּ עֲשָׂרָה.

ב נָשִׁים פְּסוּלוֹת לְעֵדוּת מִן הַתּוֹרָה. שֶׁנֶּאֱמַר: עַל פִּי שְׁנַיִם עֵדִים – לְשׁוֹן זָכָר, וְלֹא לְשׁוֹן נְקֵבָה.

ג וְכֵן הַטֻּמְטוּם וְהָאַנְדְּרוֹגִינוֹס פְּסוּלִין, מִפְּנֵי שֶׁהֵן סְפֵק אִשָּׁה. וְכָל מִי שֶׁהוּא סְפֵק כָּשֵׁר סְפֵק פָּסוּל – הֲרֵי הוּא פָּסוּל. שֶׁאֵין הָעֵד בָּא אֶלָּא לְהוֹצִיא מָמוֹן עַל פִּיו אוֹ לְחַיֵּב עַל פִּיו, וְאֵין מוֹצִיאִין מָמוֹן מִסָּפֵק וְאֵין עוֹנְשִׁין מִסָּפֵק דִּין תּוֹרָה.

ד הָעֲבָדִים פְּסוּלִין לְעֵדוּת מִן הַתּוֹרָה. שֶׁנֶּאֱמַר: וַעֲשִׂיתֶם לוֹ כַּאֲשֶׁר זָמַם לַעֲשׂוֹת לְאָחִיו. מִכְּלָל שֶׁאָחִיו כָּמוֹהוּ: מָה אָחִיו בֶּן בְּרִית, אַף הָעֵד בֶּן בְּרִית. קַל וָחֹמֶר לְעוֹבְדֵי כּוֹכָבִים: אִם עֲבָדִים, שֶׁהֵן בְּמִקְצָת מִצְוֹת, פְּסוּלִין; הָעוֹבְדֵי כּוֹכָבִים לֹא כָּל שֶׁכֵּן?!

10. See Chapters 13 and 14.
11. See Chapter 15.
12. See the Ramah (*Choshen Mishpat* 35:14) who states that in situations where male witnesses are unlikely to be found, the Rabbis ordained that the testimony of women should be accepted.
13. *Sh'vuot* 30a derives this concept from Deuteronomy 19:17: "And the two **men** will stand," implying "men," and not women. To this writer's knowledge, the commentaries have not found a prior Rabbinic source that employs the Rambam's prooftext. Indeed, the Radbaz and the *Kessef Mishneh* question the use of that prooftext, noting that the entire Torah is written using male declinations.
14. A person whose sexual organ is covered by flesh and it is impossible to detect whether he is a male or female (*Hilchot Ishut* 2:25).
15. A person who has both male and female sexual organs (*ibid.*:24).
16. See also Chapter 12, Halachah 3.
17. I.e., capital punishment or lashes.
18. We follow the principle: When a person desires to expropriate money from a colleague, the burden of proof is on him.
19. The *Kessef Mishneh* explains that this is inferred from the ruling with regard to financial penalties. If we do not impose a financial penalty when there is a doubt involved, certainly we do not inflict punishment on an individual's physical person.
20. The verse speaks about the punishment given to an *ed zomeim*, a witness who delivers false testimony against a colleague.
21. And servants are not considered full-fledged members of the covenant. As the Rambam states (*Hilchot Issurei Bi'ah* 14:17): "A servant... has already left the category of gentiles... but has not yet entered the category of Jews." See the *Or Sameach* who cites sources (e.g., *Gittin* 23b) which appear to indicate that servants are considered as

5. A person who is half a servant and half a free man[22] is not acceptable [as a witness].[23]

6. Whenever a servant has been freed, but he has not been given his bill of release,[24] he is not acceptable as a witness. Only after the bill of release reaches his hand, he immerses himself in the *mikveh*,[25] and he becomes a member of the covenant may he give testimony.

7. Minors are unacceptable as witnesses according to Scriptural Law. [This concept is derived as follows:] With regard to witnesses, [Deuteronomy 19:17] states: "And the two men will stand." [Implied is] "men," and not minors. Even if the minor was understanding and wise, he is not acceptable until he manifests signs of physical maturity[26] after completing thirteen full years of life.

If he reached the age of 20 without manifesting signs of physical maturity and on the contrary manifests physical signs of a lack of sexual potency, he is classified as a eunuch and may testify. If he does not manifest such signs, he may not testify until he completes the majority of his life,[27] as we explained in *Hilchot Ishut*.[28]

8. When a minor passes the age [of thirteen] and manifests signs of physical maturity in his upper body,[29] he need not be checked to see whether he manifested signs of physical maturity [in his lower body]. If he does not [manifest the upper signs of maturity], we do not accept him as a witness until he is inspected.[30]

When a child is thirteen years and one day[31] and manifests signs of physical maturity, but is not very familiar with business dealings, his testimony is not accepted with regard to landed property.[32] [The rationale is that] he is not precise about [such] matters because of his unfamiliarity.[33] With regard to movable property, we accept his testimony since he has reached majority.

9. A person who is mentally or emotionally unstable is not acceptable as a witness according to Scriptural Law, for he is not obligated in the mitzvot. We are not speaking about only an unstable person who goes around naked, destroys utensils, and throws stones. Instead, [the term also] applies to anyone whose mind is disturbed and continually confused when it comes to certain matters although he can speak and ask questions to the point regarding

members of the covenant although they do not have the same status as the Jewish people. Indeed, Deuteronomy 29:10-11 speaks about the covenant with God including "your wood-cutters and water-drawers," which our Sages interpret as referring to Canaanite servants.

22. For example, a servant who had been owned by two Jews in partnership and was freed by one and not freed by the other. See also *Hilchot Avadim* 7:4.

23. Because the dimension of him which is a servant involves everything that he does.

24. Although a person states that he is willing to free his servant, until he formalizes that

ה מִי שֶׁחֶצְיוֹ עֶבֶד וְחֶצְיוֹ בֶּן חוֹרִין – פָּסוּל.

ו כָּל מִי שֶׁנִּשְׁתַּחְרֵר וַהֲרֵי הוּא מְחֻסַּר גֵּט שִׁחְרוּר – פָּסוּל; עַד שֶׁיַּגִּיעַ גֵּט לְיָדוֹ, וְיֵעָשֶׂה מִכְּלַל בְּנֵי בְכְרִית, וְאַחַר כָּךְ יָעִיד.

ז הַקְּטַנִּים פְּסוּלִין לְעֵדוּת מִן הַתּוֹרָה. שֶׁנֶּאֱמַר בְּעֵדִים: וְעָמְדוּ שְׁנֵי הָאֲנָשִׁים. אֲנָשִׁים – וְלֹא קְטַנִּים. אֲפִלּוּ הָיָה הַקָּטָן נָבוֹן וְחָכָם – הֲרֵי הוּא פָּסוּל, עַד שֶׁיָּבִיא שְׁתֵּי שְׂעָרוֹת אַחַר שְׁלֹשׁ עֶשְׂרֵה שָׁנָה גְּמוּרוֹת. וְאִם הִגִּיעַ לְעֶשְׂרִים שָׁנָה וְלֹא הֵבִיא שְׁתֵּי שְׂעָרוֹת, וְנוֹלַד בּוֹ סִימָן מִסִּימָנֵי סֵרוּס – הֲרֵי זֶה סָרִיס, וְיָעִיד. וְאִם לֹא נוֹלַד בּוֹ – לֹא יָעִיד עַד רֹב שְׁנוֹתָיו, כְּמוֹ שֶׁבֵּאַרְנוּ בְּהִלְכוֹת אִישׁוּת.

ח קָטָן שֶׁהִגִּיעַ לִכְלַל שְׁנוֹתָיו שֶׁנִּרְאוּ בּוֹ סִימָנֵי בַגְרוּת מִלְמַעְלָה – אֵינוֹ צָרִיךְ בְּדִיקָה; וְאִם לָאו – אֵין מְקַבְּלִין עֵדוּתוֹ עַד שֶׁיִּבָּדֵק. וּבֶן שְׁלֹשׁ עֶשְׂרֵה שָׁנָה וְיוֹם אֶחָד שֶׁהֵבִיא שְׁתֵּי שְׂעָרוֹת וְאֵינוֹ יוֹדֵעַ בְּטִיב מַשָּׂא וּמַתָּן – אֵין עֵדוּתוֹ עֵדוּת בְּקַרְקָעוֹת, מִפְּנֵי שֶׁאֵינוֹ מְדַקְדֵּק בַּדְּבָרִים, שֶׁהֲרֵי אֵינוֹ יוֹדֵעַ. אֲבָל בְּעֵדוּת מִטַּלְטְלִין – מְקַבְּלִין עֵדוּתוֹ, הוֹאִיל וְהוּא גָדוֹל.

ט הַשּׁוֹטֶה פָּסוּל לְעֵדוּת מִן הַתּוֹרָה, לְפִי שֶׁאֵינוֹ בֶּן מִצְוֹת.
וְלֹא שׁוֹטֶה שֶׁהוּא מְהַלֵּךְ עָרֹם וּמְשַׁבֵּר כֵּלִים וְזוֹרֵק אֲבָנִים בִּלְבַד, אֶלָּא כָּל מִי שֶׁנִּטְרְפָה דַעְתּוֹ, וְנִמְצֵאת דַּעְתּוֹ מְשֻׁבֶּשֶׁת תָּמִיד בְּדָבָר מִן הַדְּבָרִים, אַף עַל פִּי שֶׁהוּא מְדַבֵּר וְשׁוֹאֵל

statement with a legal document, the servant is not formally freed and may not marry a Jewish woman.
25. Which is necessary to bring about his change of status as stated in *Hilchot Issurei Bi'ah* 13:12.
26. Two pubic hairs.
27. I.e., reaches the age of 35. For Psalms 90:10: speaks of "the years of our lives" as being "70."
28. Chapter 2.
29. Hairs in his beard or hair on his underarms.
30. To see whether he manifested signs of physical maturity in his pubic area. Even though he has reached the required age, he must also manifest physical maturity.
31. I.e., when he reaches his thirteenth birthday. After any portion of the day passes, we follow the principle (*Pesachim* 4a): "A portion of the day is like the entire day," and he is considered as thirteen and a day.
32. If, however, a child is familiar with business dealings, his testimony is accepted, even though he has just past his thirteenth birthday (*Kessef Mishneh*).
33. And we are very careful when it comes to matters involving landed property, because a person's livelihood is dependent on land (Radbaz). See *Hilchot Mechirah* 29:12-13 which mentions restrictions with regard to a youth's sale of his own landed property until he reaches the age of 20.

other matters. Such a person is considered unacceptable and is placed in the category of unstable people.

An epileptic in the midst of a seizure is unacceptable [as a witness]. When he is healthy, he is acceptable. This applies both with regard to an epileptic who has seizures only infrequently and one who continuously has seizures without having a fixed time for them, provided his mind is not continuously confused. For there are epileptics whose minds are disturbed even when they are healthy. One must ponder much [before accepting] testimony from epileptics.

10. People who are very feeble-witted who do not understand that matters contradict each other and are incapable of comprehending a concept as it would be comprehended by people at large are considered among those mentally unstable.[34] This also applies to the people who are [continually] unsettled, tumultuous, and deranged. This matter is dependent on the judgment of the judge. It is impossible to describe the mental and emotional states of people in a text.[35]

11. A deaf-mute is equivalent to a mentally unstable person, for he is not of sound mind and is [therefore] not obligated in the observance of the mitzvot. Both a deaf person who can speak and a person who can hear, but is mute [is unacceptable to serve as a witness]. Even though he sees excellently and his mind is sound, he must deliver testimony orally in court or be fit to deliver testimony orally[36] and must be fit to hear the judges and the warning they administer to him.[37]

Similarly, if a person loses the ability to speak, [38] even though his intellectual faculties have been checked as [a husband] is checked with regard to a bill of divorce,[39] he testifies in writing, and his testimony is to the point, it is not accepted at all, except with regard to [releasing] a women [from marriage], for leniency was granted so that women will not be forced to live alone.[40]

12. The blind, although they can recognize the voices [of the litigants] and know their identities, are not acceptable [as witnesses] according to Scriptural Law. [This is derived from Leviticus 5:1]: "And he witnessed or saw," [which implies that] one who can see may serve as a witness.

A person who is blind in one eye is fit to serve as a witness.[41]

34. For we assume that such a person will not be capable of giving accurate testimony. In a certain way, a feeble-minded person like this is worse than an emotionally unstable person. For an emotionally unstable person is often intellectually capable and able to perceive information; the difficulty with him involves his intemperate excesses. A simpleton, by contrast, has difficulty comprehending; that is why he is unacceptable (*Sefer Me'irat Einayim* 35:21).

35. The definition of a person as mentally or emotionally unstable is a very delicate matter, because there are times when a person is on the border of being placed in this

כָּעִנְיָן בִּשְׁאָר דְּבָרִים – הֲרֵי זֶה פָּסוּל, וּבִכְלַל שׁוֹטִים יֵחָשֵׁב. הַנִּכְפֶּה: בְּעֵת כְּפִיָּתוֹ – פָּסוּל, וּבָעֵת שֶׁהוּא בָּרִיא – כָּשֵׁר. וְאֶחָד הַנִּכְפֶּה מִזְּמַן לִזְמַן אוֹ הַנִּכְפֶּה תָּמִיד בְּלֹא עֵת קָבוּעַ. וְהוּא שֶׁלֹּא תִּהְיֶה דַּעְתּוֹ מְשֻׁבֶּשֶׁת תָּמִיד, שֶׁהֲרֵי יֵשׁ שָׁם נִכְפִּים שֶׁגַּם בְּעֵת בְּרִיאוּתָם דַּעְתָּם מְטֹרֶפֶת עֲלֵיהֶם. וְצָרִיךְ לְהִתְיַשֵּׁב בְּעֵדוּת הַנִּכְפִּין הַרְבֵּה.

י הַפְּתָאִים בְּיוֹתֵר, שֶׁאֵין מַכִּירִין דְּבָרִים שֶׁסּוֹתְרִין זֶה אֶת זֶה, וְלֹא יָבִינוּ עִנְיְנֵי הַדָּבָר כְּדֶרֶךְ שֶׁמְּבִינִין שְׁאָר עַם הָאָרֶץ, וְכֵן הַמְבֹהָלִים וְהַנֶּחְפָּזִים בְּדַעְתָּם וְהַמִּשְׁתַּגְּעִים בְּיוֹתֵר – הֲרֵי אֵלּוּ בִּכְלַל הַשּׁוֹטִים. וְדָבָר זֶה לְפִי מַה שֶּׁיִּרְאֶה הַדַּיָּן, שֶׁאִי אֶפְשָׁר לְכַוֵּן הַדַּעַת בִּכְתָב.

יא הַחֵרֵשׁ – כְּשׁוֹטֶה, שֶׁאֵין דַּעְתּוֹ נְכוֹנָה וְאֵינוֹ בֶּן מִצְוֹת. וְאֶחָד חֵרֵשׁ מְדַבֵּר וְאֵינוֹ שׁוֹמֵעַ, אוֹ שׁוֹמֵעַ וְאֵינוֹ מְדַבֵּר, אַף עַל פִּי שֶׁרְאִיָּתוֹ רְאִיָּה מְעֻלָּה וְדַעְתּוֹ נְכוֹנָה – צָרִיךְ לְהָעִיד בְּבֵית דִּין בְּפִיו, אוֹ שֶׁיִּהְיֶה רָאוּי לְהָעִיד בְּפִיו, וְיִהְיֶה רָאוּי לִשְׁמֹעַ הַדַּיָּנִים וְהָאִיּוּם שֶׁמְּאַיְּמִין עָלָיו.

וְכֵן אִם נִשְׁתַּתֵּק, אַף עַל פִּי שֶׁנִּבְדַּק בַּדֶּרֶךְ שֶׁבּוֹדְקִין לְעִנְיַן גִּטִּין וְנִמְצֵאת עֵדוּתוֹ מְכֻוֶּנֶת, וְהֵעִיד בְּפָנֵינוּ בִּכְתַב יָדוֹ – אֵינוֹ עֵדוּת כְּלָל. חוּץ מֵעֵדוּת אִשָּׁה, לְפִי שֶׁבָּעֲגוּנָה הֵקֵלּוּ.

יב הַסּוּמִים, אַף עַל פִּי שֶׁמַּכִּירִין הַקּוֹל וְיָדְעוּ הָאֲנָשִׁים – הֲרֵי אֵלּוּ פְּסוּלִין מִן הַתּוֹרָה. שֶׁנֶּאֱמַר: וְהוּא עֵד אוֹ רָאָה. מִי שֶׁהוּא רָאוּי לִרְאוֹת – הוּא שֶׁמֵּעִיד. וְהַסּוּמָא בְּאַחַת מֵעֵינָיו – כָּשֵׁר לְהָעִיד.

category and yet his testimony could be useful in enabling a woman to receive license to remarry and similar matters. Over the years, the Rabbis have frequently dealt with questions of this nature.

36. As stated in Chapter 3, Halachah 4, testimony must be delivered orally. Moreover, a person may not even sign on a legal document unless he is fit to testify orally.

As noted by the *Kessef Mishneh* and others, the Rambam's statements here are interpreted by some as an indication that if a person is fit to deliver testimony in court, he need not actually testify orally, but may instead send a record of his testimony. This understanding - both as a halachic ruling and as the interpretation of the Rambam's position - is not accepted by all authorities.

37. See Chapter 17, Halachah 2; see also *Hilchot Sanhedrin* 12:3.

38. In contrast to the individuals mentioned in the previous clause who had congenital difficulties, this person was able to speak and hear, but lost these abilities due to accident or illness.

39. See *Hilchot Gerushin* 2:16 which explains that a person whose mind is sound, but who has lost his ability to speak is asked a series of questions requiring both positive and negative answers. If it is obvious from the way he nods his head that he is responding intelligently, he is allowed to initiate divorce proceedings.

40. See *Hilchot Gerushin* 12:15, 13:28-29.

41. See *Hilchot Sanhedrin* 2:9, 11:11, which rules that a person who can see with only

CHAPTER TEN

1. The wicked are unacceptable as witnesses[1] according to Scriptural Law, as [Exodus 23:1] states: "Do not join hands with a wicked person to be a corrupt witness." The Oral Tradition interprets this as meaning: "Do not allow a wicked person to serve as a witness."[2]

Even when an acceptable witness knows that his colleague is "wicked," but the judges are unaware of his wickedness, it is forbidden for him to offer testimony together with him even though he knows that the testimony is true, for, by doing so, he is joining together with him. Thus the acceptable witness "joined hands" with the wicked person, enabling his testimony to be accepted.[3] Needless to say, it is forbidden for an acceptable witness who knows testimony concerning a colleague to testify when he knows that the other witness who testifies with him is giving false testimony.[4] [This is also implied by the verse:] "Do not join hands with a wicked person."[5]

2. What is meant by "a wicked person"? Anyone who violates a prohibition punishable by lashes[6] is considered wicked and is unacceptable as a witness.[7] For the Torah referred to a person obligated to receive lashes with the term "wicked," as [Deuteronomy 25:2] states: "If the wicked person is liable to be beaten." Needless to say, a person who is obligated to be executed by the court is unacceptable, for [Numbers 35:31] states: "He is a wicked person who is [sentenced] to die."

3. When a person commits a transgression for which he is liable to receive lashes according to Scriptural Law, he is disqualified [as a witness] according to Scriptural Law.[8] When the prohibition is Rabbinical in origin, he is disqualified by Rabbinic decree.[9]

What is implied? A person who ate the meat of an animal [cooked] in milk, carrion, a teeming animal, or the like is not acceptable as a witness according

one eye is not acceptable as a judge for cases involving capital punishment. He may, however, adjudicate cases involving monetary law.

1. It is not merely that we suspect that the wicked person may be lying and therefore, we disqualify his testimony. Instead, even in situations where we are certain that he is telling the truth, he is unacceptable as a witness (*Tzaphnat Paneach, Klallei HaTorah Umitzvot; Yayin Malchut*).
2. *Sefer HaMitzvot* (negative commandment 286) and *Sefer HaChinuch* (mitzvah 75) count this as one of the 613 mitzvot of the Torah. In that source, the Rambam cites the interpretation of the verse offered by the *Mechilta*.
3. Although our Sages extended the meaning of the verse, they did not nullify its simple interpretation.
4. I.e., he knows that the witness did not actually observe the event in question and will be lying in court.
5. The *Siftei Cohen* 34:3 questions this law, asking why shouldn't the witness testify honestly. He has information that has bearing on a case, why shouldn't he bring this information to the attention of the court?

פֶּרֶק עֲשִׂירִי

א הָרְשָׁעִים פְּסוּלִין לְעֵדוּת מִן הַתּוֹרָה. שֶׁנֶּאֱמַר: אַל תָּשֶׁת יָדְךָ עִם רָשָׁע לִהְיֹת עֵד חָמָס. מִפִּי הַשְּׁמוּעָה לָמְדוּ: אַל תָּשֶׁת רָשָׁע עֵד. וַאֲפִלּוּ עֵד כָּשֵׁר שֶׁיּוֹדֵעַ בַּחֲבֵרוֹ שֶׁהוּא רָשָׁע, וְאֵין הַדַּיָּנִים מַכִּירִין רִשְׁעוֹ – אָסוּר לוֹ לְהָעִיד עִמּוֹ, אַף עַל פִּי שֶׁהוּא עֵדוּת אֱמֶת; מִפְּנֵי שֶׁמִּצְטָרֵף עִמּוֹ, וְנִמְצָא זֶה הַכָּשֵׁר הֵשִׁית יָדוֹ עִם הָרָשָׁע עַד שֶׁנִּתְקַבְּלָה עֵדוּתוֹ. וְאֵין צָרִיךְ לוֹמַר עֵד כָּשֵׁר שֶׁהוּא יוֹדֵעַ בְּעֵדוּת לַחֲבֵרוֹ, וְיָדַע שֶׁהָעֵד הַשֵּׁנִי עִמּוֹ עֵד שֶׁקֶר, שֶׁאָסוּר לוֹ לְהָעִיד. שֶׁנֶּאֱמַר: אַל תָּשֶׁת יָדְךָ עִם רָשָׁע.

ב אֵי זֶהוּ רָשָׁע? כֹּל שֶׁעָבַר עֲבֵרָה שֶׁחַיָּבִין עָלֶיהָ מַלְקוּת – זֶהוּ רָשָׁע, וּפָסוּל. שֶׁהֲרֵי הַתּוֹרָה קָרְאָה לִמְחֻיַּב מַלְקוּת רָשָׁע, שֶׁנֶּאֱמַר: וְהָיָה אִם בִּן הַכּוֹת הָרָשָׁע. וְאֵין צָרִיךְ לוֹמַר מְחֻיַּב מִיתַת בֵּית דִּין, שֶׁהוּא פָּסוּל. שֶׁנֶּאֱמַר: אֲשֶׁר הוּא רָשָׁע לָמוּת.

ג עָבַר עֲבֵרָה שֶׁחַיָּבִין עָלֶיהָ מַלְקוּת מִן הַתּוֹרָה – הֲרֵי זֶה פָּסוּל מִן הַתּוֹרָה; וְאִם הָיָה הַחִיּוּב שֶׁבָּהּ מִדִּבְרֵיהֶם – הֲרֵי זֶה פָּסוּל מִדִּבְרֵיהֶם. כֵּיצַד? אָכַל בְּשַׂר בְּהֵמָה בְּחָלָב, אוֹ שֶׁאָכַל נְבֵלוֹת וּשְׁקָצִים וְכַיּוֹצֵא בָּהֶן, בֵּין לְתֵאָבוֹן בֵּין

He explains that he personally would interpret the command as meaning that a person should not join together with an unacceptable witness to observe testimony. For example, at a wedding, witnesses are selected to observe the consecration of the bride. If one of the witnesses selected is unacceptable, an acceptable witness should not join together with him.

The *Siftei Cohen*, nevertheless, humbly submits to the authority of the authorities of the previous generations and accepts the Rambam's ruling. He also gives support for it, explaining that since (as stated in Chapter 5, Halachah 3) when three witnesses testify about a situation, their testimony is nullified if one of them is not acceptable, there would be no value in the acceptable witness testifying.

6. See *Hilchot Sanhedrin*, Chapter 18, which outlines the criteria for the prohibitions that are punishable by lashes. The Radbaz states that any person who violates a Scriptural prohibition is disqualified as a witness even if he does not receive lashes. It appears from the gloss of his *Kessef Mishneh* to Halachah 4 that Rav Yosef Karo does not accept this ruling and in his *Shulchan Aruch* (*Choshen Mishpat* 34:2), he quotes the Rambam's wording without further clarification. The Ramah quotes the opinion of Rabbenu Yerucham who maintains that such a transgressor is disqualified by Rabbinic decree.

7. See also Chapter 12, Halachah 1, which explains that there are situations where a person is disqualified as a witness even though he is not liable for lashes. See also Halachah 4.

8. As explained in Chapter 12, Halachah 1, the person must know that he is performing a transgression to be disqualified for this lack of observance.

9. The *Shulchan Aruch* (*Choshen Mishpat* 34:3) quotes the Rambam's ruling. The Ramah, however, quotes the opinion of Rabbenu Yerucham that, to be disqualified for the transgression of a Rabbinic prohibition, a person must have a financial motive.

to Scriptural Law.[10] [This applies] whether he transgressed because of appetite[11] or [with the intent of] angering God.[12] [The same law also applies] if he desecrates the sanctity of the first day of a festival or wears a garment that is *shaatnez*, i.e., combed, spun, or woven [with wool and linen]. If he eat the meat of fowl cooked in milk, he desecrated the second day of a festival observed in the Diaspora, or wore a woolen garment in which a strand of linen was lost or the like,[13] he is disqualified by Rabbinic decree.[14] We have already enumerated[15] all the transgressions for which one is punished by lashes. And with regard to each and every mitzvah, we have already explained which matters are forbidden by Scriptural Law and which are forbidden by Rabbinic decree.

4. There are other wicked persons who are not acceptable as witnesses even though they are required to make financial restitution and are not punished by lashes.[16] Since they take money that does not belong to them lawlessly, they are unacceptable, as [Deuteronomy 19:16] states: "When a lawless witness rises up against a person...." For example, thieves and people who seize property,[17] even though they make restitution,[18] they are no longer acceptable as witnesses[19] from the time they stole or robbed onward.[20]

Similarly, a lying witness, even though his testimony was disproved with regard to financial matters[21] and he made restitution, he is still unacceptable as a witness according to Scriptural Law for all matters.[22] From when is he disqualified? From the time he testified [falsely] in court, even though his testimony was not disproved until several days later.

10. For all these are Scriptural prohibitions.
11. E.g., the non-kosher meat is less expensive than the kosher meat and the person purchases the non-kosher meat in order to save money. Such an individual is certainly suspect to accept a bribe to deliver false testimony.
12. Even though we do not suspect such a person of being willing to accept a bribe, he is nevertheless disqualified as a witness, because he is "wicked," i.e., a transgressor.

This is one of the six instances where there is a difference of opinion between the Sages, Ravva and Abbaye, and the halachah is decided according to Abbaye's opinion. In all other instances, the halachah follows Ravva's view. See *Sanhedrin* 27a.
13. I.e., he transgressed a Rabbinical prohibition like those mentioned by the Rambam.
14. See Chapter 11, Halachah 6, which distinguishes between a person disqualified as a witness by Scriptural Law and one disqualified by Rabbinic decree.
15. *Hilchot Sanhedrin*, Chapter 19.
16. See *Hilchot Sanhedrin* 18:2 which states that whenever a person is liable for both lashes and a financial penalty, he is required to pay the financial penalty and is not punished by lashes.
17. The Rambam clarifies the definition of this term later in the halachah.

The *Kessef Mishneh* and others note that in this clause, the Rambam is speaking about individuals who are disqualified according to Scriptural Law. People who seize property - as the Rambam himself states - are disqualified only according to Rabbinic Law. For this reason, there are some who maintain that a printing error crept into the *Mishneh Torah* and the proper text should read "thieves and robbers." This version appears appropriate from the later wording in the clause and indeed is found in some authoritative manuscripts. The

לְהַכְעִיס, אוֹ שֶׁחִלֵּל אֶת יוֹם טוֹב הָרִאשׁוֹן, אוֹ שֶׁלָּבַשׁ שַׁעַטְנֵז שֶׁהוּא שׁוּעַ אוֹ טָווּי אוֹ נוּז - הֲרֵי זֶה פָּסוּל לְעֵדוּת מִן הַתּוֹרָה.

אֲבָל אִם אָכַל בְּשַׂר עוֹף בְּחָלָב, אוֹ שֶׁחִלֵּל יוֹם טוֹב שֵׁנִי שֶׁל גָּלֻיּוֹת, אוֹ שֶׁלָּבַשׁ בֶּגֶד צֶמֶר שֶׁאָבַד בּוֹ חוּט שֶׁל פִּשְׁתָּן וְכַיּוֹצֵא בּוֹ - הֲרֵי הוּא פָּסוּל מִדִּבְרֵיהֶם. וּכְבָר מָנִינוּ כָּל עֲבֵרָה שֶׁחַיָּבִין עָלֶיהָ מַלְקוּת. וּכְבָר נִתְבָּאֵר בְּכָל מִצְוָה וּמִצְוָה דְּבָרִים שֶׁאֲסוּרִין מִן הַתּוֹרָה וּדְבָרִים שֶׁאֲסוּרִין מִדִּבְרֵיהֶם.

ד וְעוֹד יֵשׁ שָׁם רְשָׁעִים שֶׁהֵן פְּסוּלִין לְעֵדוּת, אַף עַל פִּי שֶׁהֵן בְּנֵי תַּשְׁלוּמִין וְאֵינָן בְּנֵי מַלְקוּת. הוֹאִיל וְלוֹקְחִים מָמוֹן שֶׁאֵינוֹ שֶׁלָּהֶם בְּחָמָס - פְּסוּלִין. שֶׁנֶּאֱמַר: כִּי יָקוּם עֵד חָמָס בְּאִישׁ. כְּגוֹן הַגַּנָּבִים וְהַחַמְסָנִים, אַף עַל פִּי שֶׁהֶחֱזִיר - פָּסוּל לְעֵדוּת מֵעֵת שֶׁגָּנַב אוֹ גָּזַל. וְכֵן עֵד זוֹמֵם, אַף עַל פִּי שֶׁהוּזַם בְּעֵדוּת מָמוֹן וְשִׁלֵּם - הֲרֵי זֶה פָּסוּל מִן הַתּוֹרָה לְכָל עֵדוּת. וּמֵאֵימָתַי הוּא נִפְסָל? מֵעֵת שֶׁהֵעִיד בְּבֵית דִּין, אַף עַל פִּי שֶׁלֹּא הוּזַם עַל אוֹתָהּ עֵדוּת אֶלָּא אַחַר כַּמָּה יָמִים.

majority of the manuscripts and all printed texts of the *Mishneh Torah*, however, follow the version found in the standard printed text.

18. The *Tur* (*Choshen Mishpat* 34) questions the Rambam's wording, asking why the thief is disqualified after he made restitution. Seemingly, once he has made restitution, he has corrected his fault and should be deemed acceptable.

The *Tur* tries to resolve the Rambam's ruling by stating that he is speaking about a situation in which the thief was compelled by the court to make restitution. Since he did not do so willingly, he is not acceptable as a witness until he takes such a step on his own initiative.

The Radbaz rejects the *Tur's* explanation, stating that the Rambam does not qualify why the thief returned the money. He could also be referring to an instance where he returned it willingly. Instead, the Radbaz offers the explanation that the intent is that the testimony he delivers between the time he testified falsely and the time he returned the money is disqualified.

The Radbaz, however, is also not satisfied with this explanation, noting that Chapter 12, Halachah 4, states explicitly that even if a thief makes financial restitution, he is disqualified until he repents. Therefore the Radbaz explains that even after a thief returns the money he stole, he is still under suspicion, for perhaps he will be willing to lie for a greater sum. This understanding is also accepted by Rav Yosef Karo in his *Kessef Mishneh* and quoted by him in the *Shulchan Aruch* (*Choshen Mishpat* 34:7).

19. For we fear that he would accept a bribe to testify falsely.

20. Hence, if he delivered testimony in court concerning another matter between the time he testified falsely and the time the falsehood is discovered, that other testimony is disqualified and the case retried. Similarly, all legal documents on which he signed are disqualified from the time he gave false testimony.

See Chapter 12, Halachah 4, which discusses when such individuals may be reinstated as witnesses.

21. If, however, he testified falsely with regard to other matters, different laws apply. Such a person is required to be lashed. After this punishment is administered, he is again acceptable as a witness.

22. In this instance as well, we fear that he will accept a bribe in order to testify falsely.

Similarly, when people are involved with loans at interest - both the borrower and the lender - if fixed interest is involved, both are disqualified according to Scriptural Law.[23] If the shade of interest is involved,[24] they are both disqualified by Rabbinic decree. Similarly, a person who transgresses the Rabbinic decrees against theft[25] is disqualified by Rabbinic decree.

What is implied? People who seize property - either landed property or movable property - without the consent of the owners, even though they pay its worth, are disqualified by Rabbinic decree.[26] Similarly, herders of their own animals[27] - both of small animals[28] and of large animals[29] - are disqualified,[30] for it can be assumed that they take liberty and steal [by] allowing their animals to pasture in fields and orchards belonging to other people. Therefore, an ordinary herder is disqualified.[31]

People who raise small animals in *Eretz Yisrael* are not acceptable [as witnesses].[32] In the Diaspora, by contrast, they are acceptable. It is permissible to raise a large animal everywhere.[33]

Generally, the collectors of the king's duty[34] are not acceptable, because it is assumed that they will collect more than what is required by the king's decree and keep the extra portion for themselves. Tax collectors,[35] by

With the term "for all matters," the Rambam is referring to *Sanhedrin* 27a which states that such a witness is disqualified even for cases involving capital punishment. We do not say that he will appreciate that these matters are more severe than mere financial questions. Instead, we suspect that will accept a bribe to testify falsely even in such cases.

23. For both are considered to have transgressed a Scriptural prohibition, as stated in *Hilchot Malveh ViLoveh* 4:2.

Rabbenu Yerucham notes that the witnesses and the guarantor to such a loan are also considered to have transgressed a Scriptural prohibition. Hence, he maintains, they should also be disqualified as witnesses. The *Kessef Mishneh* differs and explains that since they are punished for their transgression by lashes and they themselves do not receive any financial gain, there is no proof that they are not acceptable as witnesses. This understanding is also borne out by the *Maggid Mishneh* ruling in his gloss to *Hilchot Malveh ViLoveh* 4:6 and the ruling of the *Sefer Me'irat Einayim* 52:1.

24. I.e., interest forbidden by Rabbinic decree; see *Hilchot Malveh ViLoveh* 4:14. The Ramah (*Choshen Mishpat* 34:10) quotes opinions which maintain that if the interest is forbidden only according to Rabbinic Law, the borrower is not disqualified as a witness.

25. E.g., he takes an ownerless object found by a minor, deafmute, or mentally or emotionally unstable person [Ramah (*Choshen Mishpat* 34:13)].

26. Although taking property without the owner's consent violates the prohibition (Exodus 20:14) "Do not crave," *Tosafot, Sanhedrin* 25b, states that this applies only when the person does not pay the article's worth. The *Lechem Mishneh* brings support from other sources to demonstrate that the Rambam does not follow this approach.

The *Kessef Mishneh* states that since the prohibition "Do not crave" does not involve a deed, it is not punishable by lashes. Hence it does not cause a person to be disqualified by Scriptural Law.

27. But, by contrast, a person paid to herd animals belonging to a colleague is not disqualified. Since the animals are not his own, we do not suspect that he will transgress for the sake of his colleague's benefit. Instead, he will take care to pasture the animals where it is permitted to do so (see *Bava Metzia* 5b).

וְכֵן הַמַּלְוֶה בְּרִבִּית, אֶחָד הַמַּלְוֶה וְאֶחָד הַלֹּוֶה – שְׁנֵיהֶם פְּסוּלִין לְעֵדוּת. אִם רִבִּית קְצוּצָה עָשׂוּ – הֲרֵי הֵן פְּסוּלִין מִן הַתּוֹרָה, וְאִם אֲבַק רִבִּית עָשׂוּ – הֲרֵי הֵן פְּסוּלִין מִדִּבְרֵיהֶם. וְכֵן כָּל הָעוֹבֵר עַל גָּזֵל שֶׁל דִּבְרֵיהֶם – הֲרֵי הוּא פָּסוּל מִדִּבְרֵיהֶם.

כֵּיצַד? הַחַמְסָנִים, וְהֵם הַלּוֹקְחִים קַרְקַע אוֹ מִטַּלְטְלִין שֶׁלֹּא בִּרְצוֹן הַבְּעָלִים, אַף עַל פִּי שֶׁנּוֹתְנִין הַדָּמִים – הֲרֵי אֵלּוּ פְּסוּלִין מִדִּבְרֵיהֶם. וְכֵן הָרוֹעִים, אֶחָד רוֹעֵי בְּהֵמָה דַקָּה וְאֶחָד רוֹעֵי בְּהֵמָה גַסָּה שֶׁל עַצְמָן – הֲרֵי הֵן פְּסוּלִין; שֶׁחֶזְקָתָן פּוֹשְׁטִין יְדֵיהֶן בְּגָזֵל, וּמַנִּיחִים בְּהֶמְתָּן לִרְעוֹת בְּשָׂדוֹת וּפַרְדֵּסִים שֶׁל אֲחֵרִים. וּלְפִיכָךְ, סְתַם רוֹעֶה – פָּסוּל.

וּמְגַדְּלֵי בְּהֵמָה דַקָּה בְּאֶרֶץ יִשְׂרָאֵל – פְּסוּלִין; אֲבָל בְּחוּצָה לָאָרֶץ – כְּשֵׁרִין.

וּמֻתָּר לְגַדֵּל בְּהֵמָה גַסָּה בְּכָל מָקוֹם.

וְכֵן הַמּוֹכְסִין – סְתָמָן פְּסוּלִין; מִפְּנֵי שֶׁחֶזְקָתָן לִקַּח יוֹתֵר מִדָּבָר הַקָּצוּב לָהֶם בְּדִין הַמַּלְכוּת, וְלוֹקְחִין הַיֶּתֶר לְעַצְמָן.

28. I.e., sheep or goats.
29. I.e., cattle.
30. By Rabbinic decree. Similarly, all of the subsequent offenders mentioned are disqualified by Rabbinic decree unless it is stated otherwise.
31. Even if he was not seen pasturing his animals in his colleague's property, he is disqualified unless it is proved otherwise.
32. This applies even if the people raise these animals in their homes or courtyards and do not intentionally let them pasture at all. The rationale is that the animals will most likely break loose and pasture on another person's property. See *Hilchot Nizkei Mammon* 5:2,8 where the prohibition against raising such animals is discussed. As mentioned there, the prohibition was enacted as a special measure to encourage and protect the settlement of our Holy Land.
33. I.e., even in *Eretz Yisrael*. The rationale is that cattle are easier to restrain and they are more necessary for working the fields and providing milk products (*Bava Kama* 79b). Even cattle, however, may not be allowed to pasture freely without their owners taking safeguards that they will not enter other people's fields.
34. This term refers to a practice common in the Roman era in which a person would pay the tax duty for a particular region to the king in advance. He would then collect that duty - and more - from the inhabitants of that region. Since he is making a profit, and in many instances, an inordinate profit, from the inhabitants, he is considered as a robber and disqualified as a witness. The *Sefer Me'irat Einayim* 34:34 interprets this term slightly differently, explaining that it refers to customs collectors and income tax collectors. Since the rules governing these duties are not so clear cut and it is possible for the collector to overcharge, it is suspected that he will do so and keep the remainder for himself.

If such a collector is not known to have taken more than is required, he is disqualified only according to Rabbinic decree. If it is known that he took more, he is disqualified according to Scriptural Law (*Kessef Mishneh*).

In the present era, since taxes and duties are generally standardized and these standards are public knowledge, there is less possibility for wrongdoing of this nature and such individuals are not disqualified as a rule. If, however, there are situations where offenses of this type are common, the same rules would apply.
35. The collectors of a fixed head tax or property tax.

contrast, are generally considered to be acceptable. If, however, it is known that they took more than they are required to collect, even once, they are disqualified.

Similarly, those who guide the flight of doves in a settled area are disqualified, because we assume that they will steal doves belonging to others without paying for them.[36] [This ruling also applies to] merchants [of produce] in the Sabbatical year, i.e., people who [generally] are idle[37] but when the Sabbatical year arrives, they begin to do business with produce. It can be assumed that they collect the produce of the Sabbatical year and do business with it.[38]

Similarly, dice-players are [disqualified] if this is their only occupation. Since such a person does not involve himself in ordinary business pursuits, it can be assumed that his livelihood is dependent on his gambling, which is [forbidden] as "the shade of robbery."[39] The above applies not only to dice-players, but also to all those who gamble with the shells of nuts or the shells of pomegranates. Similarly, [our Sages did not disqualify] only those who train doves,[40] but also those who gamble with other animals, beasts, and fowl, saying [the owner] of the one that will outrace the other or vanquish the other will acquire [the stakes put up] by both. Similarly, other analogous types of gamblers are disqualified, provided they do not derive their livelihood from a source other than gambling.[41] All of the above are disqualified according to Rabbinic decree.

5. [The fact that] a sharecropper takes a small amount of the produce which sprouts in Nisan and in Tishrei[42] before [the harvest] is finished[43] without the

36. I.e., we suspect that this person will lead doves belonging to others from their own dovecotes to dovecotes owned by others. See *Hilchot Gezeilah* 6:7-8. As stated in that source, the prohibition applies only in a settled area. In the desert, by contrast, the doves are assumed to be ownerless and one may lead them wherever one desires.

37. The Radbaz states that with this phrase, the Rambam implies that if these individuals have another occupation, they are not disqualified even if they also do business with the produce of the Sabbatical year.

38. In the Sabbatical year, it is as if all the fields and orchards are ownerless and the produce which is in them may be taken by anyone. It may, however, be taken only for immediate consumption, but not to be hoarded and sold (see *Hilchot Shemitah* 6:1-4). Since the person transgresses this prohibition for the sake of monetary gain, we suspect that he might also accept a bribe to deliver false testimony (Radbaz).

39. See *Hilchot Gezelah* 6:10-11 where the Rambam speaks about gambling and states:

> This is robbery according to Rabbinic decree. Although the person himself consents to [the other person's] taking his money, since he is taking it for nothing, as part of the frivolous sport, it is equivalent to robbery.
>
> When a person plays dice with gentiles, he does not violate the prohibition against robbery. He does, however, violate the prohibition against occupying oneself with empty matters. It is not fitting for a person to spend any of his days occupied in anything other than words of wisdom or [pursuits that lead to] a stable world.

40. There is a slight difficulty with the Rambam's statement. As mentioned by the

אֲבָל גַּבָּאֵי מְנַת הַמֶּלֶךְ – סְתָמָן כְּשֵׁרִים. וְאִם נוֹדַע שֶׁלָּקְחוּ אֲפִלּוּ פַּעַם אַחַת יָתֵר מִן הָרָאוּי לָהֶם לִגְבּוֹת – הֲרֵי אֵלּוּ פְּסוּלִין.

וְכֵן מַפְרִיחֵי יוֹנִים בְּיִשּׁוּב – פְּסוּלִין; מִפְּנֵי שֶׁחֶזְקָתָן שֶׁגּוֹזְלִים יוֹנִים שֶׁל אֲחֵרִים בְּחִנָּם.

וְכֵן סוֹחֲרֵי שְׁבִיעִית. וְהֵם בְּנֵי אָדָם שֶׁיּוֹשְׁבִין בְּטֵלִים, וְכֵיוָן שֶׁבָּאָה שְׁבִיעִית פּוֹשְׁטִים יְדֵיהֶן וּמַתְחִילִין לִשָּׂא וְלִתֵּן בְּפֵרוֹת; שֶׁחֶזְקַת אֵלּוּ שֶׁהֵן אוֹסְפִין פֵּרוֹת שְׁבִיעִית וְעוֹשִׂין בָּהֶן סְחוֹרָה.

וְכֵן מְשַׂחֵק בְּקוּבְיָא. וְהוּא שֶׁלֹּא תִּהְיֶה לוֹ אֻמָּנוּת אֶלָּא הוּא. הוֹאִיל וְאֵינוֹ עוֹסֵק בְּיִשּׁוּבוֹ שֶׁל עוֹלָם – הֲרֵי זֶה בְּחֶזְקַת שֶׁאוֹכֵל מִן הַקּוּבְיָא, שֶׁהוּא אֲבַק גָּזֵל. וְלֹא בְּקוּבְיָא בִּלְבַד, אֶלָּא אֲפִלּוּ מְשַׂחֲקִים בִּקְלִפֵּי אֱגוֹזִים וּקְלִפֵּי רִמּוֹנִים. וְכֵן לֹא יוֹנִים בִּלְבַד אָמְרוּ, אֶלָּא אֲפִלּוּ הַמְשַׂחֲקִים בִּבְהֵמָה חַיָּה וָעוֹף, וְאוֹמֵר: כָּל הַקּוֹדֵם אֶת חֲבֵרוֹ, אוֹ כָּל הַנּוֹצֵחַ אֶת חֲבֵרוֹ – יִטֹּל בְּעָלָיו אֶת שְׁנֵיהֶן. וְכֵן כֹּל כַּיּוֹצֵא בִּשְׂחוֹק זֶה. וְהוּא שֶׁלֹּא תִּהְיֶה לוֹ אֻמָּנוּת אֶלָּא שְׂחוֹק זֶה – הֲרֵי הוּא פָּסוּל. וְכָל אֵלּוּ פְּסוּלִין מִדִּבְרֵיהֶם.

ה אָרִיס שֶׁלָּקַח דָּבָר מוּעָט מִן הַפֵּרוֹת שֶׁבִּכְּרוּ בִּימֵי נִיסָן וִימֵי תִּשְׁרֵי קֹדֶם שֶׁתִּגָּמֵר

commentaries to *Sanhedrin* 25a, there are two interpretations given to why dove-trainers are unacceptable as witnesses:
a) they steal doves, as the Rambam mentioned above;
b) they gamble by racing doves against each other, as mentioned in this clause.

Apparently, the Rambam does not see these rationales as mutually exclusive. Hence, he prohibits both types of dove trainers.

41. The Rambam's wording implies that if the person has another source of income, even if he frequently gambles, he is not disqualified. Thus it is not gambling itself, although it involves a Rabbinic prohibition, which causes him to be disqualified, but rather the fact that the person has no other source of income. As such, we suspect that he might be willing to accept a bribe to deliver false testimony.

The *Tur* (*Choshen Mishpat* 34) elaborates on this concept, stating that "since these people do not know how much a person must labor for money, causing a colleague financial loss through false testimony is insignificant in their eyes."

In his *Kessef Mishneh*, Rav Yosef Karo questions the Rambam's statements, wondering why, if gambling is equivalent to robbery, is that not alone a sufficient reason to have the person disqualified. He therefore explains that the Rambam is speaking about a person who gambles with gentiles - or is seen gambling just for sport. Since he has no other occupation, we suspect that he also gambles with Jews for profit. Hence he is disqualified as a witness. In his *Shulchan Aruch* (*Choshen Mishpat* 34:16), he quotes the Rambam's wording without emendation. See *Sefer Me'irat Einayim* 34:40.

42. Nisan is the time when fresh grain begins to be harvested, and Tishrei, the time when fruits begin to be harvested.

43. Since the harvest is not finished, he takes the license of taking some of the produce because of the extra work he performs. Although this is forbidden, he is not disqualified as the Rambam continues to explain.

The *Tur* and the Ramah (*Choshen Mishpat* 34:15) differ with the Rambam and state that this law applies if the sharecropper takes the produce after the harvest has been completed, but not before.

knowledge of the owner of the field does not cause him to be considered as a thief and he is acceptable as a witness. [The rationale is that] the owner of the field is not concerned with [such a small quantity of produce]. Similar principles apply in all analogous situations.

CHAPTER ELEVEN

1. One who does not read the Written Law, nor study the Oral Law, nor carry on ordinary social relationships[1] can be assumed to be wicked and is disqualified as a witness according to Rabbinic decree. [The rationale is that] whenever a person has descended to such a degree, it can be assumed that he will transgress most transgressions that will present themselves to him.[2]

2. For this reason, unlearned people should not be designated as witnesses,[3] nor do we accept such a person's testimony[4] unless it has been established that he observes the mitzvot, performs acts of kindness, conducts himself in an upright manner, and carries on normal social relationships. The testimony of [such a person] may be accepted even though he is unlearned and is unfamiliar with both the Written and Oral Law.

3. Thus one may conclude that any Torah scholar may be assumed to be acceptable [as a witness] unless he is disqualified, and any unlearned person may be assumed to be unacceptable[5] unless it is established that he follows just paths.[6]

4. Whoever accepts the testimony of an unlearned person before it is established [that he possesses the above positive qualities] or before witnesses come and testify that he observes the mitzvot and carries on ordinary social relations is a commoner and will be required to face judgment, for he has forfeited the financial resources of Jews on the basis of the testimony of the wicked.

5. Similarly, base people are disqualified as witnesses by Rabbinic decree. This refers to people who walk through the marketplace eating in the presence of everyone,[7] those who go unclothed in the marketplace when they are involved in ignoble tasks,[8] and the like. [The rationale is that] they are not concerned with their own shame.[9] All these people are considered as dogs; they will not be concerned with testifying falsely.

1. Our translation of the term *derech eretz*, literally, "the way of the world," is taken from the Rambam's Commentary to the Mishnah (*Kiddushin* 1:10).
2. Hence he is likely to accept a bribe to deliver false testimony.
3. I.e., to sign on a legal document or to observe a business transaction.
4. If he was designated as a witness (*Sefer Me'irat Einayim* 34:43).

מְלַאכְתָּן, אַף עַל פִּי שֶׁלָּקַח שֶׁלֹּא מִדַּעַת בַּעַל הַשָּׂדֶה – אֵינוֹ גַּנָּב וְכָשֵׁר לְעֵדוּת; שֶׁאֵין בַּעַל הַשָּׂדֶה מַקְפִּיד עָלָיו. וְכֵן כֹּל כַּיּוֹצֵא בָּזֶה.

פֶּרֶק אַחַד עָשָׂר

א מִי שֶׁאֵינוֹ לֹא בְּמִקְרָא וְלֹא בְּמִשְׁנָה וְלֹא בְּדֶרֶךְ אֶרֶץ – הֲרֵי זֶה בְּחֶזְקַת רָשָׁע, וּפָסוּל לְעֵדוּת מִדִּבְרֵיהֶם. שֶׁכָּל מִי שֶׁיָּרַד עַד כָּךְ – חֲזָקָה שֶׁהוּא עוֹבֵר עַל רֹב הָעֲבֵרוֹת שֶׁיָּבוֹאוּ לְיָדוֹ.

ב לְפִיכָךְ, אֵין מוֹסְרִין עֵדוּת לְעַם הָאָרֶץ וְאֵין מְקַבְּלִין מִמֶּנּוּ עֵדוּת.
אֶלָּא אִם כֵּן הֻחְזַק שֶׁהוּא עוֹסֵק בְּמִצְוֹת וּבִגְמִילוּת חֲסָדִים, וְנוֹהֵג בְּדַרְכֵי הַיְשָׁרִים, וְיֵשׁ בּוֹ דֶּרֶךְ אֶרֶץ – מְקַבְּלִין עֵדוּתוֹ, אַף עַל פִּי שֶׁהוּא עַם הָאָרֶץ וְאֵינוֹ לֹא בְּמִקְרָא וְלֹא בְּמִשְׁנָה.

ג נִמְצֵאתָ אוֹמֵר: כָּל תַּלְמִיד חָכָם – בְּחֶזְקַת כָּשֵׁר, עַד שֶׁיִּפָּסֵל.
כָּל עַם הָאָרֶץ – בְּחֶזְקַת שֶׁהוּא פָּסוּל, עַד שֶׁיֻּחְזַק שֶׁהוּא הוֹלֵךְ בְּדַרְכֵי הַיְשָׁרִים.

ד וְכָל מִי שֶׁיְּקַבֵּל עֵדוּת עַם הָאָרֶץ טֶרֶם שֶׁתִּהְיֶה לוֹ חֲזָקָה זוֹ, אוֹ קֹדֶם שֶׁיָּבוֹאוּ עֵדִים וְיָעִידוּ שֶׁהוּא נוֹהֵג בְּמִצְוֹת וּבְדֶרֶךְ אֶרֶץ – הֲרֵי זֶה הֶדְיוֹט, וְעָתִיד לִתֵּן אֶת הַדִּין; שֶׁהֲרֵי מְאַבֵּד מָמוֹנָן שֶׁל יִשְׂרָאֵל עַל פִּי רְשָׁעִים.

ה וְכֵן הַבְּזוּיִין פְּסוּלִין לְעֵדוּת מִדִּבְרֵיהֶם. וְהֵם הָאֲנָשִׁים שֶׁהוֹלְכִין וְאוֹכְלִין בַּשּׁוּק בִּפְנֵי כָּל הָעָם, וּכְגוֹן אֵלּוּ שֶׁהוֹלְכִין עֲרֻמִּים בַּשּׁוּק בְּעֵת שֶׁהֵן עוֹסְקִין בִּמְלָאכָה מְנֻוֶּלֶת, וְכַיּוֹצֵא בְּאֵלּוּ שֶׁאֵין מַקְפִּידִין עַל הַבֹּשֶׁת. שֶׁכָּל אֵלּוּ חֲשׁוּבִין כְּכֶלֶב, וְאֵין מַקְפִּידִין עַל עֵדוּת שֶׁקֶר.

5. Since he is unlearned, we assume that he lacks the other positive qualities mentioned in the previous halachah.
6. The Radbaz comments that this matter has been a source of error for many courts. Although our Sages state that every Jew can be assumed to be acceptable, the intent is that it can be assumed that he will not commit transgressions. It does not mean that he can be assumed to have all the positive qualities necessary for his testimony to be accepted.
7. The *Kessef Mishneh* interprets the Rambam's words as referring to a person who goes through the marketplace eating casually, exposing himself to everyone's view, as opposed to someone who eats in a private corner.
8. *Yevamot* 63b states: "There is no one more disgusting and more despicable... than someone who goes unclothed in the marketplace."
9. As indicated by Chapter 17, Halachah 2, shame is one of the essential elements necessary to discourage a person from giving false testimony (*Likkutei Sichos,* Vol. XVII).

Included are those who partake of charity given by gentiles in public.[10] Although they could derive this benefit in private, they demean themselves and accept it in public without showing concern [for their honor]. All of these individuals are disqualified according to Rabbinical decree.

6. What is the difference between a person who is disqualified as a witness according to Scriptural Law and one who is disqualified by Rabbinic decree? The testimony of a person disqualified by Scriptural Law is nullified even though it was not announced in synagogues and houses of study that he [is unacceptable].

Announcements must be made about a person who is disqualified by Rabbinic decree, by contrast, [before his testimony is disqualified].[11] Accordingly, any testimony that he gives before such announcements are made are accepted so that people [who relied on him] will not suffer a loss,[12] for they did not know that he was unacceptable, and he is disqualified only by Rabbinic decree.[13]

7. The testimony of one witness is acceptable with regard to the Torah's prohibitions,[14] even though his testimony is not accepted with regard to other matters. [This is evident from the fact that when] a wicked person known to transgress[15] slaughters an animal, his slaughter is acceptable. We accept his word when he says: "I slaughtered it according to law." When, however, a person is suspected [of violating] a particular prohibition [frequently], his word is not accepted with regard to his own matters. His word is accepted, however, with regard to others.[16]

8. For this reason, a person suspected [of violating] a particular prohibition may serve as a judge and as a witness for others. We operate under the assumption that a person will not transgress so that others will benefit.[17]

What is implied? [The word of] an unlearned person[18] is accepted if he states: "The produce of so-and-so has been tithed." [Similarly, the word of] a person who is suspected of selling the meat of a firstborn[19] is accepted if he states: "The meat which so-and-so is selling is ordinary[20] meat." Similar

10. Rashi, *Sanhedrin* 26b states that a person who receives charity from gentiles in public "desecrates the name of God for the sake of money." The intent is that by accepting the money from gentiles, the person indicates that the Jewish people are not willing to take care of him. This denigrates the honor of the Jewish people and thus of God.

As the commentaries mention, however, if a person benefits from the charity of gentiles privately or if he needs the money, and there is no other alternative but for him to take the charity in public, these words of censure do not apply. For since his livelihood is dependent on the matter, he has no option. See *Hilchot Matanot Aniyim* 8:9.

11. In this way, everyone will be advised not to rely on him.

12. For if his testimony serves as evidence concerning a loan or a sale, the lender or the purchaser will suffer financial loss if his testimony is disqualified.

13. Since his testimony is acceptable according to Scriptural Law, our Sages did not enforce their decrees in an instance which would cause people financial loss.

וּמִכְּלַל אֵלּוּ: הָאוֹכְלִין צְדָקָה שֶׁל עוֹבְדֵי כּוֹכָבִים בְּפַרְהֶסְיָא. אַף עַל פִּי שֶׁאֶפְשָׁר לָהֶן שֶׁיִּזּוֹנוּ בִּצְנְעָה, מְבַזִּים עַצְמָן וְאֵינָן חוֹשְׁשִׁין. כָּל אֵלּוּ פְּסוּלִין מִדִּבְרֵיהֶם.

ו מַה בֵּין פָּסוּל לְעֵדוּת מִן הַתּוֹרָה לְפָסוּל מִדִּבְרֵיהֶם? שֶׁהַפָּסוּל מִן הַתּוֹרָה שֶׁהֵעִיד – עֵדוּתוֹ בְּטֵלָה, אַף עַל פִּי שֶׁלֹּא הִכְרִיזוּ עָלָיו בְּבָתֵּי כְנֵסִיּוֹת וּבְבָתֵּי מִדְרָשׁוֹת; וְהַפָּסוּל מִדִּבְרֵיהֶם – צָרִיךְ הַכְרָזָה. לְפִיכָךְ, כָּל עֵדוּת שֶׁהֵעִיד קֹדֶם שֶׁהִכְרִיזוּ עָלָיו – מְקַבְּלִין אוֹתָהּ, כְּדֵי שֶׁלֹּא לְאַבֵּד זְכוּת הָעָם, שֶׁהֲרֵי לֹא יָדְעוּ שֶׁהוּא פָּסוּל, וְאֵין פְּסוּלוֹ אֶלָּא מִדִּבְרֵיהֶם.

ז עֵד אֶחָד נֶאֱמָן בְּאִסּוּרִין, אַף עַל פִּי שֶׁהוּא פָּסוּל לִשְׁאָר עֵדֻיּוֹת. שֶׁהֲרֵי רָשָׁע בַּעֲבֵרָה שֶׁשָּׁחַט – שְׁחִיטָתוֹ כְּשֵׁרָה, וְנֶאֱמָן לוֹמַר: כַּהֲלָכָה שָׁחַטְתִּי. אֲבָל הֶחָשׁוּד עַל דָּבָר – אֵינוֹ נֶאֱמָן עַל שֶׁלּוֹ, אֲבָל נֶאֱמָן הוּא עַל אֲחֵרִים.

ח לְפִיכָךְ, הֶחָשׁוּד עַל דָּבָר – יֵשׁ לוֹ לָדוּן בּוֹ וּלְהָעִיד בּוֹ לַאֲחֵרִים. חֲזָקָה אֵין אָדָם חוֹטֵא כְּדֵי שֶׁיִּהָנוּ אֲחֵרִים.

כֵּיצַד? נֶאֱמָן עַם הָאָרֶץ לוֹמַר: פֵּרוֹת פְּלוֹנִי מְתֻקָּנִים הֵם, וְנֶאֱמָן הַנֶּחְשָׁד לִמְכֹּר בְּשַׂר בְּכוֹר לוֹמַר: בָּשָׂר זֶה שֶׁמּוֹכֵר פְּלוֹנִי חֻלִּין הוּא.

14. This is a general principle. Unlike financial matters, marriage and divorce, and cases involving capital punishment, the determination of whether an object is kosher may be made on the basis of the testimony of one witness [see *Shulchan Aruch* and Ramah (*Yoreh Deah* 127:3)]. The Rambam continues, explaining that even though the testimony of a particular witness would not be accepted with regard to other matters, it is accepted with regard to questions of this nature.

15. A prohibition other than the prohibition against eating meat that is not properly slaughtered. The testimony of such a person would not be accepted in court. Thus the fact that his word is accepted in this situation serves as proof of the principle stated by the Rambam at the outset.

16. Examples of - and the rationale for - this leniency is explained by the Rambam in the following halachah.

17. When stating this law in *Hilchot Ma'aser* 13:17, the Rambam adds one proviso, that it not appear that the person making the statement is trying to perpetrate deception. For example, two produce traders who are suspect to sell untithed produce enter a city. One says: "My produce has not been tithed, but my colleague's has been tithed."

The Ra'avad differs with the Rambam's ruling and cites sources which appear to indicate that the suspect person's word is not accepted at all, not with regard to his own matters, nor with regard to those involving another person. The Radbaz and the *Kessef Mishneh* provide explanations that justify the Rambam's ruling.

18. Whose word is not ordinarily accepted with regard to questions whether his own produce has been tithed.

19. The meat of a firstborn animal cannot be eaten unless it received a blemish on its own accord. This person is suspected of slaughtering such an animal and selling it even if it did not have a blemish. Our translation is based on the gloss of the *Kessef Mishneh*.

20. I.e., meat that is not from a firstborn.

principles apply with regard to other prohibitions. For the wicked fear [the Torah's] prohibitions,[21] but they do not fear [causing others] monetary [loss].[22]

9. The Kings of Israel[23] may not testify, nor is testimony given against them, because they are strong-armed men of power who do not subjugate themselves to the yoke of the judges.[24] Testimony may be made against a High Priest, by contrast, and he may give testimony concerning the king in the Supreme *Sanhedrin*, as explained.[25]

10. Our Sages had no need to list informers,[26] *epicursim*,[27] and apostates[28] among those who are not acceptable as witnesses. For they listed only the wicked among the Jewish people. These rebellious deserters of the faith are inferior to the gentiles. Gentiles need not be saved [from a pit], but neither should they be pushed [into one][29] the pious among them[30] will receive a share in the world to come. These [deserters of the faith] should be pushed [into a pit] and should not be saved from one; they will not receive a portion in the world to come.

CHAPTER TWELVE

1. Whenever a person is disqualified as a witness for committing a transgression, he is disqualified if two witnesses testify that he committed a transgression despite the fact that they did not warn him [and hence,] he does not receive lashes.[1]

When does the above apply? When [the person] committed a transgression that is universally known among the Jewish people to be a sin, e.g., he took a false or an unnecessary[2] oath, he robbed, he stole, he ate meat from an animal that was not slaughtered in a ritual manner, or the like. [Different rules apply, however,] if the witnesses see him transgress a prohibition which he most likely violated unknowingly.[3] [In such an instance,] they must warn him. Afterwards, [if he transgresses,] he is disqualified.

What is implied? If [witnesses] saw [a person] tying or untying [a knot] on the Sabbath, they must inform him that this desecrates the Sabbath,[4] because most people are unaware of this.[5] Similarly, if they see him performing a [forbidden] labor on the Sabbath or a festival, they must inform him that the day is the Sabbath [or the festival], lest he have forgotten.

21. I.e., even if they transgress themselves, they will hesitate before causing another person to transgress.
22. They will not, however, fear causing a person monetary loss.
23. This term refers to the kings of the Ten Tribes, and by extension to the Hasmonean and Herodian kings of the Second Temple era. Different laws apply to kings of the Davidic dynasty, as stated in Chapter 1, Halachah 3, *Hilchot Melachim* 3:7.
24. In *Hilchot Sanhedrin* 2:5, the Rambam quotes this law and gives a rationale: "because this may lead to a disaster." See the notes to that halachah.
25. Chapter 1, Halachah 3.

וְכֵן כֹּל כַּיּוֹצֵא בָּזֶה מִשְּׁאָר הָאִסּוּרִין. לְפִי שֶׁאֵימַת הָאִסּוּרִים עַל הָרְשָׁעִים, וְאֵין אֵימַת הַמָּמוֹן עֲלֵיהֶם.

ט מַלְכֵי יִשְׂרָאֵל – לֹא מְעִידִין וְלֹא מְעִידִין עֲלֵיהֶן; מִפְּנֵי שֶׁהֵן אַלָּמִים, בַּעֲלֵי זְרוֹעַ, וְאֵינָן נִכְנָעִין תַּחַת עֹל הַדַּיָּנִים. אֲבָל כֹּהֵן גָּדוֹל – מְעִידִין עָלָיו, וּמֵעִיד הוּא לַמֶּלֶךְ בְּבֵית דִּין הַגָּדוֹל, כְּמוֹ שֶׁבֵּאַרְנוּ.

י הַמּוֹסְרִין וְהָאֶפִּיקוֹרוֹסִין וְהַמּוּמָרִים – לֹא הִצְרִיכוּ חֲכָמִים לְמָנוֹתָן בִּכְלַל פְּסוּלֵי עֵדוּת; שֶׁלֹּא מָנוּ אֶלָּא רִשְׁעֵי יִשְׂרָאֵל, אֲבָל אֵלּוּ הַמּוֹרְדִין הַכּוֹפְרִין – פְּחוּתִין הֵן מִן הָעוֹבְדֵי כּוֹכָבִים. שֶׁהָעוֹבְדֵי כּוֹכָבִים – לֹא מַעֲלִין וְלֹא מוֹרִידִין, וְיֵשׁ לַחֲסִידֵיהֶן חֵלֶק לָעוֹלָם הַבָּא; וְאֵלּוּ מוֹרִידִין וְלֹא מַעֲלִין, וְאֵין לָהֶן חֵלֶק לָעוֹלָם הַבָּא.

פֶּרֶק שְׁנֵים עָשָׂר

א כָּל הַנִּפְסָל בַּעֲבֵרָה, אִם הֵעִידוּ עָלָיו שְׁנֵי עֵדִים שֶׁעָשָׂה עֲבֵרָה פְּלוֹנִית, אַף עַל פִּי שֶׁלֹּא הִתְרוּ בּוֹ, שֶׁהֲרֵי אֵינוֹ לוֹקֶה – הֲרֵי זֶה פָּסוּל לְעֵדוּת.
בַּמֶּה דְּבָרִים אֲמוּרִים? כְּשֶׁעָבַר עַל דְּבָרִים שֶׁפָּשַׁט בְּיִשְׂרָאֵל שֶׁהֵן עֲבֵרָה, כְּגוֹן שֶׁנִּשְׁבַּע לַשֶּׁקֶר אוֹ לַשָּׁוְא, אוֹ גָּזַל אוֹ גָּנַב, אוֹ אָכַל נְבֵלָה וְכַיּוֹצֵא בּוֹ; אֲבָל אִם רָאוּהוּ עֵדִים עוֹבֵר עַל דָּבָר שֶׁקָּרוֹב הָעוֹשֶׂה לִהְיוֹת שׁוֹגֵג – צְרִיכִין לְהַזְהִירוֹ, וְאַחַר כָּךְ יִפָּסֵל.
כֵּיצַד? רָאוּהוּ קוֹשֵׁר אוֹ מַתִּיר בְּשַׁבָּת – צְרִיכִין לְהוֹדִיעוֹ שֶׁזֶּה חִלּוּל שַׁבָּת, מִפְּנֵי שֶׁרֹב הָעָם אֵינָן יוֹדְעִין זֶה. וְכֵן אִם רָאוּהוּ עוֹשֶׂה מְלָאכָה בְּשַׁבָּת אוֹ בְּיוֹם טוֹב – צְרִיכִין לְהוֹדִיעוֹ שֶׁהַיּוֹם שַׁבָּת, שֶׁמָּא שׁוֹכֵחַ הוּא.

26. People who collaborate with gentiles to cause Jews loss of life or property (see also *Hilchot Teshuvah* 3:6 and *Hilchot Chovel UMazik* 8:9-10).
27. As explained in *Hilchot Teshuvah* 3:8, this term refers to individuals who deny the Torah, deny prophecy, or maintain that God is not aware of man's actions.
28. Individuals who turn their back on Jewish observance (*Hilchot Teshuvah* 3:9).
29. I.e., to kill them. See *Hilchot Avodat Kochavim* 10:1; *Hilchot Rotzeach* 4:12.
30. Those who observe the seven universal laws given to Noah and his descendants (see *Hilchot Melachim* 8:10-11).

1. See *Hilchot Sanhedrin* 16:4; 12:2.
2. Note the distinctions between the two in *Hilchot Sh'vuot*, Chapter 1.
3. I.e., in a situation where we assume that he was unaware that he was transgressing as the Rambam continues to explain.
4. See *Hilchot Shabbat* 10:1.
5. *Sanhedrin* 26b and the *Shulchan Aruch* (*Choshen Mishpat* 34:4) give another

Similarly, if a person gambles continually, becomes a the collector of the king's duty, or a tax collector takes more for himself, the witnesses must inform him that a person who does this is not acceptable as a witness.[6] For the majority of the people are unaware of this matter. Similar laws apply in all analogous situations. The general principle is: Whenever it appears to the witnesses that the person committing the transgression knew that he was acting wickedly and transgressed deliberately, he is not acceptable as a witness even though he was not given a warning and [hence,] does not receive lashes.

2. A person is not disqualified as a witness because of a transgression on the basis of his own testimony. What is implied? A person comes to court and admits that he stole, robbed, or lent money at interest. Although his own statement is sufficient to obligate him to make financial restitution,[7] it does not disqualify him [as a witness]. Similarly, if he states that he ate meat from an animal that was not slaughtered in a ritual manner or had relations with [a woman] forbidden [to him], he is not disqualified until two witnesses [testify concerning the transgression]. [The rationale is that] a person is not deemed as wicked on the basis of his own testimony.[8]

Accordingly, if Shimon testifies that Reuven lent money at interest,[9] and Levi testifies: "[Reuven] lent me money at interest," Reuven is disqualified as a witness on the basis of the testimony of Shimon and Levi. Although Levi admitted that he borrowed money at interest,[10] he is not deemed as wicked on the basis of his own testimony. Hence, his word is accepted with regard to Reuven, but not with regard to himself.[11]

Similarly, if a person testifies that so-and-so sodomized him, whether against the will of the person sodomized[12] or with his consent,[13] [the person sodomized] and one other witness can join together and [through their testimony have the sodomizer condemned to] execution. [If a person states]: "So-and-so had relations with my wife,"[14] he and one other witness can join together and [through their testimony have] that person, but not the wife [condemned to] execution.[15] Similar laws apply in all analogous situations.

If a person testifies: "So-and-so sodomized my ox," he and one other witness can join together and [through their testimony have] that person [condemned to] execution.[16] [The rationale is that] a person is not considered as related to his property.[17]

3. When two people testify that a person is not acceptable [as a witness] because he committed [one of] the above mentioned transgressions and two

example: people who bury the dead on the first day of a festival. Although it is a transgression, they are under the impression that they are performing a mitzvah.

6. See Chapter 10, Halachah 4.

7. For the admission of the person himself is equivalent to the testimony of 100 witnesses (*Bava Metzia* 3a). The intent is not that his word is accepted as the testimony of witnesses, but that his admission of liability obligates him.

וְכֵן הַמְשַׂחֵק בְּקוּבְיָא תָּמִיד, אוֹ מִי שֶׁנַּעֲשָׂה מוֹכֵס אוֹ גַּבַּאי שֶׁמּוֹסִיף לְעַצְמוֹ – צְרִיכִין הָעֵדִים לְהוֹדִיעוֹ שֶׁהָעוֹשֶׂה דָּבָר זֶה פָּסוּל לְעֵדוּת. שֶׁרֹב הָעָם אֵינָן יוֹדְעִים דְּבָרִים אֵלּוּ. וְכֵן כֹּל כַּיּוֹצֵא בָּזֶה. כְּלָלוֹ שֶׁל דָּבָר: כָּל עֲבֵרָה שֶׁהַדְּבָרִים מַרְאִים לָעֵדִים שֶׁזֶּה יָדַע שֶׁהוּא רָשָׁע וְעָבַר בְּזָדוֹן, אַף עַל פִּי שֶׁלֹּא הִתְרוּ בּוֹ – הֲרֵי זֶה פָּסוּל לְעֵדוּת, וְאֵינוֹ לוֹקֶה.

ב אֵין אָדָם נִפְסָל בַּעֲבֵרָה עַל פִּי עַצְמוֹ. כֵּיצַד? הֲרֵי שֶׁבָּא לְבֵית דִּין וְאָמַר שֶׁגָּנַב אוֹ גָּזַל אוֹ הִלְוָה בְּרִבִּית, אַף עַל פִּי שֶׁמְּשַׁלֵּם עַל פִּי עַצְמוֹ – אֵינוֹ נִפְסָל. וְכֵן אִם אָמַר שֶׁאָכַל נְבֵלָה אוֹ בָּעַל אֲסוּרָה – אֵינוֹ נִפְסָל, עַד שֶׁיִּהְיוּ שָׁם שְׁנֵי עֵדִים; שֶׁאֵין אָדָם מֵשִׂים אֶת עַצְמוֹ רָשָׁע.

לְפִיכָךְ, רְאוּבֵן שֶׁהֵעִיד עָלָיו שִׁמְעוֹן שֶׁהִלְוָה בְּרִבִּית, וְהֵעִיד לֵוִי וְאָמַר: לִי הִלְוָה בְּרִבִּית – הֲרֵי רְאוּבֵן נִפְסָל בְּעֵדוּת שִׁמְעוֹן וְלֵוִי. אַף עַל פִּי שֶׁהֲרֵי הוֹדָה לֵוִי שֶׁלָּוָה בְּרִבִּית – אֵינוֹ מֵשִׂים עַצְמוֹ רָשָׁע, וְנֶאֱמָן עַל רְאוּבֵן וְאֵינוֹ נֶאֱמָן עַל עַצְמוֹ.

וְכֵן מִי שֶׁהֵעִיד שֶׁפְּלוֹנִי רְבָעוֹ, בֵּין בְּאָנְסוֹ שֶׁל נִרְבָּע בֵּין בִּרְצוֹנוֹ – הוּא וְאַחֵר מִצְטָרְפִין לְהָרְגוֹ. פְּלוֹנִי בָּא עַל אִשְׁתִּי – הוּא וְאַחֵר מִצְטָרְפִין לְהָרְגוֹ, אֲבָל לֹא לְהָרְגָהּ. וְכֵן כֹּל כַּיּוֹצֵא בָּזֶה. פְּלוֹנִי רָבַע אֶת שׁוֹרִי – הוּא וְאַחֵר מִצְטָרְפִין לְהָרְגוֹ; שֶׁאֵין אָדָם קָרוֹב אֵצֶל מָמוֹנוֹ.

ג שְׁנַיִם שֶׁהֵעִידוּ עַל אֶחָד שֶׁהוּא פָּסוּל בַּעֲבֵרָה מֵאֵלּוּ הָעֲבֵרוֹת, וּבָאוּ שְׁנַיִם וְהֵעִידוּ שֶׁעָשָׂה

8. Just as a person's testimony is not accepted with regard to his relatives, his testimony is not accepted with regard to himself. He is "his own relative" (*Sanhedrin* 9b). Nevertheless, such a person should not be appointed as a witness as an initial and preferred option [Ramah (*Choshen Mishpat* 34:28)].

9. A transgression that would disqualify him as a witness, as stated in Chapter 10, Halachah 4.

10. And that is also a transgression which disqualifies a person as a witness (*ibid.*).

11. We follow the principle *palginin diburo*, "we divide his words." We accept the portion of his statements which say that so-and-so lent money at interest; we do not accept the portion which states that the person testifying was the recipient of the loan.

12. In which instance, he would not be disqualified as a witness.

13. In which instance, were two witnesses to testify that this transpired, he would be disqualified as a witness.

14. A person's testimony is ordinarily not accepted with regard to his wife, for she is considered as his own person (Chapter 13, Halachah 3).

15. Following the principle of *palginin diburo*.

16. In this instance, the ox is also executed, for the reason the Rambam continues to explain.

17. Hence we do not require the principle *palginin diburo*.

The Ra'avad interprets *Sanhedrin* 10a, the source for the Rambam's ruling, as implying that since we do not employ the principle *palginin diburo*, the person's testimony is not others come and testify that he repented and renounced [his improper conduct] or received lashes [as punishment for the transgression], he is acceptable.[18] If, however, two [witnesses] came and contradicted [the original witnesses], saying: "He did not commit the transgression and should not be disqualified," there is an unresolved doubt if he is disqualified [as a witness or not]. Therefore he should not testify, we do not expropriate money on the basis of his testimony,[19] and he should not serve as a judge[20] until he repents.

4. Whenever a person was obligated to receive lashes, he is considered as an acceptable witness[21] again when he repents[22] or when he received lashes in court.[23] Other persons who were disqualified as witnesses because of money which they seized or stole must repent[24] even if they made financial restitution.[25] [Instead,] they are disqualified until it is known that they repented from their evil ways.

5. When is it considered that people who lend money at interest have repented?[26] When they tear up their promissory notes on their own volition[27] and manifest complete regret [over their actions] to the extent that they do not lend money at interest even to gentiles.[28]

6. When is it considered that dice-players have repented? When they break their dice on their own volition[29] and manifest complete regret [over their actions] to the extent that they do not even play without monetary stakes.[30]

accepted at all. The rationale is that since the ox is his property, he is considered an involved party and his testimony is not accepted (see Chapter 15). Since we do not accept his testimony with regard to the ox, we also do not accept it with regard to the sodomizer.
18. As stated in the following halachah.
19. For the defendant can claim: "I will pay the money when you prove that he is an acceptable witness." We do not say: "Let us follow the assumption that the witness, like all Jews, is acceptable unless it is proven otherwise," for the defendant can say: "The money is presently in my possession. Let it remain there unless it is proven that I owe it to the other person."
20. For a person disqualified as a witness is also disqualified as a judge (see Chapter 16, Halachah 4).
21. The *Siftei Cohen* 34:33 states that his word is accepted even with regard to matters which he observed before he repented.
22. Our translation follows the text suggested by the *Kessef Mishneh*. He interprets this as referring to a situation where the person does not receive lashes, because a warning was not given.

The *Sefer Me'irat Einayim* 34:72 and the *Siftei Cohen* 34:34 emphasize that the transgressor is not reinstated as a witness until testimony was given in court that he repented. Until that time, legal documents he signed are invalid. Although there are opinions which differ, this perspective is borne out by the ruling of the *Shulchan Aruch* (*Choshen Mishpat* 46:26).
23. *Hilchot Sanhedrin* 17:7 states: "Whenever a person sins and is lashed, he returns to

תְּשׁוּבָה וְחָזַר בּוֹ, אוֹ שֶׁלָּקָה - הֲרֵי זֶה כָּשֵׁר. אֲבָל אִם בָּאוּ שְׁנַיִם וְהִכְחִישׁוּם, וְאָמְרוּ: לֹא עָשָׂה עֲבֵרָה זוֹ וְלֹא נִפְסַל - הֲרֵי זֶה סָפֵק פָּסוּל.
לְפִיכָךְ לֹא יָעִיד, וְאֵין מוֹצִיאִין מָמוֹן בְּעֵדוּתוֹ, וְלֹא יָדוּן, עַד שֶׁיִּוָּדַע שֶׁעָשָׂה תְּשׁוּבָה.

ד כָּל מִי שֶׁנִּתְחַיֵּב מַלְקוּת, בֵּין שֶׁעָשָׂה תְּשׁוּבָה בֵּין שֶׁלָּקָה בְּבֵית דִּין - חוֹזֵר לְכַשְׁרוּתוֹ. אֲבָל שְׁאָר פְּסוּלֵי עֵדוּת, שֶׁהֵן פְּסוּלִין מִשּׁוּם מָמוֹן שֶׁחָמְסוּ אוֹ שֶׁגָּזְלוּ, אַף עַל פִּי שֶׁשִּׁלְּמוּ - צְרִיכִין תְּשׁוּבָה, וַהֲרֵי הֵן פְּסוּלִין עַד שֶׁיִּוָּדַע שֶׁחָזְרוּ בָּהֶן מִדַּרְכָּן הָרָע.

ה מֵאֵימָתַי חֲזָרַת מַלְוִים בְּרִבִּית? מִשֶּׁיְּקָרְעוּ שְׁטָרוֹתֵיהֶן מֵעַצְמָן, וְיַחְזְרוּ בָּהֶן חֲזָרָה גְמוּרָה שֶׁלֹּא יַלְווּ בְּרִבִּית אֲפִלּוּ לְעוֹבְדֵי כוֹכָבִים.

ו מֵאֵימָתַי חֲזָרַת הַמְשַׂחֲקִין בְּקוּבְיָא? מִשֶּׁיְּשַׁבְּרוּ אֶת פִּסִּיפְּסֵיהֶם, וְיַחְזְרוּ בָּהֶן חֲזָרָה גְמוּרָה שֶׁלֹּא יַעֲשׂוּ אֲפִלּוּ בְּחִנָּם.

his [original state of] acceptability, as [implied by Deuteronomy 25:3]: 'And your brother will be degraded before your eyes.' Once he is lashed, he is 'your brother.'"

In his *Kessef Mishneh*, Rav Yosef Karo notes that there are texts of the *Mishneh Torah* that read: "Whenever a person was obligated to receive lashes, he is considered as an acceptable witness, when he receives lashes in court." Rav Yosef Karo states that he prefers the version used above because: a) it also deals with situations where the person does not actually receive lashes, and b) it implies that if a person receives lashes, but does not repent, he is not reinstated as a witness. In his *Shulchan Aruch* (*Choshen Mishpat* 34:29), however, he does not mention repentance in this clause.

24. I.e., perform actions which indicate that he sincerely regrets his previous conduct, as the Rambam illustrates in the following halachot.

25. See the notes to Chapter 10, Halachah 4.

26. The Ramah (*Choshen Mishpat* 34:29) states that repentance is required only when a person frequently transgressed. If, however, he transgressed only once and returned the money on his own volition, that is sufficient.

27. And not because of the compulsion of the court. If the court compels them, we have no proof that they themselves regretted their actions (*Kessef Mishneh*).

The promissory notes must be torn up, because the obligation to pay interest is stated in the promissory note itself. In such an instance, the borrower is still required to return the principal. Nevertheless, the loan is given the status of a debt supported by a verbal commitment alone. As such, the creditor cannot expropriate property sold to others.

28. Although it is permitted - indeed, according to Scriptural Law, even a mitzvah - to lend to gentiles at interest, as stated in *Hilchot Malveh ViLoveh* 5:1-2, an exception is made in this instance, because of the tendency that was already ingrained in the person's character.

The *Shulchan Aruch* (*Choshen Mishpat* 34:29) adds that the lender must also return the money which he took at interest. If he does not know from whom he took the money, he should give it to the community to use for the public benefit.

29. This phrase is added on the basis of the authoritative manuscripts and early printings of the *Mishneh Torah*.

30. For we fear that this will lead to them playing for money again.

7. When is it considered that those who guide the flight of doves have repented? When they break the tools they use to snare them and manifest complete regret [over their actions] to the extent that they do not do this even in the desert.[31]

8. When is it considered that merchants [of produce] in the Sabbatical year have repented? When the Sabbatical year arrives, they are investigated [and it is discovered that they did not sell such produce].

[Expressing] regret verbally is not sufficient. Instead, they must compose [a document, stating]: "I, so-and-so, the son of so-and-so, earned 200 *zuz* from [the sale of] the produce of the Sabbatical year and this sum is given as a present to the poor."

9. When is it considered that a person suspected of benefiting[32] from [taking a false] oath has repented? When he goes to a court which does not recognize him[33] and tells them: "I am suspect [to take a false oath]." Alternatively, when he is obligated to take an oath in a court which does not recognize him with regard to a significant amount of money and he chooses to make financial restitution rather than take the oath.

Similarly, a butcher would check [the animals he slaughtered][34] by himself and market the meat who [sold] meat[35] that was *trefe* is considered like those who partake of such meat[36] and who are unacceptable as witnesses. [Such a butcher] is unacceptable as a witness until it is evident from his deeds that he regrets the evil he performed. He must wear black clothes, robe himself in black,[37] and go to a place where his identity is not known and return a lost object that is significantly valuable or acknowledge that an animal that is significantly valuable which he owned [and slaughtered] is *trefe*.

10. Similarly, a witnesses who was discovered to have lied who went to a place where he was not recognized and was offered a significant amount of money to deliver false testimony, but refused is considered to have repented and is reinstated as a witness. Similar principles apply in all analogous situations.

The Ramah (*Choshen Mishpat* 34:31) quotes opinions that state that the gamblers must also return any money that they won before they are reinstated as acceptable witnesses.

31. Where there is no question of theft involved. In this instance, as well, the Ramah (*ibid.*) quotes opinions that require that any doves stolen be returned.

32. The Ramah (*Choshen Mishpat* 34:33) emphasizes that the severe measures the Rambam requires are necessary before the person is reinstated only when the person derived financial benefit from committing a transgression. If, however, a person violates a

ז מֵאֵימָתַי חֲזָרַת מַפְרִיחֵי יוֹנִים? מִשֶּׁיְּשַׁבְּרוּ אֶת הַכֵּלִים שֶׁצָּדִין בָּהֶן, וְיַחְזְרוּ בָּהֶן חֲזָרָה גְּמוּרָה שֶׁאֲפִלּוּ בַּמִּדְבָּר לֹא יַעֲשׂוּ.

ח מֵאֵימָתַי חֲזָרַת סוֹחֲרֵי שְׁבִיעִית? מִשֶּׁתַּגִּיעַ שְׁבִיעִית וְיִבָּדְקוּ. וְלֹא חֲזָרַת דְּבָרִים בִּלְבַד, אֶלָּא כּוֹתֵב: אֲנִי פְּלוֹנִי בֶּן פְּלוֹנִי כִּנַּסְתִּי מָאתַיִם זוּז מִפֵּרוֹת שְׁבִיעִית, וַהֲרֵי הֵם נְתוּנִים בְּמַתָּנָה לַעֲנִיִּים.

ט מֵאֵימָתַי חֲזָרַת הַמּוּעָל בִּשְׁבוּעָה? מִשֶּׁיָּבוֹא לְבֵית דִּין שֶׁאֵין מַכִּירִין אוֹתוֹ, וְיֹאמַר לָהֶם: חָשׁוּד אֲנִי. אוֹ יִתְחַיֵּב שְׁבוּעָה בְּבֵית דִּין שֶׁאֵין מַכִּירִין אוֹתוֹ בְּמָמוֹן חָשׁוּב, וִישַׁלֵּם וְלֹא יִרְצֶה לְהִשָּׁבַע.

וְכֵן טַבָּח שֶׁהָיָה בּוֹדֵק לְעַצְמוֹ וּמוֹכֵר, וְיָצָאת טְרֵפָה מִתַּחַת יָדוֹ, שֶׁהֲרֵי הוּא בִּכְלַל אוֹכְלֵי טְרֵפָה שֶׁהֵן פְּסוּלִין לְעֵדוּת – הֲרֵי זֶה פָּסוּל לְעֵדוּת, עַד שֶׁיֵּרָאֶה מִמַּעֲשָׂיו שֶׁנִּחַם עַל רָעָתוֹ. וְיִלְבַּשׁ שְׁחֹרִים, וִיכַסֶּה שְׁחֹרִים, וְיֵלֵךְ לְמָקוֹם שֶׁאֵין מַכִּירִין אוֹתוֹ, וְיַחֲזִיר אֲבֵדָה בְּמָמוֹן חָשׁוּב. אוֹ יוֹצִיא טְרֵפָה מִתַּחַת יָדוֹ בְּדָבָר חָשׁוּב.

י וְכֵן עֵד זוֹמֵם שֶׁהָלַךְ לְמָקוֹם שֶׁאֵין מַכִּירִין אוֹתוֹ, וְנָתְנוּ לוֹ מָמוֹן חָשׁוּב לְהָעִיד בְּשֶׁקֶר, וְלֹא רָצָה – הֲרֵי זֶה עָשָׂה תְּשׁוּבָה, וְחָזַר לְכַשְׁרוּתוֹ. וְכֵן כֹּל כַּיּוֹצֵא בָּזֶה.

transgression that does not bring him financial gain, it is sufficient for him to make a public admission of his guilt and promise never to transgress again.

33. Making such a statement in a court that is familiar with him is not possible, for they will never require him to take an oath.

34. I.e., check to make sure that there are no lesions in the lungs or other factors that render the animal as *trefe*; alternatively, check the knife which he uses to slaughter the animal.

35. If the butcher does not sell the meat, but merely slaughters an animal for another person and tells him that it is kosher when it in fact is non-kosher, he is also disqualified as a witness. Nevertheless, since he did not garner any financial gain from his transgression, he need not undertake all the measures the Rambam continues to describe. Instead, it is sufficient for him merely to repent (*Kessef Mishneh*).

36. Since he sells non-kosher meat to others, we can assume that he partakes of it himself. This is a prohibition punishable by lashes. Hence he is disqualified as a witness (*Kessef Mishneh*).

Selling the non-kosher meat itself - even though it involves the violation of the prohibition "Do not place a stumbling block before the blind" - does not disqualify the butcher as a witness. The rationale is that this prohibition is not punishable by lashes (*ibid.*).

37. It is necessary for him to clothe and robe himself in black to humble his heart and cause him to regret having caused others to sin (*Sefer Me'irat Einayim* 34:84).

CHAPTER THIRTEEN

1. Relatives are disqualified as witnesses according to Scriptural Law, as [implied by Deuteronomy 24:16]: "Fathers shall not die because of sons." According to the Oral Tradition,[1] [the verse is interpreted as] meaning that included in this prohibition[2] is that fathers should not die because [of the testimony] of sons, nor should sons die because [of the testimony] of fathers. Similar laws apply with regard to other relatives.[3]

According to Scriptural Law, only paternal relatives are disqualified[4] - i.e., a father with his sons and grandsons,[5] paternal brothers with each other, and the sons of paternal brothers with each other.[6] Needless to say the uncles [may not testify] with their brother's sons.[7] Maternal relatives or people related by marriage are disqualified only by Rabbinic decree.[8]

2. Converts are not considered as relatives. Even two twin brothers[9] who convert[10] may testify on each other's behalf. For a convert is considered as a newborn child.[11]

3. Brothers - whether maternal brothers or paternal - are considered as one degree removed. Their sons are considered as two degrees removed. And their grandsons are three degrees removed.

1. *Sanhedrin* 27b.
2. *Sefer HaMitzvot* (negative commandment 287) and *Sefer HaChinuch* (mitzvah 589) count this as one of the 613 mitzvot of the Torah. As the Rambam states at the conclusion of the chapter, we do not disqualify relatives because we fear that they will lie on behalf of their relative. Instead, this is a Scriptural decree; Moses would not be able to testify on behalf of Jethro, his father-in-law (*Bava Batra* 159a).
3. Just as two relatives may not testify on behalf of each other; so, too, they may not testify together on behalf of someone else. Although the verse speaks about testimony in cases involving capital punishment, it applies with regard to all types of testimony.
4. As the Rambam proceeds to explain, if Jacob fathered Reuven and Shimon, Reuven fathered David, and Shimon fathered Pinchas, none of the individuals mentioned can testify on behalf of each other.
5. See Halachah 5.
6. I.e., Pinchas and David may not testify together.
7. I.e., Reuven may not testify with Pinchas.

The Family Ties Between Potential Witnesses

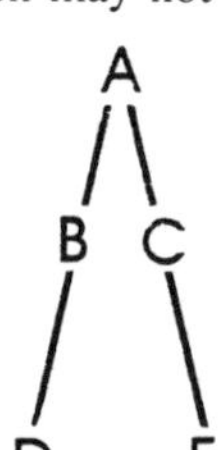

A - Jacob
B - Reuven
C - Shimon
D - David
E - Pinchas

8. The Rambam's statements with regard to maternal relatives have attracted the attention

פֶּרֶק שְׁלֹשָׁה עָשָׂר

א הַקְּרוֹבִים פְּסוּלִים לְעֵדוּת מִן הַתּוֹרָה. שֶׁנֶּאֱמַר: לֹא יוּמְתוּ אָבוֹת עַל בָּנִים. מִפִּי הַשְּׁמוּעָה לָמְדוּ, שֶׁבִּכְלַל לָאו זֶה: שֶׁלֹּא יוּמְתוּ אָבוֹת עַל פִּי בָּנִים, וְלֹא בָּנִים עַל פִּי אָבוֹת. וְהוּא הַדִּין לִשְׁאָר קְרוֹבִים.

אֵין פְּסוּלִין מִדִּין תּוֹרָה אֶלָּא קְרוֹבִים מִמִּשְׁפַּחַת אָב בִּלְבַד, וָהֵם: הָאָב עִם הַבֵּן וְעִם בֶּן הַבֵּן, וְהָאַחִין מִן הָאָב זֶה עִם זֶה, וּבְנֵיהֶן זֶה עִם זֶה, וְאֵין צָרִיךְ לוֹמַר הַדּוֹדִים עִם בֶּן אָחִיו. אֲבָל שְׁאָר הַקְּרוֹבִים מִן הָאֵם אוֹ מִדֶּרֶךְ הָאִישׁוּת – כֻּלָּן פְּסוּלִין מִדִּבְרֵיהֶם.

ב הַגֵּרִים אֵינָן בְּדִין הַקְּרוֹבִים. אֲפִלּוּ שְׁנֵי אַחִים תְּאוֹמִים שֶׁנִּתְגַּיְּרוּ – מְעִידִין זֶה לָזֶה. שֶׁהַגֵּר שֶׁנִּתְגַּיֵּר – כְּקָטָן שֶׁנּוֹלַד הוּא חָשׁוּב.

ג הָאַחִים זֶה עִם זֶה, בֵּין מִן הָאֵם בֵּין מִן הָאָב – הֲרֵי הֵן רִאשׁוֹן בְּרִאשׁוֹן. וּבְנֵיהֶם זֶה עִם זֶה – שֵׁנִי בְּשֵׁנִי. וּבְנֵי בְנֵיהֶם זֶה עִם זֶה – שְׁלִישִׁי בִּשְׁלִישִׁי.

of the commentaries, for *Sanhedrin* 28a derives the disqualification of maternal relatives from the exegesis of a verse, implying that the prohibition is of Scriptural origin. This is in fact the position of many other Rishonim.

The Radbaz (- and this interpretation also appears to fit the Rambam's Commentary to the Mishnah -) explains that although this perspective is mentioned by the Talmud, it is not accepted as halachah. The *Sefer Me'irat Einayim* 33:7 states that the Rambam interprets that Talmudic passage as an *asmachta*, i.e., a support found by the Sages for a law that was part of the Oral Tradition.

The *Kessef Mishneh* explains that the Rambam maintains - as he writes in his *Sefer HaMitzvot* (General Principle 2) - that laws derived through the principles of Biblical exegesis are *midivrei sofrim*, "from the words of the Sages." Nevertheless, such laws have the same authority as if they were stated explicitly in the Torah. See the Ramah (*Choshen Mishpat* 33:2) and commentaries where this issue is discussed.

9. Who came from the same drop of sperm (*Yevamot* 98a).

10. The *Kessef Mishneh* notes that the phrase "that they convert" implies that they converted themselves. If, however, a women converts while pregnant with twin sons, since they were born as Jews, they are disqualified from testifying on each other's behalf by Rabbinic decree. The *Siftei Cohen* 33:7 cites the Rambam's ruling in *Hilchot Issurei Bi'ah* 14:14 which states that, in such a situation, the brothers are forbidden to have relations with each other's wife by Scriptural Law. Accordingly, he maintains that they are also disqualified as witnesses by Scriptural Law. The *Be'er Heitev* 33:7, however, explains that a distinction can be made between the two instances.

11. Without any connection at all to his past. Indeed, according to Scriptural Law, a convert can marry his mother or his sister (*Hilchot Issurei Bi'ah* 14:12).

Our Sages did not decree that converts may not testify on behalf of their relatives, lest one permit native-born Jewish relatives to testify on each other's behalf, because the acceptance of witnesses is dependent on the court and a court would not make such an error (*Yevamot* 22a).

4. A person who is three degrees removed may testify on behalf of one who is one degree removed.[12] Needless to say, one who is three degrees removed may testify on behalf of one who is two degrees removed.[13] But two who are both two degrees removed,[14] and needless to say, one who is two degrees removed and one who is one degree removed[15] are both disqualified [from testifying].[16]

5. A father and his son are considered as one degree removed. Therefore a father is disqualified from testifying with his grandson.[17] With his great-grandson, i.e., the fourth generation, he is acceptable,[18] for he is of the first degree and [the great-grandson,] three degrees, removed. Similar laws apply with regard to women relatives.

What is implied? Two sisters or a brother and a sister - whether paternally or maternally related - are considered as one degree removed. Their children, whether male or female, are considered as two degrees removed and their grandchildren - including the sons of their sons and the daughters of their daughters[19] - are considered as three degrees removed. Just as we count the degrees descendants are removed for males - one degree, two degrees, and three degrees - so, too, we count the degrees for females.

6. Whenever a person is disqualified from testifying on behalf of a woman, he is also disqualified from testifying on behalf of her husband, for a husband is considered like his wife.[20] [Conversely,] whenever a person is disqualified from testifying on behalf of a man, he is also disqualified from testifying on behalf of his wife, for a wife is considered like her husband.[21]

7. Whenever two women are removed by second degrees,[22] their husbands may testify on behalf of each other.[23] If, however, [the women] are one degree removed, e.g., a man married a woman, and a colleague married her daughter,[24] [the two men] may not testify on each other's behalf.[25]

12. To refer back to the situations mentioned in Halachah 1. Jacob fathered Reuven and Shimon, Reuven fathered David, Shimon fathered Pinchas, David fathered Solomon, and Pinchas fathered Eli. Eli may testify on behalf of Reuven.

The Family Ties Between Potential Witnesses

A - Jacob C - Shimon E - Pinchas G - Eli
B - Reuven D - David F - Solomon

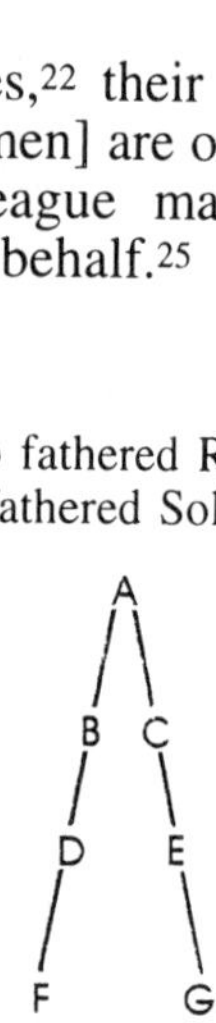

13. Eli may testify on behalf of Solomon.
14. David and Pinchas.
15. David and Shimon.
16. *Sanhedrin* 27b derives this concept from the exegesis of the verse: "Fathers shall not die because of sons." Rashi explains that since the Torah uses the plural term for both father's and sons, the implication is that several sets of relatives are involved.

ד ולְעוֹלָם שְׁלִישִׁי בְּרִאשׁוֹן – כָּשֵׁר, וְאֵין צָרִיךְ לוֹמַר שְׁלִישִׁי בְּשֵׁנִי. אֲבָל שֵׁנִי בְּשֵׁנִי, וְאֵין צָרִיךְ לוֹמַר שֵׁנִי בְּרִאשׁוֹן – שְׁנֵיהֶם פְּסוּלִים.

ה הָאָב עִם בְּנוֹ – כְּרִאשׁוֹן בְּרִאשׁוֹן הוּא. לְפִיכָךְ: הָאָב עִם בֶּן בְּנוֹ – פָּסוּל; וְעִם בֶּן בֶּן בְּנוֹ, שֶׁהוּא רְבִיעִי מִמֶּנּוּ – כָּשֵׁר, מִפְּנֵי שֶׁהוּא שְׁלִישִׁי בְּרִאשׁוֹן. וְכֵן הַדֶּרֶךְ בִּנְקֵבוֹת. כֵּיצַד? שְׁתֵּי אֲחָיוֹת אוֹ אָח וַאֲחוֹתוֹ, בֵּין מִן הָאָב בֵּין מִן הָאֵם – הֲרֵי הֵם רִאשׁוֹן בְּרִאשׁוֹן. בְּנֵיהֶם, בֵּין זְכָרִים בֵּין נְקֵבוֹת – שֵׁנִי בְּשֵׁנִי. בְּנֵי בְּנֵיהֶם אוֹ בְּנוֹת בְּנוֹתֵיהֶן – שְׁלִישִׁי בִּשְׁלִישִׁי. כְּדֶרֶךְ שֶׁאַתָּה מוֹנֶה בִּזְכָרִים רִאשׁוֹן שֵׁנִי וּשְׁלִישִׁי, כָּךְ אַתָּה מוֹנֶה בִּנְקֵבוֹת.

ו כָּל אִשָּׁה שֶׁאַתָּה פָּסוּל לָהּ, כָּךְ אַתָּה פָּסוּל לְבַעְלָהּ; שֶׁהַבַּעַל כְּאִשְׁתּוֹ. וְכָל בַּעַל שֶׁאַתָּה פָּסוּל לוֹ, כָּךְ אַתָּה פָּסוּל לְאִשְׁתּוֹ; שֶׁהָאִשָּׁה כְּבַעְלָהּ.

ז כָּל שְׁתֵּי נָשִׁים שֶׁהֵן זוֹ עִם זוֹ שֵׁנִי בְּשֵׁנִי – בַּעְלֵיהֶן מְעִידִין זֶה לָזֶה. אֲבָל אִם הָיוּ רִאשׁוֹן בְּרִאשׁוֹן, כְּגוֹן שֶׁלָּקַח זֶה אִשָּׁה וְזֶה בִּתָּהּ – אֵין מְעִידִין זֶה לָזֶה.

17. For he is considered as being two degrees removed.
18. Rabbenu Tam states that a person may not testify together with his great-grandson. The *Shulchan Aruch* (*Choshen Mishpat* 33:2) quotes both opinions and the Ramah states that Rabbenu Tam's view should be followed.
19. And needless to say, the sons of their daughters and the daughters of their sons.
20. *Sanhedrin* 28b derives this concept from the exegesis of Leviticus 18:14.
21. The opinions which disqualify a person from testifying on behalf of his great-grandson grant leniency and allow him to testify on behalf of his great-grandson's wife, provided there is no direct monetary benefit to his great-grandson involved [*Shulchan Aruch* and Ramah (*Choshen Mishpat* 33:3)].
22. To cite an example: Jacob gave birth to Dinah and Devorah, Dinah gave birth to Sarah, and Devorah, to Leah. Sarah married Abraham and Leah married Joel, Abraham and Joel may testify on behalf of each other.

A - Jacob　C - Devorah　E - Leah　G - Yoel
B - Dinah　D - Sarah　F - Abraham

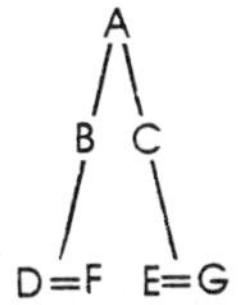

23. When relatives are distantly removed, we do not employ the concept: "A husband is considered like his wife" twice in the same instance to disqualify a witness (Radbaz).

The Ramah (*Choshen Mishpat* 33:4) quotes the *Terumat HaDeshen* who rules that the initial and preferred option is for individuals who are related by marriage in this manner not to be appointed as witnesses together or to sign a legal document together as witnesses.
24. To continue using the above example: Dinah married Joseph. Joseph and Abraham may not testify on behalf of each other.
25. Since the two women are not distantly removed, we employ the concept: "A husband is considered like his wife" twice in the same instance to disqualify a witness.

8. Similarly, the husbands of two sisters[26] are disqualified with regard to each other and are considered as one degree removed.

9. Similarly, a person should not testify on behalf of the son of his wife's sister,[27] nor on behalf of the husband of the daughter of his wife's sister.[28] He may, however, testify on behalf of the son of the husband of his wife's sister who was born to [that person] from another wife.[29]

10. Whenever [a witness] is disqualified from testifying on behalf of a colleague because he is married to [the witness'] relative, the witness may testify on behalf of the other relatives of that colleague, e.g., his son and his brother.[30] Similarly, whenever [a witness] is disqualified from testifying on behalf of a woman because she is married to [the witness'] relative, the witness may testify on behalf of her other relatives, e.g., her son and her brother.[31]

11. The father of a bride and the father of a groom may testify on behalf of each other.[32]

12. A [person's] paternal brother may testify on behalf of [that person's] maternal brother [and the maternal brother may testify on behalf of the paternal brother], for they have no connection whatsoever.[33]

What is implied? Rachel married Joseph and bore him a son Reuven. Joseph had a son, Menashe, from another wife. Joseph died and [Rachel] married Shimon and bore him Judah. Menashe and Judah may testify on each other's behalf.

13. A man and his wife are considered as being removed by one degree. Hence [a husband] may not testify on behalf of his wife's son, the wife of his wife's son, [his wife's] daughter, the husband of [his wife's] daughter, [his wife's] father, [his wife's] mother, the husband of [his wife's] mother, nor the wife of [his wife's] father.[34]

26. To refer to the above example: Devorah married Baruch. Joseph and Baruch may not testify on each other's behalf.
27. To refer to the above example, if Devorah had a son, Michael, Joseph could not testify on behalf of Michael. In this instance, after using the principle: "A husband is considered like his wife," Joseph is considered as one degree removed and Michael, two degrees removed. Hence, they are disqualified to testify on behalf of each other.
28. To refer to the above example, if Devorah had a daughter, Judith who married Judah, Joseph could not testify on behalf of Judah. In this instance, after using the principle twice: "A husband is considered like his wife," Joseph is considered as one degree removed and Judah, two degrees removed. Hence, they are disqualified to testify on behalf of each other.

The *Shulchan Aruch* (*Choshen Mishpat* 33:4) quotes the Rambam's ruling on this point, but also quotes the opinion of Rabbenu Asher who allows such testimony. The Ramah rules that Rabbenu Asher's opinion should be followed.

ח וְכֵן בַּעֲלֵי אֲחָיוֹת - פְּסוּלִין זֶה לָזֶה, וַהֲרֵי הֵן רִאשׁוֹן בְּרִאשׁוֹן.

ט וְכֵן לֹא יָעִיד לְבֶן אֲחוֹת אִשְׁתּוֹ, וְלֹא לְבַעַל בַּת אֲחוֹת אִשְׁתּוֹ. אֲבָל מֵעִיד הוּא לְבֶן בַּעַל אֲחוֹת אִשְׁתּוֹ שֶׁיֵּשׁ לוֹ מֵאִשָּׁה אַחֶרֶת.

י כָּל אִישׁ שֶׁאֵין אַתָּה מֵעִיד לוֹ מִפְּנֵי שֶׁהוּא בַּעַל קְרוֹבָתְךָ - הֲרֵי אַתָּה מֵעִיד לִשְׁאָר קְרוֹבָיו, כְּגוֹן בְּנוֹ וְאָחִיו. וְכֵן כָּל אִשָּׁה שֶׁאֵין אַתָּה מֵעִיד לָהּ מִפְּנֵי שֶׁהִיא אֵשֶׁת קְרוֹבְךָ - הֲרֵי אַתָּה מֵעִיד לִשְׁאָר קְרוֹבֶיהָ.

יא אֲבִי כַּלָּה וַאֲבִי חָתָן - מְעִידִים זֶה לָזֶה.

יב אֲחֵי הָאָח מִן הָאֵם - מְעִידִין זֶה לָזֶה, שֶׁהֲרֵי אֵין בֵּינֵיהֶן קֻרְבָה כְּלָל. כֵּיצַד? רָחֵל שֶׁנִּשֵּׂאת לְיוֹסֵף וְיָלְדָה מִמֶּנָּה רְאוּבֵן, וְהָיָה לְיוֹסֵף בֵּן מֵאִשָּׁה אַחֶרֶת וְהוּא מְנַשֶּׁה, וּמֵת יוֹסֵף, וְנִשֵּׂאת לְשִׁמְעוֹן וְיָלְדָה מִמֶּנּוּ יְהוּדָה - הֲרֵי מְנַשֶּׁה וִיהוּדָה מְעִידִין זֶה לָזֶה.

יג הָאִישׁ עִם אִשְׁתּוֹ - רִאשׁוֹן בְּרִאשׁוֹן. לְפִיכָךְ אֵינוֹ מֵעִיד לֹא לִבְנָהּ וְלֹא לְאֵשֶׁת בְּנָהּ, וְלֹא לְבִתָּהּ וְלֹא לְבַעַל בִּתָּהּ, וְלֹא לְאָבִיהָ וְלֹא לְאִמָּהּ, וְלֹא לְבַעַל אִמָּהּ וְלֹא לְאֵשֶׁת אָבִיהָ.

29. To refer to the above example: Baruch had fathered Aaron in a previous marriage. Joseph may testify on Aaron's behalf.
30. I.e., if Eliezer and Rebbeca are brother and sister and Rebbeca is married to Isaac, Eliezer may not testify on behalf of Isaac. He may, however, testify on behalf of all of Isaac's relatives. For they share no family connection at all. See Halachah 12.
31. I.e., if Eliezer's son, Dan, marries Osnat, Eliezer may testify on behalf of all of Osnat's relatives.
32. For the two individuals themselves do not share any family connection. *Sanhedrin* 28b describes them as "lids to jugs."

In their glosses to the *Shulchan Aruch* (*Choshen Mishpat* 33:6), Rabbi Akiva Eiger and the *Chatam Sofer* rule that this law applies even after *nissuin* (the consummation of the marriage bond).

See also the Ramah (*Choshen Mishpat, Ibid.*) who states that as an initial and preferred option, these individuals should not serve as judges together.
33. This law, based on *Sanhedrin* 28b, is the source for the principle stated in Halachah 10 (*Kessef Mishneh*).
34. For all these principles are one degree removed from his wife and thus two degrees removed from him. And with regard to their husbands or wives, we apply the principle: "A husband is considered like his wife and a wife is considered like her husband."

The *Sefer Me'irat Einayim* 33:15-16 emphasizes that with this halachah, the Rambam is clarifying that although we say "a husband is considered like his wife," they are not considered as the same person. For were that to be true, a husband would also not be able to testify on behalf of her grandson or grandfather according to the Rambam's perspective.

14. When a person has consecrated a woman, although the marriage bond has not been consummated, with regard to testimony, it is as if she is fully married.

To whom does the above apply? To the woman he consecrated herself; he may not testify on her behalf. If, however, he testifies on behalf of the relatives of the woman he consecrated, e.g., her sister's husband, her son or daughter, or the like, we do not disqualify him[35] until he marries her.

15. The Torah did not disqualify the testimony of relatives because we assume that they love each other, for a relative may not testify neither on his relative's behalf or against his interests. Instead, this is a Scriptural decree.[36]

For this reason [people who] love each other or who hate each other are acceptable as witnesses[37] even though they are not acceptable as judges.[38] For the Scriptural decree [disqualifies] only relatives [as witnesses].

CHAPTER FOURTEEN

1. Whenever [a witness] is disqualified from testifying on behalf of a colleague because he is married to [the witness'] relative,[1] if [that relative's] wife dies,[2] even if she left him sons, he is considered to have been released [from any connection] and is acceptable [as a witness].[3]

2. When a person knew of evidence concerning a colleague before he became his son-in-law, and then became his son-in-law, he is not acceptable. [The same law applies if a person] was in control of his senses and then became a deaf-mute, was able to see and became blind - even though he is aware of the measure of land concerning which he testifies and can define its boundaries, or was intellectually and emotionally sound and then lost control of his faculties.

If, by contrast, a person knew of evidence concerning a colleague before he became his son-in-law, became his son-in-law, and then that colleague's daughter[4] died, [the witness] is acceptable. [Similar laws apply if a person] was in control of his senses, became a deaf-mute, and then regained control of his senses, was intellectually and emotionally sound, lost control of his faculties, and then regained control of them, or was able to see, became blind, and then regained his sight.

35. For we do not assume that he has already become close to them (*Sanhedrin* 28b). The Rambam's wording implies that the initial and preferred option is not to have such a person serve as a witness. If he does, however, his testimony is not disqualified. Rabbeinu Asher is more lenient and allows the husband-to-be to serve as a witness for these people at the outset (*Sefer Me'irat Einayim* 33:17).

The Ramah (*Choshen Mishpat* 33:9) emphasizes that these laws apply with regard to a woman who was consecrated. If, however, a couple were merely engaged, the husband-to-be is not automatically disqualified. With regard to financial matters, however, it is likely that he would not be allowed to testify because he would be considered an involved party.

יד אִשְׁתּוֹ אֲרוּסָה, אַף עַל פִּי שֶׁלֹּא נִגְמְרָה הָאִישׁוּת – הֲרֵי הִיא כִּנְשׂוּאָה לְעִנְיַן עֵדוּת. [בַּמֶּה דְּבָרִים אֲמוּרִים?] בַּאֲרוּסָתוֹ עַצְמָהּ, שֶׁאֵינוֹ מֵעִיד לָהּ; אֲבָל אִם הֵעִיד לִקְרוֹבֵי אֲרוּסָתוֹ, כְּגוֹן בַּעַל אֲחוֹתָהּ אוֹ בְּנָהּ וּבִתָּהּ וְכַיּוֹצֵא בָּהֶן – אֵין פּוֹסְלִין אוֹתָהּ עַד שֶׁיִּשָּׂאֶנָּה.

טו זֶה שֶׁפָּסְלָה תּוֹרָה עֵדוּת הַקְּרוֹבִים – לֹא מִפְּנֵי שֶׁהֵן בְּחֶזְקַת אוֹהֲבִין זֶה אֶת זֶה, שֶׁהֲרֵי אֵינוֹ מֵעִיד לוֹ לֹא לְטוֹבָתוֹ וְלֹא לְרָעָתוֹ, אֶלָּא גְּזֵרַת הַכָּתוּב הוּא. לְפִיכָךְ, הָאוֹהֵב וְהַשּׂוֹנֵא – כָּשֵׁר לְעֵדוּת, אַף עַל פִּי שֶׁהוּא פָּסוּל לְדַיָּנוּת; שֶׁלֹּא גָּזְרָה תּוֹרָה אֶלָּא עַל הַקְּרוֹבִים.

פֶּרֶק אַרְבָּעָה עָשָׂר

א כָּל מִי שֶׁאֵין אַתָּה מֵעִיד לוֹ מִפְּנֵי שֶׁהוּא בַּעַל קְרוֹבָתְךָ, אִם מֵתָה אִשְׁתּוֹ, אַף עַל פִּי שֶׁהִנִּיחָה לוֹ בָּנִים – הֲרֵי זֶה נִתְרַחֵק וְכָשֵׁר.

ב מִי שֶׁהָיָה יוֹדֵעַ לַחֲבֵרוֹ עֵדוּת עַד שֶׁלֹּא נַעֲשָׂה חֲתָנוֹ, וְנַעֲשָׂה חֲתָנוֹ;
אוֹ שֶׁיָּדַע הָעֵדוּת וְהוּא פִּקֵּחַ, וְאַחַר כָּךְ נִתְחָרֵשׁ; פָּתוּחַ וְנִסְתַּמֵּא, אַף עַל פִּי שֶׁיָּכוֹל לְכַוֵּן מִדַּת הַקַּרְקַע שֶׁהוּא מֵעִיד בָּהּ וּמְסַיֵּם מְצָרֶיהָ; שָׁפוּי וְנִשְׁתַּטָּה – הֲרֵי זֶה פָּסוּל.
אֲבָל אִם הָיָה יוֹדֵעַ לוֹ עֵדוּת עַד שֶׁלֹּא נַעֲשָׂה חֲתָנוֹ, וְנַעֲשָׂה חֲתָנוֹ, וּמֵתָה בִּתּוֹ; פִּקֵּחַ וְנִתְחָרֵשׁ, וְחָזַר וְנִתְפַּקַּח; שָׁפוּי וְנִשְׁתַּטָּה, וְחָזַר וְנִשְׁתַּפָּה; פָּתוּחַ וְנִסְתַּמֵּא, וְחָזַר וְנִתְפַּתַּח – כָּשֵׁר.

36. As stated above, Moses would not be able to testify on behalf of Jethro, his father-in-law.
37. For we do not suspect that they will violate the Torah's prohibitions against testifying falsely because of their love or hatred for the other person.
38. As stated in the notes to *Hilchot Sanhedrin* 23:6, we fear that he will agree with the opinion of the person he loves and differ with that of the person he hates. Even though he will not consciously decide to deviate from the path of justice, his subconscious may motivate him to do so.

1. See Chapter 13, Halachah 6.
2. Or is divorced (*Siftei Cohen* 33:8).
3. Note, however, the guidelines spelled out in the following halachah.
The Ramah (*Choshen Mishpat* 33:12) emphasizes that if a ruling was rendered while a couple was still married and then the woman died, the case may not be reopened on the basis of the testimony that her relative may give. See, however, the gloss of the *Siftei Cohen* 33:9.
4. I.e., the witness' wife. With her death, the family connection between the witness and his former father-in-law is dissolved.

The general principle is: Whenever a person is an acceptable witness at the initial[5] and the final[6] stages, he is acceptable even though in the interim, he was not acceptable [as a witness].[7] If, however, initially he is unacceptable, even though ultimately, he would be acceptable, he is disqualified. Therefore when a person is aware of evidence as a child,[8] it is of no consequence for him to testify with regard to it when he attains majority.

3. There are matters concerning which we rely on the testimony which a person gives after he attains majority with regard to events that he observed when he was a child. [The rationale is that] these are matters of Rabbinical origin. The matters are as follows; a person's word is accepted when he states:
a) "This is the signature of my father," "...my teacher," "...or my brother," [the rationale is that] the validation of legal documents is a Rabbinic requirement;[9]
b) "I remember that when so-and-so was married, they performed the customs performed for a virgin";[10] since most women marry when virgins and a *ketubah* is a Rabbinic institution;[11]
c) "This place[12] is a *beit hapras,*"[13] for the ritual impurity associated with such a place is a Rabbinic [safeguard];
d) "We would proceed until this point on the Sabbath," because the restriction of the Sabbath limits until only 2000 cubits is a Rabbinic restriction;[14]
e) "So-and-so would leave school to immerse himself [in a *mikveh*] and eat *terumah* in the evening" or "he would receive a portion of *terumah* with us;"[15]
f) "We would bring *challah* and presents [of meat][16] to so-and-so, the priest"; [this applies when the presents were sent with] the person himself;[17]
g) "My father told me, 'This family is acceptable; this family is not acceptable";[18]

5. I.e., when he observes the event.
6. I.e., when he delivers testimony.
7. *Bava Batra* 128a derives this concept from Leviticus 5:1: "If he witnessed or saw... if he does not testify." Implied is that the person must be acceptable as a witness at the time he sees and at the time he testifies.
8. I.e., he was not acceptable as a witness when he observed the evidence.
9. As stated in Chapter 3, Halachah 4. See also Chapter 7, Halachah 2, where the Rambam qualifies this leniency, stating: "[This applies] provided he is joined by another person who [learned to] recognize these signatures while an adult."
10. See *Hilchot Ishut* 16:25 which mentions some of the details of these customs, e.g., wearing a crown or a special garment, celebrating in a particular manner.
11. As *Ibid.* 10:7 states, it is an obligation ordained by the Sages so that a man would not consider divorce a casual matter. If a woman is a virgin at marriage, her husband's fundamental responsibility is 200 *zuz,* while if she is not a virgin at marriage, his fundamental responsibility is 100 *zuz.*

The *Maggid Mishneh* (in his gloss to *Hilchot Ishut* 16:25) states that in contrast to the previous instance, in this and the latter instance, the word of the minor who attained majority is accepted even when no one else testifies together with him. The Radbaz defines the general principle as follows: Whenever the testimony of two witnesses are required, then the other witness must have observed the matter when he was an adult.

זֶה הַכְּלָל: כֹּל שֶׁתְּחִלָּתוֹ וְסוֹפוֹ בְּכַשְׁרוּת, אַף עַל פִּי שֶׁנִּפְסַל בֵּינְתַיִם - כָּשֵׁר;
תְּחִלָּתוֹ בִּפְסָלוּת, אַף עַל פִּי שֶׁסּוֹפוֹ בְּכַשְׁרוּת - פָּסוּל.
לְפִיכָךְ, מִי שֶׁהָיָה יוֹדֵעַ בְּעֵדוּת וְהוּא קָטָן, וּבָא וְהֵעִיד בָּהּ כְּשֶׁהוּא גָּדוֹל - אֵינָהּ כְּלוּם.

ג וְיֵשׁ דְּבָרִים שֶׁסּוֹמְכִין בָּהֶן עַל עֵדוּת שֶׁמֵּעִיד כְּשֶׁהוּא גָּדוֹל, הוֹאִיל וְהֵם דְּבָרִים שֶׁל דִּבְרֵיהֶם. וְאֵלּוּ הֵן הַדְּבָרִים שֶׁאָדָם נֶאֱמָן לְהָעִיד בְּגָדְלוֹ עַל מַה שֶּׁרָאָה בְּקָטְנוֹ:
נֶאֱמָן אָדָם לוֹמַר: זֶה כְּתַב יָדוֹ שֶׁל אָבִי, אוֹ שֶׁל רַבִּי, אוֹ שֶׁל אָחִי; מִפְּנֵי שֶׁקִּיּוּם שְׁטָרוֹת מִדִּבְרֵיהֶם. זָכוּר אֲנִי בִּפְלוֹנִית שֶׁנִּשֵּׂאת, וְנַעֲשָׂה לָהּ מִנְהַג הַבְּתוּלוֹת; הוֹאִיל וְרֹב נָשִׁים בְּתוּלוֹת נִשָּׂאוֹת, וּכְתֻבָּה מִדִּבְרֵיהֶם.
שֶׁהַמָּקוֹם הַזֶּה בֵּית הַפְּרָס; מִפְּנֵי שֶׁטֻּמְאָתוֹ מִדִּבְרֵיהֶם.
וְעַד כָּאן הָיִינוּ בָּאִין בְּשַׁבָּת; שֶׁצִּמְצוּם הַתְּחוּם עַד אַלְפַּיִם אַמָּה בִּלְבַד מִדִּבְרֵיהֶם.
שֶׁהָיָה אִישׁ פְּלוֹנִי יוֹצֵא מִבֵּית הַסֵּפֶר לִטְבֹּל וְלֶאֱכֹל בִּתְרוּמָתוֹ לָעֶרֶב;
וְשֶׁהָיָה חוֹלֵק עִמָּנוּ תְּרוּמָה;
וְשֶׁהָיִינוּ מוֹלִיכִים חַלָּה וּמַתָּנוֹת לִפְלוֹנִי כֹּהֵן עַל יְדֵי עַצְמוֹ;
וְאָמַר לִי אַבָּא: מִשְׁפָּחָה זוֹ כְּשֵׁרָה, מִשְׁפָּחָה זוֹ פְּסוּלָה;

Whenever the testimony of two witnesses is not required, there is no need for another witness at all.

12. I.e., this place alone and not a larger area (see *Kessef Mishneh*).

13. The term *beit hapras* refers to a field where a corpse was buried and accidentally the grave was plowed over causing the bones to be strewn over the entire field. Our Sages (see *Ketubot* 28a; *Hilchot Tumat Meit* 2:16) decreed that the area within 100 cubits of the original grave is considered as impure by Rabbinic decree.

14. As explained in *Hilchot Shabbat* 27:1, according to Scriptural Law, the Sabbath limits are 12 *mil* (a *mil* is approximately a kilometer in contemporary measure). Our Sages, however, restricted these limits to 2000 cubits. As the Rambam explains in *Hilchot Shabbat*, ch. 28, at times there can be questions regarding the determination of a city's Sabbath limits. Our present halachah is teaching that a person's word is accepted when he states that he remembers being allowed to proceed until a particular point on the Sabbath, indicating that this point was within the Sabbath limits.

15. See *Hilchot Issurei Bi'ah* 20:15 which describes this situation in slightly greater detail. By saying "he would receive a portion," the Rambam emphasizes that the person whose lineage is being questioned is not a servant, because although a servant may partake of *terumah* given his master, he is not given a portion of *terumah* himself.

16. In this context, the Hebrew term *matanot* refers particular to the forearm, jaw, and the maw, presents that must be given to a priest when slaughtering a kosher animal (*Hilchot Bikkurim*, ch. 9). There are times when the term is used in an expanded context to refer to all the priestly presents.

17. In this and the above instance, the person would be accepted as a priest, because of this testimony.

If, however, the person testifies that he remembers seeing the presents sent with others, his testimony is not accepted, for we fear that his recollections are not precise.

18. The *Kessef Mishneh* quotes Rabbenu Nissim who interprets this as referring to a

h) "We ate from the fruit-barrel brought by the brothers of so-and-so to inform others that their brother, so-and-so, married a woman who was not appropriate for him.[19]

All of the [latter four] points involve establishing a person as a priest to enable him to partake of *terumah* [that is separated at present because of] Rabbinic decree[20] or to prevent him from partaking of it.

4. [The leniency granted] in all these situations to accept the testimony of a person who reached majority with regard to what he knew when he was a minor [is not granted] when a gentile or a servant witnessed such matters and gave such testimony after he converted and was freed.[21]

5. If, before becoming a robber, a person knew of evidence concerning a colleague [and recorded that evidence in a legal document] and then became a robber, he cannot testify with regard to his signature.[22] If, however, his signature to the legal document was validated in court before he became a robber, the legal document is acceptable.[23]

Similarly, if [a witness] becomes a person's son-in-law, he may not testify concerning his signature on a legal document [involving his father-in-law]. Others, [however,] may testify concerning [the son-in-law's signature].[24] Even though the document is not validated by the court until after [the witness] becomes a person's son-in-law, it is acceptable.[25] The disqualification of a witness because of a transgression is not the same as the disqualification of a witness because of a family connection, for [a person] disqualified because of a transgression is suspected of forging [the document].[26]

6. When a legal document has only two witnesses signed upon it and they are related to each other[27] or one of them is disqualified because of a transgression, even if the document was transferred in the presence of acceptable witnesses, it is [worthless,] like a shard, because of the invalid [signatures] inside it.[28]

situation where there are two families in the same priestly clan. It is rumored that one is acceptable and one is not acceptable. We rely on the statements of the child who attained majority to determine which is acceptable and which is not.

19. See *Ketubot* 28b. In this instance as well, the *Kessef Mishneh* quotes Rabbenu Nissim as explaining that we are referring to a situation where there were already suspicions regarding the acceptability of the lineage of the family in question.

20. As the Rambam explains in *Hilchot Terumah* 1:26, from the time of the exile of the Ten Tribes onward, the obligation to separate *terumah* is Rabbinic in origin. Since the entire Jewish people do not live on the land, the regulations governing its produce do not apply according to Scriptural law. Hence certain leniencies are taken in the determination of whether or not a person is a priest. See *Hilchot Issurei Bi'ah*, ch. 20.

21. *Ketubot* 28b states that this applies even if the gentile had the intent of converting when he observed the matter of concern. We are not certain that he would be careful with regard to all the particulars involved.

The commentaries note that with regard to the Sabbath limits, the Rambam rules that

וְאָכַלְנוּ בִּקְצָצָה שֶׁל פְּלוֹנִי, שֶׁהֶאֱכִילוּנִי אֶחָיו כְּדֵי לְהוֹדִיעַ שֶׁאֲחִיהֶם פְּלוֹנִי נָשָׂא אִשָּׁה שֶׁאֵינָהּ הוֹגֶנֶת לוֹ. שֶׁכָּל אֵלּוּ הַדְּבָרִים – לְהַחֲזִיק זֶה הַכֹּהֵן לֶאֱכֹל בִּתְרוּמָה שֶׁל דִּבְרֵיהֶם אוֹ לִדְחוֹתוֹ מִמֶּנָּה.

ד כָּל אֵלּוּ שֶׁמֵּעִיד בָּהֶן הַגָּדוֹל בַּמֶּה שֶׁיָּדַע כְּשֶׁהָיָה קָטָן, אִם הָיָה עוֹבֵד כּוֹכָבִים אוֹ עֶבֶד כְּשֶׁרָאָה דְּבָרִים אֵלּוּ, וְהֵעִיד אַחַר שֶׁנִּתְגַּיֵּר וְנִשְׁתַּחְרֵר – אֵינוֹ נֶאֱמָן.

ה מִי שֶׁהָיָה יוֹדֵעַ לַחֲבֵרוֹ בְּעֵדוּת עַד שֶׁלֹּא נַעֲשָׂה גַּזְלָן, וְנַעֲשָׂה גַּזְלָן – הוּא אֵינוֹ מֵעִיד עַל כְּתַב יָדוֹ; אֲבָל אִם הֻחְזַק כְּתַב יָדוֹ שֶׁבִּשְׁטָר זֶה בְּבֵית דִּין קֹדֶם שֶׁיֵּעָשֶׂה גַּזְלָן – הֲרֵי זֶה שְׁטָר כָּשֵׁר. וְכֵן אִם נַעֲשָׂה חֲתָנוֹ – הוּא אֵינוֹ מֵעִיד עַל כְּתַב יָדוֹ, אֲבָל אֲחֵרִים מְעִידִין. אַף עַל פִּי שֶׁלֹּא הֻחְזַק בְּבֵית דִּין אֶלָּא אַחַר שֶׁנַּעֲשָׂה חֲתָנוֹ – הֲרֵי זֶה כָּשֵׁר. שֶׁאֵינוֹ דּוֹמֶה הַפָּסוּל בַּעֲבֵרָה לְפָסוּל בִּקְרִיבָה, שֶׁהַפָּסוּל בַּעֲבֵרָה חָשׁוּד לְזַיֵּף.

ו שְׁטָר שֶׁיֵּשׁ בּוֹ שְׁנֵי עֵדִים בִּלְבַד, וּשְׁנֵיהֶם קְרוֹבִים זֶה לָזֶה אוֹ אֶחָד מִשְּׁנֵיהֶם פָּסוּל בַּעֲבֵרָה, אַף עַל פִּי שֶׁמָּסַר לוֹ הַשְּׁטָר בִּפְנֵי עֵדִים כְּשֵׁרִים – הֲרֵי הוּא כְּחֶרֶס, מִפְּנֵי שֶׁהוּא מְזֻיָּף מִתּוֹכוֹ.

the word of a servant or maid-servant is accepted even if they were not freed (*Hilchot Shabbat* 28:19).

22. For, as a robber, his testimony is not acceptable.

23. We do not disqualify it because the person became a robber afterwards. Implied is that, although the person was acceptable as a witness when he signed the legal document, if he became a robber before the document was validated by the court, the document is not acceptable.

24. I.e., if the son-in-law signed the legal document before marrying the person's daughter, the document may be validated by others.

25. Although the *Shulchan Aruch* (*Choshen Mishpat* 46:35) quotes the Rambam's ruling, it also mentions the qualifying words of Rabbenu Yitzchak Alfasi who states that this leniency applies only when the legal document is in the possession of another person. If, however, it is in the possession of the witnesses, it is disqualified.

26. I.e., we fear that the unacceptable witness composed a false document and dated it falsely, writing a date that preceded his disqualification. A witness disqualified because of a family connection, by contrast, is not suspected of lying or falsifying documents. He is disqualified only because of a Scriptural decree, without any rational explanation (see Chapter 13, Halachah 15, and notes).

According to the Rambam's explanation, if the document was in the possession of others before the witness was disqualified because of his transgression, it may be acceptable even though it was not validated by the court until afterwards. This conclusion is reflected in Rav Yosef Karo's commentary in his *Kessef Mishneh* and his ruling in the *Shulchan Aruch* (*Choshen Mishpat* 46:34).

27. If, however, many witnesses signed it, it is possible that it is acceptable as stated in Chapter 5, Halachah 6.

28. When a legal document is not signed by witnesses at all and is transferred in the presence of acceptable witnesses, it is considered as binding evidence (*Gittin* 3b). The

7. [The following rule applies when a person] composes one [legal document] including testimony that he is granting all of his property to two people[29] and the witnesses [to the document] are related to one of the recipients of the present, but not related to the other. The document is not acceptable, because it is one statement of testimony.[30]

If, however, he writes in one legal document that he is giving this-and-this courtyard to Reuven and this-and-this field to Shimon, and the witnesses are related to one, but not to the other, the present given to the recipient to whom the witnesses are not related is binding.[31] Even though the two [statements are included] in one legal document, they are considered as separate testimonies. To what can the matter be compared? To a person who says: "Serve as witnesses that I gave Reuven this-and-this, that I gave Shimon this-and-this, and that I borrowed such-and-such from Levi." Although they were all included in the same legal document and there is only one person transferring the property, they are considered as three distinct statements.

CHAPTER FIFTEEN

1. Whenever a person will benefit from giving testimony, he may not give such testimony for it is as if he is testifying concerning himself.[1] Therefore when a person comes to the inhabitants of a city with a complaint concerning the [public] bathhouse or thoroughfare, none of the inhabitants of the city can testify regarding this matter nor serve as a judge regarding this matter[2] until they undertake a contractual act[3] removing themselves from [any connection to the property in question]. Afterwards,[4] they may testify or serve as a judges.[5]

signature of the unacceptable witness[es], however, causes the legal document to be disqualified. Compare to *Hilchot Gerushin* 1:15-17.

The *Shulchan Aruch* (*Choshen Mishpat* 51:3) quotes the Rambam's opinion, but also quotes the opinion of the *Baal Halachot Gedolot* and the *Tur* who refer to the explanations given in Chapter 5, Halachah 6: that perhaps the witness signed merely to fill up the empty space on the legal document. On this basis, these authorities maintain that the legal document is considered as a legal document signed by one witness. The *Siftei Cohen* 51:4 laboriously argues that even the Rambam would accept this view.

29. Without dividing the property and specifying which person receives which portion.

30. And if a portion of the testimony is nullified, the entire testimony is nullified [*Kessef Mishneh*, citing the Jerusalem Talmud (*Makkot* 1:7)].

In his *Kessef Mishneh*, Rav Yosef Karo elaborates in support of the Rambam's position although Rav Hai *Gaon* and other *Rishonim* rule differently. In his *Shulchan Aruch* (*Choshen Mishpat* 51:6), however, he mentions a leniency. If the recipient who is related to the witnesses renounces all claims to the property, the other recipient may receive his share. The *Siftei Cohen* 51:6 disputes this ruling, stating that according to the principle: "If a portion of the testimony is nullified, the entire testimony is nullified," the testimony cannot be restored by any means.

ז הַכּוֹתֵב כָּל נְכָסָיו לִשְׁנֵי בְּנֵי אָדָם בְּעֵדוּת אַחַת, וְהָעֵדִים קְרוֹבִים לְאֶחָד מִמְּקַבְּלֵי הַמַּתָּנָה וּרְחוֹקִים מִן הַשֵּׁנִי – הֲרֵי הַשְּׁטָר פָּסוּל, מִפְּנֵי שֶׁהוּא עֵדוּת אַחַת. אֲבָל אִם כָּתַב בִּשְׁטָר אֶחָד: שֶׁנָּתַתִּי לִרְאוּבֵן חָצֵר פְּלוֹנִית, וְשֶׁנָּתַתִּי לְשִׁמְעוֹן שָׂדֶה פְּלוֹנִית, וְנִמְצְאוּ הָעֵדִים קְרוֹבִים לָזֶה וּרְחוֹקִים מִזֶּה – זֶה שֶׁהֵם רְחוֹקִים מִמֶּנּוּ מַתְּנָתוֹ קַיֶּמֶת; שֶׁאֵלּוּ שְׁתֵּי עֵדֻיּוֹת, אַף עַל פִּי שֶׁהֵן בִּשְׁטָר אֶחָד. לְמָה זֶה דּוֹמֶה? לְאוֹמֵר: הֱיוּ עָלַי עֵדִים שֶׁנָּתַתִּי לִרְאוּבֵן כָּךְ וְכָךְ, וְשֶׁנָּתַתִּי לְשִׁמְעוֹן כָּךְ וְכָךְ, וְשֶׁלָּוִיתִי מִלְּוִי כָּךְ וְכָךְ; שֶׁאַף עַל פִּי שֶׁכָּתַב בִּשְׁטָר אֶחָד, וְהַמַּקְנֶה אִישׁ אֶחָד – הֲרֵי אֵלּוּ שָׁלֹשׁ עֵדֻיּוֹת שֶׁאֵינָן תְּלוּיוֹת זוֹ בָּזוֹ.

פֶּרֶק חֲמִשָּׁה עָשָׂר

א כָּל עֵדוּת שֶׁתָּבוֹא הֲנָאָה לְאָדָם מִמֶּנָּה – אֵינוֹ מֵעִיד בָּהּ; שֶׁזֶּה הוּא כְּמֵעִיד עַל עַצְמוֹ. לְפִיכָךְ, בְּנֵי הָעִיר שֶׁבָּא מְעַרְעֵר לְעַרְעֵר עֲלֵיהֶם בְּמֶרְחָץ אוֹ בִּרְחוֹב שֶׁל עִיר – אֵין אֶחָד מִבַּעֲלֵי הָעִיר מֵעִיד בְּדָבָר זֶה וְלֹא דָּן, עַד שֶׁיְּסַלֵּק עַצְמוֹ בְּקִנְיָן גָּמוּר, וְאַחַר כָּךְ יָעִיד אוֹ יָדִין.

31. Since the statements are distinct, we divide the testimony and accept the portion which is acceptable and reject the other portion.

1. A person who has a vested interest in the outcome of a judgment is likely to lie or at least distort the evidence (perhaps subconsciously) in favor of the desired result. The Rambam, however, goes further, stating that when a person has a vested interest, it is as if he is a principal in the case and he is disqualified as a witness by Scriptural Law. Even if there is no suspicion at all that he will lie, he is unacceptable. See the commentaries of the *Sefer Me'irat Einayim* 37:1 and the *Siftei Cohen* 37:1 where this subject is discussed.
2. For they have a vested interest.
3. As validated by a *kinyan suder*, the exchange of a handkerchief; see *Hilchot Mechirah*, ch. 5.
4. I.e., the fact that he was once an interested party does not disqualify him after he withdraws his interest. Although as stated in Chapter 14, Halachah 2, a witness must be acceptable both at the time he observes the matter of concern and at the time he delivers his testimony, the Rambam maintains that this principle does not apply in the present situation because the difficulty with the witness does not concern his person, but his vested interest. Hence, when he rids himself of that vested interest, he is fit to testify. *Tosafot, Niddah* 50a, differs and maintains that in this instance as well, if a person is not fit to testify when he observes the evidence, his testimony is not acceptable. This view is also cited in the *Hagahot Maimoniot*. The *Shulchan Aruch* (*Choshen Mishpat* 37:18) quotes the Rambam's position. The *Siftei Cohen* 37:32, however, mentions the other view.
5. *Bava Batra* 43a, the source for this ruling, mentions only that such an individual may serve as a judge. The Rambam extends this conclusion and applies it to witnesses as well.

2. [The following rules apply when] a [communal] Torah scroll is stolen from the inhabitants of a city. Since it is intended to be listened to [by all the members of the community], it is impossible for a person to withdraw [his share of] ownership of it.[6] [Hence,] the matter should not be adjudicated by the judges of that city, and the inhabitants of that city may not [testify to] prove [the city's ownership]. Similar laws apply in all analogous situations.[7]

3. When a person says: "Give a *manah* to the poor people of my city," the matter may not be adjudicated by the judges of that city and the inhabitants of that city may not [testify to] prove [that the pledge was made].[8]

When does the above apply? When the poor people depend upon them and they allocate charity to them. [In such a situation,] even if two members of the city promised: "We will give the fixed amount required of us [regardless]; let us testify,"[9] we do not heed their request. For they receive benefit from the fact that these poor people become wealthier[10] for [the poor] are dependent on the inhabitants of the city.[11] Similar laws apply in all analogous situations.

4. [The following rules apply when] a person raises a protest and seeks to expropriate land[12] that is owned by two partners from the possession of one of the partners. [The other partner] may not testify[13] on behalf of his partner concerning [the land][14] unless he withdraws from [ownership of the land][15] and undertakes an act of contract affirming that he gave his portion to his partner[16] and [committing himself to] reimburse him for its value if his [own] creditor expropriates it from his partner.[17] [After undertaking such an agreement,] he may testify concerning [the field]. Similar laws apply in all analogous situations.

5. [The following rules apply when] a person protests the ownership of a field. If it contains produce, a sharecropper may not testify with regard to it. For the sharecropper wishes it to remain in the possession of the owner so that he will

6. Since the person will continue to listen to the Torah being read from that scroll, he will still be deriving benefit from it remaining in the city.

The Radbaz states that, according to the Rambam, this ruling applies even when the city also possesses another Torah scroll. The *Shulchan Aruch* (*Choshen Mishpat* 7:12) and the Ramah (*Choshen Mishpat* 37:19) quote the opinion of Rabbeinu Asher who maintains that if the city has another Torah scroll, a judge or a witness may withdraw his share in the Torah scroll in question.

7. Questions involving other religious articles that are required for communal use [Ramah (*Ibid.*)].

8. As reflected in the continuation of the Rambam's statements, since the poor people are dependent upon them, when the poor people receive money from other sources, that will release their burden. Hence, they are considered to have a vested interest.

9. And thus they would have no immediate benefit from their testimony.

10. For in this way, in the future, they will not have to give them the same amount. Alternatively, the general benefit to the city will also affect them in an indirect manner.

11. When, however, the poor are supported from donations coming from outside the city,

ב בְּנֵי הָעִיר שֶׁנִּגְנַב סֵפֶר תּוֹרָה שֶׁלָּהֶן, הוֹאִיל וְלִשְׁמִיעָה הוּא עָשׂוּי שֶׁאִי אֶפְשָׁר לְאָדָם לְסַלֵּק עַצְמוֹ מִמֶּנּוּ – אֵין דָּנִין בְּדַיָּנֵי אוֹתָהּ הָעִיר, וְאֵין מְבִיאִין רְאָיָה מֵאַנְשֵׁי אוֹתָהּ הָעִיר. וְכֵן כֹּל כַּיּוֹצֵא בָּזֶה.

ג הָאוֹמֵר: תְּנוּ מָנֶה לַעֲנִיֵּי עִירִי – אֵין דָּנִין בְּדַיָּנֵי אוֹתָהּ הָעִיר, וְאֵין מְבִיאִין רְאָיָה מֵאַנְשֵׁי אוֹתָהּ הָעִיר.
בַּמֶּה דְּבָרִים אֲמוּרִים? כְּשֶׁהָיוּ הָעֲנִיִּים סְמוּכִים עֲלֵיהֶם, וּפוֹסְקִין עֲלֵיהֶן צְדָקָה. אֲפִלּוּ אָמְרוּ שְׁנַיִם מֵאַנְשֵׁי אוֹתָהּ הָעִיר: אָנוּ נִתֵּן דָּבָר הַקָּצוּב עָלֵינוּ וְנָעִיד – אֵין שׁוֹמְעִין לָהֶם; שֶׁהֲנָאָה הוּא לָהֶם שֶׁיִּתְעַשְּׁרוּ עֲנִיִּים אֵלּוּ, הוֹאִיל וְהֵן סְמוּכִין עַל בְּנֵי הָעִיר. וְכֵן כֹּל כַּיּוֹצֵא בָּזֶה.

ד קַרְקַע שֶׁבֵּין שְׁנֵי שֻׁתָּפִין שֶׁבָּא מְעַרְעֵר לְהוֹצִיאָהּ מִתַּחַת יַד הַשֻּׁתָּף – אֵינוֹ מֵעִיד לְשֻׁתָּפוֹ עָלֶיהָ; אֶלָּא אִם סִלֵּק עַצְמוֹ מִמֶּנָּה, וְקָנוּ מִיָּדוֹ שֶׁנְּתָנָהּ לַשֻּׁתָּף, וְשֶׁאִם בָּא בַּעַל חוֹב שֶׁלּוֹ וּטְרָפָהּ מִיַּד הַשֻּׁתָּף – מְשַׁלֵּם לוֹ דָּמֶיהָ, וְאַחַר כָּךְ מֵעִיד לוֹ עָלֶיהָ. וְכֵן כֹּל כַּיּוֹצֵא בָּזֶה.

ה הָעוֹרֵר עַל הַשָּׂדֶה:
אִם יֵשׁ בָּהּ פֵּרוֹת – אֵין הָאָרִיס מֵעִיד לוֹ עָלֶיהָ, שֶׁהֲרֵי רוֹצֶה הָאָרִיס לְהַעֲמִידָהּ בְּיַד

the inhabitants of the city may testify if they take precautions so that they do not have a vested interest (Radbaz).

12. I.e., he claims that the person who sold the land to the partners stole it from him and sold it illegally. Moreover, he brings witnesses to prove his claim. In such an instance, he has the right to expropriate the land and the partners must sue the thief to receive reimbursement.

13. I.e., he would be testifying that the witnesses who testified on behalf of the claimant were not acceptable because they transgressed. Hence their testimony would not be fit to take into consideration.

14. I.e., even the portion of the land belonging to the other partner.

15. He may, however, withdraw his ownership after the protest has been raised [*Shulchan Aruch* (*Choshen Mishpat* 37:1)].

16. I.e., he gives his portion to him as a present without receiving anything in return. He will lose his portion of the field regardless - for his own testimony will not avail him. Nevertheless, by giving his portion to his partner and testifying, he prevents his partner from suffering a loss.

17. We are speaking about a creditor from whom the partner borrowed money before he divested himself of a connection to the land. That creditor thus has a lien on the land and is entitled to expropriate it from the person in possession. Accordingly, the partner would still have a vested interest in keeping it in the other partner's possession. When, however, he undertakes a commitment to make restitution if the field is expropriated, it does not matter to him at all who is in possession of the field. Hence he may testify about it.

receive his portion of the crops.[18] If there is no produce in the field, he may testify [concerning it].[19]

[Different rules apply with regard to] a renter. If he brings the rent with him and says: "Let whoever is established as the owner of this field take this," he may offer testimony.[20] If, however, he already paid the rent to the owner of the field he may not testify. For if the field is expropriated by the claimant, he would have to pay him rent for all the years he dwelled in it.[21] [Hence,] he may not offer testimony. Similar laws apply in all analogous situations.

6. [The following rules apply if] Shimon borrowed money and Reuven guaranteed[22] the debt. Yehudah entered into litigation against Shimon and [sought to] expropriate landed property from his possession. If Shimon possesses another field[23] equal in value to the debt [guaranteed by Reuven], Reuven may testify with regard to the land, asserting that it belongs to Shimon. He does not derive any benefit from this, for even if Yehudah would expropriate the field, [Shimon possesses] another field from which the creditor could derive payment.[24]

Similarly, a person who purchased a field may testify on behalf of another person who purchased a field from the same seller and [affirm] that the field is his.[25] [This applies] provided the seller owns a field that is not on lien[26] that is equivalent to the value of the field acquired by the first purchaser. [In such a situation,] the first purchaser does not derive any benefit from the field remaining in the possession of the second purchaser, for even if the field he purchased is expropriated from him,[27] he may seek reimbursement from the seller and the seller possesses another field from which he could expropriate his due.

18. For if it is granted to the claimant, he is entitled to all its produce. The sharecropper receives only compensation for his expenses - and that only when the yield is sufficient to pay those expenses.

19. Even if the claimant is given the field, the sharecropper is not obligated to pay him for the previous years. Nor do we say that the sharecropper fears that he will lose the opportunity of working this field, for we assume that there are many fields of similar value available. Hence it is not considered as if he has a vested interest (*Kessef Mishneh*).

This is speaking about a situation where the sharecropper did not till the field and prepare it for sowing before the claimant demanded its return. If he had tilled the field, he may not testify, because he has a vested interest since all the work he invested will be for naught if the field is expropriated (Radbaz).

20. The *Shulchan Aruch* (*Choshen Mishpat* 37:12) states that the owner may give the rent back to the renter to enable him to bring it to court so that he may testify without any vested interest.

21. Even though he is entitled to receive reimbursement from the person who rented him the field, that requires suing him in court and no one enjoys the possibility of entering legal proceedings (*Siftei Cohen* 37:13).

22. This applies even with regard to an ordinary guarantor, not necessarily an *orev kablan* (Radbaz, *Kessef Mishneh*).

23. If, however, Shimon does not possess a field, but does possess movable property,

בְּעָלֶיהָ, כְּדֵי שֶׁיִּטֹּל חֶלְקוֹ בַּפֵּרוֹת; וְאִם אֵין בָּהּ פֵּרוֹת - מֵעִיד. אֲבָל הַשּׂוֹכֵר, אִם לָקַח הַשְּׂכִירוּת בְּיָדוֹ וְאָמַר: כָּל מִי שֶׁתִּתְקַיֵּם שָׂדֶה זוֹ בְּיָדוֹ יִטֹּל - הֲרֵי זֶה מֵעִיד; וְאִם כְּבָר נָתַן הַשְּׂכִירוּת לְבַעַל הַשָּׂדֶה - אֵינוֹ מֵעִיד. כֵּיוָן שֶׁאִם תֵּצֵא הַשָּׂדֶה לַמְעַרְעֵר - חַיָּב לִתֵּן לוֹ שְׂכַר כָּל הַשָּׁנִים שֶׁיָּשַׁב בָּהּ, אֵינוֹ מֵעִיד. וְכֵן כֹּל כַּיּוֹצֵא בָּזֶה.

ו שִׁמְעוֹן שֶׁלָּוָה, וְהָיָה רְאוּבֵן עָרֵב, וּבָא יְהוּדָה לְעַרְעֵר עַל שִׁמְעוֹן הַלֹּוֶה וְהוֹצִיא קַרְקַע מִתַּחַת יָדוֹ, אִם יֵשׁ לְשִׁמְעוֹן שָׂדֶה אַחֶרֶת כְּנֶגֶד הַחוֹב - הֲרֵי רְאוּבֵן הֶעָרֵב יֵשׁ לוֹ לְהָעִיד עַל אוֹתָהּ קַרְקַע שֶׁהִיא שֶׁל שִׁמְעוֹן. שֶׁאֵין לוֹ הֲנָאָה בָּזֶה; שֶׁאִם לְקָחָהּ יְהוּדָה - הֲרֵי שָׂדֶה אַחֶרֶת שֶׁיִּפָּרַע מִמֶּנָּה בַּעַל חוֹבוֹ.

וְכֵן לוֹקֵחַ רִאשׁוֹן מֵעִיד לְלוֹקֵחַ שֵׁנִי שֶׁלָּקַח אַחֲרָיו שֶׁזֶּה הַשָּׂדֶה שֶׁלּוֹ. וְהוּא שֶׁיֵּשׁ לַמּוֹכֵר שָׂדֶה בֶּן חוֹרִין כְּנֶגֶד דְּמֵי שָׂדֶה שֶׁל לוֹקֵחַ רִאשׁוֹן. שֶׁאֵין לְלוֹקֵחַ רִאשׁוֹן הֲנָאָה בַּעֲמִידַת זֶה הַשָּׂדֶה בְּיַד לוֹקֵחַ שֵׁנִי; שֶׁאֲפִלּוּ נִטְרַף - לוֹקֵחַ הָרִאשׁוֹן עַל הַמּוֹכֵר הוּא חוֹזֵר, וַהֲרֵי יֵשׁ לוֹ שָׂדֶה אַחֶרֶת שֶׁיִּגְבֶּה מִמֶּנָּה.

Reuven is not acceptable as a witness. For the movable property can be concealed or disposed of and the debt left to Reuven (Radbaz).

24. Hence even if the field is expropriated by Yehudah, Reuven will not suffer a loss. If, however, Shimon does not possess another field, Reuven is considered to have a vested interest in Shimon retaining possession. For if he does not possess the field, Reuven may be called upon to pay the debt (see *Bava Batra* 46b).

25. Reuven purchased a field from Shimon and afterwards, Levi purchased a field from Shimon. Yehudah then comes to Levi and claims that he, Yehudah, is the rightful owner of that field and it was stolen from him. Reuven can testify on behalf of Levi and establish him as the rightful owner of the field.

26. That is in his possession and not encumbered by any loans. In this instance, as the Rambam continues to explain, Reuven is protected, because he can always sue Shimon and expropriate the unencumbered field. If, however, Shimon does not have such a field, Reuven is considered as having a vested interest for he has no security for his purchase as we will continue to explain.

The Ra'avad adds that Shimon must designate this field as an *apotiki* for Reuven, assuring him that he will receive it if the field he purchased is expropriated. The *Shulchan Aruch* (*Choshen Mishpat* 37:14), however, does not mention this requirement. See the *Siftei Cohen* 37:18

27. I.e., Dan, a creditor of Shimon's, comes and seeks to expropriate the field Reuven purchased. Had Yehudah not prevailed against Levi, Dan would have expropriated the field Levi purchased, for that was purchased after Reuven's field. Nevertheless, even though that field is not available, Reuven will not suffer a loss, because he can rely on the unencumbered field. Hence, it makes no difference to him whether or not the field remains in Levi's possession.

If, however, Shimon does not possess an unencumbered field, Reuven would derive an advantage from the field remaining in Levi's possession. For then the creditor would expropriate Levi's field first.

CHAPTER SIXTEEN

1. [The following rule applies when] Reuven stole a field or a garment[1] from Shimon[2] and Yehudah lodges a claim against Reuven, stating that the field or the garment is his. Shimon may not testify[3] on Reuven's behalf that the field or the garment does not belong to Yehudah. [The rationale is that] Shimon desires to have the field or garment remain in the possession of Reuven who stole it from him so that he will have it returned to him from the thief.[4] For it is possible that the proof Shimon uses to expropriate it from Reuven will not enable him to expropriate it from Yehudah.[5]

Similarly, if Reuven sold or transferred as an inheritance the stolen field[6] to Levi and Yehudah lodges a claim against Levi, Shimon may not testify that it does not belong to Yehudah. For perhaps it is more comfortable for him to expropriate it from Levi.[7]

2. [The following rules apply if Reuven] sold the stolen garment[8] to Levi and Yehudah lodges a claim [concerning it]. If Reuven died, Shimon may testify that it does not belong to Yehudah.[9] [The rationale is that] this garment will never be returned to Shimon, because the purchaser acquires it because of [Shimon's] despair [of recovering] it and its change of domain.[10] Reuven, the thief, died, and thus he has no one from whom he could receive reimbursement.[11]

If, however, Reuven is still alive, Shimon may not testify even concerning a garment. For he will receive benefit from the fact that it will not remain in Yehudah's possession so that he can bring proof that Reuven stole it [and require him to] make reimbursement for it.

1. I.e., the laws apply with regard to both movable and landed property.
2. The *Tur* (*Choshen Mishpat* 37) quotes two opinions: one which maintains that this law applies even when Shimon merely suspects that Reuven stole from him, and the other that it applies only when he is certain of the matter.
3. E.g., testifying that Yehudah's witnesses are unacceptable or the like.
4. I.e., he will bring witnesses who testify that Reuven stole it from him.
5. Since he prefers having the property remain in Reuven's possession, he is considered as having a vested interest in the matter and is disqualified from testifying.
6. But not the garment, for this law does not apply with regard to movable property as stated in the following halachah. Landed property can never be stolen, but instead remains in the possession of the legal owner even when it is not in his physical possession. Hence the original owner is always expecting to receive his property (*Bava Batra* 44a and commentaries).
7. I.e., since Levi assumes the position held by Reuven. The same laws which apply with regard to testifying on behalf of Reuven apply with regard to testifying on his behalf.

From *Bava Batra* 43b, it appears that "it is more comfortable for him..." means that the claimant is a difficult person while the heir or the purchaser is easier to deal with and will surrender the property more graciously. There are some who also use this same explanation in the first clause. The Rambam, however, does not, because it is highly

פֶּרֶק שִׁשָּׁה עָשָׂר

א רְאוּבֵן שֶׁגָּזַל שָׂדֶה אוֹ טַלִּית מִשִּׁמְעוֹן, וּבָא יְהוּדָה וְעִרְעֵר עַל רְאוּבֵן וְאָמַר: שָׂדֶה זוֹ אוֹ טַלִּית זוֹ שֶׁלִּי הִיא – אֵין שִׁמְעוֹן יָכוֹל לְהָעִיד לִרְאוּבֵן שֶׁאֵין זוֹ הַשָּׂדֶה שֶׁל יְהוּדָה וְלֹא זוֹ הַטַּלִּית שֶׁל יְהוּדָה; שֶׁהֲרֵי שִׁמְעוֹן רוֹצֶה לְהַעֲמִיד שָׂדֶה זוֹ אוֹ טַלִּית זוֹ בְּיַד רְאוּבֵן, שֶׁהוּא גְּזָלָהּ מִמֶּנּוּ, כְּדֵי שֶׁיַּחֲזִירוּ לוֹ מִיַּד הַגַּזְלָן; שֶׁהֲרֵי אֶפְשָׁר שֶׁתִּהְיֶה הָרְאָיָה שֶׁל שִׁמְעוֹן, שֶׁמּוֹצִיא בָּהּ מִיַּד רְאוּבֵן, אֶפְשָׁר שֶׁאֵינוֹ יָכוֹל לְהוֹצִיא בָּהּ מִיַּד יְהוּדָה.

וְכֵן אִם מָכַר רְאוּבֵן הַשָּׂדֶה הַגְּזוּלָה אוֹ הוֹרִישָׁהּ לְלֵוִי, וּבָא יְהוּדָה לְעַרְעֵר עַל לֵוִי – אֵין שִׁמְעוֹן מֵעִיד שֶׁאֵינָהּ שֶׁל יְהוּדָה; שֶׁמָּא נַחַת רוּחַ יֵשׁ לוֹ לְהוֹצִיאָהּ מִיַּד לֵוִי.

ב מָכַר הַטַּלִּית הַגְּזוּלָה לְלֵוִי, וּבָא יְהוּדָה לְעַרְעֵר, אִם מֵת רְאוּבֵן – שִׁמְעוֹן מֵעִיד עָלֶיהָ שֶׁאֵינָהּ שֶׁל יְהוּדָה; שֶׁהֲרֵי אֵין טַלִּית זוֹ חוֹזֶרֶת לְשִׁמְעוֹן לְעוֹלָם, שֶׁכְּבָר קְנָאָהּ הַלּוֹקֵחַ בְּיֵאוּשׁ וְשִׁנּוּי רְשׁוּת, וּכְבָר מֵת רְאוּבֵן הַגַּזְלָן וְאֵין לוֹ מִמִּי יִטֹּל דָּמֶיהָ.

אֲבָל אִם עֲדַיִן רְאוּבֵן קַיָּם – אֵין שִׁמְעוֹן מֵעִיד אַף עַל הַטַּלִּית; שֶׁהֲנָאָה הִיא לוֹ שֶׁלֹּא תַּעֲמֹד בְּיַד יְהוּדָה, כְּדֵי שֶׁיָּבִיא רְאָיָה שֶׁרְאוּבֵן גְּזָלָהּ וִישַׁלֵּם דָּמֶיהָ.

unlikely that it will be "more comfortable" for the owner to deal with the thief than with the claimant (Radbaz).

8. According to the Rambam, it does not matter whether the sale precedes the legal owner's despair that the article will be returned to him or whether he despaired afterwards (*Hilchot Geneivah* 5:3). Many Ashkenazic authorities differ. See *Sefer Me'irat Einayim* 37:48.

9. As the Rambam proceeds to explain, he is not considered as having a vested interest in the matter, because the garment will never be returned to him.

10. See *Hilchot Geneivah* 5:3, *Hilchot Gezelah* 5:7, where this concept is explained. A thief himself can never acquire the stolen article while it remains in the same state as when it was stolen. And if its owner never despairs of recovering it, another person may also not acquire it. If, however, the owner despairs of recovering it and the thief sells or gives it to another person, that other person acquires the article. The thief is required to reimburse the owner for the article, but the article itself remains in possession of the person who acquired it.

The *Shulchan Aruch* (*Choshen Mishpat* 37:17) clarifies that in Talmudic times, this ruling applied only when the thief did not leave any landed property in his estate. If, however, he left landed property, that property is on lien to his debts. Hence, there is still a possibility of the original owner recovering the value of the object stolen from him. Accordingly, he is considered as having a vested interest. Moreover, in the present age, we follow the ruling of the *Geonim* who maintain that even movable property left in a person's estate is on lien to his debts. As such, as long as the thief leaves any estate whatsoever, the person from whom the property was stolen is considered as an involved party.

11. I.e., as long as they do not receive the stolen article itself as an inheritance, the thief's heirs are under no responsibility to the owner of the stolen article.

Similarly, if the garment is in the possession of Reuven's heirs, Shimon may not testify concerning it. For ultimately, if the heir retains possession, it will be returned to [the original owner].[12] Similar laws apply in all analogous situations.

3. [The following rule applies when] Reuven sold a field to Shimon without taking financial responsibility for it[13] and Yehudah issued a claim[14] to expropriate it from Shimon. Reuven may not testify concerning it on Shimon's behalf.[15] Even though he did not accept financial responsibility for [the field], he desires that it remain in Shimon's possession. For [if that is the case,] one of Reuven's creditors may come and collect it as payment for [Reuven's] debt and thus [Reuven] will not be "a wicked person [who] borrows and does not repay."[16]

4. [When, by contrast,] Reuven sold a cow or a garment[17] to Shimon and Yehudah raised a claim to expropriate it from Shimon,[18] Reuven may testify[19] that it belongs to Shimon. [The rationale is that] even if it were to remain in Shimon's possession, a creditor of Reuven does not have the right to expropriate movable property [that was sold].[20] [This applies even when the movable property] was designated as an *apoteiki*.[21]

When does the above apply? When Shimon [the purchaser] admits that the cow or the garment certainly belonged to Reuven the seller and he knows that they truly belonged to him.[22] If, however, Shimon does not acknowledge this,

12. As long as the article itself is in the heir's possession, they must return it to the original owner. Inheritance - in contrast to purchase - is not considered as a change of domain. Instead, the domain of the heir is considered as an extension of the domain of the thief (*Bava Batra, loc. cit.* and commentaries).

13. I.e., Reuven had a clause included in the contract of sale, stating that he does not accept any responsibility if the field is expropriated from Shimon the purchaser. Even if the field is taken because of a legitimate claim for which he would ordinarily be responsible, he is freed of liability because of this clause. See *Hilchot Mechirah* 19:3.

14. I.e., Yehudah claims that Reuven purchased the field from a thief before selling it to Shimon [*Tur* (*Choshen Mishpat* 37)].

The *Tur* and the Ramah (*Choshen Mishpat* 37:15) emphasize that if Yehudah's claim to the field would be effective only against Shimon the purchaser and not against Reuven, the seller, Reuven is allowed to testify on Shimon's behalf. For his creditor would have the right to expropriate the property from Yehudah, just as he could have expropriated it from Shimon.

15. E.g., by disqualifying Yehudah's witnesses.

16. Cf. Psalms 37:21. I.e., if the field is taken by Yehudah, it will not be able to be used as security for his debt. Reuven will not have such feelings if the field is expropriated from Shimon, for he can tell Shimon that by selling the field to him without accepting responsibility, it was as if he informed him of the likelihood that it would be expropriated from him.

The above applies provided Reuven does not possess another field of equivalent value in his own possession. If, however, he possesses another field, that field will be expropriated by a creditor and not the field that was sold previously. Hence, it will make

וְכֵן אִם הָיְתָה הַטַּלִּית בְּיַד יוֹרְשֵׁי רְאוּבֵן – אֵין שִׁמְעוֹן מֵעִיד עָלֶיהָ, מִפְּנֵי שֶׁסּוֹפָהּ שֶׁאִם תַּעֲמֹד בְּיַד הַיּוֹרֵשׁ לַחֲזֹר לוֹ. וְכֵן כֹּל כַּיּוֹצֵא בָּזֶה.

ג רְאוּבֵן שֶׁמָּכַר שָׂדֶה לְשִׁמְעוֹן שֶׁלֹּא בְּאַחֲרָיוּת, וּבָא יְהוּדָה לְעַרְעֵר עַל שִׁמְעוֹן וּלְהוֹצִיאָהּ מִתַּחַת יָדוֹ – אֵין רְאוּבֵן מֵעִיד לוֹ עָלֶיהָ. אַף עַל פִּי שֶׁאֵין עָלֶיהָ אַחֲרָיוּת – הֲרֵי הוּא רוֹצֶה שֶׁתַּעֲמֹד בְּיַד שִׁמְעוֹן, כְּדֵי שֶׁיָּבוֹא בַּעַל חוֹב שֶׁל רְאוּבֵן וְיִטְרְפֶנָּה בְּחוֹבוֹ, וְלֹא יִהְיֶה לֹוֶה רָשָׁע וְלֹא יְשַׁלֵּם.

ד רְאוּבֵן שֶׁמָּכַר פָּרָה אוֹ טַלִּית לְשִׁמְעוֹן, וּבָא יְהוּדָה לְעַרְעֵר וּלְהוֹצִיא מִיַּד שִׁמְעוֹן – רְאוּבֵן מֵעִיד לוֹ עָלֶיהָ שֶׁהִיא שֶׁל שִׁמְעוֹן; שֶׁאֲפִלּוּ עָמְדָה בְּיַד שִׁמְעוֹן – אֵין בַּעַל חוֹבוֹ שֶׁל רְאוּבֵן טוֹרֵף מִן הַמִּטַּלְטְלִין, וַאֲפִלּוּ הָיוּ אַפּוֹתֵיקִי. בַּמֶּה דְּבָרִים אֲמוּרִים? כְּשֶׁהָיָה שִׁמְעוֹן מוֹדֶה שֶׁזּוֹ הַפָּרָה וְהַטַּלִּית הֵם שֶׁל רְאוּבֵן הַמּוֹכֵר בְּוַדַּאי, וְהוּא יוֹדֵעַ שֶׁבֶּאֱמֶת הֵן שֶׁלּוֹ;

no difference to him whether or not Yehudah expropriates that field. As such, he is acceptable as a witness (*Kessef Mishneh*, based on *Bava Batra* 45a and commentaries).

The *Merkevat HaMishneh* differs and maintains that the Rambam follows the approach of his teacher, Rav Yosef Migash who interprets the above passage as implying that even when the seller possesses another field, he is disqualified as a witness. This view is quoted by the *Sefer Me'irat Einayim* 37:37 and the *Siftei Cohen* 37:22.

17. I.e., movable property. This also refers to an instance where Reuven did not accept financial responsibility for the sale [*Shulchan Aruch* (*Choshen Mishpat* 37:16)]. There are those who maintain that this is not necessarily the Rambam's intent, but the *Siftei Cohen* 37:25 cites *Hilchot Mechirah* 19:3 as indication that it is.

18. In this instance as well, Yehudah claims that Reuven purchased the article from a thief and Yehudah was the rightful owner [*Shulchan Aruch* (*Choshen Mishpat* 37:16)].

19. I.e., as above, he testifies to disqualify the witnesses Yehudah brings.

20. In contrast to landed property which remains in the same place and therefore its ownership is a matter of public knowledge, movable property can be transferred from hand to hand and is not as identifiable. Accordingly, our Sages did not consider it on lien to a person's debts. For if a creditor could expropriate movable property from a purchaser, no one would purchase such property, for they would always be afraid that it could be expropriated (*Bava Batra* 44b and commentaries).

21. I.e., it was specifically stated that this movable property would be used to pay the debt. Even if a contract included such a clause, the clause is not valid and the purchaser may maintain possession of the movable property. See *Hilchot Malveh V'Loveh* 18:5.

Since Reuven's creditors may not expropriate the property from Shimon, Reuven has no benefit in the property remaining in Shimon's possession Hence, he is allowed to serve as a witness on his behalf (*Kessef Mishneh*).

22. Therefore even if Yehudah's claim prevails and the property is expropriated from Shimon, Shimon does not have a claim against Reuven. For Shimon acknowledges that Reuven had the right to sell the property to him.

The *Shulchan Aruch* (*Choshen Mishpat* 37:16) does not mention this point in his statement of the law. There are commentaries that explain that since the *Shulchan Aruch* mentions that one does not accept responsibility, this point is not necessary. The *Siftei*

Reuven may not testify to deny Yehudah's right to the property. For if it is expropriated from Shimon, he will sue [Reuven] for its value, saying: "You sold me an article that did not belong to you, for witnesses came and stated that it belonged to Yehudah."[23]

When do we accept Reuven's testimony to deny Yehudah's right to the movable property and thus leave it in Shimon's possession? When witnesses come and testify that Reuven never owned landed property.[24] If, however, there are no witnesses to deliver such testimony, [Reuven] may not testify concerning a cow or a garment as well.

Why may he not testify concerning such objects? Because it is possible that he placed them on lien to his creditor by virtue of the latter's lien on landed property and in that contract stated: "That I will acquire," establishing a lien on them by virtue of the lien on the landed property.[25] Thus his creditor has the right to expropriate a cow and a garment as well. Hence, [Reuven] should not testify concerning them. For he desires to have them remain in Shimon's possession so that his creditor can come and expropriate them.[26] Similar principles apply in all analogous situations.

These matters are dependent solely on the discerning capacity of the judge and the greatness of his understanding when he comprehends the fundamental thrust of the judgments and knows how one thing leads to another, deepening his perception.[27] If he sees that a witness will derive benefit from this testimony even in an uncommon and extraordinary manner, he should not allow that person to testify.[28]

Just as a person should not testify with regard to a matter because he may have a vested interest in the case; so, too, he should not act as a judge concerning such a matter.[29] Similarly with regard to other disqualifying factors, just as they disqualify [a person as] a witness; so, too, they disqualify him as a judge.[30]

5. Therefore we do not appoint two judges to the *Sanhedrin* who are related to each other. [This applies] to both a minor *Sanhedrin*[31] and the Supreme

Cohen, however, differs and maintains that the practice cited by the *Shulchan Aruch* is not followed in all places. In the places that did not accept that practice, even if the seller does not accept responsibility, the purchaser must recognize that the property is his.

23. According to the opinion that the Rambam is speaking about a situation where Reuven the seller accepted financial responsibility, the clause is understood simply: He is considered as having a vested interest, for if his testimony is not accepted, the purchaser will sue him for the value of the property and he will have to make restitution.

According to the view that the seller did not accept financial responsibility, he will not be held liable if the seller sues him. Nevertheless, he is considered as having a vested interest. For no person desires that the people to whom he sells property have complaints against him and call him to court because of them [*Bayit Chadash* (*Choshen Mishpat* 37)].

24. For then the factors which the Rambam mentions in the following clause are not relevant.

25. As the Rambam writes in *Hilchot Malveh ViLoveh* 18:2, a lender may place all of his movable property on lien to a debt by stating in the promissory note that he establishes

אֲבָל אִם לֹא הוֹדָה שִׁמְעוֹן – אֵין רְאוּבֵן מֵעִיד לְאַבֵּד זְכוּת יְהוּדָה; שֶׁאִם תֵּצֵא מִתַּחַת יְדֵי שִׁמְעוֹן – יַחֲזֹר שִׁמְעוֹן וְיִתְבַּע דָּמִים, וְיֹאמַר לוֹ: מָכַרְתָּ לִי דָּבָר שֶׁאֵינוֹ שֶׁלְּךָ, שֶׁהֲרֵי בָּאוּ עֵדִים וְאָמְרוּ שֶׁהֵן שֶׁל יְהוּדָה. בַּמֶּה דְּבָרִים אֲמוּרִים שֶׁיָּעִיד רְאוּבֵן לְאַבֵּד זְכוּת יְהוּדָה וְיַעֲמִיד הַמִּטַּלְטְלִין בְּיַד שִׁמְעוֹן? כְּשֶׁבָּאוּ עֵדִים וְהֵעִידוּ, שֶׁהֵם יוֹדְעִים שֶׁרְאוּבֵן זֶה לֹא הָיְתָה לוֹ קַרְקַע מֵעוֹלָם; אֲבָל אִם לֹא בָּאוּ עֵדִים לְכָךְ – אַף עַל הַפָּרָה וְהַטַּלִּית אֵינוֹ מֵעִיד.

וְלָמָּה אֵינוֹ מֵעִיד עֲלֵיהֶן? שֶׁמָּא הִקְנָה אוֹתָם לְבַעַל חוֹבוֹ אַגַּב קַרְקַע, וְכָתַב 'דְּאִקְנֵי', וְהִקְנָה לוֹ מִטַּלְטְלִין אַגַּב קַרְקַע, שֶׁנִּמְצָא בַּעַל חוֹבוֹ טוֹרֵף אַף הַפָּרָה וְהַטַּלִּית; לְפִיכָךְ לֹא יָעִיד עֲלֵיהֶן, שֶׁהֲרֵי רוֹצֶה לְהַעֲמִידָן בְּיַד שִׁמְעוֹן, כְּדֵי שֶׁיָּבוֹא בַּעַל חוֹבוֹ וְיִטְרְפֵם. וְכֵן כֹּל כַּיּוֹצֵא בִּדְבָרִים אֵלּוּ.

וּדְבָרִים אֵלּוּ אֵינָן תְּלוּיִין אֶלָּא בְּדַעַת הַדַּיָּן וְעֹצֶם בִּינָתוֹ, שֶׁיָּבִין עִקַּר הַמִּשְׁפָּטִים, וְיֵדַע דָּבָר הַגּוֹרֵם לְדָבָר אַחֵר, וְיַעֲמִיק לִרְאוֹת. אִם יִמְצָא שֶׁיֵּשׁ לָזֶה הָעֵד צַד הֲנָאָה בְּעֵדוּת זוֹ, אֲפִלּוּ בְּדֶרֶךְ רְחוֹקָה וְנִפְלָאָה – הֲרֵי זֶה לֹא יָעִיד בָּהּ.

וּכְדֶרֶךְ שֶׁלֹּא יָעִיד בְּדָבָר זֶה, שֶׁמָּא נוֹגֵעַ בְּעֵדוּתוֹ הוּא, כָּךְ לֹא יָדוּן בְּאוֹתוֹ דָּבָר.

וְכֵן שְׁאָר מִינֵי פְּסוּלִין: כְּשֵׁם שֶׁפּוֹסְלִין בְּעֵדִים, כָּךְ פּוֹסְלִין בְּדַיָּנִים.

ה וּלְפִיכָךְ אֵין סוֹמְכִין בְּסַנְהֶדְרִין שְׁנַיִם הַקְּרוֹבִים זֶה לָזֶה, בֵּין בְּסַנְהֶדְרֵי קְטַנָּה בֵּין בְּסַנְהֶדְרֵי גְדוֹלָה.

this lien by virtue of the establishment of a lien on landed property. Moreover, he can include a stipulation that the lien will also include all movable property that the debtor will acquire in the future.

The *Shulchan Aruch* (*Choshen Mishpat* 37:16, 60:1) states that in the present age, the Rabbis invalidated both these stipulations and do not allow a lien on movable property at all. According to this view, the seller is allowed to testify, even if he once owned landed property. The *Siftei Cohen* 37:26, 60:4, however, differs and maintains that such stipulations are valid even at present.

26. Hence he is considered to have a vested interest, as stated in Halachah 3.

27. I.e., the disqualification of witnesses for having a vested interest is not a cut and dry matter, conforming to set rules. Instead, it is one which a judge must think over, considering all the possible ramifications.

28. The *Kessef Mishneh* states that a person is disqualified for having a vested interest only when his testimony appears to advance that interest. If he testifies against his own interest, his testimony is accepted, just as we accept the acknowledgment of liability of a person sued with owing a debt.

29. See *Hilchot Sanhedrin* 23:3 which elaborates on the care a judge must show with regard to having a vested interest in a case.

30. I.e., needless to say, the judges may not be transgressors. Nor may they be related to the litigants, the witnesses, or to each other (*Kessef Mishneh*). Similarly, all of the factors mentioned in Chapter 9, Halachah 1, disqualify a judge.

31. A court of 23 judges.

Sanhedrin.[32] With regard to the judges that are added to reach the number of seven charged with declaring a leap year as mentioned in *Hilchot Kiddush HaChodesh*,[33] it appears to me that it is of no consequence that there are relatives among them.[34]

6. Whoever is fit to act as a judge as fit to act as a witness. There are, however, some who are acceptable to act as a witness, but not to act as a judge. They include friends, enemies,[35] converts, and freed slaves.[36] Similarly, an elderly person, a eunuch,[37] a bastard, and a person with one eye[38] are acceptable as witnesses, but are not acceptable as judges as we explained.

CHAPTER SEVENTEEN

1. When many men of great wisdom and fear of God testify to a person and tell him that they saw so-and-so commit a particular transgression or borrow money from a colleague, although [the listener] believes the matter in his heart as if he saw [it actually transpire], he may not deliver testimony unless he actually sees the matter or the borrower acknowledges [the debt] verbally to him, saying: "Be a witness for me that so-and-so lent me a *maneh*." [These concepts are derived from Leviticus 5:1 which] states: "And should he witness, see, or know [of the matter]...." There is no testimony that can be established through sight or knowledge[1] [alone] except testimony involving financial matters.[2]

Whenever a person delivers testimony on the basis of the statements of others, he is a false witness and transgresses a negative commandment, as [Exodus 20:16] states: "Do not bear false witness against your neighbor."[3]

2. Therefore, we issue a warning also to witnesses [who testify regarding] financial matters.[4]

How do we warn them? We issue this warning in the presence of all [onlookers],[5] telling them the severity of bearing false testimony[6] and the shame suffered by those who deliver such testimony in this world and in the world to come.[7]

32. Israel's highest court.
33. *Hilchot Kiddush HaChodesh* 4:9-10.
34. The first three judges who make the fundamental calculations with regard to the declaration of the leap year may not be related (*Lechem Mishneh*).
35. For we fear that their love or hate of the principals may influence their subconscious thinking process. As mentioned in Chapter 13, Halachah 15, we do not suspect that a person will consciously transgress and deliver false testimony on behalf of a colleague. Similarly, we do not believe that a person will willfully deliver a wrong judgment because of his feelings for or against a particular individual. Nevertheless, there is the possibility that without knowing, his feelings will influence his decisions.
36. For a judge is not acceptable until his mother is a native-born Jewess, as stated in *Hilchot Sanhedrin* 2:9, 11:11. These individuals are, however, acceptable as witnesses.
37. For we suspect that because of the judge's age or because the eunuch never had children, they will have cruel tendencies and will not be merciful (*Hilchot Sanhedrin* 2:9).

אֲבָל אֵלּוּ שֶׁמּוֹסִיפִין עַד שִׁבְעָה לְעַבֵּר הַשָּׁנָה, כְּמוֹ שֶׁבֵּאַרְנוּ בְּהִלְכוֹת קִדּוּשׁ הַחֹדֶשׁ, יֵרָאֶה לִי, שֶׁאִם הָיָה בָּהֶן קְרוֹבִים – אֵין בְּכָךְ כְּלוּם.

ו כָּל הַכָּשֵׁר לָדוּן – כָּשֵׁר לְהָעִיד. וְיֵשׁ כָּשֵׁר לְהָעִיד, וְאֵינוֹ כָּשֵׁר לָדוּן. הָאוֹהֵב וְהַשּׂוֹנֵא, וְהַגֵּר וְהַמְשֻׁחְרָר, וְכֵן הַזָּקֵן וְהַסָּרִיס, וְהַמַּמְזֵר, וְסוּמָא בְּאַחַת מֵעֵינָיו – כְּשֵׁרִין לְהָעִיד, וְאֵינָן כְּשֵׁרִים לָדוּן דִּינֵי נְפָשׁוֹת, כְּמוֹ שֶׁבֵּאַרְנוּ.

פֶּרֶק שִׁבְעָה עָשָׂר

א מִי שֶׁהֵעִידוּ לוֹ אֲנָשִׁים רַבִּים וּגְדוֹלִים בְּחָכְמָה וּבְיִרְאָה, שֶׁהֵם אוֹמְרִים שֶׁרָאוּ פְּלוֹנִי שֶׁעָבַר עֲבֵרָה פְּלוֹנִית אוֹ שֶׁלָּוָה מִפְּלוֹנִי, אַף עַל פִּי שֶׁהוּא מַאֲמִין הַדָּבָר בְּלִבּוֹ כְּאִלּוּ רָאָהוּ – לֹא יָעִיד, עַד שֶׁיִּרְאֶה הַדָּבָר בְּעֵינָיו, אוֹ יוֹדֶה לוֹ הַלֹּוֶה מִפִּיו וְיֹאמַר לוֹ: הֱיֵה עָלַי עֵד שֶׁפְּלוֹנִי הִלְוָה לִי מָנֶה. שֶׁנֶּאֱמַר: וְהוּא עֵד אוֹ רָאָה אוֹ יָדָע; וְאֵין לְךָ עֵדוּת שֶׁמִּתְקַיֶּמֶת בִּרְאִיָּה אוֹ בִידִיעָה אֶלָּא עֵדוּת מָמוֹן. וְכָל הַמֵּעִיד מִפִּי אֲחֵרִים – הֲרֵי זֶה עֵד שֶׁקֶר, וְעוֹבֵר בְּלֹא תַעֲשֶׂה, שֶׁנֶּאֱמַר: לֹא תַעֲנֶה בְרֵעֲךָ עֵד שָׁקֶר.

ב לְפִיכָךְ מְאַיְּמִין אַף עַל עֵדֵי הַמָּמוֹן. וְכֵיצַד מְאַיְּמִין עֲלֵיהֶן? [מְאַיְּמִין עֲלֵיהֶם] בִּפְנֵי הַכֹּל, וּמוֹדִיעִין אוֹתָן כֹּחַ עֵדוּת שֶׁקֶר, וּבשֶׁת הַמֵּעִיד בָּהּ בָּעוֹלָם הַזֶּה וּבָעוֹלָם הַבָּא.

38. For judges who adjudicate cases involving capital punishment must be fit to marry into the priesthood and they must have no physical blemishes (*ibid.* 2:9, 11:11).

1. *Sh'vuot* 33b interprets testimony that is acceptable which involves sight, but not knowledge as referring to an instance where the plaintiff told the defendant: "I lent you money in the presence of so-and-so and so-and-so," the defendant asks him to bring the witnesses to testify and the witnesses testify that they saw the plaintiff give the defendant the sum mentioned, but they did not know why he gave it to him. An instance where the witnesses know without seeing is when the defendant admits the debt in their presence.
2. I.e., with regard to cases involving capital punishment or lashes, by contrast, the witness must both see and know.
3. *Sefer HaMitzvot* (negative commandment 258) and *Sefer HaChinuch* (mitzvah 37) count this as one of the 613 mitzvot of the Torah. I.e., this command does not involve only a prohibition against telling an outright lie, but also against delivering any testimony that should not be given.
4. See *Hilchot Sanhedrin* 12:3 which discusses the warning issued to witnesses in cases involving capital punishment.
5. Although the witnesses testify in private, they are given a warning in public to create a greater sense of shame and embarrassment if they are in fact lying (Radbaz).
6. *Sanhedrin* 29a relates that famine and bloodshed come to the world because of the sin of delivering false testimony.
7. *Sanhedrin, loc. cit.*, cites the example of the false witnesses hired by Izebel to testify

Afterwards, we [order] all other people[8] to go outside and leave the witness of the greatest stature inside. We say to him: "Tell [us] the basis on which you know that this person owes [money] to that person."[9] If he says: "He told me that [the borrower] said that I owe him [the money],"[10] or he says: "So-and-so told me that he owed him [money],"[11] his statements are of no consequence. [He must] say: "In our presence, [the defendant] admitted to [the plaintiff] that he owes him [the money]."

[Afterwards,] we bring in the second witness and check his testimony in this manner. If their testimony corroborates each other's, [the judges] deliberate over the matter and conclude the judgment.

3. [The following rules apply if] a person hid witnesses [against] his colleague and [that colleague] acknowledged his obligation to him in private. The witnesses saw and heard him tell him: "Certainly, I owe you this and this amount, but I am afraid you will call me to judgment tomorrow." This is not [valid] testimony[12] unless he makes the acknowledgment in the presence of witnessess.[13]

4. Whether a person acknowledged a debt to a colleague, making the admission in a sincere manner that he owes him such-and-such an amount, he told [the witnesses]: "You are my witnesses," or [he told them] "Serve as witnesses for me," they are [valid] witnesses.[14] [This applies whether] the statement is made by the borrower or whether it is made by the lender and the borrower remains silent as if he is accepting his words.[15] Needless to say, it applies if he affirmed [the appointment of the witnesses] with an act of contract, telling them: "Compose a legal document stating that I owe so-and-so this-and-this amount,"[16] or the like, [his statement] is considered as an admission and the witnesses may testify on this basis.

5. When a teacher tells a student: "You know that if they would give me all the money in the world, I would not lie. So-and-so owes me a *maneh*. I have one witness against him. [Please,] join him." If he joins him, he is a false witness.[17]

6. If he tells him: "Come and stand together with the witness. You do not have to testify, but the borrower will become frightened and panic, thinking

against Nabot. Izebel herself referred to the witnesses as "unscrupulous men" (I Kings 21:10), implying that even she who hired them looks down at them with scorn. Needless to say, in the world to come, the world of truth, they will be overwhelmed with shame.

8. This does not include the litigants themselves. For the witnesses must testify in their presence. See *Sefer Me'irat Einayim* 28:37.

9. As the Rambam states in *Hilchot Toen ViNitan* 6:1, we always ask a plaintiff and a defendant to clarify the claims they make. Similarly, the witnesses are asked to clarify their testimony.

וְאַחַר כָּךְ מוֹצִיאִין אֶת כָּל הָאָדָם לַחוּץ, וּמְשַׁיְּרִין אֶת הַגָּדוֹל שֶׁבָּעֵדִים, וְאוֹמֵר לוֹ: אֱמֹר הֵיאַךְ אַתָּה יוֹדֵעַ שֶׁזֶּה חַיָּב לָזֶה. אִם אָמַר: שֶׁהוּא אָמַר לִי חַיָּב אֲנִי לוֹ, אוֹ אִישׁ פְּלוֹנִי אָמַר לִי שֶׁהוּא חַיָּב לוֹ – לֹא אָמַר כְּלוּם, עַד שֶׁיֹּאמַר: בְּפָנֵינוּ הוֹדָה לוֹ שֶׁהוּא חַיָּב לוֹ.
וְהָיוּ מַכְנִיסִין אֶת הָעֵד הַשֵּׁנִי וּבוֹדְקִין אוֹתוֹ כָּךְ. נִמְצְאוּ דִבְרֵיהֶן מְכֻוָּנִין – נוֹשְׂאִין וְנוֹתְנִין בַּדָּבָר, וְגוֹמְרִין הַדִּין.

ג הַמַּטְמִין עֵדִים לַחֲבֵרוֹ, וְהוֹדָה לוֹ בֵּינוֹ לְבֵין עַצְמוֹ, וְהָעֵדִים רוֹאִין וְשׁוֹמְעִין שֶׁהוּא אוֹמֵר לוֹ: וַדַּאי יֵשׁ לְךָ אֶצְלִי כָּךְ וָכָךְ, אֲבָל מִתְיָרֵא אֲנִי שֶׁמָּא תְּכַפֵּנִי בַּדִּין לְמָחָר – הֲרֵי זוֹ אֵינָהּ עֵדוּת, עַד שֶׁיּוֹדֶה בִּפְנֵי עֵדִים.

ד אֶחָד הַמּוֹדֶה בִּפְנֵי עֵדִים וְאָמַר דֶּרֶךְ הוֹדָאָה: זֶה יֵשׁ לוֹ אֶצְלִי כָּךְ וָכָךְ, אוֹ שֶׁאָמַר: אַתֶּם עֵדַי, אוֹ שֶׁאָמַר: הֱיוּ עָלַי עֵדִים, בֵּין שֶׁאָמַר הַלֹּוֶה, בֵּין שֶׁאָמַר הַמַּלְוֶה וְשָׁתַק הַלֹּוֶה דֶּרֶךְ מַאֲמִין לִדְבָרָיו – הֲרֵי אֵלּוּ עֵדִים. וְאֵין צָרִיךְ לוֹמַר אִם קָנוּ מִיָּדוֹ, אוֹ שֶׁאָמַר לָהֶם: כִּתְבוּ עָלַי שְׁטָר שֶׁיֵּשׁ לָזֶה אֶצְלִי כָּךְ וָכָךְ. וְכֹל כַּיּוֹצֵא בִּדְבָרִים אֵלּוּ – הֲרֵי הֵם הוֹדָאָה וּמְעִידִין עַל פִּיו.

ה תַּלְמִיד שֶׁאָמַר לוֹ רַבּוֹ: יוֹדֵעַ אַתָּה, שֶׁאִם נוֹתְנִין לִי כָּל מָמוֹן הָעוֹלָם – אֵינִי מְשַׁקֵּר. מָנֶה יֵשׁ לִי אֵצֶל פְּלוֹנִי, וְיֵשׁ לִי עָלָיו עֵד אֶחָד, לֵךְ וְהִצְטָרֵף עִמּוֹ. אִם נִצְטָרֵף – הֲרֵי זֶה עֵד שֶׁקֶר.
ו אָמַר לוֹ: בּוֹא וַעֲמֹד עִם הָעֵד וְלֹא תָּעִיד, כְּדֵי שֶׁיִּרְאֶה הַלֹּוֶה וְיִפְחַד, וְיַעֲלֶה עַל דַּעְתּוֹ

10. But did not do so with the assurance necessary for a statement to be considered as an admission of debt. See *Hilchot Toen ViNitan* 6:7 which states that a person may admit owing other people money so that he does not appear wealthy. Such an admission is not binding in court.
11. For he must have direct knowledge of the matter, as explained above.
12. As the Rambam explains in *Hilchot Toen ViNitan* 6:7, the defendant can excuse himself saying: "I was only jesting with you." Since he was not aware of the presence of the witnesses, we do not know whether or not he was speaking sincerely.
13. I.e., witnesses whom he sees.
14. In these instances, since the plaintiff was present and the defendant made these statements with a serious intent, we cannot accept the argument that he was jesting, speaking facetiously, or made the statement so as not to appear wealthy, as the Rambam explains in *Hilchot Toen ViNitan* 7:1-2.
15. If, however, he remained silent, but appeared to mock the lender, he is not considered to have accepted them as witnesses (Radbaz).
16. This statement serves as a legal record for the loan. It does not have the strength of a promissory note unless the borrower specifically requests that it does, as stated in *Hilchot Malveh V'Loveh* 11:1.
17. As stated in Halachah 1.

that you are two witnesses and he will admit the debt on his own volition," [the student] is forbidden to stand and make it appear that he is a witness even though he does not deliver testimony. With regard to this and similar matter, [Exodus 23:7] states: "Keep distant from words of falsehood."[18]

7. A person who hires false witnesses to testify against a colleague is not liable according to a court of law,[19] but does have a moral and spiritual obligation.[20] Similarly, one witness[21] who refrains from testifying is not liable according to a court of law, but does have a moral and spiritual obligation.

CHAPTER EIGHTEEN

1. When a person delivered false testimony and witnesses testify to that fact, he is called an *eid zomeim*, "a conspiring witness."[1]

It is a positive mitzvah[2] to requite him in the manner in which he desired through his testimony to effect his colleague. If [witnesses testify] with regard to a transgression for which one is liable to be stoned to death and it is proved that they testified falsely, they are all[3] stoned. If [the transgression was punishable by] being burned to death, they are burned to death. Similar laws apply with regard to other forms of capital punishment.

If they testified [falsely] with regard to a transgression punishable by lashes, each one of them is lashed in the same manner as are all those obligated to be lashed.[4] We estimate their capacity to bear the lashes[5] and they are lashed. If they testified [falsely] to obligate the defendant to make a financial payment, we divide that amount according to the number of [lying] witnesses.[6] Each witness must pay his share. [The lying witnesses] do not receive lashes when they are required to make financial reimbursement.[7]

18. I.e., the student does not transgress the prohibition against giving false testimony, because he does not testify. Nevertheless, creating a false impression is also forbidden.
19. Since he himself did not cause his colleague financial loss - for the loss was caused by the witnesses who actually testified falsely, and they are responsible for their own conduct - he has no liability. His act is considered a secondary cause of damage (*Bava Kama* 56a and commentaries).
20. The literal translation of the Rambam's words is "He is obligated according to the laws of heaven."

The Ramah (*Choshen Mishpat* 32:2) adds several qualifications to the Rambam's ruling. Among them:
a) If the plaintiff's claim is valid, although the person who hired the witnesses was forbidden to have done so, that person does not have even a moral and spiritual obligation to the defendant.
b) If the person did not hire the false witnesses, but merely convinced them to testify, that person does not have even a moral and spiritual obligation to the defendant.
c) The Rambam is speaking about a situation where a person hired witnesses to testify on behalf of a colleague. If he hired witnesses to testify on his own behalf and expropriated money not due him by law, he is liable to make financial restitution.
21. The *Sefer Me'irat Einayim* 28:10 rules that this law applies even if two witnesses do

שֶׁאַתֶּם שְׁנֵי עֵדִים וְיוֹדֶה מֵעַצְמוֹ – הֲרֵי זֶה אָסוּר לַעֲמֹד וּלְהַרְאוֹת שֶׁהוּא עֵד, אַף עַל פִּי שֶׁאֵינוֹ מֵעִיד. וְעַל זֶה וְכַיּוֹצֵא בּוֹ נֶאֱמַר: מִדְּבַר שֶׁקֶר תִּרְחָק.

ז הַשּׂוֹכֵר עֵדֵי שֶׁקֶר לְהָעִיד לַחֲבֵרוֹ – פָּטוּר מִדִּינֵי אָדָם, וְחַיָּב בְּדִינֵי שָׁמַיִם.
וְכֵן עֵד אֶחָד שֶׁכָּבַשׁ עֵדוּתוֹ וְלֹא הֵעִיד – פָּטוּר מִדִּינֵי אָדָם, וְחַיָּב בְּדִינֵי שָׁמַיִם.

פֶּרֶק שְׁמוֹנָה עָשָׂר

א מִי שֶׁהֵעִיד בְּשֶׁקֶר, וְנוֹדַע בְּעֵדִים שֶׁהֵעִיד בְּשֶׁקֶר – זֶהוּ שֶׁנִּקְרָא עֵד זוֹמֵם, וּמִצְוַת עֲשֵׂה לַעֲשׂוֹת לוֹ כְּמָה שֶׁרָצָה לַעֲשׂוֹת בְּעֵדוּתוֹ לַחֲבֵרוֹ. אִם בַּעֲבֵרָה שֶׁחַיָּבִין עָלֶיהָ סְקִילָה הֵעִידוּ וְהוּזַמּוּ – נִסְקָלִין כֻּלָּן; וְאִם בִּשְׂרֵפָה – נִשְׂרָפִין; וְכֵן שְׁאָר הַמִּיתוֹת. וְאִם הֵעִידוּ בְּמַלְקוּת – לוֹקֶה כָּל אֶחָד מֵהֶן כִּשְׁאָר מְחֻיְּבֵי מַלְקוּת. וְאוֹמְדִין כֹּחוֹ וּמַלְקִין אוֹתוֹ.
וְאִם הֵעִידוּ לְחַיְּבוֹ מָמוֹן – מְשַׁלְּשִׁין הַמָּמוֹן בֵּינֵיהֶן לְפִי מִנְיַן הָעֵדִים, כָּל אֶחָד וְאֶחָד יִתֵּן חֵלֶק הַמַּגִּיעַ לוֹ. וְאֵין לוֹקִין בִּמְקוֹם תַּשְׁלוּמִין.

not deliver testimony. By mentioning one witness, the Rambam (and *Bava Kama* 56a, his source) are emphasizing that even in such a situation, the witness has a responsibility. Although his testimony would not obligate the defendant to make financial reimbursement - for financial responsibility is established only on the basis of the testimony of two witnesses - he would obligate the defendant to take an oath. And since it is possible that the defendant would rather pay than take the oath, the witness could have caused the plaintiff a loss.

1. The term *zomeim* has its source in Deuteronomy 19:19, which states that a witness should be punished "as he conspired to do against his colleague."
2. *Sefer HaMitzvot* (positive commandment 180) and *Sefer HaChinuch* (mitzvah 524) count this as one of the 613 mitzvot of the Torah.
3. I.e., all the witnesses who testified falsely.
4. I.e., each of the lying witnesses receives a full 39 lashes. We do not divide the 39 lashes they wished the defendant to suffer between them.
5. See *Hilchot Sanhedrin* 17:1.
Even if the person whom he testified against would have received more or less lashes, the lying witness is given the amount of lashes that he can bear.
6. *Makkot* 5a distinguishes between the penalty of receiving lashes and the obligation to make financial reimbursement, stating that as far as the defendant is concerned, money is a sum which is cumulative. He is not concerned with the number of people from whom the sum is collected. Lashes, by contrast, is a punishment and that punishment comes in a total sum; it cannot be divided.
7. I.e., although they violated the negative commandment against giving false testimony and that commandment is punishable by lashes, they are not given that punishment. The rationale is that whenever a person is liable for a financial penalty and lashes for the same transgression, he is given the financial penalty and not punished by lashes (*Makkot* 4a; *Hilchot Na'arah Betulah* 1:11; *Hilchot Sanhedrin* 18:2).

2. When does the above apply? When the witnesses were disqualified through *hazamah*. When, however, [the testimony of] two pairs of witnesses contradict each other, both testimonies are of no consequence, but neither of them receives punishment, because we do not know which pair is lying.

What is the difference between testimony which is contradicted and testimony which is disqualified through *hazamah*? A contradiction concerns the testimony itself. [One pair states]: "This is what took place," and the other pair states: "It never took place," or that conclusion was obvious from their statements. *Hazamah*, by contrast, focuses on the witnesses themselves. The witnesses who disqualify them do not know whether the event happened or not.

What is implied? Witnesses come and say: "We saw so-and-so kill a person..." or "...lend money to so-and-so on this-and-this date in this-and-this place." After they testified and the testimony was investigated, two other witnesses came and said: "On that day, we were with you and with those people the entire day and those things never happened. He never killed him," or "...He never lent him." This is considered a contradiction.

Similarly, if witnesses say: "How can you testify in this manner. Either the murderer - or the victim or the borrower or the lender - were with us on that day in another city," the testimony is considered to be contradicted. This is as if they said: "So-and-so did not kill him..." or "So-and-so did not lend him, for they were together with us and this thing did not happen." Similar principles apply in all analogous situations.

If, however, [the second pair of witnesses] say: "We do not know if so-and-so killed so-and-so on this day in Jerusalem as you say or not. We are, however, testifying that you yourselves were with us in Babylon on that date,"[8] [the first pair of witnesses] are considered as *zomeimim* and they are executed[9] or required to make financial restitution.[10] [The rationale is that] the witnesses who disqualified them did not concern themselves with the testimony itself whether it was true or false, [but with the presence of the witnesses in the place mentioned].

3. The fact that the Torah accepted the word of the latter pair of witnesses instead of that of the first pair of witnesses is a Scriptural decree.[11] Even if there were 100 in the first group of witnesses and two [witnesses] came and disqualified them [all] through *hazamah*, saying: "We testify that all 100 of you were together with us on this date in this place," [the 100 witnesses] are punished on the basis of their testimony.[12] For two witnesses are equivalent to 100 and 100 are equivalent to two.[13] Similarly, when two groups of witnesses contradict each other, we do not follow the majority instead, we nullify [the testimony of] both.[14]

4. There is no need for lying witnesses to be given a warning.[15]

8. This automatically disqualifies their testimony, for if they were in Babylon on that date, there is no way they could have observed what took place in Jerusalem.

ב בַּמֶּה דְּבָרִים אֲמוּרִים? בְּעֵדִים שֶׁהוּזַּמּוּ; אֲבָל שְׁתֵּי כִּתּוֹת הַמַּכְחִישׁוֹת זוֹ אֶת זוֹ וְאֵין כָּאן עֵדוּת – אֵין עוֹנְשִׁין אֶת אַחַת מֵהֶן, לְפִי שֶׁאֵין אָנוּ יוֹדְעִים מִי הִיא הַכַּת הַשַּׁקְרָנִית. וּמַה בֵּין הַכְחָשָׁה לַהֲזָמָה?

הַהַכְחָשָׁה – בְּעֵדוּת עַצְמָהּ. זֹאת אוֹמֶרֶת: הָיָה הַדָּבָר הַזֶּה, וְזֹאת אוֹמֶרֶת: לֹא הָיָה הַדָּבָר הַזֶּה, אוֹ יָבוֹא מִכְּלַל דְּבָרֶיהָ שֶׁלֹּא הָיָה. וְהַהֲזָמָה – בְּעֵדִים עַצְמָן, וְאֵלּוּ הָעֵדִים שֶׁהֶזְמוּם אֵינָן יוֹדְעִים אִם נִהְיָה הַדָּבָר אוֹ לֹא הָיָה.

כֵּיצַד? עֵדִים שֶׁבָּאוּ וְאָמְרוּ: רָאִינוּ זֶה שֶׁהָרַג אֶת הַנֶּפֶשׁ, אוֹ הִלְוָה מָנֶה לִפְלוֹנִי, בְּיוֹם פְּלוֹנִי בְּמָקוֹם פְּלוֹנִי; וְאַחַר שֶׁהֵעִידוּ וְנִבְדְּקוּ בָּאוּ שְׁנַיִם אֲחֵרִים וְאָמְרוּ: בְּיוֹם זֶה וּבְמָקוֹם זֶה הָיִינוּ עִמָּכֶם וְעִם אֵלּוּ כָּל הַיּוֹם, וְלֹא הָיוּ דְּבָרִים מֵעוֹלָם, לֹא זֶה הָרַג אֶת זֶה וְלֹא זֶה הִלְוָה אֶת זֶה – הֲרֵי זוֹ הַכְחָשָׁה.

וְכֵן אִם אָמְרוּ לָהֶם: הֵיאַךְ אַתֶּם מְעִידִים כָּךְ? וְזֶה הַהוֹרֵג אוֹ הַנֶּהֱרָג אוֹ הַלֹּוֶה אוֹ הַמַּלְוֶה הָיָה עִמָּנוּ בְּיוֹם זֶה בִּמְדִינָה אַחֶרֶת! – הֲרֵי זוֹ עֵדוּת מֻכְחֶשֶׁת; שֶׁזֶּה כְּמִי שֶׁאָמַר: לֹא הָרַג זֶה אֶת זֶה, וְלֹא זֶה הִלְוָה אֶת זֶה, שֶׁהֲרֵי עִמָּנוּ הָיוּ וְלֹא נִהְיָה דָּבָר זֶה. וְכֵן כָּל כַּיּוֹצֵא בִּדְבָרִים אֵלּוּ. אֲבָל אִם אָמְרוּ לָהֶם: אָנוּ אֵין אָנוּ יוֹדְעִים אִם זֶה הָרַג זֶה בְּיוֹם זֶה בִּירוּשָׁלַיִם כְּמוֹ שֶׁאַתֶּם אוֹמְרִין אוֹ לֹא הֲרָגוֹ, וְאָנוּ מְעִידִים שֶׁאַתֶּם עַצְמְכֶם הֱיִיתֶם עִמָּנוּ בְּיוֹם זֶה בְּבָבֶל – הֲרֵי אֵלּוּ זוֹמְמִים, וְנֶהֱרָגִין אוֹ מְשַׁלְּמִין. הוֹאִיל וְהָעֵדִים שֶׁהֶזְמוּם לֹא הִשְׁגִּיחוּ עַל עַצְמָהּ שֶׁל עֵדוּת כְּלָל אִם אֱמֶת הָיָה אוֹ שֶׁקֶר.

ג וְזוֹ שֶׁהֶאֱמִינָה תּוֹרָה עֵדוּת הָאַחֲרוֹנִים עַל הָעֵדִים הָרִאשׁוֹנִים – גְּזֵרַת הַכָּתוּב הוּא. אֲפִלּוּ הָיוּ הָעֵדִים הָרִאשׁוֹנִים מֵאָה, וּבָאוּ שְׁנַיִם וֶהֱזִמּוּם וְאָמְרוּ לָהֶם: אָנוּ מְעִידִים, שֶׁאַתֶּם הַמֵּאָה כֻּלְּכֶם עִמָּנוּ הֱיִיתֶם בְּיוֹם פְּלוֹנִי בְּמָקוֹם פְּלוֹנִי – הֲרֵי אֵלּוּ נֶעֱנָשִׁין עַל פִּיהֶם. שֶׁהַשְּׁנַיִם כְּמֵאָה, וּמֵאָה כִּשְׁנַיִם. וְכֵן בִּשְׁתֵּי כִּתֵּי עֵדִים הַמַּכְחִישׁוֹת זוֹ אֶת זוֹ – אֵין הוֹלְכִין אַחַר הָרֹב, אֶלָּא דוֹחִין אֶת שְׁתֵּיהֶן.

ד עֵדִים זוֹמְמִין אֵינָן צְרִיכִין הַתְרָאָה.

9. If they testified with regard to murder.
10. If they testified with regard to a loan.
11. I.e., ultimately, it is the word of these two witnesses against that of these two. Seemingly, there is no reason why one should be favored over the other (*Bava Kama* 72b; *Sanhedrin* 27a).
12. See also Chapter 20, Halachah 5.
13. Once two acceptable witnesses testify together, their testimony is binding. The fact that their are more witnesses in another group is of no consequence whatsoever. See *Makkot* 5b.
14. For there is no Scriptural decree to follow the testimony of the latter pair when the testimony of two pairs of witnesses contradicts each other.
15. The Rambam's statements here are amplified by his statements in Chapter 20, Halachah 4: "There is no concept of inadvertent action with regard to lying witnesses,

When the testimony of witnesses was first contradicted and ultimately, disqualified through *hazamah*, [the lying witnesses] are executed, lashed, or forced to make financial restitution. [The rationale is that] a contradiction is the first stage of *hazamah*.[16] It is not, however, completed.

5. [The testimony of] witnesses can be disqualified through *hazamah* only in their presence.[17] It can, however, be contradicted in their absence.[18]

When [the testimony of] witnesses has been disqualified through *hazamah* outside the presence of the witnesses, it is considered to have been contradicted.[19] Therefore if the witnesses who have been disqualified through *hazamah* die before the testimony disqualifying them is delivered in their presence, their testimony is nullified, for the [two testimonies] contradicted each other.

6. When the testimony of witnesses in cases of capital punishment was contradicted, but was not disqualified through *hazamah*, they do not receive lashes.[20] [This is true,] even if [the person whom they testified] had been killed comes himself [to court to prove the suspected murderer's innocence].[21] [The rationale is that] the prohibition is punishable by execution.[22] Hence, lashes are not given because of it. Nevertheless, the court has [the witnesses] beaten with stripes for rebellious conduct[23] according to their perception [of the severity of the matter].

7. A public announcement must be made with regard to lying witnesses.[24] What type of announcement is made? [A proclamation] is written and sent throughout every city: "So-and-so and so-and-so testified in this manner. They were disqualified through *hazamah* and executed," "...lashed in our presence," or "fined so-and-so many *dinarim*." [The necessity for this is derived from Deuteronomy 19:20:] "Those who remain shall hear and become fearful."[25]

8. The obligation of lying witnesses to make financial restitution when required is considered as a fine.[26] Therefore, they are not required to pay when they admit [their own guilt].[27]

because there is no deed involved." Since the entire purpose of a warning is to differentiate between an act performed intentionally and one performed unintentionally (*Hilchot Sanhedrin* 12:2), a warning is unnecessary.

Ketubot 33a gives a different interpretation. The lying witnesses sought to have the defendant executed without a warning. Since we are obligated to requite them as they conspired, they are also executed without a warning.

16. I.e., we do not say that since the testimony was contradicted, it was already nullified and hence is of no consequence. See *Bava Kama* 73b.

17. Since the lying witnesses become obligated for punishment or a financial penalty through *hazamah*, the testimony against them must be delivered in their presence, as stated in Chapter 3, Halachah 11.

18. For in this instance, the only effect of their testimony is to release the defendant.

19. The punishments associated with *hazamah* can be administered only when the disqualifying testimony is delivered in the witnesses' presence. The witnesses' testimony,

וְעֵדִים שֶׁהֻכְחֲשׁוּ וּלְבַסּוֹף הוּזַמּוּ – הֲרֵי אֵלּוּ נֶהֱרָגִין אוֹ לוֹקִין אוֹ מְשַׁלְּמִין; מִפְּנֵי שֶׁהַכְחָשָׁה תְּחִלַּת הֲזָמָּה הִיא, אֶלָּא שֶׁעֲדַיִן לֹא נִגְמְרָה.

ה אֵין מְזִמִּין אֶת הָעֵדִים אֶלָּא בִּפְנֵיהֶם, וּמַכְחִישִׁין אֶת הָעֵדִים שֶׁלֹּא בִּפְנֵיהֶם. וְעֵדִים שֶׁהוּזַמּוּ שֶׁלֹּא בִּפְנֵיהֶן – הֲרֵי הֻכְחֲשׁוּ. לְפִיכָךְ, אִם מֵתוּ הָעֵדִים שֶׁהֱזִמּוּם קֹדֶם שֶׁיָּזֵמּוּ אוֹתָם בִּפְנֵיהֶם – אֵין כָּאן עֵדוּת, שֶׁהֲרֵי הִכְחִישׁוּ זֶה אֶת זֶה.

ו עֵדֵי נְפָשׁוֹת שֶׁהֻכְחֲשׁוּ וְלֹא הוּזַמּוּ, אֲפִלּוּ בָּא הַנֶּהֱרָג בְּרַגְלָיו – אֵינָם לוֹקִין; מִפְּנֵי שֶׁהוּא לָאו שֶׁנִּתַּן לְאַזְהָרַת מִיתַת בֵּית דִּין, וְאֵין לוֹקִין עָלָיו. אֲבָל בֵּית דִּין מַכִּין אוֹתָן מַכַּת מַרְדּוּת כְּפִי מַה שֶּׁיִּרְאוּ.

ז עֵדִים זוֹמְמִים צְרִיכִין הַכְרָזָה. וְהֵיאַךְ הִיא הַהַכְרָזָה שֶׁלָּהֶן? כּוֹתְבִין וְשׁוֹלְחִין בְּכָל עִיר וָעִיר: פְּלוֹנִי וּפְלוֹנִי הֵעִידוּ בְּכַךְ וְכַךְ, וְהוּזַמּוּ, וַהֲרַגְנוּם, אוֹ לָקוּ בְּפָנֵינוּ, אוֹ עָנַשְׁנוּ אוֹתָן כַּךְ וְכַךְ דִּינָרִין. שֶׁנֶּאֱמַר: וְהַנִּשְׁאָרִים יִשְׁמְעוּ וְיִרָאוּ.

ח חִיּוּב הָעֵדִים זוֹמְמִים לְשַׁלֵּם בְּמָקוֹם שֶׁחַיָּבִין לְשַׁלֵּם – קְנָס הוּא, וּלְפִיכָךְ אֵין מְשַׁלְּמִין עַל פִּי עַצְמָן.

however, is disqualified even if the testimony is delivered in their absence. Since these statements have the power to disqualify their testimony if they were made in their presence, certainly they have the power to disqualify their testimony when made in their absence, for it is possible that were they made in their presence, they would admit their falsehood (*Ketubot* 20a).

The Rivash (Responsum 266) emphasizes that even in such a situation, we accept the testimony of the last pair of witnesses as true. We do not consider this as a situation where there are two pairs of witnesses whose testimony contradicts that of each other (see Chapter 22, Halachah 1). The *Noda B'Yehudah* (*Even HaEzer*, Responsum 72) does not accept this conclusion and instead interprets the Rambam's words as meaning: "There is no valid testimony at all," i.e., neither of the pairs of witnesses are accepted.

20. Although the prohibition against delivering false testimony is punishable by lashes as stated in Halachah 1, that punishment is not given in this instance for the reason the Rambam proceeds to explain.

21. This would prove without a doubt that the testimony they delivered was false.

22. I.e., were their testimony to be disqualified because of *hazamah*, they would have been executed for this is the punishment they wished to inflict upon the defendant.

23. See *Hilchot Sanhedrin* 16:3, 18:5, and notes for a definition of this punishment and the situations where it is applied.

24. I.e., as implied by the Rambam's words, after the lying witnesses are punished, a proclamation is circulated throughout the land of Israel.

25. This verse is referring to all the inhabitants of the Holy Land.

26. I.e., it is not restitution for money which they caused the defendant to lose, because he did not in fact suffer a loss. Instead, it is a fine, levied against them as a penalty for their undesirable conduct.

27. For whenever a person admits an obligation which is a fine on his own initiative, he is not held liable (*Hilchot Nizkei Mammon* 2:8).

What is implied? [The witnesses] delivered testimony and their testimony was investigated by the court. Afterwards, they both admitted: "We delivered false testimony. This person does not owe the other person anything." Or they said: "We gave testimony concerning so-and-so with regard to this-and-this [amount] and we were disqualified through *hazamah*."[28] They are not required to make restitution because of their own statements.

If, however, they said: "We gave testimony concerning so-and-so, we were disqualified through *hazamah* in the court of so-and-so and we were obligated to give him this-and-this [amount]," they are required to make financial restitution. For this is an admission of debt with regard to money that they were already sentenced to pay.[29]

If one [witness] makes such statements, he is obligated to pay his portion.[30]

CHAPTER NINETEEN

1. [The following rules apply when] two [witnesses] testify, saying: "So-and-so murdered a person in the eastern portion of the hall at this-and-this time," two [other] witnesses come and say: "You were together with us in the western portion of the hall at that time." If a person standing in the western portion could see what transpires in the eastern portion, they are not disqualified through *hazamah*. If, however, it is impossible to see [what transpires], they are disqualified through *hazamah*. We do not say perhaps the eyesight of the first pair is very powerful and they can see things which transpire at a greater distance than all other men.

Similar [principles apply] if two people testified saying: "In the morning, so-and-so committed murder in Jerusalem," and two others come and tell them: "On that day, in the evening, you were together with us in Lod." If it is possible for a person to travel, even on horseback, from Jerusalem to Lod from the morning to the evening, they are not disqualified through *hazamah*. If not, they are disqualified through *hazamah*. We do not say perhaps they found a speedy camel and were able to travel the route faster than usual. Instead, we always calculate the matter according to the known standards and disqualify them through *hazamah*.[1]

2. [The following rules apply when] two [witnesses] state: "On Sunday, so-and-so murdered a person in this-and-this place," and two [other] witnesses come and say: "On that date, you were together with us in another far removed place, but so-and-so certainly murdered [the victim] on the following day," the murderer and the first pair of witnesses are executed.[2] Even if the second [pair of witnesses] testify that he had committed the murder several days previously,[3][the above laws apply]. [The rationale is that] at the time they delivered testimony, [the murderer] had not yet been sentenced to death.[4]

28. This is speaking about a situation where a decision was not rendered by the court. Hence a financial obligation has not yet been established.

כֵּיצַד? הֲרֵי שֶׁהֵעִידוּ, וְנֶחְקְרָה עֵדוּתָן בְּבֵית דִּין, וְאַחַר כָּךְ אָמְרוּ שְׁנֵיהֶם: עֵדוּת שֶׁקֶר הֵעַדְנוּ, וְאֵין לָזֶה אֵצֶל זֶה כְּלוּם;

אוֹ שֶׁאָמְרוּ: הֵעַדְנוּ עַל זֶה בְּכַךְ וְכַךְ וְהוּזַמְנוּ – אֵין מְשַׁלְּמִין עַל פִּיהֶן. אֲבָל אִם אָמְרוּ: הֵעַדְנוּ עַל זֶה, וְהוּזַמְנוּ בְּבֵית דִּינוֹ שֶׁל פְּלוֹנִי, וְנִתְחַיַּבְנוּ לִתֵּן לוֹ כַּךְ וְכַךְ – הֲרֵי אֵלּוּ מְשַׁלְּמִין; שֶׁזּוּ הוֹדָאָה בְּמָמוֹן שֶׁנִּגְמַר דִּינוֹ לִתְּנוֹ. וְאִם אָמַר הָאֶחָד כַּךְ – מְשַׁלֵּם חֶלְקוֹ.

פֶּרֶק תִּשְׁעָה עָשָׂר

א שְׁנַיִם שֶׁהֵעִידוּ וְאָמְרוּ: בְּמִזְרַח הַבִּירָה הָרַג זֶה אֶת הַנֶּפֶשׁ בְּשָׁעָה פְּלוֹנִית, וּבָאוּ שְׁנַיִם וְאָמְרוּ לָהֶן: בְּמַעֲרַב הַבִּירָה הַזֹּאת הֱיִיתֶם עִמָּנוּ בָּעֵת הַזֹּאת: אִם יָכוֹל הָעוֹמֵד בְּמַעֲרָב לִרְאוֹת מַה שֶּׁבְּמִזְרָח – אֵינָן זוֹמְמִין; וְאִם אֵינוֹ יָכוֹל לִרְאוֹת – הֲרֵי אֵלּוּ זוֹמְמִין. וְאֵין אוֹמְרִין: שֶׁמָּא מְאוֹר עֵינֵיהֶם שֶׁל רִאשׁוֹנִים רַב, וְרוֹאִין מֵרָחוֹק יָתֵר מִכָּל אָדָם.

וְכֵן אִם הֵעִידוּ שְׁנַיִם וְאָמְרוּ: בַּבֹּקֶר הָרַג זֶה אֶת הַנֶּפֶשׁ בִּירוּשָׁלַיִם, וּבָאוּ שְׁנַיִם וְאָמְרוּ לָהֶן: בְּיוֹם זֶה בָּעֶרֶב הֱיִיתֶם עִמָּנוּ בְּלֹד: אִם יָכוֹל אָדָם לְהַלֵּךְ אֲפִלּוּ עַל הַסּוּס מִירוּשָׁלַיִם לְלֹד מִבֹּקֶר עַד עֶרֶב – אֵינָן זוֹמְמִין; וְאִם לָאו – הֲרֵי אֵלּוּ זוֹמְמִין. וְאֵין אוֹמְרִין: שֶׁמָּא כַּר קַל בְּיוֹתֵר נִזְדַּמֵּן לָהֶן וְקִפְּלוּ אֶת הַדֶּרֶךְ. אֶלָּא בְּדָבָר הַמָּצוּי הַיָּדוּעַ לַכֹּל מְשַׁעֲרִין לְעוֹלָם, וּמְזִמִּין אוֹתָן.

ב שְׁנַיִם שֶׁאָמְרוּ: בְּאֶחָד בַּשַּׁבָּת הָרַג זֶה אֶת הַנֶּפֶשׁ בְּמָקוֹם פְּלוֹנִי, וּבָאוּ שְׁנַיִם וְאָמְרוּ: בְּיוֹם זֶה עִמָּנוּ הֱיִיתֶם בְּמָקוֹם אַחֵר רָחוֹק, אֲבָל בַּיּוֹם שֶׁלְּאַחַר יוֹם זֶה הֲרָגוֹ בְּוַדַּאי; אֲפִלּוּ הֵעִידוּ הָאַחֲרוֹנִים שֶׁקֹּדֶם כַּמָּה יָמִים הֲרָגוֹ – הֲרֵי זֶה הַהוֹרֵג עִם עֵדָיו הָרִאשׁוֹנִים נֶהֱרָגִין, שֶׁהֲרֵי הוּזַמּוּ. שֶׁבָּעֵת שֶׁהֵעִידוּ שֶׁהָרַג עֲדַיִן לֹא נִגְמַר דִּינוֹ לֵהָרֵג.

29. Since a verdict has already been rendered, this is no longer considered as a fine, but as any other admission of debt.
30. I.e., half the sum he conspired to have the defendant forfeit. Although his word is not sufficient to obligate the other witness, it creates a binding obligation for his own self (*Makkot* 2b,3a).

1. Rabbi Akiva Eiger states that if, however, they explicitly claim that they found such a swift camel, we do accept their claim.
2. The murderer, because the latter pair of witnesses testified that he committed murder; the first pair of witnesses, because they were disqualified through *hazamah*.
3. And thus the defendant was already worthy of being sentenced to death before the witnesses testified against them. Nevertheless, as the Rambam continues to explain, since he had not been sentenced to death at that time, the lying witnesses are held responsible for testifying against him (see *Makkot* 5a and commentaries).
4. In contrast to the situation in the following clause.

If, however, two witnesses come on Tuesday, and say: "On Sunday, so-and-so was sentenced to death," and two others come on Tuesday and say: "On Sunday, you were together with us in this distant place, but so-and-so was sentenced to death on Friday or on Monday,"[5] these witnesses are not executed. [The rationale is that] at the time they testified, the person had already been sentenced to death.[6]

Similar principles[7] apply with regard to the payment of a fine. What is implied? Two people came on Tuesday and said: "On Sunday, [so-and-so] stole, slaughtered [the animal he stole], and was sentenced [to pay a fine of four or five times the animal's worth]."[8] Two other witnesses come and testify: "On Sunday, you were with us in a distant place, but he was sentenced on Friday" - or even if they said: "On Sunday,[9] [so-and-so] stole, slaughtered [the animal he stole], and was sentenced on Monday," the witnesses who were disqualified through *hazamah* are not required to make financial restitution. [The rationale is that] at the time they testified against him, the defendant was obligated to make financial restitution.[10] Similar laws apply in all analogous situations.

3. The witnesses to a legal document may not be disqualified through *hazamah* unless they testify in court,[11] saying: "We composed the legal document at the time stated. We did not delay [the dating of it]." If they did not say this, even though a document [composed in] Jerusalem is dated the first of Nisan and witnesses come and testify that the witnesses to the legal document were in Babylon on that date,[12] the legal document is acceptable and the witnesses are acceptable. For it is possible that they composed the legal document and postdated it, i.e., they were in Jerusalem on the first of Adar[13] and composed the legal document and postdated it, dating it the first of Nisan.[14]

[The following rules apply when, by contrast,] they said: "We signed [the document] on the date stated," and they were disqualified through *hazamah*.[15] If there are witnesses who know the day they signed the legal document or witnesses saw the legal document with their signatures on it on this-and-this date,[16] once they are disqualified through *hazamah*, they are disqualified retroactively from the date on which it is known that they signed the legal

5. Since he had already been sentenced to death, it is as if they are testifying concerning a dead man.

6. Thus it is as if he had already been executed and thus it is as if they are testifying about a dead person. Their testimony is of no consequence and hence, they are not punished (*ibid.*). See *Hilchot Mamrim* 5:12).

7. I.e., a distinction is made whether a person had already been judged as liable or not.

8. As required by Exodus 21:37.

9. They also state that the witnesses were with them in a different place on Sunday. For this reason, based on the authoritative manuscripts and early printings, there are some versions of the text which begin this quote with "On Monday."

10. If, however, they testified only concerning the transgression itself, without mentioning

אֲבָל בָּאוּ שְׁנֵי עֵדִים בַּשְּׁלִישִׁי בַּשַּׁבָּת וְאָמְרוּ: בְּאֶחָד בַּשַּׁבָּת נִגְמַר דִּינוֹ שֶׁל פְּלוֹנִי לַהֲרִיגָה, וּבָאוּ שְׁנַיִם וְאָמְרוּ: בְּאֶחָד בַּשַּׁבָּת עִמָּנוּ הֱיִיתֶם בְּמָקוֹם פְּלוֹנִי הָרָחוֹק, אֶלָּא מֵעֶרֶב שַׁבָּת אוֹ בְּשֵׁנִי בַּשַּׁבָּת נִגְמַר דִּינוֹ – אֵין עֵדִים אֵלּוּ שֶׁהוּזַּמּוּ נֶהֱרָגִין, שֶׁהֲרֵי מִכָּל מָקוֹם בָּעֵת שֶׁהֵעִידוּ עָלָיו כְּבָר נִגְמַר דִּינוֹ לַהֲרִיגָה.

וְכֵן לְעִנְיַן תַּשְׁלוּמֵי קְנָס.

כֵּיצַד? בָּאוּ שְׁנַיִם בַּשְּׁלִישִׁי בַּשַּׁבָּת וְאָמְרוּ: בְּאֶחָד בַּשַּׁבָּת גָּנַב וְטָבַח וְנִגְמַר דִּינוֹ, וּבָאוּ שְׁנַיִם וְאָמְרוּ: בְּאֶחָד בַּשַּׁבָּת עִמָּנוּ הֱיִיתֶם בְּמָקוֹם רָחוֹק, אֲבָל בְּעֶרֶב שַׁבָּת נִגְמַר דִּינוֹ; אֲפִלּוּ אָמְרוּ: בְּאֶחָד בַּשַּׁבָּת גָּנַב וְטָבַח וּמָכַר, וּבְשֵׁנִי בַּשַּׁבָּת נִגְמַר דִּינוֹ – אֵין עֵדִים אֵלּוּ שֶׁהוּזַּמּוּ מְשַׁלְּמִין, שֶׁהֲרֵי מִכָּל מָקוֹם בָּעֵת שֶׁהֵעִידוּ עָלָיו חַיָּב הָיָה לְשַׁלֵּם. וְכֵן כֹּל כַּיּוֹצֵא בָּזֶה.

ג אֵין עֵדֵי הַשְּׁטָר נַעֲשִׂין זוֹמְמִין עַד שֶׁיֹּאמְרוּ בְּבֵית דִּין: שְׁטָר זֶה בִּזְמַנּוֹ כְּתַבְנוּהוּ וְלֹא אִחַרְנוּהוּ. אֲבָל אִם לֹא אָמְרוּ כֵּן, אַף עַל פִּי שֶׁזְּמַנּוֹ שֶׁל שְׁטָר בְּאֶחָד בְּנִיסָן בִּירוּשָׁלַיִם, וּבָאוּ עֵדִים וְהֵעִידוּ שֶׁעֵדֵי הַשְּׁטָר הָיוּ עִמָּהֶם בְּבָבֶל בְּיוֹם זֶה – הַשְּׁטָר כָּשֵׁר וְהָעֵדִים כְּשֵׁרִים; שֶׁאֶפְשָׁר שֶׁכְּתָבוּהוּ וְאֵחֲרוּהוּ, וּכְשֶׁהָיוּ בִּירוּשָׁלַיִם בְּאֶחָד בַּאֲדָר כָּתְבוּ שְׁטָר זֶה שָׁם, וְאֵחֲרוּ זְמַנּוֹ וְכָתְבוּ זְמַנּוֹ בְּנִיסָן.

אָמְרוּ: בִּזְמַנּוֹ כְּתַבְנוּהוּ, וְהוּזַּמּוּ:

אִם יֵשׁ שָׁם עֵדִים שֶׁיּוֹדְעִים הַיּוֹם שֶׁחָתְמוּ עַל הַשְּׁטָר, אוֹ עֵדִים שֶׁרָאוּ זֶה הַשְּׁטָר וַחֲתִימַת יָדָם בּוֹ בְּיוֹם פְּלוֹנִי, כֵּיוָן שֶׁהוּזַּמּוּ – הֲרֵי נִפְסְלוּ לְמַפְרֵעַ מִיּוֹם שֶׁנּוֹדַע שֶׁחָתְמוּ עַל הַשְּׁטָר;

that the person had been sentenced, both the first witnesses and the defendant would be convicted by the statements of the second witnesses.

The *Kessef Mishneh* emphasizes that these laws apply with regard to fines, but not with regard to monetary obligations (e.g., debts, damages, and the like). The rationale is that a monetary obligation exists even before it was declared by the court. The obligation for a fine, by contrast, exists only when declared by a court. If the person admits his responsibility, he is not held liable.

11 . Or write this statement in the legal document itself (*Siftei Cohen* 34:12).

12 . Since witnesses in Babylon could not sign a document in Jerusalem, one might assume that the document should be disqualified. Nevertheless, this is not so as the Rambam continues to explain.

13. The month that precedes Nisan.

14. And a postdated legal document is acceptable, as stated in *Hilchot Malveh ViLoveh* 23:2,4.

15. The question discussed by the Rambam in this and the following clause is: "From when are the witnesses disqualified - from the date they testified in court or beforehand?" This is not merely an abstract point. Any legal documents that they signed and any testimony that they gave in court after the date from which their testimony is disqualified are similarly disqualified. See Chapter 10, Halachah 4.

16. I.e., a date after the date on which the document was dated, but before the time the witnesses testified in court.

document. [The rationale is that] witnesses who sign a legal document are considered as if their testimony was delivered in court from the time they signed.[17]

If, however, there are no witnesses who saw them [sign, thus giving] testimony, nor did anyone see the [signed] document beforehand,[18] [the witnesses] are disqualified only from the time they testified in court that the signature was theirs, saying: "We signed it on that date." [The rationale is that] it is possible that on the date that they testified in court, they signed a legal document that had existed for many years and they lied by saying: "We signed it on the day it was dated."[19]

CHAPTER TWENTY

1. Lying witnesses are neither executed, given lashes, nor required to make financial restitution unless both of them were fit to serve as witnesses[1] and they were both disqualified through *hazamah* after the judgment was rendered.

If, however, only one of them was disqualified through *hazamah*,[2] they were both disqualified through *hazamah* before the judgment was rendered, or after the judgment was rendered, or one of them was disqualified[3] because of family connections[4] or because he was unfit to serve as a witness,[5] the witnesses are not punished, even though they are disqualified through *hazamah* and no longer acceptable to deliver testimony in all matters of Scriptural Law.[6]

2. Although according to Talmudic logic [one might differ],[7] if the person against whom they testified was executed and then they were disqualified through *hazamah*, they are not executed.[8] [This is derived from Deuteronomy 19:19: which] speaks of: "what they conspired to do." [Implied is that] it[9] was not already done.[10] This rule is part of the Oral Tradition.

If, however, the person against whom they testified was lashed, they are lashed.[11] Similarly, if money was expropriated from one person and given to another, it is returned to its owner[12] and [the witnesses] are required to pay [the penalty].[13]

17. Accordingly, since their testimony is disqualified through *hazamah*, they are considered as lying witnesses from that date onward.
18. I.e., before the witnesses testified in court.
19. Since they did not lie previously, they are disqualified as witnesses only from that date onward.

1. If one of them is unacceptable as a witness, their testimony is no loner effective. Hence they are not punished (*Kessef Mishneh*).
2. The second pair of witnesses states that one, but not the other of the first pair were with them in a different place at the time they claim that the event transpired.
3. For the punishment was prescribed only for a pair of witnesses (Rashi, *Makkot* 5b).
4. As described in Chapter 13.

שֶׁהָעֵדִים הַחֲתוּמִים עַל הַשְּׁטָר – הֲרֵי הֵן כְּמִי שֶׁנֶּחְקְרָה עֵדוּתָן בְּבֵית דִּין בְּעֵת הַחֲתִימָה. אֲבָל אִם אֵין עֵדִים שֶׁרָאוּ עֵדוּתָן וְלֹא רָאוּ הַשְּׁטָר מִקֹּדֶם – אֵין נִפְסָלִין אֶלָּא מֵעֵת שֶׁהֵעִידוּ בְּבֵית דִּין שֶׁזֶּה כְּתַב יָדָן וְאָמְרוּ: בִּזְמַנּוֹ כְּתַבְנוּהוּ; שֶׁאֶפְשָׁר שֶׁבְּיוֹם זֶה שֶׁהֵעִידוּ בְּבֵית דִּין, בּוֹ בַּיּוֹם חָתְמוּ עַל הַשְּׁטָר שֶׁיֵּשׁ לוֹ כַּמָּה שָׁנִים, וְהֵם שִׁקְּרוּ וְאָמְרוּ: בִּזְמַנּוֹ כָּתַבְנוּ.

פֶּרֶק עֶשְׂרִים

א אֵין עֵדִים זוֹמְמִין נֶהֱרָגִין וְלֹא לוֹקִין וְלֹא מְשַׁלְּמִין עַד שֶׁיִּהְיוּ שְׁנֵיהֶם רְאוּיִין לְעֵדוּת, וְיָזֹמּוּ שְׁנֵיהֶם אַחַר שֶׁנִּגְמַר הַדִּין. אֲבָל אִם הוּזַם אֶחָד מֵהֶן בִּלְבַד, אוֹ שֶׁהוּזַמּוּ שְׁנֵיהֶם קֹדֶם גְּמַר דִּין, אוֹ אַחַר גְּמַר דִּין וְנִמְצָא אֶחָד מֵהֶן קָרוֹב אוֹ פָּסוּל – אֵין נֶעֱנָשִׁין, אַף עַל פִּי שֶׁהוּזַמּוּ וְנִפְסְלוּ לְכָל עֵדוּת שֶׁבַּתּוֹרָה.

ב נֶהֱרַג זֶה שֶׁהֵעִידוּ עָלָיו וְאַחַר כָּךְ הוּזַמּוּ – אֵינָן נֶהֱרָגִין מִן הַדִּין. שֶׁנֶּאֱמַר: כַּאֲשֶׁר זָמַם לַעֲשׂוֹת – וַעֲדַיִן לֹא עָשָׂה. וְדָבָר זֶה מִפִּי הַקַּבָּלָה. אֲבָל אִם לָקָה זֶה שֶׁהֵעִידוּ עָלָיו – לוֹקִין. וְכֵן אִם יָצָא הַמָּמוֹן מִיַּד זֶה לְיַד זֶה בְּעֵדוּתָן – חוֹזֵר לִבְעָלָיו, וּמְשַׁלְּמִין לוֹ.

5. As described in Chapters 10-12.
6. As stated in Chapter 10, Halachah 4. They are, however, acceptable in matters where leniency is granted with regard to the acceptance of testimony, e.g., testimony concerning the death of a woman's husband.
7. Our translation is based on the gloss of the *Kessef Mishneh* who states that with this phrase, the Rambam is trying to convey the following fundamental principle: Capital punishment is not given for a crime unless it is explicitly stated in the Torah. A logical proof is not sufficient.

What is the logic here? If a person who conspires to have a person executed should be executed, should not one who actually caused him to be executed.
8. From the Rambam's Commentary to the Mishnah and from the gloss of the Radbaz, it appears that although they are not executed, they should be punished by the court.
9. I.e., what they conspired.
10. I.e., the Torah prescribes punishment only in such a situation.
11. The Ra'avad and the *Kessef Mishneh* question the Rambam's source for this distinction. The *Kessef Mishneh* explains that it is possible to say that since judgment is ultimately in God's hands, had the executed party not been guilty, God would not have allowed him to be executed. Hence the lying witnesses need not be punished. Alternatively, it can be explained that the punishments inflicted by the courts are not goals in their own right, but means to bring a person to atonement. It is not fitting to give lying witnesses who had a person executed the opportunity to achieve such atonement. Since lashes is not as severe a punishment, neither of these explanations apply.
12. I.e., the plaintiff is required to return it.
13. For financial penalties are established based on Talmudic logic (*Kessef Mishneh*).

3. [The following laws apply if] there were three or even 100 witnesses. If the witnesses deliver testimony in court one after the other, each one testifying immediately after[14] his colleague and several of them were disqualified through *hazamah*, they do not receive punishment until all of them are disqualified through *hazamah*.[15]

If, however, the interval between testimonies was greater than the time it takes a student to greet a teacher, the testimonies are divided and the two who were disqualified through *hazamah* are punished. The two who testified after there was such an interlude between their testimony and that of the first pair are not punished. [This applies] even though the entire testimony is disqualified[16] because [all of the witnesses] are considered as one group[17] and when the testimony of part of a group is disqualified, the entire testimony is disqualified.[18]

4. When one [witness] delivers testimony, that testimony is investigated,[19] and the second witness states: "I also [testify] like him," "Yes, [this is what happened]," or the like, they are both executed, lashed, or subjected to a financial penalty if they are both disqualified through *hazamah*.[20] [The rationale is that] any witness who says "Yes, [this is what happened]" after his colleague testified is considered as having testified and responded to cross-examination as his colleague did.

There is no concept of inadvertent transgression with regard to lying witnesses,[21] because the transgression does not involve a deed.[22] Therefore there is no need for a warning[23] as we explained.[24]

5. Just as two witnesses can disqualify 100 witnesses through *hazamah* if the 100 testify at one time;[25] so, too, they can disqualify them through *hazamah* if they testify as 50 groups, coming two by two.

What is implied? A group of witnesses testified that Reuven killed Shimon in Jerusalem. Two witnesses came and disqualified that group through

14. As the Rambam continues to explain, the Hebrew term translated as "immediately after," *toch kidei dibur*, has a specific meaning: The time it takes a student to greet a teacher, saying: *Shalom alecha rabbi* (*Hilchot Sh'vuot* 2:17).
15. The Ra'avad questions: Since these witnesses were not disqualified through *hazamah*, why would one think that they should be punished? The Radbaz answers that the very fact that they appeared together with lying witnesses implicates them.

The *Lechem Mishneh* explains that the Rambam's intent is that even if the second pair of witnesses were also disqualified through *hazamah*, they are not punished. The rationale is that since their testimony was separated from that of the first pair and by the time they testified the defendant could have been executed because of the testimony of the first pair, their testimony is of no consequence. Hence they are not punished.
16. Thus even if there is no difficulty at all with the testimony of the last pair of witnesses, the defendant is not punished.
17. Because they saw the event together and appeared together in court.
18. The rationale for this distinction can be explained as follows: With regard to the disqualification of witnesses, everything is dependent on the testimony of the witnesses in

ג הָיוּ הָעֵדִים שְׁלֹשָׁה, אֲפִלּוּ מֵאָה, אִם הֵעִידוּ בְּבֵית דִּין זֶה אַחַר זֶה, וְהֵעִיד כָּל אֶחָד מֵהֶן אַחַר חֲבֵרוֹ בְּתוֹךְ כְּדֵי דִבּוּר, וְהוּזַמּוּ מִקְצָתָן – אֵין נֶעֱנָשִׁין עַד שֶׁיּוּזַמּוּ כֻּלָּן.
אֲבָל אִם הָיָה הֶפְסֵק בֵּין זֶה לָזֶה יָתֵר מִכְּדֵי דִבּוּר, שֶׁהוּא כְּדֵי שְׁאֵלַת שָׁלוֹם תַּלְמִיד לְרַב – הֲרֵי נֶחְלְקָה הָעֵדוּת; וְהַשְּׁנַיִם שֶׁהוּזַמּוּ – נֶעֱנָשִׁין, וְהַשְּׁנַיִם הָאֲחֵרִים, שֶׁהָיָה בֵּין דִּבְרֵיהֶן וְדִבְרֵי הָרִאשׁוֹנִים הֶפְסֵק – אֵין נֶעֱנָשִׁין. וְאַף עַל פִּי שֶׁבָּטְלָה הָעֵדוּת כֻּלָּהּ; מִפְּנֵי שֶׁהֵן כַּת אַחַת, הוֹאִיל וְנִפְסְלָה מִקְצָתָהּ – נִפְסְלָה כֻּלָּהּ.

ד הֵעִיד הָאֶחָד וְנֶחְקְרָה עֵדוּתוֹ, וְאָמַר הַשֵּׁנִי: אַף אֲנִי כָּמוֹהוּ, אוֹ שֶׁאָמַר: הֵן כַּיּוֹצֵא בָּזֶה, וְהוּזַמּוּ שְׁנֵיהֶן – הֲרֵי שְׁנֵיהֶן נֶהֱרָגִין אוֹ לוֹקִין אוֹ מְשַׁלְּמִין.
שֶׁכָּל עֵד שֶׁאָמַר אַחַר עֵדוּת חֲבֵרוֹ 'הֵן' – הֲרֵי זֶה כְּמִי שֶׁנֶּחְקַר וְהֵעִיד כְּמוֹ שֶׁהֵעִיד חֲבֵרוֹ. וְאֵין לְעֵדִים זוֹמְמִין שְׁגָגָה, לְפִי שֶׁאֵין בָּהּ מַעֲשֶׂה. לְפִיכָךְ אֵין צְרִיכִים הַתְרָאָה, כְּמוֹ שֶׁבֵּאַרְנוּ.

ה כְּשֵׁם שֶׁהַשְּׁנַיִם מְזִמִּין אֶת הַמֵּאָה אִם הֵעִידוּ הַמֵּאָה בְּבַת אַחַת, כָּךְ הֵן מְזִמִּין אוֹתָן אֲפִלּוּ הָיוּ חֲמִשִּׁים כַּת וּבָאוּ שְׁנַיִם אַחַר שְׁנַיִם.
כֵּיצַד? כַּת שֶׁהֵעִידָה עַל רְאוּבֵן שֶׁהָרַג אֶת שִׁמְעוֹן בִּירוּשָׁלַיִם, וּבָאוּ שְׁנֵי עֵדִים וֶהֱזִמּוּהָ,

court. Hence if their testimony is separated, they are not considered as a single group. Their classification as a single group, by contrast, depends on their coming to court together. Since they came together with the intent to testify, they are considered as a single group (Radbaz, *Kessef Mishneh*).

The Ra'avad (and Rashi, in his commentary to *Makkot* 6a) do not accept the Rambam's approach and maintain that even though the first pair of witnesses should be executed, if the testimony of the second pair is validated, the defendant should also be executed.

19. I.e., he is cross-examined by the court, as explained in Chapter 2.

20. I.e., despite the fact that he did not actually testify, it is considered as if he did as the Rambam proceeds to explain. See also *Hilchot Avodat Kochavim* 2:8 which states that making such statements is equivalent to actually testifying in court.

21. I.e., they receive punishment even if they committed the transgression without knowing that it was forbidden.

22. The Radbaz explains that Numbers 15:29, the source for the laws of inadvertent transgression mentions "one who *acts* inadvertently" (see *Hilchot Shegagot* 1:2). In this context (in contrast to blasphemy), speaking is not considered as an act. Hence they are not held liable.

Nevertheless, the Radbaz and the *Kessef Mishneh* offer a different rationale why these witnesses are punished without a warning: They desired to have the defendant punished although he did not receive a warning. Therefore, they should be punished without a warning.

23. See Chapter 18, Halachah 4.

24. For the entire purpose of a warning is to distinguish between a transgression committed willfully and one committed inadvertently (*Hilchot Sanhedrin* 12:2).

25. See Chapter 18, Halachah 3.

hazamah. Another group came and delivered that same testimony, that Reuven killed Shimon in Jerusalem and these same two [witnesses] arose and disqualified that group through *hazamah.* This happened a third time and a fourth time. Even if it happens 100 times, all [the other witnesses] are executed on the basis of the testimony of these two.[26]

6. When one group of witnesses testify that Reuven killed Shimon in Jerusalem and a second group come and disqualify the first group through *hazamah*, the lying witnesses should be executed and Reuven's [life] saved.[27] If a third group come and disqualify the second group through *hazamah*, the second group and Reuven should be executed[28] and the [lives of] the first group saved.[29]

If a fourth group come and disqualify the third group through *hazamah*, the third and the first groups should be executed and the [lives of] Reuven and the second group saved. Similarly, even if there are 100 groups, each one disqualifying the testimony of the previous through *hazamah*, one group's [testimony is accepted] and the other group's [testimony is disqualified].

7. When witnesses testify that a person who is *trefe*[30] murdered [a person] and then the witnesses are disqualified through *hazamah*, [the witnesses] are not executed.[31] [The rationale is that] even if they had killed him with their hands, they would not be executed, because he is *trefe*.[32]

Similarly, if witnesses who were *trefe* testified concerning a matter punishable by execution by the court and were disqualified through *hazamah*, they are not executed.[33] [The rationale is that] if [their testimony was disqualified through *hazamah*, and] the testimony of [the witnesses who] testified against them was disqualified through *hazamah*, those witnesses would not be executed, for they disqualified only a person who was *trefe*.[34]

8. [The following rule applies when] witnesses testify against another person and have him convicted in a matter that does not involve lashes, capital punishment, or a financial obligation and then [the witnesses] are disqualified through *hazamah*. They are given lashes[35] even though they did not conspire to have [the defendant] lashed or to obligate him financially.

What is implied? [Witnesses] testified that a priest was a *challal*,[36] e.g., they testified that his mother was divorced or released through *chalitzah*[37] in their

26. We do not say that they are lying and have resolved to testify against anyone who delivers testimony in this matter (Rashi, *Makkot* 5a).
27. Because the testimony of the second group exonerates him from the onus of the testimony of the first group.
28. The second group should be executed as lying witnesses who sought to have the first group executed. Reuven should be executed, because once the testimony of the second group has been disqualified, the testimony of the first group is then reinstated.
29. Because the disqualification of the second group exonerates them.
30. I.e., he has a physical ailment that will cause him to die within 12 months.

וּבָאת כַּת שְׁנִיָּה וְהֵעִידָה אוֹתָהּ עֵדוּת עַצְמָהּ, שֶׁרְאוּבֵן הָרַג שִׁמְעוֹן בִּירוּשָׁלַיִם, וְעָמְדוּ אוֹתָן הַשְּׁנַיִם וֶהֱזִמּוּהָ גַּם זוֹ הַכַּת הַשְּׁנִיָּה,

וְכֵן הַשְּׁלִישִׁית, וְכֵן הָרְבִיעִית, אֲפִלּוּ מֵאָה – כֻּלָּן הֵן נֶהֱרָגִין עַל פִּי אֵלּוּ הַשְּׁנַיִם.

ו כַּת שֶׁהֵעִידָה עַל רְאוּבֵן שֶׁהָרַג אֶת שִׁמְעוֹן בִּירוּשָׁלַיִם, וּבָאָה כַּת שְׁנִיָּה וְהֵזִמָּה אֶת הַכַּת רִאשׁוֹנָה – יֵהָרְגוּ הָעֵדִים הַזּוֹמְמִין, וְיִנָּצֵל רְאוּבֵן. בָּאָה כַּת שְׁלִישִׁית וְהֵזִמָּה אֶת הַכַּת הַשְּׁנִיָּה – תֵּהָרֵג הַכַּת הַשְּׁנִיָּה וּרְאוּבֵן, וְתִנָּצֵל הַכַּת רִאשׁוֹנָה.

בָּאָה כַּת רְבִיעִית וְהֵזִמָּה אֶת הַכַּת שְׁלִישִׁית – תֵּהָרֵג הַכַּת הַשְּׁלִישִׁית וְהָרִאשׁוֹנָה, וְיִנָּצֵל רְאוּבֵן וְהַכַּת הַשְּׁנִיָּה. וְכֵן אֲפִלּוּ הֵן מֵאָה כַּת, זוֹ מְזִמָּה אֶת זוֹ – כַּת נִכְנֶסֶת וְכַת יוֹצֵאת.

ז עֵדִים שֶׁהֵעִידוּ עַל אִישׁ טְרֵפָה שֶׁהָרַג, וְהוּזַמּוּ – אֵין נֶהֱרָגִין; שֶׁאֲפִלּוּ הֲרָגוּהוּ בִּידֵיהֶן – אֵין נֶהֱרָגִין, לְפִי שֶׁהוּא טְרֵפָה.

וְכֵן הָעֵדִים שֶׁהָיוּ טְרֵפָה, וְהֵעִידוּ בְּדָבָר שֶׁחַיָּבִין עָלָיו מִיתַת בֵּית דִּין, וְהוּזַמּוּ – אֵין נֶהֱרָגִין; שֶׁאִם יוּזַמּוּ זוֹמְמֵיהֶן – אֵין זוֹמְמֵיהֶן נֶהֱרָגִין, שֶׁלֹּא הֵזֵמּוּ אֶלָּא טְרֵפָה.

ח עֵדִים שֶׁהֵעִידוּ עַל אֶחָד, וְהִרְשִׁיעוּהוּ רֶשַׁע שֶׁאֵין בּוֹ לֹא מַלְקוּת וְלֹא מִיתָה וְלֹא חִיּוּב מָמוֹן, וְאַחַר כָּךְ הוּזַמּוּ – הֲרֵי אֵלּוּ לוֹקִין, אַף עַל פִּי שֶׁלֹּא זָמְמוּ לְהַלְקוֹת זֶה וְלֹא לְחַיְּבוֹ מָמוֹן.

כֵּיצַד? הֵעִידוּ עַל כֹּהֵן שֶׁהוּא חָלָל, כְּגוֹן שֶׁהֵעִידוּ: בְּפָנֵינוּ נִתְגָּרְשָׁה אִמּוֹ אוֹ נֶחֶלְצָה

31. Seemingly, through their testimony, they are trying to have the defendant executed. Nevertheless, despite the fact that they testify that the person who is *trefe* committed a murder, he is not executed. The rationale is that testimony must be able to be disqualified through *hazamah*. Since it is impossible to punish the witnesses "as they conspired to do to their brother," for they conspired to have a sick person executed and they are healthy, the concept of *hazamah* is not relevant, as stated in *Hilchot Rotzeach* 2:9.

32. And a person who kills a colleague who is *trefe* is not liable for execution. For it is as if he killed a dead person (*Sanhedrin* 78a; *Hilchot Rotzeach* 2:8).

33. Here also, it would appear that the intent is that since they are seeking to have the person executed, one might think that they should be executed. In fact, however, their testimony is not effective in having the defendant sentenced to death. Since they are *trefe*, there is no possibility of requiting them "as they conspired to do to their brother." For they conspired to have a healthy person executed and they are sick.

Accordingly, the *Kessef Mishneh* explains that we are speaking about a situation where the court did not recognize that the witnesses were *trefe* when it accepted their testimony.

34. Thus the punishment is not "as they conspired to do to their brother."

35. For the reasons mentioned by the Rambam in the following halachah.

36. I.e., the descendant of a priest who is not considered as a member of the priesthood, because he was conceived in relations forbidden to his father. See *Hilchot Issurei Bi'ah* 19:5.

37. Thus making his mother forbidden to his father.

presence in this-and-this place on this-and-this date. [If the witnesses] are disqualified through *hazamah*, they are punished by lashing.[38]

Similarly, if they testified that a person inadvertently killed a colleague and they are disqualified through *hazamah*, they are punished by lashing; they are not exiled.[39]

And if they testify that a person's ox killed another person and they were disqualified through *hazamah*, they receive lashes and are not required to pay an atonement fine.[40] If they testify that a person was sold as a Hebrew servant[41] and they were disqualified through *hazamah*, they receive lashes. These four rulings are part of the Oral Tradition.[42]

9. [With regard to the above matters,] our Sages received the following tradition: When two people cause a righteous person to be condemned[43] and a wicked person to be vindicated through their testimony and two others come and disqualify their testimony through *hazamah* vindicating the righteous person and condemning the wicked, the first pair of witnesses receive lashes[44] even though their condemnation of the righteous person would not have had him subjected to lashes.[45]

If, however, [witnesses] testify that a person partook of milk and meat or wore *shaatnez*, they are punished by lashes, as [implied by Deuteronomy 19:19]: "You shall requite him as he conspired."[46]

10. When two [witnesses] testify that Reuven committed adultery with the daughter of a priest, Reuven was sentenced to death by strangulation and the daughter of the priest was sentenced to be burnt to death,[47] and afterwards the witnesses were disqualified through *hazamah*, they should be executed by strangulation and not burnt to death.[48] This is part of the Oral Tradition.

Rabbi Akiva Eiger raises a question, noting that a woman who underwent *chalitzah* is only forbidden to a priest by Rabbinic decree. Hence the Ramban and others rule that lashes should not be given. Rabbi Akiva Eiger himself states that since the defendant is being disqualified according to Rabbinic decree through the testimony of the witnesses, and by giving that false testimony, they violate a Scriptural commandment, it is appropriate that they be punished by lashing.

38. We do not say that the witnesses should be considered as *challalim* themselves. This applies even if the witnesses themselves are priests. *Makkot* 2b explains this based on Deuteronomy 19:19: "And you shall requite him as he conspired to do to his brother." The obligation is to requite him, not to requite his descendants and having him declared a *challal* would be a punishment against his descendants as well as him.

39. The lying witnesses are not exiled "as [they] conspired to do to" the defendant. The rationale is that Deuteronomy 19:5 says with regard to a person convicted of inadvertent murder: "He shall flee to one of these cities." *Makkot, loc. cit.*, states: " 'He,' and not those who conspire against him.' "

40. For an atonement fine is not a monetary assessment, but rather a fine designated to bring atonement for the death of the victim. These witnesses do not need that type of atonement, for their ox did not cause death (Rashi, *Makkot, loc. cit.*; see also *Hilchot Nizkei Mammon* 10:4-5).

See also the *Ketzot HaChoshen* 38:2 which explains that even though the witness also caused the ox to be sentenced to death and no benefit to be derived from it. Nevertheless,

בְּמָקוֹם פְּלוֹנִי בְּיוֹם פְּלוֹנִי, וְהוּזַמּוּ - הֲרֵי הֵן לוֹקִין. וְכֵן אִם הֵעִידוּ עַל אָדָם שֶׁהָרַג בִּשְׁגָגָה, וְהוּזַמּוּ - לוֹקִין, וְאֵינָן גּוֹלִין. הֵעִידוּ עַל שׁוֹרוֹ שֶׁל זֶה שֶׁהָרַג הַנֶּפֶשׁ, וְהוּזַמּוּ - הֲרֵי הֵן לוֹקִין, וְאֵין מְשַׁלְּמִין אֶת הַכֹּפֶר. הֵעִידוּ עָלָיו שֶׁנִּמְכַּר בְּעֶבֶד עִבְרִי, וְהוּזַמּוּ - לוֹקִין. וְאַרְבָּעָה דְבָרִים אֵלּוּ מִפִּי הַקַּבָּלָה הֵן.

ט כָּךְ קִבְּלוּ חֲכָמִים: שְׁשְּׁנַיִם שֶׁהִרְשִׁיעוּ אֶת הַצַּדִּיק וְהִצְדִּיקוּ אֶת הָרָשָׁע בְּעֵדוּתָן, וּבָאוּ עֵדִים אֲחֵרִים וֶהֱזִמּוּם, וְהִצְדִּיקוּ אֶת הַצַּדִּיק וְהִרְשִׁיעוּ אֶת הָרָשָׁע - הֲרֵי עֵדִים הָרִאשׁוֹנִים לוֹקִים, אַף עַל פִּי שֶׁלֹּא הִרְשִׁיעוּ הַצַּדִּיק לְהַלְקוֹתוֹ.
אֲבָל אִם הֵעִידוּ עָלָיו שֶׁאָכַל בָּשָׂר בְּחָלָב אוֹ שֶׁלָּבַשׁ שַׁעַטְנֵז - הֲרֵי אֵלּוּ לוֹקִין מִשּׁוּם שֶׁנֶּאֱמַר: וַעֲשִׂיתֶם לוֹ כַּאֲשֶׁר זָמַם.

י שְׁנַיִם שֶׁהֵעִידוּ עַל רְאוּבֵן שֶׁנָּאַף עִם בַּת כֹּהֵן, וְנִגְמַר דִּין רְאוּבֵן לְחָנֵק וְדִין הַנּוֹאֶפֶת לִשְׂרֵפָה, וְאַחַר כָּךְ נִמְצְאוּ זוֹמְמִין - הֲרֵי אֵלּוּ נֶחֱנָקִין וְלֹא נִשְׂרָפִין.
וְדָבָר זֶה מִפִּי הַקַּבָּלָה.

the witnesses are lashed and not subjected to these penalties. See also the Ramban who differs and maintains that the witnesses are required to make financial restitution and are not lashed.

41. The *Nimukei Mahari* (based on *Makkot, loc. cit.*), explains that the intent is that the witnesses testify that the person stole and did not have the money to make restitution for the theft.

42. Although *Makkot, loc. cit.*, outlines how each of these concepts is derived from the exegesis of a verse, since the concepts are not derived through the Thirteen Principles of Biblical Exegesis, the exegesis is considered as only an *asmachta*. The binding obligation to fulfill these directives stems from the fact that they were transmitted through the Oral Tradition (Radbaz).

43. The Rambam is borrowing the wording of Deuteronomy 25:1-2: "And they shall validate the righteous and condemn the wicked. If the wicked man is deserving of being beaten..." which continues to speak of the punishment of lashing.

"Condemning the righteous" refers to a situation where lying witnesses caused judgment to be rendered against a righteous person.

44. In this situation, we follow the instructions of the continuation of the verse and punish the person by lashes. Delivering false testimony violates the prohibition "Do not deliver false testimony against your colleague." Nevertheless, one might think that since that prohibition does not involve a deed, it is not punishable by lashes. Hence the exegesis of the above verse is necessary. See *Makkot* 4b (Radbaz, *Kessef Mishneh*).

45. As in the four cases mentioned in the previous halachah.

46. I.e., since the lying witnesses delivered testimony concerning a transgression punishable by lashes, there is no need for a special teaching to instruct us to give them that punishment. They are requited in this manner, because this is what they "conspired to do to their brother" (*Kessef Mishneh*).

47. See *Hilchot Issurei Bi'ah* 3:3 which states that the two parties to this transgression are given different punishments.

48. *Sanhedrin* 90a derives this from Deuteronomy 19:19 which speaks of requiting a

CHAPTER TWENTY ONE

1. [The following rule applies when] witnesses testify that so-and-so divorced his wife and did not pay her the money due her by virtue of her *ketubah* and, [afterwards, these witnesses] were disqualified through *hazamah*. [Now] either today or tomorrow, when [the husband] divorces his wife, he must pay her the money due her by virtue of her *ketubah*.[1] Hence we calculate how much a person would pay for the right to collect the money due this woman by virtue of her *ketubah* [in the event she would be widowed or divorced] and [the witnesses are required to] pay this amount.[2]

[When calculating this amount,] we take into consideration [the physical state of] the woman and [the amount of] her *ketubah*. If the woman is sick or old or there is peace between her and her husband, the value for which her *ketubah* will be sold will not be the same if she is young and healthy[3] or there is strife between the couple. For such a woman is more likely to be divorced and less likely to die.

Similarly, the amount to be received for a large *ketubah* is not the same as for a small *ketubah*. For example, if her *ketubah* is for 1000 *zuz*, it might be sold for 100. If it is for 100, it will not be sold for 10 but for less.[4] These matters are dependent on the estimates of the judges.[5]

2. [Similar principles apply in the following situation. Witnesses] testify with regard to a person, saying that he is obligated to pay so-and-so 1000 *zuz* in 30 days. The borrower [admits the debt, but] says [that it is not due] until five years and 30 days. [If] the witnesses are disqualified through *hazamah*, we evaluate how much a person would pay to have 1000 *zuz* available to him for five years. This is the sum paid to the borrower.[6] Similar laws apply in all analogous situations.

3. When witnesses testify that a person's ox gored [another ox] and [afterwards,] the witnesses were disqualified through *hazamah*, they are required to pay half the damages.[7] If the ox is not worth half the damages, they are required to pay only the value of the ox. For [the fine of] half of the damages must be paid only from the body of the [goring] ox itself.[8] Therefore if they testified

lying witness, "as he conspired to do to his brother," his brother and not his sister. This, however, is an *asmachta*.

Rabbi Akiva Eiger questions what the ruling would be in a situation where the witnesses claim to have given a warning to the woman, but not to the man. He supposes that even in such a situation, they should be executed by strangulation, not burning.

1. For this reason, we do not say that the witnesses must pay the entire amount of the *ketubah*. Instead, we calculate the amount as the Rambam elaborates.
2. Rav Moshe HaCohen, the *Lechem Mishneh*, and the *Mishneh LiMelech* emphasize that the Rambam's intent is that the witnesses are required to pay the difference between the face value of the *ketubah* and the value the woman could receive for its sale immediately.

פֶּרֶק אֶחָד וְעֶשְׂרִים

א עֵדִים שֶׁהֵעִידוּ שֶׁפְּלוֹנִי גֵּרֵשׁ אִשְׁתּוֹ וְלֹא נָתַן לָהּ כְּתֻבָּה, וְהוּזַמּוּ; וַהֲלוֹא בֵּין הַיּוֹם בֵּין לְמָחָר, אִם גֵּרֵשׁ, סוֹפוֹ לִתֵּן כְּתֻבָּה –
אוֹמְדִין כַּמָּה רוֹצֶה אָדָם לִתֵּן בִּכְתֻבָּתָהּ שֶׁל זוֹ, שֶׁתִּמָּכֵר אוֹתָהּ בְּטוֹבַת הֲנָאָה, וּמְשַׁלְּמִין דְּמֵי טוֹבַת הֲנָאָה זוֹ. וּמְשַׁעֲרִין בָּאִשָּׁה וּבִכְתֻבָּתָהּ. שֶׁאִם הָאִשָּׁה הָיְתָה חוֹלָה אוֹ זְקֵנָה, אוֹ שֶׁהָיָה שָׁלוֹם בֵּינָהּ לְבֵין בַּעְלָהּ – אֵין דְּמֵי הַכְּתֻבָּה כְּשֶׁתִּמָּכֵר כְּמוֹ דָמֶיהָ אִם הָיְתָה הָאִשָּׁה בְּרִיאָה וּקְטַנָּה, אִם יֵשׁ בֵּינֵיהֶן קְטָטָה; שֶׁזּוֹ קְרוֹבָה מִן הַגֵּרוּשִׁין וּרְחוֹקָה מִן הַמִּיתָה. וְכֵן אֵין טוֹבַת הֲנָאָה שֶׁל כְּתֻבָּה הַמְרֻבָּה לְפִי טוֹבַת הֲנָאָה שֶׁל כְּתֻבָּה הַמּוּעֶטֶת; שֶׁאִם הָיְתָה כְּתֻבָּתָהּ אֶלֶף זוּז – הֲרֵי הִיא נִמְכֶּרֶת בְּטוֹבַת הֲנָאָה בְּמֵאָה, וְאִם הָיְתָה מֵאָה – אֵינָהּ נִמְכֶּרֶת בַּעֲשָׂרָה אֶלָּא בְּפָחוֹת. דְּבָרִים אֵלּוּ כְּפִי מַה שֶּׁיְּשַׁעֲרוּ הַדַּיָּנִים.

ב הֵעִידוּ עַל זֶה שֶׁחַיָּב לִפְלוֹנִי אֶלֶף זוּז עַל מְנָת לִתֵּן מִכָּאן וְעַד שְׁלֹשִׁים יוֹם, וְהַלֹּוֶה אוֹמֵר: עַד חָמֵשׁ שָׁנִים אַחַר הַשְּׁלֹשִׁים יוֹם, וְנִמְצְאוּ זוֹמְמִין – אוֹמְדִין כַּמָּה רוֹצֶה אָדָם לִתֵּן וְיִהְיוּ בְּיָדוֹ אֶלֶף זוּז חָמֵשׁ שָׁנִים, וּמְשַׁלְּמִין כֵּן לַלֹּוֶה. וְכֵן כֹּל כַּיּוֹצֵא בָּזֶה.

ג הֵעִידוּ עַל שׁוֹרוֹ שֶׁל זֶה שֶׁנָּגַח, וְנִמְצְאוּ זוֹמְמִין – מְשַׁלְּמִין חֲצִי נֶזֶק.
וְאִם אֵין הַשּׁוֹר שָׁוֶה חֲצִי נֶזֶק – מְשַׁלְּמִין דְּמֵי הַשּׁוֹר בִּלְבַד; שֶׁאֵין מְשַׁלֵּם חֲצִי נֶזֶק אֶלָּא מִגּוּפוֹ.

It is not appropriate to require them to pay only the amount the woman would receive, for they are trying to cause the husband a loss, not the woman. There are authoritative manuscripts of the *Mishneh Torah* which also point to this interpretation. See also Rashi's commentary to *Makkot* 3a.
3. And hence, likely to live for a long time and thus outlive her husband and collect the money due her by virtue of her *ketubah.*
4. People will not be willing to pay the same ratio of one tenth. Since a large sum is not involved, they are not anxious to risk their money. The Radbaz differs with the Rambam and maintains that people will be more willing to risk a smaller amount (10 *zuz*) to gain a relatively larger amount (100) than to risk a larger amount (100) for an immense sum (1000). A small amount (10), people will not consider significant; it's like buying a lottery ticket. When, however, a large outlay (100) must be made at the outset, they will hesitate.
5. And are thus variable in every time and place according to the conditions that prevail in that society.
6. For this is the amount that the lying witnesses endeavored to cause him to lose.
7. As explained in *Hilchot Nizkei Mammon* 1:2, when an ox which is not known to gore gores another ox, the owner is required to pay only half the damages it caused. Since the witnesses are required to pay the amount they conspired to cause the owner to lose, they must pay this sum.
8. The owner of an ox that gores is not obligated to pay from his own personal financial resources (*ibid.*:3). And since the owner is not required to pay more than the value of the ox, the witnesses are likewise not required.

that [the ox] consumed produce or broke utensils while walking, [the witnesses] are required to pay the full amount of the loss.[9] Similar laws apply in all analogous situations.

4. When witnesses testify that a person knocked out the tooth of his servant and then blinded [the servant's] eye,[10] if [afterwards,] the witnesses were disqualified through *hazamah*, they are required to pay the master the value of the servant[11] and the value of his eye.[12]

[A different rule applies if] they testified[13] that [the master] blinded the servant's eye and afterwards knocked out his tooth, the witnesses were disqualified through *hazamah*, and it was later discovered that [the events occurred in] the opposite order, the master knocked out his tooth and afterwards blinded him. [The witnesses] must pay the worth of the eye[14] to the servant. Similar laws apply in all analogous situations.

5. When witnesses who testified that [a woman] was warned [by her husband not to enter into privacy with another man] or who testified that she [disobeyed the warning and] entered into privacy with him are disqualified through *hazamah*,[15] they are punished by lashes. If one witness comes and testifies that she committed adultery after she was warned and entered into privacy, and that witness was disqualified through *hazamah*, [that witness] is required[16] to pay the money due her by virtue of her *ketubah*.

If there were two witnesses and they served as the witnesses for the warning, that she entered into privacy, and that she committed adultery, should they be disqualified through *hazamah*, they are required to pay the money due her by virtue of her *ketubah*;[17] they do not receive lashes.[18] Why are they not executed - they gave testimony with regard to adultery?[19] Because they did not warn [the woman].[20]

9. Since it is ordinary for oxen to cause damage in this manner, the owner would have to pay the full amount of the damages (*ibid.*:4-5). Hence the witnesses are required to pay that sum.

10. In both of these instances, the master is required to free a Canaanite servant if he inflicts these injuries upon him. Since he is required to free him for the first injury, the master would be obligated to pay him financial reimbursement for the second injury.

11. Because through their testimony, the servant would be freed.

12. Because of the financial reimbursement he would have been required to make.

The Ra'avad and others have questioned the Rambam's ruling here, noting that in *Hilchot Chovel UMazik* 4:11, the Rambam himself rules that if a person knocks out the tooth of his servant and then blinds [the servant's] eye, the master is not required to pay the servant for his eye. The rationale is that since the servant did not receive his bill of release, he is not considered as possessing an independent financial capacity. If, however, the servant seizes payment for his eye from the master, he is allowed to retain possession of what he seized. Accordingly, the Ra'avad questions why the witnesses should be held liable. If the owner would not be required to pay for the eye, why should they?

The *Lechem Mishneh* explains that the Rambam's intent is that if the owner seizes payment for the eye from the witnesses, he is allowed to retain possession. The *Emek*

לְפִיכָךְ, אִם הֵעִידוּ עָלָיו שֶׁאָכַל פֵּרוֹת אוֹ שִׁבֵּר כֵּלִים בְּדֶרֶךְ הִלּוּכוֹ - מְשַׁלְּמִין נֶזֶק שָׁלֵם. וְכֵן כֹּל כַּיּוֹצֵא בָּזֶה.

ד הֵעִידוּ עַל פְּלוֹנִי שֶׁהִפִּיל שֵׁן עַבְדּוֹ וְאַחַר כָּךְ סִמֵּא אֶת עֵינוֹ, וְהוּזַמּוּ - מְשַׁלְּמִין לָאָדוֹן דְּמֵי הָעֶבֶד וּדְמֵי עֵינוֹ.

הֵעִידוּ שֶׁסִּמֵּא אֶת עֵינוֹ וְאַחַר כָּךְ הִפִּיל אֶת שִׁנּוֹ, וְהוּזַמּוּ, וְנִמְצָא הַדָּבָר הֵפֶךְ, שֶׁהָאָדוֹן הִפִּיל אֶת שִׁנּוֹ וְאַחַר כָּךְ סִמֵּא אֶת עֵינוֹ - מְשַׁלְּמִין דְּמֵי עַיִן לָעֶבֶד. וְכֵן כֹּל כַּיּוֹצֵא בָּזֶה.

ה עֵדֵי קִנּוּי וּסְתִירָה שֶׁהוּזַמּוּ - לוֹקִין.

בָּא עֵד אֶחָד וְהֵעִיד שֶׁזָּנְתָה אַחַר קִנּוּי וּסְתִירָה, [וְנִמְצָא אוֹתוֹ הָעֵד זוֹמֵם - מְשַׁלֵּם כְּתֻבָּתָהּ.

הָיוּ שְׁנַיִם, וְהֵן עֵדֵי הַקִּנּוּי וְהַסְּתִירָה וְהַטֻּמְאָה], וְנִמְצְאוּ זוֹמְמִין - מְשַׁלְּמִין כְּנֶגֶד הַכְּתֻבָּה, וְאֵין לוֹקִין. וְלָמָּה לֹא יֵהָרְגוּ, וַהֲרֵי הֵעִידוּ בְּטֻמְאָה? לְפִי שֶׁלֹּא הִתְרוּ בָּהּ.

HaMelech states that the Rambam is indeed speaking about a situation where the master gave the servant a deed of release before damaging his eye. The Radbaz, however, gives a straightforward answer. It is very likely that the servant will seize the master's property. Hence it is considered as if the testimony of the witnesses would have caused him this loss as well.

13. *Bava Kama* 73b states that this refers to the following situation: Witnesses testified that the master knocked out the servant's tooth and blinded his eye. Afterwards, a second pair of witnesses testified that the master blinded the servant's eye and afterwards knocked out his tooth. In doing so, they wished to reduce the payment due the servant, for the damages due for the loss of a tooth are substantially lower than those due for the loss of an eye. Therefore if it is discovered that they lied, they are required to make restitution to the servant.

14. Minus the worth of the tooth.

15. For a woman to be tried as a *sotah*, her husband must issue a warning in the presence of witnesses and then witnesses must observe her entering into privacy with the other man.

16. Only one witness is involved. Nevertheless, in this instance, the testimony of one lying witness has an effect, for - as stated in *Hilchot Sotah* 1:14 - we believe the word of one witness in such circumstances. Hence the laws of a lying witness apply to him.

17. Since they say that she committed adultery, it is obvious that they wish to deprive her of the money due her by virtue of her *ketubah*. For if their intent was merely to cause her to be forbidden to her husband, that is achieved by testifying that she disobeyed the warning (*Merkevat HaMishneh*).

18. For a defendant is never required both to make financial restitution and to be lashed, as stated in Chapter 18, Halachah 1.

19. A transgression punishable by execution.

20. And since she was not warned, she could not be executed (*Hilchot Sanhedrin* 12:1-2). Hence, the witnesses were merely conspiring to cause her financial loss. Hence, that is the punishment they are subjected to.

6. If [the lying witnesses] testified that a person stole and slaughtered or sold[21] [the stolen] animal,[22] should they be disqualified through *hazamah*, they are required to pay the entire amount. If two [witnesses] testify that the person stole and two others that he slaughtered or sold [the animal], and both pairs of witnesses are disqualified through *hazamah*, the first [witnesses] are required to pay twice the animal's worth,[23] and the second pair, two or three times its worth.[24]

If the second pair alone were disqualified through *hazamah*, the thief is required to make a double payment to his victim.[25] The later witnesses must pay [the remainder of] the four and five time payment. If one of the last witnesses is disqualified through *hazamah*, the entire last testimony is negated.[26] If one of the first witnesses is disqualified through *hazamah*, the entire testimony is negated.[27] For if there is no theft, slaughtering it or selling [the animal] does not obligate the person to pay anything.[28]

7. When two [witnesses] testify that a person benefited from the produce of a field for three years[29] and are disqualified through *hazamah*, they must pay the worth of the field to its owner.[30] If two [witnesses] testify that a person benefited from the produce of a field for one year, two [others testified] that he benefited from its produce for a second year, and two [others testified] that he benefited from its produce for a third year, should they all be disqualified through *hazamah*, they divide the value of the field among themselves.[31] For although the testimony concerning the establishment of [the claimant's] right to the field involves three [separate] testimonies,[32] there is [only] one testimony with regard to disqualification through *hazamah*.[33]

For this reason, when there are three brothers and one other person, that person may join together with all three of the brothers and testify with regard to one [of the years]. Although they are three testimonies,[34] they are considered as one testimony with regard to disqualification through *hazamah*. If they are

21. I.e., in the same testimony, the witnesses mention both of these points. We are forced to say this, because the Rambam maintains (Chapter 10, Halachah 4) that the testimony of a lying witness is negated retroactively and he is disqualified from the time he testified in court. Otherwise, if the witnesses were disqualified because of their statements concerning theft, they would not be obligated with regard to their statements concerning the animal's slaughter or sale (Radbaz, *Kessef Mishneh*).
22. Thus incurring the obligation to pay four of five times the worth of the animal (Exodus 21:37).
23. The double payment obligated of any thief.
24. Since it is their testimony which causes the defendant to be obligated for the greater amount, the lying witnesses are responsible to pay that amount when they are disqualified through *hazamah*.
25. For the testimony of the first pair of witnesses obligates him.
26. As stated in Chapter 5, Halachah 3, when the testimony of one witness is disqualified, the legal power of the entire testimony is nullified. Since the testimony concerning the slaughter or the sale is nullified, the thief is held liable only for the double payment

ו שְׁנַיִם שֶׁהֵעִידוּ עַל זֶה שֶׁגָּנַב וְטָבַח אוֹ מָכַר, וְהוּזַמּוּ - מְשַׁלְּמִין אֶת הַכֹּל. הֵעִידוּ שְׁנַיִם שֶׁגָּנַב, וְהֵעִידוּ שְׁנַיִם אֲחֵרִים שֶׁטָּבַח אוֹ מָכַר, וְהוּזַמּוּ אֵלּוּ וָאֵלּוּ - הֲרֵי הָרִאשׁוֹנִים מְשַׁלְּמִין תַּשְׁלוּמֵי כֶּפֶל, וְאַחֲרוֹנִים מְשַׁלְּמִין שְׁנַיִם וּשְׁלֹשָׁה. הוּזַמּוּ הָאַחֲרוֹנִים בִּלְבַד - הֲרֵי הַגַּנָּב מְשַׁלֵּם תַּשְׁלוּמֵי כֶּפֶל, וְהָעֵדִים הָאַחֲרוֹנִים מְשַׁלְּמִין לַגַּנָּב תַּשְׁלוּמֵי אַרְבָּעָה וַחֲמִשָּׁה. נִמְצָא אֶחָד מִן הָאַחֲרוֹנִים זוֹמֵם - בָּטְלָה עֵדוּת שְׁנִיָּה. נִמְצָא אֶחָד מִן הָרִאשׁוֹנִים זוֹמֵם - בָּטְלָה כָּל הָעֵדוּת; שֶׁאִם אֵין גְּנֵבָה - אֵין הַטְּבִיחָה אוֹ הַמְּכִירָה מְחַיַּבְתּוֹ לְשַׁלֵּם כְּלוּם.

ז שְׁנַיִם שֶׁהֵעִידוּ שֶׁאָכַל שָׂדֶה זוֹ שָׁלֹשׁ שָׁנִים, וְנִמְצְאוּ זוֹמְמִין - מְשַׁלְּמִין לְבַעַל הַשָּׂדֶה דְּמֵי הַשָּׂדֶה. הֵעִידוּ שְׁנַיִם שֶׁאֲכָלָהּ שָׁנָה רִאשׁוֹנָה, וּשְׁנַיִם שֶׁאֲכָלָהּ שָׁנָה שְׁנִיָּה, וּשְׁנַיִם שֶׁאֲכָלָהּ שָׁנָה שְׁלִישִׁית, וְהוּזַמּוּ כֻּלָּן - מְשַׁלְּשִׁין בֵּינֵיהֶן. שֶׁאַף עַל פִּי שֶׁעֵדוּת הַחֲזָקָה שָׁלֹשׁ עֵדֻיּוֹת הֵן - הֲרֵי הֵן כְּעֵדוּת אַחַת לַהֲזָמָּה. לְפִיכָךְ, שְׁלֹשָׁה אַחִים, וְאֶחָד מִצְטָרֵף עִם כָּל אֶחָד וְאֶחָד, וְהֵעִידוּ בְּשָׁנָה שָׁנָה - הֲרֵי אֵלּוּ שָׁלֹשׁ עֵדֻיּוֹת, וְתִתְקַיֵּם בָּהֶן הַחֲזָקָה, וְהֵן כְּעֵדוּת אַחַת לַהֲזָמָּה;

associated with theft. The second pair of witnesses are not liable to pay, however, for financial responsibility is incurred only when both witnesses are disqualified through *hazamah* (Chapter 20, Halachah 1).

27. I.e., not only the testimony of the first pair of witnesses, but also the testimony of the second pair. Since the entire testimony is nullified, the defendant is under no financial obligation. And since only one witness was disqualified through *hazamah*, none of the witnesses are liable financially.

28. We do not have any definite knowledge that the presumed thief obtained the animal illegally. Perhaps the owner gave it to him and he slaughtered or sold an animal that belonged to him.

29. As stated in *Hilchot Toen ViNitan* 11:2, when a person claims that a field has been sold to him and produces witnesses who testify that he benefited from its produce for three consecutive years, he is presumed to be the owner.

30. For through their testimony, the plaintiff's claim to the field would have been substantiated.

31. Each of the witnesses paying one sixth.

32. Since each pair of witnesses speaks about only one year, and the claim to the field is only established when all three testimonies are joined together, one might suppose that none of the testimonies is significant in its own right. Moreover, even if the witnesses claim that they did not come to testify about the ownership of the field, merely about to whom the crops belong, we reject their claim. The rationale is that they are aware that the plaintiff is claiming ownership over the entire field and using their testimony to support his claim (*Bava Batra* 56a).

33. And hence, the value of the field is divided among all of them equally and they are not obligated to make financial restitution unless they are all disqualified through *hazamah*.

34. Despite the fact that generally the testimony of two close relatives on one matter is not accepted, in this instance the testimony is accepted, because each brother is testifying regarding a separate matter.

all disqualified through *hazamah*, the three brothers must [together] pay half the value of the field and the person who joined together with each of them must pay the [other] half of its value.

8. [Different rules apply when] an ox is declared to have a tendency to gore on the basis of the testimony of three groups of witnesses.[35] If the first and the second pair of witnesses are disqualified through *hazamah*, all [of the witnesses] are released from liability.[36] If all three [sets of witnesses] are disqualified, they are all obligated to pay for the entire damages[37] even though half-damages are paid for an ordinary ox.

When does the above apply? When [the witnesses] are all motioning to each other,[38] or they appear directly after each other,[39] or they know the identity of the owner of the ox, but do not recognize the ox itself.[40] If none of these factors are present, the first and the second group [of witnesses] are not liable, for they will say: "We came only to obligate him to pay half-damages.[41] We did not know that subsequently another group would come and cause [the ox] to be deemed as a goring ox."

9. [The following law applies when] two people testified with regard to a "wayward and rebellious son"[42] with regard to the first testimony and two others came afterwards and testified with regard to the second testimony which would cause him to be executed. If they are both disqualified through *hazamah*, the first group is lashed and not executed. [The rationale is that] they can say: "We came to have him lashed."[43] The second group, however, is executed, because it is their testimony that causes him to be executed.[44] If the second group consisted of four [witnesses]: Two said: "In our presence, he stole," and two said: "In our presence, he feasted," should they [all] be disqualified through *hazamah*, they are all executed.[45]

If two witnesses testify that a person kidnapped a Jewish person and sold him, and they were disqualified through *hazamah*, they should be executed by strangulation.[46] If two witnesses testified that [a person] kidnapped [a fellow

35. As explained in *Hilchot Nizkei Mammon*, ch. 1, when an ox has a tendency to gore (*mu'ad*), the owner is obligated to pay full damages for any injury it causes. When an ordinary ox (*tam*) causes damage by goring, by contrast, the owner is required to pay only half the amount. Witnesses must testify that an ox caused damage by goring on three occasions for the status of an ox to change.

36. I.e., they are not liable to pay the full damages required when an ox which is *mu'ad* gores. They are, however, required to pay the half-damages required for testifying that an ordinary ox gored, as stated in Halachah 3.

37. Based on the gloss of the *Kessef Mishneh*, we interpret this to mean that they are obligated to pay the decrease in the value of the ox that was caused by it being deemed as *mu'ad*. For from this point on, the owner would be obligated to pay full damages rather than half damages.

38. Since they are motioning to each other, they are obviously one group who joined together with a common intent.

שֶׁאִם הוּזַמּוּ כֻּלָּן – הֲרֵי שְׁלֹשָׁה הָאַחִין מְשַׁלְּמִין חֲצִי דְּמֵי הַשָּׂדֶה, וְזֶה שֶׁנִּצְטָרֵף עִם כָּל אֶחָד מֵהֶן מְשַׁלֵּם חֲצִי דָּמֶיהָ.

ח שָׁלֹשׁ כִּתֵּי עֵדִים שֶׁנִּתְקַיְּמוּ בְּעֵדוּתָן שֶׁשּׁוֹר זֶה מוּעָד, וְנִמְצָאת כַּת רִאשׁוֹנָה וּשְׁנִיָּה זוֹמְמִין – כֻּלָּן פְּטוּרִין. נִמְצְאוּ שְׁלָשְׁתָּן זוֹמְמִין – כֻּלָּן חַיָּבִין לְשַׁלֵּם הַנֶּזֶק; שֶׁאַף עַל פִּי שֶׁהוּא תָּם, מְשַׁלֵּם חֲצִי נֶזֶק.

בַּמֶּה דְּבָרִים אֲמוּרִים? כְּשֶׁהָיוּ כֻּלָּן רוֹמְזִין זֶה אֶת זֶה, אוֹ שֶׁבָּאוּ רְצוּפִין, אוֹ שֶׁהָיוּ מַכִּירִין בַּעַל הַשּׁוֹר וְלֹא הִכִּירוּ הַשּׁוֹר; אֲבָל אִם אֵין שָׁם אַחַת מֵאֵלּוּ – הֲרֵי כַּת רִאשׁוֹנָה וּשְׁנִיָּה פְּטוּרִין; שֶׁהֲרֵי הֵן אוֹמְרִין: לֹא בָּאנוּ אֶלָּא לְחַיְּבוֹ חֲצִי נֶזֶק, וְלֹא יָדַעְנוּ שֶׁתָּבוֹא כַּת אַחֶרֶת וְיֵעָשֶׂה מוּעָד.

ט וְכֵן שְׁנַיִם שֶׁהֵעִידוּ בְּבֵן סוֹרֵר וּמוֹרֶה עֵדוּת הָרִאשׁוֹנָה, וּבָאוּ שְׁנַיִם אַחֲרֵיהֶם וְהֵעִידוּ עָלָיו עֵדוּת הָאַחֲרוֹנָה שֶׁבָּהּ יֵהָרֵג, וְהוּזַמּוּ שְׁתֵּיהֶן – כַּת הָרִאשׁוֹנָה לוֹקָה וְאֵינָהּ נֶהֱרֶגֶת, מִפְּנֵי שֶׁיְּכוֹלִים לוֹמַר: לְהַלְקוֹתוֹ בָּאנוּ; אֲבָל כַּת הָאַחֲרוֹנָה נֶהֱרֶגֶת, שֶׁעַל פִּיהֶן בִּלְבַד הוּא נֶהֱרָג. הָיְתָה הַכַּת הָאַחֲרוֹנָה אַרְבָּעָה, שְׁנַיִם אוֹמְרִים: בְּפָנֵינוּ גָּנַב, וּשְׁנַיִם אוֹמְרִים: בְּפָנֵינוּ אָכַל, וְהוּזַמּוּ – כֻּלָּן נֶהֱרָגִין. הֵעִידוּ שְׁנַיִם שֶׁזֶּה גָּנַב נֶפֶשׁ מִיִּשְׂרָאֵל וּמְכָרוֹ, וְהוּזַמּוּ – הֲרֵי אֵלּוּ נֶחֱנָקִין.

39. The fact that they come in direct succession indicates that their intent is to have the goring ox deemed as *mu'ad* and not to have its owner required to pay for the other damages it caused.
40. In this instance, it is obvious that their intent is not to obligate the owner to pay the half-damages for the goring of an ordinary ox. For damages caused by an ordinary ox are collected only from the body of the ox itself. Since the ox is not identified, one cannot say that the witnesses had that intent. Instead, they were seeking to establish that there is a goring ox in the owner's herd. Once this is established, he is required to watch the entire herd, lest the goring ox damage other animals. See *Hilchot Nizkei Mammon* 10:3.
41. As required when an ordinary ox gores.
42. The wording is taken from Deuteronomy 21:18 which speaks of parents' efforts to discipline such a son. As explained in *Hilchot Mamrim*, ch. 7, if the son steals from his parents and buys a feast of meat and wine, they may bring him to court and have him lashed. The description of the theft by the witnesses is the first testimony mentioned in the present halachah. Afterwards, if he steals from his parents again for such a feast, they may have him executed. The description of the second theft is the second testimony mentioned here.
43. And nothing more. That was the outcome of their testimony.
44. They cannot say that they merely intended to have him lashed, because it is already public knowledge that he was lashed.
45. For the "wayward son" would not be executed unless their testimonies were combined. Hence, each of them is contributing to his execution and therefore, each deserves to be executed.
46. For, as indicated by Deuteronomy 24:7 (see *Hilchot Geneivah*, ch. 9), that is the punishment which would have been given the defendant.

Jew] and another two testified that he sold him, whether the witnesses who testified that he kidnapped or those who testified that he sold were disqualified through *hazamah*, either group which is disqualified through *hazamah* are executed.[47] [The rationale is that] kidnapping is the beginning of the conviction and condemnation to death of [the defendant].[48]

If two [witnesses] testify that [a person] sold a fellow Jew and were disqualified through *hazamah*, but there were no witnesses that he kidnapped him, [the witnesses] are not liable.[49] [The rationale is that] even if they were not disqualified through *hazamah*, [the defendant] would not have been executed, because he could have excused himself saying: "I sold my servant."

If witnesses who testify to the sale come after the disqualification of the witnesses who testified concerning the kidnapping, they are not executed.[50] [This applies] even if we see that they are motioning to each other.[51]

10. [The following laws apply if a person] spreads a libelous report about his wife,[52] bringing witnesses that she committed adultery after she had been consecrated. If her father brought witnesses who disqualified the witnesses brought by the husband through *hazamah*, [those witnesses] are executed.[53] If the husband brought witnesses who disqualified the witnesses brought by the father through *hazamah*, [those witnesses] are executed and are required to make financial restitution to the husband. They are executed, because the witnesses brought by the husband were condemned to death on the basis of their testimony. They must pay a fine,[54] because the husband was held liable to pay a fine because of their testimony. Thus they are obligated to be executed because of this person and obligated financially, because of another person.[55]

Similarly, when two people testify that a person engaged in relations with a consecrated maiden[56] and they are disqualified through *hazamah*, they are executed and are not required to make a financial payment.[57] If they said: "He engaged in relations with the daughter of so-and-so," and they are disqualified through *hazamah*, they are executed and are required to pay the fine[58] to her father.[59]

47. Although each group is testifying only about half the matter, they are still given capital punishment for the reason the Rambam explains.
48. There is no separate punishment for kidnapping alone. Hence, by testifying that a person kidnapped, a witnesses is already beginning the legal process leading to his execution and there is no other purpose for his testimony.
49. I.e., they are not even given lashes for testifying falsely, for their testimony is of no consequence.
50. For the witnesses to the sale could claim that they did not know that witnesses to the kidnapping would appear.
51. Although in Halachah 8, the fact that witnesses motioned to one an another is considered significant, a distinction can be made. Those laws involve only financial penalties and this case is one involving capital punishment. In the latter instance, we are far more stringent (Radbaz, *Kessef Mishneh*).
52. The Rambam is referring to a specific situation outlined in Deuteronomy 22:13-19 and described in detail in *Hilchot Na'arah*, ch. 3. A husband accuses his new wife of not

הֵעִידוּ שְׁנַיִם שֶׁגְּנָבוֹ, וְהֵעִידוּ שְׁנַיִם אֲחֵרִים שֶׁמְּכָרוֹ, בֵּין שֶׁהוּזַמּוּ עֵדֵי גְנֵבָה בֵּין שֶׁהוּזַמּוּ עֵדֵי מְכִירָה – כָּל כַּת מֵהֶן שֶׁהוּזַמָּה נֶהֱרֶגֶת; שֶׁהַגְּנֵבָה הִיא תְּחִלַּת חִיּוּבוֹ שֶׁל זֶה לְמִיתָה. הֵעִידוּ שְׁנַיִם שֶׁמְּכָרוֹ לְזֶה הַיִּשְׂרָאֵל, וְהוּזַמּוּ, וְלֹא הָיוּ שָׁם עֵדִים שֶׁגְּנָבוֹ – הֲרֵי אֵלּוּ פְּטוּרִין; שֶׁאֲפִלּוּ לֹא הוּזַמּוּ לֹא הָיָה זֶה נֶהֱרָג, מִפְּנֵי שֶׁיָּכוֹל לוֹמַר: עַבְדִּי מָכַרְתִּי. בָּאוּ עֵדֵי גְנֵבָה אַחַר שֶׁהוּזַמּוּ עֵדֵי מְכִירָה, אֲפִלּוּ רָאִינוּ אוֹתָן רוֹמְזִין זֶה אֶת זֶה – אֵין נֶהֱרָגִין.

י מוֹצִיא שֵׁם רַע עַל אִשְׁתּוֹ שֶׁהֵבִיא עֵדִים שֶׁזָּנְתָה כְּשֶׁהִיא אֲרוּסָה, וְהֵבִיא אָבִיהָ עֵדִים וֶהֱזִמּוּם – הֲרֵי עֵדֵי הַבַּעַל נֶהֱרָגִין. חָזַר הַבַּעַל וְהֵבִיא עֵדִים וְהֵזִמּוּ עֵדֵי הָאָב – הֲרֵי עֵדֵי הָאָב נֶהֱרָגִין, וּמְשַׁלְּמִין מָמוֹן לַבַּעַל.

נֶהֱרָגִין – מִפְּנֵי שֶׁעֵדֵי הַבַּעַל נִגְמַר דִּינָם לַהֲרִיגָה בְּעֵדוּתָן, וּמְשַׁלְּמִין קְנָס – מִפְּנֵי שֶׁנִּגְמַר דִּין הַבַּעַל לְשַׁלֵּם קְנָס בְּעֵדוּתָן, וְנִמְצְאוּ חַיָּבִין נְפָשׁוֹת לָזֶה וּמָמוֹן לָזֶה.

וְכֵן שְׁנַיִם שֶׁהֵעִידוּ עַל זֶה שֶׁבָּא עַל נַעֲרָה הַמְאֹרָסָה, וְהוּזַמּוּ – נֶהֱרָגִין וְאֵין מְשַׁלְּמִין; בָּא עַל בִּתּוֹ שֶׁל פְּלוֹנִי, וְהוּזַמּוּ – נֶהֱרָגִין, וּמְשַׁלְּמִין הַקְּנָס לְאָבִיהָ.

being a virgin. If he also brings witnesses that she committed adultery after being consecrated, her infidelity is punishable by execution.

53. For they desired to have the woman executed. The fact that they also sought to have her deprived of the money due her by virtue of her *ketubah* is not significant. For they are not punished twice - capital punishment and making financial restitution - for a wrong against the same person. See *Hilchot Na'arah* 1:13-14.

The *Kessef Mishneh* notes that in *Hilchot Chovel UMazik* 8:12, the Rambam rules that when a pursuer destroys utensils even those belonging to people other than the pursued, he is not held liable financially because he is liable to be killed. A differentiation can be made between that ruling and the present instance, because here the lying witnesses are punished "as they conspired to do to their brother," i.e., according to the punishment they desired each of the involved parties to suffer. See *Tosafot, Ketubot* 31a.

54. The 100 silver pieces which Deuteronomy 22:19 obligates the husband to pay.

55. The principle mentioned in note 53, that a person is not executed and held liable financially for the same transgression applies only when the obligations come about because of wrongs to the same person. In this instance, the witnesses sought to wrong different individuals - the witnesses and the husband - and they must receive the punishment they conspired to have each one given.

56. In which case, he is executed, as stated by Deuteronomy 22:23-24.

57. They are not required to pay the woman the money due her by virtue of her *ketubah* (see the following note). *Sanhedrin* 10a explains that this is speaking about a situation where the witnesses do not identify the woman at all in their testimony. Since she was not singled out, she would not have been held liable. Hence, the witnesses are not liable to her.

58. The Radbaz explains that this is speaking about a situation where, although it is not required, the husband wrote the woman a *ketubah* while she was consecrated, before she was married (see *Hilchot Ishut* 10:11). This is the "fine" that the woman would forfeit for engaging in relations.

59. The money is paid to her father, because he is granted any income his daughter deserves until she attains majority.

[If witnesses testify:] "So-and-so sodomized an ox," and they were disqualified by *hazamah*, they are executed, but not held liable financially.[60] [If they said]: "the ox belonging to so-and-so," they are executed and required to pay the value of the ox to its owner.[61] Similar laws apply in all analogous situations.

CHAPTER TWENTY TWO

1. [The following rules apply when] two groups of witnesses contradict each other.[1] If one witness from one group came [together] with one witness from the other group and [they both] delivered testimony concerning another matter, the testimony is of no consequence. For certainly one of them lied, but we do not know which one.[2]

If one of these groups comes alone and gives testimony and the other group comes alone and gives testimony regarding another matter, we accept the testimony of both groups individually.[3]

2. Reuven produced two promissory notes against Shimon: one for a *maneh*[4] and one for 200 *zuz*. Shimon denied [being obligated] for either of the promissory notes. The witnesses to one of the promissory notes were one of the groups whose testimonies contradicted each other and the witnesses to the other were the second group. Shimon is required to pay only a *maneh*,[5] for the bearer of the promissory note has the position of lesser strength.[6] He must take an oath concerning the remainder.[7]

It appears to me that he must take this oath concerning the remainder while holding a sacred article,[8] as is required of a person who admits a portion of

The witnesses are held liable for both capital punishment and a financial penalty, because two different people are involved: the financial penalty is for the woman's father and capital punishment is for the man and the woman.

60. Since they did not identify the ox, it is obvious that the intent of their testimony was merely to have the accused sodomizer executed. Hence, that is the punishment they are given.

61. In which instance, the ox would also be executed because of their testimony (Leviticus 20:15). Thus the two punishments result from two different involved parties.

1. As explained in Chapter 18, Halachah 2, a contradiction between two groups of witnesses refers to a situation where one group claims that an event took place, e.g., a murder was committed or a loan was given, and another group claims that the event never took place.

2. Since the testimony they originally gave contradicted each other, one of them was certainly not telling the truth. That person is not acceptable as a witness. Although we do not know which one - and hence cannot label either of them as a lying witness - we know that one of them is unacceptable. And thus when they come together, we are certain that at least one of the witnesses is unacceptable.

The *Sefer Meirat Einayim* 31:2 explains that the defendant is not even required to take

פְּלוֹנִי רָבַע הַשּׁוֹר, וְהוּזַמּוּ – נִסְקָלִין וְאֵין מְשַׁלְּמִין; שׁוֹרוֹ שֶׁל פְּלוֹנִי – נִסְקָלִין, וּמְשַׁלְּמִין דְּמֵי הַשּׁוֹר לְבַעַל הַשּׁוֹר. וְכֵן כֹּל כַּיּוֹצֵא בָּזֶה.

פֶּרֶק שְׁנַיִם וְעֶשְׂרִים

א שְׁתֵּי כִּתֵּי עֵדִים הַמַּכְחִישׁוֹת זוֹ אֶת זוֹ, שֶׁבָּא עֵד אֶחָד מִכַּת זוֹ וְעֵד אֶחָד מִכַּת זוֹ וְהֵעִידוּ בְּעֵדוּת אַחֶרֶת – אֵין כָּאן עֵדוּת; שֶׁהֲרֵי בְּוַדַּאי אֶחָד מֵהֶן שַׁקָּר, וְאֵין יָדוּעַ מִי הוּא מִשְּׁנֵיהֶן.

בָּאָה כַּת זוֹ בִּפְנֵי עַצְמָהּ וְהֵעִידָה עֵדוּת, וּבָאָה כַּת זוֹ וְהֵעִידָה עֵדוּת אַחֶרֶת בִּפְנֵי עַצְמָהּ – מְקַבְּלִין כָּל אֶחָד מֵהֶן בִּפְנֵי עַצְמָהּ.

ב רְאוּבֵן שֶׁהוֹצִיא עַל שִׁמְעוֹן שְׁנֵי שְׁטָרוֹת, אֶחָד בְּמָנֶה וְאֶחָד בְּמָאתַיִם, וְכָפַר שִׁמְעוֹן בִּשְׁנֵי הַשְּׁטָרוֹת, וְעֵדֵי שְׁטָר זֶה כַּת אַחַת מֵאוֹתָן הַשְּׁתַּיִם שֶׁהִכְחִישׁוּ זוֹ אֶת זוֹ, וְעֵדֵי הַשְּׁטָר הַשֵּׁנִי הַכַּת הַשְּׁנִיָּה – הֲרֵי שִׁמְעוֹן מְשַׁלֵּם מָנֶה, שֶׁיַּד בַּעַל הַשְּׁטָר עַל הַתַּחְתּוֹנָה, וְיִשָּׁבַע עַל הַשְּׁאָר.

יֵרָאֶה לִי, שֶׁשְּׁבוּעָה זוֹ שֶׁיִּשָּׁבַע עַל הַשְּׁאָר – בִּנְקִיטַת חֵפֶץ, כְּדִין מוֹדֶה בְּמִקְצָת;

an oath, as would be required when one witness testifies in support of the plaintiff. The rationale is that when one of a group of witnesses is disqualified, the entire testimony is of no consequence (Chapter 5, Halachah 3).

3. Since we do not know which of the groups is lying, we do not disqualify either of them. Instead, we follow the basic assumption that every Jew is acceptable as a witness (*Sh'vuot* 47b).

4. 100 *zuz*.

5. I.e., the lesser sum of the two amounts.

6. For he is trying to expropriate funds from the person in possession (see *Hilchot Malveh ViLoveh* 27:15-16). Were the promissory notes to be signed by acceptable witnesses, he would be in a position of strength. In this instance, however, since one of the groups of witnesses certainly lied and is hence disqualified, the plaintiff is put at a disadvantage.

7. After the defendant makes the smaller payment and takes the oath, the larger promissory note is destroyed by the court, so that it could not be used again [*Shulchan Aruch* (*Choshen Mishpat* 31:2)].

The *Shulchan Aruch* continues, stating that the Rambam's ruling applies only in a situation where the plaintiff demands payment for both promissory notes at the same time. If, however, he demands payment for each one individually, his claim is vindicated and the defendant is required to pay both the debts. See Halachah 4.

The Ramah adds that the defendant may require the plaintiff to take an oath that he does not possess two promissory notes. For this reason, he suggests that the plaintiff should burn the smaller promissory note so that he will at least receive payment for the larger one.

8. I.e., holding a Torah scroll or tefillin, as stated in *Hilchot Sh'vuot* 11:8.

the claim lodged [against him].[9] For there are two acceptable witnesses[10] who testify concerning a portion of the money which he denied owing entirely. And the statements of his own mouth should not have greater [legal power] than the testimony of witnesses as we explained.[11]

3. Reuven sued Levi, producing a promissory note [signed by] one of these groups of witnesses. Shimon also sued Levi and produced a promissory note [signed by] the other group. Although Levi denies both debts, both Reuven and Shimon [are given the option of] taking an oath and collecting [what they claim]. [The rationale is that] certainly one of them has [a viable claim] against him.[12] The oath required is a Rabbinic institution as is required of a storekeeper [who takes an oath to collect a claim supported by] his ledger.[13]

4. Reuven sued Shimon producing a promissory note [signed by] one of these groups of witnesses and [sued] Levi, producing a promissory note signed by the other group. If both [defendants] deny [the debts], we follow the principle: "A person who seeks to expropriate money from a colleague must prove [his claim]." Since Reuven cannot validate either of these legal documents,[14] both the promissory notes are like shards.[15] Both of the defendants are required to take [merely] a *sh'vuat heset*[16] and they are released of obligation.[17]

When does the above apply? When the two groups of witnesses come to testify at the same time. [Otherwise,] whenever a person produces a legal document containing testimony of one of these two groups, he may expropriate property based upon it. Afterwards, if either he or another person produce a legal document with testimony from the other group, it can be used to expropriate property whether from the first borrower or from any other person.[18] [The rationale is that it is as if] each of the two groups came alone and testified.[19]

9. I.e., this is a Scriptural oath, and not merely a *sh'vuat hesset* of Rabbinic origin.

10. For at least one of the groups of witnesses is acceptable.

11. As explained in *Hilchot Toen ViNitan* 4:10, when a plaintiff demands 100, the defendant denies the obligation entirely, and witnesses testify that he owes 50, the defendant is required to take a Scriptural oath concerning the remaining 50. The rationale is that just as he would be required to take such an oath had he admitted owing the 50 himself, he is required to take the oath when his obligation is established by the testimony of witnesses.

The Ra'avad and Rabbenu Nissim object to this ruling, explaining - as the Rambam states in *Hilchot Toen ViNitan* 4:4 - that when a person acknowledges a debt recorded in a promissory note, the laws concerning one who admits a portion of a debt do not apply to him. For even were he to deny the debt in this instance, his denial would not be accepted. Similarly, in the case at hand, one could claim that since there is a promissory note involved, there should be no obligation for an oath. Also, a promissory note establishes a lien against landed property and in such instances, an oath is not required.

A distinction can, however, be made. For in this instance, neither of the promissory notes have the power to enable the plaintiff to expropriate property on its basis. Hence the claim resembles one supported by a verbal commitment alone (see *Kessef Mishneh*,

שֶׁהֲרֵי עָלָיו שְׁנֵי עֵדִים כְּשֵׁרִים מְעִידִין בְּמִקְצָת הַמָּמוֹן שֶׁכָּפַר בְּכֻלּוֹ, וְלֹא תְּהֵא הוֹדָאַת פִּיו גְּדוֹלָה מֵהַעֲדָאַת עֵדִים, כְּמוֹ שֶׁבֵּאַרְנוּ.

ג הוֹצִיא רְאוּבֵן שְׁטָר עַל לֵוִי, וְעֵדָיו כַּת אַחַת מִשְׁתֵּיהֶן, וְהוֹצִיא שִׁמְעוֹן שְׁטָר שֵׁנִי עַל לֵוִי, וְעֵדָיו הַכַּת הַשְּׁנִיָּה, וְלֵוִי כּוֹפֵר בִּשְׁנֵיהֶן – הֲרֵי רְאוּבֵן נִשְׁבָּע וְנוֹטֵל, וְשִׁמְעוֹן נִשְׁבָּע וְנוֹטֵל; שֶׁבְּוַדַּאי אֶחָד מֵהֶן יֵשׁ לוֹ אֶצְלוֹ. וּשְׁבוּעָה זוֹ בְּתַקָּנַת חֲכָמִים, כְּדִין חֶנְוָנִי עַל פִּנְקָסוֹ.

ד הוֹצִיא רְאוּבֵן שְׁטָר עַל שִׁמְעוֹן, וְעֵדָיו כַּת אַחַת מֵהֶן, וְהוֹצִיא שְׁטָר שֵׁנִי עַל לֵוִי, וְעֵדָיו הַכַּת הַשְּׁנִיָּה, וְכָל אֶחָד מֵהֶן כּוֹפֵר בּוֹ – הַמּוֹצִיא מֵחֲבֵרוֹ עָלָיו הָרְאָיָה.
הוֹאִיל וְאֵין רְאוּבֵן יָכוֹל לְקַיֵּם אֶחָד מִשְּׁנֵי שְׁטָרוֹת – הֲרֵי כָּל שְׁטָר מֵהֶן כְּחֶרֶס, וּשְׁנֵי הַנִּטְעָנִין נִשְׁבָּעִין הֶסֵּת וְנִפְטָרִין.
בַּמֶּה דְבָרִים אֲמוּרִים? כְּשֶׁבָּאוּ שְׁתֵּי הַכִּתּוֹת לְהָעִיד כְּאַחַת;
אֲבָל כָּל הַמּוֹצִיא שְׁטָר שֶׁיֵּשׁ בּוֹ עֵדוּת כַּת אַחַת מִשְׁתֵּיהֶן – הֲרֵי זֶה גּוֹבֶה בּוֹ;
וְאִם הוֹצִיא אַחַר כָּךְ, בֵּין הוּא בֵּין אַחֵר, שְׁטָר שֶׁיֵּשׁ בּוֹ עֵדוּת הַכַּת הַשְּׁנִיָּה – הֲרֵי זֶה גּוֹבֶה בּוֹ, בֵּין מִלֹּוֶה הָרִאשׁוֹן בֵּין מֵאַחֵר;
שֶׁהֲרֵי כָּל כַּת מִשְׁתֵּיהֶן בָּאָה בִּפְנֵי עַצְמָהּ וְהֵעִידָה.

Radbaz). The *Siftei Cohen* 31:2, however, does not accept these resolutions and states that the Rambam's ruling applies only when the defendant does not own land.

12. Since we do not know which of the claims is valid and which is using lying witnesses, we substantiate them both.

13. See *Hilchot Malveh ViLoveh* 16:5. As the Rambam states there, this oath was instituted to appease the defendant. Since he is obligated to pay two claims and one of them is not legitimate, he is at least given the satisfaction of requiring both of the plaintiffs to take oaths.

14. Because one - and we do not know which one - is based on the testimony of lying witnesses.

15. I.e., of no value.

16. A less severe oath required by our Sages when a defendant denies entirely a claim lodged against him.

17. For each of the defendants can say: "It is the pair of witnesses on the other document that are acceptable. Those who signed my document are liars." Since we don't know which of the defendants' claims to accept - and one is certainly true - we decide in favor of both defendants. For whenever a person is trying to expropriate money, the burden of proof is upon him.

18. Rabbenu Asher and the *Tur* rule that the plaintiff must conduct the suits in two different courts. The *Shulchan Aruch* (*Choshen Mishpat* 31:3) quotes the Rambam's ruling without making this clarification.

19. For as stated in Halachah 1, when each one of the groups comes individually, their testimony is accepted.

5. [The following rules apply when] a person brings witnesses, their testimony is investigated, they were disqualified through *hazamah*, and then he brought other witnesses concerning the same claim and they were also disqualified through *hazamah*. Even [if he brings] 100 groups [who are disqualified], if afterwards, he brings other witnesses regarding that same claim and the testimony of these witnesses is found to be accurate, the case is adjudicated on this basis. Even though the plaintiff can be presumed to bring lying witnesses, we do not operate under the presumption that these witnesses are lying.[20]

When, by contrast, there is a legal document concerning which a protest has been [sustained], i.e., two [witnesses] came and said that [the plaintiff] told them to forge this legal document, we never use that legal document to expropriate [property] even if the authenticity of the signatures of the witnesses is validated.[21]

It appears to me that if the witnesses to the legal document came and testified concerning their signature,[22] [the legal document] may be used to expropriate money.

Blessed be God who provides assistance.

20. I.e., we look at the witnesses as we look at any group of witnesses, assuming that they are telling the truth.

ה מִי שֶׁהֵבִיא עֵדִים וְנֶחְקְרָה עֵדוּתָן וְהוּזַמּוּ, וְחָזַר וְהֵבִיא עֵדִים אֲחֵרִים בְּאוֹתָהּ הַטַּעֲנָה עַצְמָהּ וְהוּזַמּוּ, אֲפִלּוּ מֵאָה כַּת, וְאַחַר כָּךְ הֵבִיא עֵדִים אֲחֵרִים בְּאוֹתָהּ הַטַּעֲנָה עַצְמָהּ, וְנִמְצֵאת עֵדוּת אֵלּוּ הָאַחֲרוֹנִים מְכֻוֶּנֶת - דָּנִין עַל פִּיהֶן.

שֶׁאַף עַל פִּי שֶׁהֻחְזַק זֶה שֶׁטָּעַן טַעֲנָה זוֹ לְהָבִיא עֵדִים שַׁקְּרָנִים - הֲרֵי לֹא הֻחְזְקוּ אֵלּוּ הָעֵדִים הָאַחֲרוֹנִים שֶׁהֵן מְשַׁקְּרִין.

אֲבָל שְׁטָר שֶׁקָּרָא עָלָיו עַרְעָר, וְהוּא שֶׁיָּבוֹאוּ שְׁנַיִם וְיֹאמְרוּ: מִמֶּנּוּ שָׁאַל לְזַיֵּף לוֹ שְׁטָר זֶה, אַף עַל פִּי שֶׁנִּתְקַיֵּם הַשְּׁטָר מֵחוֹתָמָיו - אֵין גּוֹבִין בּוֹ לְעוֹלָם.

וְיֵרָאֶה לִי, שֶׁאִם בָּאוּ עֵדֵי הַשְּׁטָר וְהֵעִידוּ הֵן בְּעַצְמָן עַל כְּתַב יָדָן - גּוֹבִין בּוֹ.

בְּרִיךְ רַחֲמָנָא דְּסַיְּיעָן

21. For we assume that the plaintiff indeed had the legal document forged.

22. As the Rambam states in Chapter 8, Halachot 1 and 4, when witnesses testify with regard to their signature on a legal document, they must testify that the transaction in fact took place. Hence, we rely on their word even if the plaintiff is known to have attempted to perpetrate forgery.

The Radbaz states that even if the witnesses do not remember signing the legal document, since they remember the loan and recognize their signatures, the document is valid. We do not suspect it is a forgery.

HILCHOT MAMRIM

The Laws of the Rebellious Ones

They include nine mitzvot: three positive commandments and six negative commandments: They are:

1. To follow the directives given by the Supreme *Sanhedrin*;
2. Not to deviate from their words;
3. Not to add to the Torah, neither to the mitzvot of the Written Law, nor to their explanation which was transmitted by the Oral Tradition;
4. Not to detract from the mitzvot;
5. Not to curse one's father or mother;
6. Not to strike one's father or mother;
7. To honor one's father and mother;
8. To fear one's father and mother;
9. For a son not to rebel against his father's and mother's instruction.

These mitzvot are explained in the coming chapters.

הִלְכוֹת מַמְרִים

יֵשׁ בִּכְלָלָן תֵּשַׁע מִצְוֹת: שָׁלֹשׁ מִצְוֹת עֲשֵׂה, וְשֵׁשׁ מִצְוֹת לֹא תַעֲשֶׂה, וְזֶה הוּא פְּרָטָן:

א) לַעֲשׂוֹת עַל פִּי הַתּוֹרָה שֶׁאָמְרוּ לָנוּ בֵּית דִּין הַגָּדוֹל.
ב) שֶׁלֹּא לָסוּר מִדִּבְרֵיהֶם.
ג) שֶׁלֹּא לְהוֹסִיף עַל הַתּוֹרָה, לֹא בַּמִּצְוֹת שֶׁבִּכְתָב וְלֹא בְּפֵרוּשָׁן שֶׁלָּמַדְנוּ מִפִּי הַשְּׁמוּעָה.
ד) שֶׁלֹּא לִגְרֹעַ מִן הַכֹּל.
ה) שֶׁלֹּא לְקַלֵּל אָב וָאֵם.
ו) שֶׁלֹּא לְהַכּוֹתָם.
ז) לְכַבְּדָם.
ח) לְיָרְאָם.
ט) שֶׁלֹּא יִהְיֶה הַבֵּן סוֹרֵר וּמוֹרֶה עַל קוֹל אָבִיו וְאִמּוֹ.

וּבֵאוּר מִצְוֹת אֵלּוּ בִּפְרָקִים אֵלּוּ:

CHAPTER ONE

1. The Supreme *Sanhedrin* in Jerusalem[1] are the essence of the Oral Law.[2] They are the pillars of instruction from whom statutes and judgments issue forth for the entire Jewish people. Concerning them, the Torah promises[3] [Deuteronomy 17:11]: "You shall do according to the laws which they shall instruct you...." This is a positive commandment.[4]

Whoever believes in Moses and in his Torah[5] is obligated to make all of his religious acts dependent on [this court] and to rely on them.

2. Any person who does not carry out their directives transgresses a negative commandment,[6] as [*ibid.*] continues: "Do not deviate from any of the statements they relate to you, neither right nor left."[7]

Lashes are not given for the violation of this prohibition, because it also serves as a warning [for a transgression punishable] by execution by the court.[8] For when a sage rebels against the words of [the court], he should be executed by strangulation, as [the following verse] states: "A person who will act deliberately...."

[We are obligated to heed] their words whether they:
a) learned them from the Oral Tradition, i.e., the Oral Law,
b) derived them on the basis of their own knowledge through one of the attributes of Biblical exegesis[9] and it appeared to them that this is [the correct interpretation of] the matter,
c) instituted the matter as a safeguard for the Torah, as was necessary at a specific time. These are the decrees,[10] edicts,[11] and customs[12] [instituted by the Sages].

It is a positive commandment to heed the court with regard to each of these three matters. A person who transgresses any of these [types of] directives transgresses a negative commandment.[13] This is [derived from the continuation of the above verse in the following manner]:

1. I.e., the court of 71 judges described in *Hilchot Sanhedrin* 1:3. Since this book of the *Mishneh Torah* contains the laws pertaining to the establishment of the Supreme *Sanhedrin*, the Rambam mentions the laws governing a person who rebels against that court in the same book (Radbaz).
2. As the Rambam explains in his introduction to the *Mishneh Torah*, from the Written Law alone, it is impossible to know how to observe the mitzvot. Instead, the explanation of their particulars was conveyed by the Oral Tradition from one generation to another. In each generation, the Supreme *Sanhedrin* in Jerusalem was considered the repository of that tradition and given the authority to clarify any and all questions regarding Jewish observance. Moreover, using the accepted principles of Biblical exegesis, they could develop new laws and insights.
3. I.e., the Torah promises that there would be a High Court whose authority we are obligated to heed.
4. *Sefer HaMitzvot* (positive commandment 174) and *Sefer HaChinuch* (mitzvah 495) count this as one of the 613 mitzvot of the Torah.

There are commentaries who maintain that this mitzvah (and the negative commandment in the following halachah) apply only to the High Court which holds

פֶּרֶק רִאשׁוֹן

א בֵּית דִּין הַגָּדוֹל שֶׁבִּירוּשָׁלַיִם הֵם עִקַּר תּוֹרָה שֶׁבְּעַל פֶּה, וְהֵם עַמּוּדֵי הַהוֹרָאָה, וּמֵהֶם חֹק וּמִשְׁפָּט יוֹצֵא לְכָל יִשְׂרָאֵל, וַעֲלֵיהֶן הִבְטִיחָה תוֹרָה. שֶׁנֶּאֱמַר: עַל פִּי הַתּוֹרָה אֲשֶׁר יוֹרוּךָ – זוֹ מִצְוַת עֲשֵׂה. וְכָל הַמַּאֲמִין בְּמֹשֶׁה רַבֵּנוּ וּבְתוֹרָתוֹ – חַיָּב לִסְמֹךְ מַעֲשֵׂה הַדָּת עֲלֵיהֶן וְלִשָּׁעֵן עֲלֵיהֶן.

ב כָּל מִי שֶׁאֵינוֹ עוֹשֶׂה כְּהוֹרָאָתָן – עוֹבֵר בְּלֹא תַעֲשֶׂה, שֶׁנֶּאֱמַר: לֹא תָסוּר מִכָּל הַדָּבָר אֲשֶׁר יַגִּידוּ לְךָ יָמִין וּשְׂמֹאל.

וְאֵין לוֹקִין עַל לָאו זֶה, מִפְּנֵי שֶׁנִּתַּן לְאַזְהָרַת מִיתַת בֵּית דִּין; שֶׁכָּל חָכָם שֶׁמּוֹרֶה עַל דִּבְרֵיהֶם – מִיתָתוֹ בְּחֶנֶק, שֶׁנֶּאֱמַר: וְהָאִישׁ אֲשֶׁר יַעֲשֶׂה בְזָדוֹן וְגוֹמֵר.

אֶחָד דְּבָרִים שֶׁלָּמְדוּ אוֹתָן מִפִּי הַשְּׁמוּעָה, וְהֵם תּוֹרָה שֶׁבְּעַל פֶּה;

וְאֶחָד דְּבָרִים שֶׁלְּמָדוּם מִפִּי דַעְתָּם בְּאַחַת מִן הַמִּדּוֹת שֶׁהַתּוֹרָה נִדְרֶשֶׁת בָּהֶן, וְנִרְאָה בְעֵינֵיהֶם שֶׁדָּבָר זֶה כָּךְ הוּא;

וְאֶחָד דְּבָרִים שֶׁעֲשָׂאוּם סְיָג לַתּוֹרָה, וּלְפִי מַה שֶּׁהַשָּׁעָה צְרִיכָה, וְהֵן הַגְּזֵרוֹת וְהַתַּקָּנוֹת וְהַמִּנְהָגוֹת –

כָּל אֶחָד וְאֶחָד מֵאֵלּוּ הַשְּׁלֹשָׁה דְּבָרִים מִצְוַת עֲשֵׂה לִשְׁמֹעַ לָהֶן, וְהָעוֹבֵר עַל כָּל אֶחָד מֵהֶן – עוֹבֵר בְּלֹא תַעֲשֶׂה.

sessions in the Chamber of Hewn Stone in Jerusalem. If it holds sessions elsewhere, even when sitting with 71 judges, these mitzvot do not apply. There are, however, other authorities who differ and maintain that they apply regardless of where the court holds session. The *Sefer HaChinuch, loc. cit.*, goes even further and maintains that these mitzvot include even the obligation to heed the directives of courts in the present era.

5. I.e., any believing Jew.

6. *Sefer HaMitzvot* (negative commandment 312) and *Sefer HaChinuch* (mitzvah 496) count this as one of the 613 mitzvot of the Torah.

7. On this verse, the *Sifri* comments: "Follow them even if they tell you that left is right."

8. I.e., in the case of a rebellious elder as stated in Chapter 3. See *Hilchot Sanhedrin* 18:2 which states that when a prohibition involves capital punishment, lashes are never given for its violation.

9. E.g., the thirteen principles of Biblical exegesis stated by Rabbi Yishmael at the beginning of the *Sifra* (and quoted in the daily prayers) or other principles of this nature.

10. E.g., the prohibition against eating chicken in milk. See Chapter 2, Halachah 10.

11. E.g., the mitzvah of *eruvin*; see *Hilchot Eruvin* 1:2.

12. E.g., the recitation of *Hallel* on Rosh Chodesh (*Hilchot Chanukah* 3:7).

More particularly, in his Introduction to his Commentary on the Mishnah, the Rambam defines "decrees" as referring to practices instituted to safeguard the observance of the mitzvot, and "edicts" and "customs" as referring to practices instituted on the basis of the sages' understanding or because of mutual consent to regulate social norms or to bring people to a more complete Torah experience.

13. The Ramban (*Hasagot* to *Sefer HaMitzvot*, General Principle 1) challenges the

"According to the laws which they shall instruct you" - this refers to the edicts, decrees, and customs which they instruct people at large [to observe] to strengthen the faith and perfect the world.
"According to the judgment which they relate" - this refers to the matters which they derive through logical analysis employing one of the methods of Biblical exegesis.
"From all things that they will tell you" - This refers to the tradition which they received one person from another.[14]

3. There can never be any difference of opinion with regard to matters received through the Oral Tradition.[15] Whenever a difference of opinion arises with regard to any matter, that shows that it was not received in the tradition from Moses our teacher.

[The following principles apply] with regard to matters derived through logical analysis.[16] If the entire body of the Supreme *Sanhedrin* agrees with regard to them, their consent is [binding]. If there is a difference of opinion, we follow the majority and decide the matter according to the majority. Similarly, with regard to the decrees, edicts, and customs, if a portion [of the judges] perceived that it was necessary to issue a decree, institute an edict, or establish a custom for the people, and a portion perceived that it is not appropriate to issue this decree, institute this edict, or establish this custom, the judges should debate the matter back and forth. [Afterwards, a vote is called,] and we follow the majority and execute the matter according to [the decision of] the majority.

4. When the Supreme *Sanhedrin* was in session, there was never any [prolonged] differences of opinion among the Jewish people. Instead, if a doubt arose in a Jew's mind over any law, he would inquire of the court in his city.[17] If not, the questioner and that court - or its agents - ascend to Jerusalem and ask the court which holds sessions on the Temple Mount.[18] If they know, they will reply to him. If they do not know, everyone[19] comes to the court that holds sessions at the entrance to the Temple Courtyard.[20] If they know, they

Rambam's ruling, stating that if so, anyone who violated a Rabbinic ordinance would be liable for lashing, for in effect he would be violating a Torah commandment. Similarly, the general principle - When there is doubt regarding to a question of Rabbinic Law, we follow the more lenient position, while when there is doubt with regard to a question of Scriptural Law, we follow the more severe position - would not apply. For all matters would involve Scriptural Law.

The *Kiryat Sefer* resolves the Rambam's ruling explaining that at the outset, the Sages established their ordinances with these leniencies in mind.

In *Yayin Malchut*, the Lubavitcher Rebbe explains the difference between the Scriptural commandments and the obligation to heed the rulings of the Rabbis as follows: Scriptural commandments can involve the *cheftza* (the physical substance of the article itself); the article is forbidden. Rabbinic commandments, by contrast, can involve only the *gavra* (the person observing the commandment); he is forbidden to perform the act (*Tzafnat Paneach*, Responsum 33). Hence since with regard to a Scriptural

הֲרֵי הוּא אוֹמֵר: עַל פִּי הַתּוֹרָה אֲשֶׁר יוֹרוּךָ - אֵלּוּ הַתַּקָּנוֹת וְהַגְּזֵרוֹת וְהַמִּנְהָגוֹת, שֶׁיּוֹרוּ בָּהֶם לָרַבִּים כְּדֵי לְחַזֵּק הַדָּת וּלְתַקֵּן הָעוֹלָם;
וְעַל הַמִּשְׁפָּט אֲשֶׁר יֹאמְרוּ - אֵלּוּ דְּבָרִים שֶׁיִּלְמְדוּ אוֹתָן מִן הַדִּין בְּאַחַת מִן הַמִּדּוֹת שֶׁהַתּוֹרָה נִדְרֶשֶׁת בָּהֶן;
מִכָּל הַדָּבָר אֲשֶׁר יַגִּידוּ לְךָ - זוֹ הַקַּבָּלָה שֶׁקִּבְּלוּ אִישׁ מִפִּי אִישׁ.

ג דִּבְרֵי קַבָּלָה - אֵין בָּהֶן מַחֲלֹקֶת לְעוֹלָם. וְכָל דָּבָר שֶׁתִּמְצָא בּוֹ מַחֲלֹקֶת - בְּיָדוּעַ שֶׁאֵינוֹ קַבָּלָה מִמֹּשֶׁה רַבֵּנוּ. וּדְבָרִים שֶׁלְּמֵדִין מִן הַדִּין, אִם הִסְכִּימוּ עֲלֵיהֶן בֵּית דִּין הַגָּדוֹל כֻּלָּן - הֲרֵי הִסְכִּימוּ; וְאִם נֶחְלְקוּ בָּהֶן - הוֹלְכִין אַחַר הָרֹב, וּמוֹצִיאִין הַדִּין אַחַר הָרַבִּים. וְכֵן הַגְּזֵרוֹת וְהַתַּקָּנוֹת וְהַמִּנְהָגוֹת, אִם רָאוּ מִקְצָתָן שֶׁרָאוּי לִגְזֹר גְּזֵרָה אוֹ לְתַקֵּן תַּקָּנָה אוֹ שֶׁיַּנִּיחוּ הָעָם הַמִּנְהָג הַזֶּה, וְרָאוּ מִקְצָתָן שֶׁאֵין רָאוּי לִגְזֹר גְּזֵרָה זוֹ וְלֹא לְתַקֵּן תַּקָּנָה זוֹ וְלֹא לְהַנִּיחַ מִנְהָג זֶה - נוֹשְׂאִין וְנוֹתְנִין אֵלּוּ כְּנֶגֶד אֵלּוּ, וְהוֹלְכִין אַחַר רֻבָּן, וּמוֹצִיאִין הַדָּבָר אַחַר הָרַבִּים.

ד כְּשֶׁהָיָה בֵּית דִּין הַגָּדוֹל קַיָּם, לֹא הָיְתָה מַחֲלֹקֶת בְּיִשְׂרָאֵל. אֶלָּא כָּל דִּין שֶׁנּוֹלַד בּוֹ סָפֵק לְאֶחָד מִיִּשְׂרָאֵל - שׁוֹאֵל לְבֵית דִּין שֶׁבְּעִירוֹ. אִם יָדְעוּ - אָמְרוּ לוֹ; אִם לָאו - הֲרֵי הַשּׁוֹאֵל עִם אוֹתוֹ בֵּית דִּין אוֹ עִם שְׁלוּחָיו עוֹלִין לִירוּשָׁלַיִם וְשׁוֹאֲלִין לְבֵית דִּין שֶׁבְּהַר הַבַּיִת אִם יָדְעוּ - אָמְרוּ לוֹ; אִם לָאו - הַכֹּל בָּאִין לְבֵית דִּין שֶׁעַל פֶּתַח הָעֲזָרָה.

Commandment, the object itself becomes forbidden, we rule more stringently. With regards to a Rabbinic commandment, by contrast, since the object itself is not involved, there is room for leniency.

14. Extending back to Moses at Sinai.

15. Note the Rambam's Introduction to his Commentary on the Mishnah, where he elaborates on this subject explaining that there was never any difference of opinion among the Jewish people about which species to use on Sukkos. Although the descriptions of some of the four species in the Torah do not give clear indications which species to use, the Jewish people have always employed the same four. Similarly, in all courts throughout our people's history, "An eye for an eye" (Exodus 21:24), has always been interpreted as referring to financial payment, not actually gouging a person's eye out. These and other similar matters have always been universally accepted.

16. I.e., points derived through the accepted principles of Biblical exegesis.

17. As stated in *Hilchot Sanhedrin* 1:3-4, a court of 23 judges should be established for every city with at least 120 inhabitants. If there are less, a court of three judges is established.

18. See *Hilchot Sanhedrin* 1:3 with regard to the description of the courts mentioned in this and the following clause.

19. I.e., the questioner, the judges of his local court, and the judges of the court on the Temple Mount.

20. I.e., within the Women's Courtyard, before the Nikanor Gates that lead to the Temple Courtyard.

will reply to him, if they do not know, everyone comes to the Chamber of Hewn Stone, to the Supreme *Sanhedrin*, and presents the question. If the matter that was unresolved by all [the others] was known to the Supreme *Sanhedrin* - either as part of the Oral Tradition or because of its derivation through the principles [of exegesis] - they relate [the decision] immediately. If, however, the decision was unclear to the Supreme *Sanhedrin*, they deliberate about the matter at that time and debate it back and forth until they reach a uniform decision, or until a vote is taken. [In such a situation,] they follow the majority and then tell all the questioners: "This is the halachah." [The questioners] then all depart.

After the Supreme *Sanhedrin* was nullified, differences of opinion multiplied among the Jewish people.[21] One would rule [an article] is impure and support his ruling with a rationale and another would rule that it is pure and support his ruling with a rationale. This one would rule [an article] is forbidden and this would rule that it is permitted.

5. [The following rules apply when] there are two sages or two courts that have differing opinions in an age when there was no [Supreme] *Sanhedrin* or during the time when [the Supreme *Sanhedrin*] was still undecided concerning the matter[22] - whether in one age or in two different ages[23] - one rules that an article is pure and one rules that it is impure, one forbids [an article's use] and one permits it. If one does not know in which direction the law tends, [should the matter involve a question] of Scriptural Law, follow the more severe opinion. [If it involve a question] of Rabbinic Law, follow the more lenient opinion.

CHAPTER TWO

1. When, using one of the principles of exegesis, the Supreme *Sanhedrin* derived a law through their perception of the matter and adjudicated a case accordingly,[1] and afterwards, another court arose[2] and they perceived another rationale on which basis, they would revoke [the previous ruling], they may revoke it and rule according to their perception. [This is reflected by

21. See *Sanhedrin* 88b which states: "When the students of the Schools of Shammai and Hillel who had not studied under their masters sufficiently multiplied, differences of opinion increased among the Jewish people and it became as if there were two Torahs." See also the discussion of the matter in the Rambam's Introduction to His Commentary on the Mishnah.

22. I.e., the Supreme *Sanhedrin* had not reached a decision, and an action had to be taken immediately (see *Lechem Mishneh*).

Our translation follows the version in the standard printed texts of the *Mishneh Torah*. According to certain authoritative manuscripts and early printings, the version is "or the

אִם יָדְעוּ – אָמְרוּ לָהֶן; וְאִם לָאו – הַכֹּל בָּאִין לְלִשְׁכַּת הַגָּזִית לְבֵית דִּין הַגָּדוֹל וְשׁוֹאֲלִין.
אִם הָיָה הַדָּבָר שֶׁנּוֹלַד בּוֹ הַסָּפֵק לַכֹּל יָדוּעַ אֵצֶל בֵּית דִּין הַגָּדוֹל, בֵּין מִפִּי הַקַּבָּלָה בֵּין מִפִּי הַמִּדָּה שֶׁדָּנוּ בָּהּ – אוֹמְרִים מִיָּד;
אִם לֹא הָיָה הַדָּבָר בָּרוּר אֵצֶל בֵּית דִּין הַגָּדוֹל – דָּנִין בּוֹ בְּשַׁעְתָּן, וְנוֹשְׂאִין וְנוֹתְנִין בַּדָּבָר עַד שֶׁיַּסְכִּימוּ כֻּלָּן, אוֹ יַעַמְדוּ לְמִנְיָן וְיֵלְכוּ אַחַר הָרֹב, וְיֹאמְרוּ לְכָל הַשּׁוֹאֲלִים: כָּךְ הֲלָכָה, וְהוֹלְכִין לָהֶן.
מִשֶּׁבָּטַל בֵּית דִּין הַגָּדוֹל רָבְתָה מַחֲלֹקֶת בְּיִשְׂרָאֵל, זֶה מְטַמֵּא וְנוֹתֵן טַעַם לִדְבָרָיו, וְזֶה מְטַהֵר וְנוֹתֵן טַעַם לִדְבָרָיו; זֶה אוֹסֵר, וְזֶה מַתִּיר.

ה שְׁנֵי חֲכָמִים אוֹ שְׁנֵי בָּתֵּי דִינִין שֶׁנֶּחְלְקוּ שֶׁלֹּא בִּזְמַן הַסַּנְהֶדְרִין, אוֹ עַד שֶׁלֹּא הָיָה הַדָּבָר בָּרוּר לָהֶן, בֵּין בִּזְמַן אֶחָד בֵּין בָּזֶה אַחַר זֶה, אֶחָד מְטַהֵר וְאֶחָד מְטַמֵּא, אֶחָד אוֹסֵר וְאֶחָד מַתִּיר, אִם אֵינְךָ יוֹדֵעַ לְהֵיכָן הַדִּין נוֹטֶה: בְּשֶׁל תּוֹרָה – הַלֵּךְ אַחַר הַמַּחְמִיר, בְּשֶׁל סוֹפְרִים – הַלֵּךְ אַחַר הַמֵּקֵל.

פֶּרֶק שֵׁנִי

א בֵּית דִּין גָּדוֹל שֶׁדָּרְשׁוּ בְּאַחַת מִן הַמִּדּוֹת כְּפִי מַה שֶּׁנִּרְאָה בְּעֵינֵיהֶם שֶׁהַדִּין כָּךְ, וְדָנוּ דִין, וְעָמַד אַחֲרֵיהֶם בֵּית דִּין אַחֵר, וְנִרְאָה לוֹ טַעַם אַחֵר לִסְתֹּר אוֹתוֹ – הֲרֵי זֶה סוֹתֵר, וְדָן כְּפִי מַה שֶּׁנִּרְאֶה בְּעֵינָיו.

matter did not reach them," i.e., the decision had to be made before the matter could be taken to the High Court.

23. From the Rambam's wording, one might think that if a later court comes to a decision based on their appreciation of the subject, the principles mentioned below are followed despite the fact that a previous court had ruled differently. Even if the former court was greater in wisdom and in the number of adherents (see Chapter 2, Halachot 1-2), the latter court's decision may be followed, as stated by Rabbi Yehoshua ben Korcha in *Avodah Zarah* 7a (see *Kessef Mishneh*).

Rav Moshe HaCohen and the *Lechem Mishneh* differ and cite a responsum of the Rashba (Vol. I, Responsum 253) which states that the ruling depends on which court is greater in wisdom and in the number of adherents. The Rashba does state there is room for leniency if the matter involves a major loss. This view is cited by the Ramah (*Choshen Mishpat* 25:2).

1. I.e., not only did they teach the matter in theory, they actually had their conception applied in practice.

2. It would appear that this would apply even if the later court was lesser in wisdom and in the number of adherents than the court that made the original ruling (Radbaz).

Deuteronomy 17:9]: "To the judge who will be in that age."[3] [This indicates] that a person is obligated to follow only the court in his own generation.[4]

2. [The following rules apply when] a court[5] issued a decree, instituted an edict, or established a custom[6] and this practice spread throughout the Jewish people[7] and another court arose and sought to nullify the original order and eliminate the original edict, decree, or custom. [The later court] does not have [this authority] unless it surpasses the original court in wisdom[8] and in its number of adherents.[9] If it surpasses the original court in wisdom, but not in the number of adherents, or in the number of adherents, but not in wisdom, it cannot nullify its rulings. Even if the rationale for which the original court instituted the decree or the edict is nullified, the later court does not have the authority to negate [their rulings] unless they are greater.[10]

How is it possible that [the later court] will surpass [the original court] in number? For every [Supreme *Sanhedrin*] consists of 71 judges.[11] [The intent is] the number of sages in the generation who consent and accept the matter stated by the Supreme *Sanhedrin* without opposing it.

3. When does the above apply? With regard to matters that were not forbidden to create a safeguard for the words of the Torah, but rather [resemble] other Torah laws. [A different principle applies,] by contrast, with

3. *Rosh HaShanah* 25b states: "Would you think that a person would go to a judge that was not in his age? Instead, the intent is that he should follow the judge in his age.... Yerubaal in his generation is like Moses in his generation. Yiftach in his generation is like Samuel in his generation." Although Yerubaal and Yiftach represented - to make an understatement - less than the epitome of wisdom and righteousness, a person in their generation was enjoined to follow the rulings of their courts.

The concept that a lesser court can challenge the rulings of a previous court of greater stature appears to be supported by the Rambam's statements in his Introduction to the *Mishneh Torah* where he states that after the conclusion of the Talmud, the *Geonim* of one generation can challenge the rulings of the *Geonim* who preceded them. Nevertheless, it appears to be contradicted by his statements there that no later sage can challenge the rulings made by the Sages of the Talmud. Similarly, in the Talmud itself, it appears that the Sages of the Gemorah (the *Amoraim*) would not challenge the rulings of the Sages of the Mishnah. Thus it would seem that there were cut-off points at which the Sages of one generation would not challenge the rulings of the Sages of previous generations.

The *Kessef Mishneh* explains that it is possible to explain that, after the conclusion of the Mishnah, all the Sages accepted the general principle not to challenge the rulings of the Mishnah, and similarly, after the conclusion of the Talmud, not to challenge the rulings of the Talmud. When, however, there are no general principles of this nature in effect, the principle stated by the Rambam in this halachah applies. See also *Hilchot Sanhedrin* 6:1.

4. The *Or Sameach* relates that this principle explains why the Rambam calls the laws derived through the principles of Biblical exegesis, *divrei sofrim*, "the words of the Sages." For their interpretation is dependent upon the Sages of each generation.

שֶׁנֶּאֱמַר: אֶל הַשֹּׁפֵט אֲשֶׁר יִהְיֶה בַּיָּמִים הָהֵם – אֵינְךָ חַיָּב לָלֶכֶת אֶלָּא אַחַר בֵּית דִּין שֶׁבְּדוֹרְךָ.

ב בֵּית דִּין שֶׁגָּזְרוּ גְזֵרָה אוֹ תִקְּנוּ תַקָּנָה וְהִנְהִיגוּ מִנְהָג, וּפָשַׁט הַדָּבָר בְּכָל יִשְׂרָאֵל, וְעָמַד אַחֲרֵיהֶם בֵּית דִּין אַחֵר וּבִקֵּשׁ לְבַטֵּל דְּבָרִים הָרִאשׁוֹנִים, וְלַעֲקֹר אוֹתָהּ הַתַּקָּנָה וְאוֹתָהּ הַגְּזֵרָה וְאוֹתוֹ הַמִּנְהָג – אֵינוֹ יָכוֹל עַד שֶׁיִּהְיֶה גָדוֹל מִן הָרִאשׁוֹנִים בְּחָכְמָה וּבְמִנְיָן.
הָיָה גָדוֹל בְּחָכְמָה אֲבָל לֹא בְמִנְיָן, בְּמִנְיָן אֲבָל לֹא בְחָכְמָה – אֵינוֹ יָכוֹל לְבַטֵּל אֶת דְּבָרָיו. אֲפִלּוּ בָּטַל הַטַּעַם שֶׁבִּגְלָלוֹ גָּזְרוּ הָרִאשׁוֹנִים אוֹ הִתְקִינוּ – אֵין הָאַחֲרוֹנִים יְכוֹלִין לְבַטֵּל עַד שֶׁיִּהְיוּ גְדוֹלִים מֵהֶם.
וְהֵיאַךְ יִהְיוּ גְדוֹלִים מֵהֶם בְּמִנְיָן, הוֹאִיל וְכָל בֵּית דִּין וּבֵית דִּין שֶׁל שִׁבְעִים וְאֶחָד הוּא? זֶה מִנְיַן חַכְמֵי הַדּוֹר, שֶׁהִסְכִּימוּ וְקִבְּלוּ הַדָּבָר שֶׁאָמְרוּ בֵּית דִּין הַגָּדוֹל וְלֹא חָלְקוּ בּוֹ.

ג בַּמֶּה דְבָרִים אֲמוּרִים? בִּדְבָרִים שֶׁלֹּא אָסְרוּ אוֹתָן כְּדֵי לַעֲשׂוֹת סְיָג לַתּוֹרָה, אֶלָּא כִּשְׁאָר דִּינֵי תוֹרָה;

5. The Supreme *Sanhedrin* as indicated by the following halachah.
6. I.e., instituted a halachic practice on their own authority.
7. See Halachot 5-7.
8. In his Commentary to the Mishnah (*Ediot* 1:5), the Rambam interprets this term as meaning that the head of one court will be more renowned for his wisdom than the head of the other court.
9. The Ra'avad takes issue with the Rambam's statements, maintaining that once a decree has gain widespread acceptance within the Jewish community, it may not be nullified even by the prophet Elijah and his court. The Ra'avad's position is based on *Avodah Zarah* 36a which makes such a statement with regard to the 18 matters in which the School of Shammai's opinion was accepted over that of the School of Hillel's (see *Shabbat* 17a). The Radbaz and the *Kessef Mishneh*, however, explain that these 18 matters represent an exception to the rule (see also the notes to Halachah 3). With regard to other matters, the Rambam's ruling is accepted.
10. *Beitzah* 5b derives this concept from God's directives to the Jewish people before the Giving of the Torah. At first, He forbade sexual relations for three days in preparation for the Giving of the Torah. After the Giving of the Torah, there was a special command for the Jews to resume relations. Otherwise, although the reason for the safeguard had already been nullified - for the Torah had already been given - the original prohibition would have remained in effect.

The Ra'avad takes issue with this concept as well, stating that if the rationale for an edict or decree has been nullified, the edict or decree can be nullified even if the court which does so is lesser than the court which instituted the decree. The Radbaz and the *Kessef Mishneh*, however, support the Rambam's ruling.
11. We have been translating *biminyan*, lit. "in number," as "in the number of adherents," including the Rambam's resolution in the translation of the term from the outset. Others (the Ra'avad in his commentary to *Ediot* 1:5) interpret "in number," as "in age."

regard to matters which the court sought necessary to issue a decree and create a prohibition as a safeguard.[12] If the prohibition spread throughout the Jewish people, another Supreme *Sanhedrin* does not have the authority to uproot [the decree] and grant license even if it was of greater stature than the original [court].[13]

4. A court may, however, suspend the application of such decrees temporarily, even if it is of lesser stature than the original [court]. [The rationale is that] these decrees should not be considered as more severe than the words of the Torah itself,[14] and any court has the authority to abrogate the words of the Torah as a temporary measure.

What is implied? If a court sees that it is necessary to strengthen the faith and create a safeguard so that the people will not violate Torah law, they may apply beatings and punishments[15] that are not sanctioned by Torah.[16] They may not, however, establish the matter for posterity and say that this is the halachah.

Similarly, if they saw that temporarily it was necessary to nullify a positive commandment or violate a negative commandment in order to bring people at large back to the Jewish faith or to prevent many Jews from transgressing in other matters, they may do what is necessary at that time.[17] [To explain by analogy:] Just like a doctor may amputate [a person's] hand or foot so that the person as a whole will live;[18] so, too, at times, the court may rule to temporarily violate some of the commandments so that they will [later] keep all of them. In this vein, the Sages of the previous generations said:[19] "Desecrate one Sabbath for [a person's] sake so that he will keep many Sabbaths."

5. When a court sees it necessary to issue a decree, institute an edict, or establish a custom, they must first contemplate the matter and see whether or

12. This ruling depends on the passage from *Avodah Zarah* 36a cited above. The Rambam maintains that the reason these 18 matters were given such power is because they were instituted as safeguards (Radbaz, *Kessef Mishneh*).
13. See the *Chatam Sofer* (*Yoreh De'ah*, Responsum 13) which states that this ruling applies only when the rationale for which the safeguard was originally instituted still applies. If, however, that rationale was nullified, a court that is of greater stature than the court which instituted the decree may nullify it.
14. I.e., although there are situations where we apply the principle (*Ketubot* 83b): "The words of the Sages are more severe than the words of the Torah," this is not one of them (*Kessef Mishneh*).
15. I.e., even capital punishment as indicated by the following note.
16. In that vein, the Rambam states (*Hilchot Sanhedrin* 24:4, quoting *Sanhedrin* 46a): "An incident occurred where they had a man lashed for engaging in relations with his wife under a tree. And an incident occurred concerning a person who rode on a horse on the Sabbath in the era of the Greeks and they brought him to the court and had him stoned to death."
17. They must, however, clarify that their instructions are given only because of the immediate situation and should not be adopted as a permanent practice. The classic example of this is Elijah's confrontation of the prophets of Baal at Mount Carmel (I

אֲבָל דְּבָרִים שֶׁרָאוּ בֵּית דִּין לִגְזֹר וּלְאָסְרָן לַעֲשׂוֹת סְיָג, אִם פָּשַׁט אִסּוּרָן בְּכָל [יִשְׂרָאֵל] – אֵין בֵּית דִּין גָּדוֹל אַחֵר יָכוֹל לְעָקְרָן וּלְהַתִּירָן, אֲפִלּוּ הָיָה גָּדוֹל מִן הָרִאשׁוֹנִים.

ד וְיֵשׁ לְבֵית דִּין לַעֲקֹר אַף דְּבָרִים אֵלּוּ לְפִי שָׁעָה, אַף עַל פִּי שֶׁהוּא קָטָן מִן הָרִאשׁוֹנִים; שֶׁלֹּא יְהוּ גְזֵרוֹת אֵלּוּ חֲמוּרִין מִדִּבְרֵי תוֹרָה עַצְמָהּ, שֶׁאֲפִלּוּ דִבְרֵי תוֹרָה יֵשׁ לְכָל בֵּית דִּין לְעָקְרוֹ הוֹרָאַת שָׁעָה.
כֵּיצַד? בֵּית דִּין שֶׁרָאוּ לְחַזֵּק הַדָּת וְלַעֲשׂוֹת סְיָג כְּדֵי שֶׁלֹּא יַעַבְרוּ הָעָם עַל דִּבְרֵי תוֹרָה – מַכִּין וְעוֹנְשִׁין שֶׁלֹּא כַּדִּין; אֲבָל אֵין קוֹבְעִין הַדָּבָר לְדוֹרוֹת וְאוֹמְרִים שֶׁהֲלָכָה כָּךְ הוּא.
וְכֵן אִם רָאוּ לְפִי שָׁעָה לְבַטֵּל מִצְוַת עֲשֵׂה אוֹ לַעֲבֹר עַל מִצְוַת לֹא תַעֲשֶׂה, כְּדֵי לְהַחֲזִיר רַבִּים לַדָּת אוֹ לְהַצִּיל רַבִּים מִיִּשְׂרָאֵל מִלְּהִכָּשֵׁל בִּדְבָרִים אֲחֵרִים – עוֹשִׂין לְפִי מַה שֶּׁצְּרִיכָה הַשָּׁעָה.
כְּשֵׁם שֶׁהָרוֹפֵא חוֹתֵךְ יָדוֹ אוֹ רַגְלוֹ שֶׁל זֶה, כְּדֵי שֶׁיִּחְיֶה כֻּלּוֹ; כָּךְ בֵּית דִּין מוֹרִים בִּזְמַן מִן הַזְּמַנִּים לַעֲבֹר עַל קְצָת מִצְוֹת לְפִי שָׁעָה, כְּדֵי שֶׁיִּתְקַיְּמוּ [כֻּלָּם].
כְּדֶרֶךְ שֶׁאָמְרוּ חֲכָמִים הָרִאשׁוֹנִים: חַלֵּל עָלָיו שַׁבָּת אַחַת, כְּדֵי שֶׁיִּשְׁמֹר שַׁבָּתוֹת הַרְבֵּה.

ה בֵּית דִּין שֶׁנִּרְאָה לָהֶן לִגְזֹר גְּזֵרָה אוֹ לְתַקֵּן תַּקָּנָה אוֹ לְהַנְהִיג מִנְהָג – צְרִיכִין לְהִתְיַשֵּׁב

Kings, ch. 18). Although there is both a positive and a negative commandment that requires all sacrifices to be offered in the Temple, Elijah offered a sacrifice on Mt. Carmel to prove God's supremacy to the people. In *Hilchot Yesodei Torah* 9:3, the Rambam discusses the issue within the context of the license granted a prophet to temporarily violate the Torah's commandments, stating:

> If [the people] would have asked Elijah: "How can we violate the Torah's command,"... he would have told them: "...Anyone who offers a sacrifice outside [the Temple's premises] is liable for *karet*... [The present instance,] however, [is an exception]. I am offering a sacrifice... at God's command to disprove the prophets of Baal."

Just as a prophet is empowered to take such license based on God's command, a court may take such license based on their own perception of the situation.

18. In his gloss to this halachah, the Radbaz writes:

> The analogy is not appropriate unless we see the entire Jewish people as one body. Although their bodies separate them, since their souls are hewn out from a single source, they are like one body, for the soul is of primary importance. Know this.
>
> From our master's words, it appears that the analogy applies to the mitzvot. They are like one body and the court may nullify some [of the mitzvot] so [the people] observe the rest. Both interpretations are correct.

According to the first interpretation, the intent is that we may punish some Jews (as quoted from *Hilchot Sanhedrin*) so that the observance of the people at large will remain intact. See also *Berachot* 54a which interprets Psalms 119:126: "It is a time to act for God; they have nullified Your Torah," as "They [i.e., the Sages] may 'nullify Your Torah,' because 'it is a time to act for God.'" The intent is that the sages may violate certain Torah commandments temporarily if they feel that doing so will allow the body of the Torah to remain intact.

19. *Yoma* 85b. See the Rambam's statements in *Hilchot Shabbat* 2:1-3.

not the majority of the community can uphold [the practice].[20] We never issue a decree on the community unless the majority of the community can uphold the practice.

6. If a court issued a decree, thinking that the majority of the community could uphold it and after the decree was issued, the majority of the community raised contentions and the practice did not spread throughout the majority of the community, [the decree] is nullified.[21] [The court] cannot compel the people to accept it.[22]

7. [The following rule applies when a court] issued a decree and thought that it spread among the entire Jewish people and the situation remained unchanged for many years. If, after a long duration of time, another court arose and checked throughout the Jewish community and saw that [the observance of] this decree had not spread throughout the Jewish community,[23] it has the authority to negate [the decree][24] even if it is of lesser stature than the original court in wisdom and in number of adherents.

8. Whenever a court repeals two [decrees], it should not rush to repeal a third decree.[25]

9. A court has the authority to issue a decree and forbid something which is permitted and have its decree perpetuated for generations to come.[26] Similarly, it has the authority - as a temporary measure - to release the Torah's prohibitions.[27] What then is the meaning of the Scriptural prohibitions [Deuteronomy 13:1]: "Do not add to it[28] and do not detract from it"?[29]

[The intent is that] they do not have the authority to add to the words of the Torah or to detract from them, establishing a matter forever as part of Scriptural Law. This applies both to the Written Law and the Oral Law.[30]

20. *Avodah Zarah* 36a derives this concept from the exegesis of a verse. It is, however, logically understood. Regardless of the Sages' positive intent, instituting a practice which people at large cannot uphold will lead to a weakening - and not a strengthening - of Torah observance.

21. I.e., it is not necessary for a subsequent court to undertake a specific action to nullify the decree. If it was not accepted by the community, it is nullified automatically.

One of the classic examples of this concept is Ezra's decree that a person who had a seminal emission is forbidden to recite words of Torah until he immerses himself in a *mikveh*. Most people were unable to observe this custom and therefore it was nullified. See *Hilchot Kriat Shema* 4:8.

22. The Ramah (*Yoreh De'ah* 228:50, based on *Piskei Mahari* 292) rules that individuals also are not obligated to observe such decrees.

23. See the *Kessef Mishneh* who debates whether the intent is that the decree never spread throughout the Jewish community (as is Rashi's view) or that at his time, its observance was not widespread. The latter interpretation would lead to the conclusion that even when originally, the Jewish people had by and large observed a decree, if it is not observed in a

בַּדָּבָר וְלֵידַע תְּחִלָּה אִם רֹב הַצִּבּוּר יְכוֹלִין לַעֲמֹד בָּהֶן אוֹ אִם אֵין יְכוֹלִין לַעֲמֹד. וּלְעוֹלָם אֵין גּוֹזְרִין גְּזֵרָה עַל הַצִּבּוּר, אֶלָּא אִם כֵּן רֹב הַצִּבּוּר יְכוֹלִין לַעֲמֹד בָּהּ.

ו הֲרֵי שֶׁגָּזְרוּ בֵּית דִּין גְּזֵרָה, וְדִמּוּ שֶׁרֹב הַקָּהָל יְכוֹלִין לַעֲמֹד בָּהּ, וְאַחַר שֶׁגְּזָרוּהָ פִּקְפְּקוּ הָעָם בָּהּ וְלֹא פָּשְׁטָה בְּרֹב הַקָּהָל - הֲרֵי זוֹ בְּטֵלָה, וְאֵינָן רַשָּׁאִין לָכֹף אֶת הָעָם לָלֶכֶת בָּהּ.

ז גָּזְרוּ וְדִמּוּ שֶׁפָּשְׁטָה בְּכָל יִשְׂרָאֵל, וְעָמַד הַדָּבָר כֵּן שָׁנִים רַבּוֹת, וּלְאַחַר זְמַן מְרֻבֶּה עָמַד בֵּית דִּין אַחֵר וּבָדַק בְּכָל יִשְׂרָאֵל וְרָאָה שֶׁאֵין אוֹתָהּ הַגְּזֵרָה פּוֹשֶׁטֶת בְּכָל יִשְׂרָאֵל - יֵשׁ לוֹ רְשׁוּת לְבַטֵּל, וַאֲפִלּוּ הָיָה פָּחוֹת מִבֵּית דִּין הָרִאשׁוֹן בְּחָכְמָה וּבְמִנְיָן.

ח וְכָל בֵּית דִּין שֶׁהִתִּיר שְׁנֵי דְבָרִים - אַל יְמַהֵר לְהַתִּיר דָּבָר שְׁלִישִׁי.

ט הוֹאִיל וְיֵשׁ לְבֵית דִּין לִגְזֹר וְלֶאֱסֹר דָּבָר הַמֻּתָּר וְיַעֲמֹד אִסּוּרוֹ לְדוֹרוֹת, וְכֵן יֵשׁ לָהֶן לְהַתִּיר אִסּוּרֵי תוֹרָה לְפִי שָׁעָה, מַהוּ זֶה שֶׁהִזְהִירָה הַתּוֹרָה: לֹא תֹסֵף עָלָיו וְלֹא תִגְרַע מִמֶּנּוּ?

שֶׁלֹּא לְהוֹסִיף עַל דִּבְרֵי תוֹרָה וְלֹא לִגְרֹעַ מֵהֶן וְלִקְבֹּעַ הַדָּבָר לְעוֹלָם בְּדָבָר שֶׁהוּא מִן הַתּוֹרָה, בֵּין בַּתּוֹרָה שֶׁבִּכְתָב בֵּין בַּתּוֹרָה שֶׁבְּעַל פֶּה.

later generation, it can be nullified. The *Kessef Mishneh* does not, however, conclusively accept either interpretation.

24. The Rambam's wording implies that since the original court was under the impression that the decree had spread throughout the Jewish community, the later court must nullify the decree. It is not automatically null and void.

One of the classic examples of this concept is the actions of Rabbi Yehudah Nesiah (the grandson of Rabbi Yehudah HaNasi, the author of the Mishnah). Rabbi Yehudah and his court permitted the use of oil made by gentiles although the decree forbidding it had been issued by the students of Hillel and Shammai, a court of far greater prestige. Rabbi Yehudah surveyed the Jewish community and saw that the decree had never been observed. Therefore, he had the authority to nullify it.

25. *Avodah Zarah* 37a relates that after Rabbi Yehudah Nesiah repealed two prohibitions, some of his colleagues pressed him to repeal a third. He refused, saying that this would cause his court to develop a reputation for leniency.

26. As stated in Halachot 2 and 3.

27. As stated in Halachah 4.

28. *Sefer HaMitzvot* (negative commandment 313) and *Sefer HaChinuch* (mitzvah 454) count the prohibition against adding to the Torah as one of its 613 mitzvot.

29. *Sefer HaMitzvot* (negative commandment 314) and *Sefer HaChinuch* (mitzvah 455) count the prohibition against detracting from the Torah as one of its 613 mitzvot.

30. I.e., the interpretation of the Written Law given to Moses at Sinai - "the mitzvah" to refer to the term used by the Rambam in his Introduction to the *Mishneh Torah* - is considered as equivalent to the Written Law itself. Just as it is forbidden to add or detract from a concept explicitly stated in the Torah; so, too, it is forbidden to add or detract from the explanation of a practice conveyed by the Oral Law. The Rambam reiterates these

What is implied? The Torah states [Exodus 23:19]: "Do not cook a kid in its mother's milk." According to the Oral Tradition, we learned that the Torah forbade both the cooking and eating of milk and meat, whether the meat of a domesticated animal or the meat of a wild beast.[31] The meat of fowl, by contrast, is permitted to be cooked in milk according to Scriptural Law.[32] Now if a court will come and permit partaking of the meat of a wild animal [cooked] in milk, it is detracting [from the Torah]. And if it forbids the meat of fowl [cooked in milk] saying that this is included in "the kid" forbidden by the Scriptural Law, it is adding [to the Torah].

If, however, the court says: "The meat of fowl [cooked in milk] is permitted according to Scriptural Law. We, however, are prohibiting it and publicizing [the prohibition] as a decree, lest the matter lead to a disadvantage, [causing people to say]: '[Eating the meat of] fowl [cooked in meat] is permitted, because it is not explicitly [forbidden] by the Torah. Similarly, [the meat of] a wild animal [cooked in milk] is permitted, because it is also not explicitly [forbidden].'[33]

"And another may come and say: 'Even the meat of a domesticated animal [cooked in milk] is permitted with the exception of a goat.'[34] And another will come and say: 'Even the meat of a goat is permitted [when cooked] in the milk of a cow or a sheep. For the verse mentions only "its mother," i.e., an animal from the same species.' And still another will come and say: '[Even the meat of a goat] is permitted [when cooked] in goat's milk as long the milk is not from the kid's mother, for the verse says: "its mother."'[35] For these reasons, we will forbid all meat [cooked] in milk, even meat from fowl."

[Such an approach] is not adding [to the Torah]. Instead, it is creating safeguards for the Torah. Similar concepts apply in all analogous situations.

concepts in the ninth of his Thirteen Principles of Faith (Commentary to the Mishnah, *Sanhedrin*, ch. 10) stating:

> The ninth principle is that the Torah of Moses will never be nullified.... There can be no additions to it, nor any deletions from it - neither in its text nor in its explanation. And thus we are commanded: "Do not add to it and do not detract it from it."

(Our translation is taken from the original manuscript versions of the Rambam's Commentary to the Mishnah. The standard published text varies slightly.)

The Ra'avad harshly differs with the Rambam's explanation, stating that the Rambam's words are fit to be carried away by the wind. The Ra'avad states that any practice established as a safeguard for Scriptural Law is never considered as a prohibited addition

כֵּיצַד? הֲרֵי כָּתוּב בַּתּוֹרָה: לֹא תְבַשֵּׁל גְּדִי בַּחֲלֵב אִמּוֹ. מִפִּי הַשְּׁמוּעָה לָמְדוּ, שֶׁזֶּה הַכָּתוּב אָסַר לְבַשֵּׁל וְלֶאֱכֹל בָּשָׂר בְּחָלָב, בֵּין בְּשַׂר בְּהֵמָה בֵּין בְּשַׂר חַיָּה; אֲבָל בְּשַׂר הָעוֹף – מֻתָּר בְּחָלָב מִן הַתּוֹרָה. אִם יָבוֹא בֵּית דִּין וְיַתִּיר בְּשַׂר חַיָּה בְּחָלָב – הֲרֵי זֶה גּוֹרֵעַ;
וְאִם יֶאֱסֹר בְּשַׂר הָעוֹף וְיֹאמַר שֶׁהוּא בִּכְלַל הַגְּדִי וְהוּא אָסוּר מִן הַתּוֹרָה – הֲרֵי זֶה מוֹסִיף.
אֲבָל אִם אָמַר: בְּשַׂר הָעוֹף מֻתָּר מִן הַתּוֹרָה, וְאָנוּ נֶאֱסֹר אוֹתוֹ, וְנוֹדִיעַ לָעָם שֶׁהוּא גְּזֵרָה, שֶׁלֹּא יָבוֹא מִן הַדָּבָר חוֹבָה וְיֹאמְרוּ: הָעוֹף מֻתָּר מִפְּנֵי שֶׁלֹּא נִתְפָּרֵשׁ, כָּךְ הַחַיָּה מֻתֶּרֶת שֶׁהֲרֵי לֹא נִתְפָּרְשָׁה;
וְיָבוֹא אַחֵר לוֹמַר: אַף בְּשַׂר בְּהֵמָה מֻתֶּרֶת, חוּץ מִן הָעֵז;
וְיָבוֹא אַחֵר לוֹמַר: אַף בְּשַׂר הָעֵז מֻתָּר בַּחֲלֵב פָּרָה אוֹ הַכִּבְשָׂה, שֶׁלֹּא נֶאֱמַר אֶלָּא 'אִמּוֹ', שֶׁהִיא מִינוֹ;
וְיָבוֹא אַחֵר לוֹמַר: אַף בַּחֲלֵב הָעֵז שֶׁאֵינָהּ אִמּוֹ מֻתָּר, שֶׁלֹּא נֶאֱמַר אֶלָּא 'אִמּוֹ';
לְפִיכָךְ נֶאֱסֹר כָּל בָּשָׂר בְּחָלָב, אֲפִלּוּ בְּשַׂר עוֹף – אֵין זֶה מוֹסִיף, אֶלָּא עוֹשֶׂה סְיָג לַתּוֹרָה. וְכֵן כֹּל כַּיּוֹצֵא בָּזֶה.

to the Torah even if it is established as a permanent practice and an allusion to it from the Torah is found. According to him, addition and detractions from the Torah involve adding or detracting from the observance of certain mitzvot: e.g., wearing five or three *tzitzit* instead of the required four, or adding or subtracting a species to the four used on Sukkos. The Radbaz and the *Kessef Mishneh* support the Rambam's conception, while Rav Moshe HaCohen echoes the Ra'avad's view.

31. E.g., a deer or a buffalo which are kosher animals. The Rambam's statements have attracted the attention of the commentaries, for there is a difference of opinion among the Rabbis in *Chullin* 116a, and the Rambam (*Hilchot Ma'achalot Assurot* 9:4) and many other *Rishonim* follow the view that the meat of a wild beast that is cooked in milk is not forbidden according to Scriptural Law. Why then does he state here that it is forbidden?

The Radbaz and the *Kessef Mishneh* explain that here, the Rambam is speaking theoretically: Were the halachah to follow the opinion that the meat of a wild beast is forbidden according to Scriptural law, the ruling would be such and such. The *Merkevat HaMishneh*, however, maintains that a printing error crept into the text in *Hilchot Ma'achalot Assurot* and the text should be changed to fit the Rambam's ruling here.

32. For the verse mentions "its mother's milk," and fowl do not have milk (*Chulin* 113a).

33. This and the subsequent conclusions the Rambam mentions are all forbidden by Scriptural Law.

34. For the verse mentions explicitly a "kid," i.e., a goat.

35. I.e., interpreting the term according to its most literal meaning.

CHAPTER THREE

1. A person who does not acknowledge [the validity of] the Oral Law[1] is not the rebellious elder mentioned in the Torah.[2] Instead, he is one of the heretics[3] and he should be put to death by any person.[4]

2. Since it has become known that such a person denies the Oral Law, he may be pushed into a pit and may not be helped out.[5] He is like all the rest of the heretics who say that the Torah is not Divine in origin,[6] those who inform [on their fellow Jews],[7] and the apostates.[8] All of these are not considered as members of the Jewish people. There is no need for witnesses, a warning, or judges [for them to be executed]. Instead, whoever kills them performs a great mitzvah and removes an obstacle [from people at large].[9]

3. To whom does the above apply? To a person who denied the Oral Law consciously, according to his perception of things. He follows after his frivolous thoughts and his capricious heart and denies the Oral Law first, as did Tzadok and Beitus[10] and those who erred in following them.

[Different laws apply to] the children of these errant people and their grandchildren whose parents led them astray and they were born among these Karaities[11] and raised according to their conception. They are considered as children captured and raised by them.[12] [Such a child] may not be eager [to follow] the path of mitzvot, for it is as if he was compelled not to. Even if

1. Note the qualification of this matter in Halachah 3.
2. See Halachah 4 ff.
3. The Rambam defines the term *epicurus* (the term used here) in *Hilchot Teshuvah* 3:8. It appears, however, that here, he is not referring to the precise definition of that term, but rather to a more general conception of heresy. It must be noted that many of the authoritative manuscripts of the *Mishneh Torah* use the term *min* (see *Hilchot Teshuvah* 3:7).
4. As the Rambam continues to explain in the following halachah, a heretic should be slain. Any person may - and should - take the law into his own hands in this regard. There is no need to wait for judicial process.
5. Indeed, if the pit has a ladder, the ladder should be removed. Compare to *Hilchot Rotzeach* 4:10 which says that if it is possible, one should kill such individuals with a sword in public view.
6. I.e., there is no difference if the person denies the Oral Law or the Written Law.
7. People who seek to give gentile authorities control over the lives or the property of their fellow Jews. As stated in *Hilchot Chovel UMazik*:8:9-10, if possible, it is a mitzvah to kill such people, even in the era of exile.
8. As evident from the *Shulchan Aruch* (*Choshen Mishpat* 425:5), this terms refers to people who transgress with the intent of angering God. If, however, a person transgresses because he cannot control his desires, these severe measures do not apply.
9. Compare to *Hilchot Avodat Kochavim* 10:1 which states that these individuals "cause difficulty to the Jews and sway the people away from God." See also the Rambam's

פֶּרֶק שְׁלִישִׁי

א מִי שֶׁאֵינוֹ מוֹדֶה בַּתּוֹרָה שֶׁבְּעַל פֶּה – אֵינוֹ זָקֵן מַמְרֵא הָאָמוּר בַּתּוֹרָה; אֶלָּא הֲרֵי זֶה בִּכְלַל הָאֶפִּיקוֹרוֹסִין, [וּמִיתָתוֹ בְּכָל אָדָם].

ב מֵאַחַר שֶׁנִּתְפַּרְסֵם שֶׁהוּא כּוֹפֵר בַּתּוֹרָה שֶׁבְּעַל פֶּה – [מוֹרִידִין אוֹתוֹ] וְלֹא מַעֲלִין. וַהֲרֵי הוּא כִּשְׁאָר כָּל הָאֶפִּיקוֹרוֹסִין וְהָאוֹמְרִין אֵין תּוֹרָה מִן הַשָּׁמַיִם וְהַמּוֹסְרִין וְהַמּוּמָרִין. שֶׁכָּל אֵלּוּ אֵינָם בִּכְלַל יִשְׂרָאֵל, וְאֵין צָרִיךְ לֹא עֵדִים וְלֹא הַתְרָאָה וְלֹא דַיָּנִים, [אֶלָּא כָּל הַהוֹרֵג אֶחָד מֵהֶן – עָשָׂה מִצְוָה גְדוֹלָה וְהֵסִיר הַמִּכְשׁוֹל].

ג בַּמֶּה דְּבָרִים אֲמוּרִים? בְּאִישׁ שֶׁכָּפַר בַּתּוֹרָה שֶׁבְּעַל פֶּה בְּמַחֲשַׁבְתּוֹ וּבִדְבָרִים שֶׁנִּרְאוּ לוֹ, וְהָלַךְ אַחַר דַּעְתּוֹ הַקַּלָּה וְאַחַר שְׁרִירוּת לִבּוֹ, וְכוֹפֵר בַּתּוֹרָה שֶׁבְּעַל פֶּה תְּחִלָּה, כְּצָדוֹק וּבַיְתּוֹס וְכֵן כָּל הַתּוֹעִים אַחֲרָיו.
אֲבָל בְּנֵי הַתּוֹעִים הָאֵלֶּה וּבְנֵי בְנֵיהֶם, שֶׁהִדִּיחוּ אוֹתָם אֲבוֹתָם, וְנוֹלְדוּ בֵּין הַקָּרָאִים וְגִדְּלוּ אוֹתָם עַל דַּעְתָּם – הֲרֵי הוּא כְּתִינוֹק שֶׁנִּשְׁבָּה בֵּינֵיהֶם וְגִדְּלוּהוּ, וְאֵינוֹ זָרִיז לֶאֱחֹז בְּדַרְכֵי הַמִּצְוֹת, שֶׁהֲרֵי הוּא כְּאָנוּס.

Commentary to the Mishnah (*Chullin* 1:2) where he states that the progenitors of deviant approaches should be killed for corrupting the Torah.

10. These were two of the greatest students of Antigonus of Socho. As the Rambam states in his Commentary to the Mishnah (*Avot* 1:3), after they heard Antigonus teach: "Do not be as servants who serve their master for the sake of receiving a reward," they forsook Jewish practice, saying: "Is it just that we labor without receiving a reward?"

They began splinter sects with the intent of swaying the people after them. At first, they sought to abandon Jewish practice entirely. They saw, however, the people would not accept this and so they focused their complaints on the Oral Law, arguing that although the Written Law was of Divine origin, the Oral Law was not. Their intent, however, was to deny the entire Torah. Similarly, the individuals mentioned by the Rambam deny "the Oral Law *first*," i.e., their intent is to deny the entire connection with God and the Torah.

11. The Karaites represented a sect of deviant Jews who followed the approach of Tzadok and Beitus, rejecting the observance of the Oral Law although maintaining a certain amount of deference to Jewish tradition. In the Rambam's era, they had won the allegiance of many of the Jews in Egypt and North Africa. Their belief, however, was not perpetuated and after a brief epoch in history, they ceased to exist in significant numbers.

12. The concept of a child captured and raised by gentiles is found in *Shabbat* 68b. It is explained that when such a child comes of age and later desires to atone for his conduct, he is required to bring only one sin offering for each transgression which he performed no matter how often he repeated it (in contrast to an ordinary person who must bring a sin offering for every act of transgression he performs). He is judged more leniently and not held fully responsible for his deeds, because he was raised in a non-Jewish environment. Similarly, the Rambam is postulating, the descendants of the Karaites should not be held responsible for their transgressions, for they were brought up in an environment that drew them away from the Torah and its mitzvot.

later, he hears that he is Jewish and sees Jews and their faith, he is still considered as one who was compelled [against observance], for he was raised according to their mistaken [path].[13] This applies to those whom we mentioned who follow the erroneous Karaite path of their ancestors. Therefore it is appropriate to motivate them to repent and draw them to the power of the Torah with words of peace.[14]

4. The "rebellious elder" mentioned in the Torah,[15] by contrast, is one of the sages of Israel[16] who has received the tradition [from previous sages] and who analyzes[17] and issues a ruling with regard to the words of Torah as do all the sages of Israel. [His rebellion involves an instance when] he has a difference of opinion in one of [the Torah's] laws with the Supreme *Sanhedrin* and did not accept their views, but instead issued a ruling to act in a different manner.[18] The Torah decreed that he should be executed. He should confess his sin [before being executed][19] [so that] he will be granted a portion in the world to come.[20]

Even though he analyzes and they analyze; he received the tradition and they received the tradition, the Torah granted them deference.[21] [Even] if the court desires to forgo their honor and allow him to live, they are not allowed, so that differences of opinion will not arise within Israel.

5. A "rebellious elder" is not liable for execution unless he is a sage, [erudite enough] to issue halachic judgments who has received *semichah* from the *Sanhedrin*[22] and who differs with [that] court with regard to a matter whose willful violation is punishable by *kerait* and whose inadvertent violation requires a sin offering or with regard to *tefillin*.[23] He must direct others to act according to his ruling or act according to his ruling himself,[24] and differ with the *Sanhedrin* while they hold session in the Chamber of Hewn Stone.[25]

When, by contrast, a student who has not attained [a level of erudition that enables him to issue] halachic rulings, but, nevertheless, issues a ruling, he is not liable. [This is derived from Deuteronomy 17:8 which] states: "If a matter of judgment exceeds [your grasp]...." [Implied is that the passage concerns] only [a scholar] who is unable to grasp something which is exceedingly [difficult to comprehend].[26]

6. If a sage was an exceedingly great scholar and a member of a court and differed with [the Supreme *Sanhedrin*] and he returned home and taught others according to his [original] conception, but did not direct them to act

13. As reflected in the manuscript copies of the Rambam's Commentary to the Mishnah (*Chullin* 1:2), these words of patience and forbearance reflected a change in the Rambam's thinking. In his youth, he concluded his treatment of the subject without including them. When he rewrote his Commentary to the Mishnah in his later years and here in the *Mishneh Torah*, he felt it necessary to include them.

Contemporary Rabbinic experts have applied the Rambam's statements here to the question of how to do deal with Reform and Conservative Jews today.

וְאַף עַל פִּי שֶׁשָּׁמַע אַחַר כָּךְ [שֶׁהוּא יְהוּדִי, וְרָאָה הַיְּהוּדִים וְדָתָם – הֲרֵי הוּא כְּאָנוּס, שֶׁהֲרֵי גִּדְּלוּהוּ עַל טָעוּתָם]. כָּךְ אֵלּוּ שֶׁאָמַרְנוּ, הָאוֹחֲזִים בְּדַרְכֵי אֲבוֹתָם הַקָּרָאִים שֶׁטָּעוּ. לְפִיכָךְ רָאוּי לְהַחֲזִירָן בִּתְשׁוּבָה, וּלְמָשְׁכָם בְּדִבְרֵי שָׁלוֹם, עַד שֶׁיַּחְזְרוּ לְאֵיתַן הַתּוֹרָה.

ד אֲבָל זָקֵן מַמְרֵא הָאָמוּר בַּתּוֹרָה הוּא חָכָם אֶחָד מֵחַכְמֵי יִשְׂרָאֵל, שֶׁיֵּשׁ בְּיָדוֹ קַבָּלָה וְדָן וּמוֹרֶה בְּדִבְרֵי תוֹרָה כְּמוֹ שֶׁיָּדוּנוּ וְיוֹרוּ כָּל חַכְמֵי יִשְׂרָאֵל, שֶׁבָּאת לוֹ מַחֲלֹקֶת בְּדִין מִן הַדַּיָּנִים עִם בֵּית דִּין הַגָּדוֹל, וְלֹא חָזַר לְדִבְרֵיהֶם, אֶלָּא חָלַק עֲלֵיהֶם וְהוֹרָה לַעֲשׂוֹת שֶׁלֹּא כְּהוֹרָאָתָן – גָּזְרָה עָלָיו תּוֹרָה מִיתָה. וּמִתְוַדֶּה, וְיֵשׁ לוֹ חֵלֶק לָעוֹלָם הַבָּא. אַף עַל פִּי שֶׁהוּא דָן וְהֵן דָּנִים, הוּא קִבֵּל וְהֵם קִבְּלוּ – הֲרֵי הַתּוֹרָה חָלְקָה לָהֶם כָּבוֹד. וְאִם רָצוּ בֵּית דִּין לִמְחֹל עַל כְּבוֹדָן וּלְהַנִּיחוֹ – אֵינָן יְכוֹלִין, כְּדֵי שֶׁלֹּא יִרְבּוּ מַחֲלוֹקוֹת בְּיִשְׂרָאֵל.

ה אֵין זָקֵן מַמְרֵא חַיָּב מִיתָה עַד שֶׁיְּהֵא חָכָם שֶׁהִגִּיעַ לְהוֹרָאָה סָמוּךְ בְּסַנְהֶדְרִין, וְיַחֲלֹק עַל בֵּית דִּין בְּדָבָר שֶׁזְּדוֹנוֹ כָּרֵת וְשִׁגְגָתוֹ חַטָּאת, אוֹ בִּתְפִלִּין, וְיוֹרֶה לַעֲשׂוֹת כְּהוֹרָאָתוֹ אוֹ יַעֲשֶׂה הוּא עַל פִּי הוֹרָאָתוֹ, וְיַחֲלֹק עֲלֵיהֶן וְהֵן יוֹשְׁבִין בְּלִשְׁכַּת הַגָּזִית.
אֲבָל אִם הָיָה תַּלְמִיד שֶׁלֹּא הִגִּיעַ לְהוֹרָאָה וְהוֹרָה לַעֲשׂוֹת – פָּטוּר.
שֶׁנֶּאֱמַר: כִּי יִפָּלֵא מִמְּךָ דָבָר לַמִּשְׁפָּט – מִי שֶׁלֹּא יִפָּלֵא מִמֶּנּוּ אֶלָּא דָבָר מֻפְלָא.

ו הָיָה חָכָם מֻפְלָא שֶׁל בֵּית דִּין, וְחָלַק, וְשָׁנָה וְלִמֵּד לַאֲחֵרִים כִּדְבָרָיו, אֲבָל לֹא הוֹרָה לַעֲשׂוֹת – פָּטוּר.

14. See the conclusion of the Rambam's *Iggeret HaShmad* where he also urges a loving approach to sinners themselves, stating: "It is not appropriate to ostracize and detest those who desecrate the Sabbath. Instead, one should draw them close and encourage them to perform mitzvot.... Even if a person transgresses intentionally, when he comes to the synagogue to pray, he should be accepted and should not be abused."
15. Deuteronomy, ch. 17.
16. I.e., "the rebellious elder" must be a sage, as evident from the following halachah.
17. I.e., derives concepts using the accepted principles of Biblical exegesis.
18. As illustrated in the following halachot.
19. As is required of all those who are executed; see *Hilchot Sanhedrin* 13:1.
20. In contrast, those who deny the Oral Law are not granted a portion in the world to come (*Kessef Mishneh*, based on *Hilchot Teshuvah*, ch. 3).
21. Stating that we must follow the rulings of the majority and not deviate from them.
22. As explained in *Hilchot Sanhedrin*, ch. 4.
23. See Chapter 4, Halachah 2. The Rambam's ruling is dependent on his understanding of a difference of opinion among the Sages (*Sanhedrin* 86b, 87a).

Perhaps, *tefillin* are singled out, because "the entire Torah is equated to *tefillin* (*Yayin Malchut*).
24. If, however, he maintains that theoretically, the other sages are wrong, but refrains from giving a directive to others to act on his instructions and does not act upon them himself, he is not liable, as stated in Halachot 6 and 8.
25. I.e., the chamber outside the Temple Courtyard where they would hold court. See Halachah 7.
26. I.e., it does not apply to a scholar who lacks knowledge of more fundamental issues.

accordingly, he is not liable.[27] [This is derived from *ibid.*:12 which] states: "And the person who acts obstinately"; [i.e., the punishment is warranted] not for speaking obstinately, but for issuing a directive for action or for acting oneself.

6. If he found [the Supreme *Sanhedrin*] outside their place and rebelled against their [ruling], he is not liable. [This is derived from *ibid.*:8 which] states: "And you shall arise and ascend to that place," implied is that the place is the cause for capital punishment.

All of [the individuals mentioned above who are not executed] and anyone who acts in a similar manner, although they are not liable for execution, the Supreme *Sanhedrin* should place them under a ban of ostracism,[28] separate them from the community, subject them to corporal punishment, and prevent them from teaching their interpretation of the matter.[29]

8. How is the law applying to a rebellious elder adjudicated? When a matter is undecided because of its difficulty and a sage who [is erudite enough] to issue rulings whether with regard to a matter which he arrived at through his own reasoning or which he received from his teachers, he and the sages who differ with him ascend to Jerusalem and come to the court which [holds sessions] at the entrance to the Temple Mount.

The court tells them: "This is the law." If [the elder] listens and accepts [the ruling], it is desirable. If not, they all go to the court which holds sessions at the entrance to the Temple Courtyard. They also say: "This is the law." If [the elder] listens and accepts [the ruling], they go their ways. If not, they all go to the Supreme *Sanhedrin* in the Chamber of Hewn Stone from which the Torah emanates to the entire Jewish people, as [Deuteronomy 17:10] states: "From that place which God has chosen." The [Supreme *Sanhedrin*] tell them: "This is the law" and they all depart.

If the elder returns to his city and continues [to interpret the law] as he did previously and teaches [this interpretation] to others,[30] he is not liable. If he gave a directive for action or acted [according to his conception] himself, he is liable for execution. There is no need for a warning.[31] Even if he offers a rationale to explain his conduct, we do not heed him. Instead, once witnesses come [and testify that] he acted according to his own directive or that he directed others to perform a deed, we sentence him to death in his local court.[32] We take hold of him and bring him from that place to Jerusalem. For we do not execute him in [the presence of] his local court, nor in the presence of [the Supreme *Sanhedrin*] who left Jerusalem, but instead, bring him to the Supreme *Sanhedrin* in Jerusalem. Until the [next] pilgrimage festival, he is kept

27. The classic example of this principle is Akkavya ben Mahallel who received four teachings from his teachers which - though they represented the majority views at that time - were not accepted by the majority of the Sages in the following generation. Akkavya refused to change his conception of these laws, and yet, in deference to the majority, did not issue rulings for action according to his conception. Moreover, before

שֶׁנֶּאֱמַר: וְהָאִישׁ אֲשֶׁר יַעֲשֶׂה בְזָדוֹן. לֹא שֶׁיֹּאמַר בְּזָדוֹן, אֶלָּא יוֹרֶה לַעֲשׂוֹת אוֹ יַעֲשֶׂה הוּא בְּעַצְמוֹ.

ז מְצָאָן חוּץ לִמְקוֹמָן וְהִמְרָה עֲלֵיהֶן - פָּטוּר.
שֶׁנֶּאֱמַר: וְקַמְתָּ וְעָלִיתָ אֶל הַמָּקוֹם - מְלַמֵּד, שֶׁהַמָּקוֹם גּוֹרֵם לוֹ מִיתָה.
וְכָל אֵלּוּ וְכַיּוֹצֵא בָּהֶן שֶׁהֵן פְּטוּרִין מִן הַמִּיתָה, יֵשׁ לְבֵית דִּין הַגָּדוֹל לְנַדּוֹתָם וּלְהַפְרִישָׁן וּלְהַכּוֹתָן וּלְמָנְעָן מִלְּלַמֵּד, כְּפִי מַה שֶּׁיֵּרָאֶה לָהֶן שֶׁהַדָּבָר צָרִיךְ לְכָךְ.

ח וְכֵיצַד דָּנִין זָקֵן מַמְרֵא? בְּעֵת שֶׁיִּפָּלֵא דָּבָר וְיוֹרֶה בּוֹ חָכָם הַמַּגִּיעַ לְהוֹרָאָה, בֵּין בְּדָבָר שֶׁיֵּרָאֶה בְּעֵינָיו בֵּין בְּדָבָר שֶׁקִּבֵּל מֵרַבּוֹתָיו - הֲרֵי הוּא וְהַחוֹלְקִין עִמּוֹ עוֹלִין לִירוּשָׁלַיִם, וּבָאִין לְבֵית דִּין שֶׁעַל פֶּתַח הַר הַבַּיִת. אוֹמְרִים לָהֶן בֵּית דִּין: כָּךְ הוּא הַדִּין. אִם שָׁמַע וְקִבֵּל - מוּטָב; וְאִם לָאו - בָּאִין כֻּלָּן לְבֵית דִּין שֶׁעַל פֶּתַח הָעֲזָרָה, וְאוֹמְרִים לָהֶם גַּם הֵם: כָּךְ הוּא הַדִּין.
אִם קִבְּלוּ - יֵלְכוּ לָהֶן; וְאִם לָאו - כֻּלָּן בָּאִין לְבֵית דִּין הַגָּדוֹל לְלִשְׁכַּת הַגָּזִית, שֶׁמִּשָּׁם תּוֹרָה יוֹצֵאת לְכָל יִשְׂרָאֵל. שֶׁנֶּאֱמַר: מִן הַמָּקוֹם הַהוּא אֲשֶׁר יִבְחַר יְיָ. וּבֵית דִּין אוֹמֵר לָהֶם: כָּךְ הוּא הַדִּין, וְיוֹצְאִין כֻּלָּן.
חָזַר זֶה הֶחָכָם לְעִירוֹ וְשָׁנָה וְלִמֵּד כְּדֶרֶךְ שֶׁהוּא לָמוּד - הֲרֵי זֶה פָּטוּר.
הוֹרָה לַעֲשׂוֹת אוֹ שֶׁעָשָׂה כְּהוֹרָאָתוֹ - חַיָּב מִיתָה, וְאֵינוֹ צָרִיךְ הַתְרָאָה.
אֲפִלּוּ נָתַן טַעַם לִדְבָרָיו - אֵין שׁוֹמְעִין לוֹ.
אֶלָּא כֵּיוָן שֶׁבָּאוּ עֵדִים שֶׁעָשָׂה כְּהוֹרָאָתוֹ אוֹ שֶׁהוֹרָה לַאֲחֵרִים לַעֲשׂוֹת - גּוֹמְרִין דִּינוֹ לְמִיתָה בְּבֵית דִּין שֶׁבְּעִירוֹ, וְתוֹפְסִין אוֹתוֹ וּמַעֲלִין אוֹתוֹ מִשָּׁם לִירוּשָׁלַיִם.
וְאֵין מְמִיתִין אוֹתוֹ בְּבֵית דִּין שֶׁבְּעִירוֹ, וְלֹא בְּבֵית דִּין הַגָּדוֹל שֶׁיָּצָא חוּץ לִירוּשָׁלַיִם, אֶלָּא מַעֲלִין אוֹתוֹ לְבֵית דִּין הַגָּדוֹל שֶׁבִּירוּשָׁלַיִם.

his passing, he advised his son to accept the ruling of the majority (*Ediot* 5:6-7; *Sanhedrin* 88a).

28. See *Hilchot Talmud Torah*, chs. 6 and 7.

29. The *Maharitz Chayot* states that although this is a general guideline, in practice, the matter is left to the interpretation of every court. For that reason, Akkavya ben Mahallel was not ostracized or subjected to corporal punishment. Since Akkavya sought to minimize the discord and the lack of respect for the court that could result from different approaches being taught, he was not subjected to punishment.

30. I.e., as an abstract concept without telling people that they should conduct themselves in this manner.

31. In contrast to other cases where capital punishment is administered (*Hilchot Sanhedrin* 12:2). This ruling represents a change from the Rambam's position in his Commentary to the Mishnah (*Sanhedrin* 11:2) where he states that such a warning is required.

32. For a court of 23 judges has the authority to issue sentences of capital punishment.

under watch. During the pilgrimage festival,[33] he is executed by strangulation, as [implied by *ibid.*:13]: "And all Israel shall hear and become fearful." This indicates that [his execution] must be announced.

There are four transgressors whose [execution] must be announced publicly:[34] a rebellious elder, lying witnesses, a person who entices [others to worship idols],[35] and a wayward and rebellious son.[36] For with regard to all of them, the Torah states: "so that they will hear and become afraid."

CHAPTER FOUR

1. [A rebellious elder] who differed with the Supreme *Sanhedrin* concerning a matter whose willful violation is punishable by *kerait* and whose inadvertent violation requires a sin offering is liable for execution.[1] [This applies] whether [the court] forbids [the matter] and he permits it or [the court] permits the matter and he forbids it.[2] Even if he [bases] his statements on the received tradition, saying: "This is the tradition I received from my masters," and they say: "This is what appears to us as appropriate on the basis of logical analysis," since he differs with their ruling[3] and performs a deed or directs others to do so, he is liable. Needless to say, this applies if they also rule on the basis of their having received teachings through the Oral Tradition.[4]

Similarly, he is liable for execution if he differs with them with regard to a decree that they issued [to safeguard a prohibition] whose willful violation is punishable by *kerait* and whose inadvertent violation requires a sin offering.[5]

33. When the entire Jewish people gather together in Jerusalem. There the announcement and the execution will attract the most attention.

As evident from *Hilchot Sanhedrin*, 11:2. 13:5, executions are not held on the sacred days of the festivals, but on Chol HaMoed.

34. The Radbaz explains that the execution of these four individuals is announced publicly, because in each instance, there is a rationale that might lead one to think that the transgression is not so severe: The rebellious elder did not actually commit a transgression; he merely instructed others to. The lying witnesses are not executed if the person was executed on the basis of their testimony, only when he has not yet been executed. Hence, one might think there is room for leniency. Similarly, as will be explained, the wayward and rebellious son is not executed because of the transgressions he performed, for stealing and eating gluttonously do not make him worthy to die. Instead, the Torah appreciates the ultimate outcome of his conduct. As such, there is room to argue that, at present, there is room for leniency. And the person who entices others to idol worship can argue that he himself did not commit the transgression. Hence, to make people aware that these transgressions are indeed severe, a public announcement is made.

35. The commentaries have noted that *Hilchot Avodat Kochavim*, ch. 5, where the Rambam discusses the laws pertaining to someone who entices others to worship idols, does not mention that the execution of such a person is announced publicly. They explain that perhaps he relied on his statements here.

36. The commentaries note that *Hilchot Edut* 18:17 (which speaks about the announcement of the execution of lying witnesses) and Chapter 7, Halachah 13, of these halachot (which speaks about the announcement of the execution of a wayward and rebellious son) do not mention that these individuals should be executed during a

וְעַד הָרֶגֶל מְשַׁמְּרִין אוֹתוֹ, וְחוֹנְקִין אוֹתוֹ בָּרֶגֶל. שֶׁנֶּאֱמַר: וְכָל יִשְׂרָאֵל יִשְׁמְעוּ וְיִרָאוּ; מִכְּלָל שֶׁצָּרִיךְ הַכְרָזָה.

וְאַרְבָּעָה צְרִיכִין הַכְרָזָה: זָקֵן מַמְרֵא, וְעֵדִים זוֹמְמִין, וְהַמֵּסִית, וּבֵן סוֹרֵר וּמוֹרֶה; שֶׁהֲרֵי בְּכֻלָּן נֶאֱמַר: יִשְׁמְעוּ וְיִרָאוּ.

פֶּרֶק רְבִיעִי

א זָה שֶׁחָלַק עַל בֵּית דִּין הַגָּדוֹל בְּדָבָר שֶׁחַיָּבִין עַל זְדוֹנוֹ כָּרֵת וְעַל שִׁגְגָתוֹ חַטָּאת, בֵּין שֶׁהָיוּ הֵן אוֹסְרִים וְהוּא מַתִּיר בֵּין שֶׁהָיוּ הֵן מַתִּירִין וְהוּא אוֹסֵר – הֲרֵי זֶה חַיָּב מִיתָה. אֲפִלּוּ הוּא הָיָה אוֹמֵר מִפִּי הַקַּבָּלָה, וְאָמַר: כָּךְ קִבַּלְתִּי מֵרַבּוֹתַי, וְהֵן אוֹמְרִים: כָּךְ נִרְאֶה בְּעֵינֵינוּ שֶׁהַדִּין נוֹתֵן, הוֹאִיל וְנָשָׂא וְנָתַן עֲלֵיהֶן בַּדָּבָר, וְעָשָׂה אוֹ שֶׁהוֹרָה לַעֲשׂוֹת – הֲרֵי זֶה חַיָּב.

וְאֵין צָרִיךְ לוֹמַר אִם הֵם מוֹרִים מִפִּי הַקַּבָּלָה.

וְכֵן אִם חָלַק עֲלֵיהֶם בִּגְזֵרָה מִן הַגְּזֵרוֹת שֶׁגָּזְרוּ בְּדָבָר שֶׁיֵּשׁ בְּשִׁגְגָתוֹ חַטָּאת וּזְדוֹנוֹ כָּרֵת,

pilgrimage festival. Instead, they state that a proclamation concerning these individual's execution should be circulated among the Jewish people. This has led the *Kessef Mishneh* to conclude that according to the Rambam, only the rebellious elder must be executed at that time. This view is supported by an opinion in the *Tosefta* (*Sanhedrin* 9:1). Others, however, point to another opinion in the *Tosefta* (*ibid.* 11:3) which states that all four individuals should be executed on a pilgrimage festival.

1. *Sanhedrin* 87a derives this concept through accepted techniques of Biblical exegesis. There are two different opinions concerning the extent of the difference of opinion between the elder and the court in that Talmudic passage. In this and the following halachah, the Rambam follows one opinion (that of Rabbi Meir) and Halachah 3, his rulings relate to the other one (that of Rabbi Yehudah). See the notes to that halachah.
2. This underscores that the reason he is executed is that he is undermining the authority of the court, not because he is causing others to commit a serious transgression.
3. Our translation differs slightly from the standard published text of the *Mishneh Torah* and is based on authoritative manuscripts.
4. But they maintain that the tradition is different than that maintained by the rebellious elder.
5. The Rambam's position is not accepted by all authorities. The Ramban, in his *Hasagot* to *Sefer HaMitzvot*, General Principle 1, states that a sage is never considered a rebellious elder because of a difference of opinion with regard to a question of Rabbinic Law. For there is no point of Rabbinic Law whose willful violation is punishable by *kerait* and whose inadvertent violation requires a sin offering. *Kerait* and sin offerings are relevant only when speaking about Scriptural prohibitions.

The Radbaz supports the Rambam's position, explaining that since the prohibition against *chametz* itself is punishable by *kerait* or a sin offering, the Rabbinic safeguards against this prohibition also are included in this category. The *Kessef Mishneh* explains that these Rabbinic safeguards could lead to a situation whose willful violation is

For example, if he permits the consumption of leaven on the fourteenth of Nissan during the sixth hour or forbids deriving benefit from it in the fifth hour,[6] he is worthy of execution. Similar laws apply in all analogous situations.

2. [The above applies] whether [the rebellious elder] disputes a matter whose willful violation is punishable by *kerait* and whose inadvertent violation requires a sin offering or he disputes a matter which leads to [a situation involving a prohibition] whose willful violation is punishable by *kerait* and whose inadvertent violation requires a sin offering.

What is implied? If they disputed whether relations with a woman are adulterous or incestuous,[7] if a shade of blood would render a woman ritually impure or not, if [a woman] is impure because of birth or not, if a woman is a *zavah*[8] or not,[9] if this fat is forbidden or permitted and the like, their difference of opinion involves a prohibition whose willful violation is punishable by *kerait* and whose inadvertent violation requires a sin offering.

What is meant by a matter that will lead to [a prohibition] whose willful violation is punishable by *kerait* and whose inadvertent violation requires a sin offering. For example, [the Sages] differed concerning the declaration of a leap year, if the leap year must be declared before Purim or may be declared throughout Adar,[10] he is liable. For this leads to partaking of *chametz* on Pesach.[11] Similarly, if they differed with regard to a matter of financial law or with regard to the number of judges able to adjudicate matters of financial law, he is liable. For according to the opinion which maintains that [the defendant] is liable to [the plaintiff], everything which he expropriated from him was expropriated according to law and according to the decisions of the court. But according to the opposing view, whatever he expropriated is stolen property. If he uses it to consecrate a woman, she is not consecrated.[12] And yet according to the opinion that the person expropriated his own property, [the consecration is valid]. If another person engages in relations with her willfully, he is liable for *kerait* and if [he engages in relations with her] inadvertently, he is liable to bring a sin offering. Thus [their difference of opinion] led to a matter whose willful violation is punishable by *kerait* and whose inadvertent violation requires a sin offering.

punishable by *kerait* and whose inadvertent violation requires a sin offering. If a man consecrates a woman with *chametz* in the fifth hour of the day on the fourteenth of Nissan, according to our Sages, the woman would be consecrated, while according to the rebellious elder, she will not be. Relations with this woman is a matter whose willful violation is punishable by *kerait* and whose inadvertent violation requires a sin offering.

6. As stated in *Hilchot Chametz UMatzah* 1:8-9, the Torah prohibits partaking of *chametz* from midday of the fourteenth of Nissan onward. As a safeguard for that prohibition our Sages decreed that it is forbidden to partake of *chametz* from the beginning of the fifth hour of that day and it is forbidden to benefit from it from the beginning of the sixth hour of that day. If the rebellious elder issues directives that conflict with this decree, he is liable.

כְּגוֹן שֶׁהִתִּיר הֶחָמֵץ בְּיוֹם אַרְבָּעָה עָשָׂר בְּנִיסָן בְּשָׁעָה שִׁשִּׁית, אוֹ אֲסָרוֹ בַּהֲנָאָה בְּשָׁעָה חֲמִישִׁית – הֲרֵי זֶה חַיָּב מִיתָה. וְכֵן כֹּל כַּיּוֹצֵא בָּזֶה.

ב אֶחָד שֶׁנֶּחְלְקוּ בְּדָבָר שֶׁחַיָּבִין עַל זְדוֹנוֹ כָּרֵת וְעַל שִׁגְגָתוֹ חַטָּאת, אוֹ שֶׁנֶּחְלְקוּ בְּדָבָר הַמֵּבִיא לִידֵי דָּבָר שֶׁחַיָּבִין עַל זְדוֹנוֹ כָּרֵת וְעַל שִׁגְגָתוֹ חַטָּאת.

כֵּיצַד? נֶחְלְקוּ בְּאִשָּׁה זוֹ אִם הִיא עֶרְוָה אִם לָאו, אִם מַרְאֶה דָּם זֶה מְטַמֵּא בְּאִשָּׁה אוֹ לֹא, אִם זוֹ טְמֵאָה לֵדָה אוֹ לֹא, אִם זוֹ זָבָה אוֹ לֹא, אִם חֵלֶב זֶה אָסוּר אוֹ מֻתָּר,

וְכֹל כַּיּוֹצֵא בָּאֵלּוּ – הֲרֵי חוֹלֵק בְּדָבָר שֶׁחַיָּבִין עַל זְדוֹנוֹ כָּרֵת וְעַל שִׁגְגָתוֹ חַטָּאת.

וְכֵיצַד דָּבָר הַמֵּבִיא לִידֵי דָּבָר שֶׁחַיָּבִין עַל זְדוֹנוֹ כָּרֵת וְעַל שִׁגְגָתוֹ חַטָּאת?

כְּגוֹן שֶׁנֶּחְלְקוּ בְּעִבּוּר שָׁנָה, אִם מְעַבְּרִים עַד הַפּוּרִים אוֹ בְּכָל אֲדָר – הֲרֵי זֶה חַיָּב; שֶׁזֶּה מֵבִיא לִידֵי חָמֵץ בְּפֶסַח. וְכֵן אִם נֶחְלְקוּ בְּדִין מִדִּינֵי מָמוֹנוֹת אוֹ בְּמִנְיַן הַדַּיָּנִין שֶׁדָּנִין דִּינֵי מָמוֹנוֹת – הֲרֵי זֶה חַיָּב; שֶׁהֲרֵי לִדְבָרָיו שֶׁל זֶה שֶׁאוֹמֵר שֶׁזֶּה חַיָּב לָזֶה, כֹּל שֶׁנָּטַל מִמֶּנּוּ – כְּדִין נָטַל, וְעַל פִּי בֵּית דִּין נָטַל;

וְלִדְבָרָיו שֶׁל זֶה שֶׁאוֹמֵר פָּטוּר, אוֹ שֶׁאָמַר שֶׁאֵין אֵלּוּ רְאוּיִין לָדוּן, כֹּל שֶׁנָּטַל – גָּזֵל הוּא בְּיָדוֹ, וְאִם קִדֵּשׁ בּוֹ אִשָּׁה – אֵינָהּ מְקֻדֶּשֶׁת;

וּלְדִבְרֵי הָאוֹמֵר שֶׁלּוֹ נָטַל, הַבָּא עָלֶיהָ בְּמֵזִיד – עָנוּשׁ כָּרֵת, בְּשׁוֹגֵג – חַיָּב חַטָּאת;

וְנִמְצָא הַדָּבָר מֵבִיא לִידֵי דָּבָר שֶׁחַיָּבִין עַל זְדוֹנוֹ כָּרֵת וְעַל שִׁגְגָתוֹ חַטָּאת.

7. As an example of such a difference of opinion, *Sanhedrin* 87b speaks of a person who has relations with a daughter born from a woman whom he raped. Since the prohibition against relations with a daughter is not mentioned explicitly in the Torah (- it is instead, inferred from the prohibition against relations with one's daughter's daughter), there is room for a rebellious elder to argue that such relations are not punishable by *kerait.*

Similarly, in all the cases that follow, *Sanhedrin, loc. cit.*, gives examples of the types of differences of opinion that could arise. We will not explain all these hypothethical situations. A reader who is interested in those details should consult that source.

8. A condition involving vaginal bleeding at times other than a woman's menstrual period. Such bleeding renders the woman ritually impure.

9. In these three instances, if the woman is impure, relations with her involve a transgression whose willful violation is punishable by *kerait* and whose inadvertent violation requires a sin offering.

10. The latter view represents the halachah.

11. For the month the majority of Sages consider as the second Adar will be Nisan, according to the rebellious elder. And the month the Sages consider as Nisan will be Iyar for him. Thus he will - or instruct others to - partake of *chametz* on Pesach. Hence, the difference of opinion ultimately leads to a transgression whose willful violation is punishable by *kerait.*

12. Since the object used to consecrate her did not belong to her prospective husband, the consecration is not valid. For the stolen article must be returned and thus she never received anything for consecration.

Similarly, if their difference of opinion concerned lashes, if one person was liable to receive lashes or not, or they differed with regard to the number of judges in whose presence lashes must be administered, he is liable. For according to the opinion which says that he should not be lashed, [the court] is injuring him and [the judges] are liable to make financial restitution. Anything expropriated from them is taken according to law. But according to the opinion which says that he is liable for lashes, everything he expropriates from them is stolen property. If he uses it to consecrate a woman, she is not consecrated.[13]

Similarly, if they differed with regard to whether or not a person is obligated to pay [after making] endowment evaluations[14] or interdicted property,[15] he is liable. For according to the opinion that says that he is not liable to pay, if it is taken from him, it is stolen property and if it is used to consecrate a woman, the consecration is not valid.

Similarly, he is liable if he differed [with the majority] concerning the redemption of consecrated property, had it been redeemed or not.[16] For according to the opinion that the redemption is invalid, if [he used that article] to consecrate a woman, the consecration is not valid.

Similarly, if they differed with regard to bringing an *eglah arufah*,[17] whether a city is obligated to bring or not, he is liable. For according to those who say [that city] is obligated to bring [the calf], it is forbidden to derive benefit from it and if he uses it to consecrate a woman, the consecration is not valid. Similar [concepts apply] if they differed with regard to *orlah*.[18] And similar concepts apply with regard to *leket*,[19] *shichechah*,[20] and *pe'ah*.[21] If they differ whether it belongs to the poor or to the owner, he is liable. For according to the opinion which says that it belongs to the owner, it is stolen property in the hands of the poor and if one consecrates a woman with it, she is not consecrated.

Similarly, if [the rebellious elder] differs with the court with regard to a category of factors that impart ritual impurity, e.g., blemishes on the skin,[22] blemishes on homes,[23] or blemishes on garments,[24] he is liable. For according to the opinion that the person is pure, he is permitted to enter the Temple and partake of consecrated foods, but according to the opinion that he is impure, if he enters [the Temple] or partakes [of consecrated food] willfully, he is punishable by *kerait*, and [if he does so] inadvertently, he is liable for a sin

13. While, according to the other opinion, the consecration is valid and relations with her involve a prohibition whose willful violation is punishable by *kerait* and whose inadvertent violation requires a sin offering.

14. E.g., they differed about the endowment obligation of a child less than a month old, must the child's worth be given or not? See *Sanhedrin* 88a.

15. E.g., they differed if interdicted property (*cherem*, see Leviticus, ch. 27, *Hilchot Arachin V'Charamim*, ch. 6) whose objective was not specified should be given to the Temple treasury or to the priests. According to the opinion that it should be given to the

וְכֵן אִם נֶחְלְקוּ בְּדִינֵי מַכּוֹת, אִם זֶה חַיָּב מַלְקוּת אוֹ אֵינוֹ, אוֹ שֶׁחָלַק בְּמִנְיַן הַדַּיָּנִים שֶׁלּוֹקִין בִּפְנֵיהֶם – הֲרֵי זֶה חַיָּב; שֶׁהֲרֵי לְדִבְרֵי הָאוֹמֵר אֵינוֹ לוֹקֶה – חוֹבְלִין הֵם בּוֹ, וְחַיָּבִין לְשַׁלֵּם, וְכֹל שֶׁיִּטֹּל מֵהֶן – כְּדִין נוֹטֵל; וּלְדִבְרֵי הָאוֹמֵר בֶּן מַלְקוּת הוּא, כֹּל שֶׁיִּטֹּל מֵהֶן – גָּזֵל הוּא בְּיָדוֹ, וְאִם קִדֵּשׁ בּוֹ אִשָּׁה – אֵינָהּ מְקֻדֶּשֶׁת.

וְכֵן אִם נֶחְלְקוּ בַּעֲרָכִין אוֹ בַּחֲרָמִין, אִם זֶה חַיָּב לִתֵּן אוֹ אֵינוֹ – הֲרֵי זֶה חַיָּב; שֶׁהֲרֵי לְדִבְרֵי הָאוֹמֵר אֵינוֹ חַיָּב לִתֵּן, אִם לָקְחוּ מִמֶּנּוּ – הֲרֵי זֶה גָזֵל, וְהַמְקַדֵּשׁ בּוֹ אִשָּׁה – אֵינָהּ מְקֻדֶּשֶׁת.

וְכֵן אִם חָלַק עֲלֵיהֶן בְּפִדְיוֹן קֳדָשִׁים, אִם נִפְדּוּ אוֹ לֹא נִפְדּוּ – הֲרֵי זֶה חַיָּב; שֶׁהֲרֵי לְדִבְרֵי הָאוֹמֵר אֵין זֶה פִּדְיוֹן, אִם קִדֵּשׁ בּוֹ אִשָּׁה – אֵינָהּ מְקֻדֶּשֶׁת. וְכֵן אִם נֶחְלְקוּ בַּעֲרִיפַת הָעֶגְלָה, אִם אֵלּוּ חַיָּבִין לְהָבִיא אוֹ לֹא – הֲרֵי זֶה חַיָּב; שֶׁהֲרֵי לְדִבְרֵי הָאוֹמֵר חַיָּבִים לְהָבִיא – הֲרֵי הִיא אֲסוּרָה בַּהֲנָאָה, וְהַמְקַדֵּשׁ בּוֹ אִשָּׁה – אֵינָהּ מְקֻדֶּשֶׁת. וְכֵן אִם נֶחְלְקוּ בְּעָרְלָה. וְכֵן אִם נֶחְלְקוּ בְּלֶקֶט שִׁכְחָה וּפֵאָה, אִם זֶה לָעֲנִיִּים אוֹ לְבַעַל הַבַּיִת – הֲרֵי זֶה חַיָּב; שֶׁהֲרֵי לְדִבְרֵי הָאוֹמֵר לְבַעַל הַבַּיִת – הֲרֵי זֶה גָזֵל בְּיַד הֶעָנִי, וְאִם קִדֵּשׁ בּוֹ אִשָּׁה – אֵינָהּ מְקֻדֶּשֶׁת.

וְכֵן אִם חָלַק עֲלֵיהֶן בְּאָב מֵאֲבוֹת הַטֻּמְאָה, כְּגוֹן נִגְעֵי בָשָׂר אוֹ נִגְעֵי בָתִּים אוֹ נִגְעֵי בְגָדִים – הֲרֵי זֶה חַיָּב; שֶׁהֲרֵי לְדִבְרֵי הָאוֹמֵר טָהוֹר – מֻתָּר לְהִכָּנֵס בַּמִּקְדָּשׁ וְלֶאֱכֹל קֳדָשִׁים; וּלְדִבְרֵי הָאוֹמֵר טָמֵא, אִם נִכְנַס אוֹ אָכַל בְּמֵזִיד – עָנוּשׁ כָּרֵת, וּבְשׁוֹגֵג – חַיָּב חַטָּאת.

priests, it is his private property and can be used to consecrate a woman, while according to the other view, if it is used to consecrate a woman, the consecration is not valid.

16. I.e., their difference of opinion concerned whether the evaluation of the consecrated article's worth was carried out according to required principles and the redemption is valid, or whether those requirements where not met, and hence the redemption was invalid (*Sanhedrin, loc. cit.*).

17. A calf whose neck is broken to atone for an unsolved murder (see Deuteronomy, ch. 21).

18. The fruits produced by a tree in the first three years after it was planted. It is forbidden to benefit from these fruits. Hence according to the opinion that they are forbidden, if they are used to consecrate a woman, the consecration is not valid.

19. Produce which falls from the reapers' hands that must be left for the poor (see Leviticus 19:9, 23:22).

20. Produce forgotten by the reapers which must be left for the poor (see Deuteronomy 24:19).

21. The corners of the field which must be left for the poor (see Leviticus, *loc. cit.*).

22. The Rambam is referring to blemishes caused by *tzara'at*, a spiritual affliction resembling leprosy. See Leviticus, chs. 12-13. These blemishes render a person ritually impure.

23. As related in Leviticus, ch. 14, *tzara'at* can also affect a building. In such an instance, anyone who enters the building becomes ritually impure.

24. Similarly, as stated in Leviticus, ch. 13, *tzara'at* can also affect a garment which in turn can convey ritual impurity upon a person.

offering. Similar concepts apply if they differed with regard to the purification of a person afflicted by *tzara'at*, if he can be purified or not.[25]

Similarly, he is liable if they differ with regard to the obligation to make a *sotah* drink [the water which conveys the curse]:[26] Is a woman required to drink [the water] or is she not required? For according to the person who says that she must drink, if her husband dies before she drinks, she is forbidden to her *yevam*,[27] while according to the person who says that she is not required to drink, she may perform the rite of *yibbum*.[28] Similar laws apply in all analogous situations.

It is necessary to investigate and examine whether a difference of opinion will lead to these consequences. If it will lead to another consequence which - after a series of even 100 consequences - will bring about a situation involving a prohibition whose willful violation is punishable by *kerait* and whose inadvertent violation requires a sin offering, the [rebellious] elder is liable. [This applies] regardless of whether he ruled leniently and the others ruled stringently or he ruled stringently and they ruled leniently.[29]

3. If the difference of opinion between [the rebellious elder and the court] will not lead to such a situation, [the rebellious elder] is not liable [for execution] unless [the difference of opinion] concerns *tefillin*.[30]

What is implied? [If the rebellious elder] gave a directive to add a fifth compartment to *tefillin* making five compartments, he is liable. [This applies] provided he first made four compartments as required by law and then made a fifth compartment and attached it to the outer [compartment]. For when an outer compartment is not exposed to open space at all times, it is unacceptable.[31]

The obligation of a rebellious elder in such a matter is a law transmitted by the Oral Tradition. If, however, they differed with regard to other mitzvot, e.g., he disputed one of the laws concerning a *lulav, tzitzit*,[32] or a *shofar*, one claiming that it is unacceptable and the other claiming that it is acceptable,

25. For the same question, can that person enter the Temple and partake of consecrated foods, applies.

26. When a husband suspects his wife of committing adultery, he may warn her not to enter into privacy with a given man. If she violates this warning, she is given special water to drink. If she is in truth guilty of infidelity, she will die as a result of drinking this water. See Numbers, ch. 5.

27. The brother of her husband who must marry her if her husband died childless. See Deuteronomy, ch. 25.

28. The *Kessef Mishneh* questions the Rambam's statements, noting that although a *sotah* is forbidden to her *yevam*, that prohibition is not punishable by *kerait*, merely by lashes. (See *Hilchot Yibbum ViChalitzah* 6:19 which bears out that statement.) The *Kessef Mishneh* does not offer a resolution to the matter. Note the *Merkevat HaMishneh* who does, suggesting a situation that depends on an understanding of the intricacies of the laws regarding *yibbum*.

29. For as mentioned, our worry is not that he is releasing a stringent prohibition, but that

וְכֵן אִם נֶחְלְקוּ בְּטָהֳרַת מְצֹרָע, אִם יֵשׁ לָזֶה טָהֳרָה אוֹ אֵין לוֹ. וְכֵן אִם נֶחְלְקוּ בְּהַשְׁקָאַת סוֹטָה, אִם זוֹ צְרִיכָה לִשְׁתּוֹת אוֹ אֵינָהּ צְרִיכָה – הֲרֵי זֶה חַיָּב; שֶׁהֲרֵי לְדִבְרֵי הָאוֹמֵר צְרִיכָה, אִם מֵת הַבַּעַל קֹדֶם שֶׁתִּשְׁתֶּה – הֲרֵי זוֹ אֲסוּרָה לִיבָמָהּ; וּלְדִבְרֵי הָאוֹמֵר אֵינָהּ צְרִיכָה – מִתְיַבֶּמֶת.

וְכֵן כֹּל כַּיּוֹצֵא בָּזֶה – צְרִיכִין לִבְדֹּק וְלַחְקֹר אִם הָיְתָה מַחֲלֹקֶת זוֹ מְבִיאָה לִידֵי דָבָר זֶה, וְדָבָר זֶה מֵבִיא לִידֵי דָבָר שֵׁנִי, אֲפִלּוּ אַחַר מֵאָה דְבָרִים, אִם יָבוֹא בַּסּוֹף לְדָבָר שֶׁזְּדוֹנוֹ כָּרֵת וְשִׁגְגָתוֹ חַטָּאת, בֵּין שֶׁהָיָה הַזָּקֵן מֵקֵל וְהֵן מַחְמִירִין בֵּין שֶׁהָיָה הוּא מַחְמִיר וְהֵן מְקִלִּין – חַיָּב.

ג וְאִם לֹא תָּבִיא הַמַּחֲלֹקֶת לִידֵי כָּךְ – הֲרֵי זֶה פָּטוּר. חוּץ מִמִּצְוַת תְּפִלִּין בִּלְבַד. כֵּיצַד? הוֹרָה לְהוֹסִיף טוֹטֶפֶת חֲמִישִׁית בַּתְּפִלִּין וְיַעֲשֶׂנָּה חָמֵשׁ טוֹטָפוֹת – הֲרֵי זֶה חַיָּב. וְהוּא שֶׁיַּעֲשֶׂה בַּתְּחִלָּה אַרְבָּעָה בָּתִּים כְּהִלְכָתָן זֶה, וְיָבִיא חֲמִישִׁית וִידַבֵּק בַּחִיצוֹן; שֶׁהַבַּיִת הַחִיצוֹן שֶׁאֵינוֹ רוֹאֶה אֶת הָאֲוִיר – תָּמִיד פָּסוּל.

וְחִיּוּב זָקֵן מַמְרֵא עַל דָּבָר זֶה – הֲלָכָה מִפִּי הַקַּבָּלָה. אֲבָל אִם נֶחְלְקוּ בִּשְׁאָר מִצְוֹת, כְּגוֹן שֶׁחָלַק בְּדָבָר מִדִּבְרֵי לוּלָב אוֹ צִיצִית אוֹ שׁוֹפָר, זֶה אוֹמֵר פָּסוּל, וְזֶה אוֹמֵר כָּשֵׁר,

his directives will spur controversy among the Jewish people and prevent there being a unified halachic consensus (Radbaz).

30. As mentioned in the notes to Halachah 1, there are two different opinions in *Sanhedrin* 87a with regard to when a rebellious elder becomes liable. In Halachot 1 and 2, the Rambam followed one opinion (that of Rabbi Meir). Here his rulings relate to the other one (that of Rabbi Yehudah).

The Ra'avad differs with the Rambam, maintaining that the different opinions are conflicting and cannot be reconciled with each other. The Radbaz and the *Kessef Mishneh* justify the Rambam's position.

31. Rabbi Elazar in the name of Rabbi Ushia explains Rabbi Yehudah's perspective as follows: "He is not liable unless [the difference of opinion] concerns a matter that comes fundamentally from Scripture, but whose interpretation is Rabbinic. It must be able to add to our Sages' [interpretation of how to observe the mitzvah], and that addition must degrade [and disqualify the mitzvah]."

If at the outset, the person made five compartments, he is not making an addition that degrades; he is not fulfilling the mitzvah in the proper way from the outset. In this instance, however, the four compartments make the *tefillin* acceptable. By adding the fifth compartment in the manner described by the Rambam, he disqualifies one of the first four, thus making the *tefillin* unacceptable.

32. For unlike *tefillin*, with regard to these mitzvot, they are either acceptable or unacceptable from the outset, there is no concept of it being acceptable and then being disqualified. For to add a new strand *tzitzit* or a new species to the four for the *lulav*, one would have to undo the existing bond. And the new bond would not be acceptable from the outset (Ra'avad).

The Radbaz emphasizes that although the elder is not judged as rebellious for issuing such rulings with regard to *tzitzit* and a *lulav*, if one adds a strand or another species, one does violate the prohibition against adding to the Torah's commandments.

one claiming that the person fulfilled his obligation and the other claiming he did not fulfill his obligation, or one says: "He is pure," and the other says: "He is impure two degrees removed,"[33] [the elder] is not liable for execution.[34] Similar laws apply in all analogous situations.

CHAPTER FIVE

1. A person who curses his father and mother should be executed by stoning,[1] as [Leviticus 20:9] states: "He cursed his father and his mother; he is responsible for his death."[2] He is stoned to death whether he curses them while alive or after they died.[3] It is necessary that [his act be observed by] witnesses[4] and [they] warn [him] as is required with regard to other individuals executed by the court.[5]

The above applies to both a man and woman, and also to a *tumtum*[6] and an *androgynus,*[7] provided they reached majority, the age when they can be subjected to punishment.[8]

2. A person is not liable for execution by stoning unless he curses [his parents] with one of God's unique names.[9] If he cursed them with another term used to refer to Him,[10] he is not liable for execution by stoning. He should, [however,] be lashed, as he would be lashed for cursing any other proper Jew.[11]

3. Similarly, a person who curses his paternal and maternal grandfather[12] is considered as if he cursed any other person.[13]

4. What is the source which serves as a warning[14] against cursing one's father and one's mother? We have heard the punishment explicitly stated,[15] the warning, [however, is not stated explicitly]. [Instead,] it can be inferred from

33. I.e., he came in contact with an article or a person that came in contact with a source of ritual impurity. As the Rambam states in *Hilchot Bi'at HaMikdash* 3:15, if a person enters the Temple after coming into such contact, he is not liable for *kerait.*
34. He should, however, be punished in other ways, as stated in Chapter 3, Halachah 7.

1. *Sefer HaMitzvot* (negative commandment 318) and *Sefer HaChinuch* (mitzvah 260) count the prohibition against cursing one's parents as one of the 613 mitzvot of the Torah.

The Radbaz emphasizes that a person who curses his parents is given a more severe punishment than one who strikes them, because by cursing them he also mentions God's name in vain.

2. *Sanhedrin* 66a derives the obligation for this penalty from an analogy established between this verse and Leviticus 20:27 which mentions stoning explicitly.
3. For even after a person's death, cursing him brings negative consequences to his soul.
4. One might think that since it is likely for a person to curse his parents in the privacy of his home, the Torah would not require witnesses for it is unlikely that they be present. Hence the Rambam adds this clarification (*Kessef Mishneh*).

זֶה אוֹמֵר יָצָא יְדֵי חוֹבָתוֹ, וְזֶה אוֹמֵר לֹא יָצָא, זֶה אוֹמֵר טָהוֹר, וְזֶה אוֹמֵר שֵׁנִי לְטֻמְאָה – הֲרֵי זֶה פָּטוּר מִן הַמִּיתָה. וְכֵן כֹּל כַּיּוֹצֵא בָּזֶה.

פֶּרֶק חֲמִישִׁי

א הַמְקַלֵּל אָבִיו וְאִמּוֹ – נִסְקָל; שֶׁנֶּאֱמַר: אָבִיו וְאִמּוֹ קִלֵּל, דָּמָיו בּוֹ. וְאֶחָד הַמְקַלֵּל בְּחַיֵּיהֶן אוֹ לְאַחַר מִיתָתָן – הֲרֵי זֶה נִסְקָל. וְצָרִיךְ עֵדִים וְהַתְרָאָה, כִּשְׁאָר כָּל מְחֻיְּבֵי מִיתוֹת בֵּית דִּין.

וְאֶחָד הָאִישׁ וְאֶחָד הָאִשָּׁה, וְכֵן הַטֻּמְטוּם וְהָאַנְדְּרוֹגִינוֹס. וְהוּא שֶׁיִּהְיוּ גְּדוֹלִים שֶׁהִגִּיעוּ לִכְלַל הָעֳנָשִׁין.

ב אֵינוֹ חַיָּב סְקִילָה עַד שֶׁיְּקַלְּלֵם בְּשֵׁם מִן הַשֵּׁמוֹת הַמְיֻחָדִין; אֲבָל אִם קִלְּלָם בְּכִנּוּי – פָּטוּר מִן הַסְּקִילָה, וְלוֹקֶה כְּדֶרֶךְ שֶׁלּוֹקֶה עַל קִלְלַת כָּל אָדָם כָּשֵׁר מִיִּשְׂרָאֵל.

ג וְכֵן הַמְקַלֵּל אֲבִי אָבִיו וַאֲבִי אִמּוֹ – הֲרֵי זֶה כִּמְקַלֵּל אֶחָד מִשְּׁאָר הַקָּהָל.

ד אַזְהָרָה שֶׁל מְקַלֵּל אָבִיו וְאִמּוֹ מִנַּיִן? עֹנֶשׁ שָׁמַעְנוּ בְּפֵרוּשׁ, אֲבָל הָאַזְהָרָה הֲרֵי הִיא

5. See *Hilchot Sanhedrin* 12:2.
6. A person whose genital area is covered by a piece of flesh which prevents us from seeing his gender.
7. A person who has both male and female genital organs and whose gender is thus an unresolved matter.
8. I.e., twelve for a girl, thirteen for a boy and for a *tumtum* and *androgynus*.
9. I.e., the seven names of God that may not be erased. See *Hilchot Yesodei HaTorah* 6:2.
10. E.g., the Merciful One, the All-Knowing, or the like. Compare to *Hilchot Sh'vuot* 2:2.
11. I.e., a person who observes the Torah and its mitzvot.

The Rambam mentions the prohibition against and the punishment for cursing a fellow Jew in *Hilchot Sanhedrin* 26:1. In 26:3, he mentions that one is also liable for cursing when using a descriptive term for God.

The *Kessef Mishneh* notes that the Rambam's ruling here represents somewhat of a contradiction to his ruling in *Hilchot Avodat Kochavim* 2:7.

12. Or grandmother.
13. I.e., he is lashed, not executed. As the *Kessef Mishneh* states, a person does not owe his grandfather the same measure of honor he owes his parents.
14. I.e., an explicit negative command. For there is no verse which states: "Do not curse your parents."
15. In the verse from Leviticus cited in Halachah 1.

[Leviticus 19:14]: "Do not curse a deaf-mute." Since a person is warned not to curse any Jew,[16] his father is also included, [for] he is [also] Jewish.

5. A person who strikes his father or mother should be executed by strangulation,[17] as [Exodus 21:15] states: "One who strikes his father or his mother should certainly die." It is necessary that [his act be observed by] witnesses[18] and [they] warn [him] as is required with regard to other individuals executed by the court.

The above applies to both a man and woman, and also to a *tumtum*, and an *androgynus* provided they reached majority, the age when they can be subjected to punishment.

A person is not liable for strangulation until he wounds [his parents].[19] If he does not wound them, it is as if he strikes another Jew.[20] If he strikes them after their death, he is not liable.[21]

6. When a person strikes his father on his ear and causes him to become deaf, he is liable [for] execution.[22] [The rationale is that] it is impossible for him to become deaf without there being an [internal] wound. Instead, [we can be certain that at least] a drop of blood was released within the ear and [that] caused him to become deaf.

7. When a person lets blood for his father, or if he was a doctor and amputated flesh or a limb,[23] he is not liable.[24] Even though he is not liable, the initial and preferred option is for him not to perform the operation. Nor should he remove a thorn from the flesh of his father or mother lest he cause a bruise.

When does the above apply? When there is another person there who is capable of performing these actions. If, however, there is no one else there capable of doing this but him and they are suffering, he may let blood or amputate[25] according to the license that they grant him.[26]

8. What is the source which serves as a warning[27] against striking one's father and one's mother? We have heard the punishment explicitly stated,[28] the warning, [however, is not stated explicitly]. Since a person is warned not to strike any Jew,[29] his father and mother are also included.

9. A *shituki*[30] is liable [for cursing or striking] his mother, but not his father.

16. For as *Hilchot Sanhedrin* 26:1 states, the prohibition against cursing a deaf-mute also includes all other Jews.
17. *Sefer HaMitzvot* (negative commandment 319) and *Sefer HaChinuch* (mitzvah 48) count the prohibition against cursing one's parents as one of the 613 mitzvot of the Torah.
18. With regard to this and the other particulars mentioned in this halachah, see the notes to Halachah 1.
19. Drawing blood.

בִּכְלַל לֹא תְקַלֵּל חֵרֵשׁ. הוֹאִיל וְהוּא מֻזְהָר שֶׁלֹּא לְקַלֵּל אָדָם מִיִּשְׂרָאֵל, הֲרֵי אָבִיו בִּכְלַל יִשְׂרָאֵל.

ה הַמַּכֶּה אָבִיו וְאִמּוֹ – מִיתָתוֹ בְּחֶנֶק; שֶׁנֶּאֱמַר: מַכֵּה אָבִיו וְאִמּוֹ מוֹת יוּמָת. וְצָרִיךְ עֵדִים וְהַתְרָאָה, כִּשְׁאָר כָּל מְחֻיְּבֵי מִיתַת בֵּית דִּין. וְאֶחָד הָאִישׁ וְאֶחָד הָאִשָּׁה, וְכֵן הַטֻּמְטוּם וְאַנְדְּרוֹגִינוֹס. וְהוּא שֶׁיַּגִּיעוּ לִכְלַל עֳנָשִׁין. אֵינוֹ חַיָּב חֶנֶק עַד שֶׁיַּעֲשֶׂה בָּהֶן חַבּוּרָה; אֲבָל אִם לֹא עָשָׂה בָּהֶן חַבּוּרָה – הֲרֵי זֶה כְּמַכֶּה אֶחָד מִיִּשְׂרָאֵל. וְהַמַּכֶּה אוֹתָן לְאַחַר מִיתָה – פָּטוּר.

ו מִי שֶׁהִכָּה אֶת אָבִיו עַל אָזְנוֹ וְחֵרְשׁוֹ – חַיָּב וְנֶהֱרָג. שֶׁאִי אֶפְשָׁר שֶׁיֵּעָשֶׂה חֵרֵשׁ בְּלֹא חַבּוּרָה, אֶלָּא יָצָאת טִפַּת דָּם בִּפְנִים בָּאֹזֶן וְנִתְחָרֵשׁ.

ז הַמַּקִּיז דָּם לְאָבִיו, אוֹ שֶׁהָיָה רוֹפֵא וְחָתַךְ לוֹ בָּשָׂר אוֹ אֵיבָר – פָּטוּר. אַף עַל פִּי שֶׁהוּא פָּטוּר, לְכַתְּחִלָּה לֹא יַעֲשֶׂה. אוֹ לְהוֹצִיא סִלּוֹן מִבְּשַׂר אָבִיו אוֹ אִמּוֹ – לֹא יוֹצִיא, שֶׁמָּא יַעֲשֶׂה חַבּוּרָה. בַּמֶּה דְּבָרִים אֲמוּרִים? כְּשֶׁיֵּשׁ שָׁם אַחֵר לַעֲשׂוֹת; אֲבָל אִם אֵין שָׁם מִי שֶׁיַּעֲשֶׂה אֶלָּא הוּא, וַהֲרֵי הֵן מִצְטַעֲרִין – הֲרֵי זֶה מַקִּיז וְחוֹתֵךְ כְּפִי מַה שֶּׁיַּרְשֵׁהוּ לַעֲשׂוֹת.

ח אַזְהָרָה שֶׁל מַכֵּה אָבִיו מִנַּיִן? עֹנֶשׁ שָׁמַעְנוּ, אַזְהָרָה לֹא שָׁמַעְנוּ. הוֹאִיל וְהוּא מֻזְהָר שֶׁלֹּא לְהַכּוֹת אָדָם מִיִּשְׂרָאֵל – הֲרֵי אָבִיו וְאִמּוֹ בַּכְּלָל.

ט שְׁתוּקִי – חַיָּב עַל אִמּוֹ, וְאֵינוֹ חַיָּב עַל אָבִיו.

20. In which instance, he is liable only for a financial penalty. See *Hilchot Chovel UMazik* 5:1, *Hilchot Sanhedrin* 19:4.
21. For once a person has died, there is no concept of him being wounded.
22. Even though there is no outward sign of bleeding.
23. With the intent of healing his father.
24. *Sanhedrin* 84b uses techniques of Biblical exegesis to emphasize why actions performed for medical purposes do not make a person liable.
25. *Sanhedrin, loc. cit.*, states that we are only forbidden to perform actions that a person would not desire to have done for him.
26. Implied is that his parents must authorize his activity. *Kin'at Eliyahu* questions what would the law be if they are unconscious and he must act without permission. He maintains that if the operation is absolutely necessary, he should perform it. For a threat to life takes precedence over all the mitzvot. If it is not absolutely necessary, he should wait until his parents regain consciousness.
27. I.e., an explicit negative command. For there is no verse which states: "Do not strike your parents."
28. In the verse from Leviticus cited in Halachah 5.
29. As the Rambam states in *Hilchot Sanhedrin* 16:12; *Hilchot Chovel UMazik* 5:1.
30. In *Hilchot Issurei Bi'ah* 15:12, the Rambam defines this term as referring to a person

Although his mother is questioned and she says: "He is the son of so-and-so," he should not be executed by stoning or strangulation because of her testimony.[31]

[A person who is conceived through relations between a Jew] and a maid-servant or a gentile woman, by contrast, is not liable [for cursing or striking] his father or his mother.[32] Similarly, a convert - [even] if he was conceived outside the faith,[33] but born within the faith[34] - is not liable for cursing or striking his father.[35]

10. Just as [such a person] is not liable [for cursing or striking] his father, he is not liable [for cursing or striking] his mother.[36] [This is derived from Exodus 21:17]: "One who curses his father and mother [shall die]." [Implied is] one who is liable for [cursing] his father is liable for [cursing] his mother. Since such a person is not liable for his father, he is not liable for his mother.[37]

11. A convert is forbidden to curse or to strike his gentile father[38] or to degrade him, so that [people] will not say: "They came from a more severe level of holiness to a lesser level of holiness, for this person degrades his father."[39] Instead, he should offer him certain measures of honor.[40]

A servant, by contrast, has no connection to his natural parents.[41] His natural father is as if he was not his father with regard to all matters. This applies even if they were [both] freed.

12. When a person's father and mother are absolutely wicked and violate transgressions - even if they were sentenced to death and being taken to their execution - it is forbidden for a son to strike them or curse them.[42] If he curses them or wounds them, [however,] he is not liable.[43] If they repent, even if they are being taken to their execution, he is liable and is executed because of them.[44]

To whom does the above apply? To [the convicted person's] son.[45] If, however, an unrelated individual struck or cursed a person after he was

who knows the identity of his mother, but not of his father. *Shituki* means "one who is silenced." Rashi (*Yevamot* 37a) states that such a child is given this name, because he will call for his father and his mother will silence him.

31. Although the mother's testimony is significant in certain instances (see *Hilchot Issurei Bi'ah* 15:11), it does not have sufficient weight to have the son sentenced to death. See also *Hilchot Issurei Bi'ah* 1:20-21 where the Rambam rules that the popular conception of the matter of a person's relationship to his parents is halachicly significant.

32. For such a child is considered as having no family ties to his natural father. He is a like a servant or a gentile. If he converts, he is considered as a newborn child and has no family ties to his natural mother either. See *Hilchot Yibbum ViChalitzah* 1:4.

33. I.e., at the time of conception, his mother was not Jewish.

34. She converted before his birth.

35. This applies whether his natural father was Jewish or was a gentile who converted. The son is considered as having no family connection to him.

אַף עַל פִּי שֶׁנִּבְדְּקָה אִמּוֹ וְאָמְרָה: בֶּן פְּלוֹנִי הוּא – אֵינוֹ נִסְקָל אוֹ נֶחֱנָק עַל פִּיהָ.
אֲבָל בְּנוֹ מִן הַשִּׁפְחָה וּמִן הָעוֹבֶדֶת כּוֹכָבִים – אֵינוֹ חַיָּב לֹא עַל אָבִיו וְלֹא עַל אִמּוֹ.
וְכֵן גֵּר שֶׁהוֹרָתוֹ שֶׁלֹּא בִּקְדֻשָּׁה, אַף עַל פִּי שֶׁלֵּדָתוֹ בִּקְדֻשָּׁה – אֵינוֹ חַיָּב עַל מַכַּת אָבִיו וְקִלְלָתוֹ.

י כְּשֵׁם שֶׁאֵינוֹ חַיָּב עַל אָבִיו, כָּךְ אֵינוֹ חַיָּב עַל אִמּוֹ. שֶׁנֶּאֱמַר: וּמְקַלֵּל אָבִיו וְאִמּוֹ. אֶת שֶׁהוּא חַיָּב עַל אָבִיו – חַיָּב עַל אִמּוֹ, וְזֶה שֶׁאֵינוֹ חַיָּב עַל אָבִיו – אֵינוֹ חַיָּב עַל אִמּוֹ.

יא הַגֵּר אָסוּר לְקַלֵּל אָבִיו הָעוֹבֵד כּוֹכָבִים וּלְהַכּוֹתוֹ. וְלֹא יְבַזֵּהוּ. כְּדֵי שֶׁלֹּא יֹאמְרוּ: בָּאוּ מִקְּדֻשָּׁה חֲמוּרָה לִקְדֻשָּׁה קַלָּה, שֶׁהֲרֵי זֶה מְבַזֶּה אָבִיו. אֶלָּא נוֹהֵג בּוֹ מִקְצָת כָּבוֹד. אֲבָל הָעֶבֶד – אֵין לוֹ יִחוּס, אֶלָּא הֲרֵי אָבִיו כְּמִי שֶׁאֵינוֹ אָבִיו לְכָל דָּבָר, אַף עַל פִּי שֶׁנִּשְׁתַּחְרְרוּ.

יב מִי שֶׁהָיוּ אָבִיו וְאִמּוֹ רְשָׁעִים גְּמוּרִים וְעוֹבְרֵי עֲבֵרוֹת, אֲפִלּוּ נִגְמַר דִּינָן לַהֲרִיגָה וְהֵם יוֹצְאִים לֵהָרֵג – אָסוּר לְהַכּוֹתָן וּלְקַלְּלָם. וְאִם קִלֵּל אוֹ חָבַל בָּהֶן – פָּטוּר. וְאִם עָשׂוּ תְּשׁוּבָה – הֲרֵי זֶה חַיָּב, וְנֶהֱרָג עֲלֵיהֶן, אַף עַל פִּי שֶׁהֲרֵי הֵן יוֹצְאִין לְמִיתָה.
בַּמֶּה דְּבָרִים אֲמוּרִים? בִּבְנוֹ; אֲבָל אַחֵר שֶׁבָּא וְהִכָּהוּ וְקִלְּלוֹ אַחַר שֶׁנִּגְמַר דִּינוֹ, אַף עַל פִּי

36. Although she was Jewish when she gave birth to the child.
37. A *shituki* is not liable for cursing or striking his father, but that is because he does not know who his father is. If his father's identity was established, he would be liable. Hence he is liable for cursing or striking his mother. This child, by contrast, is considered as if he does not have a father at all. Therefore he is not liable for striking or cursing his mother (Radbaz, *Kessef Mishneh*).
38. I.e., his natural father who has not converted.
39. I.e., it would appear that becoming Jewish has minimized the convert's responsibilities for he no longer must honor his gentile father.
40. I.e., he should show him the same measure of respect as he did as a gentile.
41. I.e., a gentile has a certain measure of responsibility to his parents, for he is considered their son according to law. Hence even if he converts - at which time he is considered like a new baby - he still must continue to show them a similar degree of honor. A servant, by contrast, is considered as his master's property and thus has no connection to his natural parents. It is as if they did not conceive him. Even if his father is Jewish, the servant is not considered as his son. Compare to *Hilchot Ishut* 15:6.
42. He may not do this on his own initiative, nor may he act as an agent of the court to perform these acts, as stated in Halachah 13 (*Sanhedrin* 85b).
43. Through their violation of Torah law, it is as if they removed themselves from the Jewish people. Hence their son is not liable for violating his obligation to respect them.
44. Because their repentance restores their status. Although they are liable to die for their sins, their children are still obligated to respect them.
45. For a son is liable for cursing his parents after their death (Halachah 1). It's true that he is not liable for striking them after their death (Halachah 5), but that is only because

sentenced to death, even though he repents, he is not liable, for that person will be executed.[46] If, however, he embarrasses him, he is liable to pay a fine for embarrassing him.

13. If a person's father or mother committed a transgression punishable by lashes and the son is a court attendant, he should not lash them.[47] Similarly, if they were obligated to be placed under a ban of ostracism, he should not be the agent to apply this ban.[48] Nor should he push them or degrade them while acting as the emissary of the court[49] even though it is fit to do this to them and they have not repented.

14. A son should not serve as an agent to strike or curse [his parents] except if they entice others to worship idols.[50] For [concerning such a person], the Torah [Deuteronomy 13:9] states: "Do not have pity and do not cover up for him."[51]

15. In any situation where a person is obligated to take an oath to his son, we always endeavor that he never obligate him to take an oath that involves a curse.[52] Instead, he should have him take an oath that does not involve a curse.[53]

We already explained,[54] that when a father kills his son, none of the slain person's brothers becomes "the redeemer of the blood."[55]

The Torah showed concern not only for striking or cursing one's parents, but also for shaming them. Anyone who shames his parents, even with words alone or merely with an insinuation, is cursed by the Almighty, as [Deuteronomy 27:16] states: "Cursed be he who degrades his father and his mother." And [Proverbs 30:17] states: "The eye that mocks a father[56] and scorns the training of a mother, [the ravens... will gouge it out]." The court has the right to administer stripes for rebellious conduct[57] because of this and to punish in the manner they see fit.

CHAPTER SIX

1. Honoring one's father and mother is a positive commandment[1] of great importance, as is fearing one's father and mother.[2] The Torah equates[3] [the

there is no concept of wounding a dead person. There is, however, a concept of wounding someone going to his death.

46. As stated in Chapter 7, Halachah 9, whenever a person is sentenced to death, it is as if he was already executed. See also *Hilchot Edut* 19:2.

47. Even though he is not acting on his own, but as the agent of the court, he should not be the one charged with this responsibility.

48. For this resembles cursing (Radbaz).

49. See *Hilchot Sanhedrin* 24:5,9.

50. We have used general terms in our translation. In particular, the wording used by the Rambam has a specific connotation. A *mesit* is someone who attempts to entice an individual to worship false deities. A *madiach* is someone who attempts to lead an entire city astray. See *Hilchot Avodat Kochavim*, ch. 5.

שֶׁעָשָׂה תְּשׁוּבָה – הֲרֵי זֶה פָּטוּר, הוֹאִיל וְהוּא הוֹלֵךְ לְמִיתָה. וְאִם בִּיְּשׁוֹ – חַיָּב בִּקְנַס הַמְבַיֵּשׁ.

יג עָבַר אָבִיו וְאִמּוֹ עַל עֲבֵרָה שֶׁלּוֹקִין עָלֶיהָ, וְהָיָה הוּא חַזָּן לִפְנֵי הַדַּיָּנִים – לֹא יַכֶּה אוֹתָם. וְכֵן אִם נִתְחַיְּבוּ נִדּוּי – לֹא יִהְיֶה שָׁלִיחַ לְנַדּוֹתָם. וְלֹא יִדְחַף אוֹתָם וְלֹא יְבַזֶּה אוֹתָם בִּשְׁלִיחוּת בֵּית דִּין, אַף עַל פִּי שֶׁהֵן רְאוּיִין לְכָךְ וְלֹא עָשׂוּ תְּשׁוּבָה.

יד לַכֹּל אֵין הַבֵּן נַעֲשֶׂה שָׁלִיחַ לְהַכּוֹתוֹ וּלְקַלְּלוֹ, חוּץ מִמֵּסִית וּמַדִּיחַ. שֶׁהֲרֵי אָמְרָה תּוֹרָה: לֹא תַחְמֹל וְלֹא תְכַסֶּה עָלָיו.

טו מִי שֶׁנִּתְחַיֵּב שְׁבוּעָה לִבְנוֹ – כָּךְ רָאִינוּ בּוֹ תָּמִיד, שֶׁאֵינוֹ מַשְׁבִּיעוֹ בִּשְׁבוּעַת הָאָלָה, שֶׁהֲרֵי זֶה בָּא לְקִלְלַת אָבִיו, אֶלָּא מַשְׁבִּיעוֹ שְׁבוּעָה שֶׁאֵין בָּהּ אָלָה. וּכְבָר בֵּאַרְנוּ, שֶׁהָאָב שֶׁהָרַג אֶת בְּנוֹ – אֵין אֶחָד מֵאֶחָיו שֶׁל נֶהֱרָג נַעֲשֶׂה גּוֹאֵל הַדָּם. וְלֹא עַל הַכָּאָה וְלֹא עַל הַקְּלָלָה בִּלְבַד הִקְפִּידָה תּוֹרָה, אֶלָּא אַף עַל הַבִּזָּיוֹן. שֶׁכָּל הַמְבַזֶּה אָבִיו אוֹ אִמּוֹ, אֲפִלּוּ בִּדְבָרִים וַאֲפִלּוּ בִּרְמִיזָה – הֲרֵי זֶה אָרוּר מִפִּי הַגְּבוּרָה. שֶׁנֶּאֱמַר: אָרוּר מַקְלֶה אָבִיו וְאִמּוֹ. וַהֲרֵי הוּא אוֹמֵר: עַיִן תִּלְעַג לְאָב וְתָבֻז לִיקְּהַת אֵם וְגוֹמֵר. וְיֵשׁ לְבֵית דִּין לְהַכּוֹת עַל זֶה מַכַּת מַרְדּוּת וְלַעֲנֹשׁ כְּפִי מַה שֶּׁיִּרְאוּ.

פֶּרֶק שִׁשִּׁי

א כִּבּוּד אָב וָאֵם – מִצְוַת עֲשֵׂה גְּדוֹלָה. וְכֵן מוֹרָא אָב וָאֵם. שָׁקַל אוֹתָן הַכָּתוּב בִּכְבוֹדוֹ וּבְמוֹרָאוֹ.

51. Having one's son administer these punishments may be more painful to bear than the punishments themselves.
52. See *Hilchot Sh'vuot* 11:9.
53. I.e., he should take an ordinary oath, mentioning God's name and stating that he does not owe his son anything.
54. *Hilchot Rotzeach* 1:3.
55. Who is obligated to kill the slayer.
56. By mentioning an "eye that mocks," the prooftext emphasizes that any mocking, even a mere insinuation is considered worthy of punishment.
57. See *Hilchot Sanhedrin* 26:5.

1. *Sefer HaMitzvot* (positive commandment 210) and *Sefer HaChinuch* (mitzvah 33) count this as one of the 613 mitzvot of the Torah.
2. *Sefer HaMitzvot* (positive commandment 211) and *Sefer HaChinuch* (mitzvah 212) count this as one of the 613 mitzvot of the Torah.
3. See the Jerusalem Talmud, *Pe'ah* 1:1, which explains that the honor one is required to show one's parents exceeds that which one is required to show God, as it were (Radbaz).

honor and fear of one's parents] with the honor and fear of [God] Himself. [Exodus 20:12] states: "Honor your father and your mother," and [Proverbs 3:9] states: "Honor God from your wealth." Similarly, with regard to one's father and mother, [Leviticus 19:3] states: "A person must fear his mother and father," and [Deuteronomy 6:13] states: "And you shall fear God, your Lord." Just as He commands us to honor and fear His great name; so, too, He commands us to honor and fear our parents."

2. A person who curses his father or mother is executed by stoning and a person who blasphemes God is executed by stoning. Thus the punishment for the two is equated.

A father is mentioned before a mother with regard to honor and a mother is mentioned before a father with regard to fear to teach that they are both equal with regard to fear and honor.[4]

3. What is meant by fear and what is meant by honor? Fear [is expressed by] not standing in his place,[5] not sitting in his place,[6] not contradicting his words, nor offering an opinion that outweighs his.[7]

He should not call him by name, neither during his lifetime nor after his death. Instead, he should say: "My father and my master."[8] If his father or his teacher had the same name as others, he should call those [other people] by a different name.[9] It appears to me that one should be careful only with regard to this matter with regard to a name that is unusual and which is not used frequently by people. With regard to the names which people are generally called, by contrast, e.g., Abraham, Isaac, Jacob, Moses, and the like, one can call others by that name in any language and at any time outside [his father's] presence without thinking anything of the matter.[10]

What is meant by honoring them? One should bring them food and drink, clothe them and cover them from their own resources.[11] If a father does not have financial resources and a son does, the son is compelled[12] to sustain his father and his mother according to his capacity.[13] He should take him out and

4. *Kiddushin* 31a states that a child has a tendency to honor his mother more than his father. Therefore, his father is mentioned first with regard to this mitzvah. And his tendency is to fear his father more, so with regard to that mitzvah, his mother is given first mention.

5. I.e., taking his position in the place where elders usually stand and take counsel with each other. Alternatively, it refers to standing in his place in the synagogue [*Shulchan Aruch* (*Yoreh Deah* 240:2)].

6. I.e., the place where he dines at home.

7. Our translation is based on a responsun of the Rambam (Responsum 264). Others render the term as supporting his words. For supporting his father's decision implies that his support enhances his father's words. That is a mark of disrespect.

When quoting this law, the *Shulchan Aruch* (*op. cit.*) mentions that this applies in his father's presence. For that is a mark of disrespect. Outside his father's presence, he may differ with him or justify his father's opinion. It would appear that the Rambam himself

כָּתוּב: כַּבֵּד אֶת אָבִיךָ וְאֶת אִמֶּךָ, וְכָתוּב: כַּבֵּד אֶת יְיָ מֵהוֹנֶךָ. וּבְאָבִיו וְאִמּוֹ כָּתוּב: אִישׁ אִמּוֹ וְאָבִיו תִּירָאוּ, וְכָתוּב: אֶת יְיָ אֱלֹהֶיךָ תִּירָא. כְּדֶרֶךְ שֶׁצִּוָּה עַל כְּבוֹד שְׁמוֹ הַגָּדוֹל וּמוֹרָאוֹ, כָּךְ צִוָּה עַל כְּבוֹדָם וּמוֹרָאָם.

ב הַמְקַלֵּל אָבִיו אוֹ אִמּוֹ – בִּסְקִילָה, וְהַמְגַדֵּף – בִּסְקִילָה. הִנֵּה הִשְׁוָה אוֹתָן בְּעֹנֶשׁ. הִקְדִּים אָב לְאֵם לְכָבוֹד, וְהִקְדִּים אֵם לְאָב לְמוֹרָא. לְלַמֵּד שֶׁשְּׁנֵיהֶם שָׁוִים, בֵּין לְמוֹרָא בֵּין לְכָבוֹד.

ג אֵי זֶהוּ מוֹרָא, וְאֵי זֶהוּ כָּבוֹד? מוֹרָא – לֹא עוֹמֵד בִּמְקוֹמוֹ, וְלֹא יוֹשֵׁב בִּמְקוֹמוֹ, וְלֹא סוֹתֵר אֶת דְּבָרָיו, וְלֹא מַכְרִיעַ אֶת דְּבָרָיו.

וְלֹא יִקְרָא לוֹ בִּשְׁמוֹ, לֹא בְּחַיָּיו וְלֹא בְּמוֹתוֹ, אֶלָּא אוֹמֵר: אַבָּא מָרִי. הָיָה שֵׁם אָבִיו אוֹ שֵׁם רַבּוֹ כְּשֵׁם אֲחֵרִים – מְשַׁנֶּה אֶת שְׁמָם. יֵרָאֶה לִי, שֶׁאֵין נִזְהָר בְּכָךְ אֶלָּא בְּשֵׁם שֶׁהוּא פֶּלֶא, שֶׁאֵין הַכֹּל דָּשִׁין בּוֹ; אֲבָל הַשֵּׁמוֹת שֶׁקּוֹרְאִין בָּהֶן אֶת הָעָם, כְּגוֹן אַבְרָהָם יִצְחָק וְיַעֲקֹב מֹשֶׁה וְכַיּוֹצֵא בָּהֶן, בְּכָל לָשׁוֹן וּבְכָל זְמַן – קוֹרֵא בָּהֶן לַאֲחֵרִים שֶׁלֹּא בְּפָנָיו, וְאֵין בְּכָךְ כְּלוּם.

אֵי זֶהוּ כָּבוֹד? מַאֲכִיל וּמַשְׁקֶה, מַלְבִּישׁ וּמְכַסֶּה – מִשֶּׁל הָאָב.

וְאִם אֵין מָמוֹן לָאָב, וְיֵשׁ מָמוֹן לַבֵּן – כּוֹפִין אוֹתוֹ וְזָן אָבִיו וְאִמּוֹ כְּפִי מַה שֶּׁהוּא יָכוֹל.

would accept this distinction, because we find that he did express different halachic opinions than his father. See *Hilchot Shechitah* 11:10.

This presumption is borne out by the Rambam's ruling in *Hilchot Talmud Torah* 5:6 where he states that a person may not contradict or support the words of his teacher "in his presence."

8. This is indeed the manner in which the Rambam refers to his father in *Hilchot Shechitah, loc. cit.* The Radbaz states that if a person refers to his father as Rabbi Abraham or the like, it is acceptable.

9. For others might think that he is referring to his father, and that will compromise his father's honor (Radbaz).

Tosafot Rabbenu Asher (*Horiot* 14a) gives an example of this concept. The Sage Rabbah raised the Sage Abbaye who was his nephew. The name Abbaye was actually coined by Rabbah because Abbaye shared the same name as Rabbah's own father. Indeed, that factor is indicated by the name itself. For Abbaye is an Aramaic derivative of the Hebrew *Avi*, meaning "my father." Ravva, Abbaye's colleague, by contrast, did not refer to him as Abbaye, but instead called him by his given name: Nachmeini.

10. It would appear that within his father's presence, this is forbidden.

11. Implied is that the son does not have to use his own resources to provide for his parents.

12. I.e., the court may use physical force to compel him to provide for them.

13. I.e., he is compelled to sustain them from the money that he would donate to charity [*Kessef Mishneh*; Ramah (*Yoreh De'ah* 240:5)]. The Ramah adds that if the person has ample resources, he should be cursed if he sustains his father from money for charity.

bring him home and serve him in all the ways one serves a teacher.[14] Similarly, he should stand before him as one stands before a teacher.[15]

4. When a father was the student of his son, the father need not stand in the presence of the son.[16] The son, by contrast, must stand before his father even if he is his student.

[A son] is obligated to honor [his father] in other matters when he is carrying out his business and seeing to his concerns. What is implied? If a person went to a place because of his father's words, he should not say: "Hurry [and free] me on my own account," or "Let me go on my own account," instead "Hurry [and free] me because of my father," "Let me go because of my father."[17] Similar laws apply in all analogous situations. He should always include in his words [statements that indicate] that he is concerned with his father's honor and that he fears him.

5. [A son] is obligated to honor [his father] even after his death. What is implied? If he repeats a teaching in his father's name, he should not say: "This is what my father said." Instead, he should say: "This is what my father, and teacher - may I serve as atonement for him[18] - said."

When does the above apply? Within twelve months of his passing.[19] After twelve months, he says of him: "May he be remembered for the life of the world to come."[20]

6. Both a man and a woman are obligated to honor and fear [their parents].[21] It is only that the man has the capacity to do this and a woman is subject to another's influence.[22] Therefore if she is divorced or widowed,[23] they are both equal.

7. To what degree does [the mitzvah of] honoring one's father and mother extend? Even if [one's parent] takes his purse of gold and throws it into the sea in his presence, he should not embarrass them, shout,[24] or vent anger at them. Instead, he should accept the Torah's decree and remain silent.[25]

14. See *Hilchot Talmud Torah* 5:8 which states that all the services a servant performs for his master must be performed by a student for his teacher.
15. See *ibid.*:7 which states that a person must stand in his teacher's presence from the time he sees him until he passes from his vision.
16. Even though that would have been appropriate as a mark of deference because he is his teacher. The Radbaz questions this ruling, stating that seemingly, out of respect for his Torah knowledge, the father should show the son this mark of deference and thus they should both stand for each other. This is the position taken by the *Tur* and the *Shulchan Aruch* (*Yoreh Deah* 240:7).
17. By making such statements, he enhances his father's prestige. Conversely, if he is unsure of whether speaking in the name of his father will not produce such positive results - and certainly if he is certain that it will not - he may or should make the request in his own name [Rashi (*Kiddushin* 32b); *Siftei Cohen* 240:8-9].

וּמוֹצִיא וּמַכְנִיס וּמְשַׁמְּשׁוֹ בִּשְׁאָר הַדְּבָרִים שֶׁהַשַּׁמָּשִׁים מְשַׁמְּשִׁים בָּהֶן אֶת הָרַב. וְעוֹמֵד מִפָּנָיו כְּדֶרֶךְ שֶׁהוּא עוֹמֵד מִפְּנֵי רַבּוֹ.

ד וְהָאָב שֶׁהָיָה תַּלְמִיד בְּנוֹ – אֵין הָאָב עוֹמֵד מִפְּנֵי הַבֵּן, אֲבָל הַבֵּן עוֹמֵד מִפְּנֵי אָבִיו, אַף עַל פִּי שֶׁהוּא תַּלְמִידוֹ.

וְחַיָּב לְכַבְּדוֹ בִּשְׁאָר דְּרָכָיו בִּשְׁעַת עֲשִׂיַּת מַשָּׂאוֹ וּמַתָּנוֹ וַעֲשִׂיַּת חֲפָצָיו. כֵּיצַד? הַנִּשְׁמָע בִּדְבַר אָבִיו לְמָקוֹם – לֹא יֹאמַר: מַהֲרוּנִי בִּשְׁבִיל עַצְמִי! פָּטְרוּנִי בִּשְׁבִיל עַצְמִי! אֶלָּא: מַהֲרוּנִי בִּשְׁבִיל אַבָּא! פָּטְרוּנִי בִּשְׁבִיל אַבָּא! וְכֵן כֹּל כַּיּוֹצֵא בָּזֶה, לְעוֹלָם יְכַלֵּל בִּכְלַל דְּבָרָיו שֶׁהוּא חוֹשֵׁשׁ בִּכְבוֹד אָבִיו וְשֶׁמִּתְיָרֵא מִמֶּנּוּ.

ה וְחַיָּב לְכַבְּדוֹ אֲפִלּוּ לְאַחַר מוֹתוֹ. כֵּיצַד? הָיָה אוֹמֵר דְּבַר שְׁמוּעָה מִפִּיו – לֹא יֹאמַר: כָּךְ אָמַר אַבָּא; אֶלָּא אוֹמֵר: כָּךְ אָמַר אַבָּא מָרִי, אֲנִי כַּפָּרַת מִשְׁכָּבוֹ.

בַּמֶּה דְּבָרִים אֲמוּרִים? בְּתוֹךְ שְׁנֵים עָשָׂר חֹדֶשׁ שֶׁלְּאַחַר מִיתָתוֹ; אֲבָל לְאַחַר שְׁנֵים עָשָׂר חֹדֶשׁ – אוֹמֵר: זִכְרוֹנוֹ לְחַיֵּי הָעוֹלָם הַבָּא.

ו אֶחָד הָאִישׁ וְאֶחָד הָאִשָּׁה חַיָּבִין בְּמוֹרָא וְכָבוֹד; אֶלָּא שֶׁהָאִישׁ יֵשׁ בְּיָדוֹ לַעֲשׂוֹת, וְהָאִשָּׁה אֵין בְּיָדָהּ לַעֲשׂוֹת, שֶׁהֲרֵי רְשׁוּת אֲחֵרִים עָלֶיהָ. לְפִיכָךְ, אִם נִתְגָּרְשָׁה אוֹ נִתְאַלְמְנָה – הֲרֵי שְׁנֵיהֶם שָׁוִים.

ז עַד הֵיכָן הוּא כִּבּוּד אָב וָאֵם? אֲפִלּוּ נָטְלוּ כִּיס שֶׁל זְהוּבִים שֶׁלּוֹ וְהִשְׁלִיכוּ בְּפָנָיו לַיָּם – לֹא יַכְלִימֵם, וְלֹא יִצְעַק בִּפְנֵיהֶם, וְלֹא יִכְעַס כְּנֶגְדָּם; אֶלָּא יְקַבֵּל גְּזֵרַת הַכָּתוּב וְיִשְׁתֹּק.

18. I.e., may any misfortune to be visited upon him in the spiritual realms be visited upon me.

19. After twelve months, however, this is unnecessary, for our Sages say that even the wicked are not judged in Gehinnom for longer than twelve months. Hence, all retribution will have already been visited upon him (*Kessef Mishneh*).

20. The *Shulchan Aruch* (*Yoreh Deah* 240:9) states that one should say: "May his memory be blessed." The *Turei Zahav* 240:13 states that a combination of both expressions should be used.

21. *Kiddushin* 30b derives this concept from the fact that the command to fear one's parents uses a plural verb, implying both a man and a woman.

22. I.e., her first obligation is to her husband.

Shulchan Aruch (*Yoreh Deah* 240:17) states that a woman is not obligated to honor her father while she is married for this reason. One might infer that she is liable to fear him even when married.

23. Or if her husband consents (*Siftei Cohen* 240:19).

24. Our translation is based on the authoritative manuscripts of the *Mishneh Torah*. The standard printed text is slightly different.

25. The Rambam's words are taken from *Kiddushin* 32a. The commentaries have

To what degree does [the mitzvah of] fearing them extend? Even if one was wearing fine garments and sitting at the head of the community, if one's father and mother came, ripped the clothes, struck him on the head, and spat in his face, he should not embarrass them.[26] Instead, he should remain silent and fear the King of kings who commanded him to conduct himself in this manner. Were a mortal king to decree something which would cause him even more suffering, he would not be able to move a limb [in protest]. Certainly, this applies [when the command emanates from] He who spoke and [caused] the world to come into existence as He desired it.

8. Although these commands have been issued, a person is forbidden to lay a heavy yoke on his sons and be particular about their honoring him to the point that he presents an obstacle to them.[27] Instead, he should forgo his honor and ignore [any affronts]. For if a father [desires to] forgo his honor, he may.[28]

9. A person who strikes a son who has attained majority[29] should be placed under a ban of ostracism, for he is transgressing [the charge, Leviticus 19:14]: "Do not place a stumbling block in front of the blind."[30]

10. When a person's father or mother lose control of their mental faculties, [their son] should try to conduct his [relationship] with them according to their mental condition until [God] has mercy upon them.[31] If it is impossible for him to remain with them because they have become very deranged, he should leave them, depart, and charge others with caring for them in an appropriate manner.[32]

11. A *mamzer*[33] is obligated to honor and fear his father even though he is not liable for striking him or cursing him until he repents.[34] Even when his father

questioned this ruling, for as stated above, a son is not obligated to suffer financial loss in order to honor his father. Indeed, *Kiddushin, loc. cit.*, speaks of the purse as belonging to the father, explaining that although the son is fit to inherit that purse, since the money is presently his father's, the son may not protest. Implied is that if the purse is the son's, he may.

The *Kessef Mishneh* explains that although he is not obligated to honor his father with his own funds, he must sacrifice all the money in the world not to cause him discomfort. The *Tur* and the Ramah (*Yoreh Deah* 240:8) state that if the father has already thrown the purse into the sea, the son must remain silent. Before he throws it, however, the son may try to prevent him from doing so. The *Bayit Chadash* and the *Siftei Cohen* 240:11 state that the son may sue the father for any loss he causes him. Hence, he may not embarrass him for causing him that loss.

26. The Rambam's words are taken from *Kiddushin* 31a which cites the example of a gentile in Ashkelon who conducted himself in this manner. Our Sages explain that, in this regard, he should be looked up to as an exemplar.

27. I.e., by presenting extensive demands, he may cause them to transgress and spurn the

וְעַד הֵיכָן מוֹרָאָן? אֲפִלּוּ הָיָה לוֹבֵשׁ בְּגָדִים חֲמוּדוֹת וְיוֹשֵׁב בְּרֹאשׁ בִּפְנֵי הַקָּהָל, וּבָא אָבִיו וְאִמּוֹ וְקָרְעוּ בְּגָדָיו וְהִכּוּהוּ בְּרֹאשׁוֹ וְיָרְקוּ בְּפָנָיו – לֹא יַכְלִימֵם, אֶלָּא יִשְׁתֹּק וְיִירָא וְיִפְחַד מִמֶּלֶךְ מַלְכֵי הַמְּלָכִים שֶׁצִּוָּהוּ בְּכָךְ. שֶׁאִלּוּ מֶלֶךְ בָּשָׂר וָדָם גָּזַר עָלָיו דָּבָר שֶׁהוּא מְצַעֵר יָתֵר מִזֶּה – לֹא הָיָה יָכוֹל לְפַרְכֵּס בַּדָּבָר; קַל וָחֹמֶר לְמִי שֶׁאָמַר וְהָיָה הָעוֹלָם כִּרְצוֹנוֹ.

ח אַף עַל פִּי שֶׁבְּכָךְ נִצְטַוִּינוּ, אָסוּר לְאָדָם לְהַכְבִּיד עֻלּוֹ עַל בָּנָיו וּלְדַקְדֵּק בִּכְבוֹדוֹ עִמָּהֶם, שֶׁלֹּא יְבִיאֵם לִידֵי מִכְשׁוֹל, אֶלָּא יִמְחַל וְיִתְעַלֵּם; שֶׁהָאָב שֶׁמָּחַל עַל כְּבוֹדוֹ – כְּבוֹדוֹ מָחוּל.

ט וְהַמַּכֶּה בְּנוֹ גָּדוֹל – מְנַדִּין אוֹתוֹ, שֶׁהֲרֵי הוּא עוֹבֵר עַל וְלִפְנֵי עִוֵּר לֹא תִתֵּן מִכְשֹׁל.

י מִי שֶׁנִּטְרְפָה דַעְתּוֹ שֶׁל אָבִיו אוֹ שֶׁל אִמּוֹ – מִשְׁתַּדֵּל לִנְהֹג עִמָּהֶם כְּפִי דַעְתָּם עַד שֶׁיְּרֻחַם עֲלֵיהֶן. וְאִם אִי אֶפְשָׁר לוֹ לַעֲמֹד מִפְּנֵי שֶׁנִּשְׁתַּטּוּ בְּיוֹתֵר – יַנִּיחֵם וְיֵלֵךְ לוֹ, וִיצַוֶּה אֲחֵרִים לְהַנְהִיגָם כָּרָאוּי לָהֶם.

יא הַמַּמְזֵר חַיָּב בִּכְבוֹד אָבִיו וּמוֹרָאוֹ, אַף עַל פִּי שֶׁהוּא פָּטוּר עַל מַכָּתוֹ וְקִלְלָתוֹ עַד שֶׁיַּעֲשֶׂה תְּשׁוּבָה.

mitzvah. The *Kessef Mishneh* implies that this law is the Rambam's own deduction which he derived from the following halachah.

28. And thus a son will not be punished for failing to show the required honor; the son nevertheless fulfills a mitzvah by doing so (Radbaz, Vol. I, Responsum 524).

29. We have translated the term *gadol* according to its usual halachic meaning. The Ramah (*Yoreh Deah* 240:20) interprets this as referring to a son who has reached the age of 22 or 24.

30. As the Rambam explains in *Hilchot Rotzeach* 12:14, this command is interpreted as meaning, "Do not cause the spiritually blind to transgress." In this instance, by hitting his son after he has reached adulthood, the father is provoking him to perhaps respond in kind or to dishonor him in some way.

31. And heal them.

32. The Rambam's ruling is based on a narrative in *Kiddushin* 31b which relates how Rav Assi cared for his senile mother.

The Ra'avad differs with the Rambam's ruling, maintaining that if a son will not care for his parents, no one else will. The Radbaz supports the Rambam's ruling, explaining that the parents will take advantage of the child's obligation to respect them and make no effort to control their behavior. Other people, by contrast, will rebuke the parents severely and rather than suffer such rebuke, they will control themselves. (See, however, the *Turei Zahav* who offers a different interpretation of the Ra'avad's position.)

33. A person born out of an incestuous or an adulterous relationship.

34. For as reflected in the notes to Chapter 5, Halachah 12, a person is liable for striking and cursing his parents only when they are observant. And hence, until the father repents,

was a wicked person who violated many transgressions, he must honor him and fear him.

If he sees [his father] violate Torah law, he should not tell him: "Father, you transgressed Torah law."[35] Instead, he should tell him: "Father, is [not] such-and-such written in the Torah?", as if he is asking him, rather than warning him.[36]

12. When a person's father tells him to violate the words of the Torah[37] - whether he tells him to transgress a negative commandment or not to fulfill a positive commandment, even if all that is involved is a point of Rabbinic Law[38] - he should not listen to him, as [can be inferred from Leviticus 19:3]: "A person must fear his mother and his father and keep My Sabbaths." [Implied is that] all are obligated in honoring Me.

13. [The following laws apply when] a person's father tells him: "Draw water for me," and he has the opportunity to perform a mitzvah.[39] If it is possible for the mitzvah to be performed by others, they should perform it and he should concern himself with honoring his father.[40] For we do not negate [the observance of] one mitzvah,[41] because of [the observance of] another mitzvah. If there are no others able to perform [the other mitzvah], he should perform the mitzvah and neglect his father's honor. For he and his father are obligated to perform the mitzvah.

Torah study surpasses honoring one's father and mother.[42]

14. If a person's father tells him: "Bring me a drink of water," and his mother tells him: "Bring me a drink of water," he should overlook his mother's honor and honor his father first. For both he and his mother are obligated to honor his father.[43]

the son is not liable for execution for his deeds. He is nevertheless forbidden to conduct himself in this manner (Radbaz).

35. For rebuking his fathers in this manner would cause him aggravation (*Kiddushin* 32a).

From this ruling, the Radbaz states that it would appear that one is obligated to honor one's parents, even if they are transgressors. He notes, however, that (as the *Hagahot Maimomiot* question), *Bava Metzia* 62a appears to imply that if a person's father died without repenting, one is not obligated to honor him. Hence the Radbaz explains that the passage in *Bava Metzia*, is speaking about a situation in which the person already died. We, by contrast, are speaking about an instance when the father is alive and there is hope that he will repent. Hence, throughout his lifetime, while there is still hope that he will repent, his son is obligated to honor him.

In his *Kessef Mishneh*, Rav Yosef Karo offers a different resolution from which it appears that even if the father died without repenting, his sons are obligated to honor him, and he follows this understanding in his *Shulchan Aruch* (*Yoreh Deah* 240:18). The Ramah differs, stating that unless the father has repented, his son is not obligated to honor him during his lifetime. He may not, however, cause him aggravation.

36. The *Shulchan Aruch* (*Yoreh Deah* 240:11) quotes these words and continues: "In this manner, he will understand on his own, without being embarrassed."

אֲפִלּוּ הָיָה אָבִיו רָשָׁע וּבַעַל עֲבֵרוֹת - מְכַבְּדוֹ וּמִתְיָרֵא מִמֶּנּוּ. רָאָהוּ עוֹבֵר עַל דִּבְרֵי תוֹרָה - לֹא יֹאמַר לוֹ: אַבָּא, עָבַרְתָּ עַל דִּבְרֵי תוֹרָה! אֶלָּא יֹאמַר לוֹ: אַבָּא, כָּתוּב בַּתּוֹרָה כָּךְ וָכָךְ? כְּאִלּוּ הוּא שׁוֹאֵל מִמֶּנּוּ, וְלֹא כְּמַזְהִירוֹ.

יב מִי שֶׁאָמַר לוֹ אָבִיו לַעֲבֹר עַל דִּבְרֵי תוֹרָה, בֵּין שֶׁאָמַר לוֹ לַעֲבֹר עַל מִצְוַת לֹא תַעֲשֶׂה אוֹ לְבַטֵּל מִצְוַת עֲשֵׂה, אֲפִלּוּ שֶׁל דִּבְרֵיהֶם - הֲרֵי זֶה לֹא יִשְׁמַע לוֹ. שֶׁנֶּאֱמַר: אִישׁ אִמּוֹ וְאָבִיו תִּירָאוּ וְאֶת שַׁבְּתֹתַי תִּשְׁמֹרוּ - כֻּלְּכֶם חַיָּבִין בִּכְבוֹדִי.

יג אָמַר לוֹ אָבִיו: הַשְׁקֵנִי מַיִם! וְיֵשׁ בְּיָדוֹ לַעֲשׂוֹת מִצְוָה: אִם אֶפְשָׁר לַמִּצְוָה שֶׁתֵּעָשֶׂה עַל יְדֵי אֲחֵרִים - תֵּעָשֶׂה, וְיִתְעַסֵּק בִּכְבוֹד אָבִיו; שֶׁאֵין מְבַטְּלִין מִצְוָה מִפְּנֵי מִצְוָה. וְאִם אֵין שָׁם אֲחֵרִים לַעֲשׂוֹתָהּ - יִתְעַסֵּק בַּמִּצְוָה וְיַנִּיחַ כְּבוֹד אָבִיו; שֶׁהוּא וְאָבִיו חַיָּבִים בִּדְבַר מִצְוָה.
וְתַלְמוּד תּוֹרָה גָּדוֹל מִכִּבּוּד אָב וָאֵם.

יד אָמַר לוֹ אָבִיו: הַשְׁקֵנִי מַיִם! וְאָמְרָה לוֹ אִמּוֹ: הַשְׁקֵנִי מַיִם! - מַנִּיחַ כְּבוֹד אִמּוֹ וְעוֹסֵק בִּכְבוֹד אָבִיו תְּחִלָּה, מִפְּנֵי שֶׁהוּא וְאִמּוֹ חַיָּבִין בִּכְבוֹד אָבִיו.

37. From this statement, the Radbaz derives the ruling that a person is not considered wicked - in which instance, the son would not be obligated to heed his father at all - from merely making undesirable statements. To be placed in that category, he must perform an act of transgression.
38. For ultimately, the obligation to heed Rabbinic Law is a Scriptural command (*Kessef Mishneh*).
39. This is speaking about a mitzvah whose observance cannot be delayed, e.g., the burial of a corpse. If the observance of the mitzvah can be delayed, one should honor one's parents and then observe the mitzvah [*Kessef Mishneh*; Ramah (*Yoreh Dea'ah* 240:12)].
40. If, however, he had already begun the performance of the other mitzvah, he should complete it before concerning himself with his father's honor. For a person involved in the observance of one mitzvah is not obligated in others [*Kessef Mishneh*; Ramah (*Yoreh Dea'ah* 240:12)].
41. Honoring one's father.
42. As *Pe'ah* 1:1 states: "Torah study surpasses all [other mitzvot]." *Megilah* 16b gives an example of the relationship of Torah study to the mitzvah of honoring one's parents, stating that Jacob was punished for the 22 years in which he did not honor his father while he sojourned in Charan and tarried on the way. Although before that Jacob spent 14 years studying the Torah - and during this time, he also did not honor his father - he was not held liable for that, because "Torah study surpasses honoring one's parents."
43. See *Hilchot Ishut* 15:20 which states that a woman is obligated to honor her husband "exceedingly." The Radbaz emphasizes that if the couple are divorced, the father receives no priority over the mother. The *Shulchan Aruch* (*Yoreh Deah* 240:14) also quotes this understanding, stating that in such a situation the son may honor whomever he desires first.

15. A person is obligated to honor his father's wife even though she is not his mother throughout his father's lifetime, for this is included in honoring his father. Similarly, he should honor his mother's husband throughout her lifetime. After [his parents'] death, however, he is not obligated to honor their spouses.[44]

It is a Rabbinical decree that a person is obligated to honor his oldest brother as he is obligated to honor his father.[45]

CHAPTER SEVEN

INTRODUCTION

Deuteronomy 21:18-21 states:

> If a person will have a wayward and rebellious son who does not heed the voice of his father or the voice of his mother and they chastise him, but he does not heed them. His father and mother shall take hold of him and bring him out to the elders of his city and to the gate of his place. They say to the elders of his city: "This son of ours is wayward and rebellious. He does not heed our voice; he is gluttonous and a lush." All of the men of his city will clout him with stones, killing him, and you shall remove evil from your midst. All Israel shall hear and fear.

Our Sages (primarily in *Sanhedrin* 68b ff.) interpret this passage precisely, explaining how each term used in the passage teaches us a different concept. In the chapter that follows, the Rambam summarizes and organizes their teachings, giving us a clear-cut picture of the requirements of the mitzvah. It is important to emphasize that there is a difference of opinion among our Sages if the judgment of "a wayward and rebellious son" ever took place (*Sanhedrin* 71a). Some maintain that such a judgment was never issued. Indeed, from all the particulars mentioned by the Rambam, one can understand that it could be impossible for such a judgment to have been issued. Others maintain that they know of an instance where an individual was executed because of this transgression.

Sanhedrin 72a asks: Is eating the gluttonous meal (to be described by the Rambam) a sufficient cause for a person to be executed? In resolution, our Sages explain that the Torah considered the ultimate fate of such a person. He will be drawn after his natural tendencies and continue to steal and eat gluttonously. Ultimately, he will become a robber and slay people in order to support his habit. It is preferable, the Torah maintains, for him to be executed early in life, before he commits such severe sins.

1. It is explicitly stated that the wayward and rebellious son described in the Torah should be stoned to death.[1] Now the Torah does not administer a punishment unless a warning was issued first. Where was the warning issued? [In Leviticus 19:26]: "Do not eat upon the blood," [which can be interpreted to mean]: "Do not partake of food that will lead to the shedding of blood." This refers to the [meal] eaten by the wayward and rebellious son who is executed only because of the hateful feast of which he partook as [Deuteronomy 21:20] states: "He is gluttonous and a lush." According to the Oral Tradition, we learned that this was interpreted to mean that he ate meat and drank wine in a ravenous manner.

טו חַיָּב אָדָם לְכַבֵּד אֶת אֵשֶׁת אָבִיו, אַף עַל פִּי שֶׁאֵינָהּ אִמּוֹ, כָּל זְמַן שֶׁאָבִיו קַיָּם; שֶׁזֶּה בִּכְלַל כְּבוֹד אָבִיו.
וְכֵן מְכַבֵּד בַּעַל אִמּוֹ, כָּל זְמַן שֶׁאִמּוֹ קַיֶּמֶת; אֲבָל לְאַחַר מִיתָתָהּ – אֵינוֹ חַיָּב.
וּמִדִּבְרֵי סוֹפְרִים, שֶׁיִּהְיֶה אָדָם חַיָּב בִּכְבוֹד אָחִיו הַגָּדוֹל כִּכְבוֹד אָבִיו.

פֶּרֶק שְׁבִיעִי

א בֵּן סוֹרֵר וּמוֹרֶה הָאָמוּר בַּתּוֹרָה, הֲרֵי נִתְפָּרְשָׁה בּוֹ סְקִילָה; וְלֹא עָנַשׁ הַכָּתוּב אֶלָּא אִם כֵּן הִזְהִיר, וְהֵיכָן הִזְהִיר?
לֹא תֹאכְלוּ עַל הַדָּם – לֹא תֹאכַל אֲכִילָה הַמְּבִיאָה לִידֵי שְׁפִיכוּת דָּמִים; וְזוֹ אֲכִילַת בֵּן סוֹרֵר וּמוֹרֶה, שֶׁאֵינוֹ נֶהֱרָג אֶלָּא עַל אֲכִילָה מְכֹעֶרֶת שֶׁאָכַל.
שֶׁנֶּאֱמַר: זוֹלֵל וְסֹבֵא. מִפִּי הַשְּׁמוּעָה לָמְדוּ, שֶׁזּוֹלֵל הוּא הָאוֹכֵל בָּשָׂר בְּרַעַבְתָנוּת, וְסוֹבֵא – הַשּׁוֹתֶה יַיִן בְּרַעַבְתָנוּת.

44. The *Shulchan Aruch* (*Yoreh Deah* 240:21) states that even though there is no obligation for a son to continue to honor his step-mother after his father's death, it is proper for him to do so. The commentaries note that this ruling appears to be based on the words of Rabbi Yehudah HaNasi who, at the time of his death, instructed his sons to continue to honor their step-mother (*Ketubot* 103a).

45. In his gloss to *Sefer HaMitzvot*, the *Megilat Esther* states that from the fact that the Rambam does not qualify this ruling by stating that it applies only during the father's lifetime, we can conclude that it applies even after his death.

1. *Sefer HaMitzvot* (negative commandment 195) and *Sefer HaChinuch* (mitzvah 248) include the commandment not to act as "a wayward and rebellious son" as one of the 613 mitzvot of the Torah.

2. There are many particulars involved in [the meal for which] he is liable for eating. All of these are conveyed by the Oral Tradition. He is not liable for stoning until he steals from his father and buys meat and wine at a cheap price.[2] He must then eat it outside his father's domain, together with a group that are all empty and base. He must eat meat that is raw, but not entirely raw, cooked but not entirely cooked, as is the practice of thieves.[3] He must drink the wine as it is thinned as the alcoholics drink.[4] He must eat a quantity of meat weighing 50 *dinarim*[5] in one sitting, and drink half a *log*[6] of this wine at one time.[7]

If he stole from his father and partook of such a meal inside his father's domain,[8] or stole from others[9] and partook of this hateful meal in his father's domain or in another's domain, he is not liable. If the meal involves a mitzvah,[10] even a mitzvah of Rabbinic origin, or the meal involves a transgression,[11] even a transgression of Rabbinic origin, he is not liable. [This may be inferred from the phrase (*Ibid.*):] "He does not heed our voice"; i.e., through eating [this meal], he violates only [his parents'] command. This excludes one who [through this meal] violates the words of the Torah[12] or who partakes of it for the sake of a mitzvah.[13]

What is implied? If he partook of such a hateful meal together with a wicked company for the sake of a mitzvah, or he partook of the second tithe in Jerusalem,[14] even if they eat a meal comforting the bereaved which is a mitzvah of Rabbinic origin,[15] he is not liable. Similarly, if he ate meat from animals that were not ritually slaughtered or which were *trefe*, teeming animals or crawling animals,[16] and even if he ate on a communal fast day, a transgression of Rabbinic origin, he is not liable for execution.

3. If he partook of any type of food, but did not partake of meat,[17] even if he partook of fowl, he is not liable. If he included meat in this meal, but reached

2. For if it is expensive, it is unlikely that he will develop a habit of eating and drinking in this manner.
3. Who eat hurriedly lest they be detected and do not wait for their food to cook.
4. I.e., thinned, but not thinned in the manner that wine was ordinarily consumed. In the Talmudic era, the wines were very strong and it was customary to add water, even as much as three times the measure of the wine itself, to the wine before partaking of it.
5. According to *Shiurei Torah*, this would be approximately 200 grams, and 350 grams according to *Chazon Ish*.
6. Half a *log* is slightly more than 172 cc according to *Shiurei Torah* and 300 cc according to *Chazon Ish*.
7. The Radbaz interprets this as meaning in one mouthful. This is what is implied by the expression "eating ravenously" mentioned in Halachah 1. He states that it is possible for this to happen with regard to drinking, but it is almost impossible for a person to put that much meat in his mouth at one time. Therefore he interprets it to mean "without interruption, as if it were one mouthful, that before swallowing the first portion, he stuffed the second in his mouth."
8. This implies that he is afraid that his father will notice him. Since he still has a sense of

ב אֲכִילָה זוֹ שֶׁהוּא חַיָּב עָלֶיהָ – דְּבָרִים הַרְבֵּה יֵשׁ בָּהֶם, וְהֵן כֻּלָּן הֲלָכָה מִפִּי הַקַּבָּלָה. אֵינוֹ חַיָּב סְקִילָה עַד שֶׁיִּגְנֹב מִשֶּׁל אָבִיו וְיִקְנֶה בָּשָׂר בְּזוֹל וְיַיִן בְּזוֹל; וְיֹאכַל וְיִשְׁתֶּה חוּץ מֵרְשׁוּת אָבִיו בַּחֲבוּרָה שֶׁכֻּלָּן רֵיקָנִין וּפְחוּתִין; וְיֹאכַל הַבָּשָׂר חַי וְאֵינוֹ חַי, מְבֻשָּׁל וְאֵינוֹ מְבֻשָּׁל, כְּדֶרֶךְ שֶׁהַגַּנָּבִים אוֹכְלִים, וְיִשְׁתֶּה הַיַּיִן מָזוּג כְּדֶרֶךְ שֶׁהַגַּרְגְּרָנִים שׁוֹתִים. וְהוּא שֶׁיֹּאכַל מִשְׁקַל חֲמִשִּׁים דִּינָרִין מִבָּשָׂר זֶה בִּמְלוּגְמָא אַחַת, וְיִשְׁתֶּה חֲצִי לֹג מִיַּיִן זֶה בְּבַת אַחַת.

גָּנַב מִשֶּׁל אָבִיו, וְאָכַל אֲכִילָה זוֹ בִּרְשׁוּת אָבִיו; אוֹ שֶׁגָּנַב מִשֶּׁל אֲחֵרִים, וְאָכַל אֲכִילָה זוֹ הַמְכֹעֶרֶת בֵּין בִּרְשׁוּת אָבִיו בֵּין בִּרְשׁוּת אֲחֵרִים – הֲרֵי זֶה פָּטוּר. וְכֵן אִם גָּנַב מִשֶּׁל אָבִיו, וְאָכַל אֲכִילָה מְכֹעֶרֶת כָּזוֹ בִּרְשׁוּת אֲחֵרִים, וְהָיְתָה אֲכִילַת מִצְוָה אֲפִלּוּ מִדִּבְרֵיהֶם [אוֹ אֲכִילַת עֲבֵרָה אֲפִלּוּ מִדִּבְרֵיהֶם] – פָּטוּר. שֶׁנֶּאֱמַר: אֵינֶנּוּ שֹׁמֵעַ בְּקֹלֵנוּ – שֶׁאֵינוֹ עוֹבֵר בַּאֲכִילָה זוֹ אֶלָּא עַל קוֹלָם. יָצָא זֶה שֶׁעָבַר בָּהּ עַל דִּבְרֵי תוֹרָה, אוֹ שֶׁאֲכָלָהּ בִּדְבַר מִצְוָה.

כֵּיצַד? אָכַל אֲכִילָה זוֹ הַמְכֹעֶרֶת עִם הַחֲבוּרָה הָרָעָה שֶׁאוֹכֵל עִמָּהֶם בִּדְבַר מִצְוָה, אוֹ שֶׁאֲכָלוֹ מַעֲשֵׂר שֵׁנִי בִּירוּשָׁלַיִם, אֲפִלּוּ אֲכָלוֹ בְּתַנְחוּמֵי אֲבֵלִים שֶׁהִיא מִצְוָה מִדִּבְרֵיהֶם – הֲרֵי זֶה פָּטוּר. וְכֵן אִם אֲכָלָהּ מִנְּבֵלוֹת וּטְרֵפוֹת, שְׁקָצִים וּרְמָשִׂים, אֲפִלּוּ אָכַל בְּתַעֲנִית צִבּוּר שֶׁהִיא עֲבֵרָה מִדִּבְרֵיהֶם – הֲרֵי זֶה פָּטוּר מִן הַמִּיתָה.

ג אָכַל כָּל מַאֲכָל וְלֹא אָכַל בְּשַׂר בְּהֵמָה, אַף עַל פִּי שֶׁאָכַל אֲכִילָה זוֹ מִבְּשַׂר הָעוֹף – פָּטוּר.

shame, it is not as likely that he will become habituated to stealing. Accordingly, it is less likely that he will ultimately become a robber and murderer (*Kessef Mishneh*).

9. It will not always be possible for him to steal from others. Hence, since the habit will not be as strongly ingrained in his personality, it is possible that he will not rob and murder (*Ibid.*).

10. E.g., a meal honoring a circumcision or a marriage of which it is a mitzvah to partake.

11. E.g., the food or wine was not kosher.

12. For the phrase can be interpreted: "He does not heed our voice alone," i.e., they are not complaining that their son is transgressing the commandments, only that he is rebelling against them (Radbaz).

13. For that phrase can also be interpreted as implying "he heeds neither our voice or God's voice." Hence when he partakes of the meal while heeding God's voice, he is not liable. Alternatively, since he is performing a mitzvah while partaking of the food, his actions may not become habitual (Radbaz). The *Kessef Mishneh* suggests that this second clause is in fact the start of the following paragraph.

14. For eating the second tithe in the holy city fulfills a mitzvah.

15. See *Hilchot Evel* 13:8.

16. Which are forbidden.

17. I.e., the meat of a domesticated animal. With regard to the meat of a wild animal, e.g., deer, there is a debate among the later authorities; some hold him liable and some do not.

the sum of 50 *dinarim* by including fowl, he is liable. If he drank other beverages, but did not drink wine, he is not liable.

4. When he ate raw meat and undiluted wine, he is not liable. [The rationale is that] this is an occasional occurrence and not something that a person will be drawn after. Similarly, if he ate this meal of salted meat on the third day after it was salted,[18] or drank fresh grape juice,[19] he is not liable. For a person will not be drawn after such matters.

5. [For this transgression,] the Torah does not punish a child who has not come to the age [where he is responsible for the observance] of mitzvot.[20] Similarly, a man who has matured and is independent[21] is not stoned to death, because he ate and drank such a hateful meal.

What is implied? According to the Oral Tradition, we learned that this law concerns a youth of thirteen between the time he grew two pubic hairs[22] and the time at which his entire male organ[23] is surrounded [by pubic hair]. After the entire male organ is surrounded [by pubic hair], he is considered as independent and is not executed by stoning.[24]

6. The entire period for which a "wayward and rebellious son" is liable is only three months from the time he manifests signs of physical maturity. For it is possible that his wife will conceive and her fetus will be recognizable within three months.[25] [This is derived from Deuteronomy 21:18:] "If a person will have a wayward and rebellious son..."; [a son, and] not a "wayward and rebellious father."

Thus one may conclude that if one's pubic hair surrounds the entire organ[26] before the three months are completed, he is not liable.

7. How is the judgment of a "wayward and rebellious son" adjudicated? First, his father and mother bring him to a court of three judges[27] and tell them: "Our son is wayward and rebellious."[28] They bring two witnesses who testify that he stole from his father and bought meat and wine with what he stole and partook of the meal described above after being warned.[29] This is the first testimony.

He receives lashes as are administered to all of those who are obligated to be lashed,[30] as [Deuteronomy 21:20] states: "they chastise him, but he does not heed them." Should he steal from his father a second time and partake of such a meal, his father and mother bring him to a court of 23 judges. They

18. At which point the flavor of the salt overpowers the flavor of the meat.
19. Which has not fermented and has no alcoholic content. One opinion in *Sanhedrin* 70a interprets this as referring to grape juice that has not been left to ferment for 40 days.
20. I.e., a boy below the age of thirteen.
21. For the Torah refers to him as a "wayward and rebellious son," i.e., a son and not a man (*Sanhedrin* 68b).

וְאִם אָכַל אֲכִילָה זוֹ מִבְּשַׂר בְּהֵמָה, וְהִשְׁלִים הַחֲמִשִּׁים דִּינָרִים מִבְּשַׂר הָעוֹף – חַיָּב. שָׁתָה כָּל מַשְׁקֶה וְלֹא שָׁתָה יַיִן – פָּטוּר.

ד אָכַל בָּשָׂר חַי וְשָׁתָה יַיִן חַי – פָּטוּר; שֶׁזֶּה קְרִי הוּא, וְאֵין אָדָם יָכוֹל לְהִמָּשֵׁךְ בָּזֶה. וְכֵן אִם אָכַל בָּשָׂר מָלִיחַ בַּיּוֹם הַשְּׁלִישִׁי לִמְלִיחָתוֹ, אוֹ שָׁתָה יַיִן מִגִּתּוֹ – פָּטוּר; שֶׁאֵין אָדָם יָכוֹל לְהִמָּשֵׁךְ בָּזֶה.

ה לֹא עָנַשׁ הַכָּתוּב קָטָן שֶׁלֹּא בָּא לִכְלַל הַמִּצְוֹת. וְכֵן אִישׁ שֶׁגָּדַל וַהֲרֵי הוּא בִּרְשׁוּת עַצְמוֹ – אֵינוֹ נִסְקָל מִפְּנֵי שֶׁגָּנַב וְאָכַל וְשָׁתָה אֲכִילָה זוֹ הַמְכֹעֶרֶת. הָא כֵּיצַד? מִפִּי הַשְּׁמוּעָה לָמְדוּ, שֶׁאֵין דִּין זֶה אֶלָּא בְּבֶן שְׁלֹשׁ עֶשְׂרֵה שָׁנָה וְיוֹם אֶחָד שֶׁהֵבִיא שְׁתֵּי שְׂעָרוֹת, עַד שֶׁיַּקִּיף כָּל הַגִּיד; וְאַחַר שֶׁיַּקִּיף הַשֵּׂעָר כָּל הַגִּיד – הֲרֵי הוּא בִּרְשׁוּת עַצְמוֹ וְאֵינוֹ נִסְקָל.

ו כָּל יָמָיו שֶׁל בֵּן סוֹרֵר וּמוֹרֶה אֵינָן אֶלָּא שְׁלֹשָׁה חֳדָשִׁים מֵאַחַר שֶׁיָּבִיא שְׁתֵּי שְׂעָרוֹת. לְפִי שֶׁאֶפְשָׁר שֶׁתִּתְעַבֵּר אִשְׁתּוֹ וְיִהְיֶה עֻבָּרָהּ נִכָּר בִּשְׁלֹשָׁה חֳדָשִׁים, וְנֶאֱמַר: כִּי יִהְיֶה לְאִישׁ בֵּן סוֹרֵר וּמוֹרֶה – וְלֹא אָב סוֹרֵר וּמוֹרֶה. הָא לָמַדְתָּ, שֶׁאִם הִקִּיף הַשֵּׂעָר אֶת כָּל הַגִּיד קֹדֶם שֶׁיַּשְׁלִים שְׁלֹשָׁה חֳדָשִׁים – הֲרֵי זֶה פָּטוּר.

ז כֵּיצַד דָּנִין בֵּן סוֹרֵר וּמוֹרֶה? מְבִיאִין אוֹתוֹ אָבִיו וְאִמּוֹ תְּחִלָּה לְבֵית דִּין שֶׁל שְׁלֹשָׁה וְאוֹמְרִין לָהֶן: בְּנֵנוּ זֶה סוֹרֵר וּמֹרֶה. וּמְבִיאִין שְׁנֵי עֵדִים שֶׁגָּנַב מִשֶּׁל אָבִיו, וְקָנָה בָּשָׂר וָיַיִן בַּמֶּה שֶׁגָּנַב, וְאָכַל אוֹתָהּ אֲכִילָה הָאֲמוּרָה אַחַר הַהַתְרָאָה. וְזוֹ הִיא עֵדוּת הָרִאשׁוֹנָה. וּמַלְקִין אוֹתוֹ כִּשְׁאָר חַיָּבֵי מַלְקוּת, שֶׁנֶּאֱמַר: וְיִסְּרוּ אֹתוֹ וְלֹא יִשְׁמַע אֲלֵיהֶם.
חָזַר וְגָנַב מִשֶּׁל אָבִיו וְאָכַל אֲכִילָה זוֹ – אָבִיו וְאִמּוֹ מְבִיאִין אוֹתוֹ לְבֵית דִּין שֶׁל שְׁלֹשָׁה

22. This is the sign of physical maturity which when manifested indicates that a child has attained maturity.
23. But not the entire genital area (*Kessef Mishneh*).
24. As stated in the following halachah, we are speaking about a period of three months or less.
25. It takes, however, three months before the fetus reaches a size when it could be recognized. See Genesis 38:24. The Radbaz notes that there are situations where a fetus can be recognized before three months have passed, but this is not the norm. And the ruling follows the majority.
26. As stated in the previous halachah.
27. Who have been granted *semichah*.
28. As stated in Deuteronomy 21:20.
29. For lashes are not administered unless a warning is given.
30. See *Hilchot Sanhedrin* chs. 16-17.

bring two witnesses who testify that he stole and partook of this meal after being warned. This is the second testimony. [It is acceptable if] the first two [witnesses also deliver] the latter [testimony].

After their testimony is heard, [the youth] is examined to see if his pubic hair surrounded his entire male organ.[31] If that is not the case and it is not three months after [he became thirteen], they complete the judgment against him as is done with all those executed by the court and he is stoned to death. He is not stoned to death unless the three judges who originally [sentenced him to be lashed] are present. [This is implied by the phrase:] "This son of ours," i.e., "the one that was lashed in your presence."

8. If his father and his mother forgave him before he was sentenced,[32] he is not liable.

9. If he fled before he was sentenced [to death] and afterwards, his pubic hair surrounded [his organ], he is not liable.[33] If he fled after he was sentenced, even if he grows old, whenever he is discovered, he should be stoned to death. For whenever a person has been sentenced [to death], it is as if he has already been slain and he has no blood.

10. If his father desires [to convict him] and his mother does not, or his mother desires and his father does not, he is not [judged as] a "wayward and rebellious son,"[34] as [implied by Deuteronomy 21:19]: "His father and mother[35] shall take hold of him."

If one of [the parents] has had his arm amputated, was lame,[36] dumb, blind, or deaf, [the son] is not [judged as] a "wayward and rebellious son." [These concepts are derived as follows:] "His father and mother shall take hold of him" - This excludes [parents] with amputated arms." "And bring him out" - this excludes the lame. "They say" - this excludes the dumb. "This son of ours" - This excludes the blind.[37] "He does not heed our voice" - This excludes the deaf.[38]

11. There is a Scriptural decree that a "wayward and rebellious son" should be stoned to death. A daughter, by contrast, is not judged in this manner. [The rationale is that] she does not have the tendency to become habituated to eating and drinking.[39] [For this reason,] the Torah states: "A son," i.e., and not a daughter. A *tumtum*[40] and an *adrogynus*[41] [are also excluded].

31. Note the *Kessef Mishneh* who asks why an examination is not made before the youth is lashed. For if he is too old to be classified as a "wayward and rebellious son," there is no reason that he be lashed either.
32. I.e., although they brought him to court and initiated proceedings against him, in the midst of the trial, their mercies overwhelmed them and they forgave him. If, however, he already had been sentenced, he is executed even if his parents desire to forgive him.
33. For his body has undergone a change and he would not be held liable for this act in his present state.
34. He is not even given the first set of lashes (*Or Sameach*).

וְעֶשְׂרִים, וּמְבִיאִין שְׁנֵי עֵדִים וּמְעִידִין עָלָיו שֶׁגָּנַב וְאָכַל אֲכִילָה זוֹ הָאֲמוּרָה אַחַר שֶׁהִתְרוּ בּוֹ. וְזוֹ הִיא עֵדוּת אַחֲרוֹנָה. אֲפִלּוּ הָיוּ הַשְּׁנַיִם הָרִאשׁוֹנִים הֵם הָאַחֲרוֹנִים. וְאַחַר שֶׁמְּקַבְּלִין עֵדוּתָן בּוֹדְקִין אוֹתוֹ שֶׁמָּא הִקִּיף הַשֵּׂעָר אֶת כָּל הַגִּיד. אִם לֹא הִקִּיף וְלֹא שָׁלְמוּ לוֹ שְׁלֹשָׁה חֳדָשִׁים – גּוֹמְרִין דִּינוֹ כְּדֶרֶךְ כָּל הֲרוּגֵי בֵּית דִּין וְסוֹקְלִין אוֹתוֹ. וְאֵינוֹ נִסְקָל עַד שֶׁיִּהְיוּ שָׁם שְׁלֹשָׁה הָרִאשׁוֹנִים. שֶׁנֶּאֱמַר: בְּנֵנוּ זֶה – זֶהוּ שֶׁלָּקָה בִּפְנֵיכֶם.

ח וְאִם מָחֲלוּ לוֹ אָבִיו וְאִמּוֹ קֹדֶם שֶׁיִּגָּמֵר דִּינוֹ – פָּטוּר.

ט בָּרַח עַד שֶׁלֹּא נִגְמַר דִּינוֹ, וְאַחַר כָּךְ הִקִּיף הַשֵּׂעָר מִלְּמַטָּה – פָּטוּר. וְאִם מִשֶּׁנִּגְמַר דִּינוֹ בָּרַח, אֲפִלּוּ הִזְקִין – כָּל עֵת שֶׁיִּמָּצֵא יִסָּקֵל; שֶׁכָּל מִי שֶׁנִּגְמַר דִּינוֹ – הֲרֵי הוּא כְּהָרוּג וְאֵין לוֹ דָּם.

י הָיָה אָבִיו רוֹצֶה וְאִמּוֹ אֵינָהּ רוֹצָה, אִמּוֹ רוֹצָה וְאָבִיו אֵינוֹ רוֹצֶה – אֵינוֹ נַעֲשֶׂה בֵּן סוֹרֵר וּמוֹרֶה. שֶׁנֶּאֱמַר: וְתָפְשׂוּ בוֹ אָבִיו וְאִמּוֹ.
הָיָה אֶחָד מֵהֶן גִּדֵּם אוֹ חִגֵּר אוֹ אִלֵּם אוֹ סוּמָא אוֹ חֵרֵשׁ – אֵינוֹ נַעֲשֶׂה בֵּן סוֹרֵר וּמוֹרֶה. שֶׁנֶּאֱמַר: וְתָפְשׂוּ בוֹ – וְלֹא גִדְּמִים; וְהוֹצִיאוּ אֹתוֹ – וְלֹא חִגְּרִים; וְאָמְרוּ – וְלֹא אִלְּמִים; בְּנֵנוּ זֶה – וְלֹא סוּמִים; אֵינֶנּוּ שֹׁמֵעַ בְּקֹלֵנוּ – וְלֹא חֵרְשִׁים.

יא גְּזֵרַת הַכָּתוּב הוּא שֶׁיִּסָּקֵל בֵּן סוֹרֵר וּמוֹרֶה. אֲבָל הַבַּת – אֵינָהּ נִדּוֹנֶת בְּדִין זֶה, שֶׁאֵין דַּרְכָּהּ לְהִמָּשֵׁךְ בַּאֲכִילָה וּשְׁתִיָּה כְּאִישׁ. שֶׁנֶּאֱמַר: בֵּן – וְלֹא בַת, וְלֹא טֻמְטוּם וְאַנְדְּרוֹגִינוֹס.

35. I.e., both acting together in agreement.
36. The Meiri states that these people have a tendency to cruelty. Hence, they may not condemn their sons in this manner. The verses are merely *asmachteot*.
37. The expression "This" implies something that you can point your finger at and say: "This is it" (Rashi, *Sanhedrin* 71b).
38. This reply implies that they hear his obstinate replies to their statements to him (*Ibid.*).
39. As stated in the introduction to this chapter, a "wayward and rebellious son" is executed because of his ultimate future. We fear that he will become habituated to stealing, eating, and drinking and will ultimately become a robber and murderer. Since it is less likely for a woman to develop such habits, she is not judged in this manner.

The commentaries note that in *Sanhedrin* 69b-70a, Rabbi Simon states that a girl may develop such tendencies and support her habit through prostitution. They question why the Rambam does not mention this point. The *Kessef Mishneh* uses this as a proof that the command to kill "a wayward and rebellious son" is a Torah decree above the bounds of intellect.
40. A person whose genital area is covered with a block of flesh and whose gender cannot be determined.
41. A person with both male and female sexual organs.

12. When an operation is performed on a *tumtum*[42] and it is discovered that he is a male, he is not judged as a "wayward and rebellious son." [The rationale is Deuteronomy 21:18] states: "If a person will have a wayward and rebellious son...." [Implied is that] he must be a son[43] at the time he receives the warning.

13. An announcement must be made concerning the execution of a "wayward and rebellious son."[44] What type of announcement is made?[45] A declaration is written [and sent to] the entire Jewish people: "In this-and-this court, we stoned so-and-so because he was a 'wayward and rebellious son.'"

14. A "wayward and rebellious son" is like all others executed by the court; their estate is inherited by their heirs.[46] Even though the person's father caused him to be stoned to death, [the father] inherits all of his possessions.[47]

Blessed be God who grants assistance.

42. I.e., after he was apprehended for stealing and participating in such a feast. It would appear that if the operation is performed beforehand, he is like any other male. There are, however, authorities who do not accept this conception. They even cite manuscript copies of the *Mishneh Torah* which read "from [the beginning of]s existence" instead of "at the time he receives the warning." The latter opinion is reflected in the wording of the Rambam's source (*Bava Batra* 126b).

יב טֻמְטוּם שֶׁנִּקְרַע וְנִמְצָא זָכָר – אֵינוֹ נַעֲשֶׂה בֵּן סוֹרֵר וּמוֹרֶה. שֶׁנֶּאֱמַר: כִּי יִהְיֶה לְאִישׁ בֵּן סוֹרֵר וּמוֹרֶה – עַד שֶׁיִּהְיֶה בֵּן מִשְּׁעַת הַתְרָאָה.

יג בֵּן סוֹרֵר וּמוֹרֶה צָרִיךְ הַכְרָזָה. כֵּיצַד מַכְרִיזִין עָלָיו? כּוֹתְבִין לְכָל יִשְׂרָאֵל: בְּבֵית דִּין פְּלוֹנִי סְקַלְנוּ פְּלוֹנִי מִפְּנֵי שֶׁהָיָה בֵּן סוֹרֵר וּמוֹרֶה.

יד בֵּן סוֹרֵר וּמוֹרֶה הֲרֵי הוּא כְּכָל הֲרוּגֵי בֵּית דִּין שֶׁמָּמוֹנָם לְיוֹרְשֵׁיהֶן; שֶׁאַף עַל פִּי שֶׁאָבִיו גָּרַם לוֹ סְקִילָה – הֲרֵי הוּא יוֹרֵשׁ כָּל נְכָסָיו.

בְּרִיךְ רַחֲמָנָא דְסַיְּעָן

43. I.e., his masculinity must be obvious.
44. For the passage concludes (Deuteronomy 21:21): "All Israel shall hear and fear." The announcement is circulated after the execution.
45. Compare to similar statements in *Hilchot Edut* 18:7.
46. See *Hilchot Evel* 1:9.
47. For the "wayward and rebellious son" has no closer heir. We do not fear that he will have him executed because he desired to inherit his estate (Radbaz).

HILCHOT EVEL

THE LAWS OF MOURNING

They include four mitzvot: one positive commandment and three negative commandments:

They are:

1. To mourn for one's [close] relatives; even a priest must become impure and mourns for his close relatives.[1] A person should not mourn for individuals executed by the court. For this reason, I have included these laws in this book,[2] for they relate to the mitzvah of burying [the dead] on the day of their passing which is a positive commandment.[3]
2. For a High Priest not to become impure because of [his close] relatives;
3. For him not to enter under the same shelter as a corpse;
4. For an ordinary priest not to become impure because of a corpse except for that of his close relatives.

These mitzvot are explained in the coming chapters.

1. I.e., there are two dimensions of this mitzvah: a) for any person to mourn for his relatives; b) that despite the impurity involved, a priest must be involved in the burial of his relatives.
2. I.e., on the surface, these mitzvot are not directly related to the subject matter of this book, "The Book of Judges." Nevertheless, because of the connection mentioned by the Rambam, it is more appropriate to discuss these mitzvot here than in any other place in the *Mishneh Torah.*
3. See *Hilchot Sanhedrin* 15:8 where this mitzvah is discussed.

הִלְכוֹת אֵבֶל

יֵשׁ בִּכְלָלָן אַרְבַּע מִצְוֹת: אַחַת מִצְוַת עֲשֵׂה, וְשָׁלֹשׁ מִצְוֹת לֹא תַעֲשֶׂה, וְזֶה הוּא פְּרָטָן:

א) לְהִתְאַבֵּל עַל הַקְּרוֹבִים. וַאֲפִלּוּ כֹּהֵן מִתְטַמֵּא וּמִתְאַבֵּל עַל הַקְּרוֹבִים. וְאֵין אָדָם מִתְאַבֵּל עַל הֲרוּגֵי בֵּית דִּין. וּלְפִי זֶה כָּלַלְתִּי הִלְכוֹת אֵלּוּ בְּסֵפֶר זֶה, שֶׁהֵן מֵעֵין קְבוּרָה בְּיוֹם מִיתָה, שֶׁהִיא מִצְוַת עֲשֵׂה.

ב) שֶׁלֹּא יִטַּמָּא כֹּהֵן גָּדוֹל לִקְרוֹבִים.

ג) שֶׁלֹּא יִכָּנֵס עִם הַמֵּת בְּאֹהֶל.

ד) שֶׁלֹּא יִטַּמָּא כֹּהֵן הֶדְיוֹט לְנֶפֶשׁ אָדָם אֶלָּא לִקְרוֹבִים בִּלְבַד.

וּבֵאוּר מִצְוֹת אֵלּוּ בִּפְרָקִים אֵלּוּ:

CHAPTER ONE

1. It is a positive commandment to mourn for one's close relatives,[1] as [implied by Leviticus 10:20]: "Were I to partake of a sin offering today, would it find favor in God's eyes?"[2] According to Scriptural Law, [the obligation to] mourn is only on the first day which is the day of the person's death and burial.[3] The remainder of the seven days [of mourning] are not required by Scriptural Law. Although the Torah states [Genesis 50:10]: "And he instituted mourning for his father for seven days,"[4] when the Torah was given, the laws were renewed.[5]

Moses our teacher ordained for the Jewish people the seven days of mourning and the seven days of [wedding] celebrations.[6]

2. From when is a person obligated to mourn? When the grave is covered.[7] But until the corpse has been buried, a mourner is not bound by any of the prohibitions incumbent on a mourner.[8] For this reason, [King] David washed and anointed himself when his son died, before he was buried.[9]

3. When is the beginning of the obligation to mourn and count the seven and the thirty days of mourning for people executed by the gentile authorities who they do not allow to be buried?[10] When their relatives despair of asking permission from the king to bury them, even though they did not despair of stealing their corpses to bury them.[11]

4. When a person drowned in a river[12] or was consumed by a wild beast, [we

1. *Sefer HaMitzvot* (positive commandment 37) and *Sefer HaChinuch* (mitzvah 264) count this as one of the 613 mitzvot of the Torah. There are, however, other *Rishonim* who do not accept this concept. The *Shulchan Aruch* (*Yoreh De'ah* 398:1) quotes both these views, while the Ramah (*Yoreh De'ah* 399:13) states that the common practice is to follow the opinion that there is no Scriptural obligation for mourning. Among the distinctions between these two views is whether there is an obligation to mourn on the second day of a festival or not.

In Chapter 2, Halachah 1, the Rambam defines the term "[close] relatives" as one's "father, mother, son, daughter, brother, and sister." As will be explained there, others also include one's spouse.

2. Aaron posed this question to Moses after Moses asked him why he did not partake of a sin offering despite the fact that Aaron's sons had died that day. The Rambam maintains that the fact that mourning for his sons took precedence over partaking of the sacrifices which is a mitzvah indicates that mourning is also a mitzvah (Radbaz).

The *Kessef Mishneh* notes that this is a somewhat indirect commandment and notes that in *Sefer HaMitzvot, loc. cit.*, the Rambam quotes another source. There, he states that the mitzvah is derived from the priests' obligation to become impure while caring for their deceased close relatives.

3. I.e., according to the Rambam, for there to be a Scriptural obligation of mourning, the death and the burial must be on the same day.

4. Joseph instituted mourning for Jacob.

פֶּרֶק רִאשׁוֹן

א מִצְוַת עֲשֵׂה לְהִתְאַבֵּל עַל הַקְּרוֹבִים. שֶׁנֶּאֱמַר: וְאָכַלְתִּי חַטָּאת הַיּוֹם, הַיִּיטַב בְּעֵינֵי יְיָ. וְאֵין אֲבֵלוּת מִן הַתּוֹרָה אֶלָּא בְּיוֹם רִאשׁוֹן בִּלְבַד, שֶׁהוּא יוֹם הַמִּיתָה וְיוֹם הַקְּבוּרָה; אֲבָל שְׁאָר הַשִּׁבְעָה יָמִים – אֵינוֹ דִּין תּוֹרָה. אַף עַל פִּי שֶׁנֶּאֱמַר בַּתּוֹרָה: וַיַּעַשׂ לְאָבִיו אֵבֶל שִׁבְעַת יָמִים – נִתְּנָה תּוֹרָה וְנִתְחַדְּשָׁה הֲלָכָה.
וּמֹשֶׁה רַבֵּנוּ תִּקֵּן לָהֶם לְיִשְׂרָאֵל שִׁבְעַת יְמֵי אֲבֵלוּת וְשִׁבְעַת יְמֵי הַמִּשְׁתֶּה.

ב מֵאֵימָתַי יִתְחַיֵּב אָדָם בְּאֵבֶל? מִשֶּׁיִּסָּתֵם הַגּוֹלֵל. אֲבָל כָּל זְמַן שֶׁלֹּא נִקְבַּר הַמֵּת – אֵינוֹ אָסוּר בְּדָבָר מִן הַדְּבָרִים שֶׁהָאָבֵל אָסוּר בָּהֶן. וּמִפְּנֵי טַעַם זֶה רָחַץ דָּוִד וְסָךְ כְּשֶׁמֵּת הַיֶּלֶד טֶרֶם שֶׁיִּקָּבֵר.

ג הֲרוּגֵי מַלְכוּת שֶׁאֵין מַנִּיחִין אוֹתָן לְהִקָּבֵר, מֵאֵימָתַי מַתְחִילִין לְהִתְאַבֵּל עֲלֵיהֶן וְלִסְפֹּר שִׁבְעָה וּשְׁלֹשִׁים? מִשֶּׁיִּתְיָאֲשׁוּ לִשְׁאֹל לַמֶּלֶךְ לְקָבְרָן, אַף עַל פִּי שֶׁלֹּא נִתְיָאֲשׁוּ מִלִּגְנֹב אוֹתָן.

ד מִי שֶׁטָּבַע בְּנָהָר אוֹ מִי שֶׁאֲכָלַתּוּ חַיָּה רָעָה –

5. I.e., when there is a difference between the two, our conduct follows the commandments given at Sinai and not the conduct of the Patriarchs and their descendants.
6. I.e., although the observance of these seven days is a Rabbinic institution. Chronologically, it was given to the Jewish people at the same time as the Scriptural commandments.
7. We have translated the Rambam's words loosely. The term *golal* refers to a large stone which is placed over a grave to close it. See the Rambam's Commentary on the Mishnah (*Ohelot* 2:4).
8. See Chapter 5, Halachah 1. There are, however, certain obligations incumbent upon him because of the state of *aninut*. See Chapter 4, Halachah 6.
9. II Samuel, ch. 12, relates that when the first son which Bathsheba bore David became ill, David oppressed himself, but when the baby died, he washed and anointed himself. This was permitted because the child had not been buried.
10. In the Talmudic era, it was very common for the Romans to crucify people and leave their bodies unburied. The *Kessef Mishneh* states that if it is possible to bribe the ruling authorities to allow the corpse to be buried, then the mourning rites cannot be started.
11. For it is unlikely that they would be successful in stealing the corpses.
12. The Radbaz notes that the Rambam's wording leaves unclarified a question raised by other Rabbis. To explain: As stated in *Hilchot Gerushin* 13:16, if a person drowns in water that does not have definite boundaries, a sea or the ocean, his wife is not given the chance to remarry. There are authorities who maintain that in such a situation, mourning rites should also not be held. For if one holds mourning rites, people will be certain that he died and his wife will be allowed to remarry. This opinion is reflected in the ruling of the *Shulchan Aruch* (*Yoreh De'ah* 375:7). The Radbaz, however, does not accept this conception entirely. He explains that, according to the Rambam, since mourning is a

begin mourning for him] when we despair of finding [his corpse].[13] If his corpse was found limb by limb, we do not begin counting the days of mourning until his head and the majority of his body is found or they despair of finding [the remainder of his corpse].

5. When it is customary for people to send a corpse to another city to be buried and they do not know when the burial will take place,[14] from the time they turn back from accompanying the corpse, they are obligated to count the seven and thirty days of mourning and begin mourning rites.[15]

6. We do not mourn[16] for stillborn infants. Whenever a human[17] offspring does not live for 30 days, he is considered as stillborn. Even if he died on the thirtieth day, we do not mourn for him.[18]

7. If we know for certain that he was born after a full nine months [of pregnancy],[19] we mourn for him even if he died on the day of his birth.[20]

8. A fetus from a full term pregnancy that was stillborn, a child born in the eighth month of pregnancy who died even after living 30 days,[21] or a fetus that emerged cut or crushed even though it endured a full term pregnancy is considered stillborn. We do not observe mourning rites for them and we do not engage in activity on their behalf.[22]

9. We observe mourning rites for all of those executed by the government, even when they were executed by the government's laws and the Torah granted it license to execute them.[23] We don't withhold anything from them.[24]

Scriptural obligation, it should not be overridden because of the possibility of such an error.

13. The *Shulchan Aruch* (*loc. cit.*) states that if, after the family despaired of finding the corpse and held mourning rites, the corpse is discovered, there is no need to hold mourning rites again. The deceased's sons, however, should mourn for the remainder of the day on which the corpse was discovered.

14. *Kin'at Eliyahu* notes that today, with the advances in modern communication, it is possible to know when a corpse was buried even when it is buried in a distant place. Hence the mourners in distant places do not start the seven days of *shivah* mourning until the burial.

15. The people who accompany the corpse, by contrast, are obligated to begin mourning rites only after the burial. Thus two members of the family may complete mourning rites for the same person on different days.

16. Nor should a priest become impure (Chapter 2, Halachah 8).

17. In contrast to an animal which is considered as viable after eight days (*Shabbat* 135b).

18. The Radbaz states that this applies even when the fetus dies of unnatural causes, e.g., it is consumed by a beast of prey. Since we are not certain that the birth was viable and thus we are obligated to mourn, we follow the more lenient position.

19. I.e., the woman did not engage in relations with her husband from nine months before

מִשֶּׁנִּתְיָאֲשׁוּ לְבַקֵּשׁ. מְצָאוּהוּ אֵיבָרִים אֵיבָרִים – אֵין מוֹנִין לוֹ עַד שֶׁיִּמָּצֵא רֹאשׁוֹ וְרֻבּוֹ אוֹ יִתְיָאֲשׁוּ מִלְּבַקֵּשׁ.

ה מִי שֶׁדַּרְכָּן לִשְׁלֹחַ הַמֵּת לִמְדִינָה אַחֶרֶת לְקָבְרוֹ, וְאֵינָם יוֹדְעִים מָתַי יִקָּבֵר – מֵעֵת שֶׁיַּחֲזִירוּ פְּנֵיהֶן מִלְּלַוּוֹתוֹ מַתְחִילִין לִמְנוֹת שִׁבְעָה וּשְׁלֹשִׁים וּמַתְחִילִין לְהִתְאַבֵּל.

ו הַנְּפָלִים – אֵין מִתְאַבְּלִין עֲלֵיהֶן. וְכֹל שֶׁלֹּא שָׁהָה שְׁלֹשִׁים יוֹם בְּאָדָם – הֲרֵי זֶה נֵפֶל. אֲפִלּוּ מֵת בְּיוֹם שְׁלֹשִׁים – אֵין מִתְאַבְּלִין עָלָיו.

ז וְאִם נוֹדַע בְּוַדַּאי שֶׁנּוֹלַד לְתִשְׁעָה חֳדָשִׁים גְּמוּרִים, אֲפִלּוּ מֵת בַּיּוֹם שֶׁנּוֹלַד – מִתְאַבְּלִים עָלָיו.

ח בֶּן תִּשְׁעָה חֳדָשִׁים שֶׁנּוֹלַד מֵת, וּבֶן שְׁמוֹנָה שֶׁמֵּת אֲפִלּוּ לְאַחַר שְׁלֹשִׁים, וּמִי שֶׁיָּצָא מְחֻתָּךְ אוֹ מְרֻסָּס אַף עַל פִּי שֶׁכָּלוּ לוֹ חֳדָשָׁיו – הֲרֵי זֶה נֵפֶל; וְאֵין מִתְאַבְּלִין עֲלֵיהֶן, וְלֹא מִתְעַסְּקִין עִמָּהֶם.

ט כָּל הֲרוּגֵי מַלְכוּת, אַף עַל פִּי שֶׁנֶּהֶרְגוּ בְּדִין הַמֶּלֶךְ, וְהַתּוֹרָה נָתְנָה לוֹ רְשׁוּת לְהָרְגָן –

the child's birth until her pregnancy was detected [Rashi, *Shabbat* 136a; *Shulchan Aruch* (*Yoreh De'ah* 37:8)].

20. When a pregnancy continues for its full term, we assume that the birth was viable and that the infant died for other reasons.. Compare to *Hilchot Rotzeach* 2:7.

The Ramah (*Even HaEzer* 156:4) writes that in the present era, as long as we know that a woman has reached her ninth month of pregnancy, her child is considered as viable. Hence the mourning rites would have to be observed for such an infant.

21. The Ra'avad differs with the Rambam and maintains that we do observe mourning rites for a child born in the eighth month if it survives for more than 30 days. The difference between them depends on our Sages' statement (*Shabbat* 135a) that an infant born in the eighth month is like a stone; i.e., it will certainly die and therefore it may not be carried on the Sabbath. The Ra'avad maintains that if the infant lives 30 days, it becomes obvious that it was in fact a fetus from a seven month pregnancy that remained in the womb somewhat longer and the birth is considered viable. The Rambam does not accept such a possibility. (It must be emphasized that today, efforts are made to save all infants, even those born in the eighth month and in many instances, the doctors have been successful in enabling such infants to live.)

22. I.e., we do not arrange eulogies and funeral processions. We do, however, arrange for the fetus' burial (*Siftei Cohen* 344:6). There are, however, opinions (*Hagahot Maimoniot, Hilchot Milah* 1, note 10) which maintain that there is no mitzvah in burying a stillborn fetus.

23. I.e., even though the Torah granted such license, these individuals are not considered like those executed by the court. *Kiryat Melech* cites proof from II Samuel 11:27 which speaks of Bathsheba mourning for her husband Uriah even though he was killed as a rebel against the king.

24. I.e., the funeral and eulogies should be held in an ordinary manner. Since their

Their estate is given to the government,[25] but they are buried in their ancestral plots.

We do not, by contrast, observe mourning rites for those executed by the court.[26] We do, however, observe the rites of bitter regret (*aninut*),[27] for *aninut* is an expression of the feelings in one's heart.[28] They are not buried with their ancestors until their corpses have decomposed.[29] Their estate, however, is granted to their heirs.

10. We do not conduct mourning rites for all those who deviate from the path of the community, i.e., people who throw off the yoke of the mitzvot from their necks and do not join together with the Jewish people in the observance of the mitzvot, the honoring of the festivals, or the attendance of synagogues and houses of study. Instead, they are like free and independent people like the other nations. Similarly, we do not mourn for heretics, apostates, and people who inform on Jews to the gentiles.[30] Instead, their brothers and their other relatives wear white clothes, robe themselves in white, eat, drink, and celebrate for the enemies of the Holy One, blessed be He, have perished.[31] Concerning them, [Psalms139:21] states: "Those who hate You, O God, will I hate."

11. When a person commits suicide, we do not engage in activity on their behalf at all.[32] We do not mourn for him or eulogize him.[33] We do, however, stand in a line [to comfort the relatives],[34] recite the blessing for the mourners[35] and [perform] any act that shows respect for the living.[36]

What is meant by a person who commits suicide? Not necessarily one who climbs up on a roof, falls, and dies,[37] but rather, one who says: "I am going up to the top of the roof."[38] If we see him climb up immediately in anger or [know that] he was distressed and [see] him fall and die, we presume such a person is one who committed suicide. If, however, we see him strangled and

transgression involved disobeying the ruling authorities, their death is sufficient to atone for that transgression.

25. In punishment for rebelling against him.

26. See *Hilchot Sanhedrin* 13:6. The severity of their transgressions is so great that the additional measure of withholding mourning rites is necessary for them to gain atonement (see *Sanhedrin* 46b and commentaries). In his Commentary to the Mishnah (*Sanhedrin* 6:8), the Rambam writes that the atonement for these individuals is not granted until their corpses begin to decompose. Hence at the time of the funeral, it is not fit to mourn for them. See also Chapter 2, Halachah 8.

27. See Chapter 4, Halachah 6.

28. I.e., it is not an expression of honor for the departed and thus withholding it will not bring him atonement (see *Sanhedrin, loc. cit.*, and commentaries).

29. For we do not bury a wicked person next to a righteous one. When, however, their corpses have decomposed that is a sign that their sins have received atonement (*ibid.*). See *Hilchot Sanhedrin* 14:9.

הֲרֵי אֵלּוּ מִתְאַבְּלִין עֲלֵיהֶן, וְאֵין מוֹנְעִין מֵהֶן כָּל דָּבָר, וּמָמוֹנָם לַמֶּלֶךְ, וְנִקְבָּרִין בְּקִבְרֵי אֲבוֹתֵיהֶן.

אֲבָל כָּל הֲרוּגֵי בֵּית דִּין – אֵין מִתְאַבְּלִין עֲלֵיהֶן, אֲבָל אוֹנְנִין; שֶׁאֵין אֲנִינוּת אֶלָּא בַּלֵּב. וְאֵין נִקְבָּרִין עִם אֲבוֹתֵיהֶן עַד שֶׁיִּתְאַכֵּל הַבָּשָׂר, וּמָמוֹנָם לְיוֹרְשֵׁיהֶם.

י כָּל הַפּוֹרְשִׁין מִדַּרְכֵי צִבּוּר, וְהֵם הָאֲנָשִׁים שֶׁפָּרְקוּ עֹל הַמִּצְוֹת מֵעַל צַוָּארָן, וְאֵין נִכְלָלִין בִּכְלַל יִשְׂרָאֵל בַּעֲשִׂיַּת הַמִּצְוֹת וּבִכְבוּד הַמּוֹעֲדוֹת וִישִׁיבַת בָּתֵּי כְנֵסִיּוֹת וּבָתֵּי מִדְרָשׁוֹת, אֶלָּא הֲרֵי הֵן כִּבְנֵי חוֹרִין לְעַצְמָן, וְכֵן הָאֶפִּיקוֹרוֹסִין [וְהַמּוּמָרִים] וְהַמּוֹסְרִין – כָּל אֵלּוּ אֵין מִתְאַבְּלִין עֲלֵיהֶן; אֶלָּא אֲחֵיהֶם וּשְׁאָר קְרוֹבֵיהֶם לוֹבְשִׁין לְבָנִים וּמִתְעַטְּפִים לְבָנִים וְאוֹכְלִים וְשׁוֹתִים וּשְׂמֵחִים, שֶׁהֲרֵי אָבְדוּ שׂוֹנְאָיו שֶׁל הַקָּדוֹשׁ בָּרוּךְ הוּא. וַעֲלֵיהֶם הַכָּתוּב אוֹמֵר: הֲלוֹא מְשַׂנְאֶיךָ יְיָ אֶשְׂנָא.

יא הַמְאַבֵּד עַצְמוֹ לְדַעַת – אֵין מִתְעַסְּקִין עִמּוֹ לְכָל דָּבָר, וְאֵין מִתְאַבְּלִין עָלָיו, וְאֵין מַסְפִּידִין אוֹתוֹ. אֲבָל עוֹמְדִין עָלָיו בְּשׁוּרָה, וְאוֹמְרִין עָלָיו בִּרְכַּת אֲבֵלִים, וְכָל דָּבָר שֶׁהוּא כָּבוֹד לַחַיִּים. וְאֵי זֶהוּ הַמְאַבֵּד עַצְמוֹ לְדַעַת? לֹא שֶׁעָלָה לַגַּג וְנָפַל וָמֵת, אֶלָּא הָאוֹמֵר: הֲרֵינִי עוֹלֶה לְרֹאשׁ הַגַּג! רָאוּהוּ שֶׁעָלָה מִיָּד דֶּרֶךְ כַּעַס, אוֹ שֶׁהָיָה מֵצֵר, וְנָפַל וָמֵת – הֲרֵי זֶה בְּחֶזְקַת שֶׁאִבֵּד עַצְמוֹ לְדַעַת.

30. See *Hilchot Mamrim* 3:2 for further explanation of these terms.

31. As Proverbs 11:10 states: "At the devastation of the wicked, there is rejoicing" (*Siftei Cohen* 345:9).

Although this law is quoted by the later authorities [*Shulchan Aruch* (*Yoreh De'ah* 345:5)], in all ages, there were Rabbinic authorities who differed. For example, Rabbenu Gershom had a son who converted and yet, that sage mourned for him. (Indeed, he mourned 14 days.) Even the authorities who maintain that this practice should be upheld with regard to the deviants themselves, rule more leniently with regard to their descendants [see Ramah (*Yoreh De'ah* 340:5)]. Since they were raised without a full awareness of their Torah tradition, they are not judged as seriously for their violation of it. On this basis, there are many contemporary authorities who counsel leniency with regard to holding mourning rites for Reform and Conservative Jews today.

32. We do not even rend our garments in mourning or attend his funeral.

33. For suicide is considered a grave sin, equivalent to murder (see *Bava Kama* 91b). Hence, any act that is a token of respect for the deceased is withheld. Although mourning on the first day fulfills a Scriptural commandment, that commandment applies only when the deceased is an observant member of the Jewish community (Radbaz).

34. See Chapter 13, Halachah 1.

35. See Chapter 12, Halachah 7.

36. For they have suffered a loss and their feelings should be assuaged.

37. For perhaps he slipped and fell accidentally.

38. I.e., he states his intention to commit suicide.

hanging from a tree or slain and lying on the back of his sword, we presume that he is like all other corpses.[39] We engage in activity on his behalf and do not withhold anything from him.[40]

CHAPTER TWO

1. These are [the relatives] for whom a person is obligated to mourn according to Scriptural Law:[1] His mother,[2] his father, his son, his daughter, his paternal[3] brother and [paternal] sister. According to Rabbinic Law, a man should also mourn for his wife[4] [if she dies while they are] married.[5] And a woman should mourn for her husband. Similarly, a person should mourn for a maternal brother and sister.[6]

2. Even a priest who does not become impure for his maternal brother and sister[7] or for his paternal sister who is married, mourns for them. For his paternal sister who is married,[8] he is required to mourn by Scriptural Law.[9]

3. A person who has a son or a brother born by a maid-servant or a gentile woman should not mourn for them at all.[10] Similarly, when a person and his sons convert or a person and his mother are freed from slavery, they do not mourn for each other.[11]

Similarly, a person does not observe either the rites of *aninut* or the mourning rites for a wife whom he has consecrated, [but not married].[12] Similarly, she does not observe either of these rites for him.

39. Even though the circumstantial evidence would appear to lead to the conclusion that he committed suicide, we do not act upon that conclusion.

40. I.e., he is given a full eulogy, funeral procession, and mourning rites.

The *Shulchan Aruch* (*Yoreh De'ah* 345:3) states that a person who commits suicide because he is forced to, for example, King Saul, should be mourned.

In practice, the issue is very delicate and in many instances, even when there is much circumstantial evidence that a suicide was voluntary, Rabbis have allowed mourning rites to be held.

1. Leviticus 21:2-3 mentions that a priest is obligated to become impure while tending for the corpses of these individuals. *Mo'ed Kattan* 20b states: "Whenever a priest is obligated to become impure, others are obligated to mourn."

2. One's mother is mentioned first, because she is mentioned first in the verse.

3. See Halachah 12 on which basis we can appreciate why the Scriptural obligation is only for paternal siblings.

4. The verses from Leviticus cited above mention: *shaaro hakarov eilav* which *Yevamot* 22b interprets as referring to one's wife. The Rambam, however, maintains that this is merely an *asmachta*, a Rabbinic Law associated with a Scriptural verse, and not the direct meaning of the verse. This interpretation is borne out by the translation of the verse by Onkelos (see Halachah 6). Similarly, when the prophet Ezekiel describes the obligation for the priests to become impure (44:25), he mentions the other six relatives and not the priest's wife. Nevertheless, there are other authorities who follow the interpretation in

אֲבָל אִם רָאוּהוּ חָנוּק וְתָלוּי בְּאִילָן, אוֹ הָרוּג וּמֻשְׁלָךְ עַל גַּב סַיִפוֹ – הֲרֵי זֶה בְּחֶזְקַת כָּל הַמֵּתִים, וּמִתְעַסְּקִין עִמּוֹ וְאֵין מוֹנְעִין מִמֶּנּוּ דָּבָר.

פֶּרֶק שֵׁנִי

א אֵלּוּ שֶׁאָדָם חַיָּב לְהִתְאַבֵּל עֲלֵיהֶן דִּין תּוֹרָה: אִמּוֹ וְאָבִיו, בְּנוֹ וּבִתּוֹ, וְאָחִיו וַאֲחוֹתוֹ מֵאָבִיו. וּמִדִּבְרֵיהֶם שֶׁיִּתְאַבֵּל הָאִישׁ עַל אִשְׁתּוֹ הַנְּשׂוּאָה, וְכֵן הָאִשָּׁה עַל בַּעְלָהּ, וּמִתְאַבֵּל עַל אָחִיו וְעַל אֲחוֹתוֹ שֶׁהֵן מֵאִמּוֹ.

ב אֲפִלּוּ הַכֹּהֵן, שֶׁאֵינוֹ מִתְטַמֵּא לְאָחִיו וַאֲחוֹתוֹ מֵאִמּוֹ, וְלַאֲחוֹתוֹ הַנְּשׂוּאָה אַף עַל פִּי שֶׁהִיא מֵאָבִיו – מִתְאַבֵּל הוּא עֲלֵיהֶן.

וְאִם הָיְתָה אֲחוֹתוֹ זוֹ הַנְּשׂוּאָה מֵאָבִיו – הֲרֵי הוּא מִתְאַבֵּל עָלֶיהָ דִּין תּוֹרָה.

ג בְּנוֹ אוֹ אָחִיו הַבָּא מִן הַשִּׁפְחָה וּמִן הַנָּכְרִית – אֵינוֹ מִתְאַבֵּל עֲלֵיהֶן כְּלָל. וְכֵן מִי שֶׁנִּתְגַּיֵּר הוּא וּבָנָיו, אוֹ נִשְׁתַּחְרֵר הוּא וְאִמּוֹ – אֵין מִתְאַבְּלִין זֶה עַל זֶה. וְכֵן אִשְׁתּוֹ אֲרוּסָה – אֵינוֹ מִתְאַבֵּל עָלֶיהָ וְלֹא אוֹנֵן, וְכֵן הִיא לֹא אוֹנֶנֶת וְלֹא מִתְאַבֶּלֶת עָלָיו.

Yevamot. The *Kessef Mishneh* explains that the Rambam is following a principle which he stated on several occasions: Any concept derived through the principles of Biblical exegesis is described as Rabbinic in origin although it has the strength of Scriptural Law.

5. If, however, she has been merely consecrated, he is not required to mourn (Halachah 3). Needless to say, if he has divorced her, he is under no obligation.

6. For it is appropriate to express feelings of grief for the loss of any close relative (Radbaz).

7. According to Rabbinic decree.

8. For whom he may not become impure, as stated in Halachah 10.

9. The Ramban, the *Kessef Mishneh*, and many other authorities have questioned the Rambam's ruling in this halachah. The *Merkevet HaMishneh* offers a possible explanation, stating that the obligation to become impure on behalf of a corpse is to insure that someone takes care of that corpse's burial (see Halachah 6). For if the deceased's close relatives do not bury him, who else will? With regard to a married woman, however, there is no such fear, for her husband is obligated to bury her. Hence, no license is granted for her brothers to become impure on her behalf. On the other hand, they are obligated to mourn.

10. For the child's natural father is not considered as his father from a halachic perspective and thus the two share no family ties (*Yevamot* 22a).

11. For a convert (and a freed servant) is considered as a newborn infant with no ties to his natural parents (*ibid.*).

12. According to Jewish law, marriage is a two stage process involving: a) *erusin* - consecration, when the marriage bond is established and the woman becomes forbidden to all other men, and b) *nisu'in* - marriage, when the couple begin living together as man and

4. Whenever a person is obligated to mourn for a relative, he also mourns with that relative in his presence according to Rabbinical Law.

What is implied? If a person's grandson, his son's [maternal] brother, or son's mother[13] dies, he is obligated to rend his garments in the presence of his son and follow the mourning rites while in his presence.[14] Outside his presence, he is not obligated. Similar laws apply with regard to other relatives.[15]

5. With regard to a wife with whom one is married:[16] Although one must mourn for her, he does not mourn together with her for her other relatives with the exception of her father and her mother. He observes the rites of mourning for them in her presence.

When a man's father-in-law or mother-in-law dies, he overturns his bed[17] and observes the mourning rites together with his wife within her presence, but not outside her presence. Similarly, when a woman's father-in-law or mother-in-law dies, she observes the rites of mourning in [her husband's] presence. With regard to other relatives, by contrast, e.g., when the brother of one's wife or her son[18] dies or when the brother of one's husband or his son dies, they do not observe the mourning rites [in respect for] each other.

Similarly, it appears to me[19] that if the wife of a person's relative dies or the husband of one of his relatives, e.g., the wife of one's son or the husband of one's daughter, one need not observe mourning rites for them. Similar concepts apply in all analogous situations.

6. [See] how severe the mitzvah of mourning is! For [the prohibition against] ritual impurity is superseded[20] so that [a priest] can tend to his relatives' [burial] and mourn for them, as [Leviticus 21:2-3] states: "Except to one's flesh,[21] to whom he is close, to his mother... to her shall he become impure." This is a positive commandment;[22] if he does not desire to become impure, we force him to become impure against his will.

wife. Although at present, both of these stages commence on the same day, in Talmudic times, couples would wait a substantial period between the two.

As stated in Halachah 7 and notes, a priest does not become impure for such a wife. Hence, other men are not required to mourn.

13. Who is no longer his wife because he divorced her.

14. This is simply a measure of respect.

15. E.g., when one's grandfather dies, one observes mourning rites while together with one's father and when one's nephew dies, one observes mourning rites while together with one's brother.

The Ra'avad takes issue with the Rambam. Although he agrees that this principle applies with regard to relatives for whom one is required to mourn according to Scriptural Law, he differs when the obligation to mourn is Rabbinic, e.g., for the son's maternal brother. His rationale is that we generally do not institute a Rabbinic decree in support of another Rabbinic decree.

The Radbaz supports the Rambam's position, explaining that it could be said that just as the following halachah speaks about mourning for the parents of one's wife as a token of respect for her (although according to the Rambam, the obligation to mourn for her is

ד כָּל קְרוֹבִים שֶׁהוּא חַיָּב לְהִתְאַבֵּל עֲלֵיהֶן – הֲרֵי זֶה מִתְאַבֵּל עִמָּהֶם בִּפְנֵיהֶם מִדִּבְרֵי סוֹפְרִים.

כֵּיצַד? הֲרֵי שֶׁמֵּת בֶּן בְּנוֹ אוֹ אֲחִי בְּנוֹ אוֹ אֵם בְּנוֹ – חַיָּב לִקְרֹעַ בִּפְנֵי בְּנוֹ וְלִנְהֹג אֲבֵלוּת בְּפָנָיו; אֲבָל שֶׁלֹּא בְּפָנָיו – אֵינוֹ חַיָּב. וְכֵן בִּשְׁאָר הַקְּרוֹבִים.

ה אִשְׁתּוֹ הַנְּשׂוּאָה, אַף עַל פִּי שֶׁהוּא מִתְאַבֵּל עָלֶיהָ – אֵינוֹ מִתְאַבֵּל עִמָּהּ עַל שְׁאָר קְרוֹבִים; אֶלָּא עַל אָבִיהָ וְעַל אִמָּהּ, מִשּׁוּם כְּבוֹד אִשְׁתּוֹ, נוֹהֵג אֲבֵלוּת עֲלֵיהֶן בְּפָנֶיהָ.

כֵּיצַד? מִי שֶׁמֵּת חָמִיו אוֹ חֲמוֹתוֹ – כּוֹפֶה מִטָּתוֹ וְנוֹהֵג אֲבֵלוּת עִם אִשְׁתּוֹ בְּפָנֶיהָ, אֲבָל לֹא שֶׁלֹּא בְּפָנֶיהָ.

וְכֵן הָאִשָּׁה שֶׁמֵּת חָמִיהָ אוֹ חֲמוֹתָהּ – נוֹהֶגֶת אֲבֵלוּת בְּפָנָיו. אֲבָל שְׁאָר קְרוֹבִים, כְּגוֹן שֶׁמֵּת אֲחִי אִשְׁתּוֹ אוֹ בְּנָהּ, וְהָאִשָּׁה שֶׁמֵּת אֲחִי בַּעְלָהּ אוֹ בְּנוֹ – אֵין מִתְאַבְּלִין זֶה עַל זֶה.

וְכֵן יֵרָאֶה לִי, שֶׁאִם מֵתָה אֵשֶׁת קְרוֹבוֹ אוֹ בַּעַל קְרוֹבָתוֹ, כְּגוֹן שֶׁמֵּתָה אֵשֶׁת בְּנוֹ אוֹ בַּעַל בִּתּוֹ – אֵינוֹ חַיָּב לְהִתְאַבֵּל עֲלֵיהֶן. וְכֵן כֹּל כַּיּוֹצֵא בָּזֶה.

ו כַּמָּה חֲמוּרָה מִצְוַת אֲבֵלוּת, שֶׁהֲרֵי נִדְחָת לוֹ הַטֻּמְאָה מִפְּנֵי קְרוֹבָיו, כְּדֵי שֶׁיִּתְעַסֵּק עִמָּהֶן וְיִתְאַבֵּל עֲלֵיהֶן. שֶׁנֶּאֱמַר: כִּי אִם לִשְׁאֵרוֹ הַקָּרֹב אֵלָיו, לְאִמּוֹ וְגוֹמֵר, לָהּ יִטַּמָּא – מִצְוַת עֲשֵׂה; שֶׁאִם לֹא רָצָה לְהִטַּמָּא – מְטַמְּאִין אוֹתוֹ עַל כָּרְחוֹ.

Rabbinic); so, too, it can be said that one mourns for the relatives of one's son as a token of respect for him. Alternatively, the Radbaz explains that in this instance, our Sages gave their decrees the strength of Scriptural Law to be sure that they would be heeded.

The Rambam's ruling is quoted by Rav Yosef Karo in his *Shulchan Aruch* (*Yoreh De'ah* 374:6). The Ramah comments that in the present generation, this ruling is no longer observed. It was instituted only as a token of respect and it is customary for everyone to forgo such respect. Indeed, he writes that a person who fulfills this halachah by observing mourning rites is "one of the dolts." [Significantly, in his *Kessef Mishneh*, Rav Yosef Karo quotes similar concepts (although using less severe wording)]. The Ramah continues, however, stating that it is customary in many communities for close relatives to observe a certain dimension of mourning.

16. See Halachah 3.

17. See Chapter 5, Halachah 18.

18. From a previous marriage.

19. This expression connotes a ruling for which the Rambam has no explicit source in the previous Rabbinic literature.

20. Note the Radbaz who asks: What is unique about the mitzvah of mourning? Any positive commandment supersedes a negative commandment. See also Halachah 15.

21. This represents the Rambam's understanding of this verse and it is echoed by *Targum Onkelos*. As mentioned in the notes to Halachah 1, others translate the term differently.

22. It is not, however, considered a separate positive commandment from the commandment to mourn. Instead, they are two dimensions of the same commandment.

The *Kessef Mishneh* (in his gloss to Chapter 1, Halachah 1) explains the interrelation as

To whom does the above apply? To males who are commanded against contracting ritual impurity. [Different rules apply to] female members of the priestly family. Since they are not commanded against contracting ritual impurity,[23] they are also not commanded to become impure [when tending to their] relatives' burial. If they desire, they may become impure and if not, they do not become impure.[24]

7. A priest is forced to contract ritual impurity [to tend to] his [deceased] wife.[25] This obligation is Rabbinic in origin.[26] [Our Sages had her] considered as an unattended corpse.[27] Since she has no other heir aside from him,[28] there will be no one else to tend to her. He becomes impure only for a wife he has married. If he has [merely] consecrated her, he does not become impure for her.[29]

8. Similarly, a priest does not become impure for any of those individuals for whom we do not mourn as stated above:[30] e.g., those executed by the court, those who deviate from the ways of the community, stillborn infants, and those who commit suicide.[31]

Until when does the mitzvah to become impure apply? Until the grave is covered. Once the grave is covered, however, [the graves of one's close relatives] are like those of any other corpse. If a priest becomes impure for their sake, he should be punished by lashes.[32]

9. [A priest] should not become impure for the sake of a wife whom he is forbidden to marry.[33] Therefore if a woman heard a report that her husband died and [hence] remarried,[34] and then her [first] husband came, neither [husband] should become impure for her sake, for she is forbidden to remain married to either of them.[35]

follows: The Torah feared that since a priest is commanded to avoid contact with death, unless an explicit commandment was given to become impure, a priest would go to the other extreme and even refrain from mourning for his close relatives. Hence, to insure that he will mourn, he was commanded to become impure.

23. See Chapter 3, Halachah 11.

24. The Rambam's rationale can be explained as follows: Since an Israelite and female member of the priestly family are not obligated to maintain distance from impurity, we do not fear they will refrain from mourning. Hence, there is no obligation for them to become impure.

The Ra'avad and Rabbenu Asher differ with the Rambam, maintaining that the female members of the priestly family are also obligated to become ritually impure while tending to the corpses of their deceased relatives. The *Shulchan Aruch* (*Yoreh De'ah* 373:3) follows their opinion.

25. *Zevachim* 100a states that there was a priest called Yosef whose wife died. He did not want to become impure by tending to her - for that would disqualify him from partaking of the Paschal sacrifice - and his priestly brethren compelled him to become impure.

26. As mentioned in the notes to Halachah 1, there are many who understand this to be a Scriptural command.

בַּמֶּה דְּבָרִים אֲמוּרִים? בִּזְכָרִים, שֶׁהֻזְהֲרוּ עַל הַטֻּמְאָה; אֲבָל הַכֹּהֲנוֹת, הוֹאִיל וְאֵינָן מֻזְהָרוֹת עַל הַטֻּמְאָה, כֵּן אֵינָן מְצֻוּוֹת לְהִתְטַמֵּא לַקְּרוֹבִים; אֶלָּא אִם רָצוּ – מִתְטַמְּאוֹת, וְאִם לָאו – לֹא מִטַּמְּאוֹת.

ז אִשְׁתּוֹ שֶׁל כֹּהֵן – מִתְטַמֵּא לָהּ עַל כָּרְחוֹ. וְאֵינוֹ מִטַּמָּא לָהּ אֶלָּא מִדִּבְרֵי סוֹפְרִים. עֲשָׂאוּהָ כְּמֵת מִצְוָה; כֵּיוָן שֶׁאֵין לָהּ יוֹרֵשׁ אֶלָּא הוּא, לֹא תִּמְצָא מִי שֶׁיִּתְעַסֵּק בָּהּ. וְאֵינוֹ מִטַּמָּא אֶלָּא לִנְשׂוּאָה בִּלְבַד; אֲבָל הָאֲרוּסָה – אֵינוֹ מִטַּמָּא לָהּ.

ח וְכֵן כָּל אוֹתָן שֶׁאָמְרוּ שֶׁאֵין מִתְאַבְּלִין עֲלֵיהֶן, כְּגוֹן הֲרוּגֵי בֵּית דִּין וְשֶׁפָּרְשׁוּ מִדַּרְכֵי צִבּוּר וְהַנִּפְלִים וְהַמְאַבֵּד עַצְמוֹ לָדַעַת – אֵין הַכֹּהֵן מִטַּמָּא לָהֶן. וְעַד מָתַי מְצֻוֶּה לְהִתְטַמֵּא לִקְרוֹבָיו? עַד שֶׁיִּסָּתֵם הַגּוֹלֵל. אֲבָל מֵאַחַר שֶׁנִּסְתַּם הַגּוֹלֵל – הֲרֵי הֵן כִּשְׁאָר כָּל הַמֵּתִים, שֶׁאִם נִטְמָא בָּהֶן – לוֹקֶה.

ט אִשְׁתּוֹ הַפְּסוּלָה – אֵינוֹ מִטַּמָּא לָהּ. לְפִיכָךְ, מִי שֶׁשָּׁמְעָה שְׁמוּעָה שֶׁמֵּת בַּעְלָהּ וְנִשֵּׂאת, וּבָא בַּעְלָהּ – שְׁנֵיהֶן אֵין מִטַּמְּאִין לָהּ, שֶׁהֲרֵי הִיא פְּסוּלָה לִשְׁנֵיהֶן.

27. This term refers to the Hebrew *meit mitzvah*, literally "a corpse [that it is] a mitzvah [to bury]." See Chapter 3, Halachah 8. Just as a priest must become impure to bury an unattended corpse, he must become impure to bury his wife.

28. For one of the conditions of the marriage bond is that a husband becomes the sole heir of his wife's estate (*Hilchot Ishut* 12:3).

29. According to the Rambam, the rationale for this ruling can be explained as follows: Since he does not inherit his wife's estate until he marries her, he is not required to bury her. Instead, her heirs will perform that mitzvah.

30. Chapter 1, Halachot 6-11.

31. For some of these individuals, there are exegetical references which indicate that there is no license to become impure. In other instances, the concept is derived through deduction: Since the entire purpose of the license to become impure is to encourage the mitzvah of mourning, if there is no mitzvah to mourn, there is no license to become impure (*Kessef Mishneh*).

32. To summarize the point of this clause. A priest must attend the funeral of his close relatives; he may not visit their graves afterwards, however.

The Ramah (*Yoreh De'ah* 373:6) states that if there is a valid reason for a priest to disinter his relatives and rebury them, he may become impure while tending to their reburial until the second grave is covered.

33. E.g., a divorcee. Since he was obligated to divorce her, he is not required to mourn for her. Even if she bore him children, he may not become impure for her sake (*Siftei Cohen* 373:4).

34. Marrying a priest. Similarly, her first husband was also a priest. Otherwise, there would be no difficulty in either becoming impure for her sake.

35. See *Hilchot Gerushin* 10:7 which explains this situation in detail. The woman is not allowed to remain married to her first husband because she willingly engaged in relations with another man while married to him. She is not allowed to remain married to her

[A priest] may, however, become impure for the sake of his mother, even though she is a *challalah*[36] and he may become impure for the sake of his son, his daughter, his brother and his sister even though they are of tarnished lineage.[37] Even if they are illegitimate, he should become impure for their sake.

10. When [a priest's] sister is married[38] - even to another priest - he does not become impure for her sake, as [Leviticus 21:3] states: "his virgin sister who is close to him who has not been with a man." "Virgin" excludes a girl who has been raped or seduced. Should we also exclude a woman who attain majority[39] or a woman who lost her signs of virginity because of reasons other than relations? The Torah teaches: "who has not been with a man," i.e., [excluded is only one] who [lost her virginity] because of a man. "Who has not been with a man" - this also excludes [a sister] who has been consecrated.[40] He does not become impure for her sake even if she is consecrated to a priest.

11. If, however, [a priest's] sister is divorced after consecration, [before marriage,] he must become impure for her sake. The phrase "who is close to him" includes [a sister] divorced after consecration.

12. [A priest] does not become impure for the sake of his maternal brother and sister, as [implied by Leviticus 21:2-3]: "To his son and to his daughter, to his brother and to his sister." Just as we are speaking of a son who is fit to inherit his [father's] estate; so, too, he must be fit to inherit the estates of his brother and sister.[41]

13. [A priest] does not become impure [for the sake of relatives whose family connection is] doubtful, as [implied by Leviticus 21:3]: "to her[42] shall he become impure." He becomes impure for those whose connection is definite and not for those whose connection is doubtful. Accordingly, in an instance where children become intermingled,[43] if there is a son concerning whom there is a question whether he was born after seven months [from conception to his mother's] later [husband] or after nine months [to her] first [husband],[44] and all the like, he does not become impure for their sake[45] due to the doubt.[46]

second husband, because it was with him that she engaged in the relations that caused her to be forbidden to her first husband.

36. A *challalah* is a woman who engaged in relations that cause her to be forbidden to a priest or a woman born from such a union. We are speaking about an instance where the mother engaged in such relations after giving birth to this son (*Siftei Cohen* 373:6). Otherwise, the son is himself a *challal* and is permitted to become impure to all corpses (see Chapter 3, Halachah 11).

37. I.e., even if they are *challalim* who no longer have priestly privileges.

38. Even if she is later divorced (Radbaz; *Kessef Mishneh*).

39. And thus may have less physical signs of her virginity (see *Hilchot Issurei Bi'ah* 17:13).

אֲבָל מְטַמָּא הוּא לְאִמּוֹ אַף עַל פִּי שֶׁהִיא חֲלָלָה. וְכֵן מְטַמָּא לִבְנוֹ וּלְבִתּוֹ וּלְאָחִיו וְלַאֲחוֹתוֹ אַף עַל פִּי שֶׁהֵן פְּסוּלִין. אֲפִלּוּ הָיוּ מַמְזֵרִים – מְטַמָּא לָהֶן.

י אֲחוֹתוֹ הַנְּשׂוּאָה – אֵינוֹ מְטַמָּא לָהּ, אַף עַל פִּי שֶׁהִיא נְשׂוּאָה לְכֹהֵן. שֶׁנֶּאֱמַר: הַבְּתוּלָה הַקְּרוֹבָה אֵלָיו אֲשֶׁר לֹא הָיְתָה לְאִישׁ. הַבְּתוּלָה – פְּרָט לַאֲנוּסָה וּמְפֻתָּה. יָכוֹל שֶׁאֲנִי מוֹצִיא אֶת הַבּוֹגֶרֶת וּמֻכַּת עֵץ? תַּלְמוּד לוֹמַר: אֲשֶׁר לֹא הָיְתָה לְאִישׁ – מִי שֶׁהֲוָיָתָהּ בִּידֵי אִישׁ. אֲשֶׁר לֹא הָיְתָה לְאִישׁ – פְּרָט לַאֲרוּסָה, שֶׁאֵינוֹ מְטַמָּא לָהּ, אַף עַל פִּי שֶׁהִיא אֲרוּסָה לְכֹהֵן.

יא נִתְגָּרְשָׁה אֲחוֹתוֹ מִן הָאֵרוּסִין – מְטַמָּא לָהּ. שֶׁנֶּאֱמַר: הַקְּרוֹבָה אֵלָיו – לְהָבִיא אֶת הַמְגֹרֶשֶׁת מִן הָאֵרוּסִין.

יב אָחִיו וַאֲחוֹתוֹ מֵאִמּוֹ – אֵינוֹ מְטַמָּא לָהֶן. שֶׁנֶּאֱמַר: וְלִבְנוֹ וּלְבִתּוֹ וּלְאָחִיו וְלַאֲחֹתוֹ. מַה בְּנוֹ הָרָאוּי לִירֻשָּׁתוֹ, אַף אָחִיו וַאֲחוֹתוֹ הָרְאוּיִים לִירֻשָּׁתוֹ.

יג הַסְּפֵקוֹת – אֵינוֹ מְטַמָּא לָהֶן. שֶׁנֶּאֱמַר: לָהּ יִטַּמָּא – מְטַמָּא הוּא עַל הַוַּדַּאי, וְאֵינוֹ מְטַמָּא עַל הַסָּפֵק. לְפִיכָךְ, הַוְּלָדוֹת שֶׁנִּתְעָרְבוּ, וְהַבֵּן שֶׁהוּא סָפֵק בֶּן שִׁבְעָה לָאַחֲרוֹן אוֹ בֶּן תִּשְׁעָה לָרִאשׁוֹן, וְכֵן כֹּל כַּיּוֹצֵא בָּהֶן – אֵינוֹ מְטַמָּא לָהֶן מִסָּפֵק.

40. For the word *hoyita* (Deuteronomy 24:2) is also interpreted as a reference to consecration (*Kiddushin* 5a).
41. And one does not inherit the estates of one's maternal relatives, as stated in *Hilchot Nachalot* 1:6.
42. "To her" is seemingly an unnecessary phrase. Hence, our Sages understood it as communicating the following concept. Just as the priest is certain about the identity of "her," his sister; so, too, he must be certain about the identity of all relatives (Malbim to *Torat Kohanim*).

The Radbaz asks: Why would we think that the priest should become impure? Throughout the Torah, when there is a doubt concerning a Scriptural prohibition, we rule stringently. He explains that were it not for the verse, one might think that such a corpse is considered as unattended to. For because of the doubt involved, there will be no one with a clear-cut obligation to become impure.
43. I.e., two women, even two wives of priests, gave birth at the same time in the same place, and the babies became mixed up and neither was certain which baby was which. See *Hilchot Issurei Bi'ah* 20:4-5.
44. A woman was married and was widowed. Instead of waiting 90 days as required, she married immediately, became pregnant and gave birth within 9 months of her divorce from her first husband. We do not know if the child was conceived by her first husband (- in which instance, he is his son with regard to all matters -) or by the second husband.
45. Neither the son to the father, nor the father to the son (Rabbi Akiva Eiger).
46. The son does not become impure for the sake of his father, since he is not certain if he

Similarly, in all cases concerning divorce that involve a question concerning the validity of the divorce[47] or an invalid bill of divorce,[48], [the priest] does not become impure for the sake of [his wife].[49]

14. A priest may not become impure for the sake of a limb severed from his father while alive,[50] nor for the sake of one of his father's bones. Similarly, when one's father's bones are being collected - even if his entire backbone is intact - [a priest] may not become impure for their sake.[51]

15. If his father's head[52] is decapitated, he may not become impure for his sake. [This is implied by Leviticus 21:2:] "To his father," i.e., at a time when his [corpse] is intact and not when it is impaired.[53] Similar laws apply with regard to other relatives.

[The prohibition against contact with] ritual impurity is bypassed with regard to one's relatives; it is not released entirely.[54] For this reason, a priest is forbidden to become impure for the sake of another corpse at the time he has become impure for the sake of his relatives.[55] [This is implied by Leviticus 21:3]: "to her shall he become impure," i.e., [to her alone]. He does not become impure for the sake of others together with her. He should not say: "Since I became impure for the sake of my father, I will go gather so-and-so's bones" or "...touch so-and-so's grave."

Therefore when the relative of a priest dies, care must be taken to bury him at the edge of the cemetery, so that he will not have to enter the cemetery and become impure because of other graves when he buries his dead.[56]

is in fact his father. And if he were not to be his father, becoming impure for his sake would involve a transgression.

The commentaries raise a question: How is it possible for a priest to have such a question with regard to mourning for his wife's first husband? The only way it is possible for her to have married her second husband is for the first husband to have died. Among the answers given is that the woman never actually married him and they conceived a child in wedlock.

47. E.g., a man threw a bill of divorce to his wife and there was a doubt whether the bill of divorce was closer to her (in which instance, the divorce is binding) or closer to him (in which instance, it is not). See *Hilchot Gerushin* 5:13. In these instances, the question is one of Scriptural Law.

48. I.e., a bill of divorce that is invalidated by Rabbinic decree. See *ibid.* 10:2.

49. In the latter instance, according to Scriptural Law, the divorce is valid, and certainly, the priest is forbidden to become impure for her sake. Even in the first instance, since a question concerning a matter of Scriptural Law is involved, he is forbidden to become impure.

50. A limb severed from a living person conveys ritual impurity as stated in *Hilchot Tumat Meit* 3:1.

וְכֵן כָּל הַמִּתְגָּרֶשֶׁת סְפֵק גֵּרוּשִׁין אוֹ בְּגֵט פָּסוּל – אֵינוֹ מִטַּמֵּא לָהּ.

יד אֵין הַכֹּהֵן מִטַּמֵּא לְאֵיבָר מִן הַחַי מֵאָבִיו, וְלֹא לְעֶצֶם מֵעַצְמוֹת אָבִיו. וְכֵן הַמְלַקֵּט עַצְמוֹת אָבִיו – אֵינוֹ מִטַּמֵּא לָהֶן, אַף עַל פִּי שֶׁהַשִּׁדְרָה קַיֶּמֶת.

טו נִקְטַע רֹאשׁוֹ שֶׁל אָבִיו – אֵינוֹ מִטַּמֵּא לוֹ. שֶׁנֶּאֱמַר: לְאָבִיו – בִּזְמַן שֶׁהוּא שָׁלֵם, וְלֹא בִּזְמַן שֶׁהוּא חָסֵר. וְכֵן שְׁאָר הַקְּרוֹבִים.
הַטֻּמְאָה לַקְּרוֹבִים – דְּחוּיָה הִיא, וְלֹא הֻתְּרָה לַכֹּל. לְפִיכָךְ אָסוּר לְכֹהֵן לְהִתְטַמֵּא לְמֵת אֲפִלּוּ בְּעֵת שֶׁמִּתְטַמֵּא לִקְרוֹבָיו. שֶׁנֶּאֱמַר: לָהּ יִטַּמָּא – אֵינוֹ מִטַּמָּא לַאֲחֵרִים עִמָּהּ. שֶׁלֹּא יֹאמַר: הוֹאִיל וְנִטְמֵאתִי עַל אָבִי, אֲלַקֵּט עַצְמוֹת פְּלוֹנִי אוֹ אֶגַּע בְּקֶבֶר פְּלוֹנִי.
לְפִיכָךְ, כֹּהֵן שֶׁמֵּת לוֹ מֵת – צָרִיךְ לְהִזָּהֵר וּלְקָבְרוֹ בְּסוֹף בֵּית הַקְּבָרוֹת, כְּדֵי שֶׁלֹּא יִכָּנֵס לְבֵית הַקְּבָרוֹת וְלֹא יִתְטַמֵּא בִּקְבָרוֹת אֲחֵרִים כְּשֶׁיִּקָּבֵר מֵתוֹ.

51. The rationale for these laws is stated in the following halachah: A priest may only become impure for the sake of his relatives when their corpses are intact.

The Ra'avad - based on the ruling of Rabbenu Yitzchak Alfasi - differs with this conception. The *Shulchan Aruch* (*Yoreh De'ah* 373:9) quotes the Rambam's view.

52. Or any other limb of his body [Radbaz; *Shulchan Aruch* (*Yoreh De'ah* 373:9)].

53. Even when the head is lying next to the body, if the corpse is not whole, a priest may not become impure for its sake (*ibid.*).

54. I.e., as reflected in the Rambam's explanation, it is not as if this prohibition does not exist for the priest at this time. Instead, the intent is that the prohibition is ongoing. License is, however, granted to transgress it to bury one's dead. See a parallel ruling in *Hilchot Bi'at HaMikdash* 4:15.

55. The commentaries debate the Rambam's intent. His wording seems to imply even at the moment the priest is in contact with his relative's corpse, he may not touch another corpse. There are, however, other opinions - and the Rambam's words can also be interpreted in this manner - who maintain that at the moment he is touching his relative's corpse, he may also touch other corpses. The stringency stated by the Rambam refers to the period before the burial is completed when he may not be in contact with his relative's corpse.

56. According to the latter interpretation, the concern is when they return from the cemetery. According to the first interpretation, even on the way to the burial, there is reason for concern.

The *Shulchan Aruch* (*Yoreh De'ah* 373:7) quotes the Rambam's words without clarifying his intent. The *Tur* and the Ramah follow the second view and the *Bayit Chadash* and the *Siftei Cohen* 373:12 mention the first perspective. See also the notes to Chapter 3, Halachah 4.

CHAPTER THREE

1. With the exception of the six [relatives] mentioned in the Torah and his wife, whenever a priest becomes impure because of contact with a corpse,[1] if there are witnesses and a warning is administered, he is [punished by] lashes,[2] as [Leviticus 21:1] states: "No [one] shall contract ritual impurity for the sake of a [deceased] person among his people."

[This applies] whether one touches the corpse, stands over it, or carries it.[3] And it applies to a corpse and to all other forms of ritual impurity stemming from a corpse,[4] as [implied by] "No [one] shall contract ritual impurity for the sake of a [deceased] person among his people."[5] In *Hilchot Tumat Meit*,[6] we already described all the factors associated with a corpse that convey ritual impurity according to Scriptural Law and according to Rabbinic Law.

2. Similarly, a priest receives lashes if he touches a grave.[7] He may, however, touch clothes that touched a corpse, even though by doing so, he contracts ritual impurity [that continues] for seven days.[8]

3. Similarly, if [a priest] enters a covered structure into which ritual impurity enters,[9] he is lashed. [This applies] even though the source of impurity itself is in another building. We have already explained[10] all [the types of] "tents"[11] into which ritual impurity can enter and depart, the laws involving foliage and projections,[12] the entities which bring ritual impurity and those which interpose between ritual impurity, which involve Scriptural Law and which involve Rabbinic Law. All of this is discussed in *Hilchot Tumat Meit*.

There we explained[13] that non-Jews do not convey ritual impurity through overhangs.[14] Therefore their graves are pure and a priest may enter [their cemetery] and walk on their graves. He is forbidden only to touch impurity[15] or carry it, as we explained there.

4. [The following laws apply when] a priest enters a building where a corpse is located or a cemetery inadvertently and he is given a warning after he discovers [the fact]. If he jumps and leaves, he is not liable. If, however, he remains there for the time it takes to prostrate oneself which we explained with regard to impurity in the Temple,[16] he is lashed.

1. A priest is, however, allowed to become impure from other sources (*Hilchot Tumat Ochalin* 16:9).
2. As is appropriate for the violation of a negative commandment. *Sefer HaMitzvot* (negative commandment 166) and *Sefer HaChinuch* (mitzvah 263) count this as one of the 613 mitzvot of the Torah.
3. Covering a corpse with a portion of one's body creates a "tent," as it were, and this conveys ritual impurity (*Hilchot Tumat Meit* 1:10). Similarly, carrying a corpse, even if one does not touch it, coveys ritual impurity (*ibid.*:6).
4. E.g., blood that flowed from a corpse, bones from a corpse, a corpse that has decomposed or the like.
5. See the exegesis of this verse in the *Sifri*.

פֶּרֶק שְׁלִישִׁי

א כָּל כֹּהֵן שֶׁנִּטְמָא לְמֵת, חוּץ מִשִּׁשָּׁה מֵתִים הַמְפֹרָשִׁים בַּתּוֹרָה אוֹ אִשְׁתּוֹ, בְּעֵדִים וְהַתְרָאָה – הֲרֵי זֶה לוֹקֶה. שֶׁנֶּאֱמַר: לְנֶפֶשׁ לֹא יִטַּמָּא בְּעַמָּיו.
וְאֶחָד הַנּוֹגֵעַ בְּמֵת אוֹ הַמַּאֲהִיל אוֹ הַנּוֹשֵׂא. וְאֶחָד הַמֵּת וְאֶחָד שְׁאָר הַטֻּמְאוֹת הַפּוֹרְשׁוֹת מִן הַמֵּת. שֶׁנֶּאֱמַר: לְנֶפֶשׁ לֹא יִטַּמָּא בְּעַמָּיו. וּכְבָר פֵּרַשְׁנוּ בְּהִלְכוֹת טֻמְאַת מֵת כָּל דְּבָרִים הַמְטַמְּאִין מִן הַמֵּת מִן הַתּוֹרָה אוֹ מִדִּבְרֵיהֶם.

ב וְכֵן אִם נָגַע הַכֹּהֵן בְּקֶבֶר – לוֹקֶה. אֲבָל נוֹגֵעַ הוּא בִּבְגָדִים שֶׁנָּגְעוּ בְּמֵת, אַף עַל פִּי שֶׁמִּטַּמָּא בָּהֶן טֻמְאַת שִׁבְעָה.

ג וְכֵן אִם נִכְנַס לְאֹהֶל טָמֵא שֶׁנִּכְנְסָה לוֹ הַטֻּמְאָה – לוֹקֶה, אַף עַל פִּי שֶׁעַצְמָהּ שֶׁל טֻמְאָה בְּבַיִת אַחֵר. וּכְבָר בֵּאַרְנוּ כָּל הָאֹהָלִים שֶׁתִּכָּנֵס לָהֶן הַטֻּמְאָה אוֹ שֶׁתֵּצֵא מֵהֶן, וְדִין הַסְּכָכוֹת וְהַפְּרָעוֹת, וְכָל הַדְּבָרִים הַמְּבִיאִין אֶת הַטֻּמְאָה וְהַחוֹצְצִין בִּפְנֵי הַטֻּמְאָה, וְאֵי זֶה מֵהֶן דִּין תּוֹרָה וְאֵי זֶה מֵהֶן מִדִּבְרֵיהֶן – הַכֹּל בְּהִלְכוֹת טֻמְאַת מֵת.
וְשָׁם בֵּאַרְנוּ, שֶׁאֵין עוֹבְדֵי כוֹכָבִים מְטַמְּאִין בְּאֹהֶל, וּלְפִיכָךְ קִבְרוֹתֵיהֶם טְהוֹרִים, וּמֻתָּר לְכֹהֵן לִכָּנֵס לְשָׁם וְלִדְרֹךְ עַל קִבְרוֹתֵיהֶם. וְאֵינוֹ אָסוּר אֶלָּא שֶׁיִּגַּע בְּטֻמְאָה אוֹ שֶׁיִּשָּׂאֶנָּה, כְּמוֹ שֶׁבֵּאַרְנוּ שָׁם.

ד כֹּהֵן שֶׁנִּכְנַס לְאֹהֶל הַמֵּת אוֹ לְבֵית הַקְּבָרוֹת בִּשְׁגָגָה, וְאַחַר שֶׁיָּדַע הִתְרוּ בוֹ: אִם קָפַץ וְיָצָא – פָּטוּר; וְאִם יָשַׁב שָׁם כְּדֵי הִשְׁתַּחֲוָיָה, כְּמוֹ שֶׁבֵּאַרְנוּ בְּעִנְיַן טֻמְאַת מִקְדָּשׁ – הֲרֵי זֶה לוֹקֶה.

6. See Chapter 2 of those halachot.
7. See *Hilchot Tumat Meit* 2:15, based on Numbers 19:16, 18.
8. The clothes become an *av tumah*, a source for ritual impurity. Nevertheless, they are not considered as equivalent to the corpse itself. See *Hilchot Tumat Meit* 5:3, 13; *Hilchot Nazirut* 7:8.
9. This refers to a building next to the building where a corpse is located. There is a window or roof connecting the two through which the ritual impurity enters the structure. The *Siftei Cohen* 372:2 argues with the Rambam's ruling, maintaining that such ritual impurity is merely Rabbinic in origin. Hence lashes are not given. The *Magen Avraham* 343:2 justifies the Rambam's ruling.
10. *Hilchot Tumat Meit,* chs. 14-19.
11. As explained in those chapters, the term *ohel*, "tent," is used to describe any roof, shelter, overhang, or any substance that covers both a person and a corpse or portion of a corpse.
12. See *Hilchot Tumat Meit* 13:2.
13. *Hilchot Tumat Meit* 1:12.
14. One does, however, become impure through touching or carrying a non-Jewish corpse.
15. I.e., a corpse.
16. See *Hilchot Bi'at HaMikdash* 3:23 which speaks of the prohibition against remaining

[The following rule applies] if he entered and departed, entered and departed. If he was given a warning for each time, he is given lashes for every entrance.[17] Similarly, if he touches a corpse, is giving a warning, and then disengages himself, and afterwards, touches it and is given a warning - even [if this sequence is repeated] one hundred times, he is given lashes for each [touch].

If he was touching a corpse and did not disengage himself or was standing in the cemetery and touched other corpses, although he is given a warning several times, he receives lashes only once. For as long as he does not cease, he is continuing to desecrate [his priestly state].[18]

5. [The following rules apply when one] causes a priest to contract ritual impurity. If they both acted intentionally, the priest receives lashes and the person who caused him to contract impurity violates the prohibition against placing a stumbling block in front of the blind.[19] If the priest was not aware of the transgression and the person who caused him to contract impurity acted intentionally, that person[20] receives lashes.

6. A High Priest may not become impure for the sake of his relatives,[21] as [Leviticus 21:11] states: "He shall not become impure for his father's or mother's sake."[22] Similarly, he does not enter a shelter where there is a corpse, even the corpse of one of his relatives, as [*ibid.*:30] states: "He shall not enter [a place where] there is any corpse." [23] Thus we learn that he is liable both for not entering and for not becoming impure.

What is implied? If the High Priest touches or carries a corpse, he receives lashes for one transgression. If he[24] enters a shelter and remains there until a person dies or he enters a chest, bureau, or drawer, and a colleague comes and opens the top of this container and thus [his contact with] impurity and his entrance [into the shelter] come at the same time,[25] he receives two sets of lashes, for the prohibition against entering and for the prohibition against becoming impure.

within the Temple courtyard while impure. There it states that if a person waits in the courtyard for the period which it takes "to kneel, to prostrate oneself face down on the ground and to give thanks to God who is good, whose kindness is everlasting," he is liable.

The commentaries question: Why should he be lashed? One is not liable for lashes unless one commits a deed in violation of a transgression (*Hilchot Sanhedrin* 18:2). Here, seemingly, one's violation is passive.

Among the explanations offered to resolve this difficulty is that since he had the potential to remove himself from ritual impurity and did not do so, he is considered as if he performed a deed to contract ritual impurity (Ritbah, gloss to *Makkot* 21a). Others cite the gloss of the *Maggid Mishneh* to *Hilchot Sechirut* 13:2 which explains that whenever a transgression usually involves a deed - as a priest usually performs a deed to contract ritual impurity - one is liable for lashes even when one violates the transgression without performing a deed.

17. For each involves a separate transgression.

18. I.e., his actions are considered as a single, extended transgression. The Radbaz refers

נִכְנַס וְיָצָא, וְחָזַר וְנִכְנַס וְיָצָא, אִם הִתְרוּ בּוֹ עַל כָּל פַּעַם וָפַעַם – לוֹקֶה עַל כָּל כְּנִיסָה וּכְנִיסָה. וְכֵן אִם נָגַע בְּמֵת וְהִתְרוּ בּוֹ, וּפָרַשׁ וְחָזַר וְנָגַע וְהִתְרוּ בּוֹ, אֲפִלּוּ מֵאָה פְּעָמִים – לוֹקֶה עַל כָּל אַחַת וְאַחַת.

הָיָה נוֹגֵעַ וְלֹא פָּרַשׁ, אוֹ שֶׁהָיָה עוֹמֵד בְּבֵית הַקְּבָרוֹת וְנָגַע בְּמֵתִים אֲחֵרִים, אַף עַל פִּי שֶׁהִתְרוּ בּוֹ כַּמָּה פְּעָמִים – אֵינוֹ לוֹקֶה אֶלָּא אַחַת; שֶׁהֲרֵי מְחֻלָּל וְעוֹמֵד כָּל זְמַן שֶׁלֹּא פֵּרַשׁ.

ה הַמְטַמֵּא אֶת הַכֹּהֵן:
אִם הָיוּ שְׁנֵיהֶם מְזִידִין – הֲרֵי הַכֹּהֵן לוֹקֶה, וְזֶה שֶׁטִּמְּאוֹ עוֹבֵר עַל וְלִפְנֵי עִוֵּר לֹא תִתֵּן מִכְשֹׁל; הָיָה הַכֹּהֵן שׁוֹגֵג, וְזֶה שֶׁטִּמְּאוֹ מֵזִיד – הֲרֵי זֶה שֶׁטִּמְּאוֹ לוֹקֶה.

ו כֹּהֵן גָּדוֹל אֵינוֹ מִטַּמֵּא לַקְּרוֹבִים; שֶׁנֶּאֱמַר: לְאָבִיו וּלְאִמּוֹ לֹא יִטַּמָּא.
וְכֵן אֵינוֹ נִכְנָס עִם הַמֵּת בְּאֹהֶל, אֲפִלּוּ קְרוֹבָיו; שֶׁנֶּאֱמַר: וְעַל כָּל נַפְשֹׁת מֵת לֹא יָבֹא.
הָא לָמַדְתָּ, שֶׁהוּא חַיָּב בְּלֹא יָבֹא וְחַיָּב בְּלֹא יִטַּמָּא.
כֵּיצַד? נָגַע אוֹ נָשָׂא – לוֹקֶה אַחַת.
נִכְנַס לְאֹהֶל וְיָשַׁב שָׁם עַד שֶׁמֵּת עָלָיו הַמֵּת; אוֹ שֶׁנִּכְנַס לְשִׁדָּה תֵּבָה וּמִגְדָּל, וּבָא חֲבֵרוֹ וּפָרַע עָלָיו גַּג הַשִּׁדָּה, שֶׁהֲרֵי טֻמְאָה וּבִיאָה בָּאִין כְּאֶחָד – הֲרֵי זֶה לוֹקֶה שְׁתַּיִם: מִשּׁוּם לֹא יָבֹא וּמִשּׁוּם לֹא יִטַּמָּא.

to the difference of opinion mentioned in the notes to Chapter 2, Halachah 15, stating that according to the Rambam, it would appear that although the priest does not receive lashes, he is considered to be violating a prohibition. According to the other view mentioned there, there is no prohibition at all to come into contact with other corpses.

19. See *Hilchot Rotzeach* 12:14 which interprets this as a general prohibition, warning a person against causing a colleague to transgress.

20. Although he is not himself a priest.

21. Because of the greater sanctity associated with his position, he is given greater restrictions. He is, however, obligated to observe all the mourning rites for his relatives (Chapter 7, Halachah 6).

22. *Sefer HaMitzvot* (negative commandment 167) and *Sefer HaChinuch* (mitzvah 271) count this as one of the 613 mitzvot of the Torah.

23. *Sefer HaMitzvot* (negative commandment 168) and *Sefer HaChinuch* (mitzvah 270) count this as one of the 613 mitzvot of the Torah.

24. A High Priest; an ordinary priest, however, would be liable for only one transgression (Radbaz).

25. As long as the High Priest is in this container, he is not liable, because the container separates him from the corpse and it is as if he is not in the same place. When, however, the top of the container is removed, he is considered to have entered the place where the corpse is located and he becomes impure.

There are some who cite *Nazir* 43a which states that this is speaking about a situation where the High Priest helped the other person remove the top. Otherwise, the High Priest

7. When [the High Priest][26] became impure beforehand, and then entered a shelter [where a corpse was located], if he is warned, he should receive lashes even for this entry.[27]

8. When a priest - even a High Priest - encounters an unattended corpse[28] on the road, he is obligated to become impure for its sake and bury it. What is meant by an unattended corpse? A Jewish corpse cast away on the road without anyone[29] to bury it. This is a halachah conveyed by the received tradition.

When does the above apply? When the priest is alone and there is no one else with him; even when he calls out on the road, no one answers him. If, however, when he calls others answer, this is not considered an unattended corpse. Instead, he should call to the others and they should come and tend to [the corpse].[30]

9. If a priest and a nazirite are proceeding on a road and they encounter an unattended corpse, the nazirite should tend to it. [The rationale is that] his holiness is not of an eternal nature.[31] The priest - even an ordinary priest - should not become impure.

If a High Priest was going together with an ordinary priest, the ordinary priest should become impure. [The general principle is:] Whoever is on a higher level of holiness[32] should become impure last. When a *s'gan*[33] and the priest anointed to lead the army at war[34] encounter an unattended corpse, the priest anointed to lead the army at war should become impure, not the *s'gan*.[35]

10. When a *nasi*[36] dies, everyone - even priests - should become impure for his sake.[37] [Our Sages] had him considered as an unattended corpse, because

will not have committed a deed in his violation of these prohibitions. According to the explanations offered in note 16, however, that explanation is not necessary.

See also *Hilchot Nazirut* 5:18 which cites a similar law applying to a Nazirite and states that he must open the top "with [the Nazirite's] consent." For otherwise, the Nazirite - and the High Priest - will become impure because of factors beyond their control.

26. The Radbaz asks why the Rambam speaks about a High Priest; the same laws would also apply with regard to an ordinary priest. He explains that the Rambam is speaking about the prohibition against entering a place of impurity and that applies only with regard to a High Priest. If he would have spoke about the prohibition against incurring ritual impurity, then this ruling would also be applied to an ordinary priest.

27. As explained in the notes to Halachah 4, as long as he has ceased contact with a corpse - even though he is still ritually impure - he is liable for entering a shelter where a corpse is located (Radbaz).

28. We have translated the term according to its practical meaning. Literally, the terms the Rambam uses mean: "A corpse which it is a mitzvah [to bury]." For every Jewish corpse should be buried as soon as possible. Thus if there are no others to tend to it, even a priest or a Nazirite who would ordinarily be forbidden to touch the corpse are under obligation to bury it. *Torat Kohanim* derives the obligation for a priest to become impure for the sake of such a corpse from the exegesis of Scriptural phrases.

ז נִטְמָא מִקֹּדֶם וְאַחַר כָּךְ נִכְנַס לְאֹהֶל, אִם הִתְרוּ בּוֹ – לוֹקֶה אַף עַל הַבִּיאָה.

ח כֹּהֵן שֶׁפָּגַע בְּמֵת מִצְוָה בַּדֶּרֶךְ – הֲרֵי זֶה מִטַּמֵּא לוֹ.
אֲפִלּוּ כֹּהֵן גָּדוֹל חַיָּב לְהִטַּמֵּא לוֹ וּלְקָבְרוֹ.
וְאֵי זֶהוּ מֵת מִצְוָה? אֶחָד מִיִּשְׂרָאֵל שֶׁהָיָה מֻשְׁלָךְ בַּדֶּרֶךְ וְאֵין לוֹ קוֹבְרִין.
דָּבָר זֶה הֲלָכָה מִפִּי הַקַּבָּלָה.
בַּמֶּה דְּבָרִים אֲמוּרִים? כְּשֶׁהָיָה הַכֹּהֵן לְבַדּוֹ וְאֵין עִמּוֹ אַחֵר, וַאֲפִלּוּ קָרָא שָׁם בַּדֶּרֶךְ וְאֵין לוֹ עוֹנֶה;
אֲבָל אִם כְּשֶׁיִּקְרָא אֲחֵרִים עוֹנִים אוֹתוֹ – אֵין זֶה מֵת מִצְוָה, אֶלָּא יִקְרָא לַאֲחֵרִים וְיָבוֹאוּ וְיִתְעַסְּקוּ בּוֹ.

ט הָיוּ כֹּהֵן וְנָזִיר מְהַלְּכִין בַּדֶּרֶךְ וּפָגְעוּ בְּמֵת מִצְוָה – יִתְעַסֵּק בּוֹ הַנָּזִיר, לְפִי שֶׁאֵין קְדֻשָּׁתוֹ קְדֻשַּׁת עוֹלָם, וְאַל יִטַּמָּא בּוֹ הַכֹּהֵן, אַף עַל פִּי שֶׁהוּא כֹּהֵן הֶדְיוֹט.
הָיָה כֹּהֵן גָּדוֹל וְכֹהֵן הֶדְיוֹט – יִטַּמָּא הַהֶדְיוֹט.
וְכָל הַקּוֹדֵם אֶת חֲבֵרוֹ בְּמַעֲלָה – מִתְאַחֵר בְּטֻמְאָה.
וּסְגָן עִם מְשׁוּחַ מִלְחָמָה שֶׁפָּגְעוּ בְּמֵת מִצְוָה – יִטַּמָּא מְשׁוּחַ מִלְחָמָה, וְאַל יִטַּמָּא הַסְּגָן.

י נָשִׂיא שֶׁמֵּת – הַכֹּל מִטַּמְּאִין לוֹ, אֲפִלּוּ כֹּהֲנִים.

29. The *Turei Zahav* 374:1 emphasizes that there must be enough people besides the priest to give the person a proper burial.
30. Today with the proliferation of cell phones and satellite phones, this halachah is becoming less relevant. For in most instances, it is possible to call to others to tend to the corpse. Also, there are legal restrictions in most countries against burying a corpse oneself and a person is not obligated to place himself in danger by burying an unattended corpse. Needless to say, however, if a priest is not certain that a person is dead, he should approach him and try to offer first aid.
31. I.e., it continues only for the extent of his vow. Moreover, even if the nazirite took a vow to continue this practice indefinitely, his obligation to avoid a corpse is not an inherent dimension of his being, but an incremental factor. A priest's holiness, by contrast, is inherent to his existence (Radbaz).
32. See *Hilchot K'lei HaMikdash* 4:19 which lists various different levels of holiness among the priests.
33. The assistant to the High Priest (*ibid.*:16).
34. See *Hilchot Melachim* 7:1.
35. Although in *Hilchot K'lei HaMikdash, loc. cit.*, the Rambam rules that the priest anointed to lead the army is on a higher level, in this halachah, he relies on *Nazir* 47a which grants the *s'gan* precedence. The rationale is that if the High Priest becomes disqualified on Yom Kippur, the *s'gan* assumes his position.
36. The head of the Supreme *Sanhedrin*. See *Hilchot Sanhedrin* 1:3.
37. The Jerusalem Talmud (*Nazir* 7:1) relates that when Rabbi Yehudah HaNasi died, Rabbi Yannai announced: "There is no priesthood today."

everyone is obligated in his honor.[38] Similarly, all must observe the rites of *aninut*[39] for his sake.

11. The daughters of Aaron[40] were not warned [to avoid] the ritual impurity imparted by a corpse. [This derived from Leviticus 21:1]: "Say to the priests, the sons of Aaron...." [Implied is] "the sons of Aaron," and not "the daughters of Aaron."

Similarly, *challalim*[41] are permitted to become impure. [This is also derived from the words, "the priests,] the sons of Aaron," i.e., [to be included in the prohibition,] their priesthood must be intact.[42]

12. When a priest is a minor, the adults are warned that they should not have him contact ritual impurity.[43] If he comes to contract impurity on his own initiative, the court is not obligated to separate him [from the source of impurity].[44] His father, however, must educate him in the holiness [of the priesthood].

13. The four cubits circumscribed around a corpse are deemed impure.[45] Any priest that enters into [these] four cubits is given stripes for rebellious conduct.[46]

Similarly, if [priests] enter a *beit hapras*,[47] go to the diaspora,[48] become impure through contact with a mixture of blood,[49] a gravestone, or the stones which support the gravestone, and the like, they are given stripes for rebellious conduct, because these entities are sources [for ritual impurity] by Rabbinic decree, as we explained in *Hilchot Tumat Meit*.[50] If, however, [a priest] enters a cemetery, he receives lashes according to Scriptural Law.[51]

38. For it is not befitting for a *nasi* to be mourned merely by his family and friends. Instead, the entire Jewish people should show him respect. Everyone is considered as if he was his relative. See also Chapter 9, Halachot 2, 6, 12, and 14, which mention other mourning rites undertaken as a token of respect for a *nasi*.

There are authorities who maintain that this law is not only relevant in the Talmudic era. *Tosafot, Ketubot* 103b quotes Rabbi Chayim Cohen as stating: "Were I present when Rabbenu Tam died, I would have become impure for his sake." The Radbaz, however, questions that license. Significantly, the *Shulchan Aruch* (*Yoreh De'ah* 374:11) which mentions only the laws which are relevant in the present age, mentions the obligation to become impure for the sake of a *nasi*.

39. I.e., they should not eat meat or drink wine until his burial as stated in Chapter 4, Halachah 6.

40. I.e., women born to the priestly family.

41. Offspring born to a priest by a woman whom he is forbidden to marry (*Hilchot Issurei Bi'ah*, Ch. 19). The Radbaz and the *Siftei Cohen* 373:2 emphasize that this leniency applies only to individuals who are considered *challalim* by Scriptural Law. One who is, however, considered as a *challal* according to Rabbinic Law, e.g., a person born to a priest and a woman who performed the rite of *chalitzah*, must keep these stringencies. For according to Scriptural Law, he is a priest.

42. Thus excluding *challalim* who are considered as non-priests with regard to all matters

עֲשָׂאוּהוּ כְּמֵת מִצְוָה לַכֹּל, מִפְּנֵי שֶׁהַכֹּל חַיָּבִין בִּכְבוֹדוֹ. וְכֵן הַכֹּל אוֹנְנִין עָלָיו.

יא בְּנוֹת אַהֲרֹן לֹא הֻזְהֲרוּ עַל טֻמְאַת מֵת. שֶׁנֶּאֱמַר: אֱמֹר אֶל הַכֹּהֲנִים בְּנֵי אַהֲרֹן - וְלֹא בְּנוֹת אַהֲרֹן. וְכֵן הַחֲלָלִים מֻתָּרִין לְהִטַּמָּא. שֶׁנֶּאֱמַר: בְּנֵי אַהֲרֹן - עַד שֶׁיִּהְיוּ בִּכְהוּנָם.

יב כֹּהֵן קָטָן - הֲרֵי הַגְּדוֹלִים מֻזְהָרִים שֶׁלֹּא יְטַמְּאוּהוּ. וְאִם בָּא לְהִטַּמָּא מֵעַצְמוֹ - אֵין בֵּית דִּין מְצֻוִּין עָלָיו לְהַפְרִישׁוֹ. אֲבָל אָבִיו צָרִיךְ לְחַנְּכוֹ בִּקְדֻשָּׁה.

יג מֵת תּוֹפֵשׂ אַרְבַּע אַמּוֹת שֶׁלּוֹ לְטֻמְאָה. וְכָל כֹּהֵן שֶׁנִּכְנַס לְתוֹךְ אַרְבַּע אַמּוֹת - מַכִּין אוֹתוֹ מַכַּת מַרְדּוּת.

וְכֵן אִם נִכְנַס לְבֵית הַפְּרָס, אוֹ יָצָא חוּצָה לָאָרֶץ, אוֹ שֶׁנִּטְמָא בְּדַם תְּבוּסָה, אוֹ בְּגוֹלֵל וּבְדוֹפֵק וְכַיּוֹצֵא בָּהֶן - מַכִּין אוֹתוֹ מַכַּת מַרְדּוּת, מִפְּנֵי שֶׁהֵן אָבוֹת שֶׁל דִּבְרֵיהֶם, כְּמוֹ שֶׁבֵּאַרְנוּ בְּהִלְכוֹת טֻמְאַת מֵת. אֲבָל אִם נִכְנַס לְבֵית הַקְּבָרוֹת - לוֹקֶה מִן הַתּוֹרָה.

(see *Hilchot Issurei Bi'ah* 19:10; *Hilchot Terumah* 6:7; *Hilchot Ma'aseh HaKorbanot* 11:8).

43. *Yevamot* 114a derives this concept from the use of the similar terms *emor* and *vi'amarta* by Leviticus 21:1.

44. I.e., the Jewish community as a whole does not have the obligation to train every child in observance. Instead, the obligation is a personal one, incumbent on the child's father. See *Hilchot Ma'achalot Assurot* 17:27-28 where this issue is also discussed.

45. *Sotah* 44a explains that this is a Rabbinic decree, enacted to compel priests to keep their distance from corpses lest one accidentally, pass his hand over the corpse or the like. If, however, a barrier is erected around the corpse, this stringency need not be observed [Radbaz; *Shulchan Aruch* (*Yoreh De'ah* 371:5)]. In such a situation, he should nevertheless keep a distance of four handbreadths.

46. The punishment given for the violation of a Rabbinic decree.

47. A field in which a grave had been located, but which had been plowed over. The Sages forbade a priest from entering such a field for 100 cubits, lest he accidentally step on a small piece of bone from the corpse.

48. This applies in the era when the laws of ritual impurity were strictly observed in *Eretz Yisrael*. See *Siftei Cohen* 369:2.

49. A mixture of blood, some which was lost before the person passed away and some which drained from his corpse after his passing.

50. Chapter 2, Halachot 13-16.

51. For by stepping on a grave, he becomes impure, because he creates an *ohel*, "shelter," over the grave. The Radbaz emphasizes that this law applies only when there is no way to enter the cemetery except by walking on the graves. Different rules apply, however, if there is a path through the cemetery. In such an instance, if a priest walks within four cubits of a grave, he receives stripes for rebellious conduct and if he remains more than that distance away, he is not liable at all.

14. It is permissible for a priest to become impure through walking through a *beit hapras* or the diaspora for the sake of a mitzvah, when there is no way other than that, e.g., he went to marry or to study Torah. Even though there is someone who could teach him in *Eretz Yisrael*, [he is permitted to leave, because] a person does not merit to learn from every colleague.

Similarly, a person may incur ritual impurity that is Rabbinic in origin to show respect to other people. What is implied? If a mourner walked through a *beit hapras*, everyone[52] follows after him to comfort him. Similarly, we may walk over the coffins of the dead[53] to greet Jewish kings. [This is allowed] even to greet gentile kings, so that a distinction will be able to be made between them and Jewish kings when their glory will return to its place.[54] Similarly, [leniency is granted in] all analogous situations. Also, [a priest] may incur ritual impurity of Rabbinic origin to enter in judgment and disputation with gentiles [concerning property], for he is saving it from their hands. Similar laws apply in all analogous situations.

CHAPTER FOUR

1. These are the customs observed by the Jewish people with regard to corpses and burial. We close the eyes of the deceased.[1] If one's mouth hangs open, we tie the jaw closed. After washing [the corpse],[2] we stuff closed the orifices,[3] anoint it with different fragrances,[4] cut its hair, and dress it in shrouds of white linen[5] which are not expensive. Our Sages followed the custom of using a cloak worth a *zuz*,[6] so as not to embarrass a person who lacks resources. We cover the faces of the deceased so as not to embarrass the poor whose faces turned black because of hunger.

2. It is forbidden to bury [the dead,] even a *nasi* among the Jewish people, in silk shrouds or clothes embroidered with gold, for this is an expression of haughtiness, the destruction [of useful property],[7] and [the emulation of] gentile practices.[8]

52. I.e., even priests.
53. Since there is a handbreadth of space between the top of the coffin and the corpse, the impurity is contained and does not extend beyond the coffin according to Scriptural Law. Our Rabbis, however, ruled that according to Rabbinic Law, one contracts impurity from a coffin (*Berachot* 19b).
54. I.e., with the coming of Mashiach.

1. There is an allusion to this custom in Genesis 46:4 which relates God's promise to Jacob that Joseph would place his hands over his eyes.
2. This refers to the *taharah* procedure. The purpose is to endow the corpse with purity (*Perishah, Yoreh De'ah* 352).
3. So that air will not enter the body and cause it to decompose quickly (*Hilchot Shabbat* 26:20).

יד מֻתָּר לְכֹהֵן לְהִטַּמֵּא בְּבֵית הַפְּרָס אוֹ בְּחוּצָה לָאָרֶץ לִדְבַר מִצְוָה, בִּזְמַן שֶׁאֵין שָׁם דֶּרֶךְ אֶלָּא הִיא. כְּגוֹן שֶׁהָלַךְ לִשָּׂא אִשָּׁה אוֹ לִלְמֹד תּוֹרָה. אַף עַל פִּי שֶׁיֵּשׁ שָׁם מִי שֶׁיְּלַמְּדֶנּוּ בְּאֶרֶץ יִשְׂרָאֵל – לֹא מִן הַכֹּל אָדָם זוֹכֶה לִלְמֹד. וְכֵן מִטַּמֵּא בְּטֻמְאָה מִדִּבְרֵיהֶם לִכְבוֹד הַבְּרִיּוֹת. כֵּיצַד? אָבֵל שֶׁהָלַךְ בְּבֵית הַפְּרָס – הַכֹּל הוֹלְכִין אַחֲרָיו שָׁם לְנַחֲמוֹ. וְכֵן מְדַלְּגִין עַל גַּבֵּי אֲרוֹנוֹת שֶׁל מֵתִים לִקְרַאת מַלְכֵי יִשְׂרָאֵל. וַאֲפִלּוּ מַלְכֵי עוֹבְדֵי כּוֹכָבִים, כְּדֵי לְהַבְחִין בֵּינָם לְבֵין מַלְכֵי יִשְׂרָאֵל כְּשֶׁיַּחֲזֹר כְּבוֹדָן לִמְקוֹמָן. וְכֵן כֹּל כַּיּוֹצֵא בָּזֶה. וְכֵן מִטַּמֵּא בְּטֻמְאָה שֶׁל דִּבְרֵיהֶם לָדוּן עִם הָעוֹבְדֵי כּוֹכָבִים וּלְעַרְעֵר עִמָּהֶן, מִפְּנֵי שֶׁהוּא מַצִּיל מִיָּדָם. וְכֵן כֹּל כַּיּוֹצֵא בָּזֶה.

פֶּרֶק רְבִיעִי

א מִנְהַג יִשְׂרָאֵל בְּמֵתִים וּבִקְבוּרָה כָּךְ הוּא: מְאַמְּצִין עֵינָיו שֶׁל מֵת. וְאִם נִפְתַּח פִּיו – קוֹשְׁרִין אֶת לְחָיָיו. וּפוֹקְקִין אֶת נְקָבָיו אַחַר שֶׁמְּדִיחִין אוֹתוֹ. וְסָכִין אוֹתוֹ בְּמִינֵי בְּשָׂמִים. וְגוֹזְזִין שְׂעָרוֹ. וּמַלְבִּישִׁין אוֹתוֹ תַּכְרִיכִין תְּפוּרִין בְּחוּט שֶׁל פִּשְׁתָּן לְבָנִים. וְלֹא יִהְיוּ דְּמֵיהֶן יְקָרִים. וְנָהֲגוּ חֲכָמִים בְּסוּדָר שָׁוֶה זוּז, שֶׁלֹּא לְבַיֵּשׁ אֶת מִי שֶׁאֵין לוֹ. וּמְכַסִּין פְּנֵי הַמֵּת, שֶׁלֹּא לְבַיֵּשׁ אֶת הָעֲנִיִּים שֶׁפְּנֵיהֶם מֻשְׁחָרִין בְּרָעָב.

ב וְאָסוּר לִקְבֹּר בְּתַכְרִיכִין שֶׁל מֵשִׁי וּבִבְגָדִים הַמֻּזְהָבִין הָרְקוּמִין, אֲפִלּוּ לִנְשִׂיא שֶׁבְּיִשְׂרָאֵל; שֶׁזֶּהוּ גַּסּוּת הָרוּחַ, וְהַשְׁחָתָה, וּמַעֲשֵׂה עוֹבְדֵי כּוֹכָבִים.

4. So that the pallbearers will not be repelled by the odor of the corpse at the time of burial. The Ramah (*Yoreh De'ah* 352:4) mentions other customs.
5. Our translation follows the version of authentic manuscripts of the *Mishneh Torah*. The standard printed text reads slightly differently.
6. *Mo'ed Kattan* 27b states that this practice was initiated by Rabban Gamliel. Although as *nasi*, he obviously had ample resources, he ordered that his corpse be buried in a simple linen shroud, because in his day, the burial expenses were becoming more difficult to bear than the person's death. It had reached the point that people would simply abandon a corpse rather than bury it, because of the great expenses involved.

The Radbaz writes that at his time, this custom was discontinued and it was common for those who had the means to buy expensive shrouds. The rationale is that *Ketubot* 111b states that in the era of the Resurection, the dead will arise together with their clothes. Thus clothing the dead in elegant garments is an expression of one's faith in the coming of that era. We do not worry about the poor, because it has already become customary to bury those who cannot pay for their own funerals at the community's expense.

The *Shulchan Aruch* (*Yoreh De'ah* 352:1) and the *Siftei Cohen* 352:1 appear to suggest an intermediate position: not using expensive shrouds, but not necessarily overly simple ones either. This is the common practice today.
7. See Chapter 14, Halachah 25. See also *Hilchot Melachim* 6:10 which describes the prohibition against destroying useful property.
8. Note the prohibition against such emulation in *Hilchot Avodat Kochavim* 11:1.

We carry the dead on our shoulders to the cemetery.[9]

3. The pallbearers are forbidden to wear sandals, lest the strap of one of them snap and he hold back the performance of the mitzvah.[10]

4. We dig [burial] caves in the earth and make hollows at the side of the caves. There we bury [the corpse] with its face upward;[11] we then place the earth and the stones back in place above it. They may bury it in a wooden coffin.[12]

Those who accompany the corpse tell him: "Go in peace,"[13] as [Genesis 15:15] states: "You will go to your ancestors in peace."[14]

Markings[15] are made on the graves.[16] A tombstone is placed on the grave. For the righteous, by contrast, a tombstone is not placed, because their words [will cause them to be] remembered; a person will not [need] to visit in the cemeteries.[17]

5. A person in his deathroes is considered as a living person with regard to all matters.[18] We do not tie his cheek, stuff his orifices, nor do we place a metal utensil or a utensil that cools on his navel so that [his body] will not bloat. We do not anoint it or wash it or place it on sand or on salt until the person dies.[19]

One who touches him is considered as shedding blood. To what can the matter be compared? To a candle that is flickering; were a person to touch it, it will be extinguished. [Similarly,] anyone who closes [a dying person's] eyes as his soul expires is considered as shedding blood. Instead, they should wait some time lest he have fainted. Similarly, we do not rend our clothes because of him, uncover our shoulders,[20] recite eulogies, or bring a coffin or shrouds into the house until the person dies.[21]

9. I.e., rather than use wagons. This concept is derived from the description of Jacob's funeral procession (Genesis 50:13): "His sons carried him to the land of Canaan." At present, the custom is to transport a corpse to the cemetery in a hearse and to begin carrying the coffin shortly before the grave.

10. The Radbaz and the *Kessef Mishneh* write that this applied only in the Talmudic period when there were specific individuals designated as pallbearers. In the present age, it is customary for everyone to help carry a corpse. Hence if one person is delayed, his place will be taken by another. The Radbaz also explains that it is possible that the prohibition applies only to sandals and not to ordinary shoes.

11. This reflects the custom, still followed in most places in *Eretz Yisrael* today, to bury the corpse in the ground without a coffin.

12. Genesis 3:19 states: "To earth you shall return," and Ecclesiastes 3:20 states: "Everything is from the earth and everything returns to the earth," implying that a corpse should be placed in the earth itself. Nevertheless, since there are pores in wood, even while it is in a casket, the corpse is considered as being in contact with the earth. It is, however, preferable for the corpse to be placed in the ground itself [*Shulchan Aruch* (*Yoreh De'ah* 362:1)]. It is also customary to make two holes at the bottom of a wooden coffin to allow direct contact with the earth.

13. As a corollary to this concept, *Berachot* 64a and *Mo'ed Kattan* 29a emphasize that this

וְסוֹבְלִין אֶת הַמֵּת עַל הַכָּתֵף עַד בֵּית הַקְּבָרוֹת.

ג וְנוֹשְׂאֵי הַמִּטָּה אֲסוּרִין בִּנְעִילַת הַסַּנְדָּל, שֶׁמָּא תִּפָּסֵק רְצוּעָה מִסַּנְדָּלוֹ שֶׁל אֶחָד מֵהֶן, וְנִמְצָא מִתְעַכֵּב מִן הַמִּצְוָה.

ד וְחוֹפְרִין בֶּעָפָר מְעָרוֹת, וְעוֹשִׂין כּוּךְ בְּצַד הַמְּעָרָה, וְקוֹבְרִין אוֹתוֹ בּוֹ וּפָנָיו לְמַעְלָה, וּמַחֲזִירִין הֶעָפָר וְהָאֲבָנִים עָלָיו. וְיֵשׁ לָהֶן לִקְבֹּר בַּאֲרוֹן שֶׁל עֵץ. וְהַמְלַוִּין אוֹתוֹ אוֹמְרִין לוֹ: לֵךְ בְּשָׁלוֹם. שֶׁנֶּאֱמַר: וְאַתָּה תָּבוֹא אֶל אֲבֹתֶיךָ בְּשָׁלוֹם. וּמְצַיְּנִין אֶת כָּל בֵּית הַקְּבָרוֹת, וּבוֹנִין נֶפֶשׁ עַל הַקֶּבֶר. וְהַצַּדִּיקִים אֵין בּוֹנִים לָהֶם נֶפֶשׁ עַל קִבְרוֹתֵיהֶם, שֶׁדִּבְרֵיהֶם הֵם זִכְרוֹנָם. וְלֹא יִפְנֶה אָדָם לְבַקֵּר הַקְּבָרוֹת.

ה הַגּוֹסֵס – הֲרֵי הוּא כְּחַי לְכָל דָּבָר. אֵין קוֹשְׁרִין לְחָיָיו, וְאֵין פּוֹקְקִין נְקָבָיו, וְאֵין מַנִּיחִין כְּלִי מַתָּכוֹת וּכְלִי מֵקֵר עַל טַבּוּרוֹ שֶׁלֹּא יִתְפַּח, וְלֹא סָכִין אוֹתוֹ, וְלֹא מְדִיחִין אוֹתוֹ, וְלֹא מַטִּילִין אוֹתוֹ עַל הַחוֹל וְלֹא עַל הַמֶּלַח, עַד שָׁעָה שֶׁיָּמוּת.
וְהַנּוֹגֵעַ בּוֹ – הֲרֵי זֶה שׁוֹפֵךְ דָּמִים. לְמָה זֶה דּוֹמֶה? לְנֵר שֶׁמְּטַפְטֵף, כֵּיוָן שֶׁיִּגַּע בּוֹ אָדָם יִכְבֶּה. וְכָל הַמְאַמֵּץ עֵינָיו עִם יְצִיאַת נֶפֶשׁ – הֲרֵי זֶה שׁוֹפֵךְ דָּמִים; אֶלָּא יִשְׁהֶא מְעַט, שֶׁמָּא נִתְעַלֵּף. וְכֵן אֵין קוֹרְעִין עָלָיו, וְלֹא חוֹלְצִין כָּתֵף, וְלֹא מַסְפִּידִין, וְלֹא מַכְנִיסִין עִמּוֹ אָרוֹן וְתַכְרִיכִין בַּבַּיִת עַד שֶׁיָּמוּת.

expression should not be used when bidding a living person farewell. Instead, one should say: "Go to peace."
14. The verse communicates the prophecy that Abraham will die in tranquillity.
15. In the Talmudic era, it was customary to place an outline of lime around graves so that people who were ritually pure would not step on them.
16. Our translation follows the authoritative manuscripts and early printings of the *Mishneh Torah*. The standard printed texts follow a slightly different version.
17. Based on the Jerusalem Talmud (*Shekalim* 2:5), the *Kessef Mishneh* explains that an ordinary person is remembered by visiting his grave and therefore a tombstone is necessary to mark it. A righteous sage, by contrast, is remembered because of the Torah insights which he developed. There is no need to visit his grave. And hence, a tombstone is unnecessary.

Despite this explanation, it must be emphasized that it is common custom to place tombstones at the graves of the righteous and to go there to pray. Indeed, there is a tombstone placed at the Rambam's own grave in Tiberias.
18. I.e., a priest is not liable for entering the house. Similarly, a dying man can divorce his wife so that she will not have to undergo *chalitzah* rites.

With regard to license for a priest to enter the house: the *Shulchan Aruch* (*Yoreh De'ah* 370:1) forbids it, but the Ramah permits it.
19. As indicated by Halachah 1 and notes, these measures are intended to prevent a corpse from decomposing and producing an unpleasant fragrance and to prepare it for burial.
20. See Chapter 8, Halachah 3.
21. Lest the dying person take notice and become aggrieved. This might hasten his death.

6. When a person's dead is lying before him, he should eat in another house.[22] If he does not have another house, he should construct a partition and eat. If he does not have the materials to make a partition, he should turn away his face and eat. Under no circumstances should he recline[23] and eat or eat meat or drink wine.[24]

He does not recite the blessing [before eating], nor the grace after meals. Others do not recite the blessing[s] for him, nor is he included in a quorum of three for the recitation of grace.[25] He is free from the obligation to recite the *Shema*, pray, put on *tefillin,* or [observe] any of the mitzvot stated in the Torah.[26]

On the Sabbath,[27] he should recline, eat meat and drink wine, recite the blessing [before eating], and recite grace. Others may recite blessings for him. He is included in a quorum for grace and is obligated in all the mitzvot of the Torah with the exception of sexual relations.[28]

Once the dead is buried, he is permitted to eat meat and drink a small amount of wine to help digest the food [that he has eaten], but not in an unrestrained manner.[29]

7. We do not delay [the burial of] the dead. Instead, we hurry [to bury] him immediately. Hastening the burial is praiseworthy.[30] For one's father and mother, by contrast, it is demeaning.[31]

8. On Friday or the day before a festival[32] or when rain is drenching the coffin, it is permitted [to hurry even the funeral of one's parents]. For the person hurried the funeral only as an expression of honor for his father and mother.

Whoever delays the burial of his dead overnight violates a negative commandment,[33] unless he delays [the burial] for the honor of the dead[34] and to complete providing for his needs.

22. For eating in the presence of a corpse could be interpreted as mocking him, implying that one can partake of the pleasures of this world while the corpse cannot (*Berachot* 17b and commentaries).

We have translated *bayit* as "house." For in Talmudic times, homes were often one room structures. The term can also be rendered as "room." Halachicly, that interpretation is also acceptable.

23. As is the custom of important personages when they dine.

24. For while he is allowed to eat, he may not indulge.

25. To introduce grace with a blessing.

26. The mourner is considered as being "involved with a mitzvah," for he is concerned with the burial of his dead. And we follow the principle that a person involved with one mitzvah is not obligated in another.

The Jerusalem Talmud (*Berachot* 3:1) states that even if a person desires to be stringent with himself and observe the mitzvot, he should be restrained from doing so. It gives two rationales:

a) it implies that one is not concerned with mourning for the deceased and thus detracts from his honor;

ו מִי שֶׁמֵּתוֹ מֻטָּל לְפָנָיו – אוֹכֵל בְּבַיִת אַחֵר. אֵין לוֹ בַּיִת אַחֵר – עוֹשֶׂה מְחִצָּה וְאוֹכֵל. אֵין לוֹ דָּבָר לַעֲשׂוֹת מְחִצָּה – מַחֲזִיר פָּנָיו וְאוֹכֵל. וּבֵין כָּךְ וּבֵין כָּךְ אֵינוֹ מֵסֵב וְאוֹכֵל, וְלֹא אוֹכֵל בָּשָׂר וְלֹא שׁוֹתֶה יַיִן. וְאֵינוֹ מְבָרֵךְ וְאֵינוֹ מְזַמֵּן, וְאֵין מְבָרְכִין עָלָיו וְאֵין מְזַמְּנִין עָלָיו. וּפָטוּר מִקְּרִיאַת שְׁמַע וּמִן הַתְּפִלָּה וּמִתְּפִלִּין וּמִכָּל מִצְוֹת הָאֲמוּרוֹת בַּתּוֹרָה.
בְּשַׁבָּת – מֵסֵב, וְאוֹכֵל בָּשָׂר וְשׁוֹתֶה יַיִן, וּמְבָרֵךְ וּמְזַמֵּן, וּמְבָרְכִין עָלָיו וּמְזַמְּנִין עָלָיו. וְחַיָּב בְּכָל מִצְוֹת הָאֲמוּרוֹת בַּתּוֹרָה, חוּץ מִתַּשְׁמִישׁ הַמִּטָּה.
נִקְבַּר הַמֵּת – הֲרֵי זֶה מֻתָּר לֶאֱכֹל בָּשָׂר וְלִשְׁתּוֹת יַיִן מְעַט, כְּדֵי לְשָׁרוֹת אֲכִילָה שֶׁבְּמֵעָיו, אֲבָל לֹא לִרְווֹת.

ז אֵין מַשְׁהִין אֶת הַמֵּת, אֶלָּא מַדְחִין מִטָּתוֹ מִיָּד. וְכָל הַמַּדְחֶה מִטָּתוֹ – הֲרֵי זֶה מְשֻׁבָּח. וְעַל אָבִיו וְעַל אִמּוֹ – הֲרֵי זֶה מְגֻנֶּה.

ח הָיָה עֶרֶב שַׁבָּת אוֹ עֶרֶב יוֹם טוֹב, אוֹ שֶׁהָיוּ גְשָׁמִים מְזַלְּפִין עַל הַמִּטָּה – מֻתָּר; שֶׁלֹּא מִהֵר אֶלָּא לִכְבוֹד אָבִיו וְאִמּוֹ. וְכָל הַמֵּלִין אֶת מֵתוֹ – עוֹבֵר בְּלֹא תַעֲשֶׂה, אֶלָּא אִם כֵּן הֱלִינוֹ לִכְבוֹדוֹ וּלְהַשְׁלִים צְרָכָיו.

b) it will prevent one from taking the steps to bury the deceased as soon as possible. According to the second rationale, if there are others who are prepared to deal with the deceased's burial, the mourner himself may go to the synagogue and pray.

The *Shulchan Aruch* (*Orach Chayim* 71:1) quotes opinions which forbid a mourner to be stringent upon himself and perform mitzvot if there are others who are dealing with the corpse's burial and others which allow him this privilege. The *Shulchan Aruch HaRav* 71:1 and the *Mishnah Berurah* 71:7 state that a person in this stage of acute mourning should not observe the mitzvot under any circumstance.

27. When nothing can be done to bury the dead and outward expressions of mourning are forbidden.

28. For private expressions of mourning are required on the Sabbath. Hence, sexual relations are forbidden (Chapter 10, Halachah 1). *Tosafot, Mo'ed Kattan* 23b, refers to engaging in sexual relations at the time when one's dead is not buried as *chutzpah*, "brazen conduct."

29. Lest one become intoxicated. See Chapter 13, Halachah 8.

30. For an early burial is a measure of respect for the dead.

31. For one must mourn excessively for one's parents and arranging their funeral hastily shows a lack of respect.

32. When delaying the burial would cause it to be postponed for an additional day or more, it is considered more of an honor to bury the dead earlier than to prepare a more impressive funeral. In the present age, when corpses are held in refrigerated morgues, there are communities where even on Friday and on the day preceding a festival, funerals are postponed.

33. See *Hilchot Sanhedrin* 15:8.

34. To bring a coffin or shrouds, to enable relatives to come, or to announce his passing in outlying places [*Shulchan Aruch* (*Yoreh De'ah* 357:1)].

9. On the first day alone,[35] it is forbidden for a mourner to put on *tefillin* or to eat food of his own.[36] He must sit on a overturned bed.[37] During the remainder of the days of mourning,[38] he may eat his own food, sit on a mat or on the ground,[39] and put on *tefillin.*

What is the source which teaches that a mourner may not put on *tefillin* on the first day? [Instructions] were given Ezekiel (Ezekiel 24:17): "Your glory should be bound upon you."[40] Implied is that other people are forbidden.[41] He was instructed: "Do not eat the bread of men." Implied is that other people should eat from others on the first day and are forbidden to eat their own food.[42]

CHAPTER FIVE

1. These are the matters forbidden to a mourner on the first day according to Scriptural Law and on the remaining seven days according to Rabbinic Law.[1] He is forbidden to cut his hair, launder his clothes, wash, anoint himself, engage in sexual relations, wear shoes, perform work, study the Torah, stand his bed upright, leave his head uncovered, and greet others, eleven matters in total.[2]

2. Which source teaches that a mourner is forbidden to have his hair cut? [Leviticus 10:6] warns the sons of Aaron:[3] "Do not let [the hair of] your heads grow untended." Implied is that every mourner is forbidden to cut his hair. Instead, he lets [his hair] grow untended.[4] Just as he is forbidden to cut off his hair; so, too, he is forbidden to trim[5] his beard and any other hair on his [body]. This applies to cutting hair[6] and having one's own hair cut. If he was in the midst of a haircut and he heard that his father died, he may complete the haircut.[7] This applies to cutting hair[8] and having one's own hair cut.

Similarly, it is forbidden to cut off one's mustache or to cut one's nails with a utensil. One may, however, bite off one's nails or trim them with one's other nails.

3. Which source teaches that a mourner is forbidden to launder his clothes

35. I.e., even after the burial of the deceased when the mourner is obligated to perform mitzvot.

36. Bringing food for the mourners, particularly the *seudat havraah* (the meal of comfort served directly after the funeral; see Chapter 13, Halachah 7) is a great mitzvah. The *Perishah* (*Yoreh De'ah* 378) explains that, at this time, a mourner is overcome by his suffering and will not see to his own needs. Therefore his neighbors are commanded to tend to him.

37. The Ra'avad protests stating that he never saw a source for this custom. It is not accepted in most communities at present, as stated in *Shulchan Aruch* (*Yoreh De'ah* 387:2). See also Chapter 5, Halachot 17-18 and notes.

38. I.e., during the seven days of *shivah.*

39. In the Ashkenazic community, it has become customary to sit on low stools.

ט הָאָבֵל בְּיוֹם רִאשׁוֹן בִּלְבַד – אָסוּר לְהַנִּיחַ תְּפִלִּין וְלֶאֱכֹל מִשֶּׁלּוֹ, וְחַיָּב לֵישֵׁב עַל מִטָּה כְּפוּיָה. וּבִשְׁאָר יְמֵי הָאֵבֶל – מֻתָּר לוֹ לֶאֱכֹל מִשֶּׁלּוֹ, וְלֵישֵׁב עַל גַּבֵּי מַפָּץ אוֹ קַרְקַע, וּמַנִּיחַ תְּפִלִּין.

וּמִנַּיִן שֶׁהוּא אָסוּר בְּיוֹם רִאשׁוֹן לְהַנִּיחַ תְּפִלִּין? שֶׁהֲרֵי נֶאֱמַר לִיחֶזְקֵאל: פְּאֵרְךָ חֲבוֹשׁ עָלֶיךָ. מִכְּלָל שֶׁכָּל הָעָם אֲסוּרִין. וְנֶאֱמַר לוֹ: וְלֶחֶם אֲנָשִׁים לֹא תֹאכֵל. מִכְּלָל שֶׁכָּל הָעָם אוֹכְלִין מִשֶּׁל אֲחֵרִים בְּיוֹם רִאשׁוֹן, וַאֲסוּרִין לֶאֱכֹל מִשֶּׁל עַצְמָן.

פֶּרֶק חֲמִישִׁי

א אֵלּוּ דְבָרִים שֶׁהָאָבֵל אָסוּר בָּהֶן בְּיוֹם רִאשׁוֹן מִן הַתּוֹרָה, וּבִשְׁאָר יָמִים מִדִּבְרֵיהֶם: אָסוּר לְסַפֵּר, וּלְכַבֵּס, וְלִרְחֹץ, וְלָסוּךְ, וּלְשַׁמֵּשׁ מִטָּתוֹ, וְלִנְעֹל אֶת הַסַּנְדָּל, וְלַעֲשׂוֹת מְלָאכָה, וְלִקְרוֹת בְּדִבְרֵי תוֹרָה, וְלִזְקֹף אֶת הַמִּטָּה, וְלִפְרֹעַ אֶת רֹאשׁוֹ, וְלִשְׁאֹל שָׁלוֹם. הַכֹּל אַחַד עָשָׂר דָּבָר.

ב וּמִנַּיִן שֶׁהָאָבֵל אָסוּר בְּתִסְפֹּרֶת? שֶׁהֲרֵי הִזְהִיר בְּנֵי אַהֲרֹן: רָאשֵׁיכֶם אַל תִּפְרָעוּ. מִכְּלָל שֶׁכָּל הַמִּתְאַבֵּל אָסוּר לְסַפֵּר שְׂעָרוֹ, אֶלָּא מְגַדֵּל פֶּרַע. וּכְשֵׁם שֶׁאָסוּר לְגַלֵּחַ שְׂעַר רֹאשׁוֹ, כָּךְ אָסוּר לְגַלֵּחַ שְׂעַר זְקָנוֹ וְכָל שֵׂעָר שֶׁיֵּשׁ בּוֹ. אֶחָד הַמְגַלֵּחַ וְאֶחָד הַמִּתְגַּלֵּחַ. הָיָה מְגַלֵּחַ וְשָׁמַע שֶׁמֵּת אָבִיו – מַשְׁלִים תִּגְלַחַת שְׂעָרוֹ. אֶחָד הַמְגַלֵּחַ וְאֶחָד הַמִּתְגַּלֵּחַ.
וְכֵן אָסוּר לְגַלֵּחַ שָׂפָה, וְלִטֹּל צִפָּרְנָיו בִּכְלִי; אֲבָל בְּשִׁנָּיו, אוֹ שֶׁנּוֹטֵל צִפֹּרֶן בְּצִפֹּרֶן – מֻתָּר.

ג וּמִנַּיִן שֶׁהָאָבֵל אָסוּר לְכַבֵּס בְּגָדָיו וְלִרְחֹץ גּוּפוֹ וְלָסוּךְ?

40. These instructions were given at the time of the death of Ezekiel's wife. "Glory" refers to *tefillin* as indicated by Targum Yonaton to that verse and *Ketubot* 6b.
41. Rashi (*Sukkah* 25a) explains that when a person girds himself with glory (*tefillin*), he implies that he is not devastated by his loss.
42 . Although the Rambam speaks of this restriction as applying for the entire day, Rabbenu Asher maintains that it applies only for the first meal eaten after the burial. *Shulchan Aruch* (*Yoreh De'ah* 378:1) follows this view.

1. See Chapter 1, Halachah 1.
2. The Rambam explains each of these restrictions at length in the halachot which follow.
3. After the deaths of their brothers. They were given this command in honor of the dedication of the Sanctuary and such conduct was appropriate only at that time.
4. This also applies during the 30 days of mourning as stated in Chapter 6.
5. For shaving is forbidden, regardless; see *Hilchot Avodat Kochavim*, ch. 11.
6. I.e., even the hair of others (Radbaz).
7. For having half of one's hair cut would appear ludicrous.
8. If one is cutting someone else's hair and there is another barber in town, one should

and to wash and anoint his body? [II Samuel 14:2] states:[9] "Please conduct yourself as a mourner; please wear mourner's clothes and do not anoint yourself with oil." Washing is including in anointing oneself, for it is a preliminary step before anointing oneself as [Ruth 3:3] states: "Wash and anoint yourself."

Just as a mourner is forbidden to launder clothes; so, too, he is forbidden to wear new and freshly pressed white clothes.[10]

4. As it is forbidden to anoint one's entire body; so, too, it is forbidden to anoint a portion of one's body. To remove filth, however, it is permitted.[11] Similarly, it is forbidden to wash a portion of one's body in hot water. One may, however, wash one's face, one's hands, and one's feet - but not one's entire body - in cold water.

5. Which source teaches that a mourner is forbidden to engage in sexual relations?[12] [II Samuel 12:24] states: "And David comforted his wife, Batsheva,[13] and he came to her and lay with her." This indicates that this was forbidden beforehand.

Similarly, a mourner should not marry a woman,[14] nor should a woman marry [while mourning] even though they do not engage in relations. It is permitted for [a mourner] to remain in solitude with his wife[15] even though he is forbidden to engage in sexual relations.[16]

6. Which source teaches that a mourner is forbidden to wear shoes?[17] Ezekiel was instructed [Ezekiel 24:17]:[18] "And place your shoes on your feet." Implied is that all others are forbidden. If a person is traveling on a journey, he may wear shoes and proceed [on his way].[19] When he enters a city,[20] he should remove his shoes.

7. An allusion[21] to the prohibition against a mourner performing labor [can be derived from Amos 8:10]: "I shall transform your festivals into mourning." Just as it is forbidden to perform work on a festival; so, too, a mourner is forbidden to perform work. And just as a mourner is forbidden to perform

cease and have the other barber finish the haircut [*Kessef Mishneh*; *Shulchan Aruch* (*Yoreh De'ah* 390:2)].

9. These reflect Yoav's instructions to the wise woman of Tekoa. Although she was only feigning mourning, the fact that she followed these practices indicates that they are followed by mourners.

10. The *Shulchan Aruch* (*Yoreh De'ah* 389:3) state that this applies to colored clothes as well. The *Shulchan Aruch* (*loc. cit.*:1) also forbids using freshly laundered sheets. Wearing pressed clothes is also forbidden for the 30 days of mourning as stated in Chapter 6.

11. Similarly, the *Shulchan Aruch* (*Yoreh De'ah* 381:1-2) allows one to wash oneself in an ordinary manner to remove filth and to anoint oneself for medicinal purposes. The Radbaz quotes the Jerusalem Talmud (*Berachot* 2:6) which states that any washing that is not for pleasure is permitted.

שֶׁנֶּאֱמַר: הִתְאַבְּלִי נָא וְלִבְשִׁי בִגְדֵי אֵבֶל וְאַל תָּסוּכִי שֶׁמֶן. וּרְחִיצָה בִּכְלַל סִיכָה, שֶׁהָרְחִיצָה קוֹדֶמֶת לְסִיכָה, שֶׁנֶּאֱמַר: וְרָחַצְתְּ וָסַכְתְּ. וּכְשֵׁם שֶׁאָבֵל אָסוּר בְּכִבּוּס בְּגָדִים, כָּךְ אָסוּר לִלְבֹּשׁ כֵּלִים לְבָנִים חֲדָשִׁים וּמְגֹהָצִין.

ד אָסוּר לָסוּךְ מִקְצָת גּוּפוֹ כְּכָל גּוּפוֹ. וְאִם לְהַעֲבִיר אֶת הַזֻּהֲמָא – מֻתָּר. וְכֵן אָסוּר בִּרְחִיצַת מִקְצָת גּוּפוֹ בְּחַמִּין; אֲבָל בְּצוֹנֵן – רוֹחֵץ פָּנָיו יָדָיו וְרַגְלָיו, אֲבָל לֹא כָּל גּוּפוֹ.

ה מִנַּיִן לְאָבֵל שֶׁאָסוּר בְּתַשְׁמִישׁ הַמִּטָּה? שֶׁנֶּאֱמַר: וַיְנַחֵם דָּוִד אֵת בַּת שֶׁבַע אִשְׁתּוֹ וַיָּבֹא אֵלֶיהָ וַיִּשְׁכַּב עִמָּהּ. מִכְּלָל שֶׁהָיָה אָסוּר מִקֹּדֶם.

וְכֵן לֹא יִשָּׂא הָאָבֵל אִשָּׁה, וְלֹא תִנָּשֵׂא אִשָּׁה, אַף עַל פִּי שֶׁאֵין מְשַׁמְּשִׁין מִטָּתָן.

וּמֻתָּר לְהִתְיַחֵד עִם אִשְׁתּוֹ, וְאַף עַל פִּי שֶׁהוּא אָסוּר בְּתַשְׁמִישׁ הַמִּטָּה.

ו מִנַּיִן שֶׁהָאָבֵל אָסוּר בִּנְעִילַת הַסַּנְדָּל? שֶׁהֲרֵי נֶאֱמַר לִיחֶזְקֵאל: וּנְעָלֶיךָ תָּשִׂים בְּרַגְלֶיךָ. מִכְּלָל שֶׁכָּל הָעָם אֲסוּרִין. הָיָה בָּא בַּדֶּרֶךְ – נוֹעֵל וְהוֹלֵךְ; וּכְשֶׁיִּכָּנֵס בַּמְּדִינָה – חוֹלֵץ מִנְּעָלָיו.

ז רֶמֶז לְאָבֵל שֶׁאָסוּר בַּעֲשִׂיַּת מְלָאכָה, זֶה שֶׁנֶּאֱמַר: וְהָפַכְתִּי חַגֵּיכֶם לְאֵבֶל. מַה חַג אָסוּר בַּעֲשִׂיַּת מְלָאכָה, אַף אֵבֶל אָסוּר בַּעֲשִׂיַּת מְלָאכָה.

12. The Radbaz quotes *Mo'ed Kattan* 24a which states that there was a person who engaged in relations during the week of mourning and afterwards, wild pigs tore apart his body.
13. After the conclusion of the mourning period for their son who died.
14. This is also forbidden for the 30 days of mourning as stated in Chapter 6.
15. The *Shulchan Aruch* (*Yoreh De'ah* 383:1) states that the restrictions observed when a woman is in the *niddah* state need not be observed at this time. Although the letter of the law allows this, the Radbaz and many other authorities suggest being stringent.
16. This refers to an ordinary mourner. If, however, a couple have never engaged in relations - e.g., one of their parents dies directly after their wedding - they may not remain in solitude together [*Shulchan Aruch* (*Yoreh De'ah* 383:2)].
17. The prohibition involves only leather shoes. Shoes from other materials may be worn [*Shulchan Aruch* (*Yoreh De'ah* 382:1).]
18. In the instructions God gave him in connection with his wife's death.
19. Similarly, a person is allowed to wear shoes if there is a danger of being bitten by scorpions or for other health reasons, e.g., a woman who just gave birth [*Shulchan Aruch* (*loc. cit.*:2-3)].
20. In a city inhabited primarily by gentiles, some authorities grant license to wear one's shoes until one reaches the Jewish quarter [*ibid.*:4].
21. In contrast to the previous halachot which mention prohibitions that can be derived from the literal meaning of the verse, this prohibition is merely hinted at by the verse (Radbaz; *Kessef Mishneh*).

work; so, too, is he forbidden to engage in commercial transactions[22] and to travel from city to city on a business trip.[23]

8. For the first three days, [all mourners,] even a poor person who derives his livelihood from charity, are forbidden to perform work.[24] After that period, if [the mourner] is indigent,[25] he may perform this work privately in his home.[26] A woman may spin fabric on a spindle in her home.[27]

9. When two brothers or two partners operate one store [together] and one of them is [forced to] mourn, the store should be closed for all seven [days of mourning].[28]

10. Even activities which are permitted to be performed during *chol hamo'ed*[29] may not be performed by a mourner during the days of mourning.[30] Others[31] may, however, perform these tasks on his behalf.[32]

What is implied? If it is necessary to turn over a person's olives,[33] put pitch on his barrels,[34] or bring his flax up from the vat [where it is soaking] or his wool from the kettle [where it is being dyed],[35] he may hire someone else to perform [this task] on his behalf so that he will not suffer a loss.[36] And he may have his field irrigated in the irrigation season.

11. His sharecroppers[37] or those who hire his fields[38] may perform work in their ordinary way.[39] But donkey-drivers and camel-drivers who [rent] his animals and sailors who [rent] his ships should not perform [work].[40] If [the

22. If the mourner stands to lose a considerable amount (*davar ha'avaid*) if a transaction is not carried out, leniency may be granted for others to carry out this transaction for him as leniency is granted during *chol hamoed* [see *Hilchot Sh'vitat Yom Tov* 7:22; Radbaz; see also *Shulchan Aruch* (*Yoreh De'ah* 380:6)].
23. See Chapter 6, Halachah 2, which explains that this prohibition also applies during the thirty days of *sheloshim* mourning.
24. As evident from Chapter 13, Halachah 11, the first three days of mourning are the most intense when the mourner weeps over his dead. If he is forced to work, he will be prevented from weeping (*Kessef Mishneh*).
25. And needs to perform this work to earn his livelihood.
26. The Jerusalem Talmud (*Mo'ed Kattan* 3:5) states: "May a curse come upon his neighbors who required him to do this," i.e., who did not provide for his needs.
27. The Radbaz states that this applies even to a rich woman and even during the first three days of mourning, since it is extremely undesirable for a woman to be idle. See *Ketubot* 59b.
28. In his *Kessef Mishneh* and in his *Shulchan Aruch* (*Yoreh De'ah* 380:21), Rav Yosef Caro explains that our Sages sought to prevent public knowledge of the functioning of the partnership. Accordingly, the store must be closed. If, however, it is possible for the other partner to perform activities on behalf of the partnership in private without public knowledge, he may. The profits are then split by the two. If, however, the mourner is a well-known person and hence, any work performed on his behalf will become public knowledge, it is forbidden for his partner to perform work.

וּכְשֵׁם שֶׁהוּא אָסוּר בַּעֲשִׂיַּת מְלָאכָה, כָּךְ הוּא אָסוּר לִשָּׂא וְלִתֵּן בִּסְחוֹרָה, וְלֵילֵךְ מִמְּדִינָה לִמְדִינָה בִּסְחוֹרָה.

ח כָּל שְׁלֹשָׁה יָמִים הָרִאשׁוֹנִים אָסוּר בַּעֲשִׂיַּת מְלָאכָה אֲפִלּוּ הָיָה עָנִי הַמִּתְפַּרְנֵס מִן הַצְּדָקָה. מִכָּאן וְאֵילָךְ, אִם הָיָה עָנִי – עוֹשֶׂה בְּצִנְעָה בְּתוֹךְ בֵּיתוֹ, וְהָאִשָּׁה טֹוָה בְּפֶלֶךְ בְּתוֹךְ בֵּיתָהּ.

ט שְׁנֵי אַחִים אוֹ שְׁנֵי שֻׁתָּפִין שֶׁהָיוּ בַּחֲנוּת אַחַת, וְאֵרַע אֵבֶל לְאֶחָד מֵהֶן – נוֹעֲלִין אֶת הַחֲנוּת כָּל שִׁבְעָה.

י אֲפִלּוּ דְּבָרִים שֶׁמֻּתָּר לַעֲשׂוֹתָן בְּחֻלּוֹ שֶׁל מוֹעֵד – אָסוּר לְאָבֵל לַעֲשׂוֹתָן בְּיָדוֹ בִּימֵי אֶבְלוֹ; אֲבָל אֲחֵרִים עוֹשִׂים לוֹ. כֵּיצַד? הָיוּ זֵיתָיו לַהֲפֹךְ, וְכַדָּיו לָגוּף, וּפִשְׁתָּנוֹ לַעֲלוֹת מִן הַמִּשְׁרָה, וְצַמְרוֹ מִן הַיּוֹרָה – שׂוֹכֵר אֲחֵרִים לַעֲשׂוֹת לוֹ כְּדֵי שֶׁלֹּא יֹאבְדוּ. וּמְרַבְּצִין לוֹ שָׂדֵהוּ מִשֶּׁתַּגִּיעַ עוֹנַת הַמַּיִם.

יא הָאֲרִיסִין וְהַחֲכִירִין שֶׁלּוֹ וְהַקַּבְּלָנִין – הֲרֵי אֵלּוּ יַעֲשׂוּ כְּדַרְכָּן. אֲבָל הַחַמָּרִים וְהַגַּמָּלִים בִּבְהֵמוֹת שֶׁלּוֹ וְהַסַּפָּנִים בִּסְפִינָה שֶׁלּוֹ – הֲרֵי אֵלּוּ לֹא יַעֲשׂוּ.

29. The intermediate days of the festival when ordinary work is forbidden, but license is granted to perform work if otherwise, a person will suffer a substantial loss (see *Hilchot Sh'vitat Yom Tov* 7:1-2.
30. So that his attention will not be diverted from his mourning (Rabbenu Nissim).
31. But not his own servants or the members of his household whom he supports [Radbaz; *Shulchan Aruch* (*Yoreh De'ah* 380:4).]
32. For a wage, not merely as a favor for the mourner.
33. Before olives are pressed, they are left in the sun. First they are exposed on one side and then on the other. If they are not turned over, they will spoil.
34. To protect the oil placed inside them.
35. In both these instances, leaving the fabric to soak beyond the desired time will cause it to spoil.
36. In this halachah, the Rambam speaks about instances that apply in an agricultural society. Similar principles apply with regard to activities fundamental to a commercial society as mentioned in the notes to Halachah 7.
37. The Hebrew terms used by the Rambam include both sharecroppers who give a fixed percentage of the crops and those who give a fixed amount of produce.
38. Paying a fixed fee. The Rambam defines the three Hebrew terms used in this halachah in *Hilchot Sechirut* 8:1-2.
39. For they are working on their own behalf and not on behalf of the mourner who owns the fields.

The Radbaz and the *Kessef Mishneh* quote the Ra'avad who explains that this applies even if the rental agreement ended before the beginning of the period. In contrast to the animals or ships mentioned in the second clause, it is common to rent out land. See *Shulchan Aruch* (*Yoreh De'ah* 380:11).
40. Even though they were rented out before the person became a mourner, since the term

animals or ships] were hired out[41] or rented out previously for a specific time, [the renters] may perform work.[42]

12. A worker[43] hired by the day - even if he is located in another city - should not perform work on behalf of [the mourner].[44]

13. When a mourner was charged with doing tasks[45] on behalf of others, whether as a contractor[46] or not as a contractor, he should not perform them.[47] If his tasks were entrusted to others, they should not work on them in his home,[48] but may work on them elsewhere.[49]

14. If a mourner has litigation with a colleague, he should not prosecute the matter throughout the seven days of mourning.[50] If it concerned a matter that could lead to a loss,[51] he should appoint an agent.[52] The *Geonim* ruled in this manner.

15. Which source teaches that a mourner is forbidden to [speak] words of Torah? Ezekiel was instructed [Ezekiel 24:17]:[53] "Be silent from groaning."

16. He is forbidden to read [from] the Torah, the Prophets, and the Holy Scriptures and to study the Mishnah, the *Midrash*,[54] and the *Halachot*.[55] If many require his [instruction], he is permitted, provided he does not appoint a spokesman.[56] Instead, he should whisper to the person sitting next to him. That person should relate [the teachings] to the spokesman and the spokesman should communicate them to the people at large.

of the rental agreement was not specified originally, continuing to rent them out is considered as "work" and hence, is forbidden.

41. Employing a profit sharing agreement.

42. Since they were rented out for a specific time period, during that time period, they are considered as belonging to the renter.

43. *Mo'ed Kattan* 11b explains that this refers to a person who works the mourner's land.

44. Since the mourner's ownership of the land is common knowledge, having work performed on the land is considered as if he performed work in public.

45. Work with materials not connected with landed property, e.g., to sew clothing or to make furniture.

46. In which instance, one might think there might be room for leniency since he is not being paid specifically for the days of mourning.

47. For he is not allowed to perform work during the days of mourning.

48. Lest others think he helped perform the task or hired the person during the days of mourning.

49. For people at large will not necessarily know that these tasks are being performed, nor will they have reason to associate them with the mourner.

The *Kessef Mishneh* and the Ramah (*Yoreh De'ah* 380:18) emphasize that the work must have been contracted out before the period of mourning began.

50. For litigation, like work, will divert his attention from mourning.

וְאִם הָיוּ מְחֻכָּרִים אוֹ מֻשְׂכָּרִים מִקֹּדֶם לִזְמַן קָצוּב - הֲרֵי אֵלּוּ יַעֲשׂוּ.

יב שְׂכִיר יוֹם, אֲפִלּוּ בְּעִיר אַחֶרֶת - לֹא יַעֲשֶׂה לוֹ.

יג הָאָבֵל שֶׁהָיְתָה מְלֶאכֶת אֲחֵרִים בְּיָדוֹ, בֵּין בְּקַבְּלָנוּת בֵּין שֶׁאֵינָהּ בְּקַבְּלָנוּת - לֹא יַעֲשֶׂה. הָיְתָה מְלַאכְתּוֹ בְּיַד אֲחֵרִים: בְּבֵיתוֹ - לֹא יַעֲשׂוּ, בְּבַיִת אַחֵר - עוֹשִׂין.

יד הָיָה לוֹ דִּין עִם אָדָם - אֵינוֹ תּוֹבְעוֹ כָּל שִׁבְעַת יְמֵי הָאֲבֵלוּת. וְאִם הָיָה דָּבָר אָבֵד - עוֹשֶׂה שָׁלִיחַ. כָּזֶה הוֹרוּ הַגְּאוֹנִים.

טו מִנַּיִן שֶׁהָאָבֵל אָסוּר בְּדִבְרֵי תּוֹרָה? שֶׁהֲרֵי נֶאֱמַר לִיחֶזְקֵאל: הֵאָנֵק דֹּם.

טז אָסוּר לִקְרוֹת בַּתּוֹרָה בַּנְּבִיאִים וּבַכְּתוּבִים, וְלִשְׁנוֹת בַּמִּשְׁנָה וּבַמִּדְרָשׁ וּבַהֲלָכוֹת. וְאִם הָיוּ רַבִּים צְרִיכִין לוֹ - מֻתָּר. וּבִלְבַד שֶׁלֹּא יַעֲמִיד תֻּרְגְּמָן; אֶלָּא יִלְחַשׁ לְאַחֵר בְּצִדּוֹ, וְזֶה שֶׁבְּצִדּוֹ אוֹמֵר לַתֻּרְגְּמָן, וְהַתֻּרְגְּמָן מַשְׁמִיעַ לָרַבִּים.

51. E.g., the defendant or the witnesses are leaving the locale and it will be impossible to prosecute the matter in the future (Radbaz).

52. Just like a person may appoint an agent to perform his work for him when there is a possibility of loss (Halachah 10), he may appoint an agent to prosecute his claim. Although generally it is undesirable to have an agent prosecute a claim (*Hilchot Shluchim* 3:5), license is granted in this instance because of the extenuating circumstances.

53. In the instructions God gave him in connection with his wife's death. *Tosafot, Mo'ed Kattan* 21b associates this prohibition with the fact that Torah study engenders happiness, as Psalms 19:9 states: "The precepts of God are just, bringing gladness to the heart."

The Radbaz (in his gloss to Halachah 20) asks why in this instance we are required to emulate Ezekiel's example while in all other instances, we are required to conduct ourselves in the opposite manner. He explains that in all instances Ezekiel was given instructions that relaxed his mourning obligations and hence, we do the opposite. Here, he was given instructions that increased his mourning and hence, we certainly must follow them.

54. Based on *Mo'ed Kattan* 21a, the source for this halachah, it would appear that the Rambam is referring to the realm of study known as *Aggadah*, i.e., the homiletic teachings of our Sages.

55. Torah law.

Tosafot, loc. cit., explains that only Torah subjects that bring happiness are forbidden. The Books of *Eichah* and Job and similar prophecies of retribution are permitted. Similarly, it is permitted to study the laws of mourning. These concepts are reiterated by *Shulchan Aruch* (*Yoreh De'ah* 384:4).

56. In the Talmudic era, it was not customary for a teacher to deliver a lesson to the people himself. Instead, he would stand before them and speak to a spokesman who would, in turn, communicate the teachings to the people at large. See *Hilchot Talmud Torah* 4:3.

17. Which source teaches that a mourner should not sit on a bed?[57] [II Samuel 13:31] states:[58] "And the king arose, rent his garments, and lay on the ground."

18. [A mourner] is obligated to overturn his bed for all seven [days of mourning]. [This applies] not only to his own bed. Instead, he must overturn all the beds he has in his house. [Moreover,] even if he has ten beds in ten homes in ten cities, he is obligated to overturn all of them. Even if there are five brothers and one of them dies, all the remainder must overturn their beds.

When a bed is set aside to be used for money or for utensils, it need not be overturned. Similarly, a *dargesh*[59] need not be overturned. Instead, the straps should be released and the bed allowed to fall.

When bed posts emerge from a bed and so it is impossible to turn it over, he should turn it [on its side while] upright; this is sufficient.

If a person turned all his own beds over, but slept on beds belonging to others, on a chair, on a chest, or on the ground, he does not fulfill his obligation. Instead, he must sleep on the overturned bed.

19. Which source teaches that a mourner is forbidden to uncover his head? Ezekiel was instructed [Ezekiel 24:17]: "Do not veil [your face until] the lips." Implied is that others are obligated to cover their heads.[60] He should use the sash with which he covers his head and wind a portion of it over his mouth slightly. In this vein, Onkelos renders[61] [Leviticus 13:45]: "He should veil his face until his lips," as "He should cover himself like a mourner."[62]

20. Which source teaches that a mourner is forbidden to exchange greetings with colleagues? [Ezekiel was instructed:] "Be silent from groaning."

For the entire first three days, if someone greets him, he does not respond with greetings. Instead, he notifies him that he is a mourner. From the third day until the seventh, when a person greets him,[63] he should respond with greetings. From the seventh until the thirtieth day, he may greet others,[64] but others should not greet him[65] until after thirty days have passed. And [when he is in mourning for] his father or mother, he should not be greeted until after twelve months.

If he is forbidden to greet a colleague during the mourning period, one can certainly infer that he is forbidden to engage in lengthy talk and frivolity, as

57. In Chapter 4, Halachah 9, the Rambam writes that a mourner must sit on an overturned bed. The Radbaz explains that he is not obligated to sit on an overturned bed for all seven days of mourning. The bed must remain overturned, but the person may sit on the ground. As mentioned in the notes to that halachah, at present it is not customary to turn over beds as a sign of mourning.

The *Siftei Cohen* 387:1 states explicitly that a mourner should sit on the ground itself. It is not sufficient for him to sit on a low stool or cushion. Nevertheless, the common custom is to do the latter. Perhaps the source for leniency is the license granted for a sick or old person to sit on low stools or cushions because it is difficult for them to bear discomfort.

58. With regard to a rumor that all of King David's sons had been slain.

יז וּמִנַּיִן שֶׁאֵין הָאָבֵל יוֹשֵׁב עַל הַמִּטָּה? שֶׁנֶּאֱמַר: וַיָּקָם הַמֶּלֶךְ וַיִּקְרַע אֶת בְּגָדָיו וַיִּשְׁכַּב אָרְצָה.

יח וְחַיָּב לִכְפּוֹת הַמִּטָּה כָּל שִׁבְעָה. וְלֹא מִטָּתוֹ בִּלְבַד הוּא כּוֹפֶה, אֶלָּא כָּל הַמִּטּוֹת שֶׁיֵּשׁ לוֹ בְּתוֹךְ בֵּיתוֹ הוּא כּוֹפֶה. אֲפִלּוּ עֶשֶׂר מִטּוֹת בַּעֲשָׂרָה בָּתִּים וּבְעֶשֶׂר עֲיָרוֹת – חַיָּב לִכְפּוֹת אֶת כֻּלָּן. וַאֲפִלּוּ חֲמִשָּׁה אַחִים, וּמֵת אֶחָד מֵהֶן – כֻּלָּן כּוֹפִין אֶת מִטּוֹתֵיהֶן. הַמִּטָּה הַמְיֻחֶדֶת לְכֵלִים אוֹ לְמָעוֹת – אֵינוֹ צָרִיךְ לִכְפּוֹתָהּ. דַּרְגָּשׁ – אֵינוֹ צָרִיךְ לִכְפּוֹתוֹ, אֶלָּא מַתִּיר אֶת קַרְבִּיטָיו וְהוּא נוֹפֵל מֵאֵלָיו. מִטָּה שֶׁנַּקְלִיטֶיהָ יוֹצְאִין מִמֶּנָּה, שֶׁהֲרֵי אִי אֶפְשָׁר לְהָפְכָהּ – זוֹקְפָהּ וְדַיּוֹ. הָפַךְ כָּל מִטּוֹתָיו, וְהָיָה הוּא יָשֵׁן עַל גַּבֵּי מִטּוֹת אֲחֵרִים, אוֹ עַל גַּבֵּי כִּסֵּא, אוֹ עַל גַּבֵּי אָרוֹן, אוֹ עַל גַּבֵּי קַרְקַע – לֹא יָצָא יְדֵי חוֹבָתוֹ, אֶלָּא יָשֵׁן עַל גַּבֵּי הַמִּטָּה הַכְּפוּיָה.

יט מִנַּיִן לְאָבֵל שֶׁאָסוּר בִּפְרִיעַת הָרֹאשׁ? שֶׁהֲרֵי נֶאֱמַר לִיחֶזְקֵאל: לֹא תַעְטֶה עַל שָׂפָם. מִכְּלָל שֶׁשְּׁאָר הָאֲבֵלִים חַיָּבִין בַּעֲטִיפַת הָרֹאשׁ. וְהַסּוּדָר שֶׁמְּכַסֶּה בּוֹ רֹאשׁוֹ עוֹטֶה מִקְצָתוֹ מְעַט עַל פִּיו. שֶׁנֶּאֱמַר: וְעַל שָׂפָם יַעְטֶה, וְאֻנְקְלוֹס תִּרְגֵּם: כַּאֲבֵלָא יִתְעַטָּף.

כ וּמִנַּיִן שֶׁהָאָבֵל אָסוּר בִּשְׁאֵלַת שָׁלוֹם? שֶׁנֶּאֱמַר: הֵאָנֵק דֹּם.
כָּל שְׁלֹשָׁה יָמִים הָרִאשׁוֹנִים, מִי שֶׁנָּתַן לוֹ שָׁלוֹם – אֵין מַחֲזִיר לוֹ, אֶלָּא מוֹדִיעוֹ שֶׁהוּא אָבֵל; וּמִשְּׁלֹשָׁה וְעַד שִׁבְעָה, מִי שֶׁשָּׁאַל בִּשְׁלוֹמוֹ – מַחֲזִיר לוֹ שָׁלוֹם; וּמִשִּׁבְעָה וְעַד שְׁלֹשִׁים – שׁוֹאֵל בִּשְׁלוֹם אֲחֵרִים, אֲבָל אֲחֵרִים אֵין שׁוֹאֲלִין בִּשְׁלוֹמוֹ עַד לְאַחַר שְׁלֹשִׁים.
וְעַל אָבִיו וְעַל אִמּוֹ – אֵין שׁוֹאֲלִין בִּשְׁלוֹמוֹ עַד לְאַחַר שְׁנֵים עָשָׂר חֹדֶשׁ.
אִם בִּשְׁאֵלַת שָׁלוֹם נֶאֱסַר הָאָבֵל, קַל וָחֹמֶר שֶׁהוּא אָסוּר לְהַרְבּוֹת דְּבָרִים וְלִשְׂחֹק; שֶׁנֶּאֱמַר: דֹּם.

59. A low bed or chair with a leather base that is tied to posts by straps that is larger than a bench (the Rambam's Commentary to the Mishnah, *Sanhedrin* 2:3; *Hilchot Nedarim* 9:15).
60. The *Shulchan Aruch* (*Yoreh De'ah* 386:1) requires the observance of this practice. The Ramah, however, states that it has not been customary to observe it within the Ashkenazic community, nor is one obligated to do so.
61. In his translation of the Torah into Aramaic.
62. As reflected by the gloss of the Radbaz to Chapter 10, Halachah 1, this obligation applies only when sitting alone. When sitting with others, the mourner may uncover his face. This conclusion is quoted by the *Shulchan Aruch* (*Yoreh De'ah* 386:1).
63. As will be explained, the colleague should not greet him. If he does - because he does not know that he is a mourner or because he errs and/or forgets the law, the mourner may respond.
64. For they are in a state of well-being and composure.
65. For he has not reached a state of composure (*Mo'ed Kattan* 21b).

implied by the instruction: "Be silent." He should not hold an infant in his arms so that he will not lead him to laughter.[66] And he should not enter a place of celebration, e.g., a feasting hall or the like.[67]

CHAPTER SIX

1. According to Rabbinic Law, a mourner should observe some of the mourning practices for 30 days.[1] Which source did our Sages use as a support for the concept of 30 days?[2] [Deuteronomy 21:13] states:[3] "And she shall cry for her father and mother for a month."[4] Implied is that a mourner will feel discomfort for a month.

2. These are the practices forbidden to a mourner for the entire 30-day period. He is forbidden to cut his hair, to wear freshly ironed clothing, to marry, to [enter] a celebration of friends, and to go on a business trip to another city; five matters in all.[5]

3. What [does the prohibition] against cutting one's hair involve? Just as it is forbidden to cut any of the hair of one's body, to shave one's mustache, or to cut one's nails with a utensil through the seven days of mourning;[6] so, too, he is forbidden throughout these 30 days.

To whom does the above apply? To a man. A woman, by contrast, is permitted to remove hair after seven days[7] [although] a man must wait 30. For one's father or mother, a man is obligated to let his hair grow until it becomes noticeably long or[8] until his colleagues rebuke him [for not attending to his appearance].

66. For laughing in a state of mourning will be unseemly in the eyes of the public (*Mo'ed Kattan* 26b).
67. As stated in Chapter 6, Halachot 2 and 7, this restriction applies for a month and when one is in mourning for one's parents, for twelve months.

1. From the Rambam's wording in Chapter 10, Halachah 6, it appears that one should count the 30 days from the day of the relative's death, but Chapter 10, Halachah 8, (and this impression is also created from Chapter 7, Halachah 4) states that one should count from the day of the burial. Today, the present custom is to count the 30 days from the day of the relative's death.
2. I.e., although the practice is Rabbinic in origin, our Sages found an allusion to this practice in the Torah.
3. With regard to a *yefat to'ar*, a female captive of war.
4. The Ra'avad and the Radbaz question the Rambam's statement, noting that the Babylonian Talmud derives this concept from the exegesis of other verses. The Radbaz states that the Rambam's source is the Jerusalem Talmud. He asks, however: Why does the Rambam choose the Jerusalem Talmud over the Babylonian Talmud? Other

וְלֹא יֶאֱחֹז תִּינוֹק בְּיָדוֹ, שֶׁלֹּא יְבִיאֶנּוּ לִידֵי שְׂחוֹק. וְלֹא יִכָּנֵס לִמְקוֹם שִׂמְחָה, כְּגוֹן בָּתֵּי הַמִּשְׁתָּאוֹת וְכַיּוֹצֵא בָּהֶן.

פֶּרֶק שִׁשִּׁי

א מִדִּבְרֵי סוֹפְרִים, שֶׁיִּהְיֶה הָאָבֵל נוֹהֵג בְּמִקְצָת דִּבְרֵי אֲבֵלוּת כָּל שְׁלֹשִׁים יוֹם. וּמִנַּיִן סָמְכוּ חֲכָמִים לִשְׁלֹשִׁים יוֹם? שֶׁנֶּאֱמַר: וּבָכְתָה אֶת אָבִיהָ וְאֶת אִמָּהּ יֶרַח יָמִים. מִכְּלָל שֶׁהָאָבֵל מִצְטַעֵר כָּל שְׁלֹשִׁים יוֹם.

ב וְאֵלּוּ דְּבָרִים שֶׁהָאָבֵל אָסוּר בָּהֶן כָּל שְׁלֹשִׁים יוֹם: אָסוּר בְּתִסְפֹּרֶת, וּבְגִהוּץ, וּבְנִשּׂוּאִין, וּבְשִׂמְחַת מֵרֵעוּת, וְלֵילֵךְ בִּסְחוֹרָה מִמְּדִינָה לִמְדִינָה. הַכֹּל חֲמִשָּׁה דְּבָרִים.

ג בְּתִסְפֹּרֶת כֵּיצַד? כְּשֵׁם שֶׁאָסוּר לְסַפֵּר כָּל שְׂעַר גּוּפוֹ אוֹ לְגַלֵּחַ שְׂפָמוֹ אוֹ לָקֹץ צִפָּרְנָיו בִּכְלִי כָּל שִׁבְעָה, כָּךְ אָסוּר כָּל שְׁלֹשִׁים יוֹם.

בַּמֶּה דְּבָרִים אֲמוּרִים? בְּאִישׁ; אֲבָל בְּאִשָּׁה – מֻתֶּרֶת בִּנְטִילַת שֵׂעָר לְאַחַר שִׁבְעָה. וְהָאִישׁ – עַד שְׁלֹשִׁים יוֹם. וְעַל אָבִיו וְעַל אִמּוֹ – חַיָּב לְגַדֵּל שְׂעָרוֹ עַד שֶׁיְּשַׁלַּח פֶּרַע, אוֹ עַד שֶׁיִּגְעֲרוּ בּוֹ חֲבֵרָיו.

commentaries note that the exegesis of this verse is not found in the standard text of the Jerusalem Talmud and question the Rambam's source.

Kin'at Eliyahu states that regardless of which source the Rambam is relying upon, the Rambam is following a pattern he employs in several other places in the *Mishneh Torah*: He will rely on the most obvious Biblical source even when it is not given prominence in the previous Rabbinic writings.

5. They are described in the following halachot of this chapter.

6. See Chapter 5, Halachah 2.

7. The Rambam's ruling is based on the version of *Yevamot* 43a cited by Rabbenu Yitzchak Alfasi. The standard published version of the text differs and does not grant a woman license to cut her hair. See also tractate *Semachot*, ch. 7. Rashi and the other Ashkenazic commentaries follow the standard published version.

This difference of opinion is perpetuated by the Halachic authorities. The *Shulchan Aruch* (*Yoreh De'ah* 390:5) follows the Rambam's ruling, while the Ramah follows that of the Ashkenazic authorities.

8. The Radbaz questions the Rambam's wording and suggests that "and" should be substituted for "or." The person should let his hair grow until his colleagues rebuke him. The *Kessef Mishneh* justifies the Rambam's ruling, stating that even if the mourner's colleagues rebuke him before his hair grows uncontrollably long, he may cut it. He does require, however, that the mourner allow his hair to grow for at least 30 days. The Ramah (*Yoreh De'ah* 390:4) mentions opinions that require one to let his hair grow for three months and others that require one to let it grow for an entire year.

4. Similarly, [a mourner] is forbidden to wear new white clothes that have been ironed[9] for 30 days. This applies to both a man and a woman.[10] If they are colored and ironed, it is permitted.[11] Similarly, if they are not new although they are white and ironed, it is permitted.[12] There is no prohibition against wearing linen clothes that were ironed.[13]

After 30 days, one may wear ironed clothes, even if one is in mourning for one's father or mother.[14]

5. What does [the prohibition against] marriage involve? It is forbidden to marry a woman throughout these 30 days. It is, however, permitted to consecrate her[15] even on the day of the death [of one's relative].

When [a man's] wife dies, if he already fulfilled the mitzvah of procreation,[16] and he has someone to attend to him and he does not have young children, he may not remarry until three festivals[17] pass.[18] If, however, a person has not fulfilled the mitzvah of procreation, or fulfilled the mitzvah and has young children,[19] or does not have someone to attend to him, he is permitted to consecrate and marry immediately.[20] It is, however, forbidden for him to enter into relations with [his wife][21] until 30 days have passed.[22] Similarly, a woman who was in mourning should not enter into relations until 30 days have passed.[23]

6. A friendly get-together which a person is obligated to requite immediately[24] may be held immediately after the seven days of mourning. If, however, he is not obligated to requite [such a gathering], he is forbidden to enter one until 30 days pass.

7. When does the above apply? When [one is mourning for] other deceased

9. The translation of the term *gihutz* is a matter of debate. Some translate it as "launder," others as "iron," and still others as "press."
10. Although some early authorities (the *Baal Halachot Gedolot*) make a distinction between a man and a woman in this context, the Rambam does not see a Talmudic source that differentiates between them and hence rules as above.
11 . For in this instance, the fact that they are ironed is not as obvious.
12. Certainly, there is no prohibition against wearing laundered clothes (Radbaz).
13. For they do not appear as ironed for such a long period. The *Shulchan Aruch* (*Yoreh De'ah* 389:5) forbids also freshly ironed linen during the 30 days of mourning.
14. Although the Jerusalem Talmud (*Mo'ed Kattan* 3:8) mentions following restrictions for a year in the event of the death of one's parents in this instance as well, the Babylonian Talmud does not mention such restrictions and the Rambam bases his ruling on it.
15. Lest someone else consecrate her instead (see the Jerusalem Talmud, *Ta'aniot* 4:6). It is forbidden to hold a feast celebrating the consecration, however. For that is an extra measure of rejoicing which is inappropriate during the days of mourning [*Kessef Mishneh*; *Shulchan Aruch* (*Yoreh De'ah*392:1)]. The Ramah, however, forbids even consecration until the 30 days have passed. An engagement is permitted according to all opinions (*Siftei Cohen* 392:1).
16. I.e., he has both a son and a daughter, as stated in *Hilchot Ishut* 15:4.

ד וְכֵן אָסוּר לִלְבֹּשׁ כֵּלִים לְבָנִים חֲדָשִׁים וּמְגֻהָצִין כָּל שְׁלֹשִׁים יוֹם. אֶחָד הָאִישׁ וְאֶחָד הָאִשָּׁה.

הָיוּ צְבוּעִין וּמְגֻהָצִין – מֻתָּרִין. וְכֵן אִם לֹא הָיוּ חֲדָשִׁים, אַף עַל פִּי שֶׁהֵן לְבָנִים וּמְגֻהָצִין – מֻתָּרִין. וּכְלֵי פִּשְׁתָּן – אֵין בָּהֶן מִשּׁוּם גִּהוּץ. וּלְאַחַר שְׁלֹשִׁים יוֹם – מֻתָּר בְּגִהוּץ אֲפִלּוּ עַל אָבִיו וְעַל אִמּוֹ.

ה בִּנְשׂוּאִין כֵּיצַד? אָסוּר לִשָּׂא אִשָּׁה כָּל שְׁלֹשִׁים יוֹם. וּמֻתָּר לְאָרְשָׁהּ אֲפִלּוּ בְּיוֹם הַמִּיתָה. וּמִי שֶׁמֵּתָה אִשְׁתּוֹ:

אִם כְּבָר קִיֵּם מִצְוַת פְּרִיָּה וּרְבִיָּה, וְיֵשׁ לוֹ מִי שֶׁיְּשַׁמְּשֶׁנּוּ, וְאֵין לוֹ בָּנִים קְטַנִּים – הֲרֵי זֶה אָסוּר לִשָּׂא אִשָּׁה אַחֶרֶת עַד שֶׁיַּעַבְרוּ עָלָיו שְׁלֹשָׁה רְגָלִים; אֲבָל מִי שֶׁלֹּא קִיֵּם מִצְוַת פְּרִיָּה וּרְבִיָּה, אוֹ שֶׁקִּיֵּם וְיֵשׁ לוֹ בָּנִים קְטַנִּים, אוֹ שֶׁאֵין לוֹ מִי שֶׁיְּשַׁמְּשֶׁנּוּ – הֲרֵי זֶה מֻתָּר לְאָרְשָׁהּ וְלִכְנֹס מִיָּד, וְאָסוּר לוֹ לָבוֹא עָלֶיהָ עַד שְׁלֹשִׁים יוֹם. וְכֵן הָאִשָּׁה שֶׁהָיְתָה אֲבֵלָה – לֹא תִּבָּעֵל עַד שְׁלֹשִׁים יוֹם.

ו שִׂמְחַת מֵרֵעוּת שֶׁהָיָה חַיָּב לִפְרֹעַ אוֹתָהּ מִיָּד – מֻתָּר לַעֲשׂוֹתָהּ מִיָּד לְאַחַר שִׁבְעָה. אֲבָל אִם אֵינוֹ חַיָּב לְפָרְעָהּ – אָסוּר לְהִכָּנֵס לָהּ עַד שְׁלֹשִׁים יוֹם.

ז בַּמֶּה דְּבָרִים אֲמוּרִים? בִּשְׁאָר כָּל מֵתִים;

17. Rosh Hashanah and Yom Kippur are not considered festivals in this context [*Shulchan Aruch* (*Yoreh De'ah* 392:2)].
18. This will give him time for his first wife to fade from the forefront of his consciousness. Otherwise, even during times of intimacy, he will remember her and this will disturb his relationship with his new wife (*Nimukei Yosef*, commenting on *Mo'ed Kattan* 23a).
19. And there is no one to care for them.
20. The *Shulchan Aruch* (*loc. cit.*) rules that one may consecrate a woman immediately and marry her after the seven days of mourning.
21. The *Shulchan Aruch* (*loc. cit.*) rules that a person who has not fulfilled the mitzvah of procreation may engage in relationships after the seven days of mourning pass.
22. *Mo'ed Kattan, loc. cit.*, relates that the wife of the sage, Yosef HaCohen, died. He approached his sister-in-law in the cemetery and told her to care for her sister's children (implying that he would marry her). He did not, however, engage in relations with her until 30 days passed.
23. Note the *Kessef Mishneh* who rules that she may be consecrated and even married immediately. He asks, however: why is the woman required to wait 30 days before engaging in relations? If she is mourning for other people besides her husband, she should be permitted to engage in relations after the seven days of mourning. And if she is mourning for her husband, she is required to wait 90 days to establish clearly the parentage of any child she might conceive (see *Hilchot Gerushin* 11:20).
24. E.g., a friend held a celebration for him on the condition that he make a celebration in return immediately thereafter.

persons. [When mourning] for one's father or mother, by contrast, under all circumstances,[25] one is forbidden to enter a friendly gathering for twelve months.[26]

8. [When mourning] for all other deceased persons, one is permitted to go on a business trip immediately after 30 days pass.[27] [When mourning] for one's father or mother, by contrast, [one should not go] until his colleagues rebuke him and tell him: "Come with us."

9. [When mourning] for all other deceased persons,[28] if one desires, one may reduce his business activities.[29] If he does not desire, he need not reduce them. [When mourning] for one's father or mother, by contrast, one should reduce one's business activities.[30]

10. When a person is journeying from place to place,[31] he should minimize his commercial activity if possible. If not, he should purchase the articles he needs for his journey and articles which are necessary to maintain his existence.[32]

11. When a person's husband, wife, father, or mother was crucified in a city,[33] it is forbidden for him to dwell in that city until the flesh [of the corpse] decomposes.[34] If it is a major metropolis like Antioch, one may dwell in the other portion of the city, where one's relatives are not crucified.[35]

12. Even a portion of the seventh day[36] is considered as the entire day[37] and is counted both [as part of the seven days of acute mourning and the 30 days of mourning].[38] Therefore it is permissible to launder, to wash,[39] and to perform other activities[40] on the seventh day. Similarly, even a portion of the

25. Even if he made a commitment to hold such a celebration in the near future.
26. The Jerusalem Talmud (*Mo'ed Kattan* 3:8) states that leniency is granted with regard to a feast associated with a mitzvah. See the Ramah (*Yoreh De'ah* 391:1) who discusses this issue.
27. A distant business trip has a certain festive nature to it. Usually, one would go to county fairs and the like where there were entertainment and rejoicing. Ordinary commercial enterprises, by contrast, are permitted after the seven days of mourning (Radbaz; *Kessef Mishneh*).
28. This applies after the seven days of acute mourning, but during the 30 days of mourning (*Kessef Mishneh*).
29. For as reflected by *Hilchot Ta'aniot* 3:8, this is appropriate in times of disfavor.
30. For these 30 days.
31. This is speaking about a situation where the mourner heard about the death of his relative while he was on a business trip. Alternatively, if he left on a small business trip during the 30 days of mourning (Radbaz).
32. He may, however, purchase a large amount at one time. There is no need for him to purchase only the bare minimum (*Kessef Mishneh*).

אֲבָל עַל אָבִיו וְעַל אִמּוֹ, בֵּין כָּךְ וּבֵין כָּךְ – לֹא יִכָּנֵס לְשִׂמְחַת מֵרֵעוּת עַד שְׁנֵים עָשָׂר חֹדֶשׁ.

ח עַל כָּל הַמֵּתִים כֻּלָּן – מֻתָּר לֵילֵךְ בִּסְחוֹרָה לְאַחַר שְׁלשִׁים; עַל אָבִיו וְעַל אִמּוֹ – עַד שֶׁיִּגְעֲרוּ בּוֹ חֲבֵרָיו וְיֹאמְרוּ לוֹ: לֵךְ עִמָּנוּ.

ט עַל כָּל הַמֵּתִים כֻּלָּן – רָצָה מְמַעֵט בְּעִסְקוֹ, רָצָה אֵינוֹ מְמַעֵט; עַל אָבִיו וְעַל אִמּוֹ – מְמַעֵט בְּעִסְקוֹ.

י הַהוֹלֵךְ מִמָּקוֹם לְמָקוֹם: אִם יָכוֹל לְמַעֵט בְּעִסְקוֹ – יְמַעֵט; וְאִם לָאו – יִקְנֶה צָרְכֵי הַדֶּרֶךְ וּדְבָרִים שֶׁיֵּשׁ בָּהֶן חַיֵּי נֶפֶשׁ.

יא מִי שֶׁהָיָה בַּעְלָהּ צָלוּב בָּעִיר, אוֹ אִשְׁתּוֹ צְלוּבָה, אוֹ אָבִיו וְאִמּוֹ – אָסוּר לוֹ לִשְׁכֹּן בְּאוֹתָהּ הָעִיר עַד שֶׁיִּכְלֶה הַבָּשָׂר. וְאִם הָיְתָה עִיר גְּדוֹלָה כְּאַנְטוּכְיָא – יֵשׁ לוֹ לִשְׁכֹּן בַּצַּד הָאַחֵר שֶׁאֵינָן צְלוּבִין בּוֹ.

יב יוֹם שְׁבִיעִי – מִקְצָתוֹ כְּכֻלּוֹ, וְהוּא עוֹלֶה לְכָאן וּלְכָאן. וּלְפִיכָךְ מֻתָּר לְכַבֵּס וְלִרְחֹץ וְלַעֲשׂוֹת שְׁאָר הַדְּבָרִים בְּיוֹם שְׁבִיעִי.

33. The *Bayit Chadash* (*Yoreh De'ah* 346) states that this law does not apply when the crucifixion is carried out beyond the city limits.

34. In Talmudic times, the Romans would frequently crucify criminals - and innocent people who they termed criminals for their own reasons - and leave their bodies unburied for lengthy periods.

To dwell in the city would be considered as disrespectful to one's relative, for people will say: "His relative is crucified and he is continuing his life without mourning" (Radbaz). Others (*Nimukei Yosef* to *Mo'ed Kattan* 26b) state that the very fact that people see his relative will cause the deceased to lose respect, for people will recall that he was crucified.

35. For the people in that portion of the city may either not know about the crucifixion or might not know that the person is related to the one crucified (*Semachot* 2:13).

36. I.e., after any portion of time after sunrise, but all the mourning rites must be observed at night. The present custom is to come to the mourner's home for the morning prayers and then to order him to arise from mourning [Radbaz; Ramah (*Yoreh De'ah* 395:1)].

37. As stated in Chapter 7, Halachah 2, "since he observed mourning for a portion of the day, it is considered as if he observed [mourning] for the entire day."

38. Thus if a person buries his dead seven days before a festival begins, both the seven day and 30 day mourning periods are completed with the advent of the festival.

39. The Ramah (*Yoreh De'ah* 381:1) states that it has become customary to wait 30 days before washing with hot water. There are different customs depending on the norm in one's local community.

40. The other matters forbidden during the seven days of mourning. An exception is made with regard to sexual relations which are forbidden until nightfall (Rabbi Akiva Eiger).

thirtieth day is considered as the entire day and it is permitted to cut one's hair and iron one's clothes on that day.[41]

13. [The following laws apply when] one suffers several losses for which he is required to mourn one after the other. If his hair grows overly long,[42] he may trim it with a razor, but not with scissors.[43] He may wash his clothes[44] in water, but not with soap or using sand. He may wash his entire body in cold water, but not in hot water.

Similarly, when one suffers repeated losses for which he must mourn after arriving from an overseas journey, being released from captivity or prison, being released from a ban of ostracism under which he had being placed,[45] being absolved from a vow which he had taken, or emerging from a state of ritual impurity[46] to one of purity, he may cut his hair[47] in the midst of the period of mourning.[48] [The rationale is that] one period of mourning followed the other and the people did not have the opportunity [to care for themselves].

CHAPTER SEVEN

1. [The following rules apply when] a person receives a report that a [close] relative of his died. If he received the report within 30 days of the person's death - even on the thirtieth day itself - it is considered a proximate report. He must observe the seven days of mourning from the time he receives the report. He must rend his garments[1] and count 30 days for the prohibition against cutting one's hair and the other factors[2] [from that date]. The general principle is: The day on which he hears the report is like the day of the person's burial.[3]

If, however, a person receives a report after 30 days, it is considered as a distant report. He observes [mourning rites] for only one day and is not required to rend his garments.[4] It is as if the day of the report is both the seventh day and the thirtieth day.[5] [And we follow the principle:] A portion of the day is considered as the entire day.

41. It would appear that the same applies with regard to the other prohibitions mentioned in this chapter.
42. För he was not able to cut his hair at the conclusion of the first 30 days of mourning, because of the second period of mourning.
43. I.e., he must deviate from the ordinary manner of cutting his hair (Radbaz).
44. If he suffers two losses, the second in the week of mourning for the first.
45. A person who is under a ban of ostracism is forbidden to cut his hair as stated in *Hilchot Talmud Torah* 7:4.
46. The *Rambam Le'Am* states that a person who is ritually impure may not find someone to cut his hair lest that person contract ritual impurity. *Kina'at Eliyahu* notes that a person afflicted with *tzara'at* is forbidden to cut his hair (*Hilchot Tumat Tzara'at* 10:6). As stated in those halachot (10:8), all of the ritually impure were obligated to make it known to

וְכֵן יוֹם שְׁלֹשִׁים – מִקְצָתוֹ כְּכֻלּוֹ, וּמֻתָּר לְסַפֵּר וּלְגַהֵץ בְּיוֹם שְׁלֹשִׁים.

יג מִי שֶׁתְּכָפוּהוּ אֲבָלָיו וְהִכְבִּיד שְׂעָרוֹ – מֵקֵל בְּתַעַר, לֹא בְּמִסְפָּרַיִם.
וּמְכַבֵּס כְּסוּתוֹ בְּמַיִם, אֲבָל לֹא בְּנֶתֶר וְלֹא בְּחוֹל.
וְרוֹחֵץ כָּל גּוּפוֹ בְּצוֹנֵן, אֲבָל לֹא בְּחַמִּין.
וְכֵן מִי שֶׁתְּכָפוּהוּ אֲבָלָיו וּבָא מִמְּדִינַת הַיָּם וּמִבֵּית הַשִּׁבְיָה, אוֹ שֶׁיָּצָא מִבֵּית הָאֲסוּרִים, אוֹ שֶׁהָיָה מְנֻדֶּה וְהֻתַּר, אוֹ שֶׁהָיָה מֻדָּר וְנִשְׁאַל עַל נִדְרוֹ וְהֻתַּר, וְכָל הַיּוֹצֵא מִטֻּמְאָה לְטָהֳרָה – הֲרֵי אֵלּוּ מְגַלְּחִין בִּימֵי אֶבְלָם; הוֹאִיל וּתְכָפָם אֵבֶל אַחַר אֵבֶל וְלֹא מָצְאוּ פְּנַאי.

פֶּרֶק שְׁבִיעִי

א מִי שֶׁבָּאָה לוֹ שְׁמוּעָה שֶׁמֵּת לוֹ קָרוֹב: אִם בְּתוֹךְ שְׁלֹשִׁים יוֹם הִגִּיעָה הַשְּׁמוּעָה, אֲפִלּוּ יוֹם שְׁלֹשִׁים עַצְמוֹ – הֲרֵי זוֹ שְׁמוּעָה קְרוֹבָה, וְחַיָּב לִנְהֹג שִׁבְעָה יְמֵי אֲבֵלוּת מִיּוֹם שֶׁהִגִּיעָה הַשְּׁמוּעָה, וְקוֹרֵעַ. וּמוֹנֶה שְׁלֹשִׁים לְאִסּוּר הַתִּסְפֹּרֶת עִם שְׁאָר הַדְּבָרִים. כְּלָלוֹ שֶׁל דָּבָר: יוֹם שְׁמוּעָתוֹ הַקְּרוֹבָה – כְּיוֹם הַקְּבוּרָה.
אֲבָל אִם הִגִּיעָה לוֹ הַשְּׁמוּעָה אַחַר הַשְּׁלֹשִׁים יוֹם – הֲרֵי זוֹ שְׁמוּעָה רְחוֹקָה, וְאֵינָהּ נוֹהֶגֶת אֶלָּא יוֹם אֶחָד, וְאֵינוֹ קוֹרֵעַ. וּכְאִלּוּ יוֹם הַשְּׁמוּעָה הוּא יוֹם שְׁבִיעִי וְיוֹם שְׁלֹשִׁים, וּמִקְצָת הַיּוֹם כְּכֻלּוֹ.

others that they were ritually impure. Hence it is possible that one of the signs they employed was allowing their hair to grow long.
47. I.e., he may cut his hair in the ordinary manner. He need not use a razor (*Mo'ed Kattan* 17b).
48. Similarly, such individuals may launder their clothes in an ordinary manner [*Shulchan Aruch* (*Yoreh De'ah* 289:1)].

1. See Chapter 8.
2. Mentioned in Chapter 6.
3. Similarly, it is a mitzvah to provide him with a meal of comfort, as mentioned in Chapter 4, Halachah 9 and notes.
4. From the Rambam's wording here and in Chapter 8, Halachah 6, it would appear that if one hears a distant report concerning the death of his parents, he is not obligated to rend his garments. Rabbenu Yitzchak Alfasi and others differ and require one to rend his garments when he hears of his parent's death even if it occurred more than 30 days previously. Their view is recorded by the *Shulchan Aruch* (*Yoreh De'ah* 402:4).
5. A portion of the time he observes the mourning rites is considered as the seven days of acute *shivah* mourning and a portion as the thirty days of *sheloshim* mourning. Thus from this time onwards, none of the ordinary mourning rites must be observed (Radbaz).

The extra mourning practices one observes for parents (e.g., not cutting one's hair or going on a business trip until rebuked by one's friends) must, however, be observed within the year of mourning [*Shulchan Aruch* (*Yoreh De'ah* 402:1)].

2. What is implied by the statement: A portion of the day is considered as the entire day? Once one observed the mourning rites[6] for a certain time,[7] he is permitted to wear shoes, wash, anoint himself, and cut his hair during the remainder of the day.[8] Similarly, he has license [not to observe] any of the [mourning] rites.

3. When a person hears a proximate report in the midst of a festival or on the Sabbath[9] and after the Sabbath or after the festival, the report will become distant,[10] [the Sabbath or the festival] are counted for him. [Thus] he observes only one day of mourning after the festival or after the Sabbath. And a portion of the day is considered as the entire day as explained.

4. [The following rules apply when a close] relative of a person dies and that person does not know until he comes [to that place].[11] If he was in a close place, e.g., within ten *parseot* away,[12] and thus he could come in one day, even if he came on the seventh day, if he finds people offering comfort to the person of greatest stature in the family,[13] it is considered as if he was together with them and he counts with them the remainder of the 30 days.[14] [This applies] even if they had already begun to rise. As long as he finds comforters, [he counts with the other mourners].

If he did not find comforters, he counts for himself.[15] Similarly, if he comes from a distant place, even if he comes on the second day, he counts seven and thirty days for himself from the day he comes.[16]

5. During the first three days [of mourning], a mourner does not even go the house of another mourner.[17] From that time onward, he may go, but he does not sit together with those offering comfort, but with those receiving comfort. He should not leave the entrance to his house to go any place for the entire

6. The *Shulchan Aruch* (*Yoreh De'ah* 402:2) emphasizes that it is not necessary for the person to observe all the mourning rites. It is sufficient for him to observe one, e.g., removing his shoes or overturning his bed.
7. The Rambam uses the term *sha'ah* often translated as an "hour." In this instance, the intent is not an hour on the watch, but rather a significant amount of time, each person according to the time he sees fit. See (in related contexts) *Siftei Cohen* 389:4, 399:1.
8. *Mo'ed Kattan* 20b relates that Rabbi Chiyya heard a distant report of a relative's death. He told his attendant to remove his shoes and to take his personal articles to the bathhouse. From this, our Sages learned: a) a mourner is forbidden to wear shoes; b) one must only observe mourning rites for a distant report for one day; and c) a portion of the day is considered as the entire day and during the remainder one may bathe and the like.
9. On the festivals and on the Sabbath, those mourning rites that are public need not be observed. Those which are private, by contrast, should be observed [*Shulchan Aruch* (*Yoreh De'ah* 402:5)].
10. E.g., the Sabbath was the thirtieth day after his relative's death. This follows the ruling of the *Siftei Cohen* 402:5 which states that with regard to the proximity or distance of a report, we count from the death of the deceased and not from his burial.

ב כֵּיצַד מִקְצָת הַיּוֹם כְּכֻלּוֹ? כֵּיוָן שֶׁנָּהַג אֲבֵלוּת שָׁעָה אַחַת – כְּאִלּוּ נָהַג כָּל הַיּוֹם כֻּלּוֹ. וּמֻתָּר לִנְעֹל וְלִרְחֹץ וְלָסוּךְ וּלְגַלֵּחַ בִּשְׁאָר הַיּוֹם, וְכֵן הוּא מֻתָּר בְּכָל הַדְּבָרִים.

ג מִי שֶׁבָּאָה לוֹ שְׁמוּעָה קְרוֹבָה בְּתוֹךְ הָרֶגֶל אוֹ בְּיוֹם שַׁבָּת, וּלְאַחַר שַׁבָּת אוֹ אַחַר הָרֶגֶל נַעֲשֵׂת רְחוֹקָה – עוֹלֶה לוֹ, וְאֵינוֹ נוֹהֵג לְאַחַר הָרֶגֶל אוֹ לְאַחַר הַשַּׁבָּת אֶלָּא יוֹם אֶחָד בִּלְבַד, וּמִקְצָת הַיּוֹם כְּכֻלּוֹ, כְּמוֹ שֶׁבֵּאַרְנוּ.

ד מִי שֶׁמֵּת לוֹ קָרוֹב וְלֹא יָדַע עַד שֶׁבָּא: אִם הָיָה בְּמָקוֹם קָרוֹב, שֶׁהוּא מַהֲלַךְ עֲשָׂרָה פַּרְסָאוֹת, שֶׁאֶפְשָׁר שֶׁיָּבוֹא בְּיוֹם אֶחָד, אֲפִלּוּ בָּא בַּיּוֹם הַשְּׁבִיעִי, אִם מָצָא מְנַחֲמִים אֵצֶל גְּדוֹל הַבַּיִת, אַף עַל פִּי שֶׁנִּנְעֲרוּ לַעֲמֹד, הוֹאִיל וּמָצָא מְנַחֲמִים – עוֹלֶה לוֹ, וּמוֹנֶה עִמָּהֶן תַּשְׁלוּם שְׁלֹשִׁים יוֹם;

וְאִם לֹא מָצָא מְנַחֲמִים – מוֹנֶה לְעַצְמוֹ. וְכֵן אִם הָיָה בְּמָקוֹם רָחוֹק, אֲפִלּוּ בָּא בְּיוֹם שֵׁנִי – מוֹנֶה לְעַצְמוֹ שִׁבְעָה וּשְׁלֹשִׁים מִיּוֹם שֶׁבָּא.

ה אָבֵל בִּשְׁלֹשָׁה יָמִים הָרִאשׁוֹנִים – אֵינוֹ הוֹלֵךְ אֲפִלּוּ לְבֵית אֵבֶל אַחֵר; מִכָּאן וְאֵילָךְ – הוֹלֵךְ. וְאֵינוֹ יוֹשֵׁב בִּמְקוֹם הַמְנַחֲמִין, אֶלָּא בִּמְקוֹם הַמִּתְנַחֲמִין. וְלֹא יֵצֵא לְמָקוֹם אַחֵר מִפֶּתַח בֵּיתוֹ כָּל שַׁבָּת הָרִאשׁוֹנָה.

11. For we assume that had he known, he would have come, participated in the burial and begun the mourning rites together with the others (*Mo'ed Kattan* 21b). If, however, he was notified of the death in his own place and began observing the mourning rites on the second day, he does not shorten his obligation even if he comes to the place where the remainder of the family is mourning [*Shulchan Aruch* (*Yoreh De'ah* 375:9)].

The *Siftei Cohen* 375:11 emphasizes that this applies only when the family are mourning in the place where the deceased passed away or where he is buried. In other places, each person counts individually.

12. A *parsah* is four *mil*, approximately four kilometers in contemporary measure. It must be emphasized that due to the advances of transportation and communication in the present age, the relevance of this halachah is highly diminished, for there are few situations in which it applies.

13. I.e., the family is still observing the mourning rites.

14. I.e., he does not count the seven days of acute *shivah* mourning at all if he comes at their conclusion; or he counts only the remaining days if he comes in their midst.

15. Counting a full seven and thirty days.

16. Since it was impossible for him to have observed the entire mourning period together with his family, he is considered as a separate entity and must count himself (*Mo'ed Kattan* 21b).

17. I.e., this is forbidden even though it will not take his mind off his mourning. Needless to say, he is forbidden to go elsewhere, even to fulfill a mitzvah. This applies provided it is possible for others to fulfill the mitzvah. If that is not possible and the fulfillment of the mitzvah is dependent on the mourner, he may leave his home even on the first day (Radbaz).

first week.[18] During the second week, he may leave [his home], but should not sit in his ordinary place.[19] During the third week, he may sit in his ordinary place, but should not speak in his ordinary manner. During the fourth week, he is like any other person.

6. The High Priest is obligated [to observe] all the mourning practices, except that he is forbidden to rend the upper portion[20] of his garments,[21] to let his hair grow long,[22] or to follow the bier in the funeral procession.[23]

The entire [Jewish] people come to his house to comfort him.[24] When they bring him the meal of comfort, all of the people must sit on the ground;[25] he, by contrast, sits on a bench.[26] When they comfort him, they tell him: "We are atonement for you."[27] And he tells them: "May you be blessed from heaven."

If he desires to comfort others,[28] the deputee[29] has him positioned among the people.[30] And he tells the mourners: "Be comforted."

7. Similarly, a king is obligated [to observe] all the mourning practices, except that he does not leave his palace [in the funeral procession] for his dead.[31] Needless to say, this applies with regard to other deceased.[32] Nor does he comfort mourners. King David followed Avner's funeral procession only to show the people that he was not slain because of [David's] desire.[33]

8. No one enters the king's presence to comfort him except his servants and those who are given permission to enter. They do not have permission to speak words of comfort except what he allows them. When they serve him the meal of comfort, all of the others recline on the ground and he reclines on a *dargesh*.[34]

18. The Ramah (*Yoreh De'ah* 393:2) states that leniency can be granted in the evenings and if there is a necessity, a mourner may leave his home. On the Sabbath, all authorities grant a mourner license to attend the synagogue [*Shulchan Aruch* (*loc. cit.*:3)]. Similarly, if it is impossible to arrange communal prayers in the mourner's home, there are authorities who grant him license to attend the synagogue.
19. In the synagogue or in communal meeting places. The Ramah (*Yoreh De'ah* 393:2) states that at present, the custom is more severe. When mourning for others, one does not return to his place for 30 days and for his parents, for an entire year.
20. As an ordinary person does. The Rambam's wording implies that, as stated in *Horiot* 12b and cited in Chapter 8, Halachah 1, he should rend the lower portion of his garment.
21. Leviticus 21:10 states: "The High Priest... shall not let his hair grow uncontrolled, nor should he rend his garments." As stated in *Hilchot K'lei HaMikdash* 5:6, if a High Priest rends his garments, he is lashed for violating a Scriptural commandment.
22. As stated in *Hilchot K'lei HaMikdash, loc. cit.*, this applies at all times. He should have his hair trimmed each week.
23. Leviticus 21:12 states: "He shall not leave the Sanctuary." In *Hilchot K'lei HaMikdash, loc. cit.*:5, the Rambam states that he should remain either in his private home or in the Temple.
24. As stated in *Hilchot K'lei HaMikdash, loc. cit.*, for the High Priest, the people pass by

שְׁנִיָּה – יוֹצֵא, וְאֵינוֹ יוֹשֵׁב בִּמְקוֹמוֹ. שְׁלִישִׁית – יוֹשֵׁב בִּמְקוֹמוֹ, וְאֵינוֹ מְדַבֵּר כְּדַרְכּוֹ. רְבִיעִית – הֲרֵי הוּא כְּכָל אָדָם.

ו כֹּהֵן גָּדוֹל חַיָּב בְּכָל דִּבְרֵי אֲבֵלוּת, אֶלָּא שֶׁאָסוּר לוֹ לִקְרֹעַ בְּגָדָיו לְמַעְלָה, וּלְגַדֵּל פֶּרַע, וְלָצֵאת אַחַר הַמִּטָּה.
וְכָל הָעָם בָּאִין לְנַחֲמוֹ לְבֵיתוֹ. וּכְשֶׁמַּבְרִין אוֹתוֹ – כָּל הָעָם מְסֻבִּין עַל הָאָרֶץ, וְהוּא מֵסֵב עַל הַסַּפְסָל. וְאוֹמְרִין לוֹ כְּשֶׁמְּנַחֲמִין אוֹתוֹ: אָנוּ כַּפָּרָתְךָ. וְהוּא אוֹמֵר לָהֶם: תִּתְבָּרְכוּ מִן הַשָּׁמַיִם. וְאִם רָצָה לְנַחֵם אֲחֵרִים – הַמְּמֻנֶּה מְמַצְּעוֹ בְּתוֹךְ הָעָם, וְאוֹמֵר לָהֶם: תִּנָּחֲמוּ.

ז וְכֵן הַמֶּלֶךְ חַיָּב בְּכָל דִּבְרֵי אֲבֵלוּת, אֶלָּא שֶׁאֵינוֹ יוֹצֵא מִפֶּתַח פַּלְטֵרִין שֶׁלּוֹ אַחַר מֵתוֹ; וְאֵין צָרִיךְ לוֹמַר אַחַר מֵתִים אֲחֵרִים. וְאֵינוֹ מְנַחֵם אֲבֵלִים. וְלֹא יָצָא דָּוִד אַחַר אַבְנֵר, אֶלָּא לְהוֹדִיעַ לָעָם שֶׁלֹּא נֶהֱרַג בִּרְצוֹנוֹ.

ח אֵין אָדָם נִכְנָס לַמֶּלֶךְ לְנַחֲמוֹ, אֶלָּא עֲבָדָיו וּמִי שֶׁנָּתַן לוֹ רְשׁוּת לְהִכָּנֵס. וְאֵין לָהֶן רְשׁוּת לְדַבֵּר לוֹ דִּבְרֵי תַּנְחוּמִין, אֶלָּא כְּפִי מַה שֶּׁיַּרְשֶׁה אוֹתָם. וּכְשֶׁמַּבְרִין אוֹתוֹ – כָּל הָעָם מְסֻבִּין עַל הָאָרֶץ, וְהוּא מֵסֵב עַל הַדַּרְגָּשׁ.

him in a line at his home, in contrast to the ordinary practice which is described in Chapter 13, Halachah 1.

25. As the Rambam requires when visiting a mourner; see Chapter 13, Halachah 3.

26. As an expression of honor, he is not required to sit on an overturned bench like other mourners. He may not, however, sit on an ordinary chair.

27. I.e., "May everything that should happen to you happen to us" (Rashi, *Sanhedrin* 22b).

28. Visiting them at their homes (*Hilchot K'lei HaMikdash, loc. cit.*:4).

29. Who assists the High Priest in all matters; see *ibid.* 4:16.

30. In a manner befitting his dignity; see *ibid.* 5:4.

31. It is compromising for a king's dignity to appear before his people in mourning and bereavement (*Sanhedrin* 20a).

32. The *Kessef Mishneh*, in his gloss to *Hilchot Melachim* 2:4, states that unless the king has a reason that involves the nation at large, as David had with regard to Avner, he may not participate in funeral processions at all.

33. As related in II Samuel, chs. 2-3, after the death of King Saul, some of the tribes accepted Saul's son, Ish Boshet, as king, while the tribe of Judah followed David. Avner was the commander of Ish Boshet's forces and his monarchy was dependent on him. After a bloody civil war, Avner decided to end the bloodshed and accept David's kingship. Afterwards, Yoav - David's commander - perpetrated a ruse and slew Avner. David was extremely upset with Yoav's actions and exerted himself in public mourning for Avner to show that he had no hand in his death.

34. A low bed or chair with a leather base that is tied to posts by straps that is larger than a bench (the Rambam's Commentary to the Mishnah, *Sanhedrin* 2:3; *Hilchot Nedarim* 9:15).

CHAPTER EIGHT

1. A mourner is obligated to rend his garments for his dead,[1] as [can be derived from Leviticus 10:6]:[2] "Do not rend your garments lest you die." Implied is that others must rend [their garments].

One must rend one's garments only while standing,[3] as [II Samuel 13:31] states:[4] "And the king stood and rent his garments."

Where does one rend his garment? In front.[5] If one rends his garment from the back or from the sides or from the bottom, he does not fulfill the obligation[6] to rend his garments, with the exception of a High Priest who must rend his garment from the bottom.[7]

2. What is the required measure for the tear? A handbreadth. It is not necessary to rip apart the border of the garment.[8] One may rend his garments with a utensil.[9]

One may rend one's garments inside, not in the presence of others. Therefore he may place his hand inside his garment and tear it modestly.[10] He is only obligated to tear his upper garment.

3. For the entire seven days of mourning, he keeps the tear in front of him. If he desires to change his garments, he may. He is not required to rend the [second] garment, for any tear that is not made at the time of emotional excitement, is not a tear.

When does the above[11] apply? With regard to other deceased persons aside from his father and mother. For his father and mother, by contrast, he must rend his garment until he reveals his heart.[12] He must rip apart the border of the garment; he may not tear it with a utensil, and must tear it outside, in the presence of people at large.

He must tear all the garments he is wearing. His underwear - i.e., the garments worn next to his flesh - need not [be ripped]. If he changes his clothes, he is required to rend them for all seven days. Similarly, for his

1. *Mo'ed Kattan* 24a states that this obligation is so forceful that if a person fails to observe it, he is worthy of death.
2. This command was issued to Aaron and his sons after the death of his two sons, Nadav and Avihu.

The Ramban states that the obligation to rend one's garments is Rabbinic in origin and the verse is only an *asmachta*, a support. For the command to Aaron and his sons does not necessarily obligate everyone else. It could be interpreted that Aaron and his sons may not rend their garments, while everyone else is given that option (Radbaz).

3. The Radbaz states that the Rambam's wording implies that one does not fulfill his obligation if he rends his garment while seated. In his *Kessef Mishneh*, Rav Yosef Caro also advances that interpretation and cites other authorities who rule accordingly and he cites this decision in his *Shulchan Aruch* (*Yoreh De'ah* 340:1). As such, the person is required to rend his garment again (Ramah).

פֶּרֶק שְׁמִינִי

א אָבֵל חַיָּב לִקְרֹעַ עַל מֵתוֹ. שֶׁנֶּאֱמַר: וּבִגְדֵיכֶם לֹא תִפְרֹמוּ וְלֹא תָמֻתוּ. הָא אַחֵר – חַיָּב לִפְרֹם.
וְאֵין קְרִיעָה אֶלָּא מֵעֹמֶד. שֶׁנֶּאֱמַר: וַיָּקָם הַמֶּלֶךְ וַיִּקְרַע אֶת בְּגָדָיו.
וּמֵהֵיכָן קוֹרֵעַ? מִלְּפָנָיו.
וְהַקּוֹרֵעַ מֵאַחֲרָיו אוֹ מִן הַצְּדָדִין אוֹ מִלְּמַטָּה – לֹא יָצָא יְדֵי חוֹבַת קְרִיעָה.
אֶלָּא כֹּהֵן גָּדוֹל, שֶׁהוּא פּוֹרֵם מִלְּמַטָּה.

ב כַּמָּה שִׁעוּר הַקֶּרַע? טֶפַח. וְאֵין צָרִיךְ לְהַבְדִּיל שְׂפַת הַבֶּגֶד. וּמֻתָּר לוֹ לִקְרֹעַ בִּכְלִי.
וְיֵשׁ לוֹ לִקְרֹעַ בִּפְנִים, שֶׁלֹּא בִּפְנֵי אָדָם. לְפִיכָךְ יֵשׁ לוֹ לְהַכְנִיס יָדוֹ בִּפְנִים וְקוֹרֵעַ בְּצִנְעָה.
וְאֵינוֹ חַיָּב לִקְרֹעַ אֶלָּא בֶּגֶד הָעֶלְיוֹן בִּלְבַד.

ג כָּל שִׁבְעַת יְמֵי אֲבֵלוּת הַקֶּרַע לְפָנִים. וְאִם בָּא לְהַחֲלִיף – מַחֲלִיף, וְאֵינוֹ קוֹרֵעַ קֶרַע אַחֵר; שֶׁכָּל קֶרַע שֶׁאֵינוֹ בִּשְׁעַת חִמּוּם – אֵינוֹ קֶרַע.
בַּמֶּה דְּבָרִים אֲמוּרִים? בִּשְׁאָר הַמֵּתִים חוּץ מֵאָבִיו וְאִמּוֹ; אֲבָל עַל אָבִיו וְעַל אִמּוֹ – קוֹרֵעַ עַד שֶׁמְּגַלֶּה אֶת לִבּוֹ. וּמַבְדִּיל שְׂפַת הַבֶּגֶד. וְאֵינוֹ קוֹרֵעַ בִּכְלִי, אֶלָּא בְּיָדוֹ. מִבַּחוּץ, בִּפְנֵי כָּל הָעָם.
וְקוֹרֵעַ כָּל הַבְּגָדִים שֶׁעָלָיו. וּבֶגֶד הַזֵּעָה הַדָּבוּק לִבְשָׂרוֹ – אֵינוֹ מְעַכֵּב. וְאִם הֶחֱלִיף בֶּגֶד אַחֵר – חַיָּב לִקְרֹעַ כָּל שִׁבְעָה.

4. I.e., King David rent his clothes when he heard a report that his sons had been slain.
5. From one's collar.
6. The Ramah (*loc. cit.*:2) states that one may rend the lower hem of his garment when rending his garments for deceased persons for whom he is not obligated to mourn (e.g., one was present at the time of a person's death), but for one's relatives for whom he is obligated to mourn, he must rend his garments at the front collar.
7. See Chapter 7, Halachah 6.
8. Instead, one may leave the border whole and tear only the fabric below it. The *Shulchan Aruch* (*Yoreh De'ah* 340:12) quotes this halachah. The Ramah, however, differs and states that one is liable to rend the border for all deceased.
9. E.g., a knife or a scissors.
10. *Mo'ed Kattan* 22b states: "For all other deceased, if one desires one may rend the garment inside or one may rend it outside." The commentaries offer two interpretations of this statement: a) he may tear the garment in the privacy of his own room (Rashi); b) he may tear only the underside of the garment. It appears that the Rambam accepts both of these interpretations (*Kessef Mishneh*).
11. I.e., the leniencies mentioned in the previous clause and in the previous halachah.
12. I.e., the tear is longer than a handbreadth.
The Jerusalem Talmud (*Mo'ed Kattan* 3:8) states that this is required because he is losing the mitzvah of honoring his parents which is dependent on the heart.

father and mother, he uncovers his shoulder and takes his forearm out from his garment, revealing his shoulder and his forearm. He passes before the bier in this manner. After his father and his mother are buried, however, he is not required to uncover [his shoulder].[13]

4. A child's garments should be torn [to create] sorrow.[14]

When a dangerously ill person loses [a close relative], we do not rend his garments, nor do we notify him lest he lose control of his emotions.[15] We silence the women in his presence.[16]

5. A person should rend his garments [when] his father-in-law and mother-in-law[17] [dies] as an expression of honor for his wife.[18] Similarly, a woman should rend her garments for her father-in-law and mother-in-law as an expression of honor for her husband.

6. When a person does not have an outer garment to tear [at the time of a person's passing][19] and he obtains a garment within the seven days of mourning, he is obligated to tear it. After seven days, he is not obligated to tear it.[20] For his father and mother, he is obligated to tear it even [if he obtains it after the seven days], but within the 30 days.[21]

Whenever a person goes out wearing a torn garment before the dead implying that he tore the garment because of them, he is deceiving people and degrading the honor of the dead and the living.

7. When one tells a colleague: "Lend me your cloak so that I can visit my father who is dangerously ill," if, when he visits him, he finds that he died, he should rend the garment, mend it,[22] and return it, reimbursing [the owner] for the tear.[23] If he does not notify him that he is going to visit a person who is dangerously ill, he should not touch [the garment].[24]

13. This additional measure of mourning is included to show the intensity of his grief. See the gloss of the Radbaz to Chapter 9, Halachah 11, which explains that for one's parents one may uncover either one's left or one's right shoulder.

Although the *Shulchan Aruch* (*Yoreh De'ah* 340:16) quotes the Rambam's ruling, the Ramah (*loc. cit.*:17) writes that it is not customary to uncover one's shoulder in the present era. This is also the contemporary practice in the overwhelming majority of Sephardic communities today.

14. I.e., so that others should see and cry over the deceased's passing (Rashi, *Mo'ed Kattan* 14b). This applies even when the child is too young to be trained in the observance of the mitzvot (Radbaz).

15. For we fear that emotional aggravation might be perilous for him.

The *Siftei Cohen* 337:1 states that even if the sick person knows of his relative's passing, his garments should not be rent, because the torn garments will continually remind him of his loss.

16. Lest their mourning make him aware of his loss. The *Siftei Cohen* 337:2 states that,

וְכֵן עַל אָבִיו וְעַל אִמּוֹ – חוֹלֵץ כְּתֵפוֹ וּמוֹצִיא זְרוֹעוֹ מִן הֶחָלוּק עַד שֶׁיִּתְגַּלֶּה כְּתֵפוֹ וּזְרוֹעוֹ, וְהוֹלֵךְ כָּךְ לִפְנֵי הַמִּטָּה. וְאַחַר שֶׁיִּקָּבֵר אָבִיו וְאִמּוֹ – אֵינוֹ חַיָּב לַחֲלֹץ.

ד קוֹרְעִין לְקָטָן, מִפְּנֵי עָגְמַת נֶפֶשׁ. וְחוֹלֶה שֶׁמֵּת לוֹ מֵת – אֵין מְקָרְעִין לוֹ, וְלֹא מוֹדִיעִין לוֹ, שֶׁלֹּא תִּטָּרֵף עָלָיו דַּעְתּוֹ. וּמְשַׁתְּקִין אֶת הַנָּשִׁים מִפָּנָיו.

ה וְקוֹרֵעַ אָדָם עַל חָמִיו וְעַל חֲמוֹתוֹ, מִפְּנֵי כְּבוֹד אִשְׁתּוֹ. וְכֵן הָאִשָּׁה קוֹרַעַת עַל חָמִיהָ וְעַל חֲמוֹתָהּ, מִפְּנֵי כְּבוֹד בַּעְלָהּ.

ו מִי שֶׁאֵין לוֹ חָלוּק לִקְרֹעַ, וְנִזְדַּמֵּן לוֹ חָלוּק בְּתוֹךְ שִׁבְעָה – קוֹרֵעַ; לְאַחַר שִׁבְעָה – אֵינוֹ קוֹרֵעַ. וְעַל אָבִיו וְעַל אִמּוֹ, אֲפִלּוּ לְאַחַר שִׁבְעָה – קוֹרֵעַ כָּל שְׁלֹשִׁים יוֹם.
וְכָל הַיּוֹצֵא בְּבֶגֶד קָרוּעַ לִפְנֵי מֵתִים, כְּלוֹמַר שֶׁהוּא קָרַע עַתָּה עֲלֵיהֶן – הֲרֵי זֶה גּוֹנֵב דַּעַת הַבְּרִיּוֹת, וְזִלְזֵל בִּכְבוֹד הַחַיִּים וְהַמֵּתִים.

ז הָאוֹמֵר לַחֲבֵרוֹ: הַשְׁאִילֵנִי חֲלוּקְךָ וַאֲבַקֵּר אֶת אָבִי שֶׁהוּא חוֹלֶה, וְהָלַךְ וּמְצָאוֹ שֶׁמֵּת – קוֹרֵעַ וּמְאַחֶה, וּמַחֲזִיר לוֹ אֶת חֲלוּקוֹ, וְנוֹתֵן לוֹ דְּמֵי קִרְעוֹ. וְאִם לֹא הוֹדִיעוֹ שֶׁהוּא מְבַקֵּר לוֹ חוֹלֶה – הֲרֵי זֶה לֹא יִגַּע בּוֹ.

when a person is dangerously ill, we should not mention the death of any others, even people to whom he is not related, in his presence for that is likely to depress him.

17. But not because of any of her other relatives (*Siftei Cohen* 340:6).

18. He need not rend his garments in the same manner as his wife does. It is sufficient for him to rend them a handbreadth as one does for deceased other than one's parents (Radbaz). Although the *Shulchan Aruch* (*Yoreh De'ah* 340:4) quotes the Rambam's ruling, the Ramah explains that this practice is not observed in the present era.

19. E.g., he was wearing a garment belonging to a colleague (Ramban to *Mo'ed Kattan* 20b).

20. For this is after the period of mourning and one's garments should not be torn afterwards (*Mo'ed Kattan* 20b).

21. The Radbaz quotes opinions that mention that for one's father and mother, one should rend one's garments for a year. The *Shulchan Aruch* (*Yoreh De'ah* 340:18) states that for his father and mother, one should rend his garment "forever."

22. Generally, one may not mend a garment torn because of the passing of one's parent (Chapter 9, Halachah 1). An exception is made in this instance because we are speaking about a borrowed garment (*Nimukei Yosef*).

23. Implicit in telling the owner that his father was dangerously ill was the request to tear the garment if necessary. Nevertheless, obviously, he must reimburse the owner for his loss (*Mo'ed Kattan* 26b).

24. For he has no permission to rend it. If he tears the garment, he is considered to be stealing it - for he is taking it for a purpose for which he did not notify the owner. Hence, he is considered not to have fulfilled his obligation for rending his garments. See *Shulchan Aruch* (*Yoreh De'ah* 340:19).

8. [The following rules apply when] one has a dangerously ill person in his home, that person faints and he thinks that he has died and [hence,] he rends his garments, [the sick person regains consciousness and] then dies. If he dies immediately[25] [after the garments are torn], he need not rend [his garments] again.[26] If he dies after even a short time[27] has past, he must rend [his garments] again.[28]

Similar [concepts apply] if someone tells a person that his father died and he therefore rent his garments and then it was discovered that his son died or if someone told him that a person close to him[29] died, he thought it was his father and rent his garments and then he discovered that it was his son. If he realized the true situation immediately afterwards, he fulfilled the obligation to rend his garments. If he did not realize this until afterwards, he did not fulfill his obligation and is obligated to rend his garments again.[30]

9. When many close relatives die at once,[31] a person should rend his garments once for all of them. If his father or mother are among them, he should rend his garments once for all the others, and once for his father or mother.[32]

10. [The following rules apply when] a person's close relative dies, he rends his garments because of him and then another close relative[33] dies. If [the second relative dies] within the seven days [of mourning], he should tear his garments again.[34] If it is after the seven days, he [need] only add the slightest amount to the original tear.[35]

If a third close relative dies after the seven days of mourning for the second, [again,] he [need] only add the slightest amount to the original tear.[36] And he can continue in this manner until he reaches his navel. Once he reaches his navel, he should distance himself at least three thumbbreadths and rend [the garment again].

When [the garment] is entirely [torn] in front, he may turn it around. When its upper portion is entirely [torn], he may make the bottom the top.

If he was told: "Your father died," and he rent his garments and after the seven days [of mourning], his son died and he extended the tear, he may mend the lower tear, but not the upper tear as will be explained.[37] If he was told: "Your son died," and he rent his garments and after the seven days [of mourning], his father died, he may not merely extend the tear. Instead, he must make a new tear. For extending a tear is not sufficient for his father and mother.

25. The Hebrew expression used by the Rambam has a very specific meaning: the amount of time it takes to greet one's teacher, saying: *Shalom eleche, rabbi* (*Hilchot Sh'vuot* 2:17).

26. Since he died immediately thereafter, it is as if he died at the time the tear was made (Rabbenu Nissim, gloss to *Nedarim* 87a).

27. More than it takes to make that statement.

28. Since the person did not die until some time after the garments were torn, the tearing is not associated with the death. He need not, however, make an entirely new tear; it is

ח מִי שֶׁהָיָה לוֹ חוֹלֶה בְּתוֹךְ בֵּיתוֹ וְנִתְעַלֵּף, וְסָבוּר שֶׁמֵּת וְקָרַע, וְאַחַר כָּךְ מֵת:
אִם בְּתוֹךְ כְּדֵי דִבּוּר – אֵינוֹ חוֹזֵר וְקוֹרֵעַ;
וְאִם לְאַחַר כְּדֵי דִבּוּר מֵת – חוֹזֵר וְקוֹרֵעַ קֶרַע אַחֵר.
וְכֵן מִי שֶׁאָמְרוּ לוֹ מֵת אָבִיו, וְקָרַע, וְאַחַר כָּךְ נִמְצָא שֶׁמֵּת בְּנוֹ;
אָמְרוּ לוֹ מֵת לוֹ מֵת, וּכְסָבוּר שֶׁאָבִיו וְקָרַע, וְאַחַר כָּךְ נִמְצָא בְּנוֹ:
אִם תּוֹךְ כְּדֵי דִבּוּר נוֹדַע לוֹ אֲמִתַּת הַדָּבָר – יָצָא יְדֵי קְרִיעָה;
וְאִם לְאַחַר כְּדֵי דִבּוּר – לֹא יָצָא, וְחַיָּב לִקְרֹעַ קֶרַע אַחֵר.

ט מִי שֶׁמֵּתוּ לוֹ מֵתִים הַרְבֵּה כְּאֶחָד – קוֹרֵעַ קֶרַע אֶחָד לְכֻלָּם. הָיָה בִּכְלָלָן אָבִיו אוֹ אִמּוֹ – קוֹרֵעַ עַל כֻּלָּן קֶרַע אֶחָד, וְעַל אָבִיו וְעַל אִמּוֹ קֶרַע אַחֵר.

י מִי שֶׁמֵּת לוֹ מֵת וְקָרַע עָלָיו, וְאַחַר כָּךְ מֵת לוֹ מֵת אַחֵר: אִם בְּתוֹךְ שִׁבְעָה – קוֹרֵעַ קֶרַע אַחֵר; וְאִם לְאַחַר שִׁבְעָה – מוֹסִיף עַל הַקֶּרַע הָרִאשׁוֹן כָּל שֶׁהוּא.
מֵת לוֹ מֵת שְׁלִישִׁי אַחַר שִׁבְעָה שֶׁל שֵׁנִי – מוֹסִיף כָּל שֶׁהוּא. וְכֵן מוֹסִיף וְהוֹלֵךְ עַד טַבּוּרוֹ.
הִגִּיעַ לְטַבּוּרוֹ – מַרְחִיק שָׁלֹשׁ אֶצְבָּעוֹת וְקוֹרֵעַ.
נִתְמַלֵּא מִלְּפָנָיו – מַחֲזִירוֹ לַאֲחוֹרָיו. נִתְמַלֵּא מִלְמַעְלָה – הוֹפְכוֹ לְמַטָּה. אָמְרוּ לוֹ מֵת אָבִיו, וְקָרַע, וְאַחַר שִׁבְעָה מֵת בְּנוֹ וְהוֹסִיף – מִתְאַחֶה הַתַּחְתּוֹן וְלֹא הָעֶלְיוֹן, כְּמוֹ שֶׁיִּתְבָּאֵר. אָמְרוּ לוֹ מֵת בְּנוֹ, וְקָרַע, וְאַחַר שִׁבְעָה מֵת אָבִיו – אֵינוֹ מוֹסִיף, אֶלָּא קוֹרֵעַ קֶרַע אַחֵר; שֶׁאֵין אָבִיו וְאִמּוֹ בְּתוֹסֶפֶת.

sufficient for him to increase the existing tear a handbreadth (see Halachah 12 and notes; *Turei Zahav* 340:12; *Siftei Cohen* 240:31). All this applies with regard to other relatives; for one's parents, he is required to make an entirely new tear.
29. Without specifying that person's identity.
30. Although he rent his garments after the person's death, since he did not know the true identity of the person who died at the time he rent his garments, he has not fulfilled his obligation.
31. Or he hears about their death at the same time even though they died at different times [*Shulchan Aruch* (*Yoreh De'ah* 340:23)].
32. Giving them additional honor by showing an extra measure of grief for them. The Radbaz states that if a person loses both his father and mother at the same time, it is sufficient to rend his garments once for both of them.
33. Other than one of his parents as stated at the conclusion of the halachah.
34. Ripping the original tear another handbreadth or making a new tear at least three thumbbreadths from the first tear (*Kessef Mishneh*). For adding to an existing tear is not a sufficient expression of mourning for his relative.
35. Since the original tear could have been mended by this time, undoing the mend is considered as a new tear if a slight addition is made (*Mo'ed Kattan* 26b).
36. If, however, he dies within the week of mourning, he must make a third tear.
37. In Chapter 9, Halachah 1, which states that one may not mend clothes one tears in mourning for one's parents.

CHAPTER NINE

1. Whenever a person rends his garments after the loss of a relative other [than a parent], he may sew the tear after the seven [days of mourning] and mend it after thirty days.[1] For one's father and mother, he may sew the tear after thirty days, but may never mend it.[2] A woman should rend her garments and sew them immediately, even [when she lost] a father or mother, as an expression of modesty.[3]

2. Just as a person must rend [his garments] for [the loss of] his father and mother; so, too, he is obligated to rend his garments for [the loss of] a teacher who instructed him in the Torah,[4] a *nasi*,[5] the *av beit din*,[6] the majority of the community[7] who were slain, the cursing of God's name, the burning of a Torah scroll, [when seeing] the cities[8] of Judah, Jerusalem, and the Temple [in their destruction].[9]

3. All of these tears should be rent to the extent that one reveals his heart and they should never be mended. Although they should never be mended, they may be sewed irregularly, sewn after the sides are wound or twisted together, or sewn like ladders. All that was forbidden was Alexandrian mending.[10]

Whenever a person tears [a garment] in a place where it was sewn irregularly or sewn after the sides were wound and twisted together, his act is of no consequence. If, however, he rips [a garment] where it has been mended in an Alexandrian manner, [it is of consequence].[11]

Even if one turns a [rent] garment upside down and makes its collar its hem, he should not mend it.[12]

4. Just as the seller[13] may not mend it; so, too, the purchaser may not. Therefore the seller must notify the purchaser that this tear may not be mended.[14]

1. Sewing refers to stitching the garment in a non-professional manner in which the sides of the tear are not evenly joined. Mending it refers to repairing it in a manner that - to whatever degree possible - the tear cannot be recognized.
2. For his parent's passing is a loss that cannot be restored.
3. *Shulchan Aruch* (*Yoreh De'ah* 340:15) quotes *Mo'ed Kattan* 22b which states that a woman may sew her garment immediately because of her honor. Implied is that even when it will not be immodest for her to walk around with the tear - because she is wearing undergarments - she may mend her clothes for women feel extremely uncomfortable wearing torn garments.
4. In *Hilchot Talmud Torah* 5:9, the Rambam writes:

> When his master dies, he should rend all of his garments until he reveals his heart; he may never mend them.
> When does the above apply? With regard to one's outstanding teacher from whom one has gained the majority of his wisdom. If, however, one has not gained the majority of his wisdom from him... he should rend his garments [at his death] as he does for all the deceased for whom he is obligated to mourn. Even if he learned only one thing from him... he should rend his garments because of his [death].

פֶּרֶק תְּשִׁיעִי

א כָּל הַקְּרָעִים שֶׁקּוֹרֵעַ אָדָם עַל שְׁאָר קְרוֹבָיו – שׁוֹלֵל הַקֶּרַע לְאַחַר שִׁבְעָה, וּמְאַחֶה לְאַחַר שְׁלשִׁים. עַל אָבִיו וְעַל אִמּוֹ – שׁוֹלֵל לְאַחַר שְׁלשִׁים, וְאֵינוֹ מְאַחֶה לְעוֹלָם. וְהָאִשָּׁה קוֹרַעַת וְשׁוֹלֶלֶת מִיָּד, אֲפִלּוּ עַל אָבִיהָ וְעַל אִמָּהּ, מִפְּנֵי הַצְּנִיעוּת.

ב כְּדֶרֶךְ שֶׁקּוֹרֵעַ אָדָם עַל אָבִיו וְעַל אִמּוֹ, כָּךְ חַיָּב לִקְרֹעַ עַל רַבּוֹ שֶׁלִּמְּדוֹ תּוֹרָה, וְעַל הַנָּשִׂיא, וְעַל אַב בֵּית דִּין, וְעַל רֹב הַצִּבּוּר שֶׁנֶּהֱרַג, וְעַל בִּרְכַּת הַשֵּׁם, וְעַל סֵפֶר תּוֹרָה שֶׁנִּשְׂרַף, וְעַל עָרֵי יְהוּדָה, וְעַל יְרוּשָׁלַיִם, וְעַל הַמִּקְדָּשׁ.

ג כָּל אֵלּוּ הַקְּרָעִים קוֹרֵעַ עַד שֶׁמְּגַלֶּה אֶת לִבּוֹ, וְאֵינוֹ מְאַחֶה לְעוֹלָם. וְאַף עַל פִּי שֶׁאֵין מִתְאַחִין – מֻתָּר לְשָׁלְלָן, לְמָלְלָן וּלְלָקְטָן, וְלַעֲשׂוֹתָם כְּמִין סֻלָּמוֹת; וְלֹא אָסְרוּ אֶלָּא בְּאִחוּי אֲלֶכְּסַנְדְּרִי בִּלְבַד. וְכָל הַקּוֹרֵעַ מִתּוֹךְ הַשְּׁלָל אוֹ הַמְּלָל אוֹ הַלָּקוּט – לֹא עָשָׂה כְלוּם; אֲבָל קוֹרֵעַ מִתּוֹךְ הָאִחוּי הָאֲלֶכְּסַנְדְּרִי בִּלְבַד. אֲפִלּוּ הָפַךְ הַכְּלִי וְנַעֲשָׂה שְׂפָתוֹ לְמַטָּה – לֹא יְאַחֶה.

ד וּכְשֵׁם שֶׁהַמּוֹכֵר אָסוּר לְאַחוֹתוֹ, כָּךְ הַלּוֹקֵחַ. לְפִיכָךְ, הַמּוֹכֵר צָרִיךְ לְהוֹדִיעַ לַלּוֹקֵחַ שֶׁקֶּרַע זֶה אֵינוֹ מִתְאַחֶה.

See also Halachah 11 and notes.

5. The term *nasi* refers to the head of the *Sanhedrin* (*Hilchot Sanhedrin* 1:3). It is also used in reference to a king. From the fact that the *Shulchan Aruch* (*Yoreh De'ah* 340:17) quotes this law, one may conclude that it also refers to an outstanding Torah leader in any particular age.

6. The Sage who is second in stature in the *Sanhedrin.*

7. I.e., the majority of the Jewish people (Rashi, *Mo'ed Kattan* 26a).

8. Although the standard published texts state "the mountains of Judah," from Halachah 10, it is obvious that this is printing error.

9. This ruling definitely applies in the present age. Nevertheless, we find that there are many - even scholars of distinguished piety and knowledge - who do not rend their garments every time they visit Jerusalem beyond a 30 day interval. While an adequate halachic explanation for this lack of observance is not available, one of the ways to avoid the difficulty is to used borrowed clothes when visiting these places or to come on the Sabbath when it is forbidden to rend one's garments.

10. In which instance the tear is not noticeable on the surface of the garment.

11. Since it was mended in a manner in which the tear was not noticeable, it is as if it was being rent for the first time.

12. For the tear should remain distinct.

13. I.e., the original owner of the garment who tore it in mourning.

14. For otherwise, the seller will have deceived the purchaser. Moreover, if a person is sold a torn garment, he may not mend it until he clarifies that it was not torn in mourning.

5. What is the source that teaches that one is obligated to rend his garments at his teacher's [death] just as he rends his garments for his father? [II Kings 2:12] states:[15] "He was calling out: 'My father, my father, the chariot of Israel and its horsemen.' And then he no longer saw him. And he took hold of his garments and tore them into two halves." This teaches that one must rip apart the collar.[16]

6. What is the source that teaches that one is obligated to rend his garments at [the death of] the *nasi*, the *av beit din*, and a report that the majority of the community have been slain?[17] [II Samuel 1:11-12] relates: "David took hold of his garments and rent them as did all the people who were with him. They mourned, they cried, and they fasted until the evening for Saul - the *nasi* - for his son Jonathan - the *av beit din* - and for[18] the people of God and the House of Israel for they fell by the sword" - this is an unfavorable report.

7. What is the source which teaches that one is obligated to rend his garments when hearing the blasphemy of God's name? [II Kings 18:37] states:[19] "And Elyakim ben Chilkiyah, who oversaw the palace, Shevna, the scribe, and Yoach ben Asaf, the secretary, came to Chizkiyahu with rent garments." Just as one who hears [the blasphemy itself] must rend his garments; so, too, one who hears [the report of the blasphemy] from the listeners must rend his garments.[20]

8. The witnesses are not obligated to rend their garments when they testify in court,[21] for they already tore them when they heard the blasphemy.[22]

9. What is the source which teaches that one is obligated to rend his garments for a Torah scroll[23] that is burnt?[24] [Jeremiah 36:23-24] states:[25] "And it came to pass that when Yehudi would read three or four columns... until the entire scroll was consumed by the fire in the hearth. And neither the king nor his servants became fearful, nor did they rend their garments." Implied is that one is obligated to rend one's garments.

Similarly a torn garment may not be sold to a gentile, for we fear that he will mend it [*Tur*; *Shulchan Aruch* (*Yoreh De'ah* 340:19)].

15. When describing Elisha's conduct as Elijah was being taken to heaven. Although Elijah ascended into heaven alive and did not die, for Elisha, it was as if he was dead (*Mo'ed Kattan* 26a).

16. As one is obligated to do at the death of a parent, but not at the death of another relative (Chapter 8, Halachah 2).

17. When quoting this law, the *Shulchan Aruch* (*Yoreh De'ah* 340:36) deviates slightly from the Rambam's wording, stating: "One must rend his garments because of an unfavorable report, e.g., that the majority of the community gather for a battle, and one hears that they fled before their enemies. [This applies] even if only a minority were slain." The Ramah adds: "The same law applies if they were taken captive."

ה וּמִנַּיִן שֶׁקּוֹרֵעַ עַל רַבּוֹ כְּדֶרֶךְ שֶׁקּוֹרֵעַ עַל אָבִיו?
שֶׁנֶּאֱמַר: וְהוּא מְצַעֵק אָבִי אָבִי רֶכֶב יִשְׂרָאֵל וּפָרָשָׁיו, וְלֹא רָאָהוּ עוֹד, וַיַּחֲזֵק בִּבְגָדָיו וַיִּקְרָעֵם לִשְׁנַיִם קְרָעִים.
מִכָּאן, שֶׁחַיָּב לְהַבְדִּיל הַשָּׂפָה.

ו וּמִנַּיִן שֶׁקּוֹרְעִין עַל הַנָּשִׂיא וְעַל אַב בֵּית דִּין וְעַל שְׁמוּעָה שֶׁבָּאָה שֶׁנֶּהֱרַג רֹב צִבּוּר?
שֶׁנֶּאֱמַר: וַיַּחֲזֵק דָּוִד בִּבְגָדָיו וַיִּקְרָעֵם, וְגַם כָּל הָאֲנָשִׁים אֲשֶׁר אִתּוֹ. וַיִּסְפְּדוּ וַיִּבְכּוּ וַיָּצֻמוּ עַד הָעָרֶב, עַל שָׁאוּל – זֶה נָשִׂיא, וְעַל יְהוֹנָתָן בְּנוֹ – זֶה אַב בֵּית דִּין, וְעַל עַם יְיָ וְעַל בֵּית יִשְׂרָאֵל כִּי נָפְלוּ בֶּחָרֶב – זוֹ שְׁמוּעָה רָעָה.

ז וּמִנַּיִן שֶׁקּוֹרְעִין עַל בִּרְכַּת הַשֵּׁם? שֶׁנֶּאֱמַר: וַיָּבֹא אֶלְיָקִים בֶּן חִלְקִיָּהוּ אֲשֶׁר עַל הַבַּיִת וְשֶׁבְנָא הַסֹּפֵר וְיוֹאָח בֶּן אָסָף הַמַּזְכִּיר אֶל חִזְקִיָּהוּ קְרוּעֵי בְגָדִים. אֶחָד הַשּׁוֹמֵעַ וְאֶחָד הַשּׁוֹמֵעַ מִפִּי שׁוֹמֵעַ חַיָּבִין לִקְרֹעַ.

ח וְהָעֵדִים אֵין חַיָּבִין לִקְרֹעַ כְּשֶׁיָּעִידוּ בְּבֵית דִּין, שֶׁכְּבָר קָרְעוּ בְּשָׁעָה שֶׁשָּׁמְעוּ.

ט וּמִנַּיִן שֶׁקּוֹרְעִין עַל סֵפֶר תּוֹרָה שֶׁנִּשְׂרַף? שֶׁנֶּאֱמַר: וַיְהִי כִּקְרוֹא יְהוּדִי שָׁלֹשׁ דְּלָתוֹת וְאַרְבָּעָה וְגוֹמֵר, עַד תֹּם כָּל הַמְּגִלָּה עַל הָאֵשׁ אֲשֶׁר עַל הָאָח, וְלֹא פָחֲדוּ וְלֹא קָרְעוּ אֶת בִּגְדֵיהֶם הַמֶּלֶךְ וְכָל עֲבָדָיו. מִכְּלָל שֶׁחַיָּבִין לִקְרֹעַ.

18. Since the verse states "for" before the object of each clause, we can infer that each of these tidings is - in and of itself - sufficient to warrant the rending of one's garments (*Mo'ed Kattan* 26a).
19. With regard to Ravshakeh's - the agent of King Sannecherib, but according to tradition (*Sanhedrin* 60a) an apostate Jew - blasphemy of God's name during the siege of Jerusalem. See also Isaiah, chs. 36 and 37, which describes this event.
20. For Chizkiyahu rent his garments upon hearing the report of the blasphemy from these men (II Kings 19:1). See *Hilchot Avodat Kochavim* 2:10 which also describes the obligation to rend one's garments in this instance within the context of its discussion of the prohibition of blasphemy.
21. Who relate how the blasphemer cursed God's name in court, repeating his words; see *Hilchot Avodat Kochavim* 2:8.
22. *Sanhedrin* 60a derives this from the above narrative which relates that Chizkiyahu rent his garments, but the others did not. Why didn't they? Because they had rent them when they heard the blasphemy.
23. See also *Shulchan Aruch* (*Yoreh De'ah* 340:37) which states that the same law applies with regard to a scroll of the Books of the Prophets or *tefillin* which are burnt.
24. Similar laws apply if a scroll is torn or erased in a forceful manner. For one is mourning the desecration of God's name (*Siftei Cohen* 340:56).
25. In its description of the burning of the scroll of prophesy which Jeremiah had prepared by King Yehoyakim.

One is obligated to rend one's garments only because of a Torah scroll that was burnt arrogantly as in the incident cited. One is obligated to rend one's garments twice: once for the parchment and once for the writing, as [*ibid.*:27] states: "After the king burnt the scroll and the words."

10. What is the source which teaches that one is obligated to rend his garments [when seeing] the cities of Judah, Jerusalem, and the Temple [in their destruction]? [Jeremiah 41:5] relates:[26] "Men came from Shechem, from Shiloh, and from Samaria, eighty men with their beards shaven and their garments rent."[27]

11. Whoever is present with a dying person[28] at the time his soul expires is obligated to rend his garments even if he is not his relative.[29] Similarly, when a virtuous person[30] dies, everyone[31] is obligated to rend his garments because of him, even though he is not a sage. They tear [them] a handbreadth as other mourners do. When, however, a sage[32] dies, everyone is considered as his relative. They rend their garments for him until they reveal their hearts and uncover their right arms.[33] The house of study of that sage should be discontinued for all seven days [of mourning].[34]

Torah scholars[35] have universally accepted the custom of rending their garments for a handbreadth in respect for each other even though they are equal in stature and neither of them teaches the other.

12. Whenever a person rends his garments because of a sage who dies, as soon as he turns away from the bier,[36] he may sew it irregularly. It appears to me that when a person rends his garments for a sage, he may mend them on the following day. For even when his teacher dies, one should mourn for him for only one day,[37] either the day of his death or the day he hears the report of his death.

26. The people described in the verse had journeyed to bring sacrifices in the Temple only to find that it had been destroyed by the Babylonians.
27. See *Hilchot Ta'anit* 5:16-18 where the Rambam also discusses this obligation.
28. Man or woman [*Kessef Mishneh*; *Shulchan Aruch* (*Yoreh De'ah* 340:5)]. See *Turei Zahav* 340:2.
29. *Mo'ed Kattan* 25a explains that the passing of any person is comparable to the burning of a Torah scroll for both the Torah and the soul are called "the lamp of God" (Rashi). In his *Kessef Mishneh* and his *Shulchan Aruch* (*loc. cit.*), R. Yosef Karo cites the ruling of the Maharam of Rutenberg who states that this applies even to a Jew who transgresses, as long as he does not do so in conscious rebellion against God.
30. I.e., a person who is reputed to observe mitzvot, eschew prohibitions, and conduct himself in a moral manner [*Shulchan Aruch* (*Yoreh De'ah* 340:6)].
31. Even those people who were not present at the time of the person's death. If they encounter the corpse before its burial (or hear about the person's passing according to *Siftei Cohen* 340:12), they must rend their garments [*Shulchan Aruch* (*Yoreh De'ah* 340:6)]. The Ramah, however, quotes the *Hagahot Maimoniot* which state that although one must mourn over the death of every Jew, the custom is that only those present at the time of a person's death are required to rend their garments.

וְאֵין חַיָּבִין לִקְרֹעַ אֶלָּא עַל סֵפֶר תּוֹרָה שֶׁנִּשְׂרַף בִּזְרוֹעַ, כְּמַעֲשֶׂה שֶׁהָיָה. וְחַיָּב לִקְרֹעַ שְׁתֵּי קְרִיעוֹת: אַחַת עַל הַגְּוִיל וְאַחַת עַל הַכְּתָב. שֶׁנֶּאֱמַר: אַחֲרֵי שְׂרֹף הַמֶּלֶךְ אֶת הַמְּגִלָּה וְאֶת הַדְּבָרִים.

י וּמִנַּיִן שֶׁקּוֹרְעִין עַל עָרֵי יְהוּדָה וְעַל יְרוּשָׁלַיִם וְעַל הַמִּקְדָּשׁ שֶׁחָרְבוּ? שֶׁנֶּאֱמַר: וַיָּבֹאוּ אֲנָשִׁים מִשְּׁכֶם וּמִשִּׁילֹה וּמִשֹּׁמְרוֹן שְׁמֹנִים אִישׁ מְגֻלְּחֵי זָקָן וּקְרֻעֵי בְגָדִים.

יא כָּל מִי שֶׁעָמַד עִם הַמֵּת בִּשְׁעַת יְצִיאַת נִשְׁמָתוֹ, אַף עַל פִּי שֶׁאֵינוֹ קְרוֹבוֹ – חַיָּב לִקְרֹעַ. וְכֵן אָדָם כָּשֵׁר שֶׁמֵּת – הַכֹּל חַיָּבִין לִקְרֹעַ עָלָיו, אַף עַל פִּי שֶׁאֵינוֹ חָכָם. וְקוֹרְעִין טֶפַח כִּשְׁאָר הָאֲבֵלִים. אֲבָל חָכָם שֶׁמֵּת – הַכֹּל קְרוֹבָיו, וְהַכֹּל קוֹרְעִין עָלָיו עַד שֶׁמְּגַלִּין אֶת לִבָּם, וְחוֹלְצִין מִיָּמִין. וּבֵית מִדְרָשׁוֹ שֶׁל אוֹתוֹ חָכָם בָּטֵל כָּל שִׁבְעָה.
וּכְבָר נָהֲגוּ תַּלְמִידֵי חֲכָמִים בְּכָל מָקוֹם לִקְרֹעַ זֶה עַל זֶה טֶפַח, אַף עַל פִּי שֶׁהֵן שָׁוִין וְאֵין אֶחָד מֵהֶם מְלַמֵּד אֶת חֲבֵרוֹ.

יב כָּל הַקּוֹרְעִים עַל הֶחָכָם שֶׁמֵּת, כֵּיוָן שֶׁהֶחֱזִירוּ פְּנֵיהֶן מֵאֲחוֹרֵי הַמִּטָּה שׁוֹלְלִין. וְיֵרָאֶה לִי, שֶׁהַקּוֹרֵעַ עַל הֶחָכָם – מְאַחֶה לְמָחָר; שֶׁאֲפִלּוּ רַבּוֹ שֶׁמֵּת – אֵין מִתְאַבֵּל עָלָיו אֶלָּא יוֹם אֶחָד בִּלְבַד, אוֹ יוֹם מִיתָה אוֹ יוֹם שְׁמוּעָה.

See also *Shulchan Aruch* (*loc. cit.*) and *Siftei Cohen* 340:13 who discuss whether this obligation is incumbent on Torah scholars or not.

32. In this context, Rashi (*Mo'ed Kattan* 22b) defines this term as referring to a scholar appointed by the community to answer halachic questions. The *Shulchan Aruch* (*Yoreh De'ah* 340:7) states that it refers to a person who can provide an answer for any question in Torah law, regardless of the subject matter.

Again citing the *Hagahot Maimoniot*, the Ramah states that this custom is also not followed in the present age unless the sage who passes away is one's teacher.

33. Showing the same extra measure of respect one shows for his parents (Chapter 8, Halachah 3; Radbaz). As mentioned in the notes to that halachah, the Ramah (*Yoreh De'ah* 340:17) states that at present, the prevailing custom is not to uncover one's arm under any circumstances. This also applies with regard to the instances mentioned in the following halachot.

34. In his *Kessef Mishneh*, Rav Yosef Karo explains that this practice was instituted so that the students would eulogize and mourn over the sage. He also quotes the *Tur* who clarifies that the intent is not, heaven forbid, that his students suspend their studies, but rather that after the eulogy, they should study at home instead of collecting in the house of study. Rav Yosef Karo also quotes these concepts in his *Shulchan Aruch* (*Yoreh De'ah* 344:18).

35. I.e., even individuals who are not worthy of the title, sage. In this instance as well, the Ramah (*Yoreh De'ah* 340:8) advises leniency and does not require the tearing of garments.

36. I.e., before the burial, and certainly before the passage of the seven days of mourning in contrast to the requirements mentioned in Halachah 1.

37. The *Tur* and the *Shulchan Aruch* (*Yoreh De'ah* 242:25) state that one need not mourn an entire day; a portion of the day is sufficient.

Similarly, it appears to me that a person who rends his garments because of [the death of] the *nasi* or the like may sew them irregularly on the following day even though he may never mend them.

13. When a report comes that a sage has died,[38] we rend our garments only at the time he is eulogized. This is the honor granted to him. One may sew the garment that day and mend it on the following day.

14. When the *Av Beit Din* dies, everyone rends their garments because of him and uncovers their left arm.[39] All of the houses of study in the city are discontinued. The members of the synagogue enter the synagogue and change their places. Those who sit at the south should sit at the north and those who sit at the north should sit at the south.

15. When a *nasi* dies, everyone rends their garments because of him and uncovers both arms. All of the houses of study are discontinued. The members of the synagogue enter the synagogue on the Sabbath, call seven men to the Torah reading and depart.[40] They should not stroll in the market place,[41] but instead should sit together in families mourning the entire day.

CHAPTER TEN

1. The Sabbath is counted as one of the days of mourning.[1] [Nevertheless, the laws of] mourning are not observed on the Sabbath with the exception of private matters, e.g., veiling one's head,[2] marital relations, and washing with hot water.[3] With regard to matters which are obvious, however, the mourning laws are not observed. Instead, one may wear shoes, position his bed upright, and greet everyone.

If [the mourner] has [another] garment, he should change it.[4] He should not wear a torn garment on the Sabbath even because of his father and mother. If he does not have a garment to change, he should turn the tear to the other side.

2. When may one position his bed upright on Friday? From the afternoon onward.[5] Nevertheless, one should not sit on [the upright bed] until nightfall.

38. The *Shulchan Aruch* (*Yoreh De'ah* 340:7) states that this applies only when the report comes within 30 days of the sage's death.

39. The Radbaz (in his gloss to Halachah 11) explains that uncovering one's left arm is a greater sign of mourning than uncovering the right, because the heart is closer to the left.

40. I.e., the congregants do not pray in the synagogue, but in the home of the deceased. Nevertheless, on the Sabbath (and on Monday and Thursday), when they must read the Torah, they gather in the synagogue for that purpose alone [*Kessef Mishneh*, *Shulchan Aruch* (*Yoreh De'ah* 344:18)].

The Radbaz (and Rashi, *Mo'ed Kattan* 23a) differ and maintain that communal prayer should be suspended at this time.

וְכֵן יֵרָאֶה לִי, שֶׁהַקּוֹרֵעַ עַל הַנָּשִׂיא וְכַיּוֹצֵא בּוֹ - שׁוֹלֵל לְמָחָר, אַף עַל פִּי שֶׁאֵינוֹ מְאַחֶה עֲלֵיהֶם לְעוֹלָם.

יג חָכָם שֶׁבָּאָה שְׁמוּעָתוֹ שֶׁמֵּת - אֵין קוֹרְעִין עָלָיו אֶלָּא בִּשְׁעַת הֶסְפֵּדוֹ, וְזֶהוּ כְּבוֹדוֹ. וְשׁוֹלֵל בּוֹ בַּיּוֹם, וּמְאַחֶה לְמָחָר.

יד אַב בֵּית דִּין שֶׁמֵּת - הַכֹּל קוֹרְעִין עָלָיו, וְחוֹלְצִין מִשְּׂמֹאל, וְכָל בָּתֵּי מִדְרָשׁוֹת שֶׁבְּעִירוֹ בְּטֵלִין. וּבְנֵי בֵּית הַכְּנֶסֶת נִכְנָסִין לְבֵית הַכְּנֶסֶת, וּמְשַׁנִּין אֶת מְקוֹמָן: הַיּוֹשְׁבִין בְּדָרוֹם יֵשְׁבוּ בְּצָפוֹן, וְהַיּוֹשְׁבִים בְּצָפוֹן יֵשְׁבוּ בְּדָרוֹם.

טו נָשִׂיא שֶׁמֵּת - הַכֹּל קוֹרְעִין עָלָיו, וְחוֹלְצִין שְׁתֵּי הַיָּדַיִם מִכָּאן וּמִכָּאן, וּבְכָל בָּתֵּי מִדְרָשׁוֹת בְּטֵלִים. וּבְנֵי בֵּית הַכְּנֶסֶת נִכְנָסִין בְּשַׁבָּת לְבֵית הַכְּנֶסֶת וְקוֹרְאִין שִׁבְעָה. וְלֹא יְטַיְּלוּ בַּשּׁוּק, אֶלָּא יוֹשְׁבִין מִשְׁפָּחוֹת מִשְׁפָּחוֹת דָּוִים כָּל הַיּוֹם.

פֶּרֶק עֲשִׂירִי

א הַשַּׁבָּת עוֹלָה לְמִנְיַן אֲבֵלוּת. וְאֵין אֲבֵלוּת בְּשַׁבָּת אֶלָּא בִּדְבָרִים שֶׁבִּצְנְעָה, כְּגוֹן עֲטִיפַת הָרֹאשׁ וְתַשְׁמִישׁ הַמִּטָּה וּרְחִיצָה בְּחַמִּין; אֲבָל דְּבָרִים שֶׁבְּגָלוּי - אֵינוֹ נוֹהֵג בָּהֶן אֲבֵלוּת, אֶלָּא לוֹבֵשׁ מִנְעָלָיו, וְזוֹקֵף אֶת הַמִּטָּה, וְנוֹתֵן שָׁלוֹם לְכָל אָדָם.
וְאִם יֵשׁ לוֹ בֶּגֶד - מַחֲלִיף, וְלֹא יִלְבַּשׁ בֶּגֶד קָרוּעַ בְּשַׁבָּת, אֲפִלּוּ עַל אָבִיו וְעַל אִמּוֹ.
וְאִם אֵין לוֹ לְהַחֲלִיף - מַחֲזִיר אֶת הַקֶּרַע לַאֲחוֹרָיו.

ב מֵאֵימָתַי זוֹקְפִים אֶת הַמִּטּוֹת בְּעֶרֶב שַׁבָּת? מִן הַמִּנְחָה וּלְמַעְלָה. וְאַף עַל פִּי כֵן, לֹא יֵשֵׁב עָלֶיהָ עַד שֶׁתֶּחְשַׁךְ.

41. I.e., the suspension of the houses of prayer and study is not to relax one's religious obligations, but instead to impress people with the obligation to mourn (*Mo'ed Kattan* 23a).

1. I.e., the seven days of mourning include the Sabbath; there is no need to observe an eighth day. The rationale is that since the private aspects of the laws of mourning are observed on the Sabbath, it is included in the reckoning of the seven days.
2. This is considered a private matter. For as reflected in the notes to Chapter 5, Halachah 19, even during the week, one was not required to veil one's head in public.
3. I.e., washing one's face, hands, and feet with water that was heated before the Sabbath. Among the private matters that are forbidden on the Sabbath is also Torah study. See *Shulchan Aruch* (*Yoreh De'ah* 400:1) for details.
4. And thus wear fresh clothes in honor of the Sabbath.
5. The Halachic authorities debate whether the intent is from *Minchah Gedolah* (from half an hour after noon onward) or from *Minchah Katanah* (from nine and a half seasonal

Even when there remains only one day [for the seven days of mourning],[6] one should overturn the beds again on Saturday night.

3. On the festivals[7] and similarly, Rosh HaShanah and Yom Kippur, we do not observe any of the mourning rites at all.[8] [Moreover, whenever] anyone buries his dead even a small amount of time[9] before a festival or before Rosh HaShanah or Yom Kippur, the decree [requiring him to observe] seven days of mourning is nullified.[10]

Thus after Rosh HaShanah and Yom Kippur, [a mourner] counts 23 days.[11] After Pesach, [he counts]16 days - for the seven days of mourning are nullified and the seven days of the festival are equal to 14. Similarly, if [the deceased] was buried before Shavuos, [the mourner] counts 16 days afterwards. For even though the holiday is only one day, [since] it is a festival, it is counted as seven days.

4. When a person buries his dead before Sukkos, he should count only nine days[12] after the festival. For Shemini Atzeret is a holiday in its own right.[13] Thus the first day concludes the seven days, [then come] the seven days of the holiday, and the eighth day is considered as a festival. Thus there are 21 days.[14]

5. When a person buries his dead seven days before any one of the festivals or [seven days] before Rosh HaShanah or Yom Kippur, the decree [requiring him to observe] the 30 days of mourning is nullified. He is permitted to cut his hair and launder his garments on the day preceding the festival or Yom Kippur.[15] [The rationale is that] a portion of the day is considered as the entire day.[16] After [the holiday], he does not count any other [days of mourning].

hours after sunrise onward). See the *Kuntres Acharon* to ch. 251 in *Shulchan Aruch HaRav* which, on the basis of the Rambam's ruling in *Hilchot Tefilah* 1:5, 3;2, states that, throughout the *Mishneh Torah*, whenever the term *Minchah* is mentioned without any further description, the intent is *Minchah Katanah*, i.e., the late afternoon.

6. And thus the seven days of mourning will conclude on Sunday mourning.

7. I.e., Pesach, Shavuos, and Sukkos.

8. Since the festivals are characterized by happiness and joy, any observance of the rites of mourning is inappropriate. As *Mo'ed Kattan* 14b states, the positive commandment (Deuteronomy 16:14): "And you shall rejoice in your festivals" takes precedence over the obligation to mourn, for the obligation to rejoice is incumbent on the Jewish people as a whole.

The Rambam's wording implies that no mourning rites at all should be observed on the festivals, not even the private aspects of mourning that are observed on the Sabbath. The *Tur* and the *Shulchan Aruch* (*Yoreh De'ah* 399:1) rule that if a person did not observe the mourning rites at all before the festival, he should observe the private aspects of mourning during the festival.

9. I.e., here the intent of the word *sha'ah* is not an hour.

וְאַף עַל פִּי שֶׁלֹּא נִשְׁתַּיֵּר לוֹ אֶלָּא יוֹם אֶחָד, חוֹזֵר וְכוֹפֶה אוֹתָן בְּמוֹצָאֵי שַׁבָּת.

ג הָרְגָלִים, וְכֵן רֹאשׁ הַשָּׁנָה וְיוֹם הַכִּפּוּרִים – אֵין דָּבָר מִדִּבְרֵי אֲבֵלוּת נוֹהֵג בָּהֶן. וְכָל הַקּוֹבֵר אֶת מֵתוֹ אֲפִלּוּ שָׁעָה אַחַת קֹדֶם הָרֶגֶל אוֹ קֹדֶם רֹאשׁ הַשָּׁנָה וְיוֹם הַכִּפּוּרִים – בָּטְלָה מִמֶּנּוּ גְּזֵרַת שִׁבְעָה.

נִמְצָא מוֹנֶה לְאַחַר רֹאשׁ הַשָּׁנָה וְיוֹם הַכִּפּוּרִים שְׁלֹשָׁה וְעֶשְׂרִים יוֹם, וּלְאַחַר הַפֶּסַח – שִׁשָּׁה עָשָׂר יוֹם; שֶׁהֲרֵי בָּטְלָה גְּזֵרַת שִׁבְעָה, וְשִׁבְעַת יְמֵי הֶחָג – הֲרֵי אַרְבָּעָה עָשָׂר. וְכֵן אִם קָבַר קֹדֶם עֲצֶרֶת – מוֹנֶה אַחֲרֶיהָ שִׁשָּׁה עָשָׂר יוֹם; אַף עַל פִּי שֶׁהוּא יוֹם אֶחָד – הֲרֵי הִיא רֶגֶל וְעוֹלָה לְשִׁבְעָה יָמִים.

ד קָבַר אֶת מֵתוֹ קֹדֶם חַג הַסֻּכּוֹת – מוֹנֶה אַחַר הֶחָג תִּשְׁעָה יָמִים בִּלְבַד; שֶׁהֲרֵי שְׁמִינִי עֲצֶרֶת רֶגֶל בִּפְנֵי עַצְמוֹ, וְנִמְצָא יוֹם טוֹב הָרִאשׁוֹן מַפְסִיק שִׁבְעָה, וְשִׁבְעַת יְמֵי הֶחָג, וּשְׁמִינִי שֶׁל חַג רֶגֶל אֶחָד – הֲרֵי אֶחָד וְעֶשְׂרִים יוֹם.

ה הַקּוֹבֵר אֶת מֵתוֹ שִׁבְעַת יָמִים קֹדֶם רֶגֶל מִן הָרְגָלִים אוֹ קֹדֶם רֹאשׁ הַשָּׁנָה וְיוֹם הַכִּפּוּרִים – בָּטְלָה גְּזֵרַת שְׁלֹשִׁים. וּמֻתָּר לְסַפֵּר וּלְכַבֵּס בְּעֶרֶב יוֹם טוֹב אוֹ בְּעֶרֶב יוֹם הַכִּפּוּרִים, שֶׁמִּקְצָת הַיּוֹם כְּכֻלּוֹ, וְאֵינוֹ מוֹנֶה לְאַחֲרֵיהֶם כְּלוּם.

10. If a mourner observed the mourning rites for the briefest time before these holidays, the holiday forces him to stop that observance and he is not required to resume these rites.

11. The Radbaz explains that, according to the Rambam, even though Rosh HaShanah is followed by Yom Kippur and Yom Kippur is followed by Sukkos, since Rosh HaShanah and Yom Kippur are not festivals in the complete sense of the term, it is not appropriate that the person should have the entire mourning experience eliminated so drastically. The *Kessef Mishneh* explains that it is not appropriate that both dimensions of mourning be cut short for the same death.

The *Hagahot Maimoniot*, the *Tur*, and the *Shulchan Aruch* (*Yoreh De'ah* 399:9-10) differ and maintain that Yom Kippur and Sukkos do nullify all mourning rites. This is the universally accepted practice at present.

12. To complete the *Sheloshim* period of mourning described in Chapter 6.

13. And thus is considered as equivalent to seven days. Nevertheless, it is not considered as a festival in the sense that it has the power to nullify the *Sheloshim* mourning, because there was never any dimension of the *Sheloshim* mourning observed in a distinct manner (*Turei Zahav* 399:6).

14. In the diaspora, one need observe only eight days of mourning. Although mourning is not observed on Simchat Torah, it is also counted as one day in the *Sheloshim* reckoning [*Shulchan Aruch* (*Yoreh De'ah* 399:11)].

15. The Ramah (*Yoreh De'ah* 399:3) states that on the day before other festivals, one should perform these activities shortly before nightfall. On the day before Pesach, leniency is granted and the mourner should perform these activities shortly after midday.

16. The earlier part of the day is considered as the conclusion of the 30 day period of mourning.

If, however, he is mourning for his father or mother - even if they died more than 30 days before the festival - he may not cut his hair until it grows uncontrolled or until his friends rebuke him.[17] The festivals do not nullify this measure.[18]

6. When the sixth day of mourning falls on the day before the festival - needless to say, [this law applies] if the fifth or the third day falls on that day - he may not cut his hair. [The festival] nullifies only the decree requiring him to mourn for seven days. He is not permitted to wash, anoint himself, or perform any other practice [forbidden during the days of mourning] until the onset of the festival.[19] The festival concludes the seven days of mourning. After the festival, he concludes all 30 days[20] from the day of the death.[21] During them, he is forbidden to perform any of the five practices [mentioned in Chapter 6].

7. [The following rules apply when] the seventh day of mourning falls on the day before a festival and that day is the Sabbath.[22] The decree [requiring him to observe] the 30 days of mourning is nullified and he may cut his hair in the midst of the holiday.[23] For he was held back by forces beyond his control [since] he cannot cut his hair on the Sabbath. Similarly, one may cut one's hair after Shavuot[24] or after Rosh HaShanah and Yom Kippur, for the decree [requiring him to observe] the 30 days of mourning has been nullified and he may cut his hair whenever he desires.

8. When a person buries his dead in the midst of a festival, the laws of mourning do not apply to him.[25] He does not observe the mourning rites in the midst of the festival. Instead, after the festival he begins to count the seven days of mourning and observes all of the mourning rites at that time.[26] He counts the 30 days of *Sheloshim* from the day of the burial.[27] In the days that remain from these 30 days, he observes all the restrictions required.

9. [In the above situation,][28] in places where the holidays are observed for two days, one should count seven days from[29] the second day of the final days of

17. See Chapter 6, Halachah 3.
18. Since this dimension of mourning is not limited to the 30 day period, it is not nullified by the festivals. Similar concepts apply with regard to the other special aspects of mourning associated with the death of one's parents mentioned in that chapter.
19. On the festival, he may wash (in cold water, or with hot water during *Chol HaMoed*) for none of the mourning rites are observed during a festival as stated in Halachah 3.

The *Shulchan Aruch* (*Yoreh De'ah* 399:5) states that with regard to laundering one's clothes, one may launder them after midday, but refrain from wearing the laundered clothes until the onset of the festival. The *Shulchan Aruch* (*loc. cit.*) also mentions that there are opinions that allow one to wash shortly before the onset of the festival and the Ramah rules that it is customary to accept that view.
20. I.e., subtracting the days mentioned in Halachot 3 and 4.
21. The commentaries question why the Rambam mentions "the day of death" when he states previously that the 30 days of mourning are from the day of the burial.

וְאִם עַל אָבִיו וְעַל אִמּוֹ הוּא מִתְאַבֵּל, אֲפִלּוּ מֵתוּ קֹדֶם הָרֶגֶל שְׁלֹשִׁים יוֹם – אֵינוֹ מְגַלֵּחַ עַד שֶׁיְּשַׁלַּח פֶּרַע אוֹ עַד שֶׁיִּגְעֲרוּ בוֹ חֲבֵרָיו, וְאֵין הָרְגָלִים מַפְסִיקִין דָּבָר זֶה.

ו חָל שִׁשִּׁי שֶׁלּוֹ בְּעֶרֶב הָרֶגֶל, וְאֵין צָרִיךְ לוֹמַר חֲמִישִׁי אוֹ שְׁלִישִׁי – אֵינוֹ מְגַלֵּחַ, וְלֹא בָּטְלָה מִמֶּנּוּ אֶלָּא גְּזֵרַת שִׁבְעָה בִּלְבַד. וְאֵינוֹ מֻתָּר לִרְחֹץ וְלָסוּךְ וְלַעֲשׂוֹת דָּבָר עַד שֶׁיִּכָּנֵס יוֹם טוֹב. וְיוֹם טוֹב מַפְסִיק שְׁאָר הַשִּׁבְעָה, וּלְאַחַר יוֹם טוֹב מַשְׁלִים כָּל שְׁלֹשִׁים יוֹם מִיּוֹם הַמִּיתָה, וְאָסוּר בָּהֶן בְּכָל חֲמִשָּׁה דְּבָרִים.

ז חָל שְׁבִיעִי שֶׁלּוֹ לִהְיוֹת בְּעֶרֶב הָרֶגֶל, וַהֲרֵי הוּא שַׁבָּת – בָּטְלָה מִמֶּנּוּ גְּזֵרַת שְׁלֹשִׁים. וּמֻתָּר לְגַלֵּחַ בְּתוֹךְ הַמּוֹעֵד, שֶׁהֲרֵי אָנוּס הָיָה, וְאִי אֶפְשָׁר לוֹ לְגַלֵּחַ בְּשַׁבָּת. וְכֵן מְגַלֵּחַ אַחַר עֲצֶרֶת אוֹ אַחַר רֹאשׁ הַשָּׁנָה וְיוֹם הַכִּפּוּרִים, שֶׁהֲרֵי בָּטְלָה גְּזֵרַת שְׁלֹשִׁים, וְיֵשׁ לוֹ לְגַלֵּחַ בְּכָל עֵת שֶׁיִּרְצֶה.

ח הַקּוֹבֵר אֶת מֵתוֹ בְּתוֹךְ הָרֶגֶל – לֹא חָלָה עָלָיו אֲבֵלוּת כְּלָל, וְאֵינוֹ נוֹהֵג אֲבֵלוּת בָּרֶגֶל. אֶלָּא לְאַחַר הָרֶגֶל מַתְחִיל לִמְנוֹת שִׁבְעָה, וְנוֹהֵג בָּהֶן כָּל דִּבְרֵי אֲבֵלוּת. וּמוֹנֶה שְׁלֹשִׁים מִיּוֹם הַקְּבוּרָה, וְנוֹהֵג בִּשְׁאָר הַשְּׁלֹשִׁים בְּכָל גְּזֵרוֹת שְׁלֹשִׁים.

ט הַמְּקוֹמוֹת שֶׁעוֹשִׂין שְׁנֵי יָמִים טוֹבִים – מוֹנֶה הַשִּׁבְעָה מִיּוֹם טוֹב שֵׁנִי הָאַחֲרוֹן, אַף עַל פִּי שֶׁאֵינוֹ נוֹהֵג אֲבֵלוּת.

22. When it is forbidden to cut one's hair.
23. I.e., on Chol HaMoed, the intermediate days of the festival. Generally, this is forbidden, but leniency is granted in the present instance, because he was prevented from cutting his hair before the festival by forces beyond his control. See *Hilchot Sh'vitat Yom Tov* 7:17-18.
24. I.e., in situations when the seventh day of mourning falls on the day before any of these holidays and that day is the Sabbath.
25. For according to the Rambam, the laws of mourning should not be observed during the festival at all. The Rambam, nevertheless, rules that the expressions of grief and comfort associated with the burial should be observed during Chol HaMoed as stated in the following chapter. The *Tur* and the *Shulchan Aruch* (*Yoreh De'ah* 399:2) differ with the Rambam and state that the private dimensions of the mourning laws must be observed during the festivals.
26. The *Shulchan Aruch* (*loc. cit.*) states that certain leniencies can be observed with regard to the performance of work. After seven days pass after the death of the deceased, other people can perform the mourner's work in their own homes and the mourner's servants may perform his work in a discreet manner in his home.
27. Making no further reductions. Even when a person dies in the midst of Sukkos, Shemini Atzeret does not cause the number of days to be reduced, because he did not (fully) observe any days of mourning [*Shulchan Aruch* (*loc. cit.*)].
28. I.e., when a person dies in the middle of a festival.
29. And including the last day of the holiday.

the festival. Since its observance is a Rabbinic institution,[30] it is included in the reckoning and he need count only six days afterwards. He counts the 30 days of *Sheloshim* from the day of the burial as stated [above].

10. When a person buries his dead on the second day of a holiday which is the final day of a festival[31] or on the second day of Shavuot,[32] he should observe mourning rites, for the observance of the second day of a festival is a Rabbinic institution and the observance of mourning rites on the first day is a Scriptural obligation.[33] Hence the observance of a positive Rabbinic commandment is superseded by the observance of a positive Scriptural commandment.

If, however, one buries his dead on the second day of Rosh HaShanah, he should not observe the mourning rites. For the two days [of Rosh HaShanah] are considered as one long day, because of the rationale explained in *Hilchot Kiddush HaChodesh*.[34]

CHAPTER ELEVEN

1. Although the mourning rites are not observed at all during the festival, one should rend his garments because of his dead on a festival and uncover his shoulder.[1] Similarly, we bring the mourners bread of comfort during a festival.[2] All of the above applies during Chol HaMoed.[3] On a festival, even the second day of a festival, one should not rend his garments, uncover [a shoulder],[4] or bring bread of comfort. [5]

2. We rend our garments and uncover our shoulders during a festival only for the relatives for whom we are obligated to mourn, for a sage, an upright person, or for a person when one was present at the time his soul expired.[6]

Everyone brings the meal of comfort to his colleague for a sage during a festival in the main street of the city in the way the meal of comfort is brought for mourners. For everyone is a mourner because of him.[7]

30. And according to Scriptural Law, one should observe the mourning laws on that day.
31. I.e., Pesach or Sukkot.
32. As mentioned in *Hilchot Sh'vitat Yom Tov* 1:23, "Everything necessary [for the burial] may be performed.... With regard to a corpse, the second day of a holiday is considered like an ordinary weekday. This applies even with regard to the second day of Rosh HaShanah." As mentioned in the notes to that halachah, in the present age, it is not customary to follow this leniency and burials are usually postponed until after the holiday.
33. See Chapter 1, Halachah 1. The *Shulchan Aruch* (*Yoreh De'ah* 399:13) emphasizes that this law only applies with regard to those individuals for whom we are required to mourn according to Scriptural Law.

The *Shulchan Aruch* (*loc. cit.*) continues that the present custom is not to mourn for any relative on the second day of a festival even if the person died and was buried on that day. The Ramah states that the ruling is based on the premise that there is no Scriptural obligation to mourn.

34. *Hilchot Kiddush HaChodesh* 5:8 explains that the two days of Rosh HaShanah are considered as a single continuum of holiness since even in the time when the new moon

הוֹאִיל וּמִדִּבְרֵיהֶם הוּא - עוֹלֶה לוֹ מִן הַמִּנְיָן, וּמוֹנֶה אַחֲרָיו שִׁשָּׁה יָמִים בִּלְבַד. וּמוֹנֶה שְׁלֹשִׁים יוֹם מִיּוֹם הַקְּבוּרָה, כְּמוֹ שֶׁאָמַרְנוּ.

י הַקּוֹבֵר אֶת מֵתוֹ בְּיוֹם טוֹב שֵׁנִי, שֶׁהוּא יוֹם טוֹב הָאַחֲרוֹן, אוֹ בְּיוֹם טוֹב שֵׁנִי שֶׁל עֲצֶרֶת - נוֹהֵג בּוֹ אֲבֵלוּת. הוֹאִיל וְיוֹם טוֹב שֵׁנִי מִדִּבְרֵיהֶם, וַאֲבֵלוּת יוֹם רִאשׁוֹן שֶׁל תּוֹרָה - יִדָּחֶה עֲשֵׂה שֶׁל דִּבְרֵיהֶם מִפְּנֵי עֲשֵׂה שֶׁל תּוֹרָה.
אֲבָל אִם קָבַר בְּיוֹם טוֹב שֵׁנִי שֶׁל רֹאשׁ הַשָּׁנָה - אֵינוֹ נוֹהֵג בּוֹ אֲבֵלוּת; שֶׁשְּׁנֵיהֶן כְּיוֹם אָרֹךְ הֵן, מִטַּעַם שֶׁבֵּאַרְנוּ בְּהִלְכוֹת קִדּוּשׁ הַחֹדֶשׁ.

פֶּרֶק אַחַד עָשָׂר

א אַף עַל פִּי שֶׁאֵין אֲבֵלוּת בַּמּוֹעֵד, קוֹרֵעַ עַל מֵתוֹ בַּמּוֹעֵד וְחוֹלֵץ כְּתֵפוֹ. וּמַבְרִין אֶת הָאֲבֵלִים לֶחֶם בַּמּוֹעֵד. כָּל אֵלּוּ בְּחֻלּוֹ שֶׁל מוֹעֵד; אֲבָל בְּיוֹם טוֹב, אֲפִלּוּ בְּיוֹם טוֹב שֵׁנִי - אֵין קוֹרְעִין וְלֹא חוֹלְצִין וְלֹא מַבְרִין.

ב אֵין קוֹרְעִין בַּמּוֹעֵד וְלֹא חוֹלְצִין אֶלָּא הַקְּרוֹבִים שֶׁחַיָּבִין בְּאֵבֶל, אוֹ הַקּוֹרֵעַ וְהַחוֹלֵץ עַל הֶחָכָם אוֹ עַל אָדָם כָּשֵׁר, אוֹ מִי שֶׁהָיָה עוֹמֵד בִּשְׁעַת יְצִיאַת נְשָׁמָה. וּמַבְרִין הַכֹּל עַל הֶחָכָם בַּמּוֹעֵד לְתוֹךְ הָרְחָבָה, כְּדֶרֶךְ שֶׁמַּבְרִין אֶת הָאֲבֵלִים; שֶׁהַכֹּל אֲבֵלִים עָלָיו.

was sanctified through the testimony of witnesses, Rosh HaShanah was often observed for two days.

1. See Chapter 8, Halachot 1 and 3.
2. See Chapter 4, Halachah 9.
3. See the Ramah (*Yoreh De'ah* 340:31) which mentions that there are communities where one rends his garments only for his father and mother on Chol HaMoed.
4. Although the dead may be buried on a festival - on the first day, by gentiles, and on the second day, by Jews (*Hilchot Sh'vitat Yom Tov* 1:23) - we may perform only those activities involved with his actual burial. Rending one's garments is for the sake of the living. Hence, since it involves the performance of forbidden labor, it is not permitted on the holidays - even on the second day of the festival (Radbaz). And since it is not performed on the holidays, we postpone it until after the festival has past entirely (*Mishneh LiMelech*; *Magen Avraham* 547:3).
5. Rabbi Akiva Eiger notes that on the conclusion of the previous chapter, the Rambam states that if a person buries his dead on the second day of a festival, he is obligated to mourn. Yet as stated in this halachah, a meal of comfort is not served on a festival. Thus the implication is that mourning is more severe. Hence one would think that just as one does not mourn during Chol HaMoed, one would not serve a meal of comfort. The requirement to do so implies that serving the meal of comfort is in a different category; it resembles a eulogy.
6. I.e., we do not rend our garments for those dead for whom we observe some mourning rites as an expression of honor for the living, e.g., one's in-laws.
7. Since the entire community must mourn for him, each one brings food for another. The meal are exchanged in the main street of the city, as can be inferred from *Ketubot* 8b.

3. When we bring mourners the meal of comfort during a festival, we serve them while they are sitting on upright couches.[8] We do not recite the mourning blessing during a festival.[9] We do, however, stand in a line, comfort the mourners, and take leave of them.[10]

We do not leave the bier in the public thoroughfare lest that encourage the delivery of a eulogy. For it is forbidden to deliver eulogies and to fast during a festival.[11] Similarly, one should not gather the bones of one's father and mother[12] during a festival for this evokes mourning for the person.[13] Needless to say, this applies with regard to one's other relatives.[14]

Similarly, we do not eulogize the dead on Chanukah, Purim, or Rosh Chodesh.[15] We do, however, observe all the rites of mourning on those days.[16] It is permitted to deliver eulogies on the days which precede and which follow Chanukah and Purim.[17]

4. During a festival, the women may lament, but they do not pound their hands together in grief. On Rosh Chodesh, Chanukah, and Purim,[18] they may both lament and pound their hands together in grief; they may not, however, recite dirges on any of these days. Once the dead has been buried, they should neither lament, nor pound their hands together.

5. What is meant by lamenting? That all raise their voices in mourning together. By reciting dirges? That one recites a dirge and all respond in lament, as implied by [Jeremiah 9:19]: "to teach your daughters mourning and a woman, her friends, a dirge."

When do [all the above restrictions] apply? When ordinary people die. When, however, a Torah scholar dies, he is eulogized[19] during a festival. Needless to say, this applies on Chanukah, Purim, and Rosh Chodesh. [This does not apply] on the second day of a holiday.

8. In contrast to the ordinary practice where a mourner sits on an overturned or low chair. See Chapter 4, Halachah 9.

9. Many interpret the term "mourning blessing" as referring to the blessing given the mourners by one of the leading members of the community when they return from the funeral as related by *Ketubot* 8b. Since this blessing is recited in a public place, it is not appropriate for it to be recited during a festival lest it reduce the festive spirit (Radbaz).

Kin'at Eliyahu notes that in Chapter 13 where the Rambam describes the comforting of the mourners after the funeral, he does not mention this blessing. And in Chapter 12, Halachah 7, he states that the term refers to blessings given "in the house of a mourner." See the notes to that halachah for additional explanation.

10. See Chapter 13, Halachah 1. Ordinarily, the mourners would be accompanied by members of the company. This, however, is not appropriate during a festival. See *Mo'ed Kattan* 27a.

11. For the charge "And you shall rejoice in your festivals" also applies to Chol HaMoed and these activities will not lead to increased rejoicing.

12. I.e., gathering them from where they are buried to rebury them in another place.

13. Collecting their bones brings back memories of their passing.

ג כְּשֶׁמַּבְרִין אֶת הָאֲבֵלִים בַּמּוֹעֵד – אֵין מַבְרִין אֶלָּא עַל מִטּוֹת זְקוּפוֹת. וְאֵין אוֹמְרִין בִּרְכַּת אֲבֵלִים בַּמּוֹעֵד, אֲבָל עוֹמְדִין בַּשּׁוּרָה וּמְנַחֲמִין וּפוֹטְרִין. וְאֵין מַנִּיחִין אֶת הַמִּטָּה בָּרְחוֹב, שֶׁלֹּא לְהַרְגִּיל אֶת הַהֶסְפֵּד; שֶׁהַמּוֹעֵד אָסוּר בְּהֶסְפֵּד וּבְתַעֲנִית.

וְכֵן אֵין מְלַקְּטִים עַצְמוֹת אָבִיו וְאִמּוֹ בַּמּוֹעֵד, שֶׁאֵבֶל הוּא לוֹ; וְאֵין צָרִיךְ לוֹמַר שְׁאָר קְרוֹבִים.

וְכֵן אֵין מַסְפִּידִין אֶת הַמֵּת בַּחֲנֻכָּה וּבְפוּרִים וְלֹא בְּרָאשֵׁי חֳדָשִׁים, אֲבָל נוֹהֲגִין בָּהֶן כָּל דִּבְרֵי אֲבֵלוּת. וּמֻתָּר לִסְפֹּד לִפְנֵי חֲנֻכָּה וּפוּרִים וּלְאַחֲרֵיהֶן.

ד הַנָּשִׁים: בַּמּוֹעֵד – מְעַנּוֹת אֲבָל לֹא מְטַפְּחוֹת; וּבְרָאשֵׁי חֳדָשִׁים וּבַחֲנֻכָּה וּבְפוּרִים – מְעַנּוֹת וּמְטַפְּחוֹת. אֲבָל אֵין מְקוֹנְנוֹת לֹא בָּזֶה וְלֹא בָּזֶה. נִקְבַּר הַמֵּת – לֹא מְעַנּוֹת וְלֹא מְטַפְּחוֹת.

ה אֵי זֶהוּ עִנּוּי? שֶׁכֻּלָּן עוֹנוֹת כְּאַחַת. קִינָה? שֶׁאַחַת אוֹמֶרֶת וְכֻלָּן עוֹנוֹת אַחֲרֶיהָ. שֶׁנֶּאֱמַר: וְלַמֵּדְנָה בְנֹתֵיכֶם נֶהִי, וְאִשָּׁה רְעוּתָהּ קִינָה. בַּמֶּה דְּבָרִים אֲמוּרִים? בִּשְׁאָר הָעָם שֶׁמֵּתוּ; אֲבָל תַּלְמִיד חָכָם שֶׁמֵּת – סוֹפְדִים אוֹתוֹ בַּמּוֹעֵד, וְאֵין צָרִיךְ לוֹמַר בַּחֲנֻכָּה וּבְפוּרִים וְרָאשֵׁי חֳדָשִׁים, אֲבָל לֹא בְּיוֹם טוֹב שֵׁנִי.

14. One has an obligation to honor his parents. Although that obligation is outweighed by the happiness of the festival, it remains a factor of importance. One does not have an obligation to honor his other relatives. Hence there is no reason why he should think that he should incur the sorrow of moving their remains during a festival.
15. Although these days are not festivals according to Scriptural Law, they are days of happiness and it is inappropriate to reduce that happiness by eulogies.
16. The Radbaz and the *Kessef Mishneh* quote the *Tur* who states that on Purim, we observe only the private aspects of the mourning laws (as on the Sabbath). The rulings of the *Shulchan Aruch* on this subject appear contradictory. *Orach Chayim* 696:4 rules that the full mourning rites should be observed, while *Yoreh De'ah* 401:7 rules that only the private dimensions of these rites should be observed. Differences of opinion persist among the later authorities as well. All authorities agree that, in contrast to Scriptural festivals, Purim - and similarly, Chanukah - do not nullify the obligation to mourn.
17. *Ta'anit* 17b states that it is forbidden to eulogize on the days before the dates mentioned in "the scroll of fasts," i.e., dates which were commemorated as minor holidays in the Talmudic era. Among those dates were Chanukah and Purim. *Rosh HaShanah* 18b states: "The scroll of fasts was nullified," i.e., we no longer are bound by the restrictions mentioned there. Although *Rosh HaShanah* 19b states that this does not apply to Chanukah and Purim, this refers only to Chanukah and Purim themselves, and not to the days that precede or follow these holidays (*Kessef Mishneh*).
18. When there is no Scriptural obligation to rejoice, however, according to Rabbinic Law, they are days of happiness.
19. Similarly, women may lament and recite dirges [*Shulchan Aruch* (*Yoreh De'ah* 401:5)].

On the days when a eulogy is permitted, it is permitted only in [the deceased's] presence. Once he is buried, a eulogy is forbidden. On the day when one hears a report of his death, it is as if one is in his presence and he may be eulogized even if it is a distant report.[20]

6. A woman[21] should not have a eulogy recited for a deceased person[22] within 30 days so that the festival will not arrive when they are grieving.[23] For a deceased person will not be forgotten in less than 30 days. When does the above apply? With regard to a person who died previously. If, however, a person died within 30 days of a festival, a eulogy may be recited.[24]

7. The seven days of the wedding celebrations are comparable to a festival.[25] Thus if [a close relative] of a person - even his father or mother - dies in the middle of these days of celebration, he should complete the seven days of celebration and then observe the seven days of mourning.[26] He [also] counts the 30 days of mourning from the conclusion of the days of celebration.[27]

8. [The following rules apply when one] prepared all the necessities for [the wedding] feast, baked his bread, slaughtered his animals to enter the celebration, and then [one of his close relatives] died before he began the celebration. If he did not place the meat in water,[28] he should sell the meat and the bread, observe the seven days of mourning, and then observe the seven days of [the wedding] celebrations.[29]

If he already placed the meat in water - in which instance, it cannot be resold - the corpse is placed inside a room[30] and the groom and the bride are

20. I.e., the sage died more than 30 days previously.
21. Needless to say, this also applies to a man. The Rambam mentions women because they are more likely to arrange such an event (Radbaz).
22. Our translation is based on the Rambam's Commentary to the Mishnah (*Mo'ed Kattan* 1:5). There - and in greater detail in *Hilchot Sh'vitat Yom Tov* 6:24 - the Rambam elaborates on the rationale for this restriction. To quote *Hilchot Sh'vitat Yom Tov*: "So that the festival will not arrive when he is sad and his heart is grieved and hurting because of the memory of his agony. Instead he should remove grieving from his heart and direct his attention toward joy."
23. The *Kessef Mishneh* explains that this refers to the eulogies recited in the Talmudic era which were accompanied by loud lamenting and wails of grief. At present, when the eulogies are more controlled, these restrictions do not apply.
24. For when the death is so close, an expression of mourning will lead to a catharsis of one's grief and enable one to approach the festival with joy.
25. See *Hilchot Ishut* 10:12 which states that a man who marries a virgin bride should celebrate with her for seven days. Just as the mourning laws are not observed during a festival, they should not be observed during these days.

The commentaries question: According to the Rambam, the obligation to mourn on the first day is Scriptural in origin, while the obligation to rejoice with one's bride is Rabbinic. How could our Sages require that their decree be observed when it prevents the observance of a Scriptural commandment?

וְאֵין סוֹפְדִין אוֹתוֹ בְּיָמִים אֵלּוּ אֶלָּא בְּפָנָיו. נִקְבַּר – אֲסוּרִין בְּהֶסְפֵּד. וְיוֹם שְׁמוּעָתוֹ – כִּבְפָנָיו הוּא, וְסוֹפְדִין אוֹתוֹ, אַף עַל פִּי שֶׁהִיא רְחוֹקָה.

ו לֹא תְּעוֹרֵר אִשָּׁה עַל מֵת שֶׁלָּהּ שְׁלֹשִׁים יוֹם קֹדֶם לֶחָג, כְּדֵי שֶׁלֹּא יָבוֹא הֶחָג וְהֵם דָּוִים; שֶׁאֵין הַמֵּת מִשְׁתַּכֵּחַ מִן הַלֵּב שְׁלֹשִׁים יוֹם. בַּמֶּה דְּבָרִים אֲמוּרִים? בְּמֵת יָשָׁן; אֲבָל אִם מֵת בְּתוֹךְ שְׁלֹשִׁים יוֹם סָמוּךְ לֶחָג – מְעוֹרֶרֶת.

ז שִׁבְעַת יְמֵי הַחַתְנוּת – הֲרֵי הֵן כְּרֶגֶל. וּמִי שֶׁמֵּת לוֹ מֵת בְּתוֹךְ יְמֵי הַמִּשְׁתֶּה, אֲפִלּוּ אָבִיו וְאִמּוֹ – מַשְׁלִים שִׁבְעַת יְמֵי הַשִּׂמְחָה, וְאַחַר כָּךְ נוֹהֵג שִׁבְעַת יְמֵי אֲבֵלוּת. וּמוֹנֶה הַשְּׁלֹשִׁים מֵאַחַר יְמֵי הַשִּׂמְחָה.

ח הֵכִין כָּל צָרְכֵי הַסְּעֻדָּה וְאָפָה פִּתּוֹ וְטָבַח טִבְחוֹ כְּדֵי שֶׁיִּכָּנְסוּ לַשִּׂמְחָה, וּמֵת לוֹ מֵת קֹדֶם שֶׁיִּכָּנְסוּ לַשִּׂמְחָה: אִם לֹא נָתַן מַיִם עַל גַּבֵּי בָּשָׂר – מוֹכֵר הַבָּשָׂר וְהַפַּת, וְנוֹהֵג שִׁבְעַת יְמֵי אֲבֵלוּת, וְאַחַר כָּךְ נוֹהֵג שִׁבְעַת יְמֵי הַמִּשְׁתֶּה;
וְאִם נָתַן מַיִם עַל גַּבֵּי בָּשָׂר, שֶׁהֲרֵי אִי אֶפְשָׁר לְמָכְרוֹ – מַכְנִיסִין אֶת הַמֵּת לְחֶדֶר, וְאֶת

Rabbenu Nissim (in his gloss to *Ketubot* 3:2) offers the resolution that our Sages have the power to nullify a Scriptural commandment as long as a person does not perform a deed. Hence on the day of the burial, a person should not celebrate, but he should not mourn. The Radbaz explains that in this instance our Sages are given the license for they are not abrogating the mitzvah of mourning entirely; they are merely postponing it to a later date.

26. As is required when a person's relative dies in the midst of a festival (Chapter 10, Halachah 8).

In contrast to the situation mentioned in the following halachah, in this instance, one need not refrain from marital relations because of the laws of mourning. (This may, however, be necessary because of the *niddah* laws.)

27. The Ra'avad objects to the Rambam's ruling, questioning why the seven days of the wedding celebrations are not considered within the 30 days of mourning. After all, the Rambam states (*ibid.*) that when a person buries his dead during a festival, he counts the 30 days of mourning from the time of the burial.

The Ramban [cited by the Radbaz and the *Tur* (*Yoreh De'ah* 342)] explains that during a festival, a person observes some of the restrictions of the 30 days of mourning, for - as a measure of respect to the festival - he may not cut his hair or iron his clothes. Hence, these days can be included in the sum of the 30. With regard to the seven days of the wedding celebrations, by contrast, none of the mourning restrictions must be observed. Hence, the 30 days are counted after their conclusion.

28. I.e., begin preparing to cook it.

29. The Ra'avad objects: Since the wedding is being postponed, why is it not postponed for 30 days so that the full mourning rites will be observed? The Ramban [cited by the *Kessef Mishneh* and the *Tur* (*Yoreh De'ah* 342)] explains that since the wedding preparations have already been made and the couple's expectations have been aroused, it is not proper to postpone the wedding for such an extended period.

30. For if the burial would be held first, there would be a Scriptural obligation to mourn and it would be improper to hold the wedding (*Kessef Mishneh*).

taken to the wedding canopy. [Afterwards,] he should engage in the marital relations which are a mitzvah,[31] and then separate [from his wife].[32] He should observe the seven days of celebration and then the seven days of mourning.

Throughout [the seven days of celebration], he must observe the private aspects of the laws of mourning as is required on the Sabbath.[33] Therefore he should sleep together with other men and his wife should sleep with other women so that they do not engage in relations.[34] For these 30 days, the bride should not be prevented from wearing jewelry.[35]

In a place where it is possible to sell the meat even though it was placed in water, it should be sold and the mourning period observed first. In a place where it is impossible to sell the meat even though it was not placed in water, [the wedding] celebrations should be observed first.

When does the above apply?[36] When the father of the groom or the mother of the bride die. For if this feast is spoiled, they have no one to work [to prepare another for them]. If, however, the father of the bride, the mother of the groom, or other relatives die, one should observe the mourning period first. Only afterwards, should he enter the marriage canopy and observe the seven days of wedding celebrations.[37]

CHAPTER TWELVE

1. A eulogy[1] is an honor for the deceased.[2] Therefore we compel the heirs[3] to pay the wages of the men and women who recite laments and they eulogize him. If [the deceased] directed that he not be eulogized, we do not eulogize him.[4] If, however, he directed that he not be buried, we do not heed him, for burial is a mitzvah,[5] as [Deuteronomy 21:22] states: "And you shall certainly bury him."

2. Anyone who is sluggish with regard to the eulogy for a sage will not live long.[6] Anyone who is sluggish with regard to the eulogy of an upright person

31. This term is used to describe the first time a couple engage in relations, for this union enables them to fulfill the mitzvah of procreation.
32. And not engage in relations further.
33. See Chapter 10, Halachah 1.
34. Compare to *Hilchot Issurei Bi'ah* 22:1. Since they are just married and an external factor is preventing them from engaging in relations, this extra dimension of vigilance is required.
35. Lest she appear unattractive to her husband.
36. I.e., when do we grant the leniency to allow the wedding celebration to be held first.
37. In practice, the matter is dependent on local custom. There are certain communities where it is not customary to postpone a wedding even though relatives died beforehand and others, which are more strict in observing the mourning prohibitions. When such a problem arises, people should contact a competent Rabbinical authority familiar with the local custom.

הֶחָתָן וְאֶת הַכַּלָּה לַחֻפָּה, וּבוֹעֵל בְּעִילַת מִצְוָה וּפוֹרֵשׁ, וְנוֹהֵג שִׁבְעַת יְמֵי הַמִּשְׁתֶּה, וְאַחַר כָּךְ נוֹהֵג שִׁבְעַת יְמֵי אֲבֵלוּת.

וְכָל אוֹתָן הַיָּמִים נוֹהֵג בִּדְבָרִים שֶׁבְּצִנְעָה כְּשַׁבָּת. לְפִיכָךְ הוּא יָשֵׁן בֵּין הָאֲנָשִׁים, וְאִשְׁתּוֹ יְשֵׁנָה בֵּין הַנָּשִׁים, כְּדֵי שֶׁלֹּא יְשַׁמֵּשׁ מִטָּתוֹ. וְאֵין מוֹנְעִין תַּכְשִׁיטִין מִן הַכַּלָּה כָּל שְׁלֹשִׁים יוֹם.

הָיוּ בְּמָקוֹם שֶׁאֶפְשָׁר לְמִכֹּר הַבָּשָׂר אַף עַל פִּי שֶׁנָּתַן עָלָיו מַיִם – מוֹכֵר, וְנוֹהֵג אֲבֵלוּת תְּחִלָּה. הָיוּ בְּמָקוֹם שֶׁאִי אֶפְשָׁר לְמִכֹּר הַבָּשָׂר אַף עַל פִּי שֶׁלֹּא נָתַן עָלָיו מַיִם – נוֹהֵג שִׁבְעַת יְמֵי הַמִּשְׁתֶּה תְּחִלָּה.

בַּמֶּה דְּבָרִים אֲמוּרִים? כְּשֶׁמֵּת אָבִיו שֶׁל חָתָן אוֹ אִמָּהּ שֶׁל כַּלָּה; שֶׁאִם יַפְסִידוּ סְעֻדָּה זוֹ – אֵין לָהֶם מִי שֶׁיִּטְרַח לָהֶם. אֲבָל אִם מֵת אָבִיהָ שֶׁל כַּלָּה אוֹ אִמּוֹ שֶׁל חָתָן אוֹ שְׁאָר קְרוֹבֵיהֶם – נוֹהֲגִין שִׁבְעַת יְמֵי הָאֵבֶל תְּחִלָּה, וְאַחַר כָּךְ תִּכָּנֵס לַחֻפָּה וְיִנְהֲגוּ שִׁבְעַת יְמֵי הַמִּשְׁתֶּה.

פֶּרֶק שְׁנֵים עָשָׂר

א הַהֶסְפֵּד כְּבוֹד הַמֵּת הוּא. לְפִיכָךְ כּוֹפִין אֶת הַיּוֹרְשִׁין לִתֵּן שְׂכַר מְקוֹנְנִים וְהַמְקוֹנְנוֹת וְסוֹפְדִין אוֹתוֹ. וְאִם צִוָּה שֶׁלֹּא יִסְפְּדוּהוּ – אֵין סוֹפְדִין אוֹתוֹ. אֲבָל אִם צִוָּה שֶׁלֹּא יִקָּבֵר – אֵין שׁוֹמְעִין לוֹ; שֶׁהַקְּבוּרָה מִצְוָה, שֶׁנֶּאֱמַר: כִּי קָבוֹר תִּקְבְּרֶנּוּ.

ב כָּל הַמִּתְעַצֵּל בְּהֶסְפֵּדוֹ שֶׁל חָכָם – אֵינוֹ מַאֲרִיךְ יָמִים. וְכָל הַמִּתְעַצֵּל בְּהֶסְפֵּד אָדָם כָּשֵׁר – רָאוּי לְקָבֵר בְּחַיָּיו.

1. We have used the term eulogy for the Hebrew *hesped*, because that is its meaning in modern Hebrew. In truth, however, the term implies much more than a speech given in honor of the departed. *Hesped* was a multi-dimensional mourning experience involving the chanting of dirges and other physical expressions of grief.

2. I.e., a measure of respect that should be given him, rather than a measure of respect for the living. See *Sanhedrin* 46b which discusses this issue.

3. I.e., were it a measure of respect for the living, the heirs could elect to forgo it. Since it is a measure of respect for the dead, if they are financially capable, we compel them to show him this measure of respect. See *Sanhedrin* 46b.

4. For he has the choice to decline the honor due him.

5. See *Sefer HaMitzvot* (positive commandment 231), *Sefer HaChinuch* (mitzvah 537), and *Hilchot Sanhedrin* 15:8 where this mitzvah is discussed. See also Chapter 3, Halachah 8, *Hilchot Zechiyah UMatanah* 11:24, *Hilchot Ishut* 14:23-24.

Since it is a mitzvah to bury the person, his individual desires are of no consequence and he should be buried.

6. *Shabbat* 105b states that he is judged measure for measure. Since he did not mourn for a person whose life was cut short, his own life will be cut short.

is fit to be buried in his lifetime. Anyone who sheds tears for an upright person will have his reward for this guarded by the Holy One, blessed be He.[7]

3. We do not place a Torah scroll on the bier of a sage.[8] We do not change him from one bier to another.[9] We take his bier out only through the doorway;[10] we do not lower it to remove it through the gardens. For others, this is permitted.

4. We rise and sit no less than seven times[11] in honor of a deceased person. There should be no less than ten men who rise and sit. Only relatives should participate. This rite is carried out only on the first day, in the cemetery, in communities where it is customary to observe it.

How is this rite carried out in communities where it is customary to observe it? We have the other relatives and the members of the family who are not required to mourn stand and we recite dirges and the like in their presence.[12] Afterwards, one says: "Sit honored persons, sit." He then recites other statements [of lament] before them while they are sitting and then says: "Stand honored persons, stand." He then speaks again while they are standing and repeats this pattern seven times.

5. Just as we rise and sit in honor of men in places where this custom is observed, we observe the same rites in honor of women.[13] Never, however, do we leave the bier of a women in the public thoroughfare, for this is considered disrespectful for a woman. Instead, she is buried directly after her death.[14]

6. When a person gathers the bones [of a deceased],[15] mourning dirges and lamentations should not be recited, not should the mourning blessing or words of comfort for mourners be said. Instead, we recite only words of praise to the Holy One, blessed be He,[16] and exhortations to repentance.

7. [The following rules apply when a person] moves the coffin of a person from one place to another. If [the corpse's] backbone is intact, we stand in a line for him, recite the mourning blessing and the words of comfort for

7. *Shabbat, loc. cit.*, states that God "counts these tears and places them in His treasure stores."
8. *Mo'ed Kattan* 25a states that this would be appropriate, as if to say: "He fulfilled what is written within that." Nevertheless, this is not done, for it is not respectful to a Torah scroll to place anything else on the platform on which it is placed (see *Hilchot Sefer Torah* 10:6).
9. Instead, he is taken out on the first bier made for that purpose (*Mo'ed Kattan, loc. cit.*).
10. Even if the doorway must be widened so that the bier can pass through, we do so (*Mo'ed Kattan, loc. cit.*).
11. *Bava Batra* 100b states that this recalls the seven times the word *Hevel* ("emptiness") is mentioned in Ecclesiastes 1:2: "Emptiness of emptiness.... Everything is emptiness." (The term is mentioned actually only 5 times, but twice the plural form is used.)

וְכָל הַמּוֹרִיד דְּמָעוֹת עַל אָדָם כָּשֵׁר – הֲרֵי שְׂכָרוֹ שָׁמוּר עַל כָּךְ אֵצֶל הַקָּדוֹשׁ בָּרוּךְ הוּא.

ג אֵין מַנִּיחִין סֵפֶר תּוֹרָה עַל מִטָּתוֹ שֶׁל חָכָם. וְאֵין מְשַׁנִּין אוֹתוֹ מִמִּטָּה לְמִטָּה. וְאֵין מוֹצִיאִין מִטָּתוֹ אֶלָּא דֶּרֶךְ פְּתָחִים, לֹא שֶׁיְּשַׁלְשְׁלוּהָ דֶּרֶךְ גַּגּוֹת. וּבִשְׁאָר הָעָם – מֻתָּר לַעֲשׂוֹת.

ד אֵין פּוֹחֲתִין מִשִּׁבְעָה מַעֲמָדוֹת לְמֵת. וְאֵין עוֹשִׂין מַעֲמָד וּמוֹשָׁב בְּפָחוֹת מֵעֲשָׂרָה. וְאֵין עוֹשִׂין אֶלָּא בִּקְרוֹבִים. וְאֵין עוֹשִׂין אֶלָּא בְּיוֹם רִאשׁוֹן, וּבְבֵית הַקְּבָרוֹת, וּבְמָקוֹם שֶׁנָּהֲגוּ. כֵּיצַד עוֹשִׂין בְּמָקוֹם שֶׁנָּהֲגוּ? מַעֲמִידִין שְׁאָר הַקְּרוֹבִים וּבְנֵי מִשְׁפָּחָה שֶׁאֵינָן בְּנֵי אֵבֶל, וְאוֹמְרִין לִפְנֵיהֶם דִּבְרֵי קִינוֹת וְכַיּוֹצֵא בָּהֶן. וְאַחַר כָּךְ אוֹמֵר: שְׁבוּ יְקָרִים שֵׁבוּ! וְאוֹמֵר לִפְנֵיהֶם דְּבָרִים אֲחֵרִים כְּשֶׁהֵן יוֹשְׁבִין. וְאַחַר כָּךְ: עִמְדוּ יְקָרִים עֲמֹדוּ! וְאוֹמֵר כְּשֶׁהֵן עוֹמְדִין. וְחוֹזֵר וְאוֹמֵר כָּךְ עַד שֶׁבַע פְּעָמִים.

ה כְּדֶרֶךְ שֶׁעוֹשִׂין מַעֲמָד וּמוֹשָׁב לַאֲנָשִׁים בְּמָקוֹם שֶׁנָּהֲגוּ, כָּךְ עוֹשִׂין לְנָשִׁים. וּמַסְפִּידִין הַנָּשִׁים כָּאֲנָשִׁים בְּכָל מָקוֹם. אֲבָל אֵין מַנִּיחִין מִטַּת הָאִשָּׁה בָּרְחוֹב לְעוֹלָם, שֶׁזֶּה גְּנַאי לָאִשָּׁה, אֶלָּא סָמוּךְ לְמִיתָתָהּ קְבוּרָתָהּ.

ו הַמְלַקֵּט עֲצָמוֹת – אֵין אוֹמְרִים עֲלֵיהֶם קִנִּים וָנֶהִי, וְלֹא בִּרְכַּת אֲבֵלִים וְלֹא תַּנְחוּמֵי אֲבֵלִים. אֲבָל אוֹמְרִים עֲלֵיהֶן דִּבְרֵי שֶׁבַח לְהַקָּדוֹשׁ בָּרוּךְ הוּא וְדִבְרֵי כִּבּוּשִׁים.

ז הַמְפַנֶּה אֲרוֹנוֹ שֶׁל מֵת מִמָּקוֹם לְמָקוֹם:
אִם שִׁדְרוֹ קַיֶּמֶת – עוֹמְדִין עָלָיו בְּשׁוּרָה, וְאוֹמְרִים עָלָיו בִּרְכַּת אֲבֵלִים וְתַנְחוּמֵי אֲבֵלִים,

12. In his commentary to *Bava Batra* 100b, Rashbam states that this rite is carried out after the burial. In his commentary to *Megilah* 23b, Rashi states that the rite is carried out before burying the dead. The Rambam's Commentary to the Mishnah (*Megilah* 4:3) appears to follow Rashi's view.

In the present day, some of the formalities are relaxed, but it is customary to rise and sit down, rise and sit down, seven times after a funeral and on the way to the burial, the pallbearers and those accompanying the corpse stop seven times.

13. *Rosh HaShanah* 25a relates how Rabban Gamliel arranged a large mourning ceremony for a woman and *Megilah* 28b tells how Rafram eulogized his daughter-in-law in the syngaogue.

14. *Mo'ed Kattan* 28a derives this from the Torah's description of the death of Miriam. Numbers 20:1 states: "Miriam died there and was buried," mentioning the two facts directly after the other to imply that this should be the order. A woman's burial should follow her death.

15. To reinter them in a different grave. See *Tur* and *Shulchan Aruch* (*Yoreh De'ah* 403).

16. The *Tur* (*loc. cit.*) states one praises God for He puts a person to death and will ultimately resurrect him, lowering him to the grave and raising him up from it.

mourners. We eulogize him even if his [bones] were moved after twelve months after his death. If its backbone is not intact, we do not eulogize him. We do not stand in a line for him, nor do we recite the mourning blessing and the words of comfort for mourners.

The term "mourning blessing" refers to what is said in the mourners' home.[17] The words of comfort for mourners refers to what is said when standing in a line.[18]

8. When a person gathers[19] the bones of his father and his mother, he should mourn for them for that entire day.[20] In the evening, he should not mourn even though they are bound up in his sheet. One does not recite mourning dirges.[21]

9. We do not eulogize children. How old must a child be to be fit to be eulogized? For the children of the poor or the children of the elderly, five years old. For the children of the wealthy, six years old.[22] This applies to both boys and girls.

10. [The following rules apply when] a child dies. [If he dies within] 30 days of birth, he should be carried in one's bosom[23] and buried with one woman and two men [in attendance]. [He should] not [be buried] with one man and two women [in attendance] because of [the prohibition against men and woman] being together alone.[24] We do not stand in a line because of him, nor do we recite the mourning blessing or the words of comfort for mourners.[25]

[When a child was] a full 30 days [old],[26] [his corpse] should be carried in a small coffin that can be carried on one's forearms. We stand in a line because of him and recite the mourning blessing and the words of comfort for mourners. [A child of] twelve months is carried out in a bier.[27]

11. Whenever a corpse is taken out in a bier,[28] people at large should grieve for him.[29] Whenever it is not taken out in a bier,[30] people at large need not grieve for him. Whenever anyone is known to people at large,[31] people at

17. Some interpret this as referring to the additions that mention mourning that are made to the fourth blessing in grace (see *Hilchot Berachot* 2:8). Others interpret it as referring to blessings given the mourner by guests coming to comfort him. As mentioned in the notes to the previous chapter, based on *Ketubot* 8b, there are some who interpret the term as referring to a blessing recited in the public thoroughfare after the funeral. The Rambam, apparently, does not accept this interpretation.

18. See Chapter 13, Halachot 1and 2.

19. Or has others gather, for it is not proper for a person to gather his parents' bones himself [*Tur* and *Shulchan Aruch* (*Yoreh De'ah* 403:7-8), based on the *Evel Rabati*].

20. The *Tur* and the *Shulchan Aruch* (*loc. cit.* 403:1) state that one must observe mourning rites when the bones of any of one's close relatives are gathered. Similarly, one must rend one's garments and a meal of comfort is served.

21. Although this concept is stated in Halachah 6, the Rambam reiterates it here to teach that it applies even with regard to one's parents (*Kessef Mishneh*).

וּמַסְפִּידִין אוֹתוֹ, אַף עַל פִּי שֶׁהֶעֱבִירוּהוּ לְאַחַר שְׁנֵים עָשָׂר חֹדֶשׁ; וְאִם אֵין שִׁדְרוֹ קַיֶּמֶת – אֵין מַסְפִּידִין אוֹתוֹ, וְאֵין עוֹמְדִין עָלָיו בְּשׁוּרָה, וְאֵין אוֹמְרִין עָלָיו בִּרְכַּת אֲבֵלִים וְלֹא תַּנְחוּמֵי אֲבֵלִים. וְאֵלּוּ הֵן: בִּרְכַּת אֲבֵלִים – דְּבָרִים שֶׁאוֹמְרִים בְּבֵית הָאֵבֶל, תַּנְחוּמֵי אֲבֵלִים – שֶׁאוֹמְרִים בְּשׁוּרָה.

ח הַמְלַקֵּט עַצְמוֹת אָבִיו וְאִמּוֹ – הֲרֵי זֶה מִתְאַבֵּל עֲלֵיהֶן כָּל הַיּוֹם כֻּלּוֹ; וְלָעֶרֶב – אֵין מִתְאַבֵּל, אֲפִלּוּ צְרוּרִין לוֹ בִּסְדִינוֹ. וְאֵין אוֹמְרִין עֲלֵיהֶן קִינוֹת.

ט אֵין מַסְפִּידִין אֶת הַקְּטַנִּים. וּבֶן כַּמָּה שָׁנִים יִהְיֶה רָאוּי לְהֶסְפֵּד? בְּנֵי עֲנִיִּים אוֹ בְּנֵי זְקֵנִים – בְּנֵי חָמֵשׁ; וּבְנֵי עֲשִׁירִים – בְּנֵי שֵׁשׁ. אֶחָד זְכָרִים וְאֶחָד נְקֵבוֹת.

י תִּינוֹק שֶׁמֵּת: כָּל שְׁלֹשִׁים – יוֹצֵא בְּחֵיק, וְנִקְבָּר בְּאִשָּׁה אַחַת וּבִשְׁנֵי אֲנָשִׁים; אֲבָל לֹא בְּאִישׁ אֶחָד וּבִשְׁתֵּי נָשִׁים, מִפְּנֵי הַיִּחוּד. וְאֵין עוֹמְדִין עָלָיו בְּשׁוּרָה, וְאֵין אוֹמְרִין עָלָיו בִּרְכַּת אֲבֵלִים וְתַנְחוּמֵי אֲבֵלִים. בֶּן שְׁלֹשִׁים יוֹם גְּמוּרִים – יוֹצֵא בִּגְלוֹסְקְמָא קְטַנָּה הַנִּטֶּלֶת בָּאֲגַפַּיִם. וְעוֹמְדִין עָלָיו בְּשׁוּרָה, וְאוֹמְרִין עָלָיו בִּרְכַּת אֲבֵלִים וְתַנְחוּמֵי אֲבֵלִים. בֶּן שְׁנֵים עָשָׂר חֹדֶשׁ – יוֹצֵא בְּמִטָּה.

יא כָּל הַיּוֹצֵא בְּמִטָּה – רַבִּים מַצְהִיבִין עָלָיו; וְכֹל שֶׁאֵינוֹ יוֹצֵא בְּמִטָּה – אֵין רַבִּים מַצְהִיבִין עָלָיו.

וְכָל הַנִּכָּר לָרַבִּים – רַבִּים מִתְעַסְּקִין בּוֹ; וְכֹל שֶׁאֵינוֹ נִכָּר לָרַבִּים – אֵין רַבִּים חַיָּבִין

22. Rashi, *Mo'ed Kattan* 24b, states that a poor person will feel greater distress than a rich person at the loss of his children, for he has no other source of happiness. The passage continues, explaining that the elderly feel the loss of their children as deeply as the poor do.
23. His corpse is carried by hand to the cemetery instead of being placed in a coffin. The *Siftei Cohen* 353:2 states that it is permitted to use a coffin if one desires.
24. See *Hilchot Issurei Bi'ah*, ch. 22, which explains that this was a safeguard enacted to prevent licentious conduct. Usually, it is forbidden for many men to be together with one women unless one of them is married to her (*loc. cit.*:8). In this instance, because of the atmosphere of mourning involved, these restrictions were relaxed slightly (*Kiddushin* 80b).
25. Until a child is 30 days old, it is questionable whether his birth was viable. Accordingly, it is considered as if he was stillborn, in which instance, no mourning rites are observed for him. This applies even if we know that the pregnancy was full term [*Shulchan Aruch* (*Yoreh De'ah* 353:4)].
26. In which instance, his birth is assumed to have been viable.
27. As is an older person.
28. I.e., when a child was a year old or more.
29. I.e., attend the funeral.
30. I.e., the child was less than a year old.
31. The person would go out of his home and come in contact with his townsfolk.

large should occupy themselves with his [burial]. When one is not known to people at large, people at large need not occupy themselves with his [burial].

In a place where it is customary for women to walk before the bier, they walk before the bier;[32] [where it is customary for them to walk] after the bier, they walk after the bier.[33]

12. We do not eulogize servants and maidservants.[34] Nor do we stand in a line because of them, nor do we recite the mourning blessing nor the words of comfort for mourners. Instead, we tell [the master], "May the Omnipresent replenish your loss," as we would say if one lost an ox or a donkey.

CHAPTER THIRTEEN

1. How are mourners comforted? After the deceased is buried, the mourners gather together and stand at the side of the cemetery. All of those who attended the funeral stand around them, line after line.[1] A line may not be less than ten and the mourners are not included in the reckoning.[2]

2. The mourners stand at the left side of the comforters and the comforters pass by the mourners one by one and tell them: "May you be comforted from heaven."[3]

Afterwards, the mourner goes home. On each of the seven days of mourning, people come to comfort him. Whether new people come or not, [the others still comfort him].[4]

3. The mourner sits at the head [of the company]. The comforters are permitted to sit only on the ground,[5] as [Job 2:13] states:[6] "And they sat with him on the ground." They are not permitted to say anything until the mourner opens his mouth first,[7] as it is written (*ibid.*): "And no one spoke anything to him." And it states (*ibid.* 3:1, 4:1): "And then Job held forth.... And Eliphaz responded."

32. Since it is a funeral, we are not concerned that men may gaze upon them (*Sanhedrin* 20a and commentaries). The Jerusalem Talmud (*Sanhedrin* 2:4) states that this custom was practiced as if to say: It is because of a woman (Eve) that death was brought to the world.

33. The Jerusalem Talmud (*loc. cit.*) states that this custom has an advantage for it is more modest. The *Shulchan Aruch* (*Yoreh De'ah* 359:1) states that this is the custom that should be followed. The *Shulchan Aruch* (*loc. cit.*:2) continues, stating that even if they follow the bier, they should be prevented from entering the cemetery. Although there are communities where this advice is not followed, it is stringently adhered to in others. The *Siftei Cohen* 359:2 states that a woman's entry into a cemetery brings evil into the world.

34. *Berachot* 16b implies that were one to do so, that would detract from the praise with which one eulogizes a fellow Jew.

לְהִתְעַסֵּק בּוֹ. וּמָקוֹם שֶׁנָּהֲגוּ נָשִׁים לָצֵאת לִפְנֵי הַמִּטָּה – יוֹצְאוֹת לִפְנֵי הַמִּטָּה; לְאַחַר הַמִּטָּה – יוֹצְאוֹת לְאַחַר הַמִּטָּה.

יב הָעֲבָדִים וְהַשְּׁפָחוֹת – אֵין מַסְפִּידִין אוֹתָן, וְאֵין עוֹמְדִין עֲלֵיהֶן בְּשׁוּרָה, וְאֵין אוֹמְרִים עֲלֵיהֶן בִּרְכַּת אֲבֵלִים וְתַנְחוּמֵי אֲבֵלִים; אֶלָּא אוֹמְרִין לוֹ כְּשֵׁם שֶׁאוֹמְרִין לוֹ עַל שׁוֹרוֹ וְעַל חֲמוֹרוֹ: הַמָּקוֹם יְמַלֵּא חֶסְרוֹנְךָ.

פֶּרֶק שְׁלֹשָׁה עָשָׂר

א כֵּיצַד מְנַחֲמִין אֶת הָאֲבֵלִים? אַחַר שֶׁקּוֹבְרִין אֶת הַמֵּת מִתְקַבְּצִין הָאֲבֵלִים וְעוֹמְדִין בְּצַד בֵּית הַקְּבָרוֹת, וְכָל הַמְלַוִּין אֶת הַמֵּת עוֹמְדִין סָבִיב לָהֶן שׁוּרָה לִפְנֵי שׁוּרָה. וְאֵין שׁוּרָה פְּחוּתָה מֵעֲשָׂרָה, וְאֵין אֲבֵלִים מִן הַמִּנְיָן.

ב הָאֲבֵלִים עוֹמְדִין לִשְׂמֹאל הַמְנַחֲמִין, וְכָל הַמְנַחֲמִין בָּאִין אֵצֶל הָאֲבֵלִים אֶחָד אֶחָד, וְאוֹמְרִים לָהֶן: תְּנֻחֲמוּ מִן הַשָּׁמַיִם. וְאַחַר כָּךְ הוֹלֵךְ הָאָבֵל לְבֵיתוֹ. וְכָל יוֹם וָיוֹם מִשִּׁבְעַת יְמֵי אֲבֵלוּת בָּאִין בְּנֵי אָדָם לְנַחֲמוֹ, בֵּין שֶׁבָּאוּ פָּנִים חֲדָשׁוֹת בֵּין שֶׁלֹּא בָּאוּ.

ג הָאָבֵל מֵסֵב בְּרֹאשׁ. וְאֵין הַמְנַחֲמִין רַשָּׁאִין לֵישֵׁב אֶלָּא עַל גַּבֵּי קַרְקַע. שֶׁנֶּאֱמַר: וַיֵּשְׁבוּ אִתּוֹ לָאָרֶץ. וְאֵין רַשָּׁאִין לוֹמַר דָּבָר עַד שֶׁיִּפְתַּח הָאָבֵל אֶת פִּיו תְּחִלָּה. שֶׁנֶּאֱמַר: וְאֵין דֹּבֵר אֵלָיו דָּבָר; וּכְתִיב: אַחֲרֵי כֵן פָּתַח אִיּוֹב אֶת פִּיהוּ וְגוֹמֵר, וַיַּעַן אֱלִיפַז.

1. In this and the following halachah, the Rambam describes the custom referred to as *shurah*, "line." It is a fundamental element of the post-funeral rites.
2. Since the purpose of this custom is to comfort the mourners, the mourners should not be included in the quorum (Radbaz).
3. *Sanhedrin* 19a relates that, at the outset, the custom was that the comforters pass by the mourners as the Rambam describes. Afterwards, because of certain factors, it was ordained that the mourners should pass through the lines of comforters. Rami bar Abba states that Rabbi Yossi restored the original custom. Although the *Tur* (*Yoreh De'ah* 376) mentions this practice (albeit in brief), the *Shulchan Aruch* does not. In certain communities, the custom is observed as the Rambam describes. In others, the custom is that the mourners pass through the lines of the comforters.
4. On each of the seven days, each of the visitors should offer the traditional condolence wishes despite the fact that they offered them previously.
5. This law is not practiced today. Instead, the people who come to offer comfort sit on ordinary chairs.
6. As evident from this halachah, several of the laws of comforting mourners are derived from the account of how Job's friends came and comforted him after his children's death.
7. A person is not able to be comforted until he has regained a certain measure of composure. When he can look at others and speak to them, he is inwardly prepared to accept the consolation they offer.

Once the mourner shakes his head,[8] the comforters are no longer permitted to sit with him, so that they do not trouble him overly so.[9]

4. When a deceased person has no mourners who must be comforted,[10] ten upright men from the community at large come and sit in his place throughout the seven days of mourning.[11] Others gather around them. If there are not ten fixed people [who remain] throughout [the seven] days, [each day,] ten other people are selected and they sit in his place.

5. Everyone is obligated to stand in front of a *nasi* except a mourner and sick person.[12] To all who stand in his presence, he says: "Sit," with the exception of a mourner and sick person,[13] for that would imply: "Remain in your mourning," "Remain in your illness."

6. We sweep and we mop in a mourner's home. We wash plates, cups, pitchers, and bottles, and light lamps.[14] We do not, however, bring incense or spices.[15]

7. We do not bring the food for the meal of comfort to a mourner's home in silver or cork[16] utensils or the like, but wicker-work baskets of planed willow trees or the like so as not to embarrass a person who lacks means.[17] Similarly, beverages are not poured in clear glasses rather than colored ones[18] so as not to embarrass the poor whose wine is not of a high quality.

8. No one person should drink more than ten cups [of wine] in the house of a mourner: three before the meal, three during the meal, and four afterwards. One should not [drink] more lest he become intoxicated.[19]

8. When restating this law, the *Shulchan Aruch* (*Yoreh De'ah* 376:1) adds "in a manner in which it appears that he is dismissing the comforters."

9. For even if the people offering comfort are sincere, the sorrow is after all, that of the mourner and he must come to terms with it himself.

10. I.e., none of the seven close relatives mentioned in Chapter 1.

11. The Radbaz states that the intent is not that the ten people must stay there the entire day, but rather that they come in the morning and in the evening for a certain time.

It must be noted that the Ra'avad objects to the Rambam's ruling, stating that it does not have a Talmudic source. The *Migdal Oz* cites *Shabbat* 152b. In his *Kessef Mishneh*, Rav Yosef Karo states that the ten do not sit in the deceased's home, but instead sit in his place in the synagogue and have him recalled. In his *Shulchan Aruch* (*Yoreh De'ah* 376:3), however, he quotes the Rambam's ruling. The Ramah writes that he did not see this custom observed, but notes that the Maharil writes that it is proper to pray in the deceased's home together with a *minyan* if there are no mourners.

Kin'at Eliyahu notes that this is an example where the Rambam's ruling reflects the Kabbalistic tradition. For it is well known that in the first seven days after a person's passing, his soul frequently returns to his home.

12. A sick person may have difficulty standing because of the intensity of his illness and a mourner may have difficulty because of the intensity of his grief.

וְכֵיוָן שֶׁנִּעֲנַע בְּרֹאשׁוֹ – שׁוּב אֵין הַמְנַחֲמִין רַשָּׁאִין לֵישֵׁב אֶצְלוֹ, שֶׁלֹּא יַטְרִיחוּהוּ יוֹתֵר מִדַּי.

ד מֵת שֶׁאֵין לוֹ אֲבֵלִים לְהִתְנַחֵם – בָּאִים עֲשָׂרָה בְּנֵי אָדָם כְּשֵׁרִין וְיוֹשְׁבִין בִּמְקוֹמוֹ כָּל שִׁבְעַת יְמֵי הָאֲבֵלוּת, וּשְׁאָר הָעָם מִתְקַבְּצִין עֲלֵיהֶן. וְאִם לֹא הָיוּ שָׁם עֲשָׂרָה קְבוּעִין – בְּכָל יוֹם וָיוֹם מִתְקַבְּצִין עֲשָׂרָה מִשְּׁאָר הָעָם וְיוֹשְׁבִין בִּמְקוֹמוֹ.

ה הַכֹּל חַיָּבִין לַעֲמֹד בִּפְנֵי נָשִׂיא, חוּץ מֵאָבֵל וְחוֹלֶה. וּלְכָל הָעוֹמֵד מִפָּנָיו אוֹמֵר לוֹ 'שֵׁב', חוּץ מֵאָבֵל וְחוֹלֶה. שֶׁמַּשְׁמַע: יֵשֵׁב בְּאֶבְלוֹ, יֵשֵׁב בְּחָלְיוֹ.

ו מְכַבְּדִין וּמְרַבְּצִין בְּבֵית הָאֵבֶל, וּמְדִיחִין קְעָרוֹת וְכוֹסוֹת וְקִיתוֹנוֹת וּצְלוֹחִיּוֹת, וּמַדְלִיקִין אֶת הַנֵּרוֹת. אֲבָל אֵין מְבִיאִין שָׁם לֹא אֶת הַמֻּגְמָר וְלֹא אֶת הַבְּשָׂמִים.

ז אֵין מוֹלִיכִין לְבֵית הָאֵבֶל הַמַּאֲכָל שֶׁמַּבְרִין בּוֹ לֹא בִּכְלֵי כֶסֶף וְלֹא בִּכְלֵי שַׁעַם וְכַיּוֹצֵא בָּהֶן, אֶלָּא בִּכְלֵי נְסָרִים שֶׁל עֲרָבָה קְלוּפָה וְכַיּוֹצֵא בָּהֶן; שֶׁלֹּא לְבַיֵּשׁ אֶת מִי שֶׁאֵין לוֹ. וְאֵין מַשְׁקִין בִּזְכוּכִית לְבָנָה, אֶלָּא בִּצְבוּעָה; שֶׁלֹּא לְבַיֵּשׁ אֶת הָעֲנִיִּים שֶׁאֵין יֵינוֹתֵיהֶן טוֹבוֹת.

ח אֵין שׁוֹתִין בְּבֵית הָאֵבֶל יָתֵר עַל עֲשָׂרָה כּוֹסוֹת לְכָל אֶחָד וְאֶחָד: שְׁלֹשָׁה קֹדֶם אֲכִילָה, וּשְׁלֹשָׁה בְּתוֹךְ אֲכִילָה, וְאַרְבָּעָה לְאַחַר אֲכִילָה. וְלֹא יוֹסִיף, שֶׁמָּא יִשְׁתַּכֵּר.

13. Who rose even though they were not obligated to do so (*Kessef Mishneh*). To them, the *nasi* says: "May the Omnipresent bless you. Do not trouble yourselves" (*Nimukei Yosef to Mo'ed Kattan* 27b).

The *Shulchan Aruch* (*Yoreh De'ah* 376:2) quotes this law with regard to any scholar before whom a mourner or a sick person rise.

14. I.e., the mourner's home need not be dirty and dingy.

15. For their pleasant fragrance is a source of pleasure which is inappropriate in these circumstances.

Shulchan Aruch (*Yoreh De'ah* 378:7) states that before the funeral, if a corpse is being kept in a home, fragrances may be brought in to neutralize its undesirable odor.

16. The standard published text of *Mo'ed Kattan* 27a, the source of this halachah, and the *Tur* (*Yoreh De'ah* 378) speak of gold utensils. Perhaps the Rambam had a different version of that text.

17. I.e., our Sages did not desire that the meal of comfort be an opportunity for people to show off their wealth. As *Mo'ed Kattan, loc. cit.*, relates, such ostentatious conduct had become the ordinary practice. They felt that were that to be allowed, the poor would never bring food for the meal of comfort for they would be embarrass to show that they did not possess expensive containers. To prevent such a situation from occurring, they established a uniform standard which everyone could meet.

18. So that the wine will not be seen.

19. See *Ketubot* 8b which states that it was customary for the comforters to give the

9. We do not relate teachings [of Torah law] or homiletic insights in the home of a mourner.[20] Instead, we sit in grief.[21] In the presence of a corpse, we speak only of matters related to the corpse.[22] To be involved in Torah study in the presence of a corpse or in a cemetery is forbidden.[23]

10. One should not cry over the deceased for more than three days and one should not eulogize him for more than seven.

When does the above apply? To people at large. With regard to Torah scholars, by contrast, everything depends on their wisdom. [In any case,] we do not cry over them for more than 30 days, for we have no one greater than Moses our teacher and concerning him, [Deuteronomy 34:8] states: "[The children of Israel cried over Moses... for 30 days] and the days of crying in mourning for Moses concluded."

We do not eulogize for more than twelve months, for we have no one of greater wisdom than our holy teacher,[24] and he was eulogized for only twelve months. Similarly, if a report of a wise man's death reaches us after twelve months, we do not eulogize him.[25]

11. A person should not become excessively broken hearted because of a person's death, as [Jeremiah 22:10] states: "Do not weep for a dead man and do not shake your head because of him." That means [not to weep] excessively.[26] For [death] is the pattern of the world. And a person who causes himself grief because of the pattern of the world is a fool.

What should one do? Weep for three days, eulogize for seven, and observe the restrictions on cutting one's hair and the other five matters for 30 days.[27]

12. Whoever does not mourn over his dead in the manner which our Sages commanded is cruel. Instead, one should be fearful, worry, examine his deeds and repent.[28]

If one member of a group dies, the entire group should worry.[29] For the first three days, one should see himself as if a sword is drawn over his neck. From the third day until the seventh, [he should consider it] as if it is in the corner. From that time onward,[30] as if it is passing before him in the market

mourner to drink to drown his sorrow. Our Sages saw, however, that things were getting out of control and imposed these limits.

The *Kessef Mishneh* emphasizes that the Rambam is not requiring one to drink ten cups of wine, but rather prohibiting one from drinking more.

20. So as not to divert the mourner's attention from his grief. Moreover, the mourner is forbidden to study Torah. It is, however, customary for others who are not mourning to study *mishnayot* in honor of the deceased. Similarly, teachings that are related to mourning or recited in praise of the deceased are permitted.

21. The Radbaz states that one should be careful even with regard to talking about ordinary matters so that the mourner will not be distracted from his grief. Needless to say, frivolity is not in place. Knowing how to comfort mourners - to balance one's words so that they are allowed to release their feelings of grief, but result in feeling uplifted - is indeed a unique ability.

ט אֵין אוֹמְרִין שְׁמוּעָה וְהַגָּדָה בְּבֵית הָאֵבֶל, אֶלָּא יוֹשְׁבִין דָּוִין. וְכֵן אֵין אוֹמְרִין בִּפְנֵי הַמֵּת אֶלָּא דְבָרִים שֶׁל מֵת. אֲבָל לַעֲסֹק בְּדִבְרֵי תוֹרָה בְּפָנָיו אוֹ בְּבֵית הַקְּבָרוֹת – אָסוּר.

י אֵין בּוֹכִין עַל הַמֵּת יָתֵר מִשְּׁלֹשָׁה יָמִים, וְאֵין מַסְפִּידִין יָתֵר מִשִּׁבְעָה. בַּמֶּה דְבָרִים אֲמוּרִים? בִּשְׁאָר הָעָם; אֲבָל תַּלְמִידֵי חֲכָמִים – הַכֹּל לְפִי חָכְמָתָן. וְאֵין בּוֹכִין עֲלֵיהֶן יוֹתֵר מִשְּׁלֹשִׁים יוֹם; שֶׁאֵין לָנוּ גָּדוֹל מִמֹּשֶׁה רַבֵּנוּ, וּכְתִיב: וַיִּתְּמוּ יְמֵי בְכִי אֵבֶל מֹשֶׁה. וְכֵן אֵין מַסְפִּידִין יָתֵר עַל שְׁנֵים עָשָׂר חֹדֶשׁ. אֵין לָנוּ בְּחָכְמָה גָּדוֹל מֵרַבֵּנוּ הַקָּדוֹשׁ, וּשְׁנֵים עָשָׂר חֹדֶשׁ בִּלְבַד נִסְפַּד. וְכֵן חָכָם שֶׁבָּאָה שְׁמוּעָתוֹ לְאַחַר שְׁנֵים עָשָׂר חֹדֶשׁ – אֵין סוֹפְדִין אוֹתוֹ.

יא אַל יִתְקַשֶּׁה אָדָם עַל מֵתוֹ יָתֵר מִדַּי. שֶׁנֶּאֱמַר: אַל תִּבְכּוּ לְמֵת וְאַל תָּנֻדוּ לוֹ. כְּלוֹמַר: יָתֵר מִדַּי. שֶׁזֶּהוּ מִנְהָגוֹ שֶׁל עוֹלָם; וְהַמְּצַעֵר עַל מִנְהָגוֹ שֶׁל עוֹלָם – הֲרֵי זֶה טִפֵּשׁ. אֶלָּא כֵּיצַד יַעֲשֶׂה? שְׁלֹשָׁה לִבְכִי, שִׁבְעָה לְהֶסְפֵּד, שְׁלֹשִׁים יוֹם לְתִסְפֹּרֶת וְלִשְׁאָר הַחֲמִשָּׁה דְבָרִים.

יב כָּל מִי שֶׁאֵינוֹ מִתְאַבֵּל כְּמוֹ שֶׁצִּוּוּ חֲכָמִים – הֲרֵי זֶה אַכְזָרִי. אֶלָּא יִפְחַד וְיִדְאַג וִיפַשְׁפֵּשׁ בְּמַעֲשָׂיו וְיַחֲזֹר בִּתְשׁוּבָה. וְאֶחָד מִבְּנֵי חֲבוּרָה שֶׁמֵּת – תִּדְאַג כָּל הַחֲבוּרָה כֻּלָּהּ. כָּל שְׁלֹשָׁה יָמִים הָרִאשׁוֹנִים יִרְאֶה אֶת עַצְמוֹ כְּאִלּוּ חֶרֶב מֻנַּחַת לוֹ עַל צַוָּארוֹ; וּמִשְּׁלֹשָׁה וְעַד שִׁבְעָה – [כְּאִלּוּ הִיא] מֻנַּחַת בְּקֶרֶן זָוִית; מִכָּאן וְאֵילָךְ – [כְּאִלּוּ] עוֹבֶרֶת כְּנֶגְדּוֹ בַּשּׁוּק.

22. Eulogies in praise of him or details involving his burial.
23. *Berachot* 18a states that performing mitzvot in the presence of a corpse is "mocking the poor" (Cf. Proverbs 17:5), i.e., ridiculing the dead, as it were, by performing mitzvot which they cannot. For this reason, Torah study is forbidden. It is, however, common custom to recite Psalms in the presence of a corpse, not as study, but as prayer for his soul. See also Chapter 14, Halachah 25, which implies that when one studies in honor of the deceased, there is no prohibition.
24. Rabbi Yehudah *HaNasi*, the author of the Mishnah.
25. For the time to mourn over the tragedy has passed and our energies should be focused entirely on the future.
26. For the verse would not be prohibiting all expressions of grief.
27. Or longer in the case of the death of one's parents.

Mo'ed Kattan 27b states that when a person shows excessive grief, God chastises him: "Are you more merciful than I?" And that source states that when a person cries excessively over losing one loved one, he is likely to lose another.
28. As Ecclesiastes 7:12 states: "And the living shall take it to heart."
29. For God's judgment is extended against all of them.
30. For a year (*Mo'ed Kattan* 27b, the source of this halachah).

place. All of this is so that a person should prepare himself and repent and awake from his sleep.[31] Behold it is written [Jeremiah 5:3]: "You have stricken them, but they have not trembled." Implied is that one should awake and tremble.

CHAPTER FOURTEEN

1. It is a positive commandment of Rabbinic origin[1] to visit the sick, comfort mourners, to prepare for a funeral,[2] prepare a bride,[3] accompany guests, attend to all the needs of a burial, carry [a corpse] on one's shoulders,[4] walk before the bier, mourn, dig [a grave], and bury [the dead], and also to bring joy to a bride and groom and help them in all their needs. These are deeds of kindness that one carries out with his person that have no limit.[5]

Although all these mitzvot are of Rabbinic origin, they are included in the Scriptural commandment [Leviticus 19:18]: "Love your neighbor as yourself."[6] [That charge implies that] whatever you would like other people to do for you, you should do for your comrade in the Torah and mitzvot.[7]

2. The reward one receives for accompanying [guests] is greater than all of the others.[8] This is a statute which Abraham our Patriarch instituted and the path of kindness which he would follow. He would feed wayfarers, provide them

31. I.e., his over-preoccupation in material things and lack of sensitivity to spiritual values. Compare to *Hilchot Teshuvah* 3:4.

1. In his *Sefer HaMitzvot* (General Principle 2), the Rambam elaborates in the negation of the opinion of *Halachot Gedolot* who maintains that certain of the mitzvot mentioned are Scriptural in origin, e.g., comforting mourners and visiting the sick. The Ramban (*Hasagot* to *Sefer HaMitzvot*, General Principle 1) differs with the Rambam and supports the position of *Halachot Gedolot*.

2. The Hebrew expression used by the Rambam literally means "to take out the dead." Since the later clauses in the halachah which the details of actually carrying out a funeral, we assume that here the Rambam is speaking about the preparations for it.

The Rambam himself [*Sefer HaMitzvot* (positive commandment 231) and *Hilchot Sanhedrin* 15:8] states that burying the dead is a Scriptural commandment. Moreover, based on Chapter 3, Halachah 8, it is apparent that the resolution advanced by some - that the Scriptural obligation is incumbent on the deceased's relatives and the Rabbinic obligation on all others - is insufficient. For every Jew - even a priest - has an obligation to bury a corpse that has no others to tend to it.

Marganita Tava explains that the Scriptural obligation is to see that the burial is accomplished. The Rabbinic obligation is to become involved oneself.

3. The Hebrew expression used by the Rambam literally means "to bring a bride into [marriage]." It is not referring to the celebrations of the wedding for participation in that is mentioned in the later clauses of the halachah. Instead, it refers to helping a bride prepare to marry and set up home.

4. As was the practice in the funeral procession. See Chapter 4, Halachah 2.

5. I.e., with regard to the financial aspects of this mitzvah, there is a limit, for a person

כָּל זֶה לְהָכִין עַצְמוֹ, וְיַחֲזוֹר וְיֵעוֹר מִשְּׁנָתוֹ. וַהֲרֵי הוּא אוֹמֵר: הִכִּיתָה אֹתָם וְלֹא חָלוּ. מִכְּלָל שֶׁצָּרִיךְ לְהָקִיץ וְלָחוּל.

פֶּרֶק אַרְבָּעָה עָשָׂר

א מִצְוַת עֲשֵׂה שֶׁל דִּבְרֵיהֶם לְבַקֵּר חוֹלִים, וּלְנַחֵם אֲבֵלִים, וּלְהוֹצִיא הַמֵּת, וּלְהַכְנִיס הַכַּלָּה, וּלְלַוּוֹת הָאוֹרְחִים, וּלְהִתְעַסֵּק בְּכָל צָרְכֵי הַקְּבוּרָה: לָשֵׂאת עַל הַכָּתֵף, וְלֵילֵךְ לְפָנָיו, וְלִסְפּוֹד, וְלַחְפּוֹר, וְלִקְבּוֹר. וְכֵן לְשַׂמֵּחַ הַכַּלָּה וְהֶחָתָן, וּלְסַעֲדָם בְּכָל צָרְכֵיהֶם. וְאֵלּוּ הֵן גְּמִילוּת חֲסָדִים שֶׁבְּגוּפוֹ, שֶׁאֵין לָהֶם שִׁעוּר.

אַף עַל פִּי שֶׁכָּל מִצְוֹת אֵלּוּ מִדִּבְרֵיהֶם, הֲרֵי הֵן בִּכְלַל וְאָהַבְתָּ לְרֵעֲךָ כָּמוֹךָ – כָּל הַדְּבָרִים שֶׁאַתָּה רוֹצֶה שֶׁיַּעֲשׂוּ אוֹתָם לְךָ אֲחֵרִים, עֲשֵׂה אַתָּה אוֹתָן לְאָחִיךָ בְּתוֹרָה וּבְמִצְוֹת.

ב שְׂכַר הַלְּוָיָה מְרֻבֶּה מִן הַכֹּל. וְהוּא הַחֹק שֶׁחֲקָקוֹ אַבְרָהָם אָבִינוּ, וְדֶרֶךְ הַחֶסֶד שֶׁנָּהַג בָּהּ: מַאֲכִיל עוֹבְרֵי דְרָכִים, וּמַשְׁקֶה אוֹתָן, וּמְלַוֶּה אוֹתָן.

should not give more than a fifth of his resources to charity. But with regard to physically exerting oneself on behalf of others, there is no limit (Jerusalem Talmud, *Pe'ah* 1:1). This concept is considered so fundamental to Judaism that our Sages instituted its recitation every day, directly after the recitation of the blessings of the Torah in the morning.

6. I.e., the one Scriptural charge has many Rabbinic applications.

Likkutei Sichos, Vol. XXV, p. 75, explains that by stating that these mitzvot are included in the biblical commandment to love one's fellowman, the Rambam is implying that not only is the effect of one's deeds - that the sick be visited, the mourners be comforted, etc. - important, it is important that one carry out these deeds out of love. The recipient of his kindness must also feel the positive feelings that the giver has for him.

7. By adding the latter phrase, the Rambam implies that complete obligation of the mitzvah of loving one's fellowman applies only to one's fellow Jew, and more particularly, to observant Jews.

8. *Sotah* 46b states: "There is no measure to the reward one receives for accompanying guests." There are two dimensions to this activity. First of all, accompanying a guest lifts up that person's spirits. Secondly, it provides him with protection which in Talmudic times - and even today in certain areas - is very necessary.

It is possible to explain that accompanying guests is an activity that one performs with one's physical person, while the other deeds of kindness are performed with one's financial resources as well as with one's person. The fact that one is willing to take the extra effort and exert himself physically on behalf of another person is thus more clearly expressed in the mitzvah of accompanying wayfarers. And to refer to the previous halachah, the Rambam is speaking about "deeds of kindness that one carries out with his person."

Moreover, accompanying a guest, maintaining a connection with him even after he leaves one's house, demonstrates one's love and care. This endows all of one's previous efforts in caring for the guest with greater significance, for it shows that they were an expression of sincere love (*Likkutei Sichos,* Vol. XXV, p. 74).

with drink, and accompany them.[9] Showing hospitality for guests surpasses receiving the Divine Presence as [Genesis 18:3] states: "And he saw and behold there were three people."[10]

Accompanying them is greater than showing them hospitality. Our Sages said:[11] "Whoever does not accompany them is considered as if he shed blood."

3. We compel [people to accompany wayfarers] in the same manner as we compel them to give charity.[12] The court would prepare agents to accompany people who travel from place to place. If they were lax in this matter, it is considered as if they shed blood.[11] Even a person who accompanies a colleague for four cubits will receive a great reward.[13]

What is the extent to which a person must accompany [a colleague]? A teacher must accompany his student to the outskirts of the city.[14] A person must accompany a colleague to the city's Sabbath limits.[15] A student must accompany his teacher for a *parsah*.[16] If he was his master teacher,[17] [he must accompany him] until three *parseot*.

4. It is a mitzvah incumbent on everyone to visit the sick. Even a person of great spiritual stature should visit one of lesser stature. One may visit many times during the day. Whoever increases [the frequency of his visits] is praiseworthy provided he does not become burdensome. Whoever[18] visits a sick person removes a portion of his sickness and relieves him. Whoever does not visit [the sick] is consider as if he shed blood.[19]

5. We do not visit the sick except from the third day onward.[20] If, however, a person became ill suddenly and his illness became very severe, he should be visited immediately.

We do not visit the sick during the first three hours of the day, nor in the last three hours because [his attendants] are tending to the sick person's needs.[21]

9. As evident from the Biblical narrative in Genesis, ch. 18. See also the commentaries to Genesis 21:33.
10. Abraham was enjoying a vision of God and yet he abandoned that vision to care for the three wayfarers (*Shabbat* 127a).
11. See *Sotah* 46b (quoted by the Rambam, *Hilchot Rotzeach* 9:3) which explains that when the elders of a city bring a calf as atonement for an unsolved murder, they say "Our hands did not shed this blood." Now we do not suspect them of actually killing the person. Instead the intent is that we did not fail to provide him with accompaniment.
12. *Hilchot Matanot Aniyim* 7:10 states that a person who does not desire to give charity is compelled to give an amount appropriate to his wealth. If necessary the court seizes his property and sells it. Similarly, he is compelled to either physically accompany or pay for the accompaniment of a colleague.
13. *Sotah* 46b states that Pharaoh accompanied Abraham for four cubits and as a result merited to subjugate Abraham's descendants for four generations.
14. The term used by the Rambam has a specific halachic definition: 72 cubits and a fraction beyond the city's border.

וּגְדוֹלָה הַכְנָסַת אוֹרְחִים מֵהַקְבָּלַת פְּנֵי שְׁכִינָה, שֶׁנֶּאֱמַר: וַיַּרְא וְהִנֵּה שְׁלֹשָׁה אֲנָשִׁים.
וְלִוּוּיָם יוֹתֵר מֵהַכְנָסָתָן.
אָמְרוּ חֲכָמִים: כֹּל שֶׁאֵינוֹ מְלַוֶּה – כְּאִלּוּ שׁוֹפֵךְ דָּמִים.

ג כּוֹפִין לִלְוָיָה כְּדֶרֶךְ שֶׁכּוֹפִין לִצְדָקָה. וּבֵית דִּין הָיוּ מְתַקְּנִין שְׁלוּחִין לְלַוּוֹת אָדָם הָעוֹבֵר מִמָּקוֹם לְמָקוֹם. וְאִם נִתְעַצְּלוּ בְּדָבָר זֶה – מַעֲלֶה עֲלֵיהֶם כְּאִלּוּ שָׁפְכוּ דָּמִים.
אֲפִלּוּ הַמְלַוֶּה אֶת חֲבֵרוֹ אַרְבַּע אַמּוֹת – יֵשׁ לוֹ שָׂכָר הַרְבֵּה. וְכַמָּה שִׁעוּר לְוָיָה שֶׁחַיָּב אָדָם בָּהּ?
הָרַב לַתַּלְמִיד – עַד עִבּוּרָהּ שֶׁל עִיר.
וְהָאִישׁ לַחֲבֵרוֹ – עַד תְּחוּם שַׁבָּת.
וְהַתַּלְמִיד לָרַב – עַד פַּרְסָה.
וְאִם הָיָה רַבּוֹ מֻבְהָק – עַד שָׁלֹשׁ פַּרְסָאוֹת.

ד בִּקּוּר חוֹלִים – מִצְוָה עַל הַכֹּל. אֲפִלּוּ גָּדוֹל מְבַקֵּר אֶת הַקָּטָן. וּמְבַקְּרִין הַרְבֵּה פְּעָמִים בַּיּוֹם. וְכָל הַמּוֹסִיף – מְשֻׁבָּח. וּבִלְבַד שֶׁלֹּא יַטְרִיחַ. וְכָל הַמְבַקֵּר אֶת הַחוֹלֶה – כְּאִלּוּ נָטַל חֵלֶק מֵחָלְיוֹ וְהֵקֵל מֵעָלָיו; וְכֹל שֶׁאֵינוֹ מְבַקֵּר – כְּאִלּוּ שׁוֹפֵךְ דָּמִים.

ה אֵין מְבַקְּרִין אֶת הַחוֹלֶה אֶלָּא מִיּוֹם שְׁלִישִׁי וָהָלְאָה. וְאִם קָפַץ עָלָיו הַחֹלִי וְהִכְבִּיד – מְבַקְּרִין אוֹתוֹ מִיָּד.
וְאֵין מְבַקְּרִין אֶת הַחוֹלֶה לֹא בְּשָׁלֹשׁ שָׁעוֹת רִאשׁוֹנוֹת בַּיּוֹם וְלֹא בְּשָׁלֹשׁ אַחֲרוֹנוֹת, מִפְּנֵי שֶׁהֵן מִתְעַסְּקִין בְּצָרְכֵי הַחוֹלֶה.

15. 2000 cubits (approximately a kilometer) beyond the city's border.
16. Four *mil*; each *mil* is approximately a kilometer.
17. The person from whom he received most of his knowledge.
18. *Nedarim* 40a states that when the visitor is the same age as the sick person, he removes one sixtieth of his illness. The Rambam's statements (based on *Vayikra Rabbah* 34:1) imply that this concept applies even when the visitor is not of the same age,
19. From *Nedarim, loc. cit.*, it is apparent that one of the positive dimensions of visiting the sick is that one sees to his needs: e.g., making sure his room is neat and clean. Beyond that, one cannot underestimate the positive effect of the lift in a patient's morale accomplished by a visit.
20. From *Nedarim* 40a and commentaries, it appears that the rationale is that the sick person's enemies may become jealous of the attention he is getting and cast an evil eye against him. For this reason, relatives and close friends - whose visits would not be conspicuous - may visit immediately (*Kessef Mishneh*, based on the Jerusalem Talmud, *Pe'ah* 3:7).
21. The Radbaz notes that the Rambam ignores the reasons stated by the Talmud (*Nedarim* 40a) and instead supplies rationales of his own. The Radbaz suggests that perhaps this was motivated by the Rambam's own experience as a doctor. Significantly, the *Shulchan Aruch* (*Yoreh De'ah* 335:4) quotes the wording used by the Talmud.

We do not visit patients with stomach illnesses, eye illnesses, or headaches because the visits are difficult for them.[22]

6. When one comes to visit a sick person, he should not sit on a bed, nor on a chair, nor on a bench, nor on a high place,[23] nor above [the invalid's] head. Instead, he should wrap himself in a *tallit*, sit below his head,[24] entreat [God] for mercy on his behalf and depart.

7. It appears to me that comforting mourners takes precedence over visiting the sick. For comforting mourners is an expression of kindness to the living and the dead.[25]

8. When a person is faced with either [tending to] a corpse or a bride, he should leave the bride and occupy himself with the corpse. Thus [Ecclesiastes 7:4] states: "The heart of the wise is in the house of mourning."[26]

When a corpse and a bride confront each other on a road,[27] the corpse is turned aside before the bride.[28] Both of these should turn aside before a king[29]

9. We nullify Torah study for a funeral and for a wedding.[30] When does the above apply? When there are not enough people to care for [a corpse]. If there are enough people to care for it, [Torah study] should not nullified. Whoever does not occupy himself with Torah study is obligated to occupy himself with [the corpse].[31]

10. If there is one corpse in a city, all the inhabitants of the city are forbidden to perform work until they bury him. If there is a person [responsible][32] for tending to the needs of the funeral, the others are permitted [to work].

22. People with stomach illnesses will be embarrassed if visited and people with eye illnesses and headaches will be strained by the necessity to receive company (*Nedarim* 41a). The *Shulchan Aruch* (*loc. cit.*:8) states that although the visitor should not enter the sick person's room in these instances, he should visit his home, inquire if there are any tasks that he could perform to ease his sickness, and pray for him.

23. Based on the statements of *Tosafot* (*Shabbat* 12b), the Ramah (*Yoreh De'ah* 335:3) states that these restrictions apply only when the invalid is lying on the ground. If he is lying on a bed, the visitors may also sit on a chair or bed.

24. Next to him or at his feet. *Shabbat* 12b states that the Divine Presence rests at the head of a sick person. Therefore a visitor should not sit there and he should wrap himself in a *tallit* in reverence.

25. I.e., in addition to lifting the spirits of the living, it also shows respect for the dead.

The expression "it appears to me" indicates a conclusion reached by the Rambam without a clear source from the earlier Rabbinic literature. The Radbaz questions the Rambam's conclusion, noting that, as stated above (Halachah 4 and notes), visiting the sick is sometimes a life and death matter and that cannot be said about comforting mourners. The *Or Sameach* supports the Rambam's ruling, bringing proof from *Shabbat* 12b which mentions comforting mourners before visiting the sick in the same statement. Implied is that they are mentioned in the order of priority.

The *Siftei Cohen* 335:11 quotes the *Bayit Chadash* who states that the Rambam's

וְאֵין מְבַקְּרִין לֹא חוֹלֵי מֵעַיִם וְלֹא חוֹלֵי הָעַיִן וְלֹא מְחוֹשֵׁי הָרֹאשׁ, מִפְּנֵי שֶׁהַבִּקּוּר קָשֶׁה לָהֶן.

ו הַנִּכְנָס לְבַקֵּר אֶת הַחוֹלֶה – לֹא יֵשֵׁב לֹא עַל גַּבֵּי מִטָּה, וְלֹא עַל גַּבֵּי כִּסֵּא, וְלֹא עַל גַּבֵּי סַפְסָל, וְלֹא עַל גַּבֵּי מָקוֹם גָּבוֹהַּ, וְלֹא לְמַעְלָה מִמְּרַאֲשׁוֹתָיו. אֶלָּא מִתְעַטֵּף וְיוֹשֵׁב לְמַטָּה מִמְּרַאֲשׁוֹתָיו, וּמְבַקֵּשׁ עָלָיו רַחֲמִים וְיוֹצֵא.

ז יֵרָאֶה לִי, שֶׁנֶּחָמַת אֲבֵלִים קוֹדֶם לְבִקּוּר חוֹלִים; שֶׁנִּחוּם אֲבֵלִים גְּמִילוּת חֶסֶד עִם הַחַיִּים וְעִם הַמֵּתִים.

ח מִי שֶׁהָיָה לְפָנָיו מֵת וְכַלָּה – מַנִּיחַ אֶת הַכַּלָּה וּמִתְעַסֵּק עִם הַמֵּת. וְכֵן הוּא אוֹמֵר: לֵב חֲכָמִים בְּבֵית אֵבֶל וְגוֹמֵר. מֵת וְכַלָּה שֶׁפָּגְעוּ זֶה בָּזֶה בַּדֶּרֶךְ – מַעֲבִירִין אֶת הַמֵּת מִלִּפְנֵי הַכַּלָּה. וְזֶה וָזֶה עוֹבְרִין מִלִּפְנֵי הַמֶּלֶךְ.

ט מְבַטְּלִין תַּלְמוּד תּוֹרָה לְהוֹצָאַת הַמֵּת וּלְהַכְנָסַת הַכַּלָּה. בַּמֶּה דְּבָרִים אֲמוּרִים? בְּשֶׁאֵין לוֹ כָּל צָרְכּוֹ; אֲבָל יֵשׁ לוֹ כָּל צָרְכּוֹ – אֵין מְבַטְּלִין. וְכֹל שֶׁאֵין מִתְעַסְּקִין בַּתּוֹרָה – חַיָּבִין לְהִתְעַסֵּק עִמּוֹ.

י מֵת אֶחָד בָּעִיר – כָּל בְּנֵי הָעִיר אֲסוּרִין בַּעֲשִׂיַּת מְלָאכָה עַד שֶׁיִּקְבְּרוּהוּ. וְאִם יֵשׁ לוֹ מִי שֶׁיִּתְעַסֵּק בִּצְרָכָיו – מֻתָּרִין.

ruling applies when it is possible to visit only one of them. When it is possible to visit them both, one should visit the sick first, lest there be a task that has to be performed that will help him recuperate.

26. Similarly, Ecclesiastes 7:2 states: "It is preferable to go to the house of mourning than the house of feasting."

27. And it is impossible for both processions to pass side by side. Alternatively, even when there is room, but one would not want the two processions to meet for one will disturb the mood of the other.

28. For mitzvot involving the living take precedence over those involving the dead (*Siftei Cohen* 360:1).

29. For we are commanded to hold a king in awe (Radbaz, based on *Ketubot* 17a).

See *Semachot*, ch. 12, which states that King Agripas moved aside for a bride. The Sages praised him for his modesty and asked him to explain his conduct. He said: "I wear a crown every day. She gets only this one opportunity."

30. I.e., we are obligated to nullify our studies for these purposes (*Siftei Cohen* 361:1).

The *Shulchan Aruch* (*Yoreh De'ah* 361:2) states that this refers to attending the funeral. With regard to preparations for the funeral, it is proper that there be a burial society of select individuals who discharge this responsibility.

31. The Radbaz states that it is not customary to follow this ruling. Instead, people commonly rely on the leniency stated in the following halachah.

32. I.e., relatives and/or a burial society.

11 When a Torah scholar[33] dies, unless there are 600,000 to accompany him, we nullify Torah study for his funeral.[34] If there are 600,000, we do not nullify Torah study. If he would also teach others, there is no limit. Instead, we nullify everyone [from their ordinary activity] for his funeral.

12. We bury the dead of the gentiles,[35] comfort their mourners, and visit their sick, as an expression of the ways of peace.

13. It is forbidden to benefit from a cemetery. What is implied? We do not eat or drink, perform work, read [the Torah] or study [the Oral Law] within them. The general principle is: We do not benefit from them[36] nor act frivolously within them.[37]

A person should not walk within four cubits of a grave with *tefillin* in his hand or a Torah scroll in his arm,[38] nor should he pray there.[39] At a distance of four cubits, this is permitted.

14. When a person is transporting the bones [of a corpse] from one place to another, he should not put them in a leather sack, place them on a donkey and ride upon them,[40] because this is treating them contemptuously. If he was afraid of thieves or robbers, this is permitted.

15. We do not move a corpse from one grave to another,[41] even from a denigrating site to an honorable one. If the grave was located in another person's property,[42] the corpse may be moved even from an honorable site to a denigrating one.[43]

16. We do not bury one corpse on top of another,[44] nor do we bury two

33. See the *Siftei Cohen* 361:2 who questions whether this refers to a person who has both read the *Tanach* and studied Torah law, or if it is sufficient merely to have been involved in only one of these branches of study.

34. So that others will attend. This token of respect is granted because of the deceased's study. *Ketubot* 17a states: "Just as the Torah was brought into the world with 600,000 in attendance [at Sinai]; so, too, it [i.e., a sage who has studied it] is taken from the world with 600,000."

35. Needless to say, in a separate cemetery (Radbaz).

36. The *Shulchan Aruch* (*Yoreh De'ah* 368:1) states that it is forbidden to use the grasses which grow there. If the grasses have become overgrown and one must trim them, they should be burnt in their place.

37. This is an expression of honor for the dead (*Siftei Cohen* 368:1).

The *Biurei HaGra* explains that the prohibition against eating mentioned above stems from the prohibition against acting frivolously and the prohibition against studying stems from the prohibition against mocking the dead mentioned further in these notes. *Kin'at Eliyahu* differs and maintains that this entire clause is an explanation of the prohibition against benefiting from a cemetery stated at the outset.

38. I.e., even if he is not performing a mitzvah, carrying the religious article itself is forbidden (Radbaz).

יא תַּלְמִיד חָכָם שֶׁמֵּת, אֲפִלּוּ הָיוּ עִמּוֹ עַד שִׁשִּׁים רִבּוֹא – מְבַטְּלִין תַּלְמוּד תּוֹרָה לְהוֹצָאָתוֹ. הָיוּ שִׁשִּׁים רִבּוֹא – אֵין מְבַטְּלִין. וְאִם הָיָה מְלַמֵּד לַאֲחֵרִים – אֵין לוֹ שִׁעוּר, אֶלָּא מְבַטְּלִין הַכֹּל לְהוֹצָאָתוֹ.

יב קוֹבְרִין מֵתֵי עוֹבְדֵי כוֹכָבִים, וּמְנַחֲמִין אֲבֵלֵיהֶם, וּמְבַקְּרִין חוֹלֵיהֶם, מִפְּנֵי דַּרְכֵי שָׁלוֹם.

יג בָּתֵּי הַקְּבָרוֹת אֲסוּרִין בַּהֲנָאָה. כֵּיצַד? אֵין אוֹכְלִין בָּהֶן, וְאֵין שׁוֹתִין בָּהֶן, וְאֵין עוֹשִׂין בָּהֶן מְלָאכָה, וְלֹא קוֹרִין בָּהֶן, וְלֹא שׁוֹנִין בָּהֶן. כְּלָלוֹ שֶׁל דָּבָר: אֵין נֵאוֹתִין בָּהֶן, וְלֹא נוֹהֲגִין בָּהֶן קַלּוּת רֹאשׁ. לֹא יֵלֵךְ אָדָם בְּתוֹךְ אַרְבַּע אַמּוֹת שֶׁל קֶבֶר וּתְפִלִּין בְּיָדוֹ וְסֵפֶר תּוֹרָה בִּזְרוֹעוֹ, וְלֹא יִתְפַּלֵּל שָׁם. וּבְרָחוֹק אַרְבַּע אַמּוֹת – מֻתָּר.

יד הַמּוֹלִיךְ עֲצָמוֹת מִמָּקוֹם לְמָקוֹם – לֹא יִתְּנֵם בְּדִסְקִיָּא וְיַנִּיחֵם עַל גַּבֵּי חֲמוֹרוֹ וְיִרְכַּב עֲלֵיהֶם, מִפְּנֵי שֶׁנּוֹהֵג בָּהֶן מִנְהַג בִּזָּיוֹן. וְאִם הָיָה מִתְיָרֵא מִפְּנֵי הַגַּנָּבִים וּמִפְּנֵי הַלִּסְטִים – מֻתָּר.

טו אֵין מְפַנִּין אֶת הַמֵּת מִקֶּבֶר לְקֶבֶר, אֲפִלּוּ מִבָּזוּי לִמְכֻבָּד. וְאִם הָיָה בְּתוֹךְ שָׂדֵהוּ – מְפַנֵּהוּ אֲפִלּוּ מִמְּכֻבָּד לְבָזוּי.

טז אֵין קוֹבְרִין מֵת עַל גַּבֵּי מֵת, וְלֹא שְׁנֵי מֵתִים כְּאֶחָד, שֶׁבִּזָּיוֹן הוּא.

39. *Berachot* 18a explains that fulfilling mitzvot in the presence of the dead is "mocking the poor" (cf. Proverbs 17:5), i.e., ridiculing them, as it were, by performing mitzvot which they cannot.
40. I.e., he should not sit on the bones, but rather hang them over the side of the donkey [*Shulchan Aruch* (*Yoreh De'ah* 403:10)]. Compare to *Hilchot Sefer Torah* 10:11 which speaks of transporting a Torah scroll.
41. For the disruption of their rest is difficult for the souls to bear (Jerusalem Talmud, *Mo'ed Kattan* 2:4). The Radbaz explains that being disinterred is denigrating to the deceased.
42. And the new grave was located in property belonging to the deceased or his heirs.
43. For a soul desires that its body's eternal rest be in his own property, together with his family members (Jerusalem Talmud, *loc. cit.*; *Siftei Cohen* 363:1).
Among the other reasons license is given to disinter a corpse are:
a) to bring its remains to *Eretz Yisrael* (see *Hilchot Melachim* 5:11),
b) it was originally buried with the intent that it be moved,
c) there is a possibility that the remains will be destroyed by water or looted by gentiles [*Shulchan Aruch* (*loc. cit.*)]. Needless to say, it is permitted to disinter a corpse buried in a non-Jewish cemetery and bury him in a Jewish one. See also *Hilchot Beit HaBechirah* 7:13-14.
44. If there is six handbreadths of earth between the two, it is permitted [*Kessef Mishneh*, *Shulchan Aruch* (*Yoreh De'ah* 362:4)].

corpses together, for this is denigrating.[45] A baby who sleeps with his mother may be buried with her.[46]

17. It is not forbidden to benefit from the earth of a grave. For ordinary earth never becomes forbidden.[47] It is, by contrast, forbidden to benefit from a building which is a grave.

18. When a person builds a grave for a deceased person, the grave does not become forbidden until the corpse is placed inside.[48] Even if one places a stillborn infant in a grave, the prohibition [against benefiting from it] takes effect.

19. [The following rules apply when] a monument[49] is built for the sake of a living person[50] and a corpse[51] is placed within. If one row of bricks was added for the sake of the deceased person, it is forbidden to derive benefit from the entire [monument] even after the corpse was removed from there.[52] If one recognized the addition, one may remove it and then the remainder is permitted. If [the monument] was made for the sake of the deceased,[53] once the corpse was placed in it, it becomes forbidden even though the corpse was removed.[54]

20. When a person builds a grave for his father and then buries [his father's corpse] in another grave, he should never bury another corpse in that grave.[55] Instead, it is forbidden to benefit from this grave forever as an expression of respect for his father.

21. It is forbidden to benefit from a corpse[56] with the exception of its hair. One may benefit from [hair], because it is not his body.[57] Similarly, it is forbidden to benefit from the coffin and the shrouds.[58] There is no prohibition against benefiting from garments prepared to be used as shrouds. Even if one knitted a garment to be used for a corpse, they are not forbidden until they reach the bier which is buried with him. For designation [of an article to be used for a corpse] does not cause it to be forbidden.[59]

45. For each person should be given his own individual resting place.
46. *Semachot*, ch. 13, states that similarly, a father may be buried with his young daughters. The general principle is: Children that are permitted to sleep in the same bed as their parents may be buried with them. This principle is quoted by *Shulchan Aruch* (*Yoreh De'ah* 362:3).
47. The Ramah (*Yoreh De'ah* 364:1) quotes opinions which maintain that if one removed earth from a grave and then returned it to the grave, it is forbidden to benefit from that earth.
48. The fact that it is designated for that purpose is not sufficient cause for it to become forbidden (*Sanhedrin* 47b). This is a general principle that applies in other halachic contexts as well (e.g., the designation of compartments for *tefillin*). The designation of an object for a ritual purpose has no effect. It must actually be used for that purpose.
49. A structure over a grave. There is a question if the same rules would apply to a grave

וְקָטָן הַיָּשֵׁן עִם אִמּוֹ – נִקְבָּר עִמָּהּ.

יז עֲפַר הַקֶּבֶר – אֵינוֹ אָסוּר בַּהֲנָאָה, שֶׁאֵין קַרְקַע עוֹלָם נֶאֱסֶרֶת. אֲבָל קֶבֶר הַבִּנְיָן – אָסוּר בַּהֲנָאָה.

יח הַבּוֹנֶה קֶבֶר לְמֵת – לֹא נֶאֱסַר עַד שֶׁיִּכָּנֵס בּוֹ הַמֵּת. וַאֲפִלּוּ הֵטִיל בּוֹ נֵפֶל – נֶאֱסַר בַּהֲנָאָה.

יט נֶפֶשׁ שֶׁנַּעֲשָׂה לְשֵׁם חַי, וְשָׂם בּוֹ הַמֵּת, וְהוֹסִיף בּוֹ דִּימוֹס אֶחָד לְשֵׁם הַמֵּת, אַף עַל פִּי שֶׁפִּנָּה הַמֵּת – הַכֹּל אָסוּר בַּהֲנָאָה. וְאִם הִכִּיר אֶת הַתּוֹסֶפֶת – חוֹלֵץ אוֹתָהּ, וְהַשְּׁאָר מֻתָּר. נַעֲשָׂה לְשֵׁם הַמֵּת – כֵּיוָן שֶׁהוּטַל בּוֹ הַמֵּת נֶאֱסַר, אַף עַל פִּי שֶׁפִּנָּהוּ.

כ הַבּוֹנֶה קֶבֶר לְאָבִיו, וְהָלַךְ וּקְבָרוֹ בְּקֶבֶר אַחֵר – הֲרֵי זֶה לֹא יִקָּבֵר בּוֹ מֵת אַחֵר עוֹלָמִית, וְהַקֶּבֶר הַזֶּה אָסוּר בַּהֲנָאָה, מִפְּנֵי כְּבוֹד אָבִיו.

כא הַמֵּת אָסוּר בַּהֲנָאָה כֻּלּוֹ; חוּץ מִשְּׂעָרוֹ שֶׁהוּא מֻתָּר בַּהֲנָאָה, מִפְּנֵי שֶׁאֵינוֹ גּוּפוֹ. וְכֵן אֲרוֹנוֹ וְכָל תַּכְרִיכָיו – אֲסוּרִין בַּהֲנָאָה. אֲבָל כֵּלִים הַמּוּכָנִים לְתַכְרִיךְ – לֹא נֶאֶסְרוּ בַּהֲנָאָה. אֲפִלּוּ אָרַג בֶּגֶד לְמֵת – לֹא נֶאֱסַר עַד שֶׁיַּגִּיעַ בַּמִּטָּה הַנִּקְבֶּרֶת עִמּוֹ. שֶׁאֵין הַהַזְמָנָה אוֹסֶרֶת.

dug out from the ground. See the *Tur* (*Yoreh De'ah* 364) and commentaries. This question also applies with regard to the following halachah.

50. With the intent that when he dies, he would be buried there.

51. For whom the monument was not built.

52. If a row of bricks was not added, as long as the corpse is within the monument, it is forbidden to benefit from it. Once the corpse is removed, it is permitted [*Tur* and the *Shulchan Aruch* (*Yoreh De'ah* 364:1)].

53. I.e., after his death.

54. Since the monument was designated for the corpse and the corpse was placed there temporarily, the two influences combine to cause the monument to be forbidden forever. Note the parallel to *Hilchot Tefillin* 4:9.

55. The *Shulchan Aruch* (*Yoreh De'ah* 364:7) rules slightly more leniently, stating that the son may not be buried there, but another person may.

56. The Radbaz mentions a difference of opinion if this applies only to a Jewish corpse or also to a gentile corpse. The *Shulchan Aruch* (*Yoreh De'ah* 349:1) rules unequivocally that the ruling applies to both.

57. For the hair will remain unchanged after the person's death (see *Arachin* 7b). See also to *Hilchot Sanhedrin* 12:4 and notes. In his *Kessef Mishneh*, Rav Yosef Caro questions the Rambam's ruling and in his *Shulchan Aruch* (*Yoreh De'ah* 349:2), he rules that it is forbidden to benefit from the hair of a corpse.

58. For it was both designated and used for burial.

59. The *Siftei Cohen* 349:8 rules that, similarly, if an object was used for burial, even though it was not designated for that purpose, it is not forbidden.

22. It is forbidden to benefit from all the garments thrown upon the deceased[60] on the bier which is buried with him, so that because of them, confusion will not arise with regard to shrouds.[61]

23. If a person's father or mother were throwing garments [on the bier] in their extreme aggravation,[62] it is a mitzvah for others to save them.[63] If they reached the bier which is buried with [the corpse], we do not save them.[64]

24. We teach a person that he should not recklessly destroy property and throw it to oblivion. It is better to give it to the poor than to throw it to maggots and worms.[65] Whoever casts many articles on a deceased person violates the commandment against destroying property.[66]

25. When a king dies, we ruin the horse that he would ride upon[67] and the calf that pulls the wagon in which he would sit. We cut off its hooves from below the knee, a place that does not render it *trefe*.[68]

We convene a *yeshivah* at his grave for seven days, as [II Chronicles 32:33] states: "They honored him in his death."[69] [Our Sages interpret][70] this as [meaning:] they convened a *yeshivah* at his grave. When a *nasi* dies, we do not nullify his *yeshivah* for more than 30 days.[71]

26. When a king or a *nasi* dies, one may burn his bed and all his personal utensils. This is not considered as an Amorite[72] or destructive[73] practice. For [Jeremiah 34:5] states:[74] "You shall die in peace, and as they made pyres for your ancestors, the earlier [kings...], they will make pyres for you."

Blessed be God who grants assistance.

60. As is evident from the following halachot, it was common for the relatives of the deceased to throw garments on the bier in their grief and aggravation.
61. I.e., were they to be permitted, one might also think that the shrouds are permitted.
62. Because of their aggravation, they are willing to cause their possessions to be forbidden (Rashi, *Sanhedrin* 48a). If, however, garments are placed on a corpse with the intent that they be removed, they do not become forbidden (*Siftei Cohen* 349:8).
63. For it is a mitzvah to prevent a person's property from being lost, like it is a mitzvah to return a lost article (Rashi, *Sanhedrin* 48a).
64. Because they have already become forbidden as stated in the previous halachah.
65. I.e., to have it buried with the deceased.
66. See *Hilchot Melachim* 6:8-10 which describes this prohibition in detail. Although the strict Biblical context of the prohibition involves destroying fruit trees when besieging a city, our Sages understood the command as having a larger scope and involving all articles of value.
67. For as stated in *Hilchot Melachim* 2:1, after a king dies, no one else is allowed to ride his personal steed.
68. Injured to the extent that it will die within twelve months. If the leg was cut off above the knee, it is considered *trefe*, for it will not be able to continue to live after such an operation.
69. This refers to the tribute the Jewish people paid to King Chizkiyahu. The *Kessef*

כב כָּל הַכֵּלִים שֶׁזּוֹרְקִין עַל הַמֵּת עַל הַמִּטָּה הַנִּקְבֶּרֶת עִמּוֹ - אֲסוּרִין בַּהֲנָאָה, שֶׁלֹּא יִתְחַלְּפוּ בְּתַכְרִיכִין.

כג הָיוּ אָבִיו וְאִמּוֹ מְזָרְקִין כֵּלִים בַּחֲמָתָן עַל הַמֵּת - מִצְוָה עַל אֲחֵרִים לְהַצִּילָן.
וְאִם הִגִּיעוּ לַמִּטָּה הַנִּקְבֶּרֶת עִמּוֹ - אֵין מַצִּילִין אוֹתָן.

כד מְלַמְּדִין אֶת הָאָדָם שֶׁלֹּא יְהֵא חַבְלָן, וְלֹא יַפְסִיד אֶת הַכֵּלִים וְיַשְׁלִיכֵם לַחֲבָלָה.
מוּטָב לְתִתָּם לַעֲנִיִּים, וְאַל יַשְׁלִיכֵם לְרִמָּה וְתוֹלֵעָה.
וְכָל הַמַּרְבֶּה כֵּלִים עַל הַמֵּת - עוֹבֵר בְּלֹא תַשְׁחִית.

כה מֶלֶךְ שֶׁמֵּת - עוֹקְרִין סוּס שֶׁהָיָה רוֹכֵב עָלָיו.
וְעֶגְלָה שֶׁהָיְתָה מוֹשֶׁכֶת בַּקָּרוֹן שֶׁהָיָה יוֹשֵׁב בּוֹ - מְנַשֵּׁר פַּרְסוֹתֶיהָ מִן הָאַרְכֻּבָּה וּלְמַטָּה, מָקוֹם שֶׁאֵין עוֹשֶׂה אוֹתָהּ טְרֵפָה.
וּמוֹשִׁיבִין יְשִׁיבָה עַל קִבְרוֹ שִׁבְעָה יָמִים. שֶׁנֶּאֱמַר: וְכָבוֹד עָשׂוּ לוֹ בְמוֹתוֹ - זֶה שֶׁהוֹשִׁיבוּ לוֹ יְשִׁיבָה עַל קִבְרוֹ.
וְנָשִׂיא שֶׁמֵּת - אֵין מְבַטְּלִין יְשִׁיבָתוֹ יָתֵר עַל שְׁלֹשִׁים יוֹם.

כו מֶלֶךְ אוֹ נָשִׂיא שֶׁמֵּת - יֵשׁ לָהֶן לִשְׂרֹף מִטָּתוֹ וְכָל כְּלֵי תַּשְׁמִישׁוֹ, וְאֵין בָּזֶה דֶּרֶךְ הָאֱמוֹרִי וְלֹא מִשּׁוּם הַשְׁחָתָה.
שֶׁנֶּאֱמַר: בְּשָׁלוֹם תָּמוּת וּבְמִשְׂרְפוֹת אֲבוֹתֶיךָ הָרִאשֹׁנִים יִשְׂרְפוּ לָךְ.

בְּרִיךְ רַחֲמָנָא דְּסַיְּיעָן

Mishneh questions the Rambam's ruling, noting that the verse appears to imply that this was a special measure of honor given to Chizkiyahu because of his righteous conduct. Why then does the Rambam refer to it as standard conduct with regard to all monarchs?

70. *Bava Kama* 16b. Although it is forbidden to involve oneself in Torah study in a cemetery or in the presence of a corpse (Chapter 13, Halachah 9), as long as one is studying in honor of the deceased, there is no prohibition. Others infer that the *yeshivah* is not meant to be convened on the gravesite itself, but close to it.

71. These were the instructions which Rabbi Yehudah *HaNasi* gave before his death.

72. See *Hilchot Avodat Kochavim* 11:1 which mentions the prohibition against following gentile customs.

73. As reflected by Halachah 24, one might think that this would be forbidden. Nevertheless, *Sanhedrin* 52b states that since it is a measure of respect for a king to burn his personal items so that they will not be used by others, this is not considered as wanton destruction. It is, however, forbidden to carry out such a measure for an ordinary person [*Shulchan Aruch* (*Yoreh De'ah* 348:1)]. Such conduct would be considered as haughty (*Siftei Cohen* 348:2).

74. Communicating this prophecy to King Tzedekiah, the last king of the Davidic dynasty to have ruled. The fact that a prophet makes such statements to a righteous king indicates that the practice is permitted.

HILCHOT MELACHIM U'MILCHAMOTEIHEM

THE LAWS OF KINGS AND THEIR WARS

[This text] includes 23 mitzvot; ten positive commandments and thirteen negative commandments. They are:

1) The obligation to appoint a king in Israel;
2) The prohibition against appointing a convert [as king];
3) The prohibition against the king marrying many wives;
4) The prohibition against the king accumulating many horses;
5) The prohibition against the king amassing too much silver and gold;
6) The obligation to destroy the seven nations [living in the Land of Canaan];
7) The prohibition against allowing any one of them to remain alive;
8) The obligation to destroy the descendents of Amalek;
9) The obligation to remember what Amalek did;
10) The prohibition against forgetting Amalek's evil deeds, including his ambush against the Israelites during their journey [from Egypt to Israel];
11) The prohibition against dwelling in Egypt;
12) The obligation to offer peace to the inhabitants of a city when besieging it; to carry out the laws governing the siege as prescribed in the Torah, [in particular, the laws applying] if the enemy agrees to surrender [and those applying] if it refuses;
13) The prohibition against offering peace to Ammon and Moab, in contrast [to other nations], when besieging them;
14) The prohibition against destroying fruit-bearing trees during a siege;
15) The obligation to set up a latrine outside an army camp;
16) The obligation to carry a spike to dig with;
17) The obligation to anoint a priest to speak to the troops in the event of war;
18) The obligation to allow those who have consecrated wives, built houses, or planted vineyards to rejoice in their new status for a complete year, while releasing them from military conscription;
19) The prohibition against asking those mentioned in the previous category to perform any duties, including handling the needs of one's city or providing supplies to the troops [during that year];
20) The obligation not to become frightened, nor to flee in the midst of battle;
21) The prohibitions and obligations regarding a *yefat toar*, [a Gentile woman with whom the Torah allows relations in wartime];
22) The prohibition against selling a *yefat toar*;
23) The prohibition against subjugating her to perform menial duties after having relations with her.

These mitzvot are explained in the coming chapters.

הִלְכוֹת מְלָכִים וּמִלְחֲמוֹתֵיהֶם

יֵשׁ בִּכְלָלָן שָׁלֹשׁ וְעֶשְׂרִים מִצְוֹת: עֶשֶׂר מִצְוֹת עֲשֵׂה וּשְׁלֹשׁ-עֶשְׂרֵה מִצְוֹת לֹא תַעֲשֶׂה, וְזֶה הוּא פְּרָטָן:

א) לְמַנּוֹת מֶלֶךְ בְּיִשְׂרָאֵל.
ב) שֶׁלֹּא יְמַנֶּה מִקְּהַל גֵּרִים.
ג) שֶׁלֹּא יַרְבֶּה לוֹ נָשִׁים.
ד) שֶׁלֹּא יַרְבֶּה לוֹ סוּסִים.
ה) שֶׁלֹּא יַרְבֶּה לוֹ כֶּסֶף וְזָהָב.
ו) לְהַחֲרִים שִׁבְעָה עֲמָמִין.
ז) שֶׁלֹּא לְחַיּוֹת מֵהֶן כָּל נְשָׁמָה.
ח) לִמְחוֹת זַרְעוֹ שֶׁל עֲמָלֵק.
ט) לִזְכֹּר מַה שֶּׁעָשָׂה עֲמָלֵק.
י) שֶׁלֹּא לִשְׁכֹּחַ מַעֲשָׂיו הָרָעִים וַאֲרִיבָתוֹ בַּדֶּרֶךְ.
יא) שֶׁלֹּא לִשְׁכֹּן בְּאֶרֶץ-מִצְרָיִם.
יב) לִשְׁלֹחַ שָׁלוֹם לְיוֹשְׁבֵי הָעִיר כְּשֶׁצָּרִים עָלֶיהָ וְלָדוּן בָּהּ, כַּאֲשֶׁר מְפֹרָשׁ בַּתּוֹרָה: "וְאִם תַּשְׁלִים"; "וְאִם לֹא תַשְׁלִים".
יג) שֶׁלֹּא לִדְרֹשׁ שָׁלוֹם מֵעַמּוֹן וּמוֹאָב בִּלְבַד כְּשֶׁצָּרִים עֲלֵיהֶם.
יד) שֶׁלֹּא לְהַשְׁחִית אִילָנֵי מַאֲכָל בַּמָּצוֹר.
טו) לְהַתְקִין יָד, שֶׁיֵּצְאוּ בוֹ בַּעֲלֵי הַמַּחֲנֶה לְהִפָּנוֹת בּוֹ.
טז) לְהַתְקִין יָתֵד לַחְפֹּר בּוֹ.
יז) לִמְשֹׁחַ כֹּהֵן לְדַבֵּר בְּאָזְנֵי אַנְשֵׁי הַצָּבָא בִּשְׁעַת הַמִּלְחָמָה.
יח) לִהְיוֹת מְאָרֵס, וּבוֹנֶה בִּנְיָן, וְנוֹטֵעַ כֶּרֶם, שְׂמֵחִים בְּקִנְיָנָם שָׁנָה תְמִימָה, וּמַחֲזִירִין אוֹתָן מִן הַמִּלְחָמָה.
יט) שֶׁלֹּא יַעֲבֹר עֲלֵיהֶם לְכָל דָּבָר, וְלֹא יֵצְאוּ אֲפִלּוּ לְצָרְכֵי הָעִיר וּלְצָרְכֵי הַגְּדוּד וְדוֹמֶה לָהֶם.
כ) שֶׁלֹּא לַעֲרֹץ וְלַחֲזֹר לְאָחוֹר בִּשְׁעַת הַמִּלְחָמָה.
כא) דִּין יְפַת-תֹּאַר.
כב) שֶׁלֹּא תִמָּכֵר יְפַת-תֹּאַר.
כג) שֶׁלֹּא יִכְבְּשֶׁנָּה לְעַבְדוּת אַחַר שֶׁנִּבְעֲלָה.

וּבֵאוּר מִצְוֹת אֵלּוּ בִּפְרָקִים אֵלּוּ:

CHAPTER ONE

1. Israel was commanded to fulfill three mitzvot upon entering [the Promised] Land:[1]
a) To choose a king, as [Deuteronomy 17:15] states: "Appoint a king over yourselves;"[2]
b) To wipe out the descendants of Amalek, as [Deuteronomy 25:19] states: "Erase the memory of Amalek;"[3]
c) To build [God's] Chosen House, as [Deuteronomy 12:5] states: "Seek out His Presence and go there."[4]

2. The appointment of a king should precede the war against Amalek.[5] [This is evident from Samuel's charge to King Saul (I Samuel 15:1-3)]: "God sent me to anoint you as king.... Now, go and smite Amalek."[6]

Amalek's seed should be annihilated before the construction of the Temple, as [II Samuel 7:1-2] states: "And it came to pass, when the king dwelled in his palace, and God gave him peace from all his enemies who surrounded him, the king said to Nathan, the prophet: 'Look! I am dwelling in a house of cedar,... [but the ark of God dwells within curtains].' "[7]

Since it is a mitzvah to appoint a king, why was God displeased with the people's request of a king from Samuel?[8] Because they made their request in

1. According to most commentaries, the source of this halachah is *Sanhedrin* 20b and *Sifri, Re'eh*. However, those sources do not quote verses from the Torah to show the connection between these mitzvot and the settlement of *Eretz Yisrael*. *Midrash Tanchuma, Ki Tetzei*, sec. 15, does cite Biblical sources, however, as does the Rambam.

Many other mitzvot, including all the agricultural regulations, must be fulfilled upon entering *Eretz Yisrael*. However, those mitzvot are incumbent on every member of the nation as an individual. In contrast, the mitzvot mentioned here were commanded to the people as a collective entity. (See the conclusion of *Sefer HaMitzvot*, Positive Commandments).

The designation of the Jewish people as a *tzibbur*, collective entity, is only possible within *Eretz Yisrael*. Hence, the fulfillment of these mitzvot depends upon the Jews' presence in *Eretz Yisrael*. (See *Horiot* 3a; *Tzaphnat Pa'aneach*, Responsum 143.)

2. The Torah specifies that the Jews must appoint a king when they "come to the land that God... is giving" (Deuteronomy 17:14).

3. Here, too, Deuteronomy 25:18 states that this mitzvah is to be fulfilled "when God gives you peace... in the land."

4. In this instance as well, Deuteronomy 12:1 states "These are the rules and laws that you must carefully keep in the land that God... is giving you?' implying that the Temple will be built in that land.

In *Hilchot Beit HaBechirah* 1:1, the Rambam also mentioned the mitzvah of constructing the Temple. However, in that passage, he quoted Exodus 25:8 "And you shall make Me a sanctuary" as the Biblical source.

This apparent contradiction can be resolved as follows: The commandment in Exodus refers to the sanctuary constructed in the desert, while the present verse refers to Shilo and the Temple.

פֶּרֶק רִאשׁוֹן

א שָׁלֹשׁ מִצְוֹת נִצְטַוּוּ יִשְׂרָאֵל בִּשְׁעַת כְּנִיסָתָן לָאָרֶץ: לְמַנּוֹת לָהֶם מֶלֶךְ, שֶׁנֶּאֱמַר: "שׂוֹם תָּשִׂים עָלֶיךָ מֶלֶךְ", וּלְהַכְרִית זַרְעוֹ שֶׁל עֲמָלֵק, שֶׁנֶּאֱמַר: "תִּמְחֶה אֶת זֵכֶר עֲמָלֵק", וְלִבְנוֹת בֵּית־הַבְּחִירָה, שֶׁנֶּאֱמַר: "לְשִׁכְנוֹ תִדְרְשׁוּ וּבָאתָ שָּׁמָּה".

ב מִנּוּי מֶלֶךְ קֹדֶם לְמִלְחֶמֶת עֲמָלֵק, שֶׁנֶּאֱמַר: "אֹתִי שָׁלַח ה' לִמְשָׁחֳךָ לְמֶלֶךְ... עַתָּה לֵךְ וְהִכִּיתָה אֶת עֲמָלֵק". וְהַכְרָתַת זֶרַע עֲמָלֵק קוֹדֶמֶת לְבִנְיַן הַבָּיִת, שֶׁנֶּאֱמַר: "וַיְהִי כִּי יָשַׁב הַמֶּלֶךְ בְּבֵיתוֹ וַה' הֵנִיחַ לוֹ מִסָּבִיב מִכָּל אֹיְבָיו. וַיֹּאמֶר הַמֶּלֶךְ אֶל נָתָן הַנָּבִיא, אָנֹכִי יוֹשֵׁב בְּבֵית אֲרָזִים וְגוֹ'".

מֵאַחַר שֶׁהֲקָמַת מֶלֶךְ מִצְוָה – לָמָּה לֹא רָצָה הַקָּדוֹשׁ־בָּרוּךְ־הוּא כְּשֶׁשָּׁאֲלוּ מֶלֶךְ מִשְּׁמוּאֵל?

There are a number of levels in the fulfillment of the mitzvah of building "a house for God, prepared for sacrifices to be offered." On the most basic level, the mitzvah was fulfilled when the Sanctuary was constructed in the desert. However, the ultimate fulfillment of that commandment will be when the Temple will be constructed by the king in Jerusalem, after Amalek is annihilated (see *Lechem Mishneh; Even HaEzel*).

5. In his commentary on *Sanhedrin*, 20b, Rashi emphasized that it was necessary to fulfill these mitzvot in this sequence. Indeed, the Talmud and the Rambam emphasize this order.

6. *Sanhedrin* 20b, which is the source for this halachah, quotes a different Biblical reference for this concept. The Rambam cites his verse because it clearly demonstrates the sequence in which these mitzvot must be fulfilled.

This also teaches us a general principle regarding the composition of the *Mishneh Torah*. Although the Rambam uses the Talmud and the *Midrash* as sources, he reserves the option of employing Biblical references that are not mentioned in those texts (*Lechem Mishneh*).

7. David wanted to build the Temple only after he had fought the wars necessary to establish Israel's security.

[To briefly restate the historical background: After receiving Samuel's command, Saul waged war and utterly defeated Amalek. He slew the entire nation except for their choice sheep, and their king, Agag. The sheep and the king were taken to the prophet, Samuel. Samuel severely rebuked Saul for not fulfilling the Torah's command, and for not utterly destroying Amalek (15:23): "Because you have rejected the word of God, God has rejected you from being king." Afterwards, Samuel slew Agag.

Between his capture and execution, though, Agag was able to sire children. Thus, although Amalek ceased to exist as a nation, its seed was perpetuated. For example, Haman, the minister who tried to destroy the Jews in the Purim saga, was an "Agagite," one of Agag's descendants.]

Saul was not charged with building the Temple. This may have been because God had already rejected him, or because he was about to become embroiled in prolonged conflicts with the Philistines, which would ultimately cost him his life. When power was transferred to King David, he did establish the political security of the Jewish nation. Afterwards, he turned his attention to building the Temple, as described in the narrative cited by the Rambam.

8. As I Samuel 12:17 states: - "I will call to God, and He will send thunder and rain, so that you may know that your wickedness is great... in asking for a king."

a spirit of complaint. Rather than seeking to fulfill the mitzvah of appointing a king, they were simply intent on rejecting the Prophet Samuel [as implied by God's reply to him (I Samuel 8:7)]: "It is not you, but Me they have rejected."[9]

3. As an initial and preferred option, a king may be appointed only by a court of 70 elders,[10] together with a prophet, as Joshua was appointed by Moses and his court,[11] and as Saul and David, were appointed by Samuel of Ramah and his court.[12]

4. A king should not be appointed from converts [to Judaism].[13] This applies even if [the convert's ancestors had been Jewish] for many generations,[14] unless his mother [or father] is a native-born Israelite,[15] as [Deuteronomy 17:15] states: "You may not appoint a foreigner who is not one of yourbrethren."[16]

This does not apply to the monarchy alone, but to all positions of authority within Israel. [A convert may not serve as] an army commander, a leader of fifty, or as a leader of ten. [He may not even] supervise the allocation of water from a stream to various fields.

Needless to say, a judge or a *nasi*[17] should only be a native-born Israelite, as it is stated (*ibid.*): "Appoint a king over you from among your brethren." [This implies] that all appointments must only be "from your brethren."[18]

9. *Sanhedrin* 20b comments: "The elders of [that] generation made a proper request (I Samuel 8:6): 'Appoint a king for us to judge us.' However, the common people spoiled [the tone of the request], demanding (*ibid.* 19-20): 'Let us have a king so that we will be like all the nations...' "

10. This refers to the *Sanhedrin*, Israel's supreme court. The Rambam describes its function in *Hilchot Sanhedrin* 1:3. The appointment of the king by this court is also mentioned in that text, 5:1.

11. The mention of Joshua in this context raises a question: In Halachah 1, the Rambam stated that the appointment of a king could come only after entering *Eretz Yisrael*. Joshua was charged with leading the Jewish people before they came into the Land. Similarly, the Sages and the Rambam sometimes referred to Moses as a king (see the commentaries to Deuteronomy 33:5, *Hilchot Beit HaBechirah* 6:11), although he never entered *Eretz Yisrael*.

Accordingly, we must say that the concept of monarchy went through a number of stages. As explained above, a parallel concept may be seen regarding the mitzvah of building a Temple. The ultimate fulfillment of the mitzvah was the construction of the Temple in Jerusalem. However, before that, a Tabernacle was built to accompany the Jews through the desert, and a Sanctuary was built in Shilo. Similarly, although monarchy in its full sense was not achieved until Saul and David were anointed, Moses and Joshua may also be considered kings.

12. *Rambam LeAm* emphasizes that, as apparent from Halachah 7, the participation of the *Sanhedrin* and a prophet is only required in order to appoint a king when there is no heir to the position.

13. *Sefer HaMitzvot* (Negative Command 362) and *Sefer HaChinuch* (mitzvah 498) include this prohibition as one of the Torah's 613 mitzvot.

14. A convert is always considered a full-fledged member of the Jewish faith and is granted the same privileges and obligations as any other Jew. Nevertheless, regarding

לְפִי שֶׁשָּׁאֲלוּ בְּתַרְעֹמֶת, וְלֹא שָׁאֲלוּ לְקַיֵּם הַמִּצְוָה, אֶלָּא מִפְּנֵי שֶׁקָּצוּ בִּשְׁמוּאֵל הַנָּבִיא, שֶׁנֶּאֱמַר: ״כִּי לֹא אֹתְךָ מָאָסוּ, כִּי אֹתִי מָאֲסוּ וְגוֹ׳״.

ג אֵין מַעֲמִידִין מֶלֶךְ בַּתְּחִלָּה, אֶלָּא עַל־פִּי בֵית־דִּין שֶׁל שִׁבְעִים זְקֵנִים וְעַל־פִּי נָבִיא, כִּיהוֹשֻׁעַ שֶׁמִּנָּהוּ מֹשֶׁה רַבֵּנוּ וּבֵית־דִּינוֹ, וּכְשָׁאוּל וְדָוִד, שֶׁמִּנָּם שְׁמוּאֵל הָרָמָתִי וּבֵית־דִּינוֹ.

ד אֵין מַעֲמִידִין מֶלֶךְ מִקְּהַל גֵּרִים אֲפִלּוּ אַחַר כַּמָּה דוֹרוֹת, עַד שֶׁתִּהְיֶה אִמּוֹ מִיִּשְׂרָאֵל, שֶׁנֶּאֱמַר: ״לֹא תוּכַל לָתֵת עָלֶיךָ אִישׁ נָכְרִי אֲשֶׁר לֹא אָחִיךָ הוּא״. וְלֹא לְמַלְכוּת בִּלְבָד, אֶלָּא לְכָל שְׂרָרוּת שֶׁבְּיִשְׂרָאֵל: לֹא שַׂר־צָבָא, לֹא שַׂר חֲמִשִּׁים אוֹ שַׂר עֲשָׂרָה, אֲפִלּוּ מְמֻנֶּה עַל אַמַּת־הַמַּיִם שֶׁמְּחַלֵּק מִמֶּנָּה לַשָּׂדוֹת; וְאֵין צָרִיךְ לוֹמַר דַּיָּן אוֹ נָשִׂיא, שֶׁלֹּא יְהֵא אֶלָּא מִיִּשְׂרָאֵל, שֶׁנֶּאֱמַר: ״מִקֶּרֶב אַחֶיךָ תָּשִׂים עָלֶיךָ מֶלֶךְ״ – כָּל מְשִׂימוֹת שֶׁאַתָּה מֵשִׂים לֹא יִהוּ אֶלָּא מִקֶּרֶב אַחֶיךָ.

yichus, pedigree of lineage, a distinction is made; for example, a convert cannot marry a priest and may marry a *mamzer* (a child born from adulterous or incestuous relations). Similarly, because of this lack of *yichus*, a convert may not assume a position of authority within the Jewish people.

15. The bracketed addition was made to resolve the following difficulty: The mother of Rechavam, Solomon's son and heir, was Na'ama, an Ammonitess. If so, how could he have succeeded his father as king?

Tosafot (*Yevamot* 102a) explain that if a person's father is a native-born Israelite, he may be appointed to positions of authority, regardless of his mother's origins. Alternatively, a king's *yichus* is questioned only at the beginning of a dynasty. Once the dynasty has been established, a son may assume his father's position, even if his mother is a convert (*Noda B'Yehudah, Choshen Mishpat,* Responsum l).

16. King Herod was an Idumean, an offspring of the Edomites who were forcibly converted to the Jewish faith by King Yannai, a descendant of the Hasmoneans. Accordingly, neither he nor his descendants were qualified to serve as kings of Israel.

Herod was particularly sensitive on this issue. When he heard the Sages mention this verse, he slaughtered many of them (*Bava Batra* 3b). *Sotah* 4 1 a,b relates that Agrippas, a descendant of Herod and one of his successors, read the book of Deuteronomy to the people at the *Hakhel* gathering. As he recited the above verse, his eyes welled up with tears.

"Do not worry?" the Sages reassured him, "you are our brother." The Talmud states that God decreed the Jews' doom because of this flattery. (Though most commentaries explain that Agrippas' mother was also a convert, Rashi maintains that she was an Israelitess. Hence, he was fit to be king.)

17. *Nasi* literally means "the uplifted one." It refers to the Sage who led the *Sanhedrin* - and indeed, the Jewish nation as a whole - in the Second Temple era.

18. See *Kiddushin* 76b.

Shemaya and Avtalyon were converts. Nevertheless, they excelled in Torah knowledge to the point that they were appointed *nasi* and Head of the Supreme Court respectively. Their assumption of these positions, despite their lack of *yichus*, apparently contradicts the Rambam's statements.

5. We may not appoint a woman as king. [When describing the monarchy, the Torah employs] the male form of the word king and not the female.[19]

[This principle also applies to] all other positions of authority within Israel. Only men should be appointed to [fill] them.[20]

6. Neither a butcher,[21] barber, bath-attendant, nor a tanner should be appointed king or High-Priest.[22] This is not because of an inherent fault, but because their professions are less prestigious, and the people will always treat them lightly.[23]

A person who has served in one of these professions for [even] one day, is disqualified [for the monarchy].[24]

7. When a king is appointed, he is anointed with oil reserved for this purpose, [25]as [I Samuel 10:1] states: "And Samuel took the cruse of oil and poured it over his head.[26] [Then,] he kissed him."

Once a king is anointed, he and his descendents are granted the monarchy until eternity, for the monarchy is passed down by inheritance, as [Deuteronomy 17:20] states "Thus, he [the king] and his descendents will prolong their reign in the midst of Israel."[27]

The *Knesset HaGedolah* explains that the nation accepted Shemaya and Avtalyon as leaders, because their capabilities surpassed those of the rest of the people. In such an instance, no prohibition is involved.

Alternatively, Shemaya and Avtalyon were appointed by the Hasmonean kings. A king is granted absolute authority over the nation's internal affairs. He may appoint judges who are not acceptable according to Torah law, if he feels it necessary (*Tumim* 7:1).

19. In Jewish history, we find two examples of queens who ruled the country:

II Kings (Chapter 11) describes how Atalya, the mother of Achaziah, slew the heirs to the throne and ruled over the kingdom of Judah for seven years. Nevertheless, her assumption of the monarchy was never acknowledged by the Sages. She was always considered a murderous, idol-worshipping usurper. As soon as possible, the Priests and Sages installed Yoash, the rightful heir, on the throne.

Similarly, towards the end of the Hasmonean dynasty, Queen Salome assumed rule over the nation. She was a righteous woman who followed the guidance of her brother, the *nasi*, Shimon ben Shetach. However, neither he nor the other Sages were consulted regarding her assumption of the throne. Furthermore, there was little alternative, as the two other potential heirs to the throne were Sadducees who persecuted the Sages, and wanted to stamp out Torah practice.

20. As mentioned above, the Torah establishes a parallel between the monarchy and other positions of authority regarding the disqualification of a convert. The scope of that comparison is further extended to include the disqualification of women (*Kiryat Sefer*).

Judges (4:4) mentions that Devorah, the prophetess, served as a judge. This seems to contradict this principle. Two explanations are offered:

a) She was a prophetess, and she assumed the position because of God's decree.

b) She did not actually serve as a judge. Rather, she taught the people Torah. Since the judges' decisions were based on her teachings, it was considered as if she judged the people (*Tosafot, Niddah* 50a).

ה אֵין מַעֲמִידִין אִשָּׁה בַּמַּלְכוּת, שֶׁנֶּאֱמַר: "עָלֶיךָ מֶלֶךְ" – וְלֹא מַלְכָּה, וְכֵן כָּל מְשִׂימוֹת שֶׁבְּיִשְׂרָאֵל אֵין מְמַנִּים בָּהֶם אֶלָּא אִישׁ.

ו וְאֵין מַעֲמִידִין מֶלֶךְ וְלֹא כֹּהֵן גָּדוֹל – לֹא קַצָּב, וְלֹא סַפָּר, וְלֹא בַּלָּן, וְלֹא בוּרְסִי – לֹא מִפְּנֵי שֶׁהֵן פְּסוּלִין, אֶלָּא הוֹאִיל וְאֻמָּנוּתָן נְקָלָה, הָעָם מְזַלְזְלִין בָּהֶן לְעוֹלָם. וּמִשֶּׁיַּעֲשֶׂה בִּמְלָאכָה מֵאֵלּוּ יוֹם אֶחָד – נִפְסָל.

ז כְּשֶׁמַּעֲמִידִין הַמֶּלֶךְ, מוֹשְׁחִין אוֹתוֹ בְּשֶׁמֶן הַמִּשְׁחָה, שֶׁנֶּאֱמַר: "וַיִּקַּח שְׁמוּאֵל אֶת פַּךְ הַשֶּׁמֶן וַיִּצֹק עַל רֹאשׁוֹ וַיִּשָּׁקֵהוּ".

וּמֵאַחַר שֶׁמּוֹשְׁחִין הַמֶּלֶךְ, הֲרֵי זֶה זוֹכֶה לוֹ וּלְבָנָיו עַד עוֹלָם; שֶׁהַמַּלְכוּת יְרֻשָּׁה, שֶׁנֶּאֱמַר: "לְמַעַן יַאֲרִיךְ יָמִים עַל מַמְלַכְתּוֹ הוּא וּבָנָיו בְּקֶרֶב יִשְׂרָאֵל".

21. Recently, manuscripts of the *Mishneh Torah* have been discovered which omit this profession, replacing it with "bloodletters." Similarly, *Kiddushin* 82a, which appears to be the source for this halachah, does not mention butchers.

22. Not only the monarchy, but all other positions of authority are denied these individuals (*Kiryat Sefer*). The Talmudic passage cited above also mentions a number of other artisans, including perfume salesmen, knitters, and jewelers, professions primarily involved with women. Hence, they are also not considered sufficiently prestigious to be appointed king.

23. *Tashbetz* mentions that the Rambam included those professions which were deemed undignified in his day. Should the social norms change and these professions become considered prestigious and others undignified, these laws must also be altered.

24. *Kessef Mishneh* explains that these individuals are only disqualified if they served professionally in these capacities. If one person cut another's hair as a favor or as a school-boy's prank, he may still be appointed king.

25. This refers to the oil of anointing made by Moses, as described in Exodus 30:25. In *Hilchot Klei HaMikdash* 1:2-3, Rambam describes in detail this oil was prepared from olive oil and a mixture of spices.

In the desert, Moses used this oil to sanctify the Tabernacle's utensils. Despite its use, miraculously, the oil remained totally intact. In the following generations, it was not employed for this purpose. Rather, it was used only to anoint kings, High Priests, and the priests who led Israel's military campaigns (*Keritot* 5b). Ultimately, it was buried toward the conclusion of the First Temple era (*Hilchot Beit HaBechirah* 4:1).

26. *Hilchot Klei HaMikdash* 1:9, the Rambam wrote: "Kings of the Davidic dynasty are anointed [by pouring the oil as] a crown on their heads."

This verse describes the anointing of Saul as king. According to the Rambam, Samuel used the oil prepared by Moses for this purpose. See *Pirkei D'Rabbi Eliezer,* Chapter 17, which also mentions this opinion. This view is not, however, accepted by all commentaries. Radak states that the oil prepared by Moses was only used to anoint kings of the Davidic dynasty. In contrast, Saul was anointed with afarsimon oil, as were the kings of Israel. See Halachah 10.

27. The verse is both a blessing and a statement, implying that if its conditions are fulfilled, the king's heirs will inherit his position.

If the king leaves [only] a young son, the monarchy should be held for him until he matures, as Yehoyada did for Yoash.[28] The order of inheritance of the monarchy is the same as that governing the inheritance of property.[29] An older son is given precedence over a younger one.[30]

Not only the monarchy, but all other positions of authority and appointments in Israel, are transferred to one's children and grandchildren as inheritances forever.[31]

[The above applies] if the knowledge and the fear of God of the son is equivalent to that of his ancestors.[32] If his fear of God is equivalent to theirs but not his knowledge, he should be granted his father's position and given instruction.[33] [However,] under no circumstance should a person who lacks the fear of God be appointed to any position in Israel, even though he possesses much knowledge.[34]

Once David was anointed [king], he acquired the crown of kingship. Afterwards, the kingship belongs to him and to his male descendents forever, as [II Samuel 7: 16] states: "Your throne shall be established forever."[35] [Nevertheless, his acquisition of the monarchy was conditional],[36] applying only to the righteous among his descendents, as [Psalms 132:12] states: "If your children will keep My covenant... [their children shall also sit on your throne forever.]"

[Despite this condition,] God assured David that the monarchy would never be taken from his descendents forever,[37] as [Psalms 89:31-38] states: "If his children will forsake My Torah and cease walking in My statutes ... I will punish their transgressions with the rod and their sins with plagues.

28. After the death of Achaziah, King of Judah, Atalya, his mother, slew all his heirs and assumed the throne herself. Yoash, Achaziah's infant son, was saved. He was hidden and raised by Yehoyada, the high priest, until he was seven. At that time, he was granted the monarchy (see II Kings, Chapter l).

29. The first in line for the monarchy are the deceased king's sons, in order of age. Should none of his sons be alive, the right is passed to his grandchildren. The children of the elder son are granted preference.

If the king has no male descendents, the monarchy is given to his brothers. If they are not alive, it is granted to their sons. From them, the right to the throne passes to the deceased king's nephews (his sister's sons), then to his uncles, to his first cousins. See *Hilchot Nachalot*, Chapter 1.

30. This law is derived from II Chronicles 21:10: "And he gave the monarchy to Yehoram, for he was the first born."

King David bestowed the monarchy on Solomon, his youngest son. This raises an apparent contradiction to this principle. However, I Chronicles 22:2 relates that he was charged to do so by God: "God... chose Solomon, my son, to sit on the throne...."

31. See *Sifri, Shoftim*.

This law has been a matter of controversy throughout the years. In regard to positions of communal authority, almost all authorities accept this concept. However, controversies have frequently arisen over the inheritance of Rabbinical positions. Here, the Rambam's decision has frequently been challenged.

Maharshdam (*Yoreh De'ah*, Responsa, n. 85) states that a city must seek out the most capable Rav possible without regard to inheritance. Similarly, the *Terumat HaDeshen* (*Pesakim* 128) states "Torah cannot be inherited."

הִנִּיחַ בֵּן קָטָן – מְשַׁמְּרִין לוֹ הַמְּלוּכָה עַד שֶׁיַּגְדִּיל, כְּמוֹ שֶׁעָשָׂה יְהוֹיָדָע לְיוֹאָשׁ. וְכָל הַקּוֹדֵם בְּנַחֲלָה – קוֹדֵם לִירֻשַּׁת הַמְּלוּכָה. וְהַבֵּן הַגָּדוֹל, קוֹדֵם לַקָּטָן מִמֶּנּוּ. וְלֹא הַמַּלְכוּת בִּלְבָד, אֶלָּא כָּל הַשְּׂרָרוֹת וְכָל הַמִּנּוּיִין שֶׁבְּיִשְׂרָאֵל – יְרֻשָּׁה לִבְנוֹ וּלְבֶן־בְּנוֹ עַד עוֹלָם; וְהוּא, שֶׁיִּהְיֶה הַבֵּן מְמַלֵּא מְקוֹם אֲבוֹתָיו בְּחָכְמָה וּבְיִרְאָה. הָיָה מְמַלֵּא בְּיִרְאָה, אַף־עַל־פִּי שֶׁאֵינוֹ מְמַלֵּא בְחָכְמָה – מַעֲמִידִין אוֹתוֹ בִּמְקוֹם אָבִיו וּמְלַמְּדִין אוֹתוֹ. וְכָל מִי שֶׁאֵין בּוֹ יִרְאַת־שָׁמַיִם, אַף־עַל־פִּי שֶׁחָכְמָתוֹ מְרֻבָּה – אֵין מְמַנִּין אוֹתוֹ לְמִנּוּי מִן הַמִּנּוּיִין שֶׁבְּיִשְׂרָאֵל. כֵּיוָן שֶׁנִּמְשַׁח דָּוִד, זָכָה בְּכֶתֶר מַלְכוּת; וַהֲרֵי הַמַּלְכוּת לוֹ וּלְבָנָיו הַזְּכָרִים עַד עוֹלָם, שֶׁנֶּאֱמַר: "כִּסְאֲךָ יִהְיֶה נָכוֹן עַד עוֹלָם". וְלֹא זָכָה אֶלָּא לִכְשֵׁרִים, שֶׁנֶּאֱמַר: "אִם יִשְׁמְרוּ בָנֶיךָ בְּרִיתִי". אַף־עַל־פִּי שֶׁלֹּא זָכָה אֶלָּא לִכְשֵׁרִים – לֹא תִכָּרֵת הַמְּלוּכָה מִזֶּרַע דָּוִד לְעוֹלָם. הַקָּדוֹשׁ־בָּרוּךְ־הוּא הִבְטִיחוֹ בְּכָךְ, שֶׁנֶּאֱמַר: "אִם יַעַזְבוּ בָנָיו תּוֹרָתִי וּבְמִשְׁפָּטַי לֹא יֵלֵכוּן... וּפָקַדְתִּי בְשֵׁבֶט פִּשְׁעָם וּבִנְגָעִים עֲוֺנָם. וְחַסְדִּי לֹא אָפִיר מֵעִמּוֹ".

However, many prominent authorities (*Rivash,* Responsa 271, Ramah, *Yoreh De'ah* 245, *Maharit Algazi, Simchat Yom Tov* 6) have explained that this law applies even in regard to rabbinical positions.

The difficulties in deciding the question may be seen in the *Chatam Sofer's* lack of certainty regarding it. In his Responsa (*Orach Chayim*, Responsum 12), he at first espouses the opinion that rabbinical positions should not be handed down from father to son. However, later (Responsum 13), he reversed himself and granted the son his father's position by inheritance.

In practice, most Rabbis have reached the opinion that if the son is a capable Rabbi, though less qualified than another who seeks the position, his father's position should be awarded to him. However, if the community sees the son as incapable of filling his father's position at all, it may be given to another person.

32. Leviticus 16:32 describes the High Priest as one "who was anointed to fill the the place of his ancestor." *Torat Kohanim (Tzav)* comments: "Should he be anointed even though he does not 'fill the place' [i.e., does not equal the level of his] ancestors? No, the Torah states 'fill the place.' If he is not equal to his father, the position should be granted to someone else."

The same principles apply to the inheritance of the monarchy and to other positions of authority.

33. *Ketubot* 103b describes how Rabbi Yehudah *Hanasi* instructed that his son Gamliel be given his position, even though his knowledge was not as great as his father's.

34. The fear of God is the very foundation of the spiritual heritage of the Jewish people. Anyone who lacks that quality can never be a competent leader.

35. *Mechilta, Shmot,* states: "Until David was chosen, all Israelites were fit for the monarchy. Once he was chosen, all Israel was excluded, as [II Chronicles 13:5] states: 'God ... granted the kingdom of Israel to David forever.'"

36. *Mechilta* continues: "Three gifts were granted conditionally: *Eretz Yisrael*, the Temple, and the Davidic dynasty. What is the source for these remarks?... [Concerning the Davidic dynasty,] it is written: 'If your children will keep My covenant....'"

37. II Samuel 7:15 relates that God promised: "My grace will not depart from him, as I removed it from Saul."

Nevertheless, I will not [utterly] remove My grace from him.... [His throne shall be ... established forever.]"[38]

8. If a prophet[39] appoints a king from any other tribe of Israel and that king follows the path of Torah and mitzvot and fights the wars of God, he is considered as a king, and all the commandments associaed with the monarchy apply to him.[40]

Although the kingship was primarily given to David and one of his descendents will be serving as king, [there is halachic legitimacy to the rule of other kings]. Behold, Achiyah of Shilo[41] appointed Jeroboam and told him (I Kings 11:38): "And it shall be that if you obey[42] all that I command you... I will build you a faithful house as I built for David."[43] Similarly, Achiyah told him (*ibid.*: 36): "To his (David's) son, I will grant one tribe, so that David, My servant, will always have sovereignty before Me in Jerusalem."[44]

9. The kings of the Davidic dynasty will prevail forever (II Samuel 7:16): "Your throne shall be established forever."[45] In contrast, should a king arise from other Israelites, the monarchy will [eventually] cease from his descendents.[46] For behold, Jeroboam was told: [I Kings 11:39] "[I will afflict the House of David].... but not forever."[47]

38. Although the Davidic dynasty suffered much during its existence, it continued to rule throughout the entire First Temple period. Furthermore, the Messiah, who will renew the kingship of Israel, will also be a scion of the House of David. See Chapter 11, Halachah 4.

39. Here the Rambam does not mention the participation of the *Sanhedrin*, as he does in Halachah 3. The Radbaz states that the appointment of the king must be "by God's word." *Divrei Moshe* explains that according to law, a king must be appointed by the *Sanhedrin*. Here, however, we are not concerned with an appointment according to law. (For after the establishment of the Davidic dynasty, there is no concept of another king according to law.) Instead, the appointment of such a king is a directive for application in the immediate time (*horeat shaah*). Such directives are conveyed to a prophet from time to time and supercede Scriptural Law, as the Rambam states in *Hilchot Yesodei HaTorah* 9:3. Since the appointment is only an immediate matter, ultimately the dynasty of that king will cease as stated in Halachah 9.

40. The Jerusalem Talmud, *Horiot* 3:2, states: "The King of Israel and the King of Judah are equal in status. Neither is greater than the other."

The equal standing of the King of Israel in regard to the King of Judah may also be seen by the Rambam's statements in *Hilchot Shegagot*, regarding the sacrifice brought for committing an unintentional sin:

> Who is meant by the *nasi* mentioned in the Torah? The king, over whom no one in Israel has authority... except God, his Lord. [This applies whether the king] is of the House of David or from other tribes of Israel.
>
> If there are many kings, and none is subservient to any other, each must bring a goat (the special sacrifice brought by the king) for unintentionally committing a sin.

41. Achiyah of Shilo was considered one of the greatest spiritual figures of his age, serving as the leader of the *Sanhedrin*. See the Rambam's Introduction to the *Mishneh Torah*.

ח נָבִיא שֶׁהֶעֱמִיד מֶלֶךְ מִשְּׁאָר שִׁבְטֵי יִשְׂרָאֵל, וְהָיָה אוֹתוֹ הַמֶּלֶךְ הוֹלֵךְ בְּדֶרֶךְ הַתּוֹרָה וְהַמִּצְוָה וְנִלְחָם מִלְחֲמוֹת ה׳ – הֲרֵי זֶה מֶלֶךְ, וְכָל מִצְוֹת הַמַּלְכוּת נוֹהֲגוֹת בּוֹ; אַף־עַל־פִּי שֶׁעִקַּר הַמַּלְכוּת לְדָוִד, וְיִהְיֶה מִבָּנָיו מֶלֶךְ. שֶׁהֲרֵי אֲחִיָּה הַשִּׁילֹנִי הֶעֱמִיד יָרָבְעָם וְאָמַר לוֹ: "וְהָיָה אִם תִּשְׁמַע אֶת כָּל אֲשֶׁר אֲצַוֶּךָ... וּבָנִיתִי לְךָ בַּיִת נֶאֱמָן כַּאֲשֶׁר בָּנִיתִי לְדָוִד וְגוֹ'". וְאָמַר לוֹ אֲחִיָּה: "וְלִבְנוֹ אֶתֵּן שֵׁבֶט אֶחָד, לְמַעַן הֱיוֹת נִיר לְדָוִיד עַבְדִּי כָּל הַיָּמִים לְפָנַי בִּירוּשָׁלַיִם".

ט מַלְכֵי בֵית־דָּוִד הֵם הָעוֹמְדִים לְעוֹלָם, שֶׁנֶּאֱמַר: "כִּסְאֲךָ יִהְיֶה נָכוֹן עַד עוֹלָם". אֲבָל אִם יַעֲמֹד מֶלֶךְ מִשְּׁאָר יִשְׂרָאֵל – תִּפָּסֵק הַמַּלְכוּת מִבֵּיתוֹ, שֶׁהֲרֵי נֶאֱמַר לְיָרָבְעָם: "אַךְ לֹא כָל הַיָּמִים".

42. The Rambam's citation of the verse differs slightly from the actual text.

43. In *Sefer HaMitzvot* (Negative Commandment 362), the Rambam states that "Only a descendent of David and Solomon may be king over any believer in the Torah of Moses, our teacher." Accordingly, certain commentaries explain that when Rambam later composed the *Mishneh Torah*, he changed his views regarding the legitimacy of the kingdom of Israel. According to the explanation of *Divrei Moshe* cited above, the two positions can be reconciled.

Other commentaries also question the Rambam's acceptance of the halachic legitimacy of the kingdom of Israel. In the commentary to Genesis 49: 10, Ramban stated that the appointment of Jeroboam was only intended as a temporary measure, and that the ten tribes should later have returned to the Davidic dynasty. Ra'avad takes an intermediate view. He accepts the kings of Israel as rulers, but maintains that they should have been subservient to the kings of Judah, as the Romans possessed a Caesar and deputy Caesar.

In this context, it is appropriate to consider the Halachic legitimacy of the Hasmonean kingdom during the Second Temple period. The Rambam in *Hilchot Chanukah* 3: 1 described how: "The Hasmoneans ... delivered Israel from their hands and appointed a king from among the priests, thus returning the monarchy to Israel for more than two hundred years."

This would seem to indicate the Rambam's acceptance of the Hasmoneans as kings, despite the fact that:

a) they were not appointed by prophets; and

b) they ruled in the city of Jerusalem (see Halachah 10).

Similarly, a number of references in the Talmud (*Kiddushin* 66a, *Sotah* 41a, *Sanhedrin* 19a) imply that the Sages recognized the authority of the Hasmonean and Herodian kings. In contrast, Ramban (*ibid.*) viewed the Hasmoneans as usurpers of the monarchy. He explained that this sin alone was responsible for the tragedy and misfortune which plagued their dynasty, and cited the Jerusalem Talmud, *Horiot*, which explicitly states that a king should not be appointed from among the priests. From the Rambam's statements here, it would appear that the Rambam would share that view. For they were appointed neither by a prophet, nor the *Sanhedrin*.

44. As stated in the previous and following halachot, the monarchy was granted to David as an eternal heritage.

45. See commentary to Halachah 7 which explains that the Davidic dynasty continued in power even when the kings were not righteous.

46. The Rambam views the rule of Jeroboam and of the other kings of Israel as a

10. Kings of Israel are not anointed with the special anointing oil,[48] but with Afarsimon oil.[49] Only a descendant of David may be appointed as king in Jerusalem.[50] And only descendants of David are anointed [with the special anointing oil].[51]

11. The kings of the Davidic dynasty should only be anointed near a spring.[52]

12. A son who succeeds his father as king is not anointed unless [he assumes his position] amid a dispute [over the inheritance][53] or during a [civil] war.[54] [Under these circumstances,] he should be anointed in order to remove [all] disagreement.[55]

Therefore, they anointed Solomon because [of the claim] of Adoniyahu,[56] Jehoash, because of [the usurpation of] Atalyah,[57] and Jehoachaz, because of [the claim of his brother], Jehoyakim.[58]

temporary measure, instituted by God for a specific purpose. Accordingly, even if his descendants had all been righteous, their dynasty would not have continued forever (*Kessef Mishneh*). Ra'avad disagrees and maintains that had Jeroboam and his descendants remained righteous, their dynasty would have continued forever, alongside David's, but in a secondary status as stated above.

47. *Even HaEzel* explains the difference between the kings of Israel and those of the Davidic dynasty as follows: When a king from the kingdom of Israel dies, there is no mitzvah to appoint a king, even though there is a capable and fitting descendant from the previous dynasty. In contrast, when there is no king from the Davidic dynasty, there is a mitzvah to appoint one of his descendants if he can fill the position.

48. This refers to the anointing oil prepared by Moses mentioned in Halachah 7.

49. A fragrant oil produced by mixing olive oil and spices. Alternatively, the *Aruch HaShulchan* describes it as "a resin which exudes from the balsam trees."

50. Although other kings may legitimately rule according to halachah, as explained in Halachah 8, they may not establish their rule in Jerusalem.

This halachah raises questions about the status of the Hasmonean kings who were priests with no connection to the Davidic line. Nevertheless, they ruled in Jerusalem. See commentary to Halachah 8.

51. The use of anointing oil for any person except for a High Priest, a priest appointed to lead a military campaign, or a king of the Davidic dynasty, is a violation of one of the Torah's 365 prohibitions. See *Hilchot Klei HaMikdash* 1:5-7.

The last kings of the Davidic dynasty also were not anointed with this unique oil. The anointing oil prepared by Moses was hidden away by King Josiah along with the Holy Ark. No other anointing oil was ever prepared. See *Hilchot Beit HaBechirah* 4:1.

52. *Horiot* 12a explains that the king was anointed there as a sign that his dynasty should be perpetuated, just as a stream continues in a never-ending flow. This symbolism is only appropriate for kings of the Davidic dynasty, whose dynasty will continue forever. In contrast, the dynasties of the kings of Israel will eventually be interrupted [see Halachah 9 (*Kessef Mishneh*)].

י אֵין מוֹשְׁחִין מַלְכֵי יִשְׂרָאֵל בְּשֶׁמֶן הַמִּשְׁחָה, אֶלָּא בְּשֶׁמֶן אֲפַרְסְמוֹן. וְאֵין מְמַנִּין אוֹתָן בִּירוּשָׁלַיִם לְעוֹלָם, אֶלָּא מֶלֶךְ יִשְׂרָאֵל מִזֶּרַע דָּוִד. וְאֵין מוֹשְׁחִין אֶלָּא זֶרַע דָּוִד.

יא כְּשֶׁמּוֹשְׁחִין מַלְכֵי בֵית־דָּוִד, אֵין מוֹשְׁחִין אוֹתָן אֶלָּא עַל הַמַּעְיָן.

יב וְאֵין מוֹשְׁחִין מֶלֶךְ בֶּן מֶלֶךְ, אֶלָּא־אִם־כֵּן הָיְתָה שָׁם מַחֲלֹקֶת אוֹ מִלְחָמָה, מוֹשְׁחִין אוֹתוֹ כְּדֵי לְסַלֵּק הַמַּחֲלֹקֶת. לְפִיכָךְ מָשְׁחוּ שְׁלֹמֹה מִפְּנֵי אֲדֹנִיָּה, וְיוֹאָשׁ מִפְּנֵי עֲתַלְיָה, וּמָשְׁחוּ יְהוֹאָחָז מִפְּנֵי יְהוֹיָקִים אָחִיו.

Accordingly, King David ordered that Solomon be anointed at the Gichon Stream (1 Kings 1:33).

53. The *Kessef Mishneh* explains that David and Saul were anointed even though there was no controversy over their rule because they were the first of their lines.

In contrast, the kings of Israel are to be anointed only if there is a controversy over their assumption of the monarchy. If there is no controversy, they are not to be anointed, even though their rule initiates a new dynasty.

54. Many commentaries render *milchamah* as war. *Lechem Mishneh* interprets it as "murmuring of the people," a conflict of a lesser intensity than "dispute."

55. The Rambam writes in *Hilchot Klei HaMikdash* 1:11: "If there was a debate [concerning whom to appoint king], he is to be anointed:

a) to remove [all] disagreement; and

b) to make known that he alone is the king.'

Hilchot Klei HaMikdash describes the preparation of this special oil and its use in anointing the kings of the Davidic dynasty. Accordingly, it adds "to make known that he alone is king," which can only apply in regard to kings of the Davidic dynasty, for only they possess the essential quality of monarchy as explained above. In contrast, this phrase is omitted in *Hilchot Melachim* for that section also deals with laws of the kings of Israel.

56. 1 Kings, Chapter 1, describes Adoniyahu's abortive attempt to declare himself as David's successor.

Horiot 12a associates Solomon's anointing with that of David, his father: "David and Solomon, who were anointed with a horn of oil, merited having their dynasty endure."

The kings of the Davidic dynasty must descend from Solomon as well as David. Thus, *Sefer HaMitzvot* (Negative Commandment 362) states "There may be no king over any believer in the Torah of Moses, our teacher except from the descendants of David and Solomon."

Solomon's anointing revealed "that he alone was king." He possessed the essential quality of monarchy epitomized by David and he transferred this virtue to his children.

57. II Kings, Chapter 11, describes Atalyah's murder of the children of King Achazyahu, her assumption of the throne, and the revolt which established Joash as king.

58. Jehoachaz was younger than Jehoyakim. Nevertheless, he was given the throne, because he was more capable than his brother, and better suited to serve in his father's position.

CHAPTER TWO

1. The king must be treated with great honor.[1] We must implant awe and fear of him in the hearts of all men. The command [Deuteronomy 17:15]: "Appoint a king" [implies the obligation] to be in awe of him.[2]

We may not ride on his horse,[3] nor sit on his throne, use his scepter,[4] [wear] his crown,[5] or use any of his utensils. When he dies, they should all be burned before his [bier].[6]

Similarly, only another king is allowed to make use of his servants, maids, and attendants. Accordingly, Avishag was permitted to Solomon, but prohibited to Adoniyahu.[7]

2. However, a king's wife is forbidden to share intimacy with another person forever.[8] Even another king may not marry a king's widow[9] or divorced ex-wife.[10]

3. It is forbidden to observe him while he is naked, while he is having his hair cut, while he is in the baths, or while he is drying himself [afterwards].[11]

He may not perform *chalitzah*,[12] for [concerning that ritual,] it is said [Deuteronomy 25:9]: "And she shall spit before him." This would be disrespectful to the king.[13]

1. The king is chosen by God for his office. His function is to impress the people with their responsibility to their Creator. Accordingly, he is worthy of all the tokens of respect and honor described in this and the following halachot.
2. The Jerusalem Talmud, *Sanhedrin* 2:6 comments: "The verse states: 'You shall appoint a king.' God tells the people: 'I will not appoint the king. You must grant him this authority yourselves.'"
3. *Sanhedrin* 95a relates that if the king's life is in danger, his servants may ride on his horse to save him. For example, Avishai rode on David's horse to save him from death at the hands of the Philistines, as alluded to in II Samuel 21: 17.
4. These are obviously items specific to a king and their use by a commoner would constitute the usurpation of the king's authority.
5. The crown is more closely associated with kingship than any other royal accouterment. Accordingly, when Haman suggested that the king's crown be used to honor another person, Achasverosh refused (Esther 6:8-10).
6. It was customary to burn the king's bed and personal property, as implied by Jeremiah's prophecy to Tzedekiah (Jeremiah 34:5): "You shall die in peace, and as they made pyres for your ancestors, the earlier [kings...], they will make pyres for you."

In *Hilchot Evel* 14:26, the Rambam explains that this custom was not considered as gentile in origin. Hence, was not forbidden. Neither was it viewed as a waste of property (see Chapter 6, Halachah 10), since it was performed as an honor to the departed ruler.

7. Avishag was King David's attendant in his final days. However, David did not marry her or share intimacy with her (I Kings 1:1-4).

When David died and Solomom succeeded him, David's son Adoniyahu asked to marry Avishag (*ibid.* 2:17). Since he was a commoner and not fit to benefit from the services of a woman who had attended the king, Solomon considered this as an act of rebellion and ordered him executed.

פֶּרֶק שֵׁנִי

א כָּבוֹד גָּדוֹל נוֹהֲגִין בַּמֶּלֶךְ, וּמְשִׂימִין לוֹ אֵימָה וְיִרְאָה בְּלֵב כָּל אָדָם, שֶׁנֶּאֱמַר: "שׂוֹם תָּשִׂים", שֶׁתְּהֵא אֵימָתוֹ עָלֶיךָ. אֵין רוֹכְבִין עַל סוּסוֹ, וְאֵין יוֹשְׁבִין עַל כִּסְאוֹ, וְאֵין מִשְׁתַּמְּשִׁין בְּשַׁרְבִיטוֹ וְלֹא בְכִתְרוֹ וְלֹא בְאֶחָד מִכָּל כְּלֵי תַשְׁמִישָׁיו. וּכְשֶׁהוּא מֵת – כֻּלָּן נִשְׂרָפִין לְפָנָיו. וְכֵן לֹא יִשְׁתַּמֵּשׁ בַּעֲבָדָיו וְשִׁפְחוֹתָיו וְשַׁמָּשָׁיו, אֶלָּא מֶלֶךְ אַחֵר. לְפִיכָךְ, אֲבִישַׁג הָיְתָה מֻתֶּרֶת לִשְׁלֹמֹה וַאֲסוּרָה לַאֲדֹנִיָּה.

ב אֲבָל אִשְׁתּוֹ שֶׁל מֶלֶךְ אֵינָהּ נִבְעֶלֶת לְאַחֵר לְעוֹלָם. אֲפִלּוּ הַמֶּלֶךְ, אֵינוֹ נוֹשֵׂא אַלְמָנָתוֹ אוֹ גְרוּשָׁתוֹ שֶׁל מֶלֶךְ אַחֵר.

ג וְאָסוּר לִרְאוֹתוֹ כְּשֶׁהוּא עָרֹם וְלֹא כְּשֶׁהוּא מִסְתַּפֵּר וְלֹא כְּשֶׁהוּא בְּבֵית־הַמֶּרְחָץ וְלֹא כְּשֶׁהוּא מִסְתַּפֵּג. וְאֵינוֹ חוֹלֵץ, שֶׁנֶּאֱמַר: "וְיָרְקָה בְּפָנָיו", וְזֶה בִּזָּיוֹן.

However, Solomon would have been allowed to marry Avishag. Since David did not marry her, she was not prohibited as a king's widow (see the following halachah) and Solomon, as a king, was permitted to benefit from the services of the king's attendants.

8. *Sanhedrin* 18a explains that this prohibition applies even when a mitzvah is involved, for example, should a king die childless. In such an instance, the wife of a commoner would be obligated to marry her deceased husband's brother in order to perpetuate her husband's memory (*yibbum* in Hebrew; see Deuteronomy 25:5-6.) As mentioned in the following halachah, this mitzvah does not apply to a king's widow.

9. There is a seeming contradiction to this law in II Samuel 12:7-8 which relates how Nathan, the prophet told King David: "Thus says the Lord: ... 'I anointed you king over Israel .... I gave you your master's (Saul's) house and gave your master's women into your bosom.'"

Nevertheless, *Sanhedrin* 18a explains that the term "women" mentioned does not refer to Saul's wives, but rather, to his daughters, Merav and Michal whom David married.

10. In his commentary to the Jerusalem Talmud, *Sanhedrin* 2:3, *Mareh HaPonim* quotes the following Biblical narrative as an example of this law: When King David fled Jerusalem after the revolt of his son Avshalom, the latter had relations with David's concubines as a way of publicly casting off his authority (II Samuel 16:21-23).

Afterwards, when David returned to Jerusalem he continued to provide for the needs of these concubines, but no longer shared intimacy with them. They were (*ibid.* 20:3) "shut up to the day of their death, widows of a living husband."

Were it permissible for another man to marry a king's divorcee, David surely would have divorced them, rather than subject them to a life of loneliness.

11. Even if the king consents to the presence of others, they are forbidden to join him, for a king may never forgo his honor.

12. It is a mitzvah for a person whose brother dies childless to marry his sister-in-law and perpetuate his seed through levirate marriage (*yibbum*). If the surviving brother does not desire to marry the deceased's widow, he may free her to marry another man by performing the *chalitzah* ceremony; see Deuteronomy 25:5-10.

13. The woman's spitting is intended to embarrass her brother-in-law for not performing the mitzvah of perpetuating his brother's line. The king may not be subjected to this shame.

Even if he desires [to perform this mitzvah], he is not given the opportunity because a king's honor must be preserved even though he [is willing to] forgo it.[14]

Since he is not allowed to perform *chalitzah*, he is not eligible to participate in *yibbum*.[15] Similarly, in the event of his death, since it is forbidden to initiate *yibbum* with his wife,[16] *chalitzah* is also not performed for her.[17] Rather, she must remain in her state of attachment forever.[18]

4. Even if one of his [close relatives][19] dies, he may not leave his palace.[20] When he is served the meal of comfort,[21] the entire nation should sit on the ground and he should sit on a low couch.[22]

If he enters the Temple courtyard, and he is of David's descendants, he may sit.[23] For the only ones who may sit in the Temple Courtyard are kings of the Davidic dynasty,[24] as [II Samuel 7:18] states: "And David sat before God."[25]

5. A king should have his hair cut every day. He should dress and adorn himself in attractive and impressive garments, as [Isaiah 33:17] states: "Your eyes shall behold the king in his beauty."[26]

He sits on his throne[27] in his palace and has a crown placed on his head.[28]

When he desires, the nation must present themselves before him. They should stand before him and prostrate themselves to the ground.[29] Even a

14. Other individuals, for example, a High Priest, a *nasi*, or judge have the privilege of forgoing the honor due them. A king, by contrast, may not yield on a point of honor for there is a specific command to hold him in awe.

15 *Yevamot* 3a mentions the principle "All those who are not fit to perform *yibbum*, are not required to perform *chalitzah*." However, the converse of that principle, seemingly, the basis of this halachah, is not found in the Talmud.

Tosafot (*Yevamot* 44a) accepts this principle, but Rashi does not. Instead, he explains that a king does not perform *yibbum* because it would not be appropriate for his status for his child to be considered as his brother's.

16. For as mentioned above, a king's wife may never engage in sexual relations with another person.

17. The Rambam implies that *chalitzah* is not performed for her, because she can not engage in *yibbum*. The *Kessef Mishneh* explains that she does not perform *chalitzah*, for it is demeaning for a king's widow to perform the service of removing someone else's shoe, an essential aspect of the *chalitzah* ceremony.

18. Regardless, there would be no practical benefit from this *chalitzah*, for as mentioned above, a king's widow may not remarry.

19. I.e., his father, mother, wife, brother, sister, son, or daughter, as mentioned in *Hilchot Evel* 2:1.

20. To participate in the funeral.

Sanhedrin 20a quotes a debate among the Sages on this question. The Mishnah's first opinion, quoted by the Rambam, forbids a king from attending funerals. In contrast, Rabbi Yehudah considers the matter optional, citing King David's attendance of the funeral of Avner ben Ner (II Samuel 3: 31) as proof that a king may participate in mourning rites.

The others explain that David made an exception in this case in order to unify the nation after the civil war between his forces and those loyal to Mefiboshet, the son of King Saul. Avner had led those troops. By attending his funeral, David was able to

וַאֲפִלּוּ רָצָה – אֵין שׁוֹמְעִין לוֹ; שֶׁהַמֶּלֶךְ שֶׁמָּחַל עַל כְּבוֹדוֹ – אֵין כְּבוֹדוֹ מָחוּל. וְהוֹאִיל וְאֵינוֹ חוֹלֵץ – אֵינוֹ מְיַבֵּם. וְכֵן אִם מֵת הוּא, כֵּיוָן שֶׁאִי אֶפְשָׁר לְיַבֵּם אֶת אִשְׁתּוֹ, כָּךְ אֵין חוֹלְצִין לָהּ, אֶלָּא תֵּשֵׁב לְעוֹלָם בְּזִקָּתָהּ.

ד מֵת לוֹ מֵת – אֵינוֹ יוֹצֵא מִפֶּתַח פַּלְטֵרִין שֶׁלּוֹ. וּכְשֶׁמַּבְרִין אוֹתוֹ – כָּל הָעָם מְסֻבִּין עַל הָאָרֶץ, וְהוּא מֵסֵב עַל הַדַּרְגָּשׁ. וְאִם נִכְנַס לָעֲזָרָה וְהָיָה מִזֶּרַע דָּוִד – יֵשֵׁב; שֶׁאֵין יְשִׁיבָה בָּעֲזָרָה אֶלָּא לְמַלְכֵי בֵית־דָּוִד בִּלְבָד, שֶׁנֶּאֱמַר: "וַיָּבֹא הַמֶּלֶךְ דָּוִד וַיֵּשֶׁב לִפְנֵי ה'".

ה הַמֶּלֶךְ מִסְתַּפֵּר בְּכָל יוֹם, וּמְתַקֵּן עַצְמוֹ וּמִתְנָאֶה בְּמַלְבּוּשִׁין נָאִים וּמְפֹאָרִים, שֶׁנֶּאֱמַר: "מֶלֶךְ בְּיָפְיוֹ תֶּחֱזֶינָה עֵינֶיךָ". וְיוֹשֵׁב עַל כִּסֵּא מַלְכוּתוֹ בְּפַלְטֵרִין שֶׁלּוֹ, וּמֵשִׂים כֶּתֶר בְּרֹאשׁוֹ, וְכָל הָעָם בָּאִין אֵלָיו בָּעֵת שֶׁיִּרְצֶה, וְעוֹמְדִין לְפָנָיו וּמִשְׁתַּחֲוִין אָרְצָה.

mollify the strife and friction between the two camps (see *Hilchot Evel* 7:7).

21. After a funeral, it is customary to serve the bereaved family a meal. The food for this meal may not belong to the mourners.

22. A mourner is forbidden to sit on a normal chair. In many communities, it is customary for him to sit on the ground itself. As a token of respect, the king is allowed to sit on a low couch.

Generally, those who comfort the mourner may sit on normal chairs. In this instance, out of deference to the king, the people must sit on the ground.

23. Rashi (*Yoma* 25a) derives the prohibition against sitting in the Temple Courtyard from the verse (Deuteronomy 18:5): "For the Lord has chosen him ... to stand and to serve in the name of the Lord."

Tosafot question whether the priests are permitted to sit in the courtyard when they partake of the sacrifices of the most holy order. From the Rambam's statements, it appears that he does not permit such leniency. See *Hilchot Beit HaBechirah* 7:6 and commentaries.

24. In contrast, the kings of the kingdom of Israel were not given this honor. Indeed, *Sanhedrin* 101b relates that this differentiation was one of the reasons Jeroboam did not go to Jerusalem on the pilgrimage festivals and prevented his nation from doing so.

25. This event took place after David requested permission to build the Temple. God answered him in a vision to the prophet Nathan, informing him that David's son would build the Temple. Nevertheless, as a reward for his dedication, God promised David an everlasting dynasty.

After receiving this promise, David went to the Ark to offer his thanks to God. He exclaimed: "Who am I, 0 Lord, G-d, and what is my house that You have brought me this far." At the moment when he was granted this great honor, he displayed humility.

26. The Jerusalem Talmud, *Sanhedrin* 2:6 relates that Rabbi Yochanan went to visit the *nasi*. The latter came out to greet him wearing a simple linen garment. Rabbi Yochanan suggested that he return home and don a more attractive woolen garment for "One's eyes should behold the king in his beauty."

27. II Chronicles 29:23 refers to the throne as "the throne of God."

28. There was a unique aspect to the crown passed on in the Davidic dynasty. If a king was appropriate for his office, it would fit correctly on his head. Otherwise, it would not be able to rest upon him (*Avodah Zarah* 44a).

29. This act of homage required kneeling and bowing down with one's face to the ground as evident from the continuation of the verse from I Kings cited by the Rambam.

prophet must stand before the king and prostrate himself on the ground, as [I Kings 1:23] states: "Behold, Nathan, the prophet came before the king and prostrated himself before the king."[30]

However, a High Priest need not come before the king unless he [the High Priest] desires to do so. The High Priest need not stand before the king. Rather, the king stands before the High Priest, as [Numbers 27:21] states: "And he shall stand before Elazar, the priest."[31]

Nevertheless, it is a mitzvah for the High Priest to honor the king [by] having him seated and standing in his presence when he visits him. The king should only stand before him when he consults the *Urim* and *Tumim*.[32]

Similarly, it is a mitzvah for the king to honor students of Torah when they enter his presence. He should stand before the *Sanhedrin* and the Sages of Israel and seat them at his side.[33]

Jehosephat, King of Judah would follow this practice. Whenever even a student of a Torah scholar [would come to him,] he would rise from his throne and kiss him and address him as "My teacher and master."

When does the above apply? When the king is alone in his palace. [Then,] in private, before his servants, he should behave in this fashion.[34] However, in public, before the people at large, he should not conduct himself in this manner.[35] He should not stand before anyone. He should not speak gently and should address a person using his name alone[36] in order that the awe of him [will be implanted] in everyone's heart.[37]

6. Just as the Torah has granted him great honor and obligated everyone to revere him; so, too, has it commanded him to be lowly and empty at heart,[38] as [Psalms 109:22] states: "My heart is a void within me."[39] Nor should he treat Israel with overbearing haughtiness.[40] For [Deuteronomy 17:20] describes how "he should not lift up his heart above his brothers."[41]

He should be gracious and merciful to the small and the great, involving himself in their good and welfare. He should protect the honor of even the humblest of men.[42]

When he speaks to the people as a community, he should speak gently, as [I

30. The prophets always honored the kings even when the latter were not righteous. Accordingly, I Kings 18:46 relates how Elijah ran before Achav's chariot as a token of respect.

Though a prophet is obligated to show homage to the king, our Sages praised the kings for showing humility in their relationships with the prophets. For example, *Bamidbar Rabbah* praises Jehosephat for humbling himself before Elisha, the prophet.

31. The second chapter of *Sanhedrin* elaborates on the contrasts and similarities between these two great offices. Both were considered of great importance. In certain matters, the honor due the High Priest surpassed that due the king and in others, the king was supreme. *Horiot* 13a concludes that the king is considered supreme.

32. The stones - or the names of God - embedded in the High Priest's breastplate which served as oracles. See the conclusion of *Hilchot Klei HaMikdash*.

אֲפִלּוּ נָבִיא עוֹמֵד לִפְנֵי הַמֶּלֶךְ – מִשְׁתַּחֲוֶה אָרְצָה, שֶׁנֶּאֱמַר: "הִנֵּה נָתָן הַנָּבִיא, וַיָּבֹא לִפְנֵי הַמֶּלֶךְ וַיִּשְׁתַּחוּ לַמֶּלֶךְ". אֲבָל כֹּהֵן גָּדוֹל אֵינוֹ בָא לִפְנֵי הַמֶּלֶךְ אֶלָּא אִם רָצָה. וְאֵינוֹ עוֹמֵד לְפָנָיו, אֶלָּא הַמֶּלֶךְ עוֹמֵד לִפְנֵי כֹּהֵן גָּדוֹל, שֶׁנֶּאֱמַר: "וְלִפְנֵי אֶלְעָזָר הַכֹּהֵן יַעֲמֹד". אַף־עַל־פִּי־כֵן מִצְוָה עַל כֹּהֵן גָּדוֹל לְכַבֵּד אֶת הַמֶּלֶךְ וּלְהוֹשִׁיבוֹ וְלַעֲמֹד מִפָּנָיו כְּשֶׁיָּבוֹא לוֹ. וְלֹא יַעֲמֹד הַמֶּלֶךְ לְפָנָיו אֶלָּא כְּשֶׁיִּשְׁאַל לוֹ בְּמִשְׁפַּט הָאוּרִים. וְכֵן מִצְוָה עַל הַמֶּלֶךְ לְכַבֵּד לוֹמְדֵי הַתּוֹרָה. וּכְשֶׁיִּכָּנְסוּ לְפָנָיו סַנְהֶדְרִין וְחַכְמֵי יִשְׂרָאֵל, יַעֲמֹד לִפְנֵיהֶם וְיוֹשִׁיבֵם בְּצִדּוֹ; וְכֵן הָיָה יְהוֹשָׁפָט מֶלֶךְ יְהוּדָה עוֹשֶׂה, אֲפִלּוּ לְתַלְמִיד־חָכָם הָיָה עוֹמֵד מִכִּסְאוֹ וּמְנַשְּׁקוֹ וְקוֹרֵא לוֹ: רַבִּי וּמוֹרִי! בַּמֶּה דְּבָרִים אֲמוּרִים? בִּזְמַן שֶׁיִּהְיֶה הַמֶּלֶךְ בְּבֵיתוֹ לְבַדּוֹ הוּא וַעֲבָדָיו, יַעֲשֶׂה זֶה בִּצְנְעָה; אֲבָל בְּפַרְהֶסְיָא, בִּפְנֵי הָעָם – לֹא יַעֲשֶׂה. וְלֹא יַעֲמֹד מִפְּנֵי אָדָם, וְלֹא יְדַבֵּר רַכּוֹת, וְלֹא יִקְרָא לְאָדָם אֶלָּא בִּשְׁמוֹ, כְּדֵי שֶׁתִּהְיֶה יִרְאָתוֹ בְּלֵב הַכֹּל.

ו כְּדֶרֶךְ שֶׁחָלַק לוֹ הַכָּתוּב הַכָּבוֹד הַגָּדוֹל, וְחַיָּב הַכֹּל בִּכְבוֹדוֹ, כָּךְ צִוָּהוּ לִהְיוֹת לִבּוֹ בְּקִרְבּוֹ שָׁפָל וְחָלָל, שֶׁנֶּאֱמַר: "וְלִבִּי חָלַל בְּקִרְבִּי". וְלֹא יִנְהַג גַּסּוּת־לֵב בְּיִשְׂרָאֵל יוֹתֵר מִדַּי, שֶׁנֶּאֱמַר: "לְבִלְתִּי רוּם לְבָבוֹ מֵאֶחָיו". וְיִהְיֶה חוֹנֵן וּמְרַחֵם לִקְטַנִּים וּגְדוֹלִים, וְיֵצֵא וְיָבוֹא בְּחֶפְצֵיהֶם וּבְטוֹבָתָם, וְיָחוּס עַל כְּבוֹד קָטָן שֶׁבִּקְטַנִּים. וּכְשֶׁמְּדַבֵּר אֶל כָּל הַקָּהָל בִּלְשׁוֹן

33. By honoring the Torah, the king shows his respect for God, its Author.

34. When it is unnecessary for him to create an impression of majesty among the people, he should follow these modest practices.

35. Lest the people lose their respect for him.

36. Without any honorary titles.

37. *Ketubot* 103b relates that before Rabbi Yehudah, the *nasi*, passed away, he instructed his son Gamliel, who would assume his position: "Conduct your authority with a high hand. Cast fear into the students."

38. *Megillah* 31a states: "Where you find God's greatness, there, you find His humility." The fusion of these two qualities must also be reflected in a king. He must hold himself proudly before the nation, but remain humble in his heart.

39. Rashi (*Berachot* 61b) interprets this verse as a statement that David had entirely subdued his *yetzer hara*, evil inclination.

40. The king's behavior must inspire the people to revere him and hold him in awe. Nevertheless, it should not cause them to recoil and despise him for his pride.

41. The Jerusalem Talmud, *Sanhedrin* 2:4, explains that David's statements (Psalms 131:l): "My God, I have not made my heart haughty or my eyes lofty" refer to the time when he was anointed king by Samuel.

42. The people must dedicate themselves to the king and accept his absolute authority. Similarly, the king must dedicate himself to the people and involve himself in their concerns.

When two Sages refused to accept positions of authority out of humility, Rabban Gamliel assured them: " Don't worry. I am not giving you honor and authority, I'm making you servants [of the people]" (*Horiot* 10a).

Chronicles 28:2] states "Listen my brothers and my people...."[43] [Similarly, I Kings 12:7] states "If today, you will be a servant to these people...."[44]

He should always conduct himself with great humility. There is none greater than Moses, our teacher. Yet, he said [Exodus 16:8]: "What are we? Your complaints are not against us."[45] He should bear [the nation's] difficulties, burdens, complaints, and anger[46] as a nurse carries an infant.[47]

[Psalms 78:71] refers to [a king] as a shepherd: "to pasture, Jacob, His nation."[48] The prophets have described the behavior of a shepherd [Isaiah 40:11]: "He shall pasture His flock like a shepherd, He shall gather the lambs with His arm and carry them in His bosom."[49]

CHAPTER THREE

1. During a king's reign, he must write a Torah scroll for himself[1] in addition to the scroll which was left to him by his ancestors.[2] A court of 71 [elders] should check this scroll [by comparing it] to the Torah scroll kept in the Temple Courtyard.

If his ancestors did not leave him a Torah scroll or that scroll was lost, he must write two Torah scrolls:[3]

one, in whose [writing,] he is obligated as is every individual Israelite [and which] he places in his treasury;

the second, which should not move from his presence[4] except when he enters a lavatory, the baths, or other places in which it is not fit to read [the words of Torah].[5]

When he goes to war, this [scroll] should accompany him. When he returns,

43. The previous halachah instructed the king to refrain from "speaking gently" in public. However, that only applies when addressing an individual or small group. When the kings speaks to the entire people or their representatives, he must adopt a mild demeanor, as reflected by the manner in which David spoke to the people in the verse cited.

44. After King Solomon's death, the ten tribes who later formed the kingdom of Israel, gathered under the leadership of Jeroboam and told Rechavam, Solomon's heir: "Your father made our yoke difficult... if you will make the yoke lighter,... we will serve you."

Rechavam consulted his father's advisors who told him: "If today, you will be a servant to this people,... they will be your servants forever."

Rechavam refused to accept this advice and consulted with younger advisors who had grown up with him. They told him to deal with the people heavy-handedly and reply: "My father made your yoke heavy, I will add to your yoke." He followed their advice. When the ten tribes received this haughty reply, they revolted against Rechavam and established the independent kingdom of Israel.

45. Though the burden of leadership was entirely on his shoulders, Moses was "humble, more so than any man on the face of the earth" (Numbers 12:3). Even when the people rebelled against him in Korach's mutiny (see Numbers, Chapter 16), he patiently sought to make peace with the leaders of the rebellion.

46. The Rambam's wording closely resembles Deuteronomy 1:12.

47. Cf. Numbers 11: 12.

48. That Psalm describes how God took David "from the sheepfolds... to shepherd Jacob,

רַבִּים – יְדַבֵּר רַכּוֹת, שֶׁנֶּאֱמַר: "שְׁמָעוּנִי אַחַי וְעַמִּי", וְאוֹמֵר: "אִם הַיּוֹם תִּהְיֶה עֶבֶד לָעָם הַזֶּה וְגוֹ'"; לְעוֹלָם יִתְנַהֵג בַּעֲנָוָה יְתֵרָה. אֵין לָנוּ גָּדוֹל מִמֹּשֶׁה רַבֵּנוּ, וְהוּא אוֹמֵר: "וְנַחְנוּ מָה לֹא עָלֵינוּ תְלֻנֹּתֵיכֶם". וְיִסְבֹּל טָרְחָם וּמַשָּׂאָם וּתְלֻנּוֹתָם וְקִצְפָּם כַּאֲשֶׁר יִשָּׂא הָאוֹמֵן אֶת הַיּוֹנֵק. רוֹעֶה קְרָאוֹ הַכָּתוּב: "לִרְעוֹת בְּיַעֲקֹב עַמּוֹ". וְדַרְכּוֹ שֶׁל רוֹעֶה מְפֹרָשׁ בַּקַּבָּלָה: "כְּרֹעֶה עֶדְרוֹ יִרְעֶה, בִּזְרֹעוֹ יְקַבֵּץ טְלָאִים וּבְחֵיקוֹ יִשָּׂא וְגוֹ'".

פֶּרֶק שְׁלִישִׁי

א בְּעֵת שֶׁיֵּשֵׁב הַמֶּלֶךְ עַל כִּסֵּא מַלְכוּתוֹ, כּוֹתֵב לוֹ סֵפֶר־תּוֹרָה לְעַצְמוֹ יָתֵר עַל הַסֵּפֶר שֶׁהִנִּיחוּ לוֹ אֲבוֹתָיו. וּמַגִּיהוֹ מִסֵּפֶר הָעֲזָרָה עַל־פִּי בֵית־דִּין שֶׁל שִׁבְעִים וְאֶחָד. אִם לֹא הִנִּיחוּ לוֹ אֲבוֹתָיו אוֹ שֶׁנֶּאֱבַד – כּוֹתֵב שְׁנֵי סִפְרֵי־תוֹרָה: אֶחָד מַנִּיחוֹ בְּבֵית גְּנָזָיו, שֶׁהוּא מְצֻוֶּה בּוֹ כְּכָל אֶחָד מִיִּשְׂרָאֵל, וְהַשֵּׁנִי לֹא יָזוּז מִלְּפָנָיו, אֶלָּא בְּעֵת שֶׁיִּכָּנֵס לְבֵית־הַכִּסֵּא אוֹ לְבֵית־הַמֶּרְחָץ, אוֹ לְמָקוֹם שֶׁאֵין רָאוּי לִקְרִיאָה. יוֹצֵא לַמִּלְחָמָה – וְהוּא עִמּוֹ; נִכְנָס –

His nation." *Shmot Rabbah* 2:2 explains that God watched the kind and merciful way David pastured his father's sheep. "Such a person," God stated, "is fit to lead My people."

49. This verse refers to the manner in which God will care for the people after the Messianic redemption. These qualities must be emulated by every king.

1. Or commission others to write for him.

2. Deuteronomy 31:19 states: "Now, write for yourselves this song." Based on this verse, *Sanhedrin* 21b states that it is a mitzvah for every Jew to write a Torah scroll or have one written for him. (See also *Hilchot Sefer Torah* 7:1).

In addition to fulfilling the above command, the king is obligated to write a second Torah which will accompany him at all times. Writing this scroll is considered one of the Torah's 613 Mitzvot (*Sefer HaMitvot*, Positive Commandment 18, *Sefer HaChinuch*, mitzvah 503).

3. The obligation of the king to possess two Torah scrolls is accepted by all authorities. However, the wording used by the Rambam arouses certain questions:

Sanhedrin 21b which appears to be the source for this halachah states: "Even though a person's ancestors left him a Torah scroll, he is obligated to write one himself." Accordingly, it appears that it would be improper for a king to rely on the scroll left him by his ancestors. Rather, he should write two scrolls himself.

The *Kessef Mishneh* resolves this difficulty by explaining that a private individual may not rely on a Torah scroll written by his ancestors. He must perform the mitzvah of writing a Torah scroll himself or commission one to be written. This experience will develop a stronger connection between him and the Torah. Similarly, the king must personally write a Torah scroll. However, if the king does possess an inherited scroll, there is no need for him to write two Torah scrolls. He may rely on the scroll left him by his ancestors to use as his second scroll.

4. *Sanhedrin* 21b states that he should "wear it on his arm as an amulet, as it is written (Psalms 16:8): 'I have set God before me at all times. Since He is at my right hand, I will not be moved.'"

5. Deuteronomy 17:19, which is the source for this mitzvah, states: "It should

it should accompany him. When he sits in judgement, it should be with him. When he dines, it should be opposite him, as [Deuteronomy 17:19] states: "It should accompany him and he should read it all the days of his [life]."[6]

2. "He should not amass many wives" [Deuteronomy 17:17].[7] The Oral Tradition states that he may take no more than eighteen wives.[8]

The figure eighteen includes both wives and concubines.[9] If he takes an additional wife and has relations with her, he is [punished with] lashes.[10]

He may divorce [one of his wives] and marry another instead of the one he divorced.[11]

3. He may not accumulate many horses,[12] only what is necessary for his cavalry.[13] It is even forbidden for him [to have] one additional horse to run before him as is customarily done by other kings. If he adds [an additional horse,] he is to be lashed.

accompany him and he should read it...." Accordingly, the king's scroll need not accompany him wherever it is unseemly to study Torah (*Sanhedrin, loc. cit.*).

6. This scroll is reserved for the king's personal use. None of his subjects may study from it (*Tosefta, Sanhedrin* 4:4).

In *Hilchot Sefer Torah* 7:3, the Rambam writes: "The second [scroll] should accompany him at all times. It should not move from his presence except at night or when he enters the baths...."

The commentaries question why the Rambam excludes the night. They support their objections by quoting the *Sifri, Shoftim,* which specifically requires the king to take his Torah scroll with him at night. Similarly, from the Rambam's statements in Halachah 5 of this chapter, it would appear that the king should keep the Torah scroll with him at night as well.

Based on these questions, *Or Sameach* suggests changing the text in *Hilchot Sefer Torah* to read "even at night except when...."

7. This prohibition is counted as one of the 365 mitzvot of the Torah (*Sefer HaMitzvot,* Negative Commandment 364, *Sefer HaChinuch* 501). The Rambam discusses the ethical ramifications of this mitzvah in Halachah 6.

8. See *Sanhedrin* 21a for an explanation how this figure is derived.

9. In Chapter 4, Halachah 4, the Rambam defines a concubine as a woman singled out by the king to be his without *kiddushin* or a *ketubah.* He adds that the privilege of taking a concubine is only given a king and not a commoner.

The Ra'avad objects to the Rambam's ruling here, maintaining that the king is limited only regarding the number of his wives. He may take as many concubines as he desires. (From *Sefer HaMitzvot, loc. cit.*, it might be argued that the Rambam originally accepted the Ra'avad's opinion, and when he wrote the *Mishneh Torah,* he revised his original decision.)

Narratives from the Bible are used to support both opinions. II Chronicles 10:21 relates how Rechavam, Solomon's son and heir, took eighteen wives and 60 concubines, seeming to support the Ra'avad's opinion. However, proponents of the Rambam's opinion note that II Chronicles also states 12:14: "He (Rechavam) did evil for he did not set his heart on seeking God." Hence, his behavior cannot necessarily be accepted as a paradigm from which we may derive Torah law.

וְהוּא עִמּוֹ; יוֹשֵׁב בַּדִּין – וְהוּא עִמּוֹ; מֵסֵב – וְהוּא כְּנֶגְדּוֹ, שֶׁנֶּאֱמַר: "וְהָיְתָה עִמּוֹ וְקָרָא בוֹ כָּל יְמֵי חַיָּיו".

ב לֹא יַרְבֶּה לוֹ נָשִׁים. מִפִּי הַשְּׁמוּעָה לָמְדוּ, שֶׁהוּא לוֹקֵחַ עַד שְׁמוֹנֶה־עֶשְׂרֵה נָשִׁים – בֵּין הַנָּשִׁים וּפִילַגְשִׁים – הַכֹּל שְׁמוֹנֶה־עֶשְׂרֵה. וְאִם הוֹסִיף אַחַת וּבְעָלָהּ – לוֹקֶה. וְיֵשׁ לוֹ לְגָרֵשׁ וְלִשָּׂא אַחֶרֶת תַּחַת זוֹ שֶׁגֵּרֵשׁ.

ג וְלֹא יַרְבֶּה לוֹ סוּסִים, אֶלָּא כְּדֵי מֶרְכַּבְתּוֹ. אֲפִלּוּ סוּס אֶחָד פָּנוּי לִהְיוֹת רָץ לְפָנָיו כְּדֶרֶךְ שֶׁעוֹשִׂין שְׁאָר הַמְּלָכִים – אָסוּר. וְאִם הוֹסִיף – לוֹקֶה.

Support for the Rambam's opinion is brought from the narrative of David and Avishag (I Kings, Chapter l). Though she served David as a personal attendant, "lying in his embrace," David "shared no intimacy with her." *Sanhedrin* 22a explains that David did not marry her because he already had eighteen wives and didnot want to divorce any of them in her favor.

According to the Ra'avad's opinion, there would have been no necessity for David to exercise self-control. He could have taken her as a concubine without divorcing any of his wives. Nevertheless, proponents of the Ra'avad's opinion maintain that Avishag refused to accept that less dignified status and David respected her wishes.

Additional support for the Rambam's opinion can be derived from the verse (Deuteronomy 17:17): "He must not amass many wives lest they make his heart go astray," which is the source for this prohibition. Both wives and concubines can cause a man's heart to go astray.

10. The *Kessef Mishneh* questions why the king only incurs a penalty if he has relations with the additional wife. It would appear that he violates this prohibition as soon as he consecrates her.

In reply, the *Lechem Mishneh* explains that we must consider the reason for the prohibition: "Lest they make his heart go astray." It is the aspect of sexual relations that may cause his heart to go astray. The *Lechem Mishneh* also cites a number of examples, the prohibition against a priest marrying a divorcee, or a high priest marrying a widow (see *Hilchot Issurei Bi'ah* 17:4), where punishment is only incurred if the couple engage in sexual relations.

11. As mentioned above, *Sanhedrin* 22a notes that David could have divorced one of his wives to marry Avishag. He, nevertheless, refused to do so, because of the severity of divorce.

12. This prohibition, quoted from Deuteronomy 17:16, is one of the Torah's 365 negative commands (*Sefer HaMitzvot*, Negative Commandment 363, *Sefer HaChinuch*, mitzvah 499).

13. The king is allowed to possess as many horses as necessary for military purposes. There is no prohibition involved, even if they are only necessary to strike fear into the hearts of the enemy (Rambam, Commentary on the Mishnah, *Sanhedrin* 2:5)

In the above-mentioned text and in *Sefer HaMitzvot*, the Rambam writes that the king is allowed only one horse as his own personal steed. Hence, we have translated *merkavto* as "cavalry." However, that term may also be rendered as "chariot" According to that interpretation, the Rambam revised his decision, granting the king permission to have as many horses as necessary for his personal chariot.

4. He may not amass silver and gold[14] to keep in his [personal] treasury[15] in order to boost his pride or allow him to glorify himself.[16] Rather, he [may collect] only what is necessary to pay his soldiers, servants, and attendants.

Any gold and silver which he does accumulate [should be given] to the Temple treasury to be kept there, in readiness for the needs of the community and their wars.[17]

It is a mitzvah to accumulate [such treasure stores]. The prohibition is only against amassing personal [wealth] in his own treasure houses,[18] as [Deuteronomy 17:17] states: "He shall not amass for himself...." Should he amass [personal wealth], he is to be lashed.

5. The king is forbidden to drink [wine] to the point of intoxication,[19] as [Proverbs 31:4] states: "It is not for kings to drink wine...."[20]

Rather, he should be involved with Torah study and the needs of Israel by day and by night, as [Deuteronomy, *loc. cit.*] states: "It should accompany him and he should read it all the days of his [life]."[21]

6. Similarly, he should not be overly indulgent [in his relations] with his wives. Even if he has only one wife, he should not constantly be with her as is the practice of fools,[22] as [Proverbs 31:3] states: "Do not give your strength to women."[23]

When the Torah [forbade the king from accumulating many wives, its] emphasis was that his heart not go astray as [Deuteronomy 17: 17] warns: "lest his heart go astray."[24] His heart is the heart of the entire congregation of Israel.[25] Therefore, the verse [commanded him] to have it cleave to the Torah to a greater degree than the rest of the nation, as it is stated: "all the days of his [life]."

14. This prohibition, quoted from Deuteronomy 17:17, is considered one of the 365 prohibitions of the Torah (*Sefer HaMitzvot*, Negative Commandment 365, *Sefer HaChinuch*, mitzvah 502).

15. As the Rambam concludes, the prohibition consists not in the collection of taxes, but rather, in their use for creating his own personal fortune.

16. Pride and glory often result from the accumulation of wealth as it is written (Deuteronomy 8: 13-14): "You may amass much silver and gold..., but your heart may then grow haughty."

17. I Chronicles 29:4 relates how King David amassed a vast amount of gold and silver to be used in the building of the Temple. Similarly, in later generations, the Temple treasury contained the wealth of the nation. Accordingly, it often became the target of enemy attacks.

18. Commenting on *Sanhedrin, loc. cit.*, Rabbenu Nissim writes that a king is forbidden to amass personal wealth from taxation. However, he is allowed to accumulate a fortune from money taken as spoils of war. However, this opinion is not accepted by the *Minchat Chinuch*. See also the notes to Chapter 4, Halachah 9.

19. There is no blanket prohibition against a king's drinking wine. Indeed, *Chullin* 4b relates that it was customary for the kings of Judah to drink wine with their meals. It is intoxication that is forbidden.

ד וְלֹא יַרְבֶּה לוֹ כֶּסֶף וְזָהָב לְהַנִּיחַ בִּגְנָזָיו וּלְהִתְגָּאוֹת בּוֹ אוֹ לְהִתְנָאוֹת בּוֹ, אֶלָּא כְּדֵי שֶׁיִּתֵּן לְחֵילוֹתָיו וְלַעֲבָדָיו וּלְשַׁמָּשָׁיו. וְכָל כֶּסֶף וְזָהָב שֶׁיַּרְבֶּה לְאוֹצַר בֵּית ה׳, וְלִהְיוֹת שָׁם מוּכָן לְצָרְכֵי הַצִּבּוּר וּלְמִלְחֲמוֹתָם – הֲרֵי זֶה מִצְוָה לְהַרְבּוֹתוֹ. וְאֵין אָסוּר אֶלָּא לְהַרְבּוֹת לְעַצְמוֹ בְּבֵית גְּנָזָיו, שֶׁנֶּאֱמַר: "וְלֹא יַרְבֶּה לוֹ". וְאִם הִרְבָּה – לוֹקֶה.

ה הַמֶּלֶךְ אָסוּר לִשְׁתּוֹת דֶּרֶךְ שִׁכְרוּת, שֶׁנֶּאֱמַר: "אַל לַמְלָכִים שְׁתוֹ יָיִן". אֶלָּא יִהְיֶה עוֹסֵק בַּתּוֹרָה וּבְצָרְכֵי יִשְׂרָאֵל בַּיּוֹם וּבַלַּיְלָה, שֶׁנֶּאֱמַר: "וְהָיְתָה עִמּוֹ וְקָרָא בוֹ כָּל יְמֵי חַיָּיו".

ו וְכֵן לֹא יִהְיֶה שָׁטוּף בְּנָשִׁים. אֲפִלּוּ לֹא הָיְתָה לוֹ אֶלָּא אַחַת – לֹא יִהְיֶה מָצוּי אֶצְלָהּ תָּמִיד כִּשְׁאָר הַטִּפְּשִׁים, שֶׁנֶּאֱמַר: "אַל תִּתֵּן לַנָּשִׁים חֵילֶךָ". עַל הֲסָרַת לִבּוֹ הִקְפִּידָה תּוֹרָה, שֶׁנֶּאֱמַר: "וְלֹא יָסוּר לְבָבוֹ", שֶׁלִּבּוֹ הוּא לֵב כָּל קְהַל יִשְׂרָאֵל; לְפִיכָךְ דִּבְּקוֹ הַכָּתוּב בַּתּוֹרָה יָתֵר מִשְּׁאָר הָעָם, שֶׁנֶּאֱמַר: "כָּל יְמֵי חַיָּיו".

20. That verse continues: "Nor for princes to say: 'Where is strong drink?' Lest he drink... and pervert the judgement of any of the afflicted." *Sanhedrin* 70b interprets this verse as follows: "Is it proper for one to whom all the secrets of the world are revealed to drink wine and become intoxicated? Is it proper for one to whose door all the princes of the world gather to drink wine and become intoxicated?"

21. The king must divide his time between Torah study and caring for the welfare of the people.

The king's behavior should serve as an example to the entire nation. In that vein, the *Tosefta, Sanhedrin* 4:5 comments: "If a king of Israel, whose only involvement is for the welfare of the nation, is commanded: 'He should read it all the days of his [life];' how much more so does this apply to a common man!"

Note the commentary to Halachah 1, concerning the king's Torah study at night. See also the following halachah which explains the reason for the emphasis on the constancy of the king's Torah study.

22. This is a euphemism for sexual relations. The Rambam uses a similar expression in *Hilchot De'ot* 5:4: "Even though a person's wife is permitted to him at all times, it is fit for a Torah scholar to practice holiness and not be with his wife 'as a rooster' [i.e. over-frequently]."

23. *Hilchot De'ot* 4:19 states:

> Semen is the body's power, its life energy, and brightness of its eyes. If an excessive amount is released, the body and its strength will become depleted.... This is what Solomon implied in his wisdom [in the verse,] "Do not give your strength to women." Age will overcome a person who over-indulges in sexual relations and his vigor will be reduced.

24. *Sanhedrin* 21a states: A king may not marry even one wife if she will cause his heart to stray. If so, why did the Torah prohibit him from "amassing many wives?" Once he possesses the maximum number of wives, he is forbidden to marry any woman no matter how righteous she is.

25. Though the heart is one of the smallest organs of the body, it provides for the body's entire energy and life-force. Similarly, the king generates and controls the tone of the vitality of the entire nation. In this vein, *Bamidbar Rabbah* 19:28 states: "The leader of the generation [represents] the entire generation."

7. We have already explained[26] that kings of the Davidic dynasty may be judged and testimony may be given against them.[27]

However, in regard to the [other] kings of Israel, the Sages decreed that they neither sit in judgement or be judged.[28] They may not give testimony,[29] nor is testimony given against them. This is because they are arrogant[30] and the matter may cause a tragedy and loss to the faith.[31]

8. Anyone who rebels against a king of Israel may be executed by the king.[32]

Even if [the king] orders one of the people to go to a particular place and the latter refuses,[33] or he orders him not to leave his house and he goes out, [the offender] is liable to be put to death.[34] [The king] may execute him if he desires,[35] as [Joshua 1:18] states: "Whoever rebels against your command ... [shall be put to death]."[36]

26. *Hilchot Sanhedrin* 2:5.

27. *Sanhedrin* 19a derives this concept as follows: Jeremiah 21:12 declares: "House of David ... execute judgment in the morning" implying that the kings of the Davidic dynasty should serve as judges. Accordingly, we must assume that they could also be judged, for our Sages taught: "Correct yourself and afterwards, correct others." Were the kings themselves not subject to the scrutiny of a court of law, they would have no right to judge others.

28. *Sanhedrin, loc. cit.*, states: Why was this law enacted? Because of an incident which once occurred. The servant of Yannai, one of the later Hasmonean kings, slew another person. The Sages summoned Yannai to be present at his trial. The king complied with their request and came to the court. However, he seated himself.

Shimon ben Shetach, the presiding judge, ordered Yannai to stand, telling him: "Don't think of yourself as standing before us, but rather see yourself as standing before God."

Yannai answered him: "What do your colleagues say? I will follow their directions and not yours."

He turned to the other judges to see their reaction. They all lowered their heads. When Shimon ben Shetach saw this, he declared: "You people are concerned with your thoughts. May the Master of thought repay you." All of them died immediately. At that moment, the Sages declared: "A king does not judge, nor is he judged."

There is a slight difficulty with this halachah. On the surface, the expression, "the kings of Israel" refers to the kings of the ten tribes. They lived centuries before Yannai. If the decree was only enacted at Yannai's time, how could it affect those kings? Furthermore, on the surface, what difference does the dynasty of the king make? What is important is whether he is righteous or not.

Accordingly, the *Kessef Mishneh* explains that the Talmud's words must be interpreted as follows: The kings of Israel were not automatically disqualified from judging. However, whenever an incident similar to Yannai's occurred concerning a king of Israel, the Sages had the right to disqualify him. In contrast, since the above-mentioned verse from Jeremiah specifically associated the House of David with judgment, even in the event of a tragedy, they were not disqualified.

The *Lechem Mishneh* does not accept this view. He maintains that the Sages also had the power to disqualify kings of the House of David from judging. However, they never found cause to do so. In contrast, the kings of Israel were frequently unheeding of Torah law and hence, they were disqualified from being involved in judgment, lest a tragedy occur.

ז כְּבָר בֵּאַרְנוּ שֶׁמַּלְכֵי בֵית דָּוִד, דָּנִין אוֹתָן וּמְעִידִין עֲלֵיהֶן. אֲבָל מַלְכֵי יִשְׂרָאֵל, גָּזְרוּ חֲכָמִים שֶׁלֹּא יָדוּן וְלֹא דָנִין אוֹתוֹ, וְלֹא מֵעִיד וְלֹא מְעִידִין עָלָיו, מִפְּנֵי שֶׁלִּבָּן גַּס בָּהֶן, וְיָבוֹא מִן הַדָּבָר תַּקָּלָה וְהֶפְסֵד עַל הַדָּת.

ח כָּל הַמּוֹרֵד בְּמֶלֶךְ יִשְׂרָאֵל, יֵשׁ לַמֶּלֶךְ רְשׁוּת לְהָרְגוֹ. אֲפִלּוּ גָּזַר עַל אֶחָד מִשְּׁאָר הָעָם שֶׁיֵּלֵךְ לְמָקוֹם פְּלוֹנִי וְלֹא הָלַךְ, אוֹ שֶׁלֹּא יֵצֵא מִבֵּיתוֹ וְיָצָא – חַיָּב מִיתָה. וְאִם רָצָה לְהָרְגוֹ – יֵהָרֵג, שֶׁנֶּאֱמַר: "כָּל אִישׁ אֲשֶׁר יַמְרֶה אֶת פִּיךָ". וְכֵן כָּל הַמְבַזֶּה אֶת הַמֶּלֶךְ אוֹ

29. There is a question whether kings of the Davidic dynasty may testify or not. *Sh'vuot* 31b disqualifies a king from giving testimony. Commenting on that passage, Rashi explains that forcing the king to stand before the judges would diminish his honor. Since, as mentioned above Chapter 2, Halachah 3, a king is not allowed to yield on matters of honor, he is not be allowed to serve as a witness.

Nevertheless, the Rambam does not mention the king when discussing the individuals who are not required to testify, although he does mention the High Priest (*Hilchot Edut* 1:3). Note also the *Kessef Mishneh's* commentary.

30. In *Hilchot Sanhedrin, loc. cit.*, the Rambam states: "This is because they do not humble themselves before the words of Torah."

31. As occurred in the incident with Yannai, the king, described above.

32. Allegorically, this law can be explained as follows: As stated above, the king is the "heart" of the entire Jewish people. A limb will die if separated from the life-flow emanating from the heart. Similarly, a subject is obligated to die if he is separated from his "heart," the king.

33. *Tosafot, Kiddushin* 43a, explains that King David had the right to order the death of Uriah, the Hittite, for this reason. David ordered Uriah "go down to your house" (II Samuel 11:8). However, Uriah refused, explaining "The servants of my lord are encamped in the open fields. Shall I then go into my own house?"

Though his sentiments were noble, his refusal to obey David constituted rebellion against the king.

34. As will be explained, Shim'i ben Gera cursed King David when he fled from his son, Avshalom. Nevertheless, since he was the first to greet David after his forces were victorious, the king granted him a temporary pardon. However, before his death, he warned his son Solomon against allowing Shim'i to reach old age. Solomon ordered Shim'i to build a house in Jerusalem and remain there forever. He warned him (I Kings 2:37): "On the day that you leave, ... you will die." For three years, Shim'i heeded Solomon's command. Then, because of his own personal concerns, he left Jerusalem for one day. When he returned, Solomon ordered that he be executed as one who rebelled against the king.

35. From the Rambam's wording, it appears the matter is optional. The king is not obligated to execute the offender. Similarly, *Sefer HaMitzvot* (Positive Commandment 173) appears to leave the matter to the king's choice. Nevertheless, other authorities (*Chatam Sofer, Even HaEzer*, Responsum 151) question the matter.

On the surface, support for the Rambam's opinion may be brought from David's pardon of Shim'i as described above. On the other hand, that narrative cannot serve as conclusive evidence, for David counseled Solomon to put Shim'i to death.

36. The *Chatam Sofer*, (*Orach Chayim*, Responsum 208) questions how a matter of this serious nature can be derived from a book of the prophets. A prophet cannot create a

Similarly, anyone who embarrasses or shames the king may be executed by the king as was Shim'i ben Gera.[37]

The king may only execute people by decapitation. He may also imprison [offenders] and have them beaten with rods[38] to protect his honor. However, he may not confiscate property. If he does, it is considered theft.[39]

9. A person who negates a king's command because he was occupied with a mitzvah, even a minor one, is not liable.[40] Whose words should have precedence in case of conflict, the words of the Master or the words of the subject?[41] Needless to say, if a king decrees that a mitzvah should be negated, his words should not be heeded.[42]

10. [In all the following instances] - a murderer against whom the evidence is not [totally] conclusive,[43] or who was not warned [before he slew his victim],[44] or even [one] who [was observed by only] one witness,[45] and similarly, an enemy who inadvertently killed [one of his foes][46] - the king is granted license to execute [the killer][47] and to improve society according to the needs of the time.[48]

He may execute many on one day,[49] hang them, and leave them hanging for many days[50] in order to cast fear into the [hearts] and destroy the power of the wicked of the earth.

mitzvah which is not mentioned in the Torah itself. However, other commentaries explain that the authority of the king to execute rebels is an extension of the mitzvah to appoint a king and to revere him. Accordingly, the charge to Joshua did not represent the creation of a new command, but rather, an extrapolation of an existing one.

37. II Samuel (16:5-9) relates that when David was fleeing his son Avshalom, he came to Bachurim. "Shim'i ben Gera came out, cursing as he came. He cast stones at David... cursing as follows: '...You bloody and base man. God has returned upon you the blood of Saul...' "

Avishai ben Tzeruya said to the king: "Why should this dead dog curse the king? Let me go over and take off his head." Although David did not have him executed then, he was executed later as mentioned above.

38. As I Kings 12:11 relates, King Rechavam told the people: "My father (King Solomon) chastised you with rods." By contrast, offenders who are sentenced to lashing by a Jewish court are whipped with lashes.

39. *Hilchot Gezeilah* 5: 13 states: "Should a king confiscate a courtyard or field from one of the people unjustly, as defined by the laws which he himself legislated, behold, he is a thief."

A king's unjust seizure of his subject's property is a very serious matter. It was King Achav's murder of Navot of Yizre'el and confiscation of his property which excited the rage of the prophet, Elijah (I Kings, Chapter 21).

40. Sheva ben Bichri tried to organize a revolt against King David. David sent his general, Amassa, to gather troops to quash the revolt before it grew. "Amassa went to muster the men... but was later than the set time... assigned him" (II Samuel 20:5).

Why did Amassa tarry? Sanhedrin 49a explains that he found the men studying Torah and did not interrupt them. He reasoned: The verse (Joshua 1:18) which permits the king

הַמְחָרְפוֹ, יֵשׁ לַמֶּלֶךְ רְשׁוּת לְהָרְגוֹ כְּשִׁמְעִי בֶּן גֵּרָא. וְאֵין לַמֶּלֶךְ רְשׁוּת לַהֲרֹג אֶלָּא בְּסַיִף בִּלְבָד. וְיֵשׁ לוֹ לֶאֱסֹר וּלְהַכּוֹת בְּשׁוֹטִין לִכְבוֹדוֹ; אֲבָל לֹא יַפְקִיר מָמוֹן. וְאִם הִפְקִיר – הֲרֵי זֶה גָּזֵל.

ט הַמְבַטֵּל גְּזֵרַת הַמֶּלֶךְ בִּשְׁבִיל שֶׁנִּתְעַסֵּק בְּמִצְוֹת, אֲפִלּוּ בְּמִצְוָה קַלָּה – הֲרֵי זֶה פָּטוּר. דִּבְרֵי הָרַב וְדִבְרֵי הָעֶבֶד – דִּבְרֵי הָרַב קוֹדְמִין. וְאֵין צָרִיךְ לוֹמַר אִם גָּזַר הַמֶּלֶךְ לְבַטֵּל מִצְוָה, שֶׁאֵין שׁוֹמְעִין לוֹ.

י כָּל הַהוֹרֵג נְפָשׁוֹת שֶׁלֹּא בִרְאָיָה בְרוּרָה אוֹ בְלֹא הַתְרָאָה, אֲפִלּוּ בְּעֵד אֶחָד, אוֹ שׂוֹנֵא שֶׁהָרַג בִּשְׁגָגָה – יֵשׁ לַמֶּלֶךְ רְשׁוּת לְהָרְגוֹ וּלְתַקֵּן הָעוֹלָם כְּפִי מַה שֶּׁהַשָּׁעָה צְרִיכָה. וְהוֹרֵג רַבִּים בְּיוֹם אֶחָד, וְתוֹלֶה וּמַנִּיחָן תְּלוּיִים יָמִים רַבִּים, לְהַטִּיל אֵימָה וּלְשַׁבֵּר יַד רִשְׁעֵי הָעוֹלָם.

to execute rebels concludes: "Only be strong and brave." The word "only" always indicates an exclusion or limitation. In this context, it implies that if the king attempts to negate the words of Torah, his words need not be heeded. Though Yoav slew Amassa for violating the king's command, our Sages explain that Amassa had acted correctly.

41. *Kiddushin* 42b uses the same rationale to explain why an agent charged with the commission of a sin cannot blame the one who charged him with this act and must bear the burden of its violation himself.

42. The king's rule is intended to strengthen the observance of Torah and mitzvot, not to cause the opposite.

43. The Torah is very exact in its requirements for testimony for capital punishment. If two witnesses were both able to identify a murderer, but their testimonies were even slightly inconsistent, the defendant is acquitted (see *Hilchot Edut* 2:1).

44. To incur the death penalty a murderer must be warned that he may suffer capital punishment for his crime (see *Hilchot Sanhedrin* 12:1-2).

45. In contrast to the two witnesses required universally by Torah Law.

46. *Hilchot Rotzeach* 6:10 states: "An enemy who inadvertently kills [one of his foes] is not exiled [the punishment for manslaughter]..., we may be assured that his act was close to being willful."

47. In all these cases, though a court could not execute the offenders, if the king desired, he is granted the privilege of executing them.

There are a number of instances in the Bible where kings executed offenders despite the fact that a court would not have convicted them according to Torah law. For example, David ordered the Amalekite slain for killing Saul (II Samuel 1:15) and the sons of Rimon slain for murdering Ish-Boshet, though the only evidence against them was their own statements. According to Torah law, a person's own statements cannot be used to incriminate him. Nevertheless, David executed these offenders by virtue of his regal power.

48. Punishing wrongdoers as he sees fit.

49. In contrast, a Torah court may not try two capital cases in one day (*Hilchot Sanhedrin* 14:10).

50. Deuteronomy 21:22-23 states: "When a man is... executed, you must hang him on the gallows. However, you must not allow his body to remain on the gallows overnight.

CHAPTER FOUR

1. The king is granted license to levy taxes[1] upon the nation for his needs[2] or for the purpose of war.[3] He may also fix a duty on merchandise.[4] It is forbidden to avoid paying this duty.[5] The [king] has the right to decree that if someone does not pay these duties, his property will be seized[6] or he will be killed.[7]

[These laws are derived as follows: I Samuel 8:17] states:[8] "You will be servants to him, [the king]."[9] Previously, [Deuteronomy 20:11] states: "They shall be subject to your levy and they shall serve you." From this [association,[10] it is derived] that the king may levy taxes and fix duties.[11]

The statutes that he establishes in these and related matters are accepted as law[12] for all the matters mentioned in the Biblical passage concerning the king are rights to which the king is entitled.[13]

Rather, you must bury it on the same day." *Hilchot Sanhedrin* 15:7 relates that the hanging was only momentary. The body was hung up right before sunset and immediately taken down.

II Samuel 21:10 relates that David allowed the seven sons of Saul whom the Gibeonites hung, to remain on the gallows for several months. *Yevamot* 79a asks why the Torah's command "you must not allow his body to remain on the gallows" was ignored. It explains that the intent was to sanctify God's name. Nations would look up to the Jews when they saw the sons of kings receive such severe punishment for maltreating converts. Similarly, in all instances, should a king see the need to continue leave bodies hanging, he may do so.

1. This refers to either a head tax or an income tax.
2. Provisions for his court and household expenses. As mentioned in Halachah 3:4, the king may not amass personal wealth through taxation.
3. This is also considered a need of the nation as a whole.
4. This includes both sales tax and customs duty.
5. *Bava Kama* 113a explains that these refer to duties that were enacted directly by the king. In contrast, the Greek and Roman rulers of *Eretz Yisrael* would frequently appoint tax collectors and sell them the right to collect taxes from the people as they saw fit. There is no obligation to pay taxes of this nature.
6. Halachah 3:8 stated that the king has no right to confiscate property. However, it is possible that his power is only limited in regard to punishments meted out for affronts to his honor. In contrast, tax evasion and other monetary infractions can be punished by seizure of property.
7. As one who rebels against the king's authority, as described in Halachah 3:8.
8. This verse is part of the Biblical passage describing the rights of a king that will be explained.
9. In the same passage, Samuel had already told the people: "He will take your sons... your daughters... your servants... and your finest young men."

Thus, in telling the people they will be servants, he obviously had another implication. Hence, the meaning of that term in this context can be derived by comparison to the verse in Deuteronomy. Previously, [Deuteronomy 20:11] states: "they shall be subject to your levy and they shall serve you."

פֶּרֶק רְבִיעִי

א רְשׁוּת יֵשׁ לַמֶּלֶךְ לָתֵת מַס עַל הָעָם לִצְרָכָיו אוֹ לְצֹרֶךְ הַמִּלְחָמוֹת. וְקוֹצֵב לוֹ מֶכֶס, וְאָסוּר לְהַבְרִיחַ מִן הַמֶּכֶס, שֶׁיֵּשׁ לוֹ לִגְזוֹר שֶׁכָּל מִי שֶׁיִּגְנֹב הַמֶּכֶס - יִלָּקַח מָמוֹנוֹ אוֹ יֵהָרֵג, שֶׁנֶּאֱמַר: "וְאַתֶּם תִּהְיוּ לוֹ לַעֲבָדִים", וּלְהַלָּן הוּא אוֹמֵר: "יִהְיוּ לְךָ לָמַס וַעֲבָדוּךָ", מִכָּאן, שֶׁנּוֹתֵן מַס וְקוֹצֵב מֶכֶס, וְדִינָיו בְּכָל אֵלּוּ הַדְּבָרִים וְכַיּוֹצֵא בָּהֶן - דִּין, שֶׁכָּל הָאָמוּר בְּפָרָשַׁת מֶלֶךְ - מֶלֶךְ זוֹכֶה בּוֹ.

10. One of the thirteen principles of Biblical exegesis is *gezerah shevah*, an association between two verses on the basis of the use of a common word or phrase. In this case, the words "serve" and "servants" establish the analogy between the two verses. Just as the servitude in Deuteronomy is expressed through the payment of taxes, similarly, the servitude mentioned by Samuel can be interpreted in this fashion.

11. *Mishpat Kohen* (*Hilchot Melachim* 144:15) explains that all the privileges which are granted a king for the nation's welfare (as opposed to those granted him to protect his honor), also apply to any government aside from a monarchy. Accordingly, such governments are also empowered to levy taxes. See also *Drashot HaRan* 11.

12. The Talmud and Rabbis frequently use the expression: "The laws of the ruling kingdom are law."

13. When the people asked Samuel to appoint a king (I Samuel, Chapter 8), God told him: "Obey their request. However, warn them solemnly and relate to them the rights of the king who will reign over them." Samuel described to them in blunt terms how harshly the king could rule over the people.

Sanhedrin 20b records a debate between two *Amoraim*: Rav and Shmuel. Rav maintains that Samuel's address was intended to frighten the people and, in fact, the king is not entitled to the privileges described in that passage.

Shmuel disagrees and maintains that though Samuel obviously intended to chastise the people, nevertheless, he also conveyed a true picture the rights and privileges to which the king is entitled.

In *Hilchot Gezeilah*, Chapter 5, the *Kiryar Sefer* explains that a tax collector appointed by any king, even a gentile, is "entitled to collect taxes because 'the statutes of the kingdom are law' as derived from the Biblical passage concerning the king as explained in *Hilchot Melachim*." *Tosafot, Sanhedrin* 20b does not accept this view, maintaining that the privileges Samuel granted a king are reserved only for kings who rule over all Israel by Divine decree. Similarly, other commentaries (Rashbah, *Yevamot* 46a, Ritbah, *Bava Metzia* 73) explain that the application of the principle "the statutes of the kingdom are law" to gentile authorities stems from the king's "conquest" of the land. Just as a king takes possession of a subject from another country when he subjugates them in a war, based on a similar rationale, he is given authority over the subjects of his own kingdom.

The latter viewpoint allows us to understand the statements of the Ran (*Nedarim* 28a), that in *Eretz Yisrael*, it is impossible for anyone to rule according to the principle of "the statutes of the kingdom are law." By dwelling in any other country, a person willingly subjects himself to the rule of its king. He has the choice to accept that rule or find another homeland. In contrast, *Eretz Yisrael* is every Jew's native home. No ruler has the right to force one to leave. Accordingly, dwelling there does not necessarily constitute acceptance of the local government.

2. He may also[14] send throughout the territory of *Eretz Yisrael* and take from the nation valiant men and men of war and employ them as soldiers for his chariot and cavalry.[15] Similarly, he may appoint them as his body guard and as footmen to run before him[16] as [I Samuel 8:11] states: "He shall place them among his charioteers and his horsemen and they shall run before his chariot."[17] He may also take the choicest of them to be his servants and attendants as [*ibid.*:16] states: "He shall take... your finest[18] young men... to do his work."

3. Similarly, he may take all those that are necessary for him from [the nation's] craftsmen and [employ] them to do his work. He must pay their wages.[19] He may also take all the beasts, servants, and maids [that are necessary] for his tasks. He must pay their hire[20] or their value[21] as [*ibid.*:12-16] states: " [He will set them] to plow his ground and to reap his harvest, to make instruments of war, and gear for his chariots....[22] He will take your servants, your maids,[23] your finest young men, and your donkeys to do his work."

4. Similarly, he may take wives and concubines from the entire territory of *Eretz Yisrael*.[24] [The term] "wives" implies [women] who were married with a *ketubah* and *kiddushin*;[25] concubines, women who were not given a *ketubah* and *kiddushin*.[26]

In contrast, the perspective of the *Kiryar Sefer* which recognizes the authority of even gentile nations as stemming from the mandate granted by the Bible, would also recognize the rule of other Jews in *Eretz Yisrael* aside from the Torah appointed kings.

It is difficult to define which viewpoint the Rambam follows. In *Hilchot Gezeilah* 5:11, he writes "The statutes of the king are law... whether the king is Jewish or not." He further clarifies the matter (*ibid.* 5:18): "In which case does this apply? When the king...is accepted by the inhabitants of that land who have placed their trust in him as their lord and [consented] to be his servants." The terminology used appears to be closer to the view of the *Tosafot* and Ran.

This argument is not just a matter of theory, but is reflected in the different attitudes with which the Torah community views the secular government that presently exists in *Eretz Yisrael*. There are some who recognize the government's laws according to the principle "the statutes of the kingdom are law," while others do not accept its authority.

14. This and the following halachot continue to describe the privileges granted the king in the passage from I Samuel cited in the previous halachah.

15. It is curious why neither the Rambam nor the passage in Samuel mention the infantry. Throughout the centuries, armies were always primarily made up of these soldiers.

16. It is interesting to note that though a king could not own an extra horse to run before him (Halachah 3:3), he could employ humans for that purpose.

17. II Samuel 15:1 and I Kings 1:5 relate that when both Avshalom and Adoniyahu attempted to take control of the monarchy, they set up "horsemen and chariots and fifty men to run before them."

18. Commenting on that verse, the *Metzudot Tziyon* interprets "finest" as "most attractive."

19. By contrasting the wording used by the Rambam in this and the above halachah, the *Rambam LeAm* derives that the king's soldiers were not paid wages. Instead, they were given room and board at the king's expense.

20. If instead of purchasing them, he rents them temporarily.

ב וְשׁוֹלֵחַ בְּכָל גְּבוּל יִשְׂרָאֵל וְלוֹקֵחַ מִן הָעָם הַגִּבּוֹרִים וְאַנְשֵׁי־חַיִל, וְעוֹשֶׂה מֵהֶן חַיִל לְמֶרְכַּבְתּוֹ וּבְפָרָשָׁיו, וּמַעֲמִיד מֵהֶן עוֹמְדִים לְפָנָיו, וּמַעֲמִיד מֵהֶן אֲנָשִׁים לָרוּץ לְפָנָיו, שֶׁנֶּאֱמַר: "וְשָׂם לוֹ בְּמֶרְכַּבְתּוֹ וּבְפָרָשָׁיו וְרָצוּ לִפְנֵי מֶרְכַּבְתּוֹ". וְלוֹקֵחַ מִן הַיָּפִים שֶׁבָּהֶם לִהְיוֹת שַׁמָּשִׁים וְעוֹמְדִים לְפָנָיו, שֶׁנֶּאֱמַר: "וְאֶת בַּחוּרֵיכֶם הַטּוֹבִים... יִקָּח, וְעָשָׂה לִמְלַאכְתּוֹ".

ג וְכֵן לוֹקֵחַ מִן בַּעֲלֵי הָאֻמָּנִיּוֹת כָּל מַה שֶּׁהוּא צָרִיךְ וְעוֹשִׂין לוֹ מְלַאכְתּוֹ, וְנוֹתֵן שְׂכָרָן. וְלוֹקֵחַ כָּל הַבְּהֵמוֹת וְהָעֲבָדִים וְהַשְּׁפָחוֹת לִמְלַאכְתּוֹ, וְנוֹתֵן שְׂכָרָן אוֹ דְּמֵיהֶן, שֶׁנֶּאֱמַר: "וְלַחֲרֹשׁ חֲרִישׁוֹ וְלִקְצֹר קְצִירוֹ וְלַעֲשׂוֹת כְּלֵי מִלְחַמְתּוֹ וּכְלֵי רִכְבּוֹ וגו'. וְאֶת עַבְדֵיכֶם וְאֶת שִׁפְחוֹתֵיכֶם וְאֶת בַּחוּרֵיכֶם הַטּוֹבִים וְאֶת חֲמוֹרֵיכֶם יִקָּח, וְעָשָׂה לִמְלַאכְתּוֹ".

ד וְכֵן לוֹקֵחַ מִכָּל גְּבוּל יִשְׂרָאֵל נָשִׁים וּפִילַגְשִׁים: נָשִׁים – בִּכְתֻבָּה וְקִדּוּשִׁין, וּפִילַגְשִׁים – בְּלֹא כְתֻבָּה וּבְלֹא קִדּוּשִׁין,

21. If he purchases them.

22. The *Targum* renders this verse: "He will take farmers to plow... and craftsmen to make instruments."

23. The "servants and maids" refer to Canaanite servants who are considered the property of their master. A king may requisition them for his own use.

24. I Kings 1:3 descries how "they sought for a fair maiden throughout the entire territory of Israel" to serve as an attendant to King David.

25. According to Torah law, marriage is a two staged process. In the first stage, referred to as *kiddushin*, a man consecrates a woman as his wife. From this time onward, she may not marry another man without divorce. Sexual relations with other men are considered adultery and are punishable by death. Nevertheless, the bride and groom are not permitted to live as man and wife.

The second stage of marriage, *nissuin*, involves the consummation of the marriage and the beginning of the couple's life together. To allow for a harmonious home environment, the Sages developed basic guidelines outlining the obligations of a husband to his wife and vice versa. These responsibilities are recorded in the *ketubah*, marriage contract. Some of the *ketubah's* obligations govern the married life of a couple. Others are instituted in the event the couple divorces or the bride is widowed. The *ketubah* takes effect only after the couple complete the second stage of marriage, *nissuin*. The details of the *ketubah* are outlined in *Hilchot Ishut*, Chapter 12.

26. This definition is a point of controversy in Jewish law. Rashi in his commentary on Genesis 25:6, interprets concubines as having been consecrated to their men (*kiddushin*), but having agreed to live without a *ketubah*. Accordingly, a marriage bond has been established and relations with other men would be considered adultery.

The Rambam does not accept this view and designates a king's concubine with a unique status in Jewish law. On one hand, she is not married. On the other hand, a relationship between her and the king has been established to the point where she can no longer engage in relations with other men.

The Rambam's opinion allows us to comprehend an otherwise difficult Biblical narrative. II Samuel, Chapter 16 relates that when King David fled Jerusalem because of the rebellion of his son Avshalom, he left his ten concubines to care for the palace. When

With [the act of] *yichud* alone,[27] the king acquires her and [relations with] her are permitted him.[28]

A commoner is forbidden to have a concubine.[29] The only [similar relationship is the union with] a Hebrew maid servant after she has been designated [by her master].[30]

The king may make the concubines which he takes to his palace cooks, bakers, and perfumers as [*ibid.*:13] states: "He will take your daughters to be perfumers, cooks, and bakers.[31]

5. He may force those who are fit to serve as officers,[32] appointing them as leaders of thousands and leaders of fifties as [*ibid.*:12] states: "He shall appoint them as leaders of thousands and leaders of fifties for himself."[33]

6. He may take fields, olive groves, and vineyards[34] for his servants when they go to war and allow them to commandeer these places[35] if they have no source of nurture other than them.[36] He must pay for [what is taken].[37] This is stated in [*ibid.*:14]: "He shall take your good fields, vineyards, and olive groves and give them to his servants."

Avshalom occupied the palace, Achitofel, his counselor advised him to engage in relations with those concubines as a public act of defiance.

Avshalom followed his advice and his act strengthened his support among the people. Were the concubines to have enjoyed the status of wives, the Jewish people would never have approved of such open immorality. However, since the concubines were not considered as wives proper, though relations with them constituted a sin, it did not have the severity of adultery and hence, was not regarded as a moral affront (Radbaz).

27. Literally, *yichud* means to single out or designate. The *Rambam LeAm* maintains that the king establishes his bond with one of his concubines by designating her as his. Halachically, the term, *yichud*, means entering a private room where sexual relations could be carried out. Other commentaries maintain that the king must follow this practice in order to acquire his concubine.

28. Generally, sexual relations are not permitted without *kiddushin*. In *Hilchot Ishut* 1:4, the Rambam writes: "Anyone who has relations with a women with an immoral intent, without *kiddushin*, should be lashed according to Torah law." An exception is made for a king. He may have relations with his concubines though he has not consecrated them as wives.

29. This statement is disputed by many authorities including the Ra'avad (*Hilchot Ishut, ibid.*) and the Ramban (Responsa). The Ramban cites a number of examples of righteous men, Caleb (I Chronicles 2:46) and Gideon (Judges 8:31), who possessed concubines though they did not serve as kings. (The *Kessef Mishneh, Hilchot Ishut* resolves these incidents with the Rambam's opinion explaining that these women may have been female maid-servants.)

30. Exodus 21:8-9 states: "If she is not pleasing to her master and he does not designate her as his wife..." Implicit in the sale of the girl as a maid-servant, was the provision that her master could later designate her as a wife for himself or his son. Nothing further had to be given the girl or her father. All that is necessary is that the master declare: "You are my designated bride" (*Hilchot Avadim* 4:7).

There is a difficulty with the Rambam's statements. The manner in which a king takes a concubine resembles the consecration of a Hebrew maid-servant for in both cases, there is

אֶלָּא בְּיִחוּד בִּלְבַד קוֹנֶה אוֹתָהּ וּמֻתֶּרֶת לוֹ. אֲבָל הַהֶדְיוֹט אָסוּר בְּפִילֶגֶשׁ, אֶלָּא בְּאָמָה הָעִבְרִיָּה בִּלְבַד אַחֲרֵי יִעוּד. וְיֵשׁ לוֹ רְשׁוּת לַעֲשׂוֹת הַפִּילַגְשִׁים שֶׁלּוֹקֵחַ לְאַרְמוֹנוֹ, טַבָּחוֹת וְאוֹפוֹת וְרַקָּחוֹת, שֶׁנֶּאֱמַר: "וְאֶת בְּנוֹתֵיכֶם יִקָּח לְרַקָּחוֹת וּלְטַבָּחוֹת וּלְאֹפוֹת".

ה וְכֵן כּוֹפֶה אֶת הָרְאוּיִין לִהְיוֹת שָׂרִים, וּמְמַנֶּה אוֹתָם שָׂרֵי אֲלָפִים וְשָׂרֵי חֲמִשִּׁים, שֶׁנֶּאֱמַר: "וְלָשׂוּם לוֹ שָׂרֵי אֲלָפִים וְשָׂרֵי חֲמִשִּׁים".

ו וְלוֹקֵחַ הַשָּׂדוֹת וְהַזֵּיתִים וְהַכְּרָמִים לַעֲבָדָיו כְּשֶׁיֵּלְכוּ לַמִּלְחָמָה, וְיִפְשְׁטוּ עַל מְקוֹמוֹת אֵלּוּ אִם אֵין לָהֶם מַה יֹּאכְלוּ אֶלָּא מִשָּׁם, וְנוֹתֵן דְּמֵיהֶן, שֶׁנֶּאֱמַר: "וְאֶת שְׂדוֹתֵיכֶם וְאֶת כַּרְמֵיכֶם וְזֵיתֵיכֶם הַטּוֹבִים יִקָּח, וְנָתַן לַעֲבָדָיו".

no necessity to give the woman *kiddushin*. However, the status of the two women is totally different. Once the Hebrew maid-servant is designated as a wife, she is considered having *kiddushin* and a *ketubah*. Indeed, the Torah's description of a husband's obligations to his wife (Exodus 21:10) are taken from the passage describing the relationship with a Hebrew maid-servant.

31. Similarly, the narrative from II Samuel cited above relates how David charged his concubines with supervision of the palace in his absence.

32. Two concepts can be derived from the wording used by the Rambam:
a) A king may appoint an officer to his service against the latter's will;
b) By nature, a Jew should not desire authority and position. He must be forced to accept it.

33. Exodus 18:21 mentions a further division of authority "Leaders of thousands, leaders of hundreds, leaders of fifties, leaders of tens."

34. Fields refer to fields of grain. Thus these represent the three primary agricultural necessities. Similarly, we find the Torah frequently grouping these three together as in Deuteronomy (11:14): "You will have ample harvest of grain, oil, and wine."

35. *Tosafot*, *Sanhderin* 20b, questions this law based on the narrative of King Achav and Navot of Yizrael.

Achav desired Navot's vineyard and the latter refused to sell it to him. To satisfy Achav's desires, Izevel, his wife hired two false witnesses to testify that Navot cursed both God and the king. Navot was executed because of this testimony and Achav acquired his vineyard on the basis of the principle (Halachah 9) "The property of all those executed by the king, [belongs] to the king." Why didn't Achav take possession of the vineyard by exercising the regal privileges granted him in this halachah?

Among the resolutions offered are: a) the king may only take possession of a field or vineyard to provide food for his servants while Achav desired to take Navot's vineyard as his personal property.
b) the king is only entitled to commandeer the produce of a field or vineyard. He may not take possession of the property itself, as Achav desired (Radak).

Kin'at Eliyahu offers a resolution based on the Rambam's words. The Rambam continues: "if they have no source of nurture other than them," and in Achav's era, there was no lack of vineyards.

36. The Rambam's wording implies that the king is only allowed this right in extreme circumstances.

37. *Bava Kama* 60b mentions that David's troops paid for produce taken to feed their animals. See also the Jerusalem Talmud, *Sanhderin* 2:5.

7. He is entitled to a tenth[38] of the [produce of] the seed and the orchards[39] and the [newborn] beasts[40] as [*ibid.*:16-17] states: "He will take a tenth of your seed and your vineyards...He shall take a tenth of your sheep."

8. The Messianic king may take a thirteenth portion of all the lands conquered by Israel [as his own].[41] This will be an allotment for him and his descendants forever.[42]

9. The property of all those executed by the king, [belongs] to the king.[43] Similarly, all the treasures belonging to the kings of the kingdoms which he conquers [become the property] of the king.[44]

In regard to the other spoil which is taken. The [soldiers] may take spoil.[45] Afterwards, they must bring it to the king. He is entitled to one half of the spoil.[46] He takes this portion first.[47]

The second half of the spoil is divided between the combat soldiers and the people who remained in camp to guard the baggage. An equal division is made between them as [I Samuel 30:24] relates: "The portion of those who go down to the battle will be as the portion of those who stay with the baggage. They shall divide equally."[48]

10. All the lands that he conquers belong to him.[49] He may apportion them to

38. Commenting on the verse in Samuel, the Radak explains that the king can keep this tenth as his personal property.
39. The king's tenth comes in addition to the first tithe which must be given to the Levites (Numbers 18:21-24) and the second tithe (Deuteronomy 14:22-29) which in certain years must be eaten in Jerusalem and in other years, given to the poor.
40. Aside from this obligation, we are required to offer a tenth of the beasts born to our herds and flocks as sacrifices in the Temple (Leviticus 27:32).
41. The Radbaz cites Ezekiel 48:21 "And the remaining portion shall be for the *Nasi*" as the source for the Rambam's statements.

Other commentaries cite the Rambam's source as *Bava Batra* 122a which states that in the Messianic age, *Eretz Yisrael* will be divided up into thirteen portions. One portion will be given to each of the tribes and the thirteenth to the *Nasi*, i.e. the Mashiach.

That Talmudic passage speaks about *Eretz Yisrael* proper while the Rambam speaks about the lands to be conquered. Nevertheless, a correlation between the two statements can be made for *Pesikta Rabesi* teaches that, in the Messianic age, *Eretz Yisrael* will spread out over the entire world.
42. Becoming their personal property.
43. Therefore, in the narrative of Achav and Navot cited above, Izevel's hired witnesses testified that Navot had cursed the king. Accordingly, as explained in Halachah 3:8, he could be executed as one who rebelled against the king and his property could be taken by the king.

This law applies only to those executed for rebelling against the king. The property of a person executed for violation of one of the sins that carries the death penalty is granted to his heirs (*Hilchot Evel* 1:9).

The Radbaz (Responsa 533) writes that even a non-Jewish king is entitled to the property of those executed for rebelling against him.

ז וְיֵשׁ לוֹ מַעֲשֵׂר מִן הַזְּרָעִים וּמִן הָאִילָנוֹת וּמִן הַבְּהֵמָה, שֶׁנֶּאֱמַר: "וְזַרְעֵיכֶם וְכַרְמֵיכֶם יַעְשֹׂר וְגוֹ'. צֹאנְכֶם יַעְשֹׂר".

ח הַמֶּלֶךְ הַמָּשִׁיחַ נוֹטֵל מִכָּל הָאֲרָצוֹת שֶׁכּוֹבְשִׁין יִשְׂרָאֵל חֵלֶק אֶחָד מִשְּׁלֹשָׁה־עָשָׂר; וְדָבָר זֶה חֹק לוֹ וּלְבָנָיו עַד עוֹלָם.

ט כָּל הֲרוּגֵי הַמֶּלֶךְ – מָמוֹנָן לַמֶּלֶךְ. וְכָל הַמַּמְלָכוֹת שֶׁכּוֹבֵשׁ, הֲרֵי אוֹצְרוֹת הַמְּלָכִים לַמֶּלֶךְ, וּשְׁאָר הַבִּזָּה שֶׁבּוֹזְזִין, בּוֹזְזִין וְנוֹתְנִין לְפָנָיו, וְהוּא נוֹטֵל מֶחֱצָה בָּרֹאשׁ, וּמַחֲצִית הַבִּזָּה חוֹלְקִין אוֹתָהּ, כָּל אַנְשֵׁי הַצָּבָא בְּיַחַד עִם הָעָם הַיּוֹשְׁבִין עַל הַכֵּלִים בַּמַּחֲנֶה לְשָׁמְרָן, חוֹלְקִין בְּשָׁוֶה, שֶׁנֶּאֱמַר: "כִּי כְּחֵלֶק הַיֹּרֵד בַּמִּלְחָמָה וּכְחֵלֶק הַיֹּשֵׁב עַל הַכֵּלִים יַחְדָּו יַחֲלֹקוּ".

י כָּל הָאָרֶץ שֶׁכּוֹבֵשׁ, הֲרֵי הִיא שֶׁלּוֹ. וְנוֹתֵן לַעֲבָדָיו וּלְאַנְשֵׁי הַמִּלְחָמָה כְּפִי מַה שֶּׁיִּרְצֶה,

44. *Sanhderin* 20b considers it as a logically accepted principle that the personal property of one king should only be acquired by another king.

45. A Jewish soldier was not allowed to loot for his own personal benefit. Rather, the spoils of war were considered the property of the army as a whole and divided among them as described.

46. *Sanhderin* 20b, 21a derives this principle as follows: I Chronicles 29:22 states: "And they anointed Solomon as governor and Tzadok as [High] Priest" establishes an equation between a king and a High Priest. Accordingly, just as a High Priest is given half of the showbread, similarly, a king is given half of the spoils of war.

47. Rashi (*Sanhderin* 20b) explains that the king is entitled to select the first and better half as a token of respect and honor.

48. I Samuel, Chapter 30 relates that, in David's absence, Amalekites plundered Ziklag, the city in which he had been encamped. When he returned, David and his troops set out after the raiding party. A third of his men, faint from their journey, were unable to keep up with the pace set by David and abandoned the chase. David left any unnecessary baggage with them and resumed his pursuit.

He was able to overtake the Amalekites and rout their camp. All the spoil that the Amalekites had previously taken became David's. When he returned to the troops who had remained to guard the baggage, "the bad and worthless of those who accompanied David protested: 'Since they did come with us, we will not give them of the spoil.'"

David answered them as quoted by the Rambam. The passage concludes: "He made it a statute and ordinance for Israel to this day."

Bereishit Rabbah 43:9 explains that David continued an existing precedent. When Abraham defeated the four kings and returned with their spoil (Genesis, Chapter 14), he granted a share of the spoil to his companions, Aner, Eshkol, and Mamre, even though they did not take part in the actual battle.

49. As his personal property. This halachah refers to other kings besides the Messiah. Hence, there is a difference between this halachah and Halachah 8. Alternatively, Halachah 8 speaks about lands that Israel (i.e., the people as a whole) will conquer, while this halachah speaks about lands conquered by the king himself.

his servants and soldiers as he desires and keep the remainder for himself. In all these matters, the judgement he makes is binding.[50]

In all matters, his deeds shall be for the sake of heaven. His purpose and intent shall be to elevate the true faith and fill the world with justice, destroying the power of the wicked and waging the wars of God.[51] For the entire purpose of appointing a king is to execute justice and wage wars as [I Samuel 8:20] states: "Our king shall judge us, go out before us, and wage our wars."[52]

CHAPTER FIVE

1. A king should not wage [any other wars] before a *milchemet mitzvah.*[1] What is considered as *milchemet mitzvah*? The war against the seven nations [who occupied *Eretz Yisrael*,][2] the war against Amalek,[3] and[4] [a war] fought to assist Israel from an enemy which attacks them.[5]

Afterwards,[6] he may wage a *milchemet hareshut*, i.e. a war fought with other nations in order to expand the borders of Israel[7] or magnify its greatness[8] and reputation.[9]

2. There is no need to seek the permission of the court[10] to wage a *milchemet*

50. Since these lands become the king's personal property, he may divide them as he sees fit.

The *Minchat Chinuch* (mitzvah 497) questions the source for this halachah. The *Mishpat HaMeluchah* suggests that the Rambam's source is *Gittin* 8b which describes Syria as "territory conquered by a single individual," David. On that passage, Rashi comments that David did not conquer Syria for the sake of the entire people, but for his own needs.

51. I Kings 3:9 relates that when God granted Solomon a wish, the latter asked for "an understanding heart to judge our people." Similarly, *Kalah Rabesi*, Chapter 8 relates how royalty is acquired with 30 distinctions, among them "justice and righteousness, as (Proverbs 16:12) states: 'His throne shall be established through righteousness.'"

52. It is interesting to note that, according to *Sanhderin* 20b, this quote is taken from the words of the common people who "spoiled the tone" of the nation's request from Samuel.

The Rambam's words have the tone of a summation because this halachah concludes the laws which are directly related to the king as an individual. The following chapters discuss other issues: among them; wars, relations to gentiles, and the Messianic age.

1. The words, *milchemet mitzvah*, mean "a war which is a mitzvah." Waging each of the three wars mentioned in this halachah fulfills one of the 613 mitzvot of the Torah.

Sifri, Ekev, relates that God criticized David for conquering Syria before he conquered the totality of *Eretz Yisrael*. The conquest of *Eretz Yisrael* is a *milchemet mitzvah*, while the conquest of Syria was not. God rebuked him, "You did not drive out the Jebusites living close to your own palace and yet, you found it necessary to conquer Aram."

2. See Halachah 4.

וּמַנִּיחַ לְעַצְמוֹ כְּפִי מַה שֶּׁיִּרְצֶה; וּבְכָל אֵלּוּ הַדְּבָרִים – דִּינוֹ דִּין. וּבַכֹּל יִהְיוּ מַעֲשָׂיו לְשֵׁם שָׁמַיִם, וְתִהְיֶה מְגַמָּתוֹ וּמַחֲשַׁבְתּוֹ לְהָרִים דַּת הָאֱמֶת וּלְמַלֹּאת הָעוֹלָם צֶדֶק וְלִשְׁבֹּר זְרוֹעַ הָרְשָׁעִים וּלְהִלָּחֵם מִלְחֲמוֹת ה׳. שֶׁאֵין מַמְלִיכִין מֶלֶךְ תְּחִלָּה אֶלָּא לַעֲשׂוֹת מִשְׁפָּט וּמִלְחָמוֹת, שֶׁנֶּאֱמַר: ״וּשְׁפָטָנוּ מַלְכֵּנוּ וְיָצָא לְפָנֵינוּ וְנִלְחַם אֶת מִלְחֲמֹתֵינוּ״.

פֶּרֶק חֲמִישִׁי

א אֵין הַמֶּלֶךְ נִלְחָם תְּחִלָּה אֶלָּא מִלְחֶמֶת מִצְוָה. וְאֵי זוֹ הִיא מִלְחֶמֶת מִצְוָה? זוֹ מִלְחֶמֶת שִׁבְעָה עֲמָמִים וּמִלְחֶמֶת עֲמָלֵק וְעֶזְרַת יִשְׂרָאֵל מִיַּד צַר שֶׁבָּא עֲלֵיהֶם; וְאַחַר־כָּךְ נִלְחָם בְּמִלְחֶמֶת הָרְשׁוּת, וְהִיא הַמִּלְחָמָה שֶׁנִּלְחָם עִם שְׁאָר הָעַמִּים כְּדֵי לְהַרְחִיב גְּבוּל יִשְׂרָאֵל וּלְהַרְבּוֹת בִּגְדֻלָּתוֹ וְשָׁמְעוֹ.

ב מִלְחֶמֶת מִצְוָה, אֵינוֹ צָרִיךְ לִטֹּל בָּהּ רְשׁוּת בֵּית־דִּין, אֶלָּא יוֹצֵא מֵעַצְמוֹ בְּכָל עֵת וְכוֹפֶה

3. See Halachah 5.
4. In his commentary to the Mishnah, *Sotah* 8:6, the Rambam differentiates between the two wars previously mentioned and the war that follows. He describes the previous two wars as *chovah*, an obligation and the latter as mitzvah, fulfilling God's command. See also *Sotah* 44b.
5. Leviticus 19:16 commands "Do not stand still over your neighbor's blood." *Sefer HaMitzvot* (neg. command 297) and *Sefer HaChinuch* (mitzvah 237) interpret this verse as a mitzvah to protect a Jew's life when he is in danger. As an extension of that principle, Numbers 10:9 obligates us to "go to war against an enemy who attacks you...," promising that "you will be remembered by God and delivered from your enemies." See also *Eruvin* 45a.

This principle applies in the Diaspora, as well as in *Eretz Yisrael.* Accordingly, the *Shulchan Aruch, Orach Chayim* 229:6, relates that if gentiles attack Jews, even on the Sabbath, it is a mitzvah to organize a defense force and mount a counter-attack.

The Ramah adds that even if the enemy have not mounted their attack, but it is well known that they desire to attack the Jews, war should be waged against them. This concept has contemporary relevance as well. For example, based on this principle, many of the Rabbinic leaders in *Eretz Yisrael* declared the 1982 war in Lebanon a *milchemet mitzvah*, for the Palestinians made no secret of their desire to attack the Jews.
6. Once the totality of *Eretz Yisrael* has been conquered, Amalek annihilated, and there is no danger posed to Jewish settlements.
7. I.e., to conquer additional territory.
8. Also implied is the acquisition of wealth through plunder as obvious from *Berachot* 3b.
9. This also has a certain military value. Enhancing Israel's reputation will make other nations less eager to attack her.
10. The *Sanhderin*, Israel's highest court, composed of 71 judges.

This Halachah is derived by analysis of the wording used in *Sanhderin* 2a and 20b. In both places, the Mishnah states that the king needs the approval of the *Sanhderin* to wage a *milchemet hareshut*, implying that their approval need not be sought for a *milchemet mitzvah*.

mitzvah.[11] Rather, [the king] may go out on his own volition[12] and force the nation to go out [with him.] In contrast, he may not lead the nation out [to wage] a *milchemat hareshut* unless the court of seventy-one judges [approves].[13]

3. [The king] may burst through [the fences surrounding fields or vineyards][14] to make a road[15] and no one can take issue with him.[16]

There is no limit[17] to the road the king [may make].[18] Rather, it may be [as wide] as necessary. He need not make his road crooked because of an individual's vineyard or field.[19] Rather, he may proceed on a straight path and carry out his war.[20]

4. It is a positive commandment[21] to annihilate the seven nations [who dwelled in *Eretz Yisrael*][22] as [Deuteronomy 20:17] states: "You shall utterly destroy them."[23]

Anyone who chances upon one of them[24] and does not kill him violates a negative commandment[25] as [*ibid.*:16] states: "Do not allow a soul to live."[26] The memory of them has already been obliterated.[27]

5. Similarly, it is a positive commandment[28] to destroy the memory of

11. The Ramban (*Hosafot* to *Sefer HaMitzvot*, negative commandment 17) adds that it is also necessary for the king to consult the *urim vitumim* as oracles before embarking on any war, even a *milchemet mitzvah.*

Berachot 3a states explicitly that David would consult the *urim vitumim* before a *milchemet hareshut.* Similarly, the commentaries (Ramban, Rashi) on Numbers 27:21 explain that Joshua would consult the *urim vitumim* regarding the conquest of *Eretz Yisrael* which is a *milchemet mitzvah.*

Although here, the Rambam does not mention the *urim vitumim* in regard to either of these wars, in *Hilchot Klei HaMikdash* which describe the consultation of the *urim vitumim,* he mentions inquiring of them before setting out to wage war.

12. As explained in Halachah 7:4, the entire nation, even a groom from his marriage chamber, may be mustered for a *milchemet mitzvah.*

13. From the Rambam's words, it appears that after the nullification of the *Sanhderin*, the Jewish people are only able to fight defensive wars.

14. The bracketed additions are based on Rashi's commentary, *Sanhderin* 20b.

15. To allow for passage of his troops. Significantly, Rashi, *loc. cit.*, appears to interpret the Talmudic passage as referring to the king's right to requisition property to provide food for his troops.

16. On the contrary, a person who does so is considered as rebelling against the king and is liable to be punished accordingly.

17. To the width or length.

18. *Bava Batra* 100b relates that normally a public thorough-fare is 16 cubits wide; the highways leading to the cities of refuge, 32 cubits; and "there is no limit to the road a king may make."

19. Though, as explained in Chapter 6, Halachot 8-10, we are prohibited from wantonly destroying fruit-bearing trees, the king is allowed to proceed to his battle field without making any deviation. See also *Bava Kama* 60b.

הָעָם לָצֵאת. אֲבָל מִלְחֶמֶת הָרְשׁוּת, אֵינוֹ מוֹצִיא אֶת הָעָם בָּהּ אֶלָּא עַל־פִּי בֵּית־דִּין שֶׁל שִׁבְעִים וְאֶחָד.

ג וּפוֹרֵץ לַעֲשׂוֹת לוֹ דֶּרֶךְ וְאֵין מְמַחִין בְּיָדוֹ. וְדֶרֶךְ הַמֶּלֶךְ אֵין לָהּ שִׁעוּר, אֶלָּא כְּפִי מַה שֶּׁהוּא צָרִיךְ. אֵינוֹ מְעַקֵּם הַדְּרָכִים מִפְּנֵי כַּרְמוֹ שֶׁל זֶה אוֹ מִפְּנֵי שָׂדֵהוּ שֶׁל זֶה, אֶלָּא הוֹלֵךְ בְּשָׁוֶה וְעוֹשֶׂה מִלְחַמְתּוֹ.

ד מִצְוַת עֲשֵׂה לְהַחֲרִים שִׁבְעָה עֲמָמִין, שֶׁנֶּאֱמַר: "הַחֲרֵם תַּחֲרִימֵם". וְכֹל שֶׁבָּא לְיָדוֹ אֶחָד מֵהֶן וְלֹא הֲרָגוֹ – עוֹבֵר בְּלֹא־תַעֲשֶׂה, שֶׁנֶּאֱמַר: "לֹא תְחַיֶּה כָּל נְשָׁמָה". וּכְבָר אָבַד זִכְרָם.

ה וְכֵן מִצְוַת עֲשֵׂה לְאַבֵּד זֵכֶר עֲמָלֵק, שֶׁנֶּאֱמַר: "תִּמְחֶה אֶת זֵכֶר עֲמָלֵק". וּמִצְוַת עֲשֵׂה

20. Apparently, this Halachah applies both in regard to a *milchemet mitzvah* and a *milchemet hareshut* (*Lechem Mishneh*).
21. See *Sefer HaMitzvot* (positive commandment 187), *Sefer HaChinuch* (mitzvah 425).
22. The Canaanites, Chittites, Amorites, Girgishites, Perizzites, Chivites, and Jebusites (Deuteronomy 7:1).
23. In *Sefer HaMitzvot* (*ibid.*), the Rambam explains that these nations were to be destroyed because they were "the essence of idol-worship." Otherwise, God feared that Israel would learn from their behavior. As related frequently in the Book of Judges, Israel's hesitation in fulfilling this command showed how well-founded these fears were.
24. The use of the expression "anyone" has significant implications. At the conclusion of the section of *Sefer HaMitzvot* dealing with positive commandments, the Rambam explains that certain commandments are incumbent on the nation as a whole and others, on each person as an individual.

The commentaries explain that the mitzvah to annihilate the seven nations is incumbent on the nation as a whole. In contrast, the prohibition against allowing a Canaanite to live is an individual responsibility.
25. See *Sefer HaMitzvot*, negative commandment 49, *Sefer HaChinuch*, mitzvah 528.
26. See also the commentary to Chapter 6, Halachah 4.
27. *Sefer HaMitzvot* (positive commandment 187) states that David completed the destruction of these nations except for a small remnant who became assimilated among the other nations without preserving their identity.

In his description of this mitzvah, the Rambam touches on a point of debate. When he defined the governing principles for including a command as one of the 613 mitzvot of the Torah, the Rambam specified that a mitzvah must be a command for eternity and not for a specific time period alone. On that basis, a number of commands, for example, the command to wage war against Midian (Numbers 7:2), were excluded from this reckoning.

The Rambam explains that the command to annihilate the Canaanites should be considered a mitzvah, though it can no longer be fulfilled, because a time limit was never placed on the mitzvah itself. Had these nations' identity not been obliterated in the previous generations, we would still be obligated to destroy them today. In contrast, the mitzvah to wage war against the Midianites was only an immediate proposition. There was no mitzvah to continue this struggle in the coming generations.
28. See *Sefer HaMitzvot*, positive commandment 188, *Sefer HaChinuch*, mitzvah 604.

Amalek,[29] as [Deuteronomy 25:19] states: "Obliterate the memory of Amalek.[30]

It is also a positive commandment[31] to constantly remember their evil deeds and their ambush [of Israel] to arouse our hatred of them,[32] as [*ibid.*:17] states: "Remember what Amalek did to you." The Oral Tradition teaches: " 'Remember' - with your mouths;[33] " 'Do not forget' - in your hearts."[34] For it is forbidden to forget our hatred and enmity for them.

6. All the lands which Israel conquers [in wars led by] a king [and approved] by the court[35] are considered as conquered by the people at large.[36] Thus, they have the same status as *Eretz Yisrael*[37] which was conquered by Joshua in every regard.[38] This only applies if they were conquered after the conquest of *Eretz Yisrael* as described in the Torah.[39]

7. It is permitted to dwell [anywhere] in the entire world[40] with the exception of the land of Egypt. [Its territory includes a square of] 400 *parsah*[41] by 400 *parsah* from the Mediterranean Sea proceeding westward, bordering on the land of Kush[42] and the desert.[43] It is forbidden to dwell in this entire territory.

29. In his explanation of the mitzvah to annihilate the seven nation in *Sefer HaMitzvot*, the Rambam writes that, in contrast to the seven nations, Amalek still exists today.
30. The mitzvah to obliterate Amalek is more inclusive than that destroy the seven nations. All traces of Amalek's identity must be wiped out. Even their herds and cattle must be slain. In contrast, spoil could be taken from the seven nations . (See *Sifri, Ki Teitzei* and the commentary of Rav Yosef Caro on the *Tur, Orach Chayim* 690).
31. See *Sefer HaMitzvot*, positive commandment 189, *Sefer HaChinuch*, mitzvah 603.
32. Exodus 17:8-16 describes how Amalek attacked Israel at the beginning of the journey through the desert. Deuteronomy (*loc. cit.*) explains that Amalek did not attack Israel head on. Rather, they ambushed the stragglers who tarried behind the entire camp.

Amalek's attack had a particularly negative aspect. After the miracles of the ten plagues and the splitting of the Red Sea, no other nation would have dared to attack the Jews. Undaunted, Amalek challenged them in battle. Although they were severely beaten, they reduced the awe with which the nations had regarded the Jews.
33. *Megillah* 18a explains that we are obligated to make a verbal statement recalling Amalek's attack. Therefore, each year before Purim, the passage from Deuteronomy mentioning Amalek is read from the Torah. This time was chosen because Purim commemorates the downfall of Haman, who was a descendant of Amalek. In addition, certain communities follow the custom of reciting this passage every day.

However, by using the term "constantly" above, the Rambam implies that these readings do not represent a complete fulfillment of the mitzvah. Rather, the remembrance of Amalek must always be in our minds.
34. This is also counted as one of the Torah's 613 mitzvot (*Sefer HaMitzvot*, negative commandment 59, *Sefer HaChinuch*, mitzvah 605).
35. As mentioned in Halachah 2, the approval of the court is necessary, for these wars are *milchamot hareshut.*
36. *Hilchot Terumah* 1:2 states:

> *Eretz Yisrael* as referred to at all times is defined as lands conquered by a king of Israel or a prophet with the backing of the majority of Israel. This is referred to as a "conquest of the people at large."
>
> However, if an individual, family, or tribe of Israel go and conquer a place on their

לִזְכֹּר תָּמִיד מַעֲשָׂיו הָרָעִים וַאֲרִיבָתוֹ כְּדֵי לְעוֹרֵר אֵיבָתוֹ, שֶׁנֶּאֱמַר: "זָכוֹר אֵת אֲשֶׁר עָשָׂה לְךָ עֲמָלֵק". מִפִּי הַשְּׁמוּעָה לָמְדוּ: "זָכוֹר" – בַּפֶּה, "לֹא תִשְׁכָּח" – בַּלֵּב, שֶׁאָסוּר לִשְׁכֹּחַ אֵיבָתוֹ וְשִׂנְאָתוֹ.

ו כָּל הָאֲרָצוֹת שֶׁכּוֹבְשִׁין יִשְׂרָאֵל בַּמֶּלֶךְ עַל־פִּי בֵית־דִּין, הֲרֵי זֶה כִּבּוּשׁ רַבִּים, וַהֲרֵי הִיא כְּאֶרֶץ־יִשְׂרָאֵל שֶׁכָּבַשׁ יְהוֹשֻׁעַ לְכָל דָּבָר. וְהוּא, שֶׁכָּבְשׁוּ אַחַר כִּבּוּשׁ כָּל אֶרֶץ־יִשְׂרָאֵל הָאֲמוּרָה בַּתּוֹרָה.

ז וּמֻתָּר לִשְׁכֹּן בְּכָל הָעוֹלָם, חוּץ מֵאֶרֶץ מִצְרָיִם. מִן הַיָּם הַגָּדוֹל וְעַד הַמַּעֲרָב, אַרְבַּע־מֵאוֹת פַּרְסָה עַל אַרְבַּע־מֵאוֹת פַּרְסָה, כְּנֶגֶד אֶרֶץ כּוּשׁ וּכְנֶגֶד הַמִּדְבָּר – הַכֹּל אָסוּר לְהִתְיַשֵּׁב

own, even if it is within the land promised to Abraham, it is not considered *Eretz Yisrael* with regard to the observance of the mitzvot.

37. The *Sifri, Ekev* derives this principle as follows:

Deuteronomy 11:24 states: "Every place upon which your feet tread shall belong to you." Why is this verse necessary?

Its purpose cannot be the definition of the boundaries of *Eretz Yisrael*, for the same verse continues "Your boundaries shall extend from the desert [to] the Lebanon, from the river, the Euphrates..." Thus, we must conclude that it teaches that every place which you conquer beyond these boundaries is yours...and the mitzvot [applicable to *Eretz Yisrael*] must be kept there.

38. *Hilchot Terumah* 1:7 defines the boundaries of *Eretz Yisrael* as conquered by Joshua and the subsequent leaders as follows (see the map on page 41):

> [The southern border runs] from Rekem in the east... to the Mediterrean Sea. [The western border] is the Mediterranean Sea from Ashkelon, in the south... to Akko in the north. From Akko, one proceeds [northeastward to Kziv. The area to one's right, on the east, can generally be assumed to be of the Diaspora unless it is specifically known that it was part of *Eretz Yisrael*. The area to one's left, to the west, can generally be assumed to be part of *Eretz Yisrael* unless it is specifically known to be part of the Diaspora. From the slopes of the Umenum Mountains and to the south is *Eretz Yisrael*,... to the north, the Diaspora.

39. *Hilchot Terumah* 1:3 states: "The lands which David conquered outside of *Eretz Canaan*... are not considered *Eretz Yisrael*... even though he was a king and his deeds were approved by the *Sanhderin*....

"Why were they given a lesser status than *Eretz Yisrael*, because David conquered them before he conquered all of *Eretz Yisrael*."

See also the commentary to Halachah 1 and the *Sifri* quoted there.

40. As explained in Halachot 9-12, there is a great advantage in living in *Eretz Yisrael*. However, a Jew is not obligated to dwell there and may settle in other lands as well.

41. A *parsah* is a Persian measure of distance (parsang) approximately 4 kilometers in modern measure.

42. Modern day Ethiopia, according to most commentaries. Similarly, Ezekiel 29:10 places Kush as Egypt's southern border. *Shmot Rabbah* 10:2 relates that there were frequently border squabbles between Kush and Egypt.

43. The Sahara. Its eastern border is the lake of Alexandria (*Sefer HaMitzvot*, negative commandment 46).

In three places, the Torah warned against returning to Egypt:[44]
a) "God has told you, you must never again return on that path" (Deuteronomy 17:16);
b) "You shall not see it again" (Deuteronomy 28:68);
c) "You shall never see them again forever" (Exodus 14:13).
Alexandria is included in this prohibition.[45]

8. It is permitted to return to Egypt for the purpose of trade and commerce[46] and to [pass through] while conquering other nations.[47] The prohibition consists of settling there.[48]

Lashes are not given [as punishment for the violation] of this prohibition because at the time one enters, there is no prohibition.[49] Should he decide to settle there, there is no deed involved.[50]

It appears to me[51] that if a king of Israel would conquer the land of Egypt with the approval of the court, it would be permissible to settle there.[52] The prohibition against returning was only given to individuals[53] or to dwell there while it is under the rule of the gentiles for their behavior is more depraved than that of [the peoples of] other lands as [can be inferred from Leviticus 18:3]: "[Do not follow] the ways of Egypt...."[54]

44. *Sefer HaMitzvot* (*ibid.*) and *Sefer HaChinuch* (mitzvah 500) include this prohibition as one of the Torah's 613 mitzvot. All of the three admonitions are considered as one negative commandment.

The *Kaftor ViPerach*, Chapter 8, relates that frequently, the Rambam would sign his correspondence: "The writer who transgress three prohibitions every day."

45. *Sukkah* 51b relates that Alexander the Great massacred millions of Jews in his conquest of that city. This punishment came as retribution for their violation of this prohibition.

46. Both to buy and sell merchandise.

47. See the Jerusalem Talmud, *Sanhderin* 10:8.

48. The *Hagahot Maimoniot* notes that throughout the ages, Jews have settled in Egypt. Frequently, the Egyptian Jewish community was large, wealthy, and influential. Even the Rambam himself lived there.

The Radbaz offers a number of explanations for this phenomenon. Firstly, he mentions the opinion of the *Yereim* (309), although he rejects it as insufficient, that the prohibition consists of "returning on this way," i.e. from *Eretz Yisrael* to Egypt.

Secondly, he mentions that most of the people who settled in Egypt did not originally come for the purpose of settling there. Rather, they came to engage in trade, but economic and social pressures elsewhere caused them to make their stay permanent. Hence, their initial entry was not forbidden. In regard to the continuance of their stay, it is possible that their Torah authorities had a more lenient view than the Rambam.

In regard to the Rambam himself, the Radbaz explain that he was forced to stay in Egypt by the Sultan who appointed him as his personal physician and would not let him leave.

In the same statement, the Radbaz explains that he personally lived in Egypt for many years. He originally came for the purpose of studying Torah. He stayed to teach others and ultimately, made *aliyah* to Jerusalem.

בָּהּ. בִּשְׁלֹשָׁה מְקוֹמוֹת הִזְהִירָה תּוֹרָה שֶׁלֹּא לָשׁוּב לְמִצְרָיִם. שֶׁנֶּאֱמַר: "לֹא תֹסִפוּן לָשׁוּב בַּדֶּרֶךְ הַזֶּה עוֹד"; "לֹא תֹסִיף עוֹד לִרְאֹתָהּ"; "לֹא תֹסִפוּ לִרְאֹתָם עוֹד עַד עוֹלָם". וַאֲלֶכְּסַנְדְּרִיָּא בִּכְלַל הָאִסּוּר.

ח מֻתָּר לַחֲזֹר לְאֶרֶץ־מִצְרַיִם לִסְחוֹרָה וְלִפְרַקְמַטְיָא וְלִכְבּוֹשׁ אֲרָצוֹת אֲחֵרוֹת, וְאֵין אָסוּר אֶלָּא לְהִשְׁתַּקֵּעַ שָׁם. וְאֵין לוֹקִין עַל לָאו זֶה, שֶׁבְּעֵת הַכְּנִיסָה מֻתָּר הוּא. וְאִם יַחְשֹׁב לֵישֵׁב וּלְהִשְׁתַּקֵּעַ שָׁם, אֵין בּוֹ מַעֲשֶׂה. וְיֵרָאֶה לִי, שֶׁאִם כָּבַשׁ אֶרֶץ־מִצְרַיִם מֶלֶךְ יִשְׂרָאֵל עַל־פִּי בֵּית־דִּין, שֶׁהִיא מֻתֶּרֶת; וְלֹא הִזְהִירָה אֶלָּא לָשׁוּב לָהּ יְחִידִים, אוֹ לִשְׁכֹּן בָּהּ וְהִיא בְּיַד נָכְרִים, מִפְּנֵי שֶׁמַּעֲשֶׂיהָ מְקֻלְקָלִין יוֹתֵר מִכָּל הָאֲרָצוֹת, שֶׁנֶּאֱמַר: "כְּמַעֲשֵׂה אֶרֶץ מִצְרַיִם".

The Kabbalistic Sage, Rabbi Isaac Luria, who also lived in Egypt, explains the concept from a mystical perspective (*Pri Etz Chayim,* Section 8, Chapter 3).

Every aspect of creation possesses a Godly spark which gives it life and maintains its existence. However, the material nature of the world conceals this inner Godliness and prevents its expression. The purpose of a Jew's life is to elevate and refine the environment in which he lives, revealing the Godliness concealed in the world's physical substance.

When the Jews left Egypt after the years of bondage, they took with it all her material wealth, leaving it "as a granary without wheat, a net without fish" (*Berachot* 9b). Together with the country's material assets, they also removed her spiritual possessions, the Godly sparks allotted to that land. A Jew was forbidden to go back to Egypt because there was nothing for him to do there. All the Godliness had already been elevated.

However, with the passage of centuries, people came to Egypt from other lands, bringing with them Godly sparks from their native countries. Accordingly, there was a need for Jews to elevate these Godly sparks and hence, the Egyptian Jewish community was renewed.

49. For one may enter for commercial purposes.

50. An earthly court cannot administer punishment whenever there is no deed involved in the violation of a Torah prohibition (*Hilchot Sanhedrin* 18:2). Thought is not considered a deed. Thus, once a person is already located in Egypt, his decision to stay does not warrant punishment. Nevertheless, it does constitute a violation of a Torah command.

51. This phrase introduces a conclusion reached by the Rambam that has no explicit source in previous Rabbinic literature.

52. For then, it would no longer be considered Egypt, but rather, part of *Eretz Yisrael.*

53. Here, the word "individuals" implies people and communities other than the king and the *Sanhderin* who represent the people as a whole.

54. Many authorities (see *Minchat Chinuch*, Mitvah 500, *Chayim Sha'al*, Responsum 91) rationalize the existence of Jewish communities in Egypt as follows: The prohibition against dwelling in Egypt was instituted lest the Jews emulate the depraved behavior of the Egyptians. When Sannecherib conquered the world, he engaged in a process of mass population transfer, moving nations from one land to another to the point that none of Israel's neighbors were able to preserve their national identities.

Thus, though Deuteronomy 23:8-9 forbids marriage with an Egyptian convert until three generations pass, the Rambam maintains that this prohibition is no longer applicable. For "the Egyptians presently dwelling in the land of Egypt are of a different nationality" than those who initially inhabited that land (*Hilchot Issurei Bi'ah* 12:5).

9. It is forbidden to leave *Eretz Yisrael*[55] for the Diaspora at all times except:[56]
to study Torah;[57]
to marry;[58] or
to save [one's property] from the gentiles.[59]

[After accomplishing these objectives,] one must return to *Eretz Yisrael*.[60]

Similarly, one may leave *Eretz Yisrael* to conduct commercial enterprises.[61] However, it is forbidden [to leave with the intent] of settling permanently in the Diaspora unless the famine in [*Eretz Yisrael*] is so severe that a *dinar's* worth of wheat is sold at two *dinarim*.[62]

When do these conditions apply? When one possesses financial resources and food is expensive.[63] However, if food is inexpensive, but a person cannot find financial resources or employment and has no money available,[64] he may leave and go to any place where he can find relief.

Similarly, these authorities maintain that the prohibition against dwelling in Egypt is also dependent on the presence of the original Egyptians. Hence, since they no longer live in Egypt, a Jew is not forbidden to live there.

(The commentaries note that this opinion appears to run contrary to *Sukkah* 51b quoted above which states that the massacre perpetrated by Alexander the Great, many years after Sannecherib's conquest, took place as retribution for the Jews settling in Egypt.)

The Rambam also does not accept this view. He maintains that the prohibition stems from the land itself. As long as it is inhabited by gentiles, the nature of the land itself will impart depraved character traits to its inhabitants. (Note a similar concept in *BaMidbar Rabbah* 20:22.) Only when it will be conquered by the Jews and incorporated into *Eretz Yisrael* will this nature change.

55. There are three aspects to the uniqueness of *Eretz Yisrael*:
a) the holiness of the land. *Kelim* (1:6, quoted by the Rambam, *Hilchot Beit HaBechirah* 7:12) states that *Eretz Yisrael* is holier than all other lands. Note the *Mishnah Achronah* which explains that this holiness is a totally independent factor than the obligation to perform mitzvot there.
b) There are many mitzvot that can be fulfilled only there. In his commentary to *Bava Batra* 91a, the Rashbam writes that the prohibition against leaving *Eretz Yisrael* was instituted because by doing so, a person forsakes the mitzvot. (See also Tashbaytz, Responsum Vol. III, 200; Maharit, Vol. I, Responsa 47.)
c) God's choice of the land. "*Eretz Yisrael* is dear... for when God created the world he apportioned the other lands to the... nations, and chose *Eretz Yisrael* (*Midrash Tanchuma, Re'eh*).

56. In his *Hosafot* to *Sefer HaMitzvot* (positive commandment 4), the Ramban counts the mitzvah of conquering and settling *Eretz Yisrael* as one of the 613 mitzvot of the Torah.

The Rambam does not subscribe to this view. Though this and the following three Halachot emphasize the great importance and dearness of *Eretz Yisrael*, as evident from Halachah 7, the Rambam does not consider a Jew obligated to live there.

To explain in greater detail. According to the Rambam, the mitzvah to annihilate the seven Canaanite nations also includes the mitzvah to conquer *Eretz Yisrael*. This mitzvah is incumbent on the people as a whole. There is no mitzvah incumbent on an individual to settle in *Eretz Yisrael*. The Raman, by contrast, maintains that every person has an individual obligation to settle *Eretz Yisrael*.

ט אָסוּר לָצֵאת מֵאֶרֶץ־יִשְׂרָאֵל לְחוּצָה לָאָרֶץ לְעוֹלָם, אֶלָּא לִלְמֹד תּוֹרָה, אוֹ לִשָּׂא אִשָּׁה, אוֹ לְהַצִּיל מִן הָעַכּוּ"ם; וְיַחֲזוֹר לָאָרֶץ. וְכֵן יוֹצֵא הוּא לִסְחוֹרָה; אֲבָל לִשְׁכֹּן בְּחוּצָה לָאָרֶץ – אָסוּר, אֶלָּא־אִם־כֵּן חָזַק שָׁם הָרָעָב עַד שֶׁנַּעֲשָׂה שְׁוֵה דִינָר חִטִּין בִּשְׁנֵי דִינָרִין. בַּמֶּה דְּבָרִים אֲמוּרִים? כְּשֶׁהָיוּ הַמָּעוֹת מְצוּיוֹת וְהַפֵּרוֹת בְּיֹקֶר, אֲבָל אִם הַפֵּרוֹת בְּזוֹל, וְלֹא יִמְצָא מָעוֹת וְלֹא בַּמֶּה יִשְׂתַּכֵּר, וְאָבְדָה פְרוּטָה מִן הַכִּיס – יֵצֵא לְכָל מָקוֹם שֶׁיִּמְצָא בּוֹ רֶוַח.

Although according to the Rambam, living in *Eretz Yisrael* is not a mitzvah, a person is allowed to leave *Eretz Yisrael* only for the reasons mentioned below. The commentaries question whether the obligation to remain in *Eretz Yisrael* applies only to those who live there permanently or also, to those come as tourists or on business.

57. Permission is granted to leave *Eretz Yisrael* to study Torah because of its fundamental importance in Jewish life. One's entire Jewish practice depends on one's study.

This license is even granted when there are qualified teachers in *Eretz Yisrael* for each person's nature differs and it is necessary to find a teacher with whom he feels comfortable (*Avodah Zarah* 13a).

Many authorities grant license to leave *Eretz Yisrael* for the purpose of teaching others Torah (*Siddur Ya'avetz, Sulam Bet El* 6)

58. Marriage endows a person with stability and personal equilibrium. Similarly, it allows one to fulfill the mitzvah of "be fruitful and multiply." Hence, it was considered sufficiently important to allow one to leave *Eretz Yisrael.*

The *Shialtot D'Rabbenu Achai Gaon* maintain that Torah study and marriage are only mentioned as examples and a person may leave *Eretz Yisrael* in order to perform other mitzvot as well. However, this view is not accepted by most commentaries. They maintain that leniency was granted in these two instances alone because of their paramount importance.

59. On a number of occasions, the Talmud grants leniencies because "a person becomes overly agitated when his property is at stake." For example, because of this tendency, *Shabbat* 120a relaxes certain facets of the prohibition against moving objects from one domain to another to allow a person to save his property from fire. Based on the same principle, *Avodah Zarah* (*ibid.*) allows an individual to temporarily leave *Eretz Yisrael* to sue gentiles or rescue one's property in other ways.

60. Rav Chaninah forbade a Torah scholar from going from *Eretz Yisrael* to Babylonia to fulfill the mitzvah of *yibbum* (marrying the widow of his childless brother) because the marriage would require him to settle in the latter place (*Ketubot* 111a).

61. *Mo'ed Kattan* 14a explains that leaving *Eretz Yisrael* to do business is equivalent to leaving to obtain food. For through this commercial activity, one will be able to sustain himself and family.

62. When inflation has reached the point that basic living necessities are being sold at double their normal price, one can permanently leave *Eretz Yisrael.* It can possibly be inferred that one may leave temporarily under less severe conditions.

63. *Bava Batra* 91a mentions one opinion which allows a person to leave *Eretz Yisrael* in the face of inflation only if he cannot purchase his basic necessities. Since the Rambam does not make this qualification, we may assume he does not accept it (see *Kessef Mishneh*).

64. *Eruvin* 82b relates that once food was being sold at half the market price in Tiberias and yet, the city was filled with people starving from famine because there was no money available.

Though it is permitted to leave [*Eretz Yisrael* under these circumstances], it is not pious behavior.[65] Behold, Machlon and Kilyon[66] were two of the great men of the generation and they left [*Eretz Yisrael*] only out of great distress. Nevertheless, they were found worthy of death by God.[67]

10. Great sages would kiss the borders of *Eretz Yisrael*,[68] kiss its stones, and roll in its dust.[69] Similarly, [Psalms 102:15] declares: "Behold, your servants hold her stones dear and cherish her dust."[70]

11. The Sages commented: "Whoever dwells in *Eretz Yisrael* will have his sins forgiven as [Isaiah 33:24] states: "The inhabitant shall not say 'I am sick.' The people who dwell there shall be forgiven their sins."[71]

Even one who walks four cubits there will merit the world to come and one who is buried there receives atonement as if the place in which he is [buried] is an altar of atonement[72] as [Deuteronomy 32:43] states: "His land will atone for His people."[73] [In contrast, the prophet, Amos [7:17], used the expression] "You shall die in an impure land" [as] a prophecy of retribution.[74]

There is no comparison between [the merit of] a person who lives in *Eretz Yisrael* [and ultimately, is buried there] and one [whose body is] brought there after his death.[75] Nevertheless, great Sages would bring their dead there. Take an example, from our Patriarch, Jacob,[76] and Joseph, the righteous.[77]

65. *Pikuach Nefesh*, risk of life, supercedes observance of all the mitzvot of the Torah. However, if there is no danger to life, it is pious to remain in *Eretz Yisrael* though a certain degree of privation is involved.

66. The husband and brother-in-law of Ruth.

67. Though they left in a year of severe famine (Ruth 1:1), they were punished by death for abandoning *Eretz Yisrael*. The Alshich explains that they were punished because they were the only family that left. Though the rest of Israel also suffered severely from the famine, none considered leaving *Eretz Yisrael*.

68. Acre is on the northern border of *Eretz Yisrael*. Before he left the land or when he entered, Rav Abbah would kiss its stones as a sign of endearment (*Ketubot* 112a).

The Talmud continues, relating that "Rabbi Chaninah would lift up its stones." Rashi explains that he would remove obstacles from the streets of that city so that people coming to *Eretz Yisrael* would not receive a bad impression.

Tosafot, basing its commentary on *Midrash Tanchuma, Shelach,* relates that when Rabbi Chanina made *aliyah* from Babylonia, he frequently asked whether he had already entered *Eretz Yisrael*. No one could answer him.

To clarify the matter, he would pick up the stones and weigh them in his hands. When the stones were light, he was sure that he had not left the Diaspora. However, when he felt that the stones were heavier, he lifted them to his mouth and kissed them. "These are the stones of *Eretz Yisrael*," he exclaimed. Afterwards, he recited the verse from Psalms quoted above.

69. Rav Chiyah bar Gamda would follow this practice out of his love for the land (*Ketubot* 112b).

70. Commenting on this verse, Rashi relates that the exiles carried with them stones from Jerusalem to Babylon to build a synagogue there.

וְאַף־עַל־פִּי שֶׁמֻּתָּר לָצֵאת – אֵינָהּ מִדַּת חֲסִידוּת, שֶׁהֲרֵי מַחְלוֹן וְכִלְיוֹן, שְׁנֵי גְדוֹלֵי הַדּוֹר הָיוּ, וּמִפְּנֵי צָרָה גְדוֹלָה יָצְאוּ, וְנִתְחַיְּבוּ כְלָיָה לַמָּקוֹם.

י גְּדוֹלֵי הַחֲכָמִים הָיוּ מְנַשְּׁקִין עַל תְּחוּמֵי אֶרֶץ־יִשְׂרָאֵל, וּמְנַשְּׁקִין אֲבָנֶיהָ וּמִתְגַּלְגְּלִין עַל עֲפָרָהּ. וְכֵן הוּא אוֹמֵר: "כִּי רָצוּ עֲבָדֶיךָ אֶת אֲבָנֶיהָ, וְאֶת עֲפָרָהּ יְחֹנֵנוּ".

יא אָמְרוּ חֲכָמִים: כָּל הַשּׁוֹכֵן בְּאֶרֶץ־יִשְׂרָאֵל – עֲוֹנוֹתָיו מְחוּלִין, שֶׁנֶּאֱמַר: "וּבַל יֹאמַר שָׁכֵן חָלִיתִי, הָעָם הַיֹּשֵׁב בָּהּ נְשֻׂא עָוֹן".
אֲפִלּוּ הָלַךְ בָּהּ אַרְבַּע אַמּוֹת, זוֹכֶה לְחַיֵּי הָעוֹלָם הַבָּא. וְכֵן הַקָּבוּר בָּהּ – נִתְכַּפֵּר לוֹ, וּכְאִלּוּ הַמָּקוֹם שֶׁהוּא בוֹ, מִזְבַּח כַּפָּרָה, שֶׁנֶּאֱמַר: "וְכִפֶּר אַדְמָתוֹ עַמּוֹ". וּבְפֻרְעָנוּת הוּא אוֹמֵר: "עַל אֲדָמָה טְמֵאָה תָּמוּת".
וְאֵינוֹ דוֹמֶה קוֹלַטְתּוֹ מֵחַיִּים לְקוֹלַטְתּוֹ אַחַר מוֹתוֹ; וְאַף־עַל־פִּי־כֵן גְּדוֹלֵי הַחֲכָמִים הָיוּ מוֹלִיכִים מֵתֵיהֶם לְשָׁם. צֵא וּלְמַד מִיַּעֲקֹב אָבִינוּ וְיוֹסֵף הַצַּדִּיק.

71. *Metzudat David* interprets this verse as follows: The inhabitants of Jerusalem will not be sick because of difficulties and troubles. They will not be plagued with these for all their sins will be forgiven.

72. *Ketubot* 111a relates that being buried in *Eretz Yisrael* is like being buried under the Temple altar.

73. The Jerusalem Talmud (*Kilayim* 9:5) relates that Rabbi Eliezer and Rabbi bar Keria saw coffins being brought to *Eretz Yisrael*. The latter commented: "Why bother to bring them now? Why didn't they live in *Eretz Yisrael*? The verse (Jeremiah 2:7): 'You have come and made My land impure' applies to them."

Rebbi Eliezer answered: "As soon as they enter *Eretz Yisrael* and its dirt is placed on their coffins, they are granted atonement. The land atones for them."

The *Hagahot Maimoniot* explains that it is also customary to place earth from *Eretz Yisrael* in the graves of people buried in the Diaspora.

74. The Sages decreed that the earth of any country outside *Eretz Yisrael* is ritually impure (*Gittin* 8b).

Amatziah, priest of Bethel, wanted to banish Amos from Samaria. Amos responded to him harshly, prophesying "Your wife will be a harlot in the city. Your sons and daughters will die by the sword. You shall die in an impure land and Israel will be exiled from her land."

75. The Sage, Ulah, would frequently visit *Eretz Yisrael*. However, he died in the Diaspora. When his students informed Rav Eliezar of his passing, the latter exclaimed: "Ulah! Why was it fitting for the fulfillment of the prophesy 'you shall die in an impure land' to befall you?"

The students protested that he would be buried in *Eretz Yisrael*. However, Rav Eliezer did not accept that rationalization, replying as quoted by the Rambam (*Ketubot* 111a).

76. Who commanded Joseph to bury him in *Eretz Yisrael* (Genesis 47:30).

77. Who made the Jews swear to take his coffin with them from Egypt to *Eretz Yisrael* when they would be redeemed (Genesis 50:25). Note the comments of *Ketubot* 111a.

12. At all times,[78] a person should dwell in *Eretz Yisrael* even in a city whose population is primarily gentile, rather than dwell in the Diaspora, even in a city whose population is primarily Jewish.[79]

[This applies] because whoever leaves [*Eretz Yisrael*] for the Diaspora[80] is [considered as] if he worships idols as [I Samuel 26:19] states "They have driven me out today from dwelling in the heritage of God, saying 'Go, serve other gods.' "[81] Similarly, [Ezekiel's 13:9 prophecies of] retribution state: "They shall not come to the land of Israel."[82]

Just as it is forbidden to leave the [chosen] land[83] for the Diaspora, it is also forbidden to leave Babylon for other lands as [Jeremiah 27:22] states: "They shall be brought to Babylon and there they shall be [until I take heed of them... and restore them to this place.]"[84]

CHAPTER SIX

1. War, neither a *milchemet hareshut* or a *milchemet mitzvah*,[1] should not be waged against anyone until they are offered the opportunity of peace[2] as [Deuteronomy 20:10] states: "When you approach a city to wage war against it, you should propose a peaceful settlement."[3]

If [the enemy] accepts the offer of peace and commits itself to the fulfillment of the seven mitzvot that were commanded to Noah's descendents,[4] none of

78. Certain authorities maintain that living in *Eretz Yisrael* is only significant when the Temple is standing. *Tosafot*, *Ketubot* 110b explains that at present, when we are unsure of how to fulfill many of the agricultural laws of *Eretz Yisrael*, there is no obligation to live there. With the expression," at all times," the Rambam negates both these views.

79.The *Tosefta, Ketubot* writes that generally a high priority is placed on living in a Jewish environment. Similarly, in *Hilchot De'ot* 6:1, the Rambam writes:

> It is human nature for a person's... behavior to resemble that of the inhabitants of his country. Therefore, a person should always associate with the righteous and dwell among wise men, so that he will learn from their behavior... Similarly, if he is in a country whose ways are bad and whose inhabitants do not follow a straight path, he should go to a place whose inhabitants are righteous....

Nevertheless, these factors are of lower priority than living in *Eretz Yisrael.*

80. *Ketubot* (*ibid.*) quotes the same principle as the Rambam, but uses the expression: "Whoever lives in the Diaspora..." rather than "whoever leaves..." (The exact expression employed by the Rambam is also used by *Torat Kohanim, Behar.*) By choosing the word "leave," the Rambam emphasizes that the criticism is directed at someone who departs from *Eretz Yisrael* and forsakes the land chosen by God.

81. These statements were made by David to King Saul. He asked the king if his decision to pursue him was inspired by God or if men had urged him to that step. He continued: If they be men: "Cursed be they..., because they have driven me out..."

The commentaries declare: Saul's advisors would never have thought of having David worship idols. However, his forced departure from *Eretz Yisrael* could be equated to that sin.

82. Ezekiel prophesied against the false prophets who consoled Israel with vain visions of

יב לְעוֹלָם יָדוּר אָדָם בְּאֶרֶץ־יִשְׂרָאֵל אֲפִלּוּ בְּעִיר שֶׁרֻבָּהּ עַכּוּ"ם, וְאַל יָדוּר בְּחוּצָה לָאָרֶץ וַאֲפִלּוּ בְּעִיר שֶׁרֻבָּהּ יִשְׂרָאֵל; שֶׁכָּל הַיּוֹצֵא לְחוּצָה לָאָרֶץ, כְּאִלּוּ עוֹבֵד עֲבוֹדָה זָרָה, שֶׁנֶּאֱמַר: "כִּי גֵרְשׁוּנִי הַיּוֹם מֵהִסְתַּפֵּחַ בְּנַחֲלַת ה' לֵאמֹר לֵךְ עֲבֹד אֱלֹהִים אֲחֵרִים". וּבְפֻרְעָנִיּוֹת הוּא אוֹמֵר: "וְאֶל אַדְמַת יִשְׂרָאֵל לֹא יָבֹאוּ". כְּשֵׁם שֶׁאָסוּר לָצֵאת מֵהָאָרֶץ לְחוּצָה לָאָרֶץ, כָּךְ אָסוּר לָצֵאת מִבָּבֶל לִשְׁאָר הָאֲרָצוֹת, שֶׁנֶּאֱמַר: "בָּבֶלָה יוּבְאוּ וְשָׁמָּה יִהְיוּ".

פֶּרֶק שִׁשִּׁי

א אֵין עוֹשִׂין מִלְחָמָה עִם אָדָם בָּעוֹלָם עַד שֶׁקּוֹרְאִין לוֹ שָׁלוֹם, אֶחָד מִלְחֶמֶת הָרְשׁוּת, וְאֶחָד מִלְחֶמֶת מִצְוָה, שֶׁנֶּאֱמַר: "כִּי תִקְרַב אֶל עִיר לְהִלָּחֵם עָלֶיהָ, וְקָרָאתָ אֵלֶיהָ לְשָׁלוֹם". אִם הִשְׁלִימוּ וְקִבְּלוּ שֶׁבַע מִצְוֹת שֶׁנִּצְטַוּוּ בְּנֵי נֹחַ עֲלֵיהֶן – אֵין הוֹרְגִין מֵהֶן נְשָׁמָה, וַהֲרֵי

grandeur rather than warn them to repent and return to God. Among his curses was: "They shall not come...."

When Rav Eliezar made *aliyah*, he offered thanks to God for preventing this curse from befalling him (*Ketubot* 112a).

83. Rather than use the expression *Eretz Yisrael* as previously in the chapter, in this statement, the Rambam uses the expression," the land." He chose the terminology to emphasize the aspect of God's choice for, as will be explained, a parallel to this quality exists in regard to Babylonia.

84. The source for this law is *Ketubot* 111a. Rashi, in his commentary on that passage, explains that one is prohibited from leaving Babylon because "it is a place of Torah and *yeshivot* are located there."

By quoting the above verse as the source, the Rambam implies that the Jews should remain in Babylon, for that is the place God choose for them to be exiled until He "takes heed of them... and restores them" to *Eretz Yisrael*. Hence, just as there is a prohibition to leave *Eretz Yisrael* because it is God's chosen land, similarly, there is a prohibition to leave Babylon for that land was chosen for the Jews while in exile.

1. These terms are explained in the beginning of the previous chapter.

The *Sifri, Shoftim,* and similarly, Rashi's commentary to this verse, maintain that we are only obligated to offer a peaceful settlement in a *milchemet hareshut*, not in a *milchemet mitzvah*. (It must be noted that in *Sefer HaMitzvot*, *ibid.*, the Rambam himself accepts this view.)

Support for the Rambam's statements here can be derived from the *Midrash Tanchumah, Tzav*. Similarly, the passage from the Jerusalem Talmud (*Shivi'it* 6:1) quoted by the Rambam in Halachah 5 reinforces this statement.

2. The obligation to offer a peaceful settlement to these nations can be derived from the offer Moses extended to Sichon, king of the Amorites, one of the seven nations (Numbers 21:21-22).

3. *Sefer HaMitzvot* (positive commandment 190) and *Sefer HaChinuch* (mitzvah 527) include this as one of the 613 mitzvot of the Torah.

4. The Ra'avad maintains that in a *milchemet hareshut*, it is not necessary for the gentiles

them should be killed.[5] Rather, they should be subjugated as [*ibid.*:11] states: "They shall be your subjects and serve you."[6]

If they agree to tribute, but do not accept subjugation or if they accept subjugation, but do not agree to tribute, their offer should not be heeded. [They must] accept both.[7]

The subjugation they must accept consists of being on a lower level, scorned and humble. They must never raise their heads against Israel, but must remain subjugated under their [rule.] They may never be appointed over a Jew in any matter whatsoever.[8]

The tribute they must accept consists of being prepared to support the king's service with their money[9] and with their persons;[10] for example, the building of walls, strengthening the fortresses, building the king's palace, and the like as [I Kings 9:15-22] relates: "This is the tribute which Solomon raised to build the House of God, his own palace, the Milo, the wall of Jerusalem,... and all the store-cities which Solomon had.... All the people that remained from the Amorites... upon them did Solomon lay a tribute of bondservice until this day."[11]

In contrast, Solomon did not make bondsmen out of the children of Israel. They were men of war, his [personal] servants, his princes, his captains, the officers of his chariots, and his horsemen.[12]

2. [In the settlement he offers,] the king may propose that he is entitled to take half their financial resources. Or he may propose to take [all] their landed property and leave them their movable property; or to take [all] their movable property and leave their land.[13]

3. It is forbidden to lie when making such a covenant or to be untruthful to them[14] after they have made peace and accepted the seven mitzvot.[15]

to accept these commands. We are only required to include these commandments in the peaceful settlement offered to Amalek and the seven nations. (In *Sefer HaMitzvot*, *ibid.*, the Rambam also does not mention the seven mitzvot.)

In his commentary to the Torah (Deuteronomy, *loc. cit.*), the Ramban explains that it was not necessary for the gentiles living outside of *Eretz Yisrael* to accept the seven mitzvot for there is no way that their behavior would influence that of the Jewish people.

In contrast, the Rambam maintains that once these lands are conquered they become part of *Eretz Yisrael*. Thus, the possibility exists that Jews would settle in these countries and learn from the gentiles' behavior. Furthermore, as will be explained in Halachah 8:10, the Rambam considers acceptance of the seven mitzvot of vital importance to the gentiles regardless of the consequences to the Jews.

5. On the contrary, it is forbidden to do so as explained in Halachah 3.

6. In *Hilchot Avodat Kochavim* 10:1, the Rambam also mentions that we are prohibited against entering into a covenant with gentiles unless they abandon idol worship. However, there, he does not mention the need for subjugation.

The two statements need not be considered contradictory. *Hilchot Avodat Kochavim* may refer to a covenant made in peacetime and thus, subjugation is not required. Here, we are dealing with a situation of war. Therefore, peace should not be granted until the enemy agrees to servitude.

הֵן לָמַס, שֶׁנֶּאֱמַר: "יִהְיוּ לְךָ לָמַס וַעֲבָדוּךָ". קִבְּלוּ עֲלֵיהֶם הַמַּס וְלֹא קִבְּלוּ הָעַבְדוּת, אוֹ שֶׁקִּבְּלוּ הָעַבְדוּת וְלֹא קִבְּלוּ הַמַּס – אֵין שׁוֹמְעִין לָהֶם, עַד שֶׁיְּקַבְּלוּ שְׁנֵיהֶם. וְהָעַבְדוּת שֶׁיְּקַבְּלוּ הוּא, שֶׁיִּהְיוּ נִבְזִים וּשְׁפָלִים לְמַטָּה, וְלֹא יָרִימוּ רֹאשׁ בְּיִשְׂרָאֵל, אֶלָּא יִהְיוּ כְּבוּשִׁים תַּחַת יָדָם. וְלֹא יִתְמַנּוּ עַל יִשְׂרָאֵל לְשׁוּם דָּבָר שֶׁבָּעוֹלָם. וְהַמַּס שֶׁיְּקַבְּלוּ – שֶׁיִּהְיוּ מוּכָנִים לַעֲבוֹדַת הַמֶּלֶךְ בְּגוּפָם וּמָמוֹנָם, כְּגוֹן בִּנְיַן הַחוֹמוֹת וְחֹזֶק הַמְּצוּדוֹת וּבִנְיַן אַרְמוֹן הַמֶּלֶךְ וְכַיּוֹצֵא בוֹ, שֶׁנֶּאֱמַר: "וְזֶה דְבַר הַמַּס אֲשֶׁר הֶעֱלָה הַמֶּלֶךְ שְׁלֹמֹה לִבְנוֹת אֶת בֵּית ה' וְאֶת בֵּיתוֹ וְאֶת הַמִּלּוֹא וְאֵת חוֹמַת יְרוּשָׁלָיִם... וְאֵת כָּל עָרֵי הַמִּסְכְּנוֹת אֲשֶׁר הָיוּ לִשְׁלֹמֹה... כָּל הָעָם הַנּוֹתָר מִן הָאֱמֹרִי... וַיַּעֲלֵם שְׁלֹמֹה לְמַס עֹבֵד עַד הַיּוֹם הַזֶּה. וּמִבְּנֵי יִשְׂרָאֵל לֹא נָתַן שְׁלֹמֹה עָבֶד, כִּי הֵם אַנְשֵׁי הַמִּלְחָמָה וַעֲבָדָיו וְשָׂרָיו וְשָׁלִשָׁיו וְשָׂרֵי רִכְבּוֹ וּפָרָשָׁיו".

ב וְיֵשׁ לַמֶּלֶךְ לְהַתְנוֹת עִמָּהֶם שֶׁיִּקַּח חֲצִי מָמוֹנָם אוֹ הַקַּרְקָעוֹת וְיַנִּיחַ כָּל הַמִּטַּלְטְלִין, אוֹ הַמִּטַּלְטְלִין וְיַנִּיחַ הַקַּרְקָעוֹת, כְּפִי מַה שֶּׁיַּתְנֶה.

ג וְאָסוּר לְשַׁקֵּר בִּבְרִיתָם וּלְכַזֵּב לָהֶם אַחַר שֶׁהִשְׁלִימוּ וְקִבְּלוּ שֶׁבַע מִצְוֹת.

7. *Sifri, Shoftim* notes that the verse requires "They shall be your subjects" - i.e., subjugation, and "serve you" - i.e., pay tribute.
8. Many commentaries point to Joshua's treatment of the Gibeonites (Joshua 9:23) as the source for these principles. He forced them to be "bondmen, hewers of wood, and drawers of water forever." They were always kept in this secondary status.

Nevertheless, other commentaries differentiate; noting that the Gibeonites accepted Torah and mitzvot and thus, were included as part of the Jewish people, while these principles deal with gentiles accepting the seven mitzvot of Noah's sons.
9. As explained in Halachah 2.
10. I.e., they could be compelled to perform manual labor.
11. The Ramban (Deuteronomy, *loc. cit.*) explains that these Amorites accepted the seven mitzvot. Hence, Solomon did not violate the commandment to destroy the seven Canaanite nations by allowing them to live and serve in these capacities.
12. As mentioned in Chapter 4, Halachot 2-3, that the king has the right to conscript his subjects for these duties.
13. In Chapter 4, Halachah 9, the Rambam stated that the army may take spoil from the countries they conquer. Halachah 10 explains that the king is entitled to all the landed property of the nations that he conquers and may do with it as he desires.

In this instance, since the nation agreed to a peaceful settlement, all of their wealth is not confiscated. Nevertheless, the king is allowed to impose upon them any conditions he desires.
14. To do so would cause *Chillul HaShem*, the desecration of God's name.
15. As explained in Halachah 5, Joshua made a covenant with the Gibeonites as part of his conquest of *Eretz Yisrael.*

While pursuing King David, King Saul slew an entire village of Gibeonites. Later, they sought revenge on his sons. God told King David to agree to their request and they were allowed to kill seven of Saul's descendants. (See I Samuel 22:19, II Samuel 21:1-10.)

4. If they do not agree to a peaceful settlement,[16] or if they agree to a peaceful settlement, but refuse to accept the seven mitzvot,[17] war should be waged against them.

All males past majority should be killed.[18] Their money and their children should be taken as spoil,[19] but neither women or children should be killed,[20] as [Deuteronomy 20:14] states: "But the women and the children... [take as spoil]." "The children" refer to males below the age of majority.

The above applies to a *milchemet hareshut* [fought] with other nations.[21] However, if either the seven nations or Amalek refuse to accept a peaceful settlement, not one soul of them may be left alive as [*ibid.* 20:15-16] states: "Do this to all [the cities that ... are not the cities of these nations.] However, from the cities of these nations,... do not leave a soul alive."[22] Similarly, in regard to Amalek, [Deuteronomy 25:19] states: "Obliterate the memory of Amalek."[23]

How do we know that these [commands] are only referring to those who did not accept a peaceful settlement?[24] [Joshua 11:19-20] states:[25] "There was no city which accepted a peaceful settlement with the children of Israel except the Chivites who lived in Gibeon.[26] All the rest,[27] they conquered in battle. This was inspired by God, Who strengthened their hearts[28] to [engage] in battle against Israel so that they would be destroyed."[29] From these [statements], we can infer that a peaceful settlement was offered, but they did not accept it. [30]

5. Joshua sent three letters [to the Canaanites][31] before entering the [promised] land: At first, he sent them: "Whoever desires to flee, should flee."[32]

Afterwards,[33] he sent a second [message]: "Whoever desires to accept a peaceful settlement, should make peace."[34]

Why were they allowed to slay these blameless individuals? So that the gentile nations would not think the Jews broke their covenant with this people (*Yevamot* 79a).

Later on in our national history, we see other examples of the consequences of breaking a covenant made with other nations. Hoshea ben Elah was the final king of the kingdom of Israel. He was more righteous than all of his predecessors, yet the ten tribes were exiled in his day. II Kings (17:4) relates that the direct cause of this tragedy was Hoshea's failure to observe a pact which he made with Shalmanessar, king of Assyria.

Similarly, II Chronicles (36:13) explains that Tzedekiah, Judah's final king, broke an oath he made to Nebuchadnezzar and rebelled against him. What were the consequences? Nebuchadnezzar conquered Jerusalem, destroyed the Temple, and exiled our people from our land.

16. Deuteronomy 20:12 relates: "If they do not accept your offer of peace, you shall lay siege [to the city.]"

17. As mentioned above, in a *milchemet hareshut*, many authorities do not require the acceptance of the seven mitzvot.

18. As Deuteronomy continues (20:13) "When God... gives it into your hand, strike down all its males by the sword."

19. As the passage continues (20:14) "the women, children, animals, and all the goods in the city, you shall take as spoil."

20. Though in the war against Midian, all women above the age of three and all males even those below majority were slain (Numbers 31:17-18), that war had a specific

ד וְאִם לֹא הִשְׁלִימוּ, אוֹ שֶׁהִשְׁלִימוּ וְלֹא קִבְּלוּ שֶׁבַע מִצְוֹת – עוֹשִׂין עִמָּהֶם מִלְחָמָה וְהוֹרְגִין כָּל הַזְּכָרִים הַגְּדוֹלִים, וּבוֹזְזִין כָּל מָמוֹנָם וְטַפָּם. וְאֵין הוֹרְגִין אִשָּׁה וְלֹא קָטָן, שֶׁנֶּאֱמַר: "הַנָּשִׁים וְהַטַּף" – זֶה טַף שֶׁל זְכָרִים. בַּמֶּה דְּבָרִים אֲמוּרִים? בְּמִלְחֶמֶת הָרְשׁוּת שֶׁהוּא עִם שְׁאָר הָאֻמּוֹת, אֲבָל שִׁבְעָה עֲמָמִין וַעֲמָלֵק שֶׁלֹּא הִשְׁלִימוּ – אֵין מַנִּיחִין מֵהֶם נְשָׁמָה, שֶׁנֶּאֱמַר: "כֵּן תַּעֲשֶׂה לְכָל וְגוֹ'. רַק מֵעָרֵי הָעַמִּים... לֹא תְחַיֶּה כָּל נְשָׁמָה", וְכֵן הוּא אוֹמֵר בַּעֲמָלֵק: "תִּמְחֶה אֶת זֵכֶר עֲמָלֵק". וּמִנַּיִן שֶׁאֵינוֹ מְדַבֵּר אֶלָּא בְּאֵלּוּ שֶׁלֹּא הִשְׁלִימוּ? שֶׁנֶּאֱמַר: "לֹא הָיְתָה עִיר אֲשֶׁר הִשְׁלִימָה אֶל בְּנֵי יִשְׂרָאֵל בִּלְתִּי הַחִוִּי יֹשְׁבֵי גִבְעוֹן, אֶת הַכֹּל לָקְחוּ בַמִּלְחָמָה. כִּי מֵאֵת ה' הָיְתָה לְחַזֵּק אֶת לִבָּם לִקְרַאת הַמִּלְחָמָה אֶת יִשְׂרָאֵל לְמַעַן הַחֲרִימָם"; מִכְּלָל, שֶׁשָּׁלְחוּ לָהֶם לְשָׁלוֹם וְלֹא קִבְּלוּ.

ה שְׁלֹשָׁה כְתָבִים שָׁלַח יְהוֹשֻׁעַ עַד שֶׁלֹּא נִכְנַס לָאָרֶץ: הָרִאשׁוֹן שָׁלַח לָהֶם – מִי שֶׁרוֹצֶה לִבְרֹחַ, יִבְרַח. וְחָזַר וְשָׁלַח: מִי שֶׁרוֹצֶה לְהַשְׁלִים, יַשְׁלִים. וְחָזַר וְשָׁלַח: מִי שֶׁרוֹצֶה לַעֲשׂוֹת

intent: to "avenge the vengeance of the children of Israel" (Numbers 31:1). Accordingly, the strictures against slaying captives were relaxed to execute this vengeance.

21. To refer to the Biblical wording, "the cities that ... are not the cities of these nations," i.e. countries outside of *Eretz Yisrael.*

22. As mentioned in Chapter 5, Halachah 4, the annihilation of these nations fulfills one of the Torah's 613 mitzvot.

23. The status of Amalek differs from that of the seven nations. The mitzvah to destroy the seven nations was instituted "so that they will not teach you the revolting practices with which they worship their gods..." (Deuteronomy 20:18). Accordingly, once they abandoned those practices, there is no reason to slay them (*Sotah* 35b).

In contrast, the mitzvah to "obliterate the memory of Amalek" was instituted as retribution for Amalek's attack on the Jewish people "on the way after leaving Egypt" (Deuteronomy 25:17). Therefore, the *Mechiltah, Beshalach*, and other sources maintain that we are obligated to slay Amalek's descendants regardless of their present state. On that basis, they explain King David's execution of the Amalekite convert who brought him word of King Saul's death (II Samuel 1:13-15). Nevertheless, the Rambam obviously does not accept this view.

24. And also the observance of the seven mitzvot.

25. The following verses come at the conclusion of the description of the great wars Joshua fought to conquer *Eretz Yisrael.*

26. See the following Halachah and commentary.

27. 31 kings as described in Joshua, Chapter 12.

28. See *Hilchot Teshuvah*, Chapter 6.

29. Thus, all traces of them and their repulsive idol worship would be obliterated.

30. Had the Canaanites not been given the opportunity to choose peace, there would be no need for God to strengthen their hearts to engage in battle. They would not have had an alternative.

31. The letters were sent in the thirty three day period between the death of Moses on the seventh of Adar and the crossing of the Jordan on the tenth of Nisan.

32. The Girgishites feared God and followed this advice. God rewarded them by giving them a fine portion of land in Africa (Jerusalem Talmud, *Shivi'it* 6:1).

33. The Radbaz explains that there was no time for Joshua to wait for a reply to his first message before he sent the second. Rather, all three messages were sent at the same time.

34. As explained in the previous Halachah.

Then, he sent again: "Whoever desires war, should do battle."[35]

If so, why did the inhabitants of Gibeon employ a ruse?[36] Because originally, when he sent [the message] to them as part of all [the Canaanite nations,][37] they did not accept. They were not aware of the laws of Israel and thought that they would never be offered a peaceful settlement again.[38]

Why was the matter difficult for the princes [of Israel to accept to the point] that they desired to slay [the Gibeonites] by the sword[39] were it not for the oath [they had taken]? Because they made a covenant with them and [Deuteronomy 7:2] states "Do not make a covenant with them."[40] Rather, the laws governing their status would have prescribed that they be subjugated as servants.[41]

Since the oath was given to them under false pretenses, it would have been just to slay them for misleading them, were it not for the dishonor to God's name [which would have been caused].[42]

6. No offer of a peaceful settlement should be made to Ammon and Moav,[43] as [Deuteronomy 23:7] states: "Do not seek their peace and welfare for all your days." Our Sages declared:[44] Although it is written: "Offer a peaceful settlement," does this apply to Ammon and Moav? The Torah states: "Do not seek their peace and welfare."[45] Although it is written [Deuteronomy 23:17]: "He must be allowed to live alongside you in you midst,"[46] does this apply to Ammon and Moav? [No,][47] the Torah also forbids "their welfare."[48] Even though we should not offer them a peaceful settlement, if they sue for peace themselves, we may accept their offer.[49]

35. It is difficult to understand the reason for this rather obvious message.

36. Joshua, Chapter 9, relates that after the Jews' conquest of Jericho and Ai, the inhabitants of Gibeon:

> Acted cunningly... They took old sacks upon their donkeys, old and rent wine bottles... old, worn and patched shoes... and came to Joshua at Gilgal. They told him:... "We have come from a distant country. Therefore, make a covenant with us." Joshua made a covenant with them... and the princes of the congregation swore to them.

37. As explained in the beginning of the halachah.

38. The Ra'avad disagrees with the Rambam and explains that once the Jews crossed the Jordan, the Canaanites could no longer agree to a peaceful settlement. However, most authorities reject this view. Since the mitzvah to destroy the seven nations was instituted "so that they will not teach you the revolting practices with which they worship their gods...," there is no reason to differentiate between when their commitment would be made.

Further support for the Rambam's opinion can be brought from *Avodah Zarah* 24b which states Arvana, the Jebusite from whom King David bought the Temple site, was a Canaanite who had accepted the seven mitzvot. Thus, it appears that even after the Jews' entry into *Eretz Yisrael*, the Canaanites could have avoided being slain by accepting peace and observance.

39. As the narrative in Joshua continues (*ibid.*:18-19): "All the congregation murmured against the princes, but all the princes said to the entire congregation: 'We have sworn to them by God... therefore, we may not touch them.'"

40. The Ramban (Deuteronomy 20:11) disagrees with the Rambam and maintains that it

מִלְחָמָה, יַעֲשֶׂה. אִם־כֵּן, מִפְּנֵי מָה הֶעֱרִימוּ יוֹשְׁבֵי גִבְעוֹן? לְפִי שֶׁשָּׁלַח לָהֶם בִּכְלָל וְלֹא קִבְּלוּ, וְלֹא יָדְעוּ מִשְׁפַּט יִשְׂרָאֵל, וְדִמּוּ שֶׁשּׁוּב אֵין פּוֹתְחִין לָהֶם לְשָׁלוֹם. וְלָמָּה קָשָׁה הַדָּבָר לַנְּשִׂיאִים וְרָאוּ שֶׁרָאוּי לְהַכּוֹתָם לְפִי חֶרֶב לוּלֵי הַשְּׁבוּעָה? מִפְּנֵי שֶׁכָּרְתוּ לָהֶם בְּרִית. וַהֲרֵי הוּא אוֹמֵר: "לֹא תִכְרֹת לָהֶם בְּרִית"? אֶלָּא הָיָה דִינָם שֶׁיִּהְיוּ לָמַס עֲבָדִים, וְהוֹאִיל וּבְטָעוּת נִשְׁבְּעוּ לָהֶם, בְּדִין הָיָה שֶׁיֵּהָרְגוּ עַל שֶׁהִטְעוּם, לוּלֵי חִלּוּל הַשֵּׁם.

ו עַמּוֹן וּמוֹאָב, אֵין שׁוֹלְחִים לָהֶם לְשָׁלוֹם, שֶׁנֶּאֱמַר: "לֹא תִדְרֹשׁ שְׁלֹמָם וְטֹבָתָם, כָּל יָמֶיךָ". אָמְרוּ חֲכָמִים: לְפִי שֶׁנֶּאֱמַר, "וְקָרָאתָ אֵלֶיהָ לְשָׁלוֹם", יָכוֹל עַמּוֹן וּמוֹאָב כֵּן? תַּלְמוּד לוֹמַר: "לֹא תִדְרֹשׁ שְׁלֹמָם וְטֹבָתָם". לְפִי שֶׁנֶּאֱמַר: "עִמְּךָ יֵשֵׁב בְּקִרְבְּךָ... בַּטּוֹב לוֹ, לֹא תּוֹנֶנּוּ", יָכוֹל עַמּוֹן וּמוֹאָב כֵּן? תַּלְמוּד לוֹמַר: "וְטֹבָתָם". וְאַף־עַל־פִּי שֶׁאֵין שׁוֹאֲלִים בִּשְׁלוֹמָם – אִם הִשְׁלִימוּ מֵעַצְמָם תְּחִלָּה, מְקַבְּלִין אוֹתָן.

was permissible to establish a covenant with the Gibeonites because they had already accepted the belief in God. However, the Jews' first reply to the Gibeonites "Perhaps, you dwell among us? If so, how shall we make a covenant with you?" appears to reinforce the Rambam's view that all covenants with the Canaanites were forbidden even though they disavowed the worship of idols.

41. Rather than accepted as equals as implied by the covenant they made.

42. *Avodah Zarah* 46a explains that since the oath was taken under false premises, it was not binding. Nevertheless, the surrounding nations would think that the Jews had broken their oath. Thus, were the oath to be ignored, God's name, on which it was made, would be dishonored.

43. *Sefer HaMitzvot* (negative commandment 56) and *Sefer HaChinuch* (mitzvah 562) include this as one of the Torah's 613 mitzvot.

The prohibition was instituted as punishment for Ammon and Moav's lack of sensitivity to the Jews in their time of distress. While they were journeying to *Eretz Yisrael*, these nations "did not greet them with bread and water" (Deuteronomy 23:5).

44. *Sifri*, commenting on that verse.

45. While it is forbidden to make an overture of peace towards either Ammon or Moav, we may repay their kindness to us. Therefore, King David extended consolation to Chanon, King of Ammon after the death of his father, because the latter had protected David's family. See II Samuel, Chapter 10.

Nevertheless, even though that gesture was permitted, it did not find favor in God's eyes. He declared: "Whoever shows them mercy will ultimately be shamed."

What resulted from David's kindness? Chanon ridiculed his emissaries in public. As a consequence, Israel became engrossed in a fierce war (*BaMidbar Rabbah* 21:5).

46. This verse applies to a fugitive slave and by extension, to any gentile who is willing to accept the seven mitzvot.

47. The *Minchat Chinuch* 562 explains that even after conversion an Ammonite or Moabite may not dwell in *Eretz Yisrael.*

48. As the Rambam writes in *Hilchot Issurei Bi'ah* 12:25, after conquering most of the civilized world, Sannecherib engaged in a process of mass population transfer causing all of Israel's neighbors to lose their national identity. Thus, there are no longer any nations or individuals who can be designated as descending from Ammon or Moav.

49. The source for the Rambam's statement appears to be the above verse which forbids

7. When a siege is placed around a city to conquer it, it should not be surrounded on all four sides, only on three.[50] A place should be left [for the inhabitants] to flee[51] and for all those who desire, to escape with their lives, as it is written [Numbers 31:7]: "And they besieged Midian as God commanded Moses."[52] According to tradition,[53] He commanded them to array the siege as described.

8. We should not cut down fruit trees[54] outside a city[55] nor prevent an irrigation ditch from [bringing water to] them[56] so that they dry up, as [Deuteronomy 20:19] states: "Do not destroy its trees."[57] Anyone who cuts down [such a tree] should be lashed.[58]

[This does] not apply only in a siege, but in all situations. Anyone who cuts down a fruit tree with a destructive intent, should be lashed.[59]

Nevertheless, a [fruit tree] may be cut down if it causes damage to other trees[60] or to fields belonging to others,[61] or if a high price [could be received for its wood].[62] The Torah only prohibited cutting down a tree with a destructive intent.

9. It is permissible to cut down any non-fruit bearing tree,[63] even if one has no need for it.[64] Similarly, one may cut down a fruit bearing tree that has become old and produces only a slight yield which does not warrant the effort [required to care for it.][65]

"seeking their peace" and does not mention responding to their offer (*Minchat Chinuch, loc. cit.*).

50. The Ramban in his *hosafot* to *Sefer HaMitzvot* (positive commandments 5) considers this obligation as one of the 613 mitzvot of the Torah.

51. The Radbaz states that only in a *milchemet hareshut* should a place be left for the enemy to flee. In a *milchemet mitzvah,* no leniency of this nature should be made. The Ramban (*loc. cit.*) and the *Sefer HaChinuch* (mitzvah 527) also accept this opinion.

The *Minchat Chinuch* questions this view, asking how such a concept can be derived from the Rambam's wording. The *Toldot Adam* in his commentary on the *Sifri* explains the rationale for both opinions. According to the first view, this practice is a gesture of peace and mercy required by the Torah.

In contrast, the second view could explain that this practice was instituted for the benefit of the Jews. Were the gentiles to realize that they have no opportunity to flee, they would fight with greater savagery, as a desperate man who has no other alternative to save his life. (See also *Meshach Chochmah* on the verse from Numbers.)

52. The verse also supports the latter opinion for the war against Midian was a *milchemet mitzvah* fought with the intent of slaughtering that nation.

53. See *Sifri; Yalkut Shimoni.*

54. The laws applying to other trees are explained in the following halachah.

55. The verse from Deuteronomy begins "When you lay siege to a city." Thus, the trees in question are those growing in the orchards outside the city.

56. For this will also destroy the trees (*Sifri*).

57. The *Sefer HaMitzvot* (negative commandment 57) and the *Sefer HaChinuch* (mitzvah 529) include this as one of the Torah's 613 mitzvot. See the *Turei Zahav* (*Yoreh De'ah* 116:6) which questions why the *Tur* and the *Shulchan Aruch* do not cite this law.

ז כְּשֶׁצָּרִין עַל עִיר לְתָפְשָׂהּ, אֵין מַקִּיפִין אוֹתָהּ מֵאַרְבַּע רוּחוֹתֶיהָ, אֶלָּא מִשָּׁלֹשׁ רוּחוֹתֶיהָ; וּמַנִּיחִין מָקוֹם לַבּוֹרֵחַ וּלְכָל מִי שֶׁיִּרְצֶה לְהִמָּלֵט עַל נַפְשׁוֹ, שֶׁנֶּאֱמַר: "וַיִּצְבְּאוּ עַל מִדְיָן כַּאֲשֶׁר צִוָּה ה' אֶת מֹשֶׁה" - מִפִּי הַשְּׁמוּעָה לָמְדוּ שֶׁבְּכָךְ צִוָּהוּ.

ח אֵין קוֹצְצִין אִילָנֵי מַאֲכָל שֶׁחוּץ לַמְּדִינָה וְאֵין מוֹנְעִין מֵהֶם אַמַּת הַמַּיִם כְּדֵי שֶׁיִּיבְשׁוּ, שֶׁנֶּאֱמַר: "לֹא תַשְׁחִית אֶת עֵצָהּ"; וְכָל הַקּוֹצֵץ - לוֹקֶה. וְלֹא בְּמָצוֹר בִּלְבַד, אֶלָּא בְּכָל מָקוֹם כָּל הַקּוֹצֵץ אִילַן מַאֲכָל דֶּרֶךְ הַשְׁחָתָה - לוֹקֶה; אֲבָל קוֹצְצִין אוֹתוֹ אִם הָיָה מַזִּיק אִילָנוֹת אֲחֵרִים, אוֹ מִפְּנֵי שֶׁמַּזִּיק בִּשְׂדֵה אֲחֵרִים, אוֹ מִפְּנֵי שֶׁדָּמָיו יְקָרִים. לֹא אָסְרָה תּוֹרָה אֶלָּא דֶּרֶךְ הַשְׁחָתָה.

ט כָּל אִילַן סְרָק, מֻתָּר לָקֹץ אוֹתוֹ, וַאֲפִלּוּ אֵינוֹ צָרִיךְ לוֹ. וְכֵן אִילַן מַאֲכָל שֶׁהִזְקִין וְאֵינוֹ עוֹשֶׂה אֶלָּא דָּבָר מוּעָט שֶׁאֵינוֹ רָאוּי לְטֹרַח בּוֹ - מֻתָּר לָקֹץ אוֹתוֹ.

58. As appropriate for the violation of a negative commandment.

59. In this instance, the rationale behind the mitzvah defines one's interpretation of the halachah. The Ramban (*hosafot* to *Sefer HaMitzvot*, positive commandment 6) explains that this prohibition only applies while besieging a city. For our troops can use the trees for food or we might ultimately desire to settle in the land and benefit from the fruit. However, when our forces leave the land, they may cut down fruit trees without reservation to destroy the land.

In contrast, the *Sefer HaChinuch* explains that the purpose of this prohibition is "to love good and benefit and to cling to them... and to separate ourselves from all evil and destruction." Accordingly, the prohibition would also apply to property which belongs to gentiles.

60. This applies even to one's own trees. *Bava Kama* 92a relates that Shmuel had a date palm growing among his grape-vines which detracted from the taste of the wine they produced. Hence, he ordered his farmers to remove it.

61. *Bava Batra* 25b, 26a prohibits planting trees next to one's neighbor's field or well, lest the tree's roots destroy them. Moreover, if trees were planted too closely at the outset, one may later uproot them.

62. I.e., it would be more valuable to sell it as wood than to harvest its fruit. The Radbaz maintains that this license is only granted for an older tree that is not producing its full capacity.

63. The above mentioned passage continues (Deuteronomy, *loc. cit.*:20): "However, if you know that a tree does not produce food, you may destroy the tree."

64. The intent of this phrase is obviously not to permit wanton destruction. As mentioned in the following halachah, the prohibition against wanton destruction (*bal tashchit*) applies to all articles of value. Rather, the intent is that, with regard to non-fruit bearing trees, greater leniency can be taken than with regard to fruit trees and the restrictions mentioned in the previous halachah need not be heeded.

65. *Bava Kama* 91a explains that even without the words "if you know" in the verse quoted above it could be understood that it is permissible to cut down non-fruit bearing trees. Hence, that phrase was included with the intention of teaching a further concept; i.e., that the prohibition against cutting down fruit bearing trees only applies when it is worthwhile for their owner to maintain them. This, however, is not considered the exegesis of the

What is the yield that an olive tree must produce to warrant that it should not be cut down? A quarter of a *kav* of olives.[66] [Similarly,] a date palm which yields a *kav* of dates should not be cut down.[67]

10. [This prohibition does not apply] to trees alone. Rather, anyone who breaks utensils,[68] tears garments,[69] destroys buildings, stops up a spring,[70] or ruins food[71] with a destructive intent[72] transgresses the command "Do not destroy." However, he is not lashed.[74] Instead, [he receives] stripes for rebellious conduct[as instituted by] the Sages.[75]

11. We should lay siege to the gentiles' cities [at least] three days before the Sabbath.[76] We may engage in battle with them every day, even on the Sabbath,[77] as [Deuteronomy 20:20] states: "[against the city waging war with you] until you subjugate it." [Our Sages[78] explain: this implies] "even on the Sabbath."[79] [This applies to] both a *milchemet mitzvah* and a *milchemet hareshut*.[80]

verse to the extent that the concept is included in the Scriptural command. Instead, it is merely an allusion (an *asmachta*).

66. A *kav* is approximately 52 ounces in modern measure. Olives were very expensive and the trees require little care. Hence, it is worthwhile to maintain the tree despite this small yield.

67. These are not rigid rules, but rather, figures that can fluctuate depending on the price of fruit and cost of maintaining a tree.

68. *Shabbat* 129a relates that certain Sages would suffer severe chills after letting blood. For lack of any other fuel, they used expensive furniture as firewood. The passage continues: "Doesn't this violate the command 'Do not destroy'?" and explains that since the fire was used for the Sages' physical comfort, no prohibition is involved.

69. *Kiddushin* 32a relates that Rav Huna tore a valuable garment in front of his son to see whether the latter would lose his temper or not. Afterwards, the Sages question that statement for such an act appears to violate the prohibition under discussion. They resolve the difficulty by explaining that he ripped the garment on the seams and thus, nothing was destroyed.

70. II Kings 3:19 relates that Elisha, the prophet, instructed King Jehoram in his battle against Moav: "Destroy every good tree, stop up every stream of water, and fill every good field with stones." *Bamidbar Rabbah* 21:6 notes that such advice appears to violate the prohibition "Do not destroy" and explains that an exception is made regarding Ammon and Moav for they are lowly nations whose welfare may not be sought (see Halachah 6 above).

The commentaries explain that the prohibition applies to each element of Elisha's advice independently and quote this passage as the source for the inclusion of this phase in our halachah.

71. *Shabbat* 140b mentions an opinion that views eating and drinking expensive foods instead of cheaper ones as a violation of the prohibition "Do not destroy." The Talmud does not accept this opinion, explaining that such activities are not forbidden since one's physical pleasure is involved. Nevertheless, the fact such an issue could be raised demonstrates that the prohibition also applies to wasting food.

72. As mentioned in the previous halachah, no prohibition is involved if there is a positive reason for the deed.

וְכַמָּה יְהֵא הַזַּיִת עוֹשֶׂה וְלֹא יְקַצְּנוּ? – רֹבַע הַקַּב זֵיתִים. וְדֶקֶל שֶׁהוּא עוֹשֶׂה קַב תְּמָרִים, לֹא יְקַצְּנוּ.

י וְלֹא הָאִילָנוֹת בִּלְבָד, אֶלָּא כָּל הַמְשַׁבֵּר כֵּלִים וְקוֹרֵעַ בְּגָדִים וְהוֹרֵס בִּנְיָן וְסוֹתֵם מַעְיָן וּמְאַבֵּד מַאֲכָלוֹת דֶּרֶךְ הַשְׁחָתָה – עוֹבֵר בְּ"לֹא תַשְׁחִית", וְאֵינוֹ לוֹקֶה אֶלָּא מַכַּת־מַרְדּוּת מִדִּבְרֵיהֶם.

יא צָרִין עַל עֲיָרוֹת שֶׁל עכו"ם שְׁלֹשָׁה יָמִים קֹדֶם הַשַּׁבָּת, וְעוֹשִׂין עִמָּהֶם מִלְחָמָה בְּכָל יוֹם וָיוֹם, וַאֲפִלּוּ בְּשַׁבָּת, שֶׁנֶּאֱמַר: "עַד רִדְתָּהּ" וַאֲפִלּוּ בְּשַׁבָּת; בֵּין מִלְחֶמֶת מִצְוָה, בֵּין מִלְחֶמֶת רְשׁוּת.

Shabbat 105b compares the destruction of useful objects in a fit of anger to the worship of idols.

73. Lashing is only given as punishment for violation of a Biblical command. The extension of the scope of this prohibition to all things is Rabbinic in origin. Hence, lashes are not administered for its transgression. Rather, he receives "stripes for rebellious conduct," [as instituted by] the Rabbis.

This decision represents a reversal of the Rambam's statements in *Sefer HaMitzvot* (*ibid.*). There, he explained that lashes are given for the destruction of other valuable articles besides trees.

74. Lashes are only given as punishment for violation of a Biblical command. The extension of the scope of this prohibition to all things is Rabbinic in origin. Hence, lashes are not administered for its transgression. Rather, a violator receives "stripes for rebellious conduct," as instituted by the Rabbis.

This decision represents a reversal of the Rambam's statements in *Sefer HaMitzvot* (*ibid.*). There, he explained that lashes are given for the destruction of other valuable articles besides trees.

75. As given for the violation of a Rabbinic decree. In contrast to the Biblically ordained punishment of thirty-nine lashes for the violation of a Torah command, the extent of punishment for stripes for rebellious conduct is left to the discretion of the court. Their decision is based upon the severity of the violation, the character of the transgressor, and the circumstances involved.

76. *Hilchot Shabbat* 30:13 states that this prohibition was instituted "so that the soldiers' minds will be settled and they will not be agitated and overly preoccupied on the Sabbath."

Pikuach Nefesh, threat to life, overrides the observance of the Sabbath prohibitions. Hence, battle is permitted on Sabbath. However, to whatever degree possible, an attempt must be made to preserve the Sabbath atmosphere. Hence, by beginning the siege well before the Sabbath, the tension and frenzied activity which usually accompany the first days of a siege will not disturb the Sabbath.

77. Once a siege was begun before the Sabbath, fighting may be continued on the Sabbath. Our Sages relate that during the Maccabean revolt, the Greeks mounted an attack on the Sabbath. Unaware of the leniency allowing them to fight, our people refused to take up their arms. Thousands fell.

78. *Shabbat* 19a; see *Hilchot Shabbat*, the conclusion of Chapter 2.

79. *Hilchot Shabbat* 2:25 relates that Joshua conquered Jericho on the Sabbath.

80. Commenting on *Hilchot Shabbat* (*ibid.*), both the *Kessef Mishneh* and the *Lechem*

12. [The army] may camp anywhere.[81] A person killed in the war[82] should be buried where he falls. He acquires that place[83] in the same manner as a *meit mitzvah* acquires his.[84]

13. Four leniencies are permitted in [an army] camp:[85]
a) *Demai*[86] may be eaten.
b) There is no requirement to wash one's hands before [eating bread].[87]
c) Wood[88] may be gathered from anywhere.[89] Even if one finds [wood] that has been cut down and dried,[90] there is no objection [to taking it] for an [army] camp.[91]
d) There is no obligation to make an *eruv chatzeirot* for an [army] camp. Rather, one may carry from tent to tent and from booth to booth.[92]

The latter [is only permitted] when the entire camp is surrounded by a barrier at least ten handbreadths high,[93] for as explained in *Hilchot Shabbat*,[94] a barrier must be at least ten [handbreadths high].[95]

Just as these leniencies apply when [the army] goes out [to war], they apply when it returns.[96]

Mishneh maintain that this clause refers to the previous statement "We may engage in battle... even on the Sabbath," informing us that fighting may be continued in a *milchemet hareshut* on the Sabbath. However, the first statement of the halachah requiring us to begin the siege of a city three days before Sabbath, only holds true for a *milchemet hareshut*. In a *milchemet mitzvah*, a siege may be begun before the Sabbath.

Though that statement is not accepted by all opinions, all agree that a defensive war may be begun on the Sabbath. See *Hilchot Shabbat* 2:23, *Shulchan Aruch, Orach Chayim* 329:6.

81. The owner of the property cannot protest against the encampment.

82. The Radbaz explains that this law also applies to a soldier who died a natural death.

83. This law was instituted to prevent the owner of the property from protesting against the burial of a corpse on his land. Even though the departed's relatives could bury them elsewhere, the army may bury the corpses where they fall rather than carry them with them. However, it is questionable whether there is an obligation to bury them there.

84. The term *meit mitzvah* means a corpse which it is a mitzvah for its discover to bury. *Hilchot Evel* 3:8 states: "What is a *meit mitzvah*? A Jewish corpse cast away on the road without anyone to bury it."

When Joshua divided *Eretz Yisrael* among the tribes, he established ten conditions governing the land and its use. Among them was the provision that a *meit mitzvah* could be buried wherever he is found. There is no obligation to carry his body to a cemetery (*Hilchot Nizkei Mammon* 5:3).

85. This applies to a *milchemet hareshut* as well as a *milchemet mitzvah* (Rambam, Commentary on the Mishnah, *Eruvin* 1:10).

86. *Demai* refers to produce purchased from a common person. Our Sages were unsure whether such an individual would separate tithes properly. Hence, they required that *Terumat Ma'aser* and *Ma'aser Sheni* be separated by the purchaser of the produce. (See *Hilchot Ma'aser* 9:1-3.) There was no obligation to observe this stringency in an army camp.

87. In his Commentary on the Mishnah, *loc. cit.*, the Rambam writes "There is no

יב כְּשֶׁחוֹנִין, חוֹנִין בְּכָל מָקוֹם. וּמִי שֶׁנֶּהֱרַג בַּמִּלְחָמָה – בַּמָּקוֹם שֶׁיִּפֹּל, שָׁם יִקָּבֵר; קוֹנֶה מְקוֹמוֹ כְּמֵת־מִצְוָה.

יג אַרְבָּעָה דְבָרִים פָּטְרוּ בְּמַחֲנֶה: אוֹכְלִים הַדְּמַאי, וּפְטוּרִים מֵרְחִיצַת יָדַיִם בַּתְּחִלָּה, וּמְבִיאִין עֵצִים מִכָּל מָקוֹם. וַאֲפִלּוּ מְצָאָן תְּלוּשִׁים וִיבֵשִׁים – אֵין מַקְפִּידִין עַל כָּךְ בְּמַחֲנֶה. וְכֵן פְּטוּרִין מִלְּעָרֵב עֵרוּבֵי חֲצֵרוֹת בַּמַּחֲנֶה, אֶלָּא מְטַלְטְלִין מֵאֹהֶל לְאֹהֶל וּמִסֻּכָּה לְסֻכָּה. וְהוּא, שֶׁיַּקִּיפוּ כָּל הַמַּחֲנֶה מְחִצָּה גְבוֹהָה עֲשָׂרָה טְפָחִים כְּדֵי שֶׁתִּהְיֶה רְשׁוּת־יָחִיד, כְּמוֹ שֶׁנִּתְבָּאֵר בְּהִלְכוֹת שַׁבָּת, וְאֵין מְחִצָּה פְּחוּתָה מֵעֲשָׂרָה. וּכְשֵׁם שֶׁפְּטוּרִין מִכָּל אֵלּוּ בַּהֲלִיכָתָן, כָּךְ פְּטוּרִין בַּחֲזָרָתָן.

obligation to search for water." Seemingly, implying that if water is available, one is obligated to wash before eating. In this halachah (and similarly, in *Hilchot Berachot* 6:3) no such differentiation is made.

88. One of Joshua's ten conditions governing the use of land in *Eretz Yisrael* was that a person was allowed to gather thorns and shrubs from anyone else's field for use as firewood (*Hilchot Nizkei Mammon, loc. cit.*). Here, license is granted to take wood of a more substantial nature (*Eruvin* 17a)

89. Even though it is private property.

90. An act which obviously implies that it had been prepared by its owner for his personal use

91. The Jerusalem Talmud (*Eruvin* 1:10) allows this leniency only in a *milchemet mitzvah* and not in a *milchemet hareshut*. However, the Babylonian Talmud - and, hence, the Rambam - does not distinguish between the two.

92. According to Scriptural Law, though it is forbidden to carry in the public domain, there is no prohibition against carrying in a semi-public area, for example a courtyard. Nevertheless, to safeguard the Torah's prohibition, the Sages also forbade carrying in these areas. However, together with their prohibition, they granted a leniency, *eruv chatzeirot*, which would allow carrying in such areas.

To establish an *eruv chatzeirot*, a group of families must fence off the area in which they desire to carry with a barrier and prepare food in a centralized location. Afterwards, they may carry within the fenced off region. See *Hilchot Eruvin*, Chapter 1. The Sages allowed soldiers in an army camp to rely on the Torah law itself and did not require an *eruv*.

93. If the camp is surrounded by a barrier, the prohibition is only Rabbinic in nature and hence, is relaxed for the soldiers. However, if there is no barrier, carrying violates a prohibition of the Torah itself and is only permitted if there is a danger to life.

Similarly, no leniency is shown regarding *eruv techumim* for that prohibition has its source in the Torah itself (*Kessef Mishneh*).

94. *Hilchot Shabbat* 16:1.

95. A barrier of lesser height is not significant.

Manuscripts of the *Mishneh Torah* brought from Yemen read here: "An army camp is comprised of a minimum of ten [soldiers]." A lesser amount of soldiers are not granted these leniencies.

96. There is a certain amount of danger even when an army returns for at any moment they may be attacked by the enemy.

14. It is forbidden to defecate[97] in an [army] camp or in an open field anywhere. Rather, it is a positive commandment[98] to establish comfort facilities [for the soldiers] to defecate, as [Deuteronomy 23:13] commands: "Designate a place outside the camp [to use as a lavatory]."[99]

15. Similarly, it is a positive commandment[100] for every single [soldier] to have a spike hanging together with his weapons. When he goes out and uses those comfort facilities, he should dig with it, relieve himself, and cover his excrement, as [*ibid.*:14] states "You must keep a spike among your weapons."[101]

They must follow these practices[102] at all times, whether the ark accompanies them[103] or not,[104] as [*ibid.*:15] states: "[God walks among your camp,... therefore,] your camp shall be holy."[105]

CHAPTER SEVEN

1. In both a *milchemet mitzvah* and a *milchemet hareshut*,[1] a priest is appointed[2] to address[3] the nation before the battle. He is anointed with the oil of anointment[4] and is called, the *meshuach milchamah*.[5]

2. The *meshuach milchamah* speaks to the nation twice:[6] Once, at the border, as the army is leaving before they assume battle positions. [At that

97. *Berachot* 25a explains that the prohibition also includes urination. However, most Halachic authorities do not take notice of that statement.

98. The *Sefer HaMitzvot* (positive commandment 192) and the *Sefer HaChinuch* (mitzvah 566) include this as one of the Torah's 613 mitzvot.

99. The reason for this command is mentioned in the following halachah, so that "your camp shall be holy."

100. The *Sefer HaMitzvot* (positive commandment 193) and the *Sefer HaChinuch* (mitzvah 567) include this as one of the Torah's 613 mitzvot. However, the *Sefer Mitzvot Gadol* counts this and the previous command as one mitzvah.

101. The Torah uses the word *yetaid* which is usually rendered as "spike." However, in this instance, the Septuagint translates the term as "trowel."

102. Those mentioned in this and the previous halachah.

103. *Yoma* 75b states: "Until the Jews complained about the manna (Numbers 21), it would be totally absorbed by their systems without producing any waste. God declared: 'I wanted them to be like angels. Now, I will force them to walk three miles (the length of the camp) to perform their functions.' "

This passage obviously implies that the practices mentioned in this halachah were instituted during the Jews' journey through the desert when the ark accompanied them.

Once the Jews settled in *Eretz Yisrael*, the ark with the tablets was taken to war only once (See I Samuel, Chapter 4). According to one opinion in the Jerusalem Talmud (*Shekalim*, Chapter 6), a second ark containing the tablets broken by Moses accompanied the people to war at all times. However, the Sages do not accept this view.

104. The *Yereim* (362) states that these mitzvot only apply when the ark accompanies the Jews. The Rambam does not accept this opinion for even if the ark did not accompany them, God's presence did.

105. To quote the verse in its entirety: "[These rules are ordained] because God, your Lord, accompanies you, in the midst of your camp; to deliver you and grant you victory over

יד וְאָסוּר לְהִפָּנוֹת בְּתוֹךְ הַמַּחֲנֶה אוֹ עַל פְּנֵי הַשָּׂדֶה בְּכָל מָקוֹם, אֶלָּא מִצְוַת עֲשֵׂה לְתַקֵּן שָׁם דֶּרֶךְ מְיֻחֶדֶת לְהִפָּנוֹת בָּהּ, שֶׁנֶּאֱמַר: "וְיָד תִּהְיֶה לְךָ מִחוּץ לַמַּחֲנֶה".

טו וְכֵן מִצְוַת עֲשֵׂה לִהְיוֹת יָתֵד לְכָל אֶחָד וְאֶחָד תְּלוּיָה עִם כְּלֵי מִלְחַמְתּוֹ, וְיֵצֵא בְּאוֹתָהּ הַדֶּרֶךְ וְיַחְפֹּר בָּהּ, וְיִפַּנֶּה וִיכַסֶּה, שֶׁנֶּאֱמַר: "וְיָתֵד תִּהְיֶה לְךָ עַל אֲזֵנֶךָ וְגוֹ'". וּבֵין שֶׁיֵּשׁ עִמָּהֶן אָרוֹן וּבֵין שֶׁאֵין עִמָּהֶם אָרוֹן, כָּךְ הֵם עוֹשִׂים תָּמִיד, שֶׁנֶּאֱמַר: "וְהָיָה מַחֲנֶךָ קָדוֹשׁ".

פֶּרֶק שְׁבִיעִי

א אֶחָד מִלְחֶמֶת מִצְוָה וְאֶחָד מִלְחֶמֶת הָרְשׁוּת, מְמַנִּין כֹּהֵן לְדַבֵּר אֶל הָעָם בִּשְׁעַת הַמִּלְחָמָה. וּמוֹשְׁחִין אוֹתוֹ בְּשֶׁמֶן הַמִּשְׁחָה, וְזֶהוּ הַנִּקְרָא "מְשׁוּחַ־מִלְחָמָה".

ב שְׁתֵּי פְּעָמִים מְדַבֵּר מְשׁוּחַ־מִלְחָמָה אֶל הָעָם: אַחַת בַּסְּפָר בְּעֵת שֶׁיּוֹצְאִין, קֹדֶם שֶׁיַּעַרְכוּ

your enemy. [Therefore,] your camp must be holy. Let Him not see anything lascivious among you, lest He turn from you."

The verse gives the ultimate reason for the above practices. Were we to rely on the considerations of human decency alone, it is possible that the tensions of war would provoke a certain laxity in these matters. However, since they were instituted as respect for God's presence, they are eternally relevant for He is always with us.

In addition to the rules the verse sets down, it also contains a promise of success. God assures the people: If you will maintain your standard of holiness, I will "deliver you and grant you victory over your enemy" (*Sifri*).

1. In *Sefer HaMitzvot* (positive commandment 191), the Rambam writes that this mitzvah only applies in a *milchemet hareshut*, but not in a *milchemet mitzvah*. Accordingly, there are commentaries who maintain that this phrase should be placed at the conclusion of the previous chapter and not at the beginning of this chapter.

However, other authorities maintain that there is no need to alter the texts. In this matter, as in the issue of offering a peaceful settlement (see commentary Chapter 6, Halachah 1), the Rambam changed his opinion from that stated in *Sefer HaMitzvot*.

The *Or Sameach* brings support for the opinion that a *meshuach milchamah* is appointed even in a *milchemet mitzvah* by citing the appointment of Pinchas to that position in the war against Midian (see Numbers 31:7 and *Sotah* 43a).

2. This appointment is included by the *Sefer HaMitzvot* (*loc. cit.*) and the *Sefer HaChinuch* (mitzvah 526) as one of the 613 mitzvot of the Torah.

3. See Halachot 2 and 3.

4. The unique oil made by Moses described in Chapter 1, Halachah 7.

5. Literally, "the one anointed for the war."

Hilchot Beit HaBechirah 4:1 states that the oil of anointment was entombed together with the ark by King Josiah. Accordingly, during the latter years of the first Temple and throughout the subsequent generations, this mitzvah could no longer be fulfilled. Though Josephus and the *Sefer Chashmonim* state that Judah, the Macabee, served in this position, from a Halachic perspective, we must consider that merely an honorary title (*Minchat Chinuch* 107).

6. The primary function of the *meshuach milchamah* was to speak to the nation and

time,] he tells the nation: "Is there a man who has planted a vineyard and has not redeemed his first crop?..." (Deuteronomy 20:6).[7] When [these individuals] hear his words, they should retreat from the battlefront.[8]

[He speaks a second time] when [the army has assumed] battle positions: [Then,] he declares: "Do not be afraid. Do not panic..." (*ibid.* 20:3).[9]

3. When the armies assume battle positions and will shortly join in war, the *meshuach milchamah* stands in an elevated place before the array of the entire [army].[10] He addresses them in Hebrew:[11]

> Listen, Israel,[12] today you are about to wage war against your enemies.[13] Do not be faint-hearted.[14] Do not be afraid. Do not panic and do not break ranks before them. God, you Lord, is the One accompanying you to do battle for you against your enemies to deliver you (*ibid.* 20:3-4).[15]

These words are related by the *meshuach milchamah*. [Afterwards,] another priest of a lower rank, proclaims them to the people in a loud voice. [Then,] the *meshuach milchamah* announces:[16]

> Is there a man who has built a new house?... [Let him go home...]
> Is there a man who has planted a vineyard?... [Let him go home...]
> Is there a man who has consecrated a woman?... [Let him go home...] (*ibid.* 20:5-7).[17]

These words are related by the *meshuach milchamah*. [Afterwards,] an officer proclaims [these words] to the nation in a loud voice.[18] The officer announces on his own initiative:[19] "Is there a man who is afraid or faint-hearted? [Let him go home...]" (*ibid.* 20:8). Another officer proclaims [these words] to the people.[20]

4. After these individuals depart from the battlefront, the army is arrayed again and commanding officers are appointed at the head of the nation.[21]

inspire them before the war. In order to enhance his standing among the people and cause his words to be appreciated, he was given the honor of anointment (*Sefer HaChinuch, ibid.*).

7. The Ra'avad notes that this statement is not appropriate in a *milchemet mitzvah* for, as explained in Halachah 4, in a war of that nature, no one is freed from army service.

8. The *Kessef Mishneh* notes that in Halachah 3, this proclamation is repeated. Accordingly, he explains that first, the *meshuach milchamah* would mention the need for these individuals to return in general terms, telling them to heed the proclamations he would make later. Afterwards, at the battlefront, he would make the statements mentioned in Halachah 3. This interpretation concurs with the statement in *Sotah* 42b: "At the border, he announces: 'Listen to what will be said at the battlefield.' "

The Radbaz notes the difficulties mentioned by both the Ra'avad and the *Kessef Mishneh*. He mentions that he discovered a manuscript of the *Mishneh Torah* with a different version. That text reads:

> Once, at border, as the army is leaving before they assume battle positions: [At that time,] he tells the nation: "Is there a man who is afraid or faint-hearted?..." When [these individuals] hear his words, they should retreat from the battlefront....
> And once when [the army has assumed] battle positions: [Then,] he declares: "Do not be afraid. Do not panic..."

הַמִּלְחָמָה, אוֹמֵר לָעָם: "מִי הָאִישׁ אֲשֶׁר נָטַע כֶּרֶם וְלֹא חִלְּלוֹ וְגוֹ'" - כְּשֶׁיִּשְׁמַע דְּבָרָיו, יַחֲזֹר מֵעוֹרְכֵי הַמִּלְחָמָה; וְאַחַת בְּעוֹרְכֵי הַמִּלְחָמָה אוֹמֵר: "אַל תִּירְאוּ וְאַל תַּחְפְּזוּ".

ג עֵת שֶׁעוֹרְכִין הַמַּעֲרָכוֹת וְהֵם קְרֵבִים לְהִלָּחֵם, מְשׁוּחַ־מִלְחָמָה עוֹמֵד בְּמָקוֹם גָּבֹהַּ וְכָל הַמַּעֲרָכוֹת לְפָנָיו, וְאוֹמֵר לָהֶם בִּלְשׁוֹן־הַקֹּדֶשׁ: "שְׁמַע יִשְׂרָאֵל אַתֶּם קְרֵבִים הַיּוֹם לַמִּלְחָמָה עַל אֹיְבֵיכֶם, אַל יֵרַךְ לְבַבְכֶם אַל תִּירְאוּ וְאַל תַּחְפְּזוּ וְאַל תַּעַרְצוּ מִפְּנֵיהֶם. כִּי ה' אֱלֹהֵיכֶם הַהֹלֵךְ עִמָּכֶם, לְהִלָּחֵם לָכֶם עִם אֹיְבֵיכֶם לְהוֹשִׁיעַ אֶתְכֶם". עַד כָּאן אוֹמֵר מְשׁוּחַ־מִלְחָמָה, וְכֹהֵן אַחֵר תַּחְתָּיו מַשְׁמִיעַ אוֹתוֹ לְכָל הָעָם בְּקוֹל רָם. וְאַחַר־כָּךְ מְדַבֵּר מְשׁוּחַ־מִלְחָמָה: "מִי הָאִישׁ אֲשֶׁר בָּנָה בַיִת חָדָשׁ וְגוֹ'. וּמִי הָאִישׁ אֲשֶׁר נָטַע כֶּרֶם וְגוֹ'. וּמִי הָאִישׁ אֲשֶׁר אֵרַשׂ וְגוֹ'". עַד כָּאן מְשׁוּחַ־מִלְחָמָה מְדַבֵּר, וְהַשּׁוֹטֵר מַשְׁמִיעַ לְכָל הָעָם בְּקוֹל רָם. וְאַחַר־כָּךְ מְדַבֵּר הַשּׁוֹטֵר מֵעַצְמוֹ וְאוֹמֵר: "מִי הָאִישׁ הַיָּרֵא וְרַךְ הַלֵּבָב", וְשׁוֹטֵר אַחֵר מַשְׁמִיעַ לְכָל הָעָם.

ד וְאַחַר שֶׁחוֹזְרִין כָּל הַחוֹזְרִין מֵעוֹרְכֵי הַמִּלְחָמָה, מְתַקְּנִין אֶת הַמַּעֲרָכוֹת וּפוֹקְדִים שָׂרֵי

9. See the following halachah.
10. As Deuteronomy 20:2 states: "When you approach the battle, the priest shall step forward and speak to the people."
11. *Sotah* 42a comments that the address must be made in the holy tongue. As mentioned above, the following statements were made even in a *milchemet mitzvah.*
12. *Shema Yisrael* in Hebrew. With this expression, the priest implies that even if the Jews possessed only the merit of reciting the *Shema*, it would be sufficient to warrant victory (*ibid.*).
13. Use of the latter term reminds the soldiers that their adversaries will not show them mercy (*ibid.*).
14. The Torah mentions four commands because an army would generally employ four techniques to intimidate its foes: They raised a clamor with their shields, sounded trumpets, shouted, and had their horses neigh (*Sotah* 42b).
15. Implying that, in contrast to the gentiles who rely on physical strength, we rely on God's power.

Sefer HaMitzvot (*loc. cit.*) relates that the *meshuach milchamah* would add inspiring words of his own to further motivate the army.
16. The following statements are only made in a *milchemet hareshut.*
17. The deferments granted these individuals are discussed in Halachot 5-14 of this chapter.
18. Deuteronomy 20:5 says: "The officers shall then speak to the people and say: 'Is there a man?...'" *Sotah* 43a explains that the officer did not make these statements himself, but rather, repeated those made by the priest.
19. See Halachah 15.
20. As Deuteronomy 20:8 states: "The officers shall then continue speaking to the people: 'Is there a man?...'"
21. Deuteronomy 20:9 concludes the passage describing the mobilization of the army: "When the officers have finished speaking to the people, they shall appoint commanding officers at the head of the people."

Powerful officers with iron axes[22] in their hands are placed in the rear of each array of troops.[23] If a person wants to leave the battle, they have permission to chop off his legs,[24] for flight is the beginning of defeat.[25]

In which instances are the above-mentioned individuals sent away from the battlefront? In a *milchemet hareshut*.[26] By contrast, in a *milchemet mitzvah*, the entire [nation] must go out [to war], even a groom from his chamber, and a bride from her pavilion.[27]

5. Those who leave the battlefront include a person who builds: a house to dwell in,[28] a barn for his cattle, a woodshed, or a storage house. [A person who builds one of the latter is deferred] because those structures are also fit for dwelling.[29] Just as a person who builds [a home is deferred from military service;] so, too, one who buys [a home], receives one as a present, or inherits one should also return from the front.[30]

However, one who builds (a silo,)[31] a gatehouse,[32] an *excedra*,[33] a porch, or a house that is less than four cubits by four cubits,[34] and similarly, a person who steals a house[35] does not return [from the war.]

6. Just as a person who plants a vineyard [is deferred from military service];[36] so, too, one who plants five fruit trees, even though they are of five different species[37] [recieves a similar deferment].[38]

Sotah 44a mentions that high ranking officers were also placed at the rear of the camp to prevent flight.

22. The translation of *keshilin* as "axes" is taken from Psalms 74:6.

23. *Sotah* 44a relates that officers of this rank were also placed in the front lines of the troops to lift up all those who fall and encourage them to continue the battle. See *Kessef Mishneh*.

24. Hewing down this one individual will prevent panic from spreading throughout the troops.

25. *Sotah* 44b cites I Samuel 4:17: "And Israel fled before the Philistines and there was a great slaughter among the people" and (31:1): "The men of Israel fled before the Philistines and were felled as corpses" to illustrate this principle.

26. No deferments are granted. There are certain opinions which maintain that Levites and priests are exempted from military service based on the Rambam's statements in *Hilchot Shemitah* 13:12: "[The Levites] were separated from the manner of the world. Thus, they do not wage war as the rest of Israel."

However, most authorities explain that those statements only apply to the war to conquer *Eretz Yisrael* from the Canaanites. In other wars, the priests and Levites served in the army. They quote Halachah 8 of this chapter and Halachah 4 of the next as support of this view. I Chronicles 12:27 notes that 4,600 Levites were numbered among the troops who came to David at Hebron.

27. The phrase used by the Rambam is quoted from the Mishnah (*Sotah*, *ibid.*). It is borrowed from Joel 1:16) and employed in a different context.

The Radbaz questions the mention of women. What part do they have in a war? Furthermore, *Nazir* 59a explains that the prohibition (Deuteronomy 22:5) "No male article shall be on a woman," applies to wearing arms. Accordingly, he explains that the women would help in the preparation of food and perform other supportive functions, but would not take part in the actual fighting.

צְבָאוֹת בְּרֹאשׁ הָעָם, וּמַעֲמִידִין מֵאָחוֹר כָּל מַעֲרָכָה וּמַעֲרָכָה שׁוֹטְרִים חֲזָקִים וְעַזִּים, וְכַשִּׁילִין שֶׁל בַּרְזֶל בִּידֵיהֶם – הָרוֹצֶה לַחֲזֹר מִן הַמִּלְחָמָה, הָרְשׁוּת בְּיָדָן לַחְתֹּךְ אֶת שׁוֹקוֹ, שֶׁתְּחִלַּת נְפִילָה – נִיסָה. בַּמֶּה דְּבָרִים אֲמוּרִים שֶׁמַּחֲזִירִין אֲנָשִׁים אֵלּוּ מֵעוֹרְכֵי הַמִּלְחָמָה? בְּמִלְחֶמֶת הָרְשׁוּת, אֲבָל בְּמִלְחֶמֶת מִצְוָה, הַכֹּל יוֹצְאִין, וַאֲפִלּוּ חָתָן מֵחַדְרוֹ וְכַלָּה מֵחֻפָּתָהּ.

ה אֶחָד הַבּוֹנֶה בַּיִת לְשִׁיבְתוֹ, וְאֶחָד הַבּוֹנֶה בֵּית־הַבָּקָר, בֵּית־הָעֵצִים, בֵּית־הָאוֹצָרוֹת, הוֹאִיל וְרָאוּי לְדִירָה; וְאֶחָד הַבּוֹנֶה, וְאֶחָד הַלּוֹקֵחַ, וְאֶחָד שֶׁנִּתַּן לוֹ בְּמַתָּנָה אוֹ הַיּוֹרֵשׁ – הֲרֵי זֶה חוֹזֵר. אֲבָל הַבּוֹנֶה בֵּית־הַתֶּבֶן וּבֵית שַׁעַר אַכְסַדְרָה וּמִרְפֶּסֶת, אוֹ בַּיִת שֶׁאֵין בּוֹ אַרְבַּע אַמּוֹת עַל אַרְבַּע אַמּוֹת, אוֹ הַגּוֹזֵל בַּיִת – הֲרֵי זֶה אֵינוֹ חוֹזֵר.

ו אֶחָד הַנּוֹטֵעַ כֶּרֶם, וְאֶחָד הַנּוֹטֵעַ חֲמִשָּׁה אִילָנֵי מַאֲכָל, וַאֲפִלּוּ מֵחֲמֵשֶׁת מִינֵי מַאֲכָל. אֶחָד

28. As mentioned in Halachah 3, a person who builds a new home is deferred from military service. Deuteronomy 20:5 states: "Is there a man who has built a new house and has not begun to live in it? Let him go home, lest he die in the war and another man live in it."

By nature, a person who built a home, planted a vineyard, or consecrated a woman, thinks about these matters. In battle, he may be overcome by fear and worry that he will not benefit from his efforts. Hence, the Torah granted him a deferment in a *milchemet hareshut* (Ramban, Deuteronomy 20:4).

29. *Sotah* 43a explains that since the verse employs the verb "build," any building which is fit to dwell in causes its builder to be deferred.

30. *Sotah* (*ibid.*) relates that this concept is derived from the use of the word "man" in the above-mentioned verse. Had the verse stated: "Is there any among you who has built a new house?", the basic concept would have been understood. Adding the word "man" was used to infer these additions.

31. This term is placed in parentheses, because according to the standard printed text of *Sotah, loc. cit.*, mentions this as a structure for which a person receives a deferment. A Rabbinic source to the contrary has not been found. Hence, many have deemed it a printing error.

32. Rashi, *Sotah* (*ibid.*), explains that this refers to a watchman's booth outside a courtyard.

33. A room with four walls, but no roof. This structure was common in Greek and Roman architecture and was frequently, employed in *Eretz Yisrael* in Talmudic times.

34. A house of this size is not fit to dwell in. Similarly, the other structures mentioned in this clause are not fit to dwell in.

35. The verse states "and has not begun to live in it." The words "in it" imply that the house must be one's own (*Sotah*, *ibid.*).

36. As Deuteronomy 20:6 states: "Is there a man who has planted a vineyard and has not yet redeemed its first crop? Let him go home, lest he die in war and another man redeem it."

37. The word "planted" in the above verse includes plants of any species, not only a grapevine.

38. Rashi (*Sotah*, *ibid.*) maintains that the five trees must be planted in the manner depicted below. However, the *Tosefta* (*Sotah* 7:11) differs, allowing the trees to be

[This applies to] one who plants [a vineyard], one who extends,[39] one who grafts[40] - the extensions and graftings must be [significant enough] to obligate [the vine] in *orlah*[41] - one who buys, one who inherits, and one who received one as a present.[42] However, one who plants four fruit trees[43] or five trees that do not bear fruit[44] and similarly, one who steals a vineyard does not return [from the battlefront] because of it.[45] Also, when a vineyard [is planted] by two partners, neither may return [from the battlefront] because of it.[46]

7. Just as a man who consecrates a virgin[47] [is deferred from military service]; so, too, [a deferment is granted] to one who consecrates a widow[48] and similarly, to a man to whom a *yevamah*[49] becomes obligated. Even if there are five brothers and one of them dies, all should return [from the battlefont].[50]

If a man consecrates a wife on the condition that the *kiddushin* take effect retroactively from the day they were given after a year has passed and that time period is completed during a war, he should return [from the battlefield].[51]

8. A person who remarries his divorcee[52] and one who consecrates a woman whom he is forbidden to marry,[53] for example, a widow for a High Priest,[54] a divorcee or a woman who has undergone *chalitzah* for a common priest,[55] or a *mamzer*[56] or a *natinah*[57] to an Israelite, or an Israelitess to a *mamzer* or *natin*, should not return [from the battlefield].[58]

planted far apart, even in five different cities. The *Lechem Mishneh* presumes that the Rambam does not accept Rashi's view. Were he also to follow that opinion, it would have been necessary for him to elaborate. * * * * *

39. One of the ways of expanding a vineyard was to cut off a shoot of a vine and bury it in the ground until it grew roots and emerged as an independent plant.
40. Grafting an existing vine on the stem of another.
41. These techniques of expanding one's vineyard will only cause an individual to be deferred from army service if the resulting vines are considered as entirely new plants. Under those circumstances, they will be governed by the prohibitions of *orlah*. Hence, no benefit can be derived from their produce for the first three years of their new growth. This is necessary for the verse speaks about "redeeming one's vineyard," i.e., bringing the worth of the fruit to Jerusalem to be eaten there. *Hilchot Ma'aser Sheni* 10:14-18 discusses when a graft or a planting is considered an independent plant and when not.
42. As explained in the previous halachah, these means of acquisition can be implied from the use of the word "man" in the above-mentioned verse (*Sotah* 43b).
43. This is too small a number to be called a "vineyard."
44. Trees that do not bear fruit also cannot be called a vineyard.
45. The *Kessef Mishneh* states that there is no Talmudic source for this statement, but that it is inferred from the law regarding a stolen house in the previous halachah.
46. Neither of the partners conceives of the vineyard as his own. Hence, neither is deferred. See *Sotah* 43b, *Kessef Mishneh*, *Lechem Mishneh*.
47. Deuteronomy 20:17 states: "Is there a man who has consecrated a woman and not married her? Let him go home, lest he die in the war and another man marry her."

Similarly, Deuteronomy 24:5 relates: "When a man takes a new wife, he shall not enter military service."

According to Torah law, marriage is a two-staged process. In the first stage, referred to as *kiddushin*, a man consecrates a woman as his wife. From this time onward, she may

הַנּוֹטֵעַ, וְאֶחָד הַמַּבְרִיךְ וְאֶחָד הַמַּרְכִּיב הַבְרָכָה וְהַרְכָּבָה שֶׁהִיא חַיֶּבֶת בְּעָרְלָה. אֶחָד הַלּוֹקֵחַ, וְאֶחָד הַיּוֹרֵשׁ, וְאֶחָד שֶׁנִּתַּן לוֹ בְּמַתָּנָה. אֲבָל הַנּוֹטֵעַ אַרְבָּעָה אִילָנֵי מַאֲכָל, אוֹ חֲמִשָּׁה אִילָנֵי סְרָק, אוֹ שֶׁגָּזַל כֶּרֶם – אֵינוֹ חוֹזֵר עָלָיו. וְכֵן כֶּרֶם שֶׁל שְׁנֵי שֻׁתָּפִין, אֵין חוֹזְרִין עָלָיו.

ז אֶחָד הַמְאָרֵס אֶת הַבְּתוּלָה, וְאֶחָד הַמְאָרֵס אֶת הָאַלְמָנָה; וְכֵן אִם נָפְלָה לוֹ יְבָמָה, אֲפִלּוּ חֲמִשָּׁה אַחִים וּמֵת אַחַד מֵהֶם – כֻּלָּן חוֹזְרִין. קִדֵּשׁ אִשָּׁה מֵעַכְשָׁו וּלְאַחַר שְׁנֵים־עָשָׂר חֹדֶשׁ, וְשָׁלַם הַזְּמַן בַּמִּלְחָמָה – חוֹזֵר וּבָא לוֹ.

ח הַמַּחֲזִיר אֶת גְּרוּשָׁתוֹ, וְהַמְאָרֵס אִשָּׁה הָאֲסוּרָה עָלָיו, כְּגוֹן אַלְמָנָה לְכֹהֵן גָּדוֹל, גְּרוּשָׁה וַחֲלוּצָה לְכֹהֵן הֶדְיוֹט, מַמְזֶרֶת וּנְתִינָה לְיִשְׂרָאֵל, בַּת יִשְׂרָאֵל לְמַמְזֵר וּלְנָתִין – אֵינוֹ חוֹזֵר.

not marry another man without divorce. Sexual relations with other men are considered adultery and are punishable by death. Nevertheless, the bride and groom are not permitted to live as man and wife.

The second stage of marriage, *nissuin*, involves the consummation of the marriage and the beginning of the couple's life together.

48. Whether this is to be the first or second marriage for either of the parties involved, as long as the couple have never been married to each other, the woman is considered "a new wife" and a deferment is granted.

49. When a man dies without children, his widow is obligated to marry one of his brothers (*yibbum*) or be freed from that obligation through the *chalitzah* ceremony (see Deuteronomy 25:5-10). From the time of the deceased's passing, a halachic relationship exists between his brothers and his widow. Hence, they are deferred from military service.

50. For each of them has the potential to marry their brother's childless widow. Even if their brother is killed in the midst of the war, they are granted deferments.

51. A deferment is not granted to a man who consecrates a wife during wartime (Jerusalem Talmud, *Sotah* 8:6). Nevertheless, in these circumstances, the fact the *kiddushin* were given before the war began makes it clear that the groom did not use marriage as an excuse to free himself from military duty. Hence, the deferment is granted.

The commentaries question how King David went out to fight the Philistines after marrying Michal, daughter of King Saul (see I Samuel, Chapter 18). They explain that David had already been anointed as king by Samuel. Hence, his status differed from others and he was not bound by this mitzvah.

52. This circumstance is excluded by the Torah's use of the expression "a new wife" in Deuteronomy 24:5 (*Sotah* 44a).

53. *Sotah* (*ibid.*) explains that the Torah would not grant a deferment for a forbidden marriage.

54. Leviticus 21:14 mentions the prohibition against a High Priest marrying a widow.

55. The prohibition against a priest marrying a divorcee is mentioned in Leviticus 21:7. The Sages forbade a priest from marrying a woman who underwent *chalitzah* because the latter ritual resembles divorce (*Kiddushin* 78a, *Hilchot Issurei Bi'ah* 17:7).

56. The term *mamzer* refers to a child born from an adulterous or incestuous relationship. Deuteronomy 23:3 prohibits the marriage of a *mamzer* to a native born Israelite.

57. The term *natin* and *natinah* refer to male and female Gibeonites respectively. As

9. All those who return from the army camp, return when they hear the proclamation of the priest.[59] They must supply food and water to their brethren in the army and fix the roads [for them].[60]

10. The following should not go out to the army camp at all[61] and should not be bothered for any obligation whatsoever:[62] one who builds a house and dedicates it;[63] one who marries the woman he consecrated or his *yevamah*;[64] one who redeems his vineyard.[65] They are not conscripted until the completion of one year as [Deuteronomy 24:5] states: "He must remain free for his home for one year and rejoice with the bride he took."[66] The Oral Tradition teaches that the one-year deferment applies whether he purchased a house, married a woman, or began to benefit from the fruit of his vineyard.[67]

11. During this entire year, he is not obligated to supply [the troops] with food or water. He should not fix the roads, guard the walls or pay [the levy for] beams [for the gates] of the city,[68] as [*ibid.*] states: "He shall not enter military service or be assigned any duties."[69]

[The repetition of the prohibition teaches that] the transgression of two prohibitions are involved. [He is not obligated] to his city, nor to the army.[70]

12. If a person builds a house and rents it to others, in the event the tenants pay the rent[71] beforehand, it is considered as if he has already benefited from it.[72] If they do not pay him rent until after twelve months have passed, it is considered as if he has not yet derived benefit.[73]

mentioned above, the Gibeonites were a Canaanite nation who converted to Judaism. Despite their conversion, Joshua and later, David, forbade their marriage into the Jewish people (see *Hilchot Issurei Bi'ah* 12:22-23).

58. In all aspects excepting the prohibition against their marriage to a native-born Israelite, a *mamzer* and a *natin* are considered as Jews and hence, bound by all the Torah's mitzvot. Hence, they are also obligated to serve in the army and will not receive a deferment for a forbidden marriage. Nevertheless, although such individuals are required to serve, *Kiddushin* 76b relates that the soldiers of the House of David all had the highest pedigree of lineage. Anyone with blemished lineage was excused from service.

59. As described in Halachah 3.

60. These supportive functions are necessary for the army, yet do not involve the same danger as actual combat.

61. In contrast to the individuals previously mentioned who were required to present themselves at the army camp and perform supportive functions for the army.

62. See the following halachah. As mentioned in Halachah 4, these leniencies only apply to a *milchemet hareshut*. In contrast, in a *milchemet mitzvah*, "the entire [nation] must go out [to war], even a groom from his chamber, and a bride from her pavilion."

63. In contrast, to one who has built a home, but has not had the opportunity to dedicate it.

64. This refers to *nissuin*, the second stage of the marriage relationship, in contrast to *Kiddushin*.

65. In the first three years after a vineyard is planted, its produce is *orlah* and may not be eaten. In the fourth year, the produce is considered *neta revi'i* and must be eaten in Jerusalem. Alternatively, it may be redeemed and the money used to purchase food to be eaten in Jerusalem.

ט כָּל אֵלּוּ שֶׁחוֹזְרִין מֵעוֹרְכֵי הַמִּלְחָמָה כְּשֶׁשּׁוֹמְעִין אֶת דִּבְרֵי הַכֹּהֵן, חוֹזְרִין וּמְסַפְּקִין מַיִם וּמָזוֹן לַאֲחֵיהֶם שֶׁבַּצָּבָא, וּמְתַקְּנִין אֶת הַדְּרָכִים.

י וְאֵלּוּ שֶׁאֵין יוֹצְאִין לְעוֹרְכֵי הַמִּלְחָמָה כָּל עִקָּר, וְאֵין מַטְרִיחִין אוֹתָם לְשׁוּם דָּבָר בָּעוֹלָם: הַבּוֹנֶה בַּיִת וַחֲנָכוֹ, וְהַנּוֹשֵׂא אֲרוּסָתוֹ אוֹ שֶׁיִּבֵּם, וּמִי שֶׁחִלֵּל כַּרְמוֹ – אֵין יוֹצְאִין עַד תֹּם שָׁנָה, שֶׁנֶּאֱמַר: "נָקִי יִהְיֶה לְבֵיתוֹ שָׁנָה אֶחָת וְשִׂמַּח אֶת אִשְׁתּוֹ אֲשֶׁר לָקָח". מִפִּי הַקַּבָּלָה לָמְדוּ, שֶׁיִּהְיֶה נָקִי שָׁנָה, בֵּין לְבַיִת שֶׁקָּנָה, בֵּין לְאִשָּׁה שֶׁנָּשָׂא, בֵּין לְכֶרֶם שֶׁהִתְחִיל לֶאֱכֹל פִּרְיוֹ.

יא כָּל הַשָּׁנָה אֵין מְסַפֵּק מַיִם וּמָזוֹן, וְלֹא מְתַקֵּן דֶּרֶךְ, וְלֹא שׁוֹמֵר בַּחוֹמָה, וְלֹא נוֹתֵן לְפַסֵּי הָעִיר, וְלֹא יַעֲבֹר עָלָיו שׁוּם דָּבָר בָּעוֹלָם, שֶׁנֶּאֱמַר: "לֹא יֵצֵא בַצָּבָא וְלֹא יַעֲבֹר עָלָיו לְכָל דָּבָר" – לַעֲבֹר בִּשְׁנֵי לָאוִין, לֹא לְצָרְכֵי הָעִיר וְלֹא לְצָרְכֵי הַגְּדוּד.

יב בָּנָה בַּיִת וְהִשְׂכִּירוֹ לַאֲחֵרִים וְהִקְדִּים לוֹ שְׂכָרוֹ – הֲרֵי זֶה כְּמִי שֶׁחֲנָכוֹ. נָתַן לוֹ שְׂכָרוֹ לְאַחַר שְׁנֵים־עָשָׂר חֹדֶשׁ – הֲרֵי הוּא כְּמִי שֶׁלֹּא חֲנָכוֹ עַד עַתָּה.

66. The *Sefer HaMitzvot* (positive commandment 214) and the *Sefer HaChinuch* (mitzvah 582) count the obligation to remain free of all duties as one of the 613 mitzvot of the Torah.

The *Sefer HaChinuch* explains that this mitzvah was instituted to develop love and harmony between a man and his wife. Every two individuals possess different natures and tendencies. To overcome these differences, the Torah commands that a man and wife spend their first year together in close company, each one adopting his behavior to the other's habits and nuances. In this manner, they will become familiar with each other and their love will grow.

67. *Sotah* 43a explains that though the verse only mentions a bride and groom explicitly, the acquisition of a house and the first benefits derived from a vineyard can also be inferred.

68. The Ramban (Deuteronomy 24:5) maintains that this prohibition is incumbent on the representatives of the community or the army. They are forbidden from conscripting a groom for any services. Rabbi Eliyahu Mizrachi differs, explaining that the prohibition against leaving home is incumbent on the groom himself. This appears to be the Rambam's perspective (*Lechem Mishneh*).

69. *Sefer HaMitzvot* (negative commandment 311) and the *Sefer HaChinuch* (mitzvah 581) count this prohibition as one of the Torah's 613 mitzvot.

70. This clause is quoted from *Sotah* 44a. In *Sefer HaMitzvot*, the Rambam explains that though the Talmud mentions two prohibitions, that that expression is used for greater emphasis without necessarily implying that the two should be counted as two separate mitzvot. The Ramban disagrees and maintains that the above principle only applies when the two prohibitions are directed at the same individual. In this case, one prohibition is incumbent upon the army, and one on the community. Hence, they should be counted as two separate mitzvot.

71. For the entire year

72. And no deferment is granted.

73. Thus, he is still eligible for a deferment. Furthermore, even if twelve months have

13. [The following rules apply when a man] built a house, placed his belongings inside, and locked them [within]: If he has to spend time guarding them,[74] it is considered as if he derived benefit [from the home] and began dwelling there.[75] If he does not have to sit and guard them, he is considered as one who has derived no benefit [from his home] as of yet.[76]

14. Anyone who builds a house or plants a vineyard in the Diaspora should not return [from the battlefront] because of them.[77]

15. "Is there a man who is afraid or faint-hearted" (Deuteronomy 20:8)? [To whom does this phrase refer?[78] The phrase should be interpreted] simply, as applying to a person whose heart is not brave enough to stand in the throes of battle.[79]

Once [a soldier] enters the throes of battle, he should rely on the Hope of Israel and their Savior in times of need.[80] He should realize that he is fighting for the sake of the oneness of God's Name. Therefore, he should place his soul in his hand[81] and not show fright or fear.

He should not worry about his wife or children. On the contrary, he should wipe their memory from his heart, removing all thoughts from his mind except the war.[82]

Anyone who begins to feel anxious and worry in the [midst of] battle [to the point where he] frightens himself violates a negative commandment, as it is written (Deuteronomy 20:3): "Do not be faint-hearted. Do not be afraid. Do not panic and do not break ranks before them."[83]

Furthermore, he is responsible for the blood of the entire Jewish nation. If he is not valiant, if he does not wage war with all his heart and soul, it is considered as if he shed the blood of the entire people,[84] as [*ibid.* 20:8] states: "[Let him go home,] lest he demoralize the hearts of his brethren like his own." Similarly, the prophetic tradition explicitly states: "Cursed be he who does God's work deceitfully. Cursed be he who withholds his sword from blood." [Jeremiah 48:10].

[In contrast,] anyone who fights with his entire heart, without fear, with the intention of sanctifying God's name alone, can be assured that he will find no

passed, but the tenants have not paid their rent, the owner may still be deferred (*Lechem Mishneh*).

74. Or hires someone else for this purpose.

75. Hence, his one-year deferment begins at that time.

76. Hence he is deferred from military service accordingly.

77. A deferment is granted only for a building or planting that is a mitzvah. In *Eretz Yisrael*, these activities are intrinsic to the mitzvah of settling *Eretz Yisrael*. In the Diaspora, they are not associated with any mitzvah (Jerusalem Talmud, *Sotah* 8:4).

The commentaries question the Rambam's inclusion of this halachah. As explained in the commentary to Halachah 5:9, in contrast to the Ramban, the Rambam does not count the settlement of *Eretz Yisrael* as one of the 613 mitzvot of the Torah.

They explain that though he does not count the settlement of the land as an independent mitzvah, it is an integral part of the fulfillment of other mitzvot (see *Sefer HaMitzvot,*

יג בָּנָה בַּיִת וְנָתַן בּוֹ חֲפָצָיו וְנָעַל עֲלֵיהֶם: אִם הָיָה צָרִיךְ לְבַטֵּל עַל שְׁמִירָתָן, הֲרֵי זֶה כְּמִי שֶׁחֲנָכוֹ וְהִתְחִיל לֵישֵׁב בּוֹ; וְאִם אֵינָן צְרִיכִין לֵישֵׁב וּלְשׁוֹמְרָן, הֲרֵי זֶה כְּמִי שֶׁלֹּא חֲנָכוֹ.

יד וְכָל הַבּוֹנֶה בַּיִת אוֹ נוֹטֵעַ כֶּרֶם בְּחוּצָה לָאָרֶץ – אֵינוֹ חוֹזֵר עֲלֵיהֶן.

טו "מִי הָאִישׁ הַיָּרֵא וְרַךְ הַלֵּבָב" – כְּמַשְׁמָעוֹ, שֶׁאֵין בְּלִבּוֹ כֹּחַ לַעֲמֹד בְּקִשְׁרֵי הַמִּלְחָמָה. וּמֵאַחַר שֶׁיִּכָּנֵס בְּקִשְׁרֵי הַמִּלְחָמָה, יִשָּׁעֵן עַל מִקְוֵה יִשְׂרָאֵל וּמוֹשִׁיעוֹ בְּעֵת צָרָה, וְיֵדַע שֶׁעַל יִחוּד הַשֵּׁם הוּא עוֹשֶׂה מִלְחָמָה, וְיָשִׂים נַפְשׁוֹ בְּכַפּוֹ וְלֹא יִירָא וְלֹא יִפְחַד, וְלֹא יַחְשֹׁב לֹא בְּאִשְׁתּוֹ וְלֹא בְּבָנָיו, אֶלָּא יִמְחֶה זִכְרוֹנָם מִלִּבּוֹ וְיִפָּנֶה מִכָּל דָּבָר לַמִּלְחָמָה. וְכָל הַמַּתְחִיל לַחְשֹׁב וּלְהַרְהֵר בַּמִּלְחָמָה וּמַבְהִיל עַצְמוֹ – עוֹבֵר בְּלֹא־תַעֲשֶׂה, שֶׁנֶּאֱמַר: "אַל יֵרַךְ לְבַבְכֶם אַל תִּירְאוּ וְאַל תַּחְפְּזוּ וְאַל תַּעַרְצוּ מִפְּנֵיהֶם". וְלֹא עוֹד, אֶלָּא שֶׁכָּל דְּמֵי יִשְׂרָאֵל תְּלוּיִין בְּצַוָּארוֹ. וְאִם לֹא נִצַּח וְלֹא עָשָׂה מִלְחָמָה בְּכָל לִבּוֹ וּבְכָל נַפְשׁוֹ, הֲרֵי זֶה כְּמִי שֶׁשָּׁפַךְ דְּמֵי הַכֹּל, שֶׁנֶּאֱמַר: "וְלֹא יִמַּס אֶת לְבַב אֶחָיו כִּלְבָבוֹ". וַהֲרֵי מְפֹרָשׁ בַּקַּבָּלָה: "אָרוּר עֹשֶׂ מְלֶאכֶת ה׳ רְמִיָּה, וְאָרוּר מֹנֵעַ חַרְבּוֹ מִדָּם". וְכָל הַנִּלְחָם בְּכָל לִבּוֹ בְּלֹא פַחַד, וְתִהְיֶה כַּוָּנָתוֹ לְקַדֵּשׁ אֶת הַשֵּׁם בִּלְבָד – מֻבְטָח לוֹ שֶׁלֹּא יִמְצָא נֶזֶק וְלֹא תַגִּיעֵהוּ רָעָה,

positive commandment 153). Hence, there is an element of mitzvah involved in building a home there.

78. *Sotah* 44a cites two interpretations of this phrase: Rabbi Akiva's, as quoted by the Rambam and Rabbi Yossi's, who defines it as referring to a person who is afraid of battle lest he suffer harm as retribution for his sins. The *Sifri* quotes a different opinion for Rabbi Yossi, explaining that the verse refers to a man over the age of forty whose strength has already begun to wane.

79. Such a person is excused from serving in the army, as the verse continues: "Let him go home lest he demoralize the hearts of his brethren as his own." *Sotah* 44a explains that all the deferments mentioned above are granted so that many will leave the battlefront and thus, a faint-hearted person will not be embarrassed to depart.

A cowardly person should not try to muster false courage. The *Tosefta* (*Sotah* 7:14) states that anyone who is entitled to a deferment and does not leave the battlefront will ultimately die in the war and cause many of his brethren to fall with him.

80. *Sotah* 42a states: Our foes rely on the power of flesh and blood and we rely on the power of God.

81. I.e., be willing even to encounter danger. The phrase is borrowed from Judges 12:3.

82. Lest his preoccupation with them prevent him from fighting with all his heart. *Vayikra Rabbah* 25:2 states: "Whoever goes out to war and does not concentrate his thoughts on the battle will be killed."

83. *Sefer HaMitzvot* (negative commandment 58) and *Sefer HaChinuch* (mitzvah 525) count this prohibition as one of the Torah's 613 mitzvot. The Ramban and the Ra'avad differ, explaining that the Torah's words should be interpreted as assurances of success and not as commands.

84. The failure of one soldier to fight valiantly can endanger the entire people: Firstly, often the defense of a strategic position depends on a single individual. Furthermore, panic and fear spread easily. The cowardice of one person can engender fear in the hearts of all his colleagues.

harm, nor will bad overtake him.[85] He will be granted a proper family in Israel and [gather] merit for himself and his children forever. He will also merit [eternal] life in the world to come as [I Samuel 25:28-29] states:[86] "God will certainly make my lord a faithful house, for my lord fights the wars of God and evil will not be found with you... and my lord's soul will be bound in a bond of life with God."[87]

CHAPTER EIGHT

1. When the army's troops enter the territory of gentiles,[1] conquering them and taking them captive, they are permitted to eat meat from animals that died without being ritually slaughtered or which were *trefe*,[2] and the flesh of pigs and similar animals, if they become hungry and can only find these forbidden foods.[3]

Similarly, they may drink wine used in the worship of idols.[4] [This license is derived] by the Oral Tradition[5] [which interprets Deuteronomy 6:10-11: "God... will give you...] houses filled with all the good things" as "pigs' necks and the like."[6]

2. Similarly, [a soldier] may engage in sexual relations with a woman[7] while she is still a gentile[8] if his natural inclination overcomes him.[9] However, he

85. The Bible mentions many instances of wars in which the Jews were granted miraculous success. In the war against Midian, not one man was slain (Numbers 31:49). Similarly, in Joshua's wars to conquer *Eretz Yisrael*, the Jews suffered minimal, if any, casualties.
86. These assurances were given King David by Avigail. At the same time, she also foresaw that he would be appointed king over Israel.
87. In *Hilchot Teshuvah* 8:3, the Rambam describes the world to come: "Since there will be no death associated with this life... it is called 'the bond of life'.... This is the reward which no other reward can surpass. It is the ultimate good."

1. Some texts substitute idolaters for the latter term.
These leniencies are only permitted when the army enters enemy territory. Though certain Rabbinic obligations are relaxed within *Eretz Yisrael* (See Chapter 6, Halachah 13), all Scriptural prohibitions must be observed.
2. Implied by that term is an animal which possesses a blemish, wound, or ailment that will cause it to die within twelve months (*Chullin* 3:1).
3. The soldiers are only allowed forbidden foods if they have no alternative. However, they need not be on the point of starvation. This leniency was granted for were they required to forage for kosher food, they would place themselves in danger of enemy attack (Radbaz).
4. *Yayin Nesech* in Hebrew. The prohibition against drinking *Yayin Nesech* is included as one of the Torah's 613 mitzvot. In addition, the Sages forbade drinking all wine touched by a gentile. See *Hilchot Ma'achalot Assurot*, Chapter 11.
The Ramban (Deuteronomy 6:10) objects to this ruling, maintaining that license was only granted in regard to the Rabbinic prohibition. However, *Yayin Nesech* itself is forbidden even during wartime. Other commentaries support his argument noting that idol

וְיִבְנֶה לוֹ בַּיִת נָכוֹן בְּיִשְׂרָאֵל, וְיִזְכֶּה לוֹ וּלְבָנָיו עַד עוֹלָם, וְיִזְכֶּה לְחַיֵּי הָעוֹלָם הַבָּא, שֶׁנֶּאֱמַר: "כִּי עָשֹׂה יַעֲשֶׂה ה' לַאדֹנִי בַּיִת נֶאֱמָן, כִּי מִלְחֲמוֹת ה' אֲדֹנִי נִלְחָם וְרָעָה לֹא תִמָּצֵא בְךָ וְגוֹ'. וְהָיְתָה נֶפֶשׁ אֲדֹנִי צְרוּרָה בִּצְרוֹר הַחַיִּים אֵת ה' אֱלֹהֶיךָ".

פֶּרֶק שְׁמִינִי

א חֲלוּצֵי צָבָא, כְּשֶׁיִּכָּנְסוּ בִּגְבוּל הָעַכּוּ"ם וְיִכְבְּשׁוּם וְיִשְׁבּוּ מֵהֶן – מֻתָּר לָהֶן לֶאֱכֹל נְבֵלוֹת וּטְרֵפוֹת וּבְשַׂר־חֲזִיר וְכַיּוֹצֵא בוֹ, אִם יִרְעַב וְלֹא מָצָא מַה יֹּאכַל אֶלָּא מַאֲכָלוֹת אֵלּוּ הָאֲסוּרִים. וְכֵן שׁוֹתֶה יֵין־נֶסֶךְ. מִפִּי הַשְּׁמוּעָה לָמְדוּ: "וּבָתִּים מְלֵאִים כָּל טוּב" – עָרְפֵּי חֲזִירִים וְכַיּוֹצֵא בָהֶן.

ב וְכֵן בּוֹעֵל אִשָּׁה בְּגֵיוּתָהּ אִם תְּקָפוֹ יִצְרוֹ; אֲבָל לֹא יִבְעָלֶנָּה וְיֵלֵךְ לוֹ, אֶלָּא מַכְנִיסָהּ לְתוֹךְ

worship and anything associated with it is included among the three sins for which a person should sacrifice his life rather than transgress.

However, other authorities defend the Rambam's decision, noting that licentious sexual behavior is also one of these three sins for which for which a person should sacrifice his life and, as stated in the following halachah, soldiers are allowed relations with gentile women in wartime (*Or Sameach*).

5. See *Chullin* 17a .

6. The Ramban (*loc. cit.*) questions the Rambam's statements, noting that this verse refers to the occupation of *Eretz Yisrael* during the time of Joshua. During the entire fourteen years when *Eretz Yisrael* was settled, there was no obligation to keep any of the dietary laws even outside of a battle situation. If so, how can this license be extended to the circumstances at hand?

However, the Rambam's logic can be explained as follows: Since we see that the Torah relaxed the dietary laws entirely during the conquest of *Eretz Yisrael*, we can assume that temporary license would be granted in other conquests (Radbaz).

7. Deuteronomy 21:10-11 states:

> When you go out to war against your enemies, God will give them over to your hand, and you may take captives. If you see a beautiful woman among the prisoners and desire her, you may take her as a wife.

The Torah permits this relationship only as a concession to man's natural desires. Were the Torah to unequivocally forbid intimacy with captive women, the prohibition would probably be ignored. Hence, certain strictures are instituted so that soldiers could release their natural desires without leading to total licentiousness and a breakdown of Jewish morality and family life (*Kiddushin* 21b).

8. There are other authorities who forbid all intimacy during wartime. Relations are not permitted until the woman is brought home and undergoes the mourning procedures mentioned below. This is still a "concession" to man's natural tendencies for the soldier realizes that ultimately, he will be able to consummate his desires (Ramban, Deuteronomy, *ibid.*; Rashi commenting on *Kiddushin* 21a; Jerusalem Talmud, *Makkot* 2:6).

9. *Sefer HaMitzvot* (positive commandment 221) and *Sefer HaChinuch* (mitzvah 532)

may not engage in sexual relations with her and then, go on his way.[10] Rather, he must bring her into his home as [Deuteronomy 21:11] states "If you see a beautiful woman among the prisoners...[You shall bring her into the midst of your home...]"[11]

It is forbidden [for him] to engage in sexual relations with her a second time until he marries her.[12]

3. [Relations with] a *yefat toar* are only permitted while she is in captivity as [the verse] states " If you see... among the prisoners."[13]

[This license is permitted] whether the woman is a virgin or not, even if she is married,[14] for the gentiles' marriages are not recognized.[15]

[A number of laws are derived from the exegesis of the verse from Deuteronomy quoted above:]

"And you desire" - even though she is not beautiful.[16]

"Her" - and not another. He may not engage in sexual relations with two [women].

"You may take her as a wife" - He may not take two [women as captives with the intention of] engaging in relations with one and saving the other for his father or brother.[17]

What is the source which teaches that he may not pressure her in the midst of the war? [Deuteronomy 21:12] states: "You shall bring her into the midst of your home...." Thus, he must bring her into an (vacant)[18] place and then, engage in relations with her.[19]

4. A priest is [also] allowed relations with a *yefat toar* initially. For the Torah [only permitted relations as a concession] to [man's] natural inclination.[20] However, he is not permitted to marry her afterwards, for she is a convert.[21]

include the laws associated with relations with a captive woman, *yefat toar* in Hebrew, as one of the 613 mitzvot of the Torah.

However, though taking a *yefat toar* was permitted, the Sages looked askance at this practice. They cite the example of King David who took Ma'akah, the daughter of Talmai, King of Geshur as a captive wife. Concerning their marriage, *Midrash Tanchuma* comments:

> See what came out of their union! Avshalom, who desired to kill his father..., was born. A controversy broke out in Israel and myriads were killed, including the wisest men of the land....

10. Judaism views sexuality and responsibility as fundamentally interrelated. Were a soldier permitted to engage in sexual relations with a woman and then, abandon her without any further ties, he would begin to view sexuality as cheap and commonplace. Hence, the Torah instituted the practices described in the following halachot (Guide to the Perplexed, Vol. III, Chapter 41).

11. The *Minchat Chinuch* asks why the Rambam makes a blanket statement that the soldier is required to bring a *yefat toar* into his home. As mentioned in Halachah 5, the Sages did not approve of marriage to a *yefat toar* and were pleased when her captor did not desire her and set her free. Hence, ideally, it would seem preferable for the soldier to

בֵּיתוֹ, שֶׁנֶּאֱמַר: "וְרָאִיתָ בַּשִּׁבְיָה אֵשֶׁת יְפַת־תֹּאַר". וְאָסוּר לִבְעֹל אוֹתָהּ בִּיאָה שְׁנִיָּה עַד שֶׁיִּשָּׂאֶנָּה.

ג אֵין אִשָּׁה יְפַת־תֹּאַר מֻתֶּרֶת אֶלָּא בִּשְׁעַת הַשִּׁבְיָה, שֶׁנֶּאֱמַר: "וְרָאִיתָ בַּשִּׁבְיָה". בֵּין בְּתוּלָה, בֵּין בְּעוּלָה, בֵּין אֵשֶׁת־אִישׁ; שֶׁאֵין אִישׁוּת לְעַכּוּ"ם. "וְחָשַׁקְתָּ" – אַף־עַל־פִּי שֶׁאֵינָהּ יָפָה. "בָּהּ" – וְלֹא בַחֲבֶרְתָּהּ, שֶׁלֹּא יִבְעֹל שְׁתַּיִם. "וְלָקַחְתָּ לְךָ לְאִשָּׁה" – שֶׁלֹּא יִקַּח שְׁתַּיִם וְיִבְעֹל אַחַת, וְיַנִּיחַ אַחַת לְאָבִיו אוֹ לְאָחִיו. וּמִנַּיִן שֶׁלֹּא יִלְחָצֶנָּה בַּמִּלְחָמָה? שֶׁנֶּאֱמַר: "וַהֲבֵאתָהּ אֶל תּוֹךְ בֵּיתֶךָ" – יַכְנִיסָהּ לְמָקוֹם וְאַחַר־כָּךְ יִבְעוֹל.

ד הַכֹּהֵן מֻתָּר בִּיפַת־תֹּאַר בְּבִיאָה רִאשׁוֹנָה, שֶׁלֹּא דִבְּרָה תּוֹרָה אֶלָּא כְּנֶגֶד הַיֵּצֶר; אֲבָל אֵינוֹ יָכוֹל לְשָׂאֶנָּה אַחַר־כָּךְ, מִפְּנֵי שֶׁהִיא גִּיֹּרֶת.

lose his desire for the woman immediately, free her at that time, and never bring her home.

Possibly, the Rambam's statements can be understood on the basis of the Meiri's commentary, *Kiddushin* 21a. The Meiri writes that relations with a *yefat toar* are only permitted when the soldier intends to marry her. If he does not have that intention, all relations, even a single experience, are forbidden. (Note, however, Halachah 4 which states that a priest is permitted to engage in relations with a *yefat toar* even though he is not permitted to marry her.)

12. See Halachah 6.

13. Once a captive woman has been enslaved as a servant, intimacy with her is forbidden (*Kiddushin* 21a).

14. The word *eishet* used in the above verse can be rendered both as "woman" or "wife of." On that basis, *Kiddushin* (*ibid.*) derives this law.

15. *Sanhderin* 52b teaches that a Jew is not liable for transgression of the prohibition against adultery if he has relations with a gentile's wife. However, though a Jew is absolved for punishment for such an act, a gentile is liable. One of the seven mitzvot which the gentiles are obligated to fulfill is the prohibition against adultery. See Halachot 1 and 5 of the following chapter.

16. Though the verse mentions "a beautiful women," by using the word "desire," it implies that the attractiveness of the woman is not the determinant factor. As long as the man desires her, these laws apply (*Kiddushin*, *ibid.*)

17. He may not take even one woman for the sake of another person and not for himself (*Tosafot*, *Kiddushin* 22a).

18. This word is lacking in the printed texts of the Rambam and was added on the basis of manuscripts brought from Yemen.

19. The *Kessef Mishneh* writes that the soldier must take his captive to a city to have relations with her. Other commentaries offer different interpretations. However, all share the same basic theme. Sexual relations must be carried out in a private place without the knowledge of the other soldiers.

20. A priest also has natural desires. Were a captive woman forbidden him, he might be overcome by his instincts and violate the prohibition (*Kiddushin* 21b).

21. As mentioned in *Hilchot Issurei Bi'ah* 18:3, a priest may not marry a convert.

5. What is the procedure which a Jew must follow regarding a *yefat toar* after he had relations with her once while she is still a gentile? If she desires to enter under the wings of the *Shechinah*,[22] he may have her immersed [in a *mikveh*][23] for the purpose of conversion immediately.[24]

If she does not accept [the Jewish faith], she should dwell in his house for thirty days, as [*ibid.* 21:13] states: "She shall mourn her father and mother for thirty days." [25] Similarly, she should mourn [the abandonment of] her faith.[26] [Her captor] should not prevent her [from crying.][27]

She must let her nails grow and shave her head so that she will not appear attractive to him.[28] She must be together with him at home.[29] Thus, when he enters, he sees her; when he leaves; he sees her, so that he becomes disgusted with her.[30]

He must be patient with her so that she will accept [the Jewish faith]. If she accepts [Judaism] and he desires her,[31] she may convert and immerse herself [in the *mikveh* for that purpose,] like other converts.[32]

6. [A captor] must wait three months [before marrying his captive]: the month of mourning and two months following it.[33]

When he marries her, [he must give her] *kiddushin* and a *ketubah*.[34] If he does not desire her, he must set her free.[35] If he sells her, he violates a negative commandment,[36] as [Deuteronomy 21:14] states: "You may not sell

22. The latter phrase is a euphemism for conversion based on Boaz's blessing to Ruth 1:12: "May a full reward be granted you by God, Lord of Israel, under whose wings you have taken shelter."

Like other converts, before conversion, she must accept all the obligations of Torah and mitzvot.

23. For a woman, the conversion process involves, immersion in a *mikveh* and acceptance of the mitzvot (*Hilchot Issurei Bi'ah* 14:5-6).

24. The mourning practices described below are only necessary if the woman hesitates to adopt Torah and mitzvot. If she willingly desires to convert, none of these rites are required (*Yevamot* 47b).

25. On a number of occasions, e.g., Numbers 20:29, Deuteronomy 34:8, the Torah mentions one month as a complete period of mourning. A similar concept is expressed in Jewish law, see *Hilchot Evel* 6:1-2.

This mourning period was instituted to affect both the man and the woman: The man was intended to continually confront this woman while she was mourning. Seeing her in this state, he would lose his original desire (*Sifri,* Rashi).

From the woman's perspective, this period was an act of mercy, granting her an opportunity to release the grief and sorrow she felt about her forced abduction from her native country and her ruptured family ties. It also represented a purification process, during which the woman was cleansed of the idolatrous practices of her native land (Guide to the Perplexed, Vol. III, Chapter 41).

26. *Yevamot* 48b relates that Rabbi Akiva interprets the terms "father" and "mother" as euphemisms for idol worship. Similarly, Jeremiah 2:27 chides the people for "saying to a stock of wood: 'You are my father;' and to a stone: 'You brought me forth.'"

27. Rather, he should treat her with mercy and kindness.

ה וְכֵיצַד דִּין יִשְׂרָאֵל בִּיפַת־תֹּאַר? אַחֲרֵי שֶׁיִּבְעָלֶנָּה בִּיאָה רִאשׁוֹנָה וְהִיא בְּגִיּוּתָהּ: אִם קִבְּלָה עָלֶיהָ לְהִכָּנֵס תַּחַת כַּנְפֵי הַשְּׁכִינָה – מַטְבִּילָהּ לְשֵׁם גֵּרוּת מִיָּד; וְאִם לֹא קִבְּלָה – תֵּשֵׁב בְּבֵיתוֹ שְׁלֹשִׁים יוֹם, שֶׁנֶּאֱמַר: "וּבָכְתָה אֶת אָבִיהָ וְאֶת אִמָּהּ יֶרַח יָמִים", וְכֵן בּוֹכָה עַל דָּתָהּ וְאֵינוֹ מוֹנְעָהּ, וּמְגַדֶּלֶת אֶת צִפָּרְנֶיהָ וּמְגַלַּחַת אֶת רֹאשָׁהּ כְּדֵי שֶׁתִּתְגַּנֶּה בְּעֵינָיו. וְתִהְיֶה עִמּוֹ בַּבַּיִת. נִכְנָס וְרוֹאֶה אוֹתָהּ, יוֹצֵא וְרוֹאֶה אוֹתָהּ, כְּדֵי שֶׁיָּקוּץ בָּהּ, וּמְגַלְגֵּל עִמָּהּ כְּדֵי שֶׁתְּקַבֵּל – אִם קִבְּלָה וְרָצָה בָהּ, הֲרֵי זוֹ מִתְגַּיֶּרֶת וְטוֹבֶלֶת כְּכָל הַגֵּרִים.

ו וּצְרִיכָה לְהַמְתִּין שְׁלֹשָׁה חֳדָשִׁים: חֹדֶשׁ שֶׁל בְּכִיָּה, וּשְׁנֵי חֳדָשִׁים אַחֲרָיו. וְנוֹשְׂאָהּ בִּכְתֻבָּה וְקִדּוּשִׁין. וְאִם לֹא חָפֵץ בָּהּ – מְשַׁלְּחָהּ לְנַפְשָׁהּ. וְאִם מְכָרָהּ – עוֹבֵר

28. She was required to shave her head to diminish her beauty. This practice also served as a sign of purification and acceptance of a new status (Chizzkuni). Compare to Leviticus 14:8 which describes the initiation of the Levites, and to Numbers 8:7, which describes the purification of a Nazirite.
29. The soldier is required to bring his captive to his own home. He is not permitted to find her another dwelling in which to undergo these procedures.
30. And set her free, rather than marry her.
31. Yemenite manuscripts of the *Mishneh Torah* substitute "and she desires him" for the latter phrase. The change answers a significant question: Can the woman's captor marry her against her will or must she desire him?

The Ramban and other commentaries accept the principle that the woman's consent is not required for the marriage. Certain opinions maintain that though the Rambam differs regarding forced conversion (see below), he accepts this opinion regarding marriage. However, based on those manuscripts, it appears that after conversion, the *yefat toar* is considered as any other Jewess and cannot be married against her will.
32. The Rambam requires the captive woman to willingly accept Judaism. In contrast, the Ramban maintains that she may be converted and married against her will.
33. This three month waiting period is not instituted because of the particular circumstances associated with a *yefat toar*, but rather, is a condition imposed on every woman who converts to Judaism.

It would take three months for a woman to realize whether she was pregnant. Thus, the Sages instituted this waiting period in order to determine the pedigree of lineage of any children born to female converts. *Hilchot Gerushin* 11:21 relates that even if a gentile couple convert together, they are forced to separate for three months to differentiate between children conceived before their entry into Judaism and those conceived afterwards.

Similarly, in this instance, the captive woman must wait three months to determine when a child born to her was conceived. As mentioned in Halachah 8, even if she conceived from the original relations permitted her and her captor, that child is not considered his and hence, also has the status of a convert.
34. See Chapter 4, Halachah 4, for a definition of these terms. After her conversion, the *yefat toar*is granted all the rights possessed by any other Jewish woman.
35. In this instance as well, she is granted all the rights of any other female convert.
36. The *Sefer HaMitzvot* (negative commandment 263) and the *Sefer HaChinuch* (mitzvah 533) include this prohibition as one of the Torah's 613 mitzvot. In the Guide to

her for money."[37] Should [a captor] sell [his captive], the sale is invalidated and he must return the money.[38]

Similarly, if after having relations with her, he forces her to become a servant, he violates a negative commandment[39] from the time he makes use of her as [*ibid.*] states: *lo titamar boh.* [That phrase means] "he should not make use of her."[40]

7. Her captor must be patient with her for twelve months if she refuses to convert.[41]

If she [still] refuses [after this interval has passed], she must agree to accept the seven universal laws commanded to Noah's descendants[42] and then, she is set free. Her status is the same as all other resident aliens.[43]

[Her captor] may not marry her, for it is forbidden to marry a woman who has not converted.[44]

8. If she conceives after the initial relations [with her captor], the child has the status of a convert.[45] In no regard is he considered as [the captor's] son,[46] for his mother is a gentile. Rather, the court immerses him [in the *mikveh*] and takes responsibility for him.[47]

Tamar was [conceived] from [King David's] initial relations with a *yefat toar*,[48] but Avshalom was conceived after marriage.[49] Thus, Tamar was [only] Avshalom's maternal sister[50] and thus, would have been permitted to

the Perplexed (*ibid.*), the Rambam writes that this prohibition applies from the time the captor engages in relations with his captive (see below).

37. The *Sifri* explains that in addition to the explicit prohibitions against sale of the captive woman, she may also not be bartered, exchanged, or given to another Jew as a servant.

38. *Tamurah* 4b relates that any business transaction that violates a Torah prohibition is automatically nullified.

39. The *Sefer HaMitzvot* (negative commandment 264) and the *Sefer HaChinuch* (mitzvah 534) also include this prohibition as one of the Torah's 613 mitzvot.

In this instance as well, the prohibition begins from the time of relations, as implied by the verse (*ibid.*): "You may not sell her for money or keep her as a servant after taking advantage of her."

40. The *Sifri* notes that the root *amar* is Persian for servant and is rarely used in Hebrew.

41. A similar interval is granted to a Canaanite servant to decide whether he is willing to become circumcised and accept the mitzvot in which he is obligated (*Hilchot Milah* 1:6).

During this entire period, the captor may neither engage in sexual relations with her or use her as a servant.

42. See Halachot 10 and 11 of this chapter and Chapters 10 and 11 for an explanation of those laws.

43. The latter term is a translation of the Hebrew, *ger toshav*. As explained in Halachah 10, it refers to a gentile who accepts upon himself the observance of the seven mitzvot. The term is appropriate for such a gentile is entitled to settle in *Eretz Yisrael*. For when the Jews have undisputed rule over the land, they are forbidden to allow a gentile who has not accepted the seven mitzvot to dwell there for one moment. See *Hilchot Avodat Kochavim* 10:6, *Hilchot Issurei Bi'ah* 14:7.

בְּלֹא־תַעֲשֶׂה, שֶׁנֶּאֱמַר: "וּמָכֹר לֹא תִמְכְּרֶנָּה בַּכָּסֶף". וְאִם מְכָרָהּ – אֵינָהּ מְכוּרָה, וּמַחֲזִיר הַדָּמִים. וְכֵן אִם כְּבָשָׁהּ אַחַר שֶׁנִּבְעֲלָה, לְשֵׁם שִׁפְחָה – מִשֶּׁיִּשְׁתַּמֵּשׁ בָּהּ, עוֹבֵר בְּלֹא־תַעֲשֶׂה, שֶׁנֶּאֱמַר: "לֹא תִתְעַמֵּר בָּהּ", שֶׁלֹּא יִשְׁתַּמֵּשׁ בָּהּ.

ז לֹא רָצְתָה לְהִתְגַּיֵּר – מְגַלְגְּלִין עִמָּהּ שְׁנֵים־עָשָׂר חֹדֶשׁ. לֹא רָצְתָה – מְקַבֶּלֶת שֶׁבַע מִצְוֹת שֶׁנִּצְטַוּוּ בְּנֵי נֹחַ, וּמְשַׁלְּחָהּ לְנַפְשָׁהּ, וַהֲרֵי הִיא כְּכָל הַגֵּרִים הַתּוֹשָׁבִים; וְאֵינוֹ נוֹשְׂאָהּ, שֶׁאָסוּר לִשָּׂא אִשָּׁה שֶׁלֹּא נִתְגַּיְּרָה.

ח נִתְעַבְּרָה מִבִּיאָה רִאשׁוֹנָה – הֲרֵי הַוָּלָד גֵּר, וְאֵינוֹ בְּנוֹ לְדָבָר מִן הַדְּבָרִים, מִפְּנֵי שֶׁהוּא מִן הַגּוֹיָה; אֶלָּא בֵּית־דִּין מַטְבִּילִין אוֹתוֹ עַל דַּעְתָּם. וְתָמָר מִבִּיאָה רִאשׁוֹנָה שֶׁל יְפַת־תֹּאַר הָיְתָה; אֲבָל אַבְשָׁלוֹם נוֹלַד מֵאַחַר הַנִּשּׂוּאִין. נִמְצֵאת תָּמָר אֲחוֹת אַבְשָׁלוֹם מֵאִמּוֹ, וּמֻתֶּרֶת לְהִנָּשֵׂא לְאַמְנוֹן.

44. Deuteronomy 7:3 mentions the prohibition against marrying a gentile. It also applies to a resident alien.

45. The child only receives the status of a convert after he undergoes the conversion process. Before then, he is a gentile as any child born from relations between a Jew and a gentile woman.

46. *Yevamot* 23a comments: "A son born to you from a gentile woman is called her son and not yours." Thus, this child has no relation to his natural father in regard to inheritance or Jewish lineage.

47. *Ketubot* 12a relates that a Jewish court may convert a minor. When he comes of age, he has the right renounce the Jewish faith and return to gentile practices.

The *Or Sameach* notes that it is only necessary for the child to be immersed in the *mikveh* if the mother delays her conversion until after his birth. If she converts while pregnant, her immersion is sufficient for her child as well. Needless to say, if the child is male, he must be circumcised as a convert as well.

48. While David ruled as King of Judah in Hebron, he conquered Talmai, king of Geshur, and took his daughter, Ma'aka, as a *yefat toar* (See commentaries, II Samuel 3:3).

Ma'aka conceived from those relations and bore a daughter, Tamar. Tamar was extremely beautiful and Amnon, David's oldest son fell in love with her. He literally fell sick with love. His friends noticed him wasting away and helped him contrive a scheme to rape her.

Amnon feigned to be seriously ill and when David came to visit him, he requested that his father have Tamar prepare food for him. Unaware of Amnon's intent, David consented and sent his daughter to him. When she came, Amnon ordered all his servants to leave and took hold of the girl. She protested, begging him to marry her: "Speak to the king, for he will not withhold me from you." Amnon refused, wanting to only to fulfill his desires.

After consummating his passion, Amnon became obsessed with hate for Tamar. His despise for her exceeded his previous attraction. He sent her away rudely and paid no further attention to her. Avshalom, Tamar's brother, was enraged at the episode. He bided his time and when he had an opportunity, slew Amnon in revenge (II Samuel, Chapter 13).

49. Hence, he could have been considered David's heir.

50. The *Or Sameach* notes that Ma'aka must have converted before Tamar's birth. Thus,

Amnon.[51] This can be inferred from the statement [II Samuel 13:13]: "Speak to the king, for he will not withhold me from you."

9. A *yefat toar* who does not desire to abandon idol worship after twelve months[52] should be executed.[53] Similarly, a treaty cannot be made with a city which [desires to] accept a peaceful settlement until they deny idol worship, destroy their places of worship, and accept the seven universal laws commanded Noah's descendants.[54] For every gentile who does not accept these commandments must be executed[55] if he is under our [undisputed] authority.[56]

10. Moses only gave the Torah and mitzvot as an inheritance to Israel,[57] as [Deuteronomy 33:4] states: "[The Torah...] is the inheritance of the congregation of Jacob,"[58] and to all those who desire to convert from among the other nations, as [Numbers 15:15] states "The convert shall be the same as you."[59] However, someone who does not desire to accept Torah and mitzvot, should not be forced to.[60]

By the same regard, Moses was commanded by the Almighty to compel all the inhabitants of the world to accept the commandments given to Noah's descendants.[61]

If one does not accept these commands, he should be executed.[62] A person who [formally] accepts these [commands] is called a resident alien. [This applies]

she was considered the child's halachic as well as natural mother. Otherwise, halachically, Tamar would not have been considered her daughter and hence, would have had no relation to Avshalom.

51. For there was no relation between them.

52. The *Kessef Mishneh* questions why the captive woman is allowed to worship idols for such a long time. In no other instance is such tolerance shown. The commentaries suggest that this leniency was granted because she was forcefully possessed.

53. Regarding the captive woman's release, Deuteronomy 21:14 states: *vishilachta linafsha* which literally meaning: "You shall send her to herself." On this phrase, the *Midrash HaGadol* comments: "'Send her to herself,' but not to her gods."

54. See Chapter 6, Halachah 1.

55. See Chapter 9, Halachah 14.

56. In *Hilchot Avodat Kochavim* 10:6, the Rambam writes that no idol worshippers should be allowed to live among us "when the hand of Israel is powerful over them." The extent of the authority the Jews must yield is a matter of question among the commentaries.

It appears that throughout the Second Temple period, though Judeah existed as an independent country, the Sages did not exercise this authority. Similarly, in *Eretz Yisrael* today, there are few, if any, Torah leaders who feel justified to assume such powers.

57. Chapter 10, Halachah 9, states that a gentile who studies Torah is worthy of death at the hand of God.

58. Just as an heir becomes the legal owner of all possessions left to him, the Torah, our national heritage, belongs to each Jew, regardless of background or upbringing.

וְכֵן הוּא אוֹמֵר: "דַּבֶּר־נָא אֶל הַמֶּלֶךְ כִּי לֹא יִמְנָעֵנִי מִמֶּךָ.

ט יְפַת־תֹּאַר שֶׁלֹּא רָצְתָה לְהַנִּיחַ עֲבוֹדָה זָרָה אַחַר הַשְּׁנֵים־עָשָׂר חֹדֶשׁ – הוֹרְגִין אוֹתָהּ. וְכֵן עִיר שֶׁהִשְׁלִימָה, אֵין כּוֹרְתִין לָהֶן בְּרִית עַד שֶׁיִּכְפְּרוּ בַּעֲבוֹדָה זָרָה וִיאַבְּדוּ אֶת כָּל מְקוֹמוֹתֶיהָ וִיקַבְּלוּ שְׁאָר הַמִּצְוֹת שֶׁנִּצְטַוּוּ בְּנֵי נֹחַ, שֶׁכָּל עַכּוּ"ם שֶׁלֹּא קִבֵּל מִצְוֹת שֶׁנִּצְטַוּוּ בְּנֵי נֹחַ, הוֹרְגִין אוֹתוֹ אִם יֶשְׁנוֹ תַּחַת יָדֵנוּ.

י מֹשֶׁה רַבֵּנוּ לֹא הִנְחִיל הַתּוֹרָה וְהַמִּצְוֹת אֶלָּא לְיִשְׂרָאֵל, שֶׁנֶּאֱמַר: "מוֹרָשָׁה קְהִלַּת יַעֲקֹב", וּלְכָל הָרוֹצֶה לְהִתְגַּיֵּר מִשְּׁאָר הָאֻמּוֹת, שֶׁנֶּאֱמַר: "כָּכֶם כַּגֵּר". אֲבָל מִי שֶׁלֹּא רָצָה – אֵין כּוֹפִין אוֹתוֹ לְקַבֵּל תּוֹרָה וּמִצְוֹת. וְכֵן צִוָּה מֹשֶׁה רַבֵּנוּ מִפִּי הַגְּבוּרָה לָכֹף אֶת כָּל בָּאֵי הָעוֹלָם לְקַבֵּל מִצְוֹת שֶׁנִּצְטַוּוּ בְּנֵי נֹחַ, וְכָל מִי שֶׁלֹּא יְקַבֵּל – יֵהָרֵג. וְהַמְקַבֵּל אוֹתָם, הוּא

59. With the exception of certain restrictions based on *yichus*, pedigree of lineage, converts are granted the same privileges and responsibilities as native-born Jews. They have a full share in the Torah.

60. In the Talmudic era, the later Hasmonean kings conquered the Idumeans and forcibly converted them to Judaism. What were the results of this act? Herod, an Idumean, became King of Judeah and ruled the land as a cruel tyrant.

61. This obligation is dependent upon every individual in every era. The *Tosafot Yom Yov* (*Avot* 3:14) relates:

> As the Rambam writes, we were commanded by Moses [to compel the gentiles to accept the seven commands]. If this applies to compulsion at the point of the sword, with threats of execution,... it surely applies regarding compulsion through persuasion, to lead their hearts to the will of their Creator."

The Jews must serve as "a light unto the nations" (Isaiah 42:6) teaching them the seven mitzvot and instructing them in proper behavior (See the commentary of the Radak on the above verse). Similarly, the *Chatam Sofer* (*Choshen Mishpat,* Responsum 85) writes that it is a mitzvah to guide the gentiles in the service of God.

This particularly applies in the present age, when there is far greater communication between Jews and gentiles than ever before. The Jews should take advantage of this phenomenon. Rather than be influenced by the gentiles, they should utilize this freedom of communication to convince the gentiles to accept their seven mitzvot.

With this halachah, the Rambam begins a different section of *Hilchot Melachim.* These two halachot, and, similarly, the following two chapters, deal with the seven mitzvot the gentiles are obligated to perform. Afterwards, the final two chapters deal with the coming of Mashiach.

An important principle is implied by this sequence. Jewish thought relates that God rewards our behavior "measure for measure." One of the fundamental achievements of Mashiach will be the refinement of the gentile nations. As the prophet Tzephaniah 3:9 declares: "I will transform the peoples to a purer language that they all will call upon the name of God and serve Him with one purpose" (see Halachah 11:4). As a preparatory step to merit these rewards, we must involve ourselves in the refinement of the gentiles by motivating their acceptance of the seven mitzvot.

62. In contrast to the previous principles, this law only applies when the Jews have undisputed authority over *Eretz Yisrael*. See Chapter 9, Halachah 14.

in any place.[63] This acceptance must be made in the presence of three Torah scholars.[64]

Anyone who agrees to circumcise himself[65] and [allows] twelve months to pass without circumcising himself is considered as one of the nations.[66]

11. Anyone who accepts upon himself the fulfillment of these seven mitzvot and is precise in their observance is considered one of "the pious among the gentiles" and will merit a share in the world to come.[67]

This applies only when he accepts them and fulfills them because the Holy One, blessed be He, commanded them in the Torah[68] and informed us through Moses, our teacher, that Noah's descendants had been commanded to fulfill them previously.[69]

However, if he fulfills them out of intellectual conviction,[70] he is not a resident alien, nor of "the pious among the gentiles,"[71] nor of their wise men.[72]

63. The laws regarding resident aliens only applied while the entire Jewish people lived in *Eretz Yisrael* (*Hilchot Avodat Kochavim* 10:6). Nevertheless, in that era, a gentile could accept the obligations of a resident alien in any land.

64. Thus, comprising a court of law. The resident alien's acceptance of the seven mitzvot requires the presence of a court as does a gentile's conversion to Judaism.

65. I.e. to convert.

66. In *Hilchot Avodat Kochavim*, Chapter 10, the Rambam outlines the rules governing our relations with our fellow Jews and those governing our relations with gentiles. After a gentile has waited twelve months, his original commitment to convert is no longer taken seriously and his status reverts from that of a potential proselyte to an ordinary gentile.

The above is based on the standard published text of the *Mishneh Torah* which reads *k'min haumot*. The Yemenite manuscripts of the *Mishneh Torah* read: *kmin min haumot*, meaning "as a non-believer from the gentiles." Such an individual is subjected to harsher treatment than most gentiles.

67. This principle can be derived from the Mishnah's statement (*Sanhderin* 90a) that Bilaam will not receive a share in the world to come. It can obviously be inferred that the righteous of the gentiles will be granted a portion in that eternal good.

The *Zohar Chadash* (Ruth 78:4) relates that though the pious gentiles will merit a portion in the world to come, their portion will be separate from that of the Jewish people.

68. In the Introduction to his Commentary on the Mishnah (conclusion of section 8), the Rambam writes:

> The masses of people were created to be "company" for the wise that they not be alone... Everything in this world is only intended for the sake of a man who is complete in wisdom and deed... as implied by our Sages' statement: "All that God possesses in this world are four square cubits of Halachah."

Similarly, our Sages comment that *bereishit*, the first word of the Torah, can be broken

הַנִּקְרָא "גֵּר תּוֹשָׁב" בְּכָל מָקוֹם; וְצָרִיךְ לְקַבֵּל עָלָיו בִּפְנֵי שְׁלֹשָׁה חֲבֵרִים. וְכָל הַמְקַבֵּל עָלָיו לָמוּל, וְעָבְרוּ עָלָיו שְׁנֵים־עָשָׂר חֹדֶשׁ וְלֹא מָל – הֲרֵי זֶה כְּמִן הָאֻמּוֹת.

יא כָּל הַמְקַבֵּל שֶׁבַע מִצְוֹת וְנִזְהָר לַעֲשׂוֹתָן, הֲרֵי זֶה מֵחֲסִידֵי אֻמּוֹת הָעוֹלָם, וְיֵשׁ לוֹ חֵלֶק לָעוֹלָם הַבָּא. וְהוּא, שֶׁיְּקַבֵּל אוֹתָן וְיַעֲשֶׂה אוֹתָן מִפְּנֵי שֶׁצִּוָּה בָהֶן הַקָּדוֹשׁ־בָּרוּךְ־הוּא בַּתּוֹרָה, וְהוֹדִיעָנוּ עַל־יְדֵי מֹשֶׁה רַבֵּנוּ, שֶׁבְּנֵי נֹחַ מִקֹּדֶם נִצְטַווּ בָהֶן. אֲבָל אִם עֲשָׂאָן מִפְּנֵי הֶכְרֵעַ הַדַּעַת – אֵין זֶה גֵּר תּוֹשָׁב, וְאֵינוֹ מֵחֲסִידֵי אֻמּוֹת הָעוֹלָם וְלֹא מֵחַכְמֵיהֶם.

up into two words: *beit reishit*, "two firsts"; implying that the world was created for the sake of two things that were called "first": Israel and the Torah.

Accordingly, on one level, the purpose of the fulfillment of the seven mitzvot is to establish a stable world and a moral and hence, thriving society. However, this purpose is not an end in itself, but rather a means to allow the Jews to fulfill the Torah. Therefore, the gentiles' acceptance of the seven mitzvot must also contain an awareness of the fundamental importance of Torah.

69. Though these mitzvot were commanded well before the giving of the Torah, when the Moses received the Torah, these commandments were renewed. We see a similar example in regard to other mitzvot. In his commentary on the Mishnah (*Chullin* 7:6), the Rambam writes:

> All the [mitzvot] we fulfill should be carried out because of God's command transmitted by Moses.... We do not circumcise ourselves because Abraham circumcised himself, but because God commanded us, through Moses, to circumcise ourselves.

70. Without acknowledging them as Divine commands.

71. Thus, there are three levels in the gentiles' acceptance of their seven mitzvot: a resident alien who makes a formal commitment in the presence of a Torah court; "the pious among the gentiles," individuals who accept the seven mitzvot with the proper intent, but do not formalize their acceptance; and a gentile who fulfills the seven mitzvot out of intellectual conviction.

72. The Yemenite manuscripts of the *Mishneh Torah* substitute "but rather, of their wise men" for this phrase.

The difference between these two texts revolves around the extent in which a gentile is required to perceive his role in creation. According to the Yemenite texts, a wise man can perceive how the fulfillment of the seven mitzvot can lead to a stable society. Hence, he will commit himself to their fulfillment. However, it is piety, not wisdom, which will motivate an individual to carry them out for the sake of God and Torah.

According to the standard published text, the gentiles themselves must realize that their existence is only "for the sake of Israel and for the sake of Torah." Anyone who does not understand that concept has not reached complete wisdom.

CHAPTER NINE

1. Six[1] precepts were commanded to Adam:
a) [the prohibition against] worship of false gods;[2]
b) [the prohibition against] cursing God;[3]
c) [the prohibition against] murder;[4]
d) [the prohibition against] incest and adultery;[5]
e) [the prohibition against] theft;[6]
f) [the command to establish] laws and courts of justice.[7]

Even though we have received all of these commands from Moses and, [furthermore, they are concepts] which intellect itself tends [to accept], it appears from the Torah's words that [Adam] was commanded concerning them.

[The prohibition against eating] flesh from a living animal was added for Noah, as [Genesis 9:4] states: "Nevertheless, you may not eat flesh with its life, which is its blood."[8] Thus there are seven mitzvot.[9]

These matters remained the same throughout the world until Abraham. When Abraham arose, in addition to these, he was commanded regarding circumcision.[10] He also [ordained] the morning prayers.[11]

Isaac separated tithes[12] and ordained an additional prayer service before

1. *Sanhderin* 56a relates that Adam was commanded regarding all seven commands. Nevertheless, the Rambam choose to quote from *Bereishit Rabbah* 16:6 which mentions the seventh command, the prohibition against eating flesh taken from a living animal, as being given to Noah. It appears that the Rambam chose the latter source because man was not permitted to consume flesh at all until after the flood. Together with the license to eat meat, God explicitly forbade Noah from eating flesh from a live animal.
2. The *Midrash* derives all these six prohibitions from the exegesis of Genesis 2:16: "And God the Lord commanded to man, saying: 'You may eat of all the trees of the garden....'" As evident from Hoshea 5:11, *tzav*, "command," serves as an allusion to the worship of false gods. This prohibition is discussed in Halachah 2.
3. The mention of God's name develops an association between this verse and the prohibition against cursing God mentioned in Leviticus 24:16. This prohibition is discussed in Halachah 3.
4. The Hebrew terms translated as "to man" refer to the command against murder, as mentioned in Genesis 9:6. This prohibition is discussed in Halachah 4.
5. The word, "saying," establishes an analogy between this verse and Jeremiah 3:1 which mentions this prohibition. It is discussed in Halachot 5-8.
6. This is derived from the license granted by the verse to eat from the trees of the garden, implying that otherwise, Adam would have been forbidden to do so because the property did not belong to him. This prohibition is discussed in Halachah 9.
7. This command is inferred from the word *Elohim*. For although that term also means "Lord," Exodus 22:27 uses that term in reference to a judge. This command is discussed in Halachah 14.
8. This prohibition is discussed in Halachot 10-13.
9. Other commentaries explain that gentiles are obligated to perform other mitzvot, for example, honoring one's parents (See Rashi, Genesis 11:32) and charity (See Eichah 4:6). The Ran (*Sanhderin* 56b) relates that the number seven only applies to prohibitions. However, there are other positive commands that gentiles are obligated to fulfill.

פֶּרֶק תְּשִׁיעִי

א עַל שִׁשָּׁה דְּבָרִים נִצְטַוָּה אָדָם הָרִאשׁוֹן: עַל עֲבוֹדָה זָרָה, וְעַל בִּרְכַּת הַשֵּׁם, וְעַל שְׁפִיכוּת־דָּמִים, וְעַל גִּלּוּי־עֲרָיוֹת, וְעַל הַגָּזֵל, וְעַל הַדִּינִים; אַף־עַל־פִּי שֶׁכֻּלָּן הֵן קַבָּלָה בְּיָדֵינוּ מִמֹּשֶׁה רַבֵּנוּ, וְהַדַּעַת נוֹטָה לָהֶן – מִכְּלַל דִּבְרֵי תוֹרָה יֵרָאֶה, שֶׁעַל אֵלּוּ נִצְטַוָּה. הוֹסִיף לְנֹחַ אֵיבָר מִן הֶחָי, שֶׁנֶּאֱמַר: "אַךְ בָּשָׂר בְּנַפְשׁוֹ דָמוֹ לֹא תֹאכֵלוּ" – נִמְצְאוּ שֶׁבַע מִצְוֹת, וְכֵן הָיָה הַדָּבָר בְּכָל הָעוֹלָם עַד אַבְרָהָם. בָּא אַבְרָהָם וְנִצְטַוָּה יָתֵר עַל אֵלּוּ בַּמִּילָה. וְהוּא הִתְפַּלֵּל שַׁחֲרִית. וְיִצְחָק הִפְרִישׁ מַעֲשֵׂר וְהוֹסִיף תְּפִלָּה אַחֶרֶת לִפְנוֹת הַיּוֹם. וְיַעֲקֹב

10. Genesis 17:10 related God's command to Abraham: "This is My covenant between Me and you and your offspring... Circumcise every male."

As the Rambam writes in Chapter 10, Halachah 7, from that time onwards, the Jews were obligated to observe the mitzvah of circumcision. However, Leviticus 12:3 repeats the command to circumcise. In his Commentary on the Mishnah (*Chullin* 7:6), the Rambam explains the need for this repetition:

> All the [mitzvot] we fulfill should be carried out because of God's command transmitted by Moses... We do not circumcise ourselves because Abraham circumcised himself, but because God commanded us, through Moses, to circumcise ourselves.

At Mount Sinai, the Jews were singled out by God to be "a kingdom of priests and a holy nation." Thus, the mitzvot given then differ, in purpose as well as in number, from the mitzvot given the gentiles. The gentiles' seven mitzvot are intended to establish a stable and moral society. The purpose of the 613 mitzvot is to establish a complete bond between God and every aspect of man's personality.

Similarly, the mystical nature of the commands differ. *Kiddushin* 31a relates that one who carries out a mitzvah in fulfillment of God's command is greater than one who does so out of his own volition. Why? Because by fulfilling a mitzvah commanded by God, man steps beyond his humanity and performs deeds that are Godly in nature. This quality was granted to the mitzvot at Sinai and not beforehand. Consequently, all the mitzvot previously commanded to the forefathers had to be repeated.

11. Genesis 19:27 relates how "Abraham rose early in the morning, [hurrying] to the place where he stood before God." *Berachot* 26b infers that this applies to his morning prayers.

Kiddushin 82a states that Abraham fulfilled the entire Torah before it was given. This statement raises a question: Why does the Rambam only mention circumcision and the morning service as mitzvot which Abraham performed?

The commentaries explain that the Rambam only mentions those commands explicitly mentioned or clearly alluded to in the Torah. Furthermore, it is possible that the manner in which the Abraham and his descendants fulfilled the other commands differ from the manner in which we fulfill them today. For example, the *Zohar* writes that Ya'akov's placing the rods before Laban's sheep drew down the same spiritual energies as our donning of Tefillin.

12. Genesis 26:12 mentions how "Isaac reaped one hundred measures." *Bereishit Rabbah* 64:6 explains that he measured his crop in order to give tithes.

The Ra'avad questions why the Rambam does not count tithes as one of the mitzvot instituted by Abraham for Genesis 14:20 explicitly mentions Abraham's separation of tithes. The commentaries explain that Isaac and not Abraham, originated the mitzvah of sunset.[13] Jacob added [the prohibition against eating] the sciatic nerve.[14] He also ordained the evening prayers.[15] In Egypt, Amram was commanded regarding other mitzvot.[16] Ultimately, Moses came and the Torah was completed by him.[17]

2. A gentile who worships false gods is liable provided he worships them in an accepted manner.[18]

A gentile is executed for every type of foreign worship which a Jewish court would consider worthy of capital punishment.[19] However, a gentile is not executed for a type of foreign worship which a Jewish court would not deem worthy of capital punishment. Nevertheless, even though [a gentile] will not be executed [for these forms of worship], he is forbidden [to engage] in all of them.[20]

We should not allow them to erect a monument,[21] or to plant an *Asherah*,[22] or to make images and the like even though they are [only] for the sake of beauty.[23]

3. A gentile who curses God's name,[24] whether he uses God's unique name[25] or one of His other names,[26] in any language, is liable. This law does not apply with regard to Jews.[27]

4. A gentile who slays any soul,[28] even a fetus in its mother's womb,[29] should be executed [in retribution] for its [death].[30] Similarly, if he slew a person who

tithing produce as mandated by the Torah. Abraham tithed the booty he conquered in war. In contrast, according to Scriptural Law, the mitzvah to tithe applies only to certain agriculture products.

13. Genesis 24:63 relates how "Isaac went out in the fields to pray toward evening."

14. Genesis 32:26 relates that when Jacob was wrestling with Esau's archangel, the latter was able to dislocate Jacob's hip joint. Verse 33 continues: "Therefore, the children of Israel do not eat the displaced nerve on the hip joint." The nerve in question is the major nerve of the lower extremity, running down the back of the leg.

15. Genesis 28:11 relates that "Jacob encountered the place and spent the night there, because the sun had set." *Berachot* (*loc. cit.*) explains that implied by the Hebrew is the recitation of the evening prayers.

16. The *Kessef Mishneh* questions the source for the Rambam's statements, asking which mitzvot were commanded to Amram. Some commentaries point to the statements of the *Mechilta* (Exodus 19:10) that before the giving of the Torah, Moses reviewed the mitzvot which the Jews had been given in Egypt. Since Amram served as the leader of the people, these mitzvot were probably given to him.

Others explain that the *Mechilta* could be referring to the mitzvot of matzah, marror, and the other elements of the Passover sacrifice given to Moses and not mitzvot given to Amram. They suggest that the Rambam is referring to the mitzvot of divorce and marriage. When Pharaoh commanded the Egyptians to drown the Jewish babies, Amram divorced his wife. Later, at the suggestion of his daughter, Miriam, he remarried her.

17. As explained above, there is a difference between the mitzvot given to the gentiles and those commanded the Jews.

18. Every false god has an accepted manner in which its adherents serve it. The idol

הוֹסִיף גִּיד הַנָּשֶׁה וְהִתְפַּלֵּל עַרְבִית. וּבְמִצְרַיִם נִצְטַוָּה עַמְרָם בְּמִצְוֹת יְתֵרוֹת, עַד שֶׁבָּא מֹשֶׁה רַבֵּנוּ, וְנִשְׁלְמָה תוֹרָה עַל־יָדוֹ.

ב בֶּן־נֹחַ שֶׁעָבַד עֲבוֹדָה זָרָה – הֲרֵי זֶה חַיָּב. וְהוּא, שֶׁיַּעֲבֹד כְּדַרְכָּהּ. וְכָל עֲבוֹדָה זָרָה שֶׁבֵּית־דִּין שֶׁל יִשְׂרָאֵל מְמִיתִין עָלֶיהָ – בֶּן־נֹחַ נֶהֱרָג עָלֶיהָ; וְכֹל שֶׁאֵין בֵּית־דִּין שֶׁל יִשְׂרָאֵל מְמִיתִין עָלֶיהָ – אֵין בֶּן־נֹחַ נֶהֱרָג עָלֶיהָ. וְאַף־עַל־פִּי שֶׁאֵינוֹ נֶהֱרָג – אָסוּר בַּכֹּל. וְאֵין מַנִּיחִין אוֹתוֹ לְהָקִים מַצֵּבָה, וְלֹא לִטַּע אֲשֵׁרָה, וְלֹא לַעֲשׂוֹת צוּרוֹת וְכַיּוֹצֵא בָהֶן לְנוֹי.

ג בֶּן־נֹחַ שֶׁבֵּרַךְ אֶת הַשֵּׁם – בֵּין שֶׁבֵּרַךְ בַּשֵּׁם הַמְיֻחָד, בֵּין שֶׁבֵּרַךְ בְּכִנּוּי בְּכָל לָשׁוֹן – חַיָּב; מַה שֶּׁאֵין כֵּן בְּיִשְׂרָאֵל.

ד בֶּן־נֹחַ שֶׁהָרַג נֶפֶשׁ, אֲפִלּוּ עֻבָּר בִּמְעֵי עִמּוֹ – נֶהֱרָג עָלָיו. וְכֵן אִם הָרַג טְרֵפָה, אוֹ שֶׁכְּפָתוֹ

worshippers established many [different] services for each particular idol and image. The service of one does not resemble the service of another (*Hilchot Avodat Kochavim* 3:2). A person does not incur the death penalty unless he worships a false god in its appropriate manner.

19. In addition to the sin of serving an idol in its appropriate manner, the death penalty is also given for bowing to one, sacrificing to it, offering incense to it, or pouring libations to it, even if the idol is generally not served in that manner (*ibid.* 3:3).

20. For example, kissing the idol, embracing it, washing it, sweeping before it, and similar acts of affection and reverence (*ibid.* 3:6).

21. A structure which attracts people and motivates them to gather around it. Construction of such a structure is forbidden even as an act of reverence to God (*ibid.* 6:6).

22. A tree which is worshipped (*ibid.* 8:3). The *Zohar* (Vol. I 49b) relates that worshippers of the moon would employ such trees in their services.

23. This is not a general prohibition against all artwork. In *Hilchot Avodat Kochavim* 3:10, the Rambam explains that it only applies to sculptures of human faces. Other images and paintings, imprints, and tapestries of humans are not forbidden.

24. The Rambam uses the word *berach* which literally meaning "blesses" as a euphemism.

25. *HilchotAvodah Zarah* 2:7 explains that this refers to the name *Adonai* and, of course, the name Y-H-V-H which is only to be mentioned in the Temple.

26. The term *kinui* implies any name used to describe God and not necessarily, one of the seven names, e.g., *El* or *Shaddai* which are holy and may not be erased.

27. *Hilchot Avodat Kochavim* (*ibid.*) explains that a Jew is only liable if he mentions either the name *Adonai* or the name Y-H-V-H in the curse.

The obligation of gentiles in instances where Jews are exempt is not accepted by all Talmudic authorities (Note *Sanhderin* 56a). The *Kessef Mishneh* questions why the Rambam follows the more severe opinion.

28. Intentionally, see Halachah 10:1.

29. This refers to a person who intentionally delivered a blow to the mother which caused the fetus to die. A Jew would not be held guilty of murder for such an act (See Exodus 21:22, *Hilchot Chovel UMazik* 4:1). However, a gentile is considered liable.

It is obvious from this statement that abortion is equated with murder and is only permitted in certain instances where the mother's life is threatened.

30. Genesis 9:6 states: "He who spills human blood shall have his own blood spilled."

would have otherwise died in the near future,[31] placed a person before a lion,[32] or starved a person to death, he should be executed for through one manner or other, he killed.[33]

Similarly, one should be executed if he killed a pursuer when he could have saved [the latter's potential victim][34] by maiming one of [the pursuer's] limbs.[35] These laws do not apply with regard to Jews.

5. There are six illicit sexual relations forbidden to a gentile:[36]
a) his mother;[37]
b) his father's wife;[38]
c) a married woman;[39]
d) his maternal sister;[40]
e) a male;[41]
f) an animal.

[These prohibitions are derived from] the verse [Genesis 2:24]: "Therefore, a man shall leave [his father and his mother and cling to his wife and they shall become one flesh."][42]

"His father" - alludes to his father's wife;[43]
"his mother" - is to be understood simply;[44]
"cling to his wife" - and not his colleague's wife; [45]
"his wife" - and not a male;
"They shall become one flesh"[46] - this excludes a domesticated animal, beast, or fowl for [man] can never become "one flesh" with them.[47]

[The prohibition against relations with a maternal sister is derived from] the verse [Genesis 20:13]: "She is my sister, my father's daughter, but not my mother's. [Thus,] she became my wife."[48]

6. A gentile is liable [for relations] with [his mother even though] she was seduced or raped by his father [and never married to him]. She is, nevertheless, his mother.[49]

He is liable [for relations] with his father's wife even after his father's death.[50]

He is liable [for relations] with a male whether a minor or an adult[51] and

31. This refers to a person who is *trefe*, possessing a blemish or illness which would cause his death within twelve months. A Jew who kills such a person is not given the death penalty (*Hilchot Rotzeach* 2:8).
32. Other texts substitute "in a lion's mouth" for the latter phrase.
33. With regard to a Jew who commits such an act, *Hilchot Rotzeach* 3:10 states:

> A person who... starves a colleague to death or... sets a dog or snake upon him: in all cases of this nature, the person is not executed. Nevertheless, he is considered a murderer and the One who avenges blood will seek his blood.

34. A person is allowed to kill a person who is trying to kill or rape another individual (*Hilchot Rotzeach* 1:6-12). However, this leniency is only granted when there is no other alternative.
35. For he is not allowed to kill him. In contrast, if a Jewish pursuer kills a Jewish

וּנְתָנוֹ לִפְנֵי אֲרִי, אוֹ שֶׁהִנִּיחוֹ בָּרָעָב עַד שֶׁמֵּת – הוֹאִיל וְהֵמִית מִכָּל מָקוֹם, נֶהֱרָג. וְכֵן אִם הָרַג רוֹדֵף שֶׁיָּכוֹל לְהַצִּילוֹ בְּאַחַד מֵאֵיבָרָיו – נֶהֱרָג עָלָיו; מַה שֶּׁאֵין כֵּן בְּיִשְׂרָאֵל.

ה שֵׁשׁ עֲרָיוֹת אֲסוּרוֹת עַל בְּנֵי נֹחַ: הָאֵם, וְאֵשֶׁת הָאָב, וְאֵשֶׁת־אִישׁ, וַאֲחוֹתוֹ מֵאִמּוֹ, וְזָכוּר, וּבְהֵמָה, שֶׁנֶּאֱמַר: "עַל־כֵּן יַעֲזָב אִישׁ אֶת אָבִיו" – זוֹ אֵשֶׁת אָבִיו, "וְאֶת אִמּוֹ" – כְּמַשְׁמָעָהּ, "וְדָבַק בְּאִשְׁתּוֹ" – וְלֹא בְאֵשֶׁת חֲבֵרוֹ, "בְּאִשְׁתּוֹ" – וְלֹא בְזָכוּר, "וְהָיוּ לְבָשָׂר אֶחָד" – לְהוֹצִיא בְהֵמָה, חַיָּה וָעוֹף, שֶׁאֵין הוּא וָהֵם בָּשָׂר אֶחָד; וְנֶאֱמַר: "אֲחֹתִי בַת אָבִי הִיא אַךְ לֹא בַת אִמִּי, וַתְּהִי לִי לְאִשָּׁה".

ו בֶּן־נֹחַ חַיָּב עַל מְפֻתַּת אָבִיו וַאֲנוּסַת אָבִיו – הֲרֵי הִיא אִמּוֹ מִכָּל מָקוֹם. וְחַיָּב עַל אֵשֶׁת אָבִיו, אֲפִלּוּ לְאַחַר מִיתַת אָבִיו. וְחַיָּב עַל הַזָּכוּר, בֵּין קָטָן, בֵּין גָּדוֹל, וְעַל הַבְּהֵמָה, בֵּין

attacker under similar circumstances, "he is considered guilty of murder and obligated to die. However, he is not executed by the court" (*ibid.* 1:13).

36. There are many more relationships forbidden to a Jew. See Leviticus, Chapter 17, *Hilchot Issurei Bi'ah*, Chapters 1 and 2.

37. This applies even if she is not his father's wife. See the following halachah.

38. This applies even if she is not his mother, and even after his father's death.

39. As mentioned in the commentary to Chapter 8, Halachah 3, a Jew is not liable for adultery if he engages in relations with a gentile's wife. Nevertheless, the marriages of gentiles are significant for other gentiles and they are executed for committing adultery.

40. But not his paternal sister as obvious from the verse quoted below.

41. I.e., homosexuality.

42. This verse concludes the Torah's description of the creation of Eve and Adam's union with her. Thus, it serves as a guide for the sexual behavior of all his descendants.

43. For otherwise, there would be no need for such a prohibition for relations with males are explicitly forbidden.

44. It is interesting to note that there is no prohibition against relations with a daughter.

45. Halachah 7 explain that this refers to a woman who is married (*nissuin*) and not merely consecrated (*erusin*).

46. Give birth to children (Rashi, on Genesis, *ibid.*).

47. I.e., children can never be born from such a union.

48. Abraham made this statement to Avimelech to excuse his behavior in calling Sarah his sister rather than his wife. Abraham explained that she was like his sister (she was his father's granddaughter). However, he was allowed to marry her because they shared a common paternal ancestor, but not a common maternal ancestor.

49. This law is derived from the inclusion of two prohibitions; one against relations with one's father's wife and one against relations with one's mother. If the prohibition against relations with one's mother only applied to a woman married to one's father, only one prohibition would be necessary (*Sanhderin* 58a).

50. If not, there would be no need for this prohibition for she would be forbidden as any other married woman (*ibid.*).

51. A Jew is only liable for relations with a male nine years and over. Below that age, the Torah does not consider the child as sexually developed (*Hilchot Issurei Bi'ah* 1:14). The

with an animal whether young or old.[52] [In the latter instance,] the gentile alone is executed and not the animal.[53] We are only commanded to kill an animal with which a Jew [engaged in relations].[54]

7. A gentile is not executed for [adultery] with his colleague's wife unless they engage in relations in the normal manner[55] after she had engaged in relations with her husband at least once. However, if she was merely consecrated or had undergone a wedding ceremony, but had never engaged in relations [with her husband], one is not liable for engaging in relations with her,[56] as [Genesis 20:3] states: "For she has been possessed by [her] husband."[57]

When does the above apply? When a gentile engages in relations with a gentile woman.[58] However, a gentile who engages in relations with a [married] Jewess is liable whether their relations were carried out in a normal or abnormal manner.[59]

[Similarly,] a gentile who engages in relations with a Jewish maiden[60] who has been consecrated is stoned to death because of her as is the law regarding Jews.[61] If he engages in relations with her after she has undergone the wedding ceremony, but has not engaged in relations [with her husband], he is strangled to death as is the Jewish law.[62] However, if he engages in relations with a Jewish woman after she engaged in relations [with her husband] once, he is sentenced to be executed by decapitation[63] as if he had engaged in relations with a gentile woman.[64]

8. A gentile who singles out one of his maid-servants for one of his slaves[65] and, afterwards, engages in relations with her is executed because of her for [violation of the prohibition against] adultery.[66] However, he is not liable [for

Kessef Mishneh favors the view that the same laws apply to a gentile as to a Jew. The Radbaz maintains that a gentile is liable no matter what the age of the child.

52. The age of an animal is of no significance whatsoever. A person is sentenced to death for relations with an animal even on the day of its birth (*ibid.* 1:16).

53. The question of executing the animal was debated and left undecided by *Sanhderin* 55a. Since no decision was reached, the death penalty is not administered.

54. The animal is also executed lest it be seen in the street and the passersby comment: "See that animal! So and so was executed for having relations with it."

55. I.e., vaginal, rather than anal intercourse.

56. "Before the Torah was given, a man would meet a woman in the market-place, if both he and she desired to marry, he would bring her to his home and possess her privately, thus, making her his wife."

"Once the Torah was given, the Israelites were commanded [as follows]: Should a man desire to marry a woman, he must first acquire her in the presence of witnesses. Afterwards, she will become his wife" (*Hilchot Ishut* 1:1).

The latter paragraph describes the two stages in Jewish marriage: *kiddushin* and *nissuin*. Only a Jew is obligated to marry in this fashion. For a gentile, the law remains as it was before the giving of the Torah and the marriage bonds are established through sexual relations alone.

קְטַנָּה, בֵּין גְּדוֹלָה; וְהוּא נֶהֱרָג לְבַדּוֹ, וְאֵין הוֹרְגִין אֶת הַבְּהֵמָה; שֶׁלֹּא נִצְטַוּוּ בַּהֲרִיגַת בְּהֵמָה אֶלָּא יִשְׂרָאֵל.

ז אֵין בֶּן־נֹחַ חַיָּב עַל אֵשֶׁת חֲבֵרוֹ, עַד שֶׁיָּבוֹא עָלֶיהָ כְּדַרְכָּהּ אַחַר שֶׁנִּבְעֲלָה לְבַעְלָהּ; אֲבָל מְאֹרָסָה, אוֹ שֶׁנִּכְנְסָה לְחֻפָּה וְלֹא נִבְעֲלָה – אֵין חַיָּבִין עָלֶיהָ, שֶׁנֶּאֱמַר: "וְהִיא בְּעֻלַת בָּעַל". בַּמֶּה דְּבָרִים אֲמוּרִים? בְּבֶן־נֹחַ שֶׁבָּא עַל בַּת־נֹחַ, אֲבָל עכו"ם הַבָּא עַל הַיִּשְׂרְאֵלִית, בֵּין כְּדַרְכָּהּ, בֵּין שֶׁלֹּא כְּדַרְכָּהּ – חַיָּב. וְאִם הָיְתָה נַעֲרָה מְאֹרָסָה – נִסְקָל עָלֶיהָ כְּדִינֵי יִשְׂרָאֵל. בָּא עָלֶיהָ אַחַר שֶׁנִּכְנְסָה לְחֻפָּה וְלֹא נִבְעֲלָה – הֲרֵי זֶה בְּחֶנֶק כְּדִינֵי יִשְׂרָאֵל. אֲבָל אִם בָּא עַל אֵשֶׁת יִשְׂרָאֵל אַחַר שֶׁנִּבְעֲלָה – הֲרֵי זֶה כְּמִי שֶׁבָּא עַל אֵשֶׁת עכו"ם חֲבֵרוֹ, וְיֵהָרֵג בְּסַיִף.

ח בֶּן־נֹחַ שֶׁיִּחֵד שִׁפְחָה לְעַבְדּוֹ וּבָא עָלֶיהָ – הֲרֵי זֶה נֶהֱרָג עָלֶיהָ מִשּׁוּם אֵשֶׁת חֲבֵרוֹ. וְאֵינוֹ

57. When Avimelech took Sarah, Abraham's wife, God employed this phrase to warn him that relations with her were forbidden. From the use of the phrase "possessed by her husband" as opposed to "another man's wife" or the like, our Sages derived that the marriage bond was established through sexual relations.
58. For capital punishment in the same manner as a Jew. With regard to relations with a Jewess, a gentile sexual offender is never granted greater leniency than a Jew.
59. Leviticus 20:22 uses a plural term, *mishkavei ishah* to describe sexual relations. This expression was chosen to teach us that one is liable for two forms of intercourse, vaginal and anal (*Sanhderin* 54b).
60. The latter term refers to a virgin girl between the ages of twelve and twelve and a half.
61. See Deuteronomy 22:23-24. In this specific instance, a more severe penalty is given than in other cases of adultery.

The Jerusalem Talmud (*Kiddushin* 1:1) mentions that whenever a gentile is given the same punishment as Jews, his trial is also governed by the same laws. Generally, a gentile's trial is decided by a single judge on the basis of the testimony of a single witness. In this instance, there is obligation for twenty-three judges, two witnesses, a warning and all other elements required in capital cases involving Jews.

The Ran (*Sanhderin* 57b) does not accept this opinion. He brings proofs that the Babylonian Talmud, on which basis halachah is decided, does not differentiate between this case and other trials involving gentiles.
62. Once a couple have undergone the wedding ceremony, the penalty for adultery changes from being stoned to death to strangulation, a less severe means of execution.
63. Although a Jew would be sentenced to strangulation for the same sin.
64. In the former instances, no punishment would have been exacted for relations with a gentile woman. Hence, the offender is punished according to Jewish law. However, when a parallel offence exists among the seven mitzvot, a gentile is punished accordingly. Decapitation is considered a more severe means of execution than strangulation.
65. The slave must also have engaged in relations with the maidservant for the issue of adultery to be raised (Radbaz).
66. *Sanhderin* 57a mentions that a master should be executed for such an act. However, the reason for his execution is a matter of debate among the commentaries.

relations] with her until the matter has become public knowledge and everyone refers to her as "the wife of so-and-so, the slave."[67]

When do [relations with] her become permitted again? When he separates her from his slave[68] and uncovers her hair in the market-place.[69]

When is a gentile woman considered divorced? When [her husband] removes her from his home and sends her on her own or when she leaves his domain and goes her own way. They have no written divorce proceedings.[70]

The matter is not dependant on the man's [volition] alone.[71] Whenever he or she decide to separate, they may [and then, are no longer considered as married.][72]

9. A gentile is liable for [violating the prohibition against] theft whether he stole from another gentile or from a Jew.[73]

[This applies to] one who forcefully robs [an individual] or steals money,[74] a kidnapper,[75] an [employer who] withholds his worker's wages and the like,[76] even a worker who eats [from his employer's produce] when he is not working.[77] In all [such cases], he is liable and is considered as a robber. With regard to Jews, the law is different.[78]

Similarly, [a gentile] is liable [for stealing an object] worth less than a *p'rutah*.[79] Thus, if one gentile stole [an object] worth less than a *p'rutah* and another [gentile] stole it from him, they are both executed because of it.[80]

10. Similarly, [a gentile] is liable [for violating the prohibition against] eating a limb[81] or flesh from a living creature.[82] [This applies] regardless of the amount

Rashi maintains that there is no concept of marriage with regard to slaves. The master is violating the prohibition against theft, taking the woman he had given to his slave, but not adultery. The Rambam does not accept this view for the slave never really acquired the woman. Nor does he have the potential to do so, for "everything acquired by a servant becomes his master's property" (Radbaz).

67. The fact that the slave had relations with her is not sufficient to establish a bond between them for slaves were known for their lewdness. Their "marriage" is not recognized until the matter is publicly accepted.

68. The masculine conjugation of the verb is used implying that it is the master who performs this act.

69. Married women are obligated to cover their hair (*Shulchan Aruch, Even HaEzer* 115). Even gentiles would observe this practice.

70. A Jew who desires to divorce his wife must give her a bill of divorce (*get*). This document must be composed by a scribe with expertise and training regarding all the particular laws involved. In contrast, gentiles do not require such a document. Their separation constitutes divorce.

Modern commentaries question whether these laws still apply to gentiles in the present age when most countries have instituted formal divorce proceedings. Since these proceedings are recognized by their court system and the laws established by a country must be observed by its inhabitants, a woman may be considered married until formally divorced.

71. This differs from Jewish law. According to Scriptural Law, a husband must initiate

חַיָּב עָלֶיהָ עַד שֶׁיִּפָּשֵׁט הַדָּבָר, וְאָמְרוּ לָהּ הָעָם: "זוֹ דְּבִית עֶבֶד פְּלוֹנִי!" וּמֵאֵימָתַי תַּחֲזוֹר לְהֶתֵּרָהּ? מִשֶּׁיַּפְרִישֶׁנָּה מֵעַבְדּוֹ וְיִפְרַע רֹאשָׁהּ בַּשּׁוּק. וּמֵאֵימָתַי תִּהְיֶה אֵשֶׁת חֲבֵרוֹ כִּגְרוּשָׁה שֶׁלָּנוּ? מִשֶּׁיּוֹצִיאֶנָּה מִבֵּיתוֹ וִישַׁלְּחֶנָּה לְעַצְמָהּ, אוֹ מִשֶּׁתֵּצֵא הִיא מִתַּחַת רְשׁוּתוֹ וְתֵלֵךְ לָהּ, שֶׁאֵין לָהֶן גֵּרוּשִׁין בִּכְתָב. וְאֵין הַדָּבָר תָּלוּי בּוֹ לְבַד, אֶלָּא כָּל זְמַן שֶׁיִּרְצֶה הוּא אוֹ הִיא לִפְרשׁ זֶה מִזֶּה – פּוֹרְשִׁין.

ט בֶּן־נֹחַ חַיָּב עַל הַגָּזֵל – בֵּין שֶׁגָּזַל עַכּוּ"ם, בֵּין שֶׁגָּזַל יִשְׂרָאֵל, וְאֶחָד הַגּוֹזֵל אוֹ הַגּוֹנֵב מָמוֹן אוֹ גּוֹנֵב נֶפֶשׁ, אוֹ הַכּוֹבֵשׁ שְׂכַר־שָׂכִיר וְכַיּוֹצֵא בוֹ, אֲפִלּוּ פּוֹעֵל שֶׁאָכַל שֶׁלֹּא בִשְׁעַת מְלָאכָה – עַל הַכֹּל הוּא חַיָּב, וַהֲרֵי הוּא בִּכְלַל גַּזְלָן; מַה שֶּׁאֵין כֵּן בְּיִשְׂרָאֵל. וְכֵן חַיָּב עַל פָּחוֹת מִשְּׁוֵה־פְּרוּטָה. וּבֶן־נֹחַ שֶׁגָּזַל פָּחוֹת מִשְּׁוֵה־פְּרוּטָה, וּבָא אַחֵר וּגְזָלָהּ מִמֶּנּוּ – שְׁנֵיהֶן נֶהֱרָגִין עָלֶיהָ.

י וְכֵן חַיָּב עַל אֵיבָר מִן הֶחָי, וְעַל בָּשָׂר מִן הֶחָי, בְּכָל שֶׁהוּא.

divorce and does not need his wife's consent. In the Middle Ages, Rabbenu Gershon decreed that a woman may not be divorced against her will. However, the husband must willingly decide to grant the divorce.

72. The Rambam's statements are based on the Jerusalem Talmud (*ibid.*) which states that the gentiles "do not have divorce." The Ran (*Sanhderin* 58b) quotes an opinion which interprets that statement to mean that divorce is absolutely forbidden to a gentile couple.

73. The converse is also true. A Jew is prohibited against stealing from a gentile (*Hilchot Genevah* 1:2). However, he is not given the death penalty for such an act.

74. *Genevah* in Hebrew. In contrast to *gezeilah*, "robbery," *genevah* involves taking someone's money secretly without the owner's or the public's knowledge (*Hilchot Genevah* 1:3).

75. The command "Do not steal" in the Ten Commandments refers to kidnapping. *Sanhderin* 57a explains how this prohibition applies to gentiles.

76. For example, withholding rent due a landlord or the fee charged for the hire of a utensil or other property.

77. Deuteronomy 23:25 grants a worker the privilege of eating from the produce he is harvesting. However, this right is only given while he is actually working. Afterwards, taking from the produce is forbidden.

78. Though a Jew is also prohibited against all the above, there are different prohibitions involved. He is only labeled a robber if he forcibly taking money in the open.

79. A *p'rutah* was the smallest coin of the time. A Jew is also forbidden to steal less than this minimal amount. However, should he do so, the matter is not taken to court for surely, the owner is not concerned about the loss of such an insignificant amount (*Hilchot Gezeilah* 1:6).

80. With regard to Jews, though it is forbidden to steal from a thief, the fine the second thief is obligated to pay differs from that required of the first. See *Hilchot Genevah* 1:17.

81. The term limb implies a bone with sinews and nerves as well as meat.

82. The *Sha'agat Aryeh* explains that there is a problem implicit in the Rambam's statements: A gentile is liable for eating even the slightest amount of meat. Since it is impossible for him to eat a limb that has no meat on it whatsoever, it appears superfluous to mention two prohibitions: one against eating a limb and the other against eating meat.

involved, for [the specification of] minimum amounts only applies to Jews.[83] [A gentile] is permitted blood from a living creature.[84]

11. [The prohibition applies] to a limb[85] or flesh[86] that is separated from either a domesticated animal or a beast.[87] However, it appears to me[88] that a gentile is not executed for eating a limb [taken] from a living bird.[89]

12. Though one slaughters an animal, even if one severs the two signs [that distinguish it as having been slaughtered in a kosher manner],[90] as long as the animal moves convulsively,[91] the limbs and meat which are separated from it are forbidden to a gentile because of the prohibition against a limb from a living creature.[92]

13. All prohibitions that apply to a Jew regarding a limb from a living creature also apply to gentiles. Furthermore, there are instances where a gentile would be held liable and a Jew will not. For a gentile is liable for [partaking of] a limb or flesh from a living creature whether it is a domesticated animal or a beast, and whether it is from a kosher or non-kosher species.[93]

Similarly, for a gentile, the prohibition against [partaking of] a limb from a living creature applies to a limb or flesh which is separated from an animal that is moving convulsively even though a Jew has already severed the two signs.[94]

14. How must [the gentiles] fulfill the commandment to establish laws and courts? They are obligated to set up judges and magistrates in every major

83. A Jew is also bound by these prohibitions. However, he is not liable for punishment until he consumes a minimum measure, the size of an olive (approx. one ounce), of these forbidden foods. *Eruvin* 4a explains that the concept of minimum amounts is part of the Oral Tradition which was given to Israel alone. Hence, the gentiles are liable for eating even the slightest amount of meat.

84. Genesis 9:4, the source for the prohibition against eating flesh from a living animal, states: "You may not eat flesh with its life, which is its blood." Nevertheless, *Sanhderin* 59a relates that this verse does not prohibit a gentile from drinking blood taken from a living animal. In contrast, a Jew is prohibited against drinking all blood, whether taken from an animal before its slaughter or afterwards.

85. The term limb implies a bone with sinews and nerves as well as meat.

86. In *Hilchot Ma'achalot Assurot* (5:2), the Rambam writes:

> One is not liable for [the prohibition of] a limb from a living creature unless the limb is separated... with its flesh, sinews, and bones. However, if only flesh is separated from a living creature, [a person who eats it] is liable for [the prohibition against eating] *trefe* [meat], but is not liable for [the prohibition against] a limb from a living creature.

The *Kessef Mishneh* notes that a gentile is permitted *trefe* meat and questions why he is prohibited against eating flesh from a living animal.

The *Lechem Mishneh* replies that the prohibition for Jews and for gentiles are derived

שֶׁלֹּא נִתְּנוּ הַשִּׁעוּרִין אֶלָּא לְיִשְׂרָאֵל בִּלְבָד. וּמֻתָּר הוּא בְּדָם מִן הֶחָי.

יא אֶחָד הָאֵיבָר אוֹ הַבָּשָׂר הַפּוֹרֵשׁ מִן הַבְּהֵמָה אוֹ מִן הַחַיָּה; אֲבָל הָעוֹף - יֵרָאֶה לִי שֶׁאֵין בֶּן־נֹחַ נֶהֱרָג עַל אֵיבָר מִן הַחַי מִמֶּנּוּ.

יב הַשּׁוֹחֵט אֶת הַבְּהֵמָה, אֲפִלּוּ שָׁחַט בָּהּ שְׁנֵי הַסִּימָנִין - כָּל זְמַן שֶׁהִיא מְפַרְכֶּסֶת, אֵיבָר וּבָשָׂר הַפּוֹרְשִׁין מִמֶּנָּה, אֲסוּרִין לִבְנֵי נֹחַ מִשּׁוּם אֵיבָר מִן הֶחָי.

יג כֹּל שֶׁאָסוּר עַל יִשְׂרָאֵל מִשּׁוּם אֵיבָר מִן הֶחָי - אָסוּר עַל בְּנֵי נֹחַ. וְיֵשׁ שֶׁבְּנֵי נֹחַ חַיָּבִין וְלֹא יִשְׂרָאֵל; שֶׁבְּנֵי נֹחַ - אֶחָד בְּהֵמָה וְחַיָּה, בֵּין טְמֵאָה, בֵּין טְהוֹרָה - חַיָּבִין עָלֶיהָ מִשּׁוּם אֵיבָר מִן הַחַי וּמִשּׁוּם בָּשָׂר מִן הֶחָי. וְאֵיבָר וּבָשָׂר הַפּוֹרְשִׁין מִן הַמְפַרְכֶּסֶת, אַף־עַל־פִּי שֶׁשָּׁחַט בָּהּ יִשְׂרָאֵל שְׁנֵי סִימָנִין - הֲרֵי זֶה אָסוּר לִבְנֵי נֹחַ מִשּׁוּם אֵיבָר מִן הֶחָי.

יד וְכֵיצַד מְצֻוִּין הֵן עַל הַדִּינִין? חַיָּבִין לְהוֹשִׁיב דַּיָּנִין וְשׁוֹפְטִים בְּכָל פֶּלֶךְ וּפֶלֶךְ לָדוּן

from different verses. The verse that prohibits a gentile from eating a limb from a living creature states; "You may not eat flesh with its life," explicitly mentioning flesh.

87. Though the Torah occasionally differentiates between these types of animals, in this instance, the same laws apply.

88. Throughout the *Mishneh Torah*, the use of this expression implies that the Rambam does not have an explicit Talmudic or *Midrashic* source to substantiate his statements. However, an analysis of the different references to the subject leads to this conclusion.

89. The Ra'avad does not accept this statement and maintains that a gentile is liable for eating flesh from a living bird. He is only exempt from eating flesh from a living creeping animal, *sheretz* in Hebrew.

The Radbaz defends the Rambam's statements, noting that though *Chullin* 101b obligates Jews for eating flesh taken from a living bird, gentiles may be exempt from that prohibition. The verse which describes the gentiles' prohibition mentions, *basar* "meat." Nedarim 54b relates an argument among the Sages where meat from a bird is considered "meat" or not. Thus, though a gentile is forbidden from eating such meat, he is not executed as punishment.

90. Kosher slaughter involves slitting the gullet and the wind-pipe. Once this is done, the animal will surely die within moments.

91. After slaughter, an animal will frequently move its limbs convulsively for a short time.

92. The animal is considered alive until it stops moving. The Radbaz states that although a prohibtion exists, since the animal has been ritually slaughtered, a gentile is not executed for violating this prohibition.

93. In contrast, a Jew is only liable for eating a limb from a kosher species (*Hilchot Ma'acholot Assurot* 5:1). The prohibition against a Jew's eating such meat is derived from the verse (Deuteronomy 12:23): "Do not eat the flesh with its life." *Chullin* 102a explains that the prohibition only applies to flesh that we are permitted to eat. Such an exclusion does not apply regarding gentiles.

94. A Jew is not held liable under such circumstances. *Chullin* 121b permits a gentile to

city[95] to render judgement concerning these six mitzvot[96] and to admonish the people [regarding their observance].[97]

A gentile who transgresses these seven commands shall be executed[98] by decapitation.[99] For this reason, all the inhabitants of Shechem were obligated to die. Shechem kidnapped.[100] They observed and were aware of [his deeds], but did not judge him.[101]

A gentile is executed [on the basis of the testimony of] one witness[102] and [the verdict of] a single judge.[103] No warning [is required].[104] Relatives may serve as witnesses.[105] However, a woman may not serve as a witness or a judge for them.[106]

CHAPTER TEN

1. A gentile who inadvertently violates one of his commandments is exempt from all [punishment][1] with the exception of a person who kills inadvertently.[2] [In such an instance,] the redeemer of the blood[3] is not executed for slaying [the killer],[4] nor may the latter [seek asylum] in a city of refuge.[5] However, the court will not execute him.

When does the above apply? When he inadvertently violates a command without [sinful] intention; for example, a person who engages in relations with

eat flesh from an animal slaughtered in this fashion and the Rashbah and other authorities accept this view. However, the Rambam follows *Chullin* 33a which forbid a gentile from eating this meat.

95. *Hilchot Sanhderin* 1:1 obligates the Jews to set up courts "in every major city and town." However, that obligation applies only in *Eretz Yisrael*. In the Diaspora, they are only obligated to establish courts in every major city (*ibid.* 1:2). Similarly, gentiles need not establish courts in towns.

96. The Ramban (Genesis 34:13) disagrees and explains that the main function of these courts was not to deal with the ritual elements of these mitzvot, but rather to deal with civil cases, e.g. petty theft, wage disputes, and fraud.

97. To cite a parallel: *Tanna D'bei Eliyahu* (Chapter 11) also stresses that a court's responsibilities extend beyond the realm of judgement: "The *Sanhderin* is obligated to tie iron garters around their loins, lift their robes above their ankles... and travel throughout the villages of Israel... teaching the nation."

98. In contrast to a Jew, a gentile offender is executed for the violation of even the slightest command. As mentioned in the commentary to Halachah 1 of this chapter, the gentiles were created in order to allow for the maintenance of a stable and orderly world. All the seven commands have that intent. Hence, by violating one of those seven commands, they contradict their very purpose for existence.

99. See the commentary to Chapter 3, Hachahah 8.

100. Genesis 33:18 relates that during Jacob's return journey from Padan Aram to his father's home, he camped outside the city of Shechem. Shechem, prince of the city, kidnapped Dinah, Jacob's daughter, and raped her.

101. As retribution, Shimon and Levi, two of Jacob's sons slew every male in the entire city.

The Ramban (*ibid.*) does not accept the Rambam's interpretation of those events. He notes that Jacob severely reprimanded his sons for their behavior and did not forgive them

בְּשֵׁשׁ מִצְוֹת אֵלּוּ וּלְהַזְהִיר אֶת הָעָם. וּבֶן־נֹחַ שֶׁעָבַר עַל אַחַת מִשֶּׁבַע מִצְוֹת אֵלּוּ – יֵהָרֵג בְּסַיִף. וּמִפְּנֵי זֶה נִתְחַיְּבוּ כָּל בַּעֲלֵי שְׁכֶם הֲרִיגָה, שֶׁהֲרֵי שְׁכֶם גָּזַל, וְהֵם רָאוּ וְיָדְעוּ וְלֹא דָנוּהוּ. וּבֶן־נֹחַ נֶהֱרָג בְּעֵד אֶחָד וּבְדַיָּן אֶחָד, בְּלֹא הַתְרָאָה, וְעַל־פִּי קְרוֹבִין, אֲבָל לֹא בְּעֵדוּת אִשָּׁה, וְלֹא תָדוּן אִשָּׁה לָהֶם.

פֶּרֶק עֲשִׂירִי

א בֶּן־נֹחַ שֶׁשָּׁגַג בְּאַחַת מִמִּצְוֹתָיו – פָּטוּר מִכְּלוּם, חוּץ מֵרוֹצֵחַ בִּשְׁגָגָה, שֶׁאִם הֲרָגוֹ גּוֹאֵל הַדָּם – אֵינוֹ נֶהֱרָג עָלָיו, וְאֵין לוֹ עִיר מִקְלָט; אֲבָל בָּתֵּי־דִינֵיהֶן אֵין מְמִיתִין אוֹתוֹ. בַּמֶּה דְּבָרִים אֲמוּרִים? בְּשָׁגַג בְּאַחַת מִמִּצְוֹת וְעָבַר בְּלֹא כַוָּנָה, כְּגוֹן שֶׁבָּעַל אֵשֶׁת חֲבֵרוֹ וְדִמָּה

even on his deathbed. Had Shimon and Levi administered just and due punishment, Jacob surely would not have criticized them in this fashion.

Other commentaries defend the Rambam's opinion, explaining that Jacob did not object to the sentence administered by his sons, but rather to the guile which they employed in order to enable them to execute it (see Genesis 34: 13-25).

102. Two witnesses are required for even the slightest case in Jewish law (*Hilchot Edut* 5:1).

103. In Jewish law, capital cases are decided by 23 judges (*Hilchot Sanhderin* 5:2).

104. In contrast, a Jew is not punished for violation of a sin until he is warned that the act he is about to commit is a sin and that, in retribution, the appropriate punishment is given (*Hilchot Sanhderin* 12:1-2).

105. *Hilchot Edut*, Chapter 13 describes the relatives whose testimony is not accepted in court in cases involving Jews.

106. She is also disqualified in Jewish law (*Hilchot Edut* 9:2).

1. In contrast, a Jew is obligated to bring a sin offering for the inadvertent violation of a negative command.

Makkot 9a,b derives the exemption of a gentile from Avimelech's dialogue with God after he took Sarah (Genesis 20:3-7). God told Avimelech that he was liable to die. Avimelech protested that he did not know she was married and hence, had acted inadvertently. God replied that generally, an inadvertent offence is pardoned. However, in this instance, Avimelech would be held responsible. If his servants had not pressured Abraham concerning Sarah, he would never have said she was his sister.

2. In such an instance, a Jew is exiled to a city of refuge (See *Hilchot Rotzeach*, Chapter 5).

3. A relative of the deceased who desires to avenge his death.

4. However, he is not obligated to do so (see *Hilchot Rotzeach* 5:10).

5. The *Lechem Mishneh* notes that this applies to a gentile who has not formally accepted the responsibilities of a resident alien. In regard to a resident alien himself, *Hilchot Rotzeach* 5:4 explains that he is executed for inadvertently slaying a Jew. However, if he inadvertently kills another resident alien, he may seek asylum in a city of refuge as Numbers 35:15 states: "These six cities will be a place of refuge for the Israelites, converts, and residents among them" (*ibid.* 5:3).

his colleague's wife under the impression that she is his own wife or unmarried.[6]

If, however, one knew that she was his colleague's wife, but did not know that she was forbidden to him or it occurred to him that this act was permitted[7] or one killed without knowing that it is forbidden to kill,[8] he is considered close to [having sinned] intentionally and is executed. This is not considered as an inadvertent violation. For he should have learned [the obligations incumbent upon him] and did not.[9]

2. A gentile who is forced by another person to violate one of his commandments is permitted to transgress.[10] Even if he is forced to worship false gods, he may worship them.[11] For [gentiles] are not commanded to sanctify God's name.[12]

A gentile minor, deaf-mute, or fool[13] is never given punishment for they are not [bound by any] commandments.[14]

3. A gentile who converted, was circumcised, and immersed [in the *mikveh*],[15] and, afterwards, decided to forsake God and revert to his previous [status as] a resident alien is not granted permission to do so. Rather, he must remain as an Israelite in all matters or be executed.[16]

If he was a minor and immersed by the court,[17] he may repudiate [his conversion] when he attains majority and assume the status of a resident alien

6. In such an instance, the gentile has no intent to violate God's will. The commentaries explain that he is only freed of liability if he was misled concerning the identity of the woman with whom he engaged in relations. Otherwise, he is responsible to check to make sure no prohibition is involved.

7. Certainly, one should realize that relations with another person's wife are not permitted.

8. *Makkot* 9a relates that, in a similar circumstance, a Jew is not allowed to seek asylum in a city of refuge. Though he is not executed by the court, he must always live in dread of the redeemer of the blood (*Hilchot Rotzeach* 6:5).

9. As mentioned at the conclusion of Chapter 8, all the seven mitzvot are concepts that can and should be intellectually comprehended. Every individual should appreciate these basic statutes or, at the very least, realize the need for rules within a society and seek guidance from others.

10. In contrast, a Jew is obligated to sacrifice his life rather than transgress three sins: idol worship, murder, and illicit sexual relations. Furthermore, when the gentiles attempt to stamp out Jewish practice, we are obligated to sacrifice our lives for the performance of other mitzvot (See *Hilchot Yesodei HaTorah* 5:1-4).

Hilchot Yesodei HaTorah 5:6 relates that similar principles apply with regard to remedies. If a person is ill and can be healed by the violation of one of the Torah's commands, e.g. eating non-kosher food, he may violate that command in order to save his life or health. In this instance as well, a differentiation is made regarding the three sins mentioned above. Even if a Jew is deathly ill, he may not violate these commands.

The commentaries question whether a gentile may heal himself through the violation of the seven mitzvot. The wording used by the Rambam "be forced by another person" might imply that only under such circumstances may a gentile violate the seven commands. License is granted because he is not acting voluntarily. In contrast, the willful transgression of a command, even for the sake of a remedy, is not permitted.

שֶׁהִיא אִשְׁתּוֹ אוֹ פְּנוּיָה; אֲבָל אִם יָדַע שֶׁהִיא אֵשֶׁת חֲבֵרוֹ, וְלֹא יָדַע שֶׁהִיא אֲסוּרָה עָלָיו, אֶלָּא עָלָה עַל לִבּוֹ שֶׁדָּבָר זֶה מֻתָּר לוֹ; וְכֵן אִם הָרַג, וְהוּא לֹא יָדַע שֶׁאָסוּר לַהֲרֹג – הֲרֵי זֶה קָרוֹב לְמֵזִיד וְנֶהֱרָג; וְלֹא תֵחָשֵׁב זוֹ לָהֶם שְׁגָגָה, מִפְּנֵי שֶׁהָיָה לוֹ לִלְמֹד וְלֹא לָמַד.

ב בֶּן־נֹחַ שֶׁאֲנָסוֹ אַנָּס לַעֲבֹר עַל אַחַת מִמִּצְוֹתָיו – מֻתָּר לוֹ לַעֲבֹר. אֲפִלּוּ נֶאֱנַס לַעֲבוֹד עֲבוֹדָה זָרָה – עוֹבֵד, לְפִי שֶׁאֵין מְצֻוִּין עַל קִדּוּשׁ־הַשֵּׁם. וּלְעוֹלָם אֵין עוֹנְשִׁין מֵהֶן, לֹא קָטָן וְלֹא חֵרֵשׁ וְלֹא שׁוֹטֶה, לְפִי שֶׁאֵינָן בְּנֵי מִצְוֹת.

ג בֶּן־נֹחַ שֶׁנִּתְגַּיֵּר וּמָל וְטָבַל, וְאַחַר־כָּךְ רָצָה לַחֲזֹר מֵאַחֲרֵי ה׳ וְלִהְיוֹת גֵּר תּוֹשָׁב בִּלְבַד כְּשֶׁהָיָה מִקֹּדֶם – אֵין שׁוֹמְעִין לוֹ, אֶלָּא יִהְיֶה כְּיִשְׂרָאֵל לְכָל דָּבָר, אוֹ יֵהָרֵג. וְאִם הָיָה קָטָן כְּשֶׁהִטְבִּילוּהוּ בֵּית־דִּין – יָכוֹל לִמְחוֹת בְּשָׁעָה שֶׁיַּגְדִּיל, וְיִהְיֶה גֵּר תּוֹשָׁב בִּלְבָד. וְכֵיוָן

However, this differentiation is not accepted by all opinions. Many explain that even in this instance, a gentile may violate a command to save his life.

11. II Kings, Chapter 5 relates how Elisha, the prophet, cured Naaman, commander of the Syrian forces, of leprosy. After his miraculous cure, Naaman exclaimed "Now, I know that there is no God in all the earth except in Israel."

Naaman willingly accepted the seven commandments. However, he made one provision: "May God pardon his servant when my master goes down to the house of Rimon and prostrates himself there. For my master leans on my hand and I also prostrate myself." Elisha made no comment, seemingly indicating that his behavior was acceptable (*Sanhderin* 75a).

12. The commandment to sanctify God's name states (Leviticus 22:32): "I shall be sanctified in the midst of Israel;" implying that it only applies to Jews (Jerusalem Talmud, *Sh'vi'it* 4:3).

13. For they are not capable of taking responsibility for their conduct.

14. According to Torah law, Jewish children are not obligated to perform any mitzvot. Nevertheless, our Sages required their parents to train them in the observance of Torah and mitzvot. The commentaries question if gentiles are also obligated to train their offspring regarding their mitzvot.

15. Conversion requires these three steps (*Hilchot Issurei Bi'ah* 12:4).

16. Judaism is not a faith which is merely intellectually accepted. Rather, it constitutes an essential part of one's being and defines one's very essence. Therefore, a Jew can never leave his faith. Regardless of his behavior, he will always remain a Jew.

The same principles apply to a convert. With his acceptance of Judaism and performance of the conversion rites, he becomes a full Jew. In this regard, no distinction can be made between him and a native-born Israelite. Thus, a return to his previous status is impossible.

17. *Ketubot* 11a relates that a court has the right to take this step on the child's behalf for it is to his advantage to become part of the Jewish faith.

It must be emphasized that the court need not seek potential converts. However, if a gentile minor seeks to convert or a child's parents who have themselves converted wish their children to share their new faith, then, the court may take this step. Similarly, if the court feels that it is in the child's best interest to convert, they may convert him (*Kessef Mishneh*).

alone.[18] However, if he does not object as soon as he attains majority, he is no longer given the opportunity to object and his [status] is that of a righteous convert.[19]

Therefore, if a Jew has relations with a girl below the age of majority[20] who was immersed [in the *mikveh*] by a court,[21] the money due her as payment of her *ketubah*[22] or as a fine for raping her[23] or seducing her[24] is placed in the custody of the court until she attains majority and does not repudiate her conversion. [This step is taken] lest she take the money, attain majority, and then, repudiate her conversion. Thus, she would derive benefit as a gentile from monies to which she is only entitled according to Jewish law. [25]

4. A gentile who converts after cursing God's name, worshipping false gods, engaging in relations with a colleague's wife, or killing a fellow gentile[26] is exempt [from punishment].[27]

[In contrast,] if he converted after killing a Jew[28] or having relations with a Jew's wife, he is liable.[29] He is decapitated for [killing] the Jew[30] and strangled to death for engaging in relations with a Jew's wife.[31] [He is given the latter punishment] because the laws governing him have changed.[32]

5. It has already been explained that gentiles are always executed by decapitation[33] except in cases when one engages in relations with the wife of a Jew or a consecrated maiden. [In the latter instance,] he is stoned to death.[34]

If he engaged in relations with a Jew's wife after they married, but before they ever engaged in relations, he is executed by strangulation.[35]

18. A convert must willingly accept Judaism. Since a child is not responsible for his actions, his acceptance as a minor is not significant and he is given this choice when he attains majority.

19. The Ran (*Ketubot*, *ibid.*) questions when this objection must be made. No attention is paid to the objection if it is made when the child is a minor or after he attains majority. To require the statement to be made at the precise moment when the child reaches majority is difficult.

Thus, he concludes that the child must repudiate his conversion before attaining majority. Afterwards, if he does not resume Jewish practice before attaining majority, it is considered as if he never converted.

20. As will be explained, this applies whether they engaged in relations within or outside the context of marriage.

21. As part of the conversion process.

22. In the event the man marries her. The marriage contract includes a provision for a sum to be given the woman in the event of death or divorce.

23. Deuteronomy 22:29 requires a person who rapes a virgin girl to pay 50 silver shekels as a fine.

24. Exodus 22:15 obligates a similar fine to be paid for seducing a virgin girl. *Ketubot*, *ibid.*, specifies that these fines are only paid if the girl converts before the age of three.

25. Nevertheless, as soon as the obligation is incurred, the money is given to the court. Thus, in the case of divorce, the convert's husband will not think that he will be freed of

שֶׁלֹּא מִחָה בִּשְׁעָתוֹ – שׁוּב אֵינוֹ מוֹחֶה, אֶלָּא הֲרֵי הוּא גֵר־צֶדֶק. לְפִיכָךְ אִם בָּא יִשְׂרָאֵל עַל קְטַנָּה שֶׁהִטְבִּילוּהָ בֵית־דִּין – כֶּסֶף כְּתֻבָּתָהּ אוֹ קְנַס אוֹנֵס אוֹ מְפַתֶּה, יִהְיֶה הַכֹּל תַּחַת יַד בֵּית־דִּין, עַד שֶׁתַּגְדִּיל וְלֹא תְמַחֶה בַּגֵּרוּת; שֶׁמָּא תִטֹּל וְתַגְדִּיל וּתְמַחֶה, וְנִמְצֵאת זוֹ אוֹכֶלֶת בְּגַיּוּתָהּ מָעוֹת שֶׁאֵין לָהּ זְכוּת בָּהֶן אֶלָּא בְּדִינֵי יִשְׂרָאֵל.

ד בֶּן־נֹחַ שֶׁבֵּרַךְ אֶת הַשֵּׁם, אוֹ שֶׁעָבַד עֲבוֹדָה זָרָה, אוֹ שֶׁבָּא עַל אֵשֶׁת חֲבֵרוֹ, אוֹ שֶׁהָרַג חֲבֵרוֹ וְנִתְגַּיֵּר – פָּטוּר. הָרַג בֶּן־יִשְׂרָאֵל, אוֹ שֶׁבָּא עַל אֵשֶׁת יִשְׂרָאֵל וְנִתְגַּיֵּר – חַיָּב. וְהוֹרְגִין אוֹתוֹ עַל בֶּן־יִשְׂרָאֵל, וְחוֹנְקִין אוֹתוֹ עַל אֵשֶׁת יִשְׂרָאֵל שֶׁבָּעַל, שֶׁהֲרֵי נִשְׁתַּנָּה דִינוֹ.

ה כְּבָר בֵּאַרְנוּ, שֶׁכָּל מִיתַת בְּנֵי נֹחַ בְּסַיִף; אֶלָּא אִם בָּעַל אֵשֶׁת יִשְׂרָאֵל אוֹ נַעֲרָה מְאֹרָסָה – יִסָּקֵל. וְאִם בְּעָלָהּ אַחַר שֶׁנִּכְנְסָה לְחֻפָּה קֹדֶם שֶׁתִּבָּעֵל – יֵחָנֵק.

the obligation of a *ketubah* and the rapist or seducer will have to take responsibility for his acts immediately.

26. The same law applies to a gentile who converts after eating flesh from a living animal, stealing, or ignoring his responsibility to judge his colleagues. However, since a Jew is not given the death penalty for these sins, the Rambam did not feel it necessary to mention them.

27. Rashi (*Sanhderin* 71b) explains that he is exempt from punishment because, as a Jew, the process by which he is to be judged has changed (he must be warned, two witnesses must observe him, etc.) and his sentence is changed. He receives a more severe death penalty (for cursing God or idol worship) or no penalty at all (for killing or engaging in relations with a gentile).

Most commentaries agree that this law applies even if a gentile converted after being sentenced to death. However, some authorities maintain that in such an instance, the death sentence remains in force. They base their opinion on *Hilchot Mamrim* 7:9 which explains that a rebellious son is only executed before he attains the age of thirteen and three months. However, if he is sentenced to death before that time and flees, he is executed even after he reaches that age.

28. As a gentile, he would receive the same punishment.

29. Though the process by which he is to be judged has changed, the sentence remains the same or is lighter. Hence, he is still held responsible for his deeds.

30. As a gentile, he would receive the same punishment.

31. As a gentile, this deed would be punished by decapitation, a more severe form of execution.

32. See *Lechem Mishneh*.

A gentile who converted after stealing from a Jew must restore the stolen property. However, according to most authorities, a gentile who converted after eating flesh from a living animal is not punished by lashes as a Jew would be.

33. See Chapter 9, Halachah 14, Chapter 3, Halachah 8.

34. In the Yemenite manuscripts of the *Mishneh Torah*, the word "or" is omitted. Thus, the phrase reads "a consecrated maiden married to a Jew." This version is preferable because relations with a married Jewess are punished by decapitation as explained in Chapter 9, Halachah 7.

35. This law is also mentioned in Chapter 9, Halachah 7. Indeed, the entire halachah is

6. According to the Oral Tradition,[36] gentiles are forbidden to cross-breed animals and graft different species of trees together.[37] However, they are not executed for [violating this prohibition.][38]

A gentile who gave a Jew a blow is liable to die[39] for causing even the most minimal damage.[40] Nevertheless, he is not executed.[41]

7. Only Abraham and his descendants were commanded regarding circumcision as [Genesis 17:9-10] states: "[Keep My covenant,] you and your offspring... [circumcise every male]."[42]

The descendants of Ishmael are excluded, as implied by [Genesis 21:12]: "It is through Isaac that your offspring will be called."[43] Esau's [descendants] are also excluded,[44] for Isaac told Jacob [Genesis 28:4]: "May [God] grant Abraham's blessing to you and your descendants," implying that only he is the true offspring of Abraham who maintains his faith and his upright behavior. Thus, they [alone] are obligated in circumcision. [45]

8. Our Sages related[46] that the descendants of Keturah who are the offspring of Abraham that came after Isaac and Ishmael[47] are also obligated in circumcision.[48] Since, at present, the descendants of Ishmael have become intermingled with the descendants of Keturah,[49] they are all obligated to be circumcised[50] on the eighth day.[51] However, they are not executed for [failure to perform this mitzvah].[52]

redundant. However, it is included to summarize the laws regarding a gentile's execution. Until now, all the sins mentioned carried the penalty of execution by the court. In contrast, though some of the violations mentioned in the following halachot are punishable by death by the hand of God, an earthly court administers no retribution.

36. *Sanhderin* 56b.

37. These prohibitions are included in the category of *kilayim*. Jews are also forbidden to grow different species of crops in the same field and wear garments that combine linen and wool. See Leviticus 19:19.

38. *Sanhderin* 57a considers it an accepted tradition that gentiles are only executed for the violation of seven sins.

39. By the hand of God.

40. *Sanhderin* 58b explains that Moses killed an Egyptian taskmaster (Exodus 2:11) for violating this prohibition.

41. The Maharshah (*Sanhderin, ibid.*) states that, as above, the Sages accepted the tradition that only seven mitzvot are punishable by death. Based on that decision, he explains that Moses' act was an exception. With prophetic intuition, Moses saw that no good would ever come from this Egyptian and therefore, slew him.

42. *Sanhderin* 59a,b relates that any mitzvah which was given before Sinai and repeated at Sinai is incumbent on both Jews and gentiles. However, circumcision is not governed by this principle for, as obvious from the verse quoted, it was specifically given only to Abraham and his descendants.

This halachah is included because the Rambam wanted to contrast the obligation of the

ו מִפִּי הַקַּבָּלָה, שֶׁבְּנֵי נֹחַ אֲסוּרִין בְּהַרְבָּעַת בְּהֵמָה וּבְהַרְכָּבַת אִילָן בִּלְבַד, וְאֵין נֶהֱרָגִין עֲלֵיהֶן. וְעַכּוּ״ם שֶׁהִכָּה יִשְׂרָאֵל – אֲפִלּוּ חָבַל בּוֹ כָּל־שֶׁהוּא, אַף־עַל־פִּי שֶׁהוּא חַיָּב מִיתָה – אֵינוֹ נֶהֱרָג.

ז הַמִּילָה, נִצְטַוָּה בָּהּ אַבְרָהָם וְזַרְעוֹ בִּלְבַד, שֶׁנֶּאֱמַר: ״אַתָּה וְזַרְעֲךָ אַחֲרֶיךָ״ – יָצָא זַרְעוֹ שֶׁל יִשְׁמָעֵאל, שֶׁנֶּאֱמַר: ״כִּי בְיִצְחָק יִקָּרֵא לְךָ זָרַע״, וְיָצָא עֵשָׂו, שֶׁהֲרֵי יִצְחָק אָמַר לְיַעֲקֹב: ״וְיִתֶּן לְךָ אֶת בִּרְכַּת אַבְרָהָם לְךָ וּלְזַרְעֲךָ״, מִכְּלָל, שֶׁהוּא לְבַדּוֹ זַרְעוֹ שֶׁל אַבְרָהָם הַמַּחֲזִיק בְּדָתוֹ וּבְדַרְכּוֹ הַיְשָׁרָה, וְהֵם הַמְחֻיָּבִין בְּמִילָה.

ח אָמְרוּ חֲכָמִים, שֶׁבְּנֵי קְטוּרָה, שֶׁהֵם זַרְעוֹ שֶׁל אַבְרָהָם שֶׁבָּא אַחַר יִשְׁמָעֵאל וְיִצְחָק – חַיָּבִין בְּמִילָה. וְהוֹאִיל וְנִתְעָרְבוּ הַיּוֹם בְּנֵי יִשְׁמָעֵאל בִּבְנֵי קְטוּרָה – יִתְחַיְּבוּ הַכֹּל בְּמִילָה בַּשְּׁמִינִי; וְאֵין נֶהֱרָגִין עָלֶיהָ.

descendants of Keturah mentioned in the following halachah with the obligation of the gentiles to keep their seven mitzvot. This halachah is a necessary preface to that law.

43. The verse implies that only Isaac is considered Abraham's spiritual progeny and it is through him, that he will attain posterity. Hence, his descendants and not those of Ishmael are obligated in circumcision.

44. *Yalkut Shimoni, Toldot,* relates that Esau circumcised his descendants as long as Isaac was alive.

45. *Sanhderin* 59b derives the exclusion of Esau from Genesis 21:12. The expression "through Isaac," *biYitzchak*, can also be rendered as "in Isaac," implying "not all of Isaac." It is curious why the Rambam quotes another source when an explicit Talmudic reference exists.

46. *Sanhderin* 59b.

47. Genesis 25:1 mentions that after Sarah's death, Abraham married another woman, Keturah. She bore him six sons.

48. Since they were born after God commanded Abraham to circumcise all his descendants, they are obligated to be circumcised.

49. Both settled in the Arabian desert.

50. Because of the doubt involved in their lineage.

51. As the Jews are. Ishmael was born before Abraham's circumcision and was circumcised at the age of thirteen. Many Arabs follow the custom of circumcising their children at that age.

In Jewish law, circumcision is a two staged process involving *milah* - cutting the foreskin, and *priyah* - ripping open the thin membrane covering the crown of the penus. *Tosafot* (*Yevamot* 71b) states that Abraham (and thus, the descendants of Keturah) were not required to perform *priyah*. However, the Rambam does not make this distinction.

52. The commentaries ask a general question concerning this halachah: As explained in the notes to Chapter 5, Halachah 4, Sannecherib, king of Assyria conquered many countries and engaged in mass population transfers, thus, obliterating the national identity of most of Israel's neighbors. If so, why was the status of Keturah's descendants left unaffected?

9. A gentile who studies the Torah[53] is obligated to die.[54] They should be involved only in the study of their seven mitzvot.[55]

Similarly, a gentile who rests,[56] even on a weekday, observing that day as a Sabbath,[57] is obligated to die. Needless to say, [he is obligated for that punishment] if he creates a festival for himself.[58]

The general principle governing these matters is: They are not to be allowed to originate a new religion or create mitzvot for themselves based on their own decisions.[59] They may either become righteous converts and accept all the mitzvot or retain their statutes without adding or detracting from them.

If [a gentile] studies the Torah, makes a Sabbath, or creates a [religious] practice, a [Jewish court] should beat him,[60] punish him,[61] and inform him that he is obligated to die.[62] However, he is not to be executed.

10. We should not prevent a gentile who desires to perform one of the Torah's mitzvot[63] in order to receive reward from doing so,[64] [provided] he performs it as required.[65] If he brings [an animal to be sacrificed] as a burnt offering, we should receive it.[66]

If a gentile [who observes the seven mitzvot] gives charity, we should accept it from him. It appears to me that it should be given to the Jewish poor for the gentile [may] derive his sustenance from the Jews and they are commanded to

53. Other than their seven mitzvot.

54. At the hand of God. *Sanhderin* 59a comments: Deuteronomy 33:4 states: "The Torah which Moses commanded us is the heritage of the childen of Israel." "It is our heritage and not theirs." The passage continues, noting the connection between the word *morashah*, "heritage" and *meurasah*, "consecrated" and explains that a gentile's study of Torah is equivalent to adultery.

55. As mentioned in Halachah 8:10, the Jews have an obligation to instruct the gentiles in the performance of their seven mitzvot.

A gentile who is well versed in the particular laws involved in the observance of his seven mitzvot is worthy of more respect than a unlearned High Priest (*Sanhderin, loc. cit.*).

The seven mitzvot are by no means a narrow field of study. The Meiri (*Sanhderin, loc. cit.*) states that most elements of the Torah are included within them. For example, to observe the prohibition against the worship of false Gods correctly, one must become aware of God's unity with creation. Accordingly, a number of contemporary Sages have suggested the translation of certain basic Chassidic and Kabbalistic texts into English with the intent that they be studied by gentiles.

56. Genesis 8:22 records God's promise to Noah "As long as the earth lasts... day and night shall not cease." Yishbotu translated as "cease," can also be interpreted as "rest." Thus, *Sanhderin* 58b interprets the verse as a command prohibiting Noah's descendants from resting "day and night."

57. Rashi (*Sanhderin, ibid.*) explains that not only is a gentile is forbidden to fix a day as a day of rest, he is prohibited against taking a day off from work even to relax. In contrast, the Meiri maintains that the prohibition involves establishing a day of rest.

ט עכו"ם שֶׁעָסַק בַּתּוֹרָה – חַיָּב מִיתָה. לֹא יַעֲסֹק אֶלָּא בְּשֶׁבַע מִצְוֹת שֶׁלָּהֶן בִּלְבַד. וְכֵן עכו"ם שֶׁשָּׁבַת אֲפִלּוּ בְּיוֹם מִימוֹת הַחֹל, אִם עֲשָׂאָהוּ לְעַצְמוֹ כְּמוֹ שַׁבָּת – חַיָּב מִיתָה; וְאֵין צָרִיךְ לוֹמַר אִם עָשָׂה מוֹעֵד לְעַצְמוֹ. כְּלָלוֹ שֶׁל דָּבָר: אֵין מַנִּיחִין אוֹתָן לְחַדֵּשׁ דָּת וְלַעֲשׂוֹת מִצְוֹת לְעַצְמָן מִדַּעְתָּן; אֶלָּא אוֹ יִהְיֶה גֵּר־צֶדֶק וִיקַבֵּל כָּל הַמִּצְוֹת, אוֹ יַעֲמֹד בְּתוֹרָתוֹ וְלֹא יוֹסִיף וְלֹא יִגְרַע. וְאִם עָסַק בַּתּוֹרָה אוֹ שָׁבַת אוֹ חִדֵּשׁ דָּבָר – מַכִּין אוֹתוֹ וְעוֹנְשִׁין אוֹתוֹ וּמוֹדִיעִין אוֹתוֹ שֶׁהוּא חַיָּב מִיתָה עַל זֶה, אֲבָל אֵינוֹ נֶהֱרָג.

י בֶּן־נֹחַ שֶׁרָצָה לַעֲשׂוֹת מִצְוָה מִשְּׁאָר מִצְוֹת הַתּוֹרָה כְּדֵי לְקַבֵּל שָׂכָר – אֵין מוֹנְעִין אוֹתוֹ לַעֲשׂוֹתָהּ כְּהִלְכָתָהּ. וְאִם הֵבִיא עוֹלָה – מְקַבְּלִין מִמֶּנּוּ. נָתַן צְדָקָה – מְקַבְּלִין מִמֶּנּוּ; וְיֵרָאֶה לִי, שֶׁנּוֹתְנִין אוֹתָהּ לַעֲנִיֵּי יִשְׂרָאֵל, הוֹאִיל וְהוּא נִזּוֹן מִיִּשְׂרָאֵל, וּמִצְוָה

However, a gentile is not prohibited against taking a vacation. The Rambam appears to follow the latter opinion.

58. The observance of a festival generally implies a religious content in addition to being a day of rest. Thus, it is surely forbidden.

59. At the conclusion of Chapter 11, the Rambam notes that Christianity and Islam have certain redeeming factors for they abolished paganism and "paved the way for the coming of the Mashiach." Nevertheless, in themselves, these faiths are forbidden and may not be observed even by a gentile.

60. As mentioned in Halachah 8:10, the Jews are obligated to compel the gentiles to observe their mitzvot. When we had undisputed rule over *Eretz Yisrael*, we were able to enforce these mitzvot by administering corporal, and, when required, capital punishment. Even when we no longer have this potential, we are obligated to do whatever possible to make sure the gentiles observe the statutes the Torah established for them.

61. I.e., take economic sanctions against him.

62. By the hand of God.

63. I.e., one of the 613 mitzvot commanded to the Jews aside from Torah study and the Sabbath.

64. A person who is not commanded to fulfill a mitzvah receives less reward from God for its observance than one who is commanded. Nevertheless, even in the latter instance, God acknowledges the person's deeds and grants him blessing.

A gentile may only fulfill mitzvot for the sake of reward. He is forbidden to accept them as obligations incumbent upon him. Thus, his intent must be the very opposite of a Jew's who serves God for His sake and not for his own.

The commentaries question the source for the Rambam's statements. Some point to the statements of *Kohelet Rabbah*, Chapter 1: In the Messianic age, God will proclaim: "Whoever has never eaten pork, come and receive a reward." Many gentiles will respond and come to receive their reward.

65. He must perform the mitzvah in all of its particulars as required by Jewish law. The Radbaz explains that mitzvot which require holiness and purity, for example, *tefillin* or *mezuzah*, should be withheld from gentiles.

66. The only sacrifice a gentile is allowed to bring is a burnt offering (*korban olah*) A peace offering or meal offering is not accepted from them. Even the libations which accompany the burnt offering may not be brought by the gentile and are purchased with communal funds (*Hilchot Ma'aseh HaKorbonot* 3:2,5).

support him [if necessary].[67] In contrast, if an idolater gives charity, we should accept it from him[68] and give it to the gentile poor.[69]

11. The Jewish court is obligated to appoint judges for these resident aliens[70] to judge them according to these statutes so that the world will not become decadent.[71]

If the court sees fit to appoint the judges from [the resident aliens] themselves, they may. If it sees fit to appoint them from among the Jews, they may.

12. [The following laws apply when] two idolaters[72] come before you to [have their dispute] judged according to Jewish law.[73] If they both desire to be judged according to Torah law, they should be judged [accordingly]. If one desires [to be judged according to Torah law] and the other does not,[74] they are only forced to be judged according to their own laws.[75]

[The following laws apply when] there is [a dispute between] a Jew and an idolater: If the Jew will fare better according to their laws, they are judged according to their laws. [When the judgement is rendered, the judges] explain: "Your law obligates this judgement." If the Jew will fare better according to our laws, they are judged according to Torah law. [When the judgement is rendered, the judges] explain: "Our law obligates this judgement."[76] It appears to me that this approach is not followed in regard to a resident alien. Rather, he is always judged according to their laws.[77]

Similarly, it appears to me that in regard to respect and honor and also, in regard to charity, a resident alien is to be treated as a Jew for behold, we are commanded to sustain them as [Deuteronomy 14:21] states: "[You may not eat any animal that has not been properly slaughtered...] give it to the resident alien in your gates that he may eat it."[78] Though our Sages counseled against

67. Leviticus 25:35 states "When your brother becomes impoverished... come to his aid. Help him survive, whether he is an alien or a native [Israelite]" (see Halachah 12). Since such a gentile may benefit from Jewish generosity, charity given by him may be used for the Jewish poor.

68. *Hilchot Matanot Aniyim* 8:9 states that if a gentile king or official gives charity to the Jews, we should accept it for the sake of peace. However, if no threat of harming our relations with them is involved, it is not proper to receive charity from them (*Lechem Mishneh*).

69. Without publicizing the manner so that the gentile donor will not find out.

Two reasons are given why charity should not be accepted from gentiles:

a) The merit of their generosity will prolong their rule over the Jews (*Bava Batra* 10b).

b) The fact that Jews feel it necessay to receive charity from gentiles causes *Chillul HaShem*, the desecration of God's name, (Rashi, *Sanhderin* 26b).

70. The Radbaz emphasizes that this obligation only applies if the gentiles do not establish their own court system first.

71. The commentaries do not cite the source for this law. It is possible that it is derived from the obligation to compel the gentiles to accept the seven mitzvot mentioned in Halachah 8:10.

עֲלֵיהֶם לְהַחֲיוֹתוֹ; אֲבָל הָעַכּוּ״ם שֶׁנָּתַן צְדָקָה – מְקַבְּלִין מִמֶּנּוּ וְנוֹתְנִין אוֹתָהּ לַעֲנִיֵּי עַכּוּ״ם.

יא חַיָּבִין בֵּית־דִּין שֶׁל יִשְׂרָאֵל לַעֲשׂוֹת שׁוֹפְטִים לְאֵלּוּ הַגֵּרִים הַתּוֹשָׁבִים, לָדוּן לָהֶן עַל־פִּי הַמִּשְׁפָּטִים הָאֵלּוּ, כְּדֵי שֶׁלֹּא יִשָּׁחֵת הָעוֹלָם. אִם רָאוּ בֵּית־דִּין שֶׁיַּעֲמִידוּ שׁוֹפְטֵיהֶם מֵהֶן – מַעֲמִידִין, וְאִם רָאוּ שֶׁיַּעֲמִידוּ לָהֶם מִיִּשְׂרָאֵל – מַעֲמִידִין.

יב שְׁנֵי עַכּוּ״ם שֶׁבָּאוּ לְפָנֶיךָ לָדוּן בְּדִינֵי יִשְׂרָאֵל וְרָצוּ שְׁנֵיהֶם לָדוּן דִּין־תּוֹרָה – דָּנִין. הָאֶחָד רוֹצֶה וְהָאֶחָד אֵינֶנּוּ רוֹצֶה – אֵין כּוֹפִין אוֹתוֹ לָדוּן אֶלָּא בְּדִינֵיהֶן. הָיָה יִשְׂרָאֵל וְעַכּוּ״ם, אִם יֵשׁ זְכוּת לַיִּשְׂרָאֵל בְּדִינֵיהֶם – דָּנִין לוֹ בְּדִינֵיהֶם וְאוֹמְרִים לוֹ: כָּךְ דִּינֵיכֶם! וְאִם יֵשׁ זְכוּת לַיִּשְׂרָאֵל בְּדִינֵינוּ – דָּנִין לוֹ דִּין־תּוֹרָה וְאוֹמְרִים לוֹ: כָּךְ דִּינֵינוּ! וְיֵרָאֶה לִי, שֶׁאֵין עוֹשִׂין כֵּן לְגֵר תּוֹשָׁב, אֶלָּא לְעוֹלָם דָּנִין לוֹ בְּדִינֵיהֶם. וְכֵן יֵרָאֶה לִי, שֶׁנּוֹהֲגִין עִם גֵּרֵי תוֹשָׁב בְּדֶרֶךְ־אֶרֶץ וּגְמִילוּת־חֲסָדִים כְּיִשְׂרָאֵל, שֶׁהֲרֵי אָנוּ מְצֻוִּין לְהַחֲיוֹתָן, שֶׁנֶּאֱמַר: ״לַגֵּר אֲשֶׁר בִּשְׁעָרֶיךָ תִּתְּנֶנָּה וַאֲכָלָהּ״. וְזֶה שֶׁאָמְרוּ חֲכָמִים: אֵין כּוֹפְלִין לָהֶם שָׁלוֹם –

72. In contrast to resident aliens.
73. Though the gentiles are not obligated to follow Torah law, they may willingly accept it.
74. Preferring to be judged according to the civil laws established by gentile society.
75. There are a number of differences between Jewish business law and secular law. For example, Torah law requires two witnesses and does not accept circumstantial evidence. Similarly, the formal acts of transfer through which property is acquired differ.
76. *Bava Kama* 113a, the source for this statement, continues:

> "If there is no way to vindicate the Jew, try to trick the gentile," these are the words of Rabbi Yishmael.
>
> Rabbi Akiva states: "We should not try to trick him lest it cause the desecration of God's name."

Rabbi Akiva's opinion is accepted as halachah.
77. As mentioned above, the Rambam uses the expression "it appears to me" when he has no explicit proof for his statements in Talmudic sources. Since we are commanded to sustain a resident alien, it is logical to assume that he is judged according to a single standard even though the outcome will not necessarily benefit a fellow Jew.
78. The verse concludes "or sell it to a foreigner." *Pesachim* 21b comments that it is preferable to give the animal to a resident alien (a gentile who observes the seven mitzvot) than sell it to "a foreigner" (one who does not).

There is a slight problem with the Rambam's statements. The Talmud makes the above statements on the basis of Leviticus 25:35 which states: "When your brother becomes impoverished... come to his aid. Help him survive, whether he is an alien or a native [Israelite]."

On the surface, it would be preferable to quote that verse for it directly commands us to help a resident alien. However, there is an advantage to the verse quoted by the Rambam. It clearly distinguishes between a resident alien and an idolater.

repeating a greeting to them, that statement applies to idolaters and not resident aliens.[79]

[However,] our Sages commanded us to visit the gentiles when ill, to bury their dead[80] in addition to the Jewish dead,[81] and support their poor in addition to the Jewish poor for the sake of peace.[82] Behold, [Psalms 145:9] states: "God is good to all and His mercies extend over all His works" and [Proverbs 3:17] states: "[The Torah's] ways are pleasant ways and all its paths are peace."[83]

CHAPTER ELEVEN[1]

1. In the future, the Messianic king will arise[2] and renew the Davidic dynasty, restoring it to its initial sovereignty.[3] He will build the Temple and gather the dispersed of Israel.

Then, in his days, [the observance of] all the statutes will return to their previous state.[4] We will offer sacrifices,[5] observe the Sabbatical[6] and Jubilee years[7] according to all their particulars as described by the Torah.[8]

Anyone who does not believe in him or does not await his coming, denies not only [the statements] of the other prophets,[9] but [those of] the Torah and Moses,[10] our teacher.[11]

79. For the sake of peace, we are even allowed to greet idolaters. However, it is improper to show them the honor of repeating the greeting (*Gittin* 61a).
80. And comfort their mourners (*Hilchot Evel* 14:12).
81. Rashi (*Gittin* 61a) emphasizes that the gentiles should not be buried in the same cemetery. See *Sanhderin* 47a.
82. The Radbaz (*Hilchot Matanot Aniyim* 1:9) stresses that gentiles are only given charity when they come together with the Jewish poor. If gentiles alone ask for alms, they may be refused. Other commentaries maintain that enmity may be aroused even under such circumstances and hence, suggest giving them charity at all times.
83. The above apply only in the Diaspora or when the Jews do not have undisputed power over *Eretz Yisrael*. However, when the Jews have such power, we are not permitted to allow an idolater to dwell among us even temporarily (*Hilchot Avodat Kochavim* 10:6).

1. In the original published texts of the *Mishneh Torah*, a different heading appeared above this and the following chapter. In addition to the words *Hilchot Melachim U'Milchomoteihem* - "The laws of the kings and their wars," was added the phrase *V'Hilchot Melech HaMashiach* - "and the laws of the Messianic King."
2. The Rambam did not choose to conclude *Hilchot Melachim* and the entire *Mishneh Torah* with the subject of Mashiach merely to conclude with reassuring prophecies of the future redemption.

In his preface to the *Mishneh Torah*, the Rambam explained that his goal in the composition of the work was to summarize and outline the observance of all the mitzvot. Similarly, as explained in Halachah 4:10, the king's "purpose and intent shall be to elevate the true faith and fill the world with justice," i.e. to spread the observance of Torah and mitzvot.

בְּעַכּוּ"ם, לֹא בְּגֵר תּוֹשָׁב. אֲפִלּוּ הָעַכּוּ"ם, צִוּוּ חֲכָמִים לְבַקֵּר חוֹלֵיהֶם וְלִקְבֹּר מֵתֵיהֶם עִם מֵתֵי יִשְׂרָאֵל, וּלְפַרְנֵס עֲנִיֵּיהֶם בִּכְלַל עֲנִיֵּי יִשְׂרָאֵל, מִפְּנֵי דַּרְכֵי שָׁלוֹם. הֲרֵי נֶאֱמַר: "טוֹב ה' לַכֹּל, וְרַחֲמָיו עַל כָּל מַעֲשָׂיו", וְנֶאֱמַר: "דְּרָכֶיהָ דַּרְכֵי נֹעַם, וְכָל נְתִיבֹתֶיהָ שָׁלוֹם".

פֶּרֶק אַחַד־עָשָׂר

א הַמֶּלֶךְ הַמָּשִׁיחַ עָתִיד לַעֲמֹד וּלְהַחֲזִיר מַלְכוּת דָּוִד לְיָשְׁנָהּ, לַמֶּמְשָׁלָה הָרִאשׁוֹנָה, וּבוֹנֶה הַמִּקְדָּשׁ, וּמְקַבֵּץ נִדְחֵי יִשְׂרָאֵל, וְחוֹזְרִין כָּל הַמִּשְׁפָּטִים בְּיָמָיו כְּשֶׁהָיוּ מִקֹּדֶם. מַקְרִיבִין קָרְבָּנוֹת, וְעוֹשִׂין שְׁמִטִּין וְיוֹבְלוֹת, כְּכָל מִצְוָתָהּ הָאֲמוּרָה בַּתּוֹרָה. וְכָל מִי שֶׁאֵינוֹ מַאֲמִין בּוֹ אוֹ מִי שֶׁאֵינוֹ מְחַכֶּה לְבִיאָתוֹ – לֹא בִּשְׁאָר נְבִיאִים בִּלְבַד הוּא כּוֹפֵר, אֶלָּא בַּתּוֹרָה וּבְמֹשֶׁה רַבֵּנוּ.

The coming of Mashiach represents the most complete expression of these goals. As the Rambam explains in this and the following halachot, Mashiach will rebuild the Temple and restore the observance of all the mitzvot which cannot be fulfilled at present. Hence, a description of his coming serves as an appropriate summation for *Hilchot Melachim* and the *Mishneh Torah* as a whole (*Likkutei Sichot*).

3. The Jews will be reunited in one kingdom as the prophet, Ezekiel 37:22 states: "One king will rule over them. They will no longer be two nations" (Responsa, *Chayim Sha'al* 97).

4. *Sanhderin* 51b and *Zevachim* 45a *et al* use the expression "That halachah applies in the Messianic age," to imply that only then, will the observance of all the Torah's laws be renewed.

5. In our *Mussaf* prayers, we ask God to "Bring us up in joy to our land.... There, we will offer the sacrifices in which we are obligated."

6. In the Sabbatical year, the land in *Eretz Yisrael* must be left fallow and, throughout the world, all debts are remitted.

7. All the laws of the Sabbatical year apply. In addition, slaves are released and property reverts to its original owner.

8. According to Scriptural Law, the laws governing the Sabbatical and Jubilee years must only be observed when the entire Jewish nation is living in *Eretz Yisrael*. Thus, after the exile of the ten tribes, these mitzvot were no longer applicable. (The Sabbatical year is still observed because of Rabbinic decree. *Hilchot Shemitah* 10:8.)

With the cessation of the observance of the Jubilee year, many other mitzvot, e.g. the laws of Hebrew servants and consecrated property, also ceased (*ibid.* 10:9). Similarly, the agricultural laws governing the produce of *Eretz Yisrael, Terumah* and tithes, are also only obligatory according to Scriptural Law when the entire Jewish people live in *Eretz Yisrael*. Hence, until the Messianic age, they are only observed because of Rabbinic decree (*Hilchot Terumah* 1:26).

9. Whose works are "filled with [mention of] this matter" (Halachah 2).

10. *Hilchot Yesodei HaTorah*, Chapter 8, distinguishes between Moses' prophecies and those of the other prophets, explaining that none of the other prophets can be compared to Moses. Thus, a prophecy made by Moses in the Torah must be affirmed with greater commitment.

11. Belief in Mashiach is not sufficient. A Jew's faith is not complete unless he anxiously

The Torah testified to his [coming],[12] as [Deuteronomy 30:3-5] states:

> God will bring back your captivity and have mercy upon you. He will again gather you [from among the nations].... Even if your Diaspora is at the ends of the heavens, [God will gather you up from there]... and bring you [to the land].

These explicit words of the Torah include all the statements made by all the prophets.[13]

Reference to Mashiach is also made in the portion of Bilaam who prophesies about two anointed kings:[14] the first anointed king, David,[15] who saved Israel from her oppressors;[16] and the final anointed king who will arise from his descendants[17] and save Israel in the end of days.[18] That passage [Numbers 24:17-18] relates:[19]

> "I see it, but not now" - This refers to David;
> "I perceive it, but not in the near future;" - This refers to the Messianic king;[20]
> "A star shall go forth from Jacob" - This refers to David;[21]
> "and a staff shall arise in Israel" - This refers to the Messianic king;[22]
> "crushing all of Moab's princes" - This refers to David as [II Samuel 8:2] relates: "He smote Moab and measured them with a line;"[23]
> "decimating all of Seth's descendants" - This refers to the Messianic king about whom [Zechariah 9:10] prophesies: "He will rule from sea to sea."[24]
> "Edom will be demolished" - This refers to David as [II Samuel 8:6] states "Edom became the servants of David;"[25]
> "[Seir][26] will be destroyed" - this refers to the Messianic king as [Ovadiah 1:21] prophesies: "Saviors will ascend Mount Zion [to judge the mountain of Esau.]"[27]

waits for Mashiach to come. Mashiach's coming will initiate an age in which we will have the opportunity to fulfill all the mitzvot. Our entire life will revolve around the study of Torah and the knowledge of God. A Jew who does not desire and yearn for these goals lacks basic elements of faith.

12. *Sanhderin* 99a records an opinion which states that there will be no individual Messianic redeemer for the Jewish people. Rather, God, Himself, will redeem them. However, the majority of Sages rejected that opinion, nullifying it to the point that "a person who denies Mashiach based on that opinion denies the entire Torah" (*Chatam Sofer, Yoreh De'ah,* Responsum 356).

13. Though the prophets speak about Mashiach in greater detail, the essential message of the Messianic redemption, i.e. that Mashiach will usher in an era in which Torah and mitzvot can be fulfilled in a complete manner, is implied by the Torah's statements.

14. The word Mashiach literally means "anointed one."

15. As mentioned in Halachah 1:7, Saul was also anointed with the unique oil designated for this purpose. Nevertheless, there was a fundamental difference between the anointment of David and that of Saul. Saul was only anointed from a cruse of oil, while David was anointed from a horn implying that his dynasty would continue forever (*Megillah* 14a).

16. II Samuel 7:1 relates how "God gave him (David) rest from all his enemies." David completed the conquest of *Eretz Yisrael* and subdued the Philistines and the other nations who had previously oppressed the Jews.

17. In his Commentary to the Mishnah describing the thirteen principles of faith, the

שֶׁהֲרֵי הַתּוֹרָה הֵעִידָה עָלָיו, שֶׁנֶּאֱמַר: "וְשָׁב ה' אֱלֹהֶיךָ אֶת שְׁבוּתְךָ וְרִחֲמֶךָ, וְשָׁב וְקִבֶּצְךָ וְגוֹ'. אִם יִהְיֶה נִדַּחֲךָ בִּקְצֵה הַשָּׁמַיִם וְגוֹ'. וֶהֱבִיאֲךָ ה'". וְאֵלּוּ הַדְּבָרִים הַמְפֹרָשִׁים בַּתּוֹרָה, הֵם כּוֹלְלִים כָּל הַדְּבָרִים שֶׁנֶּאֶמְרוּ עַל־יְדֵי כָּל הַנְּבִיאִים. אַף בְּפָרָשַׁת בִּלְעָם נֶאֱמַר, וְשָׁם נִבָּא בִּשְׁנֵי הַמְּשִׁיחִים: בַּמָּשִׁיחַ הָרִאשׁוֹן שֶׁהוּא דָוִד, שֶׁהוֹשִׁיעַ אֶת יִשְׂרָאֵל מִיַּד צָרֵיהֶם, וּבַמָּשִׁיחַ הָאַחֲרוֹן שֶׁעוֹמֵד מִבָּנָיו, שֶׁמּוֹשִׁיעַ אֶת יִשְׂרָאֵל בָּאַחֲרוֹנָה. וְשָׁם הוּא אוֹמֵר: "אֶרְאֶנּוּ וְלֹא עַתָּה" – זֶה דָוִד, "אֲשׁוּרֶנּוּ וְלֹא קָרוֹב" – זֶה מֶלֶךְ הַמָּשִׁיחַ; "דָּרַךְ כּוֹכָב מִיַּעֲקֹב" – זֶה דָוִד, "וְקָם שֵׁבֶט מִיִּשְׂרָאֵל" – זֶה מֶלֶךְ הַמָּשִׁיחַ; "וּמָחַץ פַּאֲתֵי מוֹאָב" – זֶה דָוִד, וְכֵן הוּא אוֹמֵר: "וַיַּךְ אֶת מוֹאָב וַיְמַדְּדֵם בַּחֶבֶל", "וְקַרְקַר כָּל בְּנֵי שֵׁת" – זֶה הַמֶּלֶךְ הַמָּשִׁיחַ, שֶׁנֶּאֱמַר בּוֹ: "וּמָשְׁלוֹ מִיָּם עַד יָם"; "וְהָיָה אֱדוֹם יְרֵשָׁה" – זֶה דָוִד, שֶׁנֶּאֱמַר: "וַתְּהִי אֱדוֹם לְדָוִד לַעֲבָדִים וְגוֹ'", "וְהָיָה יְרֵשָׁה" – זֶה הַמֶּלֶךְ הַמָּשִׁיחַ, שֶׁנֶּאֱמַר: "וְעָלוּ מוֹשִׁיעִים בְּהַר צִיּוֹן וְגוֹ'".

Rambam writes: "Included in this principle (the belief in the Mashiach) is that there is no king in Israel except for the descendants of David and Solomon."

18. In the manuscripts and uncensored texts of the *Mishneh Torah*, the phrase "from the descendants of Esau" is substituted for the latter expression.

19. The *Kiryat Sefer* explains that the Rambam quotes this prophecy because it mentions both David and the Mashiach. Hence, we may rest assured that just as the prophecies concerning David were fulfilled, so, too, ultimately, the Messianic prophecies will also come to fruition.

However, a further intent can be ascribed to the Rambam's words. By mentioning Mashiach together with David, the Rambam implies an association between the two. David was the epitome of a Jewish king and he led the Jewish people to a much more complete observance of Torah and mitzvot.

Mashiach will "renew the Davidic dynasty." His reign will resemble David's, for he will bring the Jewish people to the ultimate level of service of God. In this context, the four parallel phrases quoted by the Rambam can be seen, not only as prophecies of David's rule and the advent of Mashiach, but as descriptions of their contributions as kings to the service of the people as a whole (*Likkutei Sichot*).

20. These two phrases refer to the very existence of David and Mashiach.

21. *Devarim Rabbah* 1:20 interprets this verse as a reference to the Mashiach. Similarly, the Jerusalem Talmud, *Ta'anit* 4:5, explains that Rabbi Akiva gave Bar Kochbah his name because of this verse.

22. A star is often used for direction and a staff is employed to prod sheep to follow the proper path. Thus, these two phrases refer to the activities of David and Mashiach to guide the people the people to a more complete performance of Torah and mitzvot. To quote Halachah 4, "He will compel all of Israel to walk in (the way of the Torah) and reinforce the breaches (in its observance)."

23. The verse continues: "He made them lie down on the ground. Those he measured with two lines were to be executed and those measured with one line, kept alive."

24. These two phrases prophesy how David and Mashiach will "fight the wars of God and be victorious."

25. The commentaries note that the verse is misquoted: Our texts read "Aram became the servants..." Perhaps, the Rambam intended to refer to II Samuel 8:14 "All of Edom became David's servants."

26. Edom's homeland.

2. Similarly,[28] with regard to the cities of refuge,[29] [Deuteronomy 19:8-9] states: "When God will expand your borders...[30] you must add three more cities."[31] This command was never fulfilled. [Surely,] God did not give this command in vain.[32]

There is no need to cite proofs from the works of the prophets for all [their] books are filled with [mention of] this matter.[33]

3. One should not presume that the Messianic king must work miracles and wonders, bring about new phenomena in the world, resurrect the dead,[34] or perform other similar deeds.[35] This is [definitely] not true.[36]

[Proof can be brought from the fact] that Rabbi Akiva, one of the greater Sages of the Mishnah, was one of the supporters of King Bar Kozibah[37] and would describe him as the Messianic king. He and all the Sages of his generation considered him to be the Messianic king until he was killed because of sins.[38] Once he was killed, they realized that he was not [the Mashiach.] The Sages did not ask him for any signs or wonders.[39]

The main thrust of the matter is: This Torah, its statutes and its laws, are everlasting. We may not add to them or detract from them.[40]

27. The prophecy continues "And the sovereignty shall be God's." These phrases relate how David and Mashiach will crush all opposing forces to the extent that no one will disturb the Jews from their fulfillment of Torah and mitzvot (see Halachah 12:4).

28. The Rambam's intention is not merely to cite another proof that Mashiach will come, but, rather, to demonstrate that he will enable the Jews to observe Torah and mitzvot in a more complete manner. Just as we see that Mashiach will enable the Jews to fulfill the mitzvah of establishing cities of refuge in the more complete manner than observed previously; so, too, he will bring the observance of all the mitzvos to consummate fulfillment (*Likkutei Sichos*).

29. Where a person who inadvertently kills a colleague must seek asylum.

30. In Genesis 15:19, God promised Abraham that his descendants would occupy the lands of ten nations. The Jews conquered seven of these nations in their occupation of *Eretz Yisrael*. The three final nations, the Keni, Kenizi, and Kadmoni will not be conquered until the Messianic age.

31. In the territory of these nations in addition to the six established in *Eretz Yisrael* and Trans-Jordan (*Hilchot Rotzeach* 8:4).

32. Hence, we may assume it is to be fulfilled in the Messianic age.

The Ari Zal (*Shaar HaMitzvot*) questions the need for cities of refuge in the Messianic age. Then, God will "cause the spirit of impurity to depart from the earth," and "nation will not lift up sword against nation." If so, why will there be a need for cities of refuge at all, and in particular, more cities of refuge that existed previously? (See also *Minchat Chinuch* 520, *Siftei Cohen*, commentary to Deuteronomy, *ibid.*)

This question can be answered based on a passage from *Yoma* 80a. The Talmud relates how after Rabbi Yishmael inadvertently committed a sin, he recorded in his notebook, "When the Temple is rebuilt, I will bring a succulent sin offering." Similarly, the cities of refuge in the Messianic age will serve as an asylum for those who killed inadvertently in the previous era.

33. See Isaiah 11:1-10, 40:1-11; Jeremiah 33:11-15; Amos 7:11-15; and many other references.

ב אַף בְּעָרֵי־מִקְלָט הוּא אוֹמֵר: "וְאִם יַרְחִיב ה' אֱלֹהֶיךָ אֶת גְּבֻלְךָ... וְיָסַפְתָּ לְךָ עוֹד שָׁלֹשׁ עָרִים וְגוֹ', וּמֵעוֹלָם לֹא הָיָה דָבָר זֶה, וְלֹא צִוָּה הַקָּדוֹשׁ־בָּרוּךְ־הוּא לַתֹּהוּ; אֲבָל בְּדִבְרֵי הַנְּבִיאִים אֵין הַדָּבָר צָרִיךְ רְאָיָה, שֶׁכָּל הַסְּפָרִים מְלֵאִים בְּדָבָר זֶה.

ג וְאַל יַעֲלֶה עַל דַּעְתְּךָ שֶׁהַמֶּלֶךְ הַמָּשִׁיחַ צָרִיךְ לַעֲשׂוֹת אוֹתוֹת וּמוֹפְתִים, וּמְחַדֵּשׁ דְּבָרִים בָּעוֹלָם אוֹ מְחַיֶּה מֵתִים וְכַיּוֹצֵא בִּדְבָרִים אֵלּוּ – אֵין הַדָּבָר כָּךְ, שֶׁהֲרֵי רַבִּי עֲקִיבָא חָכָם גָּדוֹל מֵחַכְמֵי הַמִּשְׁנָה הָיָה, וְהוּא הָיָה נוֹשֵׂא כֵלָיו שֶׁל בֶּן־כּוֹזִיבָא הַמֶּלֶךְ, וְהוּא הָיָה אוֹמֵר עָלָיו שֶׁהוּא הַמֶּלֶךְ הַמָּשִׁיחַ, וְדִמּוּ הוּא וְכָל חַכְמֵי דוֹרוֹ שֶׁהוּא הַמֶּלֶךְ הַמָּשִׁיחַ, עַד שֶׁנֶּהֱרַג בַּעֲוֹנוֹת. כֵּיוָן שֶׁנֶּהֱרַג, נוֹדַע לָהֶם שֶׁאֵינוֹ, וְלֹא שָׁאֲלוּ מִמֶּנּוּ חֲכָמִים לֹא אוֹת וְלֹא מוֹפֵת. וְעִקַּר הַדְּבָרִים כָּכָה הֵן: שֶׁהַתּוֹרָה הַזֹּאת, חֻקֶּיהָ וּמִשְׁפָּטֶיהָ לְעוֹלָם וּלְעוֹלְמֵי עוֹלָמִים, וְאֵין מוֹסִיפִין עֲלֵיהֶן וְלֹא גוֹרְעִין מֵהֶן.

34. Although the Rambam includes the resurrection of the dead as one of the thirteen principles of faith, he maintains that this miracle will not take place in the first stages of the Messianic age, but in a later era. Moreover, the resurrection will not be a miracle worked by Mashiach individually, but a change brought about by God. See *Hilchot Teshuvah*, Chapters 9 and 10, and the commentary to Chapter 12, Halachah 1-2.
35. The Yemenite manuscripts of the *Mishneh Torah* continue "as the fools say."
36. The identity of Mashiach will not be determined by miracles and wonders, but rather, as explained in the following Halachah, by his ability to lead the Jewish people to a more complete observance of Torah and mitzvot.
37. Also, known as Bar Kochbah. His name was Shimon Bar Kozibah. He adopted the name Bar Kochbah, because of the prophecy: "A star shall go forth from Jacob" (Jerusalem Talmud, *Ta'anit* 4:5).
38. Bar Kochbah led a revolt against the Romans. At first, he was successful, but, ultimately, the force of Roman military might turned the tide against the Jews. Gradually, they reconquered *Eretz Yisrael*, isolating Bar Kochbah's forces in the city of Betar. On Tisha B'Av, Betar fell and hundreds of thousands were slain, causing a national tragedy equivalent to the destruction of the Temple (*Hilchot Ta'aniot* 5:3).
39. The Ra'avad does not accept this statement. He cites *Sanhderin* 93b which states that the Sages tested Bar Kochbah to see if he possessed prophetic intuition. When he could not demonstrate this quality, they had him killed.

The difference of opinion between the Rambam and the Ra'avad revolves around a greater issue. In the following chapter, the Rambam writes: "Do not presume that in the Messianic era, the nature of the world will change.... There will be no difference between the current age and the Messianic era except [the emancipation] from our subjugation to the [gentile] kingdoms."

The Ra'avad does not accept this viewpoint and argues that Mashiach will initiate a miraculous era in which the nature of the world will change (see the commentary to those halachot). Their debate concerning the nature of the Messianic era is reflected in their conception of Mashiach, himself. The Ra'avad sees him as one who must perform wonders, while the Rambam sees him as a leader of the Jewish people who will restore their independence and motivate them to more complete Torah practice.
40. The intent of this halachah, and surely, these lines is to negate the concept shared by

4. If a king will arise from the House of David[41] who diligently contemplates the Torah and observes its mitzvot as prescribed by the Written Law and the Oral Law as David, his ancestor,[42] compels all of Israel to walk in [the way of the Torah] and rectify the breaches [in its observance],and fights the wars of God,[43] we may, with assurance, consider him Mashiach.[44]

If he succeeds in the above, builds the Temple[45] in its place,[46] and gathers the dispersed of Israel,[47] he is definitely the Mashiach.[48]

He will then improve the entire world,[49] [motivating] all the nations to serve God together, as [Tzephaniah 3:9] states: "I will transform the peoples to a purer language so that they all will call upon the name of God and serve Him with one purpose."[50]

If he did not succeed to this degree or was killed, he surely is not [the redeemer] promised by the Torah. [Rather,] he should be considered as all the other proper and exemplary kings of the Davidic dynasty who died.[51] God caused him to arise only to test the many, as [Daniel 11:35] states: "And some of the wise men will stumble, to try them, to refine, and to clarify until the appointed time, because the set time is in the future."[52]

Jesus of Nazareth who aspired to be the Mashiach and was executed by the court[53] was also [alluded to] in Daniel's prophecies, as [*ibid.* 11:14] states: "The vulgar among your people shall exalt themselves in an attempt to fulfill the vision, but they shall stumble."

Can there be a greater stumbling block than [Christianity]? All the prophets spoke of Mashiach as the redeemer of Israel and their savior who would gather their dispersed and strengthen their [observance of] the mitzvot. [In

the Christians and other false Messianic movements, that after Mashiach's coming, the observance of the mitzvot will be nullified. This concept is emphasized by the following lines taken from the Yemenite manuscripts of the *Mishneh Torah* that were stricken from the printed texts by the censor: "Anyone who adds or detracts or who reveals false interpretations of the Torah to imply that the mitzvot are not to be understood simply is surely wicked and a non-believer."

41. In this Halachah, the Rambam describes the stages in the revelation of the Mashiach and the qualities he must possess.

42. Implied in this statement is that Mashiach will be born through natural means, grow up and mature as a Torah Sage, careful in the observance of the mitzvot.

43. The uncensored printings of the *Mishneh Torah* include the phrase "defeating all the nations around him." Thus, removing the immediate obstacles to the Jews' observance of Torah and mitzvot.

44. At this stage, however, his identity cannot be absolutely ascertained.

In *Hilchot Teshuvah* 9:2, the Rambam relates that Mashiach will possess prophetic powers that approach those of Moses. However, in the present context, the Rambam does not mention these abilities because he desires to emphasize Mashiach's achievements as a Torah leader and not his individual greatness (*Likkutei Sichot*).

45. The Rambam's source is the Jerusalem Talmud, *Megillah* 1:11 and *BaMidbar Rabbah* 13:2. In contrast, Rashi and *Tosafot* (*Sukkah* 41a) and the *Midrash Tanchuma, Pekudei*, maintain that the third Temple is "the Sanctuary of God, established by Your hands." It is already completely built and is waiting in the heavens to be revealed.

ד וְאִם יַעֲמֹד מֶלֶךְ מִבֵּית־דָּוִד, הוֹגֶה בַּתּוֹרָה וְעוֹסֵק בְּמִצְוֹת כְּדָוִד אָבִיו, כְּפִי תוֹרָה שֶׁבִּכְתָב וְשֶׁבְּעַל־פֶּה, וְיָכֹף כָּל יִשְׂרָאֵל לֵילֵךְ בָּהּ וּלְחַזֵּק בִּדְקָהּ, וְיִלָּחֵם מִלְחֲמוֹת ה׳ – הֲרֵי זֶה בְּחֶזְקַת שֶׁהוּא מָשִׁיחַ. אִם עָשָׂה וְהִצְלִיחַ וּבָנָה מִקְדָּשׁ בִּמְקוֹמוֹ וְקִבֵּץ נִדְחֵי־יִשְׂרָאֵל – הֲרֵי זֶה מָשִׁיחַ בְּוַדַּאי. וִיתַקֵּן אֶת הָעוֹלָם כֻּלּוֹ לַעֲבֹד אֶת הַשֵּׁם בְּיַחַד, שֶׁנֶּאֱמַר: "כִּי־אָז אֶהְפֹּךְ אֶל עַמִּים שָׂפָה בְרוּרָה, לִקְרֹא כֻלָּם בְּשֵׁם ה׳ לְעָבְדוֹ שְׁכֶם אֶחָד". וְאִם לֹא הִצְלִיחַ עַד כֹּה, אוֹ נֶהֱרַג – בְּיָדוּעַ שֶׁאֵינוֹ זֶה שֶׁהִבְטִיחָה עָלָיו תּוֹרָה, וַהֲרֵי הוּא כְּכָל מַלְכֵי בֵית־דָּוִד הַשְּׁלֵמִים וְהַכְּשֵׁרִים שֶׁמֵּתוּ. וְלֹא הֶעֱמִידוֹ הַקָּדוֹשׁ־בָּרוּךְ־הוּא אֶלָּא לְנַסּוֹת בּוֹ רַבִּים, שֶׁנֶּאֱמַר: "וּמִן הַמַּשְׂכִּילִים יִכָּשְׁלוּ לִצְרוֹף בָּהֶם וּלְבָרֵר וְלַלְבֵּן עַד עֵת קֵץ, כִּי עוֹד לַמּוֹעֵד". אַף יֵשׁוּעַ הַנּוֹצְרִי שֶׁדִּמָּה שֶׁיִּהְיֶה מָשִׁיחַ וְנֶהֱרַג בְּבֵית־דִּין, כְּבָר נִתְנַבֵּא בּוֹ דָּנִיֵּאל, שֶׁנֶּאֱמַר: "וּבְנֵי פָּרִיצֵי עַמְּךָ יִנַּשְּׂאוּ לְהַעֲמִיד חָזוֹן וְנִכְשָׁלוּ". וְכִי יֵשׁ מִכְשׁוֹל גָּדוֹל מִזֶּה, שֶׁכָּל הַנְּבִיאִים דִּבְּרוּ שֶׁמָּשִׁיחַ גּוֹאֵל יִשְׂרָאֵל וּמוֹשִׁיעָם, וּמְקַבֵּץ נִדְחֵיהֶם וּמְחַזֵּק מִצְוֹתָן,

It is possible to resolve the two opinions: *BaMidbar Rabbah* 15:13 states that the gates to the Temple were not destroyed by our foes. Rather, they sank into the earth and will emerge when Mashiach comes. Thus, when the Temple descends from heaven, Mashiach will connect it to its gates. *Bava Batra* 53b relates that a person who affixes the doors to a building is considered as if he constructed it (*Sha'arei Zohar, Sukkot, ibid.*).

46. *Hilchot Beit HaBechirah* 1:3 specifies the Temple's location:

> There is no Sanctuary for all generations except in Jerusalem and [specifically,] on Mt. Moriah, as it is said: "And David declared: 'This is the House of God, the Lord, and this is the altar for the burnt offerings of Israel.'"

47. The ingathering of the exiles will follow the construction of the Temple. None of the major commentaries on the *Mishneh Torah* dispute this issue despite the fact that certain Talmudic and *Midrashic* passages imply that the ingathering of the exiles will precede Mashiach's coming.

48. From this point onward, his identity can no longer be disputed. Once he has accomplished these achievements, we can be certain that the Messianic era will begin.

49. As stated in Chapter 8, Halachah 10, the Jews are obligated to influence the gentiles to accept their seven mitzvot and the fundamental principles of faith they imply.

50. Isaiah 2:2 prophesies: "In the final days, the mountain of God's house will be established... and all the nations shall flow to it."

Though most published texts of the *Mishneh Torah* conclude this chapter with this paragraph. A large portion of the Rambam's text was censored and left unpublished. We have included it based on the Yemenite manuscripts of the *Mishneh Torah* and early uncensored printings. In this version, the above paragraph is found in the midst of other passages describing Christianity and Islam.

51. This passage does not refer to self-styled false Messiahs like Shabbatai Zvi or Jacob Frank, but rather to Messianic attempts supported by Torah Sages, such as Rabbi Akiva's backing of Bar Kochbah. See Malbim on the verse quoted from Daniel.

52. Ever since the destruction of the Temple, the Jews have yearned for the coming of Mashiach. The intensity of this desire has caused even our people's wisest men to err and presume that the Messianic age was imminent although its appointed time had not arrived.

53. The Jews did not actually carry out the execution for crucifixion is not one of the Torah's methods of execution. Rather, after condemning him to death, the *Sanhderin*

contrast, Christianity] caused the Jews to be slain by the sword,[54] their remnants to be scattered and humbled, the Torah to be altered, and the majority of the world to err and serve a god other than the Lord.[55]

Nevertheless, the intent of the Creator of the world is not within the power of man to comprehend, for His ways are not our ways, nor are His thoughts, our thoughts.[56] [Ultimately,] all the deeds of Jesus of Nazareth and that Ishmaelite[57] who arose after him will only serve to prepare the way for Mashiach's coming and the improvement of the entire world,[58] [motivating the nations] to serve God together as [Tzephaniah 3:9] states: "I will transform the peoples to a purer language that they all will call upon the name of God and serve Him with one purpose."[59]

How will this come about? The entire world has already become filled with the mention of Mashiach,[60] Torah, and mitzvot. These matters have been spread to the furthermost islands to many stubborn-hearted nations.[61] They discuss these matters and the mitzvot of the Torah, saying: "These mitzvot were true, but were already negated in the present age and are not applicable for all time."[62]

Others say: "Implied in the mitzvot are hidden concepts that can not be understood simply. The Mashiach has already come and revealed those hidden [truths]."[63]

When the true Messianic king will arise and prove successful, his [position becoming] exalted and uplifted,[64] they will all return and realize that their ancestors endowed them with a false heritage and their prophets and ancestors caused them to err.[65]

CHAPTER TWELVE

1. Do not presume that in the Messianic age any facet of the world's nature will change or there will be innovations in the work of creation. Rather, the world will continue according to its pattern.[1]

handed him over to the Roman authorities who executed him as a rebel against Roman rule.

54. The Rambam lived before the Spanish Inquisition and the most severe massacres perpetrated by the Crusaders. Nevertheless, even in his era, many Jews had suffered martyrdom at Christian hands.

55. This statement appears to label Christianity as the worship of false gods. That view is clearly stated in *Hilchot Avodat Kochavim* 9:4. (In some texts, that Halachah reads "Canaanites," but that is a censored version. The original text reads "Romans" and refers to the Christians.)

Other authorities (Meiri, *Avodah Zarah* 6, Maharitz Chiyot, *Kuntres Tifferet Yisrael*) express the view that belief in the trinity is considered as worshiping God together with an intermediary which is permitted to the gentiles.

56. Cf. Isaiah 55:8. The Rambam proceeds to explain that although Christianity and Islam appear to have produced negative effects, their rise was motivated by a subtle Divine intent.

וְזֶה גָּרַם לְאַבֵּד יִשְׂרָאֵל בַּחֶרֶב, וּלְפַזֵּר שְׁאֵרִיתָם וּלְהַשְׁפִּילָם, וּלְהַחֲלִיף הַתּוֹרָה וּלְהַטְעוֹת רֹב הָעוֹלָם לַעֲבֹד אֱלוֹהַּ מִבַּלְעֲדֵי ה׳. אֲבָל מַחְשְׁבוֹת בּוֹרֵא הָעוֹלָם אֵין כֹּחַ בְּאָדָם לְהַשִּׂיגָם, כִּי לֹא דְרָכֵינוּ דְּרָכָיו וְלֹא מַחְשְׁבוֹתֵינוּ מַחְשְׁבוֹתָיו; וְכָל הַדְּבָרִים הָאֵלּוּ שֶׁל יֵשׁוּעַ הַנּוֹצְרִי וְשֶׁל זֶה הַיִּשְׁמְעֵאלִי שֶׁעָמַד אַחֲרָיו, אֵינָן אֶלָּא לְיַשֵּׁר דֶּרֶךְ לַמֶּלֶךְ הַמָּשִׁיחַ, וּלְתַקֵּן הָעוֹלָם כֻּלּוֹ לַעֲבֹד אֶת ה׳ בְּיַחַד, שֶׁנֶּאֱמַר: ״כִּי אָז אֶהְפֹּךְ אֶל עַמִּים שָׂפָה בְרוּרָה לִקְרֹא כֻלָּם בְּשֵׁם ה׳ לְעָבְדוֹ שְׁכֶם אֶחָד״. כֵּיצַד? כְּבָר נִתְמַלֵּא הָעוֹלָם כֻּלּוֹ מִדִּבְרֵי הַמָּשִׁיחַ וּמִדִּבְרֵי הַתּוֹרָה וּמִדִּבְרֵי הַמִּצְוֹת, וּפָשְׁטוּ דְּבָרִים אֵלּוּ בְּאִיִּים רְחוֹקִים וּבְעַמִּים רַבִּים עַרְלֵי־לֵב, וְהֵם נוֹשְׂאִים וְנוֹתְנִים בִּדְבָרִים אֵלּוּ וּבְמִצְוֹת הַתּוֹרָה, אֵלּוּ אוֹמְרִים: מִצְוֹת אֵלּוּ אֱמֶת הָיוּ וּכְבָר בָּטְלוּ בַּזְּמַן הַזֶּה, וְלֹא הָיוּ נוֹהֲגוֹת לְדוֹרוֹת; וְאֵלּוּ אוֹמְרִים: דְּבָרִים נִסְתָּרִים יֵשׁ בָּהֶן וְאֵינָן כִּפְשׁוּטָן, וּכְבָר בָּא מָשִׁיחַ וְגִלָּה נִסְתְּרֵיהֶם. וּכְשֶׁיַּעֲמֹד הַמֶּלֶךְ הַמָּשִׁיחַ בֶּאֱמֶת וְיַצְלִיחַ וְיָרוּם וְיִנָּשֵׂא, מִיָּד הֵם כֻּלָּם חוֹזְרִים וְיוֹדְעִים שֶׁשֶּׁקֶר נָחֲלוּ אֲבוֹתֵיהֶם, וְשֶׁנְּבִיאֵיהֶם וַאֲבוֹתֵיהֶם הִטְעוּם.

פֶּרֶק שְׁנֵים־עָשָׂר

א אַל יַעֲלֶה עַל הַלֵּב שֶׁבִּימוֹת הַמָּשִׁיחַ יִבָּטֵל דָּבָר מִמִּנְהָגוֹ שֶׁל עוֹלָם, אוֹ יִהְיֶה שָׁם חִדּוּשׁ בְּמַעֲשֵׂה בְרֵאשִׁית, אֶלָּא עוֹלָם כְּמִנְהָגוֹ נוֹהֵג. וְזֶה שֶׁנֶּאֱמַר בִּישַׁעְיָה: ״וְגָר זְאֵב עִם כֶּבֶשׂ

57. I.e., Mohamed, who founded Islam.
58. Indeed, these faiths destroyed much of the paganism that existed throughout the world before their advent.
59. As mentioned above, due to censorship, these lines were taken out of context and printed as the concluding paragraph of this chapter in most published texts.
60. The coming of a Messiah is a fundamental element of Islamic as well as Christian thought.
61. The term literally means "of uncircumcised hearts." It is borrowed from Ezekiel 44:7.
62. The Christian position.
63. The Islamic view, see *Iggeret Teiman*, p.123.
64. The phrase is adapted from Isaiah 52:13: "Behold, My servant shall prosper, he shall be exalted and uplifted very high."
65. These lines are based on Jeremiah 16:19: "Nations shall come to you from the ends of the earth and say 'Surely, our fathers have inherited lies and vain things in which there is no benefit.'"

The roles Christianity and Islam will play in preparing the world for the Messianic era are also discussed in the *Kuzari*, fourth discourse, Chapter 23.

1 . These statements and similarly, the opening lines of the following halachah: "There will be no difference between the current age and the Messianic era except [the emancipation] from our subjugation to the [gentile] kingdoms" are the subject of much debate among the commentaries.

Although Isaiah [11:6] states: "The wolf will dwell with the lamb, the leopard will lie down with the young goat," these [words] are a metaphor and a parable.[2] The interpretation of the prophecy is as follows: Israel[3] will dwell securely together with the wicked gentiles who are likened to a wolf and a leopard, as in the prophecy [Jeremiah 5:6]: "A wolf from the wilderness shall spoil them and a leopard will stalk their cities." They will all return to the true faith[4] and no longer steal or destroy. Rather, they will eat permitted food at peace with Israel as [Isaiah 11:7] states: "The lion will eat straw like an ox."

Similarly, other Messianic prophecies of this nature are metaphors. In the Messianic era, everyone will realize which matters were implied by these metaphors and which allusions they contained.

2. Our Sages taught: "There will be no difference between the current age and the Messianic era except [the emancipation] from our subjugation to the [gentile] kingdoms."[5]

The simple interpretation of the prophets' words appear [to imply] that the war of Gog[6] and Magog[7] will take place at the beginning of the Messianic age.[8] Before the war of Gog and Magog, a prophet will arise to [inspire] Israel

The Ra'avad and many other commentaries maintain that Mashiach's coming will initiate a miraculous era in which the entire nature of the world will change. As the Rambam mentions, many of the Messianic prophecies appear to imply such a phenomenon.

This difference of opinion stems from a debate among the Sages, *Berachot* 34b:

> Rabbi Yochanan states: "All the prophets only prophesied regarding the Messianic age. However, the world to come [is described by the verse]: "Never has an eye seen, besides God." This contradicts [the opinion of] Shmuel who maintains: "There will be no difference between the current age and the Messianic era except [the emancipation] from our subjugation to the [gentile] kingdoms."

The Rambam follows Shmuel's opinion. Accordingly, the prophecies that appear to describe miracles must be interpreted as parables or allegories. In contrast, the Ra'avad accepts Rabbi Yochanan's opinion which interprets the Messianic prophecies simply and thus, maintains that the Messianic age will initiate a new order and nature will give way to miracles.

Several commentaries attempt to resolve the differences between the two. The Radbaz explains that the miraculous order described by the prophets will prevail only in *Eretz Yisrael*. In the Diaspora, the laws of nature will continue unchanged.

[It appears highly unlikely that the Rambam concurs with this opinion. Firstly, his blanket statement, "There will be no difference between the current age and the Messianic era," does not lend itself to a differentiation between *Eretz Yisrael* and the Diaspora.

Secondly, as mentioned in the commentary to Chapter 11, Halachah 3, the debate between these Sages concerning the nature of the Messianic era is reflected in their conception of Mashiach himself. Since the Rambam does not expect the nature of the world to change in the Messianic age, he could conceive of Bar Kochbah as a potential Mashiach even though he did not work miracles. However, Bar Kochbah lived in *Eretz Yisrael*. Thus, according to the Radbaz, he should have manifested miraculous powers.]

The *Avodat HaKodesh* offers a different resolution, explaining that though the world will follow the rules of nature, the nature of the world will return to its state before the Adam committed the sin of the tree of knowledge. That sin effected the totality of

וְנָמֵר עִם גְּדִי יִרְבָּץ" – מָשָׁל וְחִידָה – עִנְיַן הַדָּבָר, שֶׁיִּהְיוּ יִשְׂרָאֵל יוֹשְׁבִין לָבֶטַח עִם רִשְׁעֵי עכו"ם הַמְּשׁוּלִים כִּזְאֵב וְנָמֵר, שֶׁנֶּאֱמַר: "זְאֵב עֲרָבוֹת יְשָׁדְדֵם, נָמֵר שֹׁקֵד עַל עָרֵיהֶם", וְיַחְזְרוּ כֻּלָּם לְדַת הָאֱמֶת, וְלֹא יִגְזְלוּ וְלֹא יַשְׁחִיתוּ, אֶלָּא יֹאכְלוּ דָבָר הַמֻּתָּר בְּנַחַת עִם יִשְׂרָאֵל, שֶׁנֶּאֱמַר: "וְאַרְיֵה כַּבָּקָר יֹאכַל תֶּבֶן". וְכֵן כֹּל כַּיּוֹצֵא בְאֵלּוּ הַדְּבָרִים בְּעִנְיַן הַמָּשִׁיחַ הֵם מְשָׁלִים; וּבִימוֹת הַמֶּלֶךְ הַמָּשִׁיחַ יִוָּדַע לַכֹּל, לְאֵי זֶה דָבָר הָיָה מָשָׁל, וּמָה עִנְיָן רָמְזוּ בָהֶן.

ב אָמְרוּ חֲכָמִים: אֵין בֵּין הָעוֹלָם הַזֶּה לִימוֹת הַמָּשִׁיחַ אֶלָּא שִׁעְבּוּד מַלְכֻיּוֹת בִּלְבָד, יֵרָאֶה מִפְּשׁוּטָן שֶׁל דִּבְרֵי הַנְּבִיאִים, שֶׁבִּתְחִלַּת יְמוֹת הַמָּשִׁיחַ תִּהְיֶה מִלְחֶמֶת גּוֹג וּמָגוֹג, וְשֶׁקֹּדֶם מִלְחֶמֶת גּוֹג וּמָגוֹג יַעֲמֹד נָבִיא לְיַשֵּׁר יִשְׂרָאֵל וּלְהָכִין לִבָּם, שֶׁנֶּאֱמַר: "הִנֵּה אָנֹכִי שֹׁלֵחַ

creation. When that Eden-like nature is restored, many of the Messianic prophecies which we regard as miracles can be considered as natural phenomena.

The *Sheloh* (23b) suggests a third opinion. He explains that, according to Shmuel (and thus, the Rambam), there will be two periods in the Messianic age: one in which the natural order of the world will not change and a second period which will be marked by miracles.

The Rambam's inclusion of the resurrection of the dead as one of the thirteen principles of faith appears to support this opinion. There is no greater miracle and departure from the natural order than that (*Likkutei Sichot*).

See also *Iggeret Techiat HaMeitim*, Section 6, where the Rambam writes that these words do not represent a definite and final statement. Here he is defining the absolute minimum of what the Messianic era will bring. It is possible that, in fact, the Messianic era will represent a deviation from the natural order.

2. Prophets would frequently use metaphors and parables to illustrate their messages. Indeed, Numbers 23:7 uses the word *meshal*, "metaphor," as a synonym for prophetic discourse.

3. The lamb or the goat.

4. Generally, this term refers to Judaism (see *Hilchot Chagigah* 3:1,6). Both Rashi (*Avodah Zarah* 24a) and the Ran (*Derushot*, 7) state in the Messianic age, the gentiles will all convert to Judaism. However, the Rambam's wording does not imply such a change. On the contrary, Halachah 5 differentiates between "the entire world" and "Israel" indicating that even in the Messianic age, differences will exist between Jews and gentiles. Accordingly, certain texts amend this phrase to read "return in repentance."

The status of the gentiles in the Messianic age is also discussed in *Emunot V'De'ot*, in the discourse, *HaGeulah HaAtidah*.

5. See the commentary to Halachah 1. Indeed, the Yemenite manuscripts and the original printings of the *Mishneh Torah* include this paragraph as the conclusion of the previous halachah and begin Halachah 2 with the following lines. The themes of the two halachot also appear to tend to such a division.

6. The king of Magog,

7. The nation, see Genesis 10:2. Ezekiel, chapters 38 and 39, describe how "Gog will come up against the land of Israel" and how God "will exercise judgement upon him with pestilence and bloodshed."

8. Perhaps as part of "the wars of God" which, as stated in Chapter 11, Halachah 4, the Messiah will wage.

to be upright and prepare their hearts, as [Malachi 3:22] states: "Behold, I am sending you Elijah."[9]

He will not come to declare the pure, impure, or to declare the impure, pure.[10] He will not dispute the lineage of those presumed to be of proper pedigree,[11] nor will he validate the pedigree of those whose lineage is presumed blemished.[12] Rather, he will establish peace within the world as [*ibid.* 3:24] continues: "He will turn the hearts of the fathers to the children."[13]

There are some Sages who say that Elijah's coming will precede the coming of the Mashiach.[14] All these and similar matters cannot be [definitely] known by man until they occur for these matters are undefined in the prophets' [words][15] and even the wise men have no established tradition regarding these matters except [their own] interpretation of the verses. Therefore, there is a controversy among them regarding these matters.[16]

Regardless [of the debate concerning these questions], neither the order of the occurrence of these events or their precise detail are among the fundamental principles of the faith.[17] A person should not occupy himself with the *Aggadot* and the exegesis of verses concerning these and similar matters,[18] nor should he consider them as essentials, for [study of] them will neither bring fear or love [of God].

Similarly, one should not try to determine the appointed time [for Mashiach's coming]. Our Sages declared:[19] "May the spirits of those who attempt to determine the time [of Mashiach's coming] expire!"[20] Rather, one should await and believe in the general conception of the matter as explained.[21]

3. During the era of the Messianic king, once his kingdom has been established and all of Israel has gathered around him,[22] the entire [nation's] line

9. The verse concludes "before the coming of God's great and awesome day," a reference to the war of Gog and Magog which will make God's power reknown throughout the world.
10. In his Commentary to the Mishnah, *Ediot* 8:7, the Rambam writes that Moses conveyed the tradition that before the coming of Mashiach, Elijah would motivate the people to the service of God. However, he will not make any changes in the Torah. Similarly, Chapter 11, Halachah 3, states: "This Torah, its statutes and its laws, are everlasting. We may not add to them or detract from them."
11. Pedigree of lineage is an important factor in Jewish law. A person who is descended from a *mamzer* or servant may not marry a native-born Israelite. These factors are particularly important regarding priests. The Sages consider it as an accepted tradition that many people of blemished lineage have intermingled with the main body of the Jewish people and that, in the Messianic age, all questions concerning lineage will be clarified.
12. *Ediot* (*ibid.*) cites the opinion of certain Sages who maintain that Elijah's contribution will center on establishing the pedigree of lineage among the Jews. The Sages and the Rambam do not accept this view.
13. Elijah will eradicate the hatred that exists between men. Our Sages explain that the Temple was destroyed because of unwarranted hatred. When hatred, the cause of the exile, ceases, then, the exile itself will come to an end.

לָכֶם אֵת אֵלִיָּה הַנָּבִיא וְגוֹ'", וְאֵינוֹ בָא, לֹא לְטַמֵּא הַטָּהוֹר וְלֹא לְטַהֵר הַטָּמֵא, וְלֹא לִפְסֹל אֲנָשִׁים שֶׁהֵם בְּחֶזְקַת כַּשְׁרוּת וְלֹא לְהַכְשִׁיר מִי שֶׁהֻחְזְקוּ פְּסוּלִין, אֶלָּא לָשׂוּם שָׁלוֹם בָּעוֹלָם, שֶׁנֶּאֱמַר: "וְהֵשִׁיב לֵב אָבוֹת עַל בָּנִים". וְיֵשׁ מִן הַחֲכָמִים שֶׁאוֹמְרִים, שֶׁקֹּדֶם בִּיאַת הַמָּשִׁיחַ יָבוֹא אֵלִיָּהוּ. וְכָל אֵלּוּ הַדְּבָרִים וְכַיּוֹצֵא בָהֶן – לֹא יֵדַע אָדָם אֵיךְ יִהְיוּ עַד שֶׁיִּהְיוּ, שֶׁדְּבָרִים סְתוּמִים הֵן אֵצֶל הַנְּבִיאִים, גַּם הַחֲכָמִים אֵין לָהֶם קַבָּלָה בִּדְבָרִים אֵלּוּ, אֶלָּא לְפִי הֶכְרֵעַ הַפְּסוּקִים, וּלְפִיכָךְ יֵשׁ לָהֶם מַחֲלֹקֶת בִּדְבָרִים אֵלּוּ; וְעַל־כָּל־פָּנִים אֵין סִדּוּר הֲוָיַת דְּבָרִים אֵלּוּ וְלֹא דִקְדּוּקֵיהֶן עִקָּר בַּדָּת. וּלְעוֹלָם לֹא יִתְעַסֵּק אָדָם בְּדִבְרֵי הַהַגָּדוֹת, וְלֹא יַאֲרִיךְ בַּמִּדְרָשׁוֹת הָאֲמוּרִים בְּעִנְיָנִים אֵלּוּ וְכַיּוֹצֵא בָהֶן, וְלֹא יְשִׂימֵם עִקָּר; שֶׁאֵין מְבִיאִין לֹא לִידֵי יִרְאָה וְלֹא לִידֵי אַהֲבָה; וְכֵן לֹא יְחַשֵּׁב הַקִּצִּין. אָמְרוּ חֲכָמִים: תִּפַּח רוּחָם שֶׁל מְחַשְּׁבֵי הַקִּצִּים. אֶלָּא יְחַכֶּה וְיַאֲמִין בִּכְלַל הַדָּבָר כְּמוֹ שֶׁבֵּאַרְנוּ.

ג בִּימֵי הַמֶּלֶךְ הַמָּשִׁיחַ, כְּשֶׁתִּתְיַשֵּׁב מַמְלַכְתּוֹ וְיִתְקַבְּצוּ אֵלָיו כָּל יִשְׂרָאֵל – יִתְיַחֲסוּ כֻּלָּם עַל

14. Many commentaries support this opinion, explaining that Elijah will motivate the people to Teshuvah, repentance. This service will hasten the redemption for "When Israel repents, she will immediately be redeemed" (*Hilchot Teshuvah* 7:5).

15. For the prophecies can be interpreted in a number of ways.

16. See *Sanhderin* 97, 98 for different interpretations of the sequence and details of the Messianic era.

17. In contrast, the essential concept that Mashiach will come and initiate an era where we will observe Torah and mitzvot in a complete manner is counted as one of the Rambam's thirteen principles of faith.

18. I.e., the particular details of the Messianic era.

19. *Sanhderin* 97b.

20. The Sages opposed publicizing an appointed time for the Mashiach's coming, lest he not arrive at that time and many of the common people become disillusioned and abandon Jewish practice (*ibid.*).

Nevertheless, throughout Jewish history, many great Sages have fixed certain years as appropriate times for Mashiach's coming. Indeed, the Rambam himself (*Iggeret Teiman*, page 174 of the Mossad HaRav Kook edition), mentions a specific year as the appointed time when the prophetic spirit will return to Israel and the Messianic era will near.

In *Iggeret Teiman* (p. 156), the Rambam rationalizes Saadia Gaon's fixation of an appointed time for Mashiach's coming. He explains that the people's commitment to Torah and mitzvot was at a particularly low point and unless they were promised a specific time for the advent of the Messianic era, they would have lost faith entirely.

The Talmud states "all the appointed times [for Mashiach's coming] have passed and the matter is dependent on *Teshuvah* alone." Nevertheless, according to the Kabbalists, there are certain years, when there is a greater potential for Mashiach to reveal himself. By publicizing those years, the Sages intended to motivate the nation to *Teshuvah* and thus, hasten Mashiach's coming.

21. In this and the previous chapter.

22. This refers to a later stage of the Messianic redemption, when the exiles have already been gathered. Before then, Mashiach will have waged "the wars of God" and rebuilt the Temple (see Chapter 11, Halachah 3).

of descent will be established on the basis of his words and the prophetic spirit[23] which will rest upon him, as [Malachi 3:3] states: "He shall sit as a refiner and purifier."[24]

He will purify the lineage of the Levites first,[25] stating "He is a priest of defined lineage. He is a Levite of defined lineage."[26] Those[27] whose lineage he will not recognize will be lowered to the status of Israelites. This is implied by [Ezra 2:63]: "The governor[28] said to them:[29] '[They should not eat of the most holy things][30] until a priest arises [who will wear] the *urim vitumim.*'"[31] From this verse, you can infer that the prophetic spirit [will be used to] define and notify the pedigree of lineage.[32]

When he defines the lineage of the Israelites, he will make known their tribal lineage alone, stating: "He is from this tribe and he is from another tribe."[33] He will not, by contrast, state concerning a person who is presumed to be of unblemished lineage: "He is illegitimate or he is of slave lineage."[34] For the law is once a family has become intermingled [with the entire Jewish people,] they may remain intermingled.[35]

4. The Sages and the prophets did not yearn for the Messianic era in order to have dominion over the entire world, to rule over the gentiles, to be exalted by the nations,[36] or to eat, drink, and celebrate.[37] Rather, [they desired] to be free [to involve themselves] in Torah and wisdom without any pressures or disturbances,[38] so that they would merit the world to come,[39] as explained in *Hilchot Teshuvah.*[40]

5. In that era, there will be neither famine or war, envy or competition for good will flow in abundance and all the delights will be freely available as dust.[41]

23. As mentioned in *Hilchot Teshuvah* 9:2, Mashiach's prophetic abilities will approach those of Moses.

24. *Kiddushin* 71a offers two interpretations of the word "purify:" a) "smelt" - Just as a smelter extracts pure metal from an ore, Mashiach will clarify the lineage of the tribes. In contrast, in the present age, all the tribes are intermingled and no one can be sure of his origins.

b) "remove the blemish" - All families with tainted lineage who have intermingled with the Jewish people as a whole will be accepted. No notice will be made of their previous difficulties.

As apparent from the continuation of the halachah, the Rambam accepts both interpretations.

25. As the verse continues: "He shall purify the sons of Levi...."

26. The definition of the lineage of the priests and Levites is of greatest importance for their participation is necessary in the Temple services (*Kiddushin, ibid.*).

27. Who presume to be priests or Levites

28. Nechemiah.

29. Priests who could not document their pedigree of lineage.

30. I.e., because of the questions regarding their lineage, they should not consider themselves as priests.

פִּיו בְּרוּחַ־הַקֹּדֶשׁ שֶׁתָּנוּחַ עָלָיו, שֶׁנֶּאֱמַר: "וְיָשַׁב מְצָרֵף וּמְטַהֵר וְגוֹ'". וּבְנֵי לֵוִי מְטַהֵר תְּחִלָּה וְאוֹמֵר: זֶה מְיֻחָס כֹּהֵן וְזֶה מְיֻחָס לֵוִי! וְדוֹחֶה אֶת שֶׁאֵינָן מְיֻחָסִין לְיִשְׂרָאֵל. הֲרֵי הוּא אוֹמֵר: "וַיֹּאמֶר הַתִּרְשָׁתָא לָהֶם וְגוֹ', עַד עֲמֹד הַכֹּהֵן לְאוּרִים וְתֻמִּים". הִנֵּה לָמַדְתָּ, שֶׁבְּרוּחַ־הַקֹּדֶשׁ מְיַחֲסִין הַמֻּחְזָקִין וּמוֹדִיעִין הַמְיֻחָס. וְאֵינוֹ מְיַחֵס יִשְׂרָאֵל אֶלָּא לְשִׁבְטֵיהֶם, שֶׁמּוֹדִיעַ שֶׁזֶּה מִשֵּׁבֶט פְּלוֹנִי וְזֶה מִשֵּׁבֶט פְּלוֹנִי; אֲבָל אֵינוֹ אוֹמֵר עַל שֶׁהֵן בְּחֶזְקַת כַּשְׁרוּת: זֶה מַמְזֵר וְזֶה עֶבֶד!, שֶׁהַדִּין הוּא, שֶׁמִּשְׁפָּחָה שֶׁנִּטְמְעָה – נִטְמָעָה.

ד לֹא נִתְאַוּוּ הַחֲכָמִים וְהַנְּבִיאִים יְמוֹת הַמָּשִׁיחַ, לֹא כְּדֵי שֶׁיִּשְׁלְטוּ עַל כָּל הָעוֹלָם, וְלֹא כְּדֵי שֶׁיִּרְדּוּ בָּעַכּוּ"ם, וְלֹא כְּדֵי שֶׁיְּנַשְּׂאוּ אוֹתָם הָעַמִּים, וְלֹא כְּדֵי לֶאֱכֹל וְלִשְׁתּוֹת וְלִשְׂמֹחַ; אֶלָּא כְּדֵי שֶׁיִּהְיוּ פְּנוּיִין בַּתּוֹרָה וְחָכְמָתָהּ, וְלֹא יִהְיֶה לָהֶם נוֹגֵשׂ וּמְבַטֵּל, כְּדֵי שֶׁיִּזְכּוּ לְחַיֵּי הָעוֹלָם הַבָּא, כְּמוֹ שֶׁבֵּאַרְנוּ בְּהִלְכוֹת תְּשׁוּבָה.

ה וּבְאוֹתוֹ הַזְּמַן לֹא יִהְיֶה שָׁם לֹא רָעָב וְלֹא מִלְחָמָה, וְלֹא קִנְאָה וְלֹא תַחֲרוּת, שֶׁהַטּוֹבָה תִּהְיֶה מֻשְׁפַּעַת הַרְבֵּה, וְכָל הַמַּעֲדַנִּים מְצוּיִין כֶּעָפָר, וְלֹא יִהְיֶה עֵסֶק כָּל הָעוֹלָם אֶלָּא

31. As mentioned in the commentary to Chapter 5, Halachah 2, the *urim vitumim* were consulted as oracles. Thus, by use of the prophetic spirit, they could determine the priest's lineage. In the Second Temple, the *urim vitumim* were not endowed with these prophetic powers (*Hilchot Beit HaBechirah* 4:1). Hence, Nechemiah told the priests of questionable lineage to wait for the Messianic redemption when the doubt concerning their lineage could be resolved.
32. Though the Rambam maintains that Mashiach will divine the people's lineage without using the *urim vitumim*, their lineage will be established by the prophetic spirit and not by other means.
33. The knowledge of one's tribal lineage will be important in regard to the division of *Eretz Yisrael* and other matters. See Ezekiel, Chapters 47 and 48.
34. Both an illegitimate child and a slave are forbidden to marry nativeborn Israelites.
35. Mashiach will be able to identify those families whose lineage is tainted. Nevertheless, since those families have already become intermingled with the Jewish people as a whole, no restrictions will be placed upon them (*Kiddushin*, *ibid.*).
36. All the above will be realized in the Messianic era, but this is not why the Sages desired Mashiach's coming.
37. In contrast to pagan conceptions of Utopia.
38. As explained in the following Halachah.
39. In *Hilchot Teshuvah*, Chapters 8 and 9, the Rambam describes the world to come as man's ultimate reward. He interprets the world to come as a spiritual realm in which the soul will exist independent of the body. (The Ra'avad, the Ramban, and other Sages whose perspective was influenced by the Kabbalah, interpret the world to come as the period after the resurrection of the dead when the souls and bodies will both rise and live in this physical world.)
40. Chapter 9, Halachah 2.
41. The Rambam did not employ this expression simply as a metaphor for abundance. His words also imply that though physical pleasures will be available, we will not crave them.

The occupation of the entire world[42] will be solely to know God.[43]

Therefore, the Jews will be great sages and know the hidden matters,[44] grasping the knowledge of their Creator according to [the full extent] of human potential, as [Isaiah 11:9] states: "The world will be filled with the knowledge of God as the waters cover the ocean bed.[45]

This completes *Hilchot Melachim* and the entire text. Blessed be He who spoke and the world came into being as a whole, with all its particulars.

This concludes[46] the fourteenth book, the Book of Judges. It contains five Halachot and eighty one chapters.
Hilchot Sanhderin - 26 chapters,
Hilchot Edut - 22 chapters,
Hilchot Mamrim - 7 chapters,
Hilchot Evel - 14 chapters,
Hilchot Melachim - 12 chapters.
In the entire text, there are 83 Halachot and 982 chapters. Complete and perfect with praise to God, Creator of the World

Rather, we will consider them "as dust." Despite the benefit we derive from them, we will not attach any importance to them,

In Chapter 9 of *Hilchot Teshuvah*, the Rambam describes the reward received for the observance of Torah and mitzvot in similar, but not entirely parallel terms. The present passage refers to the reward to be received when the world comes to its ultimate state of fulfillment. Thus, the blessings mentioned surpass those described in *Hilchot Teshuvah* which refers to the reward that can be received at all times, not necessarily in the Messianic age (*Likkutei Sichos*).

42. Even gentiles.

43. In the Hebrew, the Rambam uses two exclusions to emphasize the total lack of involvement with other concerns.

At present, even Torah Sages should spend a certain amount of time in business endeavors to earn their livelihood rather than live off charity (*Hilchot Talmud Torah*

לָדַעַת אֶת ה׳ בִּלְבָד. וּלְפִיכָךְ יִהְיוּ יִשְׂרָאֵל חֲכָמִים גְּדוֹלִים וְיוֹדְעִים דְּבָרִים הַסְּתוּמִים, וְיַשִּׂיגוּ דַּעַת בּוֹרְאָם כְּפִי כֹּחַ הָאָדָם, שֶׁנֶּאֱמַר: "כִּי מָלְאָה הָאָרֶץ דֵּעָה אֶת ה׳, כַּמַּיִם לַיָּם מְכַסִּים".

נִשְׁלְמוּ הִלְכוֹת מְלָכִים וְהַחִבּוּר כֻּלּוֹ.

נִגְמַר סֵפֶר אַרְבָּעָה עָשָׂר וְהוּא סֵפֶר שׁוֹפְטִים.
הִלְכוֹתָיו חָמֵשׁ. וּפְרָקָיו אַחַד וּשְׁמוֹנִים.
הִלְכוֹת סַנְהֶדְרִין — שִׁשָּׁה וְעֶשְׂרִים פְּרָקִים.
הִלְכוֹת עֵדוּת — שְׁנַיִם וְעֶשְׂרִים פְּרָקִים.
הִלְכוֹת מַמְרִים — שִׁבְעָה פְּרָקִים.
הִלְכוֹת אֵבֶל — אַרְבָּעָה עָשָׂר פְּרָקִים.
הִלְכוֹת מְלָכִים — שְׁנֵים עָשָׂר פְּרָקִים.

בָּרוּךְ שֶׁאָמַר וְהָיָה הָעוֹלָם בִּפְרָטוֹ וּבִכְלָלוֹ:

3:8-9). However, in the Messianic age, there will be such abundant good that there will be no need for efforts of this nature (*Likkutei Sichot*).
44. I.e., the mystic, transcendent aspects of Torah and God.
45. The ocean contains a vast host of living beings. However, the waters cover them to the point that their individual existence is no longer perceived. Similarly, in the Messianic age, the world will continue to exist. However, every element of its existence will be permeated by the knowledge of God.

The *Mishneh Torah* begins "The foundation of all fundamental principles and the pillar of all wisdom is to know that there is a Primary Entity." Thus, the text begins and ends with the knowledge of God.

At the outset, the Rambam establishes the awareness of God as man's fundamental goal in existence. By describing the full range of our Torah practice, he gives us the tools to internalize that awareness and spread it throughout the entire world.
46. These and the following lines were composed by the Rambam, himself. Accordingly, they should be included in the printing of the *Mishneh Torah*.